MENDELSSOHN

THE CAGED SPIRIT

Mendelssohn - The Caged Spirit © Copyright 2008 by Mary Allerton-North

The author has asserted her right under the Copyright Designs and Patents Act 1988 to be identified as the author of this work.

All rights reserved. No part of this work may be reproduced or stored in an information retrieval system (other than for purposes of review) without prior written permission by the copyright holder.

A catalogue record of this book is available from the British Library

Paperback Edition: ISBN: 978-1-908028-02-0

Also available in hardback: ISBN: 978-1-908028-01-3

Published by: Forefront Publishing Ltd.
Victoria House, 26 Queen Victoria Street, Reading, Berkshire, RG1 1TG
Email: info@forefrontpublishing.co.uk Web: http://www.forefrontpublishing.co.uk

MENDELSSOHN

THE CAGED SPIRIT

*A New Approach to the Composer
and his Family*

by

MARY ALLERTON-NORTH

This book is dedicated to all the staff at Dellwood kidney dialysis unit, Reading, and the transplant centre at Churchill Hospital, Oxford, but – above all – to the unknown family who allowed my kidney transplant to be made possible.

Foreword

This is a remarkable book, by a remarkable writer, about a remarkable man. Mary Allerton-North has produced a tour de force of scholarship and insight to celebrate the life, times and musical genius of Felix Mendelssohn. It is a long time since I picked up such a biography and was unable to put it down until finished. It kept me going on train journeys, on a classical music cruise to the Baltic and many evenings when I needed mental stimulation and total enjoyment.

The author's approach is not that of the conventional biographer. As a woman and a trained psychotherapist she has approached her subject from that background, without for a moment losing sight of the composer's musicology.

Mendelssohn was in many ways complex and in many ways very simple. He was complex because of his family background: he was born into a wealthy German Jewish family at the beginning of the 19th century and by the age of seven was playing the piano, painting, writing poetry, speaking several languages and starring as a precocious athlete.

There was more to him than that. He helped revive Bach's music in Europe, he knew Goethe and although the poet was seventy and Mendelssohn only twelve when they met, they became friends.

Mary Allerton-North's love of music and her subject is patently obvious. Why else take on such a task? She undertook this work out of a combination of love for her subject and intellectual curiosity.

I recommend this engaging, page-turning book from an author who has enthusiasm, professional insight and fluency of narrative style. Mary Allerton-North has written for us what will remain for a long time to come the definitive work on a musician who can comfortably be spoken of in the same breath as Bach, Beethoven and the other greats. If you doubt that, read this book!

Henry Kelly

CONTENTS

LIST OF ILLUSTRATIONS xix

MENDELSSOHN FAMILY CHRONOLOGY. xx

INTRODUCTION AND ACKNOWLEDGEMENTS. 1

SYNOPSIS

PROLOGUE "In the Beginning..." 7

Part I
Moses Mendelssohn – 'The Modern Socrates' and 'The German Plato'. . . . 7

The story of Moses Mendelssohn is remarkable in itself. Despite his deformed spine, he walked from his home in Dessau to Berlin, with his parents' blessing, "to learn". He was eventually to become honoured throughout the cultured world, not only for his philosophical treatises and translations of Plato's works, but also for fostering greater understanding between Jew and Christian.

Part II
The Second Generation 21

Moses married Fromet Gugenheim. All their surviving children were remarkable, and each career is described.

BOOK ONE : Boy and Man Chapters 1-14

Chapter 1: "Loving and Giving" 31
Since Felix is said to have been born on a Friday, the line from the old nursery rhyme seems particularly appropriate, for this "Friday's child" was indeed loving and giving. Felix's appearance and personality are described here.

Chapter 2: "While I Rest, I Rust" 41
This was a favourite phrase of banker Abraham Mendelssohn, which he carried out to the limit as far as the education of his children – Fanny, Felix, Rebecka and Paul – was concerned. Yet the father also practised what he preached in this regard. Even leisure had to be profitable, as "doing nothing" was not to be borne.

Chapter 3: Sound Minds in Frail Bodies 55
Despite almost superhuman activity, none of the Mendelssohn children, apart from Paul perhaps, were really strong physically, especially during adulthood. Even Paul, of whom little is known, died of "a long illness" at an age that would now be regarded as too young. Fanny, Rebecka and Felix all appeared to have inherited a brain disorder from their father and, possibly, their grandfather.

Chapter 4: Leisure, at Home and Abroad 69
The Mendelssohn children did enjoy leisure pursuits, which included theatricals and reading and editing magazines. Felix, in his youth and young manhood, was an all-round athlete and sportsman besides enjoying the more cerebral pastimes.

Chapter 5: "Italy at Last!" 85
Though Felix's visit to Italy is so often described, his two sisters also visited that country. Unlike other biographies, this chapter reveals, through their letters, how each spent their time, comparing and contrasting observations from the various places – urban and rural – that were visited.

Chapter 6: Young Musicians 105
Though Felix (and, to a lesser extent, Fanny) were known as composers, any professional status was scorned by their parents. As young people, such music making was merely undertaken as amateurs in the family home. It was destined that Felix should either work in the family bank, adopt a government position or study law; Fanny's career would be wife and mother.

Chapter 7: Two Father Figures 121
As far as Felix was concerned, his music teacher, Carl Friedrich Zelter, and the poet Goethe, to whom Zelter introduced the boy, appear to have played a far greater role as surrogate fathers than Abraham Mendelssohn seemed able to do; he was more like a harsh tutor to this sensitive child.

Chapter 8: Fanny and Felix 141
As with Abraham, Leah, his mother, gave the impression not as a caring, understanding mother but a super-efficient nanny, or a matron at a boarding school. The real mother figure, for Felix, was undoubtedly his sister Fanny. She even took on this role in adult life when her brother was married and his children were little.

Chapter 9: A Family of Letter Writers 159
So much is heard about the masses of letters, which are still preserved, between family members when away from home; yet this appears to be the first time that a detailed analysis has been attempted as to what may be 'read between the lines' of this correspondence. Fascinating insights can be drawn from such a study as to the personality of each correspondent.

Chapter 10: That Money Question 173
So many myths still exist as to how rich the Mendelssohns really were. Here, probably for the first time, discussion is presented as to what is fanciful hearsay and what was reality, as regards both the financial position of the Mendelssohn Bank and the family circumstances.

Chapter 11: 'Glory to God Alone' 191
To the general public there was no doubt that Felix Mendelssohn was a strict Lutheran, simply because his father baptised the children as such, forsaking the Jewish faith. Yet, throughout his life, it is evident that Felix would have preferred to adhere to the faith of his forebears. It is equally apparent, however, that he gained much from other religions, but, above all, Felix pledged his soul to everything that was wholesome in art in all its disciplines.

Chapter 12: Free Thinkers 207
Another myth presents itself – that none of the Mendelssohn children was interested in politics. This chapter aims to prove how untrue such an idea is. Fanny and Rebecka were equally as aware as Felix and Paul of the various aspects not only of German but of European current events.

Chapter 13: Festivals, Private and Public 221
It is clear how zealously the Mendelssohns entered into the spirit of family anniversaries and other celebrations, whether at home or abroad. These included national festivals, for which Felix was invited to compose appropriate music.

Chapter 14: "Flirting Outrageously" 241
Felix is said to have had no 'sex life', though there is no doubt how thrilled he was when dancing with pretty girls, but such seemingly harmless entertainment might not have been all he enjoyed. He was, after all, a decidedly prepossessing young man.

BOOK TWO : Man of Action Chapters 15-23

Chapter 15: "The Fairies' Laureate" 259
This was the name given by Schumann to Mendelssohn, in tribute to the uncanny way in which he imagined the fairies to behave; the same applied to more menacing creatures, such as witches, or mermaids. These fantasy worlds are depicted with equal conviction for orchestra, choir, piano and solo voice.

Chapter 16: Observer of Nature and Life 271
Not only in Mendelssohn's music is the hearer aware of the part played by all five senses, but this applies equally to his watercolours and word-pictures, at home or abroad.

Chapter 17: Quest for an Opera 287
Throughout his life Felix yearned to compose an opera, as much out of duty to his father as for any other reason. Abraham's favourite composer had been Gluck, and he carried disappointment to the grave that his son had not emulated this revered personality. Though Mendelssohn's path was strewn with librettos he considered unsuitable, Felix proved himself eminently capable of writing incidental music for drama and, in his youth, musical plays (singspiels).

Chapter 18: Mendelssohn, the Renovator 303
Felix not only loved, championed and popularised Bach's music, notably by bringing his *St Matthew Passion* before the public, but he was equally enthusiastic about reviving music by Handel, Mozart, Haydn and earlier composers.

Chapter 19: Conductor and Director 315
Felix was the first to popularise the use of the baton when conducting. His achievements included directing not only musical festivals in Germany, but also the Philharmonic Society of London and the Birmingham Festival.

Chapter 20: Mendelssohn, the Soloist 337
Like Fanny, Felix was a brilliant pianist from childhood, but he also played the violin, viola and, especially, the organ; he also had a keen understanding from boyhood as to how that instrument was constructed, and was to play a vital part in advising organ builders in 19th-century England. Mendelssohn also sang, and he regarded the human voice as an instrument of equal importance to non-vocal equivalents.

Chapter 21: "A Handel and a Half" 351
This phrase, coined by Berlioz, refers to the sacred music Mendelssohn composed – not only *St Paul* and *Elijah* , but also psalm settings, cantatas and motets, as well as settings for the Anglican service.

Chapter 22: Mendelssohn as Instructor 369
Among Mendelssohn's correspondents were many potential musicians, young and old, seeking advice or presenting him with compositions to assess. Though pupils benefited from his tuition in a private capacity, his main instruction was given at the Leipzig Conservatorium, which he founded.

Chapter 23: The Highest in the Land 383
Germany comprised many states and principalities. There were, therefore, many royal houses, and from his youth Felix encountered royalty in the course of normal life. Nevertheless, he became frustrated when the King of Prussia ordered him to be appointed at court without giving a proper job specification. His sovereign demanded that Felix should compose music that no one else would have attempted or could have managed. One good result, however, was that the King gave Felix an invitation to Buckingham Palace to meet his cousin, Prince Albert, and Queen Victoria.

BOOK THREE : The Spirit Breaks Free Chapters 24-30

Chapter 24: A Mélange of Musicians 405

Part I   Mendelssohn as Music Critic 405
Unlike music critics such as Schumann or Wagner, it is only through his private correspondence that Mendelssohn's views on contemporary music are known. Perhaps he realised that some of his judgements might have appeared too harsh for comfort; yet they were invariably made with shrewdness and point.

Part II   Famous Personalities 413
Throughout his voluminous correspondence, Mendelssohn was able to describe his inevitable meetings with musical celebrities – and some fascinating descriptions are, therefore, recorded here.

Part III   Where are They Now? 429
Amongst the musicians whose names have become legendary there are people, renowned at the time, who are now unrecognised – except for the fact that Mendelssohn and his family wrote about them.

Chapter 25: "In Paradise" 437
Felix used this phrase to describe Leipzig, where he was given free rein whilst directing the Gewandhaus Orchestra and other musical institutions. Free from the oppressive environment of Berlin and the incompetence he experienced in Düsseldorf, Mendelssohn was able to come into his own in all aspects of his work as a musician.

Chapter 26: "Like an Old Married Couple" 459
Mendelssohn's marriage to Cécile Jeanrenaud must be regarded as one of the most idyllic of the 19th century. After just six weeks as a husband, Felix used this phrase when writing to Eduard Devrient, the actor and opera singer.

Chapter 27: At Home with Cécile and Felix Mendelssohn 477
Not only was Cécile a loving companion, caring deeply for her husband and children, but she was a solicitous hostess and an efficient, thrifty housekeeper. She possessed, in fact, precisely the kind of qualities needed by her hypersensitive, sometimes difficult spouse.

Chapter 28: "Dear, Good Children"..........................**495**
Cécile and Felix had five children, though their fourth child, Felix junior, never very robust, died at the age of eight. Their father loved to tell stories and play games with them, heedless of his own good clothes. He also gave them lessons in a kindly, forbearing manner, unlike his own harsh treatment from tutors and parents.

Chapter 29: The Special Relationship **509**

Part I   Mendelssohn's Musical Life in Britain *509*
Here the whole spectrum of British music is described, before, during and after Mendelssohn's ten visits to this country. Behaviour from the sublime to the ridiculous is taken into account, both at public entertainments and in the home.

Part II   1829..*526*
Mendelssohn's first visit to Britain warrants a section of its own, because there is so much to relate. Not only are his trips to Scotland and Wales covered, but the many invitations he received, from nobility downwards, since the reputation of his grandfather, Moses Mendelssohn, was still admired. Unusual experiences are included, such as Felix's visit to a phrenologist (who assessed his personality by examining the bones in his skull), and what must be the first train journey by a member of the public.

Part III   Later Visits to England...............................*542*
After 1829 Felix paid nine further visits to this country, the last, months before his death on 4th November 1847. Over this period Mendelssohn forged many loyal friendships and took opportunities of continuous invitations, both social and musical, and his popularity not only continued but increased.

Chapter 30: The Spirit Leaves its Cage........................**555**
Not only are Mendelssohn's early death and funeral described, but, where known, details of his descendants are given, together with sketches of relevant friends and acquaintances from his life, subsequent to 1847.

EPILOGUE

Retrospect

Part I The Pendulum of Fashion........................... 573
In this section the peaks and troughs of Mendelssohn's reputation are analysed, from the almost irrational fashion for his music to the contrasting decline in its popularity.

Part II Free Thought...................................... 578
So bitter – even shameful – were criticisms of Mendelssohn, both with regard to his music and to his personality, even by people he knew. Though Richard Wagner is the best-known protagonist, enmity towards Mendelssohn can even be discerned during his lifetime.

Part III Mendelssohn's Musical Legacy 590
Here, analysis is given as to how widely his music has permeated subsequent compositions, both serious and light, in a wide spectrum of this discipline.

Part IV Vivat Mendelssohn! 600
The final part of this epilogue demonstrates the various ways in which Mendelssohn is commemorated, from societies bearing his name to novels and a sports team, formed to pay tribute to the composer's little-known athletic prowess.

Index of Names and Compositions............................ 617

LIST OF ILLUSTRATIONS

1. Felix's school report, 1816 43
2. Prescription, 1846 67
3. Pencil drawing of Atrani, Italy, 1830 95
4. Sonata for Two Pianos, Mendelssohn's first known composition, 1819 113
5. Pencil drawing by Mendelssohn of waterfall at Dunkeld, Scotland, 1829 278
6. Photograph of Mendelssohn's cast of hand and baton 316
7. Letter from Felix to Charles Coventry, 1845 347
8. Mendelssohn's sketch of Cécile in milliner's shop, Strasbourg, 1837 . . . 473
9. Lithograph of the home at Lurgensteins Garten, Leipzig 479
10. Pencil drawing of Mendelssohn family group, 1844 501
11. Pencil drawing by Mendelssohn of Durham Cathedral, 1829 535
12. 'Altdeutsches Frühlingslied', Mendelssohn's last known composition, 1847 561

THE MENDELSSOHNS

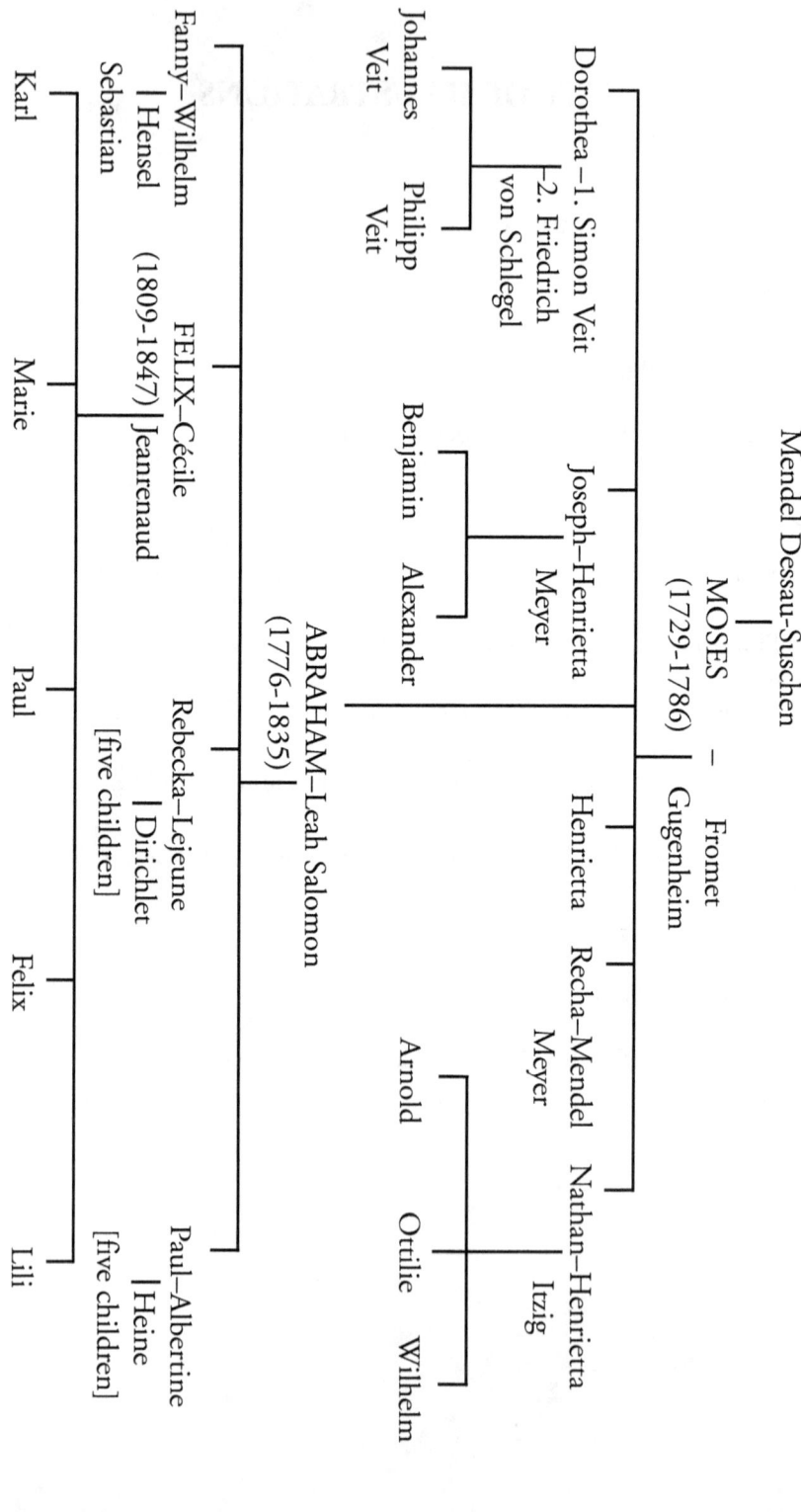

Taken from "The Mendelssohns" three generations of Genius by Herbert Kupferberg (W H Allan)

MENDELSSOHN FAMILY CHRONOLOGY

The following is adapted from a chronology in Rudolf Elvers' compilation entitled *Mendelssohn – A Life in Letters*, translated by Craig Tomlinson.

1729   Moses Mendelssohn born on 6th September.

1742   Arriving in Berlin from Dessau, he changes his name from the original Hebrew, Moses Ben Mendel, to the German equivalent.

1762   Marries Fromet Gugenheim on 22nd June.

1764   Brendel (who later named herself Dorothea) is born on 24th October.

1770   Joseph is born on 11th August.

1776   Abraham is born on 10th December.

1777   Leah Salomon is born on 26th March.

1782   Nathan Mendelssohn is born on 7th January.

1795   Joseph founds the Mendelssohn Bank, together with Moses Friedlander, later joined by Abraham.

1804   Leah Salomon marries Abraham on 26th December. The family moves to Hamburg.

1805   First child, Fanny Cäcilie, is born on 14th November.

1809   Second child, Jakob Ludwig Felix, is born on 3rd February.

1811   Third child, Rebecka, is born 11th April; family then moves to Berlin, Hamburg – originally a 'free city' – having been annexed by Napoleon.

1812   Youngest child, Paul, is born on 30th October.

1815	Felix is given rudimentary piano lessons by his mother.
1816	The Mendelssohn children are baptised as Christians on 21st March, adopting the Lutheran persuasion. Abraham visits Paris with Fanny and Felix.
1817	Cécile Charlotte Sophie Jeanrenaud, Felix's future wife, is born on 10th October.
1818	First appearance of Felix at a public concert, at nine years of age.
1819	Felix begins studies with Karl Friedrich Zelter; first known composition is written for Abraham's birthday, 10th December.
1820	Fanny and Felix become members of Berlin Singakademie on 1st October under Zelter. Felix completes his singspiel *Soldiers' Loves* (libretto purported to have been written by Carl Klingemann).
1821	Felix's second singspiel, *The Two Schoolmasters*, is completed. In October Zelter takes his daughter, Doris, and Felix to visit his old friend Goethe in Weimar.
1822	Abraham and Leah receive baptism as Lutherans in Frankfurt on 1st May, Abraham having taken his brother-in-law's name: Bartholdy. Family take holiday in Switzerland July-October.
1823	Felix is confirmed. E flat String Quartet completed. Leah's mother, Bella Salomon, gives Felix score of J. S. Bach's *Passion according to St Matthew* as a Christmas present.
1824	Felix completes Symphony No. 1, sometimes known as his String Symphony No. 13. Abraham takes Felix to spa town of Bad Doberan, where *Calm Sea and Prosperous Voyage* Overture takes root in composer's mind. Ignaz Moscheles is so impressed with Felix's piano playing that he acknowledges himself Mendelssohn's pupil, and Felix his teacher.
1825	Second visit to Paris. Abraham purchases Leipzigerstrasse 3. George Smart visits Mendelssohn home. String Octet, Op. 20, completed.
1826	Overture to *A Midsummer Night's Dream*, Op. 21, is completed.
1827	First performance of above overture in Stettin, 20th February. First and

only performance of the singspiel *Camacho's Wedding* at Royal Theatre, Berlin. From August Felix goes hiking with companions from Berlin University in southern Germany, where he meets music historian Anton Thibaut in Heidelberg. From 1827 to 1828 Felix attends lectures at the university, but, for reasons that cannot be explained, he does not take a degree.

1828　Composes cantata to commemorate the quatercentenary of Albrecht Dürer in April. Alexander von Humboldt commissions Felix in September to compose a cantata to celebrate Natural Science Day. It appears that Chopin is present at the concert, accompanied by his schoolmaster father and a colleague.

1829　Felix directs first performance of Bach's *St Matthew Passion* since 1729 on 11th March. So popular is the event that a further performance is organised for 21st March, Bach's birthday, and a third presentation is conducted by Zelter because, on 10th April, Felix departs – at last – for London. At the end of July Felix travels with Klingemann to Scotland, where his 3rd, 'Scottish', Symphony and his *Hebrides* Overture are begun. In September Felix travels to Wales via north-west England, to stay with the Taylor family, whom he met in London. On his return Felix suffers a coach accident, preventing his attending Fanny's marriage to Wilhelm Hensel on 3rd October. Felix's singspiel *Son and Stranger* is performed for his parents' silver wedding anniversary on 26th December.

1830　'Reformation' Symphony is composed in April to commemorate Martin Luther's 'Augsburg Confession', at which the theologian professed the Protestant faith. Premature birth of Sebastian, only child of Fanny and Wilhelm Hensel, on 16th June. From May Felix travels to Italy via Leipzig, Weimar, Munich, Pressburg (now Bratislava) and Vienna, to reach Venice and Florence. He arrives in Rome in November.

1831　Felix visits Naples and Pompeii, returns to Rome, and thence goes to Switzerland via Milan, where he meets Mozart's son. In September he returns to Munich, where 1st Piano Concerto is performed, and, in November, travels to Paris, where he remains until the following year.

1832　Goethe dies in Weimar on 22nd March. Zelter dies on 15th May. Also in May Rebecka marries the mathematician Peter Lejeune Dirichlet. Meanwhile, on 23rd April, Felix starts his second visit to London, where the final version of *Hebrides* Overture, Op. 26, is performed on 20th

	June. Returns to Berlin. First book of *Songs without Words* is published in London, together with the String Octet.
1833	Rungenhagen is elected on 22nd January to direct the Berlin Singakademie in succession to Zelter, by 61 votes, receiving 149 votes to Felix's 88 nominations. Having completed his 4th, 'Italian', Symphony, Felix visits London for the third time to conduct the work. He pays a further visit from June to August, this time accompanied by his father. Meanwhile, on 14th April, Felix directs the Lower Rhine Music Festival at Düsseldorf. This leads to his appointment to direct the whole musical spectrum in that city.
1834	Felix resigns his appointment at the theatre in Düsseldorf in November. He negotiates with Conrad Schleinitz and others regarding his appointment to direct the Leipzig Gewandhaus.
1835	Felix undertakes the Leipzig appointment in January. Paul marries Albertine Heine in Berlin on 27th May. Abraham Mendelssohn dies in Berlin on 19th November.
1836	Felix is granted a doctorate of law by the University of Leipzig on 8th March. His oratorio *St Paul* is performed in Frankfurt, where he meets his future wife, Cécile Jeanrenaud. Visit to sea bathing resort of Scheveningen – a 'duty' excursion with the sculptor Schadow and his son. On his return, Felix and Cécile become engaged on 9th September.
1837	Cécile and Felix are married at the French Reformed Church in Frankfurt am Main on 28th March. Felix composes a quantity of music whilst on honeymoon in the Rhine area. Felix regretfully leaves his new bride to conduct *St Paul* at the Birmingham Festival, where he also plays his 2nd Piano Concerto.
1838	First child, Karl Wolfgang Paul, is born 7th February. Summer is spent in Berlin.
1839	Felix conducts, for the first time, Schubert's 9th Symphony in C Major, 'the Great', with the Gewandhaus Orchestra on 22nd March. He directs that year's Lower Rhine Festival at Düsseldorf between May and August, and holidays with his in-laws in Frankfurt. He directs the Brunswick Festival in September, where he meets H. F. Chorley for the first time. Second child, Marie, is born in Leipzig on 7th October.

Mendelssohn Family Chronology

1840   Liszt, Hiller and Mendelssohn perform Bach's Concerto for Three Keyboards with the Gewandhaus Orchestra. Felix travels to England to conduct his *Hymn of Praise* – 2nd Symphony – at the Birmingham Festival.

1841   Third child, Paul, is born in Leipzig on 18th January. Felix conducts performance of Bach's *St Matthew Passion* at St Thomas's Church, Leipzig, on 4th April. He is named Royal Saxon Kapellmeister on 1st July, and Royal Prussian Kapellmeister on 13th October, necessitating his move to Berlin. The first stage performance of his cantata *Antigone* is given at the New Palace at Potsdam, for King Friedrich Wilhelm IV, on 29th October.

1842   Mendelssohn and Julius Rietz conduct the Lower Rhine Festival at Düsseldorf in May. From May to July Cécile and Felix visit London, where the latter is received by Queen Victoria and Prince Albert, to whom he dedicates his 'Scottish' Symphony, first performed in Leipzig and then London. He travels to Switzerland with family members between August and September. Leah dies in Berlin on 12th December.

1843   Having returned, with unparalleled relief, to Leipzig, the final version of *The First Walpurgisnacht* is performed –Berlioz attending the concert – on 2nd February. The Leipzig Conservatorium is founded on 3rd April, and Felix is made an honorary citizen of Leipzig on 13th April. The Bach monument is unveiled at St Thomas's Gate, Leipzig, on 23rd April. Fourth child, Felix, is born in Leipzig on 1st May. Mendelssohn directs a private performance of his incidental music for *A Midsummer Night's Dream*, Op. 61, at the Royal Palace, Potsdam, on 14th October. He conducts church music at Berlin Cathedral for the first time on 25th November.

1844   Eighth visit to London between April and July, where, again, Felix visits Buckingham Palace. He takes a holiday in Frankfurt with his family. He directs the Zweibrücken Music Festival from 26th July to 1st August.

1845   First performance of the E minor Violin Concerto, Op. 64, is given in Leipzig on 13th March, with Ferdinand David as soloist, Niels Gade conducting. Felix takes a vacation with his family in Freiburg-im-Breisgau in July. Fifth and last child, Elisabeth (Lili), is born in Leipzig on 19th September. First performance of music to *Oedipus at Colonus* is given at Potsdam on 1st November, followed on 1st December by music to Racine's *Athalie* at the same venue, both conducted by Mendelssohn.

1846	Felix conducts Schumann's A minor Piano Concerto on 1st January, with Clara Schumann as soloist, at the Gewandhaus. He conducts the first performance of Wagner's *Tannhäuser* Overture at the same place on 14th February. He directs music festivals in Aachen (known as the 'Jenny Lind Festival') and a similar event at Cologne in May and June. The première of the original version of *Elijah* is given on 26th August at the Birmingham Festival, for which Mendelssohn pays his ninth visit to England. He conducts the first performance of Schumann's 4th Symphony at the Gewandhaus on 3rd November.
1847	Felix makes tenth and final visit to England between April and May, conducting the revised version of *Elijah* in the Exeter Hall, London, on 16th April. Fanny dies in Berlin on 14th May. From May to October Felix has a vacation in Switzerland and parts of Germany, including Badenweiler, with Albertine and Paul. Mendelssohn dies on 4th November from a 'berry aneurysm' – similar, it may be assumed, to his father and grandfather, as well as other family members. A memorial concert is given at the Leipzig Gewandhaus on 7th November, and the burial at the Trinity Cemetery, Berlin, takes place on 8th November.
1848-52	Various of Mendelssohn's works are published posthumously.
1852	Felix junior dies in Frankfurt on 16th March.
1853	Cécile dies on 25th September in Frankfurt, where she is buried.
1858	Rebecka Dirichlet dies in Göttingen, the Netherlands, on 1st December.
1861	Wilhelm Hensel dies in Berlin on 26th November. Karl and Paul Mendelssohn publish a collection of Felix's letters. It is not clear whether it was Felix's brother Paul or his younger son who collaborated with Karl, the elder son, or whether it was the two brothers' compilation.
1874	Felix's brother Paul dies in Berlin on 21st June.

INTRODUCTION and ACKNOWLEDGEMENTS

From the earliest times, when awareness of history dawned on me, I felt an affinity with the 19th century. So much was this so that I won first prize in fancy dress parades when dressed as a Victorian girl, and – what is more – I *knew* I would win. This was not conceit, but simply because this disguise was *me* – it felt right! Felix Mendelssohn, who epitomises this period, has composed music that gives me the same feeling of oneness with that century. I first experienced this in early childhood, when my mother played 78 rpm records on a portable gramophone, known as the 'black box' on account of its appearance. One such record, entitled 'Classica', included Mendelssohn's so-called 'Spring Song' (Op. 62 No. 6).

As I gained greater knowledge of his music, my liking for it increased. However, the crucial event occurred on hearing an interval talk on BBC Radio 3 on the evening of Friday, 22nd April 1994, regarding Mendelssohn himself. During the discussion the International Mendelssohn Foundation was mentioned, whose aim has been successfully achieved: to renovate Mendelssohn's home in Leipzig. I heard that a British branch was to be formed, which I planned to join. This, though, was far easier said than done. I received no feedback, from whichever source of information I tried. I then decided to read as much as I could about this creature of so many myths. It was then that I realised his life was not all that it seemed. I discovered so many discrepancies and inaccuracies – as well as decidedly slovenly research – that there was no alternative but for me to write a new biography. I apply the line from Tennyson's poem *Maud* – "It is better to fight for the right than to rage at the ill." Rather than grumble at others' shortcomings, one should endeavour to put matters right. Hence this book, which, though never intended to be a 'definitive' biography, may – I believe – help to allow anyone who reads it, better to understand this fascinating personality.

How did the title arise? The sub-heading (*A New Approach...*) is straightforward to explain. If readers wish to study Mendelssohn's music in more minute detail, plenty of biographies have been written to make this possible, but I am not a musicologist, and any musical terms or 'jargon' that must be mentioned are explained in the text. This biography, unlike some that have been written, does not set out to unpick the stitches of his seamless music. Rather, the intention is to scrape away the veneer layered onto this character through myths and suppositions, and to reveal the true image, which did not belong to a saint but to a flesh-and-blood man.

But what about the main title, *Mendelssohn – The Caged Spirit*? In view of the fact that many biographies are simply named *Mendelssohn*, with variations such as *Mendelssohn and his World*, *Mendelssohn and his Times*, or *The Family Mendelssohn*, it seemed appropriate to find a more original title. Admittedly, George R. Marek has called his book *Gentle Genius*, but this was copied from what the composer Gabriel Fauré had named Mendelssohn, so Marek's title was not his own invention. No one but the present author has thought of *The Caged Spirit* as a title. But, surely, readers who know anything about Mendelssohn will ask, how could his spirit be called "caged"? Did he not have a privileged background, with anything he wanted immediately available to him, with money no object, because of his parents' affluence beyond most people's imagination? From what is narrated such may be true, but this is only what biographers have gleaned second-hand, in view of the fact that so much was censored regarding the Mendelssohn family. The only advantages and privileges he was given were what his strict parents thought he might need to enhance his education, without the luxury that usually accompanies such affluence. Duty and obedience were the keywords in the Mendelssohn children's harsh upbringing. Though music did play a part in family life, the parents refused to admit that their elder son had exceptional talents; his career was destined, as far as his all-powerful father understood matters, to follow his in the family bank – or, if this did not suit, to take up a legal or government post. Music was only a frivolous pastime – not a profession. Felix had no alternative but to behave with the "impeccable manners" about which we hear so often; he was driven by a lifelong quest for perfection: impossible to achieve. "Corners must not be cut," he is reputed to have reprimanded himself, even if musical notation had to be copied 12 or even 24 times, until the manuscript showed absolute correctness. Especially did this apply in the repressive environment and dull musical life of Berlin, in which city he encountered frustrations to his creativity whichever path he followed. It is, therefore, a falsehood to state that his parents encouraged their elder son "in every way" in his musical career. Even as an adult, not only were his finances looked after by his father and, after his death, by Felix's younger brother Paul, but his style of composition was constantly criticised by the Mendelssohn parents. Is it any wonder that, in view of the fact that his frail body was always too vulnerable to support his active mind, this title has been chosen?

However, there is also the 'bad press' that he has received, over and above the treatment meted out to his descendants and his own music by the Third Reich. Any praise of Mendelssohn's talent expressed by contemporaries is quoted verbatim and is not plastered with the language of hero-worship. Nevertheless, some of the expressions of admiration must be categorised as nauseating: "When Mendelssohn became a man," Stephen Stratton states, "one of the most beautiful boyhoods recorded in musical literature came to an end." Such narrative was fine for the days when the *Boys' Own* magazine exhorted its readers to the industrious life that Mendelssohn is said to have lived, but, as attitudes change, many young people are turned away from this 'wonder-child' syndrome. One is led to wonder if, indeed, such biographers would have preferred Mendelssohn to remain a boy all his life rather than become a man. However, this metamorphosis still caused drivel to be written of an even worse colour: Gisela Selden-Goth, in the introduction to her 1945 compilation of Mendelssohn's correspondence, tells her readers: "He never knew want, family quarrels, thwarted affection or the bitter battle for artistic recognition... His vitality was not rapidly sapped, as is the case with prodigies. His letters give the impression of an exceptionally happy person, centred in, and satisfied with, himself." To be fair, the compiler may not have had access to later research, the study of which creates a reverse situation to that which Selden-Goth believed to be true. Moszkowski, a recent biographer, is equally adept at laying on his praise with a shovel: "A prince of music... Germany's brightest and most attractive star... a glittering jewel in the Mendelssohn family's crown." No other German composers, it seems, aspire to such an accolade; neither do equally illustrious members of the Mendelssohn family.

There is an obverse side to the coin, however, of this false image. Adjectives are often applied to Mendelssohn's personality that reveal the biographer's distinct lack of perception. He is called "happy-go-lucky"; his music is, like his character, "lightweight", or "frivolous". He did not develop as a composer, since "he had no negative experiences to draw on in his art". He was the "darling of Europe" solely on account of "his impeccable manners". "Born with all the advantages and none of the disadvantages usually associated with the poor artist..." Not content with decrying his apparently comfortable family circumstances, Mendelssohn is taken to task for his pursuit of excellence. He evinces a "weakness" in his "distaste for opera; for panache; for Chopin's disturbing eroticism; and [for] too great a reliance on the opinions of his family and friends". "He never understood the depths of human emotion, but seemed to regard music chiefly as a means of solace and pure enjoyment." Marek and others castigate his work schedule as if this were a crime: "From his engagement to Cécile Jeanrenaud in 1836 to the 1840s" it would "weary" anyone to study Mendelssohn's career; "it would link work with more work; success upon success; tribute next to tribute..." He is even taken to task for his "ever larger register" of friends and acquaintances – "men important in their time, but now distant names". Apart from the foregoing, Mendelssohn is described by Wilfred Blunt as "unromantic". A French historian, Emile Vuillermoz, went so far as to say, "Contented nations and contented men have no history and, therefore, one should, on principle, abandon the idea of writing a life of Mendelssohn." Such an individual was "interesting but undramatic". The quotes above say more about Mendelssohn's biographers than Mendelssohn himself! Would a "contented man" have striven so assiduously to bring everything to which he applied himself to such a standard of excellence, or to assist fellow musicians and endeavour to raise funds for so many disparate causes, as Mendelssohn did? Would anyone so "unromantic" have produced such masterpieces as, say, the *Hebrides Overture*? Would anyone "undramatic" have been able to compose *The First Walpurgisnacht*? "Interesting" is an arrantly lazy word to describe this fascinating, exhilarating, multifaceted personality.

This book does not claim to be a definitive biography of Felix Mendelssohn and his family. Rather, in view of what has already been published, *The Caged Spirit* sets out to be a renovation – an attempt to put right some of the inaccuracies (either accidental or deliberate) that have been churned out and often regurgitated by subsequent biographers, who take statements at face value, without the remotest attempt to analyse them. Whenever a biography is researched, care should be taken in the use of reference sources. Though much has been written about Mendelssohn, and many of his letters zealously preserved, gaps do appear that frustrate the avid researcher. F. Max Müller states, in his memoirs, *Auld Lang Syne*, written in 1898, that there were "bitter drops" in Mendelssohn's life, "of which the world knows little and need not know anything now…as if they had never been". He speaks of "letters that are reduced to ashes and can never be produced again by friends or enemies". Müller makes the point that many people were unaware of the "struggles" through which artists – "especially musicians" – have to go, affecting Mendelssohn as much as anyone else, as, years later, this wiseacre thought it "not always commendable" to know "everything" about a celebrity. No life had been lain bare to such an extent as Mendelssohn's; "enough, and more than enough" had been written for Stratton's comfort, and anyone who wished to bring new facts to light was dismissed as "childish" and "vulgar". Today, despite the excitement over the 150th anniversary of his death, interest in his music appears to be fading into the state of oblivion and deserves constant reappraisal. This is borne out by the comments of the virtuoso violinist Luigi Alberto Bianchi, that Mendelssohn is a "forgotten composer", who admits that no serious musical study has been published. On the latter point, one is not qualified to judge, but one hopes Bianchi may be pleased with this study of Mendelssohn the man.

Though he preferred spending time with his loved ones and special friends, he did enjoy himself, as analysed in Book III, 'The spirit breaks free'. Robert Schumann's remark may be taken to heart: "The artist should beware of losing touch with society, otherwise he will be wretched, as I am." Perhaps Mendelssohn's detractors should bear this in mind when sneering at his gregarious personality. Max Müller recalls that "so bright and happy himself, he wished to see the whole world around him bright and happy". Though many of Mendelssohn's letters were circumscribed by later members of his family, the correspondence that is available must be seen as the best source of reference for his biography. They present the most delightful picture of life away from his work, particularly in London or in Frankfurt, home of his wife's family.

To conclude, a few other points are indicated as to how this book differs from

Introduction and Acknowledgements

its predecessors. H. E. Jacob, in *Mendelssohn and his Times*, believes that, in order to do justice to his subject's life, one must "leap backwards and forwards". Selden-Goth adds that "the changes from year to year… were accomplished smoothly… and it is difficult to determine points of transition from one period to another". According to Marek, "Mendelssohn entered one door as a gifted child and came out of another as a master." Such comments are far too simplistic. To avoid such confusion, *The Caged Spirit* is divided into 'pigeon-holes', each section dealing with a specific and separate aspect of Mendelssohn's life. In some respects, Mendelssohn was always childlike; in others, one wonders if his mother gave birth to a miniature adult! In existing biographies, the events of Mendelssohn's life have been 'lumped together' in one chapter – e.g. "Queen Victoria, Jenny Lind and *Elijah*" – or deal with a specific period – "An eventful year, 1824". Reminiscences of friends and contemporaries are often regurgitated wholesale, with no analysis or explanation of anything that may be difficult to understand. Neither is this book riddled with footnotes that allow the thread to be lost (unlike biographies written by authors who conform to the 'establishment' way of working) by any reader, however accustomed to following a biography.

The myth of Mendelssohn's 'Grand Tour' is exploded, despite the exaggerations of broadcasters. "All over Europe" actually includes: various parts of Germany (his homeland); Great Britain; Paris ("Paris is France", as Mendelssohn himself stated); Italy; Austria; very short periods in Belgium and what was then Hungary, but is now the Slovak Republic; Switzerland; and a duty trip to a resort in the Netherlands. For someone whose father became the Tsar's financial adviser, such travel seems distinctly limited when one thinks of the far more exotic places visited by other men of culture. Another myth is that Mendelssohn was "an ideal Victorian". However, since Queen Victoria ascended the throne in 1837, when the composer was at his peak in so many aspects of music, living for just over ten years from that date, he must be regarded as a Regency musician, spanning the reigns of George IV and William IV. Whilst on the subject of Mendelssohn and royalty, it is rarely realised that not only Felix, but other members of his family had dealings with the various royal houses of Europe; this phenomenon is discussed in Chapter 23, 'The highest in the land'. Neither do other biographies analyse, compare or contrast the various impressions, events and life experiences of other members of the Mendelssohn family. Finally, any acknowledgements, rather than being given space at the front of the book, will be cited as the text progresses. There are only a few exceptions. First, the dedicated booksellers who have supplied the majority of the material employed in compiling this book: Martin Earl of Beaconsfield; David Paramor of Newmarket; Fiennes Trotman of Beaminster, Dorset; and Andrew C. Brooks of ACB Arts. Second, Peter Ward Jones, the Music Librarian at the Bodleian Library, Oxford, for providing all the illustrations used in this book. Also Jose and Dr. Michael Keith-Lucas for their meticulous care in proof-reading this book, and Geoff Lawson, an eminent music scholar. His encyclopaedic knowledge and meticulous research has improved this book beyond recognition. Above all though I would like to thank my husband for his constant and unstinting support throughout the whole project.

Mary Allerton-North,
Reading, Berkshire.
February 2005.

PROLOGUE

"In the Beginning…"

Part I: Moses Mendelssohn – 'The Modern Socrates' and 'The German Plato'

In his memoir of the Mendelssohn family, from 1729 to 1847, Sebastian Hensel spoke with apparent pride of their 'middle-class' status, but this is too simplistic. Felix, the main subject of this book, was able to adapt himself to any stratum of society, from royalty downwards, having inherited his grandfather's ability to occupy the world of thinkers, impervious to the concept of class, with his flexible, multifaceted mind. Neither can this remarkable individual, Moses Mendelssohn, likewise, by any means, be termed 'middle-class'. A whole book could be written about each member of the three generations of Mendelssohns covered in most biographies of the composer; from what has been researched, the same applies to their successors' generation.

Moses Ben Mendel, as he was then known, was born on 6th September 1729 into the Jewish community in Dessau, eastern Germany. In the 18th century, Jews were confined to tightly knit communities, known as ghettos, in whichever city they had settled, but, to any who wished to integrate into the full social and cultural environment of his land of residence, one name above all others must be honoured. It was Moses, Son of Mendel, who was primarily responsible for Jewish emancipation from former deprivation and harsh laws. Even those who had lifted themselves out of the ghettos were prey to unjust restrictions upon their lifestyle for years to come. Because of the money they were able to make – advantageous to the Christian-governed states of which Germany consisted until 1871 – the status of 'protected' or 'court' Jew was granted. For instance, a 'body tax' was levied on any Jew seeking protection from the ever-present attacks by ignorant assailants, as Jews were prevented from carrying arms themselves. The amount of 30 ducats was charged for a journey from Berlin to Dresden – the same as for an ox to be conveyed via this route, Moses was later to write. If this, or any of the other stringent taxes was not paid immediately, Jews were threatened with expulsion from their country of residence, irrespective of the prevalent economic recession. The 'body tax' was abolished in 1813 in Dresden, but not until 1847 in Hanover. Little is known about Mendel of Dessau (surnames were not given to Jews until the

1820s) except that he was a 'sopher', or scribe, copying extracts from the Hebrew scriptures and writing letters for those who required this service. He also ran a school for poor boys of the district, aided by his sons Saul and, later, Moses. However, Moses was sent, in early childhood, to the seminary run by Rabbi Frankel. Made to rise early, he was wrapped in his cloak, against the often inclement weather.

When Moses was 14, Frankel was invited to become Chief Rabbi in Berlin. Since, at such an age, a boy was expected to make his way in the world, Moses decided to follow his revered mentor, in order to pursue further studies, living as a pedlar – one of the few employments open to Jews – selling trinkets or whatever else attracted the public. Rather than place obstacles in the way of their child's development, as many negative-minded parents are wont to do, Mendel and his wife 'Suschen' (short for Susannah) praised their son's enterprising spirit. Moses remembered his mother as an eminently patient woman, who bore with fortitude the cramped conditions and privations Jews of poor families were compelled to suffer. Suschen must also have been a thrifty housekeeper for she bestowed on Moses a gold ducat to assist his 70-mile walk from Dessau to Berlin. However, though this unexpected and unsought gift must have moved Moses greatly, of far greater value, intellectually and spiritually, would have been his father's blessing on his adventure through life.

George R. Marek describes Moses as having "an enormous nose, introspective eyes and a forehead high enough to house his knowledge", being "small, ugly and hump-backed". This deformity of the spine was caused by incessant bending to read and write as a child. (At ten years old he had composed some Hebrew poetry.) His handicap was not helped by the dim light of the ghetto conditions in which he was compelled to work. The book to which Moses attributed his deformity was *A Guide to the Perplexed*, written by the 11th-century Hebrew scholar Moses of Maimon (or Moses Maimonides). However, rather than bewail the fact that his bones had not developed enough for this unnecessary deformity to have occurred, he spent his time improving the life, social and cultural, of his co-religionists to share with them the new light he had discovered in human understanding.

It is interesting, though, that the Swiss theologian and physician Johann Caspar Lavater appears not to have set such store by his colleague's disability. In his book on physiognomy, Lavater's description of Moses is far more attractive than that of Marek. He had "a dark complexion; curly, dark hair; a vaulted forehead; dark eyes; aquiline nose; a small, pointed beard and smiling expression." Lavater actually saw the man: Marek did not. Various legends have evolved concerning Moses, Son of Mendel – some that can be verified, others that must remain apocryphal. He is said to have measured his weekly loaf into seven sections, one only for each day of the week.

On arriving, at last, at the Rosenthaler Gate, the only entry into Berlin allowed to a Jew, he was asked what business he had in that city. "Lehrnen," he replied, the only German word he knew: "to learn." An early biographer, Otto Zarek, reported that, on being asked what he had to sell, Moses replied to this insolent form of address: "Reason; a commodity with which you have no acquaintance." Once in Berlin, a merchant, Hyam (or Hermann) Bamberg, allowed Moses to sleep in his attic and invited him for meals with his household. Frankel also asked him to dine on the Sabbath and other religious festivals. However, not only was Frankel able to support him socially; he showed an even more practical approach. He recalled the boy's exemplary handwriting and asked Moses to copy some of the sections of a book he had recently compiled on the Jerusalem Talmud, a guide to the Jewish Law. For this service, he gave his pupil small sums of money to augment his income from the goods he was able to sell.

As his German progressed Moses acquired new knowledge, and the first book he read, a history of Christianity, revealed a faith that had hitherto been unknown to him. Not satisfied with German only, he learnt Latin from a book of grammar and a translation of the English philosopher John Locke's *Essay on Human Understanding*. A Dr. Reich assisted him with Latin, the lessons lasting, at first, for a quarter of an hour per day, the unwieldy process continuing for half a year. Nevertheless, it was his own motivation that drove Moses to increase his knowledge. As more people became aware of his thirst for further education, a greater number of learned men were willing to instruct him. Dr. Solomon Gumpertz, a mathematician who had gained his doctorate at Königsberg University, taught him English and French. This caused Moses to ask Frankel to lend him his copy of Johnson's *Dictionary*, which he enjoyed reading, and also Laurence Sterne's *Tristram Shandy*. Dr. Kisch, a physician from Prague, helped with Latin and very likely taught him Greek. Not only was Israel Samosz able to teach Moses Euclydian geometry and logic but, as a connoisseur of fine art, was able to guide the boy's mind into acquiring the same interest. (Samosz had disputed a theological point with the Rabbinate of Poland and had fled to Berlin.) Nevertheless, there was one subject for which Moses could see no point: history. At that time, he found it boring and merely yawned at having to study it. But this was to change, for it was essential, he perceived, if one was to make the most of one's adopted country, to know how her culture and environment had evolved and developed. Moses did not hold with the idea of a Jewish homeland; it was far more practical, he considered, to assimilate completely into whichever nation a Jew inhabited than to waste time on matters of which little was known. It was whilst contemplating such thoughts that he decided not only to adopt Germany as his home, to call himself a German, and to promote German ideas, but to alter his name. He would no longer be known as Moses Ben Mendel, but the German equivalent: Moses Mendelssohn – Moses, Mendel's Son.

In 1750, at the age of 21, a silk merchant, Isaac Bernhard, appointed Moses as tutor to his children and, once his instruction was no longer needed, employed him as book-keeper in his silk mill and, later, as manager.

Though his greater financial security in Bernhard's employment allowed Moses to purchase more books and to enjoy a greater cultural and social life, the actual work of bookkeeping did not suit his personality. It was only at a later period, after the silk business was bequeathed to Moses on Bernhard's death, that he was able to express his feelings about his erstwhile lowly position. Anyone who wished to become a serious, conscientious book-keeper – or was compelled to do so through circumstances – must "lose all wit, perception and sense", becoming "like a block of wood". He had regarded himself as nothing other than "a pack mule", rather than the racehorse whose status he had desired; the soul-destroying tasks at which he had been employed had, he considered, wasted the best years of his life.

But this is by no means true. Whenever opportunities presented themselves – even during working hours – Moses would study the writings of others, as well as putting his own thoughts into words. Once, for instance, whilst delivering a consignment of silk samples to a government official, he was kept waiting for so long that he used the sample box as a writing desk on which to make observations from discussions with Samosz. This was to become his first book, *Notes on the Emotions*, about aesthetics. At about the same time, the Swiss theologian and physician Lavater, visiting Bernhard's factory, noticed Moses working in the office. He wrote of "the Jew Mendelssohn" as "a brilliant and accomplished soul...with pleasing ideas", though with "the body of Aesop". Moses possessed "keen insight, exquisite taste and wide erudition... unaffected by praise". Herbert Kupferberg considers, that, until Moses Mendelssohn, no Jew wrote so eloquently in the German tongue.

During this time, Moses was introduced to a group who called themselves 'The Scholars' Coffee House', equivalent to London clubs, where intellectuals discussed topics of the day, but also mathematics, literature and philosophy. Friedrich Nicolai, a bookseller, had begun a periodical, *Letters on the New Literature*, though it soon became apparent that Moses Mendelssohn was the prime mover in the promotion of this publication. Though its first two issues were published anonymously, by the third edition Moses had become part of the editorial board. Its main object was to decry the Francophile attitude of King Friedrich II (Frederick the Great). The King demanded that French was to be the only language spoken at court, even calling his palace 'Sans-Souçi' – 'Without a Care'. He gathered the cream of French intelligentsia around him and dismissed German as nothing but a 'jargon'. Why, *Letters on the New Literature* asked, could a German culture not be publicised? It was as the result of an article defending the German dramatist Gotthold Ephraim Lessing that Gumpertz introduced the two men. Without Lessing's works, Marek claims, neither Goethe nor Schiller would have been inspired to augment German literature. Lessing was also to inspire John Ruskin and T. S. Eliot in their work. The article Moses had written on Lessing's behalf was prompted by his drama *The Jew*, in which the hero rescued a Christian from an attack by thieves. Professor Michaelis had written that "a noble Jew is a poetic impossibility", to which Lessing had responded that his aim, in writing the drama, had been to try to conquer such prejudice and ignorance, prompted by fear of the unknown. Jews were not bears to be baited, he argued. In this context, when Moses was once asked if he were a Jew, he had replied, "I am a man," and it was this assertion that Lessing hoped to convey.

However, the dramatist's best-known play was to be *Nathan the Wise*, based, it is universally asserted, on the personality of Moses Mendelssohn himself. The Oriental scholar Friedrich Rosen, friend of Mendelssohn's grandson Felix, would affirm that Christians should be grateful for this work, as it was instrumental in allowing Jews to take their rightful place in society; as equals in the human race, rather than, as formerly, inferior creatures. Charlotte Moscheles, born into a Jewish family herself, admired *Nathan the Wise* for its "sound reasoning" and its author for the "fine spirit" in which he wrote. Fanny Horsley, whose family (like that of Moscheles and Rosen) were lifelong friends of Mendelssohn's grandson, though still in her teens, condemned the anti-Jewish prejudice of the German hierarchy as "bigoted and shocking".

Moses could converse in English, Polish and German; the latter was his preferred mode of speech. However, he had learnt French in case he had to appear at some time before the King. Thus, when such a command was given for "that impudent Jew" to present himself at court, as his fame spread, he was prepared. He was able to respond so wittily to the anticipated harangue on the Sabbath that Lessing was inspired to include, in his drama, a scene between Nathan and the emperor, in honour of the way his now lifelong friend acquitted himself. But this was for the future. *Nathan the Wise* would not be produced in Berlin until 1773, and, though Moses must have known of Lessing's inspiration, he was always far too self-effacing to acknowledge this. Later, though, he wrote with amusement to a friend that his youngest son, named Nathan, by coincidence, would strut around calling himself 'Nathan the Wise'; "his wisdom only searches for gingerbread or other sweetmeats from the cook." As with the life of his grandson, Felix, discipline must be observed, as far as possible, when writing about the life of Moses Mendelssohn, as so many aspects occurred simultaneously but also overlapped into later periods of each facet of his life.

In 1753 the Academy of Arts in Berlin offered a prize to anyone who could write the best response to Alexander Pope's *Essay on Man*. This English man of letters had decreed that no one should mock his *Essay* until he himself made jest of it but, having died in 1744, the way was clear for somebody to refute this literary masterpiece. Thus both Lessing and Mendelssohn lampooned Pope's work, which brought the latter's name to the notice of intellectuals, culminating in a visit to the Academy to meet its head, the mathematician Maupertuis. Though his name was added to the roll of honour, it was removed by command of the King. Moses was phlegmatic, but witty, at this rebuff. He would rather, he commented, have been recognised by the intelligentsia of Germany but have his name erased at his monarch's instigation, than that the reverse situation applied. He was also glad that the name of Catherine the Great – Empress of Mother Russia – would not be contaminated, as would happen if it were placed alongside a Jew from the Fatherland. This action of Frederick the Great need not be attributed to anti-Semitism, however; more likely, it was anti-German prejudice that took effect; as Marek points out, Lessing's name was also excised from the same roll of honour. Despite this irrational attitude, Moses always recognised Friedrich II as his constitutional monarch, even going to the extent, in 1757, of writing a sermon congratulating his sovereign on a victory against Austria in the Seven Years' War. Frankel preached the sermon in the Berlin synagogue and, having been translated into English, this was the first writing of Moses Mendelssohn to be made available in London, the next year.

There is a myth that Mendelssohn applied for the post of court chaplain; this appointment of a suitable candidate depended upon the quality of the sermon. Having been informed that a text would be given him, Moses, on ascending the pulpit, found nothing but a sheet of blank paper. This inspired him to preach on the creation of the world from nothing. It must, though, be borne in mind that such a devout adherent to his faith would never have been tempted to seek a specifically Christian office. His unswerving loyalty to Judaism is proved by the 'Lavater Controversy'. The Swiss theologian could not accept that a Jew could have such superior intellect; thus, when his compatriot Charles Bonnet wrote a work *In Defence of Christianity*, Lavater dared Mendelssohn to refute the treatise. Because of the cogent, watertight counter-arguments Moses submitted, Lavater had to apologise publicly for the rashness he had displayed.

Since Moses Mendelssohn's most famous work, the translation into German of Plato's *The Immortality of the Soul*, would not appear until 1767, he was asked to review a book of poems written by the King on this subject. Rather than decrying the fact that the verses were written in French, the only language tolerated at court, he said what a pity it was that no German equivalent had been published. However, as to the argument that the soul was not immortal, this was shown to be absurd, as far as Mendelssohn understood the matter. The concept that the soul was merely mortal was similar to saying that a square was round; that a circle was square – "a mere chimera", as Moses dismissed the proposition. According to the *Dictionary*, a chimera was a monster of Greek mythology, with the head of a lion, the body of a goat and the tail of a serpent – "a fanciful horror, with no existence". In other words, there was no question, for Mendelssohn, that the soul could be anything but immortal. What is so attractive about the personality of this remarkable man is that he actually practised what he preached. Years before the translations of Shakespeare's plays by Schlegel and Tieck, Moses Mendelssohn had begun a similar project. In his correspondence the 'To be, or not to be' soliloquy from *Hamlet* is mentioned, as are also 'Ariel's song' from *The Tempest* and 'Ye spotted snakes…' from *A Midsummer Night's Dream*. Though biographers pay ample tribute to the

Prologue: Part I

later translations for inspiring the Mendelssohn grandchildren in their theatricals, their grandfather's translations must also have played a part. As for the King's view of the Shakespeare dramas, each one was nothing but "a farce" and its language fit only for "the savages of Canada".

Though Mendelssohn's financial security increased, along with his fame, one thing he desired above all was not yet granted him – a family of his own. Friends had endeavoured to find him a suitable bride, yet without success. But in 1761 plans were put in hand for his marriage. His bride was Fromet Gugenheim, daughter of a previously wealthy, but now impoverished, merchant of Hamburg, which city he visited on business. The family had heard of this remarkable Jew who wrote in German, admired his writings, and invited Moses to their home, whereupon he fell in love with Fromet. However, it took time for these feelings to be reciprocated. This attractive young lady of 33, nine years younger than Moses, was repelled by his deformed spine. Here a further anecdote must be recorded, accurate or not, as it shows how resolute Mendelssohn was in winning the hand of his bride, through his perspicacity. He explained to Fromet that the marriage of every Jewish child is made in Heaven and that he had been destined to marry a girl with a humped back, but that he had asked God to have this burden given to himself. When this had been put into effect, Fromet was "flawless and beautiful" and Moses carried her hump. Fromet was evidently so pleased with what her suitor had said that she accepted him and, in May 1761, Moses was able to seek, and eventually gain, permission (as was the law for a Jew who wished to marry) to move from Dessau to Hamburg as his permanent place of residence, and to become a married man. A further law demanded that, in order to acquire such status, a purchase had to be made from the Royal Porcelain Factory in Berlin – presumably, an article that no one else would buy. For Moses, the factory decided to sell 20 large monkeys, but this acquisition must have been preferable to an earlier law that demanded that the bridegroom purchase the carcase of a boar from the Royal Hunt.

The couple then set up home in Berlin, where their children would be born. During courtship, when apart, they wrote to each other, not the type of letters that most people would expect, but dealing with subjects of the mind – philosophy, politics, literature. Though Fromet's letters have, like the porcelain monkeys, 'disappeared', those of her betrothed remain. Unlike the precise grammar Moses used in his public writings, his letters to his bride reveal a refreshingly colloquial style; even traditional Hebrew phrases are used. In one, he recommended Fromet to read *La Nouvelle Héloïse*, but not to allow her younger sisters to do so. He also shared his joy with her of Laurence Sterne's novels, recommending her to read these. "Only when I seemed to hear the sound of the postilion did I take the opportunity to declare myself to my beloved," he wrote later.

Even on honeymoon, Moses submitted an essay to the Academy of Science, which was offering a prize of a gold medal and 50 gold ducats – a timely gift for anyone setting up home as a married man. The subject was: "What is, is right". Moses stated that philosophical and metaphysical concepts needed to be proved as thoroughly as those of mathematics. He won the prize, but, more importantly (for anyone with intellectual pride), he defeated one of the most famous contemporary philosophers – Immanuel Kant – in the contest. Later, when Kant wrote his *Critique of Pure Reason* in 1782-83, Moses was to acknowledge that he could never attain his friend's heights of erudition, whilst Kant reciprocated that he respected the zeal of Mendelssohn's quest for greater religious toleration and praised his "delicacy of perception" in his literary style. "A genius such as you," Kant declared, "will succeed in creating a new epoch of philosophy." How sad it is that such a prophecy does not appear to have come true.

Mendelssohn and Kant were to become lifelong friends, and it is appropriate here to recount an incident that must have reminded Moses of how wide a gulf still existed between what should, and what did, obtain in a society of bigotry against the unknown. Moses visited Königsberg University, where Kant was professor of philosophy, but while he was waiting in an anteroom for Kant to give his lecture some students abused Moses. It was only when the professor embraced his guest and introduced Moses to the students as a remarkable thinker that they abandoned the idea of ejecting him from the room. Marek believes this is yet another tale that has grown up regarding Moses Mendelssohn; that no philosophy student would behave in such a manner. Students are human, whatever discipline they study, and, when considering the superstition of the times, they could well have panicked at seeing not only a Jew but a person with such a disfigured body. It must have become evident, yet again, to Moses that, if bridges were to be built between Jew and Christian, he, as a Jew, would have to play his part in bringing this process to fruition.

Despite his intellectual pursuits, Moses took his domestic responsibilities as seriously. The day began for him at dawn, with prayer and meditation – probably to take advantage of the natural light, in an age in which electricity was still to be used in the home. He entered his office at 8 a.m., returning home at 3 p.m., but his real day – the part he liked best – occurred when friends, relatives and even visitors from abroad came to the Mendelssohn house. His favourite anecdote was of an early Hebrew scholar named Hiller who, when asked to recite the Law of Moses standing on one leg, simply said: "Love thy neighbour as thyself." This, Moses declared, was the only tenet that mattered, the remainder being nothing other than commentaries on the Scriptures. Nevertheless, Moses preferred to sit quietly, listening to the discussion around him, intervening, like a respected umpire, only if an argument ensued. He would sometimes ask the protagonists to rise, and, standing between them, would summarise each point, concluding that, really, each person wished to say the same thing, but in different words. Occasionally, though, when anyone sought his opinion, he would give it. Once, when a self-styled 'rabbinical expert' disputed a point from the writings of the

Prologue: Part I

11th-century Spanish philosopher Ibn Ezra, Moses replied that it would be best, in the first instance, to study the Scriptures; there would then be time enough to study the works of Ibn Ezra, though he did admit not understanding the point at issue.

In 1766 Mendel of Dessau passed away and, at about the same time, a daughter of Fromet and Moses was also taken from them. Writing to a Christian friend, Thomas Abbt, the bereaved father recalled how the little girl had grown, even in so short a time, from a tiny creature who could only sleep or cry into "a reasoning being". A son of 12 was also to be lost to the parents, but their six surviving children – three sons and three daughters – each played a distinguished part as an adult.

In 1767 Mendelssohn wrote one of his most illustrious works – *Phaedon, or the Immortality of the Soul*, his title remaining the same as Plato's treatise, which Moses converted to the modern German context rather than allowing it to represent the way of life in ancient Greece. His aim was that anyone should be able to read his translation, so straightforward was its language. Mendelssohn's version of the original was, in turn, translated into over 30 languages, including Hebrew, and became popular throughout the intellectual world, from ghetto to court, via the Sorbonne in Paris and the coffee houses of London. The Duke of Brunswick was so impressed with Moses that he tried to persuade him to live in that province. The sister of Frederick the Great discoursed with Mendelssohn on the book, even hanging the author's portrait on her wall. An English translation is even said to have crossed the Atlantic, Marek claiming that Benjamin Franklin may have possessed a copy. Kant employed the translation when writing his own treatises. Lessing called Moses the greatest Jew since Baruch (later, Benedict) Spinoza – 1632-77. He was hailed as 'the German Plato', 'the modern Socrates' and 'the third Moses', the other two being no less a person than the Old Testament lawgiver and the 12th-century Moses Maimonides, respectively.

A further epithet was conferred upon him – 'the Luther of the German Jews' – for his translation of the Scriptures. In 1768, when his Christian friend Thomas Abbt asked what would become of the Jews, Mendelssohn replied that, though they had no homeland, they still had civil rights and had to observe their traditional form of worship. The King had asked him to translate the Judaic Code of Laws into German, and this, for many years, became a model for Prussian legislation. He had campaigned for many reforms on behalf of the Jews to be put into effect. In order, however, that Jews could adhere to their creed in their new language, the Word of God had to be translated, like Plato, into German – their current mother tongue.

Though known as 'the Mendelssohn Bible', purists will say that this title is incorrect, admonishing that Christian friends, including Lessing, assisted Moses with research and translation; nevertheless, without Mendelssohn's initiative, it is doubtful if the project would have been completed. He translated the first five books of the Old Testament (the Pentateuch: Genesis, Exodus, Leviticus, Numbers and Deuteronomy), the Song of Solomon – discovered later – and the Psalms. Rather than these latter being surrounded with "mystical interpretation", Moses declared, psalms were nothing more than Hebrew poems, to be read, recited or sung to express a particular state of mind or to recognise a particular event or experience. Marek calls them "magnificent prose-poems, written from a full heart and a noble soul".

As with his translation of Plato, Mendelssohn's translations of the Holy Scriptures were straightforward enough for anyone to understand. Though they were originally meant for his own children, he soon realised that adults, who found the often abstruse message confusing, could benefit from this simplified interpretation of God's word. Moses conceived the idea of having the German characters printed alongside the original Hebrew. By this means, newly emancipated Jews would familiarise themselves with their new mother tongue, but Christians, too, would gain a different perspective from the often confused annotations of conventional theology. In England, Jew and Christian rated the work highly. Isaac Levy, Hebrew tutor to H. R. H. the Duke of Sussex, brother of William IV and uncle to the future Queen Victoria, remarked to the Horsley family, when showing his guests a Bible translated by Luther, that, in his view, Mendelssohn's translation was superior in linguistic style to that of Luther. At the time (1833), Levy was informed, both a son and grandson of the first Mendelssohn happened to be in London, whereupon Levy stated that he had heard of Felix as "a good musician". From a Christian standpoint, Mendelssohn's translation was regarded as highly as that of John Wycliffe of the 14th century, and the work was as popular in France and the Netherlands.

King Christian VII of Denmark was the first to subscribe to it from abroad. As for the refreshingly straightforward German in which Mendelssohn wrote, Franz Schubert used this version of Psalm 23 to set to his exquisite music. But, despite this new enlightenment, not everyone relished the "profane language" that Mendelssohn had used when elucidating the Scriptures. The rabbis of Altona, Posen and Prague ordered that "the German Pentateuch of Moses Dessau", as they called it, be suppressed. In Fürst, excommunication from the synagogue was threatened to anyone studying the Scriptures in such a "dangerous" language as German. In Pressburg, the highly respected Rabbi Raphael Cohen devised a series of punishments for anyone similarly occupied, and it was only the aforementioned King of Denmark that prevented such outrages from being put into action.

From the 1770s, various movements took shape to foster human understanding and freedom for the individual, the best known culminating in the anti-slavery legislation of 1833. Therefore, in view of the climate of opinion, it is not surprising to observe the greater co-operation between Jew and Christian. To this end Daniel Itzig, whose family would, in the future, inter-marry with that of Mendelssohn, played a vital part in this movement. In 1783 Mendelssohn published an essay *Jerusalem or the religious Force of Judea*, which inspired both Lavater and Kant, the

Prologue: Part I

latter so much so that, according to Marek, he was almost persuaded to become a Jew. A state or nation had no right, the pamphlet declared, to interfere in an individual's religious belief. Judaism, it proposed, was "revealed legislation" rather than a religious faith. Any creed that proclaimed one god was simply an interpretation, couched in a specific way, of the eternal truth.

For the last seven years of his life Moses suffered various attacks of dizziness, headache and general weakness. From childhood his body had been overtaxed so severely that he became physically and mentally exhausted by the time he reached his fifties. He was prescribed various 'cures' at the spa of Pyrmont and his physician ordered him complete rest – not even to read or to think. When asked afterwards what he did when there was no stimulus allowed him, he replied – perhaps in jest, but perhaps not – that he counted the tiles on the roof opposite his room. As his health worsened, and it was realised that not even the 'cure-all' properties of the spa could benefit him, Moses delegated his campaigns and pamphlet writing to young Christian colleagues, prominent among whom was Christian Döme. As European rulers, notably Joseph II of Austria, were becoming aware of the new enlightenment of Mendelssohn and his successors, the unreasonable laws against Jews were waived. Amid a spate of pamphlets on the debate between rationalism and religion, Moses wrote his book *Jerusalem, Europe and Mount Zion*, which, once and for all, explained the Judaic mode of thought. The law of the land should govern political, economic and social life; personal and spiritual life should be guided by the Holy Scriptures, he explained. This work was praised by orthodox Jews, for its adherence to traditional ritual and observance, but also by secular thinkers for its advocation of free thought.

In 1785 he wrote his final book, *Morning Hours*, in order to defend the (by then) deceased Lessing, accused by the theologian Friedrich Jacobi of having adopted the beliefs of Spinoza, who was deemed to be an atheist. Goethe and Herder were drawn into what was to become known as 'the battle of Pantheism', where the best aspects of each religious faith are adopted. In his pamphlet *To the Friends of Lessing*, Moses pointed out that, whilst Lessing had admired Spinoza, he had never become his disciple. He wrote to the deceased dramatist's brother: "He was a man who educated my soul; who acted as friend and judge in all my actions and for every line I penned." Lessing would be beside Moses in spirit, whatever he undertook in the future, just as he had been in the past.

The pamphlet was ready for delivery to Voss, the printer, on 31st December of that year. However, because it was the Sabbath, Moses postponed the errand until the following day. On returning home, he complained of a chill, caught from the atrocious weather, at the same time mentioning pains in the chest. The physician, Dr. Herz, reassured the family that there was no cause for concern, but on 3rd January 16-year-old Joseph, the eldest son, was despatched to fetch the doctor again, as his father's condition had worsened. Moses had slumped from his previous sitting posture and was now lying on the sofa, his loved ones around him and a bust of Socrates above his head. Though Herz tried to revive his patient, "…breath, pulse and life were gone…as if an angel had kissed his life away… The lamp went out for lack of oil… None but a man with his wisdom, power and self-control, moderation and inner peace could, with such a constitution, have kept the flame alight for fifty-seven years," Herz wrote.

The post-mortem cited 'apoplexy' due to 'weakness' as the cause of death; the death certificate also revealed 'cerebral apoplexy', known nowadays as 'a stroke'. It may be, however, that Dr. John O'Shea is correct in his assumption that it was a 'berry aneurysm' that caused the deaths of several of the Mendelssohn descendants, as well as the originator of the name. Joseph, as eldest son, cared for his widowed mother and was responsible also for collating his father's works. He wrote in the preface that "the enlightened spirit" of Moses could "still look upon his children and reflect that all had enough material wealth and lived an honourable life". The eldest daughter, Dorothea, wrote of their father: "Kind and mild in his wisdom…listened attentively; loved a joke, but his humour was never biting." The status of 'protected Jew' had been conferred on Moses Mendelssohn, which, at his death, was extended to his widow and children, "because of the well-known merits of your husband and father". Though such a privilege was usually conferred upon a Jew on account of financial success, this exception demonstrates how whole-heartedly the intellect of Moses Mendelssohn was valued.

On the day of his funeral, Moses was held in such deep respect among the Jews that all the shops were closed in the Jewish quarters of various cities, and no work was done; this honour was normally awarded only when a chief rabbi was buried. A huge procession followed the coffin to the Jewish Cemetery; a simple message was written in Hebrew on a stone: "Here rests Rabbi Moses of Dessau." Outside the Jewish Free School, begun in 1781, a marble tablet bore the legend: "Wise as Socrates; true to the faith of his forefathers, teaching, like him, immortality and becoming, like him, immortal." After his death, there had been discussion as to whether or not a statue of Moses should be erected in Berlin, alongside that of the philosopher Leibniz. However, in view of the vandalism perpetrated upon the statue of his grandson, Felix, in Leipzig, when the National Socialists came to power, it is as well that this did not occur in the first Mendelssohn's case.

Tributes poured in to the surviving family from most European countries, irrespective of whether the people who paid them were Jew or Christian. Jewish free schools were founded in other European communities, but that begun by Moses Mendelssohn was the forerunner. A magazine, *The Gleaner*, was begun by the writer and translator Wessely, in which issues of assimilation and the acquisition of Western culture for Jews were discussed. Though only 12 editions were published, the magazine prompted the publication of several similar periodicals. Disciples of Mendelssohn's teaching spread his philosophy throughout the German states, as well as Poland and Russia. In 1845 an article in *The Athenaeum* magazine proposed that the Mendelssohns' home in Spandauerstrasse

(Spandau Street), Berlin, should be purchased to convert it into a further school for children of poor Jewish families, but nothing more is known of the plan.

It is interesting to note that, like his father, Abraham Mendelssohn died whilst defending Lessing. In the latter instance, a dispute had arisen between Abraham and the diplomat Varnhagen von Ense, who had compared Lessing unfavourably with his literary contemporaries. Abraham, hurt at the diplomat's anger, which caused him to leave the house in undiplomatic haste, began to compose a letter explaining his views on his father's lifelong friend, and his work, but it was only after Abraham's death that his elder daughter Fanny discovered the fragment.

Part II: The Second Generation

When Moses was 33 years old he confided to Lessing how "out of sorts" he felt. The Feast of the Passover is one of the most joyous of Jewish festivals, but above all it is a family time, which accounts for his mood. Moses yearned for a family of his own. His wish was granted after his marriage to Fromet Gugenheim, and, as Kupferberg states, their house in Spandau Street, Berlin, "was always noisy with children and the tutors engaged to instruct them", as well as his own disciples, who assisted in propagating his aim for understanding between Christian and Jew, and spreading the messages from his writing. Though Marek claims Moses and Fromet had nine children, some sources – unspecified – say ten, whereas records of only eight have been discovered. Fromet gave birth to a little girl who lived till 11 months. As Moses wrote to Thomas Abbt: "Death has knocked at my door and robbed me of a child... But God be praised. Her short life was happy and full of bright promise. From a little animal who wept and slept, she grew into the bud of a reasoning creature... She showed pity, hatred, love and admiration. She understood the language of those who spoke, and endeavoured to make her thoughts known to them. You will...see in this talk the weakness of a man who, seeking comfort, finds none, save in his imagination." A boy was also born, who lived to the age of 12, but, otherwise, the other six children survived to adulthood, and the elder two – Dorothea and Joseph – reached old age. When Moses died in 1786, his brood spanned 17 years, from 22 to five years of age. In order of seniority, their names were Brendel (who renamed herself Dorothea), Joseph, Abraham, Sorel (renamed Henriette), Recha and Nathan.

Whilst Fromet and two servants saw to the children's day-to-day welfare, their education was taken in hand by Moses himself, plus tutors when required. The two elder children were given extra instruction on philosophy and religious teaching between the hour at dawn when Moses awoke and prayed, and the time he left for his office at Bernhard's premises. Though Dorothea is said to have been 'emancipated' and a free spirit, she dutifully accepted her father's only 'blind spot' in his otherwise enlightened manner of thinking. He steadfastly believed that his daughters' marriages had to be arranged and, thus, Dorothea was married at 17, in April 1781, to a young Berlin banker, Simon Veit. They had four children, two of whom, Johannes and Philipp Veit, made their name as artists of the so-called Nazarene School of painting, whose members specialised in religious subjects. But, however exemplary Simon Veit was as a breadwinner and businessman, he lacked excitement for Dorothea.

Meanwhile, along with her friends Henriette Herz and Rahel Varnhagen von Ense (as they became), Dorothea set up a salon where intellectuals – men and women, Jews and Christians – met to discuss philosophy, religion, but especially literature, and played language word games. She met Friedrich Schlegel, brother of Wilhelm (who was to translate Shakespeare's plays into German), at a soirée given by Henriette Herz. Having been a respectable married woman for 15 years, Dorothea left her husband, setting up home with Schlegel and later marrying him. This was one of the greatest scandals of the early 19th century and, because of this, the couple moved to Jena, where Schlegel took up a lecturing post at the university. Though the 25-year-old Schlegel had made attempts at conquests of women, Dorothea, described as "mannish" and having "big feet", became the love of his life – if such an impecunious, self-centred individual could be said to have loved anyone except himself. Though Henriette Herz noted Dorothea's unprepossessing physical appearance, she realised the hidden depths of "her eyes, through which, it is true, there shone the light of her lovable soul and her sparkling mind". Of the three Mendelssohn daughters, it was said how Henriette was the most beautiful; Recha the most intellectual; Dorothea the most romantic.

Schlegel then wrote a novel, *Lucinde*, in which he described his romance with Dorothea in what Kupferberg calls "terms that were rather too explicit for those times". Julius, as Schlegel called himself, "exchanges roles with Lucinde" while making love, "so that she played the masculine aggressor while he adopted a pose of feminine passivity", demonstrating Schlegel's idea of equality for the sexes. Evidently, Veit must have realised that the sexual aspect of his marriage to Dorothea was not to her liking, because he allowed her to have custody of their two surviving sons and supported them as well as Dorothea.

Lucinde has been described as "a jumbled-up succession of letters, dialogues, allegories and confessions with an erotic touch here and there". Readers were offended and confused. Some were particularly outraged by his ideas of equality of the sexes. Dorothea, too, entered the literary arena, with her novel *Florentin*, but allowed her husband to claim its editorship. Just how emancipated was this Mendelssohn daughter? As with Schlegel, Dorothea idealised Friedrich, portraying him as a romantic hero, searching throughout the world for his long-lost parents, "tasting all the delights of the senses, worshipping beauty wherever he found it", but eventually settling with a woman very similar to Dorothea herself. Although only one of the two volumes that Dorothea planned to write was published, anyone who read the novel considered it far better constructed than *Lucinde*.

Dorothea continued to write, but, whatever she produced, her husband was given the credit. She wrote of herself as serving her spouse "in all humility, as his handmaiden". Among her works were a retelling of Joan of Arc's story, "from French sources"; a biography of Marguerite de Valois; and a translation of Mme. de Staël's *Corinna*, for which Schlegel was praised for "his" erudition and skill in translation. When Dorothea contributed articles to the literary journals edited by the brothers Schlegel – and she wrote many – the letter 'D' was her only signature, whose identity readers appeared not to guess. The only cloud for Dorothea in Jena was Wilhelm's wife Caroline's dislike of this "sister-in-law". Was she jealous on account of Dorothea's authorship, or was she antipathetic to her being a Jew? Whether because of Caroline's antagonism or for some other reason, unexplained, Dorothea and Schlegel moved, in 1804, to Paris, where they married. Dorothea read the Bible, studying the Old and New Testaments, and wrote to the theologian Schleiermacher how she preferred the latter, considering the message to synchronise with the Protestant religion – it was Luther's, not Moses Mendelssohn's, translation she studied. Thus, Dorothea ("née Mendelssohn and runaway Veit", as the poet Heinrich Heine called her) became a Christian and was officially allowed to call herself by her baptismal name, rather than the obsolete Brendel. The salon over which Dorothea presided was considered even more brilliant than that of Mme. de Staël. When Henriette came to Paris and attended her sister's gatherings, it was said that "more feminine wisdom" exuded from the two daughters of Moses Mendelssohn than from any other women in that circle.

Not only did Dorothea copy her husband's writings, translate his Hindu and Sanskrit studies, keep up to date with the new books, plays and music, run her salons and write articles herself, but she also occupied herself with domestic duties, including knitting stockings and making clothes.

In 1808, tempted by the mysticism and ritual, Dorothea became a Roman Catholic and, persuading her husband to do likewise, they were married in Cologne in the new faith. Thence to Vienna, where Schlegel obtained a minor post at the imperial court. He was no longer the romantic hero, but had become a "sulky, petulant, impoverished husband". Money had dwindled. When Henriette Herz visited the Schlegels in 1811, Dorothea, who had a cold, lay shivering under bedclothes, whilst her husband drank from a carafe of wine and ate oranges as the two women talked. A similar scenario was reported by Franz Grillparzer, dramatist and friend of Beethoven and Schubert, who called on Dorothea in Rome, where she was visiting her two sons. He found the couple in the company of a priest. Whilst Dorothea was listening to his reading, Schlegel indulged himself with food and wine.

Following her husband's death, Dorothea was able to live on a small government pension from his former post in Vienna, supplemented by Philipp's earnings as a painter. Though admitting to being "old, weary and ill", her lively spirit was to remain, as witness her correspondence with Henriette Herz, in a similar circumstance to Dorothea. "We must put up with it, as the plants and flowers do," she wrote, "which…go on blooming as if it were the greatest pleasure." Dorothea died on 3rd August 1839, her latter days occupied solely in sewing and knitting: "There are too many books in the world, but I have never heard that there are too many shirts."

Joseph, 16 when his father died, was particularly close to Moses. It was he who had to fetch the doctor in his father's last illness and it was he who was tutored, with Dorothea and other young people, in the 'morning hour' lectures, and he was the only son to undertake the bar mitzvah when his father was alive. Though Moses wondered how he would make his way in the world, being too stubborn and "not gentle" (as he confided to one of the tutors), Joseph worked ably and applied himself to grasping whatever opportunity presented itself. Moses was afraid his son's bluntness and obstinacy would hold him back "unless the love of some good woman may induce him to control himself". Moses feared that, like himself, he would be "half merchant, half scholar", but "neither one nor the other", when Joseph gave up his Hebrew studies at the age of 14. However, Joseph built up the banking concern, Mendelssohn & Company, which remained in existence until 1939. The "good woman" he married was Henrietta Meyer, who bore him two sons, Alexander and Benjamin. Joseph, unlike others in his family, remained a Jew till the end, as did his son Alexander.

Joseph wrote a small book on banking that became celebrated in business circles, but his most important work was a definitive edition of his father's writings, prefaced by a concise biography and memoir (1843). In 1792 he had formed, with other young associates, an organisation, the Society of Friends, not to be confused with the more famous accurate name for the Quakers. Joseph's organisation existed to make social contacts and to provide succour in time of need for its members, as well as to promote culture and enlightenment. Their motto derived from a saying of Moses: "To seek truth; to love the beautiful; to desire good; to do the best." This benevolent society spread to Bremen, Breslau and Vienna, continuing for many years. Interested in science, Joseph helped his friend Alexander Humboldt, by then a famous naturalist. Humboldt's landlord wished to evict him and sell his house. This would mean that Alexander's fine collection of specimens would be discarded, but Joseph bought the house, so nothing was lost. Joseph attended lectures and read all he could on scientific subjects at the Berlin Polytechnic. He also conducted his own experiments and, a few days before he died at the age of 78, he was found reading a new book on algebra.

Abraham was working in Paris for a banker named Fould when Leah Salomon met him. A friend of Henriette, his sister said Abraham would never meet anyone of Leah's standard so, though he had intended to remain in Paris, the couple settled in Hamburg, where he joined Joseph's banking enterprise, running the 'sister' company. Later, Leah was to say that, though Abraham was earning a modest salary when they met, "I knew he would be able to turn my dowry to good account. My mother's ambition would not, however, allow me to be the wife of a clerk and Mendelssohn, therefore, had to enter into partnership with his brother. From which period, thank God, dates the prosperity of both." Leah was pleasant-looking when young, but, according to Marek, was "shapeless" in later years – possibly because of her style of dress. Abraham was 28, Leah 27, when they married in 1804. Like her husband, Leah was artistic, visiting art galleries, concert halls and exhibitions. She spoke English, French and Italian and had a 'nodding acquaintance' with Greek, reading Homer "in secret". She was, to Kupferberg, an "expert pianist and a good singer".

About Recha, very little information is extant. Like Dorothea, she was married off to a banker, Mendel Meyer, with whom she was unhappy. The marriage was eventually dissolved, but Recha, unlike her two sisters, never converted to Christianity. Constantly in poor health, she nevertheless founded a girls' boarding school in Altona, a town under Danish sovereignty, with a large Jewish population, adjacent to Hamburg. One of her staff was her sister Henriette, until she went to Paris to become the governess of Fanny Sebastiani, daughter of one of Napoleon's generals, who married the Duc de Praslin et Choiseul. Recha was regarded as bright and clever. Her best friend, Rachel Levin (later Mme. Varnhagen von Ense), saw Henriette as the deepest and most thoughtful of the sisters. Kupferberg spoke of her as "shying away from men", apart from what they could give intellectually. In 1799, when taking up a teaching post in Vienna, she met Bernhard Eskeles, head of a large finance house, who wished to marry her, but, though no further details are available, she refused this future Austrian baron.

Abraham, who had an apartment in Fould's mansion in the Rue Richer, invited Henriette to the house, where, renting an apartment, she kept house for her brother. It was she who introduced her brother to Leah, who, when Abraham paid a visit home, accompanied him to Hamburg, where Fromet had moved after the death of Moses.

Because there were so many wealthy people in Paris, Henriette conceived the idea of opening a school for their daughters, with which Fould agreed, allowing her to take part of his mansion for this purpose. A daughter of Moses Mendelssohn, and a German to boot, proved a suitable instructress for the parents' daughters. Henriette was fluent in English and French language and literature, as well as those of her mother tongue. Her salons were brilliant; visitors included Mme. de Staël (when not exiled to Switzerland), Benjamin Constant, the philosopher, and Spontini, whose opera *La Vestale* had made such a success.

Like Napoleon, General Horace Sebastiani was a Corsican, and he had prospered under his employer. Thus, in 1817, when his only daughter Fanny was five years old, he asked Henriette to give up her school and become her governess whilst her maternal grandmother took care of her welfare, her mother having died of a fever in Constantinople accompanying her husband on a diplomatic mission after Fanny's birth. Henriette, once his daughter married, would be handsomely provided for. Meanwhile, she would be resident at his mansion. It was the general and his mother who were responsible for Henriette becoming a Catholic, preferring their charge to have such a background. Henriette realised, too, that this would be for the best. The last barrier to conversion was removed in 1812 when Fromet passed away, but, though Henriette still had inner doubts, she became a more ardent Catholic than those who had been given the faith at birth. She even expressed in her will how she regretted not converting the whole family.

Though at first she said of Fanny: "I have not seen a child so beautiful and with more promising gifts of heart and mind," she later wrote to Abraham that, though Fanny was becoming more beautiful each day, she was not keeping pace with knowledge. Still later, she wrote, "Altogether, the only excellence in the girl is in her beauty and her amiability in heart and manners, but she is entirely without talent and inclination for learning. She has a good voice but, God knows, she sings by the sweat of my brow, for she is clearly unmusical." Her governess even presaged "some kind of disaster", once her charge had entered Parisian society: "I see it coming on like a mighty avalanche, which must destroy in one moment what I have planted and tended with such care." She was murdered by her husband, the Duc de Praslin, because of her inordinate obsession and jealousy. (For full details, see Rachel Field's book *All This And Heaven Too*, written by a niece of Mlle. Deluzy-Desportes, governess to the Praslin children in the 1840s.) There were ten suitors who sought Fanny Sebastiani's hand in marriage, with her "voluptuous figure, a complaisant temperament and an empty head – all eminent qualifications for marriage to an eligible young French nobleman". The discussion of dowry and property settlements grieved Henriette. "How such an affair (as a marriage) is transacted in great French families, God has mercifully spared you from knowing," she wrote to Abraham. In 1825 Abraham fetched his sister home, where she remained with Leah and himself until she died six years later, in 1831, at the age of 56.

Nathan, the youngest child of Fromet and Moses, must have been highly intelligent since, even when he was very little, he strutted about the house calling himself 'Nathan the Wise', after Lessing's eponymous drama. He seems, as far as the pragmatic world is concerned, to have enjoyed the most productive life. From boyhood he was interested in physics and mechanics, and he travelled to England and France to further his studies. Having become an engineer, he helped to found the Polytechnic Society in Berlin, lecturing on the 'new' science disciplines of photography and telegraphy. He invented scientific instruments, manufacturing them commercially through a grant, organised by Alexander Humboldt, from the Prussian government. Indeed, the only project that appears to have proved abortive in Nathan's life was the publication of a scientific journal, only a few copies of which ever saw the light of day.

Converting to Christianity at the age of 40 in 1823, he lived for some years in Silesia (now part of Poland), where he built factories to manufacture machinery. Nathan married Henrietta Itzig, not only related to Leah Salomon but to the poet Heine's family and to the Rothschilds. Nathan died in 1852, aged 69.

Yet, however rewarding study of the first two Mendelssohn generations proves, it is Abraham's family with which this book is concerned. Leah Mendelssohn gave birth to four children – Fanny, Rebecka, Paul and Felix – and it is the latter about whom *The Caged Spirit* is written. However great a part his forebears played, it can be stated without dispute that, had it not been for Felix Mendelssohn, little about his ancestors would be known today. Despite the insults Felix was to bear, both to his music and to the man himself, his name still shines like a beacon throughout the world.

BOOK ONE

Boy and Man

Chapter 1

"Loving and Giving"

When the Mendelssohn parents married, Abraham was 28 and Leah 27. Though it is known that the Hamburg branch of Mendelssohn Brothers & Company was founded on 1st January 1805, ten years later than its original Berlin 'parent' bank, no mention is made as to where the young couple lived for the first few weeks of marriage. They may well have set up home with Joseph and his family, for they evidently lived in one room as a beginning to their married life. Rather than writing of the future the couple hoped to build together, or their love and affection for each other, Leah writes to one of her sisters (unspecified) that their domestic arrangements are "disorganised like those of a student", with no privacy or "Berlin comfort". Leah cannot believe herself to be married, since "such status is usually accompanied by pots and pans, candelabra, mirrors and mahogany furniture". Her only comfort is the thought of Martha, her maid, "with the melodious rattle of her keys". The fact that the couple live in Hamburg – an independent city with its own government, and the second busiest port in Europe after London, capable of fulfilling so much ambition and affluence – appears irrelevant. Leah is not even thrilled by the beautiful dresses her husband has sent her from Paris, describing trying them on as "indulging myself" with these "tumultuous gowns". One is "the most wonderful, the richest, the shiniest, silk-soft robe of artfully woven Peking velvet" (colour not given); the second is "a fashionable shade of pink, interlaced with delicate white, divinely trimmed and beautifully tailored". No gratitude is given for these gowns, which must have been chosen with such care and thoughtfulness; all we hear from Leah is that "Mendelssohn was all enthusiasm; but I said such subtle and magic colours were only suitable for a reception at the court of Napoleon" and to be worn by "a young Hebe" (goddess of youth in Greek mythology). Leah did not appear to accept that this is how Abraham perceived his new bride. Also, the way Leah refers to her bridegroom elicits a jarring note; there is no mention of an endearment or 'pet' name, nor even simply "my husband" – just the cold, impersonal "Mendelssohn", as if a male business colleague is writing about him.

Nevertheless, Leah and Abraham would soon be looking at a house in the country, which they were able to buy. It had a balcony and its surroundings are "supposedly very pretty", situated beside the river Elbe near Mühlheim. All that appears to interest Leah at this point, however, is that there will be enough space for the household goods to be stored. She speaks of giving a dinner the next evening, the food to be sent in from a French restaurant to "these four little walls".

The house to which the Mendelssohns moved was No. 14 Grosse Michaelisstrasse, Hamburg. Here, three of the four children were born: Fanny Cäcilie on 14th November 1805; Jakob Ludwig Felix – invariably known by the latter name, which he used himself – on 3rd February 1809; and Rebecka on 11th April 1811. (Paul was born at Martin's Mill, Berlin, on 30th October 1812, whence the family had moved earlier that year.) Meanwhile, the Bank of Mendelssohn Brothers & Company was thriving in the independent-spirited community of Hamburg, where money was always needed to assist the flourishing commercial and industrial enterprises here and in other 'free' cities in Germany and around the Baltic. A network of branches was established in all the important cities of Europe, and even in New York. The bank's symbol was a crane, perched on a globe, with the words "I watch". Marek claims that it was Abraham himself who designed what would today be called this 'logo'. To Germans, the crane was said to bring good fortune, but opportunity played a crucial part. Apart from the 'respectable' concerns of business, the greatest wealth accrued from smuggling, seen as an economic necessity if Napoleon's 'Continental System' was to be flouted. This device was invented by Bonaparte to starve Britain into submission, by blocking the Continental ports he had conquered. Goods were stockpiled in warehouses on the various docksides, until spirited away by the German citizens whose territories had not yet fallen to Napoleon. This nefarious enterprise was, indeed, seen as nothing less than a patriotic duty. When, therefore, in 1812, Hamburg was annexed, the Mendelssohn Bank continued to help the smuggling confederacy. Abraham and his family fled to Berlin, disguised as indigent refugees, having hidden their wealth and arranged for a carriage to convey them safely to their new home.

The house to which they moved was still known as 'Martin's Mill' because, quite simply, its previous owner was named Martin and the premises were employed as a mill. Later, Abraham was to write that he "sometimes blessed Martin's Mill", in view of the way the children had developed. Meanwhile, Mendelssohn was able to equip a troop of volunteers to fight what was regarded as a war for liberty and, in 1813, he was made a Privy Councillor for this action. Neither could anything halt the progress of the bank. In 1812, Mendelssohn Brothers & Company was one of the richest finance houses in Berlin; in 1813, one of the top three in wealth and power. In 1816, Joseph and Abraham were invited by the Prussian government to negotiate the indemnity for reparations with Paris after Napoleon's defeat. This inspired rulers farther afield to seek advice and

Chapter 1: "Loving and Giving"

assistance with transactions, culminating in having the title 'Bankers to the Tsar of All the Russias' conferred upon the bank.

Four children were born to Leah and Abraham. Adolf Bernhard Marx, a former friend of the Mendelssohn children, wrote of Leah as "highly intelligent but, perhaps, a less feeling mother" than is usual. She was decidedly reserved and many guests must have found her very difficult to get to know. Though she sketched beautifully, only her most intimate friends were allowed to see the results of her work; she read Homer "in secret", perhaps fearing the scorn this might have prompted when essaying such 'masculine' literature. The more deeply this complex character is studied, the greater is the realisation that she lacked self-confidence, despite outward appearances to the contrary. This is borne out by her continual obsession with 'social climbing' – even her husband teasing her about the "aristocratic" notions she maintained. She envied her brother Jakob, who had latterly adopted the name 'Bartholdy' – the name of the former owner of the property he had purchased. It was he who, not satisfied with bullying Abraham into having the children baptised as Christians (which example the parents followed later), also compelled the family, by wily logic, to adopt the name of Bartholdy. It will be seen throughout this book what an unhealthy influence this apparently great diplomat and patron of the arts, but, truly, a nonentity, was to exert over this branch of the Mendelssohn family.

Of Fanny, the eldest child, her son, Sebastian Hensel writes that her eyes, "very dark and expressive", were her most attractive feature, but did not betray her short-sightedness. Her nose and mouth were "rather large", but she had "fine, white teeth". Her hands were those of "an excellent pianist", her movements "quick and decisive", and "her face full of life, expressing every change of emotion". She never could disguise her feelings and everyone she met soon discovered what she thought of them. Her forehead and the corners of her mouth showed wrinkles if there was someone she disliked. She delighted in meeting a true friend, but "her disgust at anything ugly, and her anger at anything she considered inferior, were intense; she could not bear dull, insipid, vain or shallow people". Indeed, her face would adopt such an expression of distress that her friends were amused. She did not relish luxuries, such as lavish food and drink, or fashionable dresses or ornamentation; all she desired were a few close friends as intelligent as herself. Fanny did, though, take sufficient pride in her appearance to disguise the malformation of her left shoulder – slightly higher than the right – by her choice of dress. Though not beautiful, "men found her looks interesting", George R. Marek claims.

Whereas this may well be correct, a further observation he makes is definitely not; he claims Fanny had "little sense of humour", but this statement implies more about Marek's distinct lack of perception than about Fanny Mendelssohn. She had a very dry wit, reminiscent of Jane Austen's novels and letters. Marek also blames Fanny's near-sightedness on the painstaking way in which she copied music "for Felix", forgetting that this task was her choice. At her birth, Leah remarked on her daughter's "Bach fugue fingers", so obsessed was she with the works of that composer. Such an observation must be attributed to the wishful thinking of a proud mother, for the hands of Johann Sebastian Bach are said to have been able to span an octave and a half.

According to Kupferberg, Rebecka was "a spritely, pretty girl, with a good singing voice". This latter characteristic is unjustly understated. Rebecka herself admitted – possibly in jest, but certainly with truth – that, had she belonged to any other family than that in which Fanny and Felix took pride of place, she could have had equal lustre in musical circles, since she was also an accomplished pianist. Rebecka was also adept at foreign languages, even learning Greek for a time, at Felix's insistence. She had many admirers, including the poet and dramatist Heinrich Heine, who visited the Mendelssohn home for the sole reason that Rebecka was there, as he claimed. From Heligoland, he wrote to the family, greeting the various members; to Rebecka, calling her "this plump little person; the dear child, so pretty, so good, every pound of her". Marek, who appears incapable of doing anything but making barbed comments about the Mendelssohn family, states that, whilst the others read "good literature", Rebecka amused herself with "fashion periodicals" and "enjoyed pampering". Certainly, she always kept up to date with fashion and was always beautifully groomed. Of Paul's looks nothing is said, but, because a daguerreotype of him exists, which is often mistaken for his elder brother, it can be deduced that his appearance resembled that of Felix. As for his character, he was the practical businessman, taking over the financial affairs of the house when his father died, and also overseeing Felix's business affairs – whether or not to the composer's advantage can be assessed in the chapters to come. Paul was a proficient 'cellist, sufficiently skilled for Felix to compose his Op. 45 'Cello Sonata and a set of variations for his brother to perform.

And so to Felix, the actual subject of this book. J. Cuthbert Hadden, in a chapter on Mendelssohn, written in the centenary year of his birth, describes him as "one of the most lovable of men, gentle as his music", his mind "pure as a mountain stream". Julius (later Sir Julius) Benedict called him "a miracle of nature". But it is Stratton who prompts the choice of title for this chapter. He gives no verification for his information, but claims that Felix was born on a Friday; it therefore seems appropriate to take the words from the old nursery rhyme, 'Friday's child is loving and giving' – which is undoubtedly true of Felix Mendelssohn. On the other hand, on calculation via an 1809 calendar, the conclusion is reached that he was born on a Saturday, whose child 'works hard for a living' –equally true of Mendelssohn.

The profile of Felix is out of sequence, which, like that of Abraham in the last chapter, is deliberate. Before the subject of this biography is described, a word seems appropriate here about the name he was given and which he preferred to 'Jakob' or 'Ludwig'. Whilst this book was in progress, the question was asked: "how is Felix the Cat getting on?" Otto Mesmer, who invented the cartoon character in

Chapter 1: "Loving and Giving"

1923, appears to have become confused; whether accidentally or by design is uncertain. The Latin word for cat is 'feles', from which the word 'feline' (cat-like) is derived. The boy's name 'Felix' means, in Latin, 'happy; fortunate; prosperous (in spirit)', and the female equivalents are 'Felicity' and 'Felicia'.

Unlike the other Mendelssohn children, far greater information exists about Felix's looks and personality. His first biographer, W. A. Lampadius, describes him as "A man of small frame, delicate and fragile-looking, yet possessing a sinewy elasticity and a power of endurance that one could hardly suppose possible. His head appeared to have been set upon the wrong shoulders..." His gait was "somewhat loose and shambling; he had a flinging [sic] motion of the limbs and a supple-jointedness, coupled with other little peculiarities of carriage (unspecified), that determined him, according to popular German tradition, as of Oriental origin. Yet his listlessness of bearing seemed to disappear entirely the moment he sat down to a pianoforte or organ." Eduard Devrient described him as of middle height, though Dr. John O'Shea defines him as measuring 162 centimetres (five feet four inches). His frame, though slender, possessed "muscular power". He was unusually sensitive, becoming excited into a frenzy when his imagination was stimulated, but restored to his "rational" mind by an "almost death-like" sleep. Whereas Devrient wrote of Mendelssohn's "pretty brown curls" as a boy, the music critic Johann Christian Lobe recalled "wavy black locks" hanging down his back. Like many who have written recollections of Mendelssohn, he describes him as "Jewish-looking". O'Shea in his book on the illnesses of the great composers tells his readers of Mendelssohn's "strikingly regular features" and "a graceful figure". In his childhood, an unnamed "distinguished teacher" as H. E. Jacob calls him, was summoned to the Mendelssohn home in an endeavour to correct the stutter manifest in Felix's speech. Leah may not have known, but Abraham must have remembered, that his own father experienced the same impediment. He might have felt ashamed that, with all the many ways in which his elder son had to strive for perfection under his guidance, nothing could be done to conquer heredity. Nevertheless, Mendelssohn still spoke throughout his life with a slight lisp; H. F. Chorley, music critic of *The Athenaeum* from 1833, remembered "this slight cloud (not to call it a thickness) caused his voice to sound like that of a friend".

It may be of interest to assess how Felix was remembered at different periods of his life. In 1822, on his return from a holiday in Switzerland, Fanny observed that Felix had become taller and stronger and that his expression and facial features had matured. This may be accounted for by the fact that his hair had been cropped; at 13, even his doting parents must have realised he was no longer a child. "Yet he is as good-looking as ever," his sister adds. A few years later, in 1829, whilst on his first visit to Great Britain, Felix was invited to stay with the Taylor family in Wales. Anne, eldest of the three daughters, submitted a memoir for the section on Mendelssohn in the first edition of *Grove's Dictionary of Music and Musicians*: "Slight of build; in figure, lithe and very light and mercurial. His look was dark and very Jewish; his face, unusually mobile and ever varying in expression; full of brightness and animation and with a most unmistakable look of genius."

Three years later, during Mendelssohn's second visit to Britain in 1832, Charles Edward Horsley, whose family became lifelong friends, wrote his own recollection: "It was a matter of wonderment [as to] how so small a body could contain so many ideas…each arranged in the most perfect and symmetrical order." Horsley recalled "his geniality; his great kindness in displaying such extraordinary gifts – both in music and in general accomplishments – the very life and soul of the entertainments" given by the Horsley family. Horsley tells of Mendelssohn's "large-mindedness towards anyone with whom he came into contact; his home and table were open to all who knew him; his advice and purse were at the disposal of all who required them" – which may, perhaps, have been far too 'open', causing many to take full advantage of his unworldliness.

At the time of his marriage in 1837, Felix is described as having hair receding from his high forehead, though what remained was still "curly and dark, with side-whiskers running past the angle of his jaw"; he had "deep, dark eyes in an olive-skinned face". As for his character, Jean Petitpierre, a descendant of Mendelssohn's wife Cécile Jeanrenaud, writes of Felix's inclination to laughter among those he loved and with whom he felt most at home. Felix "would literally twist up and wave his arms in a characteristic gesture, emphasising his expression of uncontrolled gaiety". His mirth was staunched in more formal circles by stuffing a handkerchief into his mouth. This was imitated in a tableau at a country fête to celebrate his music. When translating Mendelssohn's letter referring to this entertainment, Lady Wallace merely makes a footnote – "a habit of Mendelssohn" – giving no explanation. On this occasion, Felix would naturally not have wished to cause offence by his laughing at the efforts made by the rustics who gathered to celebrate his music. Whereas his watchwords, according to a member of the Souchay family to whom Cécile was related, were "modesty, courtesy, piety and genius", it is not unlikely that his love of laughter endeared him to the English nation as a whole; conversely, this love of eccentrics caused Felix to feel far more comfortable in England than in the more restrained Prussian environment in which he grew up.

In 1840 George Sampson, an English singer who visited Mendelssohn in Leipzig, described him as "like a beautiful picture – appropriately framed – artist and man…[he moved] with the grace of an accomplished dancer, masses of long, dark hair around his finely chiselled face". Sampson recalls "first and foremost, the pair of lustrous dark brown eyes that glowed and dilated with every deep emotion". Felix possessed "the quiet, assured manner of a master, with a reverence and benignity which combined with his somewhat Oriental tendency of feature and colour", Sampson likening him to "a prophet of Israel". When he spoke, "his English gained piquancy from his slight lisp". On 16th June 1842, Queen Victoria noted in her journal, after Mendelssohn's first visit to Buckingham Palace, "his fine,

Chapter 1: "Loving and Giving"

intellectual forehead". Joan Bulman, biographer of Jenny Lind, writes of Mendelssohn later in the decade, when the composer and singer met, as having a face "alive with intellect, the expression constantly changing, especially around the sensitive mouth". She speaks also of his short-sightedness, which, like Fanny, he must have inherited, as their father became completely blind.

Ms. Bulman writes of Mendelssohn's face that it "had a beauty no portrait painter could ever catch", and Wilfrid Blunt, in his biography *On Wings of Song*, echoes this. In fact, the most accurate portrait, based on contemporary description, is said to have been that painted at his death by his brother-in-law Wilhelm Hensel; being then completely immobile, its subtle nuances could be explored to greater effect. Stratton's attempt at description seems the least attractive, however. His "high, thoughtful forehead" was "much depressed at the temples". His dark eyes had "drooping lids, with a peculiar, veiled glance, which, through his lashes, sometimes flashed distrust; sometimes happy dreaming and expectancy". His nose was "arched and of delicate form", his lips protruded and his teeth were hidden when pronouncing sibilant consonants (e.g., the 'S' sound). He had, according to Stratton, one "solitary dark spot in his otherwise sunny disposition; he loved only in the measure with which he was loved". He quotes from Eduard Devrient, who called himself a friend and who, therefore, should have known Felix better. Devrient also wrote of this "spirit-child of fortune, unused to hardship and opposition". This, too, will be disproved. He could also be "stand-offish", according to Stratton. In order to demonstrate this failing, he quotes a recollection from Charles Horsley when meeting Mendelssohn at the home of Ferdinand David; young Horsley jumped up "in exuberant recognition", whereas Felix, in response, proffered "a cold reception: 'Sir, I do not have the honour of your acquaintance'". It is patently evident that, as Felix had arrived at that precise moment, the two would not have had the opportunity of introduction; likewise, it would have been several years since the two had previously met, in which time young Horsley must have altered in appearance and become unrecognisable to Felix. Compared with many responses to what could have been an unusual, if not unnerving, form of greeting, Mendelssohn appears remarkably polite. Once Horsley was properly introduced, however, "cordial warmth" replaced the former "frigid coldness", which could, more objectively, be seen as understandable reserve.

But how have artists represented Felix by portrait? A brief analysis seems justified here. Since there are no photographs of Mendelssohn, and only a daguerreotype of Felix's brother Paul from the 1850s, after Felix's death, portraits and sketches are the sole evidence of how he looked. In view of the change of expression from minute to minute, any attempt at depicting Felix Mendelssohn must have been very difficult. The first 'likeness' drawn of Felix was that sketched by Wilhelm Hensel in 1822, when Felix was 13. A portrait was painted by James Warren Child on Mendelssohn's first visit to Britain in 1829, but, because previously reproduced ad nauseam, this portrait is not copied here. On 2nd

December 1836, in answer to a request by the musical historian and librarian Aloys Fuchs, Felix sent him a copy of this painting, being the only portrait published at the time. He evidently viewed it with contempt, because he added: "If a decent one [portrait] ever comes out I shall send it to you at once, since you would like to have one." This attitude refutes Devrient's accusation that Felix could be "quite vain" and "liked to be the centre of attention". Yet, in the same paragraph, this 'friend' reports Felix as drawing isolation around him. His anathema to having his portrait painted or sketched bears this out. The sole exceptions apply when completely comfortable with an artist. In Rome, for instance, Horace Vernet drew a sketch of Mendelssohn "at breakneck speed", as he writes to his family. H. E. Jacob considers this to be one of the best of a collection of 16 assembled by Max Schneider of Berlin in 1953. Vernet's portrait shows "apt and charming masterliness in its execution". The "handsome brow", inherited from Moses by most members of the Mendelssohn family, is accurately reproduced; the mouth is "pleasant, but by no means feminine"; the eyelids "slightly swollen", unnoticed, according to Jacob, by any other artist – could it be that the eyelids did not show this trait when anyone else drew this subject? Vernet observed "the dark, arched eyebrows of a listener, having a close relationship with the mouth" – whatever that may mean. The hair is "curly, but not excessively so", but, Jacob asserts, the "most peculiar trait" is that Mendelssohn's face is "bathed in perspiration". In view of the hurry in which the work was effected, there is nothing "curious" about this phenomenon. Though the sitting occurred in January, Felix writes of flower girls selling violets and anemones in the streets, but, in this spring-like climate, Vernet's subject is wearing a riding cloak and cravat, more appropriate to the typically harsh weather of a Berlin January. A further portrait that passes muster among biographers is that painted by Eduard Magnus that Jenny Lind commissioned, and which was bequeathed to Mendelssohn's elder daughter, Marie, by then Mrs. Victor Benecke. Because of Jenny Lind, who commissioned the portrait, Felix would naturally have wished Magnus, another firm friend, to put his best talent into the painting.

On the whole, however, Mendelssohn's dislike of such "pretensions", as he calls them, amounted to a phobia. The committee of the Cologne Lower Rhine Festival of 1834 wished a portrait to be painted. This commission was "a project from which I gallantly defend myself, refusing either to sit or stand for the purpose", he wrote to Aloys Fuchs, the zealous collector of music memorabilia who requested Mendelssohn's "likeness". One word of praise from his family, who were present, gave him far greater "joy and delight…more truly precious to me and makes me far happier than all the publics in the world applauding me…the dearest reward for my labours". Writing to a Herr Hexte on 18th May the following year, in response to a request that a further portrait be painted, Mendelssohn stated that he would prefer, firstly, to accomplish "something to render me more worthy of my idea of such an honour", begging Hexte "to defer such a compliment until I am more deserving of it", though thanking his correspondent for the request. Again, to

Chapter 1: "Loving and Giving"

Fuchs, he cited he was able to send a sketch published by Breitkopf & Härtel and one by Simrock, informing this persistent collector, at the same time, that a third, to be published in Cologne, is not yet engraved, "and, if I have my way, this will not happen". He would have preferred to "get it down in the form of notes before it appears in the form of facial expression". He regarded the result of his inclusion in the 'Congress of Great Men' as "shameful in the extreme; I did not even sit for it". Presumably, this may have applied also to a bust modelled from life by the sculptor Rietschel and a medallion engraved by Knaurer, or a pencil drawing, which Stratton calls "charming".

However, out of so many and varied descriptions of Felix Mendelssohn, the most telling are left to conclude this synopsis. An American, Bayard Taylor, who was later to become a novelist, poet and translator of Goethe's *Faust*, met Mendelssohn towards the end of the composer's life. Taylor, then 20, was reminded of Edgar Allan Poe, born in the same year as Felix but dying two years later, in 1849. Mendelssohn's eyes shone, "not with a 'surface' light, but with a pure, serene, planetary flame". His nose had "the Jewish prominence, but without the usual coarseness", his nostrils "finely cut and flexible as an Arab's". Though Taylor had met "other families, who traced their ancestry from the House of Israel", never had he met anyone "with a face of such noble character" as that of Felix Mendelssohn. To look at him made Taylor think of how King David must have looked. Chorley, too, spoke of Mendelssohn as having "one of the most beautiful [faces] that has ever been seen", when he first met the composer at a festival in Brunswick in 1839. But what about the comment of William Makepeace Thackeray, usually so cynical and, because of this, so genuine in this instance? Whilst taking breakfast with Benjamin Hawes, brother-in-law of Isambard Kingdom Brunel (who, in turn, married Mary Horsley), Richard Doyle, illustrator and brother of the more celebrated Arthur Conan Doyle, passed on Thackeray's comment. Mendelssohn's face was "like how I imagine our Saviour's to have been". Though this was said, and repeated, Mendelssohn was nothing other than human, and his life as a boy and man are chronicled in the following chapters.

It is appropriate, in view of these comparisons with Jewish men – King David and Jesus of Nazareth – that, though professing to be a Protestant, Felix's father was never completely comfortable with his lapse from Judaism. This is demonstrated by the fact that, on 6th September 1829, the centenary of Moses Mendelssohn's birth, when a Jewish school was to be dedicated to him, Abraham took a vacation abroad, making the excuse that he cared less and less for festivals, but actually feeling ashamed of his conversion.

The cover and frontispiece illustration of this book are copied by Andrew Brooks of ACB Arts from a nineteenth century painting of Felix of unknown provenance.

Chapter 2

"While I Rest, I Rust"

The worthy concept of the 'work ethic' encapsulated in this phrase was pursued to the limit by Leah and Abraham Mendelssohn. Even leisure activities and vacations were geared for every minute to be filled with edifying pursuits. Any sign of idleness, even if misunderstood, was seen as a heinous crime. The children were compelled to rise at 5 a.m., with the luxury of an extra hour's rest on Sundays, to which Felix confided later how greatly he looked forward. As soon as he had eaten his slice of bread and butter mid-morning, Felix was ushered back to his studies with no time even to collect his thoughts. Eduard Devrient recalled how, when sitting silently (who knows what he might have been working out in his head before committing his project to paper), Leah's voice would interrupt his contemplation with the words: "Felix, why are you doing nothing?" Felix often excused the delay in replying to correspondence on account of his almost superhuman work schedule: writing to "Rodolfo", absent from Berlin, he stated that he was "made of Latin, French and arithmetic", as well as having to compose "a double sonata" as an exercise for his then music teacher, Ludwig Berger. His lessons, he tells Rodolfo, rarely ended before 8.30 in the evening.

George R. Marek speaks of Abraham Mendelssohn as ruling his own little kingdom, with Leah as his consort (who hung on every word he uttered) and his children as the subjects. 'Duty' and 'obedience' were paramount for the young people, alongside the dictum "no one was as important as a Mendelssohn", and woe betide any who sullied the name in any way. What wonder that so much is heard about Felix's "impeccable manners"; he had barely any opportunity to behave otherwise. The more money Abraham accrued, the more uncomfortable he felt with this new status, but he relished work for its own sake, which Leah felt obliged to follow. Thus, the parents projected this fear of idleness onto the children, and Felix, especially, could not break the habit, even when married to the soothing, calm-inducing Cécile Jeanrenaud.

Though Julius Schubring, in an article for an 1866 issue of *The Musical World*, stated that it might have benefited Felix had he attended boarding school, as his sensitive personality would have been toughened had he 'roughed it'. In fact, the boy did attend a local day school for two years, but no explanation is given for Abraham's removing him from there. Could it be his school reports of "good" or "very good" were not good enough for this martinet? Or perhaps his reason was more altruistic – protection from the anti-Semitic insults still prevalent. Whatever the circumstances, he tried to teach the children himself and devised a strict work schedule that included anything he could conceive. However, even Abraham Mendelssohn realised that help had to be sought, so tutors were recruited for the children's education. The curriculum included Greek, Latin and modern languages; history, general and political; mathematics, including arithmetic and Euclidian geometry; geography; and European literature, particularly that of Germany. There were, however, apart from the mammoth workload of school subjects, other lessons to be ingested. Were not the children, after all, representatives of one of the elite families of German society? The young Mendelssohn, therefore, had to behave in a way expected of such "aristocrats", as Leah wished them to become. All the social graces had to be acquired. The daughters could gain knowledge, provided they remained "feminine" and did not aspire to become "bluestockings", since Abraham abhorred such intellectual women, or besmirch the family name with scandal, like that dreadful "Schlegel woman" (aunt Dorothea). Felix did ask if Rebecka could learn Greek with him, which she did, and enjoyed the language.

It may be wondered why Henriette Mendelssohn – "Tante Jette" – was not called upon to instruct her nieces and nephews but, on second thoughts, this is completely understandable. The incisive comments she made would not have pleased her brother and sister-in-law. She warned Leah that the minds of children should be directed, not forced. Perhaps the parents may have feared Henriette's being 'too soft' with the children. As it was, Felix's brain was overtaxed, as verified by Devrient, Max Müller and other contemporaries. Felix had inherited his grandfather's thirst for knowledge and, like the ancient Greeks, thought of the word 'schola' (from which 'school' is derived), meaning 'pleasure', literally; it was, indeed, a pleasure to learn. Added to this, he took to heart Goethe's saying "as long as I exist, I must be active". Had Felix been allowed to apply his own instinct, to "dream" far more, who knows what gems of creativity would have resulted from his brilliant mind? All that can be stated is the mystery that such well-balanced, remarkably well-adjusted children emerged from this questionable upbringing.

Schubring asserted that Felix was Leah's and Abraham's favourite child. From what research has been done it appears far more likely that, if the parents favoured any, Paul, the youngest, was the one. This would be understandable, since he was far more compliant than his sisters or brother and, therefore, far less disposed to argue with his parents. Compared with letters the father wrote to his other children, to Paul he seems far more amenable. From a business trip to Paris in 1819, Abraham wrote to his six-year-old son as to whether or not the child should marry Mieke, their gardener's daughter. The father wished to "ponder" the matter and to discuss it on his return home; having had "a glimpse of this Mieke, if I find

Chapter 2: "While I Rest, I Rust"

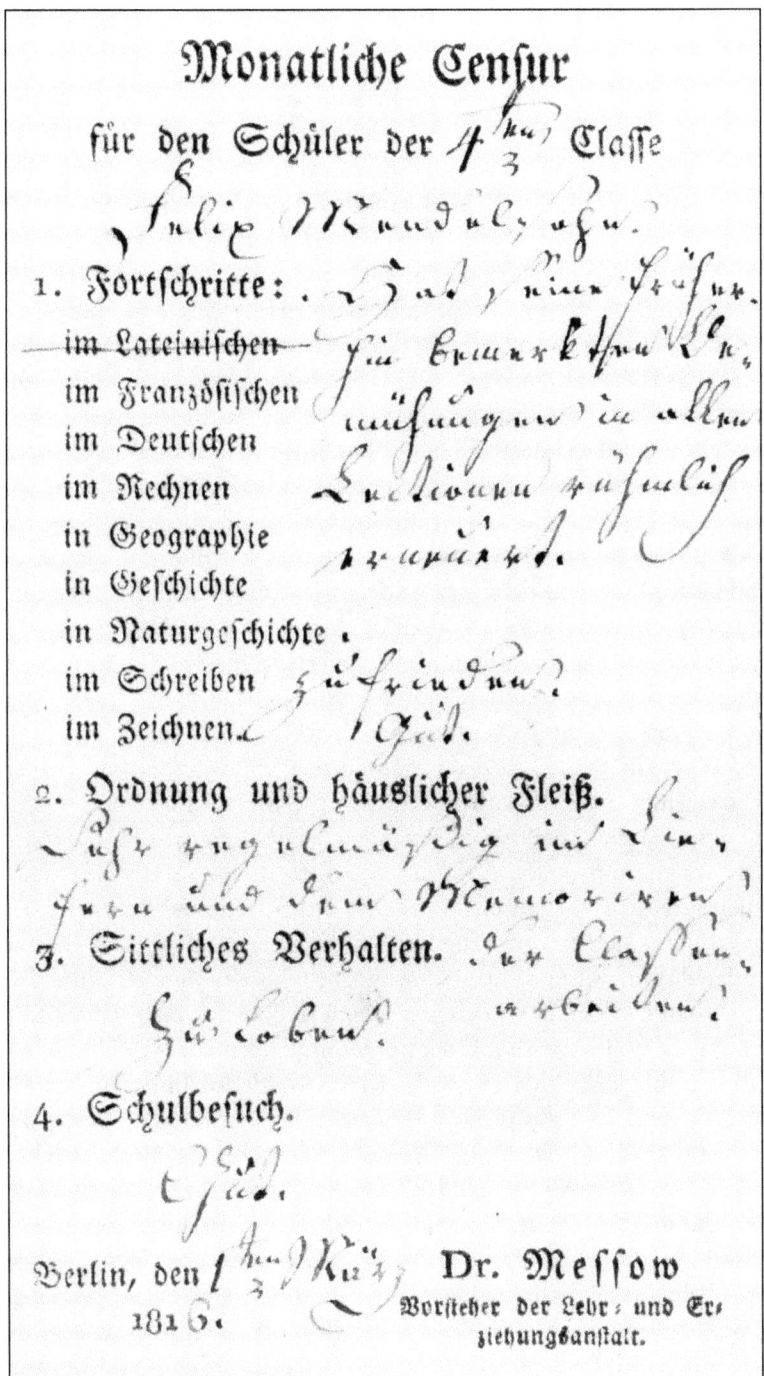

Figure 1. Felix's school report, 1816

that she is neat and clean and if you manage to behave yourself for all of 14 days, we will discuss the subject some more". To Fanny, on the contrary, he wondered why this 15-year-old daughter should have any doubt about his minding her friendship with 'H' and 'A'; she should by now have "too much sense and modesty" to allow such acquaintances to "intrude" into her personal life. On her 23rd birthday, Abraham was still not satisfied with his daughter's behaviour. She "must improve"; become "more steady" and "collected", in preparation for the only calling a woman should follow – that of wife and mother. "True economy is true liberality," Abraham admonished. Anyone who throws money away is "either a miser or an impostor", and he proceeded to give Fanny a lecture on how the weighty duties of marriage must be fulfilled. Though he did not wish to preach, she had to take his fatherly advice to heart. Progress was nothing more than progress – not an achievement – and a child's best education was to learn from the parents. Rebecka was allowed to benefit from her father's pompous humour. He praised his daughter for taking care of a squirrel – "if the weather is as horrible there (in Berlin) as it is here (in Hamburg), even a squirrelephant could not stand living out in the open" – but then he reminded this six-year-old of her mother's dictum to "work hard and be obedient and I will bring you a beautiful present, but you will have to earn it".

Neither was Felix ignored; indeed, he appears to have had to bear the brunt of his father's demanding standards of exemplary behaviour. From Amsterdam, Abraham expressed himself "very satisfied" with his son's epistles, "at least, up to now". However, he admonished his son that they "show a few slips", which would be discussed further on the father's return. "You must learn to speak better; then you will write better," Abraham reprimanded his (then) eight-year-old son. But this was not enough, apparently. Abraham hoped to receive "a truthful and pleasant diary" that Felix had to compile once his father returned home. These tasks expected of him were by no means the whole assembly of work to be completed. He translated some verses of Dante for his uncle Joseph Mendelssohn. He likewise wrote to a family friend, Dr. Caspar, about a book of poetry he had written, describing it as "yellow, with a black border and green edges". Felix asked Caspar to return the book as "there must be some wonderful things to set to music" contained therein. This was probably a joke, as he continued, "The caption reads: 'These poems shall not live long'." In 1826, ostensibly for his mother's birthday, Felix made a translation from the Latin original of Terence's *The Maid of Andros*, retaining the original metre. Not until 1862, when Sir Julius Benedict collated Mendelssohn's music, was it brought to light that it was not Heyse, Mendelssohn's tutor, but Felix himself who had translated the work. Heyse had asked his pupil if he could borrow it to make notes, but passed it off as his own work, though the initial 'F' could still be seen. Zelter suggested that Goethe should be sent a copy, with which request Felix complied on 30th September of that year. He asked Goethe to "receive this poor attempt from a schoolboy", who was "making so bold" and "taking the liberty" of sending the translation. Though Heyse had wished to make the work available to the general public, this was not Felix's intention; it was, he explained, "simply an exercise to test my abilities". It is not known how his mother received her birthday gift, but *Andria*, as it is sometimes called, bore fruit nevertheless, for Felix was awarded a place, through winning a prize for this work, at the University of Berlin. Under the all-embracing subject of aesthetics (literally, the science of beauty in the arts) he studied classics with Professor Böckh, geography with Ritter, music and philosophy with Hegel, whose style of lecturing and general idiosyncrasies, Zelter wrote to Goethe, Felix could mimic precisely. Mendelssohn's study notes are still extant in the Mendelssohn Archive in Berlin, and, though Zelter reported that it was 1827 that Felix began at university, that date is incorrect; though he did not receive a degree, he remained there from 1826 to 1829.

However, according to Julius Schubring, there was one subject Felix could never grasp: mathematics, which appears to have included astronomy. Once, for instance, when the Pole Star appeared, the pupil could not understand "the principle by which it was alone sufficient to guide us over the four corners of the globe", and the same applied to geometry and trigonometry. In view of the fact that musical notation, in which Felix excelled, is allied so closely to mathematics, it can only be deduced that Schubring could have been a poor communicator and instructor. He likewise gave a far too idyllic impression of the relationship between Felix and his father, which, he claimed, to have been "beautiful" – "very evident in the published correspondence". To be fair, however, so much more has been brought to light since this sanitised, even censored, life of the Mendelssohn household was published. If Felix ever gave his father "dissatisfaction", he was given merely "the reproving look" or "the serious, but invariably calm, rebuke". The glance from Abraham's "large, short-sighted eyes over his spectacles" commanded "the most unbounded reverence" and "utter respect" from the boy. Evidently, Abraham must have been on his best behaviour, compared with his usually unreasonable reaction to all his son endeavoured to achieve. But nothing was mentioned about love in Schubring's recollections. The therapist Philip Hodson has pointed out that it is the worst parents who demand the greatest submission, which can undermine a child's self-confidence if love and understanding are not blended with this desire for implicit obedience and respect. It may have been that neither Leah nor Abraham understood the full implications of parenthood. Any material need was supplied, if the parents thought it necessary; but the really important gifts – affection and understanding – were not available. Schubring found Felix to be "easily offended and out of sorts", and added that such "disagreeable impressions" could have been corrected by "rough treatment" meted out by boys of his own age. Such moods may well have been caused by over-exhaustion, which, fortunately, nature assuaged by allowing Felix the habit of falling asleep immediately he rested on a sofa, at whatever time of the day. Even Gisela Selden-Goth, so idealistic about the merits of Abraham Mendelssohn, admits that "his stern, patriarchal regime sometimes overshadowed the adolescence of the children, who had to refer every move to his self-confident knowledge...and Felix had to submit unconditionally to his judgement". Max Müller, too, whilst realising that Abraham Mendelssohn had "done all he could for the education of his children", considered that they should have been allowed "more time to reflect on their knowledge, or even that the mind should be given a rest, which everyone needs and deserves". It was only when Felix left home that he was able to develop a mind of his own and the self-confidence to defend his views.

In Paris, for instance, Felix actually dared to disagree with his father about his own E flat major String Quartet. Abraham barked: "Here is a piece of instrumental music which causes one to rack one's brains to discover the composer's thoughts when, in fact, he probably has no thoughts at all." Felix responded: "I love it and it depends upon the way in which it is performed." This piece, which his father was "inclined to deride", should be played "with soul and sympathy". Abraham must have been further annoyed by Felix's report of his becoming accustomed to playing in front of royalty; the Queen of France often attended concerts at the Paris Conservatoire and paid him "many compliments".

In Rome, we find Felix writing to the Baroness Pereira, Leah's sister, declining to set to music *Napoleon's Midnight Review* because he could feel nothing for the poem. Begging forgiveness for the "peculiarity" of this "inadmissible confession", Felix explained that "notes have as distinct a meaning as words" and, since he did not know whether the poem was a verse-drama or a ballad, the setting had to be right so as not to give offence. Again, on a later occasion, when the manuscript collector Aloys Fuchs wished him to set some verses of Vogl to music, Mendelssohn had to decline. He explained, on 11th November 1845, that "I am so unbelievably pressurised by...interruptions of every kind that days passed before I can have a half-hour to myself". The more work Mendelssohn undertook, the greater were the demands placed upon him. In 1839, he was obliged to write to Simrock regarding a manuscript promised during the previous year. He had, Mendelssohn explained, had no time even for leisure, but that he hoped to "free himself from debt" in terms of time, to fulfil his commission. He would, he vowed, despite popular demand, write no further *Songs without Words*. "Let the Hamburgers say what they like; there is quite a mass of such music for the pianoforte." He suggested that "another chord should be struck", resulting in a different musical genre. However, in view of several further books of 'Original Melodies for the pianoforte', as Mendelssohn called these *Songs without Words*, this decision was subsequently forgotten.

There was one aspect of musical life in which Mendelssohn would never take part. From as far back as his first visit to England in 1829, Mendelssohn vowed never to put his name to any article written for public perusal. Unlike the opinions of Schumann or Wagner, one will never find anything written by Mendelssohn in music journals; his views were solely for family and close friends. This derived from an incident in which the Belgian musicologist François-Joseph Fétis, on tour in Britain, wrote an article in *The Britannia* implying that Mendelssohn had remarked that the performance of Purcell's *Te Deum* at which they sat together had been "timid and unsatisfactory". Mendelssohn, on 8th July, wrote to the periodical in a valiant effort to make amends, saying that one was not to make judgements on one performance, and that he did not feel it appropriate to comment in public on how music was played. Besides, the warm appreciation of the English towards him "has caused such a bright period in my life, after so short a time in London". Felix wished it to be known that he wanted no misunderstanding to occur through this "painful" article, repeating his "indebtedness" to all "from whom I have received so much kindness and to whom I feel the liveliest regard".

Mendelssohn kept this vow. On 7th February 1835 he wrote to Ignaz Moscheles stating that he had been asked to edit a music journal. "Such work is undertaken for the pleasure of others," he wrote, "retaining all the annoyances for oneself." Felix found the idea "distasteful". At the same time, he sent Moscheles a copy of some songs with guitar accompaniment from "a composer", who had asked if Handel had been as good a musician as was reputed. "What better qualification for the post than that song or that question!"

Later, when the cantata *Antigone* had been composed, the musicologist Dehn wished Mendelssohn to include an article about that work for his journal *Cäcilie*. Mendelssohn's response was that he never encouraged anyone to write about his work and neither did he do so himself. He disliked the envy and intrigue propagated by such periodicals, which were read by inferior musicians but which connoisseurs ignored.

Though the musician and music critic Johann Christian Lobe was able to converse with Mendelssohn, about which he reminisced later, rarely was this possible for anyone else and, certainly, he could never be prevailed upon to address a public meeting. The publishing-house of Kistner in Leipzig invited Mendelssohn to speak at a music colloquium; he thanked them for this honour, but explained that he could not speak in public – not even for half an hour. Such engagements, would disrupt his pursuit of musical excellence. For the same reason, he declined to enter music competitions or to judge them. Mendelssohn received several invitations to award music prizes, however, but still refused to have anything to do with them. He told Ludwig Spohr that he did not know why such matters annoyed him, and he continued: "It would be sheer arrogance on my part, which I would not tolerate in others. I should be the last person to set myself up as an example and my taste as incontrovertible... God knows, possibly being guilty of the greatest injustice towards [the entrants]. So I have renounced such activity once for all and, since then, have been very happy." Throughout this book, it will be observed how surprised Mendelssohn became when receiving any type of accolade for his work. Such was his almost pathological self-effacement, which remained from childhood.

But one cannot blame his parents solely for their strict discipline of work, work and more work. On 15th July 1831 Felix wrote to Devrient from Milan reminding him that, at 22, he was not yet famous. "Had such been God's wish, this would have happened", but, as it was, he could only write as his heart dictated, leaving the rest to "he who disposes of larger matters". Felix became less and less concerned with fame and fortune or the opinions of others, so long as he did not starve by his musical activities. He would, therefore, continue to do his duty by composing what he felt was best and came from the heart. If this were achieved, his duty would have been worthwhile. It was a matter of indifference as to whether a composition brought "fame, honour, decorations or snuffboxes" to him. If Devrient was implying that Felix had neglected his duty, he accepted this as a serious reproach. What Devrient was really annoyed about, however, was the fact that Mendelssohn had not written an opera in which the actor could take the leading role; Devrient considered it "unwise" that such a masterpiece had not been composed long ago by Mendelssohn. Meanwhile, Felix had written a great deal of sacred music that he deemed of equal importance as opera. He was making progress with his cantata *The First Walpurgisnacht*, Goethe's verses having inspired him, irrespective of its success or failure as far as the public was concerned. When the public was farthest from his mind he could, in fact, compose far better music. It was Devrient's voice for which he wrote the work, and Mendelssohn wished him to play the main role of the "bearded pagan" in the cantata. When Mendelssohn returned to Berlin, he would make the acquaintance of Karl Immermann, whose poetry his mother admired so much, and, if he could not offer a successful libretto, he would see if someone in London could oblige. Whoever was chosen "must have fire and a genuine gift"; meanwhile, "I write as good music as I can and hope to make progress".

But it was not only his contemporaries who derided Mendelssohn's lack of work. Marek does not think Mendelssohn's setting of Psalm 115 or his motet *Grant Us Peace* very significant. On leaving Berlin in 1829 to tour specific parts of Europe dictated by his father, "…his genius developed haltingly… He squeezed his work hard before he could let it out of his hands. Ideas came quickly; execution slowly; approval more slowly. He had become, and was to remain, the hesitant composer." This multifaceted young man made the most of his experiences wherever he went, even if he were nothing other than a composer, leaving aside all his other interests. His father was pulling him in one direction, encouraging him to write sacred music and "to put elves and spirits on the shelf", whilst Devrient constantly nagged him to compose, if not the best, at least an opera worthy for him to display his own talents. But Felix made far greater use of his time than to produce the two pieces Marek claims.

There were times, however, when not even the workaholic Mendelssohn was able to settle to his 'duty' of a musical career. From Rome, during the carnival season, he wrote home that "all work is out of the question at present", so many distractions did Felix encounter. Nevertheless, he placated his parents by promising

Chapter 2: "While I Rest, I Rust"

that "when Lent comes, I intend to be more industrious". He planned to work on his *First Walpurgisnacht* and his 'Italian' and 'Scottish' Symphonies. The latter work "is not to my liking"; neither was he pleased with the adagio of the former, but he planned to complete it once he had arrived in Naples. "But if a brilliant idea comes to me, I shall seize it at once, quickly writing it down and finishing it." However, on 29th March, he admitted to difficulty "in returning to my misty Scottish wood", and he laid that symphony aside for the time being. "A fine day is far too great a temptation to enjoy myself than to work"; once out of doors, even Felix thought of "anything and everything but work". The warmest season in Italy lasted, he said, from 15th April to 15th May, and thoughts of Naples were on his mind. "The most prosaic people wax poetical when they speak of it." The "parties and, especially, balls" were not the only reason for his lack of progress, it must be emphasised. The orchestras were "worse than anyone could believe", lacking "good musicians and even the feeling for music. The few violinists play according to their individual tastes and make their entrances as and when they please. The wind instruments are tuned either too high or too low. They make flourishes like those heard in farmyards, but hardly as good. In short, they form a 'tin pan' orchestra, even with compositions with which they are familiar. If new musicians could be engaged and taught first principles of music, improvement could be made, but, since everyone is indifferent, there is not the slightest prospect of such a thing". Though Mendelssohn's own teeth were "set on edge" by the flute being tuned a quarter of a tone too high, no one appeared to notice the dissonance; "as there was a trill at the end, the audience applauded mechanically". Only inferior singers remained in Italy, the best travelled to Paris, London and elsewhere. From Switzerland, too, he found lack of inspiration for the same reason, and concentrated instead on sketching and exploring the landscape.

But work was a compensation when times were sad for Mendelssohn. The year 1832 saw several of his friends and acquaintances dying. On 23rd January the violinist Eduard Rietz passed away, a victim of tuberculosis. Mendelssohn dedicated his Op. 18 A major String Quintet to his deceased friend, but replaced the second movement of 1826 with a new one. On 12th February, having heard of the death of 'U', he wrote that "it is not a time for idle talk; I must work and strive to make progress". On 27th February he wrote: "People now know that I am still alive and that I intend to accomplish something; if what I do turns out to be good, they will accept it." On 22nd March Goethe died aged 83 and, as so often happens in the case of such a firm friendship, Zelter followed six weeks later.

It is evident that, once Felix ceased to be a child, his parents 'mellowed' considerably, possibly because, with increasing ill health, they began to depend on their children more and more. At their passing, he was grief-stricken in each instance. At Leah's death in late 1842, his only comfort was immersion in the profession he had chosen and loved. "What a heavenly calling art is," he wrote to Klingemann. To Herr Otter he wrote similarly: "to pursue one's own path steadily and, especially, to guard against...the squandering and frittering away of talents for the sake of outward show – a reproach...to myself... more than I might wish"; he had no inclination to travel, but to "restrict this impulse in order to strive towards a greater earnestness for my own improvement, instead of [gaining] the good opinion of others". It was his parents he had to thank. "At a time when everything else that ought to interest the mind is repugnant, empty and vapid, the smallest service to art takes hold of my innermost being...and seems a blessing sent by God... Music lives far longer than we do and is such a faithful friend." Though he was often far too upset to compose as he would like, at the loss of anyone dear to him, he gained comfort even from the mechanical, drudge-laden aspects of a musical career; "I thank God daily on my knees", particularly when Cécile or the children entered the room.

It seems appropriate here to give a synopsis of his composing schedule, from a random sample of his letters. Not all Mendelssohn's time was spent partying, despite what many chroniclers of his life lead everyone to believe. He did avail himself of quiet periods, during which compositions were produced. He reported to the family that his Op. 12 E flat major String Quartet was complete to the final movement and that he hoped to have it ready a few days hence. He was working on what would come to be known as his 'Reformation' Symphony; on his return from Scotland, his "'Scottish' Symphony and *Hebrides* Overture" were "shaping themselves"; there was also "a great deal of vocal music projected and in my head, though I take great care not to say what kind, or how, as yet"; besides all this, he was composing an organ piece to be played at Fanny's forthcoming wedding on 3rd October. Clementi, the piano makers, offered him the instrument originally loaned to him whilst in London. After his second London visit of 1832 he was surprised, on returning to Berlin, that his name had not been forgotten; this spurred him to work even harder and he said that he would bring home some further pieces he had written. He wrote to Klingemann that he was "between present and past", unable to settle properly to work, but hoped this would soon alter and that he might be inspired for new compositions, "God willing". "My family believe that the first object of my life now is to write six songs and a symphony and many other works, and I am glad that they agree with me on this point." In Paris, Mendelssohn had begun to list his works and to publish new ones in chronological order. His String Octet and quartets "might make a very good appearance"; piano arrangements, sacred music, "seven *Songs without Words* and six songs with words"; his *Calm Sea and Prosperous Voyage* Overture, after a concert in Berlin, and his D minor Symphony would be added, "if anyone is interested enough to pay for it".

In 1836 he had "scarcely been able to attend to the duties of the passing hour" but hoped Fanny and Paul would describe the performance of *St Paul* in Frankfurt. Not only did he forgo his vacation, planned for Italy and Switzerland to direct the St Cecilia Society for Schelble, but "I have to don dress clothes" to play at a concert for Adolf Marx – an invitation he could not refuse, as sentiment played a part. Even on his Rhineland honeymoon the following year (1837) he worked, having acquired a Bible and a piano – both rare commodities in Bingen; the townspeople were neither musical nor Lutheran. Though he composed various Psalm settings, he had not, at the time, written one note of his G minor Piano Concerto, to be performed at the forthcoming Birmingham Festival. He hoped that the recent death of King William IV would cause its postponement but he had since heard that the festival was to proceed after all.

Since his father's death in 1835, however, Felix had evidently realised that one could relax without committing a crime. He asked Paul, later that year, why his brother felt such unease at his comfortable life. Why, he asked, should one not enjoy or merit such happiness? Felix himself yearned for a more peaceful life, "to compose music and to leave the task of performing it to others". He could not understand why Paul expressed such anxiety, spoiling his peace of mind. In 1838, Mendelssohn wrote to Ferdinand Hiller to say that, though he had composed various works and had plans for more, piano compositions were not in his remit at the time, as he disliked writing in the genre. "I cannot even write them with success, but, if something really suitable for the piano comes into my head, why should I be afraid to write it down?" He realised that chamber music had been overlooked of late, and "I feel a great urge to do something new of this kind. I only hope that we shall not have too many foreign visitors in Leipzig this winter and that I shall not have too many honours to enjoy – which means concerts to conduct", thus hampering his own work.

On 28th November 1842 Felix had again to remind his family of the demands on his time, which prohibited him from writing as regularly as they would like. This entailed "the weekly concerts; the *extra* ones...the proof-reading of *Antigone* and the 'Scottish' Symphony – score and parts – a huge pile of letters, as well as the administration of the money for the new conservatorium and its planning" in Leipzig. "These are the principal things, which, however, branch out into a number of secondary ones." Other works were "revolving more busily in my head every day", and he hoped to turn his *First Walpurgisnacht* into a symphony-cantata, which had been put aside "for want of courage on my part" and to complete a 'Cello Sonata for Paul to play. To Fanny's delight, the King had commanded *Oedipus at Colonus* and *Athalie* to be performed in Berlin; this meant that her brother would return there to direct the performances. Rehearsals for *Elijah* were taking place in England and much copying had still to be carried out. The festival committees of Aachen, Cologne and Liège had asked Felix to direct their concerts, and the cantata *Lauda Sion* was composed for another festival. Mendelssohn could well have done with a week's respite, but this luxury was denied him. As a rule, he enjoyed entertaining Ludwig Spohr, but, on this occasion, Mendelssohn's head was "giddy" with all the activities he had to pursue – or, rather, felt unable to neglect by declining.

A further aspect of Mendelssohn's work, far too unjustly overlooked, was his constant thought for others' needs, not only by giving money but by practical help with strenuous work to organise concerts for funds to be raised. Above all, however, he was a devoted family man, so Fanny's report to Rebecka – then in Italy – of their brother's workload is amusing in its understatement: "So Felix has enough to do."

The cynic is bound to believe that Mendelssohn's quest for excellence and his selflessness towards others must have been engendered to gain reward or must have occurred through false modesty. But, the more one understands him, the more it becomes evident how untrue are these surmises.

In Paris in 1832 Felix looked forward to having his G minor 'Reformation' Symphony performed, which he "never dreamt would happen". He was asked to perform a Beethoven Sonata, but chose to play that composer's G major (No. 4) Piano Concerto, "quite unknown" in Paris at that time. His overture to *A Midsummer Night's Dream* "went quite admirably" and his A minor String Quartet was played "with fire and precision". The conductor Habeneck showed him "many little kindnesses and courtesies...and I have, for the first time, been able to introduce into the French orchestra some favourite nuances of my own". His own 1st Piano Concerto, which he called 'the Munich Concerto', was enhanced in Mendelssohn's estimation by a letter received from his former Berlin Singakademie colleague Adolf Lindblad, by then musical director in Norway. "I know few people whose judgement I respect more than his." In 1837 Felix was taken completely by surprise to be informed of his membership of the Vienna Friends of Music – and never ceased to be amazed at all the honours showered upon him by the London musical institutions. By what he wrote, however, it is plain that his head was never turned. In a letter to the publisher Simrock, thanking him for the "flattering present" that "surprised" him, on 10th October 1842, he continued that he aimed to "deserve such good and friendly feeling", which "will fill me with gratitude and pleasure for as long as I live", as "who would not prize and esteem this (approval) beyond all other recognition". Mendelssohn made the most of his relationship with the publisher, however, not for himself, but to ask Simrock to ensure that Ferdinand Hiller's music be brought to public notice, without the composer's awareness of this request; it was only after Mendelssohn's death that Hiller discovered this fact. At his last concert in Berlin, at the end of the 1844-45 season, "people kept rushing up to condole" on his departure and return to his beloved Leipzig, as Fanny reports to Rebecka. It was as much as Fanny could do not to cause a scene by bursting into tears in public, so overcome was she.

But, when all is said and done, and however much he tried to break the habit, work pursued him to the end of his life, which many say was the real cause of his early death. When Devrient, who visited Felix's family in 1845, chided his 'friend' for composing as if it was a "duty to be done", he suggested that he should wait for moments of inspiration, which appeared to come far less frequently than before. Devrient was probably correct, but missed the point as to why this was so. Many commissions – orders, in the case of King Friedrich Wilhelm IV of Prussia – were still pouring in, often from institutions not requiring anything other than 'duty' music to be written. Mendelssohn had therefore no time to write music of his own choice or preference. This was apart from all the ancillary work that had to be carried out irrespective of the actual compositions. After his ninth and penultimate visit to England in 1846, Felix wrote to Fanny that, though he was leading what he called "a vegetable existence – eating, sleeping and taking short walks", that would not do. He "ought" to be preparing the score of *Elijah* for the printers; he "ought" to be sending the German text to Bonn to allow his compatriots to perform the work, but he wished to "indulge" himself and "to be lazy for a little longer". He declined to conduct two concerts in Manchester and was so exhausted at Ostend that he broke his journey home in order to rest, as well as at Cologne and Horchheim. There, his uncle Joseph Mendelssohn "whisked me around his vineyards for an hour and a half in the broiling sun and took me at such a pace that I could not keep up with him, but felt ashamed and stopped my mouth by stuffing tender, purple grapes into it. Then, I stayed a day at Frankfurt because I was so weary and, since returning to Leipzig, I have been resting."

Chapter 3

Sound Minds in Frail Bodies

It now seems appropriate to turn to Felix's state of health, as well as that of the other family members. Heredity may have played a greater part than is realised in the Mendelssohn children's attitude to health matters. Whenever Abraham travelled with his family, he brought with him, among his retinue of servants, not only Fanny's and Rebecka's 'Fraulein' and Felix's tutor, but also the family physician. Likewise, when something was not right for Abraham Mendelssohn, he made great play of reporting the fact. From Weimar, for instance, where he and Felix visited Goethe, Abraham chided Leah for not having written for a long time. She had instead been sending letters to Paris, "where, of course, I shall be arriving much later than planned". The delay in leaving Weimar was caused by Felix's unexpected rapport with the elderly dramatist, which his father appeared to resent, rather than expressing pride. "Long summer journeys are out of the question in this weather... I shudder to think of the 30 miles to Frankfurt. My head is so full of ghosts from reading Fouqué that I think I have been bewitched and believe that the Rhine Master (the devil) has sent this weather for me," Abraham continued. Whenever anyone else was ill, however, he had little sympathy. Of Ulrike, sister of Goethe's daughter-in-law, he wrote in the same letter that he could make neither head nor tail of her "peculiar" condition. Evidently, his mother had asked Felix to report minutely on his father's condition, for Felix tells Leah of Abraham's bad cold, from which he had now recovered "with God's help, porridge and a warm stove, so that there is no cause for concern whatsoever". Though attention is focused on Abraham's health in biographies, far less is mentioned of Leah's health, apart from her heart condition, which presents itself from time to time. Nevertheless, as early as the aforementioned Swiss holiday, Felix wrote to Zelter, his music teacher, on 19th July 1822 that his mother was "slightly exhausted" by the journey via Magdeburg, Cassel and the Harz Mountains to Frankfurt am Main, but "this was not very serious, thank God". Though he and Paul had "terrible sunburn", everyone else was otherwise "fresh and healthy".

Though Dr. John O'Shea, in his writings on the illnesses of composers, gives precise details of the brain disorder – 'berry aneurysm' – that Mendelssohn and other family members inherited from their father and, one suspects, grandfather also, nothing is mentioned regarding childhood illnesses. It is evident, however, that Felix had a weak constitution, falling prey to severe colds and having little resistance to infectious diseases. Felix caught measles as a boy but, unlike most children, did not become immune to the infection, and caught the illness twice more during adulthood. His 1838 attack caused him to feel "lazy". "You cannot conceive the chaos that accumulates around me," he wrote to his family from Leipzig. For three weeks he could neither venture out of doors, nor continue with his consistently heavy correspondence. He was, however, correcting proofs of the Op. 44 String Quartets ready for publication, and carrying out "other odious tasks". Three days earlier, he apologised to Schubring for criticising his text for *Elijah*, explaining that he had "a cough and cold" that caused him to feel "more than unusually rabid". He would, nonetheless, "plough away at the soil as best I may" as regards the music, but asked Schubring to come to his assistance if no progress followed.

It is only when perusing Mendelssohn's correspondence – even a fraction of the thousands of his letters still available – that it is amazing how often 'an illness' – specific or unnamed – is revealed. Felix's utter exhaustion, or 'fatiguability', as it was clumsily translated at the time, has already been cited. However, so important was this, at least during his childhood, that the phenomenon bears repetition. The "craving for rest" that his body needed benefited the boy's mental health. In his later memoirs, Ferdinand Hiller recalled that, having wakened, Felix was able "to talk animatedly, to joke and even compose from his prone position". Another health anomaly was the blinding headaches that he experienced, with which he was plagued throughout his life. At 17, Felix wrote a letter to Adolf Lindblad, a fellow pupil at the Berlin Singakademie, explaining why he did not " jump for joy or cry out in amazement as others did" on hearing some songs the musician had composed. It might seem strange, Mendelssohn explained, but "it is the truth", so Lindblad need not feel "irritated, piqued, or shown melancholy"; Felix had "such a headache, for which he blamed eating too much pudding. Since the recipe is not known, its contents cannot be examined, but a fascinating analysis may be developed as to how great a part could be played by food allergies in Mendelssohn's health. In Scotland, too, Felix wrote from Edinburgh of the "severe headache all evening, which makes it hard for me even to think, let alone write". This was written at midnight, the day having been filled by "boat trips, galleries, churches, steam, people and smoke-stack funnels"; he excused himself for "being so brief" with his communication.

Later, on 7th August 1829, addressed from Oban, with "a view of the Hebrides", he could not go on writing, but suggested that the best part of his letter would be the bars that would eventually begin the *Hebrides* Overture. But a further experience that may well have worsened his health can be seen in this letter. "I will gladly spare you descriptions of my illness [and] the unaccommodatingly damp weather..." So frequently in his correspondence does Mendelssohn refer to a whole catalogue of almost unprecedented changes in climate that a fascinating book could

Chapter 3: Sound Minds in Frail Bodies

be written on this topic alone. No analysis has yet been made of how his health may have been impaired by the often inadequate protection against such vile weather, or how his increasing bouts of depression could have been exacerbated by this phenomenon. A further possibility for Mendelssohn's increasing mood swings might also be the coach accident he sustained on his first visit to London in 1829. Though it was his leg that was injured ostensibly, who knows what may have occurred with regard to his emotional well-being through the bizarre treatment that was meted out to him by his physician? Volume VII of the music periodical *The Harmonicon* gives a brief outline of the mishap: "On 17th September, Mendelssohn was thrown out of a cabriolet and very severely wounded in the leg, in consequence of the carriage first falling on him, then being dragged over his limb." Felix gave a more graphic account when writing home: "A stupid little gig crashed into me and robbed me of a pretty piece of skin, the accompanying flesh and black trouser cloth, etc. Dr. Kind has pitilessly condemned me to remain in bed for four or five days quietly… Inflammations are supposed to be avoided, so all I get to eat is soup and rice and fruit, like a Brahmin." His "childish scrawl" told the family that his position was "not comfortable;" he was at present "lying stretched out on the bed like a sick lapdog with a bandaged paw", able to write only by making "special arrangements", of which he gave no detail. He complained of "poultices, nauseous odours and painful bloodletting", which latter led him to the conclusion that "the soul is too much connected to the body; all the free, fresh thoughts I had have trickled into the basin, drop by drop, with my blood". Had it not been for the unstinting way in which his friend Klingemann looked after him, Mendelssohn admitted that he would have "cracked from vexation and boredom". Though he had many more visitors than he needed, his main annoyance was being unable to attend Fanny's forthcoming wedding on 3rd October, deeming his accident to have occurred at a most inopportune time. He wished her "joyful confidence" and asked her to "live and prosper…[to] shape your life so that I shall find it beautiful and homelike when I return to you". As so often when away from home, homesickness assailed Felix, even causing him to want to leave the " smoky nest" that he called his beloved London. Felix recalled "the round tea table; father's Turkish boots; the green lamps". He regretted the many invitations piled against his mirror, which he had to cancel as a result of his incapacity, and saw "my travelling cap hanging over the bed", which he looked forward to donning for his return journey. Marek, with unusually shrewd perception, states that "Mendelssohn slid from high [moods] to low and then climbed back again". This applied when he was convalescing at the home of Sir Thomas Attwood, organist at St Paul's Cathedral and a former pupil of Mozart. The country air in what was then the village of Norwood, in the county of Surrey, "must have helped Felix to recover for, instead of the earlier gloom with which he wrote home, he was able to express himself 'bold and confident' with 'bright thoughts' – no longer 'timid and anxious' if plans did not progress; he was now able to tackle 'many new projects'".

It is appropriate here to mention a similar accident that befell Abraham when he accompanied Felix on his fourth visit to London in 1833. His leg, too, had been injured but, possibly because Abraham's older body took a greater time to heal, the limb became "mortified", as Fanny Horsley described the condition when writing to her aunt, Lucy Callcott. Had gangrene set in at that period the leg would have been amputated without anaesthetic. Miss Horsley must have meant the limb had become septic – a nevertheless still serious condition. Felix cared for his father as lovingly as any wife or mother. Charlotte Moscheles observed the "dreadful state of mind" he was in, being driven "frantic", saying that he would not know how he could cope if the condition worsened. At about the same time an English visitor to Berlin suffered a similar accident, whereupon Abraham, on hearing of the predicament, wrote to Leah asking her to ensure the young man had anything he required. Kindness, he pointed out, was inherited from her mother; this should be perpetuated, and, on his return, Abraham contributed to a local hospital to provide for better nursing care. There is no doubt, Hensel considers, that Abraham Mendelssohn mellowed towards the end of his life. He may have realised that even he was vulnerable, having to depend on others because of his failing sight. An operation was discussed whereby his cataracts would be removed but, because similar eye surgery had failed on Bach and Handel, the negative decision must be understood. The Mendelssohn family very likely did not know that Charlotte Brontë took her father to Manchester for the same purpose.

Sometimes Mendelssohn's depression can be understood, through grief at the death of friend or family member; inclement weather or a cold – a sure sign of low resistance to infection and the herald of malaise for anyone, however staunchly this is denied by the recipient. Felix Mendelssohn was often far from the exuberant young man about whom so much is heard. On hearing of what turned out to be the last illness of President Verkenius of Cologne, Felix expressed himself "alarmed and distressed. Everything seems to be covered with a black veil", until the time when "those mournful images will be chased away" and health returned. Distance was made "doubly painful" when knowing there was nothing he could do to alleviate the suffering of such a "cordial and honoured friend". On learning of Zelter's death, though this was expected, Mendelssohn thought he would sustain "a serious illness" at the loss. "For the rest of the ensuing week, I could not shake off this feeling." It was only his many commitments that brought him "to myself; or, rather, out of myself", through diversion of his thoughts and with his mind fully occupied.

From Paris he wrote with anxiety to Klingemann about the cholera epidemic in Newcastle-upon-Tyne, but he himself "feel better than I used to". This changed, however, for, despite the "distractions and dissipations" that prevented him from working, he had, in order to do so, to "live in complete seclusion and face a dreadful winter". This gloom would be remedied only if his correspondent were to visit, "when we could collaborate on many musical projects". In April of 1832,

Chapter 3: Sound Minds in Frail Bodies

Felix himself is purported to have caught the disease. He called his illness 'cholera', which caused his family to panic, and they dipped his letters in a tincture devised by a local doctor. As Blunt points out, the attack, if such it was, must have been mild, because he remained in bed for ten days only.

He complained in a letter unearthed by Eric Werner to an unspecified friend: "There was always something the matter with me and, latterly, I have been really ill; had to stay in bed; have my belly massaged by an old crone; cover myself up with masses of bedclothes; sweat a lot; eat nothing; endure lots of visits and lots of sympathy; swallow enormous pills; get thoroughly bored – and so sweat out my anger and my bellyache and the cholera I was supposed to be getting."

People were said to have cholera when the illness was something else. Fanny Horsley wrote to her aunt that she suffered this usually lethal illness. Though she did suffer sickness and stomach-ache, she was well enough the next evening to read Scott's novel *Guy Mannering* and learn a Goethe song. Mama did not allow her to dine with the family, nor to visit Burlington House, home of the Royal Academy of Arts, nor to join a family excursion to the then country village of Kilburn. What was termed 'cholera' may well have been food poisoning in these two instances. An interesting article by Dr. Tom Stuttaford in *The Times* of 15th August 1996 suggests the illness may have been botulism. The article explains that the noun derives from the Latin 'botulus', meaning 'sausage', and, since Mendelssohn enjoyed this variety of food, and his symptoms tallied with botulism, as well as affecting the central nervous system, the point need not be pursued. Felix had felt "as peevish as a guinea pig and as miserable as a fish on dry land", but, once he visited London for the second time, "bliss" was all he felt.

But such "bliss" did not endure for long. A worse depression than ever assailed Felix on returning to the oppressive atmosphere of Berlin, as he wrote to Klingemann on 5th September 1832. He had "reason enough" for such a "black mood", he explained; Fanny was "constantly ailing"; his father had had "a feverish cold for some time"; his own health caused him to be "downhearted and depressed"; his stomach "rebels in a most disagreeable manner". The weather "is the most horrible that I can ever remember" [even worse than Switzerland?] "it pours the whole day long and is bitterly cold". Friends and acquaintances had died of cholera; the death of Friederike Robert, wife of Ludwig Robert the artist, caused Felix to think part of his own youth had vanished. He later wrote of "a terrible pain in my ears and headache", which came together. He complained of "the quiet monotony" of Berlin, which followed "the earlier excitement". He was annoyed by the negotiations regarding Zelter's replacement at the Singakademie, which continued "far longer than necessary". He said that they would, in the end, "appoint their Rungenhagen (Zelter's deputy) to the post – or God knows who else". Later still, writing to his friend Pastor Bauer, Felix's mood changed. He recollected his earlier "bad" state of mind, for which there was no cure (not even Bauer being able to help him). He said that "a whole mass of music is buzzing around in my head", and he looked forward to his third visit to London. There was a far deeper reason for his present state of mood swings, however; one that he dared not confide even to Klingemann, his most trustworthy friend. His father had dictated that far too long a time had passed since Felix should have put fairies and other superhuman spirits "on the shelf"; this "far too childish" series of compositions had to be replaced by something sacred – the type of music enjoyed by respectable bank managers (meaning Abraham Mendelssohn himself). Even this sole reason was enough to cause such a dark state of mind: a creative musician having his art marred completely for the sake of "duty" and "obedience" to someone else. The oratorio *St Paul* can be seen as nothing other than an answer to moral blackmail by someone who never had any intention of understanding the genius his son should have been encouraged to pursue and fulfil. All that was required of Mendelssohn by his father must have been even harder work to satisfy the almost superhuman expectations laid upon him by someone who should have known better.

In Abraham's last letter to his son, he "looks forward with impatience" to the completion of *St Paul* and "urges" Felix to finish the work. "Thus," Felix wrote to Pastor Bauer, "I will work with double zeal" to accomplish this duty. Did Abraham ever realise what fear of failure and disappointment he had inculcated into Felix from childhood, which never left him? Whatever the answer, Mendelssohn showed a far more relaxed attitude to the oratorio once he had composed it: "God will direct what is to come next". By then, Abraham had passed away. Half an hour before his death, the doctor reassured the family there was nothing amiss: there was no need to fetch Felix from Leipzig. When Fanny's husband, Wilhelm Hensel, arrived to break the sad news of Abraham's death to Felix, for days Abraham's elder son could not shed the tears that would have comforted him, so "broken and stunned" did he become. It was only when weeks had passed that he was able to pour out his grief to his old friend Julius Schubring. Wilfrid Blunt claims that Abraham's death was "undoubtedly" caused by a stroke, which was exacerbated by becoming acquainted with the correspondence between Zelter and Goethe. These had been edited and published, according to Eric Werner, by "a narrow-minded and embittered schoolmaster" – Professor Friedrich Riemer. Though Felix must have become accustomed to Zelter's outspokenness, Riemer's publication of these strictly private letters hurt him, Werner asserts; though he may well have accepted some of the ridicule of family and friends, there was no call, Felix must have felt, for allowing anyone and everyone to read them, however uncomfortably accurate they might be. Whatever Zelter was, or was not, he never lied; truth was part of his character. Whatever Leah may have felt about this publication is not known. Felix was able to write to Bauer of how "she bears her loss with such composure and dignity that we can all only wonder and admire and ascribe it to the love for her children and her wish for their happiness". He wrote to Schleinitz, municipal councillor in Leipzig and responsible for the management of the Gewandhaus, on

Chapter 3: Sound Minds in Frail Bodies

29th November 1835: "My family is so composed and calm that it is a consolation and example for me but I myself can hardly see how I shall carry on with my life. I must try to go on as he would have wished us to do if he were still with us, and only that God may grant me sufficient strength and resolve to do so." He wrote to his cousin Benjamin Mendelssohn that Abraham's wish was granted – "a quick and painless end. He departed from us without sickness or suffering, gently and peacefully, on the morning of the 19th [November] at 10.30." Abraham had spent the previous evening with his family "most cheerfully and happily, as was the custom in recent days". "The loss we have sustained cannot even be comprehended," Felix had written during the first few days of this shock. Nevertheless, despite this constant cycle of peaks and troughs in his emotional life, Klingemann, visiting Mendelssohn in Düsseldorf in 1833, wrote to the Horsley family that Felix was becoming "quite the popular man in Germany, his music selling in greater quantity than any of his contemporaries and many commissions are offered to him".

Though far less is heard of depression after *St Paul* was performed and acknowledged to be a universal success of the period, Mendelssohn still suffered from physical ailments. Even on honeymoon, his wife Cécile wrote in the diary each kept at the time: "After the meal, Felix was unwell, and remained so until three o'clock the next morning". Earlier he had complained of a similar illness from the effects of a salad he had eaten when his family had visited him in Leipzig prior to his wedding.

At the beginning of 1838 Mendelssohn wrote to Ferdinand Hiller apologising for not having sent a New Year greeting, but explained that he had "an illness" that had kept him to his room for six weeks. This entailed pains in "neck, head, etc.". His left ear was completely deaf and pain in the right ear came and went. Hiller could imagine the "agony" he suffered – frustration even more, it can be guessed – as he could hear no one speaking in the same room and neither could he hear the orchestra nor his own piano playing when he conducted. Though "all remedies" had been attempted, there was no improvement. He was anxious and hoped he would not suffer permanent deafness. A similar malady had attacked him four years previously, which also lasted six weeks; "God grant it may do the same". Felix attributed the cause to the "bitter winter weather". On 4th January 1840 he wrote to Fanny, then in Italy, that he had developed "an abominable cold and catarrh" that had kept him either in bed or confined to his room for three weeks. It is patently obvious that what his body needed was rest, which would benefit its occupant far better than any medication, but not even Cécile could persuade him to relax more. Perhaps, had he married someone with a less gentle spirit, who asserted herself more on her husband's behalf, who knows how much longer he might have lived? As it was, his doctor prescribed a "cure" at a spa but could not stop him from attending the Birmingham Festival to conduct the English version of his *Hymn of Praise* as Joseph Moore, its manager, had commanded. In the same year, however, the medical establishment did have their way in preventing Cécile accompanying her husband on his sixth visit to England. Their third child was to be born in the following January (1841), so her journey was not thought advisable. In fact, Felix must have been relieved that the mother-to-be was not with him, for, as with other such journeys, the wretched channel crossing caused Mendelssohn to arrive a day later than planned. Despite so many periods of physical illness, however, there appears to have been nothing wrong with his physical relationship with Cécile. She wrote to a cousin, on the birth of Paul, that she seemed surprised at having been married for less than four years but already having three children. The Hensel family visited Leipzig on their way home from their long vacation in Italy and encouraged Felix to follow their example. He did ponder this plan when his 1840-41 commitments at the Gewandhaus had finished for the season, but the visit never materialised.

In 1841 Felix wrote to Julius Schubring that he had been feeling lethargic for the past week, but was able to laugh at the distress of the previous year. He did not know why he felt as he did at the time; perhaps on account of the approaching spring (with its unpredictable weather) or the amount of work he had had to complete. He had conducted 15 performances since January – "enough to knock up any man", he explained. However, as with his depression that made him veer from his creative path in order to placate his father, Felix had another reason for feeling distressed that he was too frightened to admit, even to himself. He had, from the start, misgivings about his forthcoming appointment to serve the King of Prussia. Now, with continued indecision and lack of a definite remit from the court, Mendelssohn knew his instincts had been correct. But his family and friends thought otherwise. They saw Felix's new status as an ideal opportunity to excel in Berlin, to an even greater extent than in Leipzig. It was, after all, a duty to serve the sovereign – how many other of his subjects were given such an honour? Nevertheless, to conclude this sorry chronicle, Felix did use illness as a pretext for allowing himself time to compose. During his seventh visit to London in 1842, while staying with the Benecke family, he "pleaded a slight indisposition" as reason not to accompany the rest of the family on a trip down the Thames to Windsor. On arriving home, Felix greeted his hosts with one of his best-known piano pieces – his *Song without Words* Op. 62 No. 6, later known as 'Spring Song' or 'Camberwell Green', where the Beneckes lived. How often Felix used indisposition in such a way is not known. It is comforting to think that such peaceful and beautiful music could result. However, Felix was not the only one who sustained sickness. His mother's heart condition had troubled her for most of her adult life; she was, though, stoical about her suffering. This may have been the source of Felix's stubbornness in refusing time off work. Yet it is not clear whether Leah's heart condition was the cause of her death in 1842. On 10th December, Abraham's birthday, a family gathering was held at the Mendelssohn home in Berlin. "For once, we shall dance again," the matriarch commanded, and, as Felix wrote to

Chapter 3: Sound Minds in Frail Bodies

Klingemann, the party "had been livelier and merrier than it had been for many years". During the evening Leah complained of an unspecified "stomach ailment" and woke the family, though later she ordered everyone back to bed, saying she felt much better. As with Moses, and Abraham, history repeated itself; the doctor found nothing amiss with Leah, but, eventually, she lost consciousness. "She went quietly to sleep again and passed away peacefully." When the doctor had been summoned once more, he said, on this occasion, that there was no hope and the death occurred at 9.30 on the morning of the 12th, "to all appearances, without having had the slightest feeling of illness. That had always been her wish and it was like a soothing comfort to me when my brother and sisters told me about it the following evening in Berlin," Felix wrote. Why was this loyal, dutiful son not at his mother's bedside? his detractors may ask. Simply that, when Paul wrote to Felix of their mother's illness, Leah was still alive; thus, on arrival, he naturally expected to hear better news than that which greeted him. "I arrived too late, but still saw her once more," Felix explained to Klingemann. He was still not accustomed to speaking of this bitter blow to anyone who could not share his grief. "It is something that I can never forget and recover from, and [I] am equally unable to take part in what people call 'diversion'" – his only comfort was work.

It is not known how well Fanny was as a girl, but it can be ascertained that she was never a well woman. Felix mentioned her as "constantly ailing" and this resulted in her second child being stillborn. In 1837 she was unable to attend her brother's wedding through illness, suffering a miscarriage a few days after Felix's honeymoon. In 1843 she began to experience symptoms that might, with better medical knowledge, have been alleviated. Fanny wrote to Rebecka, in Italy, that her hands were less crippled than her sister imagined. "The numbness has almost disappeared and the weakness comes and goes in fits." The galvanic treatment that she was prescribed had not worked and she had therefore been advised to dip her hands "in a decoction of brandy". She had learnt that, whilst every shop in Berlin sold Schnapps, there was no distillery that produced brandy, so she needed to find how this could be acquired. As for her piano playing, sometimes she performed well, at other times "worse than a nightwatchman", and she felt no more capable of improving than when she was 14; this is hard to accept since, three years hence, "this figure will be reversed" and she would be 41. Of one thing Fanny was absolutely certain: she hoped she would never be sufficiently ill to have to consult Dr. Schönlein, whom she considered introducing to Rebecka's husband Dirichlet's mathematical colleague Jacobi "to see who can outdo the other in rudeness".

By the year 1846, Fanny had become more content with her lifestyle than ever before, but this idyllic state was not to last long. In mid-May 1847 she suffered a nosebleed, staunched by an unspecified remedy. During a choir rehearsal, preparing her brother's *First Walpurgisnacht*, she lost the use of her hands, later losing consciousness altogether, and "a rush of blood to the head killed her", her son Sebastian Hensel explained. Fanny's coffin replaced the piano in the garden room. This was covered with beautiful flowers gathered from the singer Mme. Decker's conservatory. Presumably, once Fanny had been buried, the piano was moved back into position because, when Felix visited Berlin subsequently, he saw the rooms arranged precisely as when his sister died, even to the extent of having his *First Walpurgisnacht* score placed on the music stand. Felix never recovered from the relapse he suffered on seeing this 'shrine'. His death, and the days preceding it, are described in Chapter 30, 'The spirit leaves its cage'.

Like Fanny, little is known about Rebecka's health as a girl, but it is clear she was, likewise, never well as a woman. In July 1836 she was ordered to the spa town of Franzensbad, on account of excruciating neuralgia. Though the physician had forbidden her to talk to anyone, but to take solitary walks, this rule had to be disobeyed as there were so many visitors to the spa. By the 18th she could dine out when invited, but was not to drink Hungarian wine, as it was "too exciting" on the system. August and the return of her husband from his course of lectures in Berlin, however, changed her from "feeling like a stray sheep", frightened to meet "people, kind or unkind, not knowing where next to turn", into her usual, humorous self. In Munich, on the way home, she commented that the potatoes tasted better than anywhere else she had visited, but doctors prevented her eating butter, fruit or vegetables, as they would fight with the iron still in her body from the mineral water she had imbibed at Franzensbad. A whole book could be written on the bizarre notions held by the contemporary medical profession regarding nutrition. The next year, like Fanny, Rebecka too was pregnant and unable to attend her brother's wedding. A son, Felix, was born but, on 30th November 1838, Fanny told Klingemann that her sister had lost "a beautiful boy" of 13 months. This was not all from which Rebecka suffered, however. Before, during and after the birth she experienced excruciating neuralgia. Such was her pain that, at one time, she became so delirious she "had to be held down in her bed". A recovery visit was planned to the newly fashionable resort of Heringsdorf on the Baltic, whence Fanny travelled with her sister. The first visit to the baths took place on 1st July 1839, with her commenting on "dripping hair" on emerging from this regimen. Though naturally still upset at the loss of their youngest child, Rebecka observed, eight months later, that the grass was still green and flowers still bloomed.

Whilst holidaying in Italy, Rebecka suffered a further illness, diagnosed as "black jaundice" – a more virulent form of the usual illness. Rebecka suspected that she was again expecting a child, but the doctors told her this was "impossible". It was only when Fanny realised how ill her sister was that she travelled to join her but, on the day before leaving Berlin, she suffered a nosebleed that lasted for 36 hours, according to her son, Sebastian Hensel, who described this as "salutary but not alarming" but gave no explanation. Rebecka was able to bear her illness with friends' support but, when her husband developed what Sebastian Hensel calls "Roman fever", the couple were conveyed to Florence by the artist Kaselowsky. So ill was Rebecka on the journey that all she could say, "with a shudder", was that she had been driven almost out of her mind. Fanny had equal anxiety about the youngest child of Albertine and Paul, who was dangerously ill, but, nevertheless, she set off for Italy to care for Rebecka. Though April was the anticipated time for the birth, according to her mother, little 'Flora' – short for 'Florentina' – had other ideas, arriving on 13th February 1846, in perfect health; her mother's dreadful symptoms disappeared at the same time, allowing Rebecka to recover forthwith.

Felix's wife Cécile had always had weak lungs, preventing her taking up a singing career. Even more than her in-laws, she never voiced complaints about how ill she felt, but it is surmised that she was never in robust health. She stoically coped with the pregnancies and births of the five children; their first child, Karl, appeared to give no trouble at birth, but a few days later his mother sustained a serious illness, through which Felix watched by his wife's bedside, in great anxiety, though no precise details are given as to the pattern of the illness. Before his eighth visit to London in 1844 Felix had again been anxious about his wife's health. Cécile had acquired a serious cough – "nervous, dry and trying to a degree". This was attributed to her already low resistance to infection, exacerbated by her constant nursing of the children's whooping cough, dangerous at the time before modern medication. Dr. Clarus, their Leipzig doctor, recommended a visit to Bad Ems but the doctor in Frankfurt prescribed "good country air and plenty of rest", with which Felix agreed. He therefore rented a house at Bad Soden, "two leagues" (six miles) out of Frankfurt, where wife and children were cared for by Mme. Jeanrenaud. On 29th May Fanny reported that "our fat little Paul", as Felix had called his third child, had now recovered from measles, with which the children had also been infected; Cécile had a further "inflammation of the throat". Felix, out of duty, conducted a season of Philharmonic concerts in London, but stipulated that the greatest care should be taken of his family. Sebastian Hensel asserts that Fanny appeared to be more concerned than Felix about them, but this is unfair. Cécile had begged her not to say how ill she was, so how could he know? This selfless wife wished her husband to have no anxieties on domestic matters, but to concentrate wholly on his work in London.

If only Felix had taken the same care of his own health as he advised others to do. He had written from Rome in 1831 that he hoped his brother-in-law Wilhelm Hensel's "toothache and nervous episodes" had now gone. "The man strains himself too much – I have always said so." Were he to have taken his brother-in-law's pulse, he would have diagnosed the malady and prescribed less working time; Felix evidently inherited his father's way of living: "Do as I say, not as I do". People were beginning to notice how Mendelssohn had altered since his youth. Even after his first visit to Buckingham Palace in June 1842, Queen Victoria noted in her journal the age of her guest as 35 or 36, yet he was only 33. During the winter of 1843, Cécile asked her brother, Charles Jeanrenaud, if he had read newspaper reports that her husband had become "deaf and decrepit" and that editors of an unspecified encyclopaedia had "known this for some time". He was adopting similar attitudes to his father as regards the health of others. On 10th April 1845 he wrote to his brother Paul about his mother-in-law, Mme. Heine, that he had not realised how ill she had been, thinking that "the business in the summer" before was temporary. "What is happening there?" he asked. When a Dr. Strohmeyer met Mendelssohn in the same year, he recorded in his later memoirs that Felix had "aged prematurely"; he had grown "little taller than he was as a youth. His face bore the traces of severe mental strain; his habit of keeping his eyelids closed has grown so much worse that he hardly notices his closest friends and acquaintances when he passes them in the street." On 7th March Felix wrote to Moscheles: "So little benefit is derived by the public from so many musical performances; a little better; a little worse; what does it matter? How quickly is it forgotten?" One book of studies has had more influence on music "than I know not how many morning and evening concerts during I know not how many years". The same mood is revealed in a letter to Paul of 30th October in the following year: the welter of compositions, none of which could be called "tolerably good", confirmed his wish to relinquish his public persona a few years hence. Now that Moscheles had taken over the Leipzig Conservatorium, Felix could contemplate retiring "to some pretty part of the countryside" in the summer, returning in the winter to Berlin to live with Paul and his family. He could thus compose music for his own satisfaction "in perfect harmony", with no demands made upon him by the general public. He was then working on two passages from *Elijah* that caused him "great tribulation". He had "now, at last, finished" the church liturgy that the King of Prussia had continually badgered him to compile. Devrient, who visited Felix and his wife in Dresden, noticed a "touchiness approaching the quarrelsome testiness of his father", so often accompanying a brain disorder. In Leipzig, on another occasion, Devrient noted how Mendelssohn's former "blooming, beautiful joyousness" had given place to "fretfulness – a satiety of all earthly things". Public commitments were anathema to him; though he worked feverishly, he spoke of delegating responsibility to Niels Gade for the next season's Gewandhaus concerts. Felix was "out of sympathy" with the Conservatory students, none of whom, he declared, had a grain of talent, nor showed any hope for the future of German music and composed nothing of his own but sacred music. This is hindsight, however, and unnecessarily gloomy on Mendelssohn's part, for, in 1847, Mendelssohn enjoyed – if possible – an even greater season of triumph, at least in London.

Chapter 3: Sound Minds in Frail Bodies

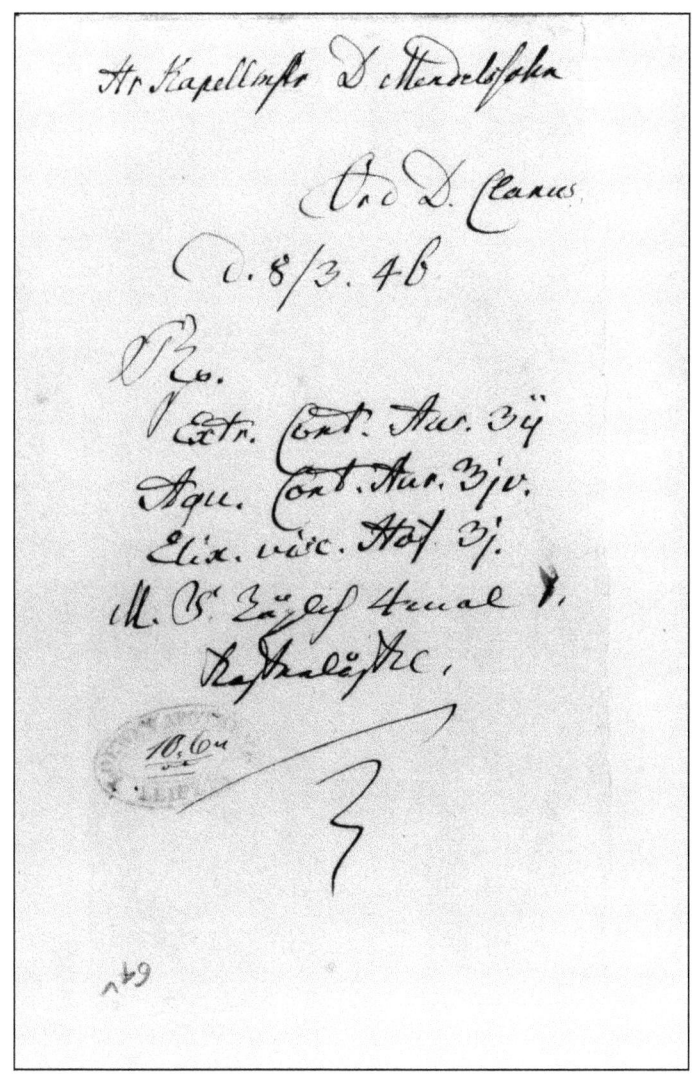

Figure 2. Prescription for Mendelssohn, 1846

Chapter 4

Leisure, at Home and Abroad

As far as any leisure pursuits of the Mendelssohn family are concerned, the earliest date that can be found is 1820, when the actor and opera singer Eduard Devrient first noticed Felix playing marbles in the street – or else the game of 'touchwood' – with companions of his own age. None of the other boys is named and neither is 'touchwood' explained, not even by biographers who regurgitate Devrient's memoirs. No dictionary appears to define the word, other than to give the usual meaning: kindling wood used in lighting fires. Devrient, who claimed to have become a firm friend, is said to have been asked by Felix, during an attack of measles, to fetch a box of building blocks with pictures that he had bestowed on the boy.

In October 1825 Abraham Mendelssohn purchased Leipzigerstrasse 3, an enormous mansion surrounded by a seven-acre park and bordering the gardens of Prince Albrecht and originally part of the King's hunting preserve. To state that such an acquisition was nothing but self-aggrandisement is unfair; like Moses before him, Abraham, too, wished to protect his children from the still prevalent physical and emotional abuse that Jews received. Now, the family could enjoy privacy in this beautiful property. Anyone who was anyone – residents of or visitors to Berlin – mingled in the brilliant salons that could now take place. The hall could accommodate several hundred guests and it is here that the celebrated Sunday concerts were organised. Leah's 'boudoir' was commandeered for theatricals, as the adjoining room, with arches, proved ideal for a theatre. On each side of the hall, suites of rooms were occupied by various people at different times. Devrient and his wife (née Thérèse Schlesinger) lived there, as did the artist Ludwig Robert and his poet wife, Friederike, as well as a Polish lady and her two nieces. When in 1829 Fanny married the artist Wilhelm Hensel, they likewise made their home there. Carl Klingemann's office of the Hanoverian Legation had occupied these premises, before he was posted to London in 1828. The garden must have inspired at least some of Felix's early music, amongst the lime trees, rose bushes, lilacs, yew alley and fountains. The 'garden house', a summer house in the grounds, was, to Sebastian Hensel, not merely a structure of bricks and mortar but "a living individual".

Fanny, however, found it too cold in the winter and despaired of having constantly to wipe the condensation from the windows. In the summer, though, concerts were held in this venue and dances in the garden, and the young people hung handmade paper lanterns on the trees.

In a letter to Klingemann of 18th June 1828, Fanny described the lawn as "bordered by magnificent roses"; the earlier lilacs and lilies of the valley had given place to strawberries – "those rosy children of nature", as she called them, one of which Paul was putting into his mouth as Fanny wrote. A space was also occupied by a laboratory in which Alexander von Humboldt studied magnetism and, with Johann Franz Encke, director of the Berlin Observatory, astronomy; he also performed experiments in this 'den'. This long-term friend of Joseph and Abraham Mendelssohn was highly popular. "Wherever he went," it was reported, "the rest of the people present would gradually form a circle round him, for every occupation and amusement soon yielded to his interesting conversation. He could go on for hours together without a pause, relating the most attractive facts from the rich source of his experience." Humboldt gave a course of lectures at the Berlin Academy of Sciences, subsequent to an earlier series on geography given at the university. By command of the King of Prussia, Fanny wrote to Klingemann, "anyone who lays claim to good breeding and fashion" was invited. Among the audience were "some beautiful spirits and some ugly ones", including "this unworthy correspondent". Such entertainment was stimulating to Fanny, who considered that women "should try to bear the scoffing" of men at such an unusual pastime. She was to attend a further course of lectures by "a foreigner, Holtai", whose audience would consist mainly of ladies, "in a room lit by gas, which is becoming very popular". Fanny wondered if "every home in Europe" would one day be fuelled from this source. In the same letter, Fanny wrote of how she missed Klingemann's "lively spirit"; his appraisal of her "embroidery, dresses, bonnets and ability to handle the German tongue so dexterously"; and she regretted his "perishing in London". She hoped he could take a few days' leave to see Konstanza Tibaldi, who had arrived at the King's Theatre. She had "all the characteristics of someone in a romantic novel – southern flair; burning power of the eyes; Juno figure; irresistible charm of languor and accent". When playing a boy's role, "no more beautiful youth can be seen"; when playing a female lead, "every sound from her mouth inspires enthusiasm". Felix, too, attended the theatre; writing to Friedrich Voigt, he described a performance of *Hamlet*, "with prohibition of clerical vestments" for the actors. The Oriental scholar Friedrich Rosen explained that, though – for Germans – *Macbeth* was the favourite Shakespeare drama, he preferred *Hamlet*, though Lessing's *Nathan the Wise* had been popular earlier.

Though Klingemann admired Fanny's thirst for knowledge, he did not wish other men to appear foolish when comparing their own intellect with hers. This need not apply, however, for she loved dancing and told him about the various balls she had attended. At one, she danced "waltzes, gallops and, the latest craze, a waltz-gallop", with an equally fashionable tune – "heard every minute of the day". The song *Lotte's Dead* had many verses, some parodies "not fit for ladies' ears", though Fanny evidently understood them. Felix, too, loved to dance equally well, but also enjoyed providing the music. Anne Taylor, eldest of the three daughters with whose family he stayed in North Wales, recalled that once, when neighbours came to dinner, "during the dancing that followed, Felix took his turn in playing quadrilles and waltzes; he was the first person who taught us gallopades".

A further pastime enjoyed in the garden house was the newspaper that Felix and Klingemann edited (before the latter went to London), but which Adolf Bernhard Marx claimed he helped to found. The sole asset was a table with a drawer, "which stood, day and night, in one of the long, shadowy arbours". Anyone, of whatever age, who wished to contribute would "creep up to the table" and present "drawings, tender poems [or] witty letters", as well as more serious articles. The winter editions were called *The Tea and Snow Times*, the summer issues *The Garden Times*, and it was from this source that the "human hyphen" legend derived. Abraham wrote in one edition: "Formerly I was known as the son of my father; now I am known as the father of my son." Another expression that Max Müller recalled Abraham uttering was: "When I was young I was called the son of the great Mendelssohn; now that I am old, I am called the father of the great Mendelssohn." Müller remembered his saying this "in a slightly Jewish accent", but woe betide anyone who dared to draw this to Abraham's attention! Julius Schubring recalled how much the father enjoyed family jokes. One such occasion occurred when four-year-old Paul "intoned a four-part canon composed that day by Felix", when the meal had finished. This caused Abraham "to burst into song and to break into laughter", order being restored only when the canon was repeated. Its translation was: "It is customary in Germany to say after the meal: 'May Heaven bless the meal.'" Felix loved teasing but, like many with this trait, did not like reciprocation of such banter. "He was never quiet for a moment," Müller recalled, "moving from chair to chair, conversing with everyone", but he could become bored very easily, looking at his watch to indicate this fact. Contemporaries often spoke of his "extremely restive and volatile temperament", whose moods were "liable to change from one extreme to another". Philip Radcliffe considers Mendelssohn to have relied "too much on nervous impulse".

There was, nevertheless, plenty of opportunity to dispense with nervous energy for, as well as dancing, Felix Mendelssohn was an all-round sportsman – except for skating, for which he found the climate too cold. Johann Droysen, in an article for *The Musical World* of 1866, gave a vivid picture of outdoor life for Felix. He went to the swimming baths in Berlin, accompanied by Klingemann, Schubring and other youths, who formed a club for which Klingemann and Mendelssohn wrote songs to be sung under the water. Droysen recalled that, though taller, stronger and three years older than Felix, his younger companion invariably ducked him whilst wrestling in the water. He remembered, too, how Felix was taught gymnastics by a pupil of the movement's founder, Friedrich Ludwig Jahn, reminding Ferdinand Hiller of "a young billy goat" in the way he ran and jumped. Droysen told of once, having been exercising on the isometric bars, Felix was called indoors to play the piano to guests. He had evidently allowed a splinter to enter his hand, which, unattended, continued to bleed, Droysen having the self-appointed task of wiping the blood from the piano keys. Felix was also an accomplished horseman and, on the one occasion when Droysen rode with Mendelssohn at Pankow near Düsseldorf, he was mightily impressed. Mendelssohn himself wrote of this excursion, "riding through the forest but stopping to listen to the birds fluttering about incessantly and warbling".

Nevertheless, the mind as well as the body had to have its exercise during leisure hours. Because Felix did not wish to study Greek alone, Rebecka joined him and was able to read Plato and the plays of Aeschylus in the native tongue. Her flair for languages allowed her, later, to help her own sons with foreign languages and, at Fanny's death, Sebastian Hensel joined the 'class'. Meanwhile, Eduard Gans taught Felix and Rebecka, prompting wry humour from Fanny: "knowing what gossips people are, this 'Platonic union' will turn into a real one", though, she wrote to Klingemann, "this half-man, half-child, half-savage is not to be thought of as a relative", despite Hensel's painting a portrait of him. Later, Rebecka became far more comfortable with Italian than German, engaging a singer, Paperini, to teach not only Walter, their elder son, but the parents themselves, from whom he – in turn – learnt German. One language Rebecka could not abide was English, saying: "yes" to everything that required a response, but, otherwise, hating both to hear and speak the language.

Whilst Marx practised drawing human faces, Felix drew landscapes, each discovering, according to this raconteur, that "the truly social art is not music, but drawing". When Rebecka took up drawing in 1830, Felix wrote to her from Vienna recommending her to make copies of his sketches of the Tyrol and the Kammergut, as she was already making of his drawings of Scottish landscapes. Felix advised her not to be too free with her eraser, as he had been. A friend of the family, Anna Frankel, having been offered this aid to perfect sketching, replied: "I don't want it", blushing at her immodesty at having to admit the eraser to be unnecessary in her art, about which Felix teased the young lady. Felix sketched anything that came to mind, earning the epithet of "a walking sketchbook" from his brother-in-law Wilhelm Hensel. Such detail was included in his drawings from nature and human activity that, whilst marvelling at his almost superhuman powers of observation, it would be understandable if the person viewing them became 'punch-drunk' with minutiae. Nevertheless, though Marek scoffs at the apparently idealistic choice of what to draw or paint ("no slums in Rome", the biographer cites), Mendelssohn had no intention of becoming a social reformer by his representations of sordid scenes and had no shame in depicting views that would, he hoped, give pleasure to anyone for whom his sketches were made. Neither was Felix unaware of his shortcomings when practising this art; this can be learnt from a remark in a letter in which he wrote of the supreme artist – far greater than the best human scene painter: "...When God Himself takes to panorama painting, he turns out strangely beautiful pictures that no one, however great the talent, and however strong the desire, could copy."

A lifelong occupation for all the Mendelssohn children was reading. A favourite author was Jean-Paul Richter, usually referred to as 'Jean-Paul'. To Felix especially, this author's novels were constant companions wherever he went. He recalled how Klingemann read to him from *Siebenkäs*, which Felix was re-reading in Düsseldorf, "reviving in me the love of my country and makes me proud to be a German. No country can boast of such a sterling fellow as Jean-Paul." On 4th February 1843 Felix suggested that Mme. Emma Preusser begin this same novel at page 26, ignoring the prologue until she had read the author's further work, and promised, if required, to send her other books by Jean-Paul for her family. As children, Felix made puns on their names, allied to those in the books they were reading; Rebecka was called 'Roebuchchen', a mixture of 'Roebuck' and Rebecka; Fanny was called 'Fish-otter' from a Jean-Paul character. Rebecka declared she would not read his *Hesperus*, however, since it was of no help to anyone who felt sad. "He only makes their burden heavier by weakening their strength", telling his readers only what they wished to hear. She preferred to read history books, which allowed one to discover people who really did triumph over adversity; later, she recommended her nephew Sebastian Hensel to read Lessing's works, but, particularly, those of their ancestor, Moses Mendelssohn.

As it was a habit to read aloud one to another, Felix asked in a letter, when abroad, if Lessing's *Antiquarian Letters* had been studied and if the family had discussed the work. But it was not solely German literature that occupied the Mendelssohn bookshelves. Such a passion raged all over Europe for the novels of Sir Walter Scott that, after his unfortunately brief meeting with the novelist, an account of which Klingemann embellished, not even the visit to Melrose Abbey could compensate Felix for the disappointing visit to Scott's home at Abbotsford (discussed later). Another British author of whom Felix was fond and whose poems he occasionally set to music was the Irishman, Thomas Moore. He asked Charlotte Moscheles if she had read his *Travels of an Irish Gentleman in Search of Religion*, said by Felix to have "gone through 70 editions at least and to have extinguished all Protestants, dissenters, nations and nationalities. It is read here by all the orthodox Catholics and praised highly. I do assure you, it is downright heavenly, like everything else of his." Another religious aspect comes to light when Mendelssohn congratulated his lifelong friend Friedrich Rosen on his translation of the Rig Vedas, the sacred hymns of the Hindu faith. Though unfamiliar with Hindi, Felix realised what a fine achievement the Oriental scholar had accomplished, and wished him joy with the long overdue work. Sadly, Rosen died the following year, 1837, of blood poisoning, so it was left to Max Müller to complete the translation.

From Düsseldorf Felix told Fanny of his reading Tasso's poems, which reminded him of Goethe's travels in Italy. Tasso's work was "dreamy, harmonious and tender". *The Death of Clorinda* was Felix's favourite, except that the finale did not please him. Neither, according to Felix, were Tancred's lamentations "true to nature"; they contained "too many clever ideas and antitheses". Though the hermit's words were meant to soothe, to Felix they were "more like censure"; had he been spoken to in such a way, he "would have killed him on the spot". He read the poems whilst in a carriage with a group of singers performing Rossini's arias and was reminded of Gluck's operas, which he thought "such genuine music" that "would never die". He wrote to Rebecka, in 1838, of reading Voss's translation of Homer's *Nausicaa* to Cécile, "repeating to her at the end of every ten verses the profound philosophical remarks" written by his younger sister during their Greek lessons as children. Later, he wrote of his wife learning English by reading Oliver Goldsmith's *The Vicar of Wakefield*. On another occasion, Felix told Paul that he was reading "that abominable thing of Diderot". Though he became ashamed of the book as he grew older, he did admit the author's genius "even in this muddy pool". He was "out of sorts" with the second part of Immermann's *Baron Munchhausen*, noting that Paul, too, refrained from praising the story, and felt as 'X' did about the author's other work in his critical article on Immermann.

At the end of his life Felix felt that Eugène Sue, whose book he was "leafing through", related "everything with the greatest precision". Apart from the books mentioned above, Felix had an inventory headed 'books owned', which included Plato and Homer in Greek; Milton and Scott in English; the complete works of Schiller and Goethe representing German literature, plus Tieck's and Wilhelm von Schlegel's translations of Shakespeare's plays; Devrient's poetry and plays were "well-thumbed"; verses of Eichendorf and Hebbel were used for song settings. Lord Byron and Robert Burns were represented, though, in the latter case, the mind boggles when contemplating Mendelssohn's forays into the poet's Scottish dialect. Felix's books included translations into German of Aeschylus, Giles Blas, Hazlitt and Dickens, whom he was to meet on his seventh London visit of 1842. Though Marek insists that Mendelssohn abhorred anything erotic, Boccaccio's *Decameron* was listed in his inventory – a present from his mother-in-law, Mme. Jeanrenaud, when he married Cécile; also listed is a 15th-century translation of *The Arabian Nights' Entertainment*. By contrast, Felix owned a Lutheran bible, with illustrations by Raphael, and, of course, everything written by his grandfather, Moses Mendelssohn.

In 1822 Abraham took his family to southern Germany and Switzerland. Though ostensibly a straightforward vacation, Wilfrid Blunt surmises that the trip was really a ruse to divert Fanny's mind from the artist Wilhelm Hensel, with whom she had fallen in love and of whom her parents disapproved. This is confirmed by a letter from 'Tante Jette', advising Fanny to enjoy herself if she could but, if not, to reflect on Goethe's words: "there must be dark leaves as well as bright flowers in a wreath". At Grosskreutz, 15 miles from Berlin, Felix was found to be missing; each member of the party believed that he was in a different coach. Heyse, Felix's tutor, having been ordered to search for the recalcitrant boy, found him walking alongside a peasant girl, having already covered ten miles on foot.

But if it is imagined that the Mendelssohns wallowed in luxury once in Switzerland, the reality was patently different, for the children at least. Writing to Carl Zelter, Felix gave a graphic account of one inn at which they stayed, converted from a herdsman's hut. These structures "are not as picturesque as might be imagined", built of "sturdy grey pine logs cleverly fitted together, their thatched roofs protected from the wind by heavy stones". Entry was difficult "because the outside is so befouled by cows that access can only be gained by walking on stones and planks thrown down by the herdsmen, over the mire". The hut where the Mendelssohn children stayed was divided into two rooms by a partition, the occupants eating in the front: "one [sitting] on a protruding bench, another on a milking stool; a third on a wooden block, a fourth having to stand behind, yelling, to make himself heard, 'I want some bread too'". The guests had to join their guides in the back room to warm themselves by the only fire: "one had cold feet; another had cold ears; while a third observed that his nose was turning purple, and all of us were desperately hungry". Lively conversation was drowned by an avalanche, the noise of which "merged with that made by a herd of reddish-brown pigs", which Felix, with evident sarcasm, described as "sweet". Apart from the firelight, the hut was "pitch black, like a bog". A ladder led to the sleeping quarters in the roof, the back room having such a low ceiling that "no one could stand properly". "After evening milking, everyone vies in snoring with the oxen and the pigs, which, I believe, also sleep in the huts. We cut a strange figure in these surroundings, what with shawls, embroidered handkerchiefs and goodness knows what other modish things. The food is also strange; chocolates and sweetmeats brought by the ladies, eaten with the herdsmen's sour cream and cheese – and all this in front of the glorious Jungfrau", in whose shelter the cows were milked in bad weather.

Nevertheless, Fanny was so overcome by the beauty of the St Gotthard Pass that she called it "God's own nature" when writing to Marianne Mendelssohn, wife of Alexander, her cousin, Joseph's son. The Devil's Bridge was at that time constructed of wood, but would be replaced, on Felix's 1831 visit, by "slender and safe granite". Even Leah climbed mountains and a guide took the family round the caves, explaining the various stalactite and stalagmite formations. All the fashionable Swiss tourist attractions were visited, but on no account would Leah agree to continue into Italy, for which Fanny yearned; presumably, the mother was afraid of meeting that impecunious fortune hunter for whom her foolish daughter had fallen. Hensel was studying in Rome, after all; easy enough for the couple to connive a clandestine liaison behind Leah's back! At Lausanne, Felix found time to work on a string quartet and his singspiel, *The Two Nephews* or *The Uncle From Boston*.

It is clear that Felix enjoyed playing 'Mr. Know-all' towards his kid brother Paul, nearly four years younger than himself: from the spa town on the Baltic, Bad Doberan, he accused Paul of making "a few huge mistakes". Felix never slept on the coach when the scenery was dull; "I close my eyes; sprawl about; open my mouth from time to time to take in fresh ideas from the air, singing out, though it is rather through my nose, so anyone who says I sleep is lying". Likewise, anyone who said he was bored in Doberan was lying: "I have so much work and, later, the theatres will be open". As for indulging in pastries: "this is too much!" Though this appeared to be the case at home, this was only to amuse everyone else; Felix preferred "good soup and tasty beef" and was "indifferent" to pastries, and was "as hungry as 500 rabbits" whether they were available or not. In all, Felix calculated, Paul had made "22 mistakes" in his "otherwise lovely little letter". Felix asked his brother's forgiveness for not describing a "good swimming party" in which he was involved, but explained that, as it was such a beautiful day, he would now sketch. Yet, despite his purported disdain of pastries, they recurred in a letter from Paris of 1825, where a plate of these delicacies was bestowed on Felix, who explained that " there is a fine art in dining" that he had learnt to appreciate in that city.

In 1828, as Abraham knew little of Paul's teachers, who were to take him and his peers on an expedition to see the iron, copper and brass foundries of Neustadt, Felix was asked to supervise the party. Fanny wrote to Klingemann, then in London, that a bill for 16 thalers had come to light, "for which I cannot account or comprehend". This is evidently an example of her dry sense of humour, for she would know perfectly well its provenance; Felix enjoyed himself with his own friends, during which get-together Ferdinand David improvised on his violin, and where, it might be guessed, Paul's educational expedition was monitored far less diligently than their father would have liked.

The same year saw Felix hiking in the Harz Mountains and the Rhineland with two colleagues from Berlin University: Gustav Magnus, a future physician, and Albert Heydemann, later a teacher and historian. In the Brocken, Heydemann imitated Ritter, their geography professor, by throwing a pebble into a stream to demonstrate its impact on water. The guide whom they employed was evidently far more interested in his brandy flask than in directing his charges, for they missed their way completely, which, Felix admitted, resulted in "strong language". "Deuce take him," Felix said of the guide, who, when threatened with belabouring with walking sticks, bleated: "Hit me, I don't care." Fortunately, a boy from a neighbouring village, chopping wood, was able to put the young men onto their proper route. Felix had plenty to say about the accommodation at which they stayed. He called Erbich "a dump", with not even a place on the map. Their fellow guests "all huddled together in blue smocks, eating roast mutton and smoking pipes", but there was no food for Felix and his companions. At the next village, to which they walked alongside a brook (which Heydemann used as a drinking fountain, filling his boots with water) and through a stubble field and marshy ground, Magnus was irritated enough to "decamp" from the inn. They slept on benches round the walls, bypassing the guest beds "out of politeness" in view of their unkempt state. "We have not shaved since leaving Berlin," Felix wrote home. Their landlady forbade them to eat "the three lumps of dough" that had been placed on the table, "so we swore by our beards that we would not". The furniture consisted of "several pictures worth about three pfennigs, a fixture supposed to be a chandelier, and a pigskin flask hanging on the door". Wherever they went, the three young men attracted attention; girls looked at them from windows opposite their lodgings. "Alley boys utter catcalls from three streets away – testimony to our popularity and white linen," Felix wrote in sarcasm. Nevertheless, "if three of the most upstanding families of Berlin knew that three of their upstanding sons were roaming around the country roads with coachmen, peasants and tradesmen, exchanging life histories with them, they would be distressed. Do not be, for the sons are as happy as larks," Felix assured his own parents. Yet, despite this euphoria, homesickness revealed itself. Felix longed for family news and admitted that "I am just a mama's boy after all". Not only did he greet his human kin, but he asked the family to say 'hello' to the lambs and to tell them not to be shorn until he returned to Berlin.

The 'Golden Sun' inn at Baden-Baden was far more comfortable than many of its predecessors, even sporting a grand piano, which Felix was invited to play. Between 40 and 50 people filled the room from the casino next door. One of the guests, a Monsieur Charpentier, a composer of French opera (as he told Felix), asked him to write music for his libretto *King Alfred*, but, at that moment, the landlord appeared and expressed displeasure that his tenants had forsaken his lucrative roulette wheel. When next Felix was asked to play the piano it was found to be missing, so a fellow guest invited the musician to his own home, the evening ending with "much carousing and a good meal at the 'Golden Sun'".

"'Heidelberg, that beautiful town, where it rains all day'; that is what the cads say," Felix wrote, quoting from a popular song of the time. "But what do I care about rain?" he continued in a letter home: "Here, there are grapes, instrument makers, periodicals, inns and Thibaut! What a man!" Justus Thibaut, as well as being a lawyer with whom Robert Schumann was later to study, had a remarkable collection of music manuscripts, yet Thibaut learnt as much from Felix as the younger from the older music enthusiast. Felix was invited to the house of Thibaut's pupil, Schröder, where, after food and wine, he was given a pipe to smoke. He then travelled to Horchheim to visit his uncle Joseph Mendelssohn and to take part in a wine festival. Though his musical experiences are described in Chapter 6, 'Young musicians', it is worth noting here that Ferdinand Hiller, whom he met in Frankfurt am Main, considered Felix to have matured beyond recognition since they had been introduced several years before; Mendelssohn had now become a man, his fellow musician declared.

Why, it may be wondered, is the next stage in Mendelssohn's travels abroad – the famous visit to London of 1829 – not mentioned here? It is precisely because this epoch-making trip was so important that a separate chapter (29) is devoted thereto – 'A special relationship'. The title of the chapter indicates that, indeed, Mendelssohn's love of Great Britain was precisely that, as he paid ten visits over the years to the land across the English Channel. On returning to Berlin, Felix and Rebecka planned an excursion to see the Passion Play that still takes place at Oberammergau in Southern Germany every ten years, but measles prevented this trip.

In 1830, Felix travelled to Austria. Graz would eventually be written off as "the most tiresome hole in the world". For want of any other means of amusement, his host took Mendelssohn to see Kotzebue's *Rehbeck*. Whereas his companion thought the drama "very good and very amusing", to Felix the production was "the most dreadful, wretched, objectionable piece" that the dramatist had written, though he did not say why. On the journey to Vienna the nights were spent "in the most disagreeable pot-houses", from where the coach departed at four o'clock the next morning. At Klagenfurt he boarded a coach whose driver promised that the next stage of the journey would take an hour, but two hours were employed on this snow-bound route. Because of his still shaky self-assertedness, a strange concatenation of events occurred for Felix. His saga was "all true and not a Klingemannesque fancy", he told his family. On the way from Salzburg, he noticed two carriages, in one of which sat "a lady – but what a lady". He belaboured the point in order that no one should think he had fallen in love, as she was elderly but had "a very charming and friendly face". This female in the black dress with a gold chain around her neck smiled "most dearly" as she handed her coachman his tip. Though his family might think he imagined it, the lady, he believed, looked straight at him. She made such an impression on "the boorish traveller in the student's cap" that he believed he recognised her and would have liked to speak to her there and then. This mysterious passenger climbed out of her carriage and hung on to Felix's coach "with an almost intimate smile". As Felix described the scene, he "was obliged to have recourse to my well-practised travelling manners, in order not to jump out and say 'My dear lady, what is your name?'", but manners triumphed. What a pity they did because, in fact, the lady was a relative of his mother, the Baroness von Pereira, as Felix discovered on enquiry, subsequently, from his coachman. After "several trying hours", Felix arrived in Vienna to learn that the Pereira party would shortly return from the spa resort of Bad Gastein and recalled a "miserable" portrait that an aunt had shown him of the Baroness, wearing the same ensemble. "God knows when I shall ever have the courage to see her again," Felix sighed. "Premonitions are dangerous things; you can have them easily, but you can only tell in retrospect that that is what they are." Had this inhibited young man plucked up the courage to speak to the baroness, who knows what course his musical path would have taken, since one of the Pereira daughters acted as Haydn's assistant in his latter years; the relatives would have thus been delighted with Mendelssohn's musicianship. As it was, all Felix could say was: "I went to bed moping", his only compensation being an opportunity to draw a sketch of the Pereira house for his mother, having had the edifice pointed out to him.

But, despite this disappointment, Mendelssohn "revelled in amusements of all kinds" in Vienna, with Adolf Marx and Franz Hauser. These included invitations to dine and to take part in musical gatherings. He visited the Burgtheater, "where plays are performed quite outstandingly". "Mlle. Müller is not doing so badly either," Felix wrote; "she bites her lips; has a sweet speaking voice as well." This soprano played a vital part in popularising the songs of Schubert. "The way everything gels makes it satisfying – more so than in Berlin." Felix lived like a Viennese citizen, " doing nothing at all and [I] spend all day occupied with so-called diversions which are, in the long run, very boring". Hauser gave Felix a book of Lutheran hymns, some of which he later set to music, and he made time to lay flowers on the tombs of Beethoven and Schubert; he must have regretted his father's intransigent attitude in denying his son the honour of meeting these two great men. This would have been completely possible, especially in view of Leah's relatives living in Austria! He also met the music librarian Aloys Fuchs and was able to aid him to build up his collection of manuscripts; Mendelssohn, too, was able to rely on this new friend for help with his own musical needs and gifts for his family.

Mendelssohn's tour of Italy and Switzerland in 1830-31 played such an important part in his life that a whole volume of letters was edited about the odyssey. Therefore a separate chapter is devoted to Mendelssohn's travels in these countries, not only on account of the vast detail but also because Fanny and Rebecka wrote profusely about their own Italian visits in 1839-40 and 1844-46 respectively. Thus, the next journey Felix made that is covered here is to Paris in 1832. His earlier vacations are described in Chapter 6, 'Young musicians', and Chapter 27, 'Musicians and other celebrities'.

Because Abraham loved Paris so much, it was felt appropriate that his two elder children should be taken there in 1816 to be given piano lessons by Mme. Marie Bigot, a former pupil of Beethoven, who later (at the age of 34) fell victim to consumption. In 1825, in order to assess just how suitable it would be for Felix to adopt his coveted musical career, which no less a celebrity than Ignaz Moscheles had advocated, Felix was presented to Cherubini at the Paris Conservatoire. Neither Schubert nor Beethoven, both still living in Vienna, were considered good enough to come into the reckoning as mentor to the son of the all-knowing Abraham Mendelssohn!

The father visited Paris again in 1830 on business. The only profit he made, he wrote to Leah, was to learn that ladies' dresses were more sober than before, being mainly white, and that their headwear was "more sensible" than the German fashion periodicals decreed. The young women wore mainly pink and "know how to dress". If Abraham made enough money by his transactions, he would buy his wife an outfit that would "scandalise" Berlin society, as it would be "too sensible" for their taste. He wrote of the Louvre, where paintings by the French School are "crowded into one room". Three pupils at a time were working on Jacques-Louis David's "horrid *Paris and Helen*", as also Raphael's *Holy Family*. Though he had seen David's *The Deluge* previously elsewhere, Abraham "cannot bear" to look at it in its new surroundings; in fact, he dismissed the whole collection in the French School exhibition as "the devil and all his clan". The only artefact to be displayed since his previous visit was the Venus de Milo, reclaimed from the Island of Milo in the 1820s. Abraham knew nothing about this sculpture except that "she has lost both her arms".

"Like all English people", Abraham visited the cemetery of Père Lachaise, 'the city of the dead', which was "becoming more vast, more important and more interesting" each day. In the Rue Ste Honoré, a cab driver told Abraham, children of 12 to 14 were fighting with sticks among the mob during the 1830 Revolution, and from Auxerre he had heard that turnpike roads were closed to avoid paying taxes to the monarch. Hummel and Meyerbeer were staying at his hotel and Hiller introduced Abraham to Hector Berlioz, whom he considered "agreeable...interesting...and more sensible than his music". The dancer Taglioni "accomplished impossibilities with grace and skill, single-mindedness and effortlessness" in her work. Abraham wondered, though, how Rossini could produce such "dissonance" in composing *William Tell*, after *The Barber of Seville* and *Otello*. He spoke of revolution engendering further revolt: "The young people want to rule and the old ones do not like it." Abraham revealed precisely the same attitude as far as Felix was concerned.

In Paris Abraham wrote that everyone was looking forward to his son's forthcoming visit, which would occur in 1832. "Hiller is the best of the Paris musicians"; Abraham claimed this composer to be the arbiter of musical taste and to be far more accomplished than, say, Chopin or Liszt, who resided there at the time! Hiller and Felix became firm friends, and, according to Schima Kaufman, it was Hiller who found lodgings for Mendelssohn next to his own in the Rue Jean-Jacques Rousseau, where Felix "shivered frightfully" after his summer in Italy. Hiller tried to reassure his friend that he would soon become accustomed to the cold of winter and warned Felix that there was nowhere as suitable for him to live. So Felix resigned himself to the situation, writing "there is no alternative but to remain and [to] add more woollens as the temperature falls". Yet Mendelssohn threw himself into the "vortex" of Parisian life, "doing nothing all day but seeing new things: the Chamber of Peers and Deputies, pictures, dio-, cosmo- and panoramas and society", as he told the German poet Karl Immermann.

Felix called upon each musician individually, since though "'numerous as the

Chapter 4: Leisure, at Home and Abroad

sands of the sea', all hating each other…they are all gossips, and what one says to another the whole corps knows the next morning". The time flew by so quickly that not a single bar of music was written. Neither had Mendelssohn seen the poet Heine, who, though in Paris, was "engrossed in liberal ideas and politics". He had written "60 'Spring Songs'", which Felix considered "genuine and truthful on the whole". Mendelssohn was "full of enthusiasm" for Mme. Malibran and, like his father, admired Taglioni, but his life was spoilt by "so many gentlemen reviling and abusing Germany. And yet they cannot speak even tolerable French; I cannot swallow that!" Though his mind was "buzzing with visits and music and politics and people", Felix made sure that Fuchs was kept up to date with musical memorabilia, and promised to send him "anything you require if it is in my power to do so". Fuchs's book of Beethoven sketches was attracting attention in Paris; he called upon "the grumbling Cherubini and the kind Herz". Outside the latter's premises a sign read: "Pianos manufactured by Henri Herz, merchants of fashion and novelties". The mystery was soon solved, however, for Herz's pianos were upstairs; the ground floor, displaying "gauze and lace and trimmings", was occupied by another entrepreneur. On entering Herz's works, Felix observed "a number of fair scholars with industrious faces". A piano bore the legend "Gold Medal for the 1827 Exhibition", which Felix found "very imposing" until he saw the same inscription on a piano at Erard's factory. "My respect seemed to diminish" – even more so when he noticed the precise detail on his own piano from Pleyel.

As regards paintings, unlike his father's grousing Felix felt that "everyone may wish for a thousand more eyes to look at these pictures", particularly those painted by Titian and Raphael.

Though Abraham wished his son to copy young gentlemen of a higher class and "make the Grand Tour", however inferior in quality and size, there was a more important purpose in his plans for his son to travel. He wished Felix to make up his mind where he would live and in which country his music would be best recognised, thereby adding lustre to the Mendelssohn name, rather than out of concern for the composer's own artistic well-being. Thus, when Felix had decided where he would best be suited, he dutifully wrote to his father, as was to be expected, but also to Zelter, proving his absolute sincerity: "People now know that I exist and have a purpose; any talent I display, they are ready to approve and accept, in order to make money from my music." He wanted, as soon as possible, to make himself completely independent of his parents' support. Felix concluded that the best location in which to achieve this was Germany, "about which there is no question". Though Berlin suited him personally, as it was where his home and family existed, yet Felix was uncertain which part of Germany would best suit his musical career. Felix was incessantly prey to exasperating self-effacement. Listing the venues at which various of his compositions were to be performed, he concluded: "but I am sure you will be sick of hearing about so many concerts", overlooking the fact that both father and mentor must have felt pride in the growing fame of son and pupil.

Yet, however loyally Felix spoke of his fatherland, no one can be fooled as to his love for another country. "I will probably [soon] have one foot in the stagecoach; the other in Calais; the third in Dover; and everything else in Bury Street with my dear old chum," he wrote to Klingemann, in anticipation of his forthcoming (second) visit across the Channel to the motherland. Nevertheless, Felix had enjoyed himself in France, despite illness and sad news of friends' deaths. "There is one great thing in Paris; not liberty, but La Taglioni. She is a real artist and dances with lovable innocence... She seems to be the only genuine musician in Paris." But, if he should discover more about her, "she will probably marry a count and leave the theatre, or become a Grande Damme, or the devil knows what". (In fact, it was not until 1847, the year of Mendelssohn's death, that Marie Taglioni left the stage, having been at the top of her profession since 1822, ten years before Felix saw her artistry.) Mendelssohn met Liszt for the first time in Paris, when, according to Hiller, Felix declared: "He has many fingers but few brains. His improvisations are miserable." But, despite this (if Felix's words were accurately reported), the two musicians socialised. Hiller recalled in later memoirs that he, Liszt, Chopin and Mendelssohn met the German pianist Kalkbrenner in a fashionable restaurant. This pompous snob boasted that he was of noble birth, but, Heine wrote, Friedrich Kalkbrenner appeared as if "thrown out by a confectioner"; his speech "almost, but not quite, concealed Berlinisms of the lowest kind". Thus, when he discovered that the four musicians were dressed in rags, like beggars, as a practical joke, Kalkbrenner was "outraged" and "too mortified to speak". Another memory recorded by Hiller concerned these four, crossing a Paris boulevard "at a late hour". Felix suddenly exclaimed: "We must do some of our jumps in Paris! Some jumps, I say! Here goes: one, two, three!" and everyone followed his fine example. Hiller revealed that his own performance was "not very brilliant", having been too "taken aback" at the idea, but he would never forget the incident.

Fanny, too, visited France, travelling to Boulogne for sea bathing, but her experiences were decidedly unfortunate. Accommodation was difficult to find on account of so many English tourists, but when the Hensels did achieve success the lodging was so dilapidated that the ceiling collapsed and let in rain. Fanny developed an eye infection that prevented her going out of doors; neither did the extortionate prices add to the enjoyment of what should have been a lovely holiday: it is hardly surprising, therefore, that Fanny referred to Boulogne with abhorrence, its only redeeming feature being the fact that friends and acquaintances congregated there. Heine complained of the "chattering ladies" in the hotel reading room, prompting him to apologise if his reading disturbed their talk. Sarah Austin, the novelist, was also staying in Boulogne; Klingemann, too, spent three days with the Hensels – the first occasion on which Fanny's husband met this family friend. They spent a night in Calais and stayed at a "pleasant" hotel at Dunkirk. The name of this latter had fascinated Fanny as a child, conjuring up "some strange Indian place", as she related to Klingemann. Travelling eastward, along a road made of shells, with the sea on the left and the downs on the right, the Hensels missed their direction and arrived at Ostend; then it was on to Bruges, which impressed Fanny greatly. The town had not changed since the Van Dyck family lived and worked there. In Ghent, the 16th-century houses were being replaced by modern buildings. At "regal", 17th-century Antwerp the party would have liked to remain longer, though they enjoyed a better social life in Brussels, meeting various friends. The Hensels paid their farewell to Belgium by visiting the town hall at Louvain, and with a trip to a private art collection.

Chapter 5

"Italy at Last"

These were the words that Felix wrote on arrival in 1830 in the land to which he had looked forward to visiting for so long. His own Italian odyssey is constantly being mentioned whenever the 'Italian' Symphony is performed, but it is little known that his sisters longed to visit Italy just as eagerly, and their observations are equally fascinating. All three shed a different light on what they experienced, both artistic and decidedly mundane. Regarding Felix's travels, two myths are perpetuated, by biographers and broadcasters. Both are incorrect. His father is given credit for organising his son's journey, which encompassed the 'Grand Tour of Europe'. His letters indicate that Felix himself organised his trips abroad, as far as his niggardly allowance from his parents would permit. As for where he visited, Italy and Switzerland were the main locations; Paris was explored because, as his father loved the city so much, Felix may have felt duty-bound to go there. Other towns in France, Belgium, Austria and what was to become Hungary were staging posts en route to a destination. Britain was a place where he worked and where most of his ideas were developed. Felix never visited Spain, Greece or Turkey like Lord Byron; he never travelled to Egypt, as the artist Baron Leighton was to do barely a few years later; neither did he venture into the Holy Land, where William Holman Hunt gained inspiration for some of his most celebrated paintings. As for the remarkable explorer James Holman, Mendelssohn's contemporary, who – though without sight – toured throughout Russia, this would have been unthinkable for Felix to undertake, even though his father became banker to the Tsar. Mendelssohn was even forbidden to visit Sicily, as Abraham decided it to be rife with bandits, thus spoiling Felix's plan to follow Goethe's Italian and Swiss travels, which had been chronicled; it was only after Abraham's death that Rebecka's family and Fanny's husband were able to discover how cultured the Sicilians actually proved to be.

Before departing from Berlin the actor Eduard Devrient asked Felix to kiss him in farewell. Though Devrient normally disapproved of two men kissing, he would recall in his 1869 memoirs, on that occasion he was glad to have done so. Then, on to Italy for Felix. His first port of call would be Venice; he felt at home even whilst driving along the roads. He described the buildings with their "roofs with convex tiles, deep windows, high white walls and lofty, square towers". He saw "chapels, brightly and colourfully painted, with flowers on every side; the monks and nuns, all symptomatic of Italy". In view of the length of time during which he had dreamt about that land, Felix expected to experience "an emotional explosion violent and startling"; instead, he felt "an indescribable sensation of pervasive content and satisfaction" at his first sight of the landscape. "The carriage seemed to fly along the smooth roads." Yet, when the time came to sleep, our traveller was annoyed by the chatter of two fellow passengers, "but my snoring finally silenced them after a time". Presumably, this was a pretence; otherwise, Felix would not have known he was snoring, had he been asleep. The coachman warned him that, once in Venice, no one would speak German, "so I took leave of my mother tongue for a long time to come". Felix planned to travel as often as possible by water, observing that the Greek, Telemachus, found this mode of transport easier than travelling by land. When he did take a boat, Felix noticed a rock with a lamp burning on it. Here, the boatman removed his hat, explaining that this was the site of the Madonna of the Tempests, who protected sailors from the "violent, dangerous storms". Felix noted all the usual tourist attractions along the canals of this ancient city state: "the theatre; St Mark's Cathedral; the lions; the Doge's palace; the Bridge of Sighs" – the title used by Thomas Hood for his moving poem written at a similar date. But what fascinated Felix most was the silence on leaving land – "no rattling wheels; no post horses or toll keepers. The obscurity of the night only enhanced my delight on hearing the familiar names and seeing the dark outline of the townscape."

On Sundays, the people wore clothing of bright colour, the women with roses in their hair, the men riding to church on donkeys; at the inns, Felix observed "idlers in the most indolent attitudes". A man placed his arm around his wife's waist, swinging her round, and, whilst "this may seem trivial", to Felix "it made a pretty effect". The atmosphere was so festive, "as if a prince were expected to make his grand entry. The town square resembled a large, gaudy transparency, with paper lanterns." Felix attended the Church of St John and St Paul (as Goethe had done in 1786), which was destroyed by fire in 1867. Of all the many paintings Felix saw in Italy, one of his favourites was Titian's *Annunciation of the Blessed Virgin* – "the most divine work ever produced by the hand of mankind", as he described it. He rowed in the Adriatic and visited the public gardens "where people lie on the grass and eat". In order to drown the noise of the band playing in St Mark's Square, Felix composed No. 6 of his Op. 19 *Songs without Words*, later to be known as 'In a Gondola'.

When Fanny visited Venice in 1839, her letters home had a more domestic slant. After the "dirty little Hotel Luna", Aulan Robert, brother of the artist Ludwig, who had taken his own life when his wife Friederike died of cholera, found rooms for the Hensels. Fanny was "not fit to be seen on account of the mosquito

Chapter 5: "Italy at Last"

bites"; her eyelids were swollen and her face, neck and hands looked as if they had been tattooed. Fanny then described the food, about which Cécile had enquired: roasts were served without gravy; the casseroles were delicious and the cheese, served with soup, was equally good. The soup itself, made with rice, macaroni or vegetables, was "monotonous", the bread "indifferent" and the butter "not fit to be eaten"; the pears were delicious, as also "a kind of biscuit named 'Invisibili'". The Venetians appeared to eat no vegetables except "a rather bad cabbage". Though good, wine was inferior to that on the mainland; and coffee was "drunk to the dregs"; Fanny chose milk, but water was her favourite beverage, which she would continue to imbibe on leaving Venice; the Venetians advised mixing water with wine. There were strawberries, even in October, but the next day the weather became so cold that a fire had to be lit in the Hensels' lodgings. Each evening the family spent an hour in a local café drinking tea and reading newspapers. Fanny complained about "the noise of the bands, the crying children and the shouts of the vendors" at a fair. "It is evident that people of a lower order congregate at such events." However, she praised the singing of a soprano and tenor, "performing correctly and with taste". A marionette theatre was "not at all bad of its kind", with "quarrels, shouting and singing" and a duel between the singers. On returning to their lodgings at 9 p.m., Fanny discovered she had lost a brooch, which her husband "absolutely found" on returning to the piazza. "Was that not lucky?" The evenings were too dark for the Hensels to row in a gondola but, like Felix, Fanny believed that Goethe's diaries of Italy should be studied; nothing had altered since his visit.

Travelling to Florence, Felix had imagined the Apennines as "richly wooded, picturesque hills", whereas they were "melancholy" and "bleak" with an occasional little stream. As the coachman drove "recklessly" along the route, Felix noticed there, and in the city itself, many vehicles containing "the most refined English ladies". In view of his present "shabby and dirty" state from the journey, he reflected that only when he could avail himself of "a little white linen and so forth" these "beautiful creatures might shake hands with me one day". Not only did he give minute details of his travels for his future memory, but, a cynic would suspect, to placate Leah and allow her to preen herself at her good fortune that she had stayed at home, rather than encountering the negative aspects of her son's journey. He wrote incessantly, for instance, of cheating coachmen and landladies. He called his present driver a "villainous knave, cheat and impostor", who directed him to "a detestable little inn" whose filth was "indescribable". It can be imagined that the stairs, "covered with dead leaves and firewood", were the most attractive part of the accommodation. Having escaped the otherwise freezing rooms, he heard peasants crowded round the kitchen stove, "babbling in their own incomprehensible dialect" and looking suspiciously at this new guest. Felix himself supervised the preparation of the soup, which, "though giving good advice on the subject", proved "inedible". Later Felix was shown "sackcloth sheets" described as "very fine linen", in which he slept "like a bear" until the next morning; "without breakfast". Asked how he had enjoyed the previous evening's "entertainment," Felix may have been hard put to know how to answer, for "a great deal of nonsense" was spoken, the topics including politics, the state of France and "abuse of my horse in German". French was used solely to converse with beggars; Felix "corrected faults in their pronunciation from my throne – a bench beside the hearth". He heard about Rationza, a small hill that incessantly vomited forth flames, which had "a singular effect in the darkness" – evidently a ploy to attract tourists.

Neither was he impressed with the *Fornarina*, except for the model's facial expression, which he realised was "a faithful reproduction" in the painting. He called the two Venuses "two spirits flying through the hall, grasping the spectators as they passed", inspiring "a feeling of piety". He visited the tower where the astronomer Galileo studied the firmament, the structure having been converted for use in winemaking. Felix examined the process of drying the grapes and the mending of casks. A girl who acted as guide escorted him to the top of the tower in order that he could see a beautiful view of the city, all the while "recounting a number of stories in her peculiar dialect, which I scarcely understood", and plying him with "sweet grapes, which I ate with great gusto". Felix lost his way whilst exploring another tower, and met "a Frenchman with green spectacles" in the same predicament, despite a map. Further innkeepers were portrayed in Mendelssohn's correspondence to detrimental effect. He vowed to pay only what he considered the proper value for goods or services "and not to pay at all if asked more than I can give". One landlady proved so stubborn that she would not even show her guest the obligatory regulations regarding customers' rights. This prompted Felix to imitate the way of life of his present locality; "using physical force" he pushed the innkeeper into an adjoining room from the passage where they had been arguing and hurried into the street. "The crowd of boys at my heels increased at every step" until "a decent-looking gentleman whom they seemed to respect" took Felix to a vine-dresser's, where a coach was organised to convey him to his next destination. But it was only when "the brave Signor" threw a handful of coins to the beggars that Felix was left in peace.

Of a play that he attended, Mendelssohn dismissed the drama as "a silly, objectionable piece that would not even please a cat". Yet, despite all his grumbles, there were enjoyable events in Florence. Felix joined the crowd at the races, followed by a masked ball at the Goldoni Theatre in the evening, arriving at his lodging at 1 a.m. with the assumption that his entertainment was over for the day. But, having seen the illuminated pergola, it was realised that gondolas were still plying the Arno in all directions, decorated with coloured lamps. A ship with green lanterns was visible but, even more brightly, the moon radiated onto the scene. Guilt caused Felix to apologise to his father for sending home a crate of wine that the sculptor Schadow had ordered. "The local wine is the most wonderful that I have yet savoured," he said to expiate his extravagance; though not expensive, he

Chapter 5: "Italy at Last"

was, nevertheless, "apprehensive" of Abraham's reaction. "Once you have opened and sampled the wine, I shall not worry any more, for you will sing my praises. It is the noblest wine I know of, and I think that you, especially, will like it very much and that it will do you good, for it is supposed to fortify the stomach." He asked that Zelter and Julius Reitz should be given "ten and five little French bottles" respectively, with a note to each recipient.

But the most exciting experience was the plethora of art galleries in Florence, as can be seen from Felix's notes on those who created the masterpieces. Titian must have been a marvellous man, enjoying life through his work, his portraits revealing him to have been "vigorous and regal". He described Domicino as "precise, austere, [yet] bright and buoyant"; Guido "pale, dignified, masterly, keen"; Langfranco "a grotesque mask; a good farfarola and reveller"; Ganearcacchi "peeping and prying"; the two Carachis "like two members of a guild"; Giorgioni "chivalrous and fantastic; serene and clear"; Caravaggio "rather commonplace and catlike"; Guarachino "handsome and affected; melancholy and dark"; Bertini "the red-haired, the stern, the old-fashioned teacher"; da Vinci "the lion"; and, in the centre, Raphael "heavenly"; Michelangelo "ugly, vigorous, malignant"; Carlo Dolci "a coxcomb"; Gerard Dau "a mere appendage among his kitchen utensils". Fanny, for whom these observations were written, was asked to notice the busts of the Medici family, "for they were [the gallery's] founder". Felix also pointed out a self-portrait of Fra Bartolomeo in a painting "falling backwards downstairs in terror, because the angel had already been painted on the canvas" without his knowledge. The paintings of churches were "beyond belief", and Fanny was asked to give her own opinion on her brother's assessments of the artists, via their portraits.

If Brunelleschi's statue outside the Duomo did not please her, Felix could not help her; the Duomo itself was written off as "not bad". His enjoyment of the Tribune Room at the Uffizi Palace found its way into Samuel Butler's novel *The Way of All Flesh*. The author wonders "how many chalks did Mendelssohn give himself for sitting, two hours at a time, and how often he looked at his watch to see when this period of reflection ended. How often did he tell himself that he was as big as any of the artists..? How vexed he became, seeing so many people pass him by without noticing him? That, if the truth be known, his two hours were not quite two hours." If Butler is joking, his jest is in thoroughly bad taste; if serious, his ignorance can be treated with the contempt it deserves. Mendelssohn, who worshipped truth, would have spent two hours in the Uffizi if he said he had; fascinated by anything relating to art of the past, in whatever form, it is utterly believable that he spent such a time in one location. All he cared about was the privilege of being able to feast on these priceless treasures, and, as likely as not, he was completely unaware of anyone else alive in the room. "Here is a place where one feels one's own insignificance and [where] one may well learn to be humble," Mendelssohn stated. Felix marvelled at the scenery, imagining Hensel calling his brother-in-law "a northern bear" at such amazement.

Whether or not Fanny did agree with her brother's assessments of the various artists is not known. Rebecka had more mundane tales to tell of Florence, however. The fact that most houses had no locks on doors in what she called this "queer, dirty little place". Coachmen, too, left much to be desired. They would not be suitable for introduction to a German drawing room, especially on Sundays, when the ladies washed more thoroughly than usual. Even when crossing a street with her skirt tucked up, coach drivers would allow the horses to throw dust in her face, or a householder would throw the contents of a dustbin (or those of a chamber-pot) at her. The family promised their coachman to return in the spring, but this pledge was given to everyone when leaving an Italian town.

But, like Fanny, Rebecka was impressed by the mosaics and the blue of the Mediterranean, and, like Felix, she planned to visit as many tourist attractions as possible. Thus, she was "bewildered" by the myriad art treasures in the Pitti Palace but, as so many saint's days occurred in Florence, art galleries were often closed – sometimes for nine days in a month. She found the theatre so luxurious when attending a Donizetti opera that she was tempted to talk through the performance rather than concentrating thereon. Rebecka observed the "red sofa, marble table and mirror in the box" where the Dirichlet family sat. A descendant of the Medici family, Countess 'S' reminded Rebecka of the "little princess" of whom Goethe had written – "small, always on the twirl and always chattering". The frescoes and statues reminded her of "one of Aunt Levy's Saturdays". Minna, the maid, could not understand why Italians never offered their guests anything to eat. Rebecka wished there were fields through which to ramble and have picnics, as in Germany. In September, snow fell, but the previous hot weather had dried up the bed of the Arno, causing it to resemble a gutter, Rebecka observed, preventing her becoming impressed with the scenery, unlike Fanny. Night followed sunset, with no twilight in between. Once, some monks in white masks with eyeholes walked by, carrying a coffin, reminding Rebecka of a painting. The Pantheon revealed memorials to Dante, Michelangelo and Galileo, on whose behalf Rebecka expressed disgust, when visiting his garden, at the way he had been debarred from propounding his scientific ideas. But the most delightful experience for the Dirichlets was the birth of Florentina, shortened to Flora, as described in Chapter 3, 'Sound minds in frail bodies'. In Milan, as he explained to Fanny in his notes before her visit, Felix saw the "millions of pictures" and the cathedral, and climbed its tower to see the beautiful view. Fanny considered the building "the most beautiful church in Italy; God himself has not created anything more wonderful", overlooking the fact that it was the architect, whom God had inspired and guided, who had achieved this feat. Rebecka and her family also took their first walk, "of course", to the cathedral. On that occasion it was the feast day of the Virgin Mary, and, thus, the pictures were illuminated. The Dirichlets and the mathematician Jacobi climbed the tower, "giving ourselves up to the influence for an hour".

For Felix, when in Milan, a milestone was his acquaintance with Mme.

Chapter 5: "Italy at Last"

Dorothea von Ertmann, an erstwhile pupil and friend of Beethoven – and innuendo from some sources implies more than this, but no proof exists. Unlike his inhibited attitude in Austria towards Mme. von Pereira, Felix took the initiative to meet General von Ertmann and his wife, having recalled their residing in Milan. When Dorothea played Beethoven's C sharp minor and D minor Piano sonatas, tears came into the general's eyes, so long had it been since he had heard his wife play. "There is not a person in Milan who would not have wished to have heard what I heard," Felix reported later. His hostess admitted that she could not recall how a Beethoven trio went, so Felix played the piece, singing the parts for violin and 'cello. The Ertmanns' kindness was "quite overwhelming" to Mendelssohn; the general took him sightseeing and Mme. Ertmann invited him to drive with her in the carriage in the afternoon. Mendelssohn dined at their house and a party was given, "with music", lasting until 1 a.m. "They are the most agreeable and cultured couple you can imagine and as much in love with one another as a honeymoon couple – yet they have been married for four and thirty years," Felix wrote to his family. General von Ertmann, "in his grey uniform, covered with orders", spoke to Felix of his campaigns "with such lucidity and liberality, the like of which I have never encountered, except from my father", placating Abraham in order to assuage any envy on his part. Fanny was likewise soothed: Mme. Ertmann sang "in a voice that emanates from the depths of her soul", but that of Fanny was "eminently superior".

Mme. von Ertmann "recounted several anecdotes about Beethoven": how, for instance, when their youngest child died, the composer shrank from visiting them, but had eventually invited Dorothea to his lodgings with the words "Let us speak to each other through music". Dorothea played Beethoven's 'Kreutzer' Sonata, Op. 47, accompanied by an Austrian cavalry officer on the violin. When he played a flourish in the manner of Paganini, Felix "almost fell off the chair with laughter at the desperate grimaces" on the general's face.

Leah had asked her son to visit Herr Teschner, whom Felix described, forgetting his usual tact, as "depressing as a thick fog. Mme. Ertmann has more soul in her little finger than that fellow has in his whole body, with his formidable moustache, behind which he seems to lie in ambush." But an entirely different contact was introduced by his hostess – Franz Xavier Wolfgang Mozart, youngest son of Wolfgang Amadeus Mozart. Haydn had promised the composer that this son would receive musical instruction from his elderly fellow musician. On this topic, Norman Lebrecht cites a diary entry of 1914 of the Irish composer Charles Villiers Stanford. When Mendelssohn played Beethoven's Piano Sonata, Op. 101 (dedicated to "my dear Dorothea"), "a modest little Austrian officer" approached the piano from his seat in a corner of the room, asking Mendelssohn to "play something by my father". On being asked his name, the man replied, "Ach, Mozart." Mendelssohn "did play Mozart for him, and for the rest of the evening". It is not known in what context Stanford included this anecdote, but Felix's letter home does not tally. It was, according to Mendelssohn himself, the hostess who asked him to play a Mozart work, otherwise her guest would be "quite upset". Felix played a piano arrangement of the *Don Giovanni* Overture, whereat the young Mozart "thawed" and requested a similar version of the overture to *The Magic Flute*. "He is a musician, heart and soul" and reminded Mendelssohn of his eminent father "in the very phrases...with their candour and simplicity" that Mozart used in his letters. His sayings "constantly recur in the son's conversation, whom no one can fail to love from the moment of introduction". Franz Mozart, in turn, introduced Mendelssohn to his own friends at Lake Como, the traveller's next destination, where he amused himself "famously" with "lively conversation" on many subjects. One of these was the love affairs of the notorious novelist George Sand, which Mendelssohn found "strange", as this matter no longer concerned anyone elsewhere. Before leaving Milan, Felix made time to improve the musical manuscript library of Aloys Fuchs in Vienna.

Writing to Ferdinand Hiller in 1837, the memory of his stay in Milan still lingered in Mendelssohn's memory. He asked how fellow musicians Liszt, Pixis and Rossini were faring in Italy and how Hiller himself enjoyed "the plains of Lombardy". He had to "drink in the air and idle away the days", as Felix had done. Fanny, Hensel and Sebastian were to visit Hiller on Lake Como on their 1839 travels in Italy, delighted to meet old friends once more. Hiller accompanied them to the Villa d'Este, "where Queen Caroline of England had lived", once her husband, George IV, had divorced her. It was, therefore, several years before Liszt's famous representation of the fountains was composed that Fanny wrote of seeing them from all directions, and ate a meal beside their cascades and sang her own setting of a poem by Hensel. The family saw the well, mentioned in Pliny's letters (including one discovered subsequent to his death), in Latin and Italian, recommending tourists to drink at the well – which the Hensels did. The next day they met a cultured gentleman, who, on learning to whom he was speaking, enquired about Felix and other musical friends in Germany, adding that he had heard "a thousand things" as to the Mendelssohns' hospitality. At first, Fanny considered Milan to be "neat and clean" with "beggars, none; fleas, fewer" but "dirt up to both ears". Grapes cost "next to nothing, peaches are too hard for eating", but she would "love to place the figs" in Rebecka's mouth. The Hensels toured the cathedral, the Brera gallery and La Scala opera house, learning the language from the laundress or waiters, finding this method more useful than studying grammar or phrase books.

At Monza the cathedral was in dire need of repair, and the palace that belonged to Frederick Barbarossa was to be pulled down. As the King of Bavaria owned it, however, Hensel was to approach him to see if it could be preserved. Padua was likewise "mouldering in decay" but, at the Church of St Antony, frescoes still showed the saint's acts; one depicted Antony teaching a child to speak, whilst another showed him mending glasses and plates. This led Fanny to remark that,

Chapter 5: "Italy at Last"

should she ever become a Catholic, Antony's was the name she would take – feminising it, presumably to "Antonia" or "Antoinette". In the chapel there could still be seen the dirt removed from the paintings by Jacopo d'Avanzi and the tables, placed one on another, used by Förster to undertake this task.

In his notes to Fanny, Felix admonished her to see everything between Genoa and Assisi, but – above all – the Church of St Francis. Of Genoa Cathedral, a journal entry for 16th August 1839 stated that, though officially its style was "Lombardo-Gothic", to Fanny the way in which the stonework was constructed resembled "a striped mattress cover". The style would be called "the ticking fashion" if she were writing a history of art. Hensel's favourite painting appeared in the Brignole Palace, that of Reubens and his wife; "with fawns and satyrs – too indecent" for Fanny's taste, her preference being for Palma Vecchio's *Adoration of the Magi*; Reubens was represented by other portraits, together with Titian and Van Dyck. The owners of the palace were portrayed "large as life and twice as fat, with their fine, white hands hanging down, standing, sitting, riding, with or without children, in enormous ruffs and the women in ugly dresses that must have been the fashion of the period". Countess Negri, in whose home the Hensels stayed, displayed portraits of her compatriots, including Christopher Columbus and Paganini. The hostess showed her guests such treasures as a cane and snuffbox that had belonged to Napoleon, and a knife and fork owned by the sculptor Benvenuto Cellini, "a pretty old harp and similar articles of the kind". In the summer house, Fanny noticed an inscription relating to George Washington. She recognised the Luini frescoes from the Brera gallery at Milan as "old friends". Of the Church of Sant Ambrogio, Hensel thought its former glory could be restored "with the removal of a few ornaments and a little dirt". Dirt also featured more dramatically in Rebecka's observations of Genoa. The hotel was said to be the best in the area, but, "really, Fanny", the place was "too bad to be discussed. Six dead; 20 dismissed as cured; the remainder uncountable." This tally referred to fleas, caught and uncaught. "Doors had to be opened with tongs. Not to mention the 'unmentionables'", the condition of which (whatever this euphemism encapsulated) "could not be contemplated". Rebecka experienced "the most dreadful nausea", cried "several times a day" and "turned sick at all I saw and smelt".

On an excursion to the neighbouring lakes the family ate breakfast under a sycamore tree and felt better than before. Though fashion demanded that Lake Como should be praised, Rebecka preferred Lake Maggiore and Lake Geneva. Driving along the road from Genoa, they reached Nevi, where the Latin poet Pindar had lived and which he called "supernatural". They spent the night at Chiavari under mosquito nets, which reminded Rebecka of the paper in which German butter and cheese was wrapped. The light, airy locality of the Gulf of Spezia, where Byron had lived and where people still spoke of what Napoleon would plan when he conquered Italy (which never happened), reminded Rebecka of fairyland. She could not understand why Fanny and her family had not deigned to visit this area.

At Carrara the buildings were made of marble from the local quarries and the workshop doors were always open so that tourists could see the craftsmen employed. A German sculptor, simply referred to as 'W', "dragged" the Dirichlets into his workshop, pledging eternal friendship to be renewed in Rome. Even the bread, lobster and fish that they were given to eat was hard enough to be made of marble and Rebecka noticed at least 20 carts that carried either newly made baths or blocks of untreated marble to the sawmills or polishing-plants. There were, though, some mishaps. Like Fanny and Felix, Rebecka also suffered seasickness on the boat excursions the family made, and she hoped the Hensels "would not be offended" on relating how they had been cheated at Modena and Lucca. At least four horses and three postilions were thrust upon them at each horse change, and, though Dirichlet argued "in his choicest Italian", the invariable excuse was that the coachmen could not read the tariff. On one stage, Rebecka was convinced that a passenger had been killed by the coach driver, and on arriving in Lucca all the hotels were occupied because a naturalists' congress was taking place. A "Signor Professore" would accommodate the family, however, and it would be "politic" to stay with them, local inhabitants told the Dirichlets. A woman who resided at the lodging sported "an extraordinary state of dress – or undress", as Rebecka wrote. Like Fanny, she herself looked as if she was suffering from scarlet fever on account of the mosquito bites on her sunburnt skin.

Though it was winter when Felix arrived in Rome, oranges hung from the trees in bright sunshine; flower girls were selling violets and anemones to the gaily clothed pedestrians in the streets. He had "more fun than ever before" at a ball and combined "gaiety and seriousness" in a way that could "only be found in Rome", evidently forgetting his visit to London the year before.

His room at No. 5 Piazza di Spagna, near the Spanish Steps, was on the first floor. The sun shone all day from the two windows and the room contained "a good Viennese grand piano"; on the table lay manuscripts and portraits of Allegri and Palestrina and a book of the Psalms in Latin. His landlord had been a captain in the French army; his daughter "possesses the most beautiful contralto voice I have ever heard" – better than that of Fanny?

He talked politics with a Prussian captain who lived on the floor above, whilst Felix's mornings were spent in work, the afternoons in sightseeing – and he found it difficult to break away from each activity. At a party given by Count Bunsen, then Prussian ambassador in Rome, the subject of "the worthy Mozart and his many sins" was discussed; Felix responded that he would willingly renounce any virtue of his own in exchange for any sin of Mozart's, and added "but I could not determine the extent of his virtues", at which the company laughed.

One place Mendelssohn avoided was the Café Greco, which Hector Berlioz, in Rome at the same time, disliked equally. The eight-foot-square room was dark and customers smoked at one side; "Artists sit around on benches, wearing broad-brimmed hats, hair covering their faces". But far worse for Mendelssohn was their criticism of the old masters whilst themselves producing "such sickly Madonnas; such feeble saints and such milksop heroes". If Felix achieved anything at that café, it would be his rudeness towards these "philistines – these judges from Hades". A cravat or a smart coat would be out of place in such surroundings, where mastiffs "see to the spread of vermin" by befouling this eating and drinking establishment.

But, when the weather broke, his previously comfortable room took on a different guise: rain poured in; the fire would not burn; foreign visitors shivered and froze; indigenous residents spoke of the climate as a national disaster. But to venture out of doors was even worse. Since Rome is built on seven hills, with smaller ones alongside, the streets slope and the rain pours towards anyone walking there, and there was, when Mendelssohn travelled to Rome, no footpath or pavement. "The Spanish Steps are flooded like the great waterworks at Wilhelmshaven" near Hamburg; "the river Tiber has burst its banks and the houses, which slope precipitously, have no waterspouts", resulting in further flooding. "One must rush into a doorway when a carriage passes and, when two vehicles meet, the gutter is the sole retreat. An abbot's umbrella knocked a peasant's hat from his head" and was filled with water when retrieved. Yet nothing prevented

Figure 3. Pencil drawing of Atrani, Italy 1830

Felix from attending parties; "The coach arrives at 5 p.m. and costs one scudo". He attended a ball at the home of the artist Horace Vernet and a party at the home of unspecified English friends. He also visited the Villa Bartholdy, telling his family that the owners had converted the salon into sleeping accommodation "with a four-poster bed – a noble, regal idea". Yet, he reflected, whatever comfort was available, just as many tourists looked forward to their own beds at home, and he was no exception.

In his notes to Fanny before her 1839-40 trip to Italy, Felix advised her to "be as weary as you like when the chanting of the Psalms takes place; it is of no matter", but said that she should hear everything in the Sistine Chapel "and compose some melodies or something". She had to "look out of every window at every convent near the Lateran", towards the Albano Hills, and "count the number of houses at Frascati in the sunshine, as it is far more beautiful there than the whole of Russia and Poland" (neither of which countries Felix ever visited.) Whereas Venice's past made Felix "out of sorts and sad", as if in a mausoleum, Rome made him feel "serious and illuminated" by her history. He had the same feelings as the ones that Goethe had expressed, and was pleased to have repeated the same sequence of his journey as the poet. He would, meanwhile, "try to acquire a new manner of painting", as he was dissatisfied with the sketches he had produced hitherto in Italy.

Felix visited a theatre to see an opera by Pacini. After the finale "the whole pit stood up, talking to each other as loudly as they could, laughing and turning their backs to the stage". Countess Samoilova fainted and had to be carried from her box. The composer left the piano and the curtain fell "amid great tumult". The ballet *Bluebeard* interrupted the opera. This was hissed, the opera booed, and, though the manager was called, he did not acknowledge the applause; Mendelssohn felt "considerably out of humour", calling the music "so wretched as to be really beneath all criticism". Whereas Pacini had been so popular that the people wished to crown him king in the Capitol, his work was now so parodied and "sung in such a ridiculous style", proving to Felix "how low a musician stands in public opinion". Mendelssohn considered Italy to be "the 'Land of Nature' rather than the 'Land of Art'". "The beautiful scenery yields far more than the vapid, tasteless theatre." Thus, Felix and his companions "ramble around, chasing each other on the Campagna and jumping fences", driving home at sunset, "weary but self-satisfied, as if we had achieved great things, which we have, if we appreciate the outings properly". He sketched and painted, not only to recall "the play of colours" but to quicken his perceptions and powers of observation.

The Hensels' visit to Rome was equally lively, but the previous journey was less satisfactory. At Ricorsi, the one stop they made en route from Florence, the hotel was "disagreeable". Two stonemasons were ousted from their beds to accommodate Fanny and her husband, whilst Sebastian had to share his bed with the family poodle; their meal was mutton from a wild sheep that had to be shot when eventually caught. Fanny was so certain that the hotel was nothing other than a

Chapter 5: "Italy at Last"

robbers' den that she would not sleep and advised Hensel and Sebastian to keep awake also. But, once in Rome, the family were so comfortable that they kept "open house", Fanny calculating that only three evenings had been spent when no guests had arrived. One evening Fanny was "provoked into sleep" when two visitors arrived late. A journal entry states of 'K': "He chases after wit, which refuses to be caught, bounding off at such a pace that he is left hopelessly behind." 'T', his companion, a Dutchman "is so unutterably dull that there should be a longer word to describe his personality, as 'dull' is too short". Yet he was "too lively for a Dutchman", whereas Ingres, head of the French Academy in Rome, was "too clumsy for a Frenchman". This proved that "a dull Frenchman is more amusing than a witty Dutchman". The Hensels saw the Church of St Paul being built and visited the Protestant cemetery, where Sebastian laid flowers on the tomb of Jakob Bartholdy, Leah's brother, for his grandmother's benefit. Another tomb was that of a Miss Bathurst, who had fallen into the river whilst riding along its bank and drowned. They visited the Scipio Palace with a Spanish monk, the baths at Caracalla, where Felix had accompanied Berlioz, and the catacombs, one passage of which had been closed 60 years before, when 50 students, exploring without a guide, had never returned above ground. Fanny found she could indulge in reverie far better in the quiet darkness than in the sunlight with the noise of the workaday world to disturb her thoughts. Though she had vowed to mention nothing in her letters about antiquities, the whole atmosphere of Rome was contagious and conducive to her enjoyment of scenes from the past.

The Hensels lodged near the Trevi Fountain, which, like their accommodation at the Baltic resort of Heringsdorf, had an out-of-tune piano. The keys were half a tone lower than normal and made "a noise like a fur cap on a woollen blanket", as Fanny described the sound. To compensate, the servant Caliban "does as much work as Heinrich, Sophie, Colberg, and Minna in Berlin and has the meal ready promptly at 1.30 p.m. and keeps the place spotless, running errands and returning like a greyhound, ready for the next task".

Caliban's schedule left him half an hour "to make speeches"; his only annoying habit was the typically Roman one of making one journey for an orange or a grain of salt. During Lent, Fanny complained of Rome's dullness, there being no ball organised. There were 12,000 bachelors or more, and Fanny wondered why St Ursula could not bring her contingent of 10, 000 virgins to join them. There was, however, an 11-year-old boy who was to join Sebastian in French lessons. As the weather became hotter, many people gave up tea drinking or having flowers in the room. Oranges varied in cost from 10, 12 or 15 for one paolo (a quarter of a franc), but were mixed together. There were few fruits so that neither preserves nor compotes – "tormented fruit", as Hensel called them – could be made. The peas were delicious and Hensel loved the fennel, which Fanny would try to cultivate on her return, though she "cannot bring my taste to appreciate" this herb. The "caporetto" (young goat) reminded Fanny of wild mutton, but, above all, she enjoyed the air in Rome.

Like her brother, Fanny visited the Villa Bartholdy, observing that the owners had added modern furniture, vases and paintings to the original treasures. By contrast, the Villa Allan, where the German archaeologist Winkelmann had lived, had been allowed to fall into disrepair, but it was now being restored to its "former order and glory". If Fanny had owned such a property, she was sure she would never let strangers in. A souvenir hunter had removed a piece of stone from a statue, so staff were employed to show visitors round. The Hensels met an Irish family named Palliser. There were "three gigantic daughters, with handsome English faces on long, slender flower stalks, who ride, paint horses and landscapes, speak French, German and Italian fluently and sing badly". There was "a tall son, a pleasant mother and a good-looking father". The mother told Fanny she had met Felix in Frankfurt, which, as singing "is not one of their prettiest accomplishments", Fanny wondered how her brother would have reacted on hearing their rendition of choruses from *St Paul*. Fanny was astonished at the Pallisers' friendliness, reflecting that this was because they were Irish, not English. She was "vexed" by the way English tourists "lived in a compact mass, making a nationality of themselves", keeping themselves apart rather than mixing with the indigenous population of Rome. Their national pride, "which allows them to do great things as a nation, seems intolerably arrogant in the individual and, when anyone takes pains to be kind, such a person is usually as clumsy as a bear". Her own shyness may not have helped matters and the proverbial English reserve may well have been unjustly mistaken for arrogance on Fanny's part. As it was, Fanny refused to play the piano at English entertainments because, however languid previously or subsequently, once the music began, "conversation becomes animated". Such lack of courtesy may have fostered the legend that England was "the land without music".

The first hour of the Dirichlets' stay in Rome was, as with all other journeys, occupied with "washing, changing clothes and eating". Rebecka then rested on her laurels – "literally true", as she had brought a quantity of this foliage from Terni. Her husband took their elder son Walter sightseeing with some German artist friends who were living in Rome. The family had hoped to stay at the Villa Bartholdy but, as with other accommodation, though 60 scudi were offered, the villa was available for a six-month term only. However, their lodging at No. 45 Via Capo da Casa was pronounced "fine, with a little dirt thrown in"; their third-floor rooms "sunny and airy and, as far as human notions go, comfortable". Fanny had asked her sister to give her love to the Albano hills, with their little white houses reminiscent of children's building bricks. The parents should take their boys to the 'Yellow Streak', where Hannibal is said to have stood.

On leaving Florence, Rebecka had written that, having seen a Dürer engraving, which had existed "before Italians knew how to paint", and a Cimabue Madonna, she would willingly forgo the tourist attractions of Rome, since one each of these

Chapter 5: "Italy at Last"

art forms was enough for her taste. Meanwhile, when Dirichlet did not "drag" her out for a walk, Rebecka warmed her back in the sunshine, turning to do the same with her hands and feet, on the balcony railings.

The family made as many excursions as Felix and Fanny had done, but Rebecka's comments were sometimes barbed. Felix had met an authority on church music named Santini, who had already translated some German works into Italian and wished to publish more manuscripts from that country. But, despite her brother's evident respect for this musician, Rebecka called an entertainment at Santini's home "a dull affair", the only interesting incident occurring when the host placed a table napkin over a bust of Palestrina, recited "a hundred sonnets" and removed the cloth once more.

The Papal Choir then sang "some ugly music". A visit to the Vatican elicited the comment that such an excursion acted like poison to anyone who suffered from rheumatism. Of the various villas, like Scott's novels, "the last is finest, though each has its own attractions". Beggars swarmed the Dirichlets' carriage, Rebecka noting particularly "a mannikin with a tiny violin" and another small individual with no legs who "jumped like a frog". Rebecka laid some flowers at the Villa Poniatowski, gathered from each of Rome's seven hills, but the display "was so lovely that I am sure no one will come and see it". They visited aunt Dorothea's son Philipp Veit, "the passage being one step beyond civilisation". Rebecka spoilt her white linen shoes, which she would never have worn in Berlin's November weather. They visited the Ham Fair with the artist Kaselowsky and his dog, "a stupid animal, without a grain of sense". Having eaten nothing all day except nuts and raisins, available everywhere, they dined on the ham they had purchased, with eggs, but, before the meal had been cleared away, guests arrived. They were dressed for the evening, "for the first time with their husbands"; Mme. Bruni wore "a velvet mantilla and a hat with feathers"; Mme. Beltay sported "an elegant French toilette". It was midnight before the guests departed and Rebecka retired to bed, only to learn that Kaselowsky's dog had vanished, to turn up later at their lodgings, where Walter and Ernst took the animal into their room.

Rebecka had not known that "so many ugly women" existed and, when driving to an excursion, she asked for the carriage blinds to be drawn, but her husband objected. Dirichlet was growing a beard, Rebecka reported, making him look like a pirate and "comical on his honest face". No music was heard but "the drumming on the piano" by English tourists, who attempted to perform the arrangement of *Robert le Diable* that rested on the music stand. Meanwhile, Fanny wrote how "fortunate" it was that Cécile and Felix had acquired the Dirichlets' servant Schumacher and occupied the Dirichlets' former home. So anxious was Fanny to find alternative accommodation for their return that "I actually dreamt that I had found a house, the only drawback being that I had to climb over the roof to gain entrance".

Of Naples, Felix was scathing. Such a small town did not warrant the title "grand city"; its only busy areas were the Toledo and the coast road to the harbour. Yet he called his lodgings at No. 13 Santicombi Santa Lucia "very lovely". He did not wish to remain, since there were too few people who contributed to the community in Naples. An acquaintance informed him that he had dealt with a shopkeeper for the past 15 years, yet he still had constantly to haggle over a few scudi "and nothing can stop it". As for the beggars, Felix's correspondence was riddled with details about these "savages", as he called them. "There are cripples, blind men...in short, wretches of every description." Even in the remotest parts, he was waylaid as soon as his carriage had reached its destination, "from every street and path. The old, white-haired men particularly distress me and such an excess of misery exceeds all belief. Even children, 30 or 40 at a time, encircle me, all wailing out their favourite phrases, rattling their jaws to show that they have nothing to eat, even when one gives them the handsomest gratuities... They give it back with the greatest indignation and then return and ask for it again." Even when glancing idly at the landscape, Felix found himself "surrounded by cripples, who make a trade of their infirmity" – and so on and so on! This negative mood might have been prompted by the intolerable heat, in which Felix felt "lethargic and disinclined for anything serious...fit only to lounge about the streets with a long face, preferring to stretch myself on the ground without thinking or wishing to do anything". Could he have envied the happy-go-lucky state of the beggars, able to get what subsistence they needed without having to resort to the tiresome work ethic?

Yet Felix did enjoy himself in Naples. He breakfasted with German artists residing there. "What could be more cheerful," he asked, "driving along the coast road with my knapsack that contains three shirts and Goethe's poems?" He and his companions dined at Baiae, visiting "ruins, ancient temples, ancient baths and other things of the kind". Among his musical experiences was a meeting with Julius Benedict, who had broken his journey in Italy on his return to London from Berlin; Mme. Fodor, though no longer singing in public, gave a recital. Mendelssohn decided, whilst in this part of Italy, nevertheless, to study nature rather than agonise over the lack of music. He therefore rose at 5 a.m. to explore outlying areas and islands, retiring at nine each evening. He saw from his window the sea and the coast of Sorrento and Vesuvius, and visited a place that his landlord did not know. Capri was "enchanting in the moonlight" and the acacia trees "give off a tranquilising scent", the fruit trees "pink-leaved", the blossom covering the foliage so thickly. The island of Nisida was his favourite, however. The scenery appeared not to have changed since Cicero visited Brutus in exile, and where he was purported to be buried. After visiting the Temple of Ceres at Paestum, the most southerly stage of his itinerary, Felix reflected that, during the year and a half since he last saw his family, he had gained "considerable experience and many new impressions" which could not fail to influence his future work. Having made full use of his time in Italy, he would "allow no opportunity to escape" in order to prove his determination to keep to his plan. He longed to hear a proper orchestra or choir

Chapter 5: "Italy at Last"

since, in Italy, "there is nothing of this kind" and his deprivation of music "leaves a sad void".

Fanny wrote in her journal on 4th February 1840 that, though oranges were still available and roses had bloomed throughout the winter, and Italy needed such little aid to produce fruit and vegetables, the more northerly lands were far more productive, because of the energy of their people. Entrepreneurs in Berlin, for instance, exported asparagus throughout the world. She wondered what would have happened had Napoleon conquered Italy – a subject often discussed within the Mendelssohn circle. France might have got on well enough without him, whilst he could have turned Italy into the "earthly paradise" it might have been, through the cultivation of the fertile soil. Fanny wrote to Rebecka how interesting she found the south of Italy and looked forward to her sister's opinion; Rebecka, wherever she lived, was "one of the few people who are receptive to impressions". At Gaeta, near Naples, Mount Vesuvius looked "uncanny" – [the excursion to the volcano is described in a later chapter, with relevance to Sebastian's birthday treat]. In fine weather, one can see as far as La Campanella, so named from the fact that bells were rung to alert neighbouring villages of the Saracens' invasion at the time of the Crusades. Underfoot was a store in which herrings were preserved, to be cooked later for meals. For Fanny, "the whole history of art" was encapsulated in the Naples museum. But, unlike the displays at the Vatican and in Munich, whose arrangement was "an art in itself", these artefacts were "stowed" indiscriminately. Nevertheless, the mosaics of animals were crafted "with great truth and correctness", whilst Hensel was "enchanted by the feeling for colour" in the paintings of houses and gardens "in the French style". Relics from Pompeii were arranged amongst shrubs and roses; one room contained frescoes, including Hercules and the Farnese bull; in another, "women feasted their eyes on the purse of Diomet", taken from the hand of a skeleton of a victim from A.D. 79, when Vesuvius erupted. Among paintings of the Holy Family, Fanny was particularly impressed with one of the Virgin's cousin Elizabeth: "no engraving could emulate this model, with such a gentle kind face of an old lady". At an art gallery two days later, Fanny marvelled at the head of a bronze horse, whose body had been used by a bishop to cast bells for his church.

Fanny's word pictures could effectively replace more conventional guidebooks to tourist attractions, so it is shameful how scantily she valued her descriptions. "To appreciate these properly" she wrote of the artefacts at the actual site of Pompeii "requires a knowledge that I do not possess [as] I cannot distinguish the various marks of character as connoisseurs are able to do... I am guided merely by my own feelings as to what is beautiful or the contrary. Therefore, my judgement is of no worth." She was fascinated by how little the humble household items had changed over the centuries: "the world did not look so very different after all, except that everything had an elegance and splendour, entirely lacking in our [own] utensils of the same kind". Fanny described dining with the Duke of Montebello, whose guests also included the English actor Charles Kemble and his daughter Fanny. The latter was "ugly and abominably dressed...very sharp and altogether very unattractive, though she spoke French very well; she is clever rather than amiable". Her voice when she sang was "fine but, like her person, without charm", though Fanny liked the father well enough. When invited to play one of Bach's keyboard concertos, Fanny Hensel felt "weak and scarcely able to manage" on the "splendid" grand piano.

At Terracino the hotel cost three scudi per night, but the Hensels had been allocated rooms belonging to the Prussian ambassador, where Lord Cavendish stayed when visiting Castellamare; he was, to Fanny, "a cultured gentleman", unlike most of the other English people she had met. The Hensels lived for three days "like royalty in a fairy tale", though they had not delivered their letters of introduction – except to the bank. Fanny observed a harbour and other buildings under construction – the first she had seen in Italy. In Amalfi they stayed in "the most curious inn on earth", having arrived "with nothing but a carpet-bag, a change of clothing and equipment for riding, driving and surveying". The three-hour journey to Capri that they had planned had had to be abandoned on account of a thunderstorm; the boatman prayed to 'Santissima Madonna' for protection. The inn at Amalfi had been converted from a monastery, whence the monks were due to return. Meanwhile, the Hensels dined on potatoes in their jackets "with great gusto", prompting the waiter to ask if they required "more potate", before exploring the town. "Flights of steps, passages, hills and quaint little alleyways" had to be negotiated, reminding Sebastian of Berlin. Hensel travelled to Ravello to study the architecture, whilst mother and son visited Salerno, where the sea looked like glass, but they could not remain because a malaria epidemic had begun in the district.

To Hensel, who could work, eat, drink and be comfortable aboard ship, the sea was blue, but, to Fanny, who – like Felix – suffered from seasickness, the furniture "walked around" and her thoughts "were doing country dances in my head". She could neither stand nor sit for five minutes at a time and even had to rest whilst writing. Fanny was awakened from a dream of home by the creaking ship; the table was upset and she found herself tossing about the cabin, after which Fanny looked forward to her "honest fatherland". Though Felix never ventured across to Sicily, Wilhelm Hensel and the Dirichlet family did allow themselves this privilege. Hensel's journey was prolonged, since two usually seaworthy steamers had broken down and the one remaining had to do the work of the three. Because of the heat, Fanny and Sebastian stayed on the mainland, Hensel being assured that no outing was really enjoyable without his company. She exhorted her husband to "drink Sicily to the dregs" but he had, when completely satisfied, to "return to your Fan and your Pep – two people who love you heartily".

Hensel took his wife's advice, making "many nice sketches and drawings" of Palermo, the capital, Messina and Taormina. He attended the Feast of Santa Rosalia

Chapter 5: "Italy at Last"

and painted the stains she was purported to bear, "which Goethe describes so prettily". Hensel found the Sicilians "liberal, cultured and wealthy," unlike the Neapolitans, whom they "detest and despise to a degree". Palermo "has more horses and carriages than London". Fanny rose at 5.30 on the morning of her husband's expected return at seven, but his ship did not arrive until two in the afternoon. Sebastian begged his mother "not to get into such a silly state of mind", arguing that Neapolitan sailors cared little for punctuality or their passengers' desire to reach their destination. Rebecka regretted leaving Palermo, but did not visit Sicily so often as her husband for fear of seasickness, though, like Hensel, she saw the Chapel of Santa Rosalia and heard the organ play and the choir sing. Meanwhile, Dirichlet visited Mount Etna and the tomb of Archimedes whilst on the island. A Don Romeo, whom Rebecka described as "the essence of politeness and having full knowledge of the area", ensured the Dirichlets were fully looked after on Sicily; Rebecka wished she had brought her paints to "daub" the "blue sky, green foreground, arches and Vesuvius".

Rebecka relished the ambience of southern Italy altogether, allowing "her vivacious and impish personality", as Sebastian Hensel described it, to express itself to the full. Nevertheless, she, like Felix before her, was plagued by beggars in Naples (but nowhere else in Italy). "If only the able-bodied men among them cultivated the land, there would be no need, with such fertile soil, to complain of cold or starvation." But the weather was unkind for the Dirichlet family, who experienced "the sirocco each morning and a thunderstorm each afternoon". As there was no room at the Villa Roma, they stayed at No. 51 Santa Lucia, so near Felix's lodging years before. Their view was obscured by a bakehouse belonging to the local barracks, but Vesuvius looked straight towards them. As Rebecka did not keep a journal, Fanny's was used by her sister to express all the observations she made. Rebecka's mystery illness, culminating in the birth of Florentina ('Flora'), must have dissuaded her from writing so much as her brother and sister had done. But, however much the Mendelssohn 'children' enjoyed Italy, they were all united in their anticipation of home. Back in what he called "old Rome" from Naples, Felix noticed vendors selling lemons and iced water in the streets, and women in light dresses, and he sat at the door of a coffee-house eating ice cream "in quantities". Yet he yearned to see his home and family again and exhorted God to grant that it would not be so long, ever again, that he stayed away. As has been seen, Fanny dreamt of home on a sea crossing and wished for her "honest fatherland". Rebecka also recalled with nostalgia the tea table and "all the familiar faces", even admitting how much she loved place names that included the word 'heim', the German for 'home' – even at the beginning of her journey to Italy.

But, for Felix, travelling had not ended, for, after his year in Italy (like a masochist), he battled with the unprecedented storms of Switzerland. His letters on this 1831 visit are full of the pure air and scenery he had sketched, but which a fellow tourist described "as if about to purchase it but finding it of so little value".

Felix found Goethe's "weak poems and even weaker letters from Switzerland...lamentable" – which, because of his own rapture at the landscape, he "cannot understand". Not even the sudden hurricane or floods daunted him. The guide informed Felix that his own family had to vacate their former home, with its beautiful and profitable garden, as it was "reduced to a wild, turbulent stream". Passengers had to leave their coach, which Felix noticed incongruously abandoned. Yet, despite the havoc wrought by the elements, Felix insisted on hiking and mountaineering. One Sunday no coaches or guides were available and, in view of the weather, everyone else stayed indoors – except Felix, who was "inspired with a wonderful sense of independence". He found the people "rude and saucy" at an inn, prompting him to say "be hanged; I will go on", exploring with the aid of his map. One is reminded of H. W. Longfellow's poem *Excelsior*, the hero of which carried "that banner with the strange device", the motto meaning 'upward'. Felix's quest seemed equally futile and pointless; neither did he have the comfort of a maiden begging him to rest his weary head upon her breast. All he was offered at "primitive" inns was a tablespoon, which "did serve the purpose" as a shoehorn. His umbrella was wrecked on a further rain-soaked adventure. Evidently, he knew nothing of this; an article recorded on 28th January 1996 that the wind always blows the rain sideways, so an umbrella user would not be kept dry in such conditions as the young man experienced. Not even today's umbrellas are made to combat unnatural weather conditions.

Yet Felix did enjoy some diversions. At a village fête in a mountain area he bought some cakes for three little girls who sang to him; he enjoyed a wrestling match, which spectacle he had never before encountered; he composed two waltzes for the daughters of a forest ranger. He composed various songs, including "my favourite one in E minor". He would like to give some English tourists "a good thrashing" on account of their attitude to the Swiss scenery: "They think everything commonplace because they themselves are commonplace". He wished to get rid of a party from Berlin because they bored him. He vied with his guide in eating, drinking and sleeping; the "trumpet and oboe sounds disturb me; he, in turn, cuts out my morning sleep". At Engelberg he discovered a copy of Schiller's *Wilhelm Tell* in a monastery, about which he rhapsodised, especially as the author had never seen Switzerland. Only a German could write as Schiller had done – "a great epoch has passed away" in contemporary literature. This was reinforced by reading a book describing Napoleon's proposed Simplon Highway, which he did not live to see completed. His correspondence showed "fire and spirit", unlike the "tame" literature of Mendelssohn's own time. Although he was "plundered infamously" he was "overjoyed" on finding, on Mont Blanc, that the innkeeper's family were "natural, honest people who could speak German" – an appropriate way to end this 'Grand Tour'. Felix could at last sing from the popular song of the time by Sir Henry Bishop: 'Home, Sweet Home.'

Chapter 6

Young Musicians

If Mendelssohn was the composer he is purported to be, why has his music been mentioned so little thus far? This lack of information is deliberate. As far as his parents were concerned, music was just a leisure pastime. Young Felix was destined either to work in the family bank or, if this did not suit, to take up a position with the Prussian government or the law. There was no intention of his selecting music as a profession.

Many biographers, erudite musicologists among them, wrongly compare Mozart with Mendelssohn as a boy, to the latter's detriment. Philip Radcliffe states that Mendelssohn's childhood inspiration was "less steady" than that of Mozart, but, if this is so, should the assertion be surprising? Leopold Mozart took young Wolfgang and his sister Maria Anna ('Nannerl') around Europe, encouraging them to display their talents for the crowned heads of the most illustrious musical capitals. Franz Liszt's father, too, was given time off by his employer to take his musically brilliant son to allow Europe's celebrities to hear him perform his pianistic feats; even Beethoven, recognising his talent, embraced the boy.

Abraham Mendelssohn, on the contrary, bullied by his brother-in-law Jakob Bartholdy, with Leah's compliance, had an almost pathological hatred of music as a profession, calling it "immoral". Fit solely for amateur status, music was merely useful to allow the Mendelssohn children to mix with affluent families around them, to be used for private entertainment only. Mozart and Liszt would have had far greater opportunity to experience the heights and depths of the musical and public world, able to develop their talents and to mature far earlier as musicians. In adulthood, Mendelssohn's music was said to be more "fitful" than that of Mozart. Again, this can be simply explained. Whereas Mozart's fertile mind was allowed to produce compositions, uninhibited by distractions, demands upon Mendelssohn's time were made by purveyors of every aspect of musical life, so it is remarkable how many compositions he wrote. Various examples can be cited of his compositions being inspired by duty and obedience to his father or to royal and civic dignitaries. Even as a boy, Felix's natural musical instincts were restricted, his intuition as to what was right for him was cramped – even clamped – by his elders and, by definition, betters.

A further myth that must be exploded is the sycophantic manner in which biographers relate how much help and encouragement the Mendelssohn parents gave their children in their musical lives, without actually explaining in what way this was achieved. Though sanitised, even censored, family letters disprove such a phenomenon. For instance, from Paris: "You say that I took the score of my quartet *in spite of your request not to*," Felix wrote to his mother, "but I am certain that I packed the score *with your approval* and you even told me that I could have the parts copied if I wanted to play it and I hope that father, who was present, will bear witness to all of this for me..." Whether or not Abraham did confirm Felix's assertion is not recorded. This was not all the 16-year-old musician, no longer a child, had to tolerate from this apparently art-loving parent: "Then you claim that I do not appreciate how much Fanny does for me. I can only assure you that the reverse is true. I cannot prove it; just believe my protestations, for I have not yet acquired the habit of lying since coming to Paris..." With regard to "the rest of the points" listed in his mother's letter, he placated her by saying that she was right and he wrong and begged pardon but, as the relevant matters are not revealed, Felix must remain the recalcitrant infant, despite possible injustice. His father, who had taken the two elder children to Paris, ostensibly to escort their aunt Henriette back to Berlin, wrote to Leah that, whereas Fanny had sent some songs that she had composed (far too ambitious for Abraham to stomach), Felix had written a fugue. All Abraham could say in mitigation was that he had not expected his offspring to set to work so earnestly or so soon. A fugue "requires reflection and perseverance". Though other musicians are praised for their early achievements, and rightly so, this does not appear to apply to Mendelssohn. Mozart's musicianship from childhood is invariably admired, as with the genius of three-year-old Saint-Saëns for playing the piano; the 14-year-old Max Bruch for composing a symphony, and other musical children could be named.

As for Mendelssohn, it has not only been suggested that he began too early to compose, but his music is branded as lacking originality. Stanley Sadie takes pride in listing the influences that infiltrated Felix's work: he appropriated the fugal technique from Bach; the rhythms and harmonic progression from Handel; the "dramatic characteristics, form and texture" from Mozart; and the instrumental technique from Beethoven. Like Sadie, Ray Longyear detects the impact of Weber, but also of the Czech composer Jan Ladislav Dussek, as having a seminal influence on Mendelssohn's music as a boy, even to the extent of giving Dussek's Op. 3 No. 10 Piano Sonata as proof, but without specifying why. Even his friend H. F. Chorley, in his *Modern German Music*, stated that his love of counterpoint caused Mendelssohn's early music to appear "hard and dry", showing "natural immaturity". Is it any wonder that this may apply, when considering the incessant 'brainwashing' with Bach's music, not only from his music teacher Carl Friedrich

Zelter, but also from his parents, especially Leah. Sadie suggests it was not until 1825, the year when Mendelssohn's Op. 20 String Octet was written, that his own musical style appeared, stimulated by the multi-disciplined curriculum laid down by his father; he overlooks the fact that physical and mental exhaustion was the norm for Felix, so demanding was the workload. Others, such as Radcliffe, imply that Mendelssohn's mature music is less inspiring than that of his youth. Again, this can be attributed to the childhood habit of constantly revising his compositions, which he later called "the old disease". Had he allowed himself to be satisfied with his first attempts, rather than trying to be superhuman in his quest for perfection, such a criticism need not have applied. R. Larry Todd's essay *Unfinished Mendelssohn* details meticulously the composer's constant revisions, scores lain aside, some of which remain in manuscript at the time of writing this book.

However, the epitome of gross misunderstanding derives from Sebastian Hensel, Felix's nephew: "Without his father, Felix would not have been the musician he became". At last, such a claim is categorically refuted, despite the 'establishment's view'. In view of the many stumbling blocks placed by his parents and the inhibitions they caused, which never forsook him throughout his life, it is remarkable what a fine triumph Felix achieved as a musician. Had his own musical instinct, intuition and talent not been stultified, it is beyond comprehension what superlative heights he could have reached. Anything Mendelssohn did achieve was through his own initiative and self-reliance, once he left the oppressive atmosphere of Berlin.

The music teachers chosen by the Mendelssohn parents had good pedigrees. Ludwig Berger had been a pupil of Muzio Clementi, who settled in London and became a famous piano manufacturer; also of John Field, the Irish-born composer and inventor of the nocturne, who eventually settled in Russia, where every pianist and composer worth the name – except Mendelssohn himself – visited him. On hearing Fanny and Felix play a piano arrangement of the ballet music in Felix's 'singspiel' *Camacho's Wedding*, Berger jumped from his seat crying, "Why, my children, you play quite first rate." On another occasion, on hearing Fanny's song from her and Felix's cycle – No. 3 of Op. 8 – Berger joked about the way Fanny had handled Grillparzer's "ponderous text". By contrast with Berger, Carl Friedrich Zelter – bluff, outspoken, caring little what offence he caused – had originally followed his father's craft as a stonemason, but, having injured his hand, pursued his special interest, the collection and performance of old music, particularly that of Bach. Through him, Mendelssohn had a direct link with that composer, since Zelter had been taught by one of Bach's pupils, Johann Kirnberger.

In view of such traditions, it can only be marvelled at the progressive versatility of Mendelssohn's music, despite criticisms from Sadie and other detractors. However, before Berger or Zelter were allocated the Mendelssohn children's musical instruction, none other than Leah took this task upon herself, giving five-minute lessons. She would sit in the room knitting whilst Fanny or Felix practised the piano. How peaceful it must have been, when the lessons began with Berger and Zelter, not to have such an insidious clicking noise in the background whilst trying to concentrate on whatever piece either was playing.

As for Zelter, though biographers give Abraham credit for choosing him as instructor for his children, it can be said that he selected himself for this task. Zelter had first met Moses, Abraham's father, at the salons of Henriette Herz, said by some to be the 'Immortal Beloved' of Beethoven's dedication. Abraham knew Zelter from boyhood, and, as his family subscribed handsomely to the Berlin Singakademie, which Zelter directed, what more suitable choice than Zelter could there have been to teach the Mendelssohn children? At his house the young Mendelssohns rehearsed what Zelter called "the bristly bits of Bach", and, as he had a collection of rare manuscripts that he zealously guarded, Felix, especially, familiarised himself with their contents and studied Forkel's biography of Bach, written in 1801. Zelter can be regarded either as a 'backwoodsman' or a spirit from an earlier age, but, whatever the view, he could not, nor did he wish to try to understand music of the 19th century. In 1816, when a friend of Goethe sent the poet some song settings by Schubert of his verses, Zelter, a lifelong friend, influenced him into ignoring Schubert's work completely, so that it was not until 1830 that Goethe heard the setting of his poem, *Erlkönig*, sung by Mme. Schröder-Devrient in Weimar. Zelter had his friend – Goethe – believe that the only settings worthy of his poetry were those by Reichardt or his own. Zelter had invited Haydn, whose music he admired, to visit Berlin, but any later music was anathema to him. Blunt wonders, in view of this attitude, why the young Mendelssohn was so popular, but the reason is patently clear. Whatever else may be laid at Zelter's door, no one could accuse him of disloyalty or sentimentality towards the past. Therefore, as Felix was Moses Mendelssohn's grandson, that was enough – especially as young Felix admired Bach so well.

Abraham, too, admired Bach above all other composers – apart, perhaps, from Gluck. Writing in 1835 to Felix after a Sunday concert where Fanny had played a Bach work, Abraham was reminded of how the composer "stood isolated from his world and surroundings, developing his own pure, mild...and...clear profundity". On the contrary, the music of Beethoven he could not or would not understand, especially his later works – an attitude with which Zelter wholly concurred. Because Felix admired Beethoven so well, this difference of opinion was a constant bone of contention between father and son. Writing later on 22nd November 1830, Felix was reminded of these disputes: his defence of the composer put Abraham in "the worst possible mood". When Abraham had "scolded Beethoven and all the romantics, he saddened me and made me impatient", Felix admitted. "Something new had come into the world and my father could not quite stomach that. It frightened him a little. As long as I insisted on talking about Beethoven and praising him his temper grew worse and worse, and, if I remember correctly, he once ordered me to leave the table..." Adolf Bernhard Marx, formerly a lawyer who had adopted a musical career, was equally loyal to Beethoven, which antagonised Abraham so much that Schima Kaufman states that he tried to discourage this musician, "ungainly in appearance" and ten years senior to Felix, from visiting Leipzigerstrasse 3. "No good could come of the friendship" between Marx and the children, as the parents still referred to the young Mendelssohns.

Marx was a regular visitor to the Sunday concerts at the Mendelssohn house and it would only be later that he and Felix would experience a rift in their companionship. For the present, the older musician was always known as 'abbé' because of his initials. Marx claimed often to have "had words" with Mendelssohn over academic topics – Dante, Raphael and, above all, Felix's interpretation of Beethoven's music. He admitted, however, that they "got nowhere", because of Marx's own lack of skill as a performer and his inability to marshal a cogent argument. This "devastating experience" aroused "an eerie feeling" in Marx's soul, according to his memoirs, especially when "the most profound and solemn things – the greatest powers of the spirit – were expressed". Of Mendelssohn himself at this period, Marx recalled him as "serious but exuberant... His long, dark hair fell over his shoulders [and his] inquisitive eyes and hesitant, soft voice" were remembered. As a pianist, "he showed the wisdom of a mature musician". Marx remembered Leah as "a highly intelligent, but perhaps less feeling, mother" who, with her background of Bach's compositions, constantly played his *Well-Tempered Clavier*; the rest of the family loved Bach, Mozart and, "to a lesser extent", Handel.

Though biographers constantly praise Abraham for organising the concerts, the only part he played was to maintain the mansion in which they were staged. Leah arranged the refreshments, but the music was selected, arranged and composed by the young Mendelssohns, Felix conducting the orchestra, standing on a stool in order to be seen and have his direction followed. Fanny played the piano, Rebecka sang and Paul, when older, played the 'cello. In 1822 Ferdinand Hiller, pupil of Hummel and the first pianist to play Beethoven's 'Emperor' Piano Concerto in E flat, who would witness Beethoven's death in 1827, thought Fanny a better pianist than Felix. Marx, however, dismissed her talent as "lacking her brother's skill and strength but, infrequently, she was first in tenderness and sense of interpretation". This assessment can be dismissed when reading other memoirs. H. F. Chorley, in his introduction to the 1863 edition of the first biography of Mendelssohn by W. A. Lampadius, states that Fanny had a "touch of the southern vivacity, which is so rare among the Germans". Music was "the very breath of life to her". Not only did she play well enough for Moscheles to say she deserved a doctorate of music, but her knowledge of music theory was almost equal to that of her brother. She had a superb contralto voice and she composed, but lived only to see 42 of her approximately 400 works published, though they were performed frequently at Leipzigerstrasse 3. When Marx first met Paul he was "still very young" and held "modestly aloof" when Felix played the piano: "with the passionate expression and short, dark curls, [he] would steal up to the piano afterwards, telling his elder brother that, in a particular bar, 'You played F; it should be F sharp'". Though Abraham was proud of his elder daughter's talent, under no circumstances did he ever allow Fanny either to play in public or to pursue a musical career during his lifetime. "Next to Fanny or Felix," Rebecka commented drily, "I would not have succeeded in attaining any such recognition;" but this was far too modest. Felix asked her to send him "some pretty verses, new or old, grave or gay" for him to set to music that would suit her voice, as he was "in the mood" to compose them. Even abroad – Italy in this instance – Felix did not forget his younger sister's musical requirements; in various letters, she described singing, especially as a member of a chorus.

But how did visitors remember the Sunday concerts? Max Müller recalled how Fanny and Felix, when playing piano duets, or extemporising at the instrument, each held the other's little finger. He also recalled how "Felix was handicapped by being made to play with his hands crossed". Again, "Mendelssohn played almost every instrument in the orchestra" and was expected to play those he liked least. If these anecdotes are true, this would account for the almost legendary talent that he showed later on, as reported by contemporaries; in view of the fact that these stories appear only in Müller's memoirs, cynics have a right to doubt their veracity. Neither is Müller the only raconteur whose anecdotes do not ring true. F. Garnett, in an article, 'Great Musicians of Yesterday', in an 1892 issue of *The Musical Times*, states that Abraham was acting quite out of character by proposing to send one of Felix's compositions to Beethoven for assessment. So terrified was Felix that, trembling with fear, he forbade his father to take such a step. Another tells of Abraham sending a carriage to fetch Weber to Leipzigerstrasse 3, after a performance of *Der Freischütz*. So much was Felix in awe of the great composer that he ran home ahead of the coach in order to hold open the carriage door for Weber. Again, no other source verifies this – except later biographies that regurgitate these tales.

Julius Benedict studied with Weber in Berlin; he was able to introduce the 12-year-old Mendelssohn to his mentor, when meeting him in the street. Felix, in turn, invited Weber home, but the composer had to decline as a rehearsal of his opera was due to take place. Benedict was a regular visitor, however, and he recalled the boy as having "auburn hair clustered in ringlets round his shoulders, with brilliant, clear eyes and a smile of innocence and candour on his lips". Any implication of femininity is abandoned by the following sentence, however. Grasping Benedict's hand, Felix suggested a race home; on arrival, he asked his mother if their new guest could play Weber's works to him, and "pushed" Benedict towards the piano "with an irresistible impetuosity". On another occasion, Benedict, five years older than Felix, recalled Mendelssohn sitting at a table writing "earnestly". On enquiry, Benedict learnt that the boy was writing out his Op. 1 Piano Quartet, straight out of his head. On completion, Felix dashed to the piano, playing from memory all Weber's repertoire he had heard on Benedict's previous visit. He then "ran into the garden, climbing high hedges with a leap...climbing the trees like a squirrel – the very picture of health and happiness". Later, Devrient was to comment on a change of appearance and dress: the "pretty brown curls" of former days had been "cut short to the neck" and he now wore "a boy's suit – an open jacket over a waistcoat that befitted his age"; yet Devrient "could not but regret his former antique appearance" having vanished.

Mendelssohn's earliest known composition was a sonata for two pianos for his father's birthday, which he wrote in 1819, when ten years old. From 1820, Mendelssohn began to keep a record of his compositions, the date and place copied in his clear, precise handwriting, almost resembling print. The notebooks in which his work was presented – 44 in all – show "the finish, polish and impeccable regard for form" that was to become the hallmark of his mature music. Whilst Chopin, Liszt and Mozart were lavished, as boys, with adulation from royalty and nobility and with gold and jewels, Mendelssohn, at a similar age, was expected to perform for no remuneration of any kind; neither did it occur to him to expect any reward. He was simply an amateur musician who played and composed, whose way in the world would be through the Prussian government or the Mendelssohn Bank. Myths perpetuated as he began to make his name away from home – and these still cling to Mendelssohn most unjustly. His family – as wealthy as the Rothschilds, it was said – were far too affluent for their son to need gratuities of any kind, since his parents were said to have lavished "everything" upon him.

Naturally, this caused resentment among his contemporaries who believed that, by not accepting any gift or money, he was merely patronising his inferiors in status; his modesty was misunderstood and misinterpreted. Thus, when Mendelssohn had become acquainted with Robert Schumann and expressed curiosity as to how a man with such wonderful musical ideas could express them in so "clumsy" a manner, Mendelssohn was challenged by his colleague's response. Had he, Schumann, been destined from early childhood to pursue a musical career, as Mendelssohn was, he could have outstripped anyone as a musician, with such financial support as Mendelssohn was said to have been given. Would Schumann have had the same view if he had known the truth? Fortunately, however, there were trusted friends who understood Mendelssohn's character. Charles Horsley stated that, however much adulation he received, Mendelssohn's "simple and modest character" never altered as one artistic triumph superseded another, only to aim yet higher in his quest for excellence. From a similar period, Anne Taylor recalled that "...there was a little shyness about him; great modesty. We knew little about his music, but the wonder of it grew upon us... We began saying to each other: 'Surely, this must be a man of genius!' He was so far from any sort of pretension or making a favour of giving his music to us" when he played for the family.

Mendelssohn first played the piano in public at Pleyel's salon in Paris, when Abraham took Fanny and his elder son to meet Mme. Bigot, a former pupil of

Beethoven, for piano tuition. He himself negotiated terms of indemnity for the Prussian government for reparation after the Napoleonic Wars. Felix played what must have been piano arrangements of concertos by Mozart and Beethoven and a sonata by the latter – eight to ten hours of complex music – from memory. His first performance with other instrumentalists occurred on 24th October 1818, when he performed Joseph Wölfl's Trio for two horns and piano with Joseph Kugel and his brother. En route to Switzerland came a concert arranged by composer and impresario Aloys Schmitt on 31st March 1822, in Frankfurt. Hiller, who lived in that city, was present at Schmitt's residence, recalling the compositions of "the little piano player with the long hair". Johann Schelble, whom they visited on the return journey and who ran Frankfurt's 'St Cecilia Society', was particularly pleased with Mendelssohn's improvisations.

Meanwhile, Felix's repertoire of compositions was multiplying. Each score was worked out in his head and transcribed onto paper only when complete – unlike the embryo sketches of Beethoven, written before the work was produced. "Everything he wrote was conceived in an unvarying spirit of the truest reverence for art and always with a clear observance of its accepted canon," W. S. Rockstro wrote. Like Benedict, Schubring recalled Mendelssohn's habit of appearing to 'copy' music onto paper and, once, when about to leave Leipzigerstrasse 3, Schubring was asked to stay, when they spoke "of all manner of things", whilst Felix continued to write what turned out to be his Grand Overture in C major (known as the Trumpet Overture, Op. 101, when published posthumously). As he wrote, "there was no looking backwards or forwards; no comparing; no humming, or anything of that kind. The pen kept going steadily on…without pausing, and we never ceased talking…" Felix's first composition to bear a date was a cantata, *Im Rührend Feierlich Tönes*, dated 13th January 1820.

However, other serious compositions were attempted before this; in 1819, he wrote to his father for more music-paper. Instead of pride and encouragement, Abraham had more important matters on his mind when replying: did Felix require "ruled, or unruled" paper, he asked – as if anyone with the free spirit of Mendelssohn would worry which he had, being able to adapt to either category. "Read over your letter before you send it," his father admonished, "and ascertain if, addressed to yourself, whether you could fully understand it and fully execute the commission contained therein." Stratton pompously takes the idea of the pedant: "Evidently, Felix had not then mastered the art of clear expression". In view of the fact that Felix's music notation "looked as if the most skilled copyist had written it", what matter whether ruled or unruled paper? The comparison between Felix's personality and that of his father is the same as distinguishing a racehorse from a carthorse – the son evidently inherited his grandfather's character. But this snub did not dissuade Mendelssohn for long. At Sécheron, near Geneva, he wrote to Zelter of revising his Op. 1 Piano Quartet, which Benedict had watched him writing. A Violin Concerto in D minor, brought to light only in the 1950s by Yehudi

Figure 4. Sonata for Two Pianos, Mendelssohn's first known composition, 1819

Menuhin, was dedicated to Eduard Rietz, as also were his Op. 4 Violin Sonata (composed in 1823 and 1824 respectively) and his Op. 20 String Octet of 1825. His *Seven Characteristic Pieces*, Op. 7, for the piano, were dedicated to Ludwig Berger and published two years later. In short, over the years "a multiplicity of compositions" followed, which included his String Symphonies, exercises for Zelter, of which Rockstro cited six; Mendelssohn's first "mature" symphony is sometimes also known inaccurately as No. 13 of his String Symphonies. Rockstro also stated "five concertos" as having been composed during Mendelssohn's childhood, but gave no further information. For the St Cecilia Society, Mendelssohn composed a motet, *Jubi Domine* (*Rejoice in the Lord*), but the real milestone occurred when a report appeared in the only English musical journal, *The Quarterly Musical Magazine and Review*, edited by Richard MacKenzie and begun in 1818.

The journalist noted that "the young Felix Mendelssohn", who "played a concerto composed by himself", was "worth noticing". A symphony by "the gifted young Mendelssohn Bartholdy" was mentioned after a concert given by Moser in 1825; "its rich invention, unity of design…promises much for his future works". A further article, in September of the same year, was copied in that journal from a German periodical. Whilst in Paris, Felix was one of the soloists in Moscheles's arrangement for 12 hands at three pianos of themes from *Der Freischütz* at a concert given in the Academie Royale. Citing his piano style and the fact that his Piano Quintet was performed, an issue of *The Harmonicon*, begun in 1823 and edited by William Ayrton, mentioned Mendelssohn and commented on "the grandson of the famous philosopher", who shows "promise of great musical excellence".

Not only did Felix sing alto with the Berlin Singakademie from the age of ten onwards, until his voice matured into that of a lyrical tenor, but a further lifelong preoccupation was with the organ – not only as a player, but gaining special knowledge of how the instrument was (or should be) built. An early letter, dated "the 3rd day of the lovely month of May 1821", asked August Wilhelm Bach about keeping an appointment for a lesson. Though no relation of the Bach family, he was a figure with stature and influence in the 19th century, accompanying for Zelter and, at his death, becoming director of the Institute of Church Music in Berlin. The lesson would be "at four o'clock" the next day, "unless there is a wedding or a confirmation to prevent this". He sent "greetings to a prelude and fugue" and also to "the principal pipes". He was "at present sweating over an organ fugue, which will come forth into the world within the next few days". From Weimar, whilst visiting Goethe, Felix wrote home on 6th November 1821: "In the morning we went to church, where half of the 100th Psalm of Handel was performed. The organ is large but weak and the St Mary organ (in Berlin) is much more powerful, though smaller. The one here has 50 ranks, 44 stops, and one 32 foot pedal…" (sic). The next year, during a visit to the Harz Mountains on the way to

Switzerland, Felix played the organ at the castle of Hallenstadt, which was "quite a task", but not through incompetence on his part; the instrument "...had ten voices, six of which did not work at all – though Zelter would have taken the organist to task"; glad that the four voices did function, he "played the miserable thing" until exhaustion overcame him. The organ in the church at Zug in Switzerland "was missing a few things. Here it splutters on G sharp; there on B flat, etc."

In August 1823, en route to visit Nathan Mendelssohn in Silesia with his father, Felix had a really interesting musical experience in Breslau. The organist, Berner, improvised on a low C, which Felix had not realised could be produced on the pedal. "With wonderful execution, Berner threw himself with all his might upon the manual", developing his theme "after a few runs", playing counter-melodies simultaneously on pedal and manual. This demonstration was taken to heart since, as an adult, Mendelssohn was not only a fine organist, according to contemporaries, but he played a crucial part in England's organ construction and playing technique. At the spa town of Bad Doberan on the Baltic a year later, he reported to Zelter on the 226-year-old instrument at the church: "The sharp keys are missing in the lower octave manual and the pedals". Though the individual registers were "quite pleasant", it was a shame that the lower manual was "almost unusable, otherwise the full organ would probably sound strong enough overall but, as it is, ...a half-dozen keys stick, so the disaster is complete. The cantor is accustomed to sing a few quarter notes [quavers] before everyone else, so he always starts off with the first note before the organist's little interludes have scarcely begun", causing Felix almost to cry out that "that was enough"; and he concluded that the instrument was too old for the task it was expected to perform.

In the same year, what must be seen as the most important breakthrough transpired for Felix's future career. In October Ignaz Moscheles, friend of Beethoven and one of the most popular composers of the time, was touring Germany and, inevitably, on appearing in Berlin, he was invited to Leipzigerstrasse 3. He was fascinated by the Sunday concerts and preserved two of their programmes, so carefully presented by the young Mendelssohns. On 28th November, for instance, Felix's "D minor String Quartet and C major String Symphony" were performed, whilst Fanny played the solo part of Bach's Keyboard Concerto and the sister and brother performed "a duet for two pianos in D minor – Arnold". (This is, most likely, Samuel Arnold, who had become organist at Westminster Abbey and who compiled the edition of Handel's works that Mendelssohn would later revise.) The fare for 20th December comprised Mendelssohn's F minor Violin Sonata, Moscheles's Duet for Two Pianos in G minor (in which Mendelssohn took part), and Hummel's G major Piano Trio, with "little Schilling" as a participant. Moscheles later called Felix "a master artist", stating that other infant prodigies of the time were merely gifted children compared with this genius.

Neither Leah nor Abraham was "of the genus 'prodigy-parents'". In fact, he observed, the Mendelssohn parents took the converse view; they feared the children's genius would dwindle as they grew older. Time and again, Moscheles tried to convince Leah and Abraham that their children's musical gifts were far too mature to desert Fanny or Felix. Though the word 'genius' was employed far too often, there was none other to describe the musical talent of either. When others were performing, Felix "in breathless excitement followed every passage and every note. His handsome face was flushed; his dark eyes sparkled with enthusiasm," Moscheles wrote. The snub that Leah must have felt herself to have received can only be imagined, when, having almost insisted that the great Moscheles humble himself to give piano lessons to her elder son, the eminent musician refused. His reason? "The boy has no need of lessons," he wrote in his diary; "if he sees anything noteworthy in my style of playing, he catches it from me at once." Later he wrote of one lesson that lasted from 2 to 3 p.m. one afternoon, when Felix was asked to play his own compositions: "I was with my master – not my pupil. He guesses my meaning before I speak." George Smart was equally impressed when this London musician visited Berlin the next year but, understandably, was not able to take the boy seriously – Felix was nothing other than an amateur with the career of merchant or something similarly unmusical before him.

After such accolades, the thought had to be lodged in Abraham's head that a musical profession had at least to be considered. Thus, rather than take his elder son to Vienna, the musical capital of the world, where two of the greatest musicians ever to exist – Beethoven and Schubert – still lived, Herr Mendelssohn knew far better. Paris was the city he had always loved and this was where Felix should be assessed; Cherubini, head of the Conservatoire, would soon put paid to such a whim, if anyone could, and the boy would come to his senses and work earnestly at a 'proper' profession, performing as an amateur and composing if he were inclined. Thus, whilst escorting his sister Henriette home from her years as governess to Fanny Sebastiani, who had married the previous year, the far-thinking, all-seeing, all-knowing Abraham Mendelssohn arranged for the mighty Maria Luigi Carlo Zenobia Salvatore Cherubini to put Felix through his paces. If this despot said "no" to the name of Mendelssohn being known throughout the musical world, then that would be that. After all, Abraham had actually met Cherubini, having attended the première of his opera *The Water Carrier*. Backstage, the composer was discovered "stalking backwards and forwards in feverish excitement, declaiming, 'This has struck home!'", Marx recalled. "The crowd was inflamed to the point of madness [because of] the suggestion of revolution" conveyed by the opera. Cherubini could be as outspoken as Zelter and even Napoleon had received the rough edge of his tongue. In 1823 the 12-year-old Liszt, though kissing his hand, had been forbidden to enter the Conservatoire, as in no circumstances was an overseas student permitted to grace this establishment. The memoirs of Hector Berlioz recount many tussles between pupil and mentor when he studied there. Though Beethoven admired Cherubini, his music was not reciprocated, being dismissed as making the Conservatoire director sneeze, but nothing more. It can therefore be imagined that, knowing this, Abraham was bound to find Cherubini to be his ally; but matters did not occur as planned. When Mendelssohn played his Op. 3 Piano Quartet, with the celebrated violinist Pierre Baillot and two others, Halévy, his pupil, refused to believe his reaction: "This boy is richly endowed; he will do well; he is doing well, but he dispenses too much silver; he puts too much material into his cloak". A Kyrie for five-part choir and orchestra was composed at the same time, Mendelssohn himself admitting it to have been "the most ambitious thing I have written"; *The Harmonicon* acknowledged the piece as "showing promise of musical excellence".

Felix had written to Zelter that the Sunday concerts had not fared so well latterly, because Eduard Rietz had painful hands and no one knew how long this condition would last. In Paris, Abraham mentioned this circumstance to a musician named Rode, to whom he exhorted his son to play, despite Felix's "cold fingers". Felix wrote home of Rode "spitting fire", but there were far pleasanter meetings with other, better-known, musicians in Paris. At Neukomm's house, a Stabat Mater was rehearsed, written by this now forgotten composer. One of the two trebles sang "in a beautiful and soft tone", but the singer with the lower voice, although equally beautiful, spoilt his voice by singing "off pitch". The singers had good diction, with "the proper amount of expression, only rarely disfigured by affectation, [but] they were sight-reading" – something for which Felix would have died rather than contemplate for himself. Neukomm, "a very good fellow", accompanied the ensemble on the newly invented 'organ espressif', which had "one gamba stop that one can cause to swell and recede by using the bellows". After each movement of the "dry but melodious composition" Neukomm experimented with "new" harmonies, "which just did not work", becoming "more and more monotonous" and more involved until, when Neukomm finally played a fugue, Felix's only comment was "BRRRRR!" As the result of a letter of introduction, Felix and his father visited Erard's piano manufacturing firm, where they were invited into the salon, where a rehearsal was in progress for a private concert. Here, among others, he met "my dear Hummel", whom he had seen in Weimar. On eventual recognition, Hummel shouted: "Hey, look! There's Felix!" and, kissing the boy, asked what had become of his pigtails. Having previously noticed his crucifix in Weimar, Mendelssohn's surmise was confirmed that Hummel was a Catholic because of the "very orthodox and serious piece" that was performed.

When an aria from Spontini's *Olympe* was to be performed, Felix "wanted to sneeze", so he "stole away" to see if some of his father's acquaintances were at home; not one was available, however. But the most significant experience of his life to date must have been a further episode in which Hummel played the main part. Having observed the state of the piano on which Felix was expected to practise in the Hôtel de l'Etoile in the Rue Caumartin, Hummel ran into the room "with four porters [and] brought me his wife's grand piano, taking our bad instrument instead". This anecdote gives real food for thought. How affluent were the Mendelssohn family, especially since Abraham brought Felix to Paris to see how his son would fare as a professional musician? Or, could the father have been so envious of his son's genius that he deliberately deprived Felix of the best "tools of his trade"? Could he have hoped this visit to Paris would allow Felix to fail his test of excellence that Moscheles had prophesied?

On his hiking holiday in the Harz Mountains with his university companions Felix was still able to gain musical experience. At a casino in Baden, presumably invited to play, the audience forsook their gaming to listen – fascinated – to the young man's recital. On a further visit the manager had had the piano moved, so that his real business could be pursued by his customers. Schima Kaufman states that "a charming Frenchwoman" attracted Felix equally as well as the piano; she also states that another piano was discovered in a different room and that Felix's playing caused "some young ladies...to shed tears of melancholy". Heydemann comforted them "and touched them in turn; Magnus preferred to talk to them, but Felix reflected on the words of Benjamin Constant and did not speak the whole evening". Since no trace of Ms. Kaufman's statements appear in any other biography of Mendelssohn, nor in his letters – even by implication – it can be assumed that both the "charming Frenchwoman" and the "young ladies" and the young men's reactions are the author's invention, but it is interesting to recount some of the nonsense that is published about Mendelssohn. However, there is no doubt about his exhilarating stay in Heidelberg. "I indulge in a 'wicked gladness'," Felix boasted on seeing Anton Thibaut on his own initiative, a whole day sooner than Leah's letter arrived, requesting her son to visit this collector of music and professor of law, with whom Schumann was later to study. "What a man!" Mendelssohn exclaimed. Because of the foul weather, he and his companions felt "very dull", but Felix visited the cathedral and was invited by Thibaut, to whom he introduced himself, to accompany him home. Mendelssohn, because of his remarkable memory, recalled that Thibaut had mentioned *Tu es Petrus* in his book, a setting of which Mendelssohn happened to be composing at the time. Though the elderly professor could not sing the motet, and neither did he know much about the history of music, he explained to Felix the provenance of all his manuscripts, "of all nationalities and periods", and "far better works" than the composition by Lotti that he lent his guest to copy. "What I liked about him was that he never asked my name. I loved music and that was enough!" Two hours elapsed before Thibaut learnt Mendelssohn's identity. Assuming him to be a student, he was invited into Thibaut's study and met a pupil, Schröder, who also invited Felix home to play his "fine grand piano" to his heart's content, "sending a dog (growling at my music) under the table". Not only was Felix allowed to smoke a pipe but he was invited to dine, a bottle of Hochheimer accompanying the meal. The invitation was reciprocated: "After this, who can deny that I am a convivial fellow". Thibaut visited the hotel "in person" where the young men from Berlin were staying and, on departing from Heidelberg, Mendelssohn and Thibaut pledged eternal friendship "based on Victoria and Bach" – though Felix had to enlighten Thibaut about the latter composer, since he knew little, despite his magnificent manuscript collection. Felix gave thanks for all he learnt from Thibaut, whose sure instinct he recognised, despite his host's limited knowledge of musical theory. "He warmed me with his passion for music; there is a glow and enthusiasm in his speech..."

But it was by no means "roses all the way" for Mendelssohn's budding profession. His Op. 1 Piano Quartet, dedicated to Prince Radziwill, and his Op. 2 Piano Quartet, dedicated to Zelter, produced "benevolent condescension" from musical journals, and the only good that was related about his Op. 4 Violin Sonata was that it did not contain the fashionable words 'Grande', 'Pathetique' or 'Melancholique' in its title. "Those who cannot accept criticisms do not deserve praise" was the verdict. Whereas, according to H. E. Jacob, Mozart "buried gutter insults" or enjoyed answering back, Mendelssohn wrote verses to express annoyance. On his mother's birthday in 1826, he produced the following:

If the composer's tone is grave,
He puts us all to sleep.
If the composer's tone is gay,
He is not one wit deep.

If the composer's tone is long,
Pity the mangey (sic) cur.
If the composer's tone is short,
Why, then, it does not stir.

If the composer's tone is clear,
Plainly, he is a fool.
If the composer is obscure,
Then send him back to school.

No matter how he turns his phrase,
Nobody is content.
Therefore, the composer must
Follow his own true bent!

(The German original was translated by Lukas von Leyden)

Mendelssohn was also criticised for the "frowns" and "faked Beethovenising" of his compositions, Marx noticing echoes of the *Coriolan* Overture in Mendelssohn's C minor Symphony. Sitting cross-legged (his customary position) in a corner of the front row of seats at a Sunday concert, Marx wrote a question mark against the initial theme of the score. The music brought to his mind "a band of imploring virgins in rippling veils". To Wagner, the *Coriolan* Overture represented "the struggle between man and woman". Jacob suggests that, in his youth, Mendelssohn "yearned to be a Beethoven, not knowing as yet how to be a Mendelssohn" – but what wonder, with so much pre-Romantic music rammed down his throat and into his ears!

If other composers' influences are heard in his music, a start has to be made somewhere, and it could well be a deliberate indication, until he discovered his own style, that Bach, Beethoven, Weber and the rest were admired by Mendelssohn and that he was actually paying tribute to these great masters who preceded him. However, Marx's quotes, which Jacob does all he can to substantiate, represent one view. It is thought by Marek that Abraham Mendelssohn disliked Marx because the latter admired Beethoven and tried too much to influence his 'pupil' (as he called Mendelssohn), wasting too much time on "sentimental trifles". Marx, in short, was not thought to be trustworthy by Abraham: "People who talk so aptly but produce nothing apt exercise a bad influence on productive talents," he is purported to have said to Devrient about their mutual acquaintance.

As Abraham Mendelssohn had at last allowed the idea to settle in his head that his elder son did have "productive talents", he did one of the most sensible things he could have done. People who mattered were taking notice despite there being none of the letters of introduction that a powerful banker could write. He therefore sought the advice of Moscheles. Now that both Schubert and Beethoven had passed away there was no one really influential in Vienna, and it was London that had superseded that city as capital of musical Europe. So, in 1829, one of the most illustrious visits was made by a musician from overseas to Britain.

Chapter 7

Two Father Figures

Contrary to received information, it was not his father who introduced the poet and dramatist Johann Wolfgang von Goethe to Felix Mendelssohn; it was Carl Friedrich Zelter who rendered this service, as was the case with Abraham himself at Strasbourg as early as 1797. On 26th October 1821 Zelter wrote to his long-term friend: "tomorrow early, I start for Wittenberg with Herr Mendelssohn's son, to attend the fête... I should like to show your face to my best pupil...before I leave this world." The fête was held to celebrate the unveiling of Gottfried von Schadow's statue of Martin Luther; Zelter's daughter Doris accompanied her father and the "lively boy of 12" who would be presented to Goethe in Weimar when the festival at Wittenberg had been concluded. "To be sure," Zelter explained, "he is the son of a Jew, but no Jew himself. His father, with remarkable self-denial, has seen to it that his children learn something and are educated properly. It would really be something if the son of a Jew turned out to be an artist." Though this remark is uncalled for in the present climate, it should be remembered that, until Zelter's time – with the exception of Solomon Rossi, a musician at the 17th-century court of Mantua – no Jew was allowed to take part in the cultural milieu of Europe. As a result of his own experiences, Goethe may well have had misgivings about the boy of whom Zelter spoke so glowingly. He had, after all, visited the Judengasse ('the Jews' Gate'), the Frankfurt ghetto, which he described as an "animal run", the streets of which were squeezed between the city wall and the castle, and "the closeness, the dirt, the swarming people; the accent of an ugly tongue" – Yiddish, a mixture of Hebrew, German, Polish and Russian. The pure Hebrew language was used wholly for reading and writing. Even had Goethe learnt of the free-spirited Mayer Rothschild's escape from this oppressive environment, to marry Golde Schnapper and to encourage their five sons to spread their wings and found branches of the Rothschild enterprise in the most prestigious cities of Europe, Goethe may have yet felt reluctance to see this boy from another Jewish family. The poet Heinrich Heine – proud throughout his life to acknowledge his Jewish faith – had travelled to Weimar to kiss Goethe's hand, reminding him that "I, too, am a poet", having sent a letter in which he "took the liberty" to enclose some verses a year and a half previously. When Heine had decided to make his pilgrimage to Weimar, he arrived in Goethe's presence "tongue-tied and stuttering about the excellence of the plums between Jena and Weimar". As may be imagined, after an attempt at friendliness, Goethe dismissed Heine curtly, as with many other visitors (according to Schima Kaufman), including Schiller.

Meanwhile, Zelter set off eastwards with daughter Doris and his "good, handsome...spirited and observant" pupil, the 12-year-old Felix. The Mendelssohn children had been reared on Goethe's works, which, because they did not bow to the dictates of fashion, found favour with Leah and Abraham on account of their timelessness. The boy's excitement can only be imagined at the prospect of meeting this demigod of whom he had heard so much. At the same time, he would escape the restrictions his parents placed upon him and would meet people who were pleased by his presence. From Leipzig, Felix wrote that he was to present a motet to "old Schicht", a musician of insufficient importance to feature in modern reference books. This, Rudolf Elvers believes, was one of several four-part motets composed by Mendelssohn that are still in manuscript. Felix also visited Professor Chladni at Kemberg, who, in the 1790s, had invented a 'Euphon' and a 'Clavcylinder' – two instruments akin to the glass harmonica that operated via a friction rod. Another instrument Felix sampled sounded like "a gentle oboe". Chladni's lodging comprised "one room that served for sleeping, working and receiving visitors". Of the inn at Kemberg, Felix wrote that Zelter complained of the too short bed; Doris was annoyed by "the bug population"; whilst Felix was "plagued by wretched feathers". However, the Hotel Russie in Leipzig was far more comfortable for the visitors. Felix wrote of drinking 'warmbier' (warm beer, as the name suggests, to which sugar and spices were added), to fight the harsh weather. A strange incident occurred in the early morning of the next day. Felix was awakened by a gentle hand resting upon him. Zelter had entered his room and, on enquiring the reason, Felix was told that his mentor had dreamt that someone had stolen his pupil away from him; "I wanted to see if you were still here". Could it have been Abraham about whom Zelter was dreaming?

Felix climbed onto the parapet of the bridge that spanned the two towers of Leipzig's main church. He visited the theatre to see a German translation of *Life is a Dream*, written by the 17th-century Spanish dramatist Calderón de la Berca. He sketched the house of Lukas Cranach, the artist. Yet, beneath all his enjoyment, Felix must have felt nervous at the thought of meeting "such superior people", as Leah referred to the Goethe household. His father, quite unnecessarily, ensured that his elder son did not forget his manners: Felix had to "speak nicely and sit properly at table"; to "speak clearly and to the point" and to "be modest and obedient". Fanny joined in: her brother had to "snap up every word that Goethe utters", keeping his eyes and ears open in order to be able to repeat everything heard and seen when he returned to Berlin, or she would have nothing to do with him. Leah wished she were a mouse, who could watch unobserved to see how her

Chapter 7: Two Father Figures

son would make out – and how badly he would behave without his parents' strict surveillance.

On 6th November 1821, Felix wrote home: "The Sun of Weimar is very friendly, but I find his portraits unlike him." Goethe showed his guest the fossil collection that one of his sons had arranged; they then took a half-hour's walk in the garden before dining. Ottilie, who had married Goethe's son August, lived in the house, as did Ulrike von Pogwisch, her sister. After the meal, Ulrike asked her host for a kiss; "I did the same," Felix reported. "Every morning I [now] receive a kiss from the author of Faust and Werther; every afternoon, two kisses from father and friend Goethe. Think of it!!!"

This is most enlightening. Reading between the lines, it appears that Felix may have wished his birth father was as demonstrative of affection as Goethe evidently proved. Not only did the elderly poet show understanding to this sensitive, gifted boy, but, like Zelter, he treated him as an equal. "In the evening they played whist," Felix continued, "and Professor Zelter, who at first played with them, explained: 'Whist means you must hold your tongue' – how very expressive! This evening, though not normally so, Goethe dined with the company." The biographer Moszkowski relates that, during this period, the elderly poet was conducting a passionate love affair with "a girl of 17" (Ottilie's sister Ulrike). It is evident that Goethe was still susceptible to attractive young women, for Felix wrote of a Mlle. Szymanowska, who was more popular than Hummel. "I was amazed and kept quiet as a mouse. It seemed to me that they have confused her pretty face with her not-so-pretty piano playing." When Felix had remained a fortnight as Goethe's guest, attracting the household "with the perfection and charm of his art", Zelter learnt that Goethe felt that "his coming did me a great deal of good, for my feelings about music are changed; I hear it with pleasure, interest and reflection".

Goethe is given far less credit as someone interested in music from biographers than he deserves. Not only, as director of Weimar's theatre, was he obliged to oversee the music of that city, but he knew what he liked and disliked and even propounded theories of his own. He presaged an idea that would be promoted by Jean Sibelius: that the different notes or musical phrases each had a colour. In the latter case, the Finnish composer visualised the key of A major as blue; C major, red; F major, green; D major, yellow; but Sibelius did not pursue his scheme further, and neither do we have any specific information about Goethe's theory in this connection. It is interesting that Mendelssohn appears to have had a similar idea. Adolf Bernhard Marx recalled the look of astonishment on Gustav Droysen's face when discussing instrumentation. "Only pure purple should be used" when debating a particular composition; "No. That shouts too loud," Felix responded, "I prefer violet." Mendelssohn always had definite ideas on the subtlety of colour in orchestration and a precise understanding of how it should sound; therefore it seems likely that he and Goethe may well have exchanged ideas on the subject.

Whilst he admitted that his sole attempt to play the Streicher piano given to him by the music critic Friedrich Rochlitz was "disastrous", Goethe did enjoy hearing others perform. When Zelter's "best pupil" was invited to oblige, Felix asked his mentor what he should play. "Whatever you can," was the response, "so long as it is not too difficult for you." Another music critic, Ludwig Rellstab, who had already heard what Felix could achieve, thought Zelter's words to be "in bad taste". He knew that "there was virtually nothing in the piano repertoire" that Mendelssohn had not mastered. (Rellstab is best remembered today for naming Beethoven's Piano Sonata Op. 27 No. 2 'the Moonlight'; for originally disparaging Chopin's music, only later to become an avid enthusiast; and for being arrested for insulting first the opera composer Gasparo Spontini and also the prima donna Mme. Sontag.) On this occasion, Rellstab recalled, after further discussion Zelter suggested "a humdrum, old-fashioned ditty with a triple figure, which Felix did not know". When Zelter had played the melody, "Felix repeated the song; then, without reflection, took the melody in both hands [in unison]...then plunged, without more ado, into the wildest allegro..." developing the piece, in each hand, with lovely contrasts. "In short, creating a torrential fantasia that poured out like liquid fire." Hummel, of whose music Rellstab was reminded – was "thunderstruck", as the passages "rumbled and dropped, like so many pearls", as Mendelssohn's small hands "worked into the masses of tone". The notes "flew by in ethereal whispers; a stream of harmonies flowed forth; surprising contrapuntal phrases were built up among them; only the rather banal melody was neglected and scarcely had a voice in the brilliant parliament of music". As may be guessed, knowing what Zelter was like, no purple prose emitted from his mouth. All he uttered were the words: "What genus of dragons were you imagining to embark on so wild a ride?"

Goethe hugged his young guest, in whose face "happiness, pride and embarrassment" were mingled. He then took Felix's head between both hands and, with "rough, kindly caresses", as Rellstab recalled, proved himself still dissatisfied. "You will not get away with that alone; you must play more before we acknowledge you fully." He asked Mendelssohn to play a minuet – "the only one" – from Mozart's opera *Don Giovanni*. This he declined, not through caprice on his part but simply in obedience to Mozart's music, realising that only an orchestra could accommodate the subtlety of the work to do it justice. To compromise, he played a piano arrangement of the Overture to *The Marriage of Figaro* by the same composer. "He began to play it with a lightness, sureness, roundness and clarity such as I have never heard before," Rellstab wrote later. "He reproduced the orchestral effects so excellently and...produced so cunningly the illusion of accompanying voices... [So] utterly enchanting...[that] it gave me such pleasure as no orchestral performance ever did." But Felix's 'test' was not yet complete. Asking him to play something he had never known, a manuscript was produced that Felix recognised, from the composer's handwriting, to be an Adagio of Mozart. "Very good," the host responded, still not satisfied; "now, let me see what you can make

Chapter 7: Two Father Figures

of this." This score, Rellstab recalled, looked "as if ink had been sprayed over it; the notes, when one could make them out, seemed to have been thrown helter-skelter onto the page", which Rellstab himself admitted to have had difficulty in deciphering. Looking over his pupil's shoulder, Zelter soon recognised the notation. "You can tell a mile off," he whispered to his fellow musicians; "Beethoven always writes as if using a broomstick and as if, afterwards, he had rubbed his sleeve over the page." Meanwhile, concentrating on the chaos of the score until he made sense of what was written, Felix recognised a setting of a poem by Goethe and played the piece with few mistakes. At a second attempt, he interrupted his recital to exclaim, "That is pure Beethoven!" As news spread regarding the young genius whom Goethe had befriended, anyone who was anyone in Weimar society wished to hear Felix perform.

However, the following incidents show that the 12-year-old Mendelssohn was precisely that – a boy of 12, with emotions to match. At a reception given by the Grand Duke of Weimar and his court, Felix was invited to show what pianistic feats he could achieve immediately after the celebrated Johann Nepomuk Hummel had performed. This musician had been a friend of Haydn and Beethoven, and a pupil of Mozart, and now he was at the peak of his career. This was too much for the unknown amateur, sheltered as he was from public appearances in the distinctly unmusical atmosphere of Berlin; Felix broke down in tears. Though Mme. Elise Polko reported that this incident took place at Leipzigerstrasse 3, this seems unlikely. There is no record of Hummel visiting Berlin at the time and, in any case, would Felix have dared to exhibit such a natural reaction in front of his parents? On another occasion, Felix was kept waiting in an ante-room whilst his name was given to the grand duke. Having "chafed and fumed for half an hour," as H. F. Chorley related, he left the grand duke's residence and "ran across the fields" back to Goethe's house. Nothing is heard as to how Ottilie, Goethe's daughter-in-law, who accompanied him, reacted. Stephen Stratton considers his behaviour "rude", without taking into account the frustration of an overactive mind with nothing to occupy it. But Hummel learnt from this freedom of spirit, despite coaxing by the servants to remain in the ante-room until summoned. Thenceforth, Hummel never allowed himself to be treated as anyone other than the highly respected musician he had become. Hitherto composers and performers were so often regarded as menials.

Nevertheless, when the grand duke and his family visited Goethe's home, Felix came into his own, as Christian Lobe recalled. Lobe, flautist with the Weimar orchestra, was summoned, with fellow musicians, to Goethe's house. Noticing three music desks placed alongside the piano, he looked at the pile of music lain ready to perform. "Studies in double counterpoint; fugues, canons and a piano quartet. The name on the scores meant nothing. The notes were written in a firm, smooth hand and, as far as I could tell at first glance, the compositions hinted at an accomplished artist." As the musicians tuned their instruments, Zelter asked that he introduce Felix, as his talent would be sure to fire their enthusiasm. "He listens avidly" to professional musicians, "and takes it all for coin of the realm," Zelter explained. As yet, "the young rapscallion is unable to differentiate between benevolent encouragement and strictly measured merit". Therefore, if the musicians praised Felix, as Zelter both wished and feared, they should do so in a moderate tempo. "Do not orchestrate your praise too loudly and do so in G major, the least colourful key"; Goethe, patting the boy's head, asked his guests to listen to what he had created. Thus, interjections of 'good' or 'bravo' and inclinations of the head were all the approval Felix received from the rapt audience. Zelter had, by his words of caution, managed to prevent what he called "those two goddamned enemies of artistic progress, vanity and conceit" on his pupil's part. Having completed his final piece, Lobe recalled, "Felix's face grew redder and redder but, giving everyone a questioning glance, [he] jumped up from the piano stool"; Goethe suggested he go into the garden to "cool off...for you are burning like fire!" Only later was it realised that the name on the scores belonged to none other than Zelter's 12-year-old pupil – the pianist and creator of that music.

Mendelssohn's G minor Piano Sonata, to be published posthumously as Op. 105, was praised by the grand duke, but also – a far greater accolade, as Felix saw it – by Johann Nepomuk Hummel. The string players, hitherto silent, had to agree that, when Mozart's genius at a similar age was discussed, Goethe could be right. Having met Mozart in 1768, Goethe declared, "He turned out imitations of his models;" Mozart's work compared with that of Mendelssohn's "bears the relationship between the prattle of a child and the conversation of a cultured adult". The art connoisseur John Julius (Viscount) Norwich admits that, even at 16, Mendelssohn's Op. 20 String Octet was superior to anything Mozart had written at a similar age. Lobe remembered that Mendelssohn, however much of a genius, was by no means a young prig. On entering the room, this boy with his "decidedly southern appearance, with thick, dark curly hair flowing down to the nape of his neck", came "prancing in, a thriving, perfectly handsome boy...slender and agile...spirit and animation sparkling in his eyes", whereas everyone else in the room bowed reverently as Goethe entered. Having played Hummel's B minor Piano Concerto at sight, "mixing genius with mischief" Felix took the bellows from the fireside and disarranged the impeccable coiffure of a lady-in-waiting. Whilst playing a Bach Fugue, Zelter asked why his pupil had not included the usual trill; "no one can play it" was his reply. On further questioning, he gave the reason, not with any conceit, but with mature self-assurance at knowing his ground: "The trill should not be there." On another occasion, Felix was asked to play "from eleven in the morning until ten in the evening", as he wrote to his family, "with two interruptions of one hour each". Again, the duke and his family were present, having visited the theatre to see "a very pretty opera" – *Charon* by Wranitzky. The repertoire included his own G minor Piano Sonata, "which he liked very much", Felix recounted, "and one for you, dear Fanny", for he never neglected to bring his

Chapter 7: Two Father Figures

sister's music to everyone's attention. He had shown some other songs to Ottilie, "who has a very pretty voice". When his daughter-in-law asked Goethe if he would like to hear them, he replied, "Yes. Yes. Very much."

As for his own musicianship, Felix was equally confiding in his elder sister: "Yesterday I played very badly, but today I shall try to play better". Indeed, he played far more than at home, his recitals lasting "seldom less than four hours" without a break; "sometimes six, seven or eight" at a stretch. Each afternoon, Goethe opened his Streicher piano with the words: "I have not yet heard you play today; now, make a little noise for me". Goethe sat alongside Felix on the piano stool, and, when the entertainment had concluded, "I ask for a kiss, or I take one. You have no idea how very good and kind he is to me..." One of his recitals included improvisations on popular songs by Körner and Eberwald; at Goethe's request Mozart's 'champagne aria' from *Don Giovanni* and 'Ipsilante waltzes' (composer unknown), celebrating a fighter for Greek independence against Turkish domination. During the latter piece, legend states, Felix was purported to have leapt from the piano to chase some young females around the room. Not only were "the spirits in the piano" awakened, as Goethe desired, but those of the audience also.

When Mendelssohn first visited Weimar, Goethe's two grandsons, Walther and Wolfgang, were aged four and two respectively. Later, Walther was to study with Mendelssohn and wrote of "that love of perfection and that dislike of anything mean or sordid, fostered and strengthened in Felix's character" under Goethe's influence. The host allowed his 12-year-old guest to study his treasures: "minerals, busts, prints, small statues and larger drawings which the Polar Star of poets possesses". Though "not much taller than father", Goethe's bearing, speech and name were imposing to Felix. "His hair is not yet white; his step is firm; his voice is mild" – when speaking to Felix. Others received a contrary impression. Felix himself admitted that "he can shout like 2,000 warriors", and this is borne out by incidents that have come down from memoirs. Goethe begged Zelter to travel alone to "that dismal hole, Jena" on the next stage of the journey, but to leave Felix at his home "for a few more days". When Zelter demurred, the host "abused him in his voice of thunder" to be silent and to obey his command "without question". As a result of this outburst, Goethe was "mobbed; everyone kissed him on hand or cheek; and anyone who could not get close enough patted and kissed his shoulder. Were he not already home, I believe we would have borne him there in triumph, as the people of Rome did with Cicero, after the first Catilinarian Epoch." To Adèle Schopenhauer, sister of the celebrated philosopher, Goethe's voice resembled someone from the Old Testament. At the theatre, when the audience laughed at a play by Ludwig Tieck, Goethe boomed into the pit that there was to be "no laughter!"

So, Zelter travelled alone with Doris, whilst Felix remained in Weimar. The attitude of his father towards Felix's admiration of Goethe as a person can only be imagined; no parent of his calibre can enjoy having an apparent rival's kindness to an offspring rammed down his throat, but there is no record of what Abraham Mendelssohn thought. Of Leah's opinion, there is evidence from correspondence with her sister-in-law, Henriette. Though it "cost me dear" to part with "my dear child", Leah realised "the advantage for the little wretch to receive a blessing from so great a man", not foreseeing that such a title would accrue to Felix himself and that many people, young or old, would treasure a blessing from Felix when he grew famous. At present, though, her son's "little journey" would be a change for him; his impulsiveness "sometimes makes him work harder than he ought to do at such an age", she added inconsequentially – though, possibly, to placate Henriette, who felt the same; and this from someone who, if Devrient is to be believed, was constantly upbraiding her elder son when he appeared to be "doing nothing!" How surprised – even, perhaps, annoyed – the parents must have been on reading Felix's report about the Goethe household: "manners are not at all stiff and formal"; the familiar pronoun 'du' ('you') is "insisted upon", as opposed to the less intimate 'sie'; and "can one refuse a glass of champagne?" from a host such as Goethe.

Yet, however mature for his years, an incident occurred at the grand duke's castle that was as frightening to Felix as to everyone else. The gamekeeper, whilst endeavouring to release a rifle from its case, accidentally shot Goethe's son, August. It was realised too late that the barrel had lodged against the trigger of another rifle, which happened to be loaded. The impact of the first rifle set off the second. As Felix reported: "The ball went through the case; through his clothes; through his hand; through his body; and right into the wall. He was not married but his mother is still alive; how sad."

However, on a happier occasion, whilst playing pencil and paper games, Adèle Schopenhauer drew and cut out some silhouettes, one of which represented Jacob's ladder, and another a scale of music notation over which a hobby horse rode. Later Goethe wrote some verses that he sent to Felix, which Karl Mendelssohn noted as remaining in his father's autograph album when, in 1874, he compiled a collection of letters between Goethe and Felix. The rhymes, roughly translated, run as follows:

When hobby horses gallop over
The lines and spaces of the score,
You'll boldly ride through music's clover
And lighten many a heart that's sore,
As you have done, with youthful charms.
We all wish you were back with us in our arms.

If witches' broomsticks can thus bound
Over the solemn score,
Ride on through wider fields of sound –

Chapter 7: Two Father Figures

The light is more and more.
As you have done, with might and main,
Then soon return to us again.

On a visit made by the family the next year, Leah heard Goethe say that Felix soothed him "like David to my Saul", referring to the Old Testament when the young harpist, through his music, banished King Saul's "evil spirits" that beset him. A young author, Stefan Schüntze, noted the rapid changes of mood that Goethe displayed. His disposition varied "for the course of one hour". He could adopt the character of "a calm, gentle sage" or "an irate autocrat"; he could be "silent", "aloof", "eloquent" or "loquacious". "Now expressing tranquillity; now displaying a fiery temper; ironically jesting or playfully teasing by turns." In short, no one could gauge from one minute to the next how Goethe might react, and this even applied to Felix on one occasion, as Baroness Gustedt noted in her memoirs. Unable to understand the import of what Goethe was saying, which caused the host to lose patience, "the boy sat frozen at the piano, unnerved by the storm" of anger that arose from Goethe. "Almost unconsciously", the baroness continued, Felix touched the keys, "as if to console himself". Evidently the poet, too, was mollified. Coming to the piano, he said "in the gentlest voice, 'You have enough. Hold onto it.'"

On Felix's 1822 visit, en route to Switzerland with his family, Goethe 's face "lit up with pleasure". Fanny likewise displayed her musical talent, not only playing works by Bach but her own settings of poems by her host. On that occasion, Goethe confided to Abraham, who had been asked by Zelter to advise his long-term friend on financial matters, that his Streicher piano had remained unopened since Felix's visit the previous year.

Meanwhile, between visits, Zelter kept Goethe in touch with his pupil's progress. Whenever he or Fanny composed a piece, each was "delighted with the other as much as if either had conquered Mexico," Zelter wrote. In 1825, he told of Mendelssohn's Op. 20 String Octet; "it really makes sense" was his cryptic assessment. Though his String Symphonies and chamber music were received coolly by a music critic, "that will not hurt him," Zelter explained, for this particular man "is an idiot, unable to find his hat when it is on his head. Felix is healthy, strong and a good swimmer – even downstream" – calling to mind that his pupil was a person as well as a superior musician. During that year Felix again visited Weimar, this time en route to Paris with his father. Goethe had a sketch drawn of this "gentle ruler of the piano", which he would display amongst his "gallery of notables". But Felix was to receive a significant gift of his own from 'the Sun of Weimar', trivial in itself, but which must have held for this 16-year-old boy far greater worth than its real value. After dinner he was handed a package tied with pink ribbon that contained a medallion on which Goethe's face was engraved. However, the accompanying inscription read "To Herr Felix Mendelssohn, 1825".

Felix was no longer regarded as a child – at least from Goethe's point of view; he was a 'herr' – a gentleman of maturity.

Readers are pitched into a contemporary way of thinking as regards the relationship between Goethe and Mendelssohn. Marek states: "It is fashionable, not to say mandatory, to read more than a genuine affection into Goethe's attitude towards a boy of 12", speaking of Felix's first visit to Weimar. Fortunately, however, even Marek has sense enough to dismiss such implications. Throughout his adult life Goethe relished the company of women, and it is clear that Felix, too, was becoming susceptible to feminine charms. Besides, though without stating categorically, he held in disdain individual homosexuals – notably George Onslow and the Count von Platen – whom he was to meet. More likely, this handsome, spirited boy may have caused Goethe to recall his own son, August, and the man he might have become, had he not followed his own path, eventually dying of drink as a feckless drifter. The disappointed father could now transfer his pride to this completely different lad, who, it was certain, would not disappoint his parents. Stemming from that point, Zelter may well have informed Goethe of the ultra-cautious upbringing that the Mendelssohn children had experienced. Goethe made up for the evident lack of encouragement and understanding that this highly intelligent, sensitive boy lacked at home.

Felix, too, like many young people, may have felt more comfortable in the company of someone other than a parent, to whom he could confide his innermost thoughts without being given negative responses in return. How refreshing it must have been for Felix to realise that no 'thou shalt nots' would pour forth from this kindly man. This talk of fatherly affection between Goethe and Felix is not a fantasy, but merely a conjecture as to what could have happened. After all, again in 1825, in a letter of 13th March, Abraham wrote to Leah that he was waiting at the hotel, after his midday meal, as his elder son was dining with Goethe. Having been invited to play his piano that morning, so excited at the prospect of the opportunity to dine and converse with the poet, rather than expressing paternal pride to Felix's mother, Abraham told Leah that their son "insisted on grabbing me round the neck, forcing me to have to drive him away". Though such behaviour does appear juvenile, Felix must have felt that he should try to show affection towards his father for the privilege bestowed upon him. All we hear is of Abraham's comfort – how he had to recuperate and rest for the next two days at their hotel, after the journey; his resentment at Ulrike's illness, cheerful in company, depressed in more intimate circles; "spoiling and pampering involved" – far more important than his son's triumph!

Neither was it Abraham Mendelssohn, but Zelter, who arranged for Felix to meet the then highly fashionable composer Ludwig Spohr at Cassel, en route to his Swiss holiday; though no mention is made in Spohr's autobiography of the visit, he was evidently impressed with Felix, who was invited to perform his Op. 1 Piano Quartet. "It was very kind of him to accompany me," Felix wrote modestly to

Chapter 7: Two Father Figures

Zelter. In turn, Spohr introduced the boy to a musician named Liste, who, though not in the usual reference books, was evidently an experienced mountaineer, with "long legs, which made paths into short cuts", when climbing with the family. On a visit to a Professor Kaiser, who had a "good piano", Felix wrote of Bach manuscripts, notably the *Well-Tempered Clavier*, which the musician "loves enthusiastically", as also "Handel's suites and many of his fugues". This opportunity occurred through an extra day spent at Zug, on account of an illness – "not very serious" – of the elder Fräulein Saling, who was travelling with the Mendelssohns.

From Bad Doberan, two years later, Felix wrote to Zelter that he had seen a charnel house where many bodies were burned, which the Oriental scholar Friedrich Rosen had recommended as a worthy tourist attraction. "This ancient but well-preserved building", about ten paces from the church, "has a small, round tower". The watchman's son guided Felix "through a tricky passage with ladders" to a staircase, leading to the top of a tower, "which was awful". A wooden structure had been "slapped on" when the original tower was struck by lightning, though the outer structure remained intact. Compared with the earlier building, this new arrangement looked "like chalk and cheese". Meanwhile, Zelter continued to correspond with Goethe about Felix's activities. It was he who brought to light the fact that it was for Leah's birthday that Felix had written *The Maid of Andros* and not his tutor Heyse. Zelter wrote of Felix's singspiel *Camacho's Wedding*, based on an incident in Cervantes's *Don Quixote*, that the work "has been lying in the King's Theatre for over a year, whilst French slop and swill is put onto the stage and the stuff hardly lasts until the next performance". On 9th March 1829 he wrote: "The boy is my only consolation. It is good that he is leaving the parental home" for his first visit to London. On 10th May 1830 Goethe learnt that Felix played the solo part in Bach's Keyboard Concerto, "as difficult as it is beautiful. Oh, I wish old Bach could have heard it!"

It was during that year that Felix paid his last visit to Weimar, on his way to Italy, but – before this – he remembered his old friend Julius Schubring, who had become a pastor at Dessau. He also visited Spohr at Cassel, who was experimenting with a new symphony. Each movement represented by its style a different period of development in the history of music. Goethe would find this fascinating, when Felix arrived in Weimar to explain this unusual idea, since he believed that music was as much a science as the study of minerals. Though Spohr's project was a failure, seeds may well have been sown in Felix's subconscious mind to start the 'historic concerts' when he came to direct the Leipzig Gewandhaus Orchestra. Meanwhile, in Dessau, Mendelssohn was asked if his *Calm Sea and Prosperous Voyage* Overture could be performed at a concert and, at "a small, select party at Rust's, a great treat", he joined in Haydn and Beethoven trios and extemporised on the latter's song 'Adelaide' and a piano arrangement of his 9th 'Choral' Symphony, as Rust had been a great friend of the composer. Felix also received some commissions from a duchess, on which he would work subsequently. He and

Schubring attempted to visit Kapellmeister Schneider, but found him to be visiting his sister, then another friend. Nevertheless, they met by chance in the village street, but Schneider continued his walk. "We felt there was something wrong," Schubring explained naively. Though Schneider had called Mendelssohn "that promising boy" on meeting him at Leipzigerstrasse 3, he had become resentful of Mendelssohn's triumph over the performances of Bach's *Passion according to St Matthew*, and his annoyance must have festered.

In Weimar, conversations with Goethe must have been fascinating to anyone else involved, since it was never known, from one topic to the next, what would be discussed. From Spontini, Goethe might ask what Felix thought of the theological disputes between the orthodox Protestants and the 'anti-Pietists'. He took Schleiermacher's view that there were pantheistic roots from the culture of ancient Greece to the teachings of Christianity. As for Hegel's dictum that, when he died, there would be no more philosophers of note, Felix had to give a 'sitting on the fence' answer, for he realised that Goethe felt the same about himself and poetry. Scott's novels were then aired, followed by a subject dear to both their hearts – "the pretty girls of Weimar". When Mendelssohn tried to thank his host for all the reminiscences and anecdotes he had recounted, all Goethe responded was that it was only because his guest was present that so many subjects came to light. These words were "wonderfully sweet" and Felix would remember his talks with Goethe for the rest of his life. In turn, Goethe confided to his daughter-in-law, Ottilie, that he had learnt much from Mendelssohn, as he had the type of mind that could combine any topic perceptively, with a new slant on the discussion, but with complete self-assurance yet absolute modesty. Posterity would remember the man of letters, not as one individual, but as "a sun, with constellations of equal importance; revolving around it" – the Sun of his Life, as he was later to write to Julius Benedict. Felix had planned to stay for two days, which he considered "no sacrifice", as his host seemed "more cheerful, amiable and communicative" than ever before.

It was at this time that Goethe commissioned the portrait for an album remembering his friends, so Felix was obliged to remain longer, until the artist Heinrich Stiehler, who spoke of Goethe in a "very kind and amiable" manner, had finished his work. Felix lived "luxuriously" meanwhile, dining each day with the elderly dramatist, and he was, naturally, asked to play the piano for him. Ottilie, though still "delicate and sometimes complaining, [was] more cheerful than formerly and quite as kind and amiable as ever". Ulrike, too, was "much pleasanter and more lovable than before", with an "innate earnestness, sureness and depth of feeling, one of the most attractive creatures that I have ever seen".

The grandchildren were "lively, industrious and obliging lads and, to hear them talking about 'grandpapa's Faust' is too sweet for words". At dinner one evening, presumably at the beginning of Mendelssohn's visit, Goethe was "silent and withdrawn; I think he wanted to see how I comported myself" after so long. On

Chapter 7: Two Father Figures

this occasion, conversation included "a ladies' choir in Weimar" and "the newspaper *Chaos*" that the ladies circulated and produced; "I have scored so high as to become a contributor," Felix wrote. Goethe laughed at the charitable work – "the ladies' intellectualisms, subscriptions and hospital work; which he seems particularly to detest" – calling on Mendelssohn to support his onslaught. "And, as I did not need to be asked twice, he speedily became just what he always was: more friendly and confiding than ever." The subject switched to Ferdinand Ries's cantata *The Robber Bride*, which, Goethe claimed, was "all that an artist in these days requires to live happily: a robber and a bride". Then followed "the melancholy for which young people yearned" – an anecdote concerning a young lady whose affections appeared to be reciprocated towards Goethe. Conversation reverted to a charity bazaar at which Felix had bought a red wallet from the handmade items for sale. Goethe asked "a great deal" about Mendelssohn's piano playing, and they discussed the "great success with my Welshmen, or Welshwomen", as Felix called his Op. 16 Fantasies composed for the Miss Taylors of Coed Du, near Mold.

On a visit to Tiefurth, as an escort for the ladies of the household, Felix was asked "not to drive to Berka, because a very pretty girl lives there and he [Goethe] did not want to plunge me into misery". Again, Mendelssohn observed that Goethe was "not one person, but several little Goethes", as anyone studying his work would discover.

Mendelssohn visited the library and saw a performance of Gluck's *Iphigenia in Aulis* at the opera house. He saw the Auerbach courtyard, "full of shops and people and surrounded by houses" with six, seven, and one with nine storeys. On Ascension Day everyone wore best attire for church. On a drive in the countryside, Felix "looked at everything". In one village, he noticed a game of bowls in progress; in another, the gardens were "gay with tulips" and he was able to purchase a bunch of lilies of the valley. Not only students, whom he met, envied his carefree state of mind. This applied also to 'President G', whose small carriage "had difficulty in containing [him] and two daughters, or wives – two women who were with him". Mendelssohn's carriage horses hardly needed to pull, yet overtook many vehicles, including that of the Russian ambassador, "travelling in such a sullen and pedestrian manner, with two large coaches drawn by four horses apiece". He did not write one bar of music all day, "but enjoyed complete idleness", ending with the sight of children "playing 'ring-around-a-rosy', like the children at home". They were in no way alarmed at the appearance of this stranger who, had the truth been known, would have liked to join in their game.

Once again Mendelssohn played to Goethe, the recital including "Bach, Haydn and Mozart, and then led him on to the present day", via Weber and his own Op. 16 and Op. 28, the so-called 'Scottish' Sonata. As regards Beethoven, Goethe showed continued stubbornness to acknowledge the composer's greatness. No emotion was caused when Mendelssohn first played the piano arrangement of his 5th Symphony, but, later, having called it "grandiose", whilst grumbling about the work, he admitted it to be "great; quite wild. It makes one feel that the house might fall down. What must it be like when all those men play together!" He questioned his guest minutely on the symphony in one of their conversations, which also included a discussion on his collection of engravings and the poet Lamartine's *Elegies*. Goethe invited many young people to the house, including "a number of Weimar beauties", but Felix felt he had to reassure the family that he never ceased to wish not to impose on his host. On Ottilie asking her father-in-law if this was so, all she received was a growl and words to the effect that he wished to learn from such an unusual guest. "I became twice as tall in my estimation when Ottilie repeated this to me", and, on parting, Felix was given a page of the *Faust* manuscript. The dedication read: "To my dear young friend F. M. B., powerfully tender master of the piano; a friendly souvenir of happy May days in 1830. W. von Goethe." He suggested "some moments of devotion", being reminded, no doubt, of the painting *Praying Family* that had made such an impression on Felix nine years before. Felix received letters of introduction for later stages of his journey to Italy, and wrote from Munich to say how useful the one to the artist Heinrich Stiehler would be. Felix showed Goethe a sketch he had made of the lambs at Leipzigerstrasse 3, which the poet found to be "well-cared-for, dainty, pretty, lovely, graceful and contented".

But, throughout his time abroad, Mendelssohn neglected neither Goethe nor Zelter, as examples of their three-way correspondence will show. "I cannot wait for the time when he gets out of the miserable, shallow swamp of Berlin and to get to Italy, where he should have gone a long time ago, in my opinion," Zelter wrote to Goethe on 10th May 1830. "There, the very stones have ears; here, the people eat pigs' ears, served with lentils." On hearing of Goethe's illness in the autumn of that year, the poet's words "I must keep well until you return" to Germany rang in Mendelssohn's ears the whole evening, to the exclusion of all else. "When he is gone, Germany will assume a very different aspect, for artists have never thought of Germany without heartfelt joy and pride in the fact that Goethe lived there. The rising generation seems, for the most part, so weak and feeble that it makes my heart sink within me... This year closes with frightening solemnity."

With greetings for Zelter's birthday, Christmas and the New Year, Mendelssohn sent the manuscript of a chorale that he had written in Venice, commenting that music never changed – unlike political events, causing mail to be delayed for weeks at a time. On 30th October Felix wrote to Zelter that he would report "anything worthy of interest". The fact that only one letter had reached his former mentor since Munich was caused by "the state of constant excitement" he experienced there and in Vienna. In Munich, "one entertainment was crowded on the heels of the next", with a party every evening and invitations to play the piano "more unremittingly than ever before". However, during the next two days, his world, which had appeared hitherto unchangeable, had now been swept away and was "quite bleak". Felix had heard no news from home for four weeks, yet was himself

Chapter 7: Two Father Figures

chided if he did not write twice a week to the family. Nevertheless, "I hurry from one enjoyment to another, hour by hour, constantly seeing something novel and fresh" whilst in Venice. The plains of Italy made "an exhilarating impression" upon him and, for two hours a day, he studied old masterpieces of art, as they meant so much to him. To Goethe and Zelter he gave details of the paintings, as in the case of his letters home, mentioning Titian's works and Giorgioni's *Girl with the Zither*; "She is lost in thought, gazing out of the picture in serious meditation, about to begin a song", which Felix felt like doing when looking at her. These pictures alone were worth his journey to Venice, "with its opulence, power and devotion to the great men who painted them, which emanate afresh each time they are studied". He heard barely any music, except that resulting from the angels in Titian's *Assumption*. They encircled Mary "with joyous shouts of welcome, one beating a tambourine gaily; another two blowing on strange, crooked flutes", another group singing – "or perhaps the music is in the thoughts of the player". Felix was seized "with solemn awe" on gazing at Titian's *Martyrdom of St Peter* at a Franciscan monastery; a figure in the painting "steals forth out of the darkness into which the long lapse of time had veiled them". He was, though, driven away by the organist's performance, out of keeping with the paintings, the service and the reverent congregation, spoiling Mendelssohn's reverie, after which he did not wish to make the organist's acquaintance. There was no such instrument in the city itself when Mendelssohn visited, "neither do the gondoliers now sing Tasso's verses".

"By this time," Zelter wrote to Goethe on 2nd November, "Felix is probably in Rome. I am very glad he is, because his mother was always against Italy. I fear he would be reduced to a jelly here in the midst of all the flatulent family gossip." Goethe wrote to Zelter on 28th June 1831: "The Herr Papa is absolutely adamant that he [Felix] should not travel to Sicily. Why should he long for something unnecessarily?" Both Goethe and Zelter tried to bend Abraham's mind on the topic, but to no avail. Later, Felix wrote to Zelter that he had been unable to write to him from Naples, having been "wandering around the mountains and gazing at the sea" for so long, but he hoped his family would allow his correspondent to see his detailed letters home. Nevertheless, he took care to "observe each separate detail" of any music he heard. That of Naples was "inferior to Rome" and, in fact, there was not a note worth remembering. Back in Rome he copied seven of the pieces used for various church services, a synopsis of which he would send his former mentor. "You cannot imagine how tiresome and monotonous the effect is, nor how harshly and mechanically they chant through the Psalms. The choir sing like a number of men quarrelling violently, shouting the same thing furiously at each other."

Zelter would be able to compare the music in the official score with how it appeared to Felix when the Berlin choir sang the same music. The parts that were "sung in the deepest emotion and reverence" turned out to be the letters of the Hebrew alphabet that precede each Lamentation, though "composed with peculiar fervour". The beautiful opening, which "sounds as if it came straight from Heaven", was simply the title. "This must be not a little repulsive to a Protestant heart... Anyone who sings 'Chapter the First' cannot possibly feel any pious emotion, no matter how beautiful the music may be." To denote the end of a ceremony, "the cardinals scrape their feet on the pavement". Though the service books explained that this symbolised the Jews seizing Christ's body, to Felix the sound resembled "the commotion in a theatre pit when a play is delayed or finally condemned". Baini's music was "devoid of life"; no one could say how the embellishments "crept" into Allegri's *Miserere* – Psalm 51 – but, in each case, the original music was "barely discernible". Though these ornaments were said to be 'traditional', Mendelssohn disputed this since "no such musical tradition can be relied upon", because "no five-part movement can be passed down by hearsay". Neither could the acoustics be held responsible for the singing, and, in such circumstances, the music depended on the availability of voices at a given time – not beforehand. A singer named Mariano came from the mountains to sing, and it was his high treble notes that caused Mendelssohn to recollect the embellishments.

A Palestrina motet was performed that Felix called "remarkable", except for the embellishment sung by the soprano, which the Italians called "an appoggiatura", reminiscent of how the elderly women sang in Berlin. It irritated him to hear "such holy and beautiful words" sung to "such drawling music... One does not find such mechanical monotony in the Scriptures; they are all truth and freshness, expressed in the most natural manner." There was no false expression, for the simple reason that there was no expression at all. He was equally irritated by the choristers' mannerisms; whereas everyone declared "how splendid" the singing was, to Felix it was "like a bad joke", by which he was "driven wild" and "out of sorts" on hearing the Spanish composer Victoria's setting of the *Passion according to St John*. He believed that the narrative should be read by a priest, according to St John's original Gospel; thus, "one could have felt oneself to be present at the scene". As Mendelssohn heard the performance, "When the people cry for Barabbas to be set free, they are very tame Jews indeed. Prayers are said for all nations but, when praying for the Jews, no one kneels and no 'Amen' is said."

From Switzerland Mendelssohn wrote that, though there was a "good" organ at the monastery at Engelberg, the monks were unaware of Bach's music. As with his family, his chief subject worthy of report was the unbelievably foul weather he appeared to have experienced almost everywhere he ventured. In short, despite the glorious scenery of Italy and Switzerland, it was the German cities that he visited which were "really, the high point of my trip, for then I realised that I was a German and wanted to live in Germany as long as I could do so... I am at home here." He did not need to learn the customs or the language, and he felt comfortable with her people, "without having to be surprised".

From Paris he wrote that music and appreciation of art were widespread in Germany whereas, elsewhere, it was concentrated into one area, but "in Germany,

Chapter 7: Two Father Figures

it is not raised to great heights, nor taken to such extremes, and, in consequence, we are able to send musicians to other countries, whilst remaining sufficiently well endowed ourselves".

On 22nd March 1832 Goethe passed away in his 83rd year. Though, at such an age, his death would have been expected, especially at a time when people normally lived for half that number of years, Felix was grief-stricken and burst into tears. "The loss of Goethe impoverishes us all," he wrote home nine days later. To Mendelssohn, Goethe was "the greatest figure in Germany's greatest period" of her cultural history; "how different our country now looks," he declared. Even Marek admits that Goethe behaved like a second father and, from a personal standpoint, Felix may well have experienced this feeling for the man whose loss not even the excitement and friendliness of Paris could alleviate.

Zelter had a different tribute to pay: "Your Excellency has, of course, precedence, but I will soon follow"; which prophecy came true far sooner than he might have anticipated. Early in May, whilst sitting on the steps of St Mary's Church in Berlin, Zelter developed a cold that turned into pneumonia, and on the 15th of that month he too passed away, and was buried on the 18th. Not only the musical world attended the funeral, but political and civic dignitaries also; the theologian Schleiermacher gave the eulogy and the Berlin Singakademie performed, directed by Zelter's deputy, Rungenhagen. Later the publishers, Trautwein, who had recently printed Bach's *St John Passion*, distributed a memoir of Goethe and Zelter. A memorial service was held on 7th June at which Mozart's Requiem and some of Zelter's own compositions were performed. On hearing news of Zelter's illness, Mendelssohn, on his second visit to London, expressed anxiety in every letter, though Abraham reassured him of Zelter's recovery. However, on hearing the ultimate tidings, Felix expressed himself as feeling that he had "lost blood", so physically weak did he feel. Like Goethe, Zelter too was regarded as part of Mendelssohn's family – more, it may be suspected, than his birth parents ever were.

When the Goethe-Zelter correspondence was published in 1834 by the lexicographer Riemann, Felix wrote to Charlotte Moscheles asking her if she knew the section 'Nicht Allein' ('Not Alone') from *Faust*, as this would help to explain the author's friendship with Zelter. Of the publication, *Goethe's Correspondence with a Child*, Abraham wrote of a "most provoking and pernicious use of the press, through which, more and more, rapidly, all illusions will be destroyed, without which life is only death. You, I trust, will never lose your illusions and [will] ever preserve your filial attachment to your father." Could this defensive remark have implied regret on Abraham's part at his lack of empathy with his elder son when compared with that of Goethe or Zelter? It is evident that, in his final years, Abraham and Felix were becoming closer one to another as father and son. When the first volume of Eckermann's biography of Goethe, *Dichtung und Wahrheit* (*Fiction and Truth*, as its English title became), Fanny commented that, unlike the memoir written by Varnhagen von Ense, this contained "a far more genuine and original picture...with no scandals".

A "far more piquant" biography could have been written, but that of Eckermann was the best since Goethe's death and her father would have appreciated it. Fanny's son, Sebastian Hensel, tantalisingly omitted what he called his mother's "cutting criticism" of von Ense's book, fearing that further scandals would erupt "with a fresh vigour" if anyone read her opinion of Goethe. Nevertheless, despite Eckermann's scandal-free volume, she considered contemporary literature more "stagnant" than at any other period during which books had been written. Felix, too, read Eckermann's biography, congratulating the author on "his faithful observation and – unlike Riemer – his delicacy... I feel just as if I hear the old gentleman speaking again...the very same words I have heard used, and I know his tone and gestures by heart", so well did Eckermann call them to mind. Though nothing more is heard of Zelter's family, Mendelssohn did contact Goethe's daughter-in-law Ottilie from time to time. H. E. Jacob makes a mockery of a letter dated 27th June 1834. To someone who understands how deeply Mendelssohn regarded the Goethe household, there appears nothing but natural, straightforward friendship in the missive. He sought news of Ulrike, from whom he had not heard for so long, and expressed a wish to meet the family once more.

Jacob, however, like a Jack Russell terrier with a rat, cannot leave the letter in peace. Having gloated over discovering it among the Mendelssohn papers in Basel, Switzerland, he wonders if Felix had been in love with Ottilie. "Heaven forbid," he answers his own question, but without explaining himself. He accuses Mendelssohn of being "a virtuoso" in "rendering consolation to women who were lonely", again not analysing his statement; "women loved to be adored", but, had Felix not "played the game by the rules" and brought "passion" into their lives, most of these women would have "found it disquieting". Naive or not, Jacob's conjecture appears ridiculous. Mendelssohn wrote again to Ottilie on 1st December 1837, evidently still as a loyal friend, but nothing more. He thanked her for a grammar book that belonged to her father-in-law; this would be a boon "to my little St Thomas's Choir pupils". Goethe's grandson, Walther, who had by then become a pupil of Felix, was reported as "physically and spiritually stronger lately and is visibly progressing in his development". In the same letter he asked, since the court was not visiting Berlin but remaining in Weimar, if the English soprano Clara Novello could sing there after leaving Leipzig; how long might Miss Novello's engagement last, and how much would she receive as her fee? He did not wish the English soprano to be given "an unfortunate impression of German musical life". He was, though, sure Miss Novello would sing "some splendid things" with which the Weimar court would be pleased. Ottilie was asked in the same letter to assist the career of the 'cellist Julius Rietz, in whatever way she could. After praising this musician fulsomely, Mendelssohn, as was his habit, begged pardon for "imposing

Chapter 7: Two Father Figures

on" Ottilie once more. "One gladly asks [a favour] on someone else's behalf that one would not think to ask for oneself." This appears to be the final letter associated with Mendelssohn and the Goethe family; neither, so far as can be proved, is Weimar mentioned again in the Mendelssohn correspondence. Yet Fanny, who badgered Felix to remember anything and everything seen and heard on his first visit to Weimar, had become thoroughly disillusioned on meeting Goethe's surviving son in 1836. She had expected such potential from this descendant but, since he fell below Fanny's expectations, she felt he did not deserve to be associated with the name of Goethe. Nothing is known of Rebecka's or Paul's opinion of the mighty dramatist.

Chapter 8

Fanny and Felix

There is no doubt that, had anyone troubled to point out to Abraham Mendelssohn that he resembled an overzealous tutor rather than a loving, caring father, or that Leah behaved more like a super-efficient nanny than a loving, understanding mother, each would have been deeply wounded; but so it appears. Fortunately, Felix was able to compensate by acquiring Zelter and Goethe as surrogate father figures. The Victorian songwriter J. P. Skelly stated that 'A Lad's best Friend is his Mother' but, as the woman who gave birth to Felix was unable to fulfil the role of best friend, a substitute had to be found. It was his sister Fanny who assumed the position of mother, giving the affection that this 'sensitive plant' needed.

According to Marek, the only woman Felix loved was Fanny, "on whom he poured out the profoundest love of which he was capable" – implying there to have been "a cognate eroticism between the two". Marek's thesis is supported by essays in the Winter 1993 issue of *Musical Quarterly*, and Wilfrid Blunt believes there was "more than a brother and sister relationship" between Fanny and Felix. He even suggests that, when Fanny became engaged to the artist Wilhelm Hensel, her brother felt "a pang of jealousy" of this "outsider", as Hensel was regarded by the Mendelssohn family. Such can be seen merely as traps into which unwary or sensation-seeking biographers have allowed themselves to fall. Friends did jest as to the date when Felix would ask Fanny to marry him but, in such a convention-ridden society as the Leipzigerstrasse 3 circle, they would be terrified of the scandal were such an event actually to occur. Brought up in such a way as to learn right from wrong at an early age, it would not have occurred to Fanny or Felix to be anything other than brother and sister. Had an incestuous liaison existed, neither would have married anyone else; Fanny would not have been so blissfully happy with Wilhelm Hensel nor Felix with Cécile Jeanrenaud. Felix and Fanny would have had no trouble in leaving their respective marriages, unlike aunts Dorothea and Recha. However, Moszkowski shows common sense: he sees Fanny as "at once, the luminous Madonna; the Mother Confessor; the eternal woman; the sounding board and the yardstick against which he [Felix] could measure his ideas, his hopes and his fears".

Fortunately for posterity, Fanny was able to bestow on Felix the mother's love and understanding that the woman who gave birth to him appeared unable to show. With this analysis in mind, the reader feels completely at ease and free from embarrassment at the often oversentimental entries in Fanny's journal and correspondence concerning her feelings towards her elder brother.

Marek bases his thesis on Fanny's remarks about her approaching wedding. (See Chapter 10). "Everything would be well – if I did not feel so unwell," she wrote on 23rd September, ten days before the wedding date. She had had a tooth extracted and, even in today's sophisticated and hygienic dentistry, the patient feels below par, whatever joyful event may be imminent. "Now I have a swollen jaw; altogether, I feel low." With what sounds like an abscess in the mouth, causing poison to enter the whole system, Fanny's state of health is hardly surprising, but Marek takes no account of this basic physical fact. "Tooth or not tooth," he declares, "it is hardly the tone one would expect from a bride-to-be in two weeks' time." If a psychological construction is to be put on this diary entry, Fanny may have been experiencing a reaction after all the years of frustration she had had to undergo, when Leah even intercepted letters from Hensel, when in Rome; now, at last, the time was upon her when happiness would be achieved for Fanny – she must have prayed that something untoward would not happen to prevent her marriage after waiting so long. As for her remark that "a bridegroom is no more than a man, after all", this could be seen as keeping her mind in balance, not to become overexcited in case anything untoward might transpire to prevent the marriage. But, if Marek's view is accurate, would Felix have liked Hensel and, despite wariness on both sides, have welcomed him so heartily?

It was a sketch Hensel had drawn that really caused Felix's suspicious attitude to change – fostered, no doubt, by his future in-laws. This showed the family circle with Felix in the centre, dressed in Highland garb, representing him on his forthcoming journey to Scotland. Indeed, Felix waxed lyrical on any drawing he liked, calling it "heavenly", and saying it gave him "warmth and joy whenever it looks at me...genial and pretty, yet true to life". A drawing of an acquaintance named Caroline, "with bearskin gloves", puzzled him: "What is the meaning of the moon with a man in it?" he asked Hensel. Fanny's portrait he felt able to criticise. Though "beautiful" and "strikingly lifelike", "in pose, dress, facial expression and whole...quality of rapturous enthusiasm" it could not be compared with the person he knew. "In her, the enthusiasm is not so much on the surface but, rather, within and shows itself...only little by little." Felix respected Hensel enough to ask him not to take offence at such sentiments. Would he have been able to express such feelings had he been jealous of his new brother-in-law? But what causes Marek to disparage Fanny's anxieties about Felix? If the quotes he uses are those of a mother figure, they are perfectly natural, especially when the hazardous travelling conditions of

Chapter 8: Fanny and Felix

the 1820s are borne in mind. Fanny must have feared that frightening place across the English Channel to which her 'son' had to return alone. As early as January 1829, Fanny noted in her journal that "Felix, our soul, is departing". In March: "I shall not know what to do without him; all will be mute and desolate." She hoped, once he had left Berlin, that Felix would receive a letter in Hamburg that she was writing, though she had sent another the previous day.

She was pleased about his new, exciting life away from home, but hoped he would make time to think of her. At Christmas 1828 she had written to Klingemann: "What shall I do without him?" and, once Felix had arrived in London, she begged that he should be allowed "many a quiet hour" to reminisce about home and family. "I know he will often be with us in his thoughts " and that Klingemann – "the alpha and omega" to her brother – "will observe that peculiar, moist sparkle in his eyes" that will result from homesickness on Felix's part. Fanny would even "feel shame" if her engagement diverted her mind from her "bereavement" at Felix's departure. "Take good care of him and let him find one warm heart for the many he leaves behind." On 14th June she sent Klingemann "a parcel of love tokens and sentimental keepsakes" for Felix as a reminder of home; but he had to receive them only when in a suitable frame of mind, not irritated "by a copyist or a fly". Is this not typical of an anxious, if overprotective, mother, whose son is leaving her care for the first time in his life – however exciting the reason? In September she expressed her feelings in a letter to Felix. Though Fanny had feared her engagement would tear them apart, "having gained a full knowledge of myself, I have come nearer to you and think even more of you, if that is possible". And again: "It is not possible that your love will decrease, for you know full well that I cannot spare one jot of it." A mother's love does not wane, however fully she loves her husband, or however well her child loves a spouse. On the 29th, four days prior to her own wedding, Fanny admitted to playing her brother's motet *Hora est*...and kissing his portrait "every few minutes". "I love you – adore you – immensely," she assured him. On 3rd April she noted in her journal how she had "helped Felix get dressed and packed" for his London odyssey. This task was not assigned to Leah, or a servant, but undertaken, without question, by Fanny herself.

But how did Felix reciprocate this filial devotion? Admittedly, on 21st July 1824 he told Fanny, "My sweet, I love you dearly," and on her 25th birthday, 14th November 1830, "I feel quite weak thinking about you," having enclosed a song as a birthday gift. Three days earlier, whilst telling her about Delphine von Schauroth, the renowned pianist he had met in Munich, he included the information that it was Fanny's portrait that gazed at him while he wrote about this other woman. Nevertheless, this 'mother and son' relationship was not all compliance on Felix's part. In 1827 he evidently resented her meddling. "Are you the Inquisition?" he asked. "Is the string on which I flutter [so] long and unbreakable?" Why, he would like to know, did she spy on him? What was she doing in his room, "prying" into his belongings? "Take care, fair flower, take care," he admonished. No explanation was given for this strange behaviour, so no analysis can be possible. Had there been a wholly innocent explanation, would Fanny not simply have sought permission, say, to borrow a book or a music sheet? It can only be assumed that Fanny was suspicious of something with which she was not happy in Felix's life. Since family correspondence was so efficiently censored, this episode must remain a mystery.

The mythology factory has decreed that, after Fanny's marriage, her love for Felix deteriorated, but evidence proves this to be false. Even when Felix himself chose a bride, Fanny continued to be as anxious as ever for her 'child's' welfare. She wrote shortly after her brother's marriage to express her regret at no longer being privy to the day-to-day happenings in his musical life; how, she asked, was the premiere of his 2nd Piano Concerto received at the 1837 Birmingham Festival? "If I could but once hear that Felix has conquered his restlessness," she wrote, she would be greatly reassured. "The constant race he runs, year after year, takes my breath away – I, who live in complete quiet." This is precisely how a lonely mother might chivvy her daughter-in-law about the recalcitrant son who appears to give no time to his former environment, but whose welfare still causes anxiety. When her 'dear Cile' received another letter Fanny would be entertaining three tedious guests, including a 'Fanny J', to luncheon, having also to make 27 further visits. She asked her 'Sunday child' to respond for the third time, continuing in the same mode a demanding parent might use. When, having nursed the children through measles and whooping cough, Cécile developed an "inflammation of the throat", Fanny appeared "more concerned than Felix about her condition", according to Jacob, but this is unjust. Knowing what she was like, Cécile may well have begged Fanny not to reveal anything to Felix (then in London for his sixth visit) about her ill health. What could he have done to alleviate the situation? In any case, Cécile would have known how strenuous a work schedule her husband would have experienced with the various demands on his time, musical and diplomatic. "God grant I may be mistaken and over-anxious," Fanny prayed, still the fretful mother, powerless to nurse her 'child'.

Marek, gloating over his thesis that there was more than a brother and sister tie between Fanny and Felix, argues that, though Leah and Abraham may or may not have guessed the truth, Rebecka certainly did. She wrote to Felix: "Last night, in lovely moonlight, during charming conversation, by the side of her most ardent betrothed, Fanny fell fast asleep. Why? Because you are not here." But need Marek be accurate in his conjecture? Might Rebecka have realised the real import of the affinity between Fanny and Felix – that she, Fanny, had taken Leah's place as his mother? In 1843 Fanny told Rebecka that Felix was "as amiable, in as good spirits, as delightful as you know him to be on his best days. I admire him afresh every day, for this quiet life together is new to me and his mind is so many-sided and so unique and interesting in every respect that one becomes accustomed to him. I do believe he becomes more lovable too, as he increases in years." As for Fanny herself, 'A' had remarked how much more amiable she had become as she had matured; a stranger had mistaken her for the wife of a government official, a M. Sevigny, causing her to feel "truly venerable", befitting the character of a woman whose child had become an adult. Again we hear the sighs of a grieving mother, once Felix's family had returned to Leipzig from Berlin in 1844. "It is very hard for me, who enjoyed the happiness of living so near him and his children... [They] are completely lost to me and I have grown so fond of them."

To Cécile, though not actually reproaching her 'daughter-in-law' for allowing Felix and the children to forsake the parental nest, Fanny made it plain what "a grievous loss" this was, especially in view of the suddenness of their departure. It had been anticipated that they would remain until Easter, when Felix would conduct a performance of *St Paul* by command of the King. "I see it all," she sighed, but without qualifying what she meant. Fanny's real son, Sebastian Hensel, believed that his mother had wished that the Mendelssohn and Dirichlet families would live together in and around Leipzigerstrasse 3, with the children growing to adulthood together. (Fanny lavished as much maternal care on Rebecka's family.) Because her sister's independent spirit – and that of her husband – would not allow them to live at Leipzigerstrasse 3, as Fanny had begged them, a house was found, No. 18 in the same street, where every detail was minutely planned and every up-to-date fixture and fitting arranged. Sebastian Hensel admitted his mother's action to be "more motherly than sisterly". Fanny had hoped, until the Dirichlets returned from Italy, that Felix, Cécile and their children would occupy Leipzigerstrasse 18. However, when Felix was obliged to stay in Berlin, Fanny had to admit how much she admired his buoyant spirit when separated from his wife. He remained for a further fortnight, whilst Hensel painted his portrait. "No doubt he will groan to his wife, nevertheless, despite his sweetness of disposition," she wrote in her journal. "I only wish he had not felt obliged to inflict so great a sacrifice upon us all, as well as upon himself." In 1846 Fanny wrote to Cécile as to how she pitied her having to spend so much time in the town in such fine weather, evidently angling for Cécile and the children to share her own "calm and pleasant life" in Berlin. She was sorry to hear of Cécile's loss of weight and appetite and that the Mendelssohns had to bear the expense of a house without a garden, and she would have loved to take care of this family, had they remained under her care.

After Fanny's death, Felix wrote to General von Webern of the comfort he had received at the sight of this "faithful, kind friend's" handwriting. "No one who has ever known my sister can forget her throughout his life... She was present [at] every moment with her kindness and love." Felix himself would "never experience any happiness without thinking how she would share it". He was "spoilt and made proud by all the riches of her sisterly love and whom I thought nothing could ever harm because, in everything, hers was always the best and leading part... It is lovely to think of such a glorious, harmonious existence [in which Fanny now resides] and that she has been spared all the adversities of advancing years..." Six weeks later, on 7th July 1847, he wrote: "A great chapter has now come to an end, for which neither the title nor the first word of the next is written; but God will put it right one day – this belongs to the beginning and the end of all chapters."

This stage of the book seems the most appropriate place to discuss Fanny's musical career in greater detail, both in regard to Felix's part in it and her own achievement. Leah's remark that Fanny and Felix were proud of one another was correct. It was to Fanny alone that he confided his musical ideas, knowing she would accept and understand them. He acknowledged – certainly in his boyhood and youth – that Fanny had a far greater awareness of the complete canon of musicianship than he. In London, on being praised for his fine piano playing, he demurred, acknowledging that his audience should first hear his elder sister before making comparison – implying that she was far superior in this respect. Such adulation was confirmed by the eminent composer Ignaz Moscheles, as has already been observed. H. F. Chorley stated that, had Fanny Mendelssohn earned her living as a pianist, she would have equalled the celebrated Clara Wieck. Whenever Felix had the opportunity to extol Fanny's accomplishments, he took it. He swelled with pride at the "unmixed delight" resulting in his playing some caprices his sister had composed (though the music may well have been enhanced by his own interpretation). In Munich a countess admired Fanny's songs, especially those set to the poetry of Grillparzer, saying that, when entertaining in future, these would be what she would sing. In displaying his sister's work, he caused himself embarrassment by agreeing with the countess in her praise. Not realising at first whose songs they were, she accused Felix of conceit, assuming they were his compositions. He showed Fanny's songs to Goethe's daughter-in-law and also to Queen Victoria. Devrient, in his *Memoirs*, wrote of Felix's "almost religious veneration" of Fanny's music. He sent her one of what the publisher Novello was to call his *Songs Without Words*, explaining that, because it was incomplete, he wanted Fanny to add a second part. Though it is observed that everyone knew which songs were composed by Fanny and which by Felix, there is room for doubt. It is clear that she had written 'Die Glückliche Fischerin' ('The Fortunate Fisher-maid'), to words by Wilhelm Müller. The 1862 edition of the catalogue of published works edited by Sir Julius Benedict stated the following: it was "a misapprehension" that Fanny had composed the whole Op. 19 song cycle, whereas it had been published in her brother's name. Six of her songs were included in Felix's Op. 8 and Op. 9, said Benedict, "but beyond [these], not one of any kind whatever". Nevertheless, despite his praise and the fact that he assisted her work to become better known by using his own name to ensure its publication, Felix was not averse to letting her know the truth as he saw it. When, for instance, he criticised two choruses Fanny had composed, he saw their faults as due to "the poetry not imposing any particular music" on Fanny's work. She had to be more discerning when choosing a text but that, if she was already taking his advice, "I had better say nothing – otherwise you would prosecute me for defamation". He mollified her by admitting that he, too, should practise what he preached with regard to his own song settings: "I am fully

Chapter 8: Fanny and Felix

aware of the beam in my own eye, [though] I would fain extract the mote from your eye, in order to relieve you at once of its presence."

Nevertheless, not always did Felix conform to the idyllic picture portrayed by biographers of "one spirit and one soul" between Fanny and himself. His sister was a separate entity and Felix had no compunction in treating her as such when her opinion differed from his own. Writing from Paris in 1825, having railed against Auber's operas and anything else he found annoying in the musical life of that city, he was made even more "furious" by his sister's apparent "prejudice" and "bias". "Though time, that kind divinity, has softened my temper and will pour balm into the wounds inflicted on you by my flaming wrath", Fanny should, nevertheless, "think a little" and consider his "entirely impartial judgement" before considering Paris the "lovely El Dorado" she had in mind. "Are you in Paris or am I?" he asked, forgetting that Fanny did accompany his father and himself in 1816 and that Abraham, valuing the French capital above any other, would have continued to build up his own experience of the place in his daughter's mind. In Munich, too, he disliked the musical environment; a neighbour displeased him particularly by "torturing the piano in the process of massacring Paganini's *La Clochette*". Not even Fanny's birthday was sacrosanct from Felix's intransigent views. He dismissed her enjoyment of a painting by Heinrich Stiehler because he disliked it and dismissed her enquiry about the "violin revolution" vis-à-vis Paganini and Lafont. Conversely, he took Fanny to task for not doing sufficient justice to Chopin's piano playing. Felix had, after all, heard him in Leipzig, when Chopin played "some of his better pieces". Had Fanny heard that recital, she, too would have realised how "entirely original" he was "yet, at the same time, so masterly that he may be called a perfect virtuoso". As it was, Chopin must have been in the wrong humour to play at his best when Fanny had heard him in Berlin.

On the whole, however, Felix regarded Fanny as his equal in music and the arts. She should know, without having constantly to be reminded, that he valued her opinion on topics such as fifths, rhythms or counterpoint. Likewise, just as he felt able to appraise her work, he would appreciate a reciprocal arrangement from Fanny, especially as regards his *First Walpurgisnacht* and *St Paul*. Since this latter was soon to be published, "a few strictures from you would come just at the right time". However, a matter that appears to have been overlooked to date is that laughter plays a part throughout the musical experience of Fanny and Felix. He reminded his sister that, when she wrote songs in a hurry, replacing them with substitutes, allowing no time to criticise any, "we would laugh together about these and other music". In what he called a "professional" letter from Paris, he took Fanny to task regarding a piece she had written for their father's birthday: "What the deuce caused you to set the G horns so high? Have you ever heard the instrument take a high G without a squeak?" Did she not know that her oboe part "growls away all pastoral feeling; all bloom"? A licence should be sought to sanction her writing the low B for the oboe and that this should be used only on special occasions, such as scenes for witches or "some great grief".

In view of such banter it is worth considering that, when writing about the Mendelssohn couple, too much seriousness may have been observed. Knowing him so well, Fanny would have realised when her brother was joking and when completely free from teasing. Felix told Fanny of a trio he had composed which, "though a trifle awkward to play", was "not really difficult", adding the words: "Seek and ye shall find", implying that, if Fanny attempted to play the composition, he knew that she would succeed with little trouble. Again, Felix wrote to Fanny that one of her songs was performed "in the Grey Room with all the engravings" in Leipzig. The last notes were sung "very prettily" by Mme. Grabau, resulting in "a hum" as the audience heard the refrain. Sterndale Bennett sent his compliments for Fanny's song, as did Felix, "against my will". This may well imply that he had been proved wrong in appearing to take his father's side in the matter of whether or not Fanny should publish her work.

Like Felix, Fanny was invited to become a member of the Berlin Singakademie under Zelter's direction; the Mendelssohn children were drilled in the music of which Zelter approved. He wanted nothing to do with Italian music, such as that of Palestrina; nor with the French Baroque style, represented by Rameau or Lully. Despite his love of all things German, Zelter disliked – almost feared – the music of Beethoven, dismissing it as "undisciplined". Weber's opera *Der Freischütz* was passed off as "ridiculous", as if this were the composer's and not the librettist's fault. His bluff, outspoken manner was a "front", so as not to appear too sentimental. Thus, "his huge face, with its long nose and furrowed cheek" would light up when he realised how greatly he had embarrassed anyone in his circle of acquaintances by his rough speech. Nevertheless, though no detail is given, it is evident that Fanny at least respected Zelter, if not actually acknowledging affection for him.

In 1828 Fanny wrote to Klingemann in London that the Singakademie finances were in such a parlous state that a concert was to be held. What she called her "symphonic association" was performed, although one singer, Herr Köpke, had to sing the bass and tenor part, since no one else was available; but, when a second performance was given, it was designated "the eighth wonder of the world". Marx, too, appears to have played a part in Fanny's musical life since, though he made no special mention of Felix's elder sister, she felt familiar enough with him to refer to him as 'Abbé' on account of his first names, Adolf Bernhard, having the initials A B. However, though the family as a whole liked his company, Abraham did not. According to Blunt, he held himself aloof from "that brilliant talker and adroit flatterer", as he called Marx. Abraham even took Devrient aside, asking him to wean Felix away from this musician whose influence, the father believed, was having a deleterious effect upon Felix. Nothing is mentioned as to Abraham's view of Marx's influence upon Fanny, which is interesting in the light of his own plans for her career – or lack of them.

Chapter 8: Fanny and Felix

Fanny was encouraged to lead a musical life, provided this was under her father's jurisdiction. He took her to Paris along with Felix in 1816, whilst negotiating the indemnity to be paid to Prussia by France after the Napoleonic Wars. The children were presented to Marie Bigot, a former pupil of Beethoven, who had been able to read at sight a rain-soaked copy of his Piano Sonata Op. 57 – the 'Appassionata' – and who was, later, to become a close friend of the composer. On 16th July 1820 Abraham wrote to his daughter that she would no longer recognise Mme. Bigot, so ill had she become with tuberculosis. Indeed, he was reminded of Heine's description of a 'Herr S' – "that beautiful soul in such a vile body". It may have been the fear of the same predicament befalling Fanny that caused Abraham's anathema to a profession for her. Loving and caring in his own way, perhaps he imagined that Fanny might also die at what was, even in the early 19th century, the comparatively early age of 34. After all, if Mme. Bigot, with a husband to provide for her and a superior talent to support herself, could succumb to such destitution, what shame would be borne by the Mendelssohn parents if Fanny pursued this absurd notion of becoming a professional musician? Fanny would have enough fulfilment in housekeeping and motherhood – now that she was, at last, allowed to become engaged to the artist Wilhelm Hensel.

At her confirmation and also on her 23rd birthday Abraham reminded Fanny of "the weighty duty of a woman". She had to "pay unremitting attention to every detail in improving the benefit of others" when embracing the "real calling" of marriage, for which she had to prepare "earnestly". Whilst in Paris, Abraham presented some of his daughter's songs to her namesake, Fanny Sebastiani, who was still in the charge of her governess, Henriette Mendelssohn. Yet Abraham still had to criticise: they were performed "so imperfectly" that their merit could not be judged. Though Tante Jette hoped her niece would send "some German songs", Fanny Mendelssohn had, in future, to compose with "lightness and naturalness"; her present repertoire was "too ambitious for the verses", according to Abraham.

But what is the verdict on Fanny's published works and what are the facts about her attitude to taking on the mantle of a public individual? So much confusion has arisen that it will take more than this discussion to discover the full picture. Rachel Leach claims that both Abraham and Felix tried to forbid Fanny from publishing and that it was her mother who wished her elder daughter to bring her work to public notice. In fact, Leah did ask Felix to persuade Fanny to take this step, so – in this regard – Ms. Leach is accurate. However, in view of other claims she propounds, it is unwise to accept her words wholesale. It was Clara, not Robert, Schumann who wrote the songs attributed to the latter, according to Ms. Leach; further, she finds it difficult to believe how Mozart found so much time to compose the mass of music he produced, therefore – her argument runs – it must have been his sister 'Nannerl' who contributed to her brother's output. Julie Anne Sadie is equally unconvincing in promoting the feminist cause. Although Fanny had "a strong self-image", she states in the same sentence that "her self-confidence was shaky". Had her self-image been as strong as is suggested, would she have admitted to feeling "less stupid" when Felix was away from Berlin, and that, were she to withdraw altogether from public life, her husband would be "very upset"?

In response to Leah's plea, Felix wrote that, as far as he was concerned, their mother's praise of Fanny's work was unnecessary; her compositions were "charming and admirable". Though he would do everything in his power "to obtain every facility for her and to relieve her, as far as I can, of any trouble. We have often discussed the subject and my opinion remains exactly the same." It was Fanny's own diffidence about which he had doubts: "I consider the publication of a work a serious matter... I maintain that no one should publish, unless one is resolved to appear as an author for the rest of one's life." In such a situation, "a succession of works is indispensable. Nothing but annoyance can be expected where one or two scores alone appear", especially if it became known that these were solely "for private circulation". He also wrote: "From my own knowledge of Fanny, I should say she has neither the inclination nor the vocation. She is too much of a woman for this. She runs her home and thinks neither of the public or the musical world, nor even music at all, until her first duties are fulfilled. Publishing would only interrupt her carrying those out and I cannot say that I approve of it. I shall not, therefore, persuade her to take this step. If she decides to publish, either on her own impulse or to please Hensel, I am, as I have said before, ready to assist her, but I cannot encourage her to do what I do not deem right myself."

Whatever the rights or wrongs of this matter, Felix, more than anyone else, knew Fanny's way of thinking and it was Fanny's own view he considered. Fanny was Leah's favourite child and it seemed unfair to her that Felix gained all the honours; the fact was overlooked that, in Berlin, he was discouraged as much as Fanny and that it was only his journeys elsewhere that allowed him to become famous.

Neither did Leah appreciate the petty intrigues of life in the harsh musical world outside Leipzigerstrasse 3. Felix, on the contrary, guessed that his sister, gentle and sweet natured as she was, would not be able to tolerate such behaviour. This was not prejudice on his part. A Leipzig friend, Friedrich Brockhaus, admitted that publishing was "repugnant" to Fanny and, as far as can be ascertained, he had no axe to grind on the subject, being objective and neutral. Feminists, such as Marcia Citron, Rachel Leach and Nancy Reich, claim that Felix was jealous of Fanny's possible success and endeavoured to thwart any rivalry. Reich quotes a letter to Mme. Kiene, sister of Marie Bigot, saying that Fanny did not appear to write such good music as she did prior to her marriage. Felix was glad, he wrote, that his sister was so fulfilled in her domestic life, and was "afraid" that she might have become a 'femme savante', like Rahel Varnhagen von Ense or Bettina Brentano von Arnim. Fanny was "not intellectual", Felix wrote to Mme. Kiene; in other words, Fanny was self-effacing and modest and – in Felix's mind – epitomised the ideal, feminine woman. He detested such behaviour as that of the Varnhagen

Chapter 8: Fanny and Felix

von Enses and Brentano von Arnim of this world, who constantly craved attention by pitting their wits against anyone and everyone – behaviour irritating in the extreme to a man of Mendelssohn's personality. As Kupferberg points out, the longer Felix lived in the real musical world, the more he realised that, talented or not, musicians existed who were only too eager to plant seeds of envy and ill will into the minds of colleagues against those they disliked or distrusted. Whereas a man could accept such intrigues, how would a woman such as Fanny handle them – especially, as Kupferberg maintains, the sheltered daughter of a banker with a famous husband and a lovely home to run, who had no need to make a living as a composer?

Though Kupferberg states that Fanny obeyed "meekly" the dictates of her father and brother, it is much more probable that this woman of good sense found it futile to argue and thereby antagonise her opponents, preferring to keep the peace. It was only later, with her husband's support, that Fanny took courage to have her compositions published. However, there could be a further justification for Felix's disapproval. A fascinating piece of unwitting testimony has come to light from an article by the feminist pianist Lucy Parham in *Classical Music Magazine*. Writing on the piano works of Clara Wieck, Ms. Parham mentions a trio that Mendelssohn particularly enjoyed. He commented that he could not believe it had been written by a woman.

Though Fanny did play her part in musical circles, she appears never to have been wholly confident, as is shown by her correspondence and journal entries. She complained to Klingemann that, since there were no musical friends in Berlin and Rebecka no longer sang, her songs had lain aside for so long that she had lost all interest in composing. She had copied two songs for the Miss Horsleys in London, but, now that Felix, "my most constructive critic", was not available so often, it was only Hensel who showed interest in her progress. She spoke of a young pianist, Théodore von Döhler, who, she predicted would be "extraordinary", – if only he could adopt a more "solid" technique.

Because Fanny had not yet heard the brilliant performances of Sigismund Thalberg, she was "doubly inspired" by the up-and-coming pianist von Döhler. Fanny admitted to envying Klingemann's Collard piano, and had envisaged buying an English instrument for herself, but, having heard the fashionable "wizards and acrobats", considered her own style "antiquated". Nevertheless, Felix's chivalry came to the rescue of Fanny's low morale; whilst he could hear his contemporaries for an hour, he could listen to his sister for a week at a time. "She has soul", an asset that every pianist must have if the audience is to be "carried along", Felix wrote. He even took time off from his honeymoon to reassure Fanny on the matter. Fanny could "cut down all those pretty fellows with ease… All this facility and coquetting no longer succeed in dazzling others, alongside you… The piano playing of 'D' is no more than Kalkbrenner could manage in his day, and will pass." Percy Scholes, of a later generation, supports Mendelssohn's view. He merely writes of Theodore von Döhler as having composed "music of a popular kind", saying nothing of his virtuosity at the piano; this, and his compositions, are now banished into limbo. As for Fanny, her brother told her that, when he and Cécile met the sculptor Schadow and his family in a hotel foyer, they were "full of enthusiasm and most excited on the subject" of the way she accompanied. Just as this belies assumptions that a rift occurred between Felix and Fanny on his marriage, it is equally untrue that he no longer sought her advice on musical topics. What, for example, did she think of his plan to play Bach's organ fugues in Birmingham? The ones he aimed to perform were "peculiarly acceptable to the English" and, when played "piano or pianissimo, both [the] preludes and fugues will allow the power of the organ to be more definite".

Though Fanny complained to Cécile that she no longer knew his compositions right from the beginning and had to assess them as a stranger, once they were put into print this was inaccurate. Felix was working on "a string trio, a piano sonata and a symphony", on which he asked her advice on 18th June 1839. Whilst staying in Frankfurt with Cécile's relatives Felix confided to Fanny that, although it was an enjoyable place to live in, he felt he could not work there. The people he met talked constantly "of music criticism, recognition, flattering testimonials, and think about themselves and fish for compliments", yet "behind people's backs they play mad pranks as much as anyone". He disparaged the "weariness and compulsion" with which the St Cecilia Society performed, rather than the "soul and love" of the Leipzig musicians.

As for her own compositions, Fanny was invariably tentative. In a letter of 28th October 1838 she wrote to Felix that she had written "a dozen pieces" that she would like him to play through, or to request one of his pupils to do so, and asked him to tell her what he thought of the compositions. Fanny explained that, because of her husband constantly encouraging her to publish, but with Felix disapproving of the project, she felt "like a donkey between two bales of hay". Even in what is claimed to have been her last letter of 1st February 1847, Fanny having been asked if she had written 'On Wings of Song' (No. 2 of her brother's Op. 34 set of songs), she wrote that "it seems some people are not clever enough to separate wheat from chaff". Because she did not wish to "show impertinence in such matters", or to acknowledge the "few little things" she had composed, Fanny proposed to "leave things in a state of darkness".

Meanwhile, Fanny told Klingemann of the first and only charity concert in which she had performed away from home. Writing on 27th February 1838, she explained that the event was "a grand affair", with "duchesses, ambassadors' wives and officers" in the audience. She was "not the least afraid", for her friends "were kind enough to take care of feeling afraid for me". That same year the Woringen family visited Berlin. Extra rooms were required for the forthcoming concert at Leipzigerstrasse 3, and some of the audience were compelled to stand.

On another occasion, Fanny related to Klingemann that a concert was to take place two days hence; then Christmas would intervene, "with trumpets and rattles". Nancy Reich claims that Fanny was "not allowed" to learn the technique of playing and composing for stringed instruments, to make contacts with anyone other than in Berlin, or to make revisions of work or to conduct and direct performances. Reich's statements are patently inaccurate. Had such been the case, Fanny would not have been able to compose as she did; neither would the family entertainments have continued, albeit with intermissions, throughout her life. Felix declared it "a sin and a shame" not to have been able to attend his sister's "musicales" or to have heard her compositions. He was equally "vexed" that Fanny had never heard his own "brilliant" subscription concerts given by the Leipzig Gewandhaus, at which Mendelssohn invited internationally renowned artistes to take part. But not every performer was a celebrity. On one occasion, Ferdinand David had noticed Mendelssohn's mother-in-law Mme. Jeanrenaud, who had arrived that evening by rail from Frankfurt. During the concert interval, despite the "shabby travelling-cloak" in which she was dressed, Felix asked her to sing Beethoven's song 'Adelaide', for which a grand piano was brought from an ante-room onto the concert platform; she sang "brilliantly", to tremendous applause. Not only did Mme. Jeanrenaud receive "a grand flourish from the trumpets"; the audience "bellowed and shouted without end. She took off her bonnet in public and pointed to her black pelisse as if to apologise for it."

Though Fanny complained to Cécile about her lack of knowledge as to Felix's day-to-day musical activities, saying that she now viewed her brother's compositions as impartially as a stranger, Felix continued to keep Fanny up to date on his doings and feelings. From Bad Soden near Frankfurt, in 1844, he asked his sister to send him "that organ piece in A major", explaining where she might find it: "either in the open shelves containing loose sheet music in the red portfolio" or "in a bound volume which lies in my cabinet, in which many similar pieces are bound together". He despised "the odious middle part" of a composition, which he had written the previous winter – but marvelled equally at "the charming beginning". He told Fanny he was to walk to Wiesbaden to visit their uncle Joseph Mendelssohn and to attend a concert given by the pianist Heinrich Dorn in Hamburg. He had heard him in London accompanying the 'cellist Alfredo Piatti, he explained; "there I clapped and cheered for them, and I want to do so again in Hamburg".

Yet Felix showed not only the same amount of affection but admiration and respect too for his younger sister Rebecka. On 4th July 1836, though full of his own concerns, before making the journey with Schadow and his son to Scheveningen in the Netherlands, he made it clear that at no time could anyone accuse him of neglecting to write to his younger sister. From Italy, it was Rebecka whom he asked to look at an engraving in which he was interested, in an art dealer's on Unter den Linden, Berlin's main shopping street. The drawing represented St John taking Mary home after the Crucifixion, originally painted by a Spanish artist, whose work was one of the most wonderful pictures Felix had ever seen. As for music, he wrote of a performance in which he had taken part in Switzerland that Rebecka would consider "pitiful" and "not too pleasant". "You do it better," he declared, referring to a German motet. On another occasion Felix wrote to Rebecka of his setting for "that gloomy thing", as he called the chorale 'O Sacred Head', which she could rehearse and perform whenever she pleased.

As for Fanny, on 4th September 1839 her greatest ambition was achieved when her journey to Italy began at last. On 2nd December she wrote that, though having had no opportunity to practise, she was invited by Herr Landsberg, a former violinist with the King's Theatre Orchestra in Berlin who had settled in Rome, to accompany him. Though Landsberg hired out his piano for two scudi per session Fanny was offered nine, but this "bargain" was declined. Fanny took part in a trio with "a beautiful lady", a Mme. Venutelli, and Landsberg. She recalled how, in Berlin, Rietz and David used to tease him, saying he would be put in prison for playing his violin on a Sunday and how the artist Spitzeder painted Landsberg's face. "Verily, how times have changed with him," she reflected. Fanny often played in order to "dissipate the dullness" of English visitors who "dropped in". Later one evening, she was able to entertain invited guests, but tried to recall to Felix the many compositions they requested of her. Among her audience was Charles Gounod, who, having won the Prix de Rome, was studying there. He asked his host to play the solo part of one of Bach's keyboard concertos ten times, but he enjoyed and admired Fanny's own compositions.

"I must not conceal from myself that the atmosphere of admiration and homage in which I have lived had something to do with my enjoyment of Rome," she wrote in her journal on departing. "Even when quite young, I was never made as much of as here, and, that this is very pleasant, nobody can deny." Fanny visited the Academy in Rome in the hope of arranging a concert, about which she was "quite passionate", but, because Ingres, its head, raised so many objections, the plan was abandoned. Meanwhile Fanny composed various pieces relating to places the family had visited, but, as she wrote to Rebecka, these were "for home use only, not to be mentioned in company". At another performance of the Bach concerto, the audience kissed Fanny's hand in admiration. Gounod, usually so voluble, was at a loss for words to express how much he appreciated the influence he gained from German music; he said later that it seemed as if a bombshell had hit him. Fanny hoped he would not become too carried away in his rapture. Had she lived, she would have realised the young composer's name would be made by his most celebrated work – his opera *Faust*. Gounod's is the best-known setting of Goethe's drama. Fanny took part in a Hummel quartet that she had learnt with Zelter years before. As far as Bach was concerned, Gounod wrote that few could interpret the work of the "old master" in a way that an audience could fully understand.

On 16th May Fanny was asked to perform once more and a subsequent journal entry expresses her shame at playing Beethoven's 'Les Adieux' Sonata more badly than ever before. This must have been because she was so sad at leaving Rome that she was unable to concentrate fully on the music. At the time of departure, packing was interrupted by "a stream of visitors" and, as was inevitable, more piano recitals. In order not to be upset once more, Fanny obliged with Beethoven's F minor Piano Sonata and, "if Bousquier would sit and listen properly", she would play the Sonata in B flat by Beethoven. "On his knees", Gounod begged her to play an adagio by Felix as well as her own compositions. The Hensels retired in a state of "pleasure, emotion and excitement" to face the day ahead. Fanny began her journal entry for 30th May at 1.30 a.m., but did not actually get to bed until three o'clock that morning. Later that day Ingres invited the family to the French Academy and Fanny had never felt so happy, playing the piano to the accompaniment of fountains in the garden. She did not think the students would understand how a musician could play a piano "from morn till dewy eve" and it was worth leaving Berlin just to show them how one could while away the time in this manner "in the most heavenly spot on earth".

When the piano was moved indoors in the evening, Fanny was assailed by "a peculiar sensation", an eerie atmosphere in which she played "as softly as possible"; everyone whispered and the smallest extraneous sound could be distinctly heard. After the meal, the guests sat on the balcony, watching the "stars, the moon, city lights, glow-worms, a meteor trailing across the sky and the lighted window of a church on a hill in the distance", which "stirred everyone with emotion". Fanny was once more asked to play, her recital interspersed with part-songs. 'They weep, they know not why' was the last music Fanny heard, at the stroke of midnight, in Italy. Ingres's embrace would have been far more conducive to Fanny's mood had the students not been present.

Rebecka would later display her pianistic skill at Landsberg's home whilst in Italy. At one recital, Mozart's music from *The Magic Flute* was performed, as also Pergolesi's *Stabat Mater*, with "the beautiful contralto voice" of Mme. Sciabatta. The singer's brother was "enchanting St Petersburg with his good looks and voice", Rebecka observed. On another occasion, an unspecified sonata was performed by Mme. Serans and "Franck", but which Franck is not detailed – the German Eduard, the Belgian Joseph or his better-known brother César, who all travelled on the continent. "[He] played in a completely different style from an amateur, even if two dozen had played it at once," Rebecka wrote. She did not mention her own part in these recitals, but this may well have been through modesty. Fanny wrote that Paul's house was graced by concerts, one of which included Felix's "beautiful A major Symphony (the 'Italian', as it came to be known). Here, "the room was crowded to suffocation, so that one was hard put not to squeeze to death at every turn [when speaking] to someone whom one knew".

After Leah's death at the end of 1842, Fanny began the Sunday concerts once more, but now, as well as arranging the music, she had to organise the lunches. She found it hard to "get into the swim" after an 18-month lapse, but "Hensel wishes it", she wrote to Rebecka. Gans played the solo part in Felix's E minor Violin Concerto but "did not fail to make a great blunder". Fanny missed Borkhardt's tenor voice, but a bass would spoil the balance in choral works, and the two voices could not be exchanged. She complained that there was a shortage of good singers and said, later, that her "second musicale" went so badly that, should her third and final concert before Christmas fare the same, she would give them up entirely. But evidently it must have been a success, for these entertainments continued. The music included "Liszt and eight variations by David, played by that little marvel, Joachim. He is not an infant prodigy but a wonderful musician." Though she had heard from gossips that her brother disliked her concerts, she would continue them "at Felix's request". When Felix arrived from Leipzig, "a grand serenade greeted him". Had Herr Woringen not apprised him of the entertainment, Felix would not have been aware of it. As a surprise, and in view of the bad weather, Fanny had had the garden house illuminated, which looked "very pretty". At the next concert, Fanny played a Beethoven piano sonata and polonaise (the latter as a duet with Felix), and also the *Midsummer Night's Dream* arrangement for piano.

In 1846 Fanny was given a new lease of life by the music critic von Keudell, who took an interest not only in her piano playing but also in her compositions. So buoyed up was she by favourable reviews in the musical press in Berlin and Leipzig regarding her piano pieces and songs that many other works poured from her pen. "Fanny Hensel is a musician in the most exalted sense of the word," one critic wrote. "In her, the happiest gifts of nature go hand in hand with the most careful cultivation of rare talents." She had never experienced such a feeling of fulfilment and contentment before, except during her visit to Italy. On 11th April, Rebecka's birthday, Fanny could not only look back to the past, but forward to the future. Her trio proved successful at a musical matinée and her journal entry for that day recorded the life that she and Hensel now enjoyed. She wrote that she was "one of the few happy people"; but went on to say that this was too good to last. Might she have had a premonition that her life on earth would soon come to an end? This prophecy came true just 14 months later.

Meanwhile, the myth of Felix's disapproval of the publication of Fanny's music can be quashed by a letter he wrote to their brother Paul in August 1847; he had written to the publisher Härtel on the matter "as planned", asking for "a precise account of the costs" to be rendered and "to send it to me as soon as possible in Berlin, for not until then can the publication of our dear sister's music be agreed and discussed". Sadly, because of the bombing Leipzig received during World War II, the archives of Breitkopf and Härtel can no longer be researched, as they were destroyed. As for Felix himself, though he sustained a most grievous blow when Fanny passed away, he had no intention of idling away his time. Once he had returned from a vacation in Switzerland and a few days in Berlin, he planned to "settle back into regular work" on a 'cello concerto to be performed by Piatti; a symphony for the new Philharmonic Hall in Liverpool; a third piano concerto; his oratorio *Christus*; and, more than any other composition, the opera *Die Lorelei*, in which Jenny Lind would play the heroine. Tragically though, none of these exciting projects was destined to materialise.

Chapter 9

A Family of Letter Writers

So much has been written about the Mendelssohn correspondence, but no analysis has been given; no 'reading between the lines' attempted. The letters are quoted at face value and any assessment that is made oscillates from one extreme to the other. Rudolf Elvers, who compiled *A Life in Letters* relating to Felix, explains that, from the time of Moses, the tradition of letter writing was continued by the Mendelssohn family and that, in Abraham's generation, this pursuit became a cult. The letters of Moses are dismissed as "striking in their eloquence", and his wit can be discovered in the prologue to this book, but it is those of Felix with which *The Caged Spirit* is primarily concerned.

Almost 7,000 Mendelssohn letters are housed in green albums at the Bodleian Library, Oxford, but this is a mere segment of those that exist worldwide, in the Mendelssohn Archive in Basel, Switzerland; Leipzig; Berlin; various parts of the United States; and many more may still come to light elsewhere. These include not only letters written by Dorothea and Henriette Mendelssohn, but, having joined the family, Leah's correspondence to her own relatives in Vienna, Stockholm, Paris and most of the German principalities. So, with this background, it is hardly surprising that the Mendelssohn children inherited this obsession (or duty) to keep in contact with relatives and friends. A fascinating picture emerges from Felix's letters of his true thoughts and feelings – often unwittingly. This applies far more than simply reading eulogies (or the reverse) by biographers or compilers of programme notes. From his earliest epistles, Felix's aunt, Henriette Mendelssohn, thought it appropriate to remind his mother that "if God spares him, his letters will, in long years to come, create the deepest interest". Those "precious relics", of which Leah had to take care, "are sacred already, as the outpourings of a mind so pure and childlike". His mother evidently took this admonishment to heart, even to the extent of dipping Felix's letters of 1831-32 from Paris in a 'tincture' to protect against cholera germs. Leah may well have felt afraid of Felix's favourite aunt, 'Tante Jette', who knew so much about the minds of young children – even more than they, the parents. However, Henriette Mendelssohn was not the only individual who idealised Felix's letters. His biographer W. S. Rockstro adopted the same attitude: "These precious offerings", as he called them, contained "a man's keen power of observation with the freshness of a child's enjoyment overflowing with natural eloquence, but bearing the stamp of literal truth in every sentence". From a later generation, Eric Werner, when describing Mendelssohn's letters from Switzerland, speaks of "a masterpiece of literature that will last as long as there are wanderers over the Swiss mountains". And, of course, the arch-rhapsodist Mme. Elise Polko had to have her say: "Anyone who does not lay aside these letters of that loving human soul [without] sincere and heartfelt gratification must be pitied, as the blind, who see no spring, or the deaf, who can hear no nightingale's note."

After all this verbiage, who dare gainsay these eulogies, but Blunt attempts so to do. Though the letters are "good", pronounces the former Eton schoolmaster, they are not as much so as Werner or Polko lead readers to believe, but he gives no analysis. But, of course, Marek can be expected to express an opinion: to him, Mendelssohn's letters "reveal a facile personality" who uses "creamy ink and a honeyed pen", employing "a cautious politeness as if to please the recipient". What Marek fails to grasp is that, certainly when writing to his parents, Felix had no alternative than to adopt this style. This is borne out by a fascinating letter he wrote to his sisters from Rome. As a "well-travelled man of the world" Felix explained how he could now understand what was required when addressing his parents, and advised Fanny and Rebecka to follow his recommendation: language should be modified, using the word "unpleasant" rather than "a scandal"; "tolerable" rather than "splendid"; Abraham had to be "indulged".

A young person should "praise what he is fond of, but...not criticise anything dear to his heart" with which he does not agree. "Anything old and venerable must be lauded; anything new must be ignored", until it has become part of the status quo. By all means the young Mendelssohns had to speak the truth, but only as far as their father could tolerate. This experiment worked for Felix, and things "got better and better and, finally, all was well again", once he had learnt how to handle his father. These rules applied particularly when Abraham was in a cantankerous mood – which Felix believed him to be when this letter was written. Abraham "likes to think himself older and more ill-tempered than he actually is, thank God, and it is up to all of us to give in to him once in a while, even if right is on our side, as he has often done". Felix had yet to find a family "even with all its weaknesses and crossness taken into account" that provided so much happiness as their own. Marek appears to be unaware of this letter, which explains the apparent style of Felix's letters home.

However, it is surprising that Wilfrid Blunt, with his wealth of schoolmasterly experience, has said nothing about the grammatical construction of sentences in Mendelssohn's letters. Mesdames M. E. von Glehn, Gisela Selden-Goth and, particularly, Lady Grace Wallace may have translated Mendelssohn's letters painstakingly and assiduously, but their English equivalent is decidedly clumsy and pedantic. Their translation reveals rambling sentences, unnecessary conjunctions and inadequate punctuation, and the sentences leap from one subject to another. Felix was expected to give minute details about everything that occurred whilst away from home, and also to tell the absolute truth at the same time. With this in mind, grammar would be the last thing on Felix's mind, despite his strict education. After all, was not Fanny, at 14, told by her father that she should know better at her age than to say there was nothing to report? She should be able to give her own views as to the day-to-day happenings in her home circle and not write about the theatre. Did it occur to this father that his sensitive elder daughter might well be too bored with matters that Abraham deemed important and that she could have written far more entertainingly about subjects that interested her? Then there was the little matter of handwriting. At six, Paul was upbraided for pressing his pen too firmly into the paper. He was told he had to hold his fingers more loosely and "sit up straight". Felix, too, complained of a poor pen, so perhaps the quality of writing materials was not thought important enough for children's use.

In a household such as that of Leipzigerstrasse 3, where children must not be indulged, any pen would serve for letter writing. Even as a young man of 20, Felix felt the need to apologise, when writing from the Literary Union Club of London, for his pen not being "worthy", but promised to make amends in his next epistle. As for Mendelssohn's actual handwriting, Marek airs his views, decrying the script as "punctilious...as if designed by a draughtsman; quite beautiful, with spacious, circular strokes for the 'H's and the 'G's, with barely a word crossed out or a line smeared; often titivated with small drawings and, finally, neatly folded and addressed". The adjective 'neat' Marek uses with sarcasm, implying that Mendelssohn was "afraid to let himself go, as if he knew his letters would become collectors' items". In passing, the 1972 price of these letters at auction made between $100 and $300, but Marek gives no detail as to their rare historic content or state of preservation. They were at that time "a favourite with private collectors all over the world". At an auction in 1996 at Sotheby's, London, the catalogue showed reserve prices ranging from £100 to £150 rising to between £1,000 and £3,000, but, in view of the auctioneers' cautiousness, a cynic should multiply these prices by ten. Felix's letters were intended solely for private, family reading but, since all the relatives were given access to these, he had to be careful not to offend anyone – hence the "care taken with his style". Felix was equally meticulous in his music notation, asking Fanny to rebuke Eduard Rietz to "free my score from ink blots, glue and red pencil marks" in future.

For his sisters and, even more, his trusted friends, he adopted a completely different style in his letters. It is from this source that readers of the future are allowed to learn what this personality was truly like. He had no need to worry about what not to say or how not to say it; thus, he was far more 'open' and relaxed. His business letters were refreshingly succinct, relaying what he had to write, but no more. There is even evidence of lapses in handwriting. For instance, Fanny Horsley, a member of a family in London with whom he maintained a lifelong friendship, wrote to her aunt Lucy Callcott, sending her a sample of Mendelssohn's "funny little hand". Nevertheless, Rosamund Brunel Gotch, a descendant of the Horsley family, in a compilation of these letters describes "the spidery script, so popular at the time" before the Penny Post began in 1840, when stamps replaced the previous system of franking. This caused thrifty letter writers to fit words into any space and any angle on the paper. Another strange phenomenon occurred in a letter dated 21st July 1829, on his first visit to Britain, when Felix and his companion Carl Klingemann shared a letter home. Whereas Klingemann, by virtue of his smaller handwriting, could accommodate more words on a page, Felix's larger script was unable to manage so many. It seems appropriate, in this section on letter writing, that Mendelssohn's most trusted friend should be introduced. Ernst Georg Carl Christoph Conrad Klingemann (known as Carl) was born in 1799, and, as a diplomat, was posted from the Hanoverian Legation to London in 1828.

His office was previously housed at Leipzigerstrasse 3, which is how he and the Mendelssohn children became acquainted. Felix stayed with Klingemann at Bury Street, Hobart Place, SW1, on his ten visits to London and it was with this diplomat that he travelled to Scotland. On 6th November 1846 Felix was to remind his friend that Montaigne, Voltaire and Jean-Paul Richter had each made the same point through characters in their books: that a person can have only one true friend – which, in Felix's case, was Klingemann. He would have congratulated his friend sooner on the news of the engagement to Sophie Rosen, half-sister to their mutual friend, the Oriental scholar, Friedrich Rosen, but for the fact of his anxiety about his elderly, faithful servant Johann Krebs. Illness had confined Krebs to bed for two months; his "vital powers suddenly sank and, to our great sorrow, he died". So valued was the Mendelssohns' servant that Klingemann "must understand we shall be in a sombre mood for a long time to come". It was to Klingemann he confided this bereavement – not to his family.

The Horsley family, too, played a vital part in Mendelssohn's letter writing. Sophie wrote to her aunt that "even in his bad books, which is a good deal to say of anyone, he is delightful", though she did not think his punctuality "particularly wonderful". As for his sister Fanny, her namesake, Fanny Horsley, told her aunt in a letter franked 21st July 1834 that she was "in awe of her piercing eyes and her severity", having – presumably – seen a portrait. She hoped, when the Hensels visited London, that the Horsleys would not meet her very often. When she learnt later from Klingemann that the proposed visit was not to take place, Miss Horsley was greatly relieved. As a postscript, she mentioned that "old Mr. Mendelssohn is to make a solitary tour of Bohemia"; but this, too, did not happen.

Despite all the rules he had to remember, even as a boy, Felix's powers of observation shone through his inhibitions. He described the lexicographer Riemer, whom he met in Weimar, as "short and fat and as round as a priest or a full moon", giving the boy "a Greek feeling". Rather than punish him, as no doubt his parents hoped would happen, Goethe merely opined that "Berliners are so forward that

Chapter 9: A Family of Letter Writers

one has to be a little rude to keep up with them", and that "any delicacy is thrown away on them". The drawings that "titivated" Felix's letters, as Marek puts it, were there for a purpose also. To the correspondent, his sketches enhanced his observations in a way that words might not have allowed. Thus, anyone not taking part in a given journey – Leah in particular, one suspects – might have been able to have a far better idea of the boy's experiences away from home and to share his adventures. Yet Mendelssohn realised that his letters had to include "the obligatory details" of life away from Leipzigerstrasse 3. It was to keep his parents happy that he included what to him must have seemed the boring minutiae of day-to-day life. On arrival in Breslau, he wrote that the journey "occurred without accident, peril, misadventure or breakdown, [so] where and how can I find any mishaps to relate? Ergo, I will begin to describe all our various adventures, even though we had none whatsoever." Later, on his first visit to London, he explained that the banker Doxat would be advised of his and Klingemann's travel plans on his return from Scotland, and it was to this poste restante address that letters should be sent. Meanwhile, he asked his parents not to be too anxious about hearing from him, as it would be "two or three weeks" before he would be able to communicate. He would, nevertheless, "continue to write on a piece of paper, be it small or large", until he found "a decent post office, in which there are several in Britain that will send letters quickly from London".

He added that he had "a whole bundle of letters of introduction to musicians, manufacturers and merchants. I will pack quickly, take a few hours' sleep…take my walking stick in my hand" (given him by the Johnston family to aid his hill climbing in Scotland) "and board the mail coach north." Philip Radcliffe points out that his aunt, Henriette Mendelssohn, appeared "over-anxious and intense", still calling her nephew "my poor boy" when he had reached the age of 20 – which is why these juvenile details would have been included. It was only with his friends that he was able to behave like an adult. Aware also of the family obsession with preserving his letters, he wrote, on his second visit to London in 1832, asking his mother to "put this letter on top of the stack of travel letters" they had already accumulated.

But, however dearly he would like to think himself a man, the more deeply his letters are researched, it becomes clear that Felix was not always the self-confident, arrogant worldly-wise legend that derives from biographers and broadcast talks. In August 1823 this 14-year-old appeared unable to make up his mind when Wilhelm von Boguslawski could visit the Mendelssohn home: "Thursday or Friday, between 4 and 7.30 p.m.", seemed suitable but, if neither date was satisfactory to him, von Boguslawski should let Felix know the date and time when the two might meet. His answer was to be "delivered by the bearer of this letter – the postman". But this was not enough for this pedant: "I shall be done [with lessons] before six, but if you are so kind as to come at 6.45 p.m., and if you wanted to spend the time with me from 5.30 on, with my family…you will receive orally the 'Bravo' for your sonata…"

On another occasion, Felix wrote to the family friend and physician Johann Caspar on 8th February 1824, asking him to accept an apology for "the hasty words, especially since they were uttered on the day of the celebration [Felix's 15th birthday] that, after all, you organised, though would have preferred not to". Felix hoped that Caspar would "please let what has passed be forgotten", but added that "no one in the orchestra repeated your remarks". There is no explanation regarding this strange incident.

From Paris, on his 1825 visit with his father, Felix was so "amazed, curious and overwhelmed" that he felt hard put to pen "a proper, well-ordered and suitable letter", though he proceeded to give enough description to satisfy the most avid news gatherer. They arrived at 8 p.m. with "spirited horses at a brisk trot" at their destination, passing an unfamiliar part of the city, the Faubourg St Lazare, where new houses had been built. This new part of Paris was seen as "fairly desolate and chaotic in some areas". The boulevards in the old district, where they stayed, were, by contrast, "a bustle" with "scurrying, screaming merriment – all the main streets gaslit, so that the names of the shops could be easily deciphered", the area being "loud and bright", like a grand celebration in Berlin.

Three days later, he could not believe he had been in Paris for such a short time, having seen and done so many new things that there was much to tell his family. Felix proffered "only a short letter" as, otherwise, he would spend until midnight writing "and, after all, it is only eight o'clock in the morning". But personal details were not to be overlooked: "I have just taken a bath in accordance with mother's express instructions and I have washed, scrubbed and scoured myself more thoroughly than can be imagined, so mother will feel reassured as far as that goes." The relatives whom Abraham and Felix encountered were "amazed" that this lad of 16 did not sit on anyone's lap, not realising how many years had elapsed since they had seen the then seven-year-old child. In London, likewise, four years later, he was in the same quandary as to what to write; having had so many new experiences, he ought really to send a journal rather than the usual letters. A characteristic that followed Mendelssohn throughout his life, but particularly when writing home, was that, having informed his correspondents that there was nothing for him to describe, he used an inordinate amount of paper and ink to convey this message. It appears that, though Felix dared not admit the fact and though he endeavoured to prove the contrary, he was far more bored in Switzerland on his 1831 visit than he had anticipated. One can almost hear the sigh of relief on departing from this land of scenery and unprecedentedly foul weather, but nothing more. In view of his turgid, dutiful prose, it is far more entertaining to read other letters from "faraway places with strange-sounding names" than those of Mendelssohn; Nikolai Rimsky-Korsakov serves as a fine example of this phenomenon. A further off-putting characteristic of Mendelssohn's letters is the sprinkling of foreign expressions, but, as Leah did the same, her son may have, albeit unconsciously, adopted this habit from his mother. It is evident also that, once he began a letter, he was driven to complete it, despite a heavy work schedule. In 1846, for instance, he wrote that, even if his epistle might appear incoherent, "fill these four pages I shall, I swear by my beard", before shutting himself away to work on *Elijah*; when this was complete, "I shall swear by my beard once more".

Felix appeared to experience profound homesickness in his letters from abroad, but there may well be a reason, independent of his own feelings, for such an admission. From Rome in 1830 he wrote to his sisters that, to placate their father, they should "praise the house frequently", and the possessions that the Mendelssohns had accumulated would no doubt be included in this outpouring. On 4th November 1834 even his mother's handwriting – her "distinct and classical characters" – reminded him of home and set him reminiscing about Leipzigerstrasse 3. He wrote of the garden, and a visit to an exhibition where he and Leah argued about a painting by the German artist Bendemann. On his walking tour of the Harz Mountains in 1827, Felix asked his family to "say hello to the lambs and tell them they may not be shorn until we return – not at all would be even better". When, later, Rebecka visited Italy, she asked Fanny to remember her to the poultry and Caro, the Hensels' poodle.

The Mendelssohn correspondence – before the age of the telephone – was a way of alleviating anxiety, though the parents applied the concept "do as I say, not as I do" in this respect. Though Leah demanded a letter twice a week, irrespective of how busy Felix might be, the same thoughtfulness was not reciprocated. From London Felix was troubled by non-receipt of news from home, which he tried not to allow to bother him, "on account of our agreement". On 27th April 1831 he wrote from Naples complaining that he had received no family news for a fortnight and trusted that nothing untoward had occurred. To Zelter, on 15th February 1832, from Paris he asked for "a few lines in return – even just a few words – so that I will know whether you would like to hear a sequel to my life and doings in Paris and whether you remain faithful and friendly towards me". He wished Zelter to say if he liked his new compositions and what he disliked about them. He asked Zelter to "lift my spirits" by letting him know how his family was faring. In Frankfurt, during his honeymoon, Felix "longed for letters" that he could answer, having not heard for "many days" from home. But not only did this anxiety apply to Felix. At Gaeta, between Rome and Naples, Fanny wrote of having received two letters: one from their cousin Marianne Mendelssohn, daughter-in-law of their uncle Joseph; the other from home – "Thank God, nothing but good news". In answer to why an earlier letter smelt of musk, Fanny surmised, "It must have lain next to some love letters at the post office, for no scent of that kind has ever come across our threshold or even greeted our noses."

On 3rd May 1840, leaving Rome, Fanny sighed: "Ah, happy they who may, and can, live here", regretting that her husband could have worked "to his heart's content", had he stayed in the French Academy. When Rebecka and her family reached Italy, Fanny twice asked her sister to give her love to the Villa Wolkonsky and asked if she had noticed the cypresses with the rose bush in the centre that spread its flowers over the foliage of the trees. In March 1844 Fanny regretted that Devrient and his wife were leaving Berlin for an appointment with the Dresden Opera and that, as Felix had returned to Leipzig, there was no one with whom she could discuss Italy with understanding. Everyone with whom she tried to discuss that country "appeared disgusted". Rebecka had sent a sketch of "Tasso's decaying oak in the sunset", which amply expressed Fanny's own feelings.

As with Felix, Rebecka was the person to whom Fanny could write nonsense without feeling embarrassed. From Rome in 1839 Fanny wrote: "I must, for once, as Felix used to say, roll in your ear and talk rubbish to you by letter." But, though her son Sebastian Hensel wrote of Felix's sketches conjuring up scenes as vividly as his letters, this applied equally to Fanny and Rebecka – their way of describing events being particularly witty. Though Fanny kept a journal from girlhood, Rebecka thought this a childish pursuit, but had to admit she found her sister's diary most useful when wishing for further details of a particular event. She was able to jot down observations, whilst leaving Fanny's more reflective commentary. "Fanny is my diary," Rebecka once declared.

Since Felix's visit to London in 1829, he explained from Rome that, in future, he would carry smaller notebooks with him, rather than the larger journal. He could then "note down in a few words what I have done, or am going to do, each day. Some [things] are written down in advance in order not to forget to do them and some written down afterwards, in order not to forget to do them later. Thus I know precisely where I have been each day, what I have taken in and, if something needs to be described in more detail, then I do so in letters to you or [represent the experience] in drawings or music. Then I do not need to write too much each day, but still do not lose track of things."

Felix compiled a journal whilst on honeymoon, Cécile writing on one side of a page, Felix on the reverse; this proved useful when making his fifth visit to London. Strangely, very little is said of Paul, there being rarely any details from biographies of the Mendelssohn family or of his letters for researchers to study.

If anyone wishes to write a thesis on climatic conditions of the time, there can be few better sources than the Mendelssohn letters. They were obsessed with the weather – possibly because it is a subject with which all can feel comfortable and on which all can agree without dispute. It may have prevented his mother, who insisted on remaining at Leipzigerstrasse 3 for the majority of her life, from feeling less resentful, knowing what frightful conditions she was missing. The poet Thomas Hood, who lived from 1798 to 1845 and was, thus, contemporary with Felix, wrote, in his poem 'November':

"No mail; no post;
No news from any foreign coast..."

Chapter 9: A Family of Letter Writers

Even during the summer months of 1829 such weather obtained in Britain; "I cannot write more as I am in a foul mood due to the unpredictable weather, which has brought on a headache." For the past week there had been "downpours, flashes of sunshine, autumn chills, stormy winds, alternating with oppressive heat; one's umbrella never dries; it is boring. I only hope it is better where you are." He could not understand how his itinerary had not reached his family, but explained that Doxat had the two addresses he would use in Scotland and Wales. He would write as often as possible, but could not communicate whilst in the Highlands. From Italy, Felix wrote that it was only when an indelible impression was left on his mind that he thought of his home and family. When "unwell, fatigued or out of sorts", he had no particular longing for his native environment. "Who can write or think with any degree of warmth," he wrote at the beginning of February 1831.

Having been so pleased to experience a whole winter without snow, he now had to give up that prospect, though his neighbours informed him that "the spring breezes will arrive in a few days' time". The weather followed him to Bella Isola (Beautiful Isle), with pouring rain and thunderclaps. "Fragrant orange blossom, blue sky, bright sun and clear lake cannot be found", and Felix complained of his "unfortunate cloak" after two days of downpour. In Switzerland he noticed "the stones, as big as stoves, Goethe's flowers and mosses", but would never forget his walks, despite the havoc surrounding him caused by floods. He had hoped to see many sights that he remembered as a boy, but all he could visualise were "the points of my umbrella", but he was not to complain of the weather, in view of the enjoyment he had experienced. His guide was "a capital fellow, singing and yodelling through the rain". Felix felt "like Orpheus in the presence of Tantalus, catching tempting glances at mountains that I have to resign myself as unable to climb". He could not "discern the finest objects" through the clouds, but he could observe "a great deal that was interesting", such as the glaciers "of fine, pure ice, [that] tumble about, and the changes of colour as the sun shines on them". He saw "the most marvellous monsters in the world", but such thoughts were lost on the inhabitants. They become alarmed when the glaciers moved "a foot and a half each day" for fear of what might happen next. Despite the damage caused by the movement of the ice, when rocks were broken, the glaciers were "splendid miracles" to Felix, the Rhône Glacier being "the most imposing I have ever seen". If nothing else could be found in Switzerland, he reflected, "It is, at all events, more than you can see in any other country."

Nevertheless, even the idealistic Felix had to admit that his family might find his notes boring. He felt guilty of his "incessant repetitions of how I sank in mud and how incessantly it rained"; how he could not write his journal for two days because it had to be dried, and likewise his clothes; how he had to warm himself by a fire (in August 1831). Fanny's family did not fare any better when the Hensels visited there en route to Italy. On arrival across the southern Alps to Ursern for the night, Fanny expressed disappointment that mist shrouded the landscape she remembered so fondly from her 1822 visit with her parents and Felix. Though the locals assured their guests that the threatening storm would pass, such was not the case. Thunder, lightning, rain and hail blew into their faces. One cannot help suspecting that so much news of bad weather must have caused Leah to rub her hands in glee, tucked safely in her comfortable home in Berlin, gloating how clever she was not to risk such adventures. Hensel set out to explore the Righi, wading through mountain streams and "jumping from rock to rock" as the paths had been washed away by the floods. But, despite the sanguine forecast of the innkeeper, the storm did not abate and Fanny called her husband's excursion "mad", on his arrival home, as he had been able to see nothing of the Swiss countryside.

Having reached Italy the Hensels were shown, on a visit to the Lateran baptistry, the well from which the woman of Samaria was purported to have drawn water, as recounted in St John's Gospel. In fact it dated from no earlier than the Middle Ages, and artists complained that the background was spoilt by the monks cutting down trees to sell as timber. But Fanny's letter was more concerned with the astonishment promoted by the foul weather. Whereas, in winter, neither warm clothes nor fires were needed, now that spring had arrived snow covered the houses and lay 12 inches thick in the streets – "regular Berlin winter in fact". The Romans were seen snowballing, whilst onlookers watched from windows. Fanny and Sebastian joined in the fun, but Hensel disliked the cold. No one had seen the like of this climatic change before; after several hours of sunshine, followed by rain, the snow remained for some days. Even at home, the weather played a part in letters. In January 1844 Fanny wrote to Rebecka, during the latter's visit to Italy, of plunging into ankle-deep snow, despite the sun, whereas it was slippery in the shade. Nature gave Berlin "everything that is disagreeable: first, a long and severe frost; then, rain, waterspouts, snow and ice". In the garden, crows made "such a prolonged and plaintive noise" the gardener, endeavouring to find the cause of the disturbance, discovered a dead bird "with his relatives singing a requiem over the corpse".

Another major topic, in Felix's letters at least, is his guilt about his delay in replying to correspondence. He wrote from Calais, en route home from his first visit to London of 1829, that his last few days there were "so crowded; the haste so great...that I lacked the leisure, composure and patience to describe everything to you", thus falling foul of his duty to write to his parents. Had Leah and Abraham been so steeped in the love of culture for which they have been given so much credit, they would have accepted and understood how little time Felix must have had for writing letters. In view of the oft-repeated anxiety in Felix's letters at the lack of news from his family, his own letter writing appears one-sided, as if compensating for his parents' lapses in this regard. As long as he carried out *his* duty, nothing else mattered. His first visit when in Florence was to the post office, and, finding three letters from home, he "celebrated at the Hotel Schneider". From Naples he was "too absorbed in work" to write and, to prove this, "will have a pleasant store of music to bring home". But this applied equally to correspondence

Chapter 9: A Family of Letter Writers

with friends and acquaintances. Eduard Hanslick, in his compilation of letters between Mendelssohn and Aloys Fuchs, cites letters to Moscheles, Ferdinand David, Hiller and others; he calls himself "a sinner", "a neglectful, lazy letter writer, who does not deserve the forbearance of his friends", and many similar self-demeaning phrases. "We are, on the contrary," writes Hanslick, "amazed at the great number of detailed letters from him...rich in content [displaying] such fresh, vivid colours." What a pity they are spoilt by his unnecessary guilt when delayed in replying. To Fuchs, for instance, he apologised for not giving details of a recital at his home, asking him "not to be angry" and to "forgive my sins of omission in correspondence". To so many people he begged them "not to be angry", assuming, no doubt, that everyone would react in the same way as his parents towards their child. To Heyse, his tutor, Felix explained his reason for non-response to letters from home: he had been "running round like mad, trying to see everything at once" in Paris. Any instructor worth the name should have been proud that his pupil took such opportunities in his new surroundings to see and do anything presented to him. To Julius Schubring he hoped that they would "not grow distant from one another" as a young man, yet their correspondence did not recommence until 1837.

To Zelter, it was evident that he did not include business letters in his correspondence. He asked his former mentor "not to be angry" at the time lapse, ignoring the fact that he had written from Munich to recommend the composer Adolf von Henselt, five years younger than Felix, to Zelter; or perhaps Mendelssohn did not consider such letters of sufficient importance to be included in his letter writing schedule. From Frankfurt in 1836 he asked Conrad Schleinitz, in charge of the financial running of the Leipzig Gewandhaus Orchestra, if he were still alive, in view of his lack of communication; "to think that I, the worst correspondent in the kingdom", should have written twice since seeing Schleinitz. "This is atrocious beyond all atrocity," he declared. On 3rd January 1841 Felix wrote of having sent off 35 letters during the past few days. As late as 1846 he felt he had to apologise for not replying sooner to Paul in thanking his brother for praising his triumph with *Elijah* in Birmingham.

It is evident that, despite his prolific letter writing, Felix Mendelssohn preferred sketching and composing in order to express his true feelings. Woe betide, even if no fault could be attributed to Felix, if an anticipated letter did not arrive on a set day. This is seen when, in 1844, Rebecka complained that she had not received a letter on her birthday, a Thursday, as expected. Letters should, and had to, be received, despite extraneous circumstances – unpredictable mail deliveries – to ensure nothing untoward had occurred. Only illness served as a good enough reason for not writing; it did not occur to the Mendelssohn parents that Felix entertained a heavy work schedule, nor that he actually disliked expressing his thoughts in words. On 12th January 1843 he was able to confide to Professor Köstlin his "instinctive dislike to pen and paper, except where music is concerned".

Would he have dared to admit such sentiments to his parents? Rather, he found other, equally justifiable reasons for lapses in communication, which would placate them more easily. From Naples he confided that his letters "are of so little value" as, because of his work, he felt unable to describe events in as much detail as they deserved. On leaving Rome he reminded them that there were so many other tasks to accomplish, tactfully omitting the fact that, unlike his father when travelling, he had no retinue of servants to deal with the mundane, day-to-day issues on his journeys abroad. From Paris he must have been particularly irritated: "…I will conclude abruptly, contrary to my usual habit. Farewell." He did not have the heart to write "such a thin, short personal letter", but he retained it until there was more to tell his family. Now, however, "I will finish, covering the page altogether". This was far more important than cutting the page into smaller sections; the sheet had to be filled – an exception to the normal rule regarding thrift in the Mendelssohn household!

He referred to his letters as "dull, dry notes", deliberately withholding them until he had something he considered worth reporting. This was dated 24th July 1836, before setting off to the seaside resort of Scheveningen in the Netherlands with Schadow and his son, a pre-arranged commitment that would take Felix away from his beloved Cécile Jeanrenaud. "My address will be 'Poste Restante The Hague'." Even in the idyllic atmosphere of Bad Soden with his family in 1844, Felix's only cloud was his having to write letters. "Forget…that I am such a lazy correspondent," he begged his sisters. Fanny, too, confessed that she did not have the patience to describe Overbeck's religious paintings, except to call them "dull, feebly poetic and slightly presumptuous", and to say that the artist himself had the "arrogance" to declare himself greater than Philipp Veit, Peter Cornelius or other "elite spirits of the day". Fanny hoped the engraver would choose a simpler design when Overbeck – "the great man" – had "turned into an old woman". In this way, "bad colouring and poor painting" could be disguised. Though her husband knew more about art than Fanny, "I bow to no authority as I too have eyes that I aim to use as much as possible." Such afterthoughts and "asides" throw far greater light on Fanny's, as well as Felix's, "dull", "stupid" letters than their authors realised.

On 22nd December 1842 Felix wrote to Paul: "The point of union is now gone where, even as children, we could always meet", Leah having passed away on the 12th. "We are children no longer, but we have enjoyed what it really is to be so. Now this is gone forever." Their mother's loss would be felt "more deeply and painfully by the family day by day". Felix felt as if he were "in a dark room, groping to find the way, hour after hour". He suggested that each write a weekly letter, thereby allowing everyone to remain up to date with family news; and, incidentally, though he did not say so, Felix's own almost superhuman work commitments would be made easier from the brunt of his correspondence. If this plan did not suit, could Fanny, Rebecka or Paul think of an alternative? However, though Albertine and Paul assured Rebecka that a letter would be written each day, she complained that none had come to hand during the past fortnight, whilst she was staying in Italy. Fanny was "touched" that her own epistles were circulated around the Mendelssohn relatives, especially as she was so candid about Italy: "A visit anywhere in that country begins pianissimo, but the longer one remains in a place it increases to fortissimo." Inconsequentially, she was reminded of how their parents would ask for the soup to be served in order to bring Paul to table at meal times. It was only towards the end of his life that Felix committed the heinous crime of letting his music supersede letter writing in importance for him. He begged Paul "not to hold it against me", on 9th July 1846. Almost a year later – four months prior to his death, in fact – Felix responded to a plea from Rebecka to Paul that their elder brother should write: "What to write I cannot think... I hope that, as the days pass, they will bring more fortitude, and so I let them flow past me in the company of Paul and in this lovely country" – Switzerland. This depression was as a result of Fanny's sudden death on 14th May of that year. On a visit the previous year, Devrient had recalled Fanny rebuking Felix for not being with her on her birthday for so many years. "Depend upon it," he vowed; he would spend the next one with her. "He kept his word," Devrient stated, but not in the expected way. On 4th November 1847, ten days before Fanny's 42nd birthday, Felix joined his sister in what Robert Schumann called "the beyond".

It is evident that what Felix preferred was conversation face to face. Despite so many letters of introduction provided by Abraham, Felix's most useful contacts were made by introducing his own personality to anyone he met. But when officials presented the young traveller to notables, he was ignored. This happened in Rome, when no one to whom Ambassador Bunsen introduced him took notice of Felix. "They even looked the other way," he wrote on 15th March 1831. He did, however, gain a half-hour's conversation with a cardinal, who volunteered that everything Meyerbeer wrote was "too learned and too scientific" for his taste; his music was "so devoid of melody that at once you knew that he was a German, and Germans, mon ami, have not the remotest conception of what melody is." The cardinal hoped to make Felix as comfortable as possible and invited him to bring as many friends along as he pleased. When he realised that anyone could attend his host's gatherings, Felix vowed "never to proffer letters of introduction to families" whom he could meet without such formality. Besides, letters could be circulated to someone by whom they were not meant to have been read. Felix became very annoyed, for example, when he had written adversely about the soprano Clara Novello. Conversation was far more likely to remain confined to the people involved. "Written words are cold vultures," he wrote during his first visit to London; "speaking is better, even if it has to be in English." To Devrient he wrote how much he looked forward to seeing him and his wife Thérèse, "when one story leads to the next". There were, however, "things that cannot be ignored in a letter", such as greeting the couple on the birth of their child, though Felix would rather have greeted the new parents with a handshake than "those tiresome old congratulations" conveyed in writing. This applied especially when Felix was too overwhelmed for words to express. To Zelter, after his visit to Goethe in 1830, despite the "elation, joy and pride" he felt, wrote that "it is difficult to say 'thanks'" for the time he had spent with their mutual friend.

On 11th February, at the birth of his own first child, he confided to Paul, on asking Albertine and himself to be godparents to Karl Wolfgang Paul, "I just do not seem to be making any headway with writing. I hope to be able to speak to you soon – to see you, make music with you, go walking – that is better than a letter. But I still must thank you for your most recent, lovely one in which you enlightened ignorant me a little about paper management. What can I do about the fact that you are so musical and [that] I can never return the favour in kind?" He expressed anxiety to the musicologist Kiesewetter in Vienna about Franz Hauser's welfare, having written two letters without response, being "quite concerned" about his friend. To President Verkenius of Cologne he asked, in view of his illness, not to read his own letter if Verkenius did not wish Mendelssohn to write so often, unaware of how comforting this must have been, judging by other correspondents. To an unnamed editor of a journal, whom he had met in Paris some years earlier, Felix wished to meet him before seeing a score from Herr Dürrner in order to gain a better knowledge of his compositions. But there was no such diffidence regarding the compositions of Herr von Boguslawski. "It was with the most heartfelt interest that I made acquaintance with your score," he wrote at his first opportunity for leisure time. "You know what affection I have had for you since childhood and for everything that has to do with you, which I shall retain my whole life long."

In conclusion, a word must be said about what Jean Petitpierre called Mendelssohn's "lively, chatty, friendly letters", and the way they were received. To his brother-in-law, Charles Jeanrenaud, Felix asked if Cherubini's opera *Medea* was to be performed in Frankfurt. He enquired if he knew the whereabouts of some miniatures by Brentano and, finally, "is there a vacant apartment in Hiller's house?" in view of the family remaining no longer in Frankfurt. The Miss Horsleys, Sophie and Fanny, were prolific letter writers to their aunt, Lucy Callcott, governess to a family in Lincolnshire and then to the Russells of Swallowfield near Reading. On one occasion Felix thanked Mrs. Horsley for some plants, or bulbs, that she had sent Leah, which their gardener had recommended to plant in the spring in order to bloom before autumn. Leah watched their progress daily. These examples give proof of such affection: Petitpierre quoting Mendelssohn's letter so long afterwards; the Horsley family sending such lovely floral remembrances. However, the final word comes from Robert Schumann via a remark made in passing to George Sampson, an English singer who visited Leipzig in 1840; if there was one thing as good as being in their host's company, it was being away from him, as one could then receive "such delightful epistles"; his sayings deserved "to be written in pure gold".

Chapter 10

That Money Question

As stated earlier, Moses Mendelssohn did not become a 'protected' Jew on account of his financial acumen, unlike others of his faith, but through his fine intellect; this privilege was also conferred on his widow and children at his death. In turn, that inherited status allowed Joseph, and – later – Abraham, to develop the family bank; but, as far as the latter is concerned, this was not the sole aid to financial security. Leah's family, also 'protected' Jews, were able to accumulate considerable wealth and, as a bride, Leah's dowry must have helped enormously to put her husband's bank onto a sound footing. Yet Abraham's father had never needed to trouble about written guarantees, or the provision of dowries when his daughters married. It was enough to say that "the word of a virtuous man is the best guarantee in the world" and, had Felix's father followed this maxim, a far pleasanter life would have been led by his children. However, Leah, browbeaten by her brother Jakob Salomon, who changed his name to Bartholdy, has much for which to answer as far as the Mendelssohns' attitude towards the acquisition of money is concerned.

In 1806, two years after Leah and Abraham married, Napoleon established the 'Continental System', whereby all ports under his control were prohibited from trading with Britain in the hope of starving her into submission. Because Hamburg was not yet annexed, this port was able to take part in what Marek calls "the biggest smuggling campaign in history". Since finance was needed, such banking houses as Mendelssohn & Company took full advantage of the situation. British goods could therefore be exported under false flags and documentation, and, despite their leader, French officials were too human not to resist bribery. A London agent reported, after the first five months of the blockade, that payments were never disturbed from Hamburg or Bremen; "there are still many methods for carrying on commercial operations," the agent declared. Not only did the banking houses supply the necessary finance, but they bought and serviced ships by which goods could be imported and exported. They sailed under flags of what were then still neutral states, about which Napoleon could do nothing. When, in 1812, Hamburg was annexed, Leah was again able to come to her husband's aid. The family, dressed as and behaving like refugees, were able to escape safely to Berlin with most of their assets, with the assistance of a friend of Leah's aunt, who happened to be the French ambassador to Prussia. Abraham was thereby able to provide money to the Prussian government and to equip a volunteer force, whilst still carrying on his nefarious smuggling enterprises. Dr. Johnson could well have had such people as Abraham Mendelssohn in mind when he coined his aphorism "patriotism is the last refuge of the scoundrel". Would Moses, with his unblemished moral code, have approved? Be that as it may, Abraham became first a municipal and, later, the King's privy councillor – an unprecedented honour for someone of Jewish descent. Whilst historians pay deserved credit to Marshal Blücher of Prussia for aiding the Duke of Wellington to win the Battle of Waterloo, he could not have achieved this without the support of such bankers as Abraham Mendelssohn. But it must not be forgotten how luck played an equal part. Abraham was not only in the right place at the right time, but he was married to the right person as far as his financial status was concerned – unlike Moses, his father.

Henriette Herz, a friend of Dorothea Mendelssohn who visited the house of Fromet and Moses, observed that Frau Mendelssohn was seen to count the almonds and raisins that remained when most guests had departed. This stemmed from the fact that, having lost the family wealth, Fromet must have learnt to be ultra-careful about every aspect of housekeeping. Like many in such circumstances, thrift tended to run to extremes. Abraham may well have inherited this parsimonious trait, which Leah followed, yet with no excuse in her case. According to Marek, Abraham was "firm of purpose, knew what he wanted, and what he wanted he got", but this applies even more so to Leah. It is she who appears to have coveted worldly wealth, taking every opportunity to enhance her social position by inviting the highest society to the Mendelssohn home.

This is how Felix has acquired the false image of riches beyond most people's imagination, thereby provoking unwarranted jealousy. Herbert Kupferberg calls the Mendelssohn family "the Rothschilds of culture", but this epithet carries no weight. Moses Mendelssohn and Meyer Rothschild did have the same background in that they each liberated themselves from the ghetto – Moses from that of Dessau, Meyer from Frankfurt – but this was as far as the similarity would remain. Meyer Rothschild's five sons were encouraged to found banking interests in different capitals of Europe, whereas only Joseph and Abraham of the Mendelssohn sons became bankers. As for culture, whilst the name of Rothschild is synonymous with art in so many ways, only Moses and his grandson Felix and granddaughter Fanny can be allied with any artistic achievement. Neither were Abraham's children allowed to share the purported Mendelssohn wealth. Whereas Chopin, Liszt and Mozart travelled all over Europe as children, in order to study or perform music, Felix was not granted such a privilege. Felix was regarded solely as an amateur displaying his talent at home for a hobby, except for visits to Paris at seven and 16, but – again – as an amateur, with no gifts of jewels, gold or entrées to European royalty. At the fortnightly concerts at Leipzigerstrasse 3, Devrient recalled Felix

Chapter 10: That Money Question

conducting the singers seated round a table, "grave and unembarrassed…as if playing a game" – which, to his parents, was the case. None of the musicians who visited in the earlier years gave much thought to his talent. Fanny wrote that the then fashionable pianist Friedrich Wilhelm Kalkbrenner "praised with taste" and "blamed candidly and amiably" when he visited Berlin in 1823, but it was only when Moscheles suggested Felix be sent to London that his professional career took root – on his own initiative.

It was only in the realm of the best tutors that Abraham Mendelssohn lavished money on his children. He wished them to follow in his own father's footsteps as an intellectual; he appeared not to be able to understand that sensitive minds might be stretched too much for their bodies to tolerate. Abraham's generation did not need to struggle as their fathers had done. As far as the children were concerned, the parents behaved as if no change had occurred in financial well-being. Anything that was seen as "extravagant" or "frivolous" was prohibited. Friendships were formed with people whom Abraham had met in his father's home, not via Abraham himself. It was Zelter who introduced Goethe to Abraham in the hope that the banker might advise the poet on financial matters. By a letter of introduction, Abraham visited Weimar in 1816, en route to Paris to negotiate the indemnity for war reparations. Having heard from Zelter about the Mendelssohn family, Goethe regretted not meeting Leah and the children on that occasion. It would be five more years before Felix met Goethe for the first time – on Zelter's initiative.

Meyer Rothschild was purported to have bequeathed £3 billion to his five sons at his death, but no record exists of the sum inherited by Felix when his father died. In any event, it was the younger son, Paul, who was recognised as 'head of the house', as stated by Fanny in a letter to Carl Klingemann of 4th February 1836. But, whatever the financial circumstances, Devrient recalled that, when visiting Leipzigerstrasse 3, apart from the building itself there was nothing to show that it had been owned by a wealthy man: the rooms were plainly furnished; the Sunday entertainments were organised "with studied plainness". John O'Shea quotes from earlier biographies to the effect that Mendelssohn "had no profound negative experiences to draw on in his art" and, because of this, did not develop as he could have done as a composer. Admittedly, earlier biographers were unaware of the truth about Mendelssohn's situation. Many composers are viewed with compassion on account of their humble beginnings, but it is not realised that Mendelssohn was placed in the same predicament; he was saddled with the myth of unprecedented affluence, and all it could acquire, at his command. It is only when careful research is undertaken and more accurate information comes to light that Felix's true position can be acknowledged. In short, either the Mendelssohn parents did not have as much money as was assumed, or they put on a 'front' of arrant parsimony and miserliness. A further puzzle is the consistent report from biographers that Abraham and Leah were such lovers of art. In view of the way Felix was treated, this appears to have applied more in the acquisition of people who had made their name in the world of the arts. One of the greatest, their son, was never taken seriously as such. Felix complained to A. B. Marx how Abraham "had once again become doubtful about Felix's profession, dissatisfied with the career of an artist, whose success would always remain uncertain". Marx would smile, pointing out "how wisely his father was acting when he encouraged him to examine himself again and again" – as if anyone of his calibre needed to undergo such bank-clerkly procedure! Marx echoed "strongly" a further dictum of Abraham: "One should only become an artist if he could not do otherwise."

But neither Leah nor Abraham can be blamed entirely for such a hiatus in their empathy with Felix's choice of profession. As mentioned previously, Marx remembered Leah as "highly intelligent though, perhaps, a less feeling mother". Decidedly reserved, never wearing her heart on her sleeve as far as affection went, she must, to her loved ones, have been very difficult to get to know. Though Leah sketched well, she rarely allowed anyone to see the result. She read Homer's works in secret; not, one suspects (as Wilfrid Blunt glibly suggests), because such a pastime was deemed too 'masculine' for a woman, but, rather, because she was too unsure of herself to demonstrate this interest to anyone. Had anyone with perception troubled to speak to her, more likely than not the observer would have realised how lacking she was in self-worth. Her evident fascination and envy with what is called 'high society' stemmed from the status of which her brother Jakob (Salomon) Bartholdy boasted. Jakob adopted the new surname from the man who sold him his property. Having bullied his sister and brother-in-law to have the children baptised as Christians, the Mendelssohns were then told to adopt the name 'Bartholdy', as Jakob had done, with the promise that – should this be put into effect – Leah would inherit all her brother's fabulous wealth. So much money had Bartholdy spent on his new property that some relatives christened it 'Little Sans-Souçi', implying that he wished to emulate the grandeur of the King's residence; less well-disposed Berliners, who had no fear of this bully, named Bartholdy's mansion 'the Jew's garden'.

In 1813 Bartholdy became Prussian consul in Rome, patronising the arts and allowing young hopefuls to study at his villa. He wrote a book on the Ancient Greek province of Mycenae and one on the Tyrolean uprising against Napoleon, but the writings for which Bartholdy is best remembered comprise his 'confidential reports', full of "plotting, scheming and conniving" – of which he suspected anyone and everyone. He believed himself to deserve far greater influence and rank than his birth, education and "unattractive bearing" would permit, doing all in his power to usurp posts to which he was never entitled. Since his diplomatic activities and acquisition of art treasures were interrupted by bouts of gambling for absurdly high stakes, it is not surprising that, at his death in 1825, all Leah inherited was a considerable debt from her brother. It can only be imagined how betrayed she must have felt by such disillusionment. When Wilhelm Hensel asked if the Mendelssohns could accommodate the frescoes from the Villa Bartholdy, Leah's

Chapter 10: That Money Question

reply was couched in an almost unbelievably negative vein, in view of the consistently asserted riches of the residents in Leipzigerstrasse 3, Berlin. Though she might have appeared "avaricious and selfish", she had to remind her prospective son-in-law that Abraham had never been rich, and it was *her* dowry that had helped develop the Mendelssohn Bank; further, it was only because she knew to what good account it would be placed that she had agreed to make it over to him through marriage. Finally, Abraham had spent so much money putting the house to rights that there would be no money available to allow these frescoes to be lodged there. Could it be that Leah would not have wished to be reminded of her humiliation, and that these perfectly cogent reasons were mere excuses to Hensel?

"Thank God," Henriette Mendelssohn wrote to Leah on 10th June 1824, "that *your* family's marriages will be new and unmixed joy to you." How much, if anything, did 'Tante Jette' surmise about the trouble caused to Fanny, having fallen in love with Wilhelm Hensel? If Leah had been such a lover of art, she would have shown far greater sensitivity than was displayed. Wilhelm Hensel, born in 1794, was 11 years older than the girl he eventually married. Son of an impoverished clergyman, Hensel arrived in Berlin having played a creditable part in the Napoleonic Wars, having been wounded several times. He had already painted portraits of Tsar Alexander I as the Archangel Michael and of Napoleon as Lucifer. This prompted Grand Duke Nicholas, heir to the Russian throne, to invite Hensel to paint the backdrops for tableaux to represent Tom Moore's *Lalla Rookh*, staged to end the celebrations of the Russian court's arrival in Berlin. The grand duchess, wishing for a memento of the entertainment, commissioned Hensel to paint portraits of the 27 participants, to be included in an album. He was also commissioned to paint a reproduction of Raphael's *Transfiguration* for the Sans-Souçi palace, and it was at an exhibition in which this work was shown that Fanny met the artist. Each fell in love with the other, which would lead anyone to foresee a 'happily ever after' ending, but this was not to be, for the next few years. Leah saw Hensel as nothing more than a fortune hunter, after the dowry with which Fanny would be provided on her marriage. When given a grant to study in Italy, it was feared that Hensel would fall under the influence of the Catholic Church, as his sister and Leah's two sisters-in-law, Dorothea and Henriette, had done. These factors carried far greater weight than the prestigious commissions Hensel was receiving and the prospects accruing therefrom.

One finds no record of the fact, but it may have been Bartholdy's meddling into this family matter that caused Leah's anxiety; whatever the circumstances, Hensel's letters were intercepted, Fanny's mother reading only what she thought fit for her elder daughter to hear. Leah declared to the prospective bridegroom that she did not consider him to have an income sufficiently dependable to provide for a Mendelssohn daughter; nor would he be able to replace his bachelor lifestyle with that of a responsible husband. Not that she expected Fanny to make a wealthy marriage, since she was "not very pretty and [had] one shoulder higher than the other" (inherited not from Leah's family, she could have added). Fanny was also short-sighted and had been brought up "modestly" – none of which factors, to Leah's mind, would allow such a fairy-tale event to occur. However, since artists were all reputed to be fickle, unfaithful and improvident and to practise all the other vices connected with these shortcomings, the couple would tire of one another and drift apart as each grew older. Then, Leah may well have asked herself, how would innocent, carefully sheltered, unprepossessing, near-sighted Fanny have managed with no husband to provide for her? Leah may also have been jealous of her elder daughter, falling in love with an artist whose work gained him access to royalty – a status the mother had never achieved. After all, whatever the situation at present, it was only Leah's dowry that had prevented Abraham from remaining a bank clerk. "I will not have you, by love letters, transporting her into a constant state of consuming passion and a yearning state of mind so strange to her character," Leah told Hensel; "I see her before me now, blooming, healthy, happy and free."

Had Hensel, like Robert Schumann, studied law, he might have been able to appeal to the court for permission to marry Fanny, as Schumann had done when wishing to marry Clara Wieck against her father's will. But Hensel chose another way of winning his bride's hand, by first winning her family's hearts. He painted portraits in an idealistic style, which pleased the Mendelssohn parents. Leah was "surprised" at her future son-in-law's "exquisite beauty of execution and fine, delicate ideas", which had "touched the family" – 'flattered' might have been a more apt verb. She had "never seen anything of the kind before, more lovely or more perfect", from Hensel or anyone else. But when it had become apparent that the love between Fanny and Hensel was to remain and, now that Bartholdy had died, there was no point in preventing their marriage, the anxious mother warned Hensel not to "fritter away" his time on "such small drawings", implying that it would be far more expedient to make more money through his art. She could not resist adding that she "could not believe" how much expression Hensel had captured in one "darling little picture". Thus, the betrothal took place on 22nd January 1829, the banns were read for the three Sundays commencing 10th September, and the wedding took place on 3rd October of that year.

Because Hensel and Fanny had been apart for five years, the bride-to-be hid at first in the shelter of her family, regarding her fiancé as a stranger. Even when he realised how faithful his bride had been throughout the years, Hensel still felt uncomfortable, in case she might be snatched from him at the last minute by someone of greater rank or wealth. Ridiculous as it may seem Hensel was even wary of Felix, so close were brother and sister, but his feelings may be understood in view of the absurd jokes about Fanny and Felix marrying. How many young men have to tolerate such innuendo as "There is many a true word spoken in jest"?

Sebastian Hensel, Fanny's son, made a tremendous effort to explain his grandparents' point of view when he later wrote his family memoirs. "They had to

Chapter 10: That Money Question

guard their daughter against every possibility of a disappointment. Neither Leah nor Abraham can be blamed for their lack of perception in appreciating Hensel's strength of character or depth of love for Fanny." Once Hensel put himself in her place, Leah had written, he would realise "how natural, just and sensible" her plea had been for him not to correspond. Though no doubt Hensel viciously denounced the mother's "barbaric action" in intercepting the love letters, "the difference in age and the uncertainty of your position" were the reasons given, though she "truly esteemed" and had "a real affection" for this untried artist; neither had she "any objection" to him personally. A man might not marry, however, until he had an assured position, "at least, to a certain degree". Abraham's views are not reported.

Felix, in London, was so anxious about the money situation regarding Fanny's wedding that he offered, "if there is not enough dowry", to "send my share for the trousseau. I cannot do any more, but you probably can, dear mother, so do it; is there not time enough?" But, fortunately, this was not necessary. On 19th September Fanny wrote to her father to thank him for the gifts he had purchased whilst on business in Hamburg and Amsterdam – beyond her wildest expectations. The embroidered materials and patterns were "so perfect that not even Nathan the Wise could have produced anything better". Her veil made such a sensation when her friends saw it, because no such fashion existed in Berlin at the time. Fanny wondered if it would make too much of a show were she to wear it, but reflected how suitable it would be "because of my red nose". The ribbons and shawls were "exquisite" and the bride-to-be wrote of visiting stores daily with her mother. She felt she should spend the whole day thanking her parents for the care they had taken of her wedding preparations.

Evidently, Felix's letter must have punctured their consciences, but Fanny would doubtless never have known of her brother's intervention. An organ piece of her own composition was played prior to the ceremony, at which Pastor Wilhelmsen gave the address. Fanny and Hensel lived in rooms at the family home, Abraham having a studio constructed where his son-in-law could work. He became a reputable artist, especially in Britain, and had several pupils, which added to his income. Fanny kept a journal from the year of her marriage, dating it from 1st January 1829 to the end of her life. Though Sebastian Hensel defended his grandparents loyally, he admitted that they could never come to terms with losing a daughter; it did not occur to this self-centred couple that, in fact, they had gained a son. Again, it was with Wilhelm's drawing skill that this unhealthy atmosphere was alleviated. Hensel drew a sketch that he entitled *The Wheel*. This depicted a circle – the Mendelssohn family – with someone endeavouring to integrate himself into it – Hensel himself. The hub represented Felix, dressed in Highland garb, referring to his proposed Scottish holiday with Carl Klingemann. So pleased was the future brother-in-law with Hensel's sketch that the family reserve eased until, eventually, the 'wheel' opened to let Hensel become part of it.

Rebecka, too, chose a husband who made his reputation by mental application and the will to work hard. In a letter, Fanny wrote that Otto Gans and Dirichlet "fight and quarrel like schoolboys", but she called the latter, her future brother-in-law, "a very handsome, amiable man, so full of fun and spirit as a student and very learned". One of 11 children, Gustav Peter Lejeune Dirichlet was born on 13th February 1805. Six years senior to Rebecka, as a boy he bought and studied books on mathematics, a discipline his parents deemed him too young to understand. "I read them until I did understand them" was his rejoinder, and, at 12, he was sent to the Gymnasium in Bonn, equivalent to a U.K. grammar school. He read history, French culture and literature, as well as his 'pet' subject. At 14 he was sent to the Jesuit college at Cologne, where he studied under both Georg Ohm, pioneer of research into electricity, and Karl Gauss, the famous mathematician. Though brilliant, Professor Gauss had no communication skills with which to teach. When a student presented Gauss with what was considered to be a new discovery, he was informed that the problem had been solved years before and, rummaging in his desk, Gauss would produce a paper to prove this. Because his parents did not believe mathematics could allow him to earn a living, Dirichlet studied law, working at this profession during the day but pursuing his favoured interest in the evenings. Eventually, however, with his parents' blessing, Dirichlet went to Paris – the then 'mathematical capital' of Europe – and, as tutor to General Foy, was enrolled in the College of France and the faculty of sciences. Foy, who, like his fellow generals Davout and Sebastiani, wished his children to study all things German, recalled Dirichlet sitting on the stove, pursuing his own studies whilst teaching his pupils.

Klingemann, as a diplomat and having met General Foy, wrote to Rebecka how pleased the parents were with their tutorial 'find'. Alexander von Humboldt had also met Dirichlet and took him seriously on his first publication for the faculty of sciences in Berlin. At Foy's death, Dirichlet returned to Germany and von Humboldt persuaded him to apply for the vacant post of instructor in mathematics at the Prussian Military Academy. At first he had been considered too young to instruct officers but, after a year's probation, he remained in the post for 27 years, until 1858. As with Fanny and Hensel, when in 1828 von Humboldt introduced this young man into the Mendelssohn household Leah resisted anything more than friendship between Rebecka and Dirichlet, until it had become evident that they had fallen in love. His lack of worldly prospects was less important than his moral wealth and ability to prove himself a loving, caring husband and father, as Leah saw the situation. How Dirichlet could achieve a higher status than that already reached in his chosen sphere is hard to imagine but, in May 1832, the couple began an idyllically happy marriage. Like the Hensels, Rebecka and her husband resided at Leipzigerstrasse 3 at the outset, having five children, three of whom survived to adulthood. For generations of mathematicians Dirichlet's name was well known, his treatise on the *Theory of Numbers* being a definitive work.

Chapter 10: That Money Question

It is fascinating to read of a conversation in 1840 between William Sterndale Bennett, Ferdinand David, Robert Schumann and their host, Mendelssohn, which the singer George Sampson recalled taking place in Leipzig. Schumann asked if Goethe had befriended Felix because he was "so successful and prosperous", having been patronising towards Beethoven and dismissive of Schubert's music altogether. Mendelssohn responded that, were it not so painful, he would have found the poet's attitude comic. "Poor Schubert," he sighed, "he always met fortune's frown – never her smile." It was "a vile doctrine", Mendelssohn asserted, to suggest, as Bennett had done, that Schubert's genius was enhanced because he was poor, though "it is true that the artist learns by suffering, because the artist is more sensitive than others and feels more deeply". Bennett's comment was, according to Sampson, "invented by a callous world to excuse its cruelty". Mendelssohn replied, "Enough suffering came even to the most fortunate, without the sordid, gratuitous misery of poverty. Poverty did not nourish or ennoble; it narrowed the vision and made one feel sordid, lowering the moral standard of an artist; one cannot get good art out of that!" Felix spoke of his parents with unrestrained gratitude for their "careful encouragement" but, above all, for their "noble, serious common sense". His mother was not a woman to allow the children to "live in a fool's paradise"; his father was "far too good a man of business to let me walk into a blind alley". Though he reminisced with nostalgia about "the musical times we had in the dear Berlin house", it was Felix who made his own reputation once he left home – especially in Britain. As for Goethe's friendship, this began when Felix was 12 and far from successful or prosperous. It was Zelter's opinion of his pupil that carried weight.

Had Leah's "serious common sense" and Abraham's astute business acumen been leavened with greater imagination and perception, Felix's spiritual well-being would have been allowed greater peace and contentment. As it was, Ludwig Spohr's first visit to London is called to mind. In 1820 the young composer sought the financial support of Nathan Rothschild, whose only response was that the music in which he was most interested was the sound of coins in his pocket, slapping that area of his person to show what he meant. The only difference was that, whereas Rothschild was honest about his musical tastes, Abraham thought he 'knew it all' and constantly found fault with his son's compositions and style. As for Leah, J. S. Bach might well have been the only composer who had ever existed. Bartholdy meddled in every aspect of Leah's family affairs, so it is not surprising that he tried to persuade his brother-in-law that music was not a suitable profession for Felix; far better that he study law, since it seemed evident that he did not want to serve his family in their bank. Combined with the hectoring from Bartholdy (on whose 'bandwagon' his parents jumped), plus his father criticising whatever he did compose when his career took wing, Felix had the constant worry about relaxing too much or, if he had no alternative but to take time off from his work, having less money than a young gentleman travelling abroad found adequate.

When completely free of any parent or father substitute, money was his main concern. He could not, for instance, understand, before setting out for Scotland, why Doxat, the banker in London, had not written to Abraham about money. "I need £30 and was given a letter of credit of £500 for the trip, for five cities," he explained. A receipt was refused by the bank, Felix being told that everything would be arranged with his father. "Please let me know if I should do anything with regard to this matter – and what?" The misunderstanding was caused on account of Felix's proposed visit to Ireland, which did not in fact take place. On arriving in Glasgow at midnight on 11th August, he put his father's mind at rest on financial affairs, despite the late hour: "Expenses have been more moderate than I thought; we have only spent £24 so far..." In Rome, however, he had spent seven florins more than he should have done; "I did not know quite exactly" the amount he was allowed, since he did not have the letter giving such instructions. This was followed by the most meticulous statement of account, which the most pedantic bank official would appreciate. He aimed to make up this deficit during the coming year but, since Felix's allowance was a guide, he hoped his father "will not take my transgression too much amiss". He tried to bear in mind his father's advice: "Not to spend money on anything needlessly, but not to deny myself anything necessary, or important, as far as possible." Yet from Vevey, Switzerland, he was able to write that he hoped to send back 100 thalers "or more" from his travel allowance.

Hensel's assertion that the Mendelssohns were of the "middle class" is borne out by a typical trait into which Felix was conditioned: to be almost ashamed of receiving any gift, money or kind; yet his own generosity compensated for this. When Leipzigerstrasse 3 was purchased, the Mendelssohn Bank was flourishing, despite the failure of various other European finance houses – Reichenbach of Leipzig and Goldschmidt of London, for example. But, in 1830, Leah wrote to Felix in Italy about his father being "weighed down by some kind of grief". He "goes about like a man depressed...gloomy and despondent. Oh God, how happy this man could be and how much happiness he could radiate." Yet "he is eternally in doubt about something deep down in his heart, nor do I know what it is that causes such constant doubt". Werner surmises that this depression arose from his regret at renouncing the Jewish faith. Marek believes that Abraham yearned to be a creative artist, rather than simply a competent banker. Though these conjectures may well be accurate and may help to explain Abraham's gloom, there is a far less complicated explanation. Abraham Mendelssohn realised that he was just as human as anyone else and just as capable of mismanagement; his Hamburg investments were lost and, to make matters worse, it was Leah's precious dowry that had perished with them. Naturally, though she wished her husband would confide in someone as to what was wrong, Leah was the last person who should know what the matter was. Hence Felix's guilt at his travels and his wish to make amends for such "careless rapture". Not only was the money lost, but the rank and status – at least, in Leah's eyes – of which she was so fond and so proud. The Mendelssohns

Chapter 10: That Money Question

not only had to be, but had to be *seen* to be, above such sordid occurrences. Wilfrid Blunt suggests that antidepressant drugs would have helped, had they existed, but to swallow his pride and discuss his feelings with someone suitable would have been a quicker, healthier and longer-lasting remedy for his tale of woe; someone who would not judge or condemn, but accept him as just as susceptible to human pitfalls as anyone else.

If Felix did manage to send back the remains of his travel allowance, he must have been ultra-thrifty in husbanding it. So often are his letters filled with swindling landlords or coachmen that his enjoyment must have been marred, except when staying in private houses, where a consistent sum for board and lodging would have been agreed in advance.

H. E. Jacob gives completely the wrong impression about Mendelssohn: he had "ships waiting for him, letters of introduction from his father" but, above all, "money he did not need to earn", being "heir to a family fortune". Yes, he did have all manner of transport awaiting him, but this was because he was such a careful planner. For this reason, he was able to assure his mother that, should the family accompany him (to Italy, as he had hoped), Felix would be able to organise everything to ease the journey. Yes, letters of introduction were written for him, but only to those people whom Abraham Mendelssohn deemed suitable. And useful contacts were forged through his own gregarious personality and initiative. As for the "large fortune", logic does lead one to assume that, as elder son, Felix would inherit the Mendelssohn money, whereas, in fact, it was Paul who became 'head of the house' after Abraham's death.

Whilst Felix was on his travels there appears no hint of even adequate wherewithal. Salzburg was, to Felix, "a dump" and "a den of ill luck". Having "ruined" two sketches of the Bavarian Alps, which he threw out of the window, he decided to "relax by climbing the Kapuzinerberg", but "that I lost my way can, of course, be assumed"; it rained "frightfully hard", which caused him to run back down the mountain for his umbrella. Wishing to see the cloister nearby he rang the doorbell, only to realise he had run out of money for the guide's gratuity, but, having seen the monk waiting expectantly, "I hastened away". On delivering mail to the post office a whole catalogue of bureaucracy was put into effect, with officials behaving "so insolently". "Hang Salzburg," he growled. He set off for Bad Ischl, where, later, Johann Strauss was to occupy a villa, but Felix could have no horses until he obtained permission from the police; this could not be granted until his passport arrived. Having walked back and forth, he eventually managed to acquire the necessary cash, as he assured his parents that, "all belongings packed; all bills and tips taken care of", he could now travel to Vienna. Though Paul was four years his junior, Felix asked if his brother was familiar with "gold florins, heavy florins, light florins, Vienna florins, standard florins and the devil and his grandmother's florins". It was here that he noticed a carriage the occupants of which he recognised but could not place; he learnt that the lady was the Baroness von Pereira, a relative of his mother, but was too diffident to introduce himself, though she looked at him as if she recognised Leah's elder son. Despite much endeavour he did not manage to see her again and, having been charged one ducat for a night's lodging at an inn, he wrote from Linz: he vowed to put "Ischl, Salzburg and the Pereiras behind me", having "sworn in English and German" at all his concatenation of mishaps.

Felix had wished to take the whole family to Italy, but Leah threw this kindness in her son's face, giving lack of money as her excuse. The real reason, however, was that she loved her home and garden too much to leave it, even for short breaks. Felix's own travel plans were marred by Abraham forbidding him to include Sicily in his Italian itinerary. Both Goethe and Zelter were angered at this intransigent attitude. No one can know now what musical inspiration Felix might have gained from this multicultural island but, to Abraham, the only places conducive to music were Paris and, later, Berlin – and that was that. Though Felix was angered at the embargo placed on his plans, he had been so conditioned into implicit obedience to his parents that he had to resign himself to visiting places that Abraham Mendelssohn approved as eminently respectable and free from bandits.

If only Abraham had known how prosperous Sicily was, and how civilised, compared with the people Felix encountered on the mainland. Whereas at first Felix found the coachman who conveyed him to Florence "almost amiable in his enthusiastic, animal nature", he turned out to be "a most villainous knave, thief and impostor". Felix was so incensed that he refused to pay the fare. In 'the blue city' itself, despite the beautiful scenery and priceless art treasures, his stay was spoilt by "incessant cheating"; neither could he discover why the local people "lied so much". Felix vowed "once for all, invariably", that he would resist every demand on his dwindling money supply, "should I be asked more than I choose to pay". Naples, too, presented a similar environment with suspicion and deceit. The Swiss, who had annoyed his father so much by their cheating, were innocent by comparison. But Felix was still expected invariably to present a well-groomed appearance. Visitors acquainted with the Mendelssohn family had evidently reported to Leah how "shabby" Felix looked, but he assured his mother that, whilst "dishevelled on the outside, I am black on the inside" – like a well-managed bank account. His evident lack of perfect grooming was apparent from an answer to Rebecka, that it would be a good idea were she to embroider some braces, his others having become "long since crippled, so please send me some". When writing a letter home from Vevey of 18th August, promising such largesse from his travel allowance, he guessed the reason for his father's depression: "Now I almost have to fear that, when all is said and done… Is there just a little less in the old iron chest [and wonder] whether you have had to curtail anything in your life… If so, it would be my bounden duty not just to put aside for myself and my family, but as a family obligation… I imagine to myself our parents do not perhaps let me know anything, on account of the lovely trip I am having."

During the last few years of Abraham's life his attitude towards Felix mellowed

Chapter 10: That Money Question

considerably. He evidently realised that the Mendelssohn family's financial embarrassment was alleviated by his elder son adopting the "immoral profession" of music, as described by Jakob Bartholdy.

The myth of Felix Mendelssohn's Croesus-like wealth may well have been perpetuated because of his lifelong ability to manage money. Unlike many in the arts, he was not a spendthrift; neither did he indulge in habits that drained his finances. Meticulous planning became a lifelong habit, ensuring that he always had enough money to survive in any situation. In 1830, en route to visit Goethe in Weimar for the last time, he was able to write from Leipzig that he had sold two string quartets: one to Marschner, who introduced him to Breitkopf & Härtel; the other to Hofmeister, who showed interest in "all the piano music I could give him". The relevant document was tactfully signed 'Felix Mendelssohn Bartholdy', in order not to antagonise his father, with whom he had had a disagreement about the addition of this name to that of Mendelssohn. The same mode of signature appeared on documents that Paul would oversee when he looked after Felix's finances. Interestingly, however, the family bank was invariably known as Mendelssohn & Company, proving that Joseph's influence triumphed in this regard. Felix learnt that not even his father's letters of introduction carried weight in some quarters and that it was his own endeavours that would allow him to thrive financially. From Venice he wrote home on 15th February 1831 that a bank "not only refused to give me any money but appeared to regard my letter as forged".

During the days before Baron von Pereira vouched for his creditworthiness, Felix and a "Herr Sternfeldt" ran around to "several other bankers, who were, unfortunately, even less polite – and it was only a matter of 100 florins – and I had to write to Eskeles to have them sent… Had Sternfeldt not given me the money, I would not have been able to do anything. An honest face gets one nowhere in Venice." Neither, it appears, did the hallowed name of Mendelssohn. As well as money for subsistence, Felix had to pay 50 scudi for a concert organised by the Duchess of Dessau with which Ambassador Bunsen would have nothing to do. "Since it is unpleasant to receive such a negative response" from the Prussian ambassador in Rome, Felix paid the full amount – 104 florins, 12 xaviers – required by the Valentine Bank in Augsburg. He asked his father to deal with the relevant transaction "by freight or whatever works best", giving his usual statement of account so that no misunderstanding could occur between father and son. From Paris he wrote to Breitkopf & Härtel on 19th April 1832, asking them to await instructions for the piano arrangements for his *Midsummer Night's Dream* Overture and the String Octet. He would send the necessary documentation from London, asking the publishers to send the copies and honorarium to his father, "A. Mendelssohn Bartholdy", rather than to Felix himself. He had to remind his father that the honorarium relating to Hofmeister's copyists remained unpaid; "as for the Duchess of Dessau, she has been kept meticulously up to date and I hope she will reimburse you as meticulously."

Even when independent of his parents, Felix felt the need to seek permission to buy anything out of the ordinary. From Düsseldorf, for instance, he asked if he might buy a horse, if Abraham did not think this purchase "too genteel" for someone as old as himself – 24.

During the same period he asked his father to send the "certified invoices" for the repair of his carriage, which had lost a wheel. He also mentioned having to borrow fifty florins from his Uncle Joseph at Horchheim, in order not to wait to pay his saddler; he asked if the sum could be reimbursed when Joseph Mendelssohn arrived in Berlin "next Monday". Felix could thus complete the details of his "complicated travel finances" to everyone's satisfaction. On 10th September 1835 he wrote as having "happily hereupon delivered myself of my letter to Hermann, [having] fulfilled my obligations, and the matter is now taken care of". Again: "I enclose three pretty announcements for the Anthology; the two together appeared in yesterday's paper here, which I bought for that reason. It cost one penny and that much the advertisements are worth; the other one I had given to me. I hope they are respectable." He asked his father, on a further occasion, to deposit £16 "or a little more, in English money", into his account. Felix also asked for a letter of credit to the bank of Woldemar Frege, with whom he had been advised to become a customer whilst in Leipzig. "Provided," he added, "that they are not more expensive than others." The letter should be sent "very soon since, having paid the rent in advance, I have only 15 thalers left, which will soon evaporate into necessities – boots, trousers, etc. I took my latchkey with me by mistake, but entrusted it to Eduard Magnus, who passed through here yesterday... I hope he will deliver it to you in good order. Whilst reminiscing about old times, he told me some stories of Paris and London that I found interesting." Evidently he did bank with Frege, whose family became friends, asking how much money Felix owed him: "It really must be put right, otherwise you will vow never to travel with musicians again, thinking them incorrigible." Felix wanted his mind to be put at rest before "they both forget about the matter" of this transaction.

Fanny, too, had inherited her parents' attitude towards money. From Paris she assured her father that the Hensels had only enough to last the month and that, since her husband's "last attack" of fever, he was less mobile than usual, so there were fewer opportunities for sightseeing. Friends had suggested that Hensel should remain *in situ* for a year in order to exhibit his work but this would be impossible. However, the fact that the Hensels were in Paris should speak for itself, and Abraham was mistaken if he thought they would not do justice to the city he loved best. Later, from Berlin, she wrote to Rebecka that her feet were soaked when walking from place to place in the rain, yet she believed it extravagant to purchase a carriage. It was "not the will of Providence", as Abraham would say. She found it "quite abominable" the way money disappeared without trace and without having anything to show for spending it. "I hope I shall not be the only member of the family who gambles", as she called spending money – being harsh with herself – and she aimed to "put a stop to this from today onwards".

On 12th March 1835, the year when Abraham died, Fanny Horsley wrote to her aunt about Felix. "At 30 [he was, in fact, 26 at the time] he must be quite the little Croesus, with private property and all", added to which, as elder son, he would be bound to inherit the "mighty fortune" that everyone claimed to exist. But all he owned was remuneration for his work, renting accommodation until he married. Joseph's eldest son Alexander Mendelssohn oversaw the family bank; Paul looked after the private assets, including Felix's financial affairs. It would appear that Felix found nothing but relief at this arrangement, as he disliked writing letters dealing with money, as uncompleted drafts reveal. He even stated to a court official how he "cursed these diplomatic letters". In a letter to Klingemann Fanny seems to have taken as a matter of course Paul's responsibility: "Paul, as head of the house, carefully supervises the affairs of the family." Yet Paul's acquisitive nature appears to have triumphed over his benevolence. In 1844, for instance, a portrait of Felix that Hensel had painted from an earlier engraving was to be purchased by Count Lvov, whose claim to fame was as composer of the tsarist national anthem. "When the painting turned out so well, Paul Mendelssohn seized upon it," the usually sycophantic Sebastian Hensel wrote in his memoirs. Neither did he leave the matter there: "The family was by nature predatory, manipulative or negative-minded." It is this rare glimpse into the Mendelssohn psyche that causes researchers to wonder why such a dearth of information is given about Paul. The part he played in the family saga may well have been censored by later chroniclers, along with much else.

Felix was "imposed upon", as Elvers expresses it, when the family took advantage of the contacts he had made through his own initiative, for them to acquire more than two dozen pianos. Aloys Fuchs in Vienna proved invaluable in his assistance. Constantly, in Hanslick's compilation of the Fuchs-Mendelssohn correspondence, precise instructions were given about quality and price of instruments, chiefly manufactured by Graf or Streicher. He wrote of one, delivered to Leipzigerstrasse 3: "The piano is quite outstanding and created the greatest possible pleasure to the whole house. It was exceptionally clear and distinct and tuneful yesterday and came across splendidly against the orchestra, to the appreciation of all" at what must have been a Sunday concert. From Düsseldorf Mendelssohn ordered a further Graf piano, on which he "cannot spend more than 300 florins". The piano Paul asked him to acquire as a wedding present for his bride, Albertine Heine, was to be "very, very beautiful, the exterior in mahogany", but without the usual brass embellishments. However, since the instrument cost 450 florins, plus freight charges, further negotiations had to take place before the asking price was finally paid. On 25th November 1833 Felix wrote to his cousin Benjamin Mendelssohn at the University of Bonn regarding a further piano purchased on his behalf. Benjamin was informed that on 6th December Conrad

Graf would ship the instrument from Vienna, which would take between 36 and 38 days to reach Bonn. "Next to the dampers it carries the words, in my handwriting: 'Chosen for Herr Felix Mendelssohn Bartholdy by Aloys Fuchs'." The piano was selected from the best Graf could supply at the time, for "Fuchs places no small store by your approval and thus took great pains to satisfy your wishes". More likely it was Felix's name that carried weight with Fuchs. When Felix visited his cousin at Christmas and played the instrument, he wrote home that "I could hardly tear myself away from it, running and rambling all over it". As in earlier transactions, no invoice was available from Arnstein & Eskeles, so this had to be investigated by Felix.

The impression of opulence may have arisen from such visitors as the theologian Julius Schubring, recommended by a letter of introduction from F. Max Müller at the University of Leipzig, who had spent some "very pleasant weeks" in Berlin and had spoken of the Mendelssohns' "extraordinarily hospitable spirit". When, therefore, Schubring studied theology under Schleiermacher in Berlin, he may well have had his view confirmed through memories of the Mendelssohns' salons. Schubring reported life at Leipzigerstrasse 3 as "brilliantly intellectual", the family "richly endowed with every kind of natural gift, as they were bountifully provided with earthly riches to a man such as myself". Müller, too, related that he "could not help receiving more than I could give". Either these guests were in awe of the luxurious surroundings of the Mendelssohn mansion, or Leah set out to impress and put on a far better show than when Devrient visited. The Mendelssohns were "harmoniously united in each other by unusual warmth of affection and congeniality of character and produced a most pleasing impression on everyone who visited their house". Evidently the acrimony between Felix and his father was hidden from anyone but the most perceptive guests. But one aspect was true to reality. The Mendelssohn family "felt little inclination to go out, being most partial, after the labours of the day, to spend the evenings in familiar fellowship with one another. Science, art and literature were equally represented" among their circle, but no mention was made of music.

Undoubtedly, Mendelssohn enjoyed himself immensely at social gatherings, but his dearest pleasure was simply to associate with friends and loved ones, either as a bachelor or, from 1837, as husband and, later, father. He wrote from Bad Soden in 1844 of his joy at "leading a very quiet life" and his increasing horror of "aristocratic acquaintances". What pleasure he found in no longer having to concern himself with "dress clothes, visiting cards, carriage [or] horses, but simply eating, sleeping, music paper and sketchbooks". The phrase "aristocratic acquaintances" may well be a misleading translation of what Felix really meant – social climbers and people with pretensions to be lions of society. Anyone who did not need to put on a show was unwaveringly admired by Mendelssohn. When visiting the Frankfurt branch of the Rothschild family, by invitation, he wrote to his family that, irrespective of the "splendid luxury" of their mansion, the

Chapter 10: That Money Question

Rothschilds applied themselves to the good of humanity that even the Philistines respect, "though they would gladly give them a good thrashing if let loose". To Felix, however, the Rothschilds' wealth was nothing but "a source of exhilaration". Nathan Rothschild, of the London branch of this remarkable family, was later to declare: "People need not praise us for our efficiency; it is this that made our money... He who can do the job better, and quicker, and more thoroughly than the next man, will always be beforehand with the world." Had Felix Mendelssohn's personality been less modest and self-effacing, such a maxim would have been apt for him to utter about himself.

Chapter 11

'Glory to God Alone'

From an early stage in his career as a composer Mendelssohn not only stated the date and place of a work, but, often, various groups of initials appeared on his compositions – 'H. D. M.', 'L. E. G. G.', or 'S. D. G.'. His parents regarded them as "mere ciphers" and not even his own children could interpret their meaning, yet compilers of memoirs and later biographers have deduced what these letters could mean. Schubring claims that 'H. D. M.' represented the German 'Hilf du mir' – 'Help thou me', a prayer to God for succour towards his music. 'L. E. G. G.' Marek interprets as meaning 'Lass es gelegen, Gott' – 'Let it succeed, God'. 'S. D. G.' – 'Soli Deo gloria' – is the Latin for the words that head this chapter. Marek claims Felix Mendelssohn's interest in religion was applied solely to the composition of oratorio and that "he was not pious". As with many statements the author propounds in his biography, *Gentle Genius*, this assertion can be completely disproved.

The poet and pamphleteer Heinrich Heine declared that many Jews converted to the Christian faith in order to obtain "an admission ticket to European culture". This cynical, yet realistic, assertion may well have applied in many instances and, indeed, some biographers suggest that, had the Mendelssohn family remained Jews, a far greater struggle would have arisen when pursuing their intellectual and cultural interests. But this overlooks the fine example of Moses Mendelssohn, who, though becoming an internationally respected man of letters and a philosopher, remained a Jew, yet brought his religion into the modern era. It was, in fact, as with many other matters, the bullying of Jakob Bartholdy that caused Abraham to have his children baptised as Lutherans. This occurred at the New Church, Berlin, on 21st March 1816, and, in view of Leah's obsession with Bach's music, the date could have been more than coincidence, being that composer's birthday. It was not until 1822 that Leah and Abraham adopted the new faith, Leah choosing the baptismal names Felicia and Paulina, the feminine equivalents of Felix and Paul. For the older children, at least, life must have become confused until the parents lived by the same rules and observances as they had been forced to follow, without an explanation.

It is fascinating to chart the pattern of behaviour inculcated by Abraham towards his children. In a postscript from Weimar, he wrote to Leah that Felix had gone to church, having not realised that the mail was due for collection; "I am finishing this for him," Abraham explained, signing himself, with no terms of endearment or affection, "Abraham Mendelssohn Bartholdy". In a letter to Fanny at her confirmation in 1818, he gave a sermon with a far more ponderous message than any she would have received from the pastor who prepared her for the ceremony. Fanny had to be "faithful, true, good, obedient, unremittingly attentive to the voice of your conscience. These [are] truths on which one's happiness depends, and I cherish a childlike faith that...fortified by this firm belief...I believe that anyone else will find the instruction and conviction to obey these tenets who seeks them with open eyes and does not voluntarily shun the light". When discussing in detail his own beliefs, Abraham admitted that he adhered to his old faith – "my Jewish unbelief", as he called it. "By pronouncing your confession of faith, you have fulfilled the claims of society and obtained the name of a Christian," Abraham exhorted Fanny. Though there were many things Abraham did not understand about religion, he believed that one should strive towards "the good, the true and the just", but, had he practised what he preached, the family would have never renounced their original faith, selling their souls to the acquisition of worldly glory and the appeasement of Jakob Bartholdy. It seems that it was of far greater importance to the Mendelssohn parents that their children gave obedience to their earthly father than to their creator.

To Felix, his father fulminated on another matter – that of his name. The musicologist Michael Steinberg sees the addition of 'Bartholdy' to the family name as a continuation of the assimilation into German life that Moses undertook, but this hypothesis is too simplistic. Moses had felt no shame – indeed, he felt proud – to remain a Jew, but the name 'Bartholdy' confirmed Abraham's adoption of Christianity. The children were troubled by the connotations implied by the new name, indicating worldly status, as opposed to the spiritual and intellectual status sought by their grandfather. Whereas artists, writers and musicians of the romantic school imagined 'Doppelgänger' or 'dual personality' figures, it can be stated that Felix was given a real one – 'Bartholdy'. This harsh, strident sound represented the money and rank that, through Abraham and later Paul, he was compelled to adopt, contrasted with the peace-loving, euphonious, contented 'Mendelssohn' character, pursuing his own path of composition. The 'Bartholdy' part of him was weighed down with duty and obedience to the demands made upon him to conduct, direct and administer tedious commitments for others. Abraham had no such perception of his son's true nature. In 1826 he had had some visiting cards printed with the name 'Felix M. Bartholdy', which his son refused. This must have angered and hurt the father, as such arrant disobedience was not forgotten.

On 8th July 1829 he wrote to Felix, then in London, informing his son that he had either "suppressed or neglected, or allowed others to suppress or neglect" the name of 'Bartholdy' from newspaper cuttings or concert programmes that the son must have sent home in pride. If Felix was to blame, "a great wrong" had been committed, with which his father was "greatly dissatisfied". Since 'Mendelssohn-Bartholdy' was too cumbersome, his recalcitrant son must use the new name. "You cannot – you must not – carry the name Mendelssohn. There can no more be a Protestant Mendelssohn than there can be a Jewish Confucius. If Felix's name is Mendelssohn, then he must be a Jew, which is contrary to fact." "Dear Felix," he pleaded, "take this to heart and act accordingly," signing himself "your father and friend".

In reply, Felix assured his father that he always tried to obey his "commands and precepts", but, if he had not, his lapse was only through carelessness, not realising that his father wished the original family name to be shelved. He had known nothing about the particular article that had upset his father so much, as it had been written a fortnight before he had arrived in London. In Britain, he was invariably addressed as 'Herr Mendelssohn', since he was linked with his grandfather, who was still highly respected there, anglicising the name as 'Mendelson', making it easier to understand and to pronounce. Thus, the British "would take any change ill. I beg you, my dear father, not to be angry with me," he continued. "The thing is done and no longer to be changed." His father pontificated that "a name must, like a garment, be appropriate for the time, place and rank" of whoever possessed it, "if it is not to become a hindrance and a laughing stock". Had Abraham realised the fact, the name Mendelssohn would shine like a beacon, throughout time, on account of its intellectual and spiritual import. J. Cuthbert Hadden reinforces this point: the name 'Mendelssohn' does not belong to Judaism, it belongs to the world, whereas the name 'Bartholdy' carries no weight.

In whatever way cynics view Mendelssohn's "piety", the fact remains that his sense of religion was woven into his whole being and into everything he did. Julius Schubring recalled what a deep feeling for religion he gleaned from his friend as each would argue the merits of his 'pet' theologian's sermons – Schubring supporting Schleiermacher, his university professor; Felix taking the side of Wilhelmssen, by whom he had been confirmed. When Schubring suggested that he would have preferred Schleiermacher to undertake Felix's instruction, Mendelssohn would have nothing said against Wilhelmssen as a mentor. He held him in "affectionate reverence", though, as far as Schubring was aware, after his confirmation on 27th September 1825 Felix did not often hear Wilhelmssen preach. Perhaps he did not feel the need for conventional sermons, gaining greater spiritual comfort from art, which he regarded as a sacred duty. According to Schubring: "Religion and veneration were enthroned in his conscience, which was why his music possessed such a magic charm."

Later, when the time came for the Hensels' son Sebastian to be confirmed, Fanny wrote to Rebecka regarding the most suitable pastor to prepare him for the ceremony. Having interviewed many clergymen, she had chosen Pastor Eysenhart – "a simple, kind, earnest man, without a trace of affectation" – for their son's instruction. Hensel, Fanny explained, left the final decision to Sebastian's mother as to who was to fulfil this role. On 10th April 1845 Felix asked Paul if he had heard Ronge preach. "Since I have read his 'Vindication', I have not the slightest regard for his character, his knowledge of art or of mankind in general." In the same letter he asked his brother if Tieck's novel *Eigensinn und Laune* had been read. Felix called this story "boring and lascivious, outdoing everything" in such a category of fiction. These two instances, juxtaposed in one letter, illustrate how highly Felix prized the love of good art above the organised rituals so often cluttering religion. With such "evil and wickedness", he felt the need to "crawl back behind the shelter of one's own four walls in order to improve one's own creativity to the glory of God". Writing in the subsequent year to Pastor Bauer regarding a book of Church history, Felix explained that, as a layman, his only view was that "the older I grow...more than ever it is the duty of everyone to be very industrious in one's own sphere and to concentrate all one's energies in accomplishing the very best of which one is capable…".

The Mendelssohn children were not averse to poking gentle fun at religious rituals, as can be seen throughout their correspondence. Felix disparaged the trend, then fashionable, "to consider 'piety' and 'dullness' synonymous". He wrote from Rome that the German clergy who had settled there "preach such fanaticism, credible in the 16th century, but quite monstrous in the present day. They all wish to make converts and abuse one another in a Christian manner, each ridiculing the beliefs of his neighbour; it is quite too sad to hear them, as if to have simplicity and to be simple were the same thing. But I am soaring too high and my father will lecture me."

Later, in 1838, in response to Professor Schirmer's implication that Mendelssohn was a saint, he stated that, though he tried to live like one, he was "not a pietist". He hoped "never to become one as long as I live", though he did "aim to live piously". He did not wish to live like "people who possess everything the world holds dear, without deriving one moment of real pleasure". He had first discovered such people in Paris. Although he enjoyed paintings by "good" artists in France, he could not believe in the sincerity of anyone who fell into ecstasies about them, whilst presuming to look down on one of Horace Vernet's paintings. In 1845, writing to Rebecka in Italy, he could not get on with 'X', whom he had met three times during the previous winter, "even with the best will on my side". Anyone who, like 'X', involved himself with the religious squabbles so prevalent at that time was liable to sever himself from former friends. "In my innermost heart, I feel uncertain as to which extreme is the most repugnant...and...cannot clearly decide between them." These theological disputes caused such as 'X' to have become "quite unsociable". Fanny was equally facetious about religious rituals. Writing to Rebecka, she related that a diplomat, Count Pourtales, had arrived with his entourage, one of whom had been recommended by a priest to ask Hensel to hear his confession. But Fanny's husband declined to fulfil this role, because he did not wish to be silent at the gathering, yet he perceived that speaking would involve him in breaking the confidentiality so important to the confessional. In any case, since the man did not understand German, his confession would have to have been translated into French. Nevertheless, Hensel toasted the company "in character with his new dignity".

Though Mendelssohn's first biographer, W. A. Lampadius, stated in 1849 that his subject was a devout Lutheran, to be followed by subsequent authors, this is only partially true. Though he set Martin Luther's prayer, 'Grant us Peace' (Op. 94) "with great vigour but with as great sweetness", H. E. Jacob maintains that Mendelssohn was receptive to the best in many faiths and denominations. From Edinburgh, Felix wrote in 1829 that the women he had met were so "worthy of note" that, if an acquaintance named Mahmood took Abraham's advice and became a Christian, Felix would "compensate for him and become a Moslem" so that he could marry all these beautiful women which Islam would permit. Though this was frivolous, Mendelssohn did follow non-Protestant religions very seriously, as is seen by his wholehearted interest in Rosen's work on the Rig Vedas; his translation of the Hindu sacred hymns which was left unfinished at his early death, but was completed by Müller.

Throughout his life, Mendelssohn was influenced more than his parents would have cared to admit by the Church of Rome. His favourite aunts, Dorothea and 'Jette', had become Catholic and his sacred music indicated his fascination for that creed. H. E. Jacob considers his choral music to have "a curiously Catholic cast". Dorn states that the setting of Ave Maria composed in Rome speaks so convincingly of the Virgin Mary's sanctity that anyone could be converted as a result of hearing the work. At Christmas 1827 Fanny wrote to Klingemann that her brother had composed a 19-part motet, *Tu es Petrus*, for her birthday. This should only be sung, Fanny considered, "in a grand church and to be performed only in the best conditions". From what Felix had said, acquaintances wondered if he were veering towards the Catholic faith. Fanny had feared that this would become 'town talk', but, fortunately, that did not happen. So popular did his motets become that not even Felix's detractors were able to have them removed from church services. Even in Nonconformist churches in Britain, choirs were able to give fine performances of Mendelssohn's motets as anthems, until the fashion changed. It is interesting to note, nevertheless, that Mendelssohn received greater remuneration for his secular than for his sacred music. From a collection of letters auctioned at Sotheby's in 1996 one learns that, for his 2nd Piano Concerto (Op. 40), Felix received £42 from Novello's but, by contrast, his Prayer for choir and orchestra sold for five guineas and his setting of Psalm 114 for 15 guineas. But, evidently, such discrepancies in fees did not trouble the composer. He confessed that, to him, neither sacred nor secular music ranked more highly than each other, "because every kind of music ought, in its own particular way, to tend to the glory of God".

Whilst Felix revered the spiritual teaching of the Roman Catholic faith, he had "never any intention" of converting. He had "harsh words to say about anyone – such as the people of Rome – who desecrate any of the ceremonies and functions of the Church of Rome". He saw a portion of Raphael's *Loggia* scratched away with unspeakable vulgarity to make room for pencilled inscriptions. "The whole base of the climbing arabesques is completely destroyed, because Italians have carved their miserable names with knives – God knows how. I saw 'Christ' scrawled beneath the Apollo of Belvedere" – in blasphemy, it is assumed, rather than any sacred connotation. He went on: "Right in the middle of Michelangelo's *Last Judgement* an altar has been erected, so large that it obscures the very centre of the picture, and it ruins the whole... Cattle are driven through the wonderful rooms of the Villa Madama, where Guilio Romano painted the frescoes, and where hay is stored. The people are indifferent and it must grieve these artists more than awful music grieves me; it is no wonder they take no pleasure in art; their spirit has probably been besieged and destroyed. They have a pope and a government, but make fun of them. They have a splendidly beautiful history, but pay no attention to it... The merriment witnessed at burial ceremonies is horrible. As the pope's coffin lay in state, the priests whispered amongst themselves and, even worse, laughed aloud. There is constant hammering on the scaffolding around the catafalque whilst masses are said for the deceased pope's soul, so that everything is drowned by the echoes from the axes and the noise made by the workmen, so that the services cannot be heard at all. As soon as the cardinals enter the conclave, satires are brought out against them. The litany is parodied but, rather than name a sin, they perform a whole opera of the cardinals' qualities in order to ridicule them. One is amorous; one a tyrant; another, a lamp-lighter. At least, in the past, the people believed in their art, their religion or their government but, nowadays, how can they be rejuvenated by art if this attitude is allowed to persist?" One thing pleased Felix: no one could spoil the winter sun, the hills or the scenery. These brought Felix far closer to the spiritual world than any human rituals, of whatever faith. His love of all things natural was borne out by a letter to his childhood friend Julius Schubring, written from Düsseldorf. He described how priests who preach "in the Elbefeld style" depressed him. They were "such disgraceful specimens in their attitude to life. They pour salt on every joy experienced by themselves and others." He called them "prosaic fault finders who think of a concert as sinful; a stroll as disturbing and pernicious; a theatre as...a sink of corruption; and the whole of spring, with its tree blossoms and its beautiful weather, as a 'Slough of Despond'." Felix may well have been reminded of an earlier occasion when, as a boy of 15, he visited the cathedral at the Baltic resort of Bad Doberan. He had written to Zelter: "After the psalms came the sermon... When he [the preacher] spoke of, say, Paradise, he practically roared, stamped his feet and beat his hands against the pulpit. By contrast, when he informed the sinners of their eternal torment, he spoke in a very soft, gentle voice." To Mendelssohn the traditions of orthodox worship were superfluous; the behaviour of many of its exponents, a sham. For anyone who had not yet come to know their creator, he could easily write a treatise on the beauty of nature to prove God's existence. The same applied to beautiful music and works of art. The provenance or purpose of a piece of music was irrelevant; all that mattered was that such composers as Lassus, Palestrina or Pergolesi gave of their best in creating the sacred piece. As for Raphael, Felix felt so drawn to him, through his paintings, that he felt able to converse with and feel affection for the artist. Particularly did he write of *The Assumption* and *The Entombment*, which he saw in Italy. Raphael must have had "such a devout, faithful and pious spirit... He knew the deepest sorrow, as well as experiencing the joys of Heaven." This could be seen from the way in which the Virgin Mary appeared as "floating on the cloud... One sees at a glance her very breathing; her awe and piety." The three angels at the right of the painting symbolised "pure, serene loveliness...the highest order of beauty". In *The Entombment*, Mendelssohn noticed how Mary Magdalene seemed to be supporting the mother of Jesus, "for fear she must die of anguish... She endeavours to lead her away, but looks round once more, evidently wishing to imprint this experience indelibly in her heart. It surpasses everything." He observed how "John suffers and sympathises with Mary"; how Joseph of Arimathea, "absorbed...in his occupation with the tomb, controls and directs the whole procedure"; how Christ himself is "lying there so tranquil, having endured to the end". Everything in the paintings "speaks to my heart and will never leave my memory". Yet he found words "more and more poor and commonplace" to describe "the thousand feelings that emanate from Raphael's work". Such an experience was not new. The previous year, 1829, in London, on seeing Titian's painting of St Ignatius Loyola at the Earl of Grosvenor's gallery (then a private collection), Felix had felt "quite Catholic", comparing the paintings with the Jews in a work by Rubens, who "looked like bears or wolves let loose".

But, despite such rapture over religious paintings, Felix, Fanny and Rebecka all gave candid opinions on the various ceremonies in Italy. When Elgar and his wife visited Rome in 1909, that composer expressed disappointment on hearing the Papal Choir from the Sistine Chapel. Fanny also, herself no mean singer, found the choir's performance "incorrect and indifferent" and viewed with disdain the way in which Mass was chanted by "the old, quavering cardinals". But, as it was a duty incumbent on the tourist, Fanny meant to observe as much of the ceremonial as possible. This was undertaken so diligently that she even attended the Armenian Orthodox church, where the music "sounded like cats".

On 2nd May Fanny attended the Greek Orthodox church for their Easter celebration, 14 days after the western Christian services had taken place. Expecting the singing to resemble that of the Armenian choir, Fanny was pleasantly surprised how "firmly and correctly" the singers performed, "fuller in tone and better in style" than the more celebrated choirs in Rome. She was particularly impressed by a three-part motet for two basses and tenor, considering it "a properly constructed composition". On the 28th, Ascension Day, the Hensels visited the Church of St John Lateran, which Fanny preferred, on account of its surroundings, to St Peter's. During the pope's benediction, Hensel mingled with the crowds in the piazza to sketch. Some peasant women recognised him from his earlier residence in Rome, to whom he gave money in exchange for their permission to draw their heads; this reminded Fanny of "a scene from the Classics". Later, the artist Elsasser gave the Hensels a sketch of the Protestant church.

Unlike Fanny, Felix had praised the Papal Choir, observing that a plainchant reminded him of Bach's B minor Mass. In fact, he had hoped to report to Zelter in a manner showing "cool and close attention" to the music, but was too overwhelmed by "sensations of reverence and piety" to be able to do so. He explained that the 15 lights around the altar signified the 12 apostles, plus the three Marys – Mary Magdalene; Mary, wife of Cleopas; and Mary the mother of Jesus – who all play a part in the Easter festival. Three psalms were sung to represent the 'three laws' – the law of nature; the Holy Scriptures; and the Gospels.

When, later, Rebecka sought her brother's advice about Holy Week, he recommended her attending the services on Wednesday, Thursday and Friday, but not to be too discouraged by the "inexpressible dullness of the innumerable psalms that they recite so abominably". A service book could be obtained anywhere, and read to follow the ceremonies, "even reading only halfway through, or not much more". Rebecka was less fatigued than anticipated, "thank Providence", when she did take part in the services. She had found the feet-washing ceremony "unpleasant", but her elder son, Walter, entered into every detail "with gusto". On one occasion, when the Sistine Chapel was not yet open, the family rested in a nearby café, but Rebecka complained about the ill manners of the other customers. During the actual service, Rebecka found the Lamentations "exquisite", though Baini's Miserere was "less impressive than that of Allegri". Though Felix's description and that in her travel guide caused Rebecka to be "moved to tears by the silent paternoster", it was not silent at all when she heard it live, "what with the coughing, blowing of noses, scraping of feet and the chattering of the Inglesi, the ceremony resembled some comedy staged to amuse the tourists". The Improperia of Palestrina reminded Rebecka of Johann Fasch's sacred music, composed 150 years later. On the recommendation of the artist Delaroche, the Dirichlet family attended Mass on Easter Saturday to hear Palestrina's setting of the service for that day. On the Sunday they attended the pope's benediction and, in the evening, took Walter to see 'the Familia', which, with the gold in the church so brilliantly illuminated, reminded Rebecka of a scene from *The Arabian Nights' Entertainment*.

At the end of 1830 Mendelssohn had written in disgust at the behaviour of the populace during the illness of Pope Paul VIII. "The pope is dying, or possibly dead by this time. 'We shall soon get a new one,' say the Italians cruelly. His death will

Chapter 11: 'Glory to God Alone'

not affect the Carnival [in February], nor the Church festivals, with their pomp and processions and fine music. They care little, provided the pope's death does not take place in February." In fact, the pope died on 1st December, to be succeeded by Gregory XVI, the festival for his enthronement ending on the day before Felix's birthday. But this was not the last to be heard of the pope. The Dirichlet family arrived in Rome on All Saints' Day, 1st November 1844. Rebecka not only observed smartly dressed people coming from church, but "castles, aqueducts, churches built on the ruins of former temples and cottages containing the fragments of former magnificence. How strange it is," she continued, "that…may be dining with the pope." Not only is it not known to whom Rebecka's ellipsis refers; neither can it be discovered what the reason was for Dirichlet's invitation to dine at the Vatican and to "kiss the pope's slipper", as Felix stated. Rebecka reported that the pontiff "had greater knowledge than Lady Summerville about mathematics and mathematicians. It must have been a sight to see Dirichlet kissing the pope's toe and Jacobi, a heretic, kissing his hand." Felix warned his sister not to divulge the satirical remarks that passed between his sisters and himself about religious ceremonies in Rome, now that Dirichlet had enhanced his family's reputation by his audience at the Vatican; otherwise such glory would be spoilt completely. Rebecka showed lapses in her religious obligation by missing the Mass on Christmas Eve as it began too late for her; neither did she attend the service on Christmas Morning, because that was too early. She would, though, hear a famous Italian preacher give a sermon at the Feast of Epiphany, whilst her husband would attend "the babel of languages" that she called the pope's blessing.

In the Church of San Lorenzo in Florence, Rebecka had been "disturbed" to hear dance music played during the service. Assisi she described as "an ultra-Catholic town". She discovered a cobbler's stall beside a chapel, together with a temple to Mithras, as in Goethe's time. Walter asked if the family could visit the Church of Santa Maria degli Angeli, which appeared "so new-fashioned" with a print by Overbrecht. Rebecka found the Church of St Francis "so ancient and so dismal" when they heard Mass; bells from neighbouring churches rang in different keys whilst, outside, beggars "in cloaks of rags stitched together as if of the royal purple" accosted the tourists, "for the souls in purgatory". The cathedral "had been built before architecture was invented". The people of Assisi appear to think no more of the pope than did the Dirichlets' cook; they were equally fearless of denigrating the government. Had the family bought as many religious pictures as they would have liked, Rebecka would have been laughed at, though Walter had been given a picture of the Madonna on a gold background. It is evident that, by the time their holiday had finished, Rebecka had had enough of Italian religion. Rome's churches were, for instance, the least of that city's attractions and she had "become sick of the colours and dress of the ceremonial". She had not realised how "strong" her Lutheran blood was – "and this I will guard".

But Felix's private spiritual life was far more ambivalent. Writing in response to

Rebecka's advice on what to do during Holy Week, whilst visiting Italy in 1844, he added a most interesting remark that gives a clue to his feelings. If she had not already done so, his sister should be sure to see the dancer Mme. Cerrito as often as possible. He then compared the often dull, morose way religious festivals were conducted with the spontaneous merrymaking observed on Jews' sacred occasions – forgetting, in his enthusiasm, that Holy Week is a sombre occasion. He wrote to Zelter that the Papal Choir was "too much for a Lutheran upbringing, superimposed by a Jewish mentality, born of Jewish parents and rooted in Jewish culture" (however strenuously his parents denied the fact, which they endeavoured to forget). In 1819 a spate of looting had taken place from the homes of newly emancipated Jews. Known as the 'Judensturm' (the 'Jews' struggle'), students in the streets of Berlin accompanied the looting with shouts of "Hep, Hep" – short for the Latin 'Hierusalym est perdita' ('Jerusalem is lost'). Even a member of the royal house took up this cry, with the additional catcall of 'Jew-boy', spitting at the feet of 10-year-old Felix. A few years later, whilst staying at the Baltic resort of Rostock, he and Fanny had stones thrown at them, with similar name-calling. Having rescued his sister, he shut himself away and wept. Not only must he have felt mortified but, even more, confused. What was so shameful about being a Jew, in view of his wise grandfather, Moses Mendelssohn, who had done so much to foster human understanding and to bring Judaism into the age of enlightenment? Why was it so important for his parents to baptise their children into the Christian faith, merely because 'Uncle Bartholdy' had dictated this step? Why had his parents' own baptism been kept such a secret? Felix had inherited his grandfather's ability to think about such matters, far in advance of his 15 years, so it is quite in order to assume that such questions would have occurred to him. Kupferberg states that, had the choice been his, as to whether he became a Christian or remained a Jew, Felix would have chosen the latter course, but, in view of his parents' unswerving insistence on obedience to their dictates and their evident fear of Leah's brother Jakob Bartholdy, this can only be a matter of conjecture, as such freedom was never allowed. The subject was 'taboo' in any case amongst the newly emancipated Jews of Germany as to their religious preference. This was borne out when Wagner became amazed at the publisher Schlesinger's openness on the subject, saying he had become a Christian on account of his wife's wholehearted commitment to that creed. Schlesinger explained that, in Germany, the subject was "anxiously avoided" for fear of causing offence to anyone unsure of their new religious lifestyle, who may have regretted the step they had taken.

But, despite this prohibition, Felix felt able to mention various matters connected with Judaism in his correspondence. From Weimar, on 20th November 1821, he used the Yiddish phrase 'eppes rares' – 'something rare' – to describe Goethe's flirtation with Ulrike von Pogwisch, younger sister of the poet's daughter-in-law Ottilie. Whilst Felix was in London in 1829, Rebecka had written that a distant relative of their grandfather, a Herr Dessauer, who had visited the

Chapter 11: 'Glory to God Alone'

Mendelssohn home, was "too much", though she was "not a Jew-baiter". In reply, her brother asked what she meant by such an expression, reminding her that, however uncultured, their relative was of their kin. As for the name 'Bartholdy', Rebecka disliked it as much as Felix, invariably signing herself, until she married, 'Rebecka Mendelssohn Bartholdy never'. However well Leah and Abraham tried to hide, and forget, their Jewish heritage Felix must have felt thoroughly relaxed in London, since, by contrast, the banking community felt no shame in preserving Jewish traditions and observances; neither did they feel the need to change their names. Each branch of the Rothschild family was highly respected, not only as shrewd financiers but as patrons of the arts, and Lionel, son of Nathan Meyer, was no exception in London, becoming a Member of Parliament in 1847. An even more illustrious parliamentarian was Benjamin Disraeli, who was to become prime minister of 'the empire on whom the sun never sets'. He had earlier written popular novels and his father, Isaac, published treatises on natural science.

As for Felix, though his father's letters of introduction may have called him 'Bartholdy', he carried his grandfather's name with pride, knowing that any fame he may have acquired was attributable in no small part to Moses Mendelssohn's unsullied reputation. Leah's family, too, was proud of its Jewish descent, to such an extent that Bella Salomon cursed her son Jakob for changing his name and faith, forbidding him to remain in the family circle. It was only when Fanny, having pleased her grandmother with her piano playing, was promised anything she could desire, on the assumption that a comparatively straightforward gift would be sought (a new dress; an item of jewellery), that the depth of feeling this aroused was revealed. Mme. Salomon must have been completely taken aback when Fanny asked simply that 'Uncle Bartholdy' might be forgiven and reinstated into the clan. One is reminded of the story in St Mark's Gospel, when King Herod's daughter Salome, having danced so exquisitely for the guests, was promised anything she craved – asking, on her mother's behalf, for the head of John the Baptist. A promise was a promise in each case and each had to be fulfilled, no matter how onerous.

However zealously the Mendelssohns attested their conversion to the Protestant faith, anti-Semitism was rife and Felix was often spat at, both behind his back and to his face. Marek states that he dismissed this in his youth, but that his sensitivity increased with maturity; there is no corroborative evidence of either assertion, however. Betty Pistor, a fellow pupil at the Berlin Singakademie, was known by her relatives as 'our music- and Jew-loving cousin', on account of her close friendship with Felix and his sisters. At the New Year of 1831 Felix confided to Klingemann that the carnival atmosphere of Rome depressed him. Serious thoughts had to be entertained at this time and one could not be afraid to do so, as these were "real days of Atonement, to be spent on one's own". When Felix was resident in Leipzig, he wondered whether a Gewandhaus concert should be postponed in view of this Jewish festival. In Paris, annoyed at being so often mistaken for Meyerbeer, Felix had his hair cut short. Kupferberg suggests that he may have envied this opera composer, whose original family name had been 'Beer' and whose father had had a synagogue built on his estate. Felix had had his birthright taken from him by his own parents, and this appears to have mattered more to him than to his brother and sisters.

The 15th Lower Rhine Festival at Düsseldorf was marred by a group calling themselves 'Die Schwarzen' ('Black People') parading in front of the concert hall bearing a placard on which was written 'Christian musicians'. The police dispersed the troublemakers and, Marek claims, the incident was ignored, even Mendelssohn being unaware of the episode. But the fact that it has been recorded subsequently must mean that some members of the festival crowd observed this behaviour.

Yet a personal insult was levied by his father that, had it been repeated to him, would have wounded Felix's pride far more deeply. Writing home, Abraham, who had travelled to the festival, had to find something about which to complain. He disliked "the Jewish character" of the slight lisp when Felix spoke, reminding him, no doubt of his own father's similar trait, and all the guilt caused by the forfeiture of his original faith. Later that year, en route to his fourth visit to London, on which Abraham joined him, Felix and his father visited Dessau and tracked down the house where Moses had been born and which had now become a school for Jewish boys. Father and son also saw the synagogue, but it is not known what reaction either experienced.

What of Felix's music? There is no question that he fulfilled his public duty as a devout Lutheran, acknowledging the tercentenary of Luther's declaration of his faith via the 'Augsburg Confession' and composing the 'Reformation' Symphony (No. 5, Op. 107) and a number of motets for use in the German and Anglican Church. Mendelssohn also resurrected much early music, sacred and secular. In this manner, he must have steered non-believers to God through his music. Marek disputes this thesis, however, claiming that "The orthodoxy of religion meant nothing to him", and saying that he was not a churchgoer either, the only pretext for attending divine service being "simply to give him the opportunity to play the organ". The initials at the head of his manuscripts were no more than ciphers "and had no depth". Marek uses a sentence from a letter written by Mendelssohn to Johann Schirmer at the Düsseldorf Academy of Arts, but takes it out of context. Because Felix admitted that he did not conform to the creed whereby the worshipper "folds his hands and expects God to work for him...[and] prattles of a call to God comparable with his earthly endeavours unable to love person or thing on earth with his own heart", it does not mean he did not absorb religion. Rather, "I strive every day to approach a goal, knowing, of course, that I shall never wholly succeed." "Felix did not pray," Marek continues, "at least, not as a ritual." It was his wife Cécile who "remained pious, adhering to the orthodox Protestant prayers, and called on God". This surmise stems from Felix once admonishing his wife "not to bother the Good Lord with trivialities". This was probably said because whatever problem may have been on Cécile's mind would very likely be solved by an earthly

Chapter 11: 'Glory to God Alone'

agency – 'God helps those who help themselves' was a highly popular concept at the time in northern Europe. Besides, Felix's whole way of life – whatever his words or actions – was proof of his unswerving love of God, and, in this as well as many other matters concerning Mendelssohn, Marek misses the point.

Gisela Selden-Goth states categorically that Mendelssohn had nothing to say about his Jewish origin: "He was far too absorbed in the shaping of his own life and career to bother about the fate of his fellow Jews. He did not think; he did not feel; he did not dream like a Jew." As usual with such statements, no analysis is given, though in the case of Ms. Selden-Goth, one can only attribute her decided lack of perception to the scarcity of information at the time of her edition of Mendelssohn's letters, in 1945. Many glimpses have escaped the strict censorship of his correspondence by later relatives regarding his Jewish empathy. "There is not a single bar of Jewish 'volksong' or synagogue music; nor did he profess any interest in such matters." If this is true, the answer must be that Mendelssohn was far too much of a 'religious free spirit' to confine himself to strictly limited boundaries in music. But is Selden-Goth's statement accurate? The author Jan Morris believes implicitly in Mendelssohn's 'Jewish music', and she is not the only one. Writing on his setting of Psalm 114, 'When Israel Out of Egypt Came', H. E. Jacob writes the following: "His blood must, for once, have throbbed fiercely when thinking of his forefathers' great transmigration from Egypt to the promised land, and it is only the plain truth to say that, in its directness and force, his music is a perfect match for the [words of] the unknown psalmist." The concert pianist Frederic Lamond was reminded of a Hebrew melody when playing Mendelssohn's Prelude and Fugue in E minor (No. 1 of his Op. 35) in 1936 at his 50th anniversary recital. The work could have been written "by a son of [one of] the prophets of Israel," Lamond declares in the programme notes, but this may be a flight of fancy on his part. Julius Schubring wrote that this prelude, composed in 1827, represented the progress of his friend August Hanstein's illness and death. Beginning in the minor key, the prelude transfers to the major and culminates in "a chorale of release". If, subconsciously, the E minor passage did remind the 18-year-old composer of a Hebrew melody and Lamond is correct in his assumption, the whole piece indicates a perceptive fusion of Judaic and Lutheran styles.

It is in Mendelssohn's oratorios that Judaism plays a greater part in understanding Mendelssohn's psyche, as regards Jewish thought. "The very best touches in his oratorios" result from "his delicate tact", Schubring reflected. In *St Paul*, for example, Mendelssohn chose words from Psalm 51 to describe the three days of blindness, "as if written on purpose" for this very occasion – far more appropriate than anything Schubring could suggest. Stanley Sadie calls the oratorio "an allegory of his own family history", whereas *Elijah* represents "his years of dissension in Berlin". If Sadie is correct, why did Mendelssohn become so depressed whilst composing *St Paul* and why is there no hint of personal bitterness in *Elijah*?

On 7th August 1834 Felix wrote to Julius Schubring that he had completed part one of *St Paul* except for the overture, which required "a heavy bit of work". He felt "all knocked about", but whether from the sultry climate, his resultant feverishness "or whatever else", he is uncertain. To Marek, Mendelssohn was "responsible for his own inner darkness", but this is far too simplistic an assertion. He gives no analysis but, to someone who has learnt to understand Felix's personality, the reason is patently clear. Many parents dump their own problems and 'hang-ups' on their offspring, and Abraham was no exception. *St Paul* was a symbol of filial duty, not to his spiritual but to his earthly father. His physical malaise was the product of emotional distress at having to write on sacred Christian (according to Abraham) themes to replace the fairy-like music of his youth and out of which he by now should have grown. As for the personal aspect of the oratorio itself, Felix's situation was completely different from that of St Paul. After all, Saul of Tarsus had been a Pharisee, a strict Jew who had persecuted the Christians, yet who had wholeheartedly accepted his conversion. Felix had likewise been born into a Jewish family but had been baptised with no choice in the matter, at an age when, though his parents may have perceived him to be too young to understand this change of faith, he could still have been aware of the alteration in routine. But, above all, Christianity had been thrust upon the Mendelssohn children for the wrong reasons – worldly, rather than spiritual, considerations. He dared not confide such thoughts to Schubring, a theologian, and hardly admitted them to himself. Mendelssohn expressed his feelings in very subtle ways, however. In response to a conversation Ambassador Bunsen repeated to Felix in Rome, for instance; on hearing that a German musician had declared *Tu es Petrus* as having revealed "a gleam of earnest purpose", Felix responded: "Oh, how I wish I were a Frenchman," if this pomposity was implied in German music. In *St Paul*, the most convincing passage is the chorus describing the stoning to death of Stephen (the first Christian martyr), by the Jews. In view of how Felix felt about some aspects of Christian worship, he may have had the same inclination. Similarly, in his *First Walpurgisnacht*, the excitement of the druids' chorus is manifest in his setting of the words 'Those stupid Christians. Let us boldly outsmart them. Come, with staves and pitchforks'.

Yet, when Mendelssohn felt completely at ease with the sacred works he composed, it is evident. The pieces he wrote for various Christian festivals are shamefully neglected and this applies, too, as regards the settings for the Anglican service. The music historian Benny Green has remarked that "music went mad in 1956" with the birth of rock'n'roll, and, sadly, Anglican and Nonconformist services have mainly followed this lead. Whilst in days gone by congregations often heard choirs singing Mendelssohn's works as anthems, this is a phenomenon that has vanished, even from the cathedral repertoire. The one exception is his *Hear my Prayer*, based on Psalm 55 and paraphrased by William Bartholomew – but not as Mendelssohn had wanted. The work was originally written for a specific soprano,

Chapter 11: 'Glory to God Alone'

Miss Ann Mounsey, for her 'sacred music concerts' at the Crosby Hall in the City of London. At the present time, the motet is mainly the property of any aspiring treble whose voice is not mature enough to manage the work. Since there appears no record of his composing for the treble voice, it can only be imagined what the composer would think of these often indifferent performances. Yet, above all, it is his settings of the psalms and his oratorio *Elijah* where Mendelssohn gives of his best. In the latter case, the sentiments are universal, whatever the listener's belief. Anyone who knows the work will easily choose a passage that gives comfort or reassurance for the particular individual. As for the psalms, Mendelssohn must have felt a particular warmth towards the man who translated these Hebrew poems into German – his grandfather, Moses Mendelssohn. As with his motets for the Christian year, fragments exist of a proposed third oratorio, *Christus*, which, though given an opus number (97), is very rarely heard. There are also many sacred pieces still in manuscript.

The words of Julius Schubring best summarise Mendelssohn's attitude to his spiritual life. Conventions and traditions of orthodox worship he viewed with disdain. His sole expression was the worship of beauty, in nature, the arts and in humanity. In his own actions, sublime or trivial, and in whatever way he behaved, "religion and veneration were enthroned in his countenance".

Chapter 12

Free Thinkers

As with religion, Marek states that Mendelssohn had no interest in politics, but, from a study of his letters, this is seen to be patently untrue. Wherever he went he read newspapers avidly and constantly kept abreast of current events. Klingemann, as a diplomat and in the centre of foreign affairs, was an impartial yet accurate source of information. Felix often sought his friend's opinion on such matters "because they interest me more than perhaps you imagine", especially regarding Germany. A fragment of a letter written to Rebecka in 1834 reads "Beckchen, I remain liberal, despite the old dragon." Since no name was given it can only be conjectured that their father is the individual to whom Felix referred. Devrient recalled that, compared with the political views of Hensel and Abraham, those of Felix were "positively revolutionary". It is evident that Felix would have preferred a united Germany and this hope remained with him throughout his life. In 1830 he complained of his country's "petty principalities; her different types of money; the coach journey that can take one and a half hours for one German mile". He would rather go to bed because he felt "dead tired", but had to watch *Fidelio* whilst in Munich. In this mood nothing could please him, even if the politicians could not be held responsible. He grumbled at the 'incessant rain and wind' in the Thuringian Forest; he had been misinformed about the coach timetable, travelling through the night to catch the next morning's mail coach, only to be told at Nuremburg that no mail would be collected that day. He was "out of patience with Germany…the whole system is enough to drive one wild. My Germany is a mad country. She can produce great people and then ignore them. She has many fine singers and intelligent artists but none modest and subordinated [enough] to render their roles faithfully and without pretensions." According to Mendelssohn Germans praised anything from abroad, only recognising native talent when acknowledged overseas. He would never, despite so many shortcomings, give up his faith in his compatriots. "Even though they cannot unite soon enough, let us hope the Germans cease their grumbling about the lack of unity and that, one day, they will begin to imitate the unity of others." Meanwhile, he would continue to compose music as long as suitable ideas came into his head, yet he still regretted that Germany did not appreciate the things in which her people excelled.

Fanny expressed irritation at her father and elder brother constantly arguing about politics as this could develop into more serious quarrels. Felix would write to Paul that he looked forward to "gossiping about politics" on his stay in Berlin in order to negotiate terms for his appointment as music director for the new King of Prussia. He admitted himself "unwilling to be one of the number [that] in the present day possess a greater number of decorations than they have written good compositions". He had no idea what return he could make for the honour to come and did not seek any such honour for himself. Neither did this interest wane when abroad. From Pressburg (now known as Bratislava, capital of the Slovak Republic), Felix wrote to ask Paul what was meant by his reference to 'the Tailors' Insurrection' in Berlin.

From Lucerne, Switzerland, the German composer Wilhelm Taubert must have been surprised at his correspondent's homily on German art. Mendelssohn allied its disorganised condition with "the truly strange, wild and troublesome attitude" prevailing in European politics. Having read some "aesthetic periodicals" after more than a year, he was "obliged to swallow the [abuse of] the scurrilous Menzel, who presumed modestly to deprecate Schiller and the supercilious Grabbe, who (modestly) deprecated Shakespeare and the philosophers who claim Schiller to be trivial. Is not this arrogant, overbearing spirit – this perverse cynicism – as hideous to you as it is to me? God help us." Did Taubert not feel, like Mendelssohn, that "the first and most indispensable quality for any artist is to feel respect for great men and to bow down in spirit before them; to recognise their merits and to endeavour not to extinguish their great flame in order that one's own feeble rush light may burn a little more brightly? If anyone is incapable of feeling true greatness, I should like to know how he intends to make me feel it…" But, realising he might have gone too far and that Taubert merely sought advice about some songs he had written, Felix explained that his annoyance stemmed from not having read anything of the kind for so long and that he was vexed that such folly continued to be written and read. Yet, despite the conflict, Mendelssohn resolved to pursue his own path quietly and told Goethe on his last birthday – 26th August 1831 – how pleased he was that he had been born early enough to meet the elderly poet and that he, Mendelssohn, was a German.

Earlier that year he wrote of the unrest in Italy. From Rome he told his family that in March the city was "not so cheerful as before", in view of some disturbances the impact of which had spread from Bologna. The streets were deserted; art galleries closed, as were the stores and the Vatican. The carnival had finished.

Everyone Felix knew had left Rome; the only news he could glean was from German newspapers, but, whatever the situation, nothing could deprive him of the glorious weather that had replaced the climate of a few weeks previously. "The hatred of the Roman people is, strangely enough, directed against the French

Chapter 12: Free Thinkers

pensioners, believing that their influence alone could easily effect a revolution. Threatening letters have been frequently sent to the Vernets." On one Sunday evening the citizens were asked to pray for the preservation of peace. Edicts, each more drastic than its predecessor, were posted in the streets warning revellers that they would be punished. Innkeepers had been asked to submit lists of foreign guests who had to present themselves to the ambassadors of their respective countries in order to vouch for their good character, though many had not troubled with this ruling. Agitators had been seen in Rome but, rather than protect any stray masquerader, the militia stood with loaded rifles in each piazza. The Swiss Guards prevented anyone from entering the colonnades of St Peter's. "The middle classes keep their doors locked, causing anyone who wishes to gain entry to have to knock three times. The poor citizens are the greatest supporters of the pope and the community of German artists have cut off their moustaches for fear of the indigenous population venting their resentment upon them, as with the French residents; when their hallmark and identification is trimmed each man looks tame in time of war," Felix commented. He had "a particular aversion for this group". He observed the contrast between "the wild gaiety" of the carnival and "the workaday atmosphere" of the present, with patrols in the streets, people arrested and "the most bitter gravity" that pervaded Rome. Though Felix recalled that his father had not wished to discuss politics on the evening of his silver wedding (26th December 1829), Felix felt he had to express his views now. He considered that the government regulations were efficiently administered and that there was no cause for alarm. The present peace was marred only by fears of what might happen, but he exhorted his family not to take notice of newspapers – especially French journals.

He reassured his family in a later letter that the displeasure of his earlier correspondence was prompted by the government's strict precautions against revolution – "and nothing more". Leah's suspicions that "something or other" happened to him were unfounded. Other visitors had expressed similar feelings and his own irritation was no exception to the thoughts of non-residents. He did, however, admit to Devrient that some music manuscripts he had taken to the customs before the mail was due to be despatched had not arrived. Having trudged "back and forth" in order to enquire their whereabouts, he was informed that "a secret correspondence in cipher was suspected", for which Mendelssohn's innocent music notation was mistaken. "I could scarcely credit such intolerable stupidity", but, as two further letters had not reached their destination, he had planned to complain to the embassy, but on reflection decided against doing so. "The letters are evidently lost, which I much regret, so my complaint will do no good." How much music might have been lost through ignorance of this nature!

Neither were Fanny's nor Rebecka's letters completely oblivious of political matters when, later, the two sisters each arrived in Italy. From Naples, Fanny was annoyed at the incessant drilling and manoeuvres by the King's soldiers, declaring that, were she their ruler, they would be given far more useful tasks to pursue than their present futile occupation. Ischia, which the Hensels reached after a three-hour journey by boat, made her imagine what the Orient would be like, with the women in Greek costume. They were greeted by "a double row of touts". The boatmen, pretending to convey their passengers ashore, "did not approach within ten yards of us". They were followed by half the population, "howling, shouting and fighting for the honour of transferring us to land. We stepped out of the boat onto the donkeys' necks and so rode out of the sea, straight onwards." Back in Naples, Fanny read with "disgust" of the removal of Napoleon's ashes from their last resting place. She stepped onto the balcony to admire the scenery in the calm moonlight to soothe her anger. She asked Felix what he thought of the political situation in France and the debates in the Chamber of Deputies. "How dark, dismal and dreary everything is – not only in foul weather," she noted in her journal. Whilst France prepared for war, the new King of Prussia refused to grant a new constitution and, "into the bargain, can be expected to do nothing for art" in Germany.

Later Rebecka was to note that the commandant at Castellana picked flowers for his guests, after which he showed them round the tower where prisoners were housed who had committed political crimes, but, though she felt ill at such a situation, nothing was ever suggested to reform it. From the spa town of Franzensbad, where she had been ordered to take a cure for neuralgia, Rebecka complained that reports were behindhand with newspapers. She knew already that Rouget de Lisle, composer of *La Marseillaise*, had died and she was asked, as the most recent visitor to the spa, what she thought of the second attempt on the life of King Louis Philippe. A child of five was entertaining everyone by playing "variations by heart", but Rebecka could not find a piano to entertain herself. "Does anything ever happen here?" she asked, looking forward to October and her reunion with her husband and sons. A family acquaintance – 'X' – would dislike Franzensbad, as she would be unable to have a clandestine affair here.

In another spa town, the fashionable Baltic resort of Heringsdorf, Fanny and Rebecka visited the nearby town of Swinemünde. They saw a Russian ship and remarked on its order and cleanliness, and "the science and skill with which it was created". On further investigation they noticed the arsenal of weapons, "like a jewel box", and the cannon resembling "pieces of drawing room furniture", leading them to the conclusion that the ship had been made ready for "organised murder". At supper-time the crew of 12 looked "with their dull, Slavonic faces" at the kettle that hung from the ceiling and the "grey broth" they were expected to eat. Yet, Fanny observed, "these creatures were not the least of the human species", and she felt like crying, rather than laughing, at their situation. "What uncivilised barbarians we shall appear to some wiser generation of the future that will have replaced war – the appeal to mere brutal forces – with international tribunals... When the time comes, people will have a right to talk about Christianity." Fanny admired the ideas of

Chapter 12: Free Thinkers

Napoleon III whereby conflicts would be settled by a European Congress. "Hensel may laugh at this pipe dream, but I am right. Women always are!"

Though, in his youth, Felix had expressed disillusionment with France, when he made his final visit there in 1832 he still had plenty about which to complain. Despite the fact that Charles X had been replaced by 'the bourgeois King', Louis Philippe, and his fascination with the acting of Mlle. Fay, the singing of Mme. Malibran and the innovative ballet performances of Mme. Taglioni, he was upset by reading in a French newspaper that "a revolution in taste" and "a musical upheaval" had occurred over the past few years in which Mendelssohn himself was purported to have "played quite a part". "Such things make me feel quite nauseated," he growled to Fanny. "At such times, I think one should be diligent, work hard and, above all, ...leave the future to God."

He attended debates in the Houses of Parliament, where they "pronounced judgement on their hereditary rights". A resolution was passed whereby "All Frenchmen of noble birth should carry the Cross of the Legion of Honour", permission not to do so to be granted only by special dispensation. "One scarcely sees a man in the street without a bit of coloured ribbon, so it is no longer a distinction." On another occasion, "votes were counted to abolish a very ancient privilege". Indeed, so irritated was he with politics as a whole, Felix wished to forget the subject "for 150 reasons", the main one being that he did not understand the French system when his companions discussed such matters. So entrenched was a 'Monsieur F.' in dogmatism, who believed himself a suitable candidate to become a minister, that Mendelssohn found it difficult to warn his colleague that "nothing will come of it". Senator Franck, as his name was subsequently revealed, "enjoys criticising others but has nothing new to add of his own to any topic". A 'Monsieur H.' (probably the poet Heine, who lived in Paris at the time) annoyed Felix not only by "hitting at Germany" but slating London in favour of Paris, which latter city he found " singular and amusing. All this I dislike because of my sincere regard for him."

A further acquaintance 'A.' had left home to join the Saint-Simon Community, "where body and soul are equally engrossed". Claude Henri de Rouvroy, Comte de Saint-Simon (1760-1825), was the first Socialist and the first to speak of a united Europe, free trade and world peace. His aim was to replace religion with science as the spiritual doctrine of the new state he wished to found. Many young Jewish intellectuals adopted his ideals but, by the time Mendelssohn arrived in Paris, after Saint-Simon's death, these original philosophies had been vitiated, causing moral decline and corruption among members. An acquaintance, 'P', had given Felix 20 copies of a pamphlet to distribute – *An Appeal to Mankind* – one of which he sent to his family. "You will find this quite enough." The pamphlet advocated that everyone should surrender a share of his property, however small, to Saint-Simon's disciples. All artists should, in future, dedicate their whole life and work to this 'religion'. "Music better than that of Rossini and Beethoven" should be composed;

artists "should paint like Raphael or Henri David. The students at the technical college take Saint-Simon's ideas seriously and it is hard to predict how far such notions will extend." The 'Fathers', as the contemporary Saint-Simonians called themselves, "place temptation in everyone's way, promising honour to one; fame to another; money to poor people and, to me, an admiring public, yet checking all effort and progress". The Saint-Simonians did not believe in hell, the devil or eternal perdition, but only in 'the brotherhood of man', yet with no means of bringing this to fruition by "duty, vocation or action". Felix attended one of their gatherings, where reports were read, praised or blamed and commands issued. "To me it was quite terrible. 'A.' is trying to procure a loan for the Community's benefit; it is a bad sign...that such a monstrous way of behaving – and in such bad prose – should ever have existed or impressed anyone. Productions at the theatre outdo one another in dramas concerning the plague, the gallows and the devil, etc.", each conveying some political message and "how the romantic school has affected all the Parisians". Only one bright spark shone out in this "catalogue of miseries, fooleries, horrors and libertinism": the actress Leontine Fay, "the perfection of grace and fascination", who "remains unsullied from the absurdities she is compelled to utter and to act". Felix reserved further discussion of his views for his return to Germany and his family.

Like many who, although revolted by a subject, remain weirdly attracted thereto, Mendelssohn had still more to write about the Saint-Simonians. Franck called to see him one morning, "revealing disclosures that shocked me so much that I resolved neither to go to see him nor to attend confederations. Early this morning, Hiller rushed in to tell me he had just witnessed the arrest of the Saint-Simonians. He wished to hear their orations, but the 'Fathers' did not arrive. All of a sudden, soldiers made their way in and requested those present to disperse as quickly as possible." One of Mendelssohn's quartets was lying sealed in the Rue Monsigny and, in view of the arrests, he feared that it would have to be played in front of a jury. But, though Mendelssohn paid no further visits to Paris, he still showed interest in its political life. In 1839 he replied to a letter from Moscheles describing Paris as "not very pleasant" by saying, "All I have heard lately from you and others does not tend to improve my opinion." The behaviour of her citizens demonstrated "vanity and outward show, assuming poses, striving to acquire decorations; to wear stiff cravats...interest in high art, but a soul replete with enthusiasm [that] does not mend matters". On the whole, he preferred "the German Philistines, with their nightcaps and tobacco".

As far as politics were concerned Felix "cannot have known himself" when visiting London. He regularly asked Klingemann how matters stood at Westminster. For this reason he was completely at home with parliamentary matters there. Fanny had asked the diplomat, before her brother's 1829 visit, how the Catholic Emancipation Bill was faring, whereby, like Nonconformists in the previous year, Roman Catholics would at last be allowed to enter the House of

Commons. Fanny teased their friend that, whenever she saw the name 'London', she scanned the appropriate article to see if *his* name appeared – just as Klingemann, when reading about the Prussian state, jokingly remarked that he would see if Fanny had been decorated or honoured. Felix reported that he, Klingemann and Rosen discussed politics at breakfast when his friends visited. On his second visit of 1832, Felix attended a debate at the Guildhall. "They ask the House of Commons to prohibit taxes and the Lord Mayor appears and says finally and once for all that he has no trust in other councillors (cheers). They are men of disgraceful principle (cheers), if it be that they have any principles at all (huge roar), and [that] Lord Grey would have to stay on (all hats tossed up into the air). Then good old Taylor gives a most delightful speech, after which the emissaries from Birmingham arrived." These would have reported progress after riots, which had prompted the eventual legislation to reform the Commons. This allowed newly prosperous industrialists and commercial magnates to become Members of Parliament.

On his fourth visit to London in 1833 Mendelssohn reported another debate, this time in the usual domain at Westminster. This concerned the removal of the last vestiges of discrimination against British Jews. On 23rd July 1833 he compared the enlightened attitudes he had witnessed in London with "the lousy edicts in Posen", Poland, where emancipation was limited to "a small elite". These edicts were disparaged in the parliament of Great Britain, "as was only right and proper," Felix averred. "*The Times* felt noble, saying that it would be much better for us." When the inevitable Jew-baiting by the reactionary element had ceased "blethering", as Felix called their histrionics, the parliamentarian who had begun the debate responded. He asked his protagonists if they had assembled to discuss the prophecies as foretold in the Scriptures, as they claimed, or whether, as was his own intent, to remember the words "Glory to God and goodwill to all mankind". Sir Robert Grant's motion was carried by 187 'ayes' to 52 'noes'. Grant's name will be familiar to anyone who still attends traditional church services in Britain, as he wrote the fine hymn "*O Worship the King, all Glorious above.*" His resolution by which Jews would be freed from any remaining prejudices was, to Felix, "noble and beautiful, and fills me with gratitude to the Heavens".

Meanwhile, in Germany, after the upheaval of the Napoleonic Wars, a period of strict adherence to convention ensued. This was known as the 'Biedermeier' era on account of an Austrian cartoonist of that name who portrayed scenes of the period. A woman's role was expected to conform to marriage, the home and children; the criteria to be followed were purity in morals and obedience towards conventional religion. As the Mendelssohn parents had always wished for this way of life, they found no difficulty in adapting to the status quo. Yet their offspring had other views. Fanny wrote to Klingemann that, having resided in London for eight years, she believed him to have forgotten "how insipid" German newspapers were at present, reporting "less than nothing" of matters abroad. Whereas Prussia was formerly in the vanguard of reform and political enlightenment, she was "disgusted" with the present outlook in politics and the arts. Others were even more rebellious for, at the end of the Lower Rhine Festival at Cologne in 1834, a revolt occurred in which many were said to have been killed, but the authorities kept this from the public. However, newspapers exaggerated the trouble, causing far greater alarm than if communication had been maintained by the government agencies.

On 23rd December of the same year Felix wrote to Klingemann that, whereas reform would remove abuses and obstructions towards progress in "life, art, politics and heaven knows what else besides", revolution "would remove everything good – and what was really good". In any case, this was, he considered "only a fashion", and he would not listen to Fanny's opinion that the playing of the violinist Lafont inspired no interest since the "revolutionary effects" of Paganini had come to the fore. "Progress is made by work alone and not by talking, which such people as revolutionaries do not believe." He hoped one day to "effect a reform in music"; he was a musician and wished to be nothing other. In 1839 he wrote to Moscheles of an insurrection in Hanover, which he followed "with great interest and which, I am sorry to say, does not reflect much credit on the German fatherland". As far as Felix was concerned, he would prefer to find a place to which one could flee "to be content, because true art could be practised" there. Felix had written to Klingemann in 1835 complaining that, during rioting that had broken out in Berlin that August, the soldiers seemed to be drunk; had sided with the mob, and paid little heed that citizens' lives were in danger, however innocent they were of the rioters' indiscriminate behaviour.

The French poet Alfred de Musset – one-time lover of George Sand – wondered why the Franco-Prussian War had not occurred in 1840, rather than 1870, in view of the ferment of feeling at the earlier date. A German historian, A. Streckfuss, wrote that anyone who admired France or anything relating thereto was assumed, by definition, to be mad in 1840; anyone whose daughter learnt French was accused of permitting her to be lured into whoredom by such an undertaking. A poet named Nikolaus Becker wrote some verses entitled 'The Rhine Song', whose first line ran: 'They shall not have it, the free German Rhine', the words 'They shall not have it' being repeated at the beginning of every verse. Various settings had been composed, including a similarly worded song in Marschner's opera *Hans Heiling* that boasted of the Rhineland wine. Felix was angered by 'La Colognaise', as the 'Rheinlied' was sometimes known, calling the words "sterile and futile". To Klingemann he wrote: "It would not be so bad if the words were altered to 'We want to keep it'. The song is sung at the court in Berlin and clubs and casinos here [in Leipzig] and, of course, the musicians pounce upon it like mad...[and it is] alluded to daily in one newspaper or another... Yesterday it was announced that I had composed the poem, whereas I would never dream of meddling in such negative sentiments. People here lie like a story book, right and left." Versions came

Chapter 12: Free Thinkers

from the pens of the Dutch composer Verhulst, and others including Schumann and Konradin Kreutzer, whose version was to be sung at a concert at the time. Felix wrote to Paul: "I could write such a letter of complaint to you... The newspapers have printed settings...including one by me... My whole name in print, but I cannot punish anyone for slander precisely because I [wish to] maintain public silence." The publishers Breitkopf & Härtel assured him that, had he set Becker's poem to music, they could have sold 6,000 copies in two months. Julius Schubring had planned to set the verses to music, but Mendelssohn dissuaded him not only from this but from his interest in politics altogether. Felix confided his abhorrence of journalists "printing every scrap of news on the subject that I might be booted across the border as a French sympathiser. Everyone is in one accord on the subject. No change is ever put into effect as to what would be good and healthy. How can anyone live and thrive in Germany in such far from gratifying conditions? We are all compelled into isolation and must, from the very first, renounce all ideas of working together, in unison... I cannot interest myself in anything that pertains to a particular era only, but prefer to compose something that is timeless. No doubt you will laugh, but I cannot help coming out with what I believe."

Neither did Fanny's interest wane in matters concerning politics. When she asked Felix whether there would be war, he replied: "How have I gained the reputation of a newsmonger? I have maintained all along, through thick and thin, Germany will have peace, despite such warlike agitation". It would be better, "with such a politicus as Paul in the family", if Fanny posed such questions to their brother. "He may say what he likes, but no war shall we have; but, when one thinks of the false speeches at the lieder circle last evening, I almost wish there could be war." In 1844 Fanny remarked that "the European powers are making faces at one another", the only difference being "that [whilst] Germany sings a cappella, thundering men-of-war accompany England's song... Though Germany is flourishing, her political situation is miserable. That fellow Eichhorn [minister of state for the arts] seems resolved to stifle any free thought." Even if a mouse stirred he became panic-stricken, "but, though that particular court official may look a fool, one must look even higher for greater foolishness". This applied especially when students were expelled from their university and professors were punished for editing a periodical unpopular with the establishment. That year Felix paid his eighth visit to England and wrote to Paul regarding "the nasty business with the radicals, which I had ample occasion to observe, and with which society cannot continue to exist". He spoke of their "inwardly corroded ideas" and, having picked up the English expression, "musically *Rotten Boroughs*" (implying corruption in parliamentary seats that were eliminated by the 1832 Reform Act). He was sorry, on Paul's as much as his own behalf, for not having been able to deliver a letter from Morgan John O'Connell to his uncle Daniel O'Connell, imprisoned in Dublin for conspiracy and sedition against the Westminster government. Shortage of time and dread of the five-day journey to Ireland prevented his visit, ostensibly to gain a doctorate of music from Dublin University. "I did not overlook the thought that it would have pleased you" to deliver O'Connell's letter, "and gave up the idea with genuine regret," he placated his brother. Klingemann stated, whilst seeing Felix onto the boat at Gravesend, that he would write to Paul on the matter.

From his holiday in Bad Soden, having returned to Germany from London, Felix wrote of the poet von Fallersleben visiting; his best-known creation was the former German national anthem 'Das Lied der Deutschen'. "All those who are entitled to do so wear a bit of ribbon in their buttonholes and are called 'geheimrat'" – equivalent to a confidential secretary in the government. "All the world is talking about Prussia and blaming her" for the general unrest, he told Klingemann. "In fact, they talk of nothing else." Paul sent Felix a pamphlet, *Wir Fragen* (*We Ask*), by Jacobi that he had heard about from the newspapers, which, were it not for Paul's kindness, would not have reached Felix for a long time. He "exulted not a little in its content" and agreed with Paul that "nothing more candid, more truthful, more noble in form and style could be desired"; the publication "is a remarkable sign of the present time in Prussia". No such pamphlet could have appeared during the previous year, but he reminded his brother that, as the work was prohibited, it remained to be seen how well its author's words would awaken an independent spirit in Germany. Both as individuals and among the community as a whole, "the great misfortune with us has always been the want of unanimity of esprit de corps". It depressed Felix to reflect that "only in time of war is Germany's path open, level and plain". If Felix's views were observed, "no one would lose and everyone gain life, power, movement and activity", which would, in turn, foster "truth, honour and loyalty" among German people. Yet, time after time, such a path was never trodden, "reasons being perpetually found for avoiding" such objectives. It was fortunate, therefore, that the author of the pamphlet "knows how to set forth what the greatest number feel, but cannot express". The lapse of a fortnight should prove whether the words had right on their side, in practice as well as theory. "God grant that this may be so." Felix asked his brother to report anything he heard in consequence of the questions asked by minister Schön, as reported in the pamphlet, which contrasted favourably with those written by Frenchmen during the previous year. "Here is, indeed, real substance...vigorous truth and inborn dignity; not merely well-bred politeness... But the work is prohibited. This is a humiliation, even amid all my delights" at such a publication.

From Italy Rebecka wrote of looking forward, on her return, to dropping in to Leipzigerstrasse for a chat with Fanny, reporting that there, too, the political situation was "very shaky" and depressing. Though some tourists told her that an insurrection had taken place in Naples, "others were mysteriously silent on the matter". Meanwhile, Fanny kept her sister informed as to what was happening in Berlin, especially as regards the art world. "We intend to organise an exhibition, but all exhibitors must expect to receive a slap in the face" in view of the myriad regulations and the organisers' negative attitude to the work displayed. Though

Chapter 12: Free Thinkers

"nothing out of the ordinary", even the flower show could boast 12,000 to 14,000 spectators. "Berlin is becoming a large town. Wilhelmplatz resembles a 'twelfth night' cake, stiff and regular; the gravel paths are firm and good." Fanny noted that "great changes are taking place in the ministry, but no one knows why". The King had granted nine million thalers for a new cathedral to be built. Fanny likened this decree to the Order of the Swan, "which rests on its laurels that it has not earned. When such announcements are made, there is an outcry; then the plan is dropped." Fanny found the new regulations for the university "irritating, self-contradictory, absurd and illogical and make my blood boil". As for Herr Walerode's pronouncement that the River Spree symbolised "calm, steady progress", Fanny "laughed for three hours straight off". Altogether, "political affairs are not in a pleasant state, exemplified by the speculation in railway shares and the plight of weavers in Silesia, though, in the latter case, individuals are doing what they can to alleviate the conditions". A letter was written by the brothers Wilhelm and Jakob Grimm to a newspaper stating that the poet von Fallersleben was "not a welcome guest" at a family birthday celebration. Students and professors were expelled, and even imprisoned, for disagreeing with the new regulations and, "in short, the government does nothing but meddle, leaving such matters as safety and health to take care of themselves". Eichhorn "seems to have sworn death to every intellectual endeavour… What a rickety state Prussia must be in, if it threatens to collapse as soon as three students form an association or three professors publish a periodical."

When Gustav Dirichlet planned to leave his Berlin appointment to take up a post in Heidelberg, Felix wrote to him "in grief". The more he reflected on the current situation, the less he trusted the political climate. Everywhere he looked, culture and intellect were "gravitating towards the larger cities, such as Berlin", and smaller places, such as Heidelberg, were being bypassed as entities where new ideas could flourish. Whilst a location such as Heidelberg might seem an agreeable place in which to live, "the residents will not remain content to continue in quiet confidence, but will strive to emulate great cities". Felix could not envisage anyone as free-spirited as his brother-in-law vacating Berlin "without the most extreme concern". If Dirichlet was dissatisfied with his present situation, or uneasy about the future, he would feel the same throughout Germany as a whole. "Such contamination spreads throughout our fatherland", and such thoughts could not be remedied simply by a change of address. "It is better not to begin a new life which holds out little prospect of improvement in itself. Such a connection as you have with Berlin is not to be dissolved by a letter and a few words, if these people believe that, by your answer, they have acquired any right over you… That which costs the greatest sacrifice is chosen so often compared with peace of mind."

On 12th October 1845 Felix wrote to Senator Bernus in Frankfurt that, when he moved there from Leipzig, as he was contemplating, he hoped either that "a nucleus of enlightened Germans will have evolved, or that the present state of affairs will have vanished", to "be entirely forgotten. Should this not happen, I fear we shall run the risk of losing our finest national characteristics – thoroughness, constancy, honest perseverance – without obtaining any substitute for them; a collection of French phrases and frivolity would be too dearly bought at such a price. Let us hope for something better." In the following year Devrient noticed, when meeting Felix and Cécile in Dresden, Mendelssohn's increasing irritability with the political situation in Germany. "It was evident that he was under the domination of the nerves of the brain," Devrient wrote in his later memoirs. This glib observation did not take into account Mendelssohn's presentiment of what was to follow, for it would be two more years before revolutions erupted all over Europe, in 1848. Not only was Mendelssohn a diligent reader of newspapers, but a profound thinker!

Even in his final year of life, 1847, he still commented on the current political situation. He wrote from Interlaken, Switzerland, "The state of affairs in Berlin is like sand, which has to be ploughed up before any fruit is produced." He further predicted that there would be, metaphorically speaking, "dense, dull, misty fogs, if not thunderstorms, in our fatherland, and many a day that could be bright and clear thus becomes sultry and grey, whereby all objects become dim and dull; indeed, vivid lightning and thunder out of the black clouds are somewhat preferable to vague mists and foggy abysses". He asked Paul about their friend General von Webern's visit to Frankfurt – "no doubt the one on the Oder", since the last letter Felix received made no mention of this visit. "Is a promotion in the offing, or is his transfer, if such it is, the result of discussion regarding the general's high reputation", or simply a vacation "away from the ideas of peace by the people who were supposed to be united in Berlin"? Mendelssohn was "unpleasantly surprised" and "found the whole affair disagreeable" on learning of this mystery. He also asked Paul what his view was on the murder of the Duc de Praslin. Did he not think of the distress Fanny would have felt at the news, in view of their aunt Henriette Mendelssohn's post as governess to the Duchess when a child? It was she who was murdered by her husband and who had earlier corresponded often with Fanny Hensel.

From Paris in 1832, as mentioned earlier in this book, Mendelssohn had written to Zelter that, whilst he appreciated the delights of Italy and Switzerland, "I have become aware that I am a German and I know that I want to live in Germany as long as I live". Though there was less beautiful scenery, Felix did not need to learn anything of her language, customs or culture. He felt comfortable without having to think about the matter and hoped to fulfil his role as a musician in his homeland. Should such a goal not be possible, which he might have suspected, Felix could live abroad, "as life is easier for a foreigner", but he hoped this would not be necessary. He had thought through the situation, especially when discussing politics elsewhere, where people disparaged Germany for having no constitution or unity; nor could he help but despise her "exaggerated modesty".

Towards the end of his life, however, Mendelssohn appeared to have had far more to fear than this aspect of German life. Though he had no precise foreboding as to his own short life, exemplified by the fact that he left no will, he dreaded what was to befall his fatherland. Like Elgar in a later generation, Mendelssohn realised a new age was dawning in which he felt more and more uncomfortable. Unlike Elgar, however, Mendelssohn, via his oratorio *Elijah*, had a positive and timeless answer – 'Be not Afraid'.

Chapter 13

Festivals, Private and Public

The Mendelssohn family was meticulous at acknowledging whatever anniversary that could be named. Birthdays in particular were a fertile source of celebration. On several occasions their parents' birthdays coincided with their offspring being away from home. From Weimar in 1825, for instance, Abraham wrote that Felix was "distressed" at being unable to greet his mother personally, since they would still be travelling. "He is quite awkward about some things, but otherwise quite tolerable," Felix's father remarked. Abraham had "made a great suggestion" that Felix send a message in advance to relay birthday wishes to his mother. Leah needed to be aware of her son's "devotion and love". "Whatever things I may think or conceive, may God grant them to you for the longest time to come." For his mother's birthday of 1828, Schubring wrote later of the verse translation of *The Maid of Andros*, about which Zelter told Goethe that, though he could not give an opinion, he considered that Mendelssohn "possessed a feeling for...nature, as well as for plastic art...capable of appreciating, with intelligence and enthusiastic admiration, the masterpieces of ancient and modern art"; but what his mother thought of the work is not recorded. When, in 1840, the Hensels visited Italy, Fanny wrote of having presented "a little composition" for her mother's birthday. On the actual day, 26th March, the Hensels and the artist Kaselowsky's family drove to the Gate of San Sebastian, the farthest extremity of the city of Rome, describing the pageantry of the wedding procession and how the brides-to-be had to make their vows in grey robes and white veils; no weddings were permitted during Lent. Leah's health was toasted with wine from Orvieto; "What could be more classical or more romantic," Fanny wrote. They dined on spring vegetable soup and roast hare and, later, whilst Hensel sketched, Fanny was asked to accompany an English musician in an aria from *St Paul* – "a rather queer performance," since the singer did not know the words, nor Fanny the music from memory. She then "played several things I did know by heart".

From Rome, Felix acknowledged his father's birthday, congratulating him the more because of his absence. He regretted not being able to greet Abraham personally but, a favourite expression of Felix's, "trees do not grow all the way up to heaven". He hoped to have completed his overture, originally called the Lonely Isle, later, universally known as the *Hebrides* or 'Fingal's Cave', in time for that date. He suggested that Abraham's date of birth – 10th December – should be marked on the score, so that his father could imagine being presented with the gift in person. He would like to bestow every day the best he had the power to give, but reflected that this should only be put into effect on a special day, such as an anniversary. Though Abraham could not read music, he would see the date on the score. In fact, the overture was not completed until 1832. When Fanny arrived in Rome in 1839, though her father had died four years earlier, she still acknowledged his birthday, saying that there was bright sunshine and that a fire was necessary only in the morning and evening.

More information comes to light regarding birthdays celebrated by Fanny. Whilst holidaying in the Harz Mountains in 1827, Felix wrote the motet *Tu es Petrus* for her, which, she wrote to Klingemann, was to be sung at the Berlin Singakademie. The next year, one of his *Songs Without Words* was presented to his sister. In the same letter she reported that a dance was held, to which "very pretty girls" were invited – presumably for her elder brother's benefit. From Rome, for her 25th birthday, Felix sent her the setting of Psalm 115, 'Not unto Us, O Lord', and further music would be arriving for her. "You know the melody well. There is an air in it which has a good ending, and the last chorus will, I hope, please you." His 1st Piano Concerto, "for Paris", began to "float in my head" and, "if Providence should grant it", he hoped he and Fanny would enjoy all these compositions together. The following year, 1831, he sent Fanny the score of a Bach chorale that Schelble, director of the St Cecilia Society of Frankfurt, had copied for his guest, rising early to have it ready for despatch. Felix wrote that the music sounded "as if angels were singing in heaven" and just right for this time, especially as he had heard of the death of his favourite aunt, Henriette Mendelssohn, and their sister Rebecka's engagement to Gustav Dirichlet. Schelble put Felix to shame "at every moment" by "some new kindness, and his clear judgement teaches me constant lessons". The organ arrangement had been made "for double pedal, eight feet; not a note is missing", Felix told his "dear little sister and musician". The St Cecilia Society would give a concert of works by "Handel, Bach, Mozart and a chorus by me", a work from his 'Roman period'. He asked Fanny and Rebecka to perform the chorale he was to send, pointing out: "At the end, when the chorale melody begins to flutter and dies out way up in the air and eventually dissolves into sound – it is surely heavenly. There are many others too, just as powerful, but...this one fits today exactly."

From Düsseldorf in 1834 Felix asked how Fanny proposed to occupy herself on her birthday. Would she make music, read newspapers or – a thought he disliked – would she be away from home? "If only we could be together now, in the evening, for, when the candles are lit – here they come with the candles [now] – I wish I were at home , even more than in the mornings." He had hoped to compose

Chapter 13: Festivals, Private and Public

a piece for Fanny's birthday, "but work has swallowed up everything" and only now was Felix able to return to routine. That afternoon he visited the artist Bendemann and his family and had to "listen to his wife's dejection, despite her own birthday, at having to visit her in-laws" in Berlin, leaving the children in Düsseldorf.

Fanny married Wilhelm Hensel on 3rd October 1829, and it was on 16th June of the following year that their only son Sebastian was born, two months premature. Felix composed a song for the new mother, "in tender mood", which was later incorporated into his Op. 30 album of *Songs without Words* as No. 2 of the set. Felix wished he could be with his sister to talk to her, but wrote from Munich: "May it please God to bestow upon you all that I hope and pray" regarding Fanny's welfare. There was so much noise around him from the guests he was entertaining that his head was bursting. Nevertheless, Felix wished the new parents "happiness and love more serene than anything I can think of". Felix congratulated his own parents on their new status as grandparents; Rebecka on being an aunt; and Paul on being a second uncle. He had wanted to throw his arms around the messenger who had delivered Fanny's letter that gave the news. He tried to compose a song for his nephew, but any attempt made by Felix resembled "stirred milk [that] turns into cheese". Felix asked Fanny to send "all the cards, newspaper articles and even the baby's rattle" as souvenirs. What would Sebastian's full name be? "Sebastian is not bad [but]," he considered, "Felix should be added. It does have something pretty about it, after all, and I think that, later, I may love the little rascal, if he carries my name. Otherwise not," he joked. He asked Fanny, again in jest, not to find "some lout" to represent him at Sebastian's baptism, "but someone who likes me, and I him". The mother "must also let the man drink a lot of chocolate as I would have done, had I been there".

Sebastian Hensel celebrated his tenth birthday in Italy and, in order for him to remember the day, Fanny and Wilhelm took their son to see Mount Vesuvius. The "most fatiguing, uphill ride" began on horseback, since there were not enough donkeys to accommodate everyone. Sebastian and his parents rode over deposits from earlier eruptions from the volcano that had spoilt vineyards, uprooted trees and caused the ground to become black. Their guide pointed out traces of lava that could be dated, which were "not quite cold". Though Hensel asked if Fanny could be carried up the ascent, she would have preferred to climb; however experienced her bearers were, they constantly slithered on loose stones and lava deposits. This "torture" lasted an hour, until they reached "Satan's headquarters – a stony, cindery plain", as Fanny described the plateau. They did not climb Vesuvius itself, but Fanny observed the different shapes the mountain adopted, depending on the angle from which it was viewed. The Hensels gazed "with curiosity, amusement and horror" into a crater. "What a diabolical mass, with its sulphurous smell; colours that are not normally seen in nature – green, yellow, red and blue, all poisonous hues – and the ashy grey at the bottom of the cauldron; the smoke now thick, now thin, rising from all the crevices, enveloping everything, while concealing nothing."

All this, changing with every turn, made up a "spectacle of horror". From one crater that they climbed a beautiful view was revealed. Fanny "preferred to sacrifice my feet" to descend, rather than be carried down. The party were smothered in smoke, ash filling their shoes at every step. "Wading, panting and stumbling" they reached terra firma. Dragging one foot in front of the other, and far behind the rest of the party, the descent was ten minutes' experience she would never forget. However, having rejoined everyone else, and resting at a hermitage where a cold meal was eaten and 'Lachrymae Christi' was drunk, Fanny was glad to be back in "civilisation". "Last, but not least, my bed was most welcoming; one appreciates such comforts after seeing the Old Gentleman (the Mendelssohns' name for the devil, i.e. Vesuvius) and his domestic arrangements." Yet, despite any discomfort, few ten-year-old boys from Germany could have experienced such an unusual birthday treat.

On 16th June 1847 Sebastian's last birthday that his uncle Felix would be able to acknowledge was, for his nephew, "the most mournful one you have yet known", Fanny having died four weeks previously on 14th May. Felix hoped that future birthdays would give Sebastian hope and comfort; that he would gain strength from the knowledge that his mother's spirit would be watching over everything he did and any ambitions he might fulfil. "May your daily steps be directed to that path towards which your mother's eyes were turned for you and that the example of her being...will go with you as long as you remain true to her memory." He also hoped that his nephew would prove himself "estimable and upright" in all he achieved.

Rebecka's birthday on 11th April 1840 was celebrated by the Hensels at the Villa Wolkonsky in Rome, where cypresses, roses and aloes grew abundantly. The evening was spent at the moonlit Coliseum, where Gounod climbed into an acacia-tree to throw branches to the party below. This reminded Fanny of the scene in *Macbeth* where Birnam Wood walked to Dunsinane, as foretold by the witches. The whole day seemed "like a poem, where every moment will live in the mind forever; it resembled *The Decameron*, where everyone did as they pleased", except that, on this occasion, "only what was proper" occurred and nothing "would have brought hesitation or shame" to Fanny, had she presented herself to the princess at the tribune in Boccaccio's story. Whilst Fanny prepared "plates and provisions", the others in the party sketched in the villa garden. Later, song settings were performed, including some by Felix and Fanny. They had intended to visit the neighbouring Villa Massini, but storms kept them indoors at the "elegantly furnished" Villa Wolkonsky. Though the guests kept jumping up to view the foul weather from the belvedere, Fanny saw a beautiful rainbow, the like of which she had never before seen: "A perfect double arch, glowing in the most intense colours, spanning my beautiful Albano Hills precisely and visible for nearly half an hour." They were able to drink coffee out of doors and the maid Jette's cooking was appreciated by all the nationalities that made up the company. As darkness fell,

Chapter 13: Festivals, Private and Public

glow-worms illuminated the rose garden and a further performance of songs took place. A tombola was then arranged, the prizes including three piano pieces composed by Fanny. The best piece was drawn by a colonel, who was not amused, his sight having almost failed, but he admired the composer nevertheless. Eduard Magnus won an engraving after Raphael but, as he was soon to leave for Germany, he did not know what to do with his prize. For those who drew blanks – sheets of notepaper with views of Rome – Fanny promised to copy further compositions for them. The impromptu fête had been one of the most satisfying Fanny had ever experienced; there were no drawbacks – even the thunderstorms added enjoyment to the proceedings. Rebecka, too, would have revelled in the celebration and Fanny had often spoken of her sister, whilst in Italy, to those who had not yet met her.

It was on Rebecka's 34th birthday, in 1845, that Felix had a marvellous piece of news to convey. The Mendelssohns' most trustworthy friend, Carl Klingemann, had become engaged to Sophie Rosen, stepsister of his deceased friend Friedrich Rosen, the Oriental scholar. The couple had met in Detmold, Felix describing Sophie as "very pretty to look at, with smooth, fair hair parted in the middle and a thorough German face: round, with blue eyes. She is also highly educated and has the same quiet, pleasant manner as her stepbrother – modesty and depth of feeling." Though she lived in England at the time, Klingemann would bring Sophie to Germany, once they were married. Like Felix, Klingemann considered very carefully before taking the decision, not even confiding in his soul mate before asking his bride for her hand. When Felix did receive the news, he "danced round the room for five minutes with joy". Felix was to compose a further book of *Songs without Words* that he would dedicate to the new bride.

It appears that not only on that occasion did poor Rebecka's birthday take second place in anyone's thoughts. Fanny recollected that her sister's anniversary coincided with the 'Landtag' or diet that was to take place in Berlin. In the previous year Fanny was far more concerned with Felix's eighth visit to London. Whilst she looked forward to Rebecka's report of how she spent the day, Fanny found the thought of Felix's departure "disgusting; I do not know how we shall get on without him", but looked forward to the summer, when the family would be reunited. As for the Dirichlet children, the only record as to any birthday celebration concerns their eldest son Walter. In Sorrento, Rebecka wrote that a donkey ride was arranged with the Nerans' children, together with "a feast of cakes and apricots". Among his presents, he received "an olive wood paintbox and some Neapolitan prints that will amuse Fanny".

As early as 1821, when Felix was 12, he wrote to Paul on his ninth birthday – 30th October – enquiring what presents his younger brother had received, and asking him to "grow tall for me, both in body and in mind, and may you soon be done with the pronouns". Felix wrote from Leipzig on his way to see Goethe in Weimar, with Zelter and daughter Doris. He asked Paul to remember him to their grandmother, Babette Salomon – Leah's mother. From Rome in 1830 Felix wished

Paul "nothing but the best". He hoped that "all the little discords" the brothers might have experienced were now behind them. He recalled an incident, three years before, when they were "quarrelling so violently one morning [that] I threw you off the chair, whereupon you scratched me; I reported you; you could not stand me, whereupon I became very angry". Though he did not remind Paul of the reason for this quarrel, Felix believed that, since that time, they had become far closer, "as if the unpredictability of both our moods had become moderated somewhat". Giving his kid brother a homily – a trait inherited, no doubt, from their father – Felix continued: "I have taken much pleasure in the course of your education and plans, and certainly hope that your lively interest and your warm sympathy in everything is not just temporary, and that there will never again be any sort of unpleasantness between us... If I can bring myself to stop myself snapping at you so horribly when you turn the page too late, and you can manage to be at home from time to time when I desire it and not go out so often, which you did when I lay abed with measles, then I am convinced of it." Since they could not correspond for a while, "it is good to shake hands (metaphorically) and wish one another something festive". Felix did feel "properly festive", imagining himself at home on Paul's special day, with all their friends. At present, however, he was in a coach on his way to Rome.

Meanwhile, if Paul's party did not take place, Felix hoped to be entertained by his brother "setting out a chair and [providing] a huge pound cake to soothe my spirits". In 1846 Felix asked if Paul was to have a cake "decorated with lights" on his birthday, and if Fanny's or Rebecka's family would be dining with Albertine and himself and – if so – where? Did Paul miss Felix and his family in Leipzig? He regretted that he could not find suitable words "in the tongue of our fatherland" to express his wishes for Paul at this time. All he could call to mind at that time showed "mediocrity or, worse, vapid superficiality parading itself". He would have thanked his brother for "the beautiful copy of Dahlmann" were it not for "the accumulation of visitors, whose enquiries and propositions were almost entirely worthless...singers, musicians, a fine heap of compositions...overflowing with the longest words; full of patriotic ardour; anything but striving after high aims, though laying claim to the highest of all".

But how did Felix himself spend his birthdays? In an early letter he thanked Fanny for her good wishes, and asked if she had heard the tale of the emperor of China, who had "written an angry letter in a brilliant red pencil". Conversely, Felix would choose "a grass-green pencil, a sky-blue one, or whatever colour a pleasant pencil ought to assume" when addressing his sister. From Italy he decided to write home two days prior to his birthday, in case he was "not in a writing mood" on the day. It was not likely, he reflected, that the Papal Band would play, as happened when a regiment serenaded him the previous year in Berlin. Notwithstanding his active social life, however, Felix had to "drive all such fancies away by hard work". He had told everyone that his birthday fell on 29th January, in order that the real

Chapter 13: Festivals, Private and Public

anniversary would "glide quietly by" unobserved. He would place Fanny's portrait beside him in the morning "and will feel happy looking at it and thinking of you". He would then "play over my military overture" (his Trumpet Overture) and would then select his favourite dish from the menu at the Lepra Restaurant. Later he wrote of the new pope's coronation. "The pope was carried to the High Altar, followed by servants wearing peacock's feathers. The people crowded to the cathedral door; the pope embraced each cardinal in turn, who each kissed his feet." Felix heard the first notes of the Papal Choir – "That was enough!" He stood among Capuchin monks. "These saintly men are far from devotional on such occasions and by no means display cleanliness." Later barrels of pitch were burnt in the streets and the Church of the Propagation of the Faith was illuminated – not because the pope had lived opposite, but on account of Felix's birthday!

Not all birthdays were joyful, however. Whilst in Paris in 1832 Felix heard of the death of his good friend, the violinist Eduard Rietz. It was as much as he could do, when breaking the sad news to Hiller, not to lose control of himself. During the next few months he would receive even worse tidings, of the deaths of Goethe and Zelter. In 1835 Fanny wrote to Klingemann on the day after Felix's birthday that parts of *St Paul* had been performed. Their father admitted that, whilst he did not have enough talent to compose such a work, his intellect did allow him to enjoy it. In 1844 Felix gave a dinner for the opera singer, Mme. Schröder-Devrient, and her mother, "who has a host of good stories". Gade and Schleinitz were also present. On the following Saturday Fanny would have more visitors to entertain for Dirichlet's birthday, but she found entertaining "such an effort", as if she "had become unaccustomed to acting as hostess". His health was drunk, nevertheless, and Mme. Schröder-Devrient, who was also invited, sang "as often as possible", including arias from Mozart's *The Marriage of Figaro* and *La Clemenza di Tito*. Felix was "grotesquely amused" at verses Hensel had written. He would treasure these, as he claimed not to possess such a gift himself.

Felix's final birthday in this world – 3rd February 1847 – appeared to have been a great success. The entertainment included a sketch performed by his wife and her sister Julie Schunck, who, as lady's maids, caused much laughter. One of the charades represented the word 'Gewandhaus'; Joseph Joachim played the G-string on his violin to represent the first syllable. For 'wand' (German for 'wall'), the relevant scene from *A Midsummer Night's Dream* was acted, and 'haus' was represented by Charlotte Moscheles, who had written that scene, knitting a blue stocking, at the same time lecturing female authors to remain in the home to pursue their domestic duties. The denouement, 'Gewandhaus', showed the Mendelssohn and Moscheles children playing toy instruments – trumpets and drums – whilst Joachim played his violin and Felix Moscheles conducted like Louis Julien (whose various ventures went bankrupt, including his 'promenade concerts' in London, half a century before those of Henry Wood). Several biographers mistakenly state that Paganini came to Felix's party but, as he had died in 1840, this cannot have been possible.

How were Felix's gifts received? Fanny wrote to Klingemann of her brother's choral work *Antiphon et Responsorium* (Op. 121) that the Berlin Singakademie would perform. He was making increasing progress in "clarity and depth" with his compositions. "His ideas take more and more a fixed direction and he already advances towards the aim he has set himself and of which he is already conscious. He has full command over all his talents...ruling, like a general, all the means of development art can offer him." Mendelssohn is rarely associated either with marches or waltzes, but each of these appears in the canon of his compositions. Two waltzes were written for a forest ranger's daughter in Switzerland and a march was composed, in 1836, for the funeral of Norbert Burgmüller, promising brother of the better-known Johann Friedrich. A second march was composed to honour the artist Peter Cornelius, whose achievements were commemorated by a festival at Dresden in 1841.

But, as regards 'compositions for special occasions and family celebrations', such pieces were omitted from Julius Benedict's original catalogue, though no explanation is given. Some critics suggest that such works were not deemed worthy of inclusion, but this does not take account of Mendelssohn's almost pathological distaste for his own work. Why should his compositions be allowed to moulder in obscure museums or, even worse, be grabbed by 'private collectors' at auction, to be hoarded and treated as trophies of acquisition, not to be shared with Mendelssohn connoisseurs? Fortunately, however, there are libraries and museums where access can be gained.

From Italy Felix wrote of a piece, "unfinished", that, according to Philip Radcliffe, contained "a rather pompous letter". As the dedication was to his father, if Felix appeared "pompous" this is quite understandable; not knowing in advance how his unpredictable father might react could have caused undue defensiveness. Mendelssohn's *Variations concertantes* (Op. 17) were dedicated to Paul. This was the first of his chamber works to allow the 'cello to play a prominent part, though no instruments 'upstaged' each other. Because of its technique, consummate skill is required to perform the work to the standard it deserves; in view of this, Paul must have been eminently capable of acquitting himself sufficiently highly for his brother to compose such a work. Yet Fanny also wrote pieces for the family. As soon as she had enough leisure time, she explained she would make a piano arrangement of her brother's *Midsummer Night's Dream* Overture – a far nicer present than a purse or pocketbooks, she believed. For Rebecka's 35th birthday, Fanny composed a trio in D minor, inspired, perhaps, by Clara Schumann's Op. 17 Trio.

But not only musical gifts were proffered by Felix and his family. Like her namesake, Fanny Horsley owned an album, in which 137 signatures were collected. That of 'Niccolò' (Paganini) contained a blot. Most of these autographs can be attributed to the diligence of Felix, who carried the album around with him

Chapter 13: Festivals, Private and Public

wherever he travelled. Abraham Mendelssohn wrote a message in French and it was only then that Miss Horsley knew his first name, having imagined it to be 'Adam' or 'Ahaziah'. The various pianos Felix had to purchase have been discussed in Chapter 10, 'That money question', but Aloys Fuchs's help was sought for musical memorabilia, details of which likewise appear in more appropriate parts of this book.

The Mendelssohn correspondence gives glimpses of birthday parties celebrated by friends and acquaintances, or acknowledgement of greetings for such events. From London, in 1829, Felix wrote to Adolf Bernhard Marx that he hoped Marx's brother would visit on his birthday. "If so, may he bring you happiness, good cheer and lasting strength and remind you that, even from a great distance, my sincerest heart is always with you and with your family." At a similar time, Johann Droysen recalled a birthday party given for him at Leipzigerstrasse 3. "After the congratulations that were roared out from everyone," he wrote to his sister. Fanny and Rebecka, "bedecked with lilacs and cornflowers" (Droysen's favourite blooms), placed on the table his favourite dish, anchovy paste, fashioned into the shape of a dolphin, with blue jewels for eyes and blades of grass sprouting from the nose to represent jets of water. Leah gave their guest a coffee maker, which must have been an early version of that appliance. In 1833 Felix wrote to Klingemann that, though he would have preferred to attend Fanny's birthday celebration, he had to pay a "duty" visit to a Mme. Beer for the same purpose. "Fanny is young and nicer than Mme. Beer," he confided to his friend. The decorations for a birthday party at Saarn, where Felix rode from Düsseldorf, comprised wreaths of flowers. His hostess, 'Mme. T.', organised "fireworks, archery and a ball". Whereas, on an earlier visit, the apple trees had been covered with blossom, they now bore "unripe, green apples". Yet there were still the same carriages and flocks of sheep: "The same noisy, merry life goes on in the blacksmith's forge; the burgher from Dettingen shaving himself just the same."

In a more southerly environment, the artist Kaselowsky's birthday was celebrated in Rome on 26th May 1844. His gifts included a straw hat; a cameo ring "that he had been ogling for some time"; some plants for his balcony; and a double opera glass. In the afternoon the party, which included Rebecka and her family, visited the Villa Pamphili, and they "had a cake and a cup in the evening". In Berlin, meanwhile, Fanny wrote to Rebecka that a "torchlight procession had been arranged in honour of Professor Böckh's birthday", to be incorporated in a festival, his students having gained permission from the Prussian authorities. However, because ten names had been removed by the police from the list of invited guests, all the professor received was "hearty congratulations", with no further celebrations. Böckh was more popular than another university professor whom Fanny met at a social evening. His students had refused to attend the latter's third lecture, and addresses had been presented to the authorities, questioning the suitability of his appointment.

Christmas was equally important to the Mendelssohn family. The earliest record of their celebrations is a letter written by Felix, home from his first visit to Weimar, in which he sent Goethe's two grandsons a 'waldteufel' each – a noisy rattle that amused children (and annoyed parents, no doubt), which could be easily purchased in the streets of Berlin. In a similarly light vein, he composed two 'Children's Symphonies', one for Rebecka and one for Paul. Sebastian Hensel states that the pieces comprised the same instruments as the 'Toy Symphony', formerly attributed to Haydn. (It has lately come to light that it was, in fact, Leopold Mozart, Wolfgang's father, who composed this work.) Hensel states, in his memoir of 1879, that, whilst one of his 'Children's Symphonies' was published, the second "was lost". Like much of Mendelssohn's output this, as far as can be ascertained, has never been performed, and no recording exists. In 1828 Fanny wrote to Klingemann in London of her preparations for the festive season. So occupied was she with embroidery that she had forgotten for the moment that any other strings existed than her silks. "Men do not realise how much work there is for women to do, as the season approaches", but her table cover was admired nevertheless. She and Rebecka were trying to instil some manners into Otto Gans of Berlin University, "which get forgotten at times". A dinner was to be given for 'the Breslau Mendelssohns' – uncle Joseph and his family.

In 1833 Mendelssohn spent Christmas with his cousin Benjamin Mendelssohn in Bonn. He planned to leave Düsseldorf on the 24th "by special coach" in the early morning, and hoped to arrive at about noon. He requested the customary "gingerbread horses, raisins and apples" and hoped to sample the Graf piano he had asked Aloys Fuchs to despatch from Vienna. "Otherwise, I am not coming," Felix had threatened in an earlier letter; "especially if you invite nasty neighbours." He planned to bring some port wine he had ordered, plus "some four-part things", as he disapprovingly called his compositions. Fuchs came to Felix's aid also in 1836 when choosing items for an album belonging to Cécile Jeanrenaud, whom Felix would "go through fire" to please. Fuchs produced autographs of Haydn, Mozart and Beethoven – a far greater surprise and delight than the prospective bridegroom anticipated. Meanwhile Fanny wrote to Cécile that two orange trees in the ante-room and one large fir tree in the blue drawing room were decorated with "little lamps" in lemon rinds. A tombola was to be arranged – "without blanks, of course" – for Hensel's pupils. Hensel's present from his wife was to be "an ounce of ultramarine" with which to paint; he had not bought this for a long time as it was very expensive in Berlin. Felix, staying with Cécile's family in Frankfurt, wrote home that he had never enjoyed the season's festivities so much. He encountered "fresh joy" at every moment of his life. His fiancée not only enjoyed the sketches but could not keep them out of her hands the whole evening. But Mme. Jeanrenaud's gift to Felix was not so highly appreciated. The portrait of Cécile was not to his liking and it was only the family's kindness in presenting it that stopped him venting his true feelings, which he did when writing to the artist 'Herr H.' in

Chapter 13: Festivals, Private and Public

Vienna. The "coarse mistakes" revealed its subject "as an ordinary young woman, flattered with a pink and white complexion, light blue eyes". The painting was quite unlike the real Cécile, who had "a natural complexion" and eyes of an unusual violet blue. "Herr H. did not adhere to truth at all" and Felix hoped that Philipp Veit's portrait would be more true to life. He found the painting "abominable" and found it difficult "not to say some impolite things", he confided to Fanny. Nevertheless, 'Herr H.' appears to have mollified Felix, admitting that Cécile's "noble countenance" would have caused difficulty to any artist in showing her true character.

When his own eldest son, Karl Wolfgang Paul, was a baby, Felix wrote to Sebastian to thank him for some chocolates, explaining that the baby would have written himself, had he not been "too dumb" to accomplish this. He also thanked the family on Cécile's behalf for her "lovely presents".

Christmas 1839 was spent by the Hensels in Italy – their first time away from home for such a festival. This caused Fanny to feel homesick but, despite this, the family made the best of the circumstances. Julie, their cook, was herself on holiday, so Fanny cooked the meals. At the market, some distance away from their lodgings, she bought "rice and pasta for the soup" and, for dessert, she made a "pound cake" that she heated in a frying pan; "ground to powder" as a result, it "was only suitable for a gentleman's wig". "Between ourselves," she wrote to Rebecka, "there is such a curiosity shop of people" that she felt unable to invite them to join the family in the festivities. She would simply "scatter a few grains of amusement among the respectable" acquaintances, but "so dull is everyone" that Fanny felt happier alone with husband and son. On the 30th, however, her Christmas appears to have been more enjoyable than had been anticipated. She wished the rest of the family could have seen the beautiful flowers at the Villa Mills, named after the English owners. In the garden was a palace purporting to have belonged to one of the Caesars and a summerhouse with lovely views, decorated by Guilio Romano, which reminded her of an enchanted castle in a fairy tale. The property was for sale "at a trifle", for anyone interested in purchasing it. For gifts, Fanny received "a little ivory-inlaid cabinet" from Hensel and, in return, she gave her husband a Veronese sketch. "People are supposed to become thin in Italy; their purses certainly do." Midnight Mass was attended at what Fanny invariably called "the Sixtine Chapel" and an advantageous place was acquired the next morning to witness the pope's blessing, which began at 8.30 a.m. "The women sit on a raised dais to see and be seen in their multicoloured bonnets and feathers," Fanny observed. "Their black veils, supposed to be obligatory, were not in evidence at all. There were so many uniforms – civic, military and clerical", as Goethe had noticed, that Fanny wondered how St Peter might have viewed such finery "put on, it seems, as if for the tourists' benefit, as if one was watching a costume drama"; but the women's voices in the congregation were far better trained than those of the Papal Choir.

In Berlin, the Christmas of 1842 was a sad occasion, being the first after Leah's death. However, Felix kept everyone amused by interrupting his work on music for the cathedral by helping Fanny and Cécile to arrange the presents, or play with the horses and dogs, returning to his music "with renewed zeal and earnestness". Fanny suggested that, another time, a picnic could be held in the garden house, as she had discovered that it could easily be heated and the weather was often mild in any case. She was to attend a rehearsal at the cathedral at New Year of her brother's setting of Psalm 98. As a rule, the crowds dissuaded her from attending services at festival-times; "to stand for long is too much a trial of faith", and she hoped to reserve a seat.

The next few years, letters from Felix report how Christmas was spent in Leipzig or Berlin. Karl, Felix's eldest son, appeared to be in his element, riding his new rocking horse before the beautifully decorated tree, blowing a toy trumpet and yelling in imitation of a coachman. Apart from two unfinished pictures, because Felix could not paint by candlelight, everything was ready, he told Rebecka on 23rd December 1843. The candles were placed in the chandeliers in the blue drawing room, to be joined next day by the tree. Large and small plants would be placed in the double window. Cécile would receive "a black satin dress; a bonnet, a few trinkets and one of my well-known, much too green, landscapes on pressed carton paper" as gifts. Paul would receive a reproduction of a landscape from the art dealer Sachse, for which he yearned. Fanny would receive a table cover, embroidered no doubt by the industrious Cécile. Hensel's gift was to be "a large ham and some claret"; Sebastian was to receive "a study lamp", and Felix's own children "some small furniture, which they need". On Christmas Day Felix was to conduct a concert in Berlin Cathedral "for the first time with an orchestra". This comprised 'To Our Salvation', (items) from Handel's *Messiah* and "a few more trifles of mine and some chorales with trombones", as he dismissed the rest of the programme. The New Year concert would be "much the same, with a variation of colour". "I must say that...so far, I do not expect much from it," he told Rebecka, though the music critic Rellstab believed "the concerts to be almost better than those of the Paris Conservatoire". On another occasion Fanny reported: "The weather, being fine for a wonder, we loitered in the streets before taking a walk. In the evening, the family played 'Black Peter' with Professor Böckh, when Sebastian was allowed to paint black moustaches on the participants."

On 25th June 1829 Felix wrote to Fanny from London that "the time is fast approaching" towards the parents' silver wedding on 26th December, for which plans would have to be made. "I have some ideas already that I have jotted down, which I will send you." Meanwhile, he asked his mother the precise date of Fanny's forthcoming wedding and if her trousseau was ready. This interested him far more than "the arrival of the empress" or many other items of news in Leah's letters. "I must find everything arranged when I return to Berlin." He aimed to dine with Fanny on the day before the wedding and expected his favourite dishes to be served. If there was no private accommodation available, Hensel was to stay at the

Chapter 13: Festivals, Private and Public

Brandenburg Hotel until his marriage. In fact, as has already been observed, a coach accident prevented Felix attending the wedding.

Meanwhile, at Leah's and Abraham's silver wedding, Felix jested that the celebrated tenor John Braham would sing; Charles Neate, Beethoven's London agent, would play a piano concerto; and a dinner would be given. "Although I approve of quiet weddings, silver weddings should be noisy," he stated. Felix could provide a steam engine as a gift, or would his parents prefer "a little Indiaman" or the front of their house to be macadamised. If none of these ideas were suitable, would Fanny write with her own suggestions, "in a systematic fashion". Meanwhile Felix was "hatching up great things" but he was "too tired from dancing" to relate them at present. The final entertainment was a singspiel, *Son and Stranger* (discussed in Chapter 17, 'Quest for an opera'). It is interesting that, whereas Mendelssohn is credited with a superhuman memory for music scores, the same does not apply to more people-related matters. At Christmas 1833 he reminded Klingemann that not only was it his parents' 28th wedding anniversary, but the third anniversary of his singspiel *Son and Stranger*. In fact he was a year too few in his calculation, the events having occurred four years previously.

Rebecka's wedding also took place whilst Felix was away from home, in 1832. Nevertheless, he wrote during his second visit to London to "the newly-weds, of whom I know only half, but will [become acquainted] and for a long time... What more could one wish for in the way of youth and talent than Dirichlet as a member of the family?" Of non-family weddings, a letter from Fanny, on her 1839-40 visit to Italy, told of a marriage of one of the Woringen daughters, for which the remaining sisters "ran errands, sewed, arranged everything...with such method... If Korff does not make Rosa, his bride, happy beyond measure, I will kill him, of a certainty." When Johann Droysen became engaged in 1834, to Marie Mendheim (originally Marie Mendel), Felix, whilst congratulating his boyhood friend, regretted the sense of loss that they would no longer remain in one another's company.

Christenings, too, played a part in family celebrations. Writing to Fanny in Italy, Felix reported that his mother and Paul attended his elder daughter Marie's baptism at the end of 1839, but this appears to be the only communication relating to his own five children, or those of Rebecka's or Paul's little ones, as far as their christenings are concerned. But it is evident that Felix was invited on several occasions to become a godfather to other friends. He congratulated Pastor Bauer on becoming a father, but had to decline attending the baptism, because he was too grief-stricken at the loss of his father a few days earlier. "If, in later years, you tell your child the names of those who were invited to this ceremony, do not omit my own from your guest list, but say to him that one of them, on that day, recommenced his life again too, though in another sense, with new purposes and wishes, and new prayers to God." By a strange coincidence, on 12th January 1843 Felix declined a similar invitation from Professor Köstlin, who had married Felix's former pupil, Josephine Lang, the year before. Though he could not be present himself, owing to his mother's recent death, Felix would be there in spirit and upbraided Köstlin for supplying so few details about his child. "You do not even mention the name your boy is to be given, whether he is fair or dark, or whether he has blue or dark eyes. My wife would be as delighted as I am to know all this and we hope that, after the christening, you will write to us with every particular."

Felix felt he should have written in a more cheerful frame of mind but, in view of his recent loss, this would be hypocritical: "During the past few weeks, my mother's loss has bowed us down with grief, from which it will take a long time to recover." Just as Felix shared his friend's joy, he hoped Köstlin might share his own sorrow and asked if his wife had composed any music recently, which is "so delightful to hear and play". But there was a far more enjoyable event: the baptism of Ignaz Moscheles's son in February 1833. On Mendelssohn's third visit to London, he was able to be present, as godfather, to Moscheles's son Felix. On 27th February, Marek relates that Felix sent "a lovely cradle song with a letter", but gives no further details. What Felix wrote to his godson may well be worth copying to congratulate any baby: "May he be prosperous (in spirit) and may he do well in whatever he does and may it fare well with him in the world." Felix Moscheles was also sent a sketch of appropriate musical instruments, with explanations as to their significance:

"His cradle song must include drums and trumpets; fiddles alone are inadequate as they are not lively enough. May happiness, joy and blessing attend the little stranger... This full orchestra consists of trumpets for when he wishes to become famous; flutes for when he falls in love; cymbals for when he grows a beard; the piano explains itself; and, if anyone plays him false, as happens to the best of us, there should be a kettledrum and the big drum in the background. This orchestra is to accompany little Felix throughout life."

He concluded that, in April, "we shall name the boy and introduce him to the world at large; it will be grand". Mendelssohn looked forward to hearing a septet composed by Moscheles, of which Klingemann sent him "11 notes", which he liked "very much indeed", and imagined what a bright, lively finale they would make. Klingemann had also given Mendelssohn an analysis of an andante Moscheles had written, but Felix realised how much better this would sound when it was played on his forthcoming visit. Fanny Horsley attended Felix's baptism, describing the baby to her aunt as resembling "a pickled walnut, with beautiful blue eyes". Three years later he had become "a sweet little boy" who should delight his namesake.

There were reports from Felix, Fanny and Rebecka relating to carnivals in Italy. On the new pope's enthronement in 1831, Felix wrote of platforms being erected; posters advertising horse racing, and samples of masks being available – none of this for any other purpose than to celebrate his birthday, he joked. A traditional ceremony was acted whereby the Jews begged to be allowed to remain in the city –

Chapter 13: Festivals, Private and Public

"a request that was refused for a further year, from the top of the hill". But, after many entreaties, their request was granted "and the ghetto assigned to them," Felix wrote home. The crowd had to wait for two hours and the Jews' oration was understood as little by him as anyone else. Later, driving along, thinking of nothing in particular, he was assailed by a shower of sweetmeats from a group of young people, notably "a very elegant young Englishwoman". On attempting to bow to the party, he was again "pelted and...clutching the confetti, I flung it back bravely" and, because "swarms of acquaintances" continued this game, his blue coat became as white as a miller's clothing when grinding flour. The 'B family' showered confetti at Felix's head "like hailstones. Thus...amid a thousand jests and jeers and horse racing and the most extravagant masks, the day came to an end. Flowers and bonbons were indiscriminately thrown." A lady in a mask presented Felix with a bouquet, which he pressed in an album to take home. In the evening the "elegant lady" could be seen sitting in a coffee house, smoking her cigar. On the Saturday Felix rode around the walls on horseback. Having changed, he "bought pocketfuls of confetti, while the people laughed at me secretly, for what reason I do not know". On arriving at the former scene of the carnival, he saw "a dour-faced man; no masks; no ladies; no coaches, which made a strange, disagreeable impression" and dampened Felix's "splendid spirits". His memories of the carnival included a ball at the French embassy and "grand entertainment" by the Spanish ambassador. In the evening the dome of St Peter's "burns in the dark, violet air" and the whole city was illuminated. "Fireworks brighten the solid, gloomy walls of the castle of San Angelo, before falling into the Tiber." The family had to ask Hensel to describe the "pomp, brilliance and animation, which surpass everything, for my pen is not equal to the task".

Unlike Felix, Fanny reported, on her visit to Italy of 1839-40, that it "showed bad form" to throw confetti at a carnival. She was, nevertheless, equally involved in aiming and receiving flowers and sweets from acquaintances, but was hard put to pursue this activity on account of difficulty in seeing the missiles through her spectacles. A party of eight attended a fête, having fun en route, placing table napkins around one another's necks, pretending to be barbers shaving each other, and eating oranges – for which the napkins must have proved very useful to catch the juice. At the monument to St Cecilia Metella, about which Felix had told Fanny and which boasted a famous echo, one of the Hensels' party imitated the shouts and singing to such a remarkable degree that it was only later that the 'real' echo was discovered. Fanny taught the remainder of the company a comic song, 'Landon is come'. They did not mix with the "dust and confusion" of the crowd, but watched this particular fête from a distance. When Rebecka's turn came to visit Italy, Fanny had to advise her younger sister to attend the artist Delaroche's ball. "One must put shyness aside, or one may lose too much." This may well have stemmed from Fanny's experience of her own stay in that country. As for Rebecka's husband on the 1844 visit, Fanny mocked Dirichlet's throwing bouquets during that year's carnival, imagining him to have displayed "a learned man's contempt for folly of all kinds", and wondered "if he ever relaxes into a smile" – even at carnival time.

Julius Schubring recalled Felix to have been a "good" dancer, his birthday celebrated by a 'masquerade' or masked ball. A friend from the previous generation, Rahel Varnhagen von Ense, wrote of Felix dancing "like a cultured gale, yet all his sisters' girlfriends flew in and out of his arms". It is understandable, therefore, that, compared with the parties at Leipzigerstrasse 3, Rebecka complained, in Italy, of her current entertainments being "dull as leather, from which an enterprising shoemaker could provide enough boots and shoes for the whole world". The family watched the carnival celebrations from their carriage, the windows of their lodging, or from the balconies of friends' houses.

On another occasion the archaeologist Winkelmann's birthday was commemorated in the Tarpelian Room. Had Rebecka been present her sister would have been "as frolicksome (sic) as a rabbit", whereas she was now "as dull as a pug on a box". Despite this mood, Fanny's observations were as pointed as ever:

"The room was painted red in the Pompeian style, so antiquely low that Dirichlet would have had to bow all the time. On a green table, a bust of Winkelmann was surrounded by a nightcap of roses and ivy that you would have described as a wreath, at which Cécile would have shivered. Even before proceedings began, everyone whispered; the solemn atmosphere made me hard put not to burst into laughter. Many Germans spoke Italian, their pronunciation being as Italian as their names. When Herr Kastner spoke, he reminded me of a sensible old horse stumbling along at every step, yet managing not to break down altogether. Herr Braun confused 'B's with 'P's, 'D's with 'T's, as he galloped through his speech. Gottfried Müller, the lion of the occasion, tried to convince his audience that, having located some ancient documents, he could identify the precise spot of a building in the forum. Realising that counter-arguments could be equally plausible, I was tempted to give my own opinion, but held back only because it was the first time I had attended such a ceremony."

When the Dirichlets' turn came to visit Italy, Rebecka, like Felix and Fanny before her, reported joining in with the Roman carnival. "The throwing of confetti, made of plaster of Paris, is the last resort. Flowers are the order of the day and the bouquets look such a pretty sight as they are thrown in many different directions."

She was caught between her husband fielding flowers and sweetmeats and Walter, her elder son, digging Rebecka in the ribs in his excitement at all the masks. Yet this merriment was spoilt by dirty handkerchiefs mingling with the flowers thrown by the crowd, and the fact that a young man was stabbed whilst trying to protect a young lady from the mêlée. Rebecka reported how the jealous husband of a Mme. Clairbourg, all too aware of the sensation his wife was making by her appearance, pelted an apparent rival with confetti; "She makes Venus look like a fishwife" was Rebecka's observation.

Chapter 13: Festivals, Private and Public

Meanwhile, how did Felix's musical contribution fit into the festival scene? Throughout his life Mendelssohn was invited to direct musical festivals, chiefly throughout Germany, but in England also. These are dealt with elsewhere in this book, but other festivals had an individual character that warrant coverage here. As early as 1824, when Felix was 15, he showed his love and admiration for musicians of an earlier era. On 5th December he commemorated the anniversary of Mozart's death in 1791 by conducting a performance of the Requiem at Leipzigerstrasse 3. A repeat was given on Abraham's birthday, the 11th of the month. These were private performances, given for family and friends, but 1828 proved a busier year for Felix. The scientist Alexander von Humboldt invited the young musician to compose a cantata for a convention, organised on behalf of the Berlin Academy of Sciences. "As von Humboldt has no ear for music," Fanny wrote to Klingemann in London, "he has asked Felix to set the work for double basses, celli, trumpets, horns and clarinets, which sounds quite original." Everyone gossiped about how much everything cost and what food there would be. "To my mind, the most vexing aspect of the convention is that no women are allowed to attend, the Rules of Mohammed being observed," Fanny wrote. Devrient sniped at Felix for "flashing off these compositions at great speed" – quite unwarranted criticism, when it is learnt that Mendelssohn was given barely six weeks to complete the work. Unlike the 39th, 40th and 41st symphonies of Mozart, which were written in a similar time-span, von Humboldt's commission was not produced 'from the heart', claimed Devrient.

Devrient may have experienced 'sour grapes' because, as an actor who fancied himself at his profession, he was not invited to take part in the convention's entertainment. Apart from the music, a feast was given at which 700 guests attended. Jeremy Siepmann, in his biography of Chopin, states that that composer accompanied a colleague of his schoolmaster father, Professor Jarocky. Chopin recognised the opera impresario Spontini at the convention, but also Zelter and Mendelssohn. Since, however, Felix was so little known at the time outside his own environment, this seems hard to believe. Whilst Chopin had been fêted by the Polish and Russian nobility, such a privilege was outside Mendelssohn's ambit.

Von Humboldt's invitation had arisen from an earlier event: the 400th anniversary celebration of Albrecht Dürer's death. Schima Kaufman claims that Abraham had "prodded" his son into composing the cantata to be performed at that festival. "It would be a great honour and the eyes of the nation would be upon him." If this is true, it is more likely that such admiration would reflect on Abraham himself, rather than his son, the father hoped. Because obedience to his father prevailed in the young composer, his heart was, again, not in the work, and he was never satisfied with the result. "Once the purpose is served," Felix vowed, "the cantata will be destroyed." But, because of its success, the threat was never allowed to be pursued. The Berlin Singakademie was decorated to reflect the lovely April weather, the ambience completed by the beautiful dresses worn by the ladies in the audience. Her brother's Trumpet Overture was performed, to be followed by Herr Tolken's three-quarter-hour speech, as Fanny reported to Klingemann. "Felix's cantata lasted an hour," she continued, "and never have I experienced such supreme entertainment – so well directed" by Felix. At the succeeding banquet Mendelssohn was made a member of the Artists' Association, which, Fanny claimed, reconciled her brother to life in Berlin. Her most exciting news, however, was that Felix had been exempted from the usual year of service in the Prussian army, the reason for which seems never to have been explained. Yet, though the Dürer cantata did not meet with its progenitor's approval, a report in the London journal *The Harmonicon* of August 1828 spoke of Mendelssohn's "symphony or, rather, overture", as well as the cantata, as having "a good style, abounding in melodies and expression". This "young man of promise" was said to be Moses Mendelssohn's nephew, rather than his grandson. The philosopher's name still had an aura of culture and enlightenment in Britain.

A further national anniversary occurred in 1830 in which Felix also played a part. On 25th May he wrote to his family that a symphony was being composed to commemorate this 300th year after the Augsburg Confession, when Martin Luther had proclaimed the Protestant faith. "Should it be named the 'Confession' Symphony, 'Symphony for a Church Festival', the 'Juvenile' Symphony, or whatever you like?" he asked Fanny. It is evident that she agreed with the first title he had suggested – the 'Reformation' Symphony – by which the work is still known. However, the proposed festival was prohibited by the then still-powerful Roman Catholic Church in Germany. Further disappointment would arise when the work was planned to be performed on Mendelssohn's 1831-32 visit to Paris. The musicians derided the symphony, calling it "too learned" and "having too little melody; of too contrapuntal a nature and lacking in colour". This collection of criticisms was quashed completely in a pre-concert talk of 1997 by Martha Kingdon-Ward. The truth, she averred, was that these musicians "made excuses for their inability to play it". Even after a performance in Berlin, however, Mendelssohn was so disappointed at the result that he refused to have the work published in his lifetime. It was not, therefore, incorporated into the orchestral repertoire until 1868, having been published in 1852 as Op. 107. Even today the 'Reformation' Symphony is far less popular than deserved. The first movement is based on the so-called 'Dresden Amen', originally composed by Johann Neumann, which Wagner deemed worthy of inclusion in his opera *Parsifal*. The second movement is a ländler, or country dance, forerunner of the waltz, danced by country dwellers at a feast. The third movement of Schubert's 9th Symphony and the trio of Mahler's first such work have similar dance rhythms. Mendelssohn's third movement leads into the finale, a theme and variations on the hymn tune 'A Safe Stronghold Our God Is Still', the best known of Luther's hymns. Mendelssohn was never satisfied with his symphony, writing to Julius Rietz on 11th February 1838 that he "could not stomach" the work and wished to burn the manuscript.

Marek, it appears, agrees with the composer, calling the work "a letdown...religiously as unconvincing as some of his other churchly works". It must be remembered, nevertheless, that these were often written at the dictates of court officials – or the whims of his father.

1840 saw a further celebration. Throughout most of Germany, the 400th anniversary of Gutenberg's invention of the printing press was commemorated – preceding William Caxton by more than 30 years. (For some reason as yet unexplained, Frankfurt, like Austria, commemorated Gutenberg's invention in 1837.) As the centre of the printing, publishing and book dealing trades, Leipzig played a full part, in which Lortzing's opera *Hans Sachs* was produced at the theatre, whilst Mendelssohn was commissioned to write a piece to be performed at the Church of St Thomas. This 'symphony-cantata', as Klingemann called it, the *Hymn of Praise*, now ranks as Mendelssohn's 2nd Symphony. W. S. Rockstro described it as "undoubtedly, one of the master's finest works. It breathes a spirit of exultant praise, which we do not find surpassed in any part of his two great oratorios." The composition might not only be a tribute to Gutenberg's genius but to Leipzig, to thank her people for making Felix so welcome and by whom his musicianship was so highly respected and valued. Philip Radcliffe calls the beginning "pompous", whilst other sections of the work are dismissed as "stodgy and oppressive". A less biased observer would substitute the words "majestic and dignified" to describe the *Hymn of Praise*. Whatever modern musicologists might think, the fact remains that the King of Saxony enjoyed the work so much that he congratulated composer and musicians alike after the performance. Joseph Moore of Birmingham, on hearing the work, invited Mendelssohn to repeat it at the forthcoming Birmingham Festival of 1840, necessitating Mendelssohn's sixth visit to Britain. For this performance, as was his habit, Felix revised the work, incorporating 'Watchman, will the Night soon pass?', which Rockstro termed "the famous song". Apparently this addition was inspired by a sleepless night. Though no reason is given, this might have been caused by Mendelssohn's anxiety over Cécile's health, since their third child Paul would be born in the following January.

Subsequent performances of the *Hymn of Praise* were given in Dresden, to which Mendelssohn travelled via the new railway from Leipzig, and a lithograph exists in the town's museum at Lausanne, Switzerland, to commemorate a performance there. But this was not the only contribution from Mendelssohn's pen to pay tribute to Gutenberg. When the inventor's statue was erected, the ceremony was enhanced by the *Festival Song*, which, though very rarely heard today, is known throughout the English-speaking world through W. H. Cummings's adaptation of one of its melodies to fit Charles Wesley's words 'Hark! The herald Angels sing'; indeed, the tune is called 'Mendelssohn'. A further piece, *To the Artists*, with words by Schiller and based on Psalm 150, was also composed for the occasion. As Felix wrote on 22nd June 1840: "I take my stand by the lamp-post [in Market Square], and David is 130 yards away with the second orchestra. It is an enormous business, with 200 male singers, 20 trombones and 16 trumpets; Spontini would scarcely complain about the second violins on this occasion." Yet the fine weather boded well for the whole festival – unlike that at Mainz, where Neukomm's music was twice interrupted by pouring rain. Indeed, as Fanny commented on reading an article in a Strasbourg newspaper: "a real 'people's festival' has taken place" in Leipzig.

Chapter 14

"Flirting Outrageously"

The meaning of the verb 'to flirt' is defined in the dictionary as: "To behave or act amorously, without any emotional commitment." So often did Mendelssohn use this phrase – until he met Cécile Jeanrenaud – that it is evident he had no shame about the kisses or flowery speeches given to the various young ladies with whom he came into contact; likewise, no doubt, they accepted such behaviour in the same light-hearted spirit. Indeed, according to Stephen Stratton, writing in 1901, "Not one breath of scandal dimmed his character", and such later biographers as Blunt, Jacob and Marek took the subject further. "He lacked the driving sexual impulse... There is no sign that carnal stings overwhelmed him... His manliness was a manliness of the drawing room, not the bedroom... One woman he did love profoundly, and that was Fanny." In his *Memoirs of a Physician* of 1875 Dr. Strohmeyer recalled that, even as late as 1837, General von Webern, a family friend, observed Felix's love for his parents as allowing "no room in his heart for another great passion" – and this was the year in which he married! Gisela Selden-Goth, in her compilation of Mendelssohn's letters, adds fuel to this myth by reflecting that "we know of no love letters written by Mendelssohn". Cécile ordered many letters to be burnt, which may account for this scarcity of amorous correspondence, plus the fact that many other letters were destroyed by later generations of the family as unworthy of such a 'saint' figure. But the lack of love letters is irrelevant, since Mendelssohn, especially when describing personal feelings, always preferred the spoken as opposed to the written word. In any case, what need was there to use words when his music spoke far more cogently when declaring his love for a woman? What more appropriate way could Mendelssohn pour out his heart than via one of his exquisite melodies? "Words only get in the way" was a favourite saying of his.

But how true are such conjectures that Mendelssohn's sex life did not exist? To quote Marek once more: "Mendelssohn was uninterested in eroticism, overt or covert, frank or smutty." If this was so, how refreshing it must have been for young ladies brought up in the same sheltered environment as Felix, realising that this personable young man's conversation, though laced with wit and amusement, was free from anything that would cause embarrassment. Yet how did this public persona tally with the private equivalent? Since boyhood "Felix had an eye for pretty girls", according to Dr. John O'Shea, and instances abound in his correspondence as to how he enjoyed dancing and how he often acted as escort to young ladies. On his first visit to Goethe at Weimar, the 12-year-old Felix wrote to his family, showing not only shrewd perception but worldly wisdom beyond his years: "Fräulein Ulrika threw herself at Goethe's neck and, as he is making love to her and she is very pretty, it all adds to the general effect." The young Mendelssohn was discovering how real men and women behaved one to another and that such scenes were not only confined to literature. From Leipzig, en route, he told his family: "Doris [Zelter's daughter] combs my unruly mane", and even when her brother was married Rebecka recalled how Felix had "behaved with Doris at the dance". There were other youthful escapades that come to light. In their chapter on Mendelssohn, J. and D. L. Thomas state: "The garden at Leipzigerstrasse 3 resembled the Garden of Eden, where 'daughters of Eve' came to bestow their admiration and flirtation on this young man." Schima Kaufman embroiders her so-called biography of Mendelssohn with fantasies of a similar nature. Yet it can be relied upon that two girls of a similar age to Felix caused havoc within his heart. Claire, elder of the two sisters, was "a spirited brunette", whilst Leila was "blonde and romantic". Rumour had it that Felix and Leila were in love but believed themselves wholly unsuspected. Felix is purported to have called the young lady 'Lorelei' on account of her long, blonde hair. These might have been the two nieces of a Polish lady who lived in rooms at Leipzigerstrasse 3. When Leila and Claire were visiting, Felix, according to Marx's widow's memoirs, persuaded her late husband to throw peaches through the window (far more romantic than the banana, as narrated by Marek). Writing home from Düsseldorf in later years, Felix recalled " paying court to that pretty Russian girl". Since most of Poland was ruled by Russia at the time, he may be forgiven for confusing the two countries.

At the same time Devrient pointed out in his recollections that Mendelssohn was ill at ease with celebrated women, singling out Bettina Brentano von Arnim and Rahel Varnhagen von Ense, friends of his aunts Dorothea and Henriette. Had Felix realised how devotedly the latter had nursed wounded soldiers in a Prague hospital, to which his family had contributed, he might have felt more amenably towards her. Undoubtedly he respected the intellects of such women; he disliked anything or anyone pretentious. He particularly disdained the manner in which everyone appeared to hang on their every word, placing such women on a far higher pedestal than he thought they deserved.

In 1827, before setting out on his walking tour in the Harz Mountains with Magnus and Heydemann, Felix stayed with the Magnus family at Sakrow, outside Berlin. There he met "a mystery girl" to whom he was attracted, so much so that his song 'Can it be?' ('Es ist wahr?') was composed, together with the String Quartet Op. 13 bearing the same melody. In the latter piece a broadcaster, whose

Chapter 14: "Flirting Outrageously"

imagination was evidently working overtime, stated that Mendelssohn's "teenage hormones" could be perceived in the rippling motif in the second movement. The more realistic observer might suggest that Felix's tears can be heard, allowing him to show his feelings without being seen to cry. Two sad events were responsible that occurred at that time, 1827. Mendelssohn's young friend August Hanstein passed away after a long illness (to commemorate which, incidentally, he wrote the Prelude in E major/minor that he later incorporated into a series of preludes and fugues, Op. 35). A far greater anguish was the death of Beethoven in the same year, and musicologists find a similarity between Mendelssohn's Op. 13 Quartet and his hero's Op. 95 and Op. 132.

Before Mendelssohn paid his first visit to London in 1829, Klingemann had written to him that "the girls look marvellous, parading in pairs...quite conscious of their charms. Even housemaids look like princesses or Hebes, but none of them know how to bake a cake." So, despite their lack of culinary skill, the 20-year-old Mendelssohn was not disappointed on meeting so many lovely young ladies. At a demonstration by Dr. Spurzheim of Franz Gall's 'science' of phrenology, in which the sitter's skull bones were studied to reveal the individual's personality traits, Felix was particularly pleased by a lady's long, blonde hair. Having asked if she was capable of stealing, or any other crime, Spurzheim asked her to unfasten these tresses. "She looked beautiful with her hair loose and, when doing it up again before the mirror, I gave three cheers for phrenology and everything about it." At one of the many dinners he attended Felix sat next to a lady whose name, he discovered, was Louise, "with beautiful brown eyes that spoke English". Felix felt very sorry for himself once she withdrew, before the cheese course had begun. A Mr. Richmond invited Felix to dine; the main reason he looked forward to this entertainment was that Richmond "has many daughters". The novelist Sarah Austin introduced Felix to her brother and his family, the Taylors, with their three daughters: Anne, Honoria and Suzanne (or Susan). Though they resided at their house in Bedford Square, Mendelssohn was invited to spend longer with the family at Coed Du, the estate they rented near Mold, north Wales.

Yet another, far more exciting female attracted Mendelssohn whilst in London. Contemporaries were fascinated by Mme. Malibran. Born a year earlier than Felix as Maria Felicia Garcia (of the illustrious family of singers), Malibran retained her first married name, though her second husband was the violinist Charles Auguste de Bériot. Not only was Mendelssohn attracted to this vivacious prima donna by her singing but, Kupferberg suggests, her off-stage antics, which included drinking, playing with dolls and dressing in men's clothes. At a party given by the Horsley family Mendelssohn could not take his eyes from Malibran's figure, "rounded to a degree of embonpoint", as Marek describes it. On a later occasion the soprano sang a sea shanty and a troubadour's song amongst her repertoire, never taking her own eyes off Mendelssohn. She asked him to play the piano, at which Felix made to slip away to another room, muttering that he could not play after hearing the diva's exquisite voice, but Malibran would have none of it and, gripping his arm, propelled Felix back to the piano. His diffidence evidently forsook him for, having never heard the melody before, Mendelssohn improvised on a Spanish song she had performed, and accompanied her in further French and Spanish songs. Felix was remarkably lucky to catch the prima donna in such a pleasant mood. The artist Eugène Delacroix wrote of her: "Her behaviour was unpredictable. Just as she might tear a handkerchief or a glove, she would tear a passion to tatters." Among her admirers, Bellini, Donizetti and Liszt could be counted, as well as the more sober Moscheles and, of all people, Abraham Mendelssohn, once he had met Malibran on his 1833 visit to London. Now that the ultra-respectable father was able to understand his son's infatuation, Felix's ardour may well have cooled, realising that there could have been nothing 'wicked' about this formerly exciting temptress. There would, therefore, be no "dangerous entanglement", as Mendelssohn senior had formerly feared.

Yet Mendelssohn's sex life in London may be probed more deeply than what mere innocent flirtations can disclose. Eric Werner unearthed a letter "hitherto unpublished" that Rosen wrote to Felix concerning a mutual female artist friend. "Her temperament, in the aggressive, erotic sense, appears to have charmed Felix, and she, his." But neither Werner nor Blunt, who regurgitates this information, chooses to elaborate on this enigmatic remark. This young man, away from home for the first time as an adult, without his parents to check his behaviour, might have been excited if a woman had the courage to take the initiative sexually. In Mendelssohn's time such forward-thinking activity would be a novelty for someone of Felix's strict upbringing, which may account for the idyllic marriage into which he would enter with Cécile Jeanrenaud in 1837. But Rosen's is not the only letter that provokes conjecture as to how innocent Mendelssohn's sex life was. In his compilation Rudolf Elvers includes a letter written by Mendelssohn himself, on 10th July 1829, to his father; "I had been about to drink a glass of wine with a lady, and was pulling the glass stopper out with great force but was very clumsy, and the bottle shattered in my hand and I cut myself a bit, but it should be noted for the record that, beforehand, I began to nod off and faint, and only then went to see Dr. Billings, a London physician "who put an English bandage on my thumb yesterday". Though, at face value, this extract appears innocent enough, a keen observer cannot help but read between the lines. Who was this mysterious "lady", and how much of a 'lady' was she, entertaining a handsome young gentleman on her own? Why did Felix find it necessary to see a doctor in order for his thumb to be bandaged, or was this an excuse to receive advice about how to prevent incurring a sexually transmitted disease? Did Felix "nod off and faint" through too much physical exertion? Was this strange incident mentioned in his letter home in order to test Abraham's reaction, or as a cathartic confession at such a deviation from the Mendelssohn code of conduct? The reader will have to imagine the reply Felix received, as this appears to have been lost.

Chapter 14: "Flirting Outrageously"

At the end of August 1829, having parted from Klingemann at Liverpool after their visit to Scotland, Felix travelled to north Wales to accept the Taylor family's invitation to Coed Du. On arriving at Chester, Felix wrote home dutifully to describe the scenery, the walks around the city walls, the towers on the horizon, and the neighbouring houses. He could not, however, resist mentioning "a girls' boarding school out for a walk". The date, late August, is puzzling, and it can only be suggested that the school was either an orphanage or that the academic year was different from today, when pupils are at home for the summer holiday. The girls were "quite pretty and I followed behind with my sketchbook". There is no record of any conversation with the girls, or of any reprimand from a schoolmistress in charge. But, if Felix yearned for feminine company, such feelings were amply rewarded on reaching Coed Du.

When Mendelssohn had first met the Taylors in London he had written of them as "an elegant, proper English family". However, on first meeting them in their country environment, the mother was riding a donkey, the two elder sisters "planting in the garden", and the youngest, Suzanne, was riding towards them from a distance, in a blue habit, "her horse clopping as she came towards us, out of breath, with a cousin behind her". Felix was delighted to see "a good English piano" in the house, which he was asked to play for the Miss Taylors, the sons being away from home with their mine-owner father. At the meal the daughters appeared in white dresses, "for which I have a decided preference". When first seeing the cousin accompanying Susan, Felix "began to hate" him. "I do nothing but flirt outrageously – and that in English," he wrote to his family. Whenever he thought about the Miss Taylors subsequently, Felix was "put in a flowery mood", remembering "the meadows, the woods, the pebbly brook with its babbling". He admitted to having become "deeply fond of the girls, and I believe this is mutual". When the father and sons returned home, Felix was asked whether he wished to go fox-hunting with the boys, or sketching with Anne, Honoria and Suzanne. "I chose the latter," Mendelssohn announced to his family. Such a decision may have been innocent, for many young men enjoyed sketching rather than fox-hunting, though the sex demarcation is interesting, since, in such novels as those of R. S. Surtees and Anthony Trollope, women are often encountered in the hunting field.

Yet, whatever flirting Felix managed did produce "three of my best compositions", as he called his Op. 16, 'Three Fantasies (or Caprices)'. These piano pieces are far too shamefully neglected in the repertoire and all three deserve greater attention. One evening, as they danced "to a band whose trumpets seemed too shrill", Suzanne pointed out the little yellow bells in her hair (*Eccremocarpus* – Blunt, a botanist – suggests; a plant recently introduced from South America to the Taylors' garden). The youngest Miss Taylor assured Felix that the plants were "fairy trumpets, and [asked] me if I could not introduce them into the orchestra... She gave it as her opinion that her trumpets might be better to dance to, so I wrote a dance for her." For Honoria, Mendelssohn wrote *The Rivulet*, "which had pleased us so much during our time together". For Anne, the third piece was inspired by a bouquet of carnations and roses. Felix wrote of this piece: "It is the best of its kind that I have composed." After his visit Felix fell asleep in the coach "and dreamt of pleasant things", but, as this adjective is so often used in Mendelssohn's correspondence for something more graphic, it may be tactful to leave his dreams to the imagination. It is evident that he still had the Miss Taylors in mind when he visited Goethe for the last time in 1830. He played the Op. 16 Caprices and, whilst in Munich, to a cousin of Mlle. Müller, to whom "I praised Susan inordinately". On his fourth visit to London in 1833 Fanny Horsley wrote to her aunt how Mendelssohn had kept singing a verse of a Charles Dibdin song, 'All on the Downs the Fleet was moored', with the line: 'O Susan, Susan, lovely Dear'. About the piano pieces he had composed, Felix had "become quite sentimental. These pieces are not lions, as Rebecka calls them, but lambs of mine." As for the story of the "fairy trumpets", the English singer George Sampson, on a visit to Mendelssohn in Leipzig in 1840, recalled that William Sterndale Bennett, who was present at the time, reminded his host of this "pretty fairy tale" he had heard "from someone", noting the little trumpet-shaped blooms that Susan had worn in her hair. Felix, by this time (1840) a respectable married man, with a growing family, was still able to acknowledge the incident with pleasure and with no embarrassment.

H. E. Jacob states categorically that "no woman ever moved him to turbulence or misery", but how true is this of Mendelssohn? The feminist author Nancy B. Reich discovered a memoir written by Ernst Rudorff regarding his mother, formerly Friederike Dorothea Elisabeth ('Betty') Pistor. Betty first became acquainted with Felix when, as a boy, he sat next to Fanny among the altos at the Berlin Singakademie. Once his voice had broken, Felix accompanied this special group at their Friday rehearsals "with great skill", as Betty remembered. Fanny and Felix had to pass Betty's home from Zelter's to their own. Once Rebecka had joined the singing group, a firm friendship developed between Betty and herself. A fortuitous circumstance allowed Felix access to the Pistor home on his own account. Pistor had outbid Zelter for a collection of early manuscripts, including some of Bach's compositions in his own handwriting. Felix offered to catalogue these treasures for Pistor, who rewarded Felix with a copy of a Bach manuscript.

All was sweetness and light until one morning in January 1828, when some friends, visiting the Pistors, broke into laughter. Hearing this from the drawing room as he entered the Pistor home, Felix became offended. The next time Betty and Felix met he treated her so coolly that Betty was perplexed. On her birthday, 13th January, which happened also to be Felix's name-day (the day on which his patron saint was commemorated), whereas Rebecka visited the Pistors, Felix did not arrive. Betty, still puzzled, could only conclude that he must have thought the laughter he had heard was directed at him. Because of the ultra-strict manner in which young ladies were reared at the time, Betty felt unable to broach the matter with Felix. He, on the other hand, a year younger than Betty, may well have felt

Chapter 14: "Flirting Outrageously"

embarrassed about the juvenile clothes he still wore and the childish style in which his hair was still arranged. That February Betty was invited to share Felix's birthday celebrations, but her father forbade her to attend, since a properly brought-up young girl was not expected to be invited by male company to such a gathering. However, Rebecka realised the true reason for this apparently absurd prohibition: it was the Mendelssohns' Jewish background, for Betty was teased by her cousins as "that music- and Jew-loving cousin". Though Pistor tried to smooth things over, Leah and Abraham felt uncomfortable about their new faith and others' ambivalence to the fact that they had once been Jews. Meeting Rebecka at the Singakademie, Betty learnt how deeply hurt Felix had become and decided to confront his mother about the ridiculous situation. Though the families continued to visit one another, no further intimacy occurred between Betty and Felix. But he did express his feelings in his favourite way – through his music, the Op. 12 String Quartet, dedicated "to B. P.". Felix had mentioned to Betty that he was composing a quartet for her, but she did not take him seriously. When it was completed, during his 1829 visit to London, Klingemann wrote to Fanny that her brother "has worked on something that makes me very happy and he was pleased that I understood it". At Coed Du Felix wrote to Klingemann of "the bouquet of carnations and roses lying near me on the score of the quartet". Did Anne Taylor guess the significance of the initials 'B. P.'? Did she mind, or was she too unworldly to allow a rival to trouble her?

At the beginning of 1830 Felix gave the manuscript of the quartet to the violinist Carl Kudelsky, who, in turn, was asked to pass it on to Ferdinand David. Kudelsky and David had each been invited by a baron to his castle in Dorpat, Estonia. On 14th April, whilst recovering from measles, Felix dictated a letter to David "in the depths of woe. Do you want to hear the latest news from Berlin? I know as little about what is going on as if I were in Dorpat... Betty Pistor is engaged – totally engaged. She is the legal property of Doktor and Professor of jurisprudence Rudorff." David was asked to alter the dedication of the manuscript to 'B. R.' "as soon as you receive confirmation of their marriage from the Berlin newspapers. It will take just a little stroke of the pen. It will be quite easy." Had Felix not already, as he stated, "given up courting girls and resolved to become an old bachelor", the news of Betty's wedding would have upset him far less than proved to be the case. Though such remarks may have emanated from the cantankerous mood of a convalescent, it is evident that Mendelssohn's feelings for Betty ran far deeper than anyone realised.

On 20th December 1831 Felix wrote home from Paris that he had gained great pleasure to hear the quartet played "with such spirit and fire". Later, at a gathering in Berlin, Felix would sit next to Marie Lichtenstein, Rudorff's piano teacher and an intimate friend of his mother. When she began to speak of Betty, Felix replied: "Yes; that was a musical soul". Though she admired "the noble youth, so ably gifted", Rudorff explains in his memoir, she bore no feeling of passion for him, "since, being a year older, she had no interest in a younger man". Presents had been exchanged "with the sincerest friendship", but, as far as Betty was concerned, this proved nothing more. Schima Kaufman states in her so-called biography: "pen and paper awaited him at the home of an unnamed young lady who lived nearby." Here Mendelssohn "composed church music, whilst eating delicious cakes". Could this young lady have been Betty Pistor? After all, her family were Swiss, which would, in view of that country's reputation, account for the delicious cakes. Part of the manuscript collection that Felix had catalogued so diligently was sold by the Leipzig publishing house of Peters in 1916 and the remainder is still preserved in the city library. The 1964 inventory includes the score of a Bach keyboard concerto autographed by Zelter and dedicated "to my dear, devoted Betty", dated 10th March 1832, barely six weeks before her mentor's death. Mendelssohn's handwritten list can also be seen, cataloguing Pistor's original manuscript collection.

Meanwhile, "In all Vienna, not a single, reasonable young lady can be drummed up," Felix wrote home on 22nd August 1830, having arrived in Austria, "so how can a man of my calibre survive for three whole weeks without a lamb? In Venice, things will be better, says Rau, but how can I survive till then! Can you not recommend someone for that purpose?" Despite this deprivation, Felix noticed "a pretty cousin" of Mlle. Müller, "in a blue dress with a bright border". It is interesting to note that, whilst Fanny was his musical adviser, it is Rebecka in whom Felix confided his love interest.

Whilst there appears to be no record of Mendelssohn's sexual experiences in Venice, the first step of his Italian travels, he did mention "a very charming night" in a gondola. But in Florence, despite Marek's insistence on Mendelssohn's being "strangely uninterested in eroticism", his thoughts were not always as 'pure' as biographers care to believe. To Paul, Felix wrote that, before leaving for Rome, he had not decided whether or not to visit the Pitti Palace again "to gaze once more at my Venus, who should not, indeed, be mentioned in front of the ladies, but whose beauty is truly divine". Yet Fanny and Rebecka would each see the same sculpture without a trace of embarrassment. A further such note appeared in Felix's synopsis of what Fanny should include in her tour of Italy in 1839-40. Referring to female portraits and sculptures in the Chiara and Borghese art galleries, he described two paintings by Titian thus: "one in a state of nature; the other, unfortunately, not so", representing earthly and heavenly love.

Schima Kaufman indulges in one of her fantasies regarding Mendelssohn's Italian tour. She writes of his "gaily coloured waistcoat, setting off his elegant figure. He was the central light, around which the most gorgeous butterflies of society fluttered, begging to be singed by the fire of his kisses and his smile, and, of course, he was not sparing." It is also from this forerunner to Mills & Boon that researchers learn of "the English beauties" whom the sculptor Thorwaldsen and the artist Vernet "discussed in anatomical terms". Jacob, Blunt and even the arch-

Chapter 14: "Flirting Outrageously"

puritan Stratton describe a young lady with whom Mendelssohn was in some way involved. From Stratton, for instance, it is learnt that "of course, there was a beautiful young lady – English this time – with whom he fell in love". It can only be described as highly vexing how serious biographers indulge in slovenly research and give no details when such tantalising statements are made. No information has as yet come to light as to who this mystery woman might have been. The only inkling, from Mendelssohn's own correspondence, is his apology for writing "in student phraseology... I have not worn a cravat for a week. I have been in the mountains where I enjoyed myself finely." He may, or may not, have been alone and a love affair may, or may not, have flourished; there is no proof or means of verification as to the facts of this trip.

At Interlaken, Switzerland, he composed some waltzes for a forest ranger's daughter but, having exhausted his supply of music paper, who knows what further pieces he might have written for her delectation? But in the following year, 1832, Mendelssohn, on his second visit to London, was introduced – probably by Moscheles – to the Horsley family, which included three daughters: Mary, Fanny and Sophie. Unlike the Swiss girl, of whom we know nothing, activities of the Miss Horsleys are well chronicled. Fanny and Sophie, then in their teens, wrote regularly to their aunt, Lucy Callcott, and many of their letters were made into a book, *Mendelssohn and his Friends in Kensington*, by a descendant, Rosamund Brunel Gotch, in 1934. Of his walk "down bright Regent Street" to the Hanover Square Rooms for a Philharmonic concert, Felix reported meeting "a couple of stunningly beautiful English girls, of whom I am quite fond, who took me along to their box". Mendelssohn found Beethoven's 'Pastoral' Symphony "easy listening alongside the pretty children". Mary, the elder sister, who married Isambard Kingdom Brunel, was then 21 and therefore too old to be called a child; thus, it is likely that Fanny and Sophie were the concert-goers on that occasion. "It is good to be here," Mendelssohn wrote on getting to know the family; "such friendly people and pretty girls are nowhere else to be found." Indeed, certainly on his early visits, Mendelssohn often visited the Horsleys at 1 High Row, Kensington Gravel Pits, where Notting Hill Gate tube station now stands. Once, though Fanny usually rose at 8.20, she changed her routine, getting up at a quarter to eight to take greater care of her appearance, as Mendelssohn was invited to take breakfast with the family at half past eight. On another visit Mendelssohn was never "so droll, brilliant, friendly and intimate". Aunt Lucy would have been "dazzled" to hear how he talked. On a walk, the wind "was so indecently obstreperous [that] mama's undergarments were on view", which Fanny and Sophie found "so distressing" that they remained behind the others. It would be interesting to learn what Felix thought of the situation. At the end, knowing that he and the Horsleys would soon part, "he looked deathly pale, with tears in his eyes".

It seems that, rather than Felix flirting with the Miss Horsleys, their feeling for him was reminiscent of a crush on this still young, but slightly older, man. On his departure from London, such phrases as "the wonderful freight on board the steamer to Rotterdam" can be seen in the Horsley letters. Fanny wrote that "a whole kingdom could not load a fleet of ships for a week, a month or a year with such precious cargo as such a great man". Mme. Elise Polko was just as fanciful as Schima Kaufman in her memoirs of Mendelssohn. Of the three "charming Horsley daughters", she describes their "gliding like the Graces through the elegant rooms as they danced". Marek likens them to characters in Jane Austen novels, but it is doubtful if Miss Austen would allow her heroines to use some of the language seen in the Miss Horsleys' correspondence. Whilst a song Felix had composed was referred to as "sweet", a German friend found the words "so shocking that he laughed so much he shook the room". In a German lesson, whilst discussing a performance of Weber's *Euryanthe*, the wrong phrase was employed to Klingemann, the instructor, at which Fanny was "mortified". Rather than using the phrase "free with my manners" in criticising the performance, the phrase "free with my morals" was used, at which he roared with laughter, especially at the young ladies' blushes.

Like the Miss Taylors, the Horsley daughters were favoured with Mendelssohn's compositions. To Sophie a book of his *Songs without Words* was dedicated, as also several other piano works, including a piano duet arrangement of his *Fair Melusine* Overture and that of the *Hebrides*. Yet the music Felix sang more than anything – apart from Dibdin's song mentioned earlier – was Weber's *Invitation to the Dance*, which would be orchestrated later by Berlioz.

Various encounters with females occurred in Germany for Felix. Chief amongst these in his young adulthood was the pianist Delphine von Schauroth, whom he met in Munich in 1830. "I am doing well and gloriously beyond all expectations. People are spoiling and pampering me with piles of sugar." A. B. Marx bore out this turn of fortune from the difficult environment of Berlin: "Felix is the darling in everyone's home. From early morning, everything is concentrated on him." Of a gathering, Felix wrote that "excellencies and counts were as thick as fowls in a poultry yard". It was there he met Delphine, then 17 – "adored here and deservedly". He flirted with her "very outrageously, following her around like a little lamb". The hostess sat the two young people together at dinner, and afterwards they played Hummel's Sonata for Four Hands "beautifully". The flirting appears to have been mutual, for Delphine asked Felix to hold the top A flat in the final movement "because my little hand cannot hold it", Felix quoted his duettist. Nevertheless, "all I want to say further is that Delphine plays very well". Yet, despite his diffidence, observers linked their names as an ideal couple to such an extent that King Ludwig I of Bavaria asked Felix if he would marry Delphine. Delphine married an English musician, Hill Handley, and, on receiving the tidings, Felix admitted himself to be "in a 'donnerwetter' (literally, 'thunder weather') mood"; he told David that, together, the couple resembled "roast beef next to vanilla ice cream".

Chapter 14: "Flirting Outrageously"

As with other female friends, music resulted – in this instance, Mendelssohn's G minor Piano Concerto, Op. 25, which was dedicated to Delphine not only during the composer's lifetime but afterwards. The last occasion was at a Mendelssohn Festival in Leipzig in 1870, when Delphine was 56 years old. Indeed, critics agreed that she played the solo part better than Mendelssohn himself had done. Fanny, curious to find out what her brother saw in this great pianist, broke her journey to Italy to visit Munich. She reported Delphine as "a very charming girl", but Felix confided to Schumann that marriage to her would have been "dangerous". Such a remark might have arisen because, so often, artistic temperaments clashed. In fact, Clara Schumann had to cease playing the piano when her husband was composing, because her practising disturbed her husband's concentration. Fortunately Felix had no such trouble with Cécile as his wife.

On his next visit to Munich in 1831, Felix wrote of 'little Miss L', to whom he gave lessons in counterpoint at noon for an hour. Felix despaired of "most masters and books" when coaching this pupil. Though, at face value, these lessons appear nothing other than prosaic, Mendelssohn's eulogy of 'little Miss L' – Josephina ('Peppi') Lang – was not the usual given by a music master about a pupil:

"She is one of the sweetest creatures I ever saw. Imagine a small, delicate-looking pale girl, with mobile, but not pretty, features; so singular and interesting that it is difficult to turn one's eyes from her, while her every gesture and word is full of talent. She has a gift for composing songs, and sings them in a way that I have never heard before, causing me the most unalloyed musical delight I have ever experienced... Every note expresses the most profound and delicate feeling... Everyone present subsides into a quiet and thoughtful mood on hearing her first notes, and each, in his own way, is deeply affected. If you could but hear her voice, you would marvel. It is so unconsciously lovely, emanating from her innermost soul, and yet so tranquil."

Though Mendelssohn and Klingemann praised Josephine Lang to the musical world, no one believed them. Since then, however, "she appears to have made the most remarkable progress. Those who are not affected by her singing have no feeling at all." So enraptured was Felix that, when asked to follow her in a performance of his own, he was unable to oblige, and declined the invitation. Yet, despite his panegyric, Mendelssohn admitted of Miss Lang that "she lacks musical culture and cannot distinguish good music from bad and thinks everything is wonderfully fine, apart from her own pieces. As she has no one to understand and guide her musical talent, she may be spoilt." Felix urged her parents not to introduce her into society, nor to allow their daughter's talents to be wasted. He hoped to send some of Miss Lang's songs to the family that were written in gratitude for his tuition. Such teaching was, according to Felix, "what she knows from nature but I have led her a little way towards good and solid music". In 1842 Miss Lang married Professor Karl Köstlin of Tübingen University and, later, Felix was asked to be godfather to their first child.

The aroma of sexual activity is once again apparent among some innocent encounters with females. In Düsseldorf, for example, Mendelssohn was alleged to have had a sexual liaison with an aristocratic widow, about which his mother was "scandalised", according to Marek (but, as seems to be the habit of biographers when treating Mendelssohn's love life, no further details are given). Blunt believes that it was the Woringen daughters who conveyed the tale of their son's questionable behaviour to his parents. Such gossip emanated from "a display of spite, characteristic of jealous females". Leah might have believed, Blunt surmises, that Felix might rush into marriage without appropriate forethought. In fact, however, because their intellects were incompatible, it was not enough that their body chemistry worked well, so whatever relationship there might have been did not last. It is interesting, however, that in 1843 Fanny wrote to Rebecka of a 'Mme. O.', the wife of a Bordeaux wine merchant, who, whilst an accomplished singer, was also "a very accomplished flirt in the style of Mme. W., but prettier". Mme. O. turned the heads of many Berlin males, though there is no record of Felix being attracted, or if Mme. W. was the actual woman purported to have shared his bed, or he hers; or, indeed, if the rumour was nothing more than malicious gossip.

Felix wrote of "a pretty girl" whom he converted from the music of Herz to the more inspiring Mozart and Beethoven. Her father was evidently pleased, for Mendelssohn was rewarded with "enough black cloth to make a suit. The painters are mad with envy at my good luck," he added. Whether the envy was ignited by the new outfit, or Felix's association with the young lady, can only be conjectured. However, Stratton points out: "There was little chance for any of his rivals when Felix was about." Another encounter resulted in Felix's own favourite work, the abysmally neglected *Fair Melusine* Overture. Though he detested Conradin Kreutzer's opera based on Grillparzer's fairy tale, Mendelssohn was captivated by Fräulein Hänel combing her long hair during the performance as the mermaid, Melusine. Perhaps, had he lived longer, Mendelssohn might have written a whole opera, once he had met Jenny Lind, for whom he began 'Die Lorelei'. In Elbefeld, whilst staying with the Bahmer family, at whose house a charity concert was given at which Felix played some of his piano music, a young lady (again, tantalisingly unnamed) drew laurel wreaths mingled with forget-me-nots around a poem, asking Felix to marry her. As with other females in Mendelssohn's life, no further information has been forthcoming.

During their marriage, Cécile demonstrated, if not outright suspicion, at least strong curiosity regarding her husband's trips away from home. "You must keep nothing from me, until your lungs are worn out," she once exhorted him prior to a visit to London. "It is doubtful," Kupferberg asserts, "whether he complied, any more than any other man." A wise, trusting wife, unable or unwilling to accompany her young, virile husband, would not think to hold him to such a pledge! It is interesting to note that Felix's friend J. W. Davison, music critic of *The Times*, warned his guest how "people are talking", Mendelssohn having been seen

Chapter 14: "Flirting Outrageously"

so often escorting Louise Bendigan to social functions. Admittedly, with his wife absent on this occasion – his eighth visit to London – it would be incongruous to see a man alone amongst couples, so his companion may have been nothing other than a friend. But could she have been the same Louise with whom Felix had dined on his 1829 visit? Whatever the facts, it is evident that a mischief-making scandalmonger might have put two and two together, making them add up to something more than four. Perhaps Davison was too cautious in the matter, or might he have been concerned, not only about Felix, but the absent wife and family he had left in Leipzig?

Whilst there is no doubt that the significant women in Mendelssohn's life were fond of him, he was regarded as a good friend, but nothing more. Yet there was an exception to this rule. Felix first met 'the Swedish nightingale' – an epithet conferred upon Jenny Lind by an Uppsala journalist in her early operatic career – at the Berlin Opera House, where Meyerbeer was in charge. He met her again at a party given by the sculptor Ludwig Wichmann, at whose house Miss Lind was staying. At the time, Mendelssohn may have been attracted by her singular lack of temperament, unlike so many contemporary prima donnas. "Among the other clumsy women who strode the stage, screaming as they strode, she was a godsend," according to H. F. Chorley. In her plain dress, Miss Lind's hair was in a simple style to match her pale, clear complexion. But Marek's observation is altogether unflattering: "She was the most controversial singing star of her own, or any other, age...a plain, snub-nosed girl of 24, austerely dressed." In other words, detractors found her unassuming appearance a 'front', masking her true character: "vain and capricious". Henry Pleasants in his book *The Great Singers* describes her as "hesitant, playing 'poor little me', pining for her northern homeland".

Such a personality must have tugged at Mendelssohn's heartstrings, for, though she had been trained by the celebrated Manuel Garcia (Malibran's brother) in Paris, Jenny had a phobia for strange lands; neither did she relish the often immoral behaviour of her opera colleagues. When Jenny was invited to the Mendelssohn home, it is recorded that Cécile "looked askance", considering this stranger as a rival for her husband's affections, but, never expressing her feelings, no scene ever took place, so far as is known. Had the couple 'had it out', it is likely that Felix would have admitted his attention lavished on Jenny was 'for her art's sake', or that 'he wanted her to feel wanted'. Jenny, feeling utterly comfortable with her mentor, could, through her interpretation of his songs and her excellence in voice projection, allow her self-confidence to attain a greater strength than ever before. Mendelssohn loved the high F sharp she could produce, and this was allowed to be demonstrated in the aria 'Hear ye, Israel' that he included in *Elijah* with this rare soprano in mind. Her biographer, Joan Bulman, states that Mendelssohn "regulated her whole career". Miss Lind had a very stubborn will of her own, and it was her own good sense that inclined her to pay heed to any advice her mentor offered. She knew, like anyone else whom Felix instructed should have known (male or female), that whatever he said would be best for her art and should be treated with the highest respect.

Mendelssohn was, therefore, able to promote her career to her best advantage, even inspiring her to come to London, where, in 1852, she settled, making England her home until her death in 1887. It was only by meeting Mendelssohn and his family that caused Jenny to realise how wonderful it would be to have a home and children of her own. Her own childhood had been unhappy, except when she sang. Her father had deserted her mother before Jenny was born. Her mother saw this unusual girl as nothing but a lucrative money-earner. This, and Jenny's inordinate sentimentality towards any charity she fancied helping, caused her to squander her money without restraint – until she married Otto Goldschmidt, a former pupil of Mendelssohn, who was able to manage her finances properly.

Joan Bulman states in her biography of Jenny Lind that "she must have fallen in love with Mendelssohn, so attractive was he, but had to repress this, the greatest emotional experience of her life". But clues may be discovered that such repression was not altogether foolproof. "When Felix improvised at the piano," Hiller recorded in his recollections, "she would be carried almost completely out of herself when gazing into his eyes, large and dark – almost black – the focal point of his beautiful, mobile, essentially Jewish face." Clara Schumann guessed Jenny's feelings also: "Because of everything she says about Mendelssohn, she loves him as much for his being a man as for his being a composer." Indeed, Jenny confided to Clara and Robert: "I thank God for sending into my life the purest, most refined artist" – crass tactlessness when addressing people of a similar calibre. Yet the confession that brings home to readers Jenny Lind's feelings for Mendelssohn more than any other was written to Judge Munthe, a Swedish friend. Acknowledging Mendelssohn's "supreme talents", Jenny added: "He is a *man!*"

No longer were audiences seen as comprising hostile, unwelcoming strangers. Under Mendelssohn's tutelage, this formerly shy soprano was filled, for the first time in her life, with the self-confidence she craved. Especially was this true once she had switched her career – again, under her mentor's instigation – from opera to oratorio. Though she could never have married him, it appears more than coincidence that Jenny chose one of Mendelssohn's pupils, Otto Goldschmidt, for a husband. His capable management of her finances must have boosted Jenny's self-confidence even more, clearing her path to become a living legend of whom, for generations, everyone would speak. Mendelssohn had always fascinated women – a fascination he was not averse to encouraging. But, when all is said and done, Cécile Jeanrenaud was the only woman he truly – deeply – loved.

BOOK TWO

Man of Action

Chapter 15

"The Fairies' Laureate"

As the English singer George Sampson remembered, it was Robert Schumann, at a gathering in Mendelssohn's home, who coined this phrase to describe his host. He was speaking particularly of Mendelssohn's *Midsummer Night's Dream* Overture, "one of the most beautiful of Mendelssohn's dreams", but Schumann also praised Felix's facility to depict witches in his songs and the cantata *The First Walpurgisnacht*. According to Kupferberg, the overture introduced Schumann "to a whole new kingdom – fairyland. Through such a unique piece of musical scenery, one is transported into a complete moonlit universe." Marcel Brion adds that the romantic school saw dreams and the subconscious as revealing far more about human nature and greater understanding than the mundane thoughts and actions of the workaday world.

So, how did this fascinating overture originate? From an early age the Mendelssohn children loved to dress up and act plays based on Wilhelm and Jakob Grimm's fairy tales; Rumpelstiltskin was a particular favourite. But Shakespeare's dramas never lagged far behind, especially when Schlegel's translations into German became available. Felix especially loved *A Midsummer Night's Dream*, and, according to Sebastian Hensel, it was the beautiful garden at Leipzigerstrasse 3 that inspired the overture to be written by this 17-year-old boy. As Sir George Grove states: "The first four notes are followed by the violins dancing away with a nimble theme, bringing the fairies into the orchestra, and fixing them there." But, in analysing the overture, truth should be disentangled from myth. The music did not take a week, or even a month, to complete. According to Hiller, "long and arduous work" went into its completion, which occurred over the greater part of a year, between lectures at Berlin University. Neither is it plausible that Felix extemporised on the piano whilst conducting an affair "with a girl of whom he was enamoured". Even at 17 Felix was a professional musician, who never allowed any distraction to disturb his concentration when writing music. A further myth is that, sitting at a table in the garden writing the score, "the evening breeze wafted to him the first four notes in sequence". What a musical breeze that must have been! More likely, it was Felix's imagination that allowed him to 'hear' these notes – just as, Sterndale

Bennett claimed Felix had confided, he "saw Shakespeare in the garden". Again, imagination took possession of Mendelssohn when absorbed in this work.

The first performance took place in the garden house at the end of August 1826. As Grove states: "Mendelssohn brought the fairies into the orchestra and left them there. At the beginning, a few wind-blown notes...magically sounded the 'open sesame' of a deep-buried fairyland. Minuscule legendary folk, with the softness of butterflies' wings, mischievously scurried through the woods on tiptoe. The same wind-blown notes usher back the world of reality – and the dream was over." Though, as Schima Kaufman reports, "the guests rubbed their dazzled eyes to make sure they, too, were not transported", there was one exception upon whom Felix relied far more than appears necessary. Whereas Zelter claimed that whatever Mendelssohn knew about music was due to his own teaching, Adolf Marx countered this assertion and endeavoured to prove this by pulling the overture's construction to pieces before its next performance. In the memoirs written by Marx's widow in 1866, she states on her late husband's behalf that it was he who prompted Felix to complete the overture, with Marx's own ideas paramount, and that Abraham Mendelssohn recognised the piece, initially, to be Marx's work. Perhaps Felix's father felt it to be more seemly that an older musician (and, by definition, a wiser person) could only be capable of such an achievement. What business had a boy of 17 in composing such a work? It would only be later that Marx had the grace to acknowledge that he was the critic only – not the creator of the overture.

Although the original work, Marx sniped, gelled with Shakespeare's play, it was Marx himself who allowed the music to gain a higher standard through his own initiative. The donkey's bray could, for instance, be more accurately represented through a change in instrumentation. An incomplete draft does exist in the Bodleian Library, Oxford, which differs markedly from the better-known transcript. Yet, despite Marx's assertions, Felix studied Shakespeare far more painstakingly than Marx had ever done, and, in view of his lifelong habit of revising his scores, it was more likely Felix himself, dissatisfied with an early attempt at the score, who revised this manuscript. During its gestation period Marx wanted nothing to do with this masterpiece, dismissing it as "pleasant and vivacious – nothing more". It was only later that Felix was encouraged to reinstate some of the passages he had originally discarded. After the rift between the two musicians in 1839, Marx invariably tried to show himself in the best light. Any criticisms were those of "a true friend", possibly playing off father and son for the latter's "own good". According to Marx's widow, Felix was, by turns, "upset, angry and hurt". Marx, surprised at Leah's coldness and Fanny's hostility towards him, did not visit the Mendelssohn home until Felix "asked him to come to his rescue". Schumann, a far more highly respected journalist than Marx, said of the overture: "It has the bloom of youth upon it, yet the mature master took his first flight via this score" into the realm of true musicianship. But Marx did admit, after a later performance, that "the new music starts here".

Chapter 15: "The Fairies' Laureate"

Apart from Marx, however, others have criticised Mendelssohn for plagiarism of Weber's overture to his opera *Oberon*, but any traces that can be heard are deliberate. Felix asked his earlier music teacher, Ludwig Berger, if it would be permissible to pay tribute to Weber in his own composition. Berger replied that already Mendelssohn's compositions surpassed those of the earlier composer. Of Weber's 'Sea-maidens' Song', notes from which Mendelssohn inserted, Jacob describes this tribute as "gentle, echoing, expressive, unforgettable, dissolving into air". How could Felix go wrong, with the memory of Weber to inspire him and the translation by August Wilhelm von Schlegel of Shakespeare's plays – the only translation used by the romantic school? Schlegel's biographer, von Brentano, explains that the translator employed up to 12 of the available English texts, painstakingly combing each to find the precise word or phrase to suit the German idiom, but to maintain the original content.

The first public performance of the *Midsummer Night's Dream* Overture took place in Stettin on the Baltic in February 1827. At the same concert Felix played the solo part with Carl Löwe in the latter's Concerto for Two Pianos. On returning home, an incident occurred that shows Felix's initiative. Their carriage overturned, but it was this 18-year-old who had the idea of how to solve the problem. He commandeered one of the horses and, being even at that stage of his life a proficient horseman, rode to seek help.

On an early visit to London Sir Thomas Attwood left a manuscript of the overture in his carriage by mistake, but Mendelssohn was able to rewrite the score from memory. It was a century later, according to Schima Kaufman, that the manuscript turned up at the Royal Academy of Music. Mendelssohn's phenomenal memory must have served him well when King Friedrich Wilhelm IV commissioned him to add various movements to the overture for a performance of the play in 1843. Critics perpetuate the myth that Felix's ability to compose had "tailed off" by that time, but how many composers have dovetailed later pieces so brilliantly with an overture written half a lifetime earlier?

The King of Prussia made it possible for Mendelssohn to lead a new generation into fairyland. The new incidental music was commissioned for a performance that took place at the Charlottenburg Palace on 14th October 1843. After the final scene, the audience, enchanted, stood for a long time – except for one individual: Mendelssohn himself. To Wagner, visiting Berlin to oversee his own opera, *The Flying Dutchman*, such an attitude was not understood at all. Having praised and congratulated Mendelssohn so fulsomely, Wagner took it to heart that Felix appeared immune to this adulation. The ill humour was justified, Wagner or no Wagner. For a start, Mendelssohn had naturally based his music on Schlegel's translation, but it was Ludwig Tieck's work that was used on this occasion. Different division of acts to the play had made a complete mockery of the music. Neither had Tieck deigned to consult Mendelssohn as to where his music should appear in the production. Thus, the Entr'acte was played before the curtain rose, which caused the phrase "between acts" to prove ridiculous. The Nocturne was played when no action occurred in the drama. Neither did Mendelssohn relish the overacting of Johann Geern as Bottom the Weaver. Max Reinhardt would have the same misgivings when his own actors played the role in the thousand productions he would direct between 1904 and 1934. To crown Mendelssohn's annoyance a long interval ensued, during which a reception was held for guests in the royal box, at which tea was served. During the whole introduction to the third act, Ferdinand David wrote, the clatter of crockery and teaspoons caused such a disturbance that Felix "became flushed, grew pale and had to exercise the utmost self-control in order to conduct the orchestra." Writing to his parents, Niels Gade, who had travelled from Leipzig with David, reported that "the music was fantastic, graceful, light, lovely, yet comic", though, like Felix, he did not enjoy the acting. After the Wedding March, the audience jumped to their feet.

In view of remarks overheard, Mendelssohn must have been reminded of his visit to Milan, where he had met Franz Xavier Mozart, one of Wolfgang Amadeus's sons, and friends. Lively discussion ensued, at which Shakespeare's plays were aired. Though his tragedies were worthy of note, Mendelssohn had been warned to have nothing to do with his comedies, especially *A Midsummer Night's Dream*. This had been translated into Italian and contained "anachronisms and childish ideas". The device of "a play within a play" – Pyramus and Thisbe – had been particularly derided. On the present occasion, it was said that the scene where the clowns took part was particularly vulgar. "How could the King, of all people," it was asked, "enjoy such a travesty of a drama, and, above all, how could Mendelssohn waste his genius composing music for such a farce?" In Milan Felix had remained "meekly silent, attempting no defence", as he had written to his family. Though no record exists, it is likely on the present occasion that he would have maintained the same disdainful mood, though, knowing his loyalty, Felix would have reminded his protagonists that, as his sovereign had commanded him to write the incidental music, he had obeyed the King as zealously as possible, despite the strange discrepancy in the staging of scenes, with which Tieck's translation did not accord.

It is often asked how Mendelssohn could have written such a brilliant piece of music at 17, yet was able to weave his incidental music around the overture so skilfully 17 years later. One answer could be that, despite his father's bullying to "put elves and spirits aside" as too childish, Mendelssohn was never able to do this. Thus, when commanded, Felix was able to re-enter fairyland, whence he was followed irresistibly. From youth, Fanny wrote, "[though] we entwined ourselves in *A Midsummer Night's Dream*, Felix made it his own, identifying with all the characters, fairy or human." The Shakespeare scholar Henry Hudson believes that the music portrayed love, beauty and delight (and humour also, he could have added), and "epitomised what is most beautiful in nature or fancy". The music critic R. C. Hersh records that the Nocturne and Scherzo, played consecutively, were among Arturo Toscanini's favourite pieces of music. This was proved by his

Chapter 15: "The Fairies' Laureate"

conducting 34 performances between 1928 and 1950. The broadcaster Spike Hughes commented on one such that it was "a realisation of the magical score...bewitching...equalled, but never surpassed, by Toscanini himself on similar occasions". As regards the Wedding March, Jean Petitpierre, a descendant of Cécile's family, waxes lyrical: "Couples use this to pledge their troth as a symbol of their wisdom in passion and their perfect love." Marek is more cynical. Having concurred with Donald Tovey that the music is "threadbare", he continues: "The strain thereon, because of its popularity, would have suffered none at all had Mendelssohn's original orchestration been allowed to remain." He was probably thinking of the organ arrangement that most couples have to tolerate, either because the bride or groom knows no better, or because the cautious organist thrusts it upon them with the rejoinder not to choose anything "too obscure" as music for the ceremony. The march came into prominence when Queen Victoria's eldest daughter chose it at her wedding to Kaiser Friedrich III at the Chapel Royal, St James's Palace, in 1858.

Of the incidental music as a whole, Jean Petitpierre declares it to be "so perfect a transformation from words to music that the stage setting is irrelevant". To Fanny her brother's score was in complete accord with Shakespeare's play, and, significantly, unlike many of his compositions, Felix appeared to find no need to revise either the overture or the later music. But praise from relatives is all very well. The finest compliment came from a fellow composer and contemporary of Mendelssohn – Hector Berlioz. Hearing a performance in Breslau, he declared he would have willingly given two years of his life if he could have written such a work. This opinion, it must be remembered, came from another lover of Shakespeare's dramas for which he wrote music: the overture to *King Lear*, the opera *Beatrice and Benedict* (based on *Much Ado about Nothing*), and music for *Romeo and Juliet*, in which Queen Mab's Scherzo is particularly reminiscent of Mendelssohn's style. A jaundiced view emanates from a Promenade concert prospectus of 1997, the 150th anniversary of Mendelssohn's death: "It is too late in the day for such a project to be planned. Apart from practical and economic considerations, today's dictator-producers would never tolerate music that, by defining atmosphere and...characters so clearly, would undermine their own authority. Mendelssohn is revealed as a superb composer for the stage, creating instant spells from simple ingredients." But evidently such criticism was bypassed when commemorating the quatercentenary of the birth of Shakespeare in 1964. A production took place, not in a conventional theatre, but on the BBC – and Mendelssohn's music was employed. This allowed the listener's imagination to play a full part in creating its own special scenery and costume.

Four performances took place, with 11 full rehearsals, of Tieck's translation and, despite the many mishaps, Felix wrote to Rebecka, in Italy with her family, as to his pleasure at the Berliners' enthusiasm "for our favourite amongst our beloved William's plays". After one performance, Paul reported that "not one ticket was unsold" but that Eckert would be able to give his sister a far better report than any newspaper could. "There was not a seat to be had for love or money," Fanny added. But the artist Eduard Magnus heard some young people discussing the authorship of the drama in a restaurant: was it Shakespeare or Tieck? The conclusion was that Shakespeare had translated the play from the original German. These youths "despised the ass's head, despite the ermine mantle spread over it by royalty".

Meanwhile, Felix complained of having to correct manuscripts from morning until night to such an extent that he felt his head would burst. He also felt a special pang of regret, at some performances and rehearsals, that Rebecka was absent. She would be so amused, especially at the mock funeral march for Thisbe, "quite in the stable of my mock preludes that used to make you laugh so". She would have been equally amused at her brother's written instructions: "Tempo, dynamics, phrasing, pedal markings in black ink and red crayon; brown ink is employed for specific instructions to the printers and green ink for alterations to the German text and stage directions." Deletions were made when parts of the original text were omitted (whereas Schlegel's translation, for which Felix wrote the music, had been divided into four acts, that of Tieck was in three). After so much work and worry, not to mention annoyance, it must have been with relief that Mendelssohn returned to Leipzig, where the still summer-laden air revived everyone.

Mendelssohn's music for *A Midsummer Night's Dream* is so popular that it is often overlooked that he wrote other pieces of music with unworldly connotations. Critics often link Shakespeare's play to his Op. 20 String Octet. Written a year earlier, this work bears the same fairy-like quality. "One is transported to that shimmering, gossamer world", as an anonymous editor of a concert programme has observed. Kupferberg calls the String Octet "so radiant and vital", and an incredible achievement for a boy of 16. Fanny wrote that it was only to herself that Felix confided his plan to create the work. "The whole piece is to be played staccato and pianissimo, the tremelandos coming in now and then, the trills passing away with the speed of lightning, everything new and strange and, at the same time, pleasing. One feels so near the world of spirits, carried away in the air, half inclined to take up a broomstick and follow the secret procession. At the end, the first violin takes flight with a feathery lightness – and all has vanished." Felix admitted that he gained inspiration from reading Goethe's description of *Walpurgisnacht* in *Faust*. This festival takes place in the Harz Mountains on the night of 30th April / 1st May. Four lines in particular caught his attention; though the translation by Sir George Grove does poor justice to the original:

> Floating cloud and trailing mist
> Bright'ning o'er us hover.
> Airs still break; the rushes shake –
> And all their pomp is over.

Chapter 15: "The Fairies' Laureate"

"I had a beautiful time writing this," Felix admitted later, adding that his String Octet was one of his favourite compositions. Along with this work, critics have ranked the scherzo movement of Mendelssohn's Op. 3 Piano Quartet that impressed Cherubini so highly when the 16-year-old Felix visited the Paris Conservatoire in 1825. Its lack of popularity compared, for instance, with the String Octet or the music for *A Midsummer Night's Dream* can only be called scandalous. Yet Adolf Bernhard Marx criticised Mendelssohn's chamber works – especially the scherzo movements – as being "too scurrying". Such a comment can only prove that Marx's imagination was far less fertile, and his personality far less perceptive, than Mendelssohn's. Such a style precisely conveyed the concept of fairies and fairy lore. Felix's love of fairyland can also be heard in his piano pieces. In a recital to commemorate his 50th anniversary as a concert pianist, Frederic Lamond included in his repertoire the last of Mendelssohn's *Seven Characteristic Pieces*, Op. 7: "Elves and gnomes are dancing on a midnight sward. The transition from E major to E minor for the eight final bars call to mind the glittering moonlight suddenly hidden by a dark, sinister cloud, causing the dancing elves and gnomes to vanish." So wrote Lamond, who compiled his own programme notes. Neither must Mendelssohn's Op. 16, Three Caprices for piano, be overlooked when discussing the life of fairyland. In the piece representing "fairy trumpets", as analysed in Chapter 14, "'Flirting outrageously'", a spray of the *Eccremocarpus* plant is drawn at the end of the score and the repeated note B represents the trumpets.

To the modern reader, a word of explanation is needed as to why there is so much talk of fairies in Mendelssohn's work. The romantic movement espoused the supernatural in all its forms; it was, therefore, no exception to include fairies in this canon and no one who did so was considered effeminate. In an autograph belonging to Fanny Horsley, Carl Klingemann had written a poem *Elves* describing these spirits dancing with fairies in the moonlight. The poem was later translated into English by E. Stanley Robinson and appears in Rosamund Brunel Gotch's compilation of letters *Mendelssohn and his Friends in Kensington*. Similarly, according to W. S. Rockstro, Mendelssohn's favourite Beethoven symphony was the Fourth, which has been described as "a fairy between two giants" – i.e., between its two giant bodyguards, the 'Eroica' and the 5th Symphony. Yet both Klingemann and Mendelssohn each epitomised manliness. In later generations, too, other decidedly masculine men – notably Sir Arthur Conan Doyle and Air Chief Marshal Lord Dowding – believed in fairies.

Another creature of mythology, equally beneficent, caught Mendelssohn's fancy: a mermaid, whose story was encapsulated in his overture *'The Fair (or Beautiful) Melusine'*. On 7th February 1834 Felix wrote to Fanny of his visit to the King's Theatre, Berlin, to see Conradin Kreutzer's opera based on Franz Grillparzer's fairy tale. As described in Chapter 14, Fräulein Hänel's image remained in Felix's mind:

"I chose the part of the subject which pleased me, exactly corresponding with the legend, and, in short, the overture came into the world and this is its pedigree."

The Leipzig public thought the overture one of his best compositions, with which Mendelssohn admitted to have agreed. Grillparzer described his own love of fairy tales as "a sense of the wonderful, combined with not wondering at wonders; being at home in the world of wonder". This could be equally applied to Mendelssohn's love of the supernatural. The story of Melusine concerns a beautiful woman who falls under a spell, whereby she is transmogrified into a mermaid every seven days, but she has made her husband, a knight, swear that he will not try to discover why she has disappeared on this seventh day. Goaded by his kin, the husband breaks his vow, causing Melusine to forsake him and their children, to live forever as a mermaid – or water nymph, as she is sometimes described.

Though Felix must have been honoured that Walter Dahms would call the overture "one of the most touching, most German works written in the realm of music", the composer did not let adulation go to his head. When Schumann first heard the work in Leipzig in December 1835, he wrote that there was no need to read Tieck's translation of the tale having listened to the music, which he described as "limpid". It conjured up "a vision of marine abysses, full of darting fish with golden scales; of pearls in open shells; of buried treasures robbed from men by the sea; of emerald castles towering one above the other". Mendelssohn rejected this "programme" synopsis and, when asked what the *Fair Melusine* was really about, his answer was "hmm – a misalliance".

Neither was Felix too concerned when negative feedback was conveyed from London, where a performance was given by the Philharmonic Society in April 1834. Klingemann wrote that, though the music was "heavenly, charming and passionate", it was "far too good" for Philharmonic audiences to appreciate. He believed that Moscheles had conducted the piece at far too slow a tempo; the instruction is 'allegro', denoting a medium pace. Charlotte Moscheles commented that the work was not popular, to which Felix replied that this would not kill him. Yet there were instances where enjoyment resulted from performances of this overture. 'Melusine' was played twice at a private gathering that Mendelssohn organised, in order for musicians to play through proofs that had arrived from the copyist. A supper of veal and bread and butter followed, supplemented by wine, "to allow them to become tipsy as they please", Felix told his family. On another occasion, an event was related to her aunt, Lucy Callcott, by Sophie Horsley in a letter of 12th March 1835. Her elder sisters, Mary and Fanny, had "considerably improved" their performance of the piano arrangement that Felix had written for them. Presumably, an earlier recital had taken place, that aunt Lucy had heard, that left something to be desired by the young pianists.

The greatest honour that Mendelssohn acknowledged was bestowed by the still-revered composer Ludwig Spohr, who acknowledged that his new overture *'Daughter of the Air'* had been inspired by *'Melusine'*. "This makes me fond of my

Chapter 15: "The Fairies' Laureate"

piece all over again," Felix wrote. He looked forward, as soon as possible, to performing Spohr's overture with the Gewandhaus Orchestra in Leipzig, and the same would apply to any other music the composer deemed suitable. "We shall all work to the best of our ability to achieve a worthy performance," Mendelssohn assured the older musician. But, however famous Spohr had become, an even greater accolade was to await the *Fair Melusine* after her creator's death. Although it is played at a tempo half that of Mendelssohn's original score, Wagner employed the precise notation to introduce his Prelude to *Das Rheingold*. It is fitting that Wagner, the self-styled arbiter of German music, should choose, however unconsciously, Mendelssohn as his guide.

Yet Felix proved not only that he was able to understand fairyland but that he was equally at ease with the malevolent world of witches. This can be heard in various of his piano pieces and songs, but especially in his setting of Hölty's poem *Hexenlied* (*Witches' Song*), No. 8 of Op. 8. Mendelssohn's music brings the poem to shuddering, shivering life through the piano accompaniment, if it is played as it should be. Shipley Douglas may well have had this song in mind when he wrote his march for brass band, *Mephistopheles*, because this later piece bears an uncanny resemblance in rhythm to *Hexenlied*.

It is strongly recommended that anyone who still clings to the myth that Mendelssohn was a milksop, composing and performing pretty pieces to amuse dainty damsels and making his compositions easy enough for these young ladies to play, should obtain a recording or indulge in the all too exclusive privilege of listening to a broadcast, or attending a concert, of *The First Walpurgisnacht*, Op. 60. Music critics have named this cantata unsurpassed in the whole of Mendelssohn's musical canon. Eric Werner regards the work as one of the best of the secular genre written in the 19th century, and H. E. Jacob goes so far as to declare that, had Mendelssohn's signature not appeared on the manuscript, it could well have been attributed to Wagner, without question. The word 'First' in the title distinguishes this work from the verses in Goethe's *Faust* that describe the same German festival. On 30th July 1799 the poet and dramatist had tried to persuade Zelter to set this poem, originally known as *Greeting Spring*, to music. However, like his contemporaries, Goethe's friend claimed not to understand the symbolism of the poem, which related to historical and political themes, nor to be aware of the context in which it was based.

Goethe's works had always been popular at Leipzigerstrasse 3, so it would hardly be surprising when Zelter's pupil sought the poet's approval to take on the task of setting this literary work to music. Felix, the thinker, soon realised the hidden depths to Goethe's manuscript. It was not a mere fantasy, but contained a universal truth that had occurred during several eras of human history. Thus, on 22nd February 1831, Mendelssohn wrote from Italy that the score was taking shape and becoming "a grand cantata". He wished to include "a tripping, mysterious chorus", admitting that "for witches, I have a particular feeling". On 28th August he wrote to Goethe, on his last birthday on earth, thanking the elderly poet for his "heavenly words. There is no need to invent music. It is there already." Mendelssohn wished to have the verses sung, once he could find a suitable choir in Berlin. All he hoped was that the cantata would demonstrate how deeply moved he had been by the poem. He would later write that the work was finished except for the overture and, when he performed it to Franz Xavier Mozart in Milan, Felix was told *The First Walpurgisnacht* should be published immediately. This, naturally, gave the composer fresh pleasure, especially considering to whom the cantata was performed – none other than Wolfgang Amadeus's youngest son.

But it would be a further 12 years before the general public was permitted to hear the composition. The overture was finished in Paris in 1832. No one but Mendelssohn, Jacob claims, could have written "such grotesque triplets when describing the witches' kitchen", reminiscent of *Macbeth* to Mendelssohn's biographer. Such an idea may not be so bizarre as first appears, because 'the Scottish play' (as actors superstitiously refer to Shakespeare's drama) was Shakespeare's best-admired play to Germans of the time. Hans Joachim Moser, in his biography of Goethe written in 1949, declares that Mendelssohn's *First Walpurgisnacht* would be suitable for performance at any Goethe festival, and added that it was a pity that the dramatist did not live to witness the first performance in 1843 – "Its romantic colour and classical control of form merge in the happiest possible manner." Moser continues, "He wrote for the people of his homeland a Mayday cantata which, hitherto, they had never possessed." Yet, as was his habit, Mendelssohn continued to be dissatisfied and made many revisions until not even he could do any more with the work. For instance, he wrote to Fanny from Düsseldorf that he did not want to bring a roll of drums into the bass or a blaze of trumpets into the treble, nor "all sorts of hobgoblins. I love my serious elements of music too well to do anything of the kind." He did not want to write anything "obvious" that imitated children's literature, "where the roofs are coloured bright red to make children aware that they are intended to be roofs".

But, eventually, on 11th December 1842 Felix wrote that a concert was to be given for the King of Saxony in which the cantata would be performed in the second half, "with which I am, nevertheless, becoming frustrated". The first half was to include the partridge and bear hunt from Haydn's *The Seasons*. His own piece, Felix confessed, was "too richly endowed with trombones and rather poor in vocal parts". The original cantata had been reconstituted "from A to Z, two arias having been added, not to mention the clipping and cutting". He wrote in a similar vein to Hiller: "In fact, it is a different work now, a hundred times better, but I am still in doubt about having it engraved." To his family he declared: "If I do not like it now, I solemnly vow to give it up for the rest of my life." Fortunately, however, his self-assurance triumphed, as can be witnessed from a report in *The Musical World* of 2nd February 1843.

The first performance by the Leipzig Gewandhaus Orchestra was hailed by the audience "with enthusiasm bordering on delirium", and several movements of the cantata were encored. At Leipzigerstrasse 3 the work was equally popular with the guests at the garden house concerts. In fact, it is significant that Fanny was rehearsing this cantata with her ladies' choir when she was taken ill, never to recover consciousness. An essayist named Steinberg quotes the lines:

> And if we are robbed of our old customs,
> Who can rob us of our light?

He sees Mendelssohn's setting of these words as comparing the old Jewish faith with the new Protestant creed. But there is an even more perceptive observation to be made. For Fanny and Felix, the "old customs" could have represented the world, with its restrictions and constraints – especially for Felix, the veto of his father whereby "elves and spirits" should be eschewed. By the end of 1847 he and his sister belonged to the light of which they would never be robbed. Malevolent spirits were no longer a force to confront; now they could enjoy fairyland or any other beautiful realm they fancied entering. Fanny and Felix were now part of the spirit world; their spirits were no longer caged.

Chapter 16

Observer of Nature and Life

From an early age Felix Mendelssohn had employed all his five senses to observe everything around him, and, the more proficient he became in drawing, painting, letter writing and composing, the more clearly this gift was revealed. Percy Young said of Elgar that, to him, music could be picked up from the air. Such a claim can be applied equally to Mendelssohn. As Anne Taylor remembered: "He observed how natural objects seemed to suggest music to him." One of the earliest examples of this perception can be noticed from his Op. 20 String Octet, written in 1825 when he was 16. Whilst, since the composer himself admitted the fact, it must be true that it was the verses describing *Walpurgisnacht* in Goethe's *Faust* that inspired him, Jacob propounds an equally plausible theory. Many guests visited Leipzigerstrasse 3, and it was not uncommon, in the warmer weather, for everyone to disport themselves in the lovely garden. On one occasion, Jacob claims, eight people were present for a lively discussion. Felix averred, possibly as what would nowadays be called 'a throwaway line', that musical notation spoke far more precisely than words. But he was to be 'hoist with his own petard'. The more he listened, the more he realised how musically the voices around him – male, female, loud, soft – could blend. Music could be created from this ensemble of sound, and the String Octet took shape in his mind. Though Ludwig Spohr had written a double string quartet and Schubert had been responsible for an octet in which instruments other than strings took part, Mendelssohn was the first to bring into existence a piece in which each string player had an individual place, but where all eight musicians made a harmonious whole.

A further example of the young composer's powers of observation can be seen in his overture to *A Midsummer Night's Dream* of 1826. Julius Schubring recalled that once, whilst he and Felix lay on the grass at Schönhausen, a wooded area outside Berlin, Mendelssohn attracted his companion's attention to a firefly that was buzzing around them. When the work was eventually performed, Felix was able to pinpoint the very place where the insect was represented: between bars 264 and 270, where the 'cellos modulated between B minor and F minor. To demonstrate the antics of the 'rude mechanicals', and especially the braying of

Bottom the Weaver with his ass's head, Mendelssohn employed the ophicleide; this would be replaced by the tuba, once the original instrument had become obsolete.

For the 1828 festival to commemorate the 400th anniversary of the death of the engraver and woodcarver Albrecht Dürer, Mendelssohn wrote his Overture in C major, later to be published as Op. 101. It was his family who coined the title 'the Trumpet Overture' by which it is known. This work, which, like many of Mendelssohn's compositions is shamefully neglected, suggests some fascinating observations made about it by contemporaries. Inspired by a visit to the spa at Bad Doberan on the Baltic four years earlier, the trumpets are given a sound as if under water, which removes their nasal, strident, brassy sound. The Swedish composer Adolf Lindblad, a former pupil with Mendelssohn at the Berlin Singakademie, called the instruments "trumpets of the deep". George Onslow, an Anglo-French composer of the time, spoke of the work "as if played through a curtain of water. [There is] something veiled about the sound – nothing to do with the forte or piano of the trumpets," he recalled in an article of 1840.

Another work, better known but still too rarely performed, also took root in Mendelssohn's mind at Bad Doberan in 1824, but, like his Trumpet Overture, it was not published until later. Felix's first visit to a seaside resort made a tremendous impression upon him. He was able to distinguish the changing colours and moods of the Baltic: "Sometimes it lies as smooth as a mirror. Sometimes it is wild and furious," Mendelssohn wrote. It is likely that he would have concurred with Matthew Arnold's dictum that "the sea is an arbiter between the inanimate and man", had he known the works of the later poet. Mendelssohn's Overture *Calm Sea and Prosperous Voyage* was based on two poems by Goethe. Schubert had set the poems as songs and Beethoven had written a cantata based on these poems, but Mendelssohn preferred instrumental music to reflect Goethe's verse. When listening to this overture, care should be taken to imagine oneself as living at the time the poems were written. A vessel is becalmed; not the idyllic phenomenon that might obtain today, but that whereby a crew of the 1820s would have been caused considerable anxiety. Thus, their gloomy foreboding is astutely perceived in the first part of this musical seascape. The slow opening ends with the sound of a flute, representing a breeze that would cause the ship to get under way and allow the minds of the crew to be eased. Subsequently the spirited sea causes great rejoicing on board and, on arrival into port, the timpani play their part to the full, and the overture ends with what can be perceived as a quiet, moving 'amen' of thankfulness that everyone has arrived safely on shore.

As described in the previous chapter, when Schumann waxed over-lyrically about the *Fair Melusine* Overture, Mendelssohn gave the same short shrift to Julius Schubring when he had the nerve to express what he felt about *Calm Sea and Prosperous Voyage*. To Schubring, the overture represented "the tones of love, approaching the goal of its desire". Sarcastically, Mendelssohn responded that the work described "some good-natured old man, sitting in the stern of a vessel,

Chapter 16: Observer of Nature and Life

blowing vigorously into the sails, so as to play his part in the prosperous voyage". But, really, all Mendelssohn wished to do was to translate Goethe's two poems into music in the most accurate way he knew how. Whenever he wished listeners to know what a composition represented, Felix ensured, by his own words, the import of his music. If the listener's imagination wandered from this description, Mendelssohn preferred his audience to keep its own counsel. But, whatever Goethe felt about Schubert's or Beethoven's settings, he enjoyed Mendelssohn's overture: "Sail well in your music," he wrote, "and may your voyages always be as prosperous as this one."

Yet Felix was reluctant to have it performed in Berlin so soon. Whilst expressing the honour Otto Gans had shown him by such an invitation, he knew that the King's Band would not allow him to conduct, and, in view of his earlier untoward experiences in Berlin, he felt it wiser to wait until he returned from abroad before bringing the work to the public. Neither was he satisfied with the overture as it stood at that time. Thus, as with so many other of his compositions, the work was revised – "30 times better than before", as he confided to Schubring. The *Calm Sea and Prosperous Voyage* was eventually published in 1832, and it was the first piece to be performed by the Gewandhaus Orchestra when Felix began his association with Leipzig.

Throughout this period of his life Mendelssohn was not backward in saying what he disliked in musical sounds. As a boy, he often played piano music by Bach or Beethoven – never his own compositions, unless he was begged specifically to do so. Regarding one such evening, he wrote: "At nine o'clock the guard marched past Leipzigerstrasse 3 en route between the barracks and the war ministry. Invariably, a tattoo was beaten during a quiet passage. I became so annoyed that, jumping up, I shouted to the guard not to indulge in such abominable, infantile tomfoolery", according to Mme. von Glehn's translation, but Felix's own German may well have been less genteel. Even at a distance the drums could be heard. "At the guard's approach, window panes rattled." As Schubring observed: "Anyone who ever heard the melting melodies played by Mendelssohn, and saw how his soul was absorbed in the magnificent creations of art, will comprehend how such discordant sounds jarred upon our reverential feelings." He continued, with increasingly pompous drivel, concerning "the drooping lids of Felix's beautiful eyes". It seems not to have occurred to the residents and guests at Leipzigerstrasse 3 to postpone the recital, or "to remove themselves from the 'evil spirits'", as Schubring called the military band who, albeit overzealous, were simply doing their duty, following the long tradition of beating the retreat.

From Switzerland Felix wrote to Zelter in 1822 complaining of "the ascending sixths, so harsh and strident nearby", when local peasants yodelled; yet, at a distance, "the sound is beautiful". He likewise despaired of the "parallel fifths" some girls were singing. "They break the rules of polite music," he sniffed. Nine years later, when returning to Switzerland, Mendelssohn was able to boast that he had mastered yodelling and was able "to shout lustily, singing several airs at the top of my voice". Whilst on this topic, though Mendelssohn wrote to Zelter that "beauty cannot be described in words" when depicting the scenery, it is strange that he composed nothing to represent this landscape, so beloved throughout his life. This may well have resulted from the decidedly unmusical ambience he found in Switzerland.

In Austria, too, music was in the doldrums under the repressive reign of Prince Metternich, now that the giants – Haydn, Mozart, Beethoven and Schubert – were no longer alive, when Mendelssohn visited this once great musical realm in 1830. Only later would Brahms, Bruckner, Mahler and Schoenberg herald another golden age for Viennese music, with Joseph Lanner, the Strauss family, von Suppé and Franz Lehár to compose more popular, but equally respected, music.

Felix enjoyed his boat trip along the Danube, from Linz to Vienna, "We flew along like an arrow. At noon the skipper promised to make the journey in a day and a half in this small, new skiff, with a gondolier's deck." Although he copied down the notes he heard from the steeples and cloisters along the route, as with Switzerland no musical ideas resulted in composition. Felix awoke to observe that "the whole starry heavens had opened up. The rowing sounds echoed more sharply. Everything was completely quiet and, all around me, nature was full of mysterious movement. Shooting stars were falling in every direction, darting back and forth on the water. The little eddies were mumbling high notes and low." Everything was so peaceful that Felix felt as if he were intruding on the 'music of the spheres'. But, as they approached the inn where they were to stay for the night, the atmosphere was completely spoilt: "A flute piped out a bad dance tune and two Hungarian officers embarked for the next stage of the journey. At Stein, I drew the notes of other bells, this time in E flat minor."

These descriptions of Austria and Switzerland demonstrate that, however fine a musician he was, much of his European tour was undertaken in obedience to his father's wishes, to ape the young men of nobler birth. Even in Italy, whence his 4th Symphony would eventually see the light of day, Felix must have regretted not visiting Sicily, with its multicultured environment that inspired other composers. On 30th April 1831 he admitted that he did not want to forgo his plan to visit that island, but reluctantly deferred to his father's exhortation. A steamer was to take passengers round the island on 4th May. These would include many Germans, among them, a diplomat: "I would have liked to see a mountain spitting fire, since naughty Vesuvius is not even smoking. Usually, my parents' wishes have coincided with my own, until now. But, against my own desires, I have crossed Sicily off my itinerary. Perhaps," he placated his father, "we shall be able to see each other all the sooner." It may be fanciful to say so, but, in view of Mendelssohn's lifelong dissatisfaction with his 'Italian' Symphony, he might have felt that a visit to Sicily would have given him even greater inspiration and more exciting musical ideas, for which he yearned. The symphony was eventually published in 1852, five years after the

Chapter 16: Observer of Nature and Life

composer's death. However he may have viewed this work, Marek describes the symphony as "a paradigm of Mendelssohn's genius, bringing his excellence to full expression. [The symphony is] exciting in the first [movement]; stately in the second; elegant in the third; jaunty in the fourth." The conductor Hilary Davan Wetton is reminded of a champagne cork popping when hearing the work. "From the very first bar, the symphony bubbles along with vitality, yet Mendelssohn is always thinking of new ideas and progressive musical techniques." Critics have stated that this does not depict the Italy of 1830-31, visited by Mendelssohn, but her past traditions – buildings, art treasures, scenery and religious ritual. The latter is represented by the second movement, sometimes known as 'the pilgrims' march'. In fact, Moscheles claimed the melody to have originated as a Czech hymn and, to anyone conversant with sacred music, similarities can be observed. The third movement, the last time a minuet and trio was to be employed in a symphony, could symbolise a yearning for the composer's love of society, so typically does it remind the listener of the type of dance that would be known at a ball of the period, before the waltz and polka became the fashion. Philistines have called the movement 'bourgeois', but without analysis. The final movement is a 'saltarello', a jumping dance, which Felix must have seen performed in the Naples area. The movement is often played too fast, whereby notes are skimped.

The symphony was part of a commission from the Philharmonic Society of London, along with his *Calm Sea and Prosperous Voyage* and Trumpet Overtures and a song for soprano, 'Infelice' ('Unhappy'). Of the symphony Mendelssohn wrote: "It cost me the bitterest moments I have ever endured," but no biographer explains this comment. His disappointment at not visiting Sicily may be one answer to this quandary. Another may derive from a letter Felix wrote to Carl Klingemann, in which he yearned for "some friend to whom I may communicate my new work and who could examine the score along with me and play a bass or flute. Whereas now, when the piece is finished, I must lay it aside on my desk without its giving pleasure to anyone. London spoils me in this respect and I can never again expect to meet such friends as I have there. Here I can only say the half of what I think and leave the best half unspoken, whereas there it was not necessary to say more than half, because the other half was a mere matter of course, and already understood."

Naples was not the only place in which Felix was plagued by beggars, as described in Chapter 5, 'Italy at last!'. A painting by Donald Wilkins of 1827, *The Pifferone*, shows these musicians, whose name derives from the 'piffero', the type of shoe they wore, and whose instrument was allied to the bagpipe, later to be used in Berlioz's symphonic work *Harold in Italy*. Very likely, Felix would have encountered these pifferone on his visit to London; he wrote of the "uproar" along his three-quarter-hour drive to the City. On another occasion, "Whilst walking along a most respectable, fog-bound street in the West End, a beggar pours forth his ditty in a deplorable voice, soon to be drowned out by the street vendors," he reported. Each morning Felix practised on his silent keyboard, but this, too, was disturbed by 'the Marylebone Band' outside his bedroom window. One morning, so exasperated did Mendelssohn become that he sent the landlord's son to ask the band to go away and entertain elsewhere, bestowing on the boy a shilling for this errand.

In Wales, too, Felix found himself annoyed by harpists in this 'land of song': "A harpist sits in the foyer of every reputable inn, playing so-called folk music at me," which he dismissed as "infamous, vulgar, out-of-tune trash". A hurdy-gurdy, whose operator Felix discovered doubled as the local barber, played simultaneously, "enough to drive me mad and give me toothache. If anyone enjoys arrangements of Beethoven's national airs, he should visit Wales to hear them, howled by shrill, nasal voices, accompanied by doltish, incompetent fingers – then try to hold his tongue. The hurdy-gurdy, having churned out the huntsman's chorus from *Der Freischütz*, another song followed, in A flat major. May 10,000 devils take all folk music, be it performed by Welsh harps, Swiss cowbells or even Scottish bagpipes." Later in the evening, when harp and hurdy-gurdy had fallen silent, Felix visited the living quarters of his host, who owned a piano. "Three daughters, who were quite pretty, entertained me with a potpourri of melodies from Auber operas and several country dances, which pleased me." Having somehow discovered that their guest was a pianist, they asked him to "favour them" at the piano. "I favoured them from my heart by racing up and down the keyboard. Having played away my toothache, the evening became more bearable."

Yet, from another part of the United Kingdom, Felix was to gain inspiration that resulted in two of his most popular compositions. In the early 19th century anyone with artistic awareness was fascinated by all things Scottish. Indeed, Goethe regarded the Waverley novels as Sir Walter Scott's finest achievement. Inevitably, therefore, the romantically inclined Mendelssohn was determined to visit what Scott called 'the land of the mountain and the flood'. Therefore, when Klingemann had been posted to London from the Hanoverian Legation, it was agreed that he and Felix would include Scotland in their itinerary when the latter visited Britain. His former music teacher, Carl Zelter, advised him to observe as much folk music as possible when abroad. Having arrived in Scotland, Zelter was told of how the national instrument, the bagpipe, "produced extraordinary music". A friend had drawn in Felix's sketchbook, in exaggeration, to demonstrate this. Yet, despite this jest, Mendelssohn attended a pibroch contest, at which the classical music of the bagpipe repertoire was performed. "Many Highlanders came in national costume from church," he wrote from Edinburgh to his family, "victoriously leading their sweethearts in their Sunday clothes, casting proud glances over the scene, with their long red beards, plaids, bonnets and plumes, bare knees, and bagpipes in their hands."

But Felix reported an even more stirring sight: that of Holyrood Palace and its environs. "Here, Mary Stuart lived in splendour and loved. We were shown a narrow little room with a winding stair. They found Rizzio, the Queen's secretary and lover, in that little room, and murdered him. The chapel is now roofless. Gorse and ivy grow there and, at that broken altar, Mary was crowned Queen of Scotland. Everything is [now] broken and mouldering and the bright sky shines in. I believe I have found today, in that old chapel, the beginning of my Scotch [sic] Symphony." As so often with Mendelssohn's compositions, critics have had a field day when reading their own interpretation of what the symphony purports to describe: there exists a warrior's lament; a gathering of the clans, whose chieftains take part in an interplay of claymore and dirk; and a Highland fling. Kenneth Loveland, writing in a concert programme of 1995, gives a better idea of the symphony's 'programme'. "The opening woodwind phrase hints at sad events. One imagines Mendelssohn walking with the betrayed ghosts of history; tragic Mary, murdered Rizzio; the ruined chapel and the surrounding countryside." Schumann, however subconsciously, may well have borne his friend's music in mind when, in 1850, he depicted the majestic façade of Cologne Cathedral in his 'Rhenish' Symphony, so strikingly does this remind the listener of Mendelssohn's work.

In his 'Italian' equivalent, Hilary Davan Wetton has described how Mendelssohn had introduced a third subject (or theme) in the first movement, rather than adhering to the first two. Likewise, in his 'Scottish' Symphony, Felix broke with tradition. Whereas a second movement was usually slow, this composition has a dance-like theme – possibly reminiscent of a melody he had heard in Scotland – that Kenneth Loveland describes as "bustling". The third movement, like the first, portrays the brooding landscape of which Mendelssohn was so fond. The final movement "has an energy that is distinctly military", according to an unnamed critic (the movement was described by Mendelssohn as an 'allegro guerrero' – 'warlike' – although the movement is headed 'allegro vivacissimo – allegro maestoso assai'). The same critic continues that this movement may well have been written to describe incidents in Scott's novels, so firmly ingrained in German minds.

Yet, though Mendelssohn worked on this symphony in the disparate climate of Italy in 1830-31, his musical inspiration had become 'fallow', as he confided to Klingemann. "The morning and evening services commissioned by Novello do not count; they are just a chore: every morning, double canons and counterpoint to my heart's content – in other words, demanding on my boredom level." He hoped, however, that Klingemann's poems would prompt him into "real work. God willing, better times may come soon." Though settled into routine, Mendelssohn saw himself as "between present and past" on his arrival home. "Every step I take, whether in the streets or in the garden, evokes dim images which I do not know where to place, as they are still too vivid." It was only when Felix had left Berlin and become wholly independent that he was able to produce his mature work. His 'Scotch' Symphony, as Mendelssohn called it, did not see the light of day until 1842, several years after he had taken up residence in Leipzig. The first performance was given there by the Gewandhaus Orchestra and, eight weeks later, in June, it was premiered in London. It was on his seventh visit there that he sought Queen Victoria's permission to dedicate the symphony to Her Majesty. In 1844 Heine, after a performance at the Paris Conservatoire, commented that "the active zeal of his friends and supporters are to be thanked. The work should be recognised by anyone with knowledge of art as genuinely beautiful and amongst his best works. But how is it," the poet continued, "that no laurel wreath wants to grow on French soil for this so deserving and highly talented artist? Mendelssohn offers us an opportunity to reflect on the great question: what is the difference between art and lies?"

A further example of crass stupidity can be seen from the journal of a New York lawyer, Templeton Strong. On 19th November 1864, having attended a performance of this work by the New York Philharmonic Orchestra, he stated that the symphony "did not have the supernatural vigour and beauty of Mozart or Beethoven, preventing the orchestra from inspiration. Mendelssohn's was a first-rate for the second-rate order." An individual opinion may be fair enough, but Strong added that he did not know why the 'Scottish' Symphony was so named, rather than, say, the 'Welsh' symphony. Strong was evidently unaware of the composer's love of Scotland and its history, or, for that matter, his dislike of Welsh

Figure 5. Mendelssohn's pencil drawing of waterfall at Dunkeld, Scotland 1829

Chapter 16: Observer of Nature and Life

music. It is not known how well, or how badly, the symphony was played on that occasion, but, at a performance by the Philharmonic Society of London, 40 or 50 bars of the adagio movement were drowned by the applause for the scherzo. Mendelssohn therefore repeated the movement, continuing to the end of the work. As with his E minor Violin Concerto, Mendelssohn's 'Scottish' Symphony is played without a break, to avoid this misunderstanding. Sir George MacFarren, who recalled this anecdote (dictated to an amanuensis through loss of eyesight), added that Mendelssohn's wife, Cécile, wanted her husband to write something for her. "M showed me the autograph. It was an octavo book bound in blue silk – I think watered – and lettered in silver on the side 'Cécile'... [He] had had the book bound and fronted with her name, having written this on paper, in pencil."

But it was not only Mendelssohn's symphony that resulted from his trip to Scotland. "In order that you may understand how extraordinarily the Hebrides affect me," Mendelssohn wrote to Fanny from Oban, "the following has come into my mind," after which the first few bars of what would become the *Hebrides* Overture followed. This was written from "one of the Hebrides" on 7th August 1829. Therefore, though biographies, broadcasters and concert programmes alike weave the picture of Mendelssohn taking a sketchbook from his pocket to write down these first few bars, on impulse, at Fingal's Cave itself, this is nothing more than a myth to perpetuate the composer's romantic image. Another fact is that Mendelssohn's overture could have been a lucky accident. Though Fingal's Cave was a popular tourist attraction, Klingemann is said to have confused the Hebrides with the Hesperides, maidens in Greek mythology, daughters of the evening, who guarded the golden apples in the Grove of Hera. This diplomat must have been disappointed that the luxurious vegetation he had anticipated was represented only by orange segments he might have found in his toddy. Nevertheless, the travelling companions set out from Oban on 8th August to see for themselves this spectacular cave.

Fingal's Cave, on the isle of Staffa, is named after Finn McCoul, a chieftain of Gaelic legend, who was purported to have driven the Norwegians from the west of Scotland, according to the poet Ossian (or Oisin). The word 'ghal' denoted a man of valour and, thus, Fingal's Cave, when literally translated from the Gaelic, means Cave of Finn, man of valour. In the 1760s James MacPherson claimed to have translated the poetry of Ossian and, although Samuel Johnson exposed MacPherson's work as fraudulent, these legends of Finn McCoul, son of Finn MacCunbail, were to fascinate Europeans for a long time to come. It was in 1782 that the botanist Joseph Banks visited Staffa, which, hitherto, only seabirds had frequented. Banks, who had sailed with Captain Cook in 1768 and had been made a Fellow of the Royal Society two years later, was to be followed to Fingal's Cave by various celebrities from the world of culture. Keats said of this strange structure: "In solemnity and grandeur [it] surpasses by far the grandest cathedral." "A temple not made by hands" was Heine's verdict. Turner would paint the cave in 1832 and

Sir Robert Peel would rhapsodise about "this cave-cathedral, placed amid the melancholy main – romantic, classical and natural, all at once". The Queen and Prince Albert would be lured to Scotland, going so far as to purchase Balmoral Castle in 1848; this holiday-home in Aberdeenshire reminded the Prince Consort of the German scenery he loved. One person, however, who appears not to have been impressed was William Wordsworth, who, in 1833 declared that the tourists spoilt the atmosphere of this once remote landscape.

It was, therefore, predictable that Mendelssohn should visit this romantic place during his journey with Klingemann to Scotland. Travelling by stagecoach to Edinburgh, the two companions broke their journey wherever the fancy took them, hiking in a westerly direction to reach Oban, and crossing to Staffa by ferry to see Fingal's Cave. "It sounds beautiful," Felix wrote home, "and looks so from pictures I have seen in guidebooks." On 8th August 1829, therefore, they boarded the steamer to view this spectacular cave, which appeared from a distance like a high, flat-topped rock, with sheer cliff faces on the east and south sides, and sloping down to the Atlantic on the north side, where the boats landed. Klingemann described Fingal's Cave as having "strange, basalt pillars, resembling the inside of a cathedral organ, black and resounding. The lower the barometer fell, the higher rose the sea. Its questing tongue licked more roughly and swirled with greater violence." Klingemann's subsequent narrative puts paid to Felix's ability to remove the sketchbook from his pocket to make his famous sound-picture of the landscape: "The ladies went down like flies and, here and there, a gentleman did the same. My companion, Felix, was terribly seasick and gets on better with the sea as an artist than does his stomach." But Mendelssohn must have recovered later, for a local aristocrat, 'Sir James', produced a bottle of wine, which "Felix fell to with a hearty quaff". On Staffa itself Felix was "in a hearty mood, scrambling on the rocks until he reached a ledge at the entrance to the cave, from which vantage point his attention was captured by nature's cathedral. Below him, the boiling sea; above him, the vaulted roof; to the sides, the columned walls."

Mendelssohn evidently had no need to describe the area. Not only did his companion supply ample verbal portraiture, but the musical narrative that followed expressed Mendelssohn's own feelings more than words or drawings ever could. The whole atmosphere of this strange landscape is encapsulated in the *Hebrides* Overture: the crash of the waves of the Atlantic onto the rocks; the grandeur of the coastline, and – above all – the various calls of seabirds. Indeed, the least imaginative listener can picture himself on Staffa. The landscape can be seen in the mind's eye; the fog and tang of seaweed assails the nostrils and the salty air can be tasted, so realistic, so true to life is Mendelssohn's overture. Turner's painting of 1832 has been called "indirect and indistinct", whereas Mendelssohn painted in his music precisely what he discerned. The Romanian sculptor Constantin Brancusi stated that an artist must be in the right frame of mind to begin a creation of any art form. Though he did not say so, intuition and inspiration must also be present

Chapter 16: Observer of Nature and Life

to the artist – and this certainly applied to Mendelssohn's *Hebrides* Overture. Kenneth Loveland considers that, together with Wagner's *Flying Dutchman* Overture, Britten's Four Sea Interludes from his opera *Peter Grimes* and Debussy's three symphonic sketches *La Mer*, Mendelssohn's overture is among the best musical seascapes. Bax's overture, *Tintagel*, could well be added to this list. The Scottish musicologist W. G. Whittaker observed that Mendelssohn was far more progressive than anyone hitherto in his musical representation of the sounds made by wind, water and seabirds, "blending them into, and combining them with the atmosphere produced by the climate, more than could have been thought possible prior to Mendelssohn". Detractors claim that the storm depicted in Beethoven's 'Pastoral' Symphony and Rossini's *William Tell* Overture are of equal merit. But these cannot be truly compared with Mendelssohn's overture, for, whereas *Hebrides* describes the sea, these other pieces are land-based.

Two copies of the manuscripts exist: one, made by Klingemann, is now in a Swedish archive; the other, by Mendelssohn, can be seen at the Bodleian Library, Oxford. But the overture was not ready until 1832. Whilst working on the score in Rome Felix wrote to Fanny: "Curses! Herr Banck from Magdeburg played me a book of songs and an Ave Maria, asking for my opinion. In reply I delivered a hypocritical speech, and a morning in Rome has been wasted." From Paris Mendelssohn still expressed dissatisfaction with the work: "The middle section, forte, in D major, is very stupid and the whole modulation savours more of counterpoint than of whale oil, seagulls and salt fish – and it ought to be exactly the reverse. I like the piece too well to allow it to be performed in an imperfect state, but hope to have it ready for England and the Michaelmas Fair at Leipzig." But once the overture was performed at a Philharmonic concert in 1832 the public took Mendelssohn to their hearts. Indeed, Jacob goes so far as to say that, like Handel before him, Felix became an adopted Englishman. Yet not only did the *Hebrides* Overture attract praise from Britain, examples can be quoted from two of the greatest German composers. "It is one of the finest pieces of music we possess," Wagner would declare; "Mendelssohn is a first-rate landscape painter and the *Hebrides* is a masterpiece." "I would gladly give all my works if I had written a piece like the *Hebrides*," Brahms would write to a friend.

When George Sampson visited Mendelssohn in Leipzig the overture was one of the topics discussed. "Almost instantly, Mendelssohn began to play as if his feelings had to express themselves in tones, rather than words. The sounds he coaxed from the piano were remarkable for their orchestral quality. Unsurpassed power lay within his delicate hands." When Sampson remarked that, to him, the overture was "made of the sounds of the sea", the composer explained that, whilst he may have had a programme in mind, even subconsciously, when writing a work, its title had to be regarded simply as an expression of feeling rather than as a representation of an actual picture. "Music cannot paint," Felix went on to explain. "A painting must leap to the eye, whereas a piece of music unfolds itself slowly. If music tried to paint, it would lose its greater glory – the power of the infinite." Mendelssohn considered Beethoven's 'Pastoral' Symphony "an outpouring of emotion, enshrining within its notes all the sweet, powerful brightness of an early summer day. To think of it," he sighed, rising to his feet, "is to be happy with the innocence of pure joy!"

The same sentiment was expressed to Cécile's relative, Marc-André Souchay, when Mendelssohn was asked what he meant by *Songs without Words*. "There is so much talk about music," he wrote in a letter of 18th October 1842; "and yet so little is said. Words do not suffice for such a purpose and, if I found they did suffice, I would, ultimately, have nothing to do with music... People often complain that music is too ambiguous, but what they should think when they hear it is so unclear, whereas everyone understands words. With me, it is exactly the reverse, not only with regard to an entire speech, but also with individual words. The thoughts that, for me, are expressed in music that I love are not too indefinite to be put into words but, on the contrary, too definite." It was not Souchay's fault if he did not understand this concept, but, rather, the fault of the words that were incapable of expressing anything better. If Mendelssohn had a particular thought in mind when composing, he would never want to tell anyone, "because", he explained, "the same thought would not mean the same thing to a different person. Only the same music can arouse the same feeling in one person as another – a feeling that is not, however, expressed by the same words... Words have many different meanings, but music we both understand in the same way. If you are not satisfied with this answer, it is, at all events, the only one that I can give – nothing, after all, more than ambiguous words."

Felix made a similar point to Julius Schubring when discussing *Elijah*. "Talking is, after all, a very different thing from writing. The few minutes with you the other day were more enlivening and stimulating than any number of letters." But, when playing his pieces on the piano, Felix could express his feelings to his greatest satisfaction.

Yet, it must be admitted, Mendelssohn appeared to adopt the precept 'Do as I say, not as I do' with regard to his compositions. Had August Hanstein not suffered a long, serious illness, after which he passed away, which upset Felix greatly when a youth of 18, how is anyone to know why he composed his E minor/E major Prelude incorporated into his Op. 35? How, if Felix had not recorded in his letters the experiences of his visit to Coed Du, what significance would his Op. 16 Three Caprices have for a listener? But, when others attempted to describe what his music meant, it was another matter entirely. His Op. 28 Fantasy in F sharp minor is sometimes known as the 'Scottish' Sonata, and whoever named the piece can be forgiven for so doing. Published before 1830, when Felix played the piece to Goethe on his last visit to Weimar, a decidedly Scottish idiom is to be observed. It is likewise understandable why some of Mendelssohn's 'Original Melodies for the pianoforte', to give them his own name, were what Novello's published as his *Songs*

Chapter 16: Observer of Nature and Life

Without Words. No. 3 of his Op. 19, known as 'Hunting Song', when played at a lively tempo, indicates galloping horses and the sound of the hunting horn. No. 6 of the same set, 'Venetian Gondola Song', truly represents the rhythm of this romantic scene. No. 3 of the Op. 62 book of melodies, 'Funeral March', was even arranged by Moscheles for a larger group of instruments than a piano for Mendelssohn's own memorial in Leipzig. As for No. 6 of the same group, known as 'Spring Song' or 'Camberwell Green', where it was written on Mendelssohn's seventh visit to London in 1842, its own story is recorded in Chapter 28, '"Dear, good children"'. No. 6 of Mendelssohn's Op. 67 book has also been given two titles, 'The Bees' Wedding' and, far more appropriate for the keen listener, 'Spinning Song', in which the bass is reminiscent of the whirring spinning wheel, used in 19th-century homes, especially on the Continent. A further No. 6, this time contained in Mendelssohn's posthumously published Book Eight, Op. 102, is named 'Children's Piece'. Anyone with imagination can hear plainly the rhythm of a skipping rope or a rubber ball bouncing.

Irrespective of Mendelssohn's view that "words get in the way of feelings", which music expresses more adequately, Felix composed far more than the 69 songs attributed to him by Marek. Neither did he discourage others from doing so. Felix congratulated Fanny on a song she had sent as being "quite different from the trifles I normally have to hear and to play from song writers here". As with the songs of the Swedish composer Adolf Lindblad, Felix admired those of Johannes Verhulst, Kapellmeister at The Hague. The songs in his mother tongue "will meet with the acknowledgement that you so well deserve. I know of no higher aim than to give music to one's homeland." As for his own songs, only verses to which he could relate were worthy of his endeavour. He was known to reject those with which he felt uncomfortable. He did not know, for instance, what style of music was most appropriate for the Baron von Pereira's poem on Napoleon's *Midnight Military Review*. A Herr Anton von Zuccalmaglio was informed that a poem he sent did not have a clear enough meaning for Mendelssohn to work at his best to set the words to music.

Though no analysis is given, Radcliffe declares that the Brahms and Schubert settings of Goethe's *Minnelied* are superior to that of Mendelssohn. All that can be suggested is to hear each setting consecutively for an individual to choose which is preferable. The only reason for Radcliffe's statement is the fatuous argument that, because of the social environment Mendelssohn occupied, his songs were sung "too often, which allowed them to cloy", forgetting that their interpretation could have been at fault when their composer was not there to correct it. As an example, Radcliffe uses Scott's *Waken, Lords and Ladies Gay*, which is never heard nowadays, so no one can rise to Mendelssohn's defence.

Apart from the songs Felix set to poems of his native land, the list includes translations from the Swedish, Spanish, French and English. As well as Scott, Burns, Tom Moore and Byron wrote verses that Felix set to music. Of the latter, he wrote to Rebecka that the first canto of his *Theramin* was "incomprehensible, the second false", when translated into German. "Can you please suggest anything better than the phrase 'half a little'?" On the whole, he considered Byron's poem "very sentimental, and I think, repeatedly, the music should have been set in G sharp minor or B major". However, since both his sisters enjoyed Löwe's setting of the same poem, Felix's attempt was abandoned, in this instance. Even Radcliffe considers the setting of *Gondola Song* superior to "the surprisingly slight equivalent of Schumann".

Yet it was with German verse that Mendelssohn came into his own. Even Radcliffe praises Goethe's *Maiden's Lament* as being "more ambitious in Mendelssohn's hands" than Schubert's setting of the same verses. Marek, on the other hand, finds Felix's songs most appealing "when at their most lyrical", but "too coy" for his taste. The page is "strewn with too many blumelein (little flowers)", overlooking the fact that, if fault there be, the poets should be held responsible, not the composer who gave access to the singing voice for the poets' benefit.

Mendelssohn dedicated songs to various people, notably Fanny and Rebecka, but also to the Miss Horsleys and to Cécile's sister, Julie Schunck (née Jeanrenaud). This latter album, Op. 34, includes what must be Mendelssohn's best-known lied, 'On Wings of Song', with words by Heine. Strangely, there is no record of his writing any songs for his wife Cécile, but this does not mean that Felix did not do so. Cécile asked that all correspondence should be burnt, and this may well have applied to music. It must also be remembered that many papers were destroyed during the war, and it may be that some stray manuscript could suddenly turn up, as has happened with various other composers of the past. On 12th June 1843, in a letter to Klingemann, Felix gave actual detail as to why he was dedicating his newly written *Songs to be Sung in the Open Air* to Jette Benecke: "I thought of her so often when composing them. The open air and the whole breath of spring and the garden, which I wish to put into the music, together with the vision of her children and herself on the lawn" at Camberwell Green. The dedication was also made "because I never wrote a second voice part without also thinking of how she complained that, with me, everything has to sound so superfine that the second parts are difficult to sing; that rankles". Mendelssohn thought a great deal about the capabilities needed for this style of part-song. "I mean to continue with this production of part-songs, as it seems the most natural music, when four people are rambling together in the woods, or in a boat, and have the melody already with them and within them. Though there is something poetic in a quartet for male voices, I consider the sound of male and female voices singing together to be even more poetical." He asked Klingemann to bring "a song or two" when next visiting Germany, suggesting topics – "some predictable; some absurd: in summer; in spring; on the water; on the grass; on a bridge; in the woods; in the garden; to the stalk; to a kind of providence; to the people of the cities of the plains; for a dance;

for a wedding; a souvenir of a romance. Any aspect of life deserves a song to represent it."

Mendelssohn's idea of composing part-songs came into being because he grew to realise that several individuals had to share the same feelings on whichever topic each was singing. Particularly does this apply to song settings relating to the landscape, especially that of his homeland. As can be expected, Klingemann's verses were often set to music, but the poems of Eichendorff became a favourite medium for Mendelssohn's songs. Strangely, though the poet had lived at a similar time to Schubert, Eichendorff appears not to feature in that composer's song settings. It was Mendelssohn who inspired later composers to use his poetry as musical settings, notably Brahms and Richard Strauss. H. E. Jacob wonders why songs concerning landscape were left to Mendelssohn to compose. After all (he gives an example), Gluck's father worked as a forester, so who more fitting, Jacob asks, to extol the idyllic qualities of the countryside? The answer can be discerned without much conjecture. For Gluck, the beautiful scenery may well have been marred by the foul weather so often encountered. Even in fine weather, the memory of icy winters and wet feet through drenching rain whilst gathering firewood or felling trees might have been recalled. Far pleasanter for Gluck would have been the reputation he made for composing operas, performed in the sophisticated European capitals and large cities. Mendelssohn, on the contrary, was a town dweller, who could choose when to visit the countryside for contemplation or to escape from the petty intrigues and jealousies he encountered in the repressive environment of his hated Berlin. He could drink in the beautiful sights and sounds of nature undisturbed in the equable climate of spring, summer and early autumn. His spirit was free – not caged – in this lovely environment.

Jacob goes so far as to say that Mendelssohn's songs were awarded the status of folk music, especially in the United States. This did not apply solely to German immigrants, he continues; Stephen Foster, by no means a mediocre songwriter himself, called Mendelssohn's setting of Eichendorff's *A Hunting Song* 'the dark green tune', singing it with his friends. When, in 1871, Leopold Damrosch founded the New York Men's Chorus, Mendelssohn's settings of landscape poetry became the choir's staple diet and the composer became known as their spiritual godfather. What a pity, in view of his wealth of songs, Mendelssohn had such trouble in writing an opera. Precisely how troublesome he found the task – however painstakingly he attempted it – is described in the next chapter.

Chapter 17

Quest for an Opera

Much space is employed in Mendelssohn biographies in criticising his inability to compose an opera worth its name, but only half the story emerges in chronicling this aspect of his musical life. Once he had come to terms with the fact that he had sired a genius, Abraham Mendelssohn did encourage his son to compose an opera to resemble, if not overshadow, his own favourite composer, Gluck. Eduard Devrient offered librettos on which Felix could work, whereby glory could be given to his own fine acting and rich baritone voice, when performing such masterpieces. But it was only towards the end of Mendelssohn's life that a suitable libretto would appear, that of Emmanuel Geibel's *Die Lorelei*, for which, having completed the work after Mendelssohn's death, Max Bruch would be given full credit.

Had Felix had the co-operation of, say, Lorenzo da Ponte or Arrigo Boito, who, respectively, assisted Mozart and Verdi so ably, or had he considered, like Wagner, writing his own librettos, matters might well have been different; but, despite his genuine endeavour to fulfil his duty to Abraham, and Devrient, Felix never achieved the success he craved. Yet it must be emphasised that neither Brahms, Chopin, Liszt nor other composers of equal merit were responsible for any opera; that Beethoven experienced considerable strain when composing *Fidelio*; and that it is only in recent years that Schubert's and Schumann's operas have been reassessed. Yet, from boyhood, Mendelssohn showed interest in opera, as is demonstrated by a letter to Georg Polchau, a friend of his mother's family, who owned a comprehensive musical library. Having sought permission, he borrowed a history of Italian opera that Forkel, better known for the first biography of J. S. Bach, had translated into German. "I assure you that the book will be returned by Friday – my honour and good name vouch for it," Felix wrote, even enclosing a receipt. "Your faithful Felix Mendelssohn will be deeply indebted were such a request granted."

After his three years away from Berlin the fact that his name was still mentioned in the musical journals spurred Felix to work harder than before to achieve operatic success: "If I cannot obtain a libretto that I like, I shall compose an opera for London," he wrote in anticipation of his 1832 visit to the English capital. "I know

I can get a commission there as soon as I choose." Likewise, during his honeymoon in 1837, he was equally keen to achieve this goal: "I have not yet heard from Hölty regarding the proposed libretto, so I shall probably compose a second oratorio. I would, though, prefer a thoroughgoing man as my librettist if I do write an opera, though whether he will appear I know not. Hitherto, I have never been able to discover him." Felix had written to Moscheles during the previous year of his wish to gain operatic credibility, "but I am afraid there is no prospect of this". Felix might well have thought to himself, but never dared to put his feelings onto paper or into the spoken word, that – now his father was dead – there was less necessity for dutiful obedience, allowing pressure to be removed from the composer.

Mendelssohn continued: "I am looking throughout Germany and elsewhere for someone to help me realise this and other musical plans, and I despair of finding him. It is absurd to think that, in all Germany, one should not be able to meet a man who knows the stage and [who] writes tolerable verses – and yet I, positively, believe there is none to be found. Altogether, this is a queer country. Much as I love it, I hate it in certain regards." In 1840 he expressed similar sentiments when writing to Ludwig Spohr. "Near or far, I can find no libretto. Those who have a genius for poetry abhor music or know nothing of the theatre. Others are acquainted with neither poetry nor music – only with boards, lights, wings and canvas. Thus, I never succeed in finding the librettist with whom I have so eagerly, yet so vainly, striven to work. I regret this more each day, but hope, at last, to meet the kind of man whose script I desire." The incessant hectoring from others cannot have helped Mendelssohn, but merely caused frustration.

Devrient continued to badger Felix on the matter, writing to him in Italy: "You are writing too much sacred music and are too greatly influenced by Bach." Such a comment demonstrates the epitome of hypocrisy, since it was none other than Devrient who exhorted Felix to revive the *St Matthew Passion* in 1829. Even in 1846, towards the end of Mendelssohn's life, Devrient continued his nagging. No wonder, Felix complained, that "people are worrying me" to put his ambition into effect. "All well and good if I could hit upon a suitable subject," he sighed. "An opera cannot be written to order if its creator is not in the right frame of mind." Had Abraham realised or known the fact, even his favourite Gluck had expressed the same feelings. If a libretto was not right in all respects, no composer, however great his talents for other genres, could be expected to write an opera. The fact that Mendelssohn excelled in works for piano; solo and duet; chamber music; works for full orchestra; the full spectrum of songs, ranging from those for solo voice to large choir; works for instruments other than the piano – none of these mattered. The blot on Mendelssohn's musical repertoire was his lack of an opera equivalent to anything else he had composed. Writing in 1901, Stephen Stratton accuses him of being autocratic and showing "impatience of restraint at rejecting so many librettos". Philip Radcliffe finds fault with his "moralising, essentially Teutonic, attitude, which, had it persisted, would never have attained the greatness of Mozart or Verdi" in opera writing. Yet who knows what Mendelssohn might have written had he lived longer? Had he been allowed to produce *Die Lorelei*, a whole cascade of operas might have followed.

One criticism did not ring true, however. According to Wagner, Mendelssohn became "disgruntled and frustrated" at his own lack of success, implying envy at that of others. If that was the case, why did he encourage Fanny when she planned to compose an opera on a libretto written by her husband? "The work must be pretty, airy and lovely throughout; very tender and beautiful." When Fanny Horsley wrote of her plan to compose what she called "an opera tragedy", Felix responded by telling her his fears that, if no orchestration was included, "I hope it will be either an opera or a tragedy but not, worse than either, a melodrama." When Marschner wrote an opera based on Devrient's libretto of the fairy tale *Hans Heiling*, Mendelssohn had nothing but praise for the work when, in 1833, it was premiered in Berlin. This is all the more to be admired, since Mendelssohn himself, having been offered the libretto, could do nothing with it. "Imagine," H. E. Jacob writes, "how Mozart or Wagner would have reacted in such a situation. They would never have forgiven themselves for letting a subject like this slip through their fingers and would have torn their rivals' work apart, since opera was their whole life." Mendelssohn did not let Devrient's libretto "slip through his fingers" but deliberately abandoned it, which, in hindsight, seems a very shrewd decision. How often is *Hans Heiling* produced today, despite its enormous popularity at the outset? For that matter, how many have heard of Heinrich Marschner, apart from serious music scholars?

In his personal life, Mendelssohn associated with people whom he valued as genuine and whom he could trust. It is therefore not surprising that, when contemplating a libretto, he was equally discriminating. He could only work on a plot that was convincing and uncontrived, as so often happened with contemporary operas. He detested most of the Parisian productions that German composers tried to imitate. Of one, he wrote that, though it resembled Auber's operas, "it is better than those of Aloys Schmitt and other Germans". Thus, as far back as 1827, whilst staying at his uncle Joseph's estate at Horchheim, Felix wrote about a possible libretto by the poet Ludwig Robert, but, on this occasion, it was his father who had had misgivings. "There is no need for anxiety," his father was reassured. "Robert and I have parted better friends than on my arrival." Though Mendelssohn had not yet decided to continue with the project, "I will not stop looking everywhere for a libretto and, sooner or later, I am bound to find one". But he did express a note of depression – "People expect something special from me" – which, he implied, he felt unable to fulfil.

In 1840 Felix wrote to Ignaz Fürst regarding an opera with which it was unjust for the librettist to accuse Mendelssohn of "raising difficulties". "On the contrary," he explained, "it is simply that I do not want to bring into the world, figuratively speaking, a child infected with a germ of disease and that it is in order to obviate subsequent infections and maladies that may have already developed. If these are, as you suggest, born with him, it is best to forget about the whole child. If the maladies admit of a remedy at all, they might be cured before they attack the whole organism. It is not the wording that has dissuaded me from working with you," Felix tried to sugar the pill, "but the whole scenario of the plot, which does not conform with my own ideas for an opera. I have given up trying to please the public taste, as this is not possible. Thus, I must follow the dictates of my own conscience, now and always." Meanwhile, Devrient never tired of trying to lure Mendelssohn into accepting a libretto from his pen. Ideas included one based on Tasso's *Gerusalima Liberata*, which Felix found too serious for the medium of opera. Devrient thought opera the ideal way for Mendelssohn to display his undoubted musical genius, but was not his own self-interest mixed with this surface goodwill? What more natural, he might have assumed, than for his loyal friend to provide him with a leading role for this superlative actor and vocalist to gain glory?

This shows that principle superseded any requests from acquaintances as far as opera writing was concerned for Mendelssohn. Felix viewed with distaste another of Devrient's suggestions, *Knight and Peasant*, about a peasants' revolt: "Any topic relating to political issues will incite the masses and produce the worst result, were the militant element to attend a performance. For God's sake, let us not have them," he barked to Devrient, referring to similar librettos. "I dread what might happen should the seeds of sedition germinate" – which had threatened to burgeon into revolution in Germany. It was the moderate temperament of Britain that attracted Mendelssohn. Karl Marx wrote that, with all her advances in industry and her drastic agricultural depressions, through bad harvests, this land across the "North Sea was ripe for revolution – except for Methodism, with its emphasis on education and self-help". By such means, anyone who followed this discipline could eventually become themselves members of the establishment, the industrial and commercial class who were superseding the aristocracy. In Germany, on the contrary, revolution had been in the air for some time. The workpeople of Berlin had rioted as early as 1389 against labour conditions, followed by linen weavers in Silesia, when soldiers were ordered to quell the rebellion, in which many people were killed. "Germany, your weavers are weaving your winding-sheet. A triple curse woven in every pleat," Heinrich Heine wrote.

Yet Devrient never gave up baiting Mendelssohn with opera plots that might please this stubborn composer. Felix wrote to Rebecka about various further suggestions that, it was hoped, would result in a mighty production in which the actor-singer would shine: "Bluebeard; King Thrustbeard; The Musk-apple; The Lorelei; a play of my own; Kohlhaas; Andreas Hofer and an episode in the Peasants' War." Each of these librettos Mendelssohn had tried to connive into a suitable setting that he thought the public might enjoy, yet not one could win his entire sympathy, Devrient recalled. "He wanted something German, noble and

Chapter 17: Quest for an Opera

cheerful." Thus, when Geibel's version of *Die Lorelei* was chosen, the plot was "inadequate", according to Devrient – an example of professional pique?

As late as March 1847 Mendelssohn wrote to Konrad Lattner to thank him for some librettos, including *Sakentale* and *Jean Beck*. Though Felix had read them, with great interest, he admitted that "the variety of projects I have already started make it impossible for me to take on the completion of an opera". He also pointed out that his forthcoming (tenth and last) visit to London would span several months and he did not know when he would be able to work on Lattner's librettos. Neither did he know where he would be staying at any given time, where correspondence could be received. In such circumstances, Mendelssohn decided to return Lattner's manuscripts. As with *Die Lorelei*, had Mendelssohn lived, Lattner's librettos might have been turned into operas; but this was not to be.

There were some subjects that did arouse Mendelssohn's inspiration, though. From Lake Zug in Switzerland, where Gessler, villain of Schiller's drama *Wilhelm Tell*, had ruled, he wrote to his family having reread Schiller's play. "I would like to bring Schiller to life in order to let you know how highly I appreciate his work", and asked for his sisters' comments on the drama, "though I dare not approach any contemporary student of literature. These gentlemen are a vast deal too wise. If I do meet one of these youthful, modern poets, who look down on Schiller and only partly approve of him, so much the worse for him, for I must infallibly crush him to death." After this outpouring Felix wrote to Devrient from Lucerne that he did not consider his own work of importance, but that he had to apply himself to composing something similar to what Schiller had achieved: "The passion, fire and fervour of *William Tell* has so enchanted and fascinated me you may forget about singing, decorations and other such things and concentrate on humanity, nature and life, and you could write the best libretto of anyone now living." If Felix did not benefit from such a work, someone else certainly would do so. "An opera can only be musical and dramatic when a vivid feeling for life is diffused through all the characters." Yet the only opera based on Schiller's play is that of Rossini and, even then, only some of the music is heard from the ballet and the popular overture to *Wilhelm Tell*. Wilhelm Taubert was apprised of Mendelssohn's desire to find the right libretto for his discerning taste. "I promise myself that, if I can only use the talents of a poet with the right amount of fire and spirit, though the right fellow has not yet appeared, I do not expect to find a giant. Yet there is nothing I more strongly covet than to write a good opera."

In Paris, Felix received a request from his parents to approach a French librettist who was to write a piece for a forthcoming festival in Berlin, in order that their son would be able to compose an opera for the occasion. As was to be expected, in view of his dislike of the contemporary fashion, Felix declined this command. In France, he pointed out, their men of letters had commitments for years to come and that, in view of his parents' opinion that some French operas were immoral (e.g. Auber's *La Muette di Portici*), he would rather set his music to the work of a German librettist. He had read the poems of Karl Immermann, about which, according to Marek, Leah "raved". A fine libretto could be produced, he assured his parents; he said that he would communicate all the theatre arrangements and that he would work seriously on the project. In London on his second visit, therefore, he read a letter from Immermann regarding a libretto based on *The Tempest*, on which Felix proposed to work as soon as he returned to Berlin. The working relationship began well enough and Mendelssohn wrote a Tyrolean song and a French march for Immermann, which he would send to Fanny for her comments as he liked the latter very well. Despite Leah's attitude, Abraham had no confidence in Immermann, calling him "unworldly" and "knowing nothing of the public's taste".

Yet every whim of Leah's had to be obeyed, and the more accustomed she became to Immermann's involvement and co-operation with Felix the more her son was browbeaten to proceed with work on *The Tempest*. "The book had been promised for May," writes Schima Kaufman, "and Felix had every reason to expect that it would be the perfect opera about which he had dreamt. Immermann's quiet taste would prevent no improper scene; no improper phrases or words to seep through to the public. He would even take Shakespeare's work and purge it of any impurities." Felix would "free the score from antique harmonies". But, once in Düsseldorf, where Mendelssohn had to work constantly with Immermann, any friendship that might have flourished was reduced to ashes. Devrient, in his later recollections, stated that the quarrel between the two artists was personal, based on nothing but concern for theatrical matters. Mendelssohn "showed a hasty and snappish temper that one would hardly have suspected in him". It is possible that Devrient may only have heard Abraham's side of the story, taking his part without asking Felix for his side in the quarrel. Theatre matters were very much connected with the rift – rather like two cooks in one kitchen, or the 'backseat driver' syndrome – but this was not the whole state of affairs. Felix wrote to Ignaz Fürst that the sculptor Schadow had a violent quarrel with Immermann, "aggravated by religious and political grounds, with wranglings, misunderstandings and petulances", in which Felix had to act as mediator. Not only was Mendelssohn working under Immermann in Düsseldorf, but he was also Schadow's tenant. But Felix's arbitration proved futile, "which is a pity, and a misfortune," he wrote, "since everyone else in the community, particularly the artists who study with Schadow, are entirely devoid of arrogance and envy, living together in true friendship." With so much stress, how could Mendelssohn write the type of opera that his parents and Devrient expected? Yet, when Immermann's libretto proved unworkable, it was Felix who had to bear the brunt of his father's anger. "I have to write my sweet little letter to Immermann," Mendelssohn confided to Klingemann, "saying that I am unable to set his libretto to music. Where shall I find inspiration for music and melody in that form of writing?"

But Felix's idea for writing an opera on *The Tempest* did not wane. On 10th December 1841 he wrote to Karl Grieffer of Leipzig, asking to meet this librettist to discuss further details. In 1846, with the French dramatist Eugène Scribe, Felix hoped to succeed in his conception of a *Tempest* opera. "It is impossible to believe that any kind of sympathy could ever have existed between composer and librettist," Felix had to conclude after yet another disillusionment. The reason for this negative remark might have been that Scribe had so often collaborated with Auber, whose operas Felix disliked to an almost irrational degree. The only result was an unsatisfactory correspondence between Mendelssohn and Benjamin Lumley, manager of Her Majesty's Theatre, London, where Scribe's libretto was to have been used when completed. Lumley – real name: Levy – was so convinced of scoring a hit with Mendelssohn's opera that he advertised it as a definite forthcoming attraction for his theatre. Unlike many operatic forays, Mendelssohn was able to choose the star who would play Miranda, the heroine of Shakespeare's original drama. Jenny Lind would play the role and, says Marek, "none other than this gentle girl" would suffice. But, despite this coup, Scribe's libretto did not please this martinet of musical taste. Why, it is cogent to ask, did Mendelssohn not take the plot from Shakespeare's translation by Schlegel, which proved so fortuitous with his *Midsummer Night's Dream* music?

In 1834 Felix had been sent the first act of a libretto by Klingemann "based", as Jacob writes, "on a bad play by Kotzebue". His enthusiasm is apparent by a drawing he made when acknowledging Klingemann's script. There was a triumphal arch with Klingemann's name written around it in capital letters, together with a laurel wreath, two crowns and a trumpet. "For once in my life," Felix wrote, "I shall have the opportunity to fulfil my ambition." He asked what type of overture would be required: "One of the fairy kind, or otherwise fantastic, and in what key?" Felix hoped that Klingemann and himself could "form a double alliance in these enterprises", but, alas, nothing came to fruition. Neither did his proposed visit take place in 1835, and the only glimmer of operatic success was his song 'Infelice', posthumously catalogued as Op. 94.

From childhood Felix had enjoyed the literature of ancient Greece and had always taken to heart the tuition given him by Heyse, Droysen, Böckh and Hegel among his instructors. It is inevitable, therefore, that Mendelssohn was led to exploring Homer for ideas for an opera. He and Droysen were planning to write a secular cantata similar to *The First Walpurgisnacht*, and, in October 1836, Droysen made some suggestions for the plot. However, either because of other musical commitments or Felix's preoccupation with his forthcoming marriage, nothing came of the project. But, on 17th October 1838, Felix took up the plan once more, suggesting episodes from Homer's *Odyssey* – "Norsicaa; the storm; falling asleep; conducting the heroes across the sea" – or the subject that had given Droysen the greatest difficulty, the ball game. "I imagine the music as having a Mozartian quality, but [it] will find its own level." On this occasion it was Droysen who released Mendelssohn from the commitment, suggesting that he compose a tone poem similar to his *Hebrides* Overture, with the possible title 'The Deep-voiced

Poseidon', but, again, nothing came of the plan. However enthusiastic Felix might have felt, Droysen was too involved with his professorship at the University of Kiel on the Baltic.

Though Ernst Wolff, quoting an earlier biography of Mendelssohn by Holten, inferred that Mendelssohn was too clever to write an opera suitable for contemporary trends, the bee still lingered in Felix's bonnet. Thus, when James Robinson Herald (pseudonym: Planché) presented him with a libretto, Mendelssohn considered the work far more seriously than hitherto. "I like the first two acts well enough," he wrote to Hiller in 1838; "the text is taken from English history of the Middle Ages, rather serious, with a siege and a famine. I am anxious to see the end of the libretto, which I expect next week. Even with this opera concerning the siege of Calais, the aid and inventiveness of a poet is wanting – and that is what I lack." During the following year the libretto that had pleased Mendelssohn originally did not turn out to be such a bright prospect after all. "The publishers are pressing me to undertake so laborious a work, which may, after all, prove vain," Mendelssohn wrote to Moscheles. "I am disposed to give up such a work as being utterly hopeless. Whether the opera be prolix, brief, detailed, sketchy or whether or not a ballet is included, are all irrelevant. Eight acts would not be enough if the opera were really good. One act would not be too few. As long as this would harmonise with the musical feeling, and general atmosphere of the work." Even before the text had been completed, Mendelssohn could tell from the general scenario that he could not continue to work on the opera. "I have thus placed the whole truth before you, and heaven grant that all these things may not deter you in writing an opera that you may entrust to me to compose, and that I may at least, through you, see a long-cherished wish fulfilled," Felix eventually wrote to Planché, after prolonged, but unsatisfactory, correspondence. "I must follow the dictates of my conscience, now and always," he added, despite the fact that this opera might have pleased public taste.

Stratton considers the librettist to have been badly served, in view of a contract having been signed, but, as the biographer gains his information from Planché's own reminiscences, only one side is given. In Mendelssohn's defence it must be remembered that the libretto for Weber's *Oberon* was written by Planché, of which only one song remains in the musical repertoire, apart from the deservedly popular overture. In 1840 Felix wrote to Fanny that, though her suggestion for an opera based on the Niebelungen legend sounded interesting, he asked her to remind him of the outline and the precise incident in the story that she considered most suitable for this medium. "I cannot recall the plot – certainly not your reference to 'sinking into the Rhine'. You will render me an invaluable service by responding to my request. Meanwhile, I shall reread the text before receiving your next letter." On 6th December Fanny thanked her brother for showing such zest towards Raupach's libretto, acknowledging that Felix's sketch was far more advanced than her own. "I find the conclusion more difficult to tackle, for who would finish an opera with so

Chapter 17: Quest for an Opera

much carnage? Yet, in view of the legend, what else is to be done?" Felix was asked to give progress reports on his work, and it is interesting to observe that even Wagner, in his autobiography *Mein Leben* (*My Life*), admitted to slow progress and hesitation owing to the complexity of the plot, and it was only by degrees that he completed his masterpiece. He considered the production of such an opera impossible in the contemporary German theatre, and it was only when his own opera house at Bayreuth was built that his ambition was achieved. In view of such an admission, Mendelssohn cannot be denigrated for shelving this project.

On 16th November 1844 Mendelssohn wrote to Professor Böttger of Brunswick on the subject of his libretto based on the tale of Genoveva. The heroine was "too passive", Felix concluded. He would prefer someone like Antigone, who triumphed over any disaster placed in her path. Having witnessed a performance of this opera in Berlin, Wagner took the same view. Indeed, though Schumann's *Genoveva* would be produced in 1850, the opera would not be presented until 1999. Therefore, rather than criticise Mendelssohn for refusing to work on this plot, he can only be praised for his shrewdness and discernment, as with his other rejected librettos. As he wrote to Rebecka: "four librettos were sent to me last week, each more ridiculous than the others. The only result is to make enemies for myself. I therefore write instrumental music and long for the unknown poet who perhaps lives close to me, or in Timbuctoo, (sic) who knows?" Why, whilst in London, could he not have researched works by – say – Tennyson or Browning, or turned to Sir Walter Scott for inspiration, or to his beloved Shakespeare?

There was a librettist in London, William Bartholomew, who was to write the text for *Elijah* and other sacred works for Mendelssohn. According to biographers, he is purported to have presented a secular libretto to the composer. Unfortunately, however, despite considerable research, no information can be found. Yet Mendelssohn did prove himself eminently capable of writing for the theatre. Whatever his shortcomings, King Friedrich Wilhelm IV must be commended for his insistence that Mendelssohn was to write several pieces for the German stage. On 21st December 1841 Mendelssohn wrote to Ferdinand David regarding *Antigone* by Sophocles, expressing pleasure that he had enjoyed reading the drama. Court officials were discussing a possible production of the cantata Mendelssohn was commanded to write. So fascinated had Felix become on studying the play and the "noble dignity" it portrayed that Tieck, who had become a municipal councillor, was asked "now or never" to write the libretto based on Sophocles's work. Fortunately, the German dramatist decided that "now" was the answer – "so I can compose to my heart's content," Felix wrote.

When rehearsals took place the chorus sang with such precision that "it was a delight to hear". But the officials at court considered the composer to be "very sly". He had written the cantata either to become a King's favourite or court fool. But the beauty and grandeur of the plot drove all else from Mendelssohn's mind, prompting him to have the work performed as soon as possible. "It is remarkable," he reflected, "how some art has remained unchanged throughout the centuries." But he did find difficulty in judging the merit of his composition in Berlin: "There are only shameless flatterers or equally shameless critics whom one meets, and there is nothing to be done for either. Both, from the very first, deprive one of all pleasure. Yet, after the performance, the learned will, no doubt, come forward to reveal to me how I should, and must, have composed, had I been a Berliner." Marek asserts that Mendelssohn derived so much pleasure from *Antigone* because it dealt with a sister who defied the law in order to pay proper tribute to a brother. This overlooks the fact that neither Fanny nor Rebecka experienced any suffering through love of Felix. More likely, it was Hegel who had influenced his pupil to love the character of Antigone, and her drama. "Of all the masterpieces of the classical and modern world, and I know nearly all of them, I consider *Antigone* to be the most magnificent and satisfying work of its kind," Hegel declared. He and Böckh had given simultaneous lectures whilst Mendelssohn was studying at Berlin University, so it is likely that Felix incorporated such propositions in his own lecture notes.

Just as Raphael had painted scenes from ancient Greece for his contemporary public, so, Mendelssohn reasoned, he too would write music for his audiences to understand. Böckh wondered how *Antigone* would have been performed at the time of Sophocles. Would music have been included? Would the various stresses of the metre have been sung or recited? At the home of Count Redern, director of the opera in Berlin, Tieck read his libretto. Devrient, who was to sing the part of Haemon the hero, Antigone's betrothed, disliked the author's "histrionics", calling them "superficial". The King, having read a German translation by Bonner, was delighted at this "new and brilliant discovery", Ambassador Bunsen reported. Tieck, therefore, decided to give readings of the play "as a forerunner to Christianity", which irritated Böckh. As for Mendelssohn's music, Tieck considered him lacking in equal merit to Haydn, whom he deemed "too noisy", and Beethoven was "beyond the pale". But Böckh defended Felix's music as "a legitimate evocation of the Attic poetic, possessing its metric and cultural origin". Far less pompously, Fanny wrote in her journal: "Felix refrained from composing music that one may have imagined to exist in ancient Greece. Rather, he constructed a bridge between the modern and the antique styles, as much as the latter was known. I found the staging quite beautiful – far nobler than an up-to-date production would be. The footlights came up from below and the curtain sank downwards, so that the actors' heads were seen first, rather than their feet. I think the modern style stupid and absurd."

According to H. E. Jacob and Tieck's biographer, Henry Lüdeke, Mendelssohn wrote to Tieck pointing out that, unlike, say, *Romeo and Juliet* or *Tristan and Isolde*, no love scene appeared in his version of *Antigone*, and that no dramatist worth his salt would have deliberately omitted such a vital aspect of drama. Even when Tieck's biography was written in 1917, the detailed correspondence between

Chapter 17: Quest for an Opera

Mendelssohn and Tieck no longer existed. Whether or not the lack of a love scene had any effect on Berlin audiences, *Antigone* was soon replaced by a further favourite of the King, Racine's *Athalie*. However, *Antigone*, French newspapers reported, became very popular among Paris audiences, each performance yielding greater applause than its predecessor. At Covent Garden, though, only 45 performances were given: "I hear great things of the production," Felix wrote to Fanny. "The chorus master's plaid trousers show below his coat. Whilst the Bacchus chorus takes place, there is a regular ballet: ballet girls and all, would you believe." A cartoon in the 18th January 1846 issue of *Punch* magazine showed a poster advertising an excursion by the Oddfellows of Birmingham to Worcester and Bristol, "returning next day with their leader, Mr. Woolley", below which a further poster read "conducted by Dr. Mendelssohn", evidently referring to his visit that year to the Birmingham Festival to conduct *Elijah*. "I laughed for three days together," Felix reported.

Of *Athalie*, for which Mendelssohn was asked to compose incidental music, Philip Radcliffe remarks, on the song 'Children of Barthe', "it comes particularly close to a chorus from *The Pirates of Penzance*." To anyone who is aware of the chronology of these pieces, the converse is true. The Gilbert and Sullivan operetta includes a chorus resembling Mendelssohn's 'Children of Barthe' in *Athalie*. In 1879, when *The Pirates of Penzance* was written, Mendelssohn had been dead for over 30 years. When he died in 1847 Sullivan was, like Frederick, the Pirate King, "just a little boy of five". But the only item now heard from *Athalie* is the War March of the Priests; thrilling when heard in its orchestral arrangement as originally written, but also stirring when arranged for brass or military band.

Oedipus at Colonus, also by Sophocles, was performed in 1845 for the King, who commissioned Mendelssohn to write incidental music, which was posthumously published as Op. 93. Fanny preferred the plays of this dramatist to those of Aeschylus, which, she said, gave her "the shivers". Felix was also commanded to compose music for performances of this latter dramatist's work. The trouble was that the *Oresteia* trilogy had to be condensed into one drama. This, Mendelssohn commented, would be difficult for any musician to accomplish, and that to set even one of the plays to music would prove difficult. The King took this perfectly rational remark as a personal slight and bitter words followed (see Chapter 23, 'The highest in the land'). It is interesting to note that, when Vaughan Williams wrote music for Aristophanes's drama *The Wasps* for a production at Cambridge University in 1909, it reflected the work of the contemporary period – the early 20th century.

Yet this chapter cannot end without discussing the singspiels (musical plays) that Mendelssohn wrote. Wilfrid Blunt states that it was as recently as 1960 that these pieces were discovered. On 2nd August 1820 Felix, a boy of 11, wrote to a family friend, the physician Johann Caspar, thanking him for "the lovely little opera, *Soldiers' Loves*", which he would do his best to complete. The scenario was already in Felix's head, and "I will summon all my muses to do honour to the words". He had chosen his soprano, tenor and bass, but Felix was aware, even at this early age, of the balance in a proper chorus and of the gap that would result if the contralto was not included: "Surely, Fanny could be catered for," he wrote to Caspar. Soon afterwards a further libretto was received from the physician, *The Two Schoolmasters*. One was named 'Kinderschreck' ('Child-frightener'), which may well have struck a personal chord with Felix, who, though highly mature for his age, was still a child. He may well have been in awe, if not actually afraid, of his various tutors, but especially his super-educator, his father. It must have been this singspiel about which he wrote from Weimar, whilst visiting Goethe: "I have not written one note of my opera since I was not inclined towards this. Laziness is a living thing." Later, however, he wrote to Fanny that he had worked "from 7 to 11" on the singspiel and had completed everything but the finale. The two operettas were performed, respectively, at Wittenberg in 1962 and Berlin in the same year, and were presented in Vienna two years later. In view of the fact that the scores are in the Bodleian Library, Oxford, it must be asked why, with a modern English translation, *Soldiers' Loves* and *The Two Schoolmasters* cannot be presented to a British public.

In 1822, Devrient recalled, he was asked to replace Carl Henning to sing the bass role in *Soldiers' Loves* and to help with rehearsals for Mendelssohn's next singspiel, *The Strolling Players*.

On 19th July Felix wrote to Zelter from Frankfurt on his way home from his family holiday in Switzerland: "I have only been able to work on my fourth opera a little." But, on 9th December of the following year, Felix was able to relate: "My opera is completed and my parents are so gracious as to let it be sung in our home, but I do hope you will be there to help with rehearsals." This singspiel was given two titles, *The Two Nephews* and *The Uncle from Boston*, and, according to Blunt, the piece was performed on Felix's 15th birthday, 3rd February 1824. On the 8th of that month Felix wrote to Caspar, whom he had evidently visited: "I was here, dearest doctor, in order to ask forgiveness for my hasty words. They were all the more inappropriate for having come on the occasion of yesterday's celebrations, which, after all, you organised (though you would have preferred not to), but please, let what is past be forgotten... I also hope that no one in the orchestra repeated your remarks." No record exists as to why the letter was written, but either a second performance was given on 7th February or Blunt is inaccurate in the first place. Neither is any further reference made to Caspar, which may, or may not, be significant.

Mendelssohn's next foray into the world of drama with music provides readers with a saga in itself. *Camacho's Wedding* concerns an incident in Miguel de Cervantes's *Don Quixote*. All the literary world of Berlin was talking about Ludwig Tieck's translation into German when Felix began this singspiel. H. E. Jacob suggests that, though it was Klingemann who first presented the libretto to his

Chapter 17: Quest for an Opera

friend, someone else may have been responsible. In fact, Felix wrote to Friedrich Voigts on 13th March 1824: "I will take pains to emulate your words. If my music cannot express all that anyone would feel at the first reading of your text, then it will not be for lack of good intentions... The more beautiful the first act, the stronger my wish to see the second." The Mendelssohns' tutor, Ludwig Heyse, would have introduced the children to Tieck's translation, so they would have known about *Camacho's Wedding* (or *The Wedding of Gamacho*, as it is sometimes written). A wealthy landowner tries to prevent a peasant from marrying a pretty girl to whom he himself is betrothed. Don Quixote (after whom the adjective 'quixotic' has come into our language) rushes in where any clear-thinking person, let alone angels, would fear to tread. He mistakes the bride, Quiteria, for his own Dulcinea, giving spice to the story through his own absurd behaviour.

Permission had been obtained from Count von Brühl, manager of the King's Theatre, Berlin, for a performance to be given for family and friends of the Mendelssohn parents. A small room was set aside, Marx sneered, "so as not to swamp the performance". As a rule, von Brühl pandered to public taste in his spectacular productions. In one such, *The Maid of Orleans* by Schiller, "the procession lasted a full half-hour, irrespective of its relevance to the drama itself". What a contrast this comparatively insignificant singspiel in two acts must have been.

Neither had von Brühl consulted Gasparo Spontini, director of the Berlin Opera, whom King Friedrich Wilhelm III had persuaded into his service after his achievements in Paris. Very few people liked this Neapolitan or his work. "Altogether, his reign was a period of false splendour," Devrient recalled, "ruinous to the spirit of German music, of which Spontini had no idea..." To Zelter he was "like a gold-king, flinging his gold at the people, breaking their heads with it". If not his lack of musical knowledge, Spontini's mannerisms gave cause for flagrant gossip; "his almost womanish vanity"; "his moss-green frock coat covered with decorations"; "his graceful attitude and the way he used his lorgnette". Percy Scholes, whose accuracy may be wholly trusted, sheds a different light upon this "man of the hour", as his contemporaries named him. Spontini was the first to provide pensions for his aged singers and, having returned to Naples in his old age, gave all his money to the poor.

Meanwhile, considerable delay ensued in producing *Camacho's Wedding*, prompting Abraham to ask Spontini what was happening about his son's singspiel, which was supposed to have been presented "soon". Spontini ordered Felix to visit him, which he did, accompanied by his father, who was "resplendant in full court dress, decorations included". He pointed to the synagogue, saying: "You have grander ideas than that cupola." He leafed desultorily through the pages of the score and, pointing out its shortcomings, Spontini concluded that it was "confusing in its far-fetchedness". This visit stung Abraham, not only for the criticism of his son's 37-page score but, even more, for the reminder of the family's Jewish origin.

According to Schima Kaufman, the solitary performance of *Camacho's Wedding* might not have taken place at all. The tenor, Blume, developed jaundice and was unwilling to take part. It was only an honorarium from Abraham that persuaded him to do so – this "worked like magic", according to Schima Kaufman, the only source of reference to give full details in her book, *Mendelssohn - A Second Elijah*.

The theologian Schleiermacher was in the audience, accompanied by Dorothea's old friend, Henrietta Herz, still attractive at 60 and supplementing her scanty income by teaching languages. Though the applause was "hearty" after the first act, it dwindled subsequently to such an extent that, when a loyal supporter called for Felix to take a bow, he was found to be missing. Kupferberg believes that Felix must have realised how badly his singspiel fitted the stage and that it was far better in manuscript. Devrient is purported to have taken father and son aside to express his foreboding for its lack of success since rehearsing it at the Mendelssohn home. Felix may have been equally disappointed at Voigts's libretto, which might well have shown up his musical talent in a bad light. His constant inhibition regarding future librettos may have stemmed from this ill-starred experience.

The failure of *Camacho's Wedding* preyed on Felix's mind as late as 1827: "Though forgotten by the public, someone will dig it up again and decide whether it will live or die. If it holds up, then the other theatres will want it. If it does not, then performances on other stages will not help any subsequent opera either." Had he realised that even the fashionable Spohr was experiencing similar trouble with Spontini regarding his own opera *Jessonda* at a similar period, Mendelssohn might have been reassured. The fact remains that, though Abraham had become acquainted with Spontini when in Paris, the debacle regarding *Camacho's Wedding* caused the Mendelssohns to break with the Berlin Opera altogether. The *Schnellpost* concluded that this singspiel was only a phase in his career, to be put aside. According to Radcliffe, this induced bitter resentment in the composer and must have added distaste to his feelings for Berlin.

Another critic considered *Camacho's Wedding* "half-baked" and said that it should not have left the Mendelssohn home. Yet a third, who had been entertained by the family, opined that the piece in no way enhanced the reputation of Councillor Mendelssohn-Bartholdy's son. Later, Felix is purported to have confided to Devrient that no praise from a newspaper gratified him as much as adverse criticism wounded him and that those who criticised his work did not know the whole truth – how the young musician was hectored into writing the singspiel, or that it would have been far better if someone who knew what the theatre required had written the libretto. Whether or not Devrient's reminiscences were his own opinions or Mendelssohn's, Felix wrote a set of verses expressing his feelings:

Chapter 17: Quest for an Opera

If the artist gravely writes,
To sleep it will beguile.
If the artist gaily writes,
It is a vulgar style.

If the artist briefly writes,
No one will care one jot.
If the artist writes at length,
How sad his hearers' lot.

Felix took heart and, in 1829, wrote *Son and Stranger* for his parents' silver wedding anniversary on 26th December. The part of Schultz was written for Hensel, who, tone-deaf, was given one note to sing throughout the play. "The look on everyone's faces made the audience guffaw with laughter as the note was whistled to him on every side", but Fanny's husband could still not manage to produce it. An even more bizarre anecdote is gleaned from Devrient's memoirs and gleefully regurgitated by Marek. Count Redern, who had replaced von Brühl, had summoned Devrient to sing at court, which would have caused him to miss the auspicious celebrations at Leipzigerstrasse 3. Some 'string-pulling' had to be achieved to allow this fine singer to forgo his court appointment. Meanwhile, Felix succumbed to a blackout. Devrient, whose imagination was fertile, to put it politely, recalled: "Mendelssohn fell into an incoherent state, becoming hysterical and babbling in English." A doctor was called and put Felix to bed, where he slept for 12 hours, appearing to remember nothing when waking the next day. To Marek, it seems these sudden "fainting spells" occurred whenever Felix was thwarted in any way: "He was extremely sensitive to criticism, rarely forgiving a harsh review, swallowing his hurt and retaining his poise to the outside world... Because he held himself in check, he fainted."

Marek colours Devrient's reminiscences with his own imagination: "Frightful scenes of brain disturbance were witnessed by the onlookers; paroxysms of anger resulted from Mendelssohn's distress." But the author's inconsistency reveals itself. If Felix held himself in check so ably, would he not have shown the same trait on this occasion, the celebration of his beloved parents' silver wedding? Would he not have bethought himself of the hard work he had put into this singspiel? Ernst Rudorff's mother, formerly Betty Pistor, recalled that the festivities began on the evening of Christmas Day, when 120 guests assembled at Leipzigerstrasse 3. On 4th January the next year the singspiel was performed at the Berlin Singakademie, which she attended and of which she would still speak with pleasure at taking part. On 13th January, Betty's birthday and Felix's name-day, Mendelssohn gave her a copy of the Hunting Song from the score: "It was written on fine, blue music paper in his own, particularly beautiful hand," Betty remembered. The first page bore a drawing by Hensel of a huntsman with his rifle. Chorley made an English translation, presumably so that it could be produced in this country. As with the other singspiels, there is no reason why, with a less clumsy form of words, *Son and Stranger* cannot be performed here. To conclude, Devrient wrote after Mendelssohn's death of his "Hamlet-like destiny" as far as his striving to compose an opera was concerned: "He wanted perfection far too much to adapt any libretto to his musical bent. When, at last, he did overcome this scruple, he sank with his fragment into the grave." This smacks of pique and self-enhancement, bearing in mind that Geibel's libretto *Die Lorelei* was preferred to his own. The constant rejection of Devrient's other librettos must have stung him equally. Mendelssohn even admitted that Marschner made a far better job than he could have done on *Hans Heiling*. Yet *Die Lorelei* did not go to the grave with Mendelssohn. Two items remain (an Ave Maria and Victuallers' Chorus, published posthumously as Op. 98). Bruch appropriated the manuscript subsequently. Scribe's libretto for *The Tempest*, a shortened version of Shakespeare's original drama, was used by Halévy in 1850 and performed at Her Majesty's Theatre. It may well be that Mendelssohn did try too hard to achieve what he (but, more especially, his father and Devrient) wanted. Evidently, this aspect of musical entertainment did not suit his personality, in view of having to collaborate with comparatively indifferent wordsmiths. In any case, what does this matter when one considers the many other successes he did achieve?

Chapter 18

Mendelssohn, the Renovator

Hector Berlioz complained that Mendelssohn was "a little too fond of the dead" yet, for someone who delighted in the operas of Gluck (a contemporary of Bach and Handel), such a statement is singularly lacking in perception. It was the romantics in particular who espoused the cause of earlier music. Schumann studied Bach's works continually and considered the music of his contemporaries "nearer to Bach than to Mozart". In 1830 he wrote of Bach's "bold, labyrinthine polyphony; the wonderous intertwining of tones". Ten years later he wrote: "This genius, who purified and invigorated me; the model of humanity, whose music I choose for my daily bread." But it was Mendelssohn, more than any composer of that period, who did most to make Bach's work more accessible to the general public. He had the rare gift to the musical world of sharing the treasures he had discovered, not as a pedant, but as a warm and admiring enthusiast. No one need be afraid of Bach's 'mathematical' notation, as some musicologists regard it; there is no need, for Mendelssohn let in the brilliant light and fresh air, so often overlooked when Bach's music is performed.

When Mendelssohn's mission began very few of Bach's works were known. Moscheles and Czerny had each played some of his keyboard music. A chamber group in Vienna had attempted his Brandenburg Concertos. Any organist worthy of the name had discovered some of the works for what Mozart called "the king of instruments". A Belgian choirmaster, Edgar Tinel, had exhorted the Catholic Church to study Bach in order to improve their singing. Even Goethe, indifferent as a rule to religion, had admitted to Zelter that "this Leipzig cantor is a phenomenon of God", acknowledging his "mystical qualities". Hegel, too, saw Bach's music as "emanating from a master whose grand, truly Protestant piety, yet learned genius, we have only lately come to value properly". J. N. Forkel wrote the first biography of Bach in 1802, followed by that of E. T. A. Hoffmann, which the romantics admired, and C. J. P. Spitta. Yet very little of Bach's music existed in print. A shining exception was *The Art of Fugue*, which Bach's son, Carl Philipp Emmanuel, had published in 1755, allowing 30 copies to be printed. Later in the century musicians, such as Leopold Mozart, saw great difficulties in bringing Bach's manuscripts to the public. Nothing but chaos and confusion would result, it was said, if Bach's handwritten scores were made accessible for wider circulation. Especially did this apply to his choral works, where the limited resources of most choirs would be inadequate to cope with them. Whilst Weber admitted that Bach's settings of Christ's Passion, as narrated by the four evangelists, were ripe for revival, he could think of no one capable of bringing such a project to fruition. A. B. Marx had tried to persuade the publisher Schlesinger to have Bach's manuscripts printed, suggesting that the 3,000 thalers the enterprise would cost was a sound investment compared with the prestige it would yield.

Mendelssohn can be said to have had direct links with J. S. Bach. All the aunts on his mother's side played the composer's keyboard music long before it had become universally popular. Felix's aunt, Sarah Levy, was an especially accomplished harpist and had been a pupil of Wilhelm Friedemann, Bach's eldest son, and a patron of the better-known C. P. E. Bach. If this were not enough, Zelter had studied with Johann Kirnberger, who had studied, in turn, with Bach himself. The Mendelssohn children could not have helped but be encouraged to "drink in Bach with their mother's milk", as a radio broadcaster put it. Zelter continued this pattern, inviting Felix, Fanny and Rebecka to his home on Fridays to practise "the bristly bits of Bach". It was in this environment that Felix became familiar with his instructor's library of manuscripts that he had collected.

Before describing the remarkable event that took place in 1829, when Mendelssohn brought the *Passion according to St Matthew* (hereinafter referred to as the *St Matthew Passion*) to the public, two myths must be laid to rest. Whilst Eduard Devrient's memoirs of 1869 are entertaining, care should be taken in accepting everything he wrote. The score that Felix employed had not been used by a cheese merchant to wrap a customer's purchase; neither was there any contumely between Zelter and Felix as to whether permission could be granted to borrow the manuscript from his precious library. Zelter was never involved, and neither would his manuscript have been contaminated by cheese stains but retained, like all his other treasures, in a pristine condition. Felix received a manuscript of the *St Matthew Passion* from his grandmother, Bella (or Babette) Salomon, for Christmas 1823. Having studied the work, during the years 1827 and 1828, 12 choristers were gathered to rehearse Bach's choral masterpiece at Leipzigerstrasse 3, despite Julius Schubring's contention that Bach was "too dull" for public taste. Among the singers was Thérèse Schlesinger and her husband Eduard Devrient, as may be guessed.

"Things went miserably at the start, because of the illegibility of notes and text," Devrient's wife wrote. "Yet the singers were so moved that we felt we had been transported into a new world of music." As an old lady, Betty Rudorff (née Pistor) recalled to her son how excited she had felt at this revival, in which, like everyone else, she played an active part. "Mendelssohn's magnificent and eloquent interpretation of the orchestral accompaniment at the piano created the indescribable impression that each individual instrument was speaking in the most expressive tones. From rehearsal to rehearsal the music seemed to become greater, more powerful and more gripping to the participants." Other incidents cannot have helped but inspire these amateurs in their quest. Fanny wrote that the Swiss publisher Nägeli's edition of the B minor Mass was "a triumph for the Berlin enthusiasts and Nägeli deserves well of his undertaking". In 1828 Felix met the music librarian Justus Thibaut in Heidelberg, "whose collection contains music of many nationalities and periods", but who was unfamiliar with Bach's works. On parting Thibaut "swore eternal friendship, based on the music of Luis de Victoria and Johann Sebastian Bach", to whom Felix had the privilege of introducing this otherwise erudite musician.

In October 1828 it occurred to Devrient that there would be great potential in a public performance of the *St Matthew Passion*, in which he, it went without saying, would play Christ, in order to demonstrate his fine acting and vocal aptitude. A private performance took place at the Mendelssohn home but, when he suggested that such a work could be presented at the Berlin Singakademie, doubts reared their negative heads from all directions. Leah, Abraham, Zelter and Marx expressed reservations on behalf of the committee, but it was Felix himself who was the most cautious on the subject. So little did he believe the project could be achieved that he threatened to play the score "on a rattle or a penny trumpet", Devrient recalled. When he suggested that Felix should conduct the Passion, his answer was: "The deuce I shall!" But Devrient played his trump card. He reminded Felix of his artistic duty "to bring to light this most important moment in German music". Since Felix had such a thorough knowledge of the work, he was the only person suited to wield the baton.

Devrient described the morning on which they set out to seek Zelter's approval. He called at Leipzigerstrasse 3 and exhorted Paul to wake his elder brother, which he did by placing his arms under Felix's shoulders. "Mendelssohn was dreaming about music," Devrient wrote. "Speaking in a Berlin accent, he was heard to say: 'Stop it! I always said so. It's sheer squawking.'" More likely, he was disturbed by the hue and cry around him in that state between sleep and wakefulness. Devrient continued: "I remember the large, white writing table in his little workroom, where his breakfast awaited him, his coffee keeping warm on the stove." He exhorted Felix to eat a good breakfast and not to interrupt what he had to say. "With excellent humour and a capital appetite, he went at it," Devrient remembered. Mendelssohn must be the first to be credited with producing what would today be called 'a corporate image'. He and Devrient each wore a white waistcoat, black trousers and cravat, and yellow chamois leather gloves – "very important", Fanny mocked this latter accessory, which Leah called "too extravagant". So much was this the case that Devrient is purported to have had to lend Felix the money to buy the gloves. Dressed alike, Mendelssohn realised, though Devrient sneered at their "Bach uniform", the team would present a far more credible appearance when calling on Zelter and the soloists to invite participation in the forthcoming production than if they were haphazardly clad.

The first soloist to be approached was the soprano Mme. Anna Milder-Hauptmann, who had played Leonore when Beethoven's *Fidelio* was premiered and of whom Haydn had once remarked that "she has a voice to shake a house". Carl Adam Bader, the operatic tenor, was asked to sing the evangelist, St Matthew, and, as a bass normally sings the part of Jesus of Nazareth, Devrient reserved that role for himself. On 7th March 1829 Mendelssohn invited Friedrich Schneider, Kapellmeister at Dessau, to the first performance of the Passion. Schneider had commented to Schubring about "the promising boy", but nursed resentment and annoyance at Felix's enthusiasm for Bach's music, as he was unacquainted with the Passion settings. This attitude rankled for years afterwards, so that Schneider could never bear to hear any of Bach's Passion music performed. Even the Mendelssohn home was anathema to this musician, who, when Felix visited Schubring at Dessau in 1830, would still not greet him. Yet an impartial observer can understand Schneider's hostility towards Mendelssohn and all he stood for. The first performance was to take place on 11th March, so, especially in pre-railway conditions, with bad roads and possible encounters with criminals en route, four days' notice does appear unreasonable for anyone – especially anyone so important – to travel between Dessau and Berlin. Perhaps someone else gave Felix a metaphorical dig in the ribs for the letter to be written. Nevertheless, despite Spontini doing all he could to prevent the performance from taking place, Mendelssohn triumphed on that auspicious day. As Betty Rudorff recalled to her son: "The amiability of this master of conducting did not fail to charm everyone. On no single occasion throughout rehearsals did he lose his patience. Nor did we, the executants, ever feel tired of our task."

Though Mendelssohn's romantic concept of the Passion has been belittled by musicologists, any changes he made were put into effect simply to cater for the limited resources with which he had to work. Neither would any audience, to his knowledge, have tolerated a four-hour performance, as stipulated by Bach. Felix's adaptation was so exemplary that not even Bach himself, it has been suggested, would have been able to detect, without studying the manuscript thoroughly, where alterations had been made. Fanny wrote in her journal that the audience sat so quietly that they might have been in church, but, at the end, such tremendous enthusiasm was witnessed that encores were requested. As Jacob states: "Never had a divine service been so much of a concert, nor ever a concert such a divine service." It was evident that a second performance was necessary to accommodate the many who had not been able to obtain tickets for the original; "The same crowds, only larger," Felix wrote to Klingemann.

Even the seats in the lobby and the small rehearsal room behind the orchestra were sold out as a result of the second performance, held on Bach's birthday, 21st March. The Berliners were still not satisfied, however; the *St Matthew Passion* had to

Chapter 18: Mendelssohn, the Renovator

be performed a third time, "by tumultuous request". This took place on Good Friday, 17th April, replacing the traditional *Death of Jesus* by Carl Graun, a contemporary of Bach. Despite the dignity and solemnity, a humorous incident took place. After the second performance Zelter, who appears to have claimed the credit for Mendelssohn's success, gave a supper at his home, at which Felix and Devrient sat at the head of the table. A gentleman who behaved in far more familiar a manner than Mme. Devrient liked sat next to her. He endeavoured to ply her with wine, which she refused, apart from toasting the artistes at the appropriate time. He held her laced sleeve in a relentless grip, "to protect it", she stated, "making free with many other gallantries towards her". So annoyed did she become that Felix was asked whom "this idiot" might be. Holding a handkerchief to his mouth, presumably to prevent his laughter being noticed, Mendelssohn replied that that "idiot" was the celebrated philosopher Hegel. This proves that philosophers are not always ensconced in ivory towers, but resort occasionally to human behaviour.

Praise arose from every side for these performances. Even Spontini, forgetting Mendelssohn's ill-fated singspiel *Camacho's Wedding*, had to acknowledge that "never have we heard so perfect a performance. If a few details were spoiled by the few, this was never the conductor's fault. His extraordinary achievement was accomplished through his devotion and unique talent." By the time of the third performance, which Zelter conducted, Felix had set off for his first visit to London, and, coincidentally, Bader, the tenor, was visiting the same location simultaneously. Stürmer, his replacement as the evangelist, excelled himself, especially as he claimed to dislike Bach's music. During the interval he expressed surprise at seeing traces of tears in his wife's eyes. "I have no shame about this," she responded, "since all the men around me cried also." Later, however, Schubring reported with gratification, "the music really did affect him." However, with Zelter in charge, Fanny, writing to her brother the next day, 18th April, found the need to express criticism of the performance. "Now forgetting to take up his baton, to which he is unaccustomed; now forgetting to give the chorus their proper cues; Milder-Hauptmann became mixed up in her most important solo; but, all in all, the public thought it was a great performance." For Marek, such a letter "can be taken for what it is – a glow of satisfaction on her brother's part; propaganda of love. If Felix was not there, it [Zelter's performance] would not be very good."

There was no need for Fanny to compare this third performance detrimentally with the previous two that Felix had conducted. As a professional who had been equally involved with the Passion revival from the outset, she naturally wished to expect everything to go well, so any shortcomings must have been disappointing in view of the family's respect for Zelter's usually high musical accomplishment.

Meanwhile, in London, Bader greeted Felix in the street with the cry, "Here you are. When are we to sing the Passion again?"

The profits that had accrued were donated to found 'industrial schools': institutions where girls from poor families could learn the useful craft of needlework. Whilst there was no thought of academic education, such a scheme was very forward for the time. Mendelssohn's work for Bach's revival did not end with his *St Matthew Passion*. Nevertheless, in narrating Mendelssohn's achievements, negative criticism has to be included if an impartial assessment is to be given. The musicologist Alfred Einstein derogates the romantic conception of "the greatest and holiest work...transplanted to the concert hall; shortened; mutilated; completely modernised", and is equally dismissive of Zelter's opinion of what Mendelssohn achieved. "He rendered it practical for the abilities of the singers," Zelter had written. Also, as there was no organ available at the Berlin Singakademie, Mendelssohn had to contrive its sound by using various combinations of instruments in the orchestra. But what matter whether Bach's work is performed in a sacred or secular edifice? The music of "the greatest and most profound of composers, if his music is performed with the proper spirit, supersedes any venue or audience or performers". Despite this over-romanticised conception of the *St Matthew Passion*, as critics see it, half the audience left during the first part of a performance at Königsberg in 1832; the people remaining spoke of it as "out of date rubbish". Marek jumps on this bandwagon, giving it as his opinion that the work would have been heard sooner or later, had there been no Mendelssohn; but is this the case? Marek then retracts his previous sentiments: "He turned the light on, shining it on a monument that stood half in the shadows. He destroyed the fear of approaching this super-lifelike creation. He stimulated the willingness to understand."

Apart from a few grumbles, however, overwhelming acclaim poured forth as a result of Mendelssohn's triumph. Performances of the *St Matthew Passion* took place in Breslau, Cassel, Dresden, Frankfurt and Stettin, irrespective of the ill-starred fiasco at Königsberg. Bach Societies were formed in Berlin and London. In 1875 Jenny Lind, with husband Otto Goldschmidt, a former pupil of Mendelssohn's Leipzig Conservatorium, formed the London Bach Choir. Mendelssohn's revival of the Passion remained the version on which the work was performed for almost 100 years; but this was just the beginning for the popularisation of Bach's music. In all, Mendelssohn edited 48 of his predecessor's manuscripts, and an edition was published simultaneously in Leipzig and London in 1845. His working copies are now accommodated at the Bodleian Library, Oxford. These show how painstaking Mendelssohn had been in ensuring meticulous accuracy when compared with Bach's originals. The most objective scholars have to admit that no alteration was made to the actual text to Bach's works, notably the *St Matthew Passion*. Adolf Marx had what Richard Middleton calls "an anonymous edition" printed, that comprised the settings of the St Matthew and the St John Passions, together with six Bach cantatas, but gives no explanation as to how Marx was able to claim credit if the edition was anonymous. Could Mendelssohn have had greater influence in the project than has been acknowledged?

Chapter 18: Mendelssohn, the Renovator

Later composers with disparate styles would all be drawn to Mendelssohn's work in reviving early music. Brahms, Gounod, Max Reger and even Wagner all benefited by the indelible impression printed on their art through Mendelssohn. Betty Pistor had considered the Bach revival to be "an historic artistic event of the first and foremost significance. Everyone, whether musician or member of the audience, experienced a purer, more profound or sacred artistic inspiration." Fanny concurred, saying that 1829 was likely to "form an epoch in the annals of music".

Though Mendelssohn's involvement with Bach's works has become a legend, it is less recognised how much he helped to popularise the work of other earlier composers. At Christmas 1828 Fanny wrote to Klingemann that her brother was preparing Handel's opera *Acis and Galatea* for a forthcoming performance at the Berlin Singakademie. Between that year and 1830 he composed additional accompaniments for the opera, at the same time working on Handel's 'Dettingen' Te Deum, having to compensate for the missing organ at that venue. However, he had no option but to advise the Handel Society of London, on a later visit, that the organ was the only instrument suitable for an English performance, whereas, in Germany, "wind instruments are added to fill the void"; but he did not regard these as convincing. An interesting letter was written to Zelter concerning these Handel scores. "Many alterations are still to be made," he wrote on 8th January 1829, "particularly with regard to the frequent and overtly long arias in the opera and translation into German of the original English text." For the Singakademie performance Felix omitted "the F major aria in 3/8 time, together with several long arias preceding it", as being "not very appealing". Before continuing with the 'Dettingen' Te Deum, Felix would have had to obtain the English text. "I will then get started on the work right away."

Whilst in Italy, Felix set to work to revive Handel's oratorio *Solomon*, for which the Italian musician Santini gave him the manuscript. He begged his sisters to say nothing of a possible performance, "for Herr Topp, or some other little person, will come along and give the thing a coiffure with flutes, and spoil the first noisy stage effect". In 1832 Felix asked Klingemann for a copy of the English text, so that the oratorio could be performed at the Berlin Singakademie during that winter. Though the text arrived, Rungenhagen rehearsed the German translation and felt the time to be too short to alter his schedule. "My whole plan is turned to water," Felix was obliged to confide in Klingemann. Nevertheless, Rungenhagen had to admit that the German text showed weaknesses when translated, so Mendelssohn lent him one that Klingemann had made.

Biographers have stated that Felix never sought help when revising early music – or, for that matter, any other project. This is disproved by a letter in which he asked Rebecka to check a copy of his translation into German of Handel's *Alexander's Feast*. She was asked to let him know of "any improvements you can suggest to rhymes that are rugged or deficient", but was also told that the English idiom and meaning should not be sacrificed. He even admitted to taking notice of his father's counsel in this regard: "If I cannot rectify old faults, I can at least refrain from committing new ones," he replied. It is clear that Fanny and Rebecka took an equally active and intelligent interest in their brother's work. Fanny told Klingemann that she had attended a performance of Handel's *Israel In Egypt* at the Berlin Singakademie. "Only those in the know," she continued, "would realise how sadly this once reputable institution is deteriorating under faithful old Rungenhagen's direction. Fortunately, the public, their faces hard as flint, cannot discern the differences between present-day performances and those directed by Felix in 1829."

In 1836 Mendelssohn asked if Fanny knew the Coronation Anthem *Zadok the Priest*, performed at every coronation in London since 1727. "The beginning is one of the finest that not only Handel, but anyone, ever composed." Sadly, at the performance in Frankfurt of which he wrote, "the performers could not master it, but they are far too busy to grieve much over that". It is evident that the choir's attempts at this fine music were decidedly mediocre, for he continued: "The remainder, once the introduction ends and the choir begin to sing, is very dry and commonplace." What a pity he was never able to attend the ceremonies in Westminster Abbey that would allow his opinion to be altered.

In 1837 Felix suggested that Fanny and her choir should rehearse Handel's *Theodora*. "The work is not adaptable for a large ensemble, but has some spirited choruses and arias... Some parts, such as the final chorus, are as fine as anything you have ever heard by Handel." However, the German translation was "perfectly absurd" to Felix, so that he suggested that a new translation be made. In 1844 Fanny witnessed a further performance of *Israel in Egypt*, this time at Berlin Cathedral with Felix directing. Despite this, she had viewed the actual production with "apprehension, so far from perfection" were the musicians. Indeed, had seats not been reserved for the Mendelssohn family – "and other aristocracy", as Fanny mocked – she might not have been present. But the building was "crowded to the doors" and she must have been impressed with the "splendid" organ accompaniment that Felix had composed. "I never wish to hear an orchestral accompaniment without this addition," she declared. As an accomplished singer herself, she detailed the nuances of the various voices, concluding with the statement that "though a gross mistake was made during the first recitative, all went beautifully otherwise".

A further task for Felix was to correct the edition of Handel's works compiled by Samuel Arnold in the 18th century. This 36-volume edition was presented to Mendelssohn by the festival committee at Cologne in 1834. It was "bound in green leather in the usual, distinguished English fashion", as he wrote to Fanny, "with the title and contents in gold letters on each volume spine". When Chopin visited him in Leipzig these volumes proved "an almost childlike delight" to Mendelssohn's guest. Upon scanning these manuscripts at random, Felix discovered "a great aria from Samson, quite unknown to me, which yields in beauty to none of Handel's

Chapter 18: Mendelssohn, the Renovator

other works". He was "enchanted and charmed" by the gift and looked forward with pleasure to what the set of volumes would provide. Felix might not have been so enthusiastic, had he known the amount of time he would have to spend in correcting the "many errors" contained in these volumes. A further revocation of the myth that Mendelssohn never sought assistance from anyone can be demonstrated by his asking Sterndale Bennett to help him with editing the series, as a result of Breitkopf & Härtel's wish to republish Arnold's compilation. Felix suggested that Bennett seek advice from Handel scholars in London and research his manuscripts in the Royal Library. Bennett carried out his duties painstakingly and wrote to Mendelssohn on 17th October 1839, stating that more questions needed to be answered regarding the edition. As late as 10th March 1845 Bennett was asked to check the score of *Israel in Egypt* and to seek further help elsewhere if necessary. "I feel keenly the onus and responsibility that you have taken upon yourself and acknowledge with deep gratitude your assistance on the project." In the previous year, during Mendelssohn's eighth visit to London, the Handel Society requested him to edit that oratorio, thus allowing "the untouched Handel" to be made available at last. On 8th December Mendelssohn asked Sir George MacFarren, secretary of the society's council, to arrange for the King of Saxony to receive some Handel scores, in order that the monarch's interest might be fostered in the work of this composer, who was born in Halle, Saxony. The King might then become a subscriber to the Handel Society. Apart from writing a suitable organ accompaniment and a piano equivalent were no organ available, Felix had to deal with matters of far greater triviality regarding the society's council. He was, for instance, dragooned into arbitrating on the vexed question of the correct gender of the oboe. In a minute of 30th June 1845 it was mooted that 'oboe' had been "falsely declined". "In future," it continued, "all manuscripts should be printed correctly, indicating that 'oboe' is masculine and that singular and plural are the same." One of the council members was Sir Henry Bishop, the composer of such songs as 'Home, Sweet Home', 'My Pretty Jane' and 'The Mistletoe Bough'.

Meanwhile, the King of Saxony had agreed to become a society member, the subscription money to be administered by Ambassador Bunsen via Klingemann, his employee in London. "The proofs of the Handel manuscripts should be sent to Frankfurt, where I shall be staying, but the many, quite ridiculous errors, due to carelessness on the engraver's part, must be corrected and great care must be taken in this task. I cannot put my name to anything unworthy of Handel." Were Felix to become a member, his subscription should be deducted from his fee for the work he had already undertaken, the fee to be sent from the publishers, Messrs. Buxton, to his brother Paul's bank (in other words, the Mendelssohn Bank). However, Felix wrote to MacFarren as an individual rather than as secretary of the society that he had no room for any further manuscripts. (Though this august institution was founded in 1843, it was to lapse mid-century.)

It is more appropriate to discuss Mendelssohn's further interest in earlier music in the next chapter, 'Conductor and Director', and in Chapter 25, 'In Paradise', which considers Mendelssohn's musical activities in Leipzig. Meanwhile, to return to the chronology of Mendelssohn's interest in pre-romantic music, on 19th May 1830, en route to his last visit to Goethe, he wrote from Leipzig that an auction of Bach manuscripts was to take place. He asked Abraham to apprise Zelter and Rietz of the event, in case either wished to bid for any of the items for sale. Though some of the lots were "beyond doubt", Felix was not gullible enough to be taken in by everything. A score of the *St Luke Passion* was not by Bach but by Georg Philipp Telemann. Despite the auctioneer's vain efforts to convince him otherwise, Felix recognised "the beautiful and graceful hand" of the composer, contemporary with Bach. In any case, the score was merely a copy, with Bach's name written thereon, whereas, to Zelter, only an original would interest him. On arrival in Italy Felix discovered that Bunsen, the Prussian ambassador, owned a score of the *St Matthew Passion* and that the publisher Trautwein was planning to print Bach's *Passion according to St John*. When the St Matthew score was shown to the Papal Choir, Felix was told that such a work would be impossible to undertake by human voices, "at least in Rome".

As with Devrient's recollections, those of Mme. Polko should be treated with care if an accurate account of Mendelssohn's life is to be maintained. However, some of her anecdotes can be regarded as authentic. In 1832, for instance, Felix sent to Moscheles an 88-page book containing sketches by Beethoven for his *Missa Solemnis* of 1823. Like other such manuscripts, this may well have been supplied by Aloys Fuchs from Vienna, for family or friends. In answer to a request from Klingemann, Mendelssohn sent a copy of "Bach's Second Passion" for William Horsley's choir to perform as "something in the school way". He also sent a work by Lassus, along with "other insignificant music" that he had discovered in Cologne. But not everything of an earlier era appealed to Mendelssohn. Of Beethoven's cantata *Glorreiche Augenblick*, performed when three monarchs met at the Congress of Vienna in 1815, he wrote to Hiller in 1837: "This grand music is spoilt by the wording, whereby 'heller glauz' is made to rhyme with 'Kaiser Franz', followed by a great flourish of trumpets, yet Haslinger has written even more stupid verses. In praise of music, 'poesy' is made to rhyme with 'harmony' and the flourish of trumpets comes in even more stupidly."

Though Felix later became a revered authority on early works, in April 1838 he had to admit to Fuchs that the only item in Samuel Arnold's compilation of Handel works of which he had any knowledge was his *Dixit Dominus*. Neither could he recall a Mozart aria to which Fuchs had referred. The score of his 'Litanie' that Schleinitz had sent him "has two piano movements but no arias". On 6th January 1840 Felix pointed out to the Leipzig publisher Peters how many errors existed in a copy of Bach's Prelude and Fugue in G minor, at which they would be "amazed". "Poor Bach would have taken the printers to task quite severely" on that account. "The subject of the fugue is seen to have the eighth note once on page 7, twice on page 8 and even three times on page 9." Felix neither owned the original nor knew its whereabouts, "but I am not yet convinced that I have found all the mistakes" in the Peters copy. "I own a handwritten copy, but this is far more accurate. I can correct several errors by knowing how Bach composed. The extra note, for instance, gives the fugue altogether dreadful middle voices and harmonies underneath, especially in the last two systems. If, therefore, you can do anything by way of apology to this honourable fellow, Bach's disciple would be obliged." In December 1846 Mendelssohn wrote to Klingemann about editing Bach's B minor Mass and asked if his friend, like himself, recalled Zelter's Friday rehearsals. The manuscript that Felix received from Dresden "bears a dedication to the Elector of Saxony from Bach, 'in the most noble devotion'. I have weeded out numerous errors from the score...though I have often noticed them, they have never until now...been corrected. This mechanical, but interesting work is very welcome." But it was not all Bach and Handel for Mendelssohn. He wrote to the publishers Simrock asking if they knew of another manuscript of Mozart's *Magic Flute* Overture. If not, could the publisher's copy, with which he was familiar, be reproduced and proofs supplied. "The opera may [then] descend to posterity in its unvitiated form", as opposed to that which later included alterations not of Mozart's volition. Mendelssohn went on: "If young musicians were to study the latter, a false impression of Mozart's thoughts might be received. It is a positive duty to prevent this, since even the undeniably bad passages [in Mozart's and Schikaneder's work] deserve to be retained. As the opera has become a household work, the text should not be modernised but, if this should occur, a contemporary version should be placed alongside the original. In no case should it be entirely banished. Otherwise, fidelity to the deceased master is not properly observed, irrespective of any flaws in the libretto."

Simrock was asked to "say a few words" to Herr Hermann as to whether or not the plates of the original were to be issued. "I shall then be the first, but not the last, of your clients, to thank you for this assistance."

Mozart featured again in a letter to Moscheles in 1845. "I have received a copy of the 'Jupiter' Symphony (No. 41 in C major), together with a separate sheet of paper containing 11 bars. Though these close the adagio movement, they have been crossed out on the manuscript and added three bars later towards the end. I consider this a happy alteration and hope it will amuse you." He called the repetition "one of the most delightful passages in the whole symphony". Other letters featured in Mendelssohn's correspondence concerned more obscure music. He thanked Horsley for editing an unspecified manuscript on his behalf. "It is not a curiosity or old rubbish," he explained, "otherwise I should not have sent it." He wrote to Mme. Steffens stating that he could have heard her father Johann Reichardt's song "not only twice, but to continue throughout the whole evening. It was a true, genuine German song, such as no other nation has... One finds nothing better, perhaps greater...this must be the case for all time, and it must cause you such joy... Many a young musician on hearing Reichardt's music...will not do better than by following all the books on instruction and all the examples of the present day." Though the musical historian Dr. Burney respected the songs of this composer, those of Schubert, Schumann, Brahms, Mahler, Richard Strauss and, to a shamefully lesser extent, Mendelssohn have taken precedence over Reichardt's once popular lieder, and it can only be wondered if the panegyric to this composer's daughter was simply written from politeness and even nostalgia for the past, since Goethe and Zelter admired his music.

It was Reichardt who wrote that, had Bach "possessed the sublime sense of truth and the deep feeling of expression that Handel yielded, he would have been greater, but, as it is, Bach, being merely more industrious and cleverer than his contemporary, he might have superseded Handel in his composition". It is not known what Mendelssohn thought of this homily. Even as a boy, however, he loved Bach's music, but he had no time for screeds of words to express feelings for this venerable master. As a man of action, Felix preferred to prove his admiration by bringing Bach's works, and those of other earlier composers, into the light, either by his own achievements or his encouragement of other publishers to do so. He never allowed the early scores to be reproduced 'parrot-fashion', but studied them meticulously, not only to ensure accuracy but to highlight the subtle nuances in the music. In his greatest triumph, the resurrection of the *St Matthew Passion*, he observed how "the sea of suffering" was represented by violins imitating waves; how, in the scene where the crown of thorns was placed on Jesus's head, the notes demonstrated the thorns in their sharp, pointed staccato; he observed the "jabbing, lashing beats" when Jesus was scourged.

George Sampson, visiting Mendelssohn in 1840, was reminded of the great event. "One man, greater even than Bach, was worthy to suffer the supreme tragedy of all," Mendelssohn murmured, as if to himself, when the subject was discussed. When the host played a piano version of the Passion, Sampson wrote: "Though at first tentative, the chords grew gradually into the most strangely moving music I have ever heard. Its complex, swelling phrases gradually drew together and rose up in one great major chord. No one spoke. I felt as if some mighty spirit had been evoked and that its unseen presence overwhelmed us." It is evident that, rather than gloating of his remarkable achievement, as some musicians would have done, Mendelssohn had, through all the years that had intervened between 1829 and Sampson's visit, remained awe-stricken. "On departing," Sampson recalled, "he confided, too overcome with emotion to continue, as to how he wished posterity to remember him, 'not as a master, but as a servant, for, in my way, I have tried...to serve the great men before me – Mozart, Haydn, Beethoven, Schubert – but Bach most of all. Even if every note of my writing should perish, perhaps future generations will think kindly of me, remembering that it was I, a Jew by birth, who gave back to Christianity that imperishable setting of the tragedy and glory.'"

Chapter 19

Conductor and Director

Although Ludwig Spohr claimed in his autobiography to have been the first to conduct with a baton at a Philharmonic Society concert in 1820, this appears not to be the case. Musicologists of the 1970s discovered that, as early as 1798, Haydn conducted a performance of his oratorio *The Creation* in this manner, whilst, in 1810, Daniel Tork "sawed the air so energetically that he tended to strike the chandelier above his head [with his baton], bringing down a rain of glass" at a concert in Halle. Barry Sterndale Bennett, a descendant of the composer, William Sterndale Bennett, owns a baton originally wielded by Weber. But it was Mendelssohn who really popularised this mode of conducting, though Berlioz adapted to employing the baton with equal dexterity and skill. Originally a roll of music paper was used, or a violin bow, to keep order but, as more than one conductor was often in charge of an ensemble, chaos resulted until the baton came into prominence. It was Mendelssohn who insisted that only one conductor held sway. Hermann Levy points out that, in order to conduct to an exemplary standard, a musician should learn from youth to apply himself to this accomplishment. Mendelssohn was unusually fortunate in this regard, having plenty of opportunity to learn the art of conducting at the Leipzigerstrasse 3 concerts. Even though, at first, he was obliged to stand on a low stool so that his orchestra could see him, his savoir faire and flawless technique never let him down. As an adult, since it was unthinkable to stand with his back to the audience, Mendelssohn stood at right angles to the orchestra, turning his head as required, "his eyes flashing the cues to each group of instruments". His memory was so remarkable that he did not need a score for reference – though, for the sake of etiquette, one was always provided.

Julius Benedict wrote that, when Mendelssohn's "magnetic figure" appeared on the podium, "it was as if electric fluid was loosed". No one, it seems, knew better than Mendelssohn what was required from an orchestra, or how to achieve it, even if sarcasm was employed towards his musicians. Once, for instance, at a rehearsal of Beethoven's 8th Symphony, progress was not as good as he would have liked in the allegretto movement. Smiling he admonished his orchestra that, though, to a man, each could play and compose a scherzo, he would like to hear what Beethoven had written, as that "had some merit". Still not satisfied, he asked for a repetition of a passage, but "no" was the response. The musicians would only be satisfied if the movement was played from the beginning, which was performed "with the utmost delicacy and finish", Benedict reported. Felix congratulated his orchestra: "What would I have given had Beethoven heard his own work, so well understood and so magnificently performed."

Joseph Joachim wrote of Mendelssohn's "indescribably electrifying influence" over his orchestra. "He communicated his spirit and his wishes...by gestures and signs that were scarcely perceptible, but eloquent. Neither was he ever guilty of showiness. Whereas some conductors threatened with their sceptres to thrash the score, the orchestra and even the audience," Felix never indulged in such antics. His authority ruled by deeds, not words. As Schumann recorded: "Mendelssohn never allowed anyone to forget who was in charge. Schumann's wife Clara wrote of Mendelssohn's gestures as "sharp, decisive, but barely visible...a glance at the leader; a slight look, this way or that, sufficed. When pleased with a performance from his orchestra, he let them know it by nodding his head and pushing out his lower lip."

Yet Mendelssohn was not a saint. Sometimes his behaviour as a conductor was something less than unblemished. On one occasion, when Spontini was absent and Felix was asked to replace him, the orchestra "tested" him by "playing up", as children do when someone other than their regular parent is looking after them. Mendelssohn stood the nonsense for one rehearsal, then fined them. "Now," he wrote to his family, "they regard me as another Spontini and, instead of being

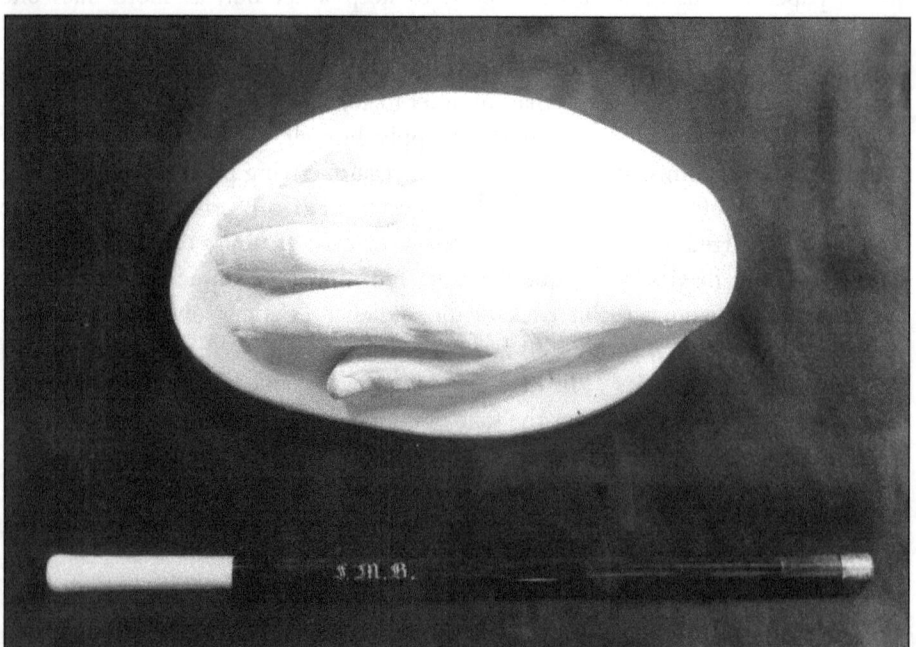

Figure 6. Photograph of cast of Mendelssohn's hand and baton

naughty, they are obedient." At Düsseldorf he became so angry when rehearsing the incidental music to Beethoven's *Egmont* that he tore the manuscript in two, and it was only subsequently that he expressed anguished regret to his family. When, at a rehearsal of his own *Hymn of Praise*, a trombonist named Queisser introduced an ornament at the beginning of his second bar, Felix thanked him politely but then rebuked him for not following the precise scoring. Wagner accused him of "racing through the piece" in his *Essay On Conducting*, with reference to Beethoven's Eighth Symphony. Kupferberg calls the essay "an anti-Semitic tract", unfit to be taken seriously. Felix was meticulous in observing a composer's score. Like Toscanini subsequently, Mendelssohn carried out a composer's instructions; otherwise, what was the point of reading and studying a manuscript in the first place?

To Mendelssohn, conducting was not simply a matter of beating time, but included holding the musicians' attention and correcting any bad habits into which they might have lapsed, or about which they may not have known. His style has been summarised as including "clarity, avoidance of excessive sentimentality or exaggerated showiness", his favourite expression being "that is not written". His creed was to reveal a real sense of colour in the music, so that his orchestra could "see" what was required. To demonstrate this, he played over a piece on the piano before tackling the orchestral work. Wagner's assertion that Mendelssohn would take a work too quickly has become a myth, perpetuated ad nauseam by biographers and repeated, parrot-fashion, by programme compilers and broadcasters. But how true is this assertion? Julius Schubring, when discussing a performance at the Mendelssohn home of Haydn's Symphony No. 82, 'The Bear', recalled how "a new light was shed for me" on the slowness of the final movement. "Hitherto, I had always heard the final movement without much interest, but, on this occasion, it was a most pleasing piece of composition. Good old Papa Haydn must not be hurried." At other performances, "the orchestra kept continuing to hurry but, with an iron will and beating the time most forcibly with his stick, he held back until even the faithful Eduard Rietz, the leader, began to grumble."

It was, according to Schubring, only after Felix's triumph when reviving Bach's *St Matthew Passion* in 1829 that he regularly wielded a baton to conduct. Previously "he had stated his opinion from the piano or the tenor's desk", reminding Devrient of "a little field-marshal leading his troops". "The baton gave him a more independent bearing," Schubring continued. This prosaic theologian also gave Weber credit for the inspiration he gave Mendelssohn, having attended rehearsals of the opera *Euryanthe* in Berlin. "He spoke with astonishment as to what he [Weber] could do with a strange orchestra." Yet, with such musical gifts, his own imagination must have played a greater part. As far as Jacob is concerned, Mendelssohn did "even more than Mozart to explore the potential for new instrumentation, though adhering to tenets from the past". At 21 Felix wrote: "No one can forbid me to enjoy and develop all that the great masters have left behind them, for there is no sense in beginning at the beginning again, but it must be a development to the best of one's ability, not a lifeless repetition of what has already been." Three years later his thinking had not altered: "Men must come...who will continue along the [same] road. They will lead others forward, or else back, though it really should be called forward, to what is old and right." There was, in fact, nothing new to Mendelssohn's mind; only variations of, and differences between, old and new styles.

In 1830 Mendelssohn was offered the new position of professor of music at Berlin University, which he declined. According to Radcliffe, Felix considered himself "too highly strung and volatile" to teach. More likely, the young man, still only 21, felt it expedient to decline the appointment on account of the hostility he knew he would receive from the Berlin establishment in view of his lack of experience for undertaking such an onerous task. He might also have been conscious of his Jewish ancestry and the prejudice that would ensue. Instead, he made what is erroneously known as 'the Grand Tour', returning to Berlin in 1832. Despite the puddings eaten at the home of Heinrich Bärmann, virtuoso clarinettist and friend of Weber, Mendelssohn disliked "all the insincerity that is such a social element in south Germany" when he stayed in Munich. He dreaded the fact that a concert of his own works was arranged and must have been relieved that, during the Oktoberfest, it was "out of the question" to hire an orchestra and concert hall. But this proved no impediment for, on 18th October, he reported that the concert proceeded "far more successfully than I expected". The piano extemporisations he was obliged to perform, and the speech he was expected to make, must have proved popular for, as Felix wrote to his family, "none of the 80 musicians, nor the extra cor anglais players and trumpeters I had engaged from the military authorities, asked for one kreutzer. Thus, the receipts for the benefit of the poor will be very large."

In Paris, too, conducting was included in Felix's itinerary, chiefly at the conservatoire under Habeneck: "A mere catalogue of all I have done and all I still have to do will suffice for today," yet he wrote minute details filling reams of paper to his family. On 17th February 1832 he attended a church where Beethoven's life was commemorated but where, incongruously, his own String Octet was performed: "This is the strangest thing the world ever yet heard" was his verdict. "Yet I could not refuse and, to some degree, I enjoyed the thought of being present as the Low Mass was read during the scherzo. I can scarcely imagine anything more absurd than a priest at the altar and my scherzo going on." An article in *Le Figaro* summarised Paris as "the grave of all reputations, for no one there admires anything". Paganini, Felix wrote, "yawned at me. He does not seek to please much" when meeting the violinist. Yet, having gained so much experience in his youth, Mendelssohn was able to speak with authority as to what was required from a conductor. Of what was then known as Beethoven's 'new' (Second) Symphony, written in 1803, the tempo was "altogether too fast". Of the manner in which

Habeneck directed the performance, he wrote: "[He] made himself quite miserable, stamping his feet and hitting the stand with his bow so hard that it wobbled, moving his whole body – none of these antics being of any use. The orchestra simply would not slow down, rushing so much that, eventually, they were almost tumbling over one another. Why," he growled in exasperation, "can the beat not be given via the baton? I have heard nothing so extraordinary and wonder if good music is hiding in Paris... The situation becomes worse from day to day."

According to Schima Kaufman, seeing an empty place where a tympanist should have sat, Mendelssohn "sprang upon the stage and beat a roll of drums as fine as any tabor of the old guard". At a subsequent concert, when Kalkbrenner was to be present, "he did everything in his power to get me out of the way". Indeed, though friendly to his face, the musical world of Paris "was ready to tear him to pieces, the moment his back was turned", Kaufman states. Indeed, the only place Felix was genuinely loved and respected at that time, and throughout his life, was London, where he paid his second visit in 1832. He confided to Klingemann from Berlin that he found difficulty in getting back into the spirit of what passed for music in that city. He attended an entertainment that he described as "tame and lame until Bernhard Klein began to tell his bad jokes". At a meeting of the Academy of Arts, Felix witnessed "a genuine blossoming of Philistines. The treasurer announced that, since the proceeds had not amounted to much, he deemed it inappropriate to submit a statement of expenses." Neither was there "one fresh face or one pretty girl" at a popular festival Felix attended. "Out of sheer exasperation, I bought a ticket for the Elysium, costing eight groschen. There were fireworks, illuminations, rope dancers, but not one decent person to look at. My spirit of adventure became overwrought and I vowed never to set eyes on festivals, the academy, or the Elysium again in this city."

So why was Mendelssohn so depressed at returning home? The answer was simple. Abraham had ordered him to curtail his second, highly successful, visit to London, in order to undertake what was felt to be a really exciting, ambitious step on the musical ladder – the directorship of the Berlin Singakademie. It had been founded in 1791 by Christian Fasch, who directed the institution until his death in 1800, when Zelter replaced him. During his reign, 19 members of the Mendelssohn family became involved in the Singakademie. It was not surprising, therefore, when Zelter died of pneumonia on 13th May 1832, that Felix was destined, as far as his parents were concerned, to fill the vacant post of director. Had not Zelter himself expressed the wish that this should be so? Had not he asked Felix to deputise for him during his last illness? However, although he had become a good friend rather than an instructor to whom Felix confided his musical ideas and sought advice regarding composition, Zelter had died whilst Mendelssohn was in London, and Carl Rungenhagen had taken the reins of power. Thus Abraham had exhorted Felix to return to Berlin. On 18th May, before he knew of Zelter's death, Felix asked if this was necessary, and not a figment of his father's imagination. "I will offer him [Zelter] every service within my power, of every kind, and try to relieve him of his labours for as long a period as is required... It is my duty to do so." Felix pointed out that he could not undertake this role without consulting Zelter, or anyone else who had replaced him, since it would be unfair to the future director otherwise. Although he would be delighted to fulfil this honour, Felix would be even more pleased were Zelter to recover and remain in his post. When he did learn of Zelter's death, Felix wrote: "These times are hard... The news is always present in its sad reality."

Klingemann recalled how "floods of letters arrived" to drag Mendelssohn away from London and back to Berlin. "The whole Mendelssohn clan thought Felix was the heir apparent, and that was that." However, to the establishment, Rungenhagen was a 'safe' choice for director and Felix knew that whatever experiments he may have wished to make in bringing the musicians to his own high standard would not be popular. Yet it was not for his son's genius that Abraham wished him to accept the post, since no pride in Felix's achievements to date entered the picture. Rather, it was Leah, and Fanny too, as likely as not, who wished him to remain in Berlin; and, besides, what a fillip to the Mendelssohn name! To think that one of this superior family, so steeped in music for so long, had become director of this august institution. In order to have a neutral ally, Devrient was summoned to persuade Felix to adopt this, his rightful course, and that it was simply his duty to obey his parents.

But Felix expressed his doubts. In answer to Fanny's criticism of Rungenhagen, Felix countered: "One musician is different from another. They are all better than some tenors dressed in priests' garb of black and with trousers," and added that the Singakademie post was nothing more than a sinecure "suitable for advanced years...a harbour of refuge". Felix preferred to gain independence by writing music of his own. "All I hope," he concluded, "is that they will find a man who will fulfil his duties with as much zeal as old Zelter." On 1st June he reminded his father of the professorship of music at Berlin University into which he had been "pushed into applying" three years earlier. Neither did he wish to accept the meagre salary offered by the Singakademie, "with influence to match". On 4th August, after visiting that latter institution, he told William Horsley of the "feelings of melancholy" he experienced at Zelter's absence "from what had been the best organisation in Berlin". Though Felix would have loved to hear Horsley's new compositions, "no new music is now being performed, and any that is would be full of errors".

Nothing appears to have altered when, on 18th January 1833, "Berlin's music is in dire straits," Felix confided. "It is only when non-Berliners, such as Neukomm and Marschner, conduct their own works that productions are enjoyable." The orchestration in Handel's oratorios was "improved by tedious imitations and sentimental dissonance. Flutes and clarinets are added indiscriminately, rather than with care and delicacy, as shown by Mozart. One cannot imagine how sad the hall

Chapter 19: Conductor and Director

looks without Zelter and Rietz (who had also passed away in 1832). The foundation is gone, yet all the drawbacks remain and stand out glaringly," Felix continued. "If they [the Singakademie committee] want to have me, let them make their offer and I will accept or not – but, probably, nothing will happen."

Even at Leipzigerstrasse 3 matters were no better. Of a musical entertainment organised by Fanny, her brother wrote to the Horsley family that "the guests' faces were so black and awful that I thought I must have done something radically wrong", until Fanny, more accustomed to the Berlin environment, laughed at his qualms. It was only later that Felix discovered the apparently grim silence denoted rapt attention, unlike the "lively chatter" of concert-goers in England at the time. Nevertheless, Moscheles was invited to visit Berlin from 17th to 19th October. As well as many parties, a successful concert was held at the opera house and three further benefit concerts were planned. Mendelssohn had originally intended that any profits would be donated to the Singakademie but, in view of the forthcoming election, it was the fund for indigent musicians that benefited. Though Mendelssohn was accused of self-promotion when his works were included in musical entertainments, it is more likely that whoever looked after the funds suggested that more money would accrue from Felix's compositions, compared with those of, say, Beethoven or Bach. The music critic Ludwig Rellstab wrote that such concerts were more meaningful than a whole year of performances of earlier music. Herr Mendelssohn, he continued, had shown himself to be "an extraordinary piano virtuoso of the highest calibre; an instrumental composer of genius and diligence, and a skilful orchestral conductor" – but none of this praise was good enough for the Berlin Singakademie.

It was proposed that Rungenhagen and Mendelssohn become co-directors, which the latter would not countenance. Felix wanted the position to be decided solely by constitutional means. At the outset, the committee of 20 had rejected 13 applicants, who had either been nominated or put themselves forward for the post of director. Devrient, who organised the election, was among this gallimaufry of applicants. On 22nd January 1833 the full membership, as opposed to the board, were asked to cast their votes – 115 junior members on the Wednesday; 385 full members on the Thursday. The situation was farcical, however, for only members of two years' standing and older women were allowed to vote. Thus only 240 votes were recorded: 148 for Rungenhagen; 88 for Mendelssohn; and four for Grahl. Rungenhagen was therefore elected by 60 votes and the status quo remained at the Berlin Singakademie. Since records were destroyed in World War II, Devrient's memoirs are the only source of reference now available.

"So long as the majority was undecided, names were called quietly and properly. But, when Rungenhagen had been proved the winner in this contest, his name was shouted with an offensive triumph," Devrient reported. By contrast, Mendelssohn's name was uttered "in a desponding, pitying tone", and the "frequent laughter" caused Devrient, he claimed, to protest, having become "indignant". Cautioned "not to make a useless disturbance", Devrient confessed himself "weak enough to follow their advice". This he regretted to the date of his memoirs – 1869. Mendelssohn was offered the deputyship, but he declined. According to a commentator named William Little, Mendelssohn's "bitterness began to calcify. He was stung and humiliated at being outgunned by a contender of such colourless and minimal talent." Rockstro concurred; "This was a failure which annoyed him," he said of Mendelssohn; and subsequent biographers continue to adhere to this misunderstanding. Apart from Zelter's tuition, Mendelssohn never set store by what happened in the musical milieu of Berlin. He certainly never wanted the directorship of the Singakademie, unless Zelter had invited him to accept it. He contested the election only to placate his parents and Devrient's badgering. He had enough nous to realise, young as he was, that an establishment figure would be bound to triumph over a visionary and a "new broom" such as himself.

Eric Werner contends that Felix's defeat was nothing more than an example of the contumely between Jew and Christian in early 19th century Berlin. This is based upon a remark, heard by Devrient, by one of the gentlemen choristers that was tactlessly repeated to Abraham. "It was an unheard-of thing to thrust a Jewish lad upon their conductor." A far more plausible reason for Mendelssohn's defeat might have been that the Singakademie members found Rungenhagen's compositions and low standards far more comfortable to stomach than Mendelssohn's quest for perfection, as far as humanly possible. If anyone heard Felix's choral works they would have found them far more exciting and challenging for choristers with imagination and ambition – neither of which applied to Rungenhagen's choir. Still today they have the reputation of being 'difficult, if not impossible', even by choirs with unparalleled experience compared with Singakademie members of the 1830s. Leah corroborated this view: "The older members (i.e., those who were allowed to vote) want only the traditional and cannot reconcile themselves to seeing a lively young man at the head."

Faithful old Rungenhagen remained at the helm for almost 18 years. Rockstro stated that the Mendelssohn family, taking Felix's defeat as a personal insult, resigned en bloc, taking with them all their backing. This can be disproved, for, whilst the Mendelssohns' financial stake in the Singakademie may have been withdrawn, Leah's sister Sarah Levy, when she died in 1854, left her splendid music library to the institution. Yet Felix did have pleasant interludes during this period. To Klingemann he described his room "where, with my beloved objects around me, I can work in peace". Pictures included a portrait of Bach over the piano; one of Rebecka alongside that of Beethoven, and a couple of Raphaels, so that the wall is rather a medley. On my bedside table there is a bottle of eau de Cologne in a basket, particularly admired by my relatives. There are three little travel diaries, some wallets, sketchbooks, a paintbox and a couple of landscapes on which I am working. On the other side of the room is my old piano without strings, which you certainly remember, together with a new instrument. A chest of drawers contains old letters, amongst which I have just discovered one from you, which begins: 'It is a great and good thing that you are coming...' This referred to Mendelssohn's first visit to London of 1829, the letter having been received in Hamburg, whence he had sailed. Also in the room were "many potted plants, books, tables, several chairs and a lot of dust on the floor. If you do not know by now what my place is like, it is not my fault. All my clothes still smell strongly of coal and half of me is still over there, in England." But Felix could not imagine having lived away from home for three years, apart from short snatches of time in Berlin.

An enjoyable incident was the visit, en route to Russia, of Heinrich and Carl Bärmann, father and son, to Berlin. Felix was asked to compose a piece that could be performed during their tour. The result was his Op. 113 *Konzertstück* for clarinet, basset-horn and piano, which bears the inscription 'Grand Duet for choux pastry and whipped cream' – his reward for finishing the work "before 5 p.m.". As a result of its success Mendelssohn was asked to write a similar piece, which was published, like Op. 113, posthumously, as Op. 114. At about the same time Felix was given what is termed 'a patent' for membership of the Berlin Academy of Fine Arts and Sciences, at the behest of his father (more for family glory than for any proof of talent his son might have shown). "This is contained in a formidable red case," Felix wrote, "together with a very ancient statue and a complimentary letter, hoping that I would return to Berlin, where my productions are so highly praised, as elsewhere."

Meanwhile, Mendelssohn's compositions continued to be performed at the Singakademie during his absence from Berlin. In 1838, for instance, *St Paul* was given for the first time, and in 1842, having – at last – been awarded membership, Felix himself was invited to conduct the same oratorio. Yet Werner writes of a "conspiracy of silence" regarding the lack of recognition towards his music in Berlin as a whole. Felix, on that account, experienced "traumatic effects, catastrophic for him, of which he was at first unconscious". The exception was his revival of Bach's *St Matthew Passion*, but this was a "flash in the pan", for which Zelter took most of the credit. It is true that the saying 'A prophet is without honour in his own country' applied without doubt to Mendelssohn in Berlin, despite his family's prestige. The only environment in which he felt comfortable was his home, but even there he was deemed nothing more than an amateur.

In 1833 Felix was invited to conduct the Lower Rhine Festival at Düsseldorf, probably by Franz von Woringen, whose family were friends of the Mendelssohns. Felix explained his schedule meticulously to the head of the festival committee. He aimed to pay his third visit to London "in late April at the latest", travelling to Düsseldorf en route to discuss arrangements and returning thence from London on 16th May. "I believe conductors have arrived only a week in advance for the previous festivals." Felix expressed his "deep gratitude" to the committee "for the delightful honour and confidence placed in me. It is every musician's duty and pleasure to take part in such an event." Whilst in London, he had shown a picture of Düsseldorf to the Horsley family, "where I am to live in the Belgrave Square of the town. I will promenade from one till three, dressed in a fine coat, large moustaches and a fine riding whip in my hand," he joked. His real intention was to work hard, and, since his father would be present, any such frivolity would be out of the question in any case.

Of the festival's social side, Abraham gave a fascinating description to his family, who remained in Berlin. The audience consumed "sandwiches and May wine during the long concert intervals". So popular was the event that visitors were obliged to sleep "eight or nine to the room" at hotels and guest houses. "People flocked to the 1,300-seat concert hall, one mile from the city centre, in carriages, farm carts or on foot." Felix "desisted from the horrible process of turning from the piano" during the performances. A further innovation occurred when "audiences were called to their places by a flourish of trumpets from the orchestra" – a forerunner of Wagner's similar practice at Bayreuth. "The hall measured 130 feet in length, 70 feet wide, but only 27 feet in height. Situated in a large, shady garden, adjoining a restaurant, the building [was] entirely without ornament, with whitewashed walls. One-third of the space was reserved for the orchestra and choristers."

As for the music, to give the first concert a lively start, Felix's own "martial-sounding" Trumpet Overture, Op. 101, was performed, followed by Handel's oratorio *Israel in Egypt*, in which Mendelssohn revived the original instrumentation, which had fallen out of fashion. He had studied this via a book compiled by the composer himself. Felix had rehearsed his musicians for more than a week beforehand and, two days prior to the performance, the rehearsal lasted from 8 a.m. to 10 p.m. Yet the dress rehearsal, to which the public was invited, still did not satisfy this martinet, so that a further practice was called on the morning of the concert. Other highlights included Beethoven's 'Pastoral' Symphony, his 6th, which, although known to musical circles in London, Vienna and Berlin, was new to Düsseldorf. At the committee's insistence a cantata by Ernst Wolff appeared on the programme. Another piece, *The Power of Music* by Peter von Winter, was dismissed by Abraham as "deathly dull and guaranteed to put one to sleep". Conversely, Beethoven's *Leonore* No. 3 Overture, though virtually unknown, was "stimulating and most effective to everyone". But, though Abraham was evidently proud of his son's triumph, he reverted to the social scene. "Ladies carried roses and carnations under scarves or music stands, ready to shower the director at the finale. One of Woringen's daughters rushed to the rostrum to place a laurel wreath on Felix's head", which he removed. On replacing the wreath, "he bowed with it intact, to avoid offence". Abraham was reminded of the family legend of Saul Wahl, "the one-night King of Poland," from whom Mendel of Dessau had claimed descent. In 1588, when the previous King had died without an heir, two factions emerged, causing Saul to renounce the crown. Future Mendelssohn generations regaled everyone with this legend, which Kupferberg states "still appears in Jewish and Polish folklore". To Abraham, Felix was emulating their purported ancestor "with his kingly bearing".

Felix certainly allowed his father to be treated like royalty, for, unlike the majority of guests, there was no scrimmaging for accommodation for Abraham Mendelssohn. Woringen had been persuaded to receive Abraham as his personal guest, "for the sake of your bright eyes", as he was informed later by his host. Felix gained a reputation for concocting the May cup 'Maitrank', consumed during the festival. A newspaper reported the frightful heatwave, despite which "gentlemen had travelled from a distance and still wore their sensible, German suits, in which they perspired so freely that the temperature was reminiscent of Africa". Indeed, the intense heat made patrons wonder if the festival would be cancelled. Nevertheless, on 26th May at 6 p.m., when the first concert began, the auditorium was full to capacity.

However well Abraham enjoyed the festivities, there was fault to find with the way his son acquitted himself: "When he made a speech, his Jewish intonation was frowningly observed." To Abraham, musical festivals were, hitherto, a time for meeting acquaintances and for chatting during rehearsals. But, right from the start of this festival, his son changed all that. No untoward behaviour would be tolerated. "I am neither able, nor willing, to shout," he explained. Orchestra and singers must listen in absolute silence in order to listen to what he had to say, and to obey implicitly his instructions. It was their duty, for the sake of art, Felix admonished. "The moment he taps his baton and says something," Abraham wrote, "there is a general 'Pssst', followed by deep silence. It is miraculous that 400 people of differing nationalities, backgrounds and ages let themselves be led as if they were children."

So successful was 'Herr Felix', as he was called, that he was given the post of directing Düsseldorf's music for three years, with leave of absence from May to October. Whereas many people were given a title without an office, the reverse situation applied to Mendelssohn, which pleased Abraham. This strange reasoning can only be conjectured. Perhaps he was glad that his son could remain dependent upon his dictates. At a banquet, Felix's new position was announced, and the sculptor Wilhelm von Schadow gave a ball. A laurel wreath was again placed on Mendelssohn's head and the chorus 'Hail, the conquering Hero comes', from Handel's oratorio *Judas Maccabaeus*, was sung. Though the wine flowed, Abraham remained abstemious, as did his son on this occasion. The party ended at 2 a.m. with singing, into which Abraham was drawn despite himself. Exhausted, he slept for the next 24 hours, irrespective of an unprecedented further concert, put on owing to the demand for tickets.

In accepting the appointment for his three-year term Felix wrote to the mayor, taking scrupulous care with his title: 'Most esteemed Herr Lord Mayor, Your Excellency'. Thanking him for the ring bestowed upon him by the festival committee, Felix said: "I am equally grateful for the friendship with which it was given to me and the kind words which accompanied the ring." He assured the mayor, Herr Joseph von Fuchsius, that his memory of the festival "is among the most precious of my musical life and will not leave me, as also the uncommon pleasure thereof at this splendid gift".

Mendelssohn's contract was to include the organising of church music, directing further Lower Rhine Festivals in Düsseldorf, as well as giving concerts during the 1833-34 season. The fee would be 600 Rheinthalers. The good burgers of Düsseldorf wished to emulate Weimar as a city of culture, and a promising start had been made in this regard. Schadow had founded the Academy of Arts, to which students enrolled from many parts of Germany. Karl Immermann had founded a national theatre, and Marek believes that it may have been he who had recommended Mendelssohn for the musical directorship of Düsseldorf. Thus, on 6th September 1833, Felix wrote to Schubring that, though he planned to fulfil his official duties conscientiously, he hoped to find time and leisure to write music of his own. On arriving at Düsseldorf on 19th September Felix found that the tenants had not yet moved from Schadow's home, where he was to lodge. Thus Mendelssohn had to live at a hotel (a converted shop) in a room "so diminutive", as he wrote to Moscheles, that visitors had to crowd into the street to gain entry and, as there were so few chairs, guests were often required to sit on Felix's bed. Interestingly, for the offspring of such an apparently affluent family, Felix said of his room that it was "as if I were living at home in Berlin".

Rockstro reported: "The whole period of Mendelssohn's term at Düsseldorf was beset by many serious difficulties." The Church dignitaries would not listen to reason and had to be superseded. Music had deteriorated to such an extent generally that anything new that Mendelssohn introduced was met with apathy by the townspeople. In the theatre the situation was even worse. Although Felix threw himself wholeheartedly into work under Immermann, a fatal coldness developed between them. As late as 19th April 1834, Felix wrote to von Boguslawski "I have been so busy coping with the system, which is still disorderly", that letter writing had had to be shelved. He sought Devrient's advice as to which singers to engage. He required "an efficient soprano, with enthusiasm in the voice – and nothing else". In other words, glamour, with all its accompanying distractions, did not signify. Later, in response to the singer's suggestions, Felix wrote: "Fräulein Grosser can roast in the musical inferno for turning her poetic soul from us for 500 thalers. How miserable are the devils that we know." But he was able to write with pride to Ignaz Fürst after a musical entertainment: "If you could hear their enthusiasm, it would do your heart good." Whenever Immermann wrote a piece for Felix to set to music, volunteers painted scenery to accompany it.

To the Horsley family Felix wrote that the repertoire of his choir included *Israel in Egypt*, *Judas Maccabaeus*, *Samson* and *Alexander's Feast*, as well as choruses from *The Creation* and Weber's *Oberon*. A Cherubini mass would be performed on Good Friday (1834), to be followed in the evening by the music of Lassus. Felix was particularly pleased by the standard to which Handel's works were performed. To Schubring Felix listed, as well as the Cherubini mass, one by Beethoven and two cantatas by Bach, and he said he would send a further one that Moritz Hauptmann had transcribed in Leipzig from an original manuscript. But it was not all sweetness and light. "Of course, much is left to be desired" regarding a performance of Handel's 'Dettingen' Te Deum, written after the victory at the Battle of Dettingen in 1742 (the last occasion, incidentally, when British royalty – King George II – led the troops in person).

Even at the beginning of his Düsseldorf period Felix might well have had forebodings as to how matters would shape themselves. His first concert, on 22nd November 1833, St Cecilia's Day, included his own G minor Piano Concerto and Handel's *Alexander's Feast*, composed to commemorate the patron saint of music. "I think the performance will sound good, but there is a great deal to do," Felix wrote. The same applied to Beethoven's incidental music for Goethe's drama *Egmont*. It was on this occasion that, during the rehearsal, so annoyed did Mendelssohn become with his musicians' inability to keep to the correct tempo that he tore the score in two: "They are more fit for babies' milk. They like to belabour each other in the orchestra. This I do not choose that they do in my presence." However, after his vandalism, perpetrated "for the first time in my life", his musicians "played with much more expression. I heard something of Beethoven's for the first time. Especially did this apply to the march and the 6/8 movement, where Clerchen meets Egmont." In wet weather, he reported, "the violinists carry their instruments under their coats, but wholly unprotected when the weather is fine. If you heard me conduct this orchestra, not even four horses would bring you there a second time. Music commitments have to be fulfilled in the mornings, because every citizen of Düsseldorf is drunk by 4 p.m." On 12th October 1834 Felix threatened to submit his resignation to the mayor if the organist at St Maximilian's Church was not replaced. "So incompetent has he become that I find it so unpleasant to see the effects on the performers and myself going entirely to waste." All Felix could employ to comfort himself was the thought that "at least the pieces are being heard".

But there were shafts of sunshine in Mendelssohn's term at Düsseldorf. On 16th November 1834 he gave details of a successful concert. Items had included Weber's *Oberon* Overture "again"; a "symphonia" by the younger Burgmüller; "an aria sung by Mme. Dautler; a 'cello concerto performed by Julius Rietz; and an elegy by Romberg, which Paul likes". (Probably, this was Bernhard Romberg, "a 'cellist of high repute", according to Percy Scholes.) Songs by Beethoven and Felix were represented, among other obscure pieces, now forgotten. Rietz conducted Mendelssohn's *Rondo brillant* "very well" and the concert ended with "a damned duet by Mercadante – are we not fashionable? The room was packed, the ladies so elegant, and no one was eating bread and butter and apples. A 'grande soirée' followed, with all Their Excellencies and all their fancy speeches." Fanny Horsley wrote that the length of Mendelssohn's concerts suited her far better than "the 20 pieces" served up by London orchestras.

Mendelssohn strove to unearth manuscripts of earlier music that he considered suitable to be performed; hence he travelled to Cologne, Elbefeld and other German towns with well-stocked music libraries that might yield the treasures he sought. Herr Polchau was approached. Surely, Felix must have thought, this friend of the Bach and Salomon families would be amenable to his borrowing, or even copying, Mozart's arrangement of Handel's opera *Acis and Galatea*. Was it not, after all, from that source that his own manuscript of the *St Matthew Passion* had originated, given to Felix by his grandmother at Christmas 1823? But no, Polchau would not oblige, and it was Aloys Fuchs, loyal as ever, who sent his own manuscript from Vienna. It was from Fuchs that Mendelssohn sought guidance as to what was right and what was wrong regarding the many rumours that arose from the new discoveries of Beethoven scores. Was there, Felix asked, a tenth symphony? Fuchs assured him that no such piece existed (though the Philharmonic Society of London, whose archives are now with the British Library, possessed some sketches from the 1820s by the composer).

Meanwhile, Immermann wished his new theatre to resemble that at Weimar and expected his new director to behave like Napoleon; he disliked any counter-argument to his own views. Immermann ordered musicians to be engaged, which task Mendelssohn eventually refused to undertake, in view of the aggravation it caused. Two contracts had to be arranged for each musician with a 'fight to the death' regarding salaries. Those auditioned proved "troublesome". "They refuse to sit at their music desks. Then an aunt of a very wretched performer who was not engaged in the orchestra appeared. The wife of another musician, likewise rejected, appeared with two young children to intercede on her husband's behalf. Others played so utterly beneath contempt that I really could not agree to take any of them. Looking utterly humble, they went quietly away, miserable at having lost their bread. The wife then returned weeping. Out of 30 musicians, only one felt sufficiently satisfied to sign his contract. The remainder bargained and haggled for an hour at least, before they were made to understand that there was only a limited amount to pay them. These were four of the most horrendous days I have ever spent, until Klingemann arrived and understood the situation." The singers were drunk, causing Felix to "speak with authority", resulting in further rebellion. "I then had to shout at them like the boots at an inn. Mlle. Butler became hoarse... I thereupon made up my mind to abdicate my role as concert master, three weeks after the opening of the theatre."

For the first time in public, Felix conducted an opera, Mozart's *Don Giovanni*, in December 1833. "From first to last, everyone concerned threw themselves into it, heart and soul," he reported. However, with the 20 rehearsals that Felix felt to be necessary, expenses were incurred that caused the theatre lessees to raise ticket prices for the forthcoming performance. Felix continued, "When the curtain rose on the first night, some malcontents in the audience cried wildly for Signor Dorossi and made a tremendous disturbance. After five minutes, order was restored and we began going splendidly through the first act, constantly accompanied by applause. But, lo and behold, as the curtain rose on the second act, the uproar broke out afresh, with redoubled vigour and persistence. Well, I felt inclined to hand over the whole concert to the devil… I should have liked to break the heads of some of those fellows. The curtain rose and fell four times, extraneous to scene shifting, before the performance ended." Unless he received an apology, Felix threatened to resign from the theatre forthwith. Four days later, he was talked out of taking such a step. "People I met were unable to talk of anything else" but what he called "this Grande Scandale". The ringleaders were sent to the director; then to the president, "who blew them up tremendously. Soldiers who had taken part in the riot were treated likewise by their commanding officer."

The "fatal coldness" between Immermann and Mendelssohn grew until, eventually, Felix, after so many exasperating setbacks, resigned, forgoing what salary remained to him. But this was not the end of the matter. His father gave him what Yorkshire people would call 'a rollicking'. How could his son, with such inadequate knowledge of the theatre, judge what was required in this specialised art form? Felix had undertaken these duties voluntarily, but had let them overwhelm him. What really angered Abraham more than anything else, however, was that "you have made an enemy of a man who, at all events, policy should have taught you not to despise". Through such rashness, "you will have offended and lost friendship of many respectable people". Paul, in his later compilation, added a note that readers of the Mendelssohn letters would realise from that epistle: "What an impartial and incorruptible judge Felix had for a father." Devrient took Abraham's part, probably in his own interests, anticipating what glory he would gain through his acting and singing roles. In his memoirs he observed how much better Felix could have handled the situation.

In a letter, Mendelssohn explained his position to Rebecka, whom he knew would understand if no one else could do so. No decision had ever been made as to the allocation of duties, he explained. Immermann, who objected to attending to all the administration, allowed it to land in Felix's lap, along with his musical activities. It is hardly surprising, therefore, that Felix "fretted and fumed at so many distractions. Each morning, my doorbell rings at every bar" when indulging in the rare luxury of composing his own music; there were "choristers to be scolded; stupid musicians to be taught; seedy musicians to be engaged, and, when this has gone on the whole day, and when I realise that all these things are for the sole benefit of Düsseldorf, I am provoked". He concluded that, "having beaten a hasty retreat, I feel myself to be a person once more". Yet there were enjoyable social interludes for Felix. Klingemann visited him, relaying all his news to the Horsley family: "Klingemann is full of Düsseldorf and Mendelssohn," Lucy Callcott was informed by her niece Fanny Horsley. He had bought a chestnut mare, after obtaining permission from his father. "I can imagine him [Felix] walking, trotting, cantering, galloping or running away, or being run away with," she continued. It was an acquaintance who suggested this purchase. "Everyone admires this animal, which I ride through storms, but, though a good leaper, the horse is shy. Once, seeing flashes of lightning, [she] started so violently that I felt quite sorry for her." At home, he was "driven almost to distraction" by a pianist in the next room, "who practises for two hours each day, making the same mistakes and playing Rossini's aria at such a phlegmatic tempo". He bethought himself, however, that she might find his own practising irritating. "I sometimes hear her teacher, or her mother, strike the right note 17 times in succession. At night she develops some old barrel organ tune that can be recognised by a single note. I know all her pieces by heart the moment she strikes the first chord."

To Ignaz Fürst Felix wrote of a forthcoming feast, "where the whole town will drink wine, as if this were not the case every day". To his family he reported "a real treat" when the actor Seydelmann played the part of Nathan the Wise, the hero of Lessing's eponymous drama. He wished "a hundred times" that his father could have watched the performance with him. Unhappily, however, the next day "I could have had a war to the knife" regarding this production. "Schadow became irritated and a gentleman from Berlin declared that, viewed from a dramatic angle… I did not argue the point at all for, where there is such a difference of opinion on any subject, even about first principles, there is nothing to be done." Apart from home life, Felix fulminated: "Berliners have stopped dead and gone backwards… People have grown more narrow-minded than ever. The best of them have passed away; others, who once conceived fine plans, are now happy Philistines" – a word Felix often used when speaking of the arts.

Felix's cousin Alexander Mendelssohn claimed to have delivered some port wine to their mutual cousin Benjamin in Bonn, for Felix to collect. "Confess," he joked; "did you take it for ordinary old Ahrbleichart and drink it up? If not, would you care to send it to me." A 'contract' was arranged between Felix and the Miss Horsleys, whereby he was to give them a piano arrangement of his *Fair Melusine* Overture in exchange for some household items, for which an inventory was compiled. On receipt of these the morning was devoted to putting his room in order, having spent the night and risen at 6 o'clock that morning to complete his part of the bargain. For the rug he had received he wrote that he should have written three overtures, so pleased was he. "I would guess that some of its patterns are Persian, representing Herr Musik Direktor. A little table cover bears the Indian crows'-feet design and splendid colours… How the yellow was inserted no one can understand." These Oriental patterns might have been suggested by Friedrich Rosen. Felix continued: "Where, in God's name, did you find the candleholder everyone admires?" On receipt of a further parcel, containing music and "what seems like ironwork", this prompted "a row" with the customs, as it contained no name or sender's address.

Chapter 19: Conductor and Director

It would be tedious to catalogue, year on year, the prolific amount of music festivals that Mendelssohn directed, so a few significant jottings must suffice. His experiences in Leipzig and his ten visits to England are covered elsewhere. Meanwhile, Lower Rhine Festivals took place in Aachen and Cologne, as well as Düsseldorf. At the 1834 Aachen Festival Hiller's oratorio *Deborah* was the chief item on the programme. Having heard "a movement or two", Felix dismissed it as "subordinate to Handel". However, having endured an 11-hour coach journey from Düsseldorf, causing him, not surprisingly, to be "cross and impatient", extenuation must be allowed. The main feature of the Cologne Festival of 1835, which Felix was invited to direct, was Handel's *Solomon*, on which he had worked whilst in Italy, having composed an organ accompaniment. A further item worthy of attention was C. P E. Bach's cantata *Morgengesang* (*Morning Song*), which Felix considered to be "so romantic and poetical that, each time I hear it, I feel more touched than charmed". The work was "admirable" and gave "great pleasure" to anyone who heard it. "The work must be adapted to suit the resources available", but Mendelssohn felt gratitude to "such a noble man as Reichardt" for his adaptation of the original score. Though the committee "scarcely consented to its inclusion", it was borne in upon them what a fine work the cantata proved to be. Whereas Leah opined that her son had become "less handsome and less lively" on his return to Berlin, Bendemann and Hildebrandt, each painting a portrait of Felix on the committee's behalf, both observed that the sitter's expression changed so often whilst being painted. The Mendelssohn family attended that festival, but Leah fell ill en route from Cologne to Düsseldorf.

Mme. Polko, whose anecdotes should be taken with a huge canister of salt, recorded that Felix summoned a doctor friend to attend his mother, "who had frightened everyone by collapsing… Felix, having watched over her for two whole days, was utterly exhausted. There he lay, his noble forehead bent down, his dark eyelashes resting on his cheeks, his well-cut lips gently closed; pale and breathing softly – a most charming picture." If this fanciful author is to be believed, Rebecka, "this lovely girl, sewed her brother's shirtsleeves to the sofa where their mother had lain. On waking, Felix found himself held fast to the couch", where guests observed "his embarrassed and laughing face".

At the 1838 Cologne Festival the first performance of Felix's festival song *To the Artists*, with words by Schiller, was presented at the Gürzenich concert hall. "It sounded very jolly," Mendelssohn wrote, dismissing the composition. The next day, however, the 2,000-strong choir, as Felix stated, sounded "penetrative and massive" and the entire audience applauded throughout the whole festival. When his *Volklied* (*Folk Song*) was heard, Felix was "overwhelmed by joy". "The organ was most effective in Handel's works," he wrote to Hiller, "but, in those of Bach, even more so." Some early music he had discovered "is still wanting to excite interest". On his return to Leipzig Felix promised to relate "many stories, far too insignificant to be put into print".

At Düsseldorf the following year *St Paul* was performed. Felix was far less impressed with the Ritterhall at which the concert took place than he had anticipated, writing to Hiller that it was "hot and close". Mme. Polko in her memoirs recorded how Fanny, sitting among the altos, "corrected an error in one of the choruses". In the English periodical *The Musical World*, Klingemann reported having "never heard such glorious singing". There were 364 choristers and 173 musicians. To Hiller, Felix proved to be "a lively and agreeable host...centre of the whole proceedings, introducing everyone to everyone, knowing who would mix with whom in a party spirit". Klingemann brought J. W. Davison with him, soon to become music critic of *The Times*. In his recollections he wrote that, when he had a headache, Felix crooned "poor fellow; poor fellow", stroking Davison's forehead, "his soft voice soothing as effectively as the stroking motion". Of Beethoven's *Leonore* Overture No. 3, seldom heard in Cologne at that time, Fanny wrote: "A rare piece... The orchestra played it as one man; all its nuances; all its hidden meanings revealed."

The main feature of the 1839 Festival consisted of the three female singers whom Mendelssohn had engaged. "Elise Polko excelled herself in her narrative; Augusta von Fassmann, the most aristocratic soprano ever to have played the part of the Countess Donna Anna (in Mozart's *Marriage of Figaro*) sang 'Dove Sono'; Sophie Sohl, was the nightingale of contraltos, and Clara Novello, whose enchanting voice, so fresh and redolent of spring as her face and disposition, sang like a glad, exultant lark, harbinger of that season." Whilst no record can be found as to how Felix viewed the first two singers, he was, as some biographers have been, far less complimentary of the latter than Mme. Polko, as is noted elsewhere in this book.

In September of that year Mendelssohn met someone who was a prime mover in championing his music: Henry Fothergill Chorley, music critic of *The Athenaeum* since 1833. Visiting Germany for the first time, in order to report on the Brunswick Festival, he recalled "a clean, civil little boy, escorting me from my hotel [The Blue Angel] to the concert hall, a converted church. A weak, tame contralto, with a profusion of fair ringlets" followed Beethoven's 5th Symphony with an aria from *St Paul*, 'The Lord is Mindful of His own'. Chorley continued: "At dawn, the first day of three, the auditorium was almost three-quarters full, with a decidedly mixed assembly of concert-goers. Next to the woman of fashion dressed elegantly enough to grace an English ballroom were gypsy-coloured women displaying beads and picturesquely decorated pendant streamers of ribbon. A comely youth, tight-laced in his uniform, every hair of his moustache trimmed and trained to the agony of perfection, was squeezed against a dirty, savage, half-naked student, his wild hair halfway down his back; his velveteen jacket fastened at the waist by one button, revealing that neither shirt nor waistcoat were underneath. The orchestra, by contrast, had an effective appearance of uniformity. The ladies wore white...their sole decoration, a nosegay. The audience merged into one entity,

Chapter 19: Conductor and Director

not on account of the Duke of Brunswick's presence, but as a result of Mendelssohn. Eyes turned when he entered."

On Mendelssohn's desk, alongside the customary score, was "a bouquet of flowers and...a paper containing those delicacies [in which] every good German housewife is skilled", to obviate the need for Felix to search for refreshment. After the concert, Chorley continued: "Ladies threw bouquets at the conductor and...a laurel wreath was placed on Felix's head." A ball took place in the evening and Mendelssohn was invited to give an organ recital at the cathedral after the festival. Chorley observed that the instrument "had a doleful, worm-eaten case". At Mecklenburg-Strelitz Mendelssohn again conducted *St Paul* and Haydn's *Creation*, amongst smaller works. Chorley found the event "a signal illustration of the twin concepts of gentleness and simplicity in German music". The duke was evidently impressed, for he placed his attendants and officials at Mendelssohn's disposal to avoid disturbance. The next year Felix wrote to Paul in far less sanguine mood about a festival in Hamburg: "The people of Hamburg are *not* planning on my baton at their music festival. At least, it does not seem that Herr Grund is kindly disposed towards me, [but] I have heard things to that effect before." No explanation can be found for the 'bad odour' inculcated by the Hamburg establishment.

At Eppstein in 1844 a large organ was installed in the church, resulting in a festival of dedication. For Felix and his family, a real party atmosphere was witnessed. Mendelssohn reported: "As the party journeyed, heads innumerable – all, I suspect, more or less tipsy – shouted out loud 'Vivat!' to me." The ladies wished to stop at an inn for coffee, which Felix opposed, presumably to hurry the journey along, "so we ate pound cake in the carriage". The innkeeper drove them to Zweibrücken on the first stage of their route, where a Herr Piaskus gave them breakfast "and very fine wine". On the next stage of the excursion "we dined at a glorious castle in the Vosges Mountains... Cannons were fired to demonstrate the echo and champagne was drunk, and, at every fresh toast, the cannons were discharged anew. Good wine was imbibed at St Johann, where we slept. Herr Bull's cellars cannot be described... Those who have not paid a visit to Herr Bull...do not know what Forster is... From nine o'clock in the morning we were never quite steady until the evening. Herr Breiting will not be in as good a state as Pompeii". Nevertheless, Felix, despite his alcoholic indulgence, was able to recall that "the rooms were elegant, hung with pictures...a fine, new piano by Streicher and a pretty woman who selects the grapes". Neither did so much merrymaking inhibit performances of *The First Walpurgisnacht* and *St Paul* at the festival.

In 1842 Corelli Hill had founded the New York Philharmonic Orchestra, and, three years later, Felix was invited to conduct a season of concerts. It is a matter of opinion whether or not this was a backhanded compliment. It was Spohr who was first approached but, having turned 60, this highly fashionable musician refused to leave Germany, so Mendelssohn, next on Hill's list, was asked. Hill had conducted *St Paul* with the New York Sacred Music Society, and the *Midsummer Night's Dream* music was presented at the third concert of the orchestra's inaugural season. Felix, far younger than Spohr, found plausible reasons himself to decline such a prestigious offer. Had he been invited sooner, he stated, he might have accepted but, at present, he needed to rest after so many demands having been made upon him, and, in any case, his youngest son, Felix, was ill. Besides, he wished solely to write his own music, "sans journeys, sans festivals, sans everything". He did, later, confide the real reason for not crossing the Atlantic – "We Germans do not like the sea" – when the American poet and novelist Bayard Taylor visited him in Germany. It is interesting to observe that neither Beethoven, Schubert, Schumann nor Brahms journeyed anywhere that involved sea crossings, confining themselves to mainland Europe, so it must be regarded as a real privilege that Mendelssohn made ten visits to the United Kingdom.

At the Liège Festival Mendelssohn's cantata *Lauda Sion*, based on Psalm 64, was premiered. Commissioned by a M. Mathis-Greyseman, he was asked to conduct the work in preference to Felix, "out of sensitivity towards his feelings", as it was reported. One rehearsal only was organised, owing to the tight budget. Neither were any women allowed to take part at St Martin's Church, so a treble was engaged to sing the soprano role. To Radcliffe, the cantata suggests "perfunctory and official rejoicing" and is reminiscent to him of Brahms's '*German Requiem*', the first performance of which would not take place until 1869 – 23 years after the cantata and 22 years after Mendelssohn's death.

At the 1846 Aachen Festival, however painstakingly Felix worked, his name was either ignored or taken for granted, since, for a long time, it had been known as 'the Jenny Lind Festival'. "She took the audience by storm in Haydn's *Creation*," it was reported. On Whit Sunday a rehearsal extended from 10 in the morning until 2 p.m., and, after a banquet, a further rehearsal took place between five and nine that evening. It was at this event that Mendelssohn, hoping to take "a normal bath", was made so drowsy by spa water "that I was hard put to keep awake whilst proceedings ensued".

His social life was "a whirl", rising at 6.30 in the morning, not retiring to sleep until 12.30 or one the following day. Mendelssohn spent a day with a Herr Kuhlmann, reminiscing about times past. "A few dear, good people never change, thank God," he declared. It was at the home of this host that Felix met the legendary widow Clicquot, who promised him two dozen bottles of her famous champagne every year thereafter. Sadly, it was only the year before he died, so the annual gift was not continued after 1847. Before the festival, Mendelssohn had taken a few days' holiday, sailing along the Rhine with Jenny Lind – and, of course, her companion, Mlle. Johannsen. It was there that he first mentioned *Elijah* and became Miss Lind's unofficial business manager, advising on useful contacts, scanning the contracts she had to sign and generally suggesting what she should sing at future concerts. It might have been after one of their discussions that Jenny decided to make the change in her singing career from opera to oratorio, which occurred in 1847. A further event that had been arranged was a visit to Sweden, where Jenny's friends, Herr Geiger and his family, had invited him. However, both Geiger and Mendelssohn were destined not to meet again, for each passed away in 1847.

Chapter 20

Mendelssohn, the Soloist

Sadly, neither piano rolls nor recordings exist from Mendelssohn's time, so any assessment of Felix's ability as a soloist can only be made from contemporary sources. Whilst some recollections may be tinged with envy, or an overworked imagination, others can be given due credit for impartiality and accuracy. An example of the first type of reminiscence is that of A. B. Marx. According to him Fanny "often despaired" when her brother played his own compositions at Leipzigerstrasse 3. "After the third or fourth repetition, one could observe that, with each successive performance, he sped up the tempo, often significantly...which expression of growing excitement and impatience was not always appropriate. Much more dubious was the influence of his pleasure-laden environment and the constant company of his sisters' young female friends." Such a narrative smacks of jealousy after Marx's rift with Mendelssohn. Why should not a talented pianist show off his prowess to his peers, especially when, as an amateur, he was exhorted – nay, ordered – to do so by his adult family and friends? Yet, on a later occasion, at his parents' home, he played on the "old, broken-winded Broadwood", from which he could still coax "melody, sweetness, soul and power to flow".

In Italy Julius Benedict recalled Mendelssohn's piano playing as "remarkable... He played one theme, adding a second, a third and a fourth, weaving them simultaneously in the most brilliant way, polishing each phrase and modulation like a diamond cutter at work on a priceless stone, chipping away at ideas until they were fine-honed into a pleasing whole." Though senior to him, Benedict had idolised Mendelssohn from their youth, and continued to do so. Yet, on Felix's first visit to London in 1829, a newspaper reporter, who would, at the time, have barely had the chance of meeting him, wrote of this 20-year-old guest: "[He is] a piano player of almost transcendent talent, which becomes more admirable when something of the man is known. His modesty binds him to the success with which he has cultivated it... In the art of playing, he is lost to everything but the instrument before him."

No one could accuse Mendelssohn of false modesty. When anyone praised him, he would express genuine astonishment. "Did you like it?" he would ask. "That makes me very happy." This trait persisted throughout his life, proving that childhood experiences can be ingrained in a personality. Cynics must be reminded, especially those who have read sycophantic profiles of the parents, that all the Mendelssohn children – even Paul, the favourite – had to live with constant carping from Leah and fault-finding by Abraham. It is evident that the love of the arts with which these parents have been credited did not include recognition of the already mature talents of their remarkable offspring. Indeed, it is only when they became adult that praise was grudgingly bestowed. Neither is it wise to accept what celebrated critics have said, without careful consideration. Sir Charles Hallé, for instance, never gave him credit for the same pianistic virtuosity as Thalberg and Liszt. Whilst, at face value, this assertion might appear negative, Mendelssohn, had he lived, would have acknowledged the remark as a compliment. He never wanted to be known as a virtuoso. Hans von Bülow expressed surprise that Felix "did not employ the arpeggio to announce his virtuosity at the piano", missing the point, as Hallé had done, that different pianists employed different styles to display their musicianship.

Clara Schumann, internationally renowned pianist herself, whose criticisms were candid and shrewd, sometimes harsh, recalled Mendelssohn's piano playing in her memoirs thus: "He would sometimes take the tempo very quickly, but never to the prejudice of the music. Of mere effect on performances, he knew nothing. He could carry everyone with him in the most incredible manner. Music streamed from him in all the fullness of his inborn genius, always stamped with nobility and beauty... One even almost overlooked those spiritual gifts, fire, invention, soul, comprehension." Altogether, Mme. Schumann declared Mendelssohn "the greatest pianist of the time". Ferdinand Hiller wrote in a similar vein: "Mendelssohn's musicianship was one of the most delightful things in my artistic life. Listeners were overwhelmed by [his] ardour, soulfulness, inspiration and intelligence... Mendelssohn played as a lark sings, because it was his nature." This latter memoir derives from someone who, like Marx, developed a rift in his friendship with Felix. Unlike him, however, Hiller was never bitter when recollecting events from the past.

Of Mendelssohn's application to the piano keys, the following examples may be cited from his contemporaries' memoirs. In old age, Joseph Joachim still recalled how Felix "electrified the keyboard". Senator Souchay, albeit a relative of Cécile's, was always trustworthy in his recollections: in this instance, he wrote of Felix's "slender fingers [that] appeared to have a life of their own as they danced on the keys". Charles Salaman, another celebrated pianist, remembered how "Mendelssohn's fingers sang"; the critic and former chorister J. E. Cox recalled how "spellbound" listeners became when Felix gave piano performances. "But," cynics will answer, "of course such praise would be forthcoming. Mendelssohn had such an easy, comfortable life, filled with luxury." How true is this? From childhood, Felix was compelled to pursue an unstinting work schedule, in which he had to

Chapter 20: Mendelssohn, the Soloist

make time for musical activities – except when obliged to play for friends and relatives. This gruelling pursuit of work, in obedience to his sense of duty, stayed with him for the rest of his life. It was unremitting, consistent effort that ensured his genius might prosper.

However, glimpses of his human feelings can be observed. On his first visit to London, in 1829, the concert hall was empty and "echoed with every footstep". As the Clementi piano was locked, Felix daydreamed about "the old grey instrument on which the fingers of several generations must have wandered. I lost myself in a world of strange fantasies and dwelt in time, until people began to come in." As 2 p.m. approached, Felix realised he had not touched the keys to practise. "The hall contained more people than ever before for a London concert. Nothing but ladies' gay bonnets and frightful heat." Ladies unable to acquire seats in the audience sat on the platform. "I was overcome with panic," he wrote – until his recital began. "I think I was actually feverish until the gay bonnets gave me a nice reception, very attentive and quiet (which, for this talkative concert public, is a rare thing)." Because the piano was "excellent and had a light touch", Mendelssohn was soon able to shake off his "tremors", as he described his apparent stage fright. "I calmed down completely and was amused to see the bonnets become agitated at every little flourish, which reminded me, and many others, of the wind in a tulip bed. Many ladies on the platform were very lovely." To add to Felix's sense of bonhomie, Sir George Smart, who promoted the concert, "took a pinch of snuff". Afterwards, Felix was able to report that "the concert went pretty well and the audience made a great deal of noise when it was over".

After another recital Felix complained of having had his fill "of tedious notes... I have had enough of that dry C and must play Beethoven again." In an early edition of his biography of Mendelssohn, Stratton claims that Charles Neate, Beethoven's London agent, first played the composer's 5th (E flat) Piano Concerto, the 'Emperor', in 1820; it was actually Mendelssohn who introduced London audiences to the work in 1829, for which he received brilliant notices. "A pleasurable electric shock passed through his hearers, and held them spellbound," a journalist reported. It is interesting to note that, whereas Liszt sight-read a score when playing this concerto, Mendelssohn was able to apply his memory to perform the work. But, of Beethoven's five concertos for piano and orchestra, his 4th in G major appears to have been Felix's favourite. "Having thought of my mother," he wrote on one occasion, [I] never played the work so well. The first cadenza and the return of the orchestra after it, pleased me extraordinarily, and the audience, apparently, more so." In Paris he played the same concerto with the Conservatoire Orchestra under Habeneck, in the presence of the Queen, and Rockstro wrote of a further performance in London in 1844: "The delicacy of the piano was perfect. Every note penetrated to the remotest corner of the room. At the rehearsal, two days earlier, Mendelssohn had developed the magnificent[ly] extravagant extempore cadenza. His skill never failed him when he gave the reins to his exuberant fancy." As with this coup of 24th June 1844, that of 27th April 1847 was remembered for years afterwards. In 1898 Wilhelm Kuhe, professor of piano at the Royal Academy recalled: "Mendelssohn raised his hand to prevent Costa from lifting his baton and was heard to say, 'Not yet. Not yet.'" Later, Felix confided to Sir George MacFarren "that he wished to do his best to please two ladies in the audience – Queen Victoria and Jenny Lind".

To the serious researcher, biographies need to be studied with care. Rockstro, for example, wrote of Mendelssohn having played Beethoven's 1st Piano Concerto, "not then known in Leipzig", but this is inaccurate. The *Gewandhaus Orchestra Statistics*, published by Breitkopf & Härtel, record this and the composer's 2nd Concerto having been played as early as 1802 and the following year. Therefore, some elderly Leipzigers might well have cast their minds back to that period on hearing Mendelssohn's performance. The *Statistics* also note Felix's last public performance at the piano, playing the same composer's 'Kreutzer' Sonata, Op. 47, with Ferdinand David on 19th July 1846.

Mozart, too, was represented among Mendelssohn's piano recitals. On 13th May 1832 Felix wrote a cadenza for the K. 271 Piano Concerto, No. 9, when, once again, he "electrified" the audience. As a consequence Paganini, who was also in London at the time, invited Mendelssohn to play duets with him. However, the violinist had to undergo jaw surgery and this exciting entertainment never happened. Afterwards, when Charles Horsley congratulated Felix in Hyde Park, Mendelssohn answered: "The audience likes octaves, so I played them."

It is interesting to chart Felix's growing self-confidence, once he began to leave home. From Weimar he was able to tell his family that "I played for two hours one afternoon; partly Bach fugues; partly I followed my own fancies". On hearing the 12-year-old's improvisations, Goethe was heard to remark that, having heard Mozart at a similar age, he had written nothing comparable. "This little man borders on the miraculous." Yet the young Mendelssohn never expressed anything but surprise at any praise, especially from strangers. Having read an article in *The Times* on his first visit to London with his morning tea, he wrote home: "I felt devilishly proud how well the concert-going public like me." This must have boosted his morale to such an extent that he even had the temerity to imply that the well-meaning letters of introduction from his father were superfluous, so many acquaintances had he made via his own musicianship.

At a soirée in Munich he wrote to Zelter: "Young ladies played their piano pieces nicely, except that they tried to break their fingers with juggling tricks and rope dancing feats." When Felix was asked to play, he chose Beethoven's C sharp minor Sonata, Op. 27, No.2, (later to be known as 'Moonlight') warning his audience, "Well, if you get bored, it serves you right." The next morning the countess summoned her music teacher and asked if she could learn to play "some good, really good music, by Beethoven or Weber". Mendelssohn was dubbed 'a prophet in the desert', once the story spread through the musical population of

Chapter 20: Mendelssohn, the Soloist

Munich. "I was tempted to give a sermon, to exhort the Munich musicians to encourage better taste among the populace." Felix's letter to Zelter continued: "The countess vowed to improve and, since that time, I play only what I really like, however serious, and everyone listens to me with attention."

At a party in Rome given by the artist Horace Vernet, Mendelssohn was asked to entertain the other guests at the piano. Since his host's favourite was Mozart's *Don Giovanni*, he extemporised on themes from that opera, "gliding into Weber's *Konzertstück*". Vernet was so delighted that "I rarely experienced such praise". It was on this occasion that Mendelssohn's portrait was painted. Vernet was barely able to keep the surprise from Felix until they entered the room where a canvas was prepared. Yet Felix did not neglect his own compositions, and it was in Italy that he worked on what he called his 'German' concerto, No. 1 in G minor, to be performed in Munich and dedicated to the pianist Delphine von Schauroth. On a later visit to Munich "the audience applauded so much that Mendelssohn had to be called back to acknowledge the ovation, but declined". David Bishop points out that, until the Second World War, audiences clapped between movements in symphonies and concertos. Felix's ungracious behaviour may well have stemmed from this irritating intrusion, for, like his later E minor Violin Concerto and 'Scottish' Symphony, this concerto is played without a break between movements.

Writers of reference books and music critics dismiss Mendelssohn's compositions as "too easy", "suitable only for students", if not "frivolous and lightweight". Wendy Thompson, in a concert programme of 13th November 2000, quotes Berlioz's fantasy: "Because this concerto (G minor) was so popular at a competition, when the last student prepared to play it the piano played by itself." To support her claim, Ms. Thompson falls into the trap of repeating Felix's own words: "A hastily sketched matter." Anyone conversant with his personality, and his speed of composition, knows how unjust he was to himself. When played properly, with the enjoyment and fun that Mendelssohn would have applied, the work differs completely from versions performed as if attending Leah Mendelssohn's "pleasant" tea parties.

The 'Munich' concerto was enjoyed in Paris, but, on Mendelssohn's second visit to London in 1832, Klingemann hailed it "a triumph… Once again, I felt, as everyone, full of emotion, like a young mother, when the silly grey-haired people approached *me*, as if I had played or written it… The cause of art has been furthered much more." 'Dilettanti' of *The Harmonicon* wrote of the performance as "more astonishing than ever witnessed to date".

Mendelssohn's 2nd Piano Concerto, Op. 40, was composed for the Birmingham Festival of 1837, where it was premiered, for which Felix's favourite Erard piano was provided. "They prevented me taking my seat at the instrument for a long time and offers were bestowed upon me from all sides," Felix reported.

On 25th May 1832, at a concert organised by a M. Mori, Mendelssohn introduced his *Capriccio brillant*, Op. 22, for piano and orchestra. In a Promenade

Concert programme note, Joan Chissell points out that, like several of his compositions, the piece changes from minor to major (vice versa in some cases). At Elbefeld, whilst searching for early music in the libraries, museums and churches, he was invited to take part in a concert. On that occasion he improvised on themes from Weber's *Oberon*. As so often, Felix deprecated his extemporisation as having "not much merit in it". Yet he was applauded enough to gratify anyone and was invited to return to perform at a charity concert in the following winter. "When Felix improvised," Hiller recalled, "he resembled a centaur, using the piano as a horse."

On 22nd April 1838, at a concert given in Leipzig by a Mme. Botgerschreck, "an excellent contralto persecuted me to play the piano", for which he composed a rondo "not one note of which had been written until two days before, but which will be rehearsed this morning for this evening's performance". This became his *Serenade and Allegro Giocoso*, Op. 43. In 1841 he published his Op. 54 *Variations sérieuses*. Though he had written to Hiller of composing a similar work in the same style, Klingemann was informed that, as Felix liked that first piece so much, he would compose "a further set in E flat and another in B flat".

When Davison apprised Mendelssohn that his Piano Trio Op. 49 was to open a concert, Felix begged MacFarren to ensure that an Erard piano would be made available. In this connection Felix wrote to Moscheles that, after five years of performing on his own Erard, on tour and at home, "owing to frequent shiftings and, possibly, some bad treatment, the instrument is not fit for use either at public recitals or private entertainments. I want an instrument with a perfectly even and precise tone. Though the tone has maintained its original power and beauty, I shall be pleased for the defective parts and the mechanism to be put to rights, as I believe no sacrifice too great to preserve an instrument with such a splendid tone." Though Chopin preferred the more delicate tone of a Pleyel piano, other musicians, such as Liszt, Verdi and Wagner, employed Erard pianos in their later years, which leads it to be suspected that Mendelssohn set the fashion.

It was not only as a soloist that Mendelssohn excelled. From youth he and Fanny entertained with piano improvisations at Leipzigerstrasse 3. As Felix Moscheles wrote in his father's biography: "The two elder children performed all manner of musical extravagances, jointly or severally, on two pianos, to the mystification and amazement of their father" (but no mention is made of praise from Leah or Abraham).

During his first visit to England, in 1829, Mendelssohn's uncle Nathan had asked if his nephew would help to raise funds for flood relief in Silesia, where he lived. A grand concert was therefore arranged, one of whose items was a concerto for two pianos by Moscheles. Reporting the rehearsal, which Charlotte Moscheles and 'Herr Collard', the piano manufacturer, attended, Felix "had a heavenly time of it with the piano arrangement. I padded, stitched in sleeves *à la* Mameluke, and tailored a brilliant concerto." Felix wrote the tutti for the full orchestra; Moscheles composed the cadenza. (The full purport of the concert is given in Chapter 29, 'The special relationship'.)

On 1st June 1832 Mendelssohn, on his second visit to London, joined Moscheles once more in Mozart's Concerto for Two Pianos. "Each pianist introduced his own cadenza," related *The Harmonicon*, "with musical skill and execution that certainly none in the present day could surpass, and very few would dream of rivalling." A year later, at the newly renovated Hanover Square Rooms in Regent Street, the two musicians entertained with a piano duet composed of themes from Weber's opera *Preciosa*, based on Cervantes's novel *The Gypsy Girl*. The staid *Morning Post* recorded "rapturous plaudits" from the audience, but Moscheles's son, (and Mendelssohn's godson) Felix Moscheles's recollections are far more worthy of repeating: "Like a ball, an idea would be tossed and caught, hurled boldly into the air; delicately suspended by one; recaptured by the other, analysed, dissected, then, perhaps, carried off triumphantly into other worlds, in a new form, by the four hands, often sounding like...one soul. Though sometimes they stumbled, they would quickly retrieve the situation. They reached around, amongst and into each other's fingers."

But neither Moscheles nor Fanny were the only duettists with whom Mendelssohn performed. George Sampson recalled how, in 1840, Sterndale Bennett and the host amused the other guests. "The two began to romp like schoolboys at the piano. The simple duet was woven into a brilliant fantasia around a melody set to a poem by Heine about Jack Frost and the flowers dancing like fairies." Back in London, for his eighth visit, a real extravaganza took place, when Mendelssohn and Moscheles joined with Sigismund Thalberg in one of Bach's Concerto for Three Keyboards. Since this virtuoso pianist was unaccustomed to perform in any other guise than as a soloist, Mendelssohn was able to shine even more than usual. For his cadenza he improvised on six songs that Mme. Malibran had made her own. "Beginning softly," Charles Horsley later wrote in *The Choir* magazine, "he ended with a hurricane of notes. The cadenza lasted a full five minutes", which the unimaginative Stratton dismisses as "an exaggeration". Yet Horsley claimed that he did not exaggerate when writing of Mendelssohn's talent. "His mastery at the piano was little short of miraculous. His powers of execution were quite as great as those of Rubinstein or Liszt; his touch and tone not exceeded by Thalberg or Chopin... I do not in the least exaggerate when I assert that, of all pianoforte players before and since his time, Mendelssohn stands by far at the apex of greatness." But, Horsley continued, Felix was equally superlative as an organist: "Many happy afternoons were spent in hearing his interpretation of Bach's fugues. His wonderful extemporisations and...his own sonatas and other organ pieces still existing in his memory... I have heard most of the greatest organists of my time – English, German and French – but in no respect have I ever known Mendelssohn excelled, either in creative or executive ability... His feet were equally as active as his hands and...produced a result which, at that time, was quite unknown in England,

and undoubtedly laid the foundation for a school of organ playing...that...placed English organists on the highest point attainable in their profession."

Later critics have dismissed Mendelssohn's organ works as imitating those of the 18th century, but have they listened carefully enough to the scope of harmonies that earlier composers did not create? Stratton compares several organists favourably with Mendelssohn. These include Rinck, Adolf Hasse, Julius André, Thomas Adams and Samuel Wesley. To the lay enthusiast of organ playing, only the latter is remembered today – and erudite organ scholars may also care to argue this statement. Neither is it known what mechanical skills these favourites of Stratton possessed, but the contrary is true of Mendelssohn. From boyhood Felix had an uncanny knowledge of how an organ worked, how it was constructed, and what was right or wrong. From August 1820 Zelter arranged for August Wilhelm Bach, a member of the Singakademie, but not related to the illustrious Bach family, to give lessons to the 11-year-old Mendelssohn. Written "on the third day of the lovely month of May" 1821, Felix wrote to 'Herr Bach' promising to be at the tower "punctually at four with my sister, as you permitted, unless the appointment may not be kept on account of a wedding or confirmation". From Weimar Felix informed his parents that an organ he saw (and might have played), "though larger, with 50 ranks, 44 stops, and a 32-foot pedal", was "weaker and less powerful" than the one at St Mary's Church in Berlin. In 1822, whilst on a family holiday in Switzerland, he wrote to Zelter of having played organs at Apfensell and Zug: the latter was "in the worst possible condition, but delightful"; that at Berne Cathedral was "a truly great instrument, with 53 stops, several of 15 feet in the manual, 32 in the pedal, and eight bellows, which, however, leak and often make the old organ sing; also, two pipes on the 16-foot principal rattle together murderously". At Bulle, in the canton of Freiburg, he found the organ "in very good condition, with only one fault: the pedal reached to the high A only, as the B and C are missing, so nothing of Bach's can be played on it, despite its 28 stops and two manuals. All the stops work, because Messer, the [organ] builder, lives in the town. The man, who has completed his 64th assignment in Geneva, dresses like a peasant, with his pale grey coat and large shoes."

In Chapter 6, 'Young musicians', Felix's vacation at the Baltic resort of Bad Doberan is described, but it is appropriate here to add an interesting anecdote. At Breslau, during that vacation, Schima Kaufman relates, Felix's uncle, Nathan Mendelssohn, paid the organist eight groschen to allow his nephew to play the instrument. When in 1829, therefore, the family were asked to help with funds for the flood relief in Silesia, it was Felix's guilty conscience that caused him to plan his London concert (cited in Chapter 29, 'A special relationship', and the present chapter).

On Mendelssohn's last visit to Weimar, in 1830, Goethe arranged for him to play the cathedral organ. Zelter had apprised him of the repairs, which had been made to a higher standard than any other instrument to his knowledge. "The pedal pipe is fitted deep into its housing," Felix confirmed. "The full organ sounds mighty and strong; the tone does not tremble in the least, proving that there must be plenty of wind. The pedal is in perfect proportion to the manual and there is no lack of beautiful, soft voices of various pitches." Asked by the organist to choose "something scholarly and something for the public", having himself chosen the more complex repertoire, he admitted to Zelter that "this was nothing to be proud of. The available pieces had enough modulations to make one giddy, but [there was] nothing unusual."

He played Bach's D minor Toccata, remarking that "this was popular but, at the same time, scholarly". A manservant asked Mendelssohn to cease playing, "since my employer could not study as required on a weekday". This anecdote amused Goethe when his guest repeated it.

At St Peter's Church in Munich Felix wrote to Zelter of "intending to practise footwork in a few Bach fugues, about which the bearer of this letter will be able to tell you more". But it was not always the case that Mendelssohn's recitals gave him contentment. At Kalkbrenner's rooms in Paris, when asked to play, the Bach preludes he chose were pronounced "wonderfully pretty" and one, in A minor, reminded his audience of an aria from a Monsigny opera: "Everything went green and blue before my eyes". It is worth asking if Mendelssohn was colour-blind, since it is far more usual to 'see red' when angry, whereas green or blue are regarded as soothing, restful colours.

Church organs played an equally important part in Mendelssohn's 1831 visit to Switzerland. At Engelberg he had heard the monks "intoning nocturnes with a splendid, deep-sounding B [that resonated] down the valley". Having been invited to play for a service, he wrote to Zelter: "The first two pieces went rather well." He was accompanied by monks "playing a double bass and violins. An old, decayed rustic played an old, decayed oboe. At a distance, two more puffed contentedly at two large trumpets with large tassels. The cantor sang a solo, conducting with a stick as thick as my arm. It is impossible not to like these people, for they play with plenty of zeal." Having been asked to play a congregation in and out of church on another occasion, "I played a march repugnant to me," Felix reported to Zelter. The monks asked for a private recital, at which Felix played a fantasia, "but, sadly, I could not recall the piece enough to convert it into musical notation" for his former mentor's benefit. "Though the monks know nothing of Bach, it was the first time I got my hands on a decent instrument."

It seems appropriate to mention whilst discussing Switzerland that it would be there, in 1847, that Mendelssohn bade farewell to his organ playing. He had discovered an organ in an old church at Ringberg near Interlaken, to which he and Chorley, who was visiting Mendelssohn, journeyed by boat. The church was empty except for a peasant boy, whom Chorley and Mendelssohn persuaded (with a few coins, no doubt) to blow the bellows for the recital to begin. "I could not help contrasting this occasion with the last time I had heard him playing to an audience of thousands at Exeter Hall" in London. "Listening to the long, rich chains of sound, I was reminded of words by Milton: 'Such sound could bring all heaven before the eyes.' Such things must come to an end," Chorley prophesied.

Mendelssohn had described Sargans as "a wretched hole", but Julius Rietz had told him of a "fabulous" organ that he had the opportunity to play. From Saarn he wrote to Professor Werden that "the organist's wife gave me a glass of schnapps [and] explained that her husband had so many enemies, who did not wish him to continue in that post. She hoped that, through his own judgement, I would prove him wrong. Like Solomon, I could have put to shame all those talkers; wrangling and discord are to be found everywhere." On reaching that church Felix found that the organ had been built at great expense, "but there was no way of reaching it, except by dark, narrow stairs". On asking the reason for such poor access, Mendelssohn was told: "No one could run up from the church to see the organ. One's neck could be broken in several places; neither was there any window, and, to me, it resembled a poultry yard. If the church authorities were so cautious about security, would a lock and key not have made better sense?"

On honeymoon in the Rhineland Mendelssohn composed three organ pieces that he soon aimed to publish: "I hope that one, or even two or three, will be particularly well received." These were eventually included in his Op. 37, comprising various preludes and fugues written between 1833 and 1839, dedicated to Sir Thomas Attwood, organist of St Paul's Cathedral and a former pupil of Mozart. At a similar time, Felix asked Fanny to find a piece he had composed for her wedding: "I need it, as I have promised an English publisher a whole book of organ pieces, and, as I was writing out one after another, that old one suddenly recurred to me. I love the beginning, but detest the end and I am completely rewriting it with another choral fugue, but I should like to compare it with the original."

During his correspondence with Coventry's, the publishers to whom he had promised these organ pieces, he was able to send some Bach fugues to England. He considered that, out of the 59 extant, only nine were known as yet to English musicians. Of his own work, Mendelssohn published what have become known as his Organ Sonatas, Op. 65, written between 1839 and 1845. The term 'sonata' was used because Felix did not know what the often used English term 'voluntary' meant. Reference books state that the term implies ability to play the given piece before, during or after divine service. Scholes adds that the organist can improvise or extemporise on an original theme and be free to use the piece for a special occasion or for a normal service. In Frankfurt, whilst staying with Cécile's family, Felix not only composed but practised, writing to Fanny that his pedalling was "becoming more tolerable". Fanny was asked to study the Riedel edition of Bach's fugues, "especially the one in G major. Natural and simple as these are, I feel quite in love with them and played them over at least 50 times yesterday. How the left hand glides and turns, but how gently it dies away towards the close. It [the G major Fugue] pleases me beyond all others."

Though Felix had, throughout his musical life, applied his gifts to raise funds for good causes, one of his own dreams came true on 21st April 1843, when the Bach monument was erected in Leipzig. Mendelssohn gave two organ recitals at the Church of St Thomas, where Bach himself had been Kapellmeister. Of the first, Schumann wrote that "letters of gold would be required to describe it appropriately". He continued: "How well Mendelssohn understands the treatment of Bach's royal instrument. Many may have reflected on the wonderful sounds,

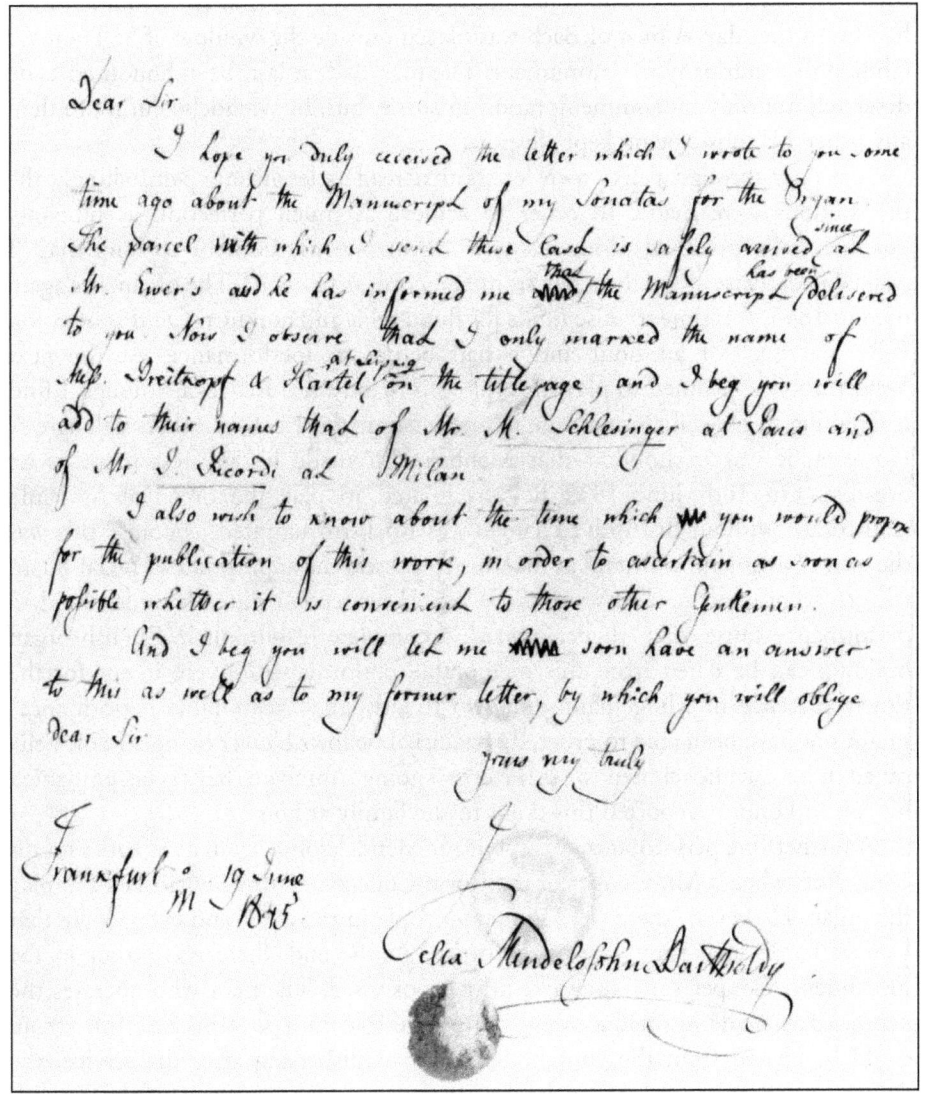

Figure 7. Letter from Felix to Charles Coventry, 1845

thinking that there is nothing greater in music and the two-fold mastery displayed when one musician gives expression to another's work. Fame and honour to young and old – Mendelssohn and Bach alike." By contrast, it is amusing to repeat what Mme. Elise Polko had to say about the recitals given by her hero. "Sacred awe pervaded the souls of the hearers and tears rushed to the eyes of those who had long since ceased to weep. It was no wonder-musician giving the concert, but Bach himself." The elderly critic Rocklitz embraced Mendelssohn, declaring, like Simeon, when Jesus of Nazareth was presented to him in the temple, that he, too, was now prepared for his soul to depart in peace, having experienced such a superlative performance. He would not hear anything "so fine and sublime" as he had heard that day. A bust of Bach was placed outside the window of St Thomas's Church to accompany the monument. The man had, at last, been honoured as he deserved, not only by commemoration in stone, but, by Mendelssohn more than any other, his music being kept alive.

It is only through Felix's own letters that readers learn how painstakingly the preparations were made. In order to achieve as much perfection as humanly possible, Felix practised assiduously, sitting in one position for so long that "I walked pedal-wise along the street from St Thomas's Church". The organ was again used in 1845, this time to raise funds for flood relief in Frankfurt. On this occasion Felix practised for an hour and a half before his performance. At the next opportunity he planned to play his Op. 65 to Fanny and Rebecka, "though I find it fatiguing to play all six at a time in one session, and I believe others will agree". However, it was in London that Mendelssohn made his greatest mark as an organist. On 10th June 1833 he was invited to play the organ at St Paul's Cathedral, "without disruptive changes", as Rockstro narrated, "because this was the only instrument in Britain at the time to possess the appropriate G pedal-board (sic) to accommodate Bach's works. So much excitement did this unusual aid to performance cause, that, thenceforward, a complete revolution in English organ building can be dated from this memorable performance." Were it not for the timely presence of Klingemann and two friends, the "memorable performance" might not have been able to proceed. The usual bellows blower being absent, Felix called in his own henchmen to set the organ going. Abraham, having accompanied his son to London, reported this event to the family at home.

A further fine performance was spoilt for Mendelssohn, again at St Paul's on his 1837 visit, when a Mr. Cooper of the Royal College of Arms invited Felix to play the organ. However, "there were so many people in the choir and everywhere that I could hardly make my way to the organ. At the end, there was no air in the instrument. Cooper runs away like a man possessed. The man who operates the bellows also made himself scarce – the beadle told him to – because not a soul could be chased from the church. Rather than dispersing after the service, the congregation increased." Mendelssohn commented on the "spirit of the English public"; the English words 'spirit' and 'public' were incongruously mixed into the otherwise German text of his letter home. "There was a tremendous outcry, as if something really important had happened. From all corners could be heard cries of 'shame' when the organ could no longer function. Three or four clergymen gave the beadles what for in front of all the people, and Cooper cursed also" (having presumably returned to the scene). Mendelssohn described the beadles and other church officials as "the gentlemen who walk about in bombazine gowns".

But the most rewarding experiences for Mendelssohn during his London visits must have been his recitals at Christ Church, Newgate Street in the City. In 1837 he had the privilege of meeting Samuel Wesley, known as the 'father of English organists', who happened to be in the congregation. Barely a month would elapse before this veteran would pass away, on 11th October of that year. Wesley praised Mendelssohn's technique as demonstrating "a purity and originality of thought". The church possessed a newly built organ, for which Hill & Company of London were responsible, the construction of which was supervised by John Gauntlett. Organist at Westminster Abbey and a lawyer by profession, Gauntlett was a prime mover in English organ building. His treatise on organ technique was reproduced in the 15th September issue of *Music and Letters* for 1837, but his ultimate claim to fame, according to the reference books, is having composed "at least 10,000 hymn tunes".

Like the organ at St Paul's Cathedral, that at Christ Church had a C pedal, and this innovation would be built into the new organ at Birmingham's town hall. When visiting the 'second city' that year, where *St Paul* was to be performed at the Birmingham Festival, Mendelssohn naturally gave a recital on the new instrument. His repertoire included Bach's Fugue in E flat, based on the hymn tune known as 'St Anne', which Stratton believes to have been the first occasion for a Birmingham audience to hear a work by that composer. Rockstro wrote that Felix also included an extemporisation on themes from Handel's *Solomon* and "a concerto by Mozart" (presumably at the piano).

During his 1840 visit to London Mendelssohn gave a recital at another new organ, this time at St Peter's, Cornhill, as well as repeating his earlier triumph at Christ Church, Newgate Street. Recitals at City churches were repeated in 1842. On one occasion he wrote home: "They have asked a little too much of me... I thought for a few moments that I would suffocate, so great was the crowd and the pressure around my bench at the organ. Then, too, several days later, I had to play at Exeter Hall before 3,000 people, who shouted 'Hurrah' and waved their handkerchiefs and stamped their feet till the hall quaked. At that moment I felt no bad effects, but next morning my head was dizzy and I felt that I had had a sleepless night." At St Paul's Cathedral Felix was intrigued when the congregation sang a hymn "to Haydn's tune". Originally derived from Haydn's 'Emperor' string Quartet, Op. 76, No. 3, Austria adopted the tune as her national hymn, later to be appropriated by Germany.

As far as English congregations were concerned, the most likely words

Mendelssohn would have heard would have been 'Glorious Things of Thee are Spoken', or 'Praise the Lord! Ye Heavens, adore Him'. After the service Felix used this fine tune, sometimes still known as 'Austria', as an improvisation. Four days later he employed the same melody "to extemporise a long and elaborate fugue". Rockstro continued: "The piece began with a long treble A on the organ swell that developed into the most ingenious and delightful harmony, gliding through G sharp to G, to F sharp. Sitting at the eastern end of the building I whispered to Vincent Novello that it must be a cipher that must mean something, with which Novello agreed." But only Mendelssohn could have provided the answer to this puzzle, had there actually been one. Felix became very irritated when anyone tried to "read something" into his compositions that was not there.

Evidently, church ambiences appear not to have suited Mendelssohn's constitution, for Rockstro accused the crowd of having had the "bad taste" to press into "the limited space of the organ loft". Felix was obliged to cease in mid-flow, in order to get some air. "Having recovered, though still looking pale, he joked with his friends: 'You thought it was a cipher; I know you did.'"

On 5th May 1847, during Mendelssohn's tenth and final visit to London, he played at a concert sponsored by Prince Albert. Included in the repertoire was "a fugue on the name 'Bach'", the B flat representing 'H' in German musical notation. No further details are given, except that Stratton decries the organ as "wretched and out of tune". Despite this, however, Chorley wrote in *The Athenaeum* that the recital was "one of the marvels of the season". The next day Felix paid his last visit to Buckingham Palace and played "for two hours" to the royal family.

Not only was Mendelssohn a genius, but he was full of praise for fellow musicians who warranted such admiration. Of Frederick Gunton, organist at Chester Cathedral, Felix declared him to have had "a touch like velvet". Many other examples can be cited, as may be observed throughout these chapters. There are far too many eulogies by people of sound judgement, when discussing not only his piano and organ playing but also his accomplishment on the violin and other instruments, to be dismissed as false. But Stratton is still dissatisfied. He maintains that it was nothing more than his "magnetic personality that riveted audiences to him". To this often pompous biographer it is "often difficult to rekindle enthusiasm [for Mendelssohn's achievements]. The many stories recorded need not be retold in this biography." Fortunately, readers are free to judge for themselves regarding Mendelssohn as a soloist – and, indeed, every other aspect of his musical, and personal, life.

Chapter 21

"A Handel and a Half"

This was the phrase Hector Berlioz coined to describe Mendelssohn as a composer of sacred music, not only his two complete oratorios, *St Paul* and *Elijah*, but the many smaller pieces that flowed from his pen throughout his lifetime. Under Zelter's supervision, Felix was given a thorough grounding in music for religious occasions. Joining the Berlin Singakademie, with Fanny, in 1820 as an alto, he transferred in 1824 to the tenor section and began to conduct the choir. On 31st March 1828 Haydn's *Creation* was performed, to be followed by Bach's *St Matthew Passion* on 15th April and Graun's oratorio *Jesus* on the 20th. But this was never enough for Mendelssohn. As Leon Botstein points out, "Mendelssohn's sacred music was written to demonstrate, and prove, his love of God, which, as a true believer, he wanted to share", without turning people away by ramming religion down anyone's throat, or bragging of his faith. Felix himself added an ancillary reason for his choice of compositions in this genre: "to purify and restore the public taste" in sacred music. Mendelssohn was no religious prig. To Pastor Bauer he confided: "Aesthetic [and, he could have added, theological] discourses make me silent and dejected." Through music, Felix found a way of communicating widely, but, as Botstein states, "with rare insight, immediacy and intensity. He did not wish to create distance between his audience and performers and himself, but won their trust through affection, lightness, refinement and clarity." This is still noticeable today, when the dictates of fashion do not hold sway to prevent Mendelssohn's sacred music from being performed or recordings made.

Regularly, Mendelssohn's sacred music appeared in the repertoire of the Singakademie. When that august institution moved to new premises in 1827, his Te Deum was premiered; in 1828 *Tu es Petrus* was performed, and, a year later, *Hora est*. Having heard a performance of this work in Berlin, a journalist, 'J. T.', reported in the 23rd November 1829 issue of *Harmonicon* that the motet was "of intense interest and delight". From Rome Felix wrote to his family of having composed the motet *Mittel Wir im Leben Sind*: "It either growls angrily or whistles darkly." This warning might have been given because he anticipated what Abraham would think of the piece (No. 3 of his Op. 23, Three Sacred Pieces). Having heard the *Ave Maria*, No. 1 of this set, Felix received his father's verdict: "Too learned and complex". According to Abraham, such an opinion was borne out on hearing a performance at the family home, when even Rebecka was "confused" as the piece was "too abstrusely modulated". Abraham's final onslaught was that Felix's music "did not accord with the simple, pious spirit of the words". Mendelssohn's response can only be regarded as almost saintly in the forbearance he showed. Having had "long familiarity" with the setting, his father, after "one indifferent performance", had "taught me the truth". In other words, Felix allowed his father to think himself right in his judgements. Fortunately, if ever his *Ave Maria* is heard, others can appreciate the progressive harmonies and subtle cadences of the work. Another Mendelssohn composition of the same period that is even less often heard was his setting of the Lutheran chorale *Vom Himmel Hoch*. Whereas settings are heard from earlier composers at Christmas, that of Mendelssohn is virtually ignored.

Like his grandfather, psalms played a vital part in Felix's life. Just as Moses translated some of these into German from the original Hebrew, his grandson made new and highly individual settings of these poems. Of Psalm 2, published posthumously with Psalms 22 and 43 in his Op. 78, Fanny wrote the following to Rebecka: "I wonder what will be said about the music – that is, if people listen at all… He smuggles in part-singing with the least notice from officials [in Berlin]. A man of such moral influence may even improve the taste of these Philistines and blockheads." When the setting was performed, it was spoilt for Fanny by the sermon given by Pastor Strauss, which she called "miserable beyond description", adding: "Perhaps Felix ought to preach as well as compose and conduct, but this is too much to expect." Of the sermon she had heard, she commented that "it is futile to expect perfection when the priest has no sense".

An eccentric Englishman, Charles Bayles Broadley, hoped to publish privately a metrical version of the psalms. To this end, he asked Moscheles, his teacher, to act as intermediary between Mendelssohn and himself in order that Felix receive a commission to write settings for Psalms 13, 100 and 126. In a letter of 20th December 1840 Felix stated that, though unfamiliar with the Anglican service, his work on Psalm 13 "gave me greater pleasure than I anticipated", and asked permission for the German translation to be published simultaneously with the English original. On 9th February of the following year Moscheles was able to tell Felix that his pupil had received "joy and special pleasure at the noble, self-controlled, pure and sacred presentation". Particularly did Broadley like the way Felix had set the words "weak and fainting" for the contralto to sing. The music built up into a climax in which the choir joined. Broadley and his wife were "moved to rapture" at its first performance and hoped that a second one would take place "in York Cathedral".

Charlotte Moscheles found Broadley's manner "a fussy, meddlesome annoyance," explaining how "no paper is too fine; no engraver too good, and he constantly plagues my husband with this edition". Evidently, Felix had to restrain himself when declining to add a short, introductory prelude. "But, with the best will in the world, I could not write a short prelude to suit the piece without altering the whole form and giving it a pretentious colouring it should not have. I would rather leave it to the organist to tumble his fingers around at random, making it as long or short as he likes, and as rich or poor as he can manage." The letter in which Broadley had requested the prelude has been described as "comical and one of the numerous documents bearing witness to his half-deranged nature". It is therefore hardly surprising, given so much trouble, that Mendelssohn wrote to Simrock, on 4th March 1841, to negotiate publication of the German text independently of Broadley's requirements. Though Spohr and Moscheles set the remaining psalms for Broadley, this persistent gentleman had not finished with Mendelssohn.

On 18th November 1842, in answer to an offer of ten guineas to write an orchestral accompaniment to Psalm 13, he agreed to "try to fit an orchestral dress onto the piece and, if I succeed, will send it to you without delay". A fugal finale was added, which Felix described as "the best piece of the whole". When the work was completed on 5th January 1843, Leah's death having delayed the matter, Broadley described it as "exceedingly beautiful", adding that "it is often performed at the command of Her Majesty at the Chapel Royal, Windsor", (Moscheles having arranged the orchestral accompaniment for the organ.) Still not satisfied, Broadley requested Felix "to write on a piece of paper about the size of this note[paper] a few bars for a lady's autograph album". Mendelssohn granted this request, at the same time telling Broadley that his fugue was a gift.

Length has been given to this saga to show just how painstaking and caring Mendelssohn was when dealing with commissions, however obscure or how much of a nuisance his patron was. The same may be applied to the motet *Hear my Prayer*, based on Psalm 55. As early as 1840 Mendelssohn declared himself to have been "haunted" by the words. "The noble language of the scriptures...seems to call for an appropriate setting." But it was not until four years had passed that the motet came into existence. It was William Bartholomew, who was to write the English text for *Elijah*, who was responsible for the paraphrase of Psalm 55. Miss Ann Mounsey, whom Bartholomew married, made the work popular via her sacred music concerts at Crosby Hall in the City of London. The second half, beginning 'O for the Wings of a Dove', has become particularly popular when trebles warble this air, with their mothers, aunts and grandmas drooling over how 'yootifully' their relative caterwauled and screeched through it. Mendelssohn composed it for a mature female soprano, after all! Ruskin felt it his duty, whilst lecturing on Sir Joshua Reynolds, to digress, in 1857, accusing an Oxford chorister of "having the face and voice of an angel, but no handkerchief". Not only is the woman's voice able to express self-assurance when singing the solo; through her maturity – experience of life – she is able to give the proper interpretation and feeling to the work, far more than can a pre-pubescent treble. In 1846 Felix wrote to Moscheles of setting 'Lauda Sion' (Psalm 64) to music for the forthcoming Liège Festival. It is worth commenting on Mendelssohn's unbiased spirit for religion, since he never confined himself to the Lutheran faith alone. For instance, the Council of Trent had allowed Thomas Aquinas's paraphrase to be used in Roman Catholic services when it met between 1343 and 1363. (Further reference is made to the actual performance in Chapter 19, 'Conductor and director'.) Stratton considers Mendelssohn's psalm settings "important", but particularly does he like Psalm 114. "It reaches the height of creativity in its loftiness, as with his other eight-part choral works." But, for whatever reason, probably self-doubt, Mendelssohn's works from his Op. 78 to Op. 121 were not published until after his death. Amongst these was his Op. 96, Hymn for contralto, chorus and organ. Though the vocal arrangement had been available since 1843 the organ accompaniment, which takes the form of a three-part canon, was not published until 1852.

Mendelssohn composed settings for the Anglican service (posthumously published as part of Op. 111 and 121). At first he appeared diffident, in a letter to Novello about his Te Deum, having "never composed anything" for the Anglican Church. Was the commission still required and what fee was charged by English composers for such works? He believed the Te Deum was "not unworthy of being published", although any future pieces would be "better". Were it not for his asking about Novello's family, Felix "would not venture to give you the trouble of reading so bad an English as this is," he wrote. It was, in fact, Ewers who published the work, asking their Edward Buxton if a copy could be sent to Novello, who had requested one "by a curious coincidence". "There must not be a German translation made of this piece... It is written for your own service," Buxton was apprised. "If they wish to do so on their own account, I cannot help it, but I will not authorise publication by...any...publisher in Germany. If there are faults in the English words or musical accents, I wish you to correct them. But first...can I say 'English Service' on the title-page, or must it be 'Service for the English Church?'" As a matter of interest, the fee for Mendelssohn's Te Deum, together with his Op. 66 Trio, was £30.

When discussing *St Paul*, one of its best analyses would appear to be an article, written for a performance of 1872, by George Grove, reproduced in early editions of his *Dictionary of Music and Musicians*. For Kupferberg, the oratorio pays homage to Bach's *St Matthew Passion*, but is "toned down and easier to take, the dramatic element diluted; the rugged mass smoothed away". The passages of character and nobility in *St Paul* "cause it to deserve a better fate than the oblivion into which it is consigned" when Kupferberg's book was published. Blunt, however, considers dramatic opportunities to have been missed. What, he conjectures, could not have been made when Paul and Silas escaped from prison, or of the trial at Caesarea? Blunt deprecates the influence of Bach and Handel, though admitting that "both critics and the public enjoyed the female voices and woodwind instruments in the words 'Saul, why persecutest thou me?'" Conversely, Charles Horsley considered

Chapter 21: "A Handel and a Half"

that there had been "no opportunity for dramatic treatment", except "the raving of the Jews, the taunts of Stephen and the outpourings of Paul". To Horsley, the oratorio revealed "a stern, uncompromising, early Christian colouring". He continued that "the dramatic tendency of Elijah will remain the chief secret of his [Mendelssohn's] popularity. The whole oratorio might be placed on the stage with the greatest propriety, with scenery, costumes and dramatic action." Horsley's observations give a clue to Mendelssohn's own feelings on his two completed oratorios, and it has been agreed by many critics that, as well as having greater dramatic potential, *Elijah* is "true Mendelssohn". The listener can tell how comfortable the composer feels with the work, whereas *St Paul* is another matter entirely.

No one has yet explained why, when writing his first oratorio, Mendelssohn suffered such depression, but a plausible reason may be easily understood. Though Felix would not have dared admit the fact, even to himself, *St Paul* was a 'duty' work, to placate and mollify his earthly father, composing other sacred works for his spiritual creator. To Julius Schubring Felix wrote "a half-dry and serious letter but, such has been the character of this present period, and so, to a certain extent, I have grown like it". He posed various queries to the theologian, whose text Mendelssohn was originally to set to music. He wished, for instance, to include a chorale in the scene with Ananias, but had been dissuaded "by various people", notably Adolf Bernhard Marx. Nevertheless he asked Schubring to supply "all the hymns and passages" that related to Paul's life and teaching "in order to enter fully into the spirit of the words, and the music will then follow". He expressed anxiety that "the oratorio will be in character with, and based upon, the New Testament". Originally, Stratton states, Devrient was asked to help with the text but, "unable to cope", he declined.

Therefore, in July 1834 Schubring was informed that he had made "the best suggestions I have yet received…little by little, things have come into the same order as I find them in the Bible. That remains, after all, the best way." Felix hoped to have finished *St Paul* by the following year, 1835. He even read a history of Christianity when studying the text, taking it with him whilst riding or rambling, "poring over it, even oblivious of the rain". He studied Greek history in order to familiarise himself with the period in which Paul had lived. Still not satisfied, he discussed the work with a canon at Cologne Cathedral, whilst searching for early music to be performed at his Düsseldorf concerts. He began to work on the project "that very morning, taking up my Bible in the disorder of my room. I soon became so engrossed that I could hardly force myself to finish the other projects that I absolutely had to complete first."

Though Felix promised to let Schubring know in the following spring as to how the oratorio was progressing, "some compositional problems came up that really bothered me," he reported. Yet, though Mendelssohn blamed himself for his delay, he was not the only tardy correspondent. "It was hardly right of you not to notify me, in a short letter or a postcard," he wrote angrily about the new addition to Schubring's family. "I received news of the birth third-hand. Still, a pastor such as yourself is hardly allowed to take vengeance or hold a grudge," Felix joked, "though I well deserve such lack of communication." Felix likewise enabled himself to jest with the Horsley family about a Handel festival they had attended at Westminster Abbey between 24th and 28th June of that year. He commented on "the 40 voices that sounded like 14" and the "trombonisation" of Handel's music, "as if the composer himself did not know enough about instrumentation. I can imagine the gentleman usher carrying a white staff, wearing a red riband and, indeed, a white costume." As for his own work, Felix had "not included any trombones, and only two of the choruses have any trumpets. Thus, I shall become an enemy of Birmingham's brassware industry and a friend of invalid trombonists." Meanwhile, "there are two piles of music paper on my writing table, one blank, the other comprising the completed score. I hope to have the work [*St Paul*] finished by May [1835], when I will visit England for a month or longer." But Mendelssohn's proposed visit did not take place for a further two years.

Despite this show of light-heartedness, Felix still felt obliged to seek his father's advice on the oratorio. He believed an explanation was required as to why Paul did not appear in the scene where Stephen was stoned to death. He was determined to adhere to the text of the Acts of the Apostles, in which none of Paul's words appear. A further rebuke by Abraham was answered similarly: though the original text was long, a recitative did not last more than two minutes, and the whole section, including the choruses, "should last no more than a quarter of an hour". However, at the end of Paul's conversion, Felix mollified his father: "The music becomes more and more difficult, though the words are fewer." This may well have stemmed from Mendelssohn's feeling of unease with that subject, compared, say, with the stoning of Stephen, in which he really comes into his own. Saul of Tarsus, after all, accepted the tenets of Christianity without apparent demur, whereas Felix and his siblings were never given such a choice, Uncle Jakob Bartholdy having thrust the idea of conversion upon Felix's parents for a purely materialistic, not a spiritual, reason. However subconsciously, or convincingly, he might have denied it, Mendelssohn's representation of Stephen being stoned to death might well have been a demonstration of his own anger at having been forbidden to practise as a Jew, and – what is more – to have had to embrace another faith for the wrong motives.

On 20th July Felix acknowledged a text from Ignaz Fürst, reminding him that "the Scriptures are simpler, shorter and more condensed" than the words presented to him. However, tactful as ever, Felix expressed gratitude for Fürst "preparing the ground that allowed me to begin". On 4th November Felix wrote to the family that he would like someone to hear the oratorio as far as it had been completed. Though friends had approved, Fanny, "with her thick eyebrows and criticisms", should give her opinion of the work. "The first part is completed; the second part is in my head

Chapter 21: "A Handel and a Half"

up to the point where Paul is thought to be Jupiter and the people wish to offer him sacrifices." Even though the work would be ready for performance at Frankfurt and the Lower Rhine Festival at Düsseldorf in 1836, Felix was still dissatisfied and continued to work on the score, "because I propose to publish it in as perfect a form as possible". Though he considered the beginning of the first part and the end of part two " three times as good as before", he had worked on the oratorio for two years and would be "more than glad when I can work on something else". He thanked Rebecka for her praise, "the dearest and best that I can ever hear", and his audiences concurred. Perhaps this quest for perfection was to pay tribute to Abraham, who had died in December 1835.

To Spohr Felix wrote that the piano arrangement of *St Paul* was "one of the most tedious tasks I have ever had to undertake and have often been beside myself over the tiresome and imperceptible progress I have made, despite my best intentions. But, now that the whole work, up to the final chorus, is out of the stable – or, rather, into the printer's – I hope I shall be finished with the thing." To his family he admitted: "How glad I shall be that something therein pleases you. Do you think father would have found it agreeable? You should tell me." To Moscheles Felix confided "how the task of revision is beginning to weigh heavily upon me, yet I wish to make the whole of the oratorio as good as the best parts and to have my ideas as clearly expressed as possible. I am more and more attracted to other work and wish I could look back on the oratorio as finally completed." He would have liked, for example, to write "a few symphonies during the next few years", as well as to satisfy his late father's craving for an opera to be produced – an obsession that would forever plague Felix's conscience.

Fanny travelled with Paul's wife Albertine to Düsseldorf to hear the premiere of *St Paul*, and she wrote in her journal how her brother had "struck the right note" with Bach's chorale 'Sleepers wake!', declaring this introductory item "a great stroke of wit". She found the scene of Paul's conversion "so beautiful; so surprising; so touching that I know nothing in music to equal it". (Even the precious Bach came into that category, it appears.) "The noise and applause were so tremendous that I believe, had mother been present, she could not have borne the emotion." With regard to his use of female voices to represent God, "Had not The Acts mentioned female missionaries as having spread God's word?" Felix responded. "I must make no mistake in employing this text to the letter as far as humanly possible."

Critics have argued that the stoning of Stephen was given too much attention in act one. Mendelssohn explained that, in view of the fact that this took place, as well as the martyrdom of Paul, he had followed the Scriptures meticulously and that both were therefore portrayed, irrespective of how well or badly his audiences could tolerate repetition of these events. "What a pity it is," he wrote to Schleinitz, "that you were not present to witness the love and goodwill of the audience and the wonderful fire of the performers. Yet," he added, "there were individual passages, especially in the solos, that might have annoyed you. I can imagine your face through the mechanical manner of one indifferently executed aria and your breaking forth with a dressing down on hearing 'the Apostles of the Gentiles'." Schleinitz would have been "charmed" at the only chorale and "thrilled at the spontaneous applause". Felix reiterated his wish to strive for the best, on thinking of his father. "I will endeavour to place myself in the listeners' minds. Many parts caused me so much pleasure; others, not so much; but [I] learnt a lesson from it all and hope to succeed the next time I write an oratorio."

After a performance in Leipzig Schubring suggested that the voice of the man taking the part of Christ was "too thin" and that the phrase 'Why persecutest thou me?' should be sung by a four-part chorus, with which Felix agreed. "After looking at me for a long time," Schubring wrote, "he said: 'Yes, and the worthy theologians would cut me up nicely, for wishing to deny and supplant Him who rules from the Dead'." Schubring answered on their behalf: "They know that the transfigured Lord of heaven and earth has a different voice from that of mere mortals." Thus Felix altered the relevant recitative, "and how powerful was the effect". Droysen also wrote to Felix after a performance at Kiel in 1841, calling it "the triumph of Protestant music since the time of Bach and Handel". On a performance at Durkheim two years later, Mendelssohn was able to pronounce it "the greatest ever in Germany to date"; a Herr Oberhover "sang with more intelligence than I have yet heard". Yet, despite all the august seriousness, Felix must have been amused at Herr Sternfeld conducting with a sausage as a baton and, during the first part, the kettledrum player belaboured his instrument so vigorously that the drumstick broke in two. He confessed to Fanny that the remark he had made "whilst drinking punch at 2 a.m. must be heard from my own lips, strictly private from Sebastian".

Eventually, *St Paul* was performed in 41 different places in Germany, as well as in the Netherlands, Denmark, Poland and Switzerland and all over the English-speaking world. In Britain, when King Charles II came to the throne in 1660, music had begun to reappear after Cromwell's Puritan attitude prohibited it. For charitable purposes, the sermon gave place to Bible stories told in song - the oratorio, which reached its peak in the 18th and 19th centuries. As secular music was banned in Lent this became a most useful substitute. It was performed not only in churches, but theatres and other concert venues. With the growth of turnpike roads and – later – railways, travelling became far easier. This allowed good musicians to perform at the increasing number of musical festivals in the expanding towns and cities of the land. Handel's *Messiah* and Haydn's *Creation* had become especially popular with choirs. Though Mendelssohn's oratorios were sometimes considered 'too conservative for their date', *St Paul* and, particularly, *Elijah* joined their earlier counterparts in popularity. When, in 1836, *St Paul* was performed at St Peter's Church, Liverpool (the third performance to be given after Frankfurt and Düsseldorf), tickets were sold out days before and the most illustrious singers were engaged.

Stratton is specific about the date of this English premiere. Sir George Smart conducted the oratorio on Friday 7th October "to a crowded hall". Though *The Musical World* enthused, "*The Times* gave it a lukewarm reception, Stratton contends, "possibly on account of the alterations and errors that occurred by comparison with the German performances." The Revd J. E. Cox recalled that, in order to put the audience into a more accommodating frame of mind, "choruses from Handel's *Judas Maccabaeus* began the proceedings because, it was surmised, everyone was accustomed to that work". A private recital of choruses was given at the Royal Pavilion, Brighton, in front of Queen Adelaide, wife of William IV. German herself, she must have felt very much at home on hearing a work by her compatriot. However, the truly auspicious performances took place in London and Birmingham in 1837.

Mr. Joseph Moore, manager of the Birmingham Festival and a button maker by trade, visited Germany to discuss arrangements with Mendelssohn whereby his oratorio was to be the main feature of this event. Felix therefore committed himself to his fifth visit to England for 1837, but, when the time approached, he had married and had to curtail his blissful honeymoon with Cécile – "all for the sake of a musical festival", as he complained to Fanny. Though Mendelssohn loved England and its people, he found himself counting the days until his return to Leipzig, even to the extent of hoping to travel direct from Birmingham to Calais and looking forward to the German wine. To make matters worse, a performance had been planned for Exeter Hall in London, an earlier one having taken place there on 7th March. The Birmingham Festival had tried to prevent the later one from happening before their own treat, fearing a financial loss. This resulted in what Felix called "unseemly" correspondence. Trouble was circumvented by Mendelssohn taking a seat in the Exeter Hall audience rather than conducting the oratorio. *The Musical World* gave a glowing review of this 12th September performance, despite several arias having been omitted. This was to allow the good people of Birmingham to hear Mme. Catalani and other notable singers of the time.

Meanwhile, Felix had been asked by Adolf Bernhard Marx to write the words for his own oratorio, *Moses*. However, Marx objected to so many chorales being included and wished to have nothing further to do with his (then) friend's endeavours; *St Paul* had been criticised on the same grounds as early as Mendelssohn's time in Paris, when Johann Schelble had commissioned him to write the oratorio for his St Cecilia Society in Frankfurt. Marx had agreed originally to write the text for *St Paul* but, because of the dispute over the superfluity of chorales, the friendship was severed. Eventually he threw all the correspondence he had received from Mendelssohn into the Tiergarten Lake in Berlin. He contended that "these Lutheran hymns" were out of keeping with biblical times. It might never have occurred to Marx that, with regard to *St Paul*, Felix may have had good reason to incorporate these "Lutheran hymns" into his oratorio. As this was written at his father's behest, what would be more appropriate than to pay tribute to

Abraham in this manner? Only Marx's side of the dispute is now available via his widow's memoirs.

Mozart's first biographer, Otto Jahn, wrote an article on *St Paul*, as well as a later analysis of *Elijah*. Mendelssohn, he pointed out, had intended to write a trilogy, including a third oratorio, *Christus*, of which only a few recitatives and choruses survive as Op. 97. As early as 14th July 1837 Mendelssohn had written to Schubring of a new oratorio for the Lower Rhine Festival at Düsseldorf in 1839. Schubring had suggested St Peter as being a possible subject: "The two chief apostles and pillars of the Christian Church could be promoted against one another." If Felix followed the New Testament as he wished, Christ would have to play the main part, he replied, thus lessening the impact made by Peter. The events in Peter's life, on the other hand – his denial of Jesus; his repentance; his acceptance of the keys of heaven; and his preaching at Pentecost – would be suitable material for an oratorio. Felix had already conceived the two parts, the first chronicling the events from the disciples leaving their nets to Jesus naming Simon as Peter; the second part covering the Crucifixion, Peter's denial and repentance and the outpouring of the Holy Spirit at Pentecost. "Subsequently," Schubring recalled, "Mendelssohn never exchanged one word with me on that oratorio, though we had often discussed St Peter and John the Baptist. What I told Mendelssohn about Nicodemus...interested him to a considerable degree, and, from what escaped him, I am inclined to believe he intended to turn it, at some time or other, to musical account."

Felix also discussed John the Baptist with Pastor Bauer, wondering how anything could "be written for the time before Christ's birth", since the liturgy of the Lutheran Church made no provision for such material to be set to music. All he could suggest was "a mere concert item, evoking a devotional mood". Bach's settings of the passion were sung "as independent pieces of music for edification", and Felix knew of no other sacred music than that sung by the Papal Choir in Rome. "There, however, music is a mere accompaniment, subordinate to the sacred rituals... the waxed candles, incense, etc. If it be that type of church music that you need," he told Bauer, "I am unable to find a connecting link that would allow this to be put into effect. When composing an oratorio, one principle must be maintained – the progressive history of persons or events – so as not to render the subject vague." Mendelssohn could well have answered his father by this wise counsel. As with other aspects of music, Felix received a homily on the oratorio from this all-knowing sage. Had Handel lived at that time, 1835, would he have written oratorios in that idiom? "Rarely, if they have to be written in the style of today," Abraham opined. He pronounced *Messiah* and *The Creation* "very remarkable phenomena, combining profound depths with cheerful efficiency...and genuinely religious influence... The combination of the playful...with the most noble and sincere feeling of gratitude." Such oratorios required no large orchestras, "without even an organ and yet, to the satisfaction and delight of everyone". By

Chapter 21: "A Handel and a Half"

"everyone", it may well be deduced that the name Abraham Mendelssohn could be substituted.

With so many sources of advice and criticism, it is remarkable that Felix gained so much strength and willpower to rise above these negative, unimaginative attitudes. Felix realised that he could never write anything better than Handel's *Messiah*, which chronicles the prophecies of Isaiah, ending with Christ's Resurrection. Neither could he emulate Bach's passion settings. He therefore chose subjects never before contemplated, *St Paul* and *Elijah*, for his most powerful sacred works. Though his father might well have regretted his defection from the faith of his forebears, there is plenty of evidence to prove that Felix certainly did so. With *Elijah*, Mendelssohn was able to identify his affinity with Judaism and, thereby, together with his psalm settings, wrote his most convincing sacred music. Even Marek acknowledges this fact, despite denigrating Mendelssohn's other religious compositions. After 1842, when both Leah and Abraham had passed away, Felix had no need to pander to the duty and obedience his parents expected from him and could write an oratorio based on his own religious needs.

The Story of Mendelssohn's Oratorio, Elijah, by F. G. Edwards of *The Musical World*, is still the definitive work employed by musicologists to gain the best sources of information and background. Other articles worth pursuing have been written by Joseph Bennett in Edwards's periodical relating to Mendelssohn's revision of *Elijah*. Julius Schubring's memoirs state that "a considerable amount of preliminary study had been undertaken, before I knew anything about the new oratorio. Mendelssohn always proved himself a thoughtful artist... He also rejected much that was suggested, being so well acquainted with his Bible, from which he obtained a great deal of valuable material. He was pleased that he should, without any further introduction, have commenced the oratorio with the voice of Elijah and marked the overture as the second movement." Hiller supported Schubring, recalling Mendelssohn "deep in his Bible" one evening, from which he read, "in a gentle and agitated voice, a passage from the First Book of Kings: 'And behold, the Lord passed by.' 'What a fine line this would be in an oratorio,' Felix exclaimed." In an essay, Martin Stehelin gives a further source of inspiration for Felix. In a hymnal of 1829 some verses described Christ's voice crying out: "It is finished", as recorded in St John's Gospel. Mendelssohn wrote a recitative based on these words, 'It is enough', whereby Elijah declared his victory over death. Grove had this and Bach's aria from the St John Passion sung to him. "The spirit is the same in both," he wrote to his friend Edith Oldham, "but, how much finer is that of Mendelssohn's to that of Bach. There is so much more...colour and it is so much more dramatic, without losing any of the religious feelings and sentiment" of the earlier work.

Yet another source for *Elijah* may be cited. In 1828, 23 'Elijah Sermons' were published, which ran into seven editions between then and 1903. Their author, Friedrich Wilhelm Krummacher, was the son of a pastor in the French Reformed

Church in Frankfurt. Since the father of the girl Mendelssohn married, Cécile Jeanrenaud, had also been a pastor at that church, it can be assumed that Felix met the Krummacher family. Goethe, who had read the sermons, pronounced them "narcotic, pacifying too much the congregation whose members had suffered distress". Goethe and Mendelssohn may well have included the 'Elijah Sermons' among their eclectic discussions when they met in Weimar in 1830. It is, therefore, not surprising that, on Felix's fifth visit to England in 1837, the subject was broached of a new oratorio, with "some [themes] in jest; some in earnest: St Peter; Og of Bashan; and Elijah".

Though Klingemann had begun work on the last-named subject, his heart was never in the script, which was lain aside. Thus Felix approached Schubring, who had written the German text for *St Paul*. On 2nd November 1838 he wrote to the theologian saying that "the text is so well assembled that only the music is needed". Schubring was asked to proceed with the text "when time permits" and to send him the draft when complete. "Elijah was a great and mighty prophet," Felix continued, "such as we might require again in our own day: energetic and zealous; but also stern, wrathful and gloomy – a stark contrast to the court myrmidons and popular rabble." He required "no epic narrative to be introduced" and Elijah's presentation "must be as spiritual as possible".

On 6th December Schubring was informed that the oratorio was "on a much firmer footing. Such people as Elijah should be shown as acting and speaking with fervour but not, for heaven's sake, to become mere musical pictures, but people, in a positive, practical world as we see in every chapter of the Old Testament. At present the pagans and pagan priests fall before me like shadows, or misty forms, whereas, to satisfy me, they should be solid, robust men." Schubring had wished to incorporate New Testament material, but Mendelssohn objected to the inclusion of the Transfiguration, where Christ appears with Moses and Elijah, or to allow Peter, James and John, who witnessed this scene, to be represented in the oratorio. Could this be that, though a devout Lutheran in public, he regarded himself as a Jew at heart? A far more mundane reason could be that the New Testament personalities would appear in *Christus*, Mendelssohn's third, incomplete, oratorio, which he might have been considering at that time.

On 28th November 1842 Felix again wrote to Schubring with the completed score of *Elijah*, asking him to "study the whole thing carefully and write in the margin a great many beautiful arias, reflecting pithy utterances, choruses and all sorts of things, and let me have it back as soon as possible". But it was not until the summer of 1845, when Joseph Moore invited Mendelssohn to compose a new oratorio for the following year's Birmingham Festival, that *Elijah* finally took shape. "I began once more to plough up the soil," Felix wrote. Not only had he pored over the Bible but he had met a decidedly earthly singer, Jenny Lind, for whom the soprano role would be written. Joanna Maria Lind-Fellborg, as Miss Lind was really named, was – as has been cited in Chapter 14 – "an enigma". It is only when Joan

Chapter 21: "A Handel and a Half"

Bulman's biography is studied that her character rings true. Miss Lind really did dislike false praise and insincere people, preferring the countryside and, once she found it, a peaceful home environment and domestic happiness. Such a personality must have aroused Mendelssohn's fellow feeling, as well as his ability to appreciate her musical talents. The fact that he had, at last, discovered a true artist means that nothing further need be said. Jenny would have been almost physically hurt had she read some assessments of her personality. In his book *The Great Singers*, Henry Pleasants describes her as "smug and prim, ready to deplore and condemn anything [of which] she did not approve". Her almost pathological shyness and "little girl lost" appearance were said to have been a "front" towards her public. She knew, it has been argued, how well her charming, "simple country girl" ways would be admired by her audiences.

If *St Paul* was described as "unconvincing", the same cannot be said of *Elijah*, and Mendelssohn appears to have supported this view. To William Bartholomew he wrote, regarding the English text, "I hope you will give your best English words, as translator, for I feel so much more interest in this work than for my others, and I only wish it may last so with me." On 17th January 1846 Felix was able to tell Joseph Moore that "every day I am making greater progress, but the work…will not be ready until further months have passed, but, even then, this will be five months more than the proposed date"; he added that he hoped to finish the oratorio as soon as his other commitments had been finalised. He then expressed doubts as to engaging Jenny Lind. Whilst he regarded her as "without hesitation, the absolutely first singer of the day and, perhaps, for many days to come", he did not feel able to undertake the negotiations that would bring her to Birmingham. He wrote: "I am aware of the many engagements of all sorts by which she is surrounded and how little likely it is that I can get a positive answer from her," having already spoken to Jenny in response to a letter from Moore. "She said she would not go to England…that it was impossible, etc., etc." Having twice declined such an invitation, Felix made no further enquiry at that time. Though it is undoubtedly true that Miss Lind's commitments might have prevented her singing the role specifically written for her voice – and especially her "high F sharp" – her plans could have been rescheduled, especially as Mendelssohn was so influential in her artistic life. But this was not the deepest concern in her own mind. As has been discussed in Chapter 14, "Flirting outrageously", Jenny not only admired Felix as a superlative musician but loved him as a man, irrespective of his blissful marriage and home life. She was either too frightened to take part in *Elijah* at Birmingham, in case she spoilt the performance, or her phobia for strange surroundings overcame her, however confident she felt in Mendelssohn's company. Biographers, such as Marek, describe how capricious she could be when anything did not go according to plan. Whatever the 'whys?' or 'wherefores?', Mme. Caradori-Allan was recommended by the festival committee to replace Miss Lind in the 1846 premiere of *Elijah*.

This soprano, once magnificent but now past her peak, took exception to the aria 'Hear ye, Israel', complaining that "it is not a lady's song". If, Felix retorted, Madame did not feel able to sing the aria, he would find someone to take her place. This redoubtable lady of 46, who had sung oratorios for years but whose voice was now "slightly worn", made a further demand. Unable to manage the high F sharp included on Jenny's account, Mme. Caradori-Allan insisted that Mendelssohn lower the key by a whole tone. The logistical issues involved in altering all the orchestral parts made this unthinkable.

The baritone Joseph Staudigl and the tenor Charles Lockey pleased the composer particularly. On 9th July Felix was able to write to Paul how "a few weeks ago, I was quite worried about it all, but slowly, I am beginning to look forward to it". Thus he and the musicians travelled to 'Brummagem' (as Felix referred to the Midlands city, reflecting how he had heard the citizens refer to it) in 1846, on a 'Mendelssohn Special' train that he hired. Felix encouraged newspaper critics whom he knew would give favourable reviews to attend rehearsals and to examine the score. In his way, Kupferberg states, they would have no alternative but to praise the oratorio in their columns. For the performance, on 26th August, Birmingham Town Hall was crowded with ticket-holders for the 3,000 places, "who mingled with lookers-on, and the inevitable vendors", whose wares, though not specified, can be left with little difficulty to the imagination.

As Mendelssohn mounted the podium and took up his baton that morning in 1846, "the sun broke through the clouds", whence graphic descriptions were printed in newspaper columns, from which legends were derived. "It seemed to illuminate the vast edifice in honour of the bright and pure being who stood there, the idol of all beholders. Never was there a more complete triumph; never a more thorough and speedy recognition of a great work of art" as *Elijah*, Davison of *The Times* blazoned to his readers. To Jenny Lind, Felix wrote that this was the best performance he had ever heard of any of his works, "with such go and swing in the way everyone sang, played and listened". Did Jenny have a guilty conscience that she had not taken part herself?

According to contemporary accounts, Mendelssohn received the overwhelming amount of praise "with all his calm, customary lack of vanity". An hour afterwards, at Moore's house, he replied to Horsley's congratulations with the humble words: "I know you liked some of *Elijah*; tell me what you do not like." It was, indeed, through suggestions by Horsley that Felix was prompted to revise the oratorio for an anticipated performance in 1847. One such example, Horsley claims, was the substitution of an unaccompanied trio of sopranos to sing the aria 'Lift thine Eyes' with a duo accompanied by the orchestra. *Elijah*'s complete overhaul caused Moscheles to ask if the composer was trying to make his already beautiful work still more beautiful. From Leipzig Mendelssohn wrote to Klingemann how little he had realised that so much revision was required before the 1847 performance. "Unluckily," Stratton remarks dryly, "some composers never find out this kind of

Chapter 21: "A Handel and a Half"

thing at all." Of Mme. Caradori-Allan, Felix wrote: "She sang in a manner so pretty, so pleasant, so elegant, but so out of tune, so breathless, so soulless." Compared with how this once fine soprano used to sing, Mendelssohn's blood was made to boil, as he declared. The contralto Maria Hawes acquitted herself "with musicianship and intelligence" but "had not the voice to fill the hall. I disliked her cold, breathless coquetry in the music; her actual performance was more important than her vocal execution." To his old friend Livia Frege he wrote asking why, being able to sing the arias from memory, she had not accompanied him to Birmingham. "It is not fair to make people's mouths water when their hunger cannot be satisfied. You would have loved the rich, full sounds of the orchestra and the huge organ, combined with the power of the choir, who sang with honest enthusiasm in the resonance of the grand, giant hall." Lockey, Staudigl, a second soprano and a second contralto were singled out as "singing with peculiar spirit and the utmost fire and sympathy, not only doing justice to the loudest passages but to the softest piano, in a manner that I have never heard before". As for "the kindly, hushed but enthusiastic audience, I doubt if they will ever witness such a fine performance" as took place that day.

On 8th November 1846 Felix assured Schubring that, judging by his comments in the margin, he had a far better idea of what was required in the text than anyone. On 6th December Felix confided to Klingemann how he hoped "the full vigour" he had put into the revision of *Elijah* would "eliminate successfully many things that disturbed me at the first performance". Having revised one of the most difficult parts, that of the widow, he hoped Klingemann would be satisfied with his alterations. "The role of Elijah has become much more important and musical in this part... Unfortunately, I only discovered these things post-festum... I hope to be able to express more precisely what I wish for the work and I intend to review everything that does not suit me perfectly with the greatest care, and then to begin something new."

The widow's part has certainly made its mark on the present-day conductor Richard Hickox. He believes this to be "the most operatic part in oratorio altogether", and that *Elijah* is really "a religious opera". Whatever derogatory critics and biographers say, Mendelssohn did achieve his burning ambition – and his father's wish – to write an opera. It is shameful that so many "wooden", "dull" and "lifeless" performances of *Elijah* are attributed to Mendelssohn himself, wrecking the composer's reputation. Such "lethargic and banal" presentations of his sacred music are contemplated with a yawn. When, conversely, a diligent choir leader rehearses an equally enthusiastic choir, "fantastic and exciting" results are produced. From contemporary accounts, only the latter occurred when Mendelssohn himself directed a performance of his, and others', works – sacred or secular.

On 11th April 1847 Felix, accompanied by the young violinist Joseph Joachim, arrived on his tenth and final visit to London, to conduct *Elijah* on the 17th at Exeter Hall. Felix was upset by what Benedict called the "most unruly and inefficient" choir, made up of amateur musicians and chiefly manual workers from the Sacred Harmonic Society. According to Max Müller, in London at the time, Felix let his temper get the better of him on the afternoon before the performance, fulminating that he would not conduct "all these tailors and shoemakers. They cannot do it and they will not practise... Elijah is too much for them." To Müller, Exeter Hall, opened in 1830 and existing until 1907 where the Strand Palace hotel is now situated, was the best place for choral music to be heard. Though, to idealists, the far-sighted plan by which working people were encouraged to sing was a fine concept, its disadvantage was that the choristers knew by heart such works as *Messiah* and *Judas Maccabaeus*, thus skipping rehearsals in order to give priority to their normal employment. A vicious circle arose, as absence meant that anything new (and certainly anything needing greater practice) could not be undertaken as thoroughly as the director or composer would have preferred. It was the lack of discipline that the usually democratic Mendelssohn resented and it was only on his being informed that the Queen and Prince Albert would attend the forthcoming performance that caused his temper to abate. Extenuation must be given for his outburst, as he was thoroughly exhausted. Indeed, having been asked to stay in London longer, he declared that another week would kill him.

Chorley wrote of the performance as being "such as entirely to confuse outline, form, texture, light and shade throughout the greater part of the work". This prompted a letter to *The Athenaeum* from a chorister, citing too few rehearsals for such a slovenly performance, and the fact that so few scores were available that participants had to share those that did exist. But the singing of Miss Birch and Miss Dolby was praised. "I was there," Müller recalled. "The hall was crowded. Mendelssohn, who conducted, now and then made a face, but no one else noticed what was wrong. Had he lived and been able to hear *Elijah* sung by the same choristers, in later years, he would not have made a fuss." This is borne out by the novelist George Eliot having been seen to weep with joy at a subsequent performance of the oratorio at this venue. In her journal, Queen Victoria noted that the items she particularly liked from *Elijah* were 'Hail our Cry, O Baal', 'Cast thy Burden', "the chorus descriptive of the fire coming down", and 'Holy, Holy, Holy'. "The recitative might be shortened, but the whole is a splendid work," the Queen added.

Though Mendelssohn believed how right he had been in revising *Elijah*, and in deciding "not to rest until the whole work is as good as I can make it", the 1846 performances caused it to be known as 'Elijah's Year', and, as late as 1901, Stratton could still write of the Birmingham performance as "the cream of choral singing" and the oratorio as "a beacon work on the shores of time". "As the hall filled with sunlight, the galleries gay with ladies like tulip bowls, Mendelssohn exercised such power over the musicians, moulding them to his will...actually laughing them to perfection," reported *The Times*. "At the end, a long continuous volley of plaudits, vociferous and deafening, as if enthusiasm, unchecked, had burst its bonds and

Chapter 21: "A Handel and a Half"

filled the air with shouts of excitement." Mendelssohn's thoughtfulness is exemplified when, at the first rehearsal, Grattan Cook, an evidently experienced oboist, complained that he had been given no solo. The composer thereupon inserted a long-held C for the oboe, to be played whilst the youth sang when asked to see if rain had fallen after the drought. A further example can be cited of Mendelssohn's generous spirit when a later performance was given for the benefit of Dr. Stimpson, who had done such sterling work during the Birmingham Festival. The composer defrayed his expenses and donated his fee towards the funds.

But what of Jenny Lind? Percy Young, in his biography of Elgar, mentions that she was expected to sing in a performance of *Elijah* in Worcester Cathedral in 1848. Though Lockey and Staudigl took part, Miss Lind's role was sung by Clara Novello, but no reason is given for Jenny's absence. It was possible that she was still traumatised by Felix's death of the previous year. However, in 1849, on 3rd February, when he would have reached the age of 40 had he lived, she sang at a performance of the oratorio at the College Hall, Worcester, in aid of the local infirmary, for which £850 was raised. Was the date pure coincidence, or chosen by astute planning? During that year the prima donna finally left her operatic career behind, to concentrate fully on oratorio, as Mendelssohn had advised.

However, despite the glory of the late 1840s, it was the Birmingham Festival performance that was commemorated on the precise date – 26th August – 150 years later; not in Birmingham, but at the Royal Albert Hall Promenade Concert season of 1996. This would have delighted the composer, who loved London more than anywhere in the world, apart from Leipzig.

Chapter 22

Mendelssohn as Instructor

From his youth Felix was expected to give advice and help to budding musicians, however senior the individual was to this young fountainhead of musical acumen. One such correspondence lasted for 19 years, between 1823 and 1842, when such "lessons by post" were abandoned – but not by Felix. Wilhelm von Boguslawski, a government official, first sought Felix's judgement on a symphony he had written. Six years younger, Mendelssohn set to work to analyse the music, pointing out its good and bad points as impartially as anyone with many more years' experience. Nevertheless, Boguslawski was urged to persevere with counterpoint – the converse of what Telemann would have exhorted. "Keep away from all fellows who believe in counterpoint, rather than imagination. Music ought not to be an effete and occult science; a sort of black magic," he had written. This demonstrates how stringently the then 14-year-old Felix was influenced by his parents' obsession with reality – and the influence Zelter breathed into his pupil's mind. Indeed, Bruno Hake, who compiled this correspondence, finds several 'Zelterisms' in that letter. No mention is made, for instance, of the melody or use of instrumentation, but instead there is an assessment of the "formal structure" of the symphony, together with its "purity"; how the score was "to the point" and the theme "must show simplicity and tidiness", its ideas to be carried through so as to be "skilful in their plan". Hake sees "the schoolmaster raising his head, taking offence at the unusual boldness of the work", and speaking, like Zelter, in a tone that was "strict and pedantic". But one aspect of the letter escaped parental censorship: he simply signed the letter 'Felix Mendelssohn' – no 'Bartholdy'!

In 1832 Felix was asked to criticise a further work of Boguslawski, which Hake considers to have been an overture. "If you recognise my writing, you will throw the remains of my letter into the waste-paper basket unread, or at least, read it with displeasure, comparable with the last time I beat you at chess," Felix warned. Though, again, Boguslawski's work gave Felix "great pleasure", his "open opinion" had been sought. Thus: "I would have preferred it if some things had been done differently...some things do not seem quite right." There followed a catalogue of errors, which, to anyone who respected Mendelssohn's instruction and took it seriously, need not have been included. Felix hoped that the older man would not take what he had written "the wrong way" and hoped pieces "along the same lines and in the same thoroughbass" would be produced. A year later, on 16th November 1833, though he was glad that Boguslawski was still composing, he wished, on that occasion, his correspondent had not sent him a particular piece to analyse. "There is a trend of judgement that I do not like anywhere, least of all by musicians. A master carpenter knows exactly how the joints must lie and how to smooth rough pieces of wood. But, before reaching that stage, he becomes an apprentice, then a journeyman." Felix detested "the cold reason required for a practical form of work", preferring to praise or rebuke as a pupil progressed or developed musical talent. Boguslawski was asked "not to show this letter to anyone, or to call me to account for it, like so many chess games won or lost". However tactful and courteous Felix remained towards this pupil, it is evident that Boguslawski was destined to remain an apprentice, and it can only be wondered why Mendelssohn continued to encourage him in his compositions. If someone as celebrated as Max Müller was dissuaded to dispense with musical composition and to continue as a philosopher and linguist, was there some arcane explanation why Boguslawski was not put out of his misery in the same manner?

It was evident that, however much he failed to express the mood, Felix was becoming exasperated with this enigmatic pupil: he exhorted Boguslawski not to expect a letter during the forthcoming winter. "Many and varied tasks await me...that I cannot seem to get down to letter writing, and times will only get worse, not better", for such a duty. Nevertheless, when this persistent government attorney produced an opera, *Elfino*, with a libretto by Ludwig Tieck, Mendelssohn, though limited for time, "played the work through to myself at the piano and sang and acted it out, and I would have been applauding as a member of an audience, too, at a great many points". He would say what was right and wrong with the piece, were he sure that Boguslawski would not misinterpret what was said. "It is precisely this love of every artistic production," Felix concluded, "that I demand of every artist... Compliments do not do the trick... What matters in the end is...whether one has achieved the greatest possible development. So do not let yourself be dissuaded...from continuing to work... The work and the joy in it are result enough... It must always give me great pleasure to recognise and pay tribute to your progress."

On 11th March 1842 Mendelssohn mentioned "several successful passages" in Boguslawski's latest offering, yet no heed appears to have been paid to the correction of errors. Though the pupil applied himself to experimenting with new and larger works, Bruno Hake states that "time and again" these same mistakes occurred, of which Mendelssohn "never tired of reminding him". Again Felix wrote: "There is nothing more disagreeable to me than criticism of a person's nature or talent. It creates ill feeling and confusion and does no good... One can only keep silent on this subject." Rather than theorising, Mendelssohn preferred to work with a pupil, allowing ideas and thoughts of his own to be developed through the instructor's influence. Felix preferred his pupils to dissect the whole work before putting pen to paper, so that a convincingly expressed idea would materialise. "In every fresh piece," Mendelssohn had written in 1838, "I learn better to write what is exactly in my heart – which is, after all, the only rule I know. If I am not adapted to popularity, I will not try to acquire, nor to seek after it."

Similar sentiments were encouraged in other musicians. Carl Eckert was admonished: "What really matters is to express what is felt and experienced in one's own breast and uttered from the depths of one's heart. Character and life are displayed here. You must work and go on working at this. Go deeper into your inner being… Let criticism and intellect rule as much as you please in all outward questions and forms but, in all inner and original thoughts, let heart and feelings alone supervene." Though Eckert submitted some 'songs without words' and an overture, nothing is heard of either today. To Eduard Franck, director of the Berne Conservatoire, who sent him an étude, Mendelssohn wrote encouraging him to "go on working, as this is the best thing anyone can do, because one work is not enough to achieve success. Your purpose should be to produce a succession of compositions, all aiming towards one point. To achieve progress is your only function and a duty which God has imposed on a serious artist, through the talents the Creator has bestowed. Fulfil it, then, for I believe that the happiness of life lies entirely in this, and cannot be attained without it, and its omission would be a very great sin." The only advice Felix was able to offer on the one piece Franck submitted was to "pursue your path and continue your labours".

Though Franck, no relation to the Belgian composer César Franck, achieved status as "professor in various conservatoires", he is not mentioned as a composer, or a celebrated musician. Johann Kelz, on the contrary, who sent Mendelssohn a series of fugues, and was told how "I cannot give a first prize, as each has something to recommend it", did succeed as a popular 'cellist. Adolf Lindblad, a fellow pupil with Mendelssohn at the Berlin Singakademie, was able, later, to compose some Swedish songs. He evidently benefited from his colleague's advice: "what *you* think should be the most important thing for *you*" was all that mattered when being creative. Why did Mendelssohn ignore such wise counsel when planning his own compositions? Young as he was, Felix valued receiving from would-be composers "such serious pieces against the trend for such silly trifles that tickle the ear on all sides", as he had written to Kelz on 7th July 1826. This concept was also revealed to Lindblad and a further composer, simply referred to as 'A'. To the latter, Mendelssohn praised the "many unmistakable traces of talent" in an overture submitted. This trend gave Felix "much pleasure". He would have liked, nevertheless, to see "more definite ideas worked out in the composition", but he would also have liked "to become more musically acquainted" with 'A' – not forgetting, however, to point out, in a painstaking but sympathetic way, the various shortcomings of the piece, hoping such remarks to be "unnecessary in the future".

Mendelssohn never wished "to shout down anyone who seeks my advice", and, to Wilhelm Taubert, he wrote from Lucerne in 1831 that he would like to be treated as a friend rather than a tutor. "Such formality makes me almost nervous, as I do not know what to say in response. I will tell you, frankly and freely, my honest opinion. Thus, I think we should give one another good counsel" as regards compositions. Yet Mendelssohn was discerning in his judgement when responding to requests for tuition. Although Stratton glibly brushes aside his refusal to accept Professor Naumann's son Emil as due to Mendelssohn's "inability to teach", it is more likely that, having assessed the boy's character, he realised him to have been too immature as yet to leave the parental home. Meanwhile, the professor's work received as much constructive assistance as could be mustered.

Compared with earlier compositions, "your present output gives me extreme gratification, as it shows much to be unreservedly commended". Though Felix hoped for "something vigorous and good" to result, "it is only you who can ensure that this will occur". Having seen the influence of Naumann's tutor, Franz Nesser, in his work, Mendelssohn recommended him to follow his instructor's advice. "You must attend assiduously, making the most of the time when you can, and must learn." As for Naumann's piano playing: "This will improve if correct time is maintained, concentrating on steadfastness and clearness." Though lack of time prevented his writing at greater length, Mendelssohn analysed Naumann's C major Capriccio as "more original" than his E minor equivalent, whereas "a great deal pleases me about your sonata. As you apply Goethe's words to me, and call me a master, I can only reply further in Goethe's words: 'Learn soon to know wherein he falls. True art and not its type revere.'"

Another parent who required a reply was a Frau Franck, who nursed an evident ambition for her son. What, if any, relationship she may have had with the professor at Berne, or any other of the same name, is not known. However ambitious his mother might have been, the son did not relish music lessons. Having written earlier about her hopes for the future, Mendelssohn gave short shrift to the persistent mama. "As he has not practised during the whole time since Düsseldorf [about a year], I have declined to teach him, saying that he must first show some diligence, without which the separation from his family will come to nothing." The only course his mother should pursue was to let her son decide for himself as to how important a musical career would be to him. "As a result, he decided to stay in Breslau and we parted on completely good terms." Whilst on the subject of Breslau, Felix remembered a young relative, asking his uncle Nathan "if Arnold still has a taste for music and, if so, is he still cultivating it?" No details can be found as to how Arnold fits into the contemporary Mendelssohn family tree. The only Arnold Mendelssohn mentioned in reference books is a later composer, mainly of church music, born in 1899 and best remembered as a pupil of Paul Hindemith.

Of Sebastian Hensel's 'Op. 1', Felix wrote to Fanny: "When all examinations come to an end, learning will begin in earnest, which will be delightful. Though no reward is received for applying oneself, it forms part of my creed to have nothing to do with worldly wealth; only spiritual contentment and well-being through worthwhile work, accomplished to the best of my ability." Fanny did not need to worry, her brother reassured her, about his nephew's 'Op. 1', or about composing a second work, which advice must be repeated to Sebastian. Incidentally, no details are extant about Sebastian Hensel's musical prowess – not even his biography of *The Family Mendelssohn* makes mention of any such experience.

Robert Franz, whose songs may still be heard, was another musician whom Mendelssohn criticised on submitting a song. On 15th September 1845 Felix wrote, whilst acknowledging Franz's skill as a lyricist, "which I, too, would like to be able to do, this is exactly what I did not discern clearly enough. I do not know what to say" about the song submitted at that time. However, Mendelssohn promised to meet Franz when he visited Halle. "Then, we can talk, or argue at great length to our heart's content." Mendelssohn's letter may appear jaundiced, but, in view of what reference books reveal about Robert Franz, this might have been a strangely twisted admission of rivalry, albeit subconscious. Franz's songs were admired not only by Liszt and Schumann but by Mendelssohn himself. Indeed, since many of these were written for the mezzo-soprano voice, Fanny might well have sung them. Whereas Mendelssohn often praised musicians in his letters fulsomely, even with sycophancy, when he did discover gold among the dross of potential musicians there is no doubt of his generosity of action and sincerity of words. When Mendelssohn first met Jenny Lind in Berlin she was already a celebrated opera diva. But, despite her earlier glory, it was in oratorio that she came into her own. It was Mendelssohn who advocated this change of musical genre and showed her what was right for her personality. Miss Lind had previously considered retiring from the opera stage, with so much false glitter and even 'immorality', of which she so strongly disapproved. Felix also fostered her interest in lieder, which she sang to perfection – notably those of Schubert, Schumann and Taubert, but those of her mentor even more so. He also reorganised her disorderly business and financial structure, giving her the confidence not only to feel at ease in formerly hostile countries, such as Austria and England, but to take audiences by storm wherever she sang.

The 'Artists' Concerts', originally introduced into the Lower Rhine Festival at Düsseldorf in 1833, were ideal venues in which Miss Lind could excel. Her peak in this regard was witnessed at Whitsuntide in Aachen in 1846, where the audience was "driven to delirium" by her performances. As well as oratorio (see Chapter 19, 'Conductor and director'), Jenny sang songs by Adolf Lindblad, her compatriot, and Felix's 'On Wings of Song' and his 'Spring' songs. "The musicians were all so uplifted, so animated, so artistically moved by Lind's singing and manner," Felix wrote to Franz Hauser, "that the whole thing became a delight; a general success, with everyone working together." As the former prima donna was so punctual at rehearsals, she was ordered to rest by Mendelssohn, until needed. However, apathy set in among the musicians, so that even the conductor became lethargic, "until, thank God, Jenny Lind appeared, when the necessary interest and good humour returned to us and things moved again".

Fanny reported to Rebecka, in Italy, in 1844 about "a charming little Hungarian lad", and added that Ferdinand David "can teach him nothing more". This rare being, whom Felix had discovered, became, like Jenny Lind, a legend in his lifetime. Even today the name Joseph Joachim is spoken with awe among music connoisseurs. Fanny had first met this lad of 14 whilst accompanying a party to Berlin for a performance of Mendelssohn's *Midsummer Night's Dream* music. Fanny found Joachim "very sensible" and considered his residence at the Rheinischerhof "very natural and proper". As with so much about Mendelssohn's life, yet another myth must be laid to rest. Whereas commentators on music speak of Brahms's name in conjunction with that of Joachim, it is Mendelssohn to whom credit should redound for initiating the young violinist's career. Though Brahms and Joachim became firm friends, this occurred only later in adulthood.

Jenny Lind and Joseph Joachim can truthfully be considered exceptions to the rule of meting out instruction to run-of-the-mill pupils, however keenly they might have appreciated Mendelssohn's teaching. Charles Horsley became a pupil of Mendelssohn from 1841 to 1843. Having met the family on his second visit to London in 1832, Felix had, reluctantly, discouraged Horsley's father from sending compositions for the Berlin Singakademie to perform now that Rungenhagen had become director. Whereas Zelter had ensured that this institution had been the finest of its kind, "many errors now occur" under the new head. Mendelssohn took a keen interest in the young people, threatening, jokingly, to judge the Miss Horsleys' compositions "harshly – woe to any fifths". Several pieces were dedicated to the these girls, and Felix asked to see the drawings for which another brother, John Callcott Horsley, had been awarded a medal by the Royal Academy. However, it was Charles who gained the most from Felix's instruction. On 17th January 1839 the parents were encouraged to send their son to study with Moritz Hauptmann in Leipzig. "The musician has no mannerisms; is this an English word?" he asked. "Once the boy becomes accustomed to Hauptmann's reserve and the ice is broken, he will find his warmth all the more genuine and will thank you for taking up my suggestion."

On 15th March Felix wrote further to the father, William Horsley, "who I am proud to call 'friend'", that Charles should be encouraged to concentrate on piano playing rather than composing. Mendelssohn showed almost pathetic tact. "He plays too well, almost, not to play better. He rushes through difficult passages in order the more quickly to reach smoother ones." Mendelssohn suggested that Horsley should practise exercises, "which he is not inclined to do. Though his touch is improving, the stiffness in his fingers will take time to allow him to become a talented pianist." Whilst Horsley had been dissuaded from composing,

Chapter 22: Mendelssohn as Instructor

Mendelssohn admitted his endeavours to be "pure. His ideas flow naturally. Neither do they possess the frivolities or lack of harmony seen as 'modern' and 'lovely'. His frankness and good nature make him popular with everyone he meets and he is very fond of Cécile – which is mutual."

Writing later, Horsley recalled that he was "not taught in a formal manner", but visited the Mendelssohn home three times a week, having been asked to practise particular pieces between these lessons. Bach and Beethoven featured in Horsley's repertoire. Mendelssohn would either criticise the way a piece was played or, more frequently, play them to his pupil. Horsley's favourite tuition took place during walks, when they "would invariably converse on musical subjects". One of Felix's favourite haunts was "a little inn in a forest near Leipzig, the Rosenthal". Discussion could revolve around "a Beethoven symphony, a Mozart opera, a Handel oratorio, a Bach fugue, Mendelssohn analysing the work and the idea behind it; the ingenuity of the instrumentation or the sublimity of the counterpoint. Pupils were invariably invited to rehearsals at the Gewandhaus, for which scores would be provided. These were expected to be studied thoroughly, as a result of which an examination would follow as to the construction and peculiarities" of a given work. At no time until the Leipzig Conservatorium was founded could Horsley recall Mendelssohn receiving a fee for a pupil's tuition.

Max Pirani states that Mendelssohn had hoped to found his conservatorium as early as 1840, when the King of Saxony had enthused about his *Hymn of Praise*, written to commemorate the 400th anniversary of printing. This is borne out by a letter of 8th April of that year, in which Felix asked von Falkenstein, who administered the city's finances, if a legacy bequeathed to the corporation by a Herr Blümner could be used "for the erection and maintenance of a basic music academy in Leipzig". Up to that time, he pointed out, "music has never received the smallest aid from any quarter", though the Leipzigers had enjoyed music, new and old, for the past 50 years. "Blümner himself cherished a great love for...all the arts and always devoted attention to musical conditions here. Leipzig has a deep-felt need" for an establishment in which music could be studied conscientiously "and with an earnest mind" for tutors and pupils alike. He stressed the long musical tradition in Leipzig – secular and sacred – and pointed out how suitable a location the city was for such an institution. Were the request to be granted, "a new impetus to musical life will result, the effects of which will be speedily and enduringly disseminated", to everyone's benefit. "This is not a pipedream, but a properly formulated plan", which was enclosed with Mendelssohn's letter. But fate, and his inordinately selfish family, intervened to prevent such a mission coming into being for a further three years.

Mendelssohn was commanded by the new King of Prussia, Friedrich Wilhelm IV, to become the court musical director in Berlin. The concatenation of circumstances relating to this appointment is described in Chapter 23, 'The Highest In The Land'. However, Felix was at last able to write to his family on 11th

December 1842 – the day before his mother passed away – that "please God, the new school in Leipzig should begin in February next year, with ten sinecures", as he called his scholarship pupils. As for the remaining students, "if they wish to learn, [they] must pay 75 thalers per annum". This was the only information Felix could give at that time: "The rest can only be taught through experience and trial."

Thus, in January 1843 Mendelssohn was given full rein and loyal support by his staff. "Seldom have people worked with such warmth, goodwill and harmony as at the Leipzig Conservatorium," contemporary reports observed. Mendelssohn's friendship and courtesy were invariably reciprocated and this attitude of mutual helpfulness was perpetuated after his death. Jacob believes this to have been because each member of his team, so carefully selected by Mendelssohn, enjoyed a settled home and family life, with no need for unsatisfactory love affairs or antisocial modes of behaviour that would divert these thorough professionals from their work. In March, on Hiller's advice that a really excellent singer had to be engaged to teach the students, Felix asked if such an individual existed in Germany. In any case, he pointed out, it would be "hard work" to persuade Leipzig's Treasury to include such a post in the budget, even though this appointment was "even more necessary than anyone else" on his staff. Meanwhile 34 pupils had enrolled and, until the new buildings were ready, rooms at the Gewandhaus were used. Felix "would have to talk about 6/8 chords three or four times a week, but I am quite willing to do this for the love of the cause". Mendelssohn and Schumann would teach piano composition and technique; Ferdinand David would do likewise for the violin; Moritz Hauptmann – "the most revered contrapuntalist in Europe", as Rockstro termed him – would instruct in harmony and counterpoint; Carl Becker was to teach the organ and Christian Pohlenz had been chosen as the singing tutor, but he passed away before the conservatorium opened. For that discipline, classes were therefore shared between Mme. Grabau and Herr Böhme. Though the elders of Leipzig wished the institution to expand, allowing students to undertake more theoretical training, Mendelssohn considered that, for the time being, two rooms at the Gewandhaus were sufficient for tuition and practice.

Upon the official opening, on 3rd April 1843, a journalist, Paul Stöcklin "expected great things" from the new venture, which he saw as "a profound and truthful influence for modern Germany – the greatest achievement of Mendelssohn's life". Felix was awarded the freedom of Leipzig by the corporation, "the letters patent reposing in a beautiful silver-gilt box". In *The Athenaeum*, Henry Chorley suggested that British cities and towns should honour in a similar manner anyone who had allowed so much civic pride to accrue to their locality. On 30th April Mendelssohn was able to write to Moscheles in London: "A famous beginning has been made. Applications from students arrive daily and the number of instructors has been increased." Though his pupils would "compose and theorise", there was nothing more efficacious to Mendelssohn than "thorough, steady practising, strict time and the knowledge of all solid tasks – the noblest things which can, and should, be taught. From these, all other knowledge follows. Yet I do not wish to render art a mere handicraft." To this end, in addition to the subjects already mentioned, the history of music and Italian were included in the curriculum, so that the many musical terms encountered would be easily understood.

As a tutor, Mendelssohn was "keen and stimulating" and, Grove observed, he "insisted that any pupil who showed a gleam of talent should not be prevented from entering the Conservatorium through lack of funds". In a memorandum, Mendelssohn pointed out that the best students were often found to be those with no financial support to allow for private tuition and that scholarships had to be provided for such candidates. A prime example whom he bore in mind was Joseph Joachim, who was awarded a free place at this school of excellence. Bruno Hake calls the Leipzig Conservatorium "the first modern institution of higher learning in music, which...by the strictest demands made on its students...lifted them high above the craftsmanlike level of artistic performance". Felix had written to Conrad Schleinitz expressing similar sentiments on 1st August 1838: "I cannot agree that one profession is preferable to another. To whatever a man gives his heart, that becomes a noble vocation. The only occupation I dislike is one where all individuality disappears and whose employees are allowed no freedom of personality... The best part of every calling, and which should be common to all, is to give utterance to one's best thoughts, which should become more and more worthy of being expressed. All the rest is immaterial."

Though Mendelssohn had been commanded by the King of Prussia to found an academy of music in Berlin, which came to naught, he was now able, through the Leipzig institution, to put his ideas into effect. As Hake writes: "correctness and discipline, sharp and clear, were the basic principles, both in teaching and study." Mendelssohn added: "If the artist's highest potential is to be achieved, he must adopt purely spiritual aims. Applying talent for its own sake would prove detrimental to art." According to Bruno Hake: "Every word the master spoke, based as it was on rich experience, deep insight and vision, was worth its weight in gold. Mendelssohn possessed the rare gift of expressing himself briefly, clearly and incisively, without mincing matters", when discussing the business of the Conservatorium.

But, despite so much talk of tutor-student discipline, humour infiltrated itself into the lessons. Writing to Moscheles regarding a composition, Felix averred: "My favourite is the fairy tale for children, so gracious and graceful, especially when the bass repeats the melody, down, down, down, like a fat bassoon, or one of the other growling instruments." During thoroughbass exercises, Felix Moscheles recalled, Mendelssohn "would make charming pen-and-ink drawings". Were his students aware of this lapse in their tutor's own discipline? Did they, on the contrary, experience fear of the barbed comments he could have been writing about themselves? Moscheles reported that a young female pupil was given the rough edge of Mendelssohn's tongue on account of her unruly red hair, which she was asked, in no uncertain terms, to rearrange into a more seemly style. On the surface, such a reprimand was in order, if professionalism and discipline was to be applied; but could there have been more in Felix's mind? Herr Doktor Mendelssohn, though he would not have dared admit the fact, was still susceptible to feminine charms and looks. However blissfully happy in his marriage, he might well have shown annoyance, reflected on the unfortunate young lady, that such untoward thoughts had not abated, causing greater disturbance to his libido than was proper.

Stratton cites the incident of "that unfortunate girl student, whose hair was not amenable to the rule of the hairpin", as an example of Mendelssohn's "contempt and satire", overlooking that slovenliness in appearance was equally to be disdained in Mendelssohn's opinion as poor workmanship. Not only the female sex was singled out for such verbal opprobrium. Rockstro recalled "a handsome young Pole" [possibly Wasielewski, who later was to write Schumann's first biography], "who, due to the fashion of his homeland, allowed his jet-black hair to hang halfway down his neck". Mendelssohn, "with a merry laugh", ordered the student to have his hair cut short. "One of the best pianists in the class", the Pole played with such emotion his hair fell over his shoulders. "At the next lesson there was not a student who would not have gladly had his hair cut, in order to win the smile with which he was rewarded for his devotion in parting from his pride and joy."

A further anecdote in Rockstro's biography refers to the time when Mendelssohn, during his absence at the 1846 Aachen Festival, asked each pupil to compose a string quartet. On his return, one student handed in his attempt, at the head of which score the word 'Charivari' was written. This noun is defined in the dictionary as: "Rough, harsh notes; hubbub of discordant sounds; a mock serenade to a newly married couple, applying pots, kettles and the like." 'Charivari' was used as the title for a French satirical magazine, equivalent to *Punch*, which, in turn, was known as 'the London Charivari'. In complete contradiction, a lovely perfume was so named in recent years. Rather than displaying temper, Mendelssohn became "deeply hurt", explaining that, as a man whose time was so occupied, did the student really expect him to waste it on a composition that had been declared "rubbish"? "If you are not in earnest," Felix concluded, "I can have nothing further to say to you." Nevertheless, the work was analysed as thoroughly as the other contributions, "while the culprit stood by, as white as a sheet, well knowing that not a member of the class would speak to him for many a long day to come".

The most fascinating account of life at the Leipzig Conservatorium occurs in the 1883 biography of Mendelssohn written by William Smyth Rockstro. Though at times nauseatingly sycophantic, Rockstro's book is a useful adjunct for anyone studying the musical life of 1840s Leipzig. There is no explanation as to why he changed his name from Rackstraw to a more exotic one, but, as principal of the Royal College of Music, he may have feared ridicule as the result of Ralph Rackstraw, a character in Gilbert and Sullivan's *HMS Pinafore*. Rockstro's story as to how he came to meet Mendelssohn is well worth repeating. In 1842 there lived in London a Mr. Emmett, who allowed serious students access to his remarkable collection of manuscripts. On a visit, Rockstro queried the authenticity of a score that Emmett had recently purchased at an auction. Because Emmett had no sight, he suggested Mendelssohn, whom he knew well, should be visited. Thus, "without the loss of a minute", he and Rockstro set off to Denmark Hill, where Felix was staying during his seventh trip to London. On arrival at the home of Cécile's relatives, the Benecke family, "the guests were received with enormous welcome". Mendelssohn "explained in the most minute detail the peculiarities of the handwriting", which undoubtedly had belonged to Bach, and pronounced it "genuine, without a moment's hesitation". In view of Rockstro's evident enthusiasm and his rapt attention to what Mendelssohn had to say, the young musician was asked his future plans: "He spoke so warmly of Leipzig that, henceforth, a visit to the Gewandhaus became the dream of our life." (Rockstro had a confusing habit of speaking of himself in the plural.)

In 1845, "at Pentecost", as he quaintly called Whitsuntide, Rockstro visited the Mendelssohn family, who were staying with the Jeanrenauds in Frankfurt. Again he was welcomed warmly, the internationally famous composer behaving "as unaffectedly as his youngest child, taking great delight in the sunshine and flowers". Mendelssohn took Rockstro to see Thorwaldsen's statue of Goethe and the dramatist's birthplace in Hirschgraben. Felix suggested they attend "an open-air concert" that evening. "In an unfrequented part of the public gardens, a nightingale sang. 'He sings here every evening,' Mendelssohn explained, 'and I often come to hear him.'" Felix gained inspiration for new works in this sheltered spot. "'Whenever an idea occurs to me, I get a feeling like this,' and he twisted his hands rigidly and nervously in front of his breast, 'and, when that happens, I know I must write.'" Rockstro was then asked if he would care to hear some organ sonatas Mendelssohn had just written – later to be published as Op. 65.

Punctually at 10 a.m., as arranged, Rockstro presented himself at St Catherine's Church. "The whole set of six were played from the neatly written manuscript with the crispness with which the double bass player Dragonetti performed his most highly finished pizzicato. One other, who had been quietly listening, left us at the church door." Later, Rockstro was asked whether he would like to study Félicien David's composition *The Desert*, or Mendelssohn's own Piano Trio, soon to be published as Op. 66, whilst Felix occupied himself with currently outstanding work. The latter composition was chosen and, halfway through his perusal of the score, Mendelssohn reappeared to discuss Rockstro's forthcoming studies in Leipzig. (Félicien David was a French composer not related to Ferdinand David.)

As Ferdinand David would be leaving for London that evening, it was suggested that he and Rockstro travel together and that the young pupil could be introduced to everyone whom he would be likely to encounter during his studies. When David arrived the trio was performed "with as much effect as on its subsequent introduction to the general public at the Gewandhaus". Rather than the formal 'Leben sie wohl' ('live well'), uttered when the speaker is unlikely to see the person again, 'auf Wiedersehen' ('on seeing again') was Mendelssohn's parting response. Felix hoped to be in Leipzig by the end of the year and looked forward to seeing his new pupil as much as he could. David was given a box of cigars, whilst Rockstro was rebuked "for insufficient defences against the cold night air" and an old scarf was supplied. "'Let me wrap this round your throat,' he gasped, having run into the house to collect it and hurried back to the carriage. 'When you get to Leipzig, you can leave it on the coach.'" This did not happen because, when Rockstro came to write his biography, "the dear remembrance of a happy time lies on the table, not having been worn for many a year". Nevertheless, the Frankfurt weather cannot have been too inclement, for a further gift was "a basket of early fruit for the journey".

Whilst he was studying at the Conservatorium that came to be known as 'the Mendelssohnium', notes made by Rockstro were retained, to appear in his biography. Felix took two classes per week in piano technique, and also in composition, each Wednesday and Saturday afternoon. Contemporary pupils included: Otto Goldschmidt, who was later to marry Jenny Lind and, with her, founded the London Bach Choir; Johann Kalliwoda, a Czech composer, whose work is still heard occasionally; and Wilhelm von Wasielewski. The first piece Rockstro recalled analysing was Hummel's D minor Septet. "As each student received an instantaneous proof of his want of sonority, I can still recall the look of blank dismay on their faces." Their tutor showed how the piece should be played, with "grand chords in both forte and piano passages" that were "peculiarly impressive". As each pupil "tried and failed to succeed in this exercise, which he explained with microscopic minuteness and clearness of expression, in order that no student had any doubt as to his meaning, this lesson was priceless. Though his occasional vehemence intimidated the already timid student, he was so perfectly just, so sternly impartial, that consternation soon gave place to confidence – confidence [progressing] to boundless affection."

In 1839 Mendelssohn had explained to Professor Naumann, who had asked if his son might become Mendelssohn's pupil, "I do not know if it is my lack of patience but, on personal experience, the fact remains that I do not succeed in teaching. Occasionally young people have remained with me, but any improvement they have derived was through studying music together, through unreserved communication and casual conversation on various subjects, and also from discussions. This is better than anything else for early youth" – and, he might well have added, for pupils of any age. Yet, because the strictest discipline was the rule, such casual tuition was channelled, in the Leipzig Conservatorium, into a proper basis for learning, and Mendelssohn's admission of impatience proves during these years that he was far too hard on himself when discussing his lack of ability to teach. In any case, for anyone who expects such a high standard, it must be highly irritating to have to repeat a fact more than once to a deliberately inattentive or unwilling pupil. Sows' ears cannot be turned into silk purses if the individual has no wish to learn. If Felix did have cause to lose his temper, pupils at 'the Mendelssohnium' realised that it was for their own benefit. On the other hand, anyone who was seen to be striving towards excellence was amply rewarded by his confidence in and assistance towards that individual.

Carl Reinecke contrasts the teaching methods of Mendelssohn with those of Schumann. "Very free with his comments", Felix gave "clear expression in sharp but concrete criticism so that, in a quarter of an hour, one could glean enough hints on musical rules for an entire lifetime". Schumann, by comparison, "proved to be rather uncommunicative in his personal dealings with the eager disciples of his art". Yet Wilhelm von Wasielewski found the latter "more confiding and encouraging than Mendelssohn, who may, admittedly, have been forced to adopt a certain reserve on account of the unbelievable crowd of people who sought him out", and who, perhaps, tried to maintain the gulf that a person in authority must allow to exist if respect from pupils and staff is to remain. A further anecdote from Rockstro's biography demonstrates Felix's method of teaching. "Once he played three Cs, constructing an enchanting little melody", moulding the three notes into a 'song without words'. On another occasion, having become dissatisfied with an exercise devised by Rockstro, Mendelssohn said in English: "I call that modulation very ungentlemanlike." Though Hauptmann taught harmony and counterpoint, Mendelssohn supervised the more advanced pupils in these disciplines. No one was allowed to include a 'rest' in the stave but had to insert a genuine note, until the whole exercise was completed in red chalk on the blackboard, unless an exception presented itself to this strict rule. Rockstro found himself in such a dilemma. "'Can you not find a note?' Mendelssohn asked. 'Not one that can fit in with the rules,'" was Rockstro's reply. What a surprise the student must have had when, expecting a sarcastic harangue in a voice of thunder, all he received was a hearty laugh, with the response: "'How pleased I am with your answer, for I cannot find one either.' It was a case of checkmate"; Rockstro preened himself on such cleverness.

No one knew, from one lesson to the next, what form it would take. Sometimes a poem would be presented for each pupil to set to music. Each student might, on another occasion, be asked to compose a motet or set some verses of a psalm to music, ready for the next lesson. "You must listen to good singers," was a favourite exhortation from Mendelssohn. "You will learn far more from them than from any piano players you are likely to hear." Sometimes, "a seriously detailed examination" was set, to assess progress, during which Felix "spared neither time nor endeavour to make it as complete as possible". No record is given of how any student fared, nor of any comments by the tutor as a result of such an ordeal, as some would have found it. The only exception was a remark by this paragon Rockstro, who "had the honour" of having his double string quartet performed in July 1846, when Ferdinand David and Joseph Joachim played the first violins.

Mendelssohn's memory for music was a legend, during and after his life. This can be proved when "an English pupil", possibly Charles Horsley, asked how much of Handel's music Felix could recall without a score. "Every note," Mendelssohn replied, not with conceit, but stated as a simple fact. After his death the music critic Rellstab was asked by the King of Prussia if such a phenomenon could apply. Rellstab responded that everything the King had heard about Mendelssohn was completely accurate. Not only did he know, note for note, music that he enjoyed, but, equally, this applied to works he disliked – and to those compositions to which he had never devoted full attention. As for his own work, he never put pen to paper until he was absolutely satisfied with it, having worked out the music in his head. But, with so much mental activity, even Mendelssohn was not invincible, so that it became evident that not even he could continue to dedicate himself so strenuously to promote the standard of musical excellence in Leipzig.

Proving himself human after all, Felix delegated his responsibilities at the Gewandhaus to Niels Gade, and to Ignaz Moscheles as regards the Leipzig Conservatorium.

Of the latter, Rockstro wrote that he "sacrificed his high place in the musical world of London", but how much of a sacrifice was this to Moscheles? His descendant, Henry Roche, gives what appears a more accurate analysis: "The new director saw himself as fulfilling a sacred trust committed to his care by his dead friend", and it cannot be disputed that, had the roles been reversed, Mendelssohn would have carried out the same obligation, unstintingly, for Moscheles.

Chapter 23

The Highest in the Land

It was not until 1871 that Germany became a united country. Before that date there were many states and principalities, some large, some very small indeed, each having a royal house. Thus, at the time such authors as the Brothers Grimm were writing their fairy tales, with their myriad princes or princesses, kings and queens, such royal personages did exist in quantity. It follows, therefore, that a family such as the Mendelssohns – Abraham with his banking interests and Leah with her craving for social prestige – was likely to come into contact as a matter of course with royalty. The first instance of Felix's encounter with royalty appears to have been in 1822, on his way home from a visit with his father to uncle Nathan Mendelssohn in Silesia. Having played at a charity concert, there was no jewellery, gold watches or money for the 13-year-old – simply a posy "presented by a pretty girl". It was only later that his mother wrote to Henriette Mendelssohn, Abraham's sister, boasting that the young girl was, in fact, a princess. In another letter to the same correspondent, Leah boasted of another princess asking for the loan of some compositions Felix had written. It is evident, in view of such beginnings, that Felix soon learnt to accept such meetings with self-effacement, but also with humour.

In 1830 he wrote home from Munich of an evening at the theatre at which King Ludwig I of Bavaria attended. "He must," Felix reported, "have become bored with the incessant playing of 'God save'", as he called the anthem that Weber incorporated into his *Jubilee Overture*. At a further gathering that the King attended Felix was reminded of "a choir. For every one man, there were 30 ladies." At the same court a year later he "gingerly" showed his 1st Piano Concerto to Herr von Schauroth, father of the brilliant pianist Delphine, expressing surprise to his family that the piece was to be played.

Felix attended the coronation of the new King of Hungary whilst on his so-called 'Grand Tour'. Proceedings began in Pressburg (now Bratislava, capital of the Slovak Republic, where Hummel was born), when the militia shouted "Vivat!" outside Felix's window; "I was able to push through the crowd in tremendous uproar, whilst the ladies watched the unbelievably brilliant magnificence of the pageant. The King swore an oath of allegiance from a dais covered with cloth in the Hospitallers Square." These drapes would later be torn down to be used by the public for the making of garments. "The crowd yelled [for the drapes], as if roasting on a spit. Others swarmed like ants onto a coach, occupying box, roof and wheel spokes. Though the grenadiers tried to hold back the crowd, they were powerless." Felix had his hat snatched "without ceremony" by an elderly spectator hoping to gain a better view of the procession; it was then "flattened into the size of a cap".

As for the celebrations, Felix's descriptions are completely reminiscent of a fairy tale. A fountain poured forth "Hungarian wine, red and white" and, after all the "trumpeters, drummers, servants, heralds and all that class", came the nobility. Count Sándor, whom Felix called "mad", was "covered in diamonds, real aigrette feathers and embroidered velvet", his horse "caparisoned in gold". As they galloped along the street, the count "prodded his horse with an ivory sceptre, causing the animal to rear and to bound at every prod", Felix observing that "the Hungarians ride like the devil".

Sixty more officials rode by, "all in the same fantastic splendour, with brightly coloured turbans, amusing moustaches and dark eyes". One rode a white horse "covered with a gold net"; another was mounted on a grey, "with diamond-studded accoutrements; then, a rider on a black horse with purple cloth; one was clad from head to foot in sky blue covered with thickly appliquéd embroidery of gold, except for a white turban and a white robe; another was dressed in cloth of gold and a purple dolman: each horseman more richly attired than his predecessor". Then came the guards with Prince Esterhazy, "dazzling in gems and pearl embroidery", accompanied by "the high golden mitres of the bishops, with all their coloured jewels, their crucifixes glittering in the sunshine like a thousand stars". For children watching such a spectacle, it would have been easy to believe in fairy tales.

It was not only as a spectator that Felix met the royal families. In Düsseldorf, at a fête, triumphal arches were erected and the neighbouring houses were decorated. People cheered for the Crown prince "again and again". He arrived on the Sunday evening at his hunting lodge, "passing under all the triumphal arches, the illuminations, the pealing of bells and the firing of cannons, with an escort of burgher guards, between lines of soldiers and to the sound of martial music", he gave a dinner, to which Felix was invited. "I amused myself famously, being very jovial" amongst his literary and artistic contemporaries. "The Crown prince was as gracious as possible and shook hands with me." Yet, despite such a friendly gesture, Felix found the court itself "proper, polite and polished, and every time you move your elbow you nudge an Excellency", standing in the middle of the room, "with my citizen's heart and my aching head". However, he survived enough to extemporise, when invited, on "royal themes, for which I was highly commended by the Queen".

In 1834 Felix wrote of "leading a gay life" (at a time when the adjective had

Chapter 23: The Highest in the Land

none of its modern connotations), as he described himself "casting aside all cares...full of fun and jollity." His activities appear to have consisted of "eating, sleeping, occasionally riding and bathing". Whilst indulging in the latter pastime, an amusing incident took place. In the cool of the evening, after a hot, sultry day, Felix discovered a rock on the banks of the Ruhr "placed there as if by some sultan". Not only did this allow shade, but it became a suitable place to undress. All would have been fine for him and the two companions, except that the Queen of Bavaria passed by in her barge: "Graf S. presented all the clergy and officials to the Queen. As I had no swimming attire, I felt obliged to dive into the river." Thus, not only the royal party's, but his own embarrassment, was saved. This anecdote, reminiscent of a disingenuous juvenile rather than a man of the world of 25, may disclose a secret fondness for Her Majesty, which, when considered against a further meeting, proved mutual. At a recital Felix had given, the same lady remarked on his power to carry away the audience. No one could think of anything else than his fine playing. "I apologised for having carried away Her Majesty," he wrote home.

It was not only Felix who came into contact with royalty. In 1836 Rebecka had been ordered to take a cure for neuralgia at Franzensbad. Regarding Otho, King of Greece, "the whole people, high and low, stared at him in the street... He passed by and talked to the 'R's near us, so I could see him very well indeed. His appearance is most significant." Another monarch, the King of Wittenberg, became involved with the Mendelssohn family in 1844. The artist Elsasser, who lived in Italy, had painted a picture for him, but the King had offered far too small a price for the painting. Paul was anxious to acquire Elsasser's painting and "has decided to send a bill of exchange for one hundred Louis d'or to Valentini, to be paid at once to Elsasser, if he will let him have the picture," Fanny wrote to Rebecka, then in Italy. "I am very much afraid," Fanny continued, "that this over-scrupulous man will not make up his mind to send it to us... But perhaps, when the King hears that private individuals have offered a far higher price, he may be induced to give more himself. I should be so glad if Paul got the picture." Paul's wish was granted, for which the artist thanked him, sending the painting, once a copy had been made for the King of Wittenberg, "which will carry a note on its reverse that states the original has been purchased".

Yet such encounters are trivial compared with the experiences of Wilhelm Hensel, Fanny's husband. Though Marek passes him off as "a handsome, but indigent artist", this dismissal is far from just. Apart from his painting, it is he who must be given credit for encouraging Fanny to compose and to perform in public, for the first and only time, at a charity concert in 1838, taking the solo part in her brother's G minor Piano Concerto. A synopsis is given of Hensel's early life of painting in Chapter 10, 'That money question'. Now, however, since his marriage and his ability to work in the studio that Abraham had had built, his artistic technique improved beyond recognition. Formerly, through lack of money,

Hensel's sketches were "stiff and sharp"; now, they became "more free and broad", according to his son Sebastian. Whereas he scratched out the colours in earlier days, if light was required, leaving bare the white paper, he could now purchase white paint to allow the right effect in his pictures.

In 1836 Fanny was presented with a copy of his painting *Miriam leading the March of the Children of Israel*, as she pedantically described the title. The original was purchased by Queen Victoria, to hang amongst the Rembrandts and Van Dycks in the Royal Collection. Later, Hensel was asked to make pencil drawings of the Queen, Prince Albert and their eldest son, the Prince of Wales, later to become King Edward VII. King Friedrich Wilhelm IV of Prussia asked to see the sketches.

In 1838 Hensel was able to achieve what Felix was never able to do – attend the coronation of the young Queen. Hensel's description is one of the most enlightening for a historian to study and it is regrettable that, apart from Hensel's son, no other biographer of the Mendelssohn family has covered this event. Hensel had set off for London on 27th May with a view to exhibiting his new work. Whereas none of the art dealers showed interest, the young Queen was enthusiastic. Thus, *Miriam* joined what Hensel called "the heroes of art" – Raphael, Rubens, among other "greats" – in the Royal Collection. Since anyone and everyone who had pretensions to fashion copied what the royal family did, "with the help of God and good fortune", as Hensel realised, further opportunities would allow him other commissions. The Duchess of Sutherland wanted a figure from the *Miriam* painting to be reproduced, and Lord Egerton followed her example, requesting a scene from a ball given by the Duke of Devonshire on the eve of Waterloo in 1815 that had been represented in paint. This had been described in Cantos 21 and 22 of Byron's *Childe Harold*. It was through this circumstance that Hensel obtained a ticket for the coronation, on 28th June 1838. He made a sketch of "the fair young girl entering Westminster Abbey, passing along the line of red-coated guardsmen". Hensel imagined himself in the Middle Ages as he saw the Queen's mediaeval costume – "A glimpse of sunlight had settled on such a pretty picture" – and he saw this as a happy omen: "I prayed that the young sovereign will enjoy a worthy reign."

That evening, after the dress rehearsal, Hensel dined quietly and mingled afterwards among the crowds, in order to gather material for future work. Early the next morning carriages could be seen "rolling about" along the neighbouring streets, decorated with greenery; "I could imagine how Shakespeare must have pictured a similar scene as described in Macbeth, when Birnam Wood marched to Dunsinane, as the witches had predicted." At 5.15, Hensel continued, "the children of the nobility were dragged from bed to make the journey to the Abbey before the crush ensued. Ice was brought from wherever water could be frozen [before the advent of the refrigerator]. Irish oxen were paraded through the streets to be roasted and consumed on plates, dishes or without these orthodox eating accessories." Hensel was invited to watch the procession "in an ideal vantage

Chapter 23: The Highest in the Land

point", outside the Westminster Hospital. Julius Benedict invited Hensel to dine and to meet musical colleagues at a house he had taken in Piccadilly. These included the baritone Lablache, singing teacher to the young Queen, and the celebrated soprano, Mme. Grisi.

On the whole the crowds behaved well, though Hensel did observe the recently established Metropolitan Police "grabbing an occasional collar, brutally in manner, without reason and pushing the unfortunate individual into another part of the crowd" for committing the heinous crime of being pushed beyond the cordon in the first place. The cavalry controlled the "press of humanity" in a far more authoritative manner than the "futile piece of meddling" Hensel considered the police to have effected. "I saw more drunken women than men in the same state", one of whom his neighbour was able to pacify "by familiar jokes and a few boxes on the ear". Whereas some of the aristocracy were hissed, others, notably the Duke of Wellington, the Austrian ambassador and, ironically, Marshal Soult (a former enemy, being one of Napoleon's generals), were loudly cheered. "The Belgian ambassador, Prince De Ligne, received fewer greetings, whilst General Sebastiani (to whose daughter Henriette Mendelssohn had been governess) was overlooked altogether." Hensel was particularly delighted with "the most beautiful six horses with their rich harness, the carriages and grooms covered with fine embroidery". But, most outstanding of all for Hensel was "the fairy-like carriage, supported by tribunes with their tridents," bearing the Queen, "bowing right and left", to the Abbey. All that could be seen from the crowds were handkerchiefs and hats waving, the roar "drowning the sound of bells, trumpets and drums". Hensel had to pinch himself to ensure that he was not dreaming, so splendid was the procession, "as if from a tale in *The Arabian Nights' Entertainment.*"

Everyone was in place within the hour and, as Hensel progressed "into the solemn obscurity" of the Abbey, he observed further soldiers in mediaeval costume. "Their cheeks suggested beer; their noses whisky and claret." Hensel admitted having spent less money that day than any other whilst in London. Before setting out, tea and coffee were served with "eggs, etc.". The luncheon comprised "beef, ham, jellies, ices, etc.". Sadly, no mention is made of the actual ceremony. But, though the scenes he had witnessed that day would remain with him for the rest of his life, he would not have liked to repeat the feeling he experienced during the evening. After all the excitement of the day, he found this an anticlimax and would have loved his wife to have travelled with him.

It turned out that Hensel did not feel it worthwhile to describe the full details of the coronation ceremony, "since all the newspapers, British and foreign", covered the events in full detail, which the Mendelssohn relatives would be bound to have read from cover to cover. On 18th September Fanny expressed thanks to Klingemann that her husband had arrived home, albeit one day later than anticipated, owing to a measles epidemic in Hamburg that caused panic.

Hensel was later to associate with royalty in the person of King Friedrich

Wilhelm IV of Prussia who was crowned in 1840. Fanny had it in mind that the new King was "always willing to give money to those who need it", and her husband was asked to approach him on behalf of the artist Elsasser, who, by that time, was gravely ill. This idea stemmed from the fact that Felix had sought his help on behalf of a young musician from Mecklenburg, "speaking of his music in very high terms", resulting in the provision of 200 thalers to enable the young Mecklenburger to study in Berlin. Felix was addressed as "some being from another sphere" in gratitude. "Indeed, it is the most natural flow of gratitude I have ever heard," Fanny wrote. "This is only one out of a thousand pretty, touching, amusing and out-of-the-way things that have happened to Felix."

It was a different situation between the King and Felix's own career. The musicologist Michael Steinberg claims that it was through the recommendation of von Humboldt and Ambassador Bunsen that the sovereign commanded Mendelssohn to serve him at the Prussian court. Felix at first declined, saying he did not wish to involve himself in disputes between Church and State, but would compose music for the King. Eventually, however, minister von Massow asked Paul to negotiate with Felix regarding the appointment. Felix did not like the idea of "losing my despotism", as he jokingly termed his directorship over the Leipzig musicians, having gained so much prestige, credibility and respect for that city's musical life. Freedom and independence were of far greater importance to Felix than all the pomp entailed in serving a king, or the 3,000 thalers per annum that were promised for that post.

The Mendelssohn family were full of hope for the future, after the many disappointments of the old King's reign. When Fanny heard from her mother of the new King's accession, she wrote: "We shall see many changes. Let us hope they will be for the best." Matters did augur well initially. Conscription, in existence since 1819, was abolished and three of the 'Göttingen Seven', banished from their university posts for so-called sedition against the government, were reinstated. Meyerbeer had been summoned from Paris to replace Spontini at the Berlin Opera. The Brothers Grimm were to visit Berlin shortly, and the poet Rückert was to be given an appointment at court. Were Rebecka to have lived under the Pope's jurisdiction, she wrote, she would be "the most loyal of Protestants, even if only because the King has brought Felix onto the Berlin stage".

But such an idyllic atmosphere did not last. Reforms of the constitution and parliament that were promised did not come into effect, leading, in 1848, to revolution in Berlin – a pattern that was taken up all over mainland Europe. The artist Peter Cornelius had been given a court appointment but, as Fanny confided to her journal, "he does not seem the most appropriate person to further the revival of German art. He continually copies the frescoes of Schinkel, whose mind has completely gone", and she wondered whether there would be any cultural renaissance in Berlin as far as art was concerned. "Newspapers are as poor as ever. Philistinism is rampant." Rebecka complained that the King's birthday was

Chapter 23: The Highest in the Land

celebrated with dinners, addresses from schoolchildren and that everything was "heavy and dull". The only features of the whole scene she found attractive were "the moonlight and the sun, which replaced it at 3.30 a.m. the following morning". Indeed, the situation was succinctly summarised by the Austrian chancellor, Prince Metternich. Unless he was wrong, and this redoubtable person was never wont to admit such a human failing, he called the new King "a fine and imaginative dreamer". There was a distinction between what he planned and what was actually to take effect. As with many such individuals, however grand the ideas and ideals he possessed, they never became reality. King Friedrich Wilhelm IV preferred not to carry out plans in which something might go amiss.

Though Wilfrid Blunt recommends Marek's and Eric Werner's biographies of Mendelssohn for anyone to study the concatenation of circumstances relating to Mendelssohn's ill-starred appointment, in this book Felix's own letters are used. At face value, the King's project must have seemed exciting and fulfilling for such a free-spirited individual as Felix Mendelssohn. The proposed Academy of the Arts and Sciences would comprise four faculties: art, sculpture, architecture and music, which latter Mendelssohn was to direct. Apart from the 3,000 thalers per annum he would receive as his salary, he would be given the title of Kapellmeister. His remit would include the organisation of all music in Berlin, and a Conservatorium would be founded, in which students would be expected to perform with the Court Theatre and at concerts. Mendelssohn would also be asked to compose new works for the King's private entertainment. The new sovereign had been disappointed that such a man, from such a prestigious family, had chosen to "exile himself" in Leipzig, as Kupferberg describes Felix's sojourn in that city. The time was long overdue for this internationally renowned composer and conductor to be "brought back to his own environment".

According to Rockstro: "One after another, the cavalcade of petty annoyances soon proved that the grandiose scheme, as conceived by the King, would be impracticable to be put into effect. As Mendelssohn had foreseen initially...he found everything in so unsatisfactory a condition that he felt compelled to tender his resignation from the King's service." Paul visited his brother in Leipzig, to whom Felix stated his view that Paul's letter demanded "mature deliberation"; Felix would have preferred to make his decision before the interview with von Massow. Though he valued the honour conferred upon him, he would have liked it if his job specification had been more clearly defined before accepting the post. "You will perceive that I can accept the proposals only when they either define every point or confine themselves to my personal, rather than to my official, situation. If the two are blended, then I cannot agree to undertake them. You must clear the compass to allow me to pursue as clear a path as possible." He stipulated that he would have nothing to do with any concerts unless he had full control in directing the orchestra, as in Leipzig and elsewhere, and he had to have unqualified support from whoever might be relevant; "I delay my commitment from day to day, because such a step must be final." When eventually Mendelssohn did arrive in Berlin, the contrast can only be imagined between the well-ordered musical life of Leipzig and the "official blundering" that completely paralysed that of Berlin, which Rockstro describes as "a fiasco".

As for the Academy, so glowingly promised, it was only after Mendelssohn's lifetime that this came into existence for Berlin. Writing to Klingemann, his most trusted friend, Felix found his move to Berlin "one of the sourest apples a man can eat, yet eaten it must be". On 13th February 1841 Felix wrote of "time and people standing still... There are weeks when everything seems to run about like billiard-balls – making cannons; losing and winning hazards." On 19th June he asked Paul "not to be angry" at his inability to fix a date for his return to Berlin from Leipzig. "God willing, the recent cavilling is now coming to a definite end." Though his salary had been settled, the further details of his employment had still not been arranged. Though Paul accused Felix of "hair-splitting" over the term 'Kapellmeister', which he had not chosen for his own glory, but for the respect and credibility that his appointment would be given, "it is not right to portray something as coveted when offered to someone who is in no way involved, as you appear to have done... Time is being wasted and I foresee...that I shall lose the coming summer, which I should like to have spent in travelling... I solemnly oblige you not to take another single step in this matter, in particular, not to say anything at court. This would look like pressurising and even the appearance of this must be avoided."

Later the same year Mendelssohn composed a cantata, *Antigone*, at the King's command, which, like much of his music, has become shamefully neglected. It was Professor Böckh who introduced the sovereign to the plays of Aeschylus and Sophocles. Böckh had often visited the Mendelssohn home and, as Felix attended his lectures, it would have been natural for him to discuss these dramas with the professor and to become familiar with them. Sophocles's *Antigone* was premiered on 28th November 1841, in Potsdam. A medallion was ordered by the King to be cast, commemorating this event; on one side Mendelssohn and the 68-year-old librettist Ludwig Tieck were represented, with the original playwright on the obverse. Though people from as far afield as England and Russia came to the performance, the Berliners soon became tired of the work. But Droysen waxed lyrical on the piece. "You must have penetrated to this innermost core of this ancient splendour...something no musician has yet accomplished," he wrote to Felix. Not only did Böckh introduce the King to *Antigone* but he suggested that only Mendelssohn was capable of composing the required music. A theatre journal wrote of the cantata: "The play must not be a mere masterly and brilliant court festival... The work is intended for...the whole public." To Droysen, Felix confessed that he wrote the piece for his own amusement – an experiment to see if he could compose music suitable for this centuries-old drama.

But, though time progressed, Mendelssohn's position at court did not. His

Chapter 23: The Highest in the Land

frustration can only be imagined. He was hampered not only by the lack of employment in the King's service, but at having to adopt a tactful front on the matter towards the King's ministers, and his own family. No one, least of all himself, knew what would happen next; neither had he any power to push matters along. He even had to wait for the King to commission him to write any music.

Not only Mendelssohn but other celebrities were treated in such a cavalier fashion by the King of Prussia. Any bright ideas would remain just that, only to be shelved when practical difficulties (real or imaginary) ensued. From Interlaken, where he took a holiday, Mendelssohn wrote that he did not know if he would remain in Berlin for good or for a few weeks only: "The whole affair has been so topsy-turvy recently that I can no longer tell up from down and I am becoming quite perplexed and confused whenever I try to think about what I ought to do. When I return, things will no doubt work out, but do not be angry with me for the long period of uncertainty. I cannot help it."

To von Massow Felix wrote excusing the King on account of the welter of correspondence with which he would have to deal, but he sought a further interview with the monarch: "I will, meanwhile, await your response in some other place, where I can be useful and efficient for the moment, until either the new building is complete or until the King requires my services elsewhere, when I would consider it a great happiness to hasten back and to exert my best energies for such a sovereign, whose mandates in themselves show the highest regard for an artist". Court officials were reminded by Mendelssohn on another occasion that the King had summoned a choral ensemble "to serve as a rallying-point and pattern...gradually to elevate and ennoble church music and to ensure its greater development". A further group of musicians had also been engaged "to support grand performances of oratorios, ...which will produce the most solemn and noble effect", such as had occurred at the jubilee celebration at St Nicholas Church. Meanwhile, since Felix had been given no work from His Majesty, he sought permission to return to Leipzig, in which case his salary would be halved, he requested. Whenever called upon, he vowed, "with the utmost zeal and to the best of my ability...for as long as I take advantage of this freedom from work", to be aware of "all the favours so lavishly bestowed on Your Majesty's most devoted servant...till death".

The King, via von Massow, awarded Felix the title of general musical director, which would allow him to "hold his own against Meyerbeer in Berlin". But there was still no definite work schedule to accompany this designation. "I can no longer endure the state of suspense in Berlin," he wrote to Klingemann. This occupational rootlessness depressed him so much that "I requested to be told plainly that I should do nothing, or to be told exactly what to do", and he asked for an interview to submit his resignation from the King's service. This prompted a strong response, as Felix reported: "The King was very displeased with me and it was his intention to take his leave in very few words." However, in Leipzig, the announcement came that the 20,000 thalers so long promised could be used to found the Conservatorium there. "Once this is established, I may well say that I have been the means of procuring a permanent advantage for music here. If they begin anything worthwhile in Berlin, I can settle there with a clear conscience."

Once her recalcitrant son had made up his mind to flee the maternal nest, Leah wept so copiously that Felix was compelled to continue to work in Berlin as often as possible. He wrote to Klingemann of his mother's "demand" for letters, which made him "distraught". It was evident, however often Felix reminded her, that Leah had no idea how heavy her son's workload in Leipzig was. On 12th December 1842 his mother passed away. Felix wrote to Klingemann of how his sisters wept at his departure for Leipzig, which was greeted "in ill will, however thankful this might be to me. I could not have believed that news would affect them so strongly. You know how calm mother generally was and how seldom she allowed anyone to get a real glimpse into her heart. Therefore, it was doubly and trebly painful for me to cause her such unhappiness, and yet I could not do otherwise." It might be that Leah had had a premonition that she would not see her son again, but could not bring herself to tell him of this before she died.

Felix was now able to live where he pleased and to travel when required, so long as he was available to compose music for his sovereign. His interview was arranged "at the King's house", via von Massow, whom Felix called "the kindliest friend in Berlin". Though not even the King could force Felix to live in Berlin, his departure would cause "heartfelt regret". Afterwards, Felix reported that "the King must have been in an extraordinarily good mood for, instead of being angry with me, I have never seen him so amiable and confiding. His plans have been frustrated and there would be a void that no one else could fill," the King had admitted. When Mendelssohn was asked to recommend a successor, Ludwig Spohr was his suggestion as the most suitable. However, comfortably ensconced in his position as Kapellmeister at Cassel, the ageing musician declined the Berlin appointment. Before Leah died, Felix had considered bringing to Berlin one movement each of his incidental music from *Oedipus at Colonus* and the *Midsummer Night's Dream*, the overture of which, written 17 years previously, dovetailed so beautifully with his current work. Though each had been commissions from the King, "I wonder how well such musical experiments will be received, in view of the usual repertoire [Berlin] audiences are obliged to hear". Such an example was a composition by the British ambassador, the Earl of Westmorland. "You will again say that I am cynical," he warned his mother, "but you must be indulgent towards my own ideas, so closely bound up with my life and art." Spohr, Felix added, must be congratulated on his common sense for refusing the King's appointment. What Felix called "this tedious, everlasting affair" was making him angry, as he confided to his brother. A further communication from von Massow "irritated me so much that it almost made me ill, and I do not feel right yet". Further clauses had been added to what served as a contract, "which show, in the clearest possible light, all

Chapter 23: The Highest in the Land

the difficulties to which I formerly alluded, the existence of which Herr von Massow denies". Felix had considered writing to His Majesty direct, but thought better of it, preferring to shelve the whole rigmarole into which he had been dragged.

Regarding the commissions, Felix wrote "in a friendly manner, but which cost me four of the most angry, disturbing and tiresome days". Biographers of Mendelssohn constantly take him to task for allowing his music to lose its "sparkle and originality" of former years during his period in the King's 'service'. "Neither did he compose so much music as he should have done," adds Marek. On the contrary, in view of so much disorientation for such a sensitive artist, it is remarkable how much music *did* come from Mendelssohn's pen in these later years. Name any of his better-known music, and it can be seen that, with a few exceptions, it is in these years that they were written. Indeed, in view of such emotional upheaval, it is surprising that he was able to undertake any work of his own at all. Felix himself admitted to Paul that he found inspiration difficult, "except to sketch the Jungfrau in Indian ink" whilst taking a much needed holiday in Switzerland; "the mountain is, I think, excellent but, again, I have utterly destroyed the pines in the foreground." Though not precisely "in a black mood", he wrote to Sir George MacFarren in London, "I am certainly in a half-grey one." Even in Leipzig, "with wife, children, chairs, table, piano and everything", the thought of his time with the Prussian court still depressed him. He tried to compose a 'cello sonata for Paul (still in manuscript at the time of writing this book) and this is when the music for Racine's *Athalie* was planned, as he wrote to Klingemann. "The original French drama has to be translated into German for the private order and the private use of the King of Prussia... There are many things in it to be combed out and brushed up. If, from time to time, I carry out some of these musical ideas on which nobody else wants to break his teeth, it is because I think he will be satisfied and let me live where and how I like, and thus we shall both benefit."

Felix asked his brother about the "mischief surrounding *Athalie*", which did not receive its premiere until 1845 and is given very short shrift by Radcliffe and Marek, who dismiss the music as "very undistinguished" and "pompous". The fact was, though, that a king's servant had to please his sovereign, which, in view of the Prussian ethos, is why such comments might be justified. (For further details of this, and other commissions, please see Chapter 17, 'Quest for an opera', in which Mendelssohn's incidental music is discussed.) Felix, meanwhile, had become so insecure as to whom he could trust that he even wrote to ask Paul if he could stay, whilst in Berlin, at his former home, Leipzigerstrasse 3. It appears that, contrary to the usual process of law, it was Paul, the younger brother, who had inherited the Mendelssohn mansion. On this occasion the King had commanded Felix to direct the music for Prussia's 1,000th anniversary celebrations. Though, as was his wont, Felix put all his energy and skill into this task, he still abhorred "all the annoyances and vexations" of so much "tiresome correspondence... All this is very confusing and I do not like it at all," he wrote to Paul. "It is true that his [the King's] head must also be in a daze and he seems to take all imaginable trouble about the affair [but] I need to bring the whole everlasting paperwork for your inspection, which we can read together when we meet." Felix hoped when the celebrations had ended, to have a dinner with the King "and a satisfactory discussion about business". A chorale Felix had written "appears [to be] just what the King wishes. At all events, it furnishes an opportunity for a complete understanding."

Rebecka, having heard the work, considered it "symbolic of his own affairs, which remain unresolved and are likely to be so for the next 1,000 years". Whilst in Italy she had heard from a Scotsman that Felix was to oversee Berlin Cathedral's music, she wrote to Fanny. Her sister responded that such a decision had been ratified, "so there will be good music in Berlin during the coming winter", especially as Felix would have less work with the Berlin Opera, as their building had been burnt down. As regards Felix's sarcasm concerning the personnel with whom he was obliged to work at the Opera, "we scarcely know how to stop laughing". Of a performance she had attended, conducted by Felix, she wrote to Rebecka: "The costume worn by A could only be described as a paraphrase...of black silk, trimmed with fur, resembling that of a tortoiseshell cat. The sleeves revealed the wearer's bony arms; the black velvet breeches arranged like those of a lunatic. The whole thing was evidently intended to be artistic, but succeeded in being so hideous that I really could not take my eyes off her."

At a soirée Fanny recounted how Felix had to conduct Lord Westmorland's "ridiculously childish symphony, betraying a smile of sarcasm during the performance". Fanny's continued yearning for her brother to remain in Berlin can still be perceived after Leah's death. "Felix never gives way to temper as he used and, if he so remains, the family cannot be thankful enough for having him in Berlin." But, for Mendelssohn himself, his joy and relief can only be imagined on returning to his own little kingdom of Leipzig, where he was allowed to rule supreme as far as music was concerned. Just as he had yearned to return 'home', his people looked forward with unalloyed pleasure to the end of 'King Felix's' exile. Ferdinand David immediately handed over the "baton as if it were a sceptre to its rightful guardian. Just as he had composed his setting of Psalm 95 in thankfulness for his marriage, so Felix completed his Violin Concerto, Op. 64, to thank David, his concert master, for all his work during the composer's absence. The King of Saxony commanded a performance of the *Hymn of Praise*, which went "with such precision that it was a joy to listen to it," Mendelssohn reported. During the interval Felix was summoned by the sovereign and, to reach him, "was obliged to walk through a double row of ladies". Felix continued: "He conversed with me for some time in the most good-natured and friendly manner and spoke very well about music." During the second half of the concert Mendelssohn heard murmurings from the audience to the effect that the King wished to see him again. Mendelssohn

Chapter 23: The Highest in the Land

continued, "He came up to my desk and spoke to me in a most animated manner and with such cordiality and warmth that I really did feel pleased and honoured. He mentioned the particular passages he liked best, thanked all the singers and then departed, whilst the whole orchestra, and the whole audience, made the best bows and curtsies they could possibly manage. There arose a hubbub of confusion like Noah's Ark. Perhaps he would grant the 20,000 thalers that I long ago petitioned might be given for music here. In that case, I can honestly say that I have rendered a good service to the music of Leipzig."

Since that occasion, no one could imagine what impetus had been given to the musical life in Leipzig by the King's "cordial and kind appreciation". Not only had he shown "pure, kind and natural feelings in his demeanour, but his praise was not comprised of mere words solely, but he facilitated a number of things for us that were not thought of formerly. Visitors from Dresden appear at every concert. Singers vie with one another to appear in Leipzig from Saxony's chief city [Dresden]." The King of Saxony asked Felix to improvise at a concert there, and, as Gluck's opera *Iphigenia in Aulis* had been performed the previous evening, Mendelssohn concocted a potpourri of its themes, though he had not heard the opera for seven years. Such a feat of memory must have impressed the King, for he vowed to make Felix Kapellmeister at Dresden. But this was impossible and, even as late as 7th January 1844, Felix was still in the King of Prussia's domination, though he was determined that the "delightful harmony" that Leipzig engendered would not be marred by any misunderstanding between court officials and himself. He trusted that Paul would empathise with any doubts on the matter and he had to understand that, despite any anger Felix had expressed, he hoped, at some future date, to live "at your house". But Mendelssohn's sister Fanny had to admit how "I hate having to be civil to such inferior court officials". She reported to Rebecka how Felix had to accompany a "Mme. O." in a French song at a party given by von Massow, followed by "an Italian duet and other trash. The guests chattered the whole way through his trio, which had been requested. Felix did not even show temper" at such a travesty. "On the whole, in fact, he has never been so even-tempered as he is at the present time, though he has had a good deal to try him." However, after a party given by Devrient, so popular at court, "his rage lasted for three days" at the "uncommonly stupid" scenes from *Bluebeard* that were acted. As for minister Eichhorn, "though he may be a fool, one must look higher for greater foolishness". The more diligently Felix tried to fulfil his obligations at court the more obstacles were put in his way, and, though she missed the presence of her brother's children, Fanny realised how "absolutely normal" Felix's attitude had been. "To stay on such slippery ground is impossible in such circumstances. He does not wish to be an indifferent, doubtful, secretly discontented servant of the King."

What turned out to be the last straw for Felix versus the King was the command not only to compose music for the *Oresteia* of Aeschylus, comprising the

Agamemnon, the *Choephori* and the *Eumenides*, but that the trilogy had to be telescoped into one drama. Felix declared that no musician could carry out such a commission, and that though he might be prepared to lose the King's opinion of him he certainly was not prepared to lose his own self-respect by attempting the task. This caused anger at court. Müller demanded peremptorily, in the King's name, that orders should be obeyed without question, misunderstanding Mendelssohn's reason for this disobedience and perceiving Felix to have committed a personal slight against his sovereign. Bunsen, "in a kindly spirit", explained how hurt the King had become. He was not prepared to let the matter drop, though, and, if Mendelssohn would not oblige, someone else would be given the commission. Tieck recognised Felix's "character and genius", but his stubbornness left "a painful impression upon everyone concerned". Bunsen admonished Mendelssohn that "we should all assist in supporting this noble ruler in his great, good and grand idea", signing himself "your unchangeable friend".

Why, it must be wondered, was Mendelssohn so reluctant to break away from what was, to all intents and purposes, slavery to the King's commands? With so much moral blackmail from his family and pressure from the Prussian court, he could be said, in today's vernacular, to have been in a 'no-win' situation. Added to this, A. B. Marx (according to his widow's memoirs) asked his erstwhile friend to wait until the unsympathetic court officials had been replaced. "In vain did I try to reason with him," Marx is purported to have declared. Even Klingemann expressed caution at such a "hasty" decision to resign from court. Entrenched as he was in diplomatic protocol, he might have feared the detrimental effect such a foolish decision would have on Felix's future career. On 10th January 1845 Mendelssohn wrote to Rebecka: "I cannot cling onto such a position with a clear conscience, in view of such inept organisation that I have no power to reform." Only the King could put any improvements into effect for Berlin's artistic well-being, and he, Felix excused his sovereign, because he "has too many other matters on his mind".

Therefore, once the edict was signed to allow Mendelssohn to return to his former life in Leipzig, he received "a pretty serenade", according to Fanny, on leaving Berlin. "The whole population was in distress at his return to Leipzig, but all, or nearly all, made some contribution to make him go."

Though Felix received the Order of Merit from the King of Prussia – given also, later, to Liszt, Rossini and Wagner – far smaller tributes moved him more. For instance, whilst walking with some friends at Offenbach, a toll keeper asked if Herr Mendelssohn was in the party. When this was confirmed he refused to accept the requisite toll money, which he paid from his own resources. It turned out that the toll keeper belonged to a music society, and prized Mendelssohn's music highly. "Hm. I like this better than the King's award," the composer remarked. Returning to Leipzig, at his first Gewandhaus concert Felix was "greeted by a flourish of trumpets and drums and a storm of applause from the audience". No wonder

Chapter 23: The Highest in the Land

Fanny was able to confide to her journal how her brother had "once again become lovable".

Yet, despite his true feelings towards the King (which, by that time, might have mellowed), on 17th October 1847, less than a month before he died, Mendelssohn dedicated his oratorio *Elijah* to his sovereign, sending a grovelling letter. Felix was "taking the liberty of laying, with the utmost reverence, the enclosed first copy of the score, at your feet, not only with the deepest and innermost gratitude, which makes this my duty, but to prove how constantly I strive to be more and more worthy of your generosity". Mendelssohn had hoped, he explained, to present his original version to the King in person but, having been detained in Leipzig through illness, did not want to wait until the revised *Elijah* was published. "I am, therefore, making so bold," Felix concluded, "in sending the original score through the mail. With deepest reverence from Your Majesty's humble servant." There appears to be no record as to how moved, or guilt-ridden, the King must have felt on hearing of Mendelssohn's death on 4th November 1847, or how deeply he appreciated his good fortune in engaging a man of such genius, tact and patience to serve him.

Whatever his shortcomings, the people of England must pay a debt of gratitude for one thoughtful gesture, for it was Friedrich Wilhelm IV of Prussia who gave Felix a letter of introduction to his relative, Prince Albert. Thus began several visits to Buckingham Palace for Mendelssohn. There were no doubts as to his suitability to meet the Queen and Prince Consort. Ambassador Bunsen, now Prussian representative in London, knew Felix well, as did many at whose houses he had dined – bishops, aristocrats and celebrities of the time. There was also a further individual, not acknowledged in Mendelssohn biographies to date. Miss Marianne Skerrett, a friend of the Horsley family, happened to be Queen Victoria's private secretary. According to the artist, Edward Landseer, if anything at the palace went amiss, whether involving a crowned head of Europe or the lowliest kitchen maid, the command went forth: "Send for Miss Skerrett", who invariably put the matter right. This redoubtable lady could well have "put in a word or two" on Felix's behalf, having known of him through visits to the Horsleys.

Much has been written about music and the royal houses of Germany. When, therefore, the Hanoverian dynasty ruled the United Kingdom, it is logical that such a pastime would be inherited. George III patronised Bach's son, Johann Christian, known as 'the London Bach', and the Prince of Wales, later to become George IV, was praised by Haydn not only as "the handsomest man on God's earth" but because his 'cello playing was "quite talented". Prince Albert's compositions became celebrated, and are still played, although the French ambassador, Guizot, is purported to have slept through a performance. The young Queen nudged the diplomat's elbow, at which Guizot nodded to the prince in approval – and promptly fell asleep again. As a princess, Victoria was taught to sing by the legendary Luigi Lablache. On one occasion he is said to have sung a note "from piano to forte and back again, at the same time drinking from a glass, followed by a chromatic scale and, finally, blowing out a candle – all in one breath". This story could be apocryphal, since no singer worth the name allows an audience to hear when a breath is taken.

Before its first London performance, on 14th June 1842, Mendelssohn's 'Scottish' Symphony was played at a private concert, together with opera fantasies arranged for the piano by Thalberg. As the Prince Consort attended the event, it could well have been on this occasion that Felix's first invitation to Buckingham Palace was extended. Whereas, according to Jeremy Siepmann's biography of Chopin, when that composer was asked to play for the Duchess of Sutherland "the Queen wore her diamonds and orders", there was no such pomp and ceremony for Mendelssohn. Having escorted her guest to the drawing room, her first comment referred to the havoc caused by a draught, which had blown loose-leaf papers from a music portfolio lying on the table. Papers had spread over the floor, almost touching the organ pedals. Kneeling, the Queen set to work to tidy the disorder, "which, by the way, made a very pretty feature in the room," Felix wrote to his family. Prince Albert helped his wife to accomplish this task, "and I, too, was not idle," Felix wrote with pride. The Prince Consort explained how the organ stops worked and, asked by the Queen to play something, obliged with a chorale, played "by heart, with pedals, so charmingly, clearly and correctly that many an organist could have learnt something. The Queen, having finished her work, sat beside him and listened, very pleased." It must have been this incident that the Princess Royal, their eldest daughter, recalled when, as a very young child, she remembered having heard a few chords from the melody.

An acquaintance named Grahl had informed Felix that Buckingham Palace was "the only friendly English home that is really comfortable", yet Mendelssohn admitted to knowing others equally comfortable in London. He found the Queen "so pretty and charming; so youthful; so shyly friendly and courteous, and she speaks good German". She apologised for wearing a house-dress rather than anything more glamorous, but explained that the family were due to travel to their country house at Claremont for a holiday that afternoon. "The Queen knows all my music so well – the four books of *Songs without Words*; those with words; the symphony and the *Hymn of Praise* and *St Paul*." Thus, when Felix was asked to play to the royal couple, he began with a part of this oratorio, 'How Lovely are Thy Messengers', in which they joined before the aria had finished. "They began to sing the chorus very well and, all the time, Prince Albert managed the stops so expertly for me. First the flute, then full at the forte [and] the whole register at the D major part. Then he produced such an excellent diminuendo with the stops, and so on till the end of the piece, all from memory, with which I was heartily pleased." When Felix was asked to improvise, a discrepancy arose as to which themes were to be employed. "We gave him two," Queen Victoria recorded in her journal; 'Rule, Britannia!' and the Austrian national anthem... Really, I have never heard anything so beautiful." With the right hand Mendelssohn played one melody, the

Chapter 23: The Highest in the Land

other with the left hand. However, Felix himself, when writing to his family (and he should know), stated that he played 'Gaudeamus Igitur', the student song that the prince would have known (later to be used in the finale of Brahms's *Academic Festival* Overture and Lützow's *Forest Hunt*). Such extemporisations were "somewhat difficult, but remonstrances were out of the question" for, "since they gave me the themes, I had to be able to play them".

Several of his *Songs without Words* were included in this recital, and his "Serenade" – presumably Op. 43. As a matter of interest, the Prince of Wales, later Edward VII, would be born later that year, on 9th November; thus, though biographers speak of the Queen and her husband listening to the concert, their eldest son, so recently conceived, could well have ingested the music. Felix then described the "great gallery" to which he was led, "in which many portraits were hanging, which did not displease me". His 'Scottish' Symphony was "received by one and all with a degree of amiability and kindness which exceeds anything I have ever known in the way of hospitality. All this sometimes makes my head feel quite bewildered and confused, and I have to pull myself together, in order that I do not lose all self-control." A piano arrangement was made of the symphony for the Queen and Prince Consort to play as a duet. According to the Queen's journal, this arrangement was played at Claremont on Christmas Eve of that year.

But Mendelssohn's visit was not completely devoid of embarrassment. "After a little begging from her husband that the Queen should show off her voice, the song 'Spring Thoughts' was selected." Enquiries revealed that it had already been despatched to Claremont. The Queen then summoned "Lady N-N – I did not catch her name; the bell was rung, the servant sent after the music, but returned embarrassed". Thwarted, Her Majesty was heard to remark: "This really is most unseemly," Felix reported. "Nevertheless, rummaging among the music, I found my first set of songs, so, naturally, I begged Her Majesty to choose one, rather than the Gluck suggested by Prince Albert, to which she kindly agreed." However, it was one of Fanny's songs that was chosen, known in English as 'In Italy'. Apart from a D natural, as opposed to a D flat, in the third stanza, "the Queen sang beautifully in tune, in strict time, and with very nice expression...in a really charming style, and the last long G I have never heard sung better, purer or more naturally by any amateur". Later Felix could not resist asking his hostess to sing one of his own songs, to which she agreed, "provided I gave her plenty of help". 'At Parting' was chosen, which was "sung, really, without a mistake, with charm, feeling and expression. The Queen explained she was nervous," Felix continued, "otherwise she would have had a very long breath" – the result of tuition from Lablache, as likely as not. This remark arose because Mendelssohn, not wishing to be too ingratiating, merely thanked her initially, which the Queen interpreted as disapproval of her style of singing. "So I praised her heartily with the best conscience in the world."

Prince Albert then sang 'Death, the Reaper', but whether the guest's attention wandered can only be conjectured. Mendelssohn observed that, near the piano, "an enormous rocking horse" was positioned, along with "two large birdcages, pictures on the walls, beautifully bound books on the tables and music on the piano". From one of the birdcages a further embarrassment occurred. Before the Queen sang she had asked if a parrot could be removed from the room, as its screech was louder than she could sing. Though a servant was summoned to remove the offending bird, and though the Prince of Coburg volunteered for this duty, it was left to Mendelssohn to accomplish the task. "Allow me," he begged, "and, as no one negated this plea, I lifted the heavy cage out to the astonished servants. If Dirichlet calls me an aristocrat, this must be corrected. I swear that I am a greater radical than ever." "Poor Mendelssohn was quite exhausted," the Queen noted in her journal. Felix noted that, as a rule, when improvising, he played "so dreadfully badly and, had this occurred on the present occasion, I would have been vexed, but, without any arrogance at all, I really improvised so well. I was in the mood for it and played for a long time and enjoyed it." Having left the palace, he continued his description of this auspicious visit. "I saw the beautiful carriage waiting, with its scarlet-clad outriders and, in a quarter of an hour, the flag was lowered." The Queen left the palace at "30 minutes past three", contemporary newspapers reported. As for Felix, "I walked back through the rain to Klingemann's and enjoyed more than anything giving a piping hot account to him and Cécile", who had travelled to London with her husband but, for some reason that has never been explained, did not accompany him to Buckingham Palace.

Whilst the Queen busied herself with the missing music, Prince Albert had given Felix a box containing a ring on which 'VR, 1842' was engraved. The prince explained that the Queen had wished their guest to receive this gift. They also expressed a desire for him to visit the palace again when he was next in London – a trip that would take place in 1844.

On his eighth visit the Queen confided to her journal how she found Mendelssohn to be "such an agreeable, clever man and his countenance beams with intelligence and genius". On 10th June her journal noted that seven of Mendelssohn's *Songs without Words* were performed at the palace, one of which had not yet been published. Felix had arranged one of his Op. 85 sets of melodies as a piano duet for the Queen and Prince Albert, but, as Roger Nichols states in his compilation *Mendelssohn Remembered*, "a simplified upper part for the Queen", who was "having difficulty with the original", was substituted. How accurate this may be can only remain a matter of conjecture, in view of so many assessments of her pianistic gifts. The *Midsummer Night's Dream* music was performed at a concert that evening, when the Queen, Prince Albert and the King of Saxony were in the audience.

On his final visit to England, in 1847, Felix was again invited to the palace. The most significant event is recorded by Felix Moscheles, in the biography of his father. "Having listened as enthusiastically as ever to his music", the Queen asked if there was any request she could fulfil for her guest. She must have been delighted

Chapter 23: The Highest in the Land

as well as surprised when Mendelssohn's answer came. He asked the Queen if he could visit the nurseries to see her children. "The Queen led the way and the two were soon deep in [conversation relating to] children's clothes, diets and ailments." What a pity Felix had no opportunity to discuss education. His wise counsel, from his own experience as a child, and as father of his own children, would have been patently beneficial in enabling 'Bertie', the future Edward VII, to have been far better understood by his parents – an understanding that never appeared to exist.

To conclude this summary of the Mendelssohn family's association with royalty, it is fitting to repeat the tribute that Prince Albert wrote on his copy of *Elijah*.

"To the noble artist who, though encompassed by Baal-worshippers, by his genius and study has succeeded, like another Elijah, in faithfully preserving the worship of true art, once more habituating the ear, amid the giddy world of empty, frivolous sound, by the pure tones of sympathetic feeling and legitimate harmony. To the Great Master who, by the tranquil current of his thoughts, reveals to us the gentle whisperings, as well as the mighty strife, of the elements. Written in grateful remembrance. Albert. Buckingham Palace."

Mendelssohn would have done well to show such a fine eulogy to the King of Prussia and his court, but his self-effacing personality would never have allowed such forwardness to occur. Let this strange monarch and his ways be confined to the pages of history. All that matters to posterity is how warmly Mendelssohn was appreciated, and his music valued, by our own royal family and that he was allowed to know, before his death, what a loyal following he commanded – and this was not an ephemeral trick of fashion. Their eldest daughter, 'Vicky', the Princess Royal, learnt to love Mendelssohn's music. In fact, it was she who, for her wedding to the future Kaiser Friedrich III in 1858, chose the Wedding March from Mendelssohn's incidental music for *A Midsummer Night's Dream*. Queen Alexandra, wife of Edward VII, had a musical box made for her, one of whose tunes was another favourite from Mendelssohn's pen – the melody 'On Wings of Song'. Such memories live on!

BOOK THREE

The Spirit Breaks Free

Chapter 24

A Mélange of Musicians

Part I – Mendelssohn as Music Critic

On 7th February 1835 Felix wrote to Moscheles regarding an invitation to edit a music periodical: "Such work will require me to please everyone and to keep all annoyances to myself. I find this idea distasteful." A few days later, to the same correspondent, Felix wrote of some songs sent by a budding musician, who asked if Handel's work was as fine as reputed. "Would he not do as an editor, with these songs and this question?" Mendelssohn commented. Such scathing judgements demonstrate why Felix preferred to keep his opinions to himself, rather than exposing them to public scrutiny. It is only through his letters to his family, but, particularly, to intimate friends such as Moscheles, that Mendelssohn's views on contemporary music can be discovered.

From boyhood Felix knew his own mind and did not mince words, especially to express his dislikes. When, for instance, Abraham took his son to Paris, to be grilled by the all-powerful Cherubini (who would, it was hoped, put a stop to the nonsense of this banker's son becoming a professional musician), his views on Parisian opera were jaundiced in the extreme. At the prospect of seeing Rossini's *Otello*, Felix was "awaiting a sensation. Hardly. Though the violins played well and together, I found the woodwind and brass mediocre, the basses out-and-out bad. I would hardly call it an outstanding performance at all." As for Mme. Pasta, the heroine, "however much fire and life she put into her acting, and her wealth of embellishments, and however pretty she looked, her voice is raw and indistinct; her intonation slovenly, lacking a sharp, crisp delivery." In view of Mendelssohn's later admiration for this prima donna, it must be assumed that she, or Felix, had an off day when he wrote this letter. His criticisms of a French version of Weber's *Der Freischütz* were equally harsh. The production was "miserable, infamous, vile, lousy and boring. In short, a complete outrage. Never in all my life have I dreamt of such a scandal. The tempi were faulty; the 'Chorus of the Bridesmaids' was taken too fast; Agathe's aria [was] cut and changed completely."

Ferdinand Hiller considered Mendelssohn's youthful opinions to be "overripe, if not arrogant". Former schoolmaster Wilfrid Blunt concurs: "This little gentleman was getting above himself." Yet, though Hiller believed that his arrogance would mellow, Felix's thoughts never altered as regards Parisian opera. He had never felt comfortable with the works of Auber, calling them "not at all musical; full of intrigue and effect, [making them] lucrative". To Klingemann Felix described one, unspecified, production as featuring "a young girl [who] divests herself of her garments and sings an aria to the effect that the next day, at this time, she will be married". Of Meyerbeer's *Robert le Diable* Felix gave the narrative in detail; it appears that he only watched the opera because his beloved Taglioni, the celebrated ballet dancer, took the heroine's role. "The plot involved nuns presenting themselves, one after another, to seduce the hero until, at last, the abbess succeeds. The same hero is conveyed to the apartment of the one he loves, whom he casts off, in an attitude of which the public here approve and the Germans will probably do the same. She then implores his mercy in a grand aria. Taglioni acts the ghostly nun who wants to seduce fat Nourrit. The tenor is coaxed into kissing and hugging her, to public delight. Some nuns, who look like pug-dogs and tom-cats compared with the sweet young child Taglioni, would like to do some seducing. I would just like to do away with all the music and take the place of Nourrit, who is having such a good time. No doubt Taglioni would not consider this too much amiss either, for the devil appears in the opera. This is romance and imagination enough for the Parisians. Were it not for two brilliant seduction scenes, no effect whatsoever would be produced."

In short, despite Taglioni's dancing and Mlle. Fay's acting, which Felix also admired, the whole French opera scene was dismissed as "bankrupt". The same appears to have applied to music as a whole in that country. In response to Fanny's exhorting him to convert his audience to appreciating good music, he became exasperated: "Remember, my dear child, that such people do not know a note of *Fidelio* and believe Bach to be nothing but a wig stuffed with learning." Nothing had changed on his visit of 1831-32. At a party Felix had his sleeve tugged with excitement at the news that "something of a symphony" was to be performed. This turned out to be a movement from one of his own string quartets: "Isn't it famous that my quartet should be played in the classroom of the conservatoire and that the people are practising their fingers off to play it."

Though the Paris Conservatoire Orchestra was the best Felix had ever heard, not even this satisfied the young martinet: The trumpets were "unsure in the high notes...the timpani muffled like the sound of the kettledrums. The hall is very small, so that every error can be noticed, and with such small audiences the music is heard twice as loudly and the detail twice as precisely as in a large auditorium", which accounted for the thorough rehearsals that were undertaken. Though Beethoven's symphonies did come to be enjoyed, this would be to the detriment of earlier masters: "They speak of Haydn as if he wore a powdered wig and of Mozart as if he were a simpleton... I cannot stand the way Haydn and Mozart are

Chapter 24: A Mélange of Musicians

denigrated. It drives me mad." Yet neither was the Parisians' love of Beethoven genuine: "His symphonies are like exotic plants. They do not really look at them, except as a curiosity that, like a plant, should someone examine the petals, [they] would discover that they belong to a well-known family or species." Several Beethoven quartets were performed by "full orchestra", 28 violins and no wind instruments, "in order to have something new by him". Felix had been asked to arrange some piano sonatas for this ensemble, "but I delivered such a pretty lecture to them that, no doubt, they have given up on such an idea". As for the opera houses, no German equivalent was as dilapidated as the Opéra Comique. When Cherubini was asked why none of his operas was performed, he replied that he did not know how to direct them without an orchestra, singers or dancers.

Yet there is extenuation for Mendelssohn's harsh judgements. Highly regarded musicologists all concur that, at that time, music in Paris was at its nadir. The Italian Orchestra, based at the Academie Royale was "quite good, but in no way outstanding".

The salons could only produce "potpourris" on opera themes. Genuine musicians had either "withered, or constantly complain about Paris and Parisians, cursing up a storm". The organ at the Church of Saint Sulpice was, Felix had been told, the finest in Europe. "So it would be, if it were to be renovated at a cost of 30,000 francs. Those who have not heard it can hardly conceive the effect at present, like a chorus of all old women's voices with clumsy bells clanging all the time." What a pity Mendelssohn did not live to witness the glories to come, when the church became more famous for its organists than anything else. "Paris *is* France," Felix wrote to Zelter, "and anyone who wishes to excel studies at the conservatoire. Otherwise, there is scarcely a tolerable orchestra in the whole of France... There is as good as no music at all in the rest of her cities."

Vienna, the former musical capital of Europe, was in the same parlous state when Mendelssohn visited the city in 1830. Under the repressive regime of Prince Metternich the giants had all passed away, with no one as yet to take their place. The fashion was for music by Czerny, Kalkbrenner, Clementi and John Field, attractive in their way, but not to be compared with their magnificent predecessors. Again, Felix's depressing views can be understood, especially when it is realised what opportunities he could have had were his father less intransigent in believing that Paris was the "be all and end all" for musical tuition. Did not Leah have many relatives in Vienna who could have helped him if asked? Might it not have been the young Mendelssohn, and not Liszt, two years his junior, who had played the piano with Beethoven in the audience and been given the maestro's blessing and embraced as "a boy of great promise", which happened to Liszt.

Felix regarded Italy's musicians as "similar to those in the second-rate cities of Germany, but harsher and less correct", and looked forward to hearing "a proper orchestra and choir, because I am musician enough to realise that the lack of it leaves a sad void". At the opera "the violinist beats the four quarters of each bar with a thin candlestick, which is more often distinctly heard than the voice, and sounds like the accompaniment of castanets, only louder. The voices are never together and every little instrumental solo is decorated with old-fashioned flourishes. These pervade the whole performance, which is entirely devoid of genius, fire and spirit. The Italian singers are the worst I have ever heard, except in Italy." Again, Felix found good reason to express such a demoralising situation. "This is natural, since how can such institutions flourish in such poverty and lack of capital. The era of worthwhile musicians in Italy has long vanished. The public nowadays pays scant attention to music, treating it with the same indifference, lack of homage and respect, as anything else. Any talented musician takes up residence abroad, where reputation is valued, music appreciated and, above all, something profitable and spiritually inspiring may be learnt. Even Tamborini [sic] will return to Italy, once he realises how his voice has deteriorated." Though Felix refers to that singer as a bass, Percy Scholes calls him a baritone, with "versatility and flexibility of voice range". But even in his beloved London Felix wrote of "bear basses and semi-bear tenors". In a performance of Rossini's *Otello*, Donzelli "ranted".

Whilst in Rome Mendelssohn was invited to sing with the tenor section of the Papal Choir. "I sang better from the leading chorister's score than the tenor himself," he admitted to Zelter. His attacks "were very uncertain" in masses by Allegri and Palestrina. As for the choir as a whole, Felix dismissed them as "poor", and neither was the congregation as devout as he would have liked. However, the atmosphere of St Peter's Church was heavenly. "The sounds were reflected from above and every corner of the building, mingling, dying away and, altogether, producing the most wonderful music, one chord melting into the next. What no musician would dare, St Peter's achieved... When one hears musicians saying that there is nothing to be gained musically from Rome...I would like to rub their noses on the capital of a column, for this is where the music can still be found. What do I care if the wretched bassoons squeak in the orchestra... There are more divine things here than one can grasp in a lifetime, so the bad music can disturb me very little, but, for the sake of truth, I must confess that it really is bad."

When some songs by Benedetto Marcello, a contemporary of Bach and Handel, were sung, Fanny was told that the singers were not of the same standard as "your own well-drilled, properly prepared choir, and, since you are a serious musician, their performance would not have amused you, had you been present. The ladies pressed forward, insistent on singing together, whereas the particular item was for sopranos only. The tenor next to me rambled about in the most curious regions, taking over the second tenor's part, which I sang, reverting to his own higher register. The choir sang soprano-falsetto, but switched to first bass. The director quacked out an order for all to sing, but to no avail, so he smiled sorrowfully across at me... The pianist constantly lost his place, often being one bar behind, or one in front. Thus we sang with the most complete anarchy, breaking into a chorus of loud laughter."

Chapter 24: A Mélange of Musicians

Not even Germany escaped Mendelssohn's acid comments. On a hike with Magnus and Heydemann, friends from Berlin University, uncle Joseph Mendelssohn was visited at Horchheim. Gottfried Weber, the music theoretician spoke of Beethoven as if he were "a farmer [discussing] a sick cow who did not get enough rock salt, having become half as crazy as ever he was, and having felt sorry for Beethoven as a result". Yet Felix disliked anyone who limited himself to preferring one composer: "I cannot bear anyone who likes Beethoven only, Palestrina only, Mozart only, Bach only. Give me all four, or none at all." Of Handel he derogated "the different compartments into which he placed his music for whichever occasion it was needed: there was a pigeon-hole for warlike music; another for heathens, a third for religion and so on". But he never condoned the embellishing of Handel's music: "If not deemed rich enough, flutes and clarinets were added, not with the delicacy and care applied by, say, Mozart. Audiences love the thoughtless hurry with which such music is performed. They crowd into the room for the 'old' works", although, as he wrote to Fuchs, Felix was gratified at the applause he received when performing one of Bach's keyboard concertos on the piano at a charity concert. Mendelssohn was always interested in contemporary music. He scorned the common attitude to the so-called "mad" sonatas of Beethoven that had so recently been brought to the public's notice: "I am sure the audience objected to them far more than the musicians did." On another occasion Felix asked his friend Moscheles if he had heard anything new. "I have heard nothing I like... Musicians in Leipzig would like to begin where Beethoven left off. They can clear their throats as he did, and cough as he coughed, but that is all."

He had heard a book of mazurkas and other pieces by Chopin, for instance, but these were "so mannered they were hard to stand". Hiller had written two books of songs that "would have been better unwritten. I wish I could admire such music, but it is [so] rarely or little to my taste that I cannot." Some modern composers made Felix think of "riding on horseback through wet fields after rain. They may dash along splendidly, even if splashed, but, when they try to walk, they become stuck fast in the mud." From Berlin in 1833 Felix wrote to Klingemann of a piano recital by a "Mme. B", "who is not handsome and wears wide, hanging sleeves when playing all kinds of variations by Herz... Why should one be obliged to listen for the 30th time to such piano music. Such entertainment gives me less pleasure than rope dancers or acrobats, who at least cause barbarous excitement at the fear of their necks being broken, or escaping such a calamity, whereas those who perform such feats of agility on the piano do not endanger their lives, only our ears, in which I have no interest. The public are supposed to demand the type of piano playing practised by Mme. B, but I am a member of the public, and I demand the reverse."

On the other hand, of provincial German orchestras, Felix told Zelter of that of Stuttgart, which played together "so completely, beautifully and perfectly, in a way about which one can only dream". Symphonies were performed each year at subscription concerts. "In the summer, the conductor has so little to do that he and his wife set off for a few days' walking across country, with some underwear and a tobacco pipe, returning via the hillside vineyards. Though everyone grumbles at his absence, no one will leave the orchestra at any price." In Frankfurt things were done "in a far more businesslike, dignified, cosmopolitan manner," Felix recorded. "But it is not nearly so much fun as in Stuttgart." The St Cecilia Society "work with such precision and enthusiasm" under Schelble "that it is a delight to listen to them. The choir of 200 meet weekly, but the director has a group that meet at his home each Friday evening that consists of 30 voices. Little by little they prepare his favourite compositions, which he does not dare to give directly to the larger horde." But, on his return in 1836, Felix told Moscheles that the musicians were "quite shameful. Considering the size and importance of the town... But the fact is, they do nothing, and it were better that they did not live in the same place as each other, for they grumble and brood over their grievances, or ask how much anything costs, before deciding to take action. It is enough to drive one to depression. Where so many musicians congregate, the authorities should be forced to give the people of Germany a little music – not just their philosophies about it."

In Düsseldorf, so frustrated had Mendelssohn become with its musical life, that he even became blasé about the convivial spirit of the city. At one fête "the whole town will drink wine, as if that were not the case every day". On returning from Elbefeld, where Felix had played at a charity concert and searched its library and churches for early music, he told the family: "I found everyone drinking champagne at the inn. I drank chocolate. They danced in the frightful heat, and became tipsy as usual. Beasts were exhibited; there were puppets; and cakes were baked in the public thoroughfares." But any idea of the discipline Felix sought "lies in the womb of time". Of his work in Düsseldorf he wrote: "Two such years are more taxing and wearing than four steady ones in a calm environment and that, though I might compose more, I can make no inward progress in such a situation" (see Chapter 19, 'Conductor and Director', for further reference to his Düsseldorf period). To Aloys Fuchs, the music manuscript collector in Vienna, Felix apologised for his inability to send anything new, "for there are no significant musicians on the Rhine".

On an early visit to London, Mendelssohn compared music in England with that in Germany. "Here, they pursue music like a business – calculating, avaricious, bargaining – and, truly, a great deal is lacking, but personnel and public are still gentlemen – otherwise they would be expelled from polite society, a category in which our own dear Royal Chamber Musicians are too often lacking." The German music festivals are shabby. Their court officials are princes of whining, full of vanity, ignorance, crudeness and emptiness, against whom I feel bitter as gall, because they do not possess the quality that, in England, I even expect from my shoemaker. They are not even honest, yet they appear to be such sensitive souls, who supposedly live only for art. English musicians by contrast are miserable dross.

Chapter 24: A Mélange of Musicians

They do not speak of the concept of an apple pie – that it consists of crust and apples – but, instead, they just cheerfully gobble it up, rather than analysing or discussing its potential. In short, may the devil take a lot of things." The "apple pie" idea is, of course, a metaphor for how music was discussed.

According to Schima Kaufman, Felix "quarrelled violently with many of the opera singers, striking them from his list of performers for concerts at the Mendelssohn home, but no source of reference is given, and such information as she gives does not ring true when balanced against Felix's own correspondence. Of a performance of Gluck's *Armide* under Spontini's direction, Felix wrote of the "great mass of thoroughly trained musicians and singers, the splendid house full to suffocation and the beautiful music". But, on another occasion, audiences were criticised for "such operas as *The Postillon* being given the same applause as that of Gluck the next evening". With one evening's fare Mendelssohn was highly irritated. "Up came the curtain. I saw before me India, with all her pariahs, palm trees and prickly plants. Then comes death and murder, so I must weep bitterly… Then follows a farce, at which I must laugh. No. This I cannot stand, but would rather stay at home with my own family."

Of choral music, sacred and secular, the following examples are cited from Mendelssohn's correspondence: "Bavarian churches, Catholic or Protestant, do not permit music, because it is said to desecrate the services, yet chorales are becoming almost obligatory in the Berlin theatres, which I find very strange." On 23rd October 1840 the Lieder Circle held their 25th anniversary concert, "but I felt so angry, as if I were a young boy," he told Fanny the next day. "Though they sang falsely, they spoke even more so, praising our German fatherland and the good old German fashion for singing." After his sixth visit to London, that year, 1840, he had vowed not to let anything distress him, and he told Fanny "not to fall into a passion as you do about the art exhibitions"; even in his beloved Leipzig such promises could not be kept. "Cécile, who sat beside me, had to keep on saying: 'Dear husband, do be calm,' especially when a work of mine was performed. They also played some quartets and, invariably, they bungled the very same passage from ten years ago."

Though a performance of Weber's *Oberon* was "beyond conception, never having fared better than that occasion", he had to state his negative opinion of the Berlin choral hierarchy. To Ferdinand David Felix wrote in 1844: "The most important aspect, which is overlooked, is an innate vigour and enthusiasm. These people are singing, playing and listening in a style of the utmost refinement and detachment. Real joy is lacking… There is no shortage of goodwill, but…no genuine feeling; no sincere conviction. I could tell you a fine tale of the musical life in Berlin and its participants one day, when we play billiards…or wherever else we find a cheerful place for a chat." In another letter, the court musicians were dubbed "a bunch of court servants impossible to hold accountable, so little rapport can I gain with them".

To President Verkenius of Cologne Felix confided: "There is scarcely a place in Germany in which I feel as little at home as here... As in my youth, the compulsion to move elsewhere [from Berlin] still applies... The Berliners abuse and revile the committees they themselves have elected, and like them to remain in their old form. The whole tendency of the musicians...is as little directed at the practical. They play merely so that they can talk about it, before and afterwards, so that discussions are better and wiser than anywhere else in Germany, but the music is more defective... Unfortunately, there is very little to discuss with regard to music and its deficiencies, and I have no idea how such a sorry state can be remedied. I hear blunders and wrong notes that can emanate only from the grossest carelessness on the musicians' part. These royal functionaries cannot be brought to account because of their privileged position." No notice was taken when a fault was mentioned, and Mendelssohn's deep sigh of resignation can be almost heard. One of his trios was performed "10 or 20 times, when the same errors were made, and the same blunders in the accompaniment and tempo". Because Spontini had conducted the orchestra for so long, it was at his door that Felix laid such slovenliness. "Spohr would be the best person to bring the musicians to order, but, because this is the case, he will not be elected. As for the Berlin Singakademie, each member considers himself superior to the director. But there also it is all talk, with no exertion of will to improve. Though everyone speaks of wanting beauty in music, all that can be heard is mediocrity."

Mendelssohn did not only spend time penning his harsh words; he took action. When Felix was commanded to play the solo part in a Mozart piano concerto at Potsdam, the musicians were so out of time and tune that, after an hour's rehearsal, he decided to improvise on themes from Weber and Mozart, asking their director, a schoolmaster, to apprise the audience of this change in the programme – and the reason for the alteration thereto. When, in 1837, Hummel died and Moscheles asked Felix what he thought about his friend's accepting the vacant appointment in Weimar, Mendelssohn's reply is telling: "Your skill and talent would be worthy assets to German music, and I would wish you well. However, as far as I am aware, the culture and intellect of Weimar is confined to the grand duchess and her court, a relic of former days. It would be madness for such a fine musician to forfeit your present high position and reputation in London, for the littleness that Weimar can offer by comparison." Neither would Charlotte Moscheles, Felix believed, like the German state, but he suggested that they visit Weimar to see how well, or badly, the atmosphere suited them. It is significant that it was only when Moscheles was asked by Felix himself to supersede him as director of the Leipzig Conservatorium that the older musician left London.

In view of his privately printed remarks about contemporary music and musicians, it is not surprising that Mendelssohn eschewed all editorships of periodicals, or forbore to write articles for these journals. Though an absolute martinet about telling the truth, Felix would never think of embarrassing his musical colleagues in public. His credo can be summarised by his letter to Conrad Schleinitz in which he accepted his appointment in Leipzig: "You can imagine, since it is my only desire to further the cause of music along the path that seems right to me, for that reason, I would gladly accept a calling that would place the means of my doing so within my reach." With such a high ideal, Mendelssohn felt no need to edit or contribute to musical journals. He preferred to let his own work, in all its compartments, speak for itself.

Part II – Famous Personalities

From boyhood Felix knew what he liked, and disliked – which applied equally to inanimate objects, topics for conversation, and people. His first journey away from home is covered in Chapter 7, 'Two father figures', when he visited Goethe in Weimar in 1821. During the following year, when the Mendelssohns visited Switzerland, Felix was given a letter of introduction by Zelter to meet Ludwig Spohr, then at the height of his popularity as a fashionable composer. Strangely, however, this meeting is not mentioned in Spohr's autobiography, which his family completed on his death in 1859. In an effort to be helpful, Stratton propounds reasons for this omission. Spohr "may have been occupied with his opera *Jessonda*, which was hampered by Spontini in Berlin, but this took place in 1825, three years hence. "He may not have realised what a brilliant star was to come into the ascendant," Stratton tries again. "If he did, he might have felt envious, or frightened, that his pre-eminent position was to be usurped." Were this so, would Spohr have invited Felix to play his piano quartet, which Rudolf Elvers believes to have been Mendelssohn's Op. 1? Would he have introduced Felix to the musician Anton Liste, whom Spohr declared to be "a good musician and an even more outstanding hiker", who guided the family around Switzerland?

Throughout the years, various proofs of friendship between Spohr and Mendelssohn can be cited. Felix visited the older musician en route to see Goethe in Weimar for the last time in 1830. In 1845 Felix begged Spohr "not to be angry with me" for dedicating his trio, Op. 66 to him, which Moritz Hauptmann assured Mendelssohn would be well received. Felix "would like to have had the honour" to write a longer piece, since "nothing seems good enough to me and neither, in fact, does the trio". He looked forward "beyond all measure" to perform some of Spohr's works when available from the copyists. Spohr's cantata *Die Kreuzfahrer* had been rehearsed "with 200 voices and an organ to supplement the orchestra", and his Concerto for String Quartet and Orchestra had been performed with David, Sachse, Gade and Wittmann as the four string players. Though the piece was rehearsed with piano accompaniment, as Spohr had instructed, Felix had to admit that "the orchestral accompaniment was not entirely free of mistakes". Despite this,

Felix commented, "I wish you could have heard it, for I have never known such a performance; I fancy that you, too, would have been happy with it."

Fortunately, Mendelssohn's meeting with Spohr of 1846 was, unlike their first meeting, recorded in the autobiography. An evening is mentioned in which two of Spohr's quartets were performed by musicians including Mendelssohn and Wagner, who "read from the score with countenances expressive of their delight". This might well have taken place in Leipzig where, according to Rockstro, Spohr was "treated with the utmost honour, entirely because Mendelssohn admired his music". The whole Conservatorium class was paraded before Spohr, and, at a party given by Mme. Voigt, further chamber music was performed; David, Joachim and the composer took part, Gade and Felix playing the viola parts. Rockstro had never heard such a fine performance, "the only exception having been at the Beethoven Rooms in London", where Spohr himself led the first violins, Joachim leading the second group of these instruments.

Another musician to whom Felix was introduced on his 1822 Swiss holiday was Ferdinand Hiller, two years younger; on this occasion, Aloys Schmitt introduced his favourite pupil to the young guests. Fanny described Hiller as "open-hearted and frank in manner". During a visit to the Swan Hotel Fanny played Hummel's *Rondo Favori*. This "little pianist with the long hair", as Hiller was known, was more impressed with Felix's sister's piano playing than that of her brother. However, in a letter, Fanny admitted to having "broken down, so nervous had I become". Felix impressed Hiller far more by his violin playing in a piece by Schmitt, "though his bravura passages were rather sketchy. On Mendelssohn's visit to Paris of 1831-32 Hiller was living there (as covered in Chapter 4, 'Leisure, at home and abroad').

The next time Felix and Hiller met was when, in 1836, Mendelssohn directed the St Cecilia Society on Schelble's behalf: "We have much to discuss, which is interesting to both of us, but I find him – what shall I call it? –not sufficiently single-minded. By nature, he loves Bach and Beethoven above all others and would therefore prefer to adopt the gravest style of music. On the other hand, he likes Rossini, Auber, Bellini, etc., and, with such a catholicity, no one can make real progress. This is the topic of all conversation, which stimulates me to spend so much time with Hiller and, if possible, to extend some influence over him through my mode of thinking."

Mendelssohn did try to persuade Hiller to return to Germany from Paris, so it must have pleased him when they met in Frankfurt. Hiller's music, Felix had declared, was "becoming mannered...unless you return to the musicians, ...who will praise, criticise or stimulate you, rather than such a gifted and bright fellow [as yourself] engaging in the nonsense of Parisian melancholy". Mendelssohn confided to Klingemann that Hiller's *Faust* Overture was "horribly weak... This is not good."

There is no record of Felix pointing out to the composer himself why the overture did not come up to the ideals of this ultra-disciplined musician, but, with

Chapter 24: A Mélange of Musicians

such criticisms, it is little wonder that a rift developed between Hiller and Mendelssohn. To Conrad Schleinitz Felix wrote: "It was impossible for me to go calmly to bed, having parted from such a friend as you in anger, ...but I have really lost confidence in his talent...which has often put me into a bad mood of late." On a later occasion, to the same correspondent, Felix declared: "You disagree with me...but I cannot depart from what I feel so strongly... It is becoming hard for me not to lapse into a certain bitterness whenever I think of the whole miserable affair in which I have been involved with Hiller. I do not want to be bitter, or to say one word too many... No matter how I try to turn my eyes and forget it, the whole thing is odious and, for that very reason, there is no cure but silence and distance. Fire on it!" Nevertheless, Gustav Magnus was able to bring Felix up to date regarding gossip in Paris and London on a visit to Leipzig. Hiller, Mendelssohn was informed, had published a piano version of Halévy's *The Jewess*, "and, in keeping with everything I see or hear of him, he has jumped on the great Parisian bandwagon altogether. [He] will probably take things as far as Halévy, Meyerbeer or Hérold, becoming universally praised in the next ten years – and despised ten years later."

During the 1825 visit to Paris Felix had met other celebrities who lived there. "Since my arrival," he explained to his tutor, Heyse, in apology for a delay in writing, "I have been running around like mad, trying to see and experience everything at once." Halévy's brother, who had translated Horace's *Odes* into French, was teaching Felix Latin: "He is a most remarkable man, allowing me to pronounce the language in the good, German way." This was hardly a tactful remark to his tutor, who, presumably, had other ideas on how Latin should be pronounced. To Fanny, who tried to calm her brother when fulminating against the musical life of Paris, he thundered: "Are you in Paris, or am I?" He evidently felt disheartened, especially in view of the idealised build-up his father would have given regarding that city. Why, he must have wondered, was Abraham so void of discernment? Blunt accuses Felix of jealousy towards Rossini, Meyerbeer and Liszt. This may well have been true. In the case of Rossini, Mendelssohn might have lumped his operas with those of Auber and others whose work was equally abhorrent. Meyerbeer's father, originally named Beer, actually had a synagogue on his family estate, where he worshipped, whereas Felix was not permitted to practise the faith into which he was born. As for Liszt, it can only be imagined what resentment Felix must have nursed, once he knew how Count Esterhazy allowed his employee, Liszt's father, to escort his talented son around Europe to display his pianistic virtuosity. What a contrast with the young Mendelssohn, who was introduced to inferior musicians with a view to his discouragement to indulge in such an "immoral profession", as Abraham saw it.

It would be 11 years later, when Mendelssohn again met Rossini in Frankfurt, that the two musicians understood one another better. Had Abraham lived another year he might have been enlightened as to what Rossini had to say of German music, vis-à-vis Italian musicians. The Germans, according to the veteran opera composer, were more at ease writing orchestral and instrumental music, whereas Italians had greater empathy with opera and choral music. But, in 1825, Felix regarded Rossini as "puzzling; a mixture of roguishness, superciliousness and ennui, with long side-whiskers, wide as a church door, elegantly dressed, surrounded by all the ladies, answering their attempts to entertain him, only with a little smile – and there you have the Great Maestro Windbag". At a soirée given by a Countess Rumford "the famous Rossini," Felix reported, "sat at the piano and accompanied Mozart's 'Ave Verum Corpus'... But he, as a learned composer, wanted to make suspensions before all the dissonances... When the music is playing, the ladies gossip and jump from one seat to the next, as if they were playing musical chairs... At the end, they all clap for joy that they have a few minutes' relief [from the music]."

Felix was invited to improvise, after which Rossini complimented him "many times". The audience appeared to enjoy the young man's performance but, for the cynical Felix: "with four trifles, six coquetries and several runs, one can play the silliest stuff through without thinking... I howl with the pack, or I am sweet as the most cloying confectionery and the audience is as courteous in either case... This, and the heat, became so uncomfortable that we slipped away, leaving our tea stranded, which was served at precisely midnight." The "we" referred to Felix and his father, but no record is extant as to the latter's opinion of this gathering.

In 1836 Rossini had been invited to the wedding of his close friend Lionel Rothschild, and it was at that illustrious mansion that Felix was invited to dine. On this occasion Rossini was described as "big, fat and in the sunniest disposition of mind. I really know so few men who can be so amusing and witty, when he chooses. He keeps us laughing the whole time... It will be quite too much fun to see Rossini obliged to admire Sebastian Bach." The last sentence referred to the fact that the elder statesman of music was invited to a performance by the St Cecilia Society, who were to sing Bach's works, including the B minor Mass. It was evident that Rossini enjoyed German hospitality whilst in Frankfurt: "Once he had received the wine list at the Rhein Hotel, the waiter was obliged to show him the way to his room each night, or he would never manage to find it." Meanwhile, he regaled Felix with tales of Paris and her musicians. "He claims to all the deepest respect for all the men of the day," Mendelssohn reported to his family, "which you might really believe had you no eyes to see his clever face. Intelligence, animation and wit sparkle in all his features and in every word he utters. Whoever does not consider him a genius ought to hear him expatiate in this way."

On 30th June of that year Felix wrote to Conrad Schleinitz how Rossini had enjoyed the *Fair Melusine* and *Hebrides* overtures, as well as Bach's music as performed by the St Cecilia Society. Felix was invited by Rossini to Italy, "where I can obtain as much pretty music as I want, and just as many pretty girls. The Germans, he said, have overly large feet. I said I did not think so." Presumably this latter remark, next to the mention of pretty girls, refers to the myth that a man with unusually large feet is purported to be more virile than his smaller-footed companion. A serenade was played for Rossini's benefit, "very badly, coming close to being messed up completely". After such a performance, "the rascal said that there were two kinds of music, one depending upon the performer, which had always been loathsome to him, the second depending upon the language of the heart – his favourite type of music, that had just been played, at which the performers were all delighted and told him how charming he was. Had he told them they should have played it better, he would have been called an arrogant wretch. Should one remain an honest man?"

Hiller recalled that, at that period, Rossini had lost much of his earlier corpulence and, through years of Paris society, he had reverted from being "a haughty Italian" to a "dignified, gracious and charming man of the world, enchanting everyone with his irresistible amiability. He beamed with health and happiness, displaying the power of the singer and the wit of the humorist." Yet, as with Berlioz in Italy, Felix loathed Rossini's teasing. Whilst playing his F sharp minor Capriccio, Op. 5, "Rossini muttered something between his teeth that I pretended not to hear," Hiller recalled. "I was assailed by a tirade of abuse from Felix." Rossini had said that Mendelssohn's composition "smelt of Scarlatti", but that had been in 1825 when Felix was a boy of 16, and Hiller's recollection did not need to be taken seriously in his mature years.

Much detail is given of Cherubini in Chapter 6, 'Young musicians', so that only a few words need be employed upon this august ruler of the Paris Conservatoire. "Cherubini is like an extinct volcano," Mendelssohn is purported to have declared; "still throwing out occasional sparks and flashes, but now almost entirely covered by ashes and slag." In fact, though Marek and others attribute this aphorism to Felix, it is Klingemann who is given the credit by Rudolf Elvers. Mendelssohn did consider the old man's music "wizened and dried up, like the musician himself", with which Halévy concurred: "If Cherubini makes a grimace on hearing a new piece of music [by a pupil], everyone knows it must have been altogether outstanding." One of his students was asked if he were a painter, whilst another was told, "You will never create anything". Abraham had met the conservatoire director in earlier days, and he still lived in Abraham's favourite city. Felix was, therefore, presented to Cherubini, despite the fact that many of Leah's relatives lived in musical Vienna, and Schubert and Beethoven were still alive in this musical capital of Europe.

Another musician whom Felix met in Paris was Friedrich Kalkbrenner, who had had the privilege of visiting Leipzigerstrasse 3. "He praises tastefully and blames candidly and amiably," Fanny observed, when she and Felix had played a piano duet for him. However, in 1825 Mendelssohn had another view of Kalkbrenner: "The man has become quite romantic and purloins themes and ideas from Hiller; writes pieces in F sharp minor [which key was often employed by Felix himself],

417

and practises every day for several hours... Every time I see him he enquires after my charming sister, whom he likes so much and who has such a fine talent for playing and composing," he told Fanny. "I invariably reply [that] she has not given up music, is very industrious and that I love her very much, which is all true."

On Felix's later visit to Paris "Kalkbrenner played his new 'Dream' Piano Concerto... He explained beforehand that it begins with hazy dreams, then comes an episode of despair, then a declaration of love and fidelity, then a military march. No sooner did Herz hear this than he, too, came up with a romantic piece for the piano, likewise explaining it beforehand. First came a conversation between a shepherd and a shepherdess, then a thunderstorm, then a prayer, evening bells and, finally, a military march. Though you may not believe the fact, Kalkbrenner played his piece wonderfully beautifully and with an affability, elegance and perfection that nothing can rival," Felix told Zelter. In response to a letter from Moscheles describing a soirée given by the same musician some time later, Felix wrote: "I see and hear it all. The anxiety to shine at the piano; the greed for a poor little round of applause; the shallowness that underlines it all is as pretentious as if such petty exhibitions were of worthwhile importance. To read about it is more than enough for me."

Of the Anglo-French composer George Onslow Felix reported: "He became quite distracted when I played a piano arrangement of Beethoven's *Fidelio* Overture to him on a bad piano. He scratched his head, added the orchestration in his mind and, at last, sang with me, growing quite mad with delight." The compositions of Count Sigismund Neukomm, whom Felix met at a similar time, were "charming but mediocre, and have no power, no fire". Of one of Neukomm's overtures William Horsley was told: "I would say a German word, but I am too polite to write, but one of your daughters can translate." Later Felix wrote to Klingemann: "Neukomm is behaving just as one would expect, and he is just the right man for spinsters, for he is one so himself. His extraordinary gentility, in contrast with the Berliners, produces an exotic effect and would be completely wasted if I did not make notes about it in my memory or in my diary. Recently he read me a beautiful lecture on morals, in which I was exhorted to be cheerful and happy. I listened patiently to that. When I get to be an old man I shall know how to be like Neukomm, but all the time I wished him at the bottom of the sea. He is too boring."

When Neukomm's oratorio *The Ten Commandments* was performed at the Berlin Singakademie the chorus 'Thou shalt not Commit Adultery' sounded "excellent. But," added Felix, "the single girls do not understand what they are singing about. The married ones do not care. 'Thou shalt not Steal' rose and rose like thunder and the composer can be sure of a medal for art, or science, or education. All this disgusts me, when a fellow keeps steering for such goals, whilst pretending to be a philosopher with high standards. There is more poetry in the Horsleys than Neukomm could dream of." Referring Moscheles to Neukomm's

Chapter 24: A Mélange of Musicians

works, Felix found it "astonishing that a man of such taste and cultivation could not write more elegant and refined music". He added that "his music is carelessly written, even commonplace, with his feckless use of trombones, that should be used sparingly, compared with Handel's use of kettledrums and trumpets, which are pleasing. Neukomm would be far better employing this style of instrumentation than his over-exotic manner, which stimulates the audiences into becoming used to all this cayenne pepper of contemporary composers."

Felix mocked in a similar vein at Cherubini's opera *Ali Baba*. Whilst "quite enchanted" with the piece as a whole, "I lament his use of the new, corrupt, Parisian fashion, in which the instruments are nothing and the effect everything; where three or four trombones are flung around, as if the audience had skins of parchment instead of the drums. His finale ends with hideous chords and a tumultuous crash, to which it grieves me to listen." When compared with his earlier work, "[it] is between a living man and a scarecrow". But it is evident that Felix had a love-hate relationship with Paris. Writing in 1839 to Mme. Kiene, sister of Mme. Bigot (by then deceased), friend and pupil of Beethoven, who gave Mendelssohn lessons as a child, he said: "I find Parisian music too modern, too clever, too piquant and the environment in which it is performed too cold and very seldom natural. I wonder what the musicians gain from the lifestyle they are obliged to pursue?" He would, despite these shortcomings, "like to visit Paris once more and see Baillot and any of the others who may remember me". But this never happened.

Nonetheless, between these Paris visits Mendelssohn met many other celebrities. Goethe had, for instance, given him a letter of introduction to the artist Heinrich Stiehler in Munich, whom Felix found to be "kind and amiable". At the time the artist was painting *The Young Fishergirl*, inspired by an exhibition in Berlin that, though Stiehler disliked it, made a sensation. "The painting was treated in far too sensuous a manner," he had claimed, but Felix did not know how this could have been avoided. "If you are to have the figure of a woman rising fresh from the water, at the same time singing and speaking in a lovable manner, she must be charming, and the fisherman to whom she beckons must be a graceful youth, whereas his pictures seem to be based on another conception." Though still in the form of a sketch, Stiehler's *Head of a Nymph* was "so exquisite and pretty that she is sure to please any man". The artist had been commissioned by King Ludwig I of Bavaria to paint portraits of the most beautiful women in Munich, for the sovereign's gallery of beautiful womanhood (Schönheitsgallerie). Needless to say, Felix reported to his family, Stiehler was delighted with such an assignment: "No wonder the ladies pay him no end of attention and will do everything to please him, in order that their portraits will appear in the gallery." (Not only, they must have realised, would the artist be gratified but, even more important to their egos, so would the King.)

Whilst, as a man, Felix's most exciting encounter must have been with the pianist Delphine von Schauroth (see Chapter 14, '"Flirting outrageously"'), as a musician his most edifying association would have concerned Heinrich Bärmann, the brilliant clarinettist, for whom Weber wrote concertos and other works. "Having corrected proofs until one o'clock, I visit Scheidel's coffee house in the Kaufinger Gate, where I know each person by heart and know him to be in the same place every day...[after which] Bärmann usually departs with me for the forthcoming concert. After a walk, we have cheese and beer when I return to work." At one entertainment that Mendelssohn hosted Bärmann played a Beethoven work, along with a second clarinettist, plus basset-horn and bassoon players, for whom the piece had been arranged.

Though music was moribund in Vienna, as may be deduced from Mendelssohn's correspondence, he took every opportunity that presented itself to meet anyone who was anyone in that erstwhile celebrated musical capital. On three occasions, when writing to Zelter, he was interrupted: "Levy, a horn player, ordered me to compose a serenade for his instrument to accompany a voice, to be sung outside the window of some beautiful young lady. Then Berk arrived to toss off some violin variations, so that the window panes shattered and applauded. Then Herr Rau came to invite me to dinner and to play in a quartet." Among the guests was the virtuoso pianist Sigismund Thalberg, whose name appears throughout Mendelssohn's letters. It was Thalberg who pioneered the 'three hands' piano technique, whereby the melody is played in the middle of the piano, its accompaniment occurring in the higher and lower notes. Another celebrity of the time was the music publisher Tobias Haslinger, who asked if his services were required by his young guest. Fanny was therefore asked to send the score of his Op. 18 String Quintet: "You will not find it in the bookcase. Rietz has it. You must thank lucky old Eduard for the copy and tell him I will copy the piano arrangements, as I have for Schlesinger. If Rietz addresses me as 'My dear, good friend, your stinginess', it is certainly he who is writing." Felix hoped to see Leah's relatives, the Pereira family, famous bankers of Vienna (covered in Chapter 4, 'Leisure, at home and abroad').

But, for Felix, the past was of equal importance with the present. His most moving experience was to lay flowers on the graves of Beethoven and Schubert, whose coffins would be later transferred to a more auspicious cemetery. Another link with the past was a meeting with the collector of rare music manuscripts, Aloys Fuchs. Like Thalberg, Fuchs played a major part in the Mendelssohn correspondence. Felix was often responsible for additions to Fuchs's treasure house of musical memorabilia, whilst, in turn, Fuchs was often called upon to arrange for pianos to be presented to Felix's friends and relatives. Not only this, but, through this remarkable gentleman, Felix was able to acquire music as yet unheard at the various festivals he was asked to direct. One of the rarest manuscripts was a treatise on Gluck's music, still extant in the Friends of Music Museum in Vienna. It was solely by chance that a Herr Piering, who had associated with Gluck in his latter days,

Chapter 24: A Mélange of Musicians

had given the manuscript to Fuchs, who had sought memorabilia on the opera composer for a long time. Since anything in Gluck's handwriting was extremely rare, even in the early 19th century, Fuchs termed the treatise "the jewel in the crown" of his collection. Gluck had treated his work so haphazardly, destroying many of his own scores once they had been copied and put into print.

In Milan, Felix realised he had no need for letters of introduction from his father because, when taking the initiative himself to meet influential people, he was better served in furthering his career. It was here that Mendelssohn met General Ertmann and his wife Dorothea, to whom Beethoven had dedicated his Piano Sonata Op. 101. An intimate friend of the composer – "probably more", Marek implies – the Ertmanns made Felix completely at ease in their exalted company, introducing him to Franz Xavier Mozart, the composer's youngest son (see Chapter 5, '"Italy at last!"').

In Rome, Count Bunsen, Prussian ambassador, introduced Mendelssohn to Sir Thomas Brisbane, the soldier after whom the Australian city was named. It was with reluctance that Felix had to interrupt his "fascinating conversation about places he had visited in the Near East" to witness the induction of the new Pope. Ambassador Bunsen also introduced Felix to the Danish sculptor Bertel Thorwaldsen: "a man – a lion," Felix wrote, "whom I admire tremendously. His nature is so superior and gentle, kind and mild. He has recently completed a statue of Lord Byron, sitting amongst some ancient ruins, his feet resting on the capital of a column. The poet is gazing into the distance, evidently about to write something on the tablet he holds in his hand. He is depicted, not in Roman costume, but in simple, modern dress, which I do not think spoils the effect. The statue has the natural, easy pose, yet the poet looks gloomy and elegiac, but not affected... Never did a piece of sculpture make such an impression upon me. Every week I gaze upon the statue, entering Babylon in imagination, along with the poet." In Thorwaldsen's studio Felix was privileged to see the preparatory sketches for the statue of Copernicus, a commission from the people of Warsaw to have their greatest philosopher and astronomer represented. Felix was particularly impressed by the contrast between the "usual, narrow, thin, pretty statues" and the art of his new friend. Felix was invited to play the piano to the sculptor, which must, in turn, have stimulated or soothed him, whichever mood applied.

Whilst in Naples Felix met Donizetti, whom he despised. However, he had to admit that "whether cheered or hissed, no matter. For he has been paid just the same and can go about enjoying himself but, should his reputation suffer, he will have to do real work, which will be disagreeable to him. Sometimes he spends three weeks on an opera, taking great pains on an aria or two that will please the public. He can then afford to amuse himself some more and, once again, write trash." If anyone dismisses this view as 'sour grapes', the reader might have a point, because Donizetti's operas have stood the test of time and are becoming increasingly performed. As is described in Chapter 17, 'Quest for an opera', Mendelssohn was never destined to achieve such heights in that musical genre. At the end of his life, however, he mellowed enough to allow himself to admit to Chorley how well he admired Donizetti's *Daughter of the Regiment*. Nor, when in Naples, was he too proud to socialise with the opera composer. On one occasion he met Mme. Fodor, a former prima donna who had taught Mme. Sontag. Fodor was "very kind and amiable towards me", Felix wrote home, "and her singing has given me such pleasure. It is easy to see how Mme. Sontag has learnt from her, and I count myself most fortunate to have met Mme. Fodor. She keeps her voice in excellent condition, singing most prudently and judiciously, though no longer as full and free as formerly."

The musician who was to become a titan in his profession, whom Felix met in Italy, was Hector Berlioz. Having won the Prix de Rome at the third attempt with his orchestral work *Sardanapale*, which he disliked, Mendelssohn congratulated Berlioz on his good taste for disliking it. Indeed, in his early career Berlioz received short shrift from the more musically experienced Mendelssohn. "Wretched", "atrocious" and "boring" were epithets given to Berlioz's compositions of the time, and surprise was expressed that "his attempts to go stark, staring mad have not succeeded". Of his overture *Les Francs-Juges* Mendelssohn wrote to Moscheles: "His orchestration is such a frightful muddle; such an incongruous mess that one feels like washing one's hands after touching this score. It is such a shame to set murder, wailing and misery to music. Though his judgement of others' music is so clever, so good, so correct, and so thoughtfully sensible, yet he does not perceive that his own music is such nonsensical rubbish that it makes me feel so melancholy." Of the final movement, 'The Witches' Sabbath', of the *Symphonie Fantastique* Felix told his family: "The poor artist goes to the devil, where the audience would love to have gone long ago. Then all the orchestra have a hangover and vomit music, causing one to feel most uncomfortable." Since such acerbic comments were not meant for public scrutiny, it is unfortunate that Paul allowed the letter to escape the usual strict censorship. Having seen the letter, it is not surprising that Berlioz was deeply hurt: "So, that is what our Rome friendship amounts to," he declared in his memoirs. Yet, extenuation of Mendelssohn's vitriolic pen might be made. Berlioz's memoirs have been called "eminently suspect" by the music critic Jeremy Siepmann and were written, according to the Pelican *History of Music*, "by a forgivable, but imaginative, liar". Had Mendelssohn lived longer he might well have come to admire the music of Berlioz. Neither did Berlioz acknowledge the unstinting help Mendelssohn gave the French composer when he visited Leipzig.

Ferdinand Hiller wrote that Felix admitted not to have understood the music of Berlioz, and this could have applied equally to his personality: "An excitable, cymbal-rolling individual, bursting with ideas and usually infatuated with some girl or other. By nature garrulous and unruly," Felix described him, disparaging his "Byronic attitude" on another occasion. The dictionary definition of this adjective reads: "Imitating the temperament Lord Byron is said to have displayed – cynical,

Chapter 24: A Mélange of Musicians

yet romantic." This attitude, Mendelssohn noticed, was employed particularly to attract women, who, in turn, were fascinated by this young man. Could it be that the strait-laced Felix (still adopting the ideas ingrained in him by his parents) might have envied this freer spirit? Neither did Felix like the way Berlioz teased his companion, or, rather, Felix disliked being teased on specific topics. At the baths at Caracalla in Rome, for instance, Berlioz, as was his wont, mocked the Bible, comparing the rewards of good behaviour on earth with those higher, but less worldly, benefits of the hereafter. At that very moment Felix missed his footing, as a result of which he was precipitated to the bottom of a deep, ruined staircase. "You take that for an example of divine justice," Berlioz mocked. "I blaspheme. You fall." From the look on Mendelssohn's face, Berlioz recounted later to the musician Stefan Heller, "I realised I must have gone too far." Rather, Felix might have been too physically shocked and bruised to have the spirit to parry this thrust.

Like Mendelssohn, Berlioz abhorred the Caffè Greco in the Via Condotti, calling the establishment "the most odious imaginable. Dark, dirty and ill-lit. The patrons all sit there killing time and smoking abominable cigars" – and berating true art, he might well have added. The French poet Théophile Gautier frequented the café and called Berlioz "an exasperating eagle", but he admired Mendelssohn, as man and musician. Berlioz agreed, despite their differences in personality. As regards music: "Everything I have heard by him delights me. I firmly believe he has one of the highest talents of this epoch", and he admitted to Hiller how well each got on with the other, having many interests in common. Each admired Goethe, Shakespeare, Beethoven and Gluck; of the latter Felix wrote home: "I often feel so annoyed at his posturing and feel like taking a huge bite out of him until, at that moment, he [Berlioz] begins to rave about Gluck." Again: "When Berlioz abuses Haydn and Mozart, I want to murder him, but this is prevented when he sings arias from Gluck's operas."

At the Villa Medici, where Berlioz was studying, he played Astarte's aria from Gluck's opera *Telemaco*. Unacquainted with the piece, Felix thought it had been written by their contemporary, Vincenzo Bellini. On another, similar, occasion, Felix was made to look a fool by Berlioz. "No true musician should require a metronome to gauge the beat of any music and, if he does, he must be a real dunce," Felix expostulated. On playing Berlioz's *King Lear* Overture, Felix asked for the right tempo to be made manifest, therefore proving himself to be the dunce of equal magnitude with other musicians devoid of the metronome. "He would not admit it, but this annoyed him," Berlioz recalled later.

At a concert in Paris in 1846 the *Midsummer Night's Dream* music was performed, causing Berlioz to write that he would "willingly embrace" its composer; "I belong to you, heart and soul", which fellow feeling did not wane after Mendelssohn's death. On 19th May 1852 J. W. Davison of *The Times* reported on a performance of the 'Italian' Symphony that Berlioz conducted. "With great devotion, every tempo was gauged perfectly." It is a matter of debate that "there should have been a little more of Berlioz in Mendelssohn's character", as Marek states.

Another French musician who won the Prix de Rome was Charles Gounod, whom Fanny first met in Italy. He became "intoxicated" with her piano playing, as Kupferberg describes his feeling, especially with her interpretation of Bach and Beethoven. It was inevitable, therefore, when Gounod visited Germany later, that the Hensels gave him a letter of introduction to Felix. "My reception at his hands was wonderful," the young man recalled. "I use the word deliberately to describe the manner in which a man of such standing welcomes a lad who must have seemed to him to have been no more than a schoolboy." In fact, Gounod was only nine years younger than Mendelssohn. Felix showed "the liveliest and most sincere interest...and was full of the most valuable words of support and encouragement", enquiring about Gounod's studies and compositions and asking him to play some of his piano pieces. Although the Gewandhaus season had finished for the summer, Mendelssohn reconvened the musicians for Gounod's benefit. The 'Scottish' Symphony was performed and Gounod received the score, "on which a few friendly words were written". One of his own pieces, Mendelssohn admonished, sounded like Cherubini. This caused Gounod to endeavour to cultivate his own style: "I shall not be content until I have written something that sounds like Gounod."

Fanny had admired not only Gounod's intelligence but his "infinite gentleness and delicacy" when she had first met him in Rome, and, no doubt through the Mendelssohns' influence, the seeds were sown in Germany for what would become Gounod's best-loved work, his opera *Faust*, premiered in Paris in 1859 and performed in New York and London four years later. In the latter case, according to Charles Chilton, the most unlikely venue saw its premiere: the Canterbury Music Hall, in south-east London.

Though, according to Jeremy Siepmann's biography, Chopin first met Mendelssohn in Berlin at a Spontini opera, whilst travelling with his father to von Humboldt's scientific congress in 1828, it was during Felix's 1831-32 Paris visit that the two musicians really met. Kalkbrenner had tried to take the new arrival under his wing. Felix, observing Chopin's lack of confidence, exhorted him to have nothing to do with Kalkbrenner's instructions and to allow his own musical genius to develop in its own way. At a concert at the Salle Pleyel Chopin played his E minor Piano Concerto and some mazurkas and nocturnes, after which Felix led the applause from the enraptured audience, according to Hiller's memoirs. The next time Chopin and Mendelssohn met was at Aachen, where Hiller's oratorio *Deborah* was performed. Mendelssohn wrote: "I noticed a man with a moustache reading the score, who turned out to be Hiller himself. He ran into my arms and almost hugged me to death for joy." The next day, Hiller, Chopin and Mendelssohn "betook ourselves to the piano, [on which] I had the greatest enjoyment. They have both improved in execution and, now, Chopin as a pianist is one of the finest of

Chapter 24: A Mélange of Musicians

all. He produces new effects like Paganini on his violin and achieves such wonderful passages that no one would have previously thought possible. Yet both imitate the Parisian, impassioned, spasmodic style, too often losing sight of time and sobriety and of true music. I, on the contrary, do so, perhaps, too little. Thus, we all learn from and improve one another. This causes me to feel like a schoolmaster."

The three musicians returned to Düsseldorf and it must have been at that time that a piano recital was held at Schadow's house where Felix lodged. Hiller and Felix were asked to perform, as was the custom, whilst Chopin sat in a corner. Hiller's memoirs record that he was "inordinately shy and spoke in a whisper, staying close to my side". When the guest was asked to display his talents Chopin was "reluctant at the outset, but, after a few bars, the company fell silent. Schadow was astonished at this virtuoso, declaring that he had never heard such a performance before." Yet, though many encores were begged, it was not all piano playing. Early in the evening, "a game of bowls was played, followed by coffee". The next day the three journeyed to Cologne and, having shown his companions the bridge over the Rhine and the Church of the Apostles, Felix shouted "Adieu" and pursued his quest for early music in the city's library and churches.

At Leipzig a Chopin Festival was arranged, at which the guest was warmly welcomed. "It is so pleasant to be once more in the company of a true musician," Felix wrote to his family. "He is so unlike those semi-virtuosi and semi-classicists who gladly combine the honours of virtue with the pleasures of vice… Though far asunder we may be in our different spheres, I can still get on famously with such a person, but not with those semi-demi people." Chopin asked his host to play through *St Paul* on the piano and, during the interval, obliged with his own études and "a new concerto", as well as some nocturnes that Felix had learnt by heart. If Felix would compose a new symphony in his honour, Chopin promised to return to Leipzig – probably a jest.

"On this we took an oath in the presence of three witnesses, but we shall see whether we both adhere to our word." The Arnold edition of Handel's works, presented to Felix by the Cologne Festival committee, was "a source of quite childish delight to Chopin". To Moscheles, Felix acknowledged that "our friendship is flourishing", calling Chopin "certainly the most gifted of them all, and his playing has real charm". But, during the next year, 1836, Rebecka had a different experience. Chopin was present at Marienbad, which Rebecka visited for a health cure. Though his physician and the Polish countess with whom he was staying tried to persuade Chopin to play, he would not – "not even for Mendelssohn's sister", as Rebecka grumbled. "Chopin was suffering too much from nerves," Rebecka and her husband were informed. Very little is heard of Chopin after that time, as far as his friendship with Felix was concerned, but Cécile must have been delighted to receive his autograph for her album.

Another visitor to Leipzig was Franz Liszt, in 1840. On Felix's last visit to Paris he had played Mendelssohn's 1st Piano Concerto from memory. "A miracle. A real miracle," Felix had enthused. "It could not have been played more beautifully." However, though Marcel Brion records this incident, he does not give the full story. Hiller, better acquainted with Liszt, warned Felix that, once the pianist had played anything to perfection, he would spoil any subsequent performance of the same piece by adding his own embellishments. Any seeds of hostility that might have lurked in Mendelssohn's mind concerning Liszt were allowed to grow. To Moscheles Felix confided that he found one of Liszt's compositions "depressing", having put it aside with indifference. "But if that sort of stuff is noticed, even admired, it is surely provoking, but is that the case? I do not believe that anyone impartial takes an interest or a pleasure in discords. Whether a few writers puff the piece matters little. Their articles will leave no more trace than the composition."

Though, having entertained the Hungarian composer for a fortnight in 1840, "Liszt is a warm-hearted man and an admirable artist", as Felix wrote to his family in Berlin; "...but, unhappily, his behaviour here towards the public has not made a favourable impression. The whole wrangle gives one the feeling of listening to a peroration from two people, both of whom are wrong and one of whom would fain interrupt at every word." The "wrangle" of which Felix spoke, concerned the inflated ticket prices for Liszt's concert, for which his publicist, a Herr Kermann, must be held responsible. It was ostensibly to this individual that the hisses were directed from the audience whilst Liszt's transcription of Schubert's 'Erlkönig' had concert-goers standing on their seats with excitement. His fantasia on themes from Donizetti's *Lucia di Lammermoor* "drove them mad". Newspapers were "full of explanations, counter-explanations, criticisms, complaints and all kinds of stuff dragged in, totally unconnected with music, so that his [Liszt's] stay here caused almost as much annoyance as pleasure, though the latter was often great beyond words." Felix organised a fine public relations coup. In order that Leipzigers could meet this fascinating visitor in an informal atmosphere, a soirée was held at the Gewandhaus, to which 350 guests were invited, independently of the concert schedule. Hiller, Liszt and Mendelssohn played the solo piano parts in Bach's Concerto for Three Keyboards. The *Calm Sea* overture was performed, not through the composer's conceit but because Mendelssohn considered it a 'lucky' piece and a good omen. Liszt's triumphs were repeated, plus a chorus from *St Paul* – "and the devil and his grandmother", as Felix wrote later. "The people were so delighted and played and sang with such enthusiasm, and swore that they had never enjoyed a jollier evening, so my object was most happily effected in such an agreeable manner. This atmosphere cannot have helped but be boosted by the cakes and wine that were served." Felix could have added that his own gregarious personality and facility for putting everyone at their ease must have played their part.

"Notwithstanding his unpalatable contribution to the newspapers, I am thoroughly impressed both by his playing and his striking personality," Felix confided to Moscheles. To his family, Felix wrote that, whereas he rated Thalberg as "more nearly perfect as a virtuoso... The man has such incredibly powerful hands and such practised light fingering that it is unique", Liszt, on the contrary, "possesses a certain suppleness and flexibility in his fingertips, as well as a thoroughly musical feeling that cannot be equalled... His directness, his stupendous technique and expertise, allow him to surpass anyone." When Paul saw the celebrated pianist in November of the same year, Felix sought his brother's opinion. "Have you heard him often, or only that one time?" he asked. Paul had mentioned "Liszt's coffee hour" and had complained about the musical taste of Hamburg's citizens. Jean Petitpierre states that Felix had accused Liszt of "constantly and deliberately clowning", which would not have pleased the sober-sided Paul. "Dressed in the height of fashion" for a concert performance, Mendelssohn called him "a spectacle". Neither did Liszt's transcription of Beethoven's *Pastoral* Symphony meet with Felix's approval. The violinist Joseph Joachim recalled Liszt playing a piano version of Mendelssohn's E minor Violin Concerto "with a lighted candle between his middle and forefinger". Liszt was regarded as having "such a childishly naive way of laughing". This was epitomised when, at a smart restaurant he laughed, Hiller recalls, "when he realised that the meal was far more expensive than the lavish entertainment Mendelssohn had hosted".

Max Müller recalled how Liszt, dressed in national costume, "looking wild and Hungarian", played "something special" at Mendelssohn's home. The piece turned out to be a national folk song "with variations, each more incredible than its predecessor, Liszt all the while swinging to and fro on the piano stool". A guest whispered to the host: "Now, Felix, we may as well pack up. Nobody can play like that." Liszt then asked Mendelssohn to follow him at the piano which, as was his custom, he declined to do at first, but, eventually, he obliged, "provided that Liszt would not be angry" with his performance. Having never heard the work, "he played it so accurately that only Liszt might have discerned any differences", or errors. This display included Liszt's "grandiose moves and extravagant gestures", along with the theme and full complement of variations. Consternation was caused in the audience, as everyone present feared the maestro's reaction. "But he laughed, applauded enthusiastically and admitted that not even he could accomplish such a piece of bravura." Liszt not only gave a second recital – the concept he himself had coined – but, after a short visit to Dresden, made a third appearance to raise money for the Musicians' Pension Fund.

Richard Wagner was another titan with whom Mendelssohn came into contact during his Leipzig years. He is discussed in Chapter 26, '"In paradise"', which deals with Leipzig, and 'Free thought', Part II of the Epilogue. This present chronicle, therefore, concludes with Mendelssohn's most intimate friend amongst his contemporaries, with whose music Felix's is so often linked – Robert Schumann. On 4th November 1835, when Felix conducted his first Gewandhaus concert, Schumann wrote to Clara Wieck, the celebrated pianist whom he was later to marry: "He [Mendelssohn] is for me the artist most worthy of veneration – the new Mozart." This friendship was enhanced by their mutual love of Bach, by whose music they were each inspired. Of Schumann's physical appearance the English singer George Sampson gives a succinct description: "A sturdily-built man of 30 years or thereabouts... His long, straight hair was brushed back from a broad, intelligent brow and his thoughtful, far-looking eyes intensified the impression he gave of force and original power." Though Bruno Hake called Schumann "taciturn and brooding; engaged in struggle throughout his entire life, having travelled down lonely roads", Max Müller admitted his having "a nature that liked to be left alone...and would shrink from the too demonstrative happiness of others".

However, like Mendelssohn, Schumann was at his best when in the company of a few intimate friends whom he loved and trusted. Thus, at Felix's home, Sampson's description reflects this side of the composer: "He had an air of courage, resolution and good humour", and it was he who pointed out to Sampson that the pictures on Mendelssohn's walls were the host's own creations. "Mendelssohn does everything well," he confirmed, prompting Ferdinand David to warn the English guest not to attempt to play Felix at billiards, unless he had had vast experience of the game. When, in 1840, Clara and Robert Schumann married they often played chamber music with Felix, and the two men were to be seen strolling in Leipzig's public gardens, listening to Johann Strauss the Elder's orchestra playing dance music. Indeed, according to Marcel Brion, in his book *Schumann and the Romantic Age*, it was this type of entertainment by which the composer was lured to Vienna.

At the time of which Sampson wrote, Schumann had jested that "the youth, beauty and intellect of Leipzig were all in the same room", but that he would leave others to decide which quality applied to whom. David responded that "Schumann and Mendelssohn divided the firmament of Leipzig between them". Felix stated that Schumann wrote the best music criticism. David retorted that, were he to write less, he could compose more music. "The cobbler should stick to his last," he continued. This dictum might well have been passed on to the students of the Conservatorium, once it had been founded, for the same aphorism was taken seriously by Arthur Sullivan, who was to study there. Yet, without Schumann's music criticism, much unwitting testimony would have been lost to posterity. Schumann's lifelong cry was "Chopin and Mendelssohn", overlooking his own place amongst the giants of the 19th century. "He considered himself neither rival nor equal of Mendelssohn," Hake observed. As Schumann himself declared: "There should be no rivalry, as I know my place. Mendelssohn and I differ about this sometimes, but who could quarrel with him?" Felix's music, to Schumann, was "as pellucid as clear water, whereas I like to baffle listeners; to leave them something with which to struggle".

The highest accolade that Schumann could offer was to add Mendelssohn to his 'League of David' (the 'Davidsbund'), a band of brothers whose purpose was 'to fight the Philistines of art'. Felix was given the name 'Meritis', in acknowledgement of his merit as an artist of the highest calibre. A sentence gleaned from papers recovered after Schumann's death read: "Meritis conducted a concert of works by Mendelssohn." Schumann saw it as his duty to promote his friend's music, to the detriment, it must be said, of his own work. But, in view of Felix's almost pathological modesty, the music journalist can be said to have single-handedly revealed to the otherwise uninitiated just what qualities were to be found in Mendelssohn's versatile range of compositions. Fortunately, despite the blatant abuse Felix's reputation was later to receive, Schumann's praise has survived all subsequent vilification.

Part III – Where are They Now?

This section of the chapter concerns the unpredictability of musical fashion. Indeed, it is accurate to state that, were it not for the correspondence of Fanny, Felix and Rebecka, the individuals mentioned here would not be known today. In some instances, not even the most painstaking reference books acknowledge their existence. A further point to be considered is that, contrary to so much misunderstanding, Mendelssohn did not associate solely with celebrities but showed interest – as did his sisters – in musicians who, even at that time, did not crave fame.

On 22nd September 1831 Felix recommended to Zelter a 17-year-old student who hoped to study with Hummel in Weimar. It is only within the last few years that the music of Adolf von Henselt is becoming recognised, especially his Piano Concerto. As von Henselt was due to visit Berlin, Mendelssohn promised to give Zelter news of their many friends, via this young musician: "I have already apprised him of Berlin's music and, in so doing, have made his mouth water, as I am now causing my own to do." As director of the Singakademie, Felix asked Zelter to introduce von Henselt to the Friday concerts and to familiarise him with the music of Bach: "Though not very well acquainted, I know from everything I hear that Henselt is certainly worthy of your hospitality and is a very talented and unassuming young man." Percy Scholes dismisses von Henselt in six lines. After stating his dates of birth and death, the sole information given is that he was "a brilliant piano virtuoso pupil of Hummel, [and he] exploited his possibilities in large numbers of compositions, especially 24 studies".

Another young musician whom Mendelssohn 'discovered' on his fourth visit to London in 1833 was the 16-year-old William Sterndale Bennett, to whom Scholes feels able to devote almost half a column, not on account of his musical output, but because his name survives as a competent administrator, for which service he was knighted. Born in Sheffield in 1816, Bennett had studied at the Royal Academy of Music in London since the age of 11. It was at a pupil's concert that he performed his Piano Concerto, with which Felix was impressed. As a boy he had sung the part of Cherubino, the page, in *The Marriage of Figaro*, about which the press had been hostile: "In every way, a blot on the whole place," one critic described his prowess as a singer. He therefore concentrated, wisely, on becoming a pianist and composer, as a result of which Mendelssohn invited him to Leipzig, not as a pupil, but as a friend. Bennett's music is said to resemble that of Mendelssohn but, to anyone who admires the latter, such observers show kindness to Bennett, in view of his bland, pale imitations of Felix's style. It can be said that it was only because this leading light showed so much interest in Bennett that his name and reputation are allowed to live today. "From the cocoons of the school, such a brilliant butterfly has taken wing that we fain would follow as it bathes in the ether, taking from, and giving to, the flowers," Schumann eulogised on Bennett's arrival in Leipzig. But, sadly, like a butterfly, the English composer's potential faded. England had still to wait for the epoch in which her golden era – the days of the Tudors and Stuarts – would return. Handel, though a naturalised Englishman, was originally a German, and it would not be until the turn of the 20th century that the rich vein of English music would flourish. Though Felix introduced his guest to his musical circle, a letter home from Bennett reveals what he thought of one musician: "I have met a very nice fellow, whose name is Schumann, but whose music is too eccentric." Bennett met Clara Wieck, who played his E minor Piano Concerto "like a witch", showing an uncanny realisation of what was required from the piece. His host played Mozart's D minor Piano Concerto "as written". There was no need for Mendelssohn to substitute a cadenza of his own; he chose to retain Mozart's original. Felix provided Fuchs with a letter from Bennett to augment his musical collection and even promised a manuscript from the budding musician.

Bennett was also asked to assist with correcting the Arnold edition of Handel's works, and Felix tried to secure for him the professorship of music at Edinburgh University. The position was awarded, rightly or wrongly, to Henry Hugh Pierson, who, shortly after the appointment, resigned to live in Germany, dying in 1871. Yet Bennett had the honour to be buried in Westminster Abbey. Various descendants have helped to keep his name alive. The ballads of T. C. Sterndale Bennett – notably *Leanin'* and *The Carol Singers* – can be heard on nostalgia programmes. Joan Sterndale Bennett was a leading soprano at such venues as The Players' Theatre, and Barry Sterndale Bennett is a trustee of the International Mendelssohn Foundation of the United Kingdom, whose Leipzig parent preserved Mendelssohn's home at Goldschmidtstrasse, Leipzig.

In 1834 Felix asked his childhood friend Julius Schubring if a musician named Seelmann had composed anything further. As for Adolf Bernhard Marx, Felix regretted that he had broken off his engagement, but added: "Some of his compositions that he has published displease me, to my great distress." To Fanny he wrote of "your interest in the faithful Eckert, who is a sound, practical musician...the most good-natured and by far the most inoffensive, and these are two precious qualities. Anyone not so [i.e. possessing such qualities] ought to be abused, from the Lord Chamberlain to the cobbler." To Eckert himself Felix wrote "You have won honour and esteem for your talent and character, so important at the present time. Without talent, nothing can be done and, without character, just as little. Day after day one notices this in people of the highest capability, who yet accomplish nothing. I pray Heaven to bestow the same attributes upon you that have been granted during the past few years, but it is through one's own will that they can flourish. Heaven can merely plant these seeds in the spirit of an individual... Every wild animal has its own special skin and roar, so I continue to roar in my own tones. Work daily, hourly and unremittingly... The most important point is to bring into existence the highest that obtains in your nature and feelings, which no one except yourself can know of or possess."

After such a worthy homily (condensed for the sake of space), it is fascinating to discuss an entirely different character in Mendelssohn's life. Felix did not concern himself solely with conventional music making. He asked his family to meet Josef Gusikov, who gave "brilliant" performances on a home-made instrument resembling a xylophone, consisting of two wooden sticks on a bed of straw. When Gusikov did visit Berlin, and Leah became acquainted, she found his features "interesting", noting that "his garb betokens his orthodoxy". Perhaps it was his Jewish faith that caused Felix to befriend Gusikov, rather than his musical accomplishments: "He is such a phenomenon, inferior to no virtuoso in the world, delighting me more with his instrument of wood and straw than many pianists are able to please me." Having heard the unusual musician in Leipzig, David and Schleinitz wished to speak with him in another room: "The whole group of Polish Jews followed in our wake, anxious to hear our eulogies. When we went to the side room, they pressed forward so quickly that David and Schleinitz were left in the rear and the door [was] shut right in their faces," Felix reported. "Then all the Jews stood quite still, waiting to hear the compliments Gusikov was about to receive. At first I could not speak for laughter." Though others than Felix cultivated Gusikov, his career ended with his early death at the age of 31, from tuberculosis, scourge of rich and poor alike until the 20th century.

Of Niels Gade Felix wrote: "There can scarcely be anything greater than to hear fine music... Would that it came less seldom." Of Gade's 1st Symphony Felix stipulated: "The work must be performed, so that everyone can hear it properly." On 3rd March 1843 Mendelssohn outdid himself in eulogising this young Dane: "No one henceforth will speak of Gade's works with anything but the most heartfelt esteem and [I will] receive with open arms all his future compositions, which will be assiduously studied and joyfully hailed by all friends of music in this town." Felix even wrote to the King of Prussia about this young musician: "His music shows unmistakable talent and genuine musical feeling that resembles an oasis in the desert. His sacred music inspires me with the strong hope that the composer may accomplish something really important in this sphere." Were Gade to be given the opportunity to study in Berlin, Felix continued, "Nothing will be wanting for the development of his talent, except pecuniary resources." A grant of 200 thalers per year for two years was suggested, which would be supplemented by Gade's willingness to teach. "With his modest ideas and simple mode of life, he will make progress and, by his industry, secure his livelihood in the meantime... Gade would be made happy for life; all obstacles would be removed and one more happy man would be made happier", this last phrase referring to Mendelssohn himself. The King did oblige, allowing Gade to benefit from whatever music Berlin could offer.

Mendelssohn chose Gade to replace him as director of the Gewandhaus in 1846, but this was not entirely altruistic. Though Schumann had hoped to occupy this post, a non-German was deliberately selected to avoid the anticipated factionalism that could have occurred among the indigenous musicians, who vied with one another for the prestigious appointment. By such a shrewd choice, much antagonism and resentment was avoided. Gade would make his mark subsequently as head of the conservatory at Copenhagen, by teaching Denmark's most important composer, Carl Nielsen. Gade's own music is rarely performed today and, when this does happen, it is, like Bennett's, a watered-down version of Mendelssohn's style. Though Gade's Symphony was dedicated to his mentor, Mendelssohn's prophecy is uncanny: "No one will follow your career with warmer sympathy, nor anticipate your future work with more anxiety and hope." Even music scholars write of Gade's music as influenced to a large extent by that of Schumann and Mendelssohn.

Felix had much to say that was negative about musicians, individually and collectively, of whom, fortunately, nothing is now heard. "There are many fine singers and intelligent artists, but none sufficiently modest or self-effacing to render their roles faithfully or without pretension. Marselline introduces all sorts of flourishes into scenes. Jeaquino is a blockhead." But not only performers received the rough edge of Mendelssohn's pen: "The minister is a simpleton and, when a German such as Beethoven writes an opera, then comes a German such as Stuntz or Poissl, or whoever else, [and] strikes out the ritornello or 'similar and unnecessary passages'. Another German adds a trombone passage to his symphonies; a third declares that Beethoven is 'overloaded' and the great man is done for." Yet, despite this catalogue of woes, Mendelssohn still loved Germany herself. Fanny admired Mariani's performance in *Lucia di Lammermoor*, particularly the way he produced his voice, and his "simple style". Felix considered him, "though still wonderful, less good than formerly". As with Frank, editor of a musical journal, he denigrated the public who read his criticism, and "praise weak points and berate anything of true merit. Such attitudes annoy me enough to believe physical injury to have been inflicted upon me."

Mendelssohn argued with the Berlin Cathedral personnel that "unless matters improve [regarding Berlin's music], such a state of affairs will never be worth

Chapter 24: A Mélange of Musicians

anything". Neither did Felix relish having to perform four motets by "the English ambassador", the Duke of Westmorland, "plus a magnificat and six waltzes" by the same individual. "My horror of aristocratic acquaintances has, if possible, increased and you would laugh to see me plunging about in an effort to escape the nets of the English ambassador. Though he has hooked me for one dinner, he will not do so twice, that I vow," he wrote to Fanny. To Rebecka he wrote how "we stay at home in our own family circle, and that is much the best". After one of his forays into Berlin's social life, Felix compared the way in which the actor Seydelmann was treated there with his visit to Leipzig: "The King of Saxony forbade a performance of *The Robber* [his best-known role]. David harangued him, book in hand, arguing for an hour and dragooning me into seeing the actor's performance in Berlin." On another occasion he and Cécile were compelled to leave the theatre, as they disliked the drama so much.

After dining Fanny attended a concert in Berlin, singling out the Millanolla sisters as her chief enjoyment. The elder, aged thirteen, "played the violin exquisitely"; the younger, aged nine, "cleverly. They are causing a sensation with their short, white dresses and, respectively, long dark plaits and curly hair like that of a cherub." The only instance that the name Millanolla is heard today is because H.M. Coldstream Guards chose for their quick march the melody that bears the same name, which is used on ceremonial occasions.

Felix exhorted Fanny to hear Thalberg perform on his forthcoming visit to Berlin. "Anyone who has heard such perfection has heard everything," he wrote. "His musicianship inspires one afresh to set to work more industriously. You should study particularly his fantasias for the piano, with their astonishing difficulties. His embellishments and his taste for their execution are supported by know-how and confidence. He yields to no one in lightness and dexterity of fingering and the strength of his wrists is incredible." Just as their father admired the flautist Philippe Drouet, "snatches of whose airs he sang after dinner and which either of us had to play to him", Thalberg was equally modest. According to Felix, "his straightforward simplicity does not allow him to read the criticisms from music periodicals". Mendelssohn wished Thalberg's concert success, but suggested to his sister that she might promote his popularity "by inviting him to play beforehand", which would be appreciated.

"I wish I had as thorough a belief in my own ideas as the great R. [von Redern, director of the Berlin Opera] in supposing the ceremony planned for Devrient will induce him to stay for all time in Berlin," Fanny wrote to Rebecka. "This is so unspeakably stupid that the art world of Berlin will be scratching each other's eyes out for six months afterwards." But Hensel's good sense prevailed, so that Devrient's farewell (on taking up a new appointment at Dresden) took the form of a presentation solely, at the Hotel Russie where he was staying. He was given a "beautiful" vase, with the contributors' names inscribed on its pedestal. Wagner made a speech, during which he broke down. This was followed by what Fanny called "a simple repast", but where "champagne flowed freely at the general expense, as von Redern put it. I dread to see the bill, which, at the time of writing, is still hanging over the meal, like the sword of Damocles, but Devrient was very happy."

A dinner was given the next evening, during which another gift – this time unspecified – was presented by his colleagues at the Berlin Opera. "So, altogether, the two final days of Devrient's stay in Berlin were very pleasant." Earlier in the week the Danish sculptor Thorwaldsen was honoured. A series of tableaux chronicling his life and work "resulted in the most preposterous blunders", Fanny reported. "A speech was made by my handsome friend Reumont, followed by a dithyramb by the great Rungenhagen, a cantata in the style of *Antigone* by Kopisch and Taubert was then performed. The Academy Hall was beautifully decorated with a cleverly modelled statue in the centre by Kiss. Imagine the display, though 'embarrassment' would be a more appropriate word, of the notables of Berlin, when it was discovered that, by accident, neither the King nor his court had been invited to the ceremony. Not a mouse, not even a chamberlain, appeared in the royal box. Afterwards my dinner guests and I laughed at the stewards' attitudes unmercifully, which they deserved, though we felt more like crying. I wonder why such a commemoration could be held, when its mistakes were not foreseen and prevented." Why, when both Devrient and Thorwaldsen appear so prolifically in the Mendelssohn correspondence, is neither remembered today?

A further celebrity of the time to whom such present-day oblivion applies was Devrient's relative, Mme. Schröder-Devrient, the prima donna, now only in evidence to readers of biographies for that era. Fanny mentioned Wagner's *Flying Dutchman*, in which she took part as Senta. She also mentioned Countess Rossi, the former Mme. Sontag, who had come out of retirement "and still sings exquisitely". Having become weary of constant tales of 'Mme. O.' "and her French romances", Sontag decided to make her own presence felt. As court etiquette did not permit such an unprecedented appearance to occur immediately, von Massow and von Redern agreed to arrange a contest to see who would be the most ready for the concert; von Massow won, inviting the court and the Mendelssohn family to attend the performance. Felix accompanied each soprano in a solo and the two together in a duet. Sontag sang "with as much grace and finish" as in her heyday. As for Mme. O., Fanny claimed, "it must have been her pretty face that prevented her causing a fiasco". She looked forward to hearing the tenor Mariani sing, as also "our Roman friend" Sciabatta: "A fine voice goes a long way for me."

Fanny reported leading "a most dissipated life, with several engagements per day and a party on four consecutive evenings". At one of these Miss Birch sang, "her soprano voice reminding me of Clara Novello". Mme. Decker also sang, having given two soirées, one of which was attended by the Duke of Mecklenburg and his theatre director. The concerts at Leipzigerstrasse 3 recommenced and "proceeded apace". At one of these, "22 carriages filled the forecourt, with at least eight

Chapter 24: A Mélange of Musicians

princesses and Liszt in the room". At one such concert, the Belgian 'cellist Adrian Servais took part. Though Scholes speaks of his "high reputation in Europe", Fanny appears not to have been so impressed: "His music, which he may well have composed himself, was spoilt for me. We watched with amused curiosity the different emotions that struggled for mastery over his face and, however well his music was played, I shall not be tempted to hear it a second time. I am becoming more and more critical." This attitude may well have resulted from Fanny's increasing experience and self-confidence in writing her own music. For such an improvement, credit should be given to Herr von Keudell, whose name, if for no other reason, should be unearthed from the rubbish heap on which otherwise forgotten individuals have been jettisoned. Having returned from Italy she must have wondered if she would meet anyone with as fine an ear for music as Gounod, who truly appreciated her musicianship. But von Keudell, a diplomat and, later, ambassador to Rome, really took an interest in his hostess's concerts, but, of more importance, in Fanny's compositions: "He keeps my music alive and active, as Gounod did once. He takes immense interest in everything I write, draws attention to any shortcomings (and is generally in the right too). His advice is always worth taking and his benevolent but careful criticism [is] always worth heeding." It may well have been von Keudell who selected Fanny's most suitable works for publication when two rival publishers vied with each other to bring her compositions to public notice.

Chapter 25

"In Paradise"

This phrase was used often when Felix described his life in Leipzig, where he took up residence in order not only to direct the already famous Gewandhaus Orchestra but to take responsibility for the whole musical life of that city. Whereas Liszt complained that Leipzig lacked both countesses and princesses, Schumann found a different aristocracy, as he called the "150 booksellers, 50 printing works and 30 periodicals". He could well have added the musical tradition, which, since Mendelssohn's arrival in Leipzig, had become the jewel in Europe's cultural crown, as in the days of Bach and Telemann. On 20th September 1835 Felix wrote confirming his arrival in his new environment, but also described his situation. He proposed to stay at an inn, so as not to impose on Abraham's friend, the singer Franz Hauser, for more than a week. However, this altruistic plan came to naught, for each lodging was worse than its predecessor: "I saw only the stairways in some of them, before turning quickly away, having been asked to pay 30 thalers for a sitting room and bedroom on the third floor, for the impending fair gives people strange ideas about prices."

However, Felix eventually found suitable accommodation, which, though "exceedingly expensive", was "most charming and comfortable, and thus the cost is justified...two elegant rooms on the second floor in the best part of town". In this new home, adjacent to the promenade and the fashionable public gardens, Felix was able to set his mind to composing. Indeed, "during the past three days here, I have done good work". Though he was charged 20 thalers per month, "the neighbours are friendly. There is morning sunlight, large, solidly closing windows, elegant curtains and wallpaper, a red sofa and a large stove." Felix was always pleased to return to his rooms, preferring to stay indoors than to go out. "Believe it or not," he wrote to his family, "I rise at seven and am at work at eight, having finished my breakfast in the sunshine." This habit had begun whilst staying with Hauser, who "woke me with the most gentle sound he could coax from his viola, after which a barber called to shave me".

Felix had been offered 1,000 to 2,000 florins to direct the opera in Munich, but declined once he had learnt of the Leipzig appointment. After his untoward experiences in Berlin, and especially Düsseldorf, he wrote to Conrad Schleinitz making sure of his new directorship. He did not wish to usurp anyone who deserved the appointment more than himself. He was even prepared to reduce his salary to between 400 and 600 thalers, depending upon how satisfied the management would be with his work at the Gewandhaus. A further 1,000 thalers would accrue from his work with the choir of St. Thomas's Church. Another advantage would be that, with the exception of the winter concert season, Felix could travel whenever he pleased, when required. His main reason for accepting such a prestigious post was not worldly, though, but spiritual, as stated in his letter to Conrad Schleinitz, president of the music and fine arts committee in Leipzig: "Since it is my only desire to further the course of music along the path that seems right to me, you can imagine that, for this reason, I would gladly accept a calling that would place the means of my doing so within my reach."

Rudolf Elvers suggests that it was publisher Friedrich Kistner who recommended Felix for each of these Leipzig appointments, but, in view of his untoward experience of the election for director of the Berlin Singakademie, which still seared his emotions, Mendelssohn ensured that all arrangements would be watertight before pursuing his new career. As early as 13th January 1835 Mendelssohn sought his father's blessing on the forthcoming venture, marshalling several arguments were this ultra-cautious, intransigent man to refuse this privilege. After July, he pointed out, the only reason to remain in Düsseldorf "will be to do my own work in peace", which Felix could undertake equally well elsewhere. Most of all, however, "I have an impulse to be seen and heard in the great world and to hear and see, before tying myself down". Fortunately, Abraham had no alternative than to see reason, but Felix was still dissatisfied. Before any further negotiations could take place, Felix made certain that there was no other individual who had a prior claim to these sources of employment, and who could usurp the position. This settled to Felix's satisfaction, he wrote to privy councillor Rocklitz, who also happened to be a celebrated music critic, giving his ideas as to the forthcoming season's repertoire. On 5th May Schleinitz was apprised of similar views, to be relayed to other members of the management committee.

Mendelssohn's reception in Leipzig was "far beyond all expectations Felix wrote to his family and, if this continues, the winter should be very pleasant indeed". From the large garden attached to his lodging he could hear "the strings playing my overture so clearly...unlike those at Düsseldorf". He looked forward to the following week's rehearsal, when he was to be "ceremoniously introduced to the elite of Leipzig...at which Rocklitz will want to deliver a very long speech, I suspect". Though Mendelssohn had been prepared to play his *Fair Melusine* Overture, the management, with – according to Felix – "much wisdom and forethought", suggested that "I must not toss off everything at the first concert as if the pieces were merely clever trifles". Thus, on 4th November 1835 the Gewandhaus season began with Weber's shamefully neglected overture, *Ruler of the*

Chapter 25: "In Paradise"

Spirits. Opera arias were performed, including Cherubini's 'Ali Baba', "never before played by the orchestra", and an unspecified Beethoven symphony. At subsequent concerts, works by Mendelssohn included the *Calm Sea* Overture, his G minor Piano Concerto, and his *Fair Melusine* Overture.

Only one cloud marred Mendelssohn's otherwise idyllic life in Leipzig. On 19th November his father passed away, causing Felix to ask Schleinitz if the concert on the 25th could be conducted in his absence. Though he would have preferred to return to Leipzig [from Berlin] on the Monday, ever thoughtful for others, despite his own grief, Felix offered to travel on the previous day (see Chapter 3, 'Sound Minds in Frail Bodies'). Meanwhile, he had confided to Julius Schubring his private thoughts on musical life in Europe. At the time, Vienna was nothing more than "a dissolute den of eating and drinking", and Berlin consisted of "nothing but barracks and sand". However assiduously Mendelssohn had tried to bring the music of Düsseldorf to a high standard, he met "nothing but quarrelling and perpetual strife and petty criticism" among his colleagues. "Leipzig will be something really special," Felix vowed, pledging himself "to be of as much service in the cause of good music as lies within my power". Apart from the usual duties he would undertake, he would give precedence to resurrecting the music of "Leipzig's elder statesman of art", Johann Sebastian Bach. Neither would he give any concert for his own benefit. "Pecuniary considerations would be of less importance to me were it not for my parents, who, I think rightly, exact from me that I should follow my art as a professional and gain my livelihood therefrom... I acknowledge the propriety of what my parents insist on so strictly."

The Gewandhaus Orchestra – so named after the building in which it was housed: 'the cloth-hall' – had been founded in 1781, and it was Heinrich Matthai who had brought the orchestra to the standard at which Mendelssohn found it. However, since his predecessor had passed away, Felix vowed to maintain Matthai's standard and to improve upon it. In view of the sterling work already apparent, there would, Felix realised, be little difficulty in this achievement. All that was needed would be to augment this already fine ensemble. In 1802, according to the Gewandhaus statistics, the orchestra comprised 33 musicians; in 1839 the number was augmented to 50. Mendelssohn lured Ferdinand David from his post at Dorpat, Estonia, to become concert master (leader) of the Gewandhaus Orchestra. Mendelssohn was concerned equally with the Orchestra's welfare, having instigated a higher salary scale and put a pension fund into operation, whereby the musicians could live more comfortably once they had retired or had had to resign through illness. Neither were the widows and children forgotten of those musicians who had already died, and, indeed, Mendelssohn often helped out such individuals from his own resources. Felix also begged the management to reward Christian Pohlenz, a former conductor, still living at the time, for his past services.

When Mendelssohn arrived in Leipzig a city of 45,000 inhabitants, second in importance only to Dresden in the state of Saxony, audiences expected and appreciated "well-behaved" music, such as that composed by Ludwig Spohr and – some biographers carp – Mendelssohn himself. Though Felix gave the public what they required, his spirit of adventure prompted him to have 'new' music performed. Chamber groups, which had, to date, played in private houses, were now encouraged to perform at the Gewandhaus. At one such performance David and Felix played Bach's *Chaconne*. For these innovations, Mendelssohn was awarded a Doctorate of Law by the University of Leipzig. Although, in 1834, the Academy in Berlin had made him a member, he would never have expected to be allowed to call himself Herr Doktor Mendelssohn, nor to be so addressed.

Felix entered with unfeigned enthusiasm into Leipzig's musical life and social activity. It would not be long before the illustrious Paris Conservatoire Orchestra would be obliged to bow before its more easterly rival and, even after his death, the names 'Mendelssohn' and 'Leipzig' would not only be spoken with awe and pride by anyone so musically inclined but with love by anyone associated with the Gewandhaus or the Leipzig Conservatorium. No wonder Rebecka declared, when visiting her brother, how "perfectly admired" he was becoming. Charles Horsley bore out this remark: in Leipzig "Mendelssohn's fame was at its zenith... His orchestra...and its performances of all the great works, particularly Beethoven's symphonies, were celebrated as the most complete to have been given to date." The Gewandhaus concerts covered the period from Michaelmas week (around 29th September) to Easter of the succeeding year. Though the management was entrusted, via a constitution, to oversee the orchestra, it was Mendelssohn's jurisdiction, as director, that ruled. These Thursday concerts were of shorter duration than those that Horsley called the "selection of incongruous pieces" that obtained at the time; "the ear was not tired out" by Mendelssohn's entertainments. "Audiences were able to return home...with a perfect sense of enjoyment of the feast of sound that had been so discriminately set before them." Invariably, a symphony occupied the second half of a concert, but, during the part before the interval, young musicians were positively encouraged to play solo parts, where appropriate. Such individuals as a violinist named Eckart and a pianist named Kufferath are recalled by Horsley. Likewise, any piece of music that pleased Felix "was sure to find its way into the concert programme and [be] given an admirable interpretation". There were two rehearsals per week and a chamber concert, in addition to the Gewandhaus concert proper.

Always a stickler for the truth, Mendelssohn made it plain how his musicians could cope with a piece, or what difficulties might arise. To Johann Schneider, Kapellmeister at Dessau, for instance, he reported how "the orchestra played at their best and acquitted themselves without mistakes" in a symphony he had written; "the scherzo and last movement were almost completely impeccable". However, Felix had to administer tact and caution regarding an oratorio from the same composer's pen. "This cannot be performed at present, as the amateur singers appear to be lacking in spirit and initiative, and to have the choruses performed by

Chapter 25: "In Paradise"

the Choir of St. Thomas's Church alone would appear ill-advised, since the music seems more suitable for female voices", whereas the St. Thomas choristers were male. "It has not been possible to perform a larger choral work during the winter," Felix continued, "and I almost fear that this deficit will not soon be made up." Though Schneider's Symphony pleased him, could it be that Felix used his refusal as an excuse for not having the oratorio performed? How many people – musicians or listeners to music – have even heard of Schneider today, except when studying such 'greats' as Mendelssohn?

The day-to-day activities of Mendelssohn's life present a schedule that would put most people to shame who bleat as to how busy they are. The first few months of 1836 serve as an example. Throughout his life Felix kept in touch with Aloys Fuchs in Vienna. In January he asked for Lachner's 'Prize' Symphony to be performed at a concert on 20th March, the finale to his first Gewandhaus season: "A prompt performance here would be good enough to publicise the work." An auction that Felix had hoped to attend on Fuchs's behalf had been postponed and, since "I have a number of travel plans to work out", he could not render this service for his friend. However, Felix was able, meanwhile, to send Fuchs "two songs by Rihm and a canon by Attwood", promising to pass on Fuchs's requests to Kistner.

Hiller was another correspondent whom Felix felt required a letter. His D minor Overture, "despite the most beautiful of opening passages", needed "many amendments" to be made to the piece as a whole, despite the "repeated and careful" rehearsals undertaken by the Gewandhaus Orchestra. As was his custom, Felix apologised for writing with such candour: "I realise [that] no one else would allow me to write in such a way." He hoped Hiller would not take offence, but wondered if his interest in composing had dwindled, and perceived that other musicians might have the same idea. "Only you know how to apply and develop such a talent, in order to improve it." So certain was Felix of Hiller's musical gifts that he wished them to be fostered, but, in view of the limbo into which his music has fallen, it might be wondered, because of his crowded working life, why Mendelssohn should make time to write such epistles.

"I had to conduct three concerts yesterday," Felix wrote to the family, "as well as having to perform Mozart's [Piano] Concerto, K. 466. The cadenza made such an impression on the audience that an elderly man told me later that he had heard Mozart play the concerto, but that not since that day had he heard anyone produce such good cadenzas as I did yesterday", and he promised to send Fanny a copy of the score. Guessing how painstakingly Felix applied himself, the work would have had to be practised until such a perfectionist would be satisfied with his interpretation of the work. On 11th February, according to Rockstro, a performance of Beethoven's 9th Symphony was given that, again, would have needed considerable work from the orchestra and singers. The performance had "an effect quite unknown to the audience" until then.

"There is so much running and chasing around," Felix complained to Fuchs, with regard to his work commitments, "that I have no time for myself – much less a letter." This was borne out by the fact that, though Felix must have needed a holiday (which he hoped to take in Genoa, "with sea bathing"), this was cancelled and never took place. Not only was he invited to direct the Lower Rhine Festival at Düsseldorf in 1836, where his oratorio *St Paul* would be premiered, but his old friend Johann Schelble was taken ill. Felix was therefore summoned to Frankfurt-am-Main to conduct a further performance of the oratorio, as well as other works, with the St. Cecilia Society. Although this was seen as a brief interruption in his Leipzig career, Schelble passed away, which kept Felix longer in Frankfurt. But such a commitment was handsomely rewarded. The cancellation of his holiday was irrelevant when compared with the beautiful girl with whom he fell in love – and married within ten months of meeting her (described in Chapter 26, "Like an old married couple"). Meanwhile, Mendelssohn's almost superhuman work schedule continued in 1837. On 4th January Sterndale Bennett's 1st Piano Concerto was performed with the composer as soloist. "In Leipzig, no one talks of anything else," Felix wrote to Fanny. Bennett had an overture ready for performance at a subsequent concert, while Wilhelm Molique, violinist and former pupil of Spohr, played "exquisitely" at a recent one. Two of Hiller's overtures were to be presented to Leipzig audiences and Spohr's *Daughter of the Air* Overture, inspired by Felix's *Fair Melusine*, was to be published. Mendelssohn also aimed to have Prince Radziwill's *Faust* music performed and Mme. Gressini had agreed to sing in Leipzig. In view of such musical activity, "the good people of Berlin can hold their tongues", Felix told his family. On 10th January Felix wrote to Hiller that "six symphonies lie before me", all of which hoped for the honour of a Gewandhaus premiere. "God knows what they may be. I would rather not know. Not one of them pleases me and there is no one to blame but myself. Good heavens, should these Kapellmeisters not be ashamed of themselves and search their own hearts. What artistic pedantry they all possess. The living spark, of which they speak so often, leaves ruin everywhere." Evidently Felix yearned for Frankfurt and his lovely Cécile, whom he married on 27th March.

Hiller, before the rift occurred, was Felix's adviser, despite his apparent "dwindling interest" in music. He was asked to "look through the six preludes and fugues to be published in February", as Op. 35. This compilation was begun ten years earlier with the Prelude in E minor, chronicling the illness and death of August Hanstein. "I fear these pieces will not be much played," Felix wrote, and, sadly, like many of his works, he proved to be accurate, since it is only among Mendelssohn connoisseurs that they are known today. In the same letter, Felix wrote of three organ fugues, eventually published as Op. 37, in 1839, with other pieces. "Heaven grant that some spirited piano piece may come to me to efface this unpleasant depression."

Evidently this must have occurred, for several books of *Songs without Words* were published during that year, together with a variety of other compositions. Though

Chapter 25: "In Paradise"

this barely needs to be said, Mendelssohn's depression lifted once he returned to Frankfurt to marry Cécile Jeanrenaud. Chapter 26 covers the wedding tour of the Rhine and his fifth visit to London, ostensibly to conduct *St Paul* at the Birmingham Festival and the premiere of his 2nd Piano Concerto.

In February 1838 another milestone was reached for the musical audiences of Leipzig: Mendelssohn's 'historic concerts' began. So popular were these programmes that the doors to the ante-room had to be opened to accommodate the concert-goers. The penultimate concert in the 1837-38 season included works by Righini and Naumann as well as still little-known compositions by Bach and Handel, together with Haydn's 'Farewell' Symphony, No. 45. "To the great delight of the public, the musicians literally blew out their candles and went off one by one, the first violins alone remaining... It is a curious, melancholy little piece", composed by Haydn as a hint to his employer, Prince Esterhazy, that a holiday was long overdue for his musicians. "Next time," Felix wrote to Rebecka, "we are to have Mozart, whose C minor [Piano] Concerto I am to play, and also, for the first time, a quartet from his unfinished opera *Zaïde*. Then comes Beethoven and, to complete our set of 20 concerts, we are left with two for every kind of modern work." A concert extraneous to the Gewandhaus season included the four overtures written by Beethoven for his opera *Fidelio*: "Nowhere, other than at the Gewandhaus, and under such a conductor, could such an idea have been happily carried out," Rockstro recalled. Felix was also responsible for bringing to his chamber music audience a Haydn trio, "whose beauty filled listeners with amazement", published "long ago" by Breitkopf & Härtel.

To Mendelssohn, history did not consist solely of music from the past. It was a living, thriving phenomenon. It was not therefore, patronising, but genuinely exciting for him to promote contemporary music. Johannes Verhulst, Kapellmeister at The Hague, submitted an overture that, though originally resembling that of Weber's *Der Freischütz*, had been improved and "will now find many friends and, I hope, will soon appear in print. At least, to me, it seems completely worthy of being published," Felix wrote to the composer. He also anticipated a further Verhulst overture to be given at a subsequent concert. On 2nd December the 19-year-old Clara Wieck was invited to perform the final movement of Chopin's 1st Piano Concerto to end the concert, and to include a caprice by Thalberg. If the "esteemed Fräulein" would accept this invitation, "it will round off the year nicely". Not only was Clara celebrated throughout Europe as a pianist, and would relish the thought of the Leipzig audience to hear her play; an added incentive was that Robert Schumann, the man she would marry in the following year, lived there, and, despite her father's objections to her future husband, they would meet openly.

In the 1839-40 Gewandhaus season two other works new to the Leipzig audience were heard. On 11th April 1839 Wagner's Symphony in C major was performed. Because this occurred once only the composer never came to terms with the fact, and even accused Mendelssohn of destroying the score. Though no reference is extant, either in the Gewandhaus or Mendelssohn family archives, Felix was far too professional a musician and far too scrupulous a man to perpetrate such vandalism, and this can be proved. Percy Young records in his biography of Sir George Grove that, at a concert given on 29th November 1887, the symphony was performed "to an almost empty St James's Hall" in London.

Later in 1839 another symphony in C major was given its first performance, to be repeated on several occasions throughout the season. In Vienna Robert Schumann visited Ferdinand, Franz Schubert's brother, who showed him music that had lain buried and neglected since the composer's death in 1828. Schumann had no doubt as to whom the score of Schubert's 9th Symphony – subsequently called the 'Great C major' – should be despatched. Mendelssohn wrote to Moscheles of "the most remarkable and interesting symphony of Franz Schubert. It is without doubt one of the best works we have heard to date. Bright, fascinating and original throughout. It stands quite at the head of his orchestral works." It is thanks to Schumann and to Mendelssohn that this remarkable work came to public notice. Though an attempt had been made to perform the work in Vienna in the year Schubert died, no one then understood this music. So popular was the first Leipzig performance on 9th September 1839, however, that three further repeats were demanded.

During this period singers were not neglected. Miss Clara Novello was engaged to sing with the Gewandhaus Orchestra for the 1838-39 season. But her appearance produced "a vast amount of rivalry and bad artistic feeling... When really good musicians condescend to deprecate one another, to be malicious and to sting in secret, I would as soon renounce music altogether, or, rather, I should say, musicians." The reply from his trusted friend led Felix to believe that "the world is not so bad after all", adding: "I wish I could be like you, seeing good in everything and endeavouring to amend anything adverse, and, like you, be a little more mild, just, judicious and many other things." But, despite what Felix might have thought of 'La Novello', she was evidently a favourite of Hiller. Felix wrote to him in Italy, where he was living with his mother, saying: "I imagine you sitting by Lake Como...lounging about with Liszt and paying court to La Novello, who I hear is now in Milan, taking lessons. Is she still your favourite and what do you think of her singing and looks?" Another English singer who visited Leipzig during that season was Mrs. Alfred Shaw (née Mary Postone), who had sung the contralto solos in *St Paul*. However competently she sang in her native tongue, this redoubtable lady knew no German, nor very much French, so Cécile and Felix had to act as interpreters. To make matters worse, "the thoroughgoing downright people of Leipzig talk in their own dialect". As if this were not enough, three further English visitors arrived, all of whom had to be looked after. He gave himself time to relax by reading the works of Ephraim Lessing. "This celebrated fellow makes me feel quite fresh again, though Germany fares badly when reading his letters to my

Chapter 25: "In Paradise"

grandfather [Moses Mendelssohn]." Yet it was not music making alone that absorbed the mind of this remarkable director.

His musicians' welfare, collective and individual, was of equal importance to Mendelssohn. A clarinettist named Drobisch, who had served 19 years with the Gewandhaus Orchestra, had petitioned councillor Porsche to take up a post as copyist to supplement his income, and, to add weight to this request, he asked Mendelssohn to support his application. Felix obliged, pointing out that Drobisch "had survived, or existed, hitherto, on a pension of eight thalers, plus a minimum stipend from the Church of St. Thomas. Could Drobisch's needy family be given support from the object of his desire?" Felix could never be accused of deserving the epithet 'grovelling lickspittle'. He addressed eminent dignitaries by their titles, however pompous they might seem, by virtue of the respect he held for their office, rather than to the individual who occupied the post. Felix worked conscientiously at every aspect of his work, however tired or ill he became. Despite a second attack of measles in 1838 he carried on working; "I could scarcely do anything else but take an occasional rest," he excused himself, but still he berated himself for "laziness", notwithstanding the fact that his Op. 44 String Quartets were written at that time, together with his Op. 45 Sonata for Piano and 'Cello. Other works composed during this period, as Felix reported to Moscheles, were "a psalm setting, some songs without words, some songs with words…and a symphony in B". He would speak about this on his sixth visit to London in 1840, Moscheles was informed. (Most likely this could have been the *Hymn of Praise*, written in 1840 for Leipzig's commemoration of 400 years of Gutenberg's printing press.) Felix also mentioned a trio in D minor, which Schumann called "the master trio of the age". Its first movement possessed "concerto-like brilliance; the second movement has some of the sweetest songs without words; the scherzo, a light and airy invention, so characteristic of the composer; the finale combines Schubertian strength with Mendelssohn's own subtle harmonies". At this time also incidental music for Victor Hugo's *Ruy Blas* – or 'Rwy Blas', as Marek insists on naming it. Though considered "quite a pleasure" at the outset, Felix later disparaged the work, consistently referring to the piece as the 'Pension Fund Overture'. The theatre trustees commissioned Mendelssohn to write the overture and a song for this production, to be given in aid of the pension fund for retired and infirm performers and their families. As Felix disliked the play only the song was presented at first, but the trustees insisted on hearing the overture because this was required for a fund-raising event. Felix's conscience troubled him, as always in such circumstances, but he never liked the work, dismissing it as "perfectly horrible".

In the *New Musical Journal*, which Schumann edited from 1834, he wrote: "In Leipzig…German music blossoms to such a degree that, without arrogance, it [the Gewandhaus under Mendelssohn's direction] can compete with the richest and largest orchestras…of all the other cities." The Zollverein (or Customs Union), which came into existence during the same year, allowed the railway system to develop so that, by 1840, all the cities west of the river Oder and the Polish border were linked together. Such a convenient means of access allowed Leipzig to become an even greater city of culture than hitherto, which many visitors were able to appreciate more easily at first hand. Especially must this have applied to the never-flagging work for which Felix was responsible. In February 1840 Felix took part in four concerts in one week, plus a "quartet soirée", a concert at Hiller's lodgings and a performance of Mozart's Concerto for Two Pianos, "with two grand cadenzas", the soloists being Hiller and himself. Then came a further "quartet soirée" that included "a new rondo by Spohr", another similar musical entertainment, a meeting of the Lieder Circle and a ball. "Yet, despite this, everyone complains that I live in such a retired manner," Felix wrote to Paul. "Latterly, I have become quite tired of music and think I must take to painting once more." At a gathering given in honour of Liszt (see Chapter 24, 'A mélange of musicians'), he, Hiller and Felix played the Bach D Minor Concerto for Three Keyboards, which was played at a further performance on 19th October by Felix, Moscheles and Clara Schumann.

Yet, there were many frustrations when plans went awry. Apart from the fiasco of his appointment at the Prussian court (covered in Chapter 23, 'The Highest In The Land'), smaller pinpricks upset Mendelssohn's orderly plans. He was obliged to ask Count Baudissin to send his own score and parts for a concerto from Paris, as – unbelievably – none were available in Leipzig. Added to this was the nuisance of arranging which train would transport the music, in view of the short notice of the performance: "If a later train than the 6 p.m. be preferred," Felix wrote, "I must request that a courier deliver the music, either to my home or the Gewandhaus." A further irritation occurred when unwelcome musicians persisted in seeking an interview with Mendelssohn. As a rule, he had no hesitation in recommending suitable musicians to the Gewandhaus Orchestra, via its management; equally, he knew whom he did not want. A 'cellist named Breuer, whom Felix had heard in Düsseldorf, an "excellent" horn player and an "altogether outstanding oboist" did not come into the present category. A Herr Buber, who fancied himself as an opera singer, approached this kind-hearted director for advice. Mendelssohn's tact can be gathered from the letter Buber received: "Any singer," Felix pointed out, "must have a strong larynx, otherwise he could ruin not only the voice but his whole life, if he persisted in pursuing such a career. Zeal and a desire to succeed are not enough. An opera singer must have a voice that will carry in an auditorium." Whatever Buber might have been told by anyone else, Mendelssohn found his voice "too small and unconvincing. I am obliged to write to you in this way for the sake of your own well-being." Three days later, Felix heard, this potential opera star had shot himself, unable either to accept that his voice was unsuitable for such a strenuous application, or to find the courage to change direction in his career.

It was at this time also that Felix lost two of his long-standing friends, not from death, as so often happened, but because, in each case, a rift developed between the companions from Felix's youth. Adolf Bernhard Marx had asked Mendelssohn to

Chapter 25: "In Paradise"

write the text for his oratorio *Moses*, whereas he would write the music. Having studied life in ancient Egypt, the oratorio had become an obsession with Marx. Dissatisfied with what Felix had produced, Marx wrote his own text and, visiting Leipzig, asked his friend to have the work published. Marx sang part of the oratorio but, asked to desist from doing so by Mendelssohn, Marx, on his return to Berlin, became so outraged that he threw all Felix's letters, accumulated over the years, into the Tiergarten Lake. Though Marx's widow wrote of the success that accrued when *Moses* was conducted by Liszt in Weimar, Schumann had a different opinion: "Such a distinguished musicologist should have known better than to foist such an inferior work onto Mendelssohn." Like Marx, Hiller could do no wrong in Mendelssohn's eyes. Two of his oratorios, *Jeremiah* and *The Destruction of Jerusalem*, were to be performed at the Gewandhaus. "I feel as much anxiety as if they were my own – or even greater anxiety," Felix wrote to Fanny. Perhaps because Hiller had recently lost his mother, and was lonely, rather than staying for a week in Leipzig, as planned, he remained with the Mendelssohns for the whole winter. Each sat at one table to work; the arrangement proved ideal when composing small pieces but, when larger works were involved, this became a problem, which might have been the reason for arguments between Felix and Hiller. Felix even asked Simrock to publish the oratorios, but this did not happen for 20 years and they were not rediscovered until Max Reger unearthed them at the beginning of the 20th century.

A more cheerful meeting for Felix was with Moscheles and Chorley, with whom he travelled back to Leipzig from his sixth visit to London. Chorley sustained an accident that rendered him lame and unable to leave his hotel room. To cheer him, Felix and Moscheles had a piano delivered, on which each played for the invalid. Once Chorley had become mobile, a musical evening was arranged at the Gewandhaus in his honour. A performance was given for elderly and infirm musicians of the *Hymn of Praise*. "I do not want it to be performed in the imperfect style of Birmingham, owing to an illness," Felix wrote to Klingemann, but no explanation is given whose indisposition was meant." Four new movements are to be added and I have also improved the three symphonic parts, which are now being copied. As an introduction to the chorus 'Der Nacht ist Vergangen' ('The Night is Past'), I have found words in the Bible that could not be more beautiful, nor better adapted to the music... Not only shall I send the piece into the world as a symphony-cantata, but I am also seriously thinking about resuming *The First Walpurgisnacht*, which has been stored away for so long, ...finishing the work and finally getting rid of it. Though I do not think it worthy to be performed, I am so fond of it."

As a result of the *Hymn of Praise* performance 500 thalers were distributed to the fund, donated by the town council: "The sum is small...but I feel satisfied to disburse these funds and hope this grant can be repeated in the future, thus rendering a real service to the musicians, whether they thank me or not."

In 1841 Bach's *St Matthew Passion* was performed in its original home, St. Thomas's Church, with as great a triumph as in 1829, but, unlike the productions of the earlier year, Mendelssohn could do as he pleased, having larger musical resources. Arias and recitatives that were omitted in 1829 could now be heard. Though important later performances took place, especially that of 1843, Bach scholars suggest that, however much the work may have been modernised, through the use of contemporary instruments to replace those that had become obsolete, the 1829 performances should be counted as being of greater importance than their successors.

Fanny was recommended by Felix to read Rückert's translations of "some eastern poetry, which contain the most beautiful and interesting descriptions I have read for a long time. If this book does not delight you beyond measure, I shall never recommend one to you again." Strangely, however, despite such a panegyric, there appear to be no song settings of this poetry in the catalogue of Mendelssohn's works, for that, or any other period, of his musical output. However, new works from other composers were brought to the fore. On 23rd April 1841 Julius Rietz was informed that his works had been performed "with universal applause and unanimous appreciation from musicians and public alike, even during rehearsals". The concert audience "had sat quiet as mice" before the performance, "and never made a sound. Even towards the end, I noticed the smiling faces and nodding heads of the orchestra. There is always something genuinely artistic in your orchestral works, about which I am happy from the first bar, and they captivate and interest me to the very end." As for George MacFarren's *Chevy Chase* Overture, even Wagner enjoyed the piece. After his final Philharmonic Society concert in London of 1855 he would write of its "curiously wild and passionate element, which made it a pleasure to conduct". This praise was spoilt, however, by his reference to "the Steeplechase Overture", which Cosima Wagner misspelt "Chevy Chace". On 13th January 1843 Felix told Fanny of a new symphony by the Danish composer Niels Gade: "You should hear this most original, most earnest and sweet-sounding symphony." The work was performed on 18th February "to the lively and unalloyed delight of the public, who broke out into the loudest applause at the end of each of the four movements. There was great excitement from the audience after the scherzo, and the clapping of hands seemed interminable. After the adagio, the same [applied]... It was to me a source of great delight, as great as if I had written the work myself." To Gade, Felix wrote: "In your work, I feel nothing but pure delight in all its admirable beauty. You have won the admiration of the mighty public, who truly love music, as your permanent friends." As Gade was to visit Leipzig, "I hope...to express my thanks more fully and clearly in person, rather than by my empty written words". Gade's *Ossian* Overture was also performed (with other of his works), Felix enjoying its "local colour, dreamy melancholy and heroic pathos".

But Felix sometimes had to obey his management as to what could, or could

Chapter 25: "In Paradise"

not, be performed. To MacFarren, for instance, he had to explain that, though he would have liked to perform his new symphony, the authorities considered that too many such works had been included in the repertoire for the season and that one more might be one too many for the audience to digest. Felix believed that English music would, in time, be appreciated in Germany – and, in fact, this prophecy came true at the beginning of the 20th century with the music of Elgar. Though MacFarren's Sonata *Ma Cousine*, dedicated to Miss Emma Pendixon, could be performed "without wrong notes", there was too little time for real justice to be done with this work. He assured MacFarren that *Chevy Chase* had been received with "cordiality...and performed with delight and enthusiasm, which bodes well for many musical treats from you".

Readers can be excused for imagining that Mendelssohn cared only for works that would disappear into oblivion, but this is not the case. In 1842 Schumann's Piano Quintet Op. 44 won immediate approval. One evening, at the composer's home, Clara, who was to play the piano part, was taken ill, so Felix took her place. As this was the first time it had been played, before the public knew of the quintet, Felix could not have had much opportunity to familiarise himself with the work, yet he played the piano part from memory. In the same year Mendelssohn wrote to Edward Buxton, the London publisher, in an attempt to promote his friend's cantata *Paradise and the Peri*, the words for which were taken from Tom Moore's *Lalla Rookh* At last, this work has been recognised and is occasionally performed. He accompanied Clara in her husband's *Andante and Variations* for two pianos on another occasion. Though Schumann had been an enthusiastic pianist, he had tried to invent a device with which to stretch the span of a pianist's fingers on the keyboard, but crippled his hand in attempting the experiment.

At a personal level, it is worth recording that, prior to the 1842-43 Gewandhaus season, Felix had written to Schleinitz to ask if the usual Thursday pattern could be waived during November to account for the Day of Atonement, a hallowed Jewish festival. How many apparently devout Protestants would think of acknowledging this sacred time for a different faith? Or could it be that Felix, always a Jew at heart, wished to observe this festival himself, as loyally as his enforced conversion would allow? In 1842 another personal trauma assailed him. On 12th December, the day after Abraham's birthday, Leah passed away. Felix reminisced with the family and his *Song without Words*, Op. 62 No. 1, was written at this time. The concert pianist Frederic Lamond wrote of the "subdued melancholy, unrequited love and poignant grief" expressed in the piece. Since Felix's was an idyllically blissful marriage, the outpourings of his feelings as witnessed by the melody can only have been his sadness – and guilt, perhaps – at Leah's death, and the fact that they never had the opportunity to understand one another.

A concert was given for the King of Saxony at the end of 1842, "who swears death and destruction to all the Herrs and hares throughout the countryside.

Works will include 'the Partridge' and 'the Bear Hunt' from Haydn's *The Seasons* (how touching). The second half will comprise my own *First Walpurgisnacht*, in a somewhat different garb, indeed, from the former one, which was somewhat too richly endowed with trombones and rather poor in the vocal parts." When the piece was eventually performed, on 2nd February 1843, the English journal *The Musical World* reported "several encores and enthusiasm approaching delirium" from the audience. Also at the King of Saxony's invitation, Mendelssohn conducted *St Paul* in Dresden and composed a march for the event, when a statue to King Friedrich Augustus I was erected. Whereas the march was for male voices and brass accompaniment, Wagner wrote a march for the same occasion for voices alone. According to the latter composer's autobiography *Mein Leben* (*My Life*), his was "simple and heartfelt and totally eclipsed the inferior one [by Mendelssohn], with its complex artificialities". The June 1906 issue of *The Musical World* found nothing complex or artificial in Mendelssohn's tribute. Rather, he was praised for the "legendary ingenuity, weaving 'God Save the King' with the Saxon national anthem subtly into the harmonic texture of the piece".

On 9th March 1843 the centenary of the original Leipzig orchestra was celebrated, for which Felix chose works by previous cantors at St. Thomas's Church. Moritz Hauptmann conducted his own Kyrie and Gloria, Felix conducted his own setting of Psalm 114. Sadly, in what today would appear to have been an oversight, one of the most prominent composers of his generation in Leipzig, Georg Philipp Telemann, was overlooked. However, his contemporary, J. S. Bach, was given pride of place. His music was not the only commemoration of Bach's life. "If they wish to honour Handel in Halle, Mozart in Salzburg, Beethoven in Bonn by forming good orchestras and performing their works perfectly and intelligently, then I am their man... My present hobby-horse is the improvement of the musicians' lot in our orchestra. If, after no end of letter writing, soliciting and importuning, I have succeeded in getting their salaries raised by 500 thalers (and, before I leave them, I mean to get them double that amount), if this is granted, I will not mind setting up a monument to Sebastian Bach in front of St. Thomas's Church. You will be touched at how much heart the musicians put into their work and strive to do their best."

Evidently, the authorities did raise the salaries and the Bach monument was erected at Mendelssohn's instigation. According to Marek, Felix was asked "to help" in this project, but his letters reveal that he played a far greater part than merely helping. "The monument looks very handsome," Felix was able to tell his family on 11th December 1842. "The scaffolding has been removed, so that the pillars, smaller columns, scrolls and, above all, the bas-reliefs and antiquarian features sparkle in the sun and give me great delight. The structure, with its elegant decorations, is really typical of the old fellow. Cedars are planted around it and a Gothic-style seat will be placed in front. We are anxious...to avoid the present-day pompous style of phraseology, ...which is so much the fashion." Bach's birthday,

Chapter 25: "In Paradise"

21st March, was the original date for the unveiling of the monument in 1843, but it was almost a month later, on 20th April, before Felix was able to invite the council officials to a concert at which some of Bach's motets were performed, to be followed by the ceremony. "I will ensure that the necessary seats are reserved in the innermost circle, adjacent to the monument," he informed these august persons. A stonemason named Hiller, no relation to the composer, and a sculptor named Knaur were responsible for the edifice, supervised by the artists Bendemann and Hübner, long-standing friends of Felix. On 8th May Mendelssohn sent councillor Fleischer the 113 thalers for the railings around the monument, thanking him at the same time for "your goodwill in having the plaza designed, by which you have beautified and distinguished the environs".

How did the craftsmen find the money to build the structure? It is from Felix's correspondence that the answer is found. "Although my expenses were considerable, I gained a profit of 300 thalers" from organ recitals at St Thomas's Church, where Bach had presided 100 years earlier. "I practised for eight days consecutively, so that my legs became so stiff that I walked organ pedal in the street and could not stand properly." All Felix's dedication proved worthwhile, especially when it was learnt that Bach's one surviving grandson, Wilhelm Friedrich Ernst Bach, was in the audience.

It is appropriate to juxtapose old with new. Bach had been almost reverently commemorated, but, in 1844, a link was forged between Mendelssohn and a boy of 13. A former pupil of Professor Böhm in Vienna, even at that age, he was a brilliant violinist. However, unlike many "child stars", he was to become one of music's legends. Most people think of Joseph Joachim, son of a Hungarian wood merchant, as being associated with Brahms, two years his junior. It is forgotten, or not even known, that it was Mendelssohn who first took the young musician seriously and promoted his career. Joachim accompanied Felix in Beethoven's Op. 47 'Kreutzer' Sonata in the Mendelssohn home. In old age (Joachim lived until 1907) he recalled Schumann sitting in a corner of the room, pointing to the stars that shone through the open window and patting the boy's knee, asking, "Do you think they know up there that a young boy down here has been accompanying Mendelssohn?" At a concert organised by the soprano Pauline Viardot, Malibran's sister and herself a soprano of repute, Joachim played a rondo by Bériot, Malibran's widower and a pioneer of the Franco-Belgian school of violin playing.

With regard to Mendelssohn's appointment at the Prussian court, Marek implies that it was his own fault, for clinging so long after the original year that had been agreed for the term of this post. What would anyone else have done but remain, with so many false promises and abortive decisions as to what would be achieved: constant haranguing from court officials; continuous weeping by the family at the slightest hint of returning to Leipzig; and friends begging him to "stick with it"? (See Chapter 23, 'The Highest in the Land', for a full discussion). Felix celebrated his spiritual homecoming by completing one of his best-loved works, his E minor Violin Concerto, Op. 64. He had written what Marek calls "a little concerto" in D minor and one for violin, piano and strings, when a youth, but it was in 1838 that this new composition was conceived. On 30th July of that year Felix had written to Ferdinand David from Frankfurt: "I would like to write a violin concerto for you for next winter. One in E minor runs in my head, the beginning of which gives me no peace." On 30th November Felix told Moscheles of "a new concerto, at present swimming around in my head in a shapeless condition, but how it is to end, and what will be in the middle, heaven alone knows." R. Larry Todd, who has studied Mendelssohn manuscripts in the Bodleian Library, believes that the seed of this concerto grew from a piano concerto in E minor "on which Mendelssohn had ruminated" in his youth. However, the "next winter" of which Felix spoke came and went and it was not until 1840 that any further reference was made to the concerto. Felix played what was to become his Op. 64 at a gathering in his home, where the English singer George Sampson, Sterndale Bennett and Schumann were present. Bennett declared, on hearing the melodies, that he was reminded of the Garden of Eden – Adam represented by Beethoven's concerto, Mendelssohn's taking the role of Eve. Beethoven's work has been described as "heroic; epic"; that of Mendelssohn, "a lyrical poem". However, these prosaic descriptions are far less imaginative than those of Bennett. Beethoven's 'Adam' is 'masculine' in aspect; Mendelssohn's 'Eve' is, by contrast, 'feminine', giving a balanced whole nowadays when each concerto is combined on one recording.

On 17th December 1844 Felix, still diffident, sought "the favour" of David's advice on many technical details regarding the concerto. Alterations and revisions had been made "before sending the manuscript irrevocably to Breitkopf & Härtel for publication". Felix suggested that Gade should study the final score. "Do not laugh at me too much. I feel ashamed. I cannot help it; I am just groping around. 'Thank God the fellow has done with his concerto,' you will say." But the work received its premiere at the Gewandhaus, with David as soloist and Gade conducting, in Mendelssohn's absence through illness. Was this genuine, or 'diplomatic', in view of his strange anxiety?

In 1994 the Paganini specialist Alberto Luigi Bianchi played on this fact when performing the original score of Mendelssohn's E minor Concerto. This performance followed a convoluted search, which led Bianchi eventually to a Polish monastery, where the 'true' concerto was discovered. In fact, this unrevised score can be studied far nearer home, in the Bodleian Library, Oxford. "Mendelssohn must have been weak to alter it," Bianchi declared. Musicologists, jumping on this bandwagon, believe that the concerto was sabotaged, "probably by David", but this cannot be countenanced. Unswervingly loyal to Mendelssohn, both as a friend and a musician, he did his best at the Gewandhaus and would never have thought of such an unprofessional, unworthy action. It makes far better sense to suggest that the concerto was deliberately revised because David,

Chapter 25: "In Paradise"

competent as he might have been, was not capable of tackling the far more technically perfect original. If not, why did Fanny write to Rebecka that David had taught Joachim, a lad of 13, with years in front of him to improve his technique and gain experience of playing the violin, "all he knew"?

However pleasing the revised version might be, the original concerto is far more satisfying technically to the soloist and, to the listener, far more enjoyable. In each case, innovations can be observed from the earlier equivalents. The cadenza, during which the soloist is expected to display talent, is integrated into the first movement at the beginning of the recapitulation - a novel procedure. As with the 'Scottish' Symphony and the 1st Piano Concerto, the movements are played without a break, linked together, in each case, by a 'bridge' passage.

David played the concerto on a Guarneri violin, later to be acquired by the Lithuanian virtuoso Jascha Heifetz. A second performance, again with David as soloist, took place on 23rd October 1845: "I should have informed you long ago of the success with which I first publicly performed your violin concerto," David wrote to Mendelssohn. "It fulfils to the highest degree all demands that one might make on a concert piece, and violinists cannot be sufficiently grateful for this gift... May the great success of this work so please you that you will again think of us forlorn violinists"; but this did not happen. On 10th November it was Joachim's turn to play the work. In 1906, the year before he died, Joachim declared that the Germans had four violin concertos. The greatest was that by Beethoven; next came that by Brahms, with its superior technical skill. Max Bruch "wrote the richest and most enchanting of the four"; but the dearest of them all, "the heart's jewel", was that by Mendelssohn. Neither Bach's masterpiece, nor the considerable output of Spohr, evidently passed muster.

Chopin and Liszt both visited Leipzig, as discussed in 'Famous personalities', Part II of Chapter 24. Another visitor was Hector Berlioz, a concert of whose works was presented, and a performance of his *King Lear* Overture was repeated at a charity event. Felix, certainly in young manhood, had an ambivalent attitude to the music of this composer. Writing of his *Symphonie Fantastique*, after listening, evidently, to a mediocre performance: "Though the work is an uncouth, craggy, bare-faced [example of] impudence, it could have [had] some go about it, and be amusing." Of Felix, Berlioz recalled in his memoirs that he was "as prickly as a porcupine and one does not know how to get hold of him without hurting one's hand". With such an attitude Berlioz had doubts, on his first tour of Germany, of any welcome in Leipzig. Therefore, on receiving Felix's cordial invitation, he had to apologise for not including a visit to his colleague on that itinerary, writing: "I love you as much as I admire you and that is saying a lot." Felix was reassured.

However, in 1843, Berlioz did arrive, and Fanny, visiting simultaneously, wrote in her journal of the concessions her brother had to make. In one piece a harp was required, but, with no harpist available, Felix suggested the then defunct ophicleide as a substitute, which Berlioz, not surprisingly, considered "worthless". Felix himself played the piano to compensate. In his *Romeo and Juliet*, albeit a charity performance, the bass singer was dismissed as "one of the large and flourishing class of musicians who are ignorant of music". The performance had to be abandoned, depriving the charitable institution of much-needed funds.

Yet Schumann must have been the first to praise his *Grande Messe des Morts*, especially the Offertorium. This caused Berlioz to praise him as "one of the most justly renowned composer-music critics in Germany". Not only Schumann appreciated the work. When Berlioz was taken ill, a physician, rather than asking for a fee, instructed the composer to write a few bars of this requiem for him. Evidently Berlioz enjoyed his stay in Leipzig for, inspired by Fennimore Cooper's *Last of the Mohicans*, popular at the time, Berlioz asked his host to exchange 'tomahawks' (batons), writing: "To Chief Mendelssohn, Great Chief. We are pledged to exchange tomahawks. Mine is rough-hewn; yours, too, is plain. Only squaws and pale-faces love ornate weapons. Be my brother and, when the Great Spirit sends us to hunt in the Land of Souls, may our warriors hang our tomahawks side by side at the Great Door of the Council Chamber." Whereas Berlioz's 'tomahawk' was "a large cudgel of lime wood, with the bark still on, Felix's was a pretty, light stick of whalebone, covered with leather", as Fanny wrote in her journal. Whatever may be said of Berlioz's memoirs, there is no question that Fanny Hensel, a stickler for truth, can be trusted to have been patently accurate in what she recalled.

Chopin, Liszt and Berlioz notwithstanding, the 1845-46 Gewandhaus season was, according to Rockstro "particularly brilliant". Clara Schumann played the solo part in Henselt's Piano Concerto at one concert, in which she also played a fugue by her husband and two of Felix's *Songs without Words*, Nos. 3 and 4 of Op. 67, not then published. Miss Helen Dolby was engaged for the season. A particular favourite vocalist of Felix, this contralto later married the French tenor Prosper Sainton, and was known as Mme. Sainton-Dolby. "She performed with great success, not only in the higher forms of classical music, but also in familiar phases of English art, as yet unknown in Germany," Rockstro reported in his quaint manner, with no further explanation. But, however much of a celebrity Miss Dolby appeared, Mendelssohn also introduced a soprano whose fame was remembered throughout the 19th century and who, in the succeeding one, was still a legend. Having been summoned to Berlin by the King of Prussia, in order to direct *Oedipus at Colonus* at Potsdam and *Athalie* at Charlottenburg, Felix returned to Leipzig on 1st December with none other than 'the Swedish nightingale', Jenny Lind, who made her debut on the 4th of that month. Clara Schumann was once heard to remark, quite unjustly, that "one song from Miss Lind gave her greater popularity" than the years of her own many appearances in public. Miss Lind did cause "a furore" with her arias from Bellini's *Norma*, however, and her presentation of songs by Mendelssohn. It was at this concert that prices were raised from the usual ½ of a thaler to 1½, causing Otto Goldschmidt, a student at the Conservatorium, to protest – to no effect. Fortunately for Goldschmidt, not only was he able to acquire a ticket on what would now be called the black market but, later, he actually married the prima donna and became her eminently successful business manager.

At this concert Felix played his own 1st Piano Concerto and some *Songs without Words*, together with a prelude and interlude, "such as only the composer could improvise. These spur-of-the-moment choices were twice re-demanded, the melody sending an electric thrill through everyone's heart in the room, his modulation never to be forgotten by anyone who heard it," Rockstro recalled. Afterwards, Jenny was "serenaded at her window by 300 amateurs, accompanied by wind instruments and torchlight". The publisher Brockhaus, a relative of Wagner, at whose house Miss Lind was staying, gave her a tankard of champagne to hand round, but, overcome by shyness, Jenny handed the tankard to Ferdinand David, who did the honours. Asking what she should do to acknowledge such adulation, Felix suggested that a few simple words would suffice, but, again, through her self-consciousness, she asked Mendelssohn to oblige on her behalf. Escorting Jenny into the circle of musicians, Felix explained that they would have to imagine him to have metamorphosed into the prima donna. "Thank you from the bottom of my heart," he responded. "But, having now fulfilled my honourable commission, I am again transformed into the Leipzig music director. In that capacity I say: 'Long life to Jenny Lind.'"

Jenny returned to Leipzig in the spring but, rather than accepting a benefit for herself, any profits were donated to the fund for families of deceased and infirm musicians. That concert took place on Easter Day, 12th April 1846, in which Jenny sang arias by Mozart and Weber. At a rehearsal the boys of St. Thomas's Church missed their cue, so intent were they on following the soprano's scale passages. "At the 107th bar Mendelssohn brought down his baton, which resulted in complete silence", but, rather than becoming annoyed, Felix joined in the merriment. The concert itself was so popular the main hall was "crammed to suffocation" and the adjoining room, where a buffet was to be served, had to accommodate the concert-goers who could not find a seat in the auditorium. David presented Jenny with a silver tray, towards the purchase of which all the Gewandhaus musicians had contributed. It was on this occasion that Mendelssohn played the piano for the last time in public, which Rockstro called "sadly memorable". Having played a Beethoven violin sonata with David, he vacated the seat at the piano, inviting Clara Schumann to take his place. She played one of Felix's *Songs without Words* and a scherzo her husband had written.

Felix paid tribute to a Herr Velten, who had died before his musical output really developed. In condoling with his family, he wrote: "In him, a true genius has passed away, who only required life and health to develop that genius, to be a source of joy and pride to his father." Velten's works were, to Felix, "very superior, compared with those I see each day. There shines forth in every part a striving after progress and the promise of a genuine vocation, along with the most perfect development. When you rejoice with your son, it is to be hoped there is still music, with no more sorrow or parting."

New works from living composers continued to play a part in the Gewandhaus repertoire. Mendelssohn was the first to conduct Wagner's *Tannhäuser* Overture, in February 1846. Natalia Planer, Wagner's stepdaughter, wrote of "the small Jew, slippery as an eel, who mutilated and damaged the overture". Wagner himself called the performance "ill-humoured", prophesying that the gulf would be widened between those who promoted his own "music of the future" and the backwoodsmen who still had the stupidity to ally themselves with Mendelssohn's music. However, even Marek admits that Felix was far too much of a professional to allow likes or dislikes to influence him when presenting new music. As for Schumann, when he met Wagner in Dresden he confided to Felix that, "though undoubtedly a clever fellow, with bold and original ideas, he can write no more than four consecutive bars that are either melodious or correctly produced, but I cannot express such sentiments publicly, as I would be accused of jealousy by Wagner".

There were undoubted successes during this period. Clara scored a triumph with Schumann's Piano Concerto, which Mendelssohn had premiered in 1845. This applied equally to her husband's 2nd symphony, performed at the Gewandhaus on 4th November 1846, which was subsequently reorchestrated and renumbered as No. 4 in 1851. Neither did Felix neglect his own output. As well as *Elijah* he produced a set of songs to poems by Eichendorff. It is strange that, though this poet was born in 1788, and was 40 when Schubert died, it was Mendelssohn who initiated his poetry to be set to music, opening up a rich vein that ended with Richard Strauss's exquisite Four Last Songs in 1948.

Felix realised, having conducted the Lower Rhine Festival at Düsseldorf in 1846, that he still bore the scars of his residence there in the 1830s. He wrote of "unpleasant associations that sober me". Though he had done all he could to recommend Julius Rietz for the vacant post, even asking Paul to try to negotiate on his behalf, he now spoke of his colleague's wishing to leave that town, having been treated so badly by the authorities. "I hope he does too," Felix affirmed. Everyone he knew had now altered and had become quite unrecognisable in Düsseldorf. The ambience of the Festival was "neither polished, orderly or friendly". Two glee clubs, which each serenaded him, were "in too much dispute with one another, rather than joining together".

Though, in theory, Mendelssohn should have had more opportunity to take a well-deserved rest, having delegated responsibility for the Gewandhaus Orchestra to Gade and for the Conservatorium to Moscheles, Felix wrote: "There is still much work to be accomplished in Leipzig." In earlier years he had planned to retire to Switzerland, but now he wished to live in Frankfurt and, on 12th October 1846, he asked Senator Bernus to find such a house for his family, or he would have one built. "As soon as I have won the right to live solely for my own work, composing,

Chapter 25: "In Paradise"

conducting and playing in public only occasionally, depending upon how much I enjoy it, then, assuredly, the way I think now [I shall] go to Frankfurt. The sooner that occurs, the happier I shall be. I have undertaken many musical activities from a sense of duty, never from inclination. I hope before many years are over, to turn up as a house-builder." Felix reminded Jenny Lind of a conversation they had had on their Rhine journey returning from the Aachen Festival of that year. "You were quite right. In two or three years at the most, I think I shall have done my duty here, after which I should scarcely stay any longer. Perhaps I might prefer...somewhere very pretty, where I can compose all day long as much as I like, but, really, you will have to sing to me sometimes." To Klingemann he wrote in a similar vein as to Bernus, that "duties have become distasteful [and that] all engagements are fulfilled with the greatest reluctance and unwillingness". Felix believed that the time had come, and might have already passed, "when I shall put all public commitments on the shelf... and let existence continue as best it may. A piece of paper gives me far greater pleasure when filled with musical notation than any success at conducting or performing in public."

Felix had planned to discuss his future with Klingemann, either at his residence "or strolling through Chelsea", and hoped to bring not only some new music to London, but Cécile also. At the end of 1847 it was fate that decided what Mendelssohn's future would be. He had no opportunity to make any decisions as to how his life would continue. It came to an end. His mortal remains would be buried in the family vault in Berlin, his spirit free at last in what Schumann called "the beyond". However, some bright stars did appear on Mendelssohn's horizon in Leipzig. After his final visit to Switzerland, Mendelssohn discovered with pleasure that Broadwoods of London had sent him a new piano. Further commissions poured into his home. The Philharmonic Society of London wanted a new symphony from him. A 'cello concerto was to have been written for Alfredo Piatti, who, with Joachim, would make such a name for himself in London. A work was required for the opening of the Philharmonic Hall in Liverpool in 1849, the successor to which was opened in 1996. There were commissions for Frankfurt and other German cities, but the most important related to the United Kingdom.

It is fascinating to wonder, had the discussion taken place with Klingemann, whether Felix would have followed his compatriot – Handel – to London, or the singer he admired the most – Jenny Lind – to Great Malvern. Though Mendelssohn was a loyal German, it is evident how dearly he loved his home across the English Channel, where he paid ten visits and made so many trusted friends.

Chapter 26

"Like an Old Married Couple"

Though Abraham Mendelssohn had died at the end of 1835, "not an hour passes without thinking of...my master in art and life," Felix confided to Pastor Bauer in 1836. "My father was so good to me...I was devoted to him with my whole soul," Julius Schubring was told. Nevertheless, to Klingemann, a diplomat rather than a theologian, Felix adopted a more positive frame of mind: "A new life must begin for me...the old life is severed. I must be like my father and [I aim to] fulfil his desire and marry and raise a family and to emancipate myself from the subjective world of romantic fantasy and to attain the solid ground of ethical responsibility." Biographers give credit to Fanny, who exhorted him to "find a wife", but it is evident from his own letters that the subject was already in Felix's mind. However much he might have promised, as it is claimed, to perpetuate the Mendelssohn dynasty, and however earnestly he desired to fulfil his father's wish, on meeting Cécile Jeanrenaud all such theoretical striving and pompous rhetoric became irrelevant. Felix Mendelssohn was in love! Neither was this state of mind an infatuation, albeit the period of courtship lasted less than a year. Wiseacres might well have warned the pair "Marry in haste; repent at leisure", but to neither Cécile nor Felix did this apply. This is proved by the words Felix wrote to Devrient six weeks after the marriage. Felix knew that this girl of 18 was the only wife he wanted, to share his home, and, in time, when nature decided, to be the mother of his children.

Felix had always enjoyed flirting as a bachelor, but this no longer applied on coming to Frankfurt. His mind was wholly committed to becoming a married man; his sole concern was that this lovely young lady should concur. On 18th June 1836 Felix arrived to conduct *St Paul* with the St. Cecilia Society for his old friend Johann Schelble, who was ill, thereby forgoing a much-needed holiday in Italy. On an earlier visit Mendelssohn had praised this musical association: "The singers work with such enthusiasm and precision that it is a delight to listen to them. The choir of 200 meets weekly, but the director has a group who meets at his home each Friday evening that consists of 30 voices... The female singers are far more enthusiastic than the men...women are much more community-minded than men." But, in 1836, rumour had spread that, if no improvement were made to the society, it would be disbanded should Schelble's illness continue. He had dreaded "the lukewarm attitude of members", as he confided to Felix. However, through the latter's energy, the singers were galvanised into a new spirit of endeavour, as a result of their new director's "electrifying" presence and his "invariable good temper and kindness".

When Felix had prepared *St Paul* for publication he wrote to Schleinitz that, for a whole week, "I shall do nothing in the way of work". He would "eat cherries; draw; walk with Schlemmer; lunch and dine with Hiller; read what Eckhard has to say about Goethe; meet a few pretty girls; bathe in the Main each morning, which flows beneath my window". He looked forward to playing trios on the next evening with relatives of the Schunck family, who lived in Leipzig, "to whom I am indebted for the pleasant company with which they have provided me". As was Mendelssohn's habit, ingrained from his parents, "pleasant" was a decidedly mild adjective. The company – or, rather, one special individual – attracted Felix immensely. Not only was he charmed by the sweet voice of Cécile Jeanrenaud, but by her looks even more so. But this was not love at first sight for Cécile. She had no intention of pursuing a singing career; her lungs would have been too weak had she planned to do so, in any case. As for her idea of Mendelssohn, about whom she had heard, a totally misguided picture emerges from a letter written to a cousin: "I imagine a stiff, disagreeable, jealous man, seated at the organ, with a green velvet skullcap on his head, playing tedious fugues." When, therefore, this decidedly prepossessing bachelor of 27 visited the house so often, Cécile assumed that it was her widowed mother, still a lively, highly attractive woman, to whom Felix was attracted. Her husband, Pastor Jeanrenaud, had died of pneumonia and overwork when the children were young. Indeed, it has been suggested by Gustave Kobbé that Cécile, her sister Julie and brother Charles teased their mother for her cleverness at netting such an eligible "catch" as Felix.

No one was more surprised than Cécile, therefore, when Felix swallowed his diffidence to reveal his true feelings towards the girl herself. Hiller recalled how, lying on the sofa or walking in the moonlight, Felix would "pour out his heart about her in the most charmingly frank and artless way, often full of fun and gaiety, then, again, with deep feeling, but never with any exaggerated sentimentality or uncontrolled passion... One could hardly get him to talk of anything else that did not, in some way, touch upon her." Once their courtship had become an open secret it was watched with curiosity and interest by the whole of Frankfurt society, and, as Hiller declared, "many remarks that I heard showed me that to possess such genius, culture, fame, amiability, fortune and to belong to a family of such consideration and celebrity is, to certain circles, hardly enough to enable a man to raise his eyes to a girl of patrician birth, but I do not think anything of the sort ever came to Mendelssohn's ears". Hiller's description of Cécile as "patrician" depends by which standpoint such an adjective is viewed. Her mother had married a self-

Chapter 26: "Like an Old Married Couple"

effacing but highly gifted pastor of the French Reformed Church, but her own family were merchants of high repute.

Cécile's mother's family, the Souchays, had business interests extending as far afield as Egypt, with enterprises in Milan, London and Manchester, as well as Frankfurt am Main. Therefore, rather than choosing "a countess, if not a duchess" for his bride, as the Miss Horsleys had conjectured, Felix married into a family whose background was similar to his own, except that the Souchays' commercial standing extended to the 17th century, which might well have caused resentment, even envy, to the social-climbing Leah Mendelssohn. In his book *Mendelssohn and his Times* H. E. Jacob states that the ideal of German womanhood was based on Queen Louise of Prussia and that anyone who fell below this yardstick was, if not exactly ostracised, met with disdain. Though presumably accurate for indigenous Germans, it need not have applied either to Cécile or Felix. The Souchays were an old Huguenot family; the Jeanrenauds Swiss. Mme. Jeanrenaud's mother was known, before her marriage, as 'Miss Sophie Barwell, la belle Anglaise'. As for Felix, his inheritance came from a more easterly direction and, as Jewish traditions and ideas remained with him, despite his conversion, there was no need for either to follow German fashion. Cécile was Mendelssohn's idea of femininity, and this sufficed.

When describing this exquisite young lady, accounts are confusing. Jean Petitpierre, a descendant of the Jeanrenaud family, writes of her: "At 16, her exquisite figure and carriage drew everyone's gaze. Her deep blue eyes were shaded by long lashes and crowned by velvet eyebrows, which shone with a radiant gentleness. It was impossible to see a more beautiful head of brown hair, a fresher complexion or a more perfectly oval face." Mme. Polko opined that, "at the sight of her, the same state of intoxication resulted, for Felix, as that by opium, except the distress of a hangover" – as if either this prim raconteur or the self-disciplined Felix would have known about this narcotic. To Marek, Cécile was "blonde and blue eyes; her skin tawny; figure full and soft, but not heavy; an ideal for a painting of a Victorian girl". The same author calls her "pink and white in soul". Sterndale Bennett called Cécile "the handsomest girl I have ever met, except aesthetically", but refrained from giving any enlightenment on the last phrase. To Schumann, she was given the epithet "that lovely foreign rose".

The sculptor Schadow described Cécile's face as "so pure and lovely, a loveliness so apparent from the time she entered a room". Her various portraits that Rockstro studied "give nothing like an adequate idea of the charm and expression of manner which, once seen, could never afterwards be forgotten". No wonder Felix was so disappointed when he received a portrait of his bride-to-be at Christmas 1836, "showing an ordinary young woman, flattered, with not a spark of poetry about it". The painting so often reproduced in Mendelssohn biographies has been said "to make her look like a china doll". Sadly, though Wilhelm Hensel had a high reputation for sketching with the utmost accuracy people who had died, when

Cécile became one of his subjects her looks had, by that time, become so haggard, through illness, that the posthumous portrait belies altogether her living profile. What a pity that, though Louis Daguerre had become an eminent exponent of reproducing 'likenesses' on metal plates, and even Henry Fox Talbot had begun to practise the art of photography during her life, no such reproduction of Cécile's true features exists.

Of her personality, George Sampson remembered a "beautiful and charming girl", but this says nothing. Later biographies pay short shrift to Mendelssohn's wife. "She was not an exciting creature," Marek opines. "A lackadaisical Lorelei... She was never very strong, never very demanding... She wanted to be petted, to be treated tenderly, to be made a fuss over." Especially as readers become acquainted with her, this assessment of Cécile is unjust. Naturally, any woman brought up so carefully as she had been would expect to be treated in such a fashion, but her personality encompassed far more than this effete dismissal. Even Sebastian Hensel, her husband's nephew, was uncomplimentary at first sight: "Not a striking person in any way; neither extraordinarily clever, brilliantly witty nor particularly accomplished." However, "an aura of gentleness surrounded her. Her influence was as gentle and soothing as the open sky or running water." Devrient recalled how "she spoke little, never with animation, in a low, soft voice". Gustave Kobbé states that the words put into King Lear's mouth by Shakespeare, "My precious silence", applied to Cécile. Indeed, the old proverb "still waters run deep" sums up her character.

For such a highly charged, hypersensitive individual as Mendelssohn, these qualities were precisely those he required in a bride. Such a self-possessed woman felt no need to compete with the ultra-clever women who, in any case, Felix disliked. Neither did she try to make a fool of herself by doing so. Had she been familiar with the English proverb "empty vessels make the most noise" she might well have taken it to heart. Not even her mother could truly fathom this veiled personality. Writing to Paul Mendelssohn on 1st July 1848, eight months after Felix's death, Mme. Jeanrenaud pronounced: "From childhood, Cécile's nature has always been gentle, but a little secretive. One has always had to guess more than what she actually expresses."

It would have been better, Marek states, had Felix married Clara Schumann, Constanze Mozart, Giuseppina Verdi or Cosima Wagner; but, evidently, he does not have the perception to analyse Felix's personality. For Mendelssohn, Cécile was precisely the woman he wanted and needed: an excellent hostess, warmly welcoming to visitors; a thrifty housekeeper, but without Leah's parsimony; and, above all, a loving, caring wife and mother. For the first time in his life, Felix could relax with a companion who understood him. No longer need he play the gallant, flirting, whirling young ladies around a dance floor, or trying to avoid any sexual impropriety. Neither did he need to indulge in games of verbal tennis with intellectual women such as Rahel Varnhagen von Ense or Bettina Brentano, whom

Chapter 26: "Like an Old Married Couple"

Devrient said Felix disliked. No scenes were caused by clashes of 'artistic temperament', as might well have occurred between Felix and the ladies selected by Marek.

Blunt, who harks back to his former profession of schoolmaster, compiles a school report on Cécile. This nonentity was "reasonably talented as an artist and not particularly musical, though she sang in a fashionable ladies' choir". Marek is given credit for having almost uncanny powers when reading the handwriting in the honeymoon diary kept by Felix and Cécile. Marek adds that "she never inspired Felix to write any music of consequence". Such criticisms are irrelevant.

One of the most revealing recollections was given by Eduard Souchay regarding his niece: "Rather than initiate a topic of conversation, she cleverly guided the threads of discussion, whether as hostess or guest... She received all the admirers and musicians recommended to him. Rather than show her intelligence at interviews with these gentlemen, she allowed them to guess at it. They preferred that... After meeting her, no one went away dissatisfied." It is appropriate here to quote what Joanna Richardson said about Emily Tennyson, wife of the Poet Laureate, and Percy Young's assessment of Alice Elgar, wife of the composer, as both these statements apply equally to Cécile Mendelssohn. "Emily knew her sphere and, in her refusal to leave it, lay her genius as a wife." Though Alice Elgar hoped to pursue her own career as an author, "saw her role as wife to Edward, as caring for his every need, musical and domestic. 'The care of a genius is enough of a life's work for any woman,' she had written."

Despite what Blunt says, Cécile was a better artist than was realised, but, like Emily Tennyson and Alice Elgar, Frau Mendelssohn lived to fulfil her true vocation, for so she considered the responsibility of living for her husband. Jacob states that "the Mendelssohns' marriage was the very model of passionlessness". Felix behaved "so incredibly" when courting Cécile that "it seemed that he would never take off his gloves". In an effort to score points in belittling Felix's manliness, Marek, too, adopts this attitude, saying: "His passion was no different in the bedroom than [in] the drawing-room"; but how does he know? The letters between the couple when Felix was away from home were burnt at her request. Initially the young bachelor must have felt obliged to behave in a circumspect manner, in view of the young lady's upbringing. Thoroughly sheltered from the world, Felix would in no way wish to offend or frighten Cécile, or her mother. He had to earn his place in the Jeanrenaud and Souchay families' good books, however he would have liked to behave. Neither did it help that he and Cécile were two of a kind, each diffident, preferring to hide their feelings rather than be humiliated or make fools of themselves. Nevertheless, on 2nd December Felix wrote to Fuchs, once the wedding was planned, seeking his friend's help in supplying something suitable for Cécile's autograph album: "Out of love for one's bride, one would happily leap into the fire, no less." This declaration does not square with the lack of passion written about so often by those who do not know the truth. Once the marriage had taken place, Cécile and Felix were blessed with three children in four years (Cécile gave birth to five in all, four of whom survived to adulthood. See Chapter 28 "Dear, Good Children").

Before his marriage Felix lodged at Schelble's residence in the Schöner Aussicht (Beautiful Prospect). "I am living with two suitcases and a hatbox outside the other set of rooms. There is a grand piano, plenty of music, complete rest and undisturbed tranquillity, and I have had a very kind reception," he wrote at the beginning of his sojourn. Though he vowed to apply himself to the tasks in hand, "all I have been able to do at the outset is to admire the view and to sun myself each morning. Idleness is so pleasant and agrees with me so much." Besides directing the St. Cecilia Society, "I have to don my dress clothes to play at Marx's concert. I could not possibly refuse this invitation." He reminisced about the period during 1830 for him and Marx. "Sentiment played a part...our music at Eskeles', our playing at billiards, and driving to Baden am Wien in a fiacre. He is beyond doubt the very finest of all violoncello players."

Felix loved to ramble among "the fruitful richness of the verdant gardens and fields, with the beautiful blue hills in the background and the forest on the farther side – a delight to the heart – and herbs, flowers, blackberries and strawberries". So much did he enjoy the outdoor life that he even declined an invitation to a ball at the Rothschilds', but was thrilled to have been asked. He did, however, dine there one evening to meet Rossini, a guest at Charlotte Rothschild's wedding. "I must spend a whole evening describing this meeting to you in a hotel room alone sometime," Felix wrote to Schleinitz in Leipzig. Felix's cousin Alexander Mendelssohn visited Frankfurt with his three sons, when an excursion was arranged to the watchtower at Mainz, returning to Frankfurt on foot. Hiller's mother sometimes lent her carriage for outings, to which Felix was invited. Once, however, so angry did he become with their coachman, Hiller wrote in his memoirs, that "he jumped from the vehicle, letting forth a torrent of abuse to the driver, and planned to walk the rest of the way. It was we who suffered, mother becoming quite upset on the journey home." Nothing is known as to why this "towering rage" occurred, or whether any apology was given to Frau Hiller, if to no one else.

It was "that Schlegel woman", as Leah still referred to Dorothea, her sister-in-law, who introduced Felix to Cécile, although he had already noticed her in the St. Cecilia Choir. Eduard Souchay realised that "something significant" was happening between his beautiful niece and this brilliant young nephew of Frau von Schlegel, at whose home the couple officially met. Felix was soon made welcome at the Jeanrenauds' residence. Their courtship must have proceeded smoothly, although, as mentioned earlier, Cécile assumed that it was her mother to whom this young man was attracted, and felt safer than might otherwise have been the case, even when alone in his company. "Would mother have welcomed such a man at their home had any scandal been uncovered about him?" Cécile must have pondered. Such a beautifully brought-up young lady would never have been allowed to

Chapter 26: "Like an Old Married Couple"

associate with anyone who had a mistress lurking in the background, or who consorted with women of ill repute. Indeed, so convinced is Jacob that Felix had had no such blemish on his reputation that he calls Cécile "the woman without precedence". Mme. Jeanrenaud wrote to an aunt that she hoped her daughter's behaviour would remain exemplary "in the land of malice and coquetry [Frankfurt society]" in which the Jeanrenauds lived.

Marek states that Felix was attracted to Cécile primarily because "she looked English", but he could have added that she had been steeped in manners and customs, as well as the language, of that country by her English governess, Miss Bury. On 2nd July Felix confided to Rebecka: "I can neither compose, write letters or play the piano, only sketch a little, so much in love am I." At the end of the month "Felix did a most peculiar thing – he fled"; but such a statement indicates only what slovenly research Marek must have undertaken in writing his biography. For some time past, Felix had arranged to accompany Schadow and his son to the Dutch seaside resort of Scheveningen.

Before taking any new step, Abraham had ingrained into his son the habit of caution, to look before he leapt, so what more natural to analyse his feelings for the girl he loved? This trip to the Netherlands seemed the most appropriate venue, away from Berlin, Leipzig or Frankfurt, for such self-analysis. Was he really ready to become a husband and, he hoped, a father? Could he handle the fact that Leah might disapprove of the girl he wished to marry? Would Cécile accept him, for that matter, and how would he cope if she did not? Would it be fair to this evidently frail young woman to put her through the tortures of childbearing in the 1830s? Would he mind if Cécile pursued her own career, as his father had done vis-à-vis Fanny? Would Cécile mind having to travel for the sake of his work? Would his own work be inhibited? This thought would be called to mind later, when Schumann had confided how, when Clara was practising, he was prevented from concentrating on his compositions. Thus, with all these questions spinning round in his head, Felix left for his "sea bathing duty" at Scheveningen.

There was one memento Mendelssohn was able to bring with him on his journey north that gladdened his heart. The St. Cecilia Society had presented Felix with what Marek calls "his toilet kit" – an exquisitely crafted travelling case. "It has three compartments," Felix wrote to his family, "with every variety of shaving, grooming and writing instrument of silver and ivory, lined with velvet and that special English solidity that I like so much. Its elegance and splendour resemble a gift more suitable for a prince travelling incognito than a musician." What really pleased him was the inscription "To F. M. B. and Cecilia". Was this not a propitious omen for the years to come? Felix had arranged to help Schadow's young son with his Latin, whilst taking the prescribed course of treatment, which lasted three weeks. However, as he wrote to Hiller, this was only a small part of the assignment that awaited Felix: "I have to mend the boy's pens, cut his bread and butter, and make tea each morning and evening. Today I had to coax him into the water, because he screamed so with his father, he was so frightened." The reward for this nursemaiding was a sprained ankle. A further irritation was caused by a man who approached Felix speaking "in a mixture of Dutch and German, with the words, 'Ah, here is where you collect your magical ideas', with no introduction or explanation of his purpose in addressing me". Had the stranger shown any interest in music, Felix "would have been touched and would have endeavoured to give suitable advice". Felix had not written home "until I have something worth communicating. I do not know how to bear the separation from the nice girl about whom I wrote to you last time, and her charming family." With less tact than appears politic, Felix called his visits to the Jeanrenaud family "the first truly bright hours of the year, with whom I have felt freer and happier than for a long time". Later he wrote: "I would gladly send Holland, its sea, its bathing machines, the Kursaal and its visitors to the devil."

But the 21 daily sessions at the mineral baths did finish, and Felix, before proposing to Cécile, asked his mother's blessing on his hoped-for marriage: "If you tell me that you are once more ready to trust me entirely and [to] offer me the full liberty I have enjoyed in former years, you will make me very happy. You may rest assured that I will not abuse your confidence, which I have, perhaps, done something to deserve." In answer to the inevitable questions his mother asked regarding this rival to her affections, as she might have considered Cécile, Felix admitted: "I know very little about her, or she about myself." He was, however, able to furnish details of the Souchay relatives, and to report that Cécile "has been educated at home with the utmost care and tenderness by her mother". He asked Leah to keep his new love the closest secret. "Say nothing to anyone, especially anyone in Frankfurt, as it may destroy my whole chance" of being accepted as a husband. To Rebecka Felix felt able to bare his soul more freely: "I am more deeply in love than ever I was in my life before, and I do not know what to do... I intend...to see this charming girl once more, before I return to Leipzig, but I have no idea whether she likes me or not. Neither do I know what to do to make her like me. But one thing is certain. To her I owe the first happiness I have enjoyed this year... When I am away from her, I am always sad." Should she wish to know more about her future sister-in-law, Rebecka should write poste restante to The Hague. His reason for secrecy is quite understandable. He was so terrified that this vision of loveliness, in looks and personality, would reject him and, should anyone realise how he felt, his humiliation would be unbearable to contemplate. Felix hoped his suspense would soon be at an end "and that I shall then know whether we are to be anything, or nothing, to each other". Such agonising brought a reply of refreshing common sense from Rebecka: "You let slip something to the effect that you would 'try to get married'. Do you wish to enlarge your imagination through love, or do you love her for her own sake? You have twice told me [that] you do not know what to do... Then decide. Amen."

Felix returned to Frankfurt "fresh and hopeful again" after his spa treatment at

Chapter 26: "Like an Old Married Couple"

Scheveningen, which must have had greater benefit than he realised at the time. In August 1841 he would write to the Leipzig banker, Woldemar Frege, who was to undertake a similar 'cure': "Though the cure appears ineffective at first to relieve the sorrows of the spirit, I pray that you will eventually be strengthened and revived. That the baths tire you and, at the same time, excite the nerves, as you write, seems only natural to me, for things were exactly the same with me when I was in Scheveningen. It cost me such an effort even to write a letter and, at times, eating seemed too much trouble, and only sleep was comfortable. But the good, truly curative results made their appearance after the first two weeks at the baths." Felix advised his friend to "occupy yourself professionally again as soon as possible, even if, at the beginning, you find it intolerable, for, after all, the only possible human consolation is to be found in ceaseless, continued work". This might have been a lesson learnt from Felix's own experiences at Scheveningen. To people of his temperament, boredom causes as much depression as sadness or fear.

Despite his legal status as an adult Felix had vowed not to think of marriage, but, thankfully, for posterity and for Mendelssohn's personal comfort, armed with his mother's sanction, Cécile accepted Felix's proposal. Jacob states that she "whispered" her consent when the proposal took place under beech trees in the forest adjacent to the Taunus Mountains outside Frankfurt. Rather than the usually stilted, almost pompous epistles Felix wrote to his family, the present letter was that of a free-spirited, uninhibited outpouring of a man in love: "At the moment…all that I can write to you is that I have become engaged to Cécile Jeanrenaud. My head is spinning with what I have experienced today [9th September 1836]. It is now already far into the night. I do not know what else to say, but I had to write to you how blessed and happy my life is." A postscript conveyed Mme. Jeanrenaud's wish to be observed "that it would not be desirable to make it public for a while. Therefore, I ask you not to mention it to anyone." Perhaps this plea for secrecy might have arisen so that the bride's mother would have more time to accustom herself to 'losing her daughter' to the possessive, clannish Mendelssohn matriarch, who might well dominate the gentle, complaisant Cécile.

According to Marek, Leah had become "suspicious", perhaps because her undesirable sister-in-law, Dorothea von Schlegel, had introduced the bride to her precious son. "Why," Leah might have wondered, "did I not find the right girl for him, from a family of whom I approved?" A letter Leah wrote to Ferdinand David throws more light on her thoughts: "Felix is engaged to be married. [Whilst] I cannot deny myself the pleasure of personally communicating to you, Felix's excellent friend, the news, which is a matter of such happiness to us all, as an affectionate mother, you cannot imagine how strange it is to me not to know either his bride-elect or any of her numerous relations. Nor can I even recollect the name of the family." Had Leah deigned to travel as Felix had wished her to do, such an oversight might have been remedied. Perhaps Leah might not have wanted to learn about the prestigious Souchays and their Jeanrenaud relatives. Fanny, plus a sedative from the doctor, endeavoured to reassure her mother: "He must have found someone worth having, for he is not without taste. Why do the names Jeanrenaud or Souchay come to mind?" Fanny wrote in her journal. "Did Ferdinand David's engagement to a Russian princess inspire Felix to shake himself out of his state of doubt and ask for Cécile's hand?" Once Rebecka knew of her brother's engagement she scanned the Frankfurt newspapers to see the announcement "about the famous musician, Felix Mendelssohn". The only news of importance she gained was "that the cotton market is flat, and news of the Stock Exchange".

Rebecka had always taken a lively interest in Felix's love life and this new turn of events was no exception: "Write me a real love letter," she implored, "about the girl who fascinates you so much. How does she look, walk, talk, and, above all, is she musical? My claim on your love I will not renounce for any beloved in the whole world." To Cécile, Rebecka wrote: "I do not say that there are not husbands who love their wives as much as Felix loves you, but I have never seen one so much in love before. However, I can understand it for, though I am not your husband, I am a little in love with you myself." In answer to Rebecka's question as to how musical her new sister-in-law might be, like all young ladies of fashion, it is clear that Cécile had learnt at least the rudiments of piano playing. As she wrote to a cousin: "Julia and I had to supervise the practice of the little rabble of the Benecke children" – relatives whom she visited in Heidelberg. "One needs a lot of patience to listen to their little fingers scampering about [the keys] and see all the funny faces these youngsters pull when counting [the bars]: 'Hélène, don't screw up your mouth. What's that face for? Sit up straight.' The child is making progress, though, because she is very eager to improve." Though she sang with the St. Cecilia Society, the saint's namesake was certainly diffident about her musical skill. She wrote in the same letter about their new director being "indulgent" with "our chirpings", adding, apropos her cousin's pianistic talent, "I hear you play with Herr Mendelssohn [in Leipzig]. I would never have the courage for that." Despite Blunt's dismissal of her artistic accomplishments, others have compared Cécile with Wilhelm Hensel, and this comparison is uncanny. Each had a clergyman father whose widow lived a far longer time than their spouses, who each died very young. The only difference was that, whereas Hensel had to struggle to achieve his artistic career, Cécile remained an amateur, in the true sense of the word, throughout her life. But, had she wished or needed, her sketches show how much of a professional Cécile could have become.

Schumann was the first to congratulate Felix, once the news was announced. The betrothed was "like a cooling drink to my restless spirit, with her serene and cheerful disposition". Of Mendelssohn, Schumann wrote: "Mendelssohn has a bride and his thoughts are constantly taken up with her. He gains in charm and greatness of soul. Not a day goes by without his coming up with at least a couple of thoughts that could instantly be engraved in gold. A few days ago he said

Chapter 26: "Like an Old Married Couple"

wistfully: 'Ah, Schumann. How sad it would have been if I were to pass that house by,' referring to the Souchay-Jeanrenaud residence" in Frankfurt's Fahrthor (Thoroughfare). Max Müller recorded in his memoirs that, though rumour had spread that Felix was to marry, no one knew the identity of the bride. However, at the end of a Gewandhaus concert in which Müller had sung in the chorus and had remained in the hall, friends teased Felix about his approaching marriage. "But, though his beaming face betrayed him, he would say nothing. But at last he sat at the piano and extemporised on the chorus from *Fidelio*, 'He who a pure Bride has won'." Gustave Kobbé states that the choir had actually sung this chorus. "As Mendelssohn took up the baton, the audience burst into applause, which continued for a long time."

Once the engagement had become public property, Cécile and Felix were given the privilege of taking lunch alone at the bride's home. Cécile confirmed her forthcoming marriage in a letter to her cousin, Cornaille Schunck: "confirmed by a name you will know well that you will find below mine". To her brother, Charles, she wrote: "I love another man besides you, with all my heart." Felix added that he hoped to receive "brotherly love" from Charles. On the 19th her cousin was told: "The whole of Frankfurt can talk of nothing else" but the betrothal, but "I feel a secret shame at so much unsought and unaccustomed publicity. Looking in the mirror, I feel myself to have altered during the past few days and that everything is upside down in my heart", and Mme. Jeanrenaud concurred that "everything is very gay with us".

At Christmas Felix gave his fiancée an album containing autographs and sketches, to which additions were made throughout their marriage. What Marek's information does not reveal, however, is the untiring work involved in collecting the many priceless items contained in this treasure store, now in the Bodleian Library, Oxford. On 18th November Felix wrote to Aloys Fuchs: "Cécile is so good and beautiful that I would fall in love with her all over again every day, if I had not already done so on the first day." In consequence, he would like "up front, as an introduction, autographs of Mozart and Beethoven. This request is a big one." But such a demand was not too big for Fuchs, who sent, from his own collection, not only autographs from the two composers requested but one by Haydn in addition. "Joyfully surprised", Felix acknowledged "the great sacrifice you have made...to part with these priceless treasures", and realised what respect Fuchs had for him when such gifts were bestowed so unstintingly. Felix reciprocated by augmenting his friend's collection with, *inter alia*, a copy of Handel's *Dixit Dominus* from the only surviving manuscript he had discovered in the Royal Library in London. Hanslick, who collated their correspondence, stated that Felix had copied this "to while away the time" whilst recovering from his coach accident. The question remains, however, as to whether permission had been given, or, more likely, whether Mendelssohn had copied the work from memory. Felix was also able to solve a puzzle regarding Mozart's *Lamentations*, omitted from Köchel's catalogue of the composer's works. This particular piece was, Felix explained, "a litanie that Mozart had written, but [was] still unpublished".

Ludwig Spohr composed "a pretty song, perfectly suited to my fiancée's voice, which will bring her great joy". Among the visits paid by the engaged couple, aunt Dorothea was included. Cécile called her "a tall and beautiful lady". Bendemann, the artist who was to paint her portrait, was "the most distinguished of that sphere in all Düsseldorf", where so many German artists lived. Biographers maintain that, though Rebecka liked her well enough, Fanny showed jealousy towards her prospective sister-in-law, but extracts from her writings disprove such a myth. Cécile was, to Fanny, "slender, with strikingly beautiful and delicate features". Was this an assessment by someone who nursed jealousy? Even her dry sense of humour came to the fore: on being told that the couple had to make 162 calls on friends and relatives in Frankfurt, she calculated that "this superhuman duty would have taken 20 visits per day for one week to accomplish. Were this ritual to be repeated after the wedding, certain reasons, which modesty prevents my mentioning, make me think that Leipzig would be a very good idea, since you will not know so many people" – and their fulfilled sex life would not be inhibited, she implied. Fanny asked if either Cécile or Felix could have developed a cold, or sprained an ankle, to prevent so many calls having to be made. Felix replied: "I was bound by my beard to comply and nothing could have exempted us." During the Christmas holiday final arrangements were made for the wedding, to take place at the French Reformed Church in Frankfurt on 27th March 1837. When Felix returned to Leipzig, Cécile wrote: "I have been thoroughly spoilt by his presence but, now that he is far away, my mood has nothing of the rosy hue of my notepaper. Why should that horrible thing, separation, exist?" On 4th January Felix confided to Fanny how glad he was that the New Year had begun: "I cannot believe the contrast between the present time and the start of the past year. How low were my spirits when I heard the clock strike midnight, to herald 1836", having sustained the loss of his father at the end of 1835. "God willing, we shall be married at eleven o'clock." On 24th March Felix wrote of the "many things of which I have to take care. Until yesterday, the papers were still not in order, for the gentlemen in Frankfurt are even more narrow-minded and difficult than usual, but, yesterday, a letter from Schleinitz arrived, supplying all the proper attestations: that I am not yet married; that I am not a vagrant, and such nonsense, and now everything is set for Tuesday, God willing."

Of the wedding itself Peter Ward Jones, who has edited the Mendelssohns' honeymoon diary, states that little is known, appearing to regard Jean Petitpierre's account as suspect. However, recollections from Senator Souchay and Ferdinand Hiller do provide useful information, which rings true. Chains were placed around the approach to the church to prevent anyone entering who had not been invited to the ceremony. This could well have been a safety measure, for "carriages thronged the Fahrthor" where the bride's family lived, "bringing myriads of flowers,

Chapter 26: "Like an Old Married Couple"

as well as guests to the wedding". The congregation sang verses from Psalm 92 and, according to Hiller, Pastor Howard conducted the exchange of vows, which Felix made in French: "It was extraordinary to hear so fundamentally German an artist expressing himself in French at this solemn moment. The simplicity of the ceremony and the young couple were so attractive in every way, and [they] combined to captivate and move every heart." Pastor Appel, with whom Cécile's father had worked, preached the sermon, which the bride thoughtfully copied for her cousin Alphonse, who could not attend the wedding. As a surprise at the reception, held at the bride's home, Hiller had composed a piece, which a ladies' choir sang. Despite the inordinate sources of help of which Marek boasts, he still asks why none of the Mendelssohn family, except Aunt Dorothea, came to the wedding. It is evident that Rebecka had wished to do so. Felix was accused of avoiding the introduction of his birth family to his in-laws, but this was not the case. Leah visited Leipzig shortly before the wedding but, in view of her phobia of travelling – exacerbated, no doubt, by her heart condition – she might not have wished to make a further journey to Frankfurt so soon afterwards. Paul preferred to concentrate on business commitments, rather than take time off to see his brother married. As for Fanny and Rebecka, each was pregnant and each underwent untoward symptoms. This could well have been a further reason for Leah's non-appearance, caring for her two daughters – and, incidentally, obviating the need to meet "that Schlegel woman", who, still lively in her 71st year, had mellowed considerably since her rebellious youth.

The young Herr and Frau Mendelssohn set off on their Rhineland honeymoon at 5.30 that evening for Mainz, the first stage of their journey, Felix having booked at the best hotel and having had a "blue and brown" carriage designed. No plans were made as to the precise itinerary on account of the unpredictable weather. Tantalisingly, no indication is given by either party as to the wedding night, but this, and others, must have gone well. On 29th March the diary reveals: "Rose at ten in the morning. Took a walk to the citadel, where Felix sketched." On 31st March the hotel at Worms exuded "no trace of comfort". But, despite the cold room, "one thing was agreeable, which I shall refrain from mentioning".

The couple's health was not always of the best. After dinner on 29th March "Felix was unwell and remained so until 3 o'clock in the morning". It transpired that an ingredient in the salad had caused this disorder, as had occurred similarly in Leipzig, as he reminded his mother. The couple walked a great deal when sightseeing, causing Mme. Jeanrenaud to have misgivings about the exhaustion her daughter might experience. Cécile had trouble with a tooth; having been filled, the cement came out one morning. "I had to spend the whole day at home. The piano was brought upstairs. Felix looked after me, despite which I passed a dreadful night and did not doze off until about 5 o'clock." The next day "I had the most dreadful pain", to alleviate which "the kind landlady sent figs, saffron and milk up to me. Felix had the dentist summoned, who turned out to be ill himself. The pain eased (nothing new under the sun) and I went to sleep on the sofa", but the tooth still had to be extracted. Various other ailments were mentioned in this diary. "Felix complained of pains at Freiburg." For the first time in her life Cécile became dizzy at the top of a tower at Strasbourg. "Last evening's indisposition" caused Felix such anxiety that he consulted a doctor. Later, having been satisfactorily reassured, Felix "expressed joy and happiness". There could not have been much amiss, for the couple walked to the ramparts and ate "an enjoyable lunch".

Wherever the couple visited the post office was invariably a port of call, to enquire for mail, especially from Leipzigerstrasse 3. On 9th April it was evident that all was not well in Berlin. Fanny had suffered a miscarriage, and Rebecka, too, was decidedly unwell during her pregnancy. So anxious had Cécile become that she added her own postscript to a letter from Felix: "Please comfort my Felix and me, soon, with news, for we are anxious on account of our dear sisters. Please, please, dear mother, grant our wish and pardon my haste, as the bell is now ringing for the evening meal." Felix, too, wished for further communication to provide information on this, the only cloud on his radiant horizon: "You cannot imagine how good I feel and how sweet life is with my dear Cécile. We are enjoying these altogether blissful, happy weeks to the full and one day after the next flies by without any plan, except to be a happy couple. This we follow carefully."

Yet there is record of a lover's tiff. From the joint diary entry for 24th April, in Freiburg im Breisgau, it appears that Felix forgot his status as a married man. "Felix flirted with Fräulein Rehfuss and bought her some violets." On this occasion, Felix's eyes wandered to another peasant girl selling flowers, and he cast a backward glance at her a couple of times. "After that, it only needed a few casual facial expressions and words to make me quite stubbornly melancholy and jealous... My thoughts became more and more gloomy, and he more and more exasperated. Meanwhile it had started to rain and we sat beside the inn door, mute as two fish... Felix's questions and irritation made me more and more silent. I did nothing but weep, tormenting him and myself... Only when back home did we become our old selves again. I told Felix my absurd thoughts, and he was once more kind and affectionate towards me. I made a firm resolution never to be sulky without giving my husband a reason. Felix spent all evening playing all my favourite pieces to me so beautifully. Thus was the matrimonial quarrel settled." Felix added a postscript: "Do not be angry with me, dear Cécile."

A particularly enjoyable excursion was to Strasbourg and the "splendid" cathedral. Despite his earlier grumbling about France, Felix was pleased to be back once more "among all its different customs and people, with French spoken, good food and manners, such polite customs officials and postilions...the French signs with their big, wide letters...and 50 sous for a guide. It all begins at the border." Felix played the Silbermann organ, the first time Cécile had seen inside such an instrument. She made "some lovely purchases", having sought advice as to the best shops to visit. At luncheon music was played, "including butchered Strauss waltzes.

Chapter 26: "Like an Old Married Couple"

The uncouth men ate and talked in an unseemly manner... As it was Rebecka's birthday, her health was drunk."

Felix did not relinquish his routine despite his honeymoon. He wrote a "little allegretto", as Radcliffe calls it, for Cécile's album, a string quartet (which would become part of his Op. 44), some *Songs without Words* and his setting of Psalm 42. He sketched scenes of town and countryside. A picture exists of Mme. Picot's milliner's shop in Strasbourg, and others of various inns, reproduced in Peter Ward Jones's compilation of the Mendelssohns' honeymoon diary. Cécile made a drawing of Mainz. One of their many walks entailed "strolling through primrose-filled meadows en route to a paper mill at Freiburg". On another walk Cécile plucked violets, leaning over a gate to obtain a buttonhole for her new husband. Not to be outdone, Felix picked roses and hyacinths (sic) for their room, which his wife pressed into her album once the flowers had dried.

At Heidelberg the couple met various friends and family, including Mme. Jeanrenaud. Schlemmer persuaded Felix to give an organ recital at the Church of the Holy Spirit. They heard all the Berlin gossip from the Schadow family; how

Figure 8. Mendelssohn's sketch of Cécile in milliner's shop, Strasburg, 1837

Spontini "had destroyed and ruined everything, causing himself vexation and anxiety, like an ill-assorted marriage, where parties are in the wrong when they come to blows", yet he would continue for some years more to rule the opera scene.

Cécile did not play the compliant young daughter-in-law when Leah harangued her and had no compunction in correcting her mother-in-law's misunderstandings. Having been accused of dousing her letter with a musk perfume, she replied on 28th May: "I very much refute the charge of musk perfume which you made against me. Really, dear mother, I do not know how I came to deserve it. There is truly no one who hates this scent as much as I do and I cannot imagine at all how the unfortunate letter may have suggested it. In truth, you could suspect the postman sooner than myself. In any case, dear mother, if you had not done so already, burn it immediately, so that I am not the cause of headaches or unpleasant feelings." This incident is reminiscent of Felix's similar experience whilst in Italy. Perhaps Leah might have been allergic to this powerful scent, or its erotic implications could have caused feelings not conducive to the life of a woman of utmost probity. In the same letter Cécile thanked Leah for "the long list of Felix's linen... Yet, with a few repairs, everything will be fit for the English journey, and as he does not look in the least untidy, but always appears like the 'finest gentleman', you need not take the trouble to send the things here. I will receive the items in Leipzig with double delight when the need is greatest." Cécile was always conscientious in laundering or mending her husband's clothing. Such care caused Felix to appear "rarely...as cheerful as in these past few days and, in the face, one really notices it. Everyone says he looks so prosperous and well and aunt Schlegel says she has never seen him like it in her whole life." Evidently the young Frau Mendelssohn enjoyed rubbing her mother-in-law's nose in the existence of "that Schlegel woman".

A strange incident appears in Rockstro's biography of Felix. He states that, whilst on honeymoon, Felix "narrowly escaped drowning", but gives no further detail. Neither is such a seemingly important incident recorded elsewhere. Peter Ward Jones believes that an acquaintance must have become muddled and reported this story, unaware of the real scenario. Felix did, in fact, complain of his body being chilled after bathing in the river Main, about which his mother reprimanded him, but nothing further occurred. On 14th July Felix wrote to Julius Schubring of "a change for the better" in his life and invited his old friend to visit Leipzig during the forthcoming winter. Even at this early stage in his life Felix confided to Hiller how he disliked conducting and directing, and said he would prefer to be composing his own music solely, but "I find a certain charm in working within an organised structure", such as that offered by Leipzig. He wrote of how much the St. Cecilia Society was deteriorating, "not through the fault of any individual, but because the soil here is far from favourable to music, though all the better for apples, cherries, wine and other good things". He explained further on 29th May how "the call went out for experienced singers, good, dependable musicians,

Chapter 26: "Like an Old Married Couple"

obliging leaders who needed just a little piano playing, a little goodwill, a little knowledge. Scarcely anyone has come forward to take on Schelble's directorship." Though Neukomm "decidedly accepted the post, I decidedly declined it". Hiller found the work "troublesome" and chose to live in Italy with his mother. "In short, there is no one to perpetuate the right, true and noble spirit in which it [the society] was begun... No one who can understand Handel, Bach and other such people are superior to what they themselves can do or say." Felix was grieved that all Schelble's hard work was coming to naught. "If Ferdinand Ries takes over, he, I consider, is deficient in such a role." In September Felix decided to have nothing further to do with the St. Cecilia Society, and at the same time his blissful honeymoon came to an end. He had promised to direct the Birmingham Festival that year, and not even the old friends he had made in London could assuage the low spirits he sustained without Cécile by his side. So much did this apply that, on his return to Leipzig, he wrote: "Behind me was fog but, in front, brilliant sunshine" – metaphorically and literally.

Chapter 27

At Home with Cécile and Felix Mendelssohn

"The minute details of the pure and elevated happiness which Mendelssohn enjoyed in his intimate, domestic relations are expressly withheld as being the peculiar treasures of his family." So runs the preface, painstakingly and clumsily translated by Lady Grace Wallace, of the compilation of Mendelssohn correspondence between 1833 and 1847 made by Felix's brother Paul and his nephew Karl. Fortunately, anyone who wishes to probe more deeply into life between Cécile and Felix has other sources of reference, rather than having to heed such sanctimonious guff. From Scheveningen Felix wrote to Hiller: "Some ladies from Leipzig parade along the promenade, their hair coming down in a fine dishevelled state. I suppose I ought to make love to them." Then, remembering his hopes, soon to be fulfilled, of becoming a married man, he added: "Do not show this letter to anyone. It should be destroyed, or, preferably, burnt, or may you be hanged or roasted!" By "anyone", Felix especially meant Cécile or her relatives, whom Hiller often met. So terrified was the young swain that his truly beloved would marry someone else that not one word of doubt was to be breathed of this paragon of virtue. Even when married, Felix confided to his mother-in-law: "I refrain from walking with my wife in the street on account of the continuous stares of passers-by. Not a man we encounter does not open his eyes wide. Cécile modestly laughs, assuring me that such behaviour is not meant for herself."

Such passion did not wane as time elapsed. "Every hour is like a festival," Felix wrote, again to Mme. Jeanrenaud, on his return from England in 1837. "Every day brings a succession of joy and happiness and I once more know what it is to value life." The sentiments were similar to other correspondents, such as Devrient: "With a lovely home and an open view of fields, gardens and the city towers, I feel so serenely happy, so calmly joyous, as I have never felt since leaving my parents' home", and it is to this correspondent that, after barely six weeks of marriage, Felix considered himself to be part of "an old married couple". Nothing changed when the couple were obliged to remain apart. From Berlin, serving the King of Prussia, Felix wrote to his wife on her birthday, 10th October: "How much I long to speak to you, to kiss you, to spend the whole day with you, to gaze upon you, to enjoy the festive occasion... Were I with my dear, good Cécile, I would kiss you...and kiss you again, and you would have to take notice of my presence, because I would not leave you in peace, through my love and joy on your birthday. I shall take the earliest train to Leipzig on Saturday, where I belong with my darling, wonderful Cécile, my birthday child." On another occasion, when Cécile was visiting her family and Felix was obliged to remain in Leipzig, he wrote: "Time hangs heavily", and asked his "treasure" why she did not write "even a few lines. Is this revenge for my stupid joke in Nuremberg?" (no explanation of which can be found). "If I am to live a long time without you, I shall be physically ill. As it is, I have no appetite, merely swallowing a few bites because one has to eat. I do not enjoy anything." He even unburdened himself to Mme. Jeanrenaud: "When I am with her, I do not understand how indispensable to my life, every moment of it, she is. But when I am not with her, the absence becomes heavier to bear. I count the hours until I can see her again – her, without whom I no longer know joy or happiness. In three weeks' time, with God's help, I shall be reunited with Cécile and the children, for whom I yearn. Then, nothing will keep us apart."

Such letter writing was not one-sided. When Felix was allowed, at last, to return to Leipzig permanently, having served with such frustration at the Prussian King's court in Berlin, Cécile congratulated him on being allowed to reinstate himself "where your extraordinary talent to lead and influence people, so that they fulfil your wishes, would be valued once more." And again: "Like a children's fairy tale, a dream has come true. I shall bear the separation patiently, fixing my eyes on a ray of light in a gloomy November. It is a matter of indifference where I live, so long as you are contented and happy, as I am with you. [However], so desolate am I that all the charms of the world cannot improve the situation. This sounds exaggerated, but all that I write is true, and not just a momentary mood, but the result of all my thoughts."

As a bachelor, Felix's first home consisted of rooms at Reichels Garten, but, on marriage, the couple moved to Lurgensteins Garten that faced St Thomas's School and Church, adjacent to the city gates. Hiller remembered the drawing room, dining room, large salon and two bedrooms. A wide range of information exists regarding food in the Mendelssohn home. According to Hiller, who stayed one winter, rather than one week as arranged, breakfast at 8.30 consisted of coffee, white bread and butter. Felix, however, preferred plain bread, which "he preferred to dunk into his coffee, the same as any other schoolboy, as he has always done". Lunch lasted "no longer than necessary", on account of Felix's heavy work schedule. At dinner, host and guests would sit round the table, "chatting, not smoking, after the evening meal had been eaten". Unless Cécile had music to copy for Gewandhaus concerts, Felix would suggest that he and Hiller share the table to compose but, after a fortnight, it became evident that this plan was proving unworkable. Hiller, therefore, worked and slept at his own lodgings, where Felix had formerly lived, but took meals with the Mendelssohns. Hiller gave no details

Chapter 27: At Home with Cécile and Felix Mendelssohn

as to what menu was served at the Mendelssohns' table, but other sources give an idea of the type of food enjoyed by Cécile and Felix. Their honeymoon diary records a lunch in Strasbourg comprising "Julienne [soup] of mixed vegetables; maître d'hôtel potatoes; Roquefort cheese; and an omelette soufflé". Veal garnished with plums was another favourite and, as a luxury, larks with apple sauce were consumed. Confectionery was always to play a part in Felix's diet. On a visit to Leipzig Fanny produced a layer cake for a farewell party for Cécile's Schlemmer relative, who was leaving for Frankfurt. 'Baumkuchen' – literally 'tree-cake': cake formed into the shape of a tree – often featured at entertainments. Yet another member of the cake hierarchy is cited by Herbert Kupferberg. On a visit to Berlin Felix asked on his wife's behalf if anyone other than a Jew was allowed to make the 'butter cake' he relished so much, and, if not, why not?

Good wine featured equally fulsomely in anecdotes of the Mendelssohns' cuisine. Felix was "partial to a glass" with his main meal and "sometimes he asked his companions to sample a special vintage, which our host would produce with great delight and swallow with immense satisfaction". He was eminently capable also of concocting his own brew, as Rockstro recalled. On New Year's Eve 1845 "a perfect little supper [was] served at small tables around the room. As the clock struck midnight, Mendelssohn toasted each guest in turn, touching each glass with his own, greeting them with his indescribable smile, having produced some choice

Figure 9. Lithograph of the home at Lurgensteins Garten, Leipzig

old wine reserved for the occasion." Later Felix produced his 'Maitrank' ('May drink'), comprising "hock and Mosel, mixed in certain artistic proportions with Waldmeister (woodruff) and sugar, which he called 'the True Jack' ('der Wahr Jakob') for the benefit of his English guests". Julie Schunck and her husband (Cécile's sister and brother-in-law) regarded this mixture "the best of its kind ever sampled". On 9th July of the following year, Felix asked Paul if Scholz and Kuhnert could "take back the bottles for red wine, of which I have a multitude and then, could they send back to me some of them filled?" To save trouble for Paul, Felix suggested the wine merchants contact him direct; "they must answer at once, as almost no red wine can be found". Thus Mendelssohn's wine cellar remained well stocked, added to which Mme. Clicquot promised, after the 1846 Aachen Festival, to send two dozen bottles of her celebrated champagne each year.

Wagner suggested that Mendelssohn should join the Temperance Movement because his compositions could in no way equate with the "music of the future". Though this was meant as a jibe, Felix's personality might well have fitted this concept of moderation and self-discipline. Felix drank solely from a small glass, and only a limited quantity of alcohol passed his lips at a time. Neither could he abide drunkenness, especially from people he respected, and whom he thought should know better than to indulge in such lack of self-control. When friends took Felix to a smoky tavern he noticed Ludwig Devrient, a fine actor like his brother Eduard, "quite unrecognisable from his usual self, declaiming speeches of Falstaff, Shylock and King Lear, embracing a barrel". He then "stretched out on the table, like a corpse", Julius Bab relates in his book on the Devrient family. So disgusted was Felix that, in order to avoid vomiting in public, he had to escape into the fresh air.

But, again, inconsistency is to be found in the life of this almost superhuman individual. Once, at an entertainment, Felix wrote to Rebecka complaining of a headache through having consumed "212 glasses of punch". Evidently guilt overcame him, for he added: "Pray, cut off this [last] part [of my letter] before sending it to Rome", where Fanny was staying. "A younger sister may be entrusted with such a confidence, but an elder one, [especially] in such a papal atmosphere – not on your life."

When the Woringen sisters persuaded Rebecka to accompany them to Leipzig, she confessed herself "ill at ease" on first meeting Cécile; Fanny still tended to perpetuate the role of mother figure towards Felix and his bride. "You are so fortunate in your choice," she wrote. "This child, with her lovely eyes and tranquil disposition, will, most likely, cure your fits of irritability altogether." Paul does not appear to have been particularly sociable, visiting only to discuss business matters with his brother, when required. However his brother and sisters felt about Cécile, Gustave Kobbé has no doubt of the position: "She was just the woman to grace the home such a fastidious musician would want to establish."

However, this young wife was not only a charming, welcoming hostess. Cécile adapted to the responsibilities placed upon her with the aplomb of an experienced

Chapter 27: At Home with Cécile and Felix Mendelssohn

matron, rather than a young bride. Not only was Felix able to reassure his mother that meals were cooked better than before, since leaving the precincts of Leah's abode, but he reported to his brother-in-law, Charles Jeanrenaud, how efficiently Cécile coped with builders' annoyances. This ensured the home was furnished comfortably, but she also purchased many household items that, in his bachelor state, Felix did not think necessary: "fruit dishes, salad bowls and [extra] knives and forks" were listed in this new inventory. As a mother-to-be, Cécile had to prepare for the new baby in addition, and many hours must have been passed in sewing and knitting, for no ready-made babywear or bedding would have been available to buy. Though servants were engaged to do the rough work, these, too, had to be cared for. Kindness was the only way to earn respect and loyalty and, for the young Mendelssohns, love abounded between employer and staff. When Moscheles dedicated his Six Songs, Op. 97, to Cécile, Charlotte, his wife, congratulated "the excitable, effervescent Mendelssohn" on his "having met with a wife so gentle, so exquisitely feminine. You are perfectly matched." Though servants are not mentioned specifically in biographies of the Mendelssohn family, various snippets of information appear in correspondence. Fanny mentioned Heinrich and Schumacher, a real character, whom Rebecka wrote of as "acting as head of the party on her trip to Italy". When, en route, the Dirichlets visited cousin Franz Mendelssohn, "he gave me a book of Schumacherisms". Evidently he, too, must have been well acquainted with this servant and his sayings. Eventually Cécile and Felix employed him, but their favourite was Johann Krebs. Once, when this manservant was ill, Cécile even related to him the events of an evening's entertainment. Johann also accompanied Felix on his 1844 visit to London, and the children loved him especially. During his last illness Felix was grief-stricken and, at his death, found among his belongings, "which were in the most excellent order", a letter containing his last will. "No man – no poet, indeed – could have written anything so beautiful, earnest and touching," Felix wrote to Klingemann. Johann's mother and sister did not arrive until the day before the funeral, which distressed Cécile, who could not offer enough words of condolence to the relatives of such a beloved servant.

After Berlioz visited Leipzig he wrote an article for the French *Journal des Débats*, quoting a letter from Felix. Cécile was highly amused when Felix remarked in a letter to Rebecka: "It is a wonder no mention is made of Jette and Crystel" – the children's nursemaids, to whom Berlioz apparently took a fancy. In the same epistle Minna, the maid, was reminded "not to forget her brown sauces", and Felix continued: "Hanna has now married her tailor and sometimes calls on us, when we give her a meal."

Just as Felix and his wife were treated as her son and daughter-in-law by Fanny, readers can be forgiven for assuming that Rebecka was also her daughter, rather than her younger sister. When describing the almost sacrosanct ritual of spring-cleaning that was in progress at Leipzigerstrasse 3, it would seem that Rebecka, an equally fastidious homemaker, had never experienced such a task herself: "The carpets are up, the floors have not yet been waxed, the curtains are all in the wash and there are brooms, dustpans and hand-brushes all over the house." Labour-saving appliances – vacuum cleaners, floor polishers, washing machines or electric irons – would not become available to anyone until the 20th century. Carpets had to be beaten with a device invented for the purpose; beeswax had to be manually applied to floors in such residences as Leipzigerstrasse 3, where dances took place; curtains, as with other household items and clothing, were placed in a tub and agitated manually with a dolly stick to remove the dirt. Ironing was done by hand, once the washing had been wrung through the mangle, the irons being heated on the stove. Though Fanny's servants would undertake these tasks, Fanny would have had to ensure that the right calibre of employee was engaged.

As for life in professional households in Leipzig, an accurate picture can be gained through a letter written to Moscheles by Felix. A home "with seven or eight rooms, plus kitchen and appurtenances (sanitary arrangements), would cost 300 to 350 thalers to maintain. Servants' wages are 100 to 110 thalers. Male domestics earn between three and 12 thalers per annum. A good cook would expect to receive 32 thalers; a similar wage would apply for a housemaid and a lady's maid, particularly if she could sew and make dresses"; the sewing machine would be invented after Felix's death. Nothing is mentioned about children's servants – nannies, governesses or tutors – but, as Moscheles's children were older than Felix's, this might not have been necessary. Though Marek calls the household accounts "orderly, as that of a Swiss bank", implying that Felix had had them tabulated by a bank employee, this is not the case: "These figures were taken from my wife's housekeeping books," Felix stated categorically to Moscheles. "Male servants are not much in demand here," Felix continued, "so I think you would scarcely need one" – a contradiction from his family's own employment of manservants. Though Felix calculated that a professional family could live comfortably on 1,000 to 2,000 thalers per annum, "I cannot predict what you would gain from music lessons. When I arrived in Leipzig, there was no precedent on which costs could be based. Mme. Schumann-Wieck charged two thalers but, at that price, found few pupils, mostly foreigners spending a short time here. If, therefore, you were to charge one and a half thalers, I believe you would be overrun with applicants." This income, plus his salary at the Conservatorium and fees for his own compositions, would allow Moscheles's capital to remain intact, to be invested or used otherwise, as required. "I do not think that, in any way, I have been over-optimistic in giving you these estimates. I certainly gauged them, after due consideration, based on my own experience in Leipzig."

As for Moscheles's furniture, "there should be no duties involved when transporting it from London". Other comparisons between England and Germany are to be found in the letters of Sophie and Fanny Horsley. Friedrich Rosen, a mutual friend of the Horsley family and Felix, told Mrs. Horsley that English

Chapter 27: At Home with Cécile and Felix Mendelssohn

servants were far more trustworthy and conscientious than their German equivalents. Evidently, he did not meet Johann Krebs or any other of the Mendelssohn servants. Rosen also found that, whilst English tradesmen delivered goods to the household, this did not happen in Germany. Whereas, in Leipzig at least, "rates and taxes are next to nothing – eight or nine thalers will cover these", in Britain at a similar date a slogan was coined: "Taxes are paid in sorrow; rates in anger". "Wood for fires and the kitchen stove costs 200 thalers for a family of five," Felix continued to Moscheles, "which I find expensive." When this letter was written, the Mendelssohn family comprised seven – Cécile, Felix and five children, though the youngest boy, Felix, died later.

Moscheles was a regular visitor to Leipzig and recalled that, in the evenings, host and guests either read newspapers or played music. If chamber groups were not available, piano duets sufficed. It must have been during these hours that Cécile occupied herself so industriously with her needlework. At the Mendelssohn Museum at Goldschmidtstrasse, where the Mendelssohn's moved from the Lurgensteins Garten, her beautifully embroidered cushions and fire screens can still be seen. In late 1840 a soirée was held at the Gewandhaus on the eve of his departure, with 400 guests. As so many people wished to bid farewell to this popular visitor, Moscheles was unable to finish his meal before having to set off. Cécile, therefore, handed his dessert to him through his carriage window. During the same year George Sampson had been given a letter of introduction by Klingemann to visit Leipzig. This singer from England was most impressed with his reception.

Mendelssohn's study at the Lurgensteins Garten was "plainly a musician's workroom, yet it had a note of elegance". When George Sampson visited Leipzig in 1840 he was surprised at the tidiness of the room, and wrote: "Musicians are not a tidy race, but here I found none of the admired disorder that one associates with an artist's sanctum. There was no litter. The well-used piano could be reached without having to negotiate books and papers. Even the chairs were free from encumbrances." In view of his self-confessed muddle at Düsseldorf (see Chapter 19, 'Conductor and director'), it can only be deduced that, on Sampson's visit, Cécile's influence must have been brought to bear in making Felix's Leipzig study so orderly. Of Cécile herself, Sampson remembered "a beautiful, charming girl, who welcomed her guests warmly". Talk centred on Clara Wieck, the celebrated pianist whom Schumann would marry in September of that year, when Clara was 21. Felix called her "a charming young lady and an excellent musician, well worth all the struggle. I know you will be very happy." Her father had, for several years, done all he could to hamper the marriage of his brilliant daughter to "that reprobate", as Wieck dismissed poor Schumann. Fortunately, however, Schumann had studied law before adopting music as a profession, so was able to appeal to the court to marry Clara. "Though Wieck is much worried, Clara and I will marry this year," he proclaimed.

Charles Horsley was another visitor from London whose reminiscences are worthy of attention. He recalled an invitation to dine with the Mendelssohns to meet Sigismund Thalberg, the virtuoso pianist, who had arrived the previous evening. After dinner Thalberg played his Fantasia on themes from Bellini's opera *La Sonnambula*, with "chromatic runs in octaves" – Thalberg's own invention. "Mendelssohn was much struck by the novel effect and the ingenuity produced" in this piece, still in manuscript. Having arrived the next day at 2 p.m. as instructed, Horsley heard Felix playing passages from the Fantasia. "I waited for at least half an hour, listening in wonderment. On [my] entering, Mendelssohn laughed and asked me to listen: 'Is this not almost like Thalberg?' and continued to improvise, based on all the double scales." Horsley claimed that the sixth *Song without Words* in Book Four, dedicated to Sophie Horsley, "contains an accompaniment somewhat founded on this idea". Horsley continued: "Mendelssohn's life in Leipzig was that of a true artist. Rising early, he was usually at work by ten in the morning. He was most regular in addressing letters, professional and private, from his large correspondence." Rehearsals usually took place "in the forenoon" and, after his one o'clock lunch with the family, Felix pursued his own projects until the evening, "which, when not at a concert, he spent regularly with his wife and family". During the week of Horsley's departure for London, a party was held at the Gewandhaus at which the *Hymn of Praise* was performed. This was the first time that Sophie, who had joined her brother, had heard the work. On the evening before his departure, the guests included Clara and Robert Schumann and Fanny Hensel, who was visiting her brother and his family. "Felix's sister played brilliantly, showing much of her brother's fire and style – a most intellectual and talented person."

Of Fanny's accomplishment, Felix wrote: "I will tell you another time how much your piano playing pleased everyone, and it is still discussed." Not only did she acquit herself at the piano. On her first visit to Leipzig Fanny brought two songs, "one in F major, with a variation, and an even prettier one in C major", for which Felix thanked her. What of Felix's own musical output? Though Marek dismisses any inspiration Cécile gave her husband, this appears untrue. According to Hiller: "Her wholehearted support and encouragement never wavered... Felix maintained that his own piano playing was enhanced by the highly expert opinions of his wife, whose appreciation and judgement were always full of wisdom." Friedrich Brockhaus, the Leipzig publisher and relative of Wagner, bears out this testimony: after a Gewandhaus concert he wrote of Cécile: "Her joy was mirrored in her eyes, an apparition that can only be called beautiful and upon which I could gaze forever." And, of Felix: "Since his marriage, a stronger spirit seems to have possessed him."

Hiller claimed to have assisted Mendelssohn in his compositions: during the 1839-40 Gewandhaus season, when the Op. 49 Piano Trio was written, whilst praising its "fire and spirit" and "masterly character" Hiller derided its broken chords as old-fashioned compared with the 'new' music of Liszt and his disciples, with whom Hiller had associated and by whom he had been influenced when living in Paris. Hiller recalled his "small triumph" when Felix admitted that the trio "might be altered, leaving it as a small reminder of you". On another occasion Hiller found Felix one evening, having worked for four hours on a part-song, "in such a state of feverish excitement" that the guest became alarmed. "Twenty attempts at the score were scattered over the desk, any one of which would have satisfied anyone else." Sensibly, Hiller suggested Mendelssohn should "sleep on it", pointing out that "four minutes would suffice, as likely as not, to complete the task the next morning that the wasted four hours of time and effort had failed to do the previous evening". Ernst Wolff, in his centennial biography of Mendelssohn's birth (1909), recounts that the sleepless night resulted in Felix's setting of 'The Huntsman's Farewell', words by Eichendorff, "which would be known by a whole new generation who would otherwise have not known Mendelssohn's music, since it [that song setting] has become almost a national folk song", according to the biographer.

The heavier his workload the greater the number of demands that were made on Felix. Thus omissions had to be amended. In 1839, for instance, he had to apologise to Simrock for the delay in submitting a manuscript promised during the previous year. "I want to make my work as perfect as possible, but still have no time for leisure, but hope to free myself from this debt", by which he meant the despatch of this manuscript. He continued: "I intend, despite popular demand, to write no more *Songs without Words*. Let the people of Hamburg say what they will. There is quite a mass of such music for the pianoforte. Another chord should be struck, I say." But either Felix forgot this pledge, or the popularity of his 'Original Melodies for the pianoforte', as he named them, was too great to resist. Five further books of these pieces would be published in his lifetime or posthumously. Yet he showed embarrassment at this style of music, the title of which Novello's invented on his behalf. At an entertainment Felix heard Taubert playing some of these melodies: "Upon my honour, it is crazy to plagiarise someone, as he does myself. He tears me to pieces, adding all sorts of rubbish of his own." Neither, he told his family in the same letter, did the two books of Cramer's Studies satisfy him completely: "There are some very pretty ones among them, each of which bear titles that, in a few cases, are so silly and naive that I have to laugh out loud." What would he have thought of his own *Songs without Words* being given their own titles: 'Spring Song', 'The Bees' Wedding' and the like?

When George Sampson visited he was privileged to hear the germ of what was to become Felix's Op. 64 Violin Concerto in E minor. Having begun the work in 1838, Felix explained that, at the present time, he would like to discuss further details with Ferdinand David, for whom it would be written, and the violinist had brought the score with him. David predicted that the Concerto would be "something great", Sampson recalled. "Though there are oceans of music for violin and orchestra, there is only (spreading his arms wide to demonstrate the point) only one big Concerto for the solo violin (meaning that by Beethoven). Now, there will be two." This comment requires a word of explanation. Paganini's violin concertos were kept secret at the time, and are only now coming to the forefront of this genre. Those by Bach, Vivaldi and other of their contemporaries were barely known; those by Viotti, Vieuxtemps or Spohr appear not to have merited mention; but it is surprising that Mozart's five masterpieces were not considered. Those by Brahms, Bruch, Tchaikovsky and their successors were yet to be written.

As for Felix's manuscript, Sampson continued: "The violin gave out a beautiful melody that soared passionately, yet gracefully, above an accompaniment. Simple at first, but gradually growing more intense and insistent, until a great climax was reached, after which the solo violin sank to a low, whispering murmur, whilst the piano played above it a succession of delicate and graceful phrases... The playing of the two musical masters was beyond description." Felix explained to his audience that he had never intended to rival Beethoven in writing his Concerto, but, on asking for his guests' comments, Sterndale Bennett made the most profound remark ever likely to be heard by a Mendelssohn connoisseur: "I am reminded of the Garden of Eden. Just as there is something essentially masculine about Beethoven's Concerto, yours is exquisitely feminine. You have mated your Eve with Beethoven's Adam. The tribe of violin concertos shall increase and multiply and become as the stars of heaven in abundance." Bennett ended his peroration "waving his hands in blessing".

Despite Felix's onerous work schedule, life was not always serious. On 8th December 1840 a joke was played on Frau Härtel, wife of the Leipzig publisher. The epistle apologised for her husband's delayed homecoming: "The undersigned married couple do discharge our obligations and legal duty to attest that, only by means of urgent compunction, and not without judicial remonstration, could Herr Raymond Härtel be detained for several hours at the aforementioned house at Lurgensteins Garten. May this attestation serve as a legally binding alibi for him, in the eyes of the lonely hearth of his marriage, and contribute towards mediation in any possible legal quarrels that may arise in consequence. Such is the wish of...", with the full signatures of Cécile and Felix. Presumably Härtel called at the Mendelssohn home to discuss business but, knowing his generous hostess and host, he might well have been given a meal, at which good wine was included. The letter, couched in mock legalese, would have been sent on ahead to reassure Frau Härtel of her husband's safety. Since the telephone was not even invented until 1876, and would not come into prominence until the 20th century, to send a servant with a note was the simplest way of conveying a message. Other relaxations included playing billiards at the local café, at which Felix was defeated on five occasions. "I do not do this very often," he reassured his family; "such indulgences are only for my holiday enjoyment."

As for their actual holidays, Cécile and Felix usually went to Frankfurt, the

Chapter 27: At Home with Cécile and Felix Mendelssohn

adjacent spa, Bad Soden, or stayed in Switzerland, but there were exceptions. After the Lower Rhine Festival at Düsseldorf, "which all three of us will attend – four if Hanna is to be included – we shall be guests at Julie's (Cécile's sister's) wedding. Thence to Bingen to sample some wine and on to Horchheim to see uncle Joseph (Mendelssohn). After that we shall follow the advice of the weather, the pocketbooks, etc..." Of his appearances at the musical festivals in Vienna and Oxford, Felix knew nothing: "The newspapers are sending me there to conduct an oratorio of 2,000 persons, as I hear, and about which I have already received a number of enquiries from German musicians, who want me to take them along, although I have yet to hear one single word from London, Oxford or anywhere else, which is not unusual. I would like to be known as a reliable man."

In the summer of 1842 Cécile and Felix stayed in Interlaken, at the same inn where his family had resided in 1822. It was understandable, therefore, that Felix reminisced with Leah about events of the past. Did his mother recall how he had sketched the walnut tree outside the window, but that Paul had poured a glass of water over the drawing? "I have sketched the same tree, better than before, but not as well as it should be done." When, in 1831, he had tried to stay at that inn, "the same landlady refused to give me lodgings, so shabby did I look. I believe this was my only vexation during the whole of that trip, but now we are people of consequence, having arrived by carriage, with Friedrich on the box." Though the landlady had aged, she was still recognisable by her deportment. Though many new houses had been built, other scenic features had not changed. "The river Aar still gurgles and glides, rapid, smooth and green as before, and the Jungfrau retains her elegant, graceful outline, resembling silver horns." Felix, "building castles in the air", fancied himself owning a country house outside Lausanne, Vevey, Lucerne or Interlaken itself, "with a vineyard and pastureland". Rather than keeping a journal as before, Felix sketched as often as possible, aiming to complete one each day. "I sit facing the mountain, and not until the picture is ruined do I leave off painting." His impressions were quite different from those on his earlier visits: "Whereas I ran off to every jagged mountain and meadow, I now see everything with Cécile, and want to remain in the same place for months."

An excursion was planned to the Lauterbrunnen "at full moon", returning via Furka, Grimsel, Lake Lucerne and the Rigi to Interlaken. "Then, away from this country of countries, back to Germany, where things are not really so bad after all." From Zurich Felix wrote to his family: "I have discovered my old guide [Michael] of 1831. He is now landlord of the Crown Inn at Meiringen." Leah was asked to recommend the inn to anyone who planned to visit the area and John Murray would be asked to include it in his next Swiss edition of his legendary *Red Guides*. "Michael now has a fine house, a very pretty wife and five children, for whom I bought a few little trifles and toy soldiers at Untersee, and thus we had a very enjoyable meeting after 11 years. He brought me the words of the song in G minor that he had sung on the last occasion, the melody of which I still recall." Learning of the proposed visit to the Lauterbrunnen, Michael planned to accompany them, entrusting the care of his inn to a friend. "Thus, the next morning, Michael, with mountain staff and blouse, led the horses and the ladies past some awkward and dangerous terrain. A haymaker called out: 'Oho, Michael, you haven't given up being a guide yet, then?' Michael confided that, though relinquishing the job of guide was difficult, his wife and children became anxious at the danger involved."

Though enjoying so much to travel himself, Felix was ever thoughtful on behalf of other relatives and friends who journeyed for health, business or pleasure. He expressed relief when Rebecka had found rooms for his Leipzig banker friend Woldemar Frege and his wife, the soprano Livia Gerhardt. At the fashionable Baltic resort of Heringsdorf, accommodation was always in short supply, so Felix had been anxious when a 'cure' had been suggested at this spa town. "I hope your wife will soon recover, though the difficult test will not be completed until your return to Leipzig. The new railway will make travelling less irksome." Mendelssohn himself had been taking a similar cure near Berlin at the same time as the Freges: "I found the routine wearisome and was as idle as a sloth for the first two weeks. But, in the first few hours [when] I set myself to work, I made great progress in all manner of new things. I have also turned to painting again and lead a regular, relaxed existence." Felix was pleased that a grand piano had been installed at the Freges' lodging "and that Livia is keeping herself occupied with music. I am sending several musical items, some handwritten, some printed, through which you may like to play and sing sometimes." When Rebecka had visited the same spa, "she had found singing difficult or impossible. How can this be imagined?"

Ferdinand David and his wife were also in Felix's mind whilst he was confined to Berlin, pursuing his servitude at the Prussian court. On 17th October 1842 his friend and deputy was exhorted to let Mendelssohn know immediately that Frau David was "out of danger" from an unspecified illness. Felix was also called upon to solve practical problems. When, in 1844, Devrient was summoned to superintend the theatre at Dresden, the celebrated actor recalled in his memoirs how Mendelssohn offered him "plenty of trunks and packing cases, if you do not have enough already, stroking my hand as he spoke". When the Hensels planned to visit Frankfurt Felix's help was once again sought, this time with regard to suitable accommodation: "There are plenty of rooms facing north, with a window and a capital light. Though I cannot promise you an actual studio like the one at the garden house, I shall find you something suitable where you can work."

It seems appropriate here to mention Cécile's occupation with painting. Though not a professional like her brother-in-law, Wilhelm Hensel, contemporaries regarded her as highly accomplished; too much so, perhaps, from her husband's point of view. There is no doubt that he approved of her sketching the hyacinths and tulips that grew among the cherry, peach, pear and almond trees in the garden of Leipzigerstrasse 3, and everything was fine with her "painting Alpine roses" (sic) when in Switzerland. However, when away from home taking rehearsals

Chapter 27: At Home with Cécile and Felix Mendelssohn

or working with the Gewandhaus or the Conservatorium, Cécile could not resist taking the opportunity to complete a sketch left unfinished by her husband. For such an accomplished artist as Mendelssohn, this must have caused irritation, even if this was never voiced. Only Felix's "placid temperament" is recorded in biographies towards his beloved Cécile, not only when "interfering" in his sketches, but when his music took second place in her order of preference: "Whenever I wish to please my wife I play her favourite compositions, which are those that you have written," he wrote to Chopin on 3rd November 1844, asking, at the same time for his autograph to place in Cécile's album. "Forgive me for this tiresome request among the many with which you must be inundated." Though the autograph was proffered, "somehow, it took about a year," Marek snipes. Nevertheless, Chopin's autograph did arrive and can now be seen, with so many other such treasures, in this album at the Bodleian Library, Oxford.

Meanwhile, though adopting a Spartan front, Leah was never really well. She may have disliked to travel because of her indifferent heart condition, having been taken ill on various trips away from home. Even in her safe haven, Leipzigerstrasse 3, she still allowed matters to upset her, about which a mother would have been expected to be excited. When, for instance, news of Felix's wedding was announced, "she put herself into such a state of collapse that Fanny begged the doctor to administer a sleeping draught". In view of such circumstances, the Mendelssohn children may not have been so surprised at Leah's death as acquaintances who did not know her. Fanny was able to report to Rebecka in Italy later that the cemetery was in good order and the trees thriving. "The drawing room has been changed so much that you will not recognise it on your return." Fanny had been invited to a dinner for Schadow's 81st birthday at Kroll's Restaurant. "Since eclipses and leap years are more frequent than such social functions, I must rush out in haste to buy a gown, cap, collar, etc. and hope nothing will prevent my attending." Fanny also related the sad fate of a government official, Mme. Herz, who, despite her years, "fell from the 16th or 17th stair, right over the balustrade, part of which she carried with her onto the stone pavement below. When the terrified bystanders wanted to pick her up and carry her upstairs, she refused all help. Anyone else would have been killed outright, but all old Diefenbach could find were a few bruises, and in three days she was all right again." In the same letter Fanny gave a glowing account of the garden. "Flourishing in the May sunlight, the newly mown lawn looks like emeralds. In the evenings Albertine and I have taken to sitting out of doors on the pretty new garden chairs, where the only sounds are the Bacchia balls and the games of the grown-up children, which divert everyone from the political situation so dire in Prussia." Once Rebecka and her family returned from Italy, "spectacles will be needed to see any greenery. The lilac trees will look like tobacco and the grass plots will have vanished like fairy tales, allowing you to think that my description was just a fancy. Yet it is true."

Whenever Cécile visited Berlin she loved the opera, especially Spontini's productions, as a result of which she was "overwhelmed by the mass of sound and dazzled by its glitter". Felix must have found it galling indeed to hear such praise, unless he had mellowed by that time, in view of his own untoward experience with *Camacho's Wedding* (see Chapter 17, 'Quest for an opera'). Fanny, too, enjoyed the Berlin Opera, and was only discouraged by the hot weather from seeing "two Kotzebue dramas and a ballet" one evening. But the fine building was destroyed by fire on the following night, as Fanny reported to Rebecka: "I explored my old friend [the opera house] with Albertine before eight o'clock the next morning, to confirm that there was no hope of saving the place. All that remained was the shell, and the two iron programme cases on either side of the door, bills for the previous evening's programme and the gilt-lettered date, 1743. The statues fell with a crash as the firemen dismantled them with a hook devised for the purpose. Inside was a confusion of smoke, water, timber and rubble... If I were King, I would have the premises rebuilt in the same style, with up-to-date arrangements... But why have an opera house today, when opera is a thing of the past?"

Apart from Leipzig and London, Felix's favourite place for relaxation was Frankfurt. "I do nothing but bathe, sketch, play the piano or the adjacent organ and walk," Felix wrote to Klingemann. To his family, Felix's news was similar: having worked each morning, "the evenings are occupied by going into society or staying at home, the most charming society of all... I am leading the most joyous life imaginable." A fête the Mendelssohns attended in the neighbouring forest was described as "unique of its kind". An entertainment was included, with "the audience sitting on camp stools, hampers or lying on the moss". At the interval "strawberries, cherries, oranges, ice cream, raspberry syrup and wine were served on the most delicate china". At the end there was "an excellent supper, with all kinds of good dishes and wine, served from a table decorated with flowers and brilliantly illuminated. Though the trees had become dark and stern, the people underneath them became noisier and merrier as the evening progressed." The caterers had remained until dark but missed their way to their wagon. After the musical items, some of which were "shouted, rather than sung", Felix concluded: "I know now how songs ought to be sung in the open air, and I hope to write a further book of these."

Another such entertainment consisted of tableaux, by the St. Cecilia Society, of Felix's works: his *Midsummer Night's Dream* music; a girl sang his setting of Goethe's *Suleika*; a scene from his singspiel *Camacho's Wedding* – "three dancing couples, admirably costumed, behind whom was a pathetic Don Quixote". A figure of Felix himself then made his appearance, "a youth in a small cravat and a large shirt collar, singing 'Can it be?'". Then came a tableau of *St Paul* and a chorus from Psalm 42, "but I was wondering how they were to represent the panting hart, and who was to attempt it". A further representation of Mendelssohn appeared, "in an inspired attitude, writing music and chewing away at his handkerchief. By his side, a lovely St. Cecilia with a wreath." Evidently, whoever had prepared the scenes

Chapter 27: At Home with Cécile and Felix Mendelssohn

knew of Felix's habit of stuffing a handkerchief into his mouth to restrain laughter when inappropriate. "I believe my ink should be red when describing the representation of my music and myself." Yet a third fête consisted of "ham sandwiches placed on a mossy stone, with 20 singers performing their little store of duets". On another occasion the party was joined by Professor Böckh of Berlin University, "a Jewish dentist from Berlin and an unknown, not great, but big, man".

In 1844 Felix held a "family congress", with Paul playing the most important part, during which he gave his reasons for wishing to remain at Bad Soden for a year, rather than "no longer conducting or performing in public as a soloist". He could not reconcile his court position with his own beliefs as to what was right for him: "I am the head of a musical institution the power in which rests solely with the king and the organisation of which I have no power to alter," he wrote to Rebecka. The family "will not recognise me, so healthy I feel and how well I enjoy life at this resort, which boosts my feeling of good health". Rebecka's husband, Gustav Dirichlet, commented on how well Felix looked, "younger, stronger and fitter" than before, as well as noticing "the large beard" that he had grown. Dirichlet wanted to ask so many questions of Felix that his cravat had to be tied through shortage of time, as they were to visit Mme. Jeanrenaud that evening.

Among other visitors were the poets von Fallersleben and Lenau, whom Felix accompanied part of the way home in the evenings. "We find fault with the system of the world, utter prophecies about the weather, and are unable to predict what England will do in the future. The list of visitors comes out every Saturday, as regularly as *Punch* does with you," he wrote to Klingemann. Of the day-to-day happenings Felix wrote of "violets and green peas, too dear for my liking"; of rising at 6 a.m. "yet [I] sleep for nine and a half hours"; of drinking at the local spa known as 'the champagne spring'. Felix wrote of "the confectioners, from whom we can buy thread and shirt buttons... The postman calls early...asking if we require anything, and brings back my linen the next day" (presumably from the nearest laundry), and "the policeman, husband of our cook". On a shopping expedition the Mendelssohns bought "four-poster beds and a selection of brushes and brooms", in addition to the more mundane "roasted coffee, sugar, butter and milk". Cécile sought advice regarding a replacement milkman, "as the present one is no good at all".

The spring weather had caused the river Main to "bubble under the bridge, springing and rushing along, flinging around the great blocks of ice, as if to say: 'Away with you! We have done with you for the present!' to the winter season, showing that it has preserved both strength and youth under its icy covering. It runs along twice as rapidly and it leaps along twice as high as in the sober days of the past season. The quay by the river is black with people." But Felix found it "pitiable". Rather than writing about the poetry of spring: "All I can do is to discuss the economies the season brings – wood, light, how much sweeter everything smells; how many more things there are to eat; that the ladies have resumed their brightly coloured dresses and that the steamers are sailing down the river." The warmer weather brought unprecedented flooding, causing rich and poor alike to suffer. Old Mme. Souchay (Cécile's grandmother) was marooned on the upper floor of her home and had to be rescued. A large section of the buttress supporting the bridge fell into the river. Felix asked if this could remain *in situ* until his sisters had seen this evident tourist attraction when they next visited. In response, Mendelssohn was informed that the masonry would not be removed and that the request from such a celebrity would add weight to this decision.

The work situation was ambivalent; Felix had an invariably heavy workload, but social events were mixed into it with equal enjoyment. He paid a visit to a Herr Kiengel for "good music, on the Wednesday of the past week in the forenoon", despite having "a great deal to do that morning". When the other guests expressed regret that there was no alto, Felix obliged "in a falsetto voice, the old gentleman sitting in his dressing gown at the piano... Good red wine followed...I stayed until half past one and could not resolve to depart. Could I have spent such evenings in Paris or Berlin?" He wrote to Klingemann of "my peaceful life in the solitude I desire. Thanks be to God, my wife and children are well. I have plenty of work, so what more can anyone need? I do not ask heaven to grant me anything more." The only cloud on his horizon was having to avoid "the Philistine social gatherings that flourish and thrive in Leipzig, into which I am enticed to take part, losing much time and pleasure, though I have succeeded pretty well in getting rid of them. I now plan to have a very pleasant period of domestic rest." Yet, to Charlotte Moscheles, he wrote complaining "how hard driven I am with work. Since January there has been an uninterrupted succession of musical events. The Leipzigers are so very sociable that one is hardly allowed a quiet evening at home. Our own house has become a lively centre, too. We invite our friends, and they return the compliment. We speak German, French and English, all in one breath and, all the while, the orchestra is fiddling, trumpeting and drumming every day, whilst one is expected to sit for an hour and a half at dinner to sing four-part songs to a roast beef accompaniment." Yet, despite so much social activity, Felix wrote to his family on 20th October 1843: "I am at my desk from morning until evening, correcting scores, so that my head aches, with no time to catch the Saturday mail, in order to answer my correspondence, by which I mean that hateful word 'business'. I have nothing about which to write, except oboes and trumpets, and they do not bear description."

Later, in 1846, Felix heard that Moscheles had been earmarked to conduct the Birmingham Festival at which his own *Elijah* was to be premiered. At first this caused surprise but, later, as he told the London publisher Edward Buxton, "the letter came from wheels within wheels. Otherwise, I would not have taken it seriously." Did Buxton know the full facts?

When summoned to Berlin Felix tried to make the best of his unsatisfactory situation to Klingemann: "The King invited me to dine. The Queen asked me to

Chapter 27: At Home with Cécile and Felix Mendelssohn

make a piano arrangement of my *Hymn of Praise*, which I have done. In this way, nearly two months have passed since I arrived, but I know no more about what I am supposed to be doing than I did before and, if anything, even less. The only advantage as I see it is that I can live at Leipzigerstrasse 3, quite retired, and with no one to bother about. I sketch and drink mineral water, which agrees with me, and spend the evenings contentedly with the family." Though the King had what he called "an urgent desire" for Sophocles's *Antigone* to be set to music, "nothing is definite. We talked about it four months ago." Nevertheless, "I am going to work on the project, as it means a great deal to me to bring the piece to fulfilment. I am hustling, rushing and pushing people as much as I can. At least, if nothing comes of it, I shall have done my part and then, next year, I shall retire to my jolly home in Leipzig...and will be justified in the eyes of my mother, brother and sisters, but I cannot stay in a place that is not for me."

Fanny wrote to Rebecka: "Heinrich [her servant] has such eccentric ideas about table arrangements that I must lay the places in the morning and prepare the music for next Sunday's concert. Besides being invited to dine with Paul and his family... Altogether, there is so much noise and confusion around me that I cannot find one quiet moment to conclude this letter." Despite the "flat spin" in which Fanny found herself, "we set to work on an immense fish, a ditto turkey and an excellent [wine] cup. Felix was in high spirits, Ambassador Bunsen in raptures, but Hensel was not in the mood to give his customary witty toasts, as he had heard that Thorwaldsen had passed away." The Hensels' poodle, Caro, won his spurs by helping the nightwatchman catch a man lurking in one of the outbuildings. "He may have planned to burgle the house, as No. 1 next door suffered that fate. Felix was amused because I gave Winter (the nightwatchman) a thaler and a plate of roast mutton to the dog."

It was whilst in Berlin that Felix met Jenny Lind, who was staying with the sculptor Ludwig Wichmann and his wife, who gave a soirée to which Felix was invited. Not only did friendship flourish but, more important, empathy towards each other's art. There was nothing of Felix becoming a Svengali to Jenny's Trilby O' Ferrall. Mendelssohn was never power-hungry, as with George Du Maurier's character; neither was Jenny like the hypnotised young singer whom her impresario turned into an international prima donna. Jenny had already gained years of experience as an opera singer. Never happy in a strange environment, she found Mendelssohn "incredibly friendly and polite", at the same time recognising his "great talent". Joan Bulman, Jenny Lind's biographer, expressed surprise that, once in Leipzig, Cécile's attitude became "a little cool and strained". If these were the only feelings she showed, bearing in mind how fond Jenny had become of Felix, it can only be marvelled at her attitude. His letters to Miss Lind were no more than courteous. He addressed her as "My Dear Fräulein", commiserating on her sprained ankle that confined her indoors for three weeks. She was often troubled by migraine and nervous collapse, having, like Felix, fallen victim to headaches from childhood. "Cordial messages from Cécile" were invariably included. "The children think of you daily and hourly, as do their parents" was another message. He confided to her his wish: "All I want is a quire of music paper, no need to conduct anything I do not care for and [to] be altogether independent and free. It will be a few years indeed before this can take place." Signing himself "Your friend" to Jenny, this meant more than was intended. When Friedrich Brockhaus met her in Leipzig, he opined: "She has such a beautiful character, yet she is not happy." He had a presentiment that she would leave the opera stage to become a wife and mother after she had witnessed the idyllic domestic life the Mendelssohns had made for themselves. Though she could never give birth to Mendelssohn's children, it is significant that Jenny did the next best thing by marrying one of his pupils, Otto Goldschmidt, and was blessed with a son and daughter from this marriage. What joy there must have been when, in 1846, Mendelssohn heard that Moscheles had agreed to replace him as director of the Leipzig Conservatorium: "We are all well and looking forward with impatience to your next letter," Felix wrote, "which is to bring us the welcome news that you are coming. When this happens, I shall drain my best bottle of wine and cap it with a cup of champagne." Though music still played a vital part in the Mendelssohns' home life, another aspect, glimpsed only minutely in biographies to date, deserves a chapter of its own – the joys and sorrows, fun and anxieties, created by the Mendelssohn children.

Chapter 28

"Dear, Good Children"

On Felix's first visit to London in 1829 a phrenologist, Dr. Spurzheim, examined the bones of his client's skull to deduce what characteristics emerged. One of Spurzheim's assertions was that Mendelssohn loved children. This was borne out two years later when, in June 1831, Felix wrote to Fanny on the birth of her only child, Sebastian Hensel; enclosing a *Song without Words*, he said how her news "warms me to the depths of my heart" and that, one day, he, too, would like to have a family of his own. In 1833, however, when visiting his godson, Felix Moscheles, Fanny Horsley reported to her aunt how "he frightened the child by making a dreadful noise with throat and mouth" and, on being reproved for his unorthodox welcome to the baby, "he gained equilibrium and played a new rondo". It is evident that, as a bachelor, Felix had no idea of the best way to approach his godson.

However, this incident must have been forgotten, if Felix Moscheles's memoirs are to be given credence. He spoke often in his father's biography of the ball games in Regent's Park and how agilely Felix senior could run. By that time Mendelssohn had children of his own, the first of whom, Karl Wolfgang Paul, was born on 7th February 1838. Cécile must have conceived in May 1837, having been married on 28th March of that year. In August Felix wrote to his mother that "it is the third month with her, as the experts say". Because the honeymoon diary the couple shared coincides with Cécile's first pregnancy, readers are able to gain far more information about this than the four later events of this nature.

On 13th June, for instance, "Felt unwell. Felix took care of and pampered me prettily, as did mother." The next day a Dr. Lejaune gave her medicine "that, like a child, I take with hideous grimaces". On 5th July Cécile felt "definitely unwell and, after lunch, took my medicine again, with dreadful grimaces. What a strange business [caused by] such a small person." No details are given as to the content of the medicine but, in view of today's ideas, it must be suspect as to its necessity. A letter to Leah is worth quoting, which Cécile wrote on 25th June: "Felix read me a story by Hoffmann about the imprints children receive from their mother before they are born. This gave me the idea of consulting the good witch with whom you were in contact before Felix was born. In truth, it often appears to me unnatural how everything flows from his hand. It is at least very different from my own character." Modern psychologists may laugh at such a notion, talking instead about the part that each parent plays in the formation of a child's personality and the vital effect of nurture and heredity from both parents' genes.

Though the couple reported themselves to be "in excellent health and spirits", the mother-to-be experienced unusual lethargy, due, perhaps, to the medicine she imbibed so dutifully. This might have contained laudanum, an opium compound that enhanced sleep. "I am so tired that the first tree trunk, stone or even the hard ground must serve as a seat", whilst undertaking the "long walks" so regularly the order of the day. Indoors, too, matters were no different: "the smell of the pigments, together with the heat", caused her to fall asleep whilst trying to paint. At a drawing lesson and a subsequent piano lesson "I could do nothing right," she confided. Marek and other biographers take Cécile to task for her apparent indolence but, to Leah, she explained her situation: "Whenever I try to occupy myself, within half an hour mother or Felix come to me and admonish me about the constant stooping or sitting" – as opposed, presumably, to lying in bed. "Whenever she suffers a headache or is too tired not to retire early, I feel unable to take up any occupation," Felix added. Cécile's life consisted, apart from "going for long walks", of "I really do nothing at all but eat, drink...sleep and awaken again to [a] renewed, almost animal-like existence".

Despite the burden of worry concerning his young wife's condition, Felix was obliged to travel to England for his fifth visit in September 1837, to direct *St Paul* at that year's Birmingham Festival and fulfil other music engagements in London. It must therefore only be imagined how he rejoiced when eventually reading her part of their diary for 3rd September: "During the past ten days I have felt life stir within me for the first time. It is far too great a delight to be my Felix's wife"; and, she must have thought, "to be the mother of his child". Two days later, having shopped with her mother in the morning, "did not work much in the afternoon, as my back hurt. Read and reread Felix's letter 100 times and rejoiced that [despite his hectic schedule] he had not forgotten me." On a visit to an art exhibition the artist Stiehler mistook Cécile for an unmarried girl, her dress, presumably, hiding her expanding figure. Food cravings are also noted, in particular ice cream. As this was naturally produced in those pre-mechanised days, it is likely it would have proved nutritious for mother and baby alike.

Between 27th September, the date when the diary ended, and 7th February, when the Mendelssohns' first child was born, not much is known about Cécile's well-being. The one exception appears to be a letter written by Felix on 1st December to Ottilie von Goethe, with whose family the couple maintained contact: "The mother is as healthy and rosy-cheeked as when you last saw her." Nevertheless, although apparently contented to the outside world, Cécile might well have been scared, not only by the old wives' tales that thoughtless women still put about, but by real alarms. At the time of the Mendelssohns' wedding both

Chapter 28: "Dear, Good Children"

Fanny and Rebecka were pregnant. Fanny soon miscarried, which, through lack of news from Berlin, caused much anxiety to her brother and sister-in-law. As for Rebecka, both during and after the birth, agonising neuralgia overwhelmed her, causing delirium, as a result of which her doctor prescribed a 'cure' at the spa town of Franzensbad (see Chapter 3, 'Sound minds in frail bodies'). On 30th November 1838 Fanny wrote to Klingemann: "My sister has just lost a beautiful boy at 13 months old", whom the parents had named Felix after his uncle. Despite so much distress to her sisters-in-law, Cécile gave birth herself to a son.

Four days afterwards Leah was informed that "old Carus (a celebrated Leipzig physician) has just visited and reports no trace of fever and that all is well with mother and child". Though, "God willing", Felix "could look forward to her complete recovery", this was not to be. God's will was irrelevant, for human incompetence and poor hygiene must have caused Cécile's unspecified illness. This could have been post-natal eclampsia, which, through blood poisoning, can cause hallucinations, delirium and fever. Even with the ultra-hygienic conditions of today, care must still be taken that such a traumatic condition does not occur.

Once the mother had recovered Felix could still recall his anxiety, as he wrote to Mme. Kiene, sister of Mme. Bigot, his early piano teacher and pupil of Beethoven: "I constantly watched by my wife's bedside, noting any change in her condition", but no details were forthcoming. Not even commentators say how her face looked – a vital indication as to the state of an individual's illness. Felix was full of his new status as a father: "It is such a dear and warm feeling to look at such a tiny little fellow, who has brought into the world his mother's blue eyes, little button nose and peaceful disposition," he wrote to Hiller. "He knows us so well when his mother enters the room and then, when he lies at her breast and drinks like mad, and both enjoy it so, I cannot help myself. I am beside myself with happiness." Felix wrote similarly to Klingemann, telling his old friend how "delightful" his situation was, "and I hope that you, too, will manage it [fatherhood] one day". He described how baby Karl cried; how he enjoyed his feeds and how, young as he was, Cécile was convinced that their son beat time with his hands. "All these are joys to me." In the days when no ante- or post-natal care existed, and when fathers' classes or their attendance at the birth was unthinkable, it is remarkable how well adjusted Felix was to this new member of his family. Neither was his love for Karl a temporary matter, to be shelved once the novelty of fatherhood had palled. In July, five months after his birth, Felix wrote again to Hiller: "My boy is fat and merry and takes after his mother in looks and manner, which is an inexpressible delight to me, because it is the best thing he can do."

Neither was Cécile reluctant to eulogise her baby son. To her brother, Karl's godfather Charles Jeanrenaud, she wrote: "I think he resembles you with his dark hair and dark blue eyes and [he] gurgles comfortably when asleep." Later, during the winter, she wrote: "He yelled 'Oooooh' on seeing snow for the first time, imagining visions of snowballing and tobogganing." In preparation for the baptism

Felix invited Albertine and Paul to visit Leipzig once Mme. Jeanrenaud had returned to Frankfurt. He hoped the spring weather would continue, "because the rooms prepared for you cannot be heated and are uncomfortable" should a cold spell present itself. Whereas the Romans had invented a central heating system, it would not be until the 20th century that homes were so heated, initially as a luxury. In the Mendelssohns' time rooms were heated by coal and wood fires only when in regular use.

After the baptism the young family moved to Berlin for the summer, whilst Felix honoured his commitment to conduct the Lower Rhine Festival in Cologne. Meanwhile, Cécile had the opportunity to observe her in-laws. Despite their pretensions to a devout Lutheran creed, and accompanying mode of behaviour, she noted that the Mendelssohns still adhered to the traditions of German Jews of the period in all their actions and character traits. To Hiller Felix wrote of how "life in Berlin is most pleasant. Every evening we debate and discuss politics and make music." They had received only three invitations to visit other houses, "and need only hear as much music as we please". As an epidemic of measles erupted the parents and baby Karl hurried back to Leipzig, but the father succumbed to this infection, which prevented his conducting *St Paul*, the task being delegated to Ferdinand David. H. E. Jacob takes Felix to task for his "trepidation" over the forthcoming birth of each of his children, and his "immoderate joy" when these had been safely accomplished. But is this fair, when taking into account the conditions that appertained during his lifetime? It is only in comparatively recent times that fathers have been encouraged to attend antenatal classes and to be present at the birth. In Felix's time, such matters were wholly outside a man's domain. Women, too, knew little of how their bodies functioned, so pain in childbirth was a duty to be endured, and, indeed, the word 'labour' is still used to describe the process of giving birth. It would not be until 1847, when Queen Victoria insisted on receiving the new drug, chloroform, to alleviate her discomfort, that matters were made easier. In any case, there were no breathing or relaxation exercises to help matters along. For a sensitive man such as Felix, he might have felt guilty for causing his wife such trauma, however irrational this thought may appear, at his selfish pleasure when the child was conceived. Added to this, Felix had to endure watching his wife's illness taking its course once Karl was born. He, too, was responsible for this, he might have perceived. "I cannot put into words all I went through during that time," he wrote to Hiller. Especially must this have applied when Dr. Carus had given Cécile such a clean bill of health four days after Karl's birth. Only a callous, insensitive father would not have shown "immoderate joy", once everything had settled into a harmonious, straightforward routine.

Fortunately, as far as anyone is aware, no such post-natal illnesses assailed Cécile when her other four children were born. Though family planning was becoming fashionable through the aegis of Thomas Malthus and others, whereby the time of

Chapter 28: "Dear, Good Children"

a child's birth could be clinically contrived, it is likely that Moses Mendelssohn's traditions were followed, and such a modern phenomenon was not practised in the Mendelssohn household. In this case, nature must have been highly imaginative, for not only did Karl arrive four days after his father's birthday, but their second child, Marie, was born on 2nd October 1839, in good time for Cécile to enjoy her own date of birth, the 10th of that month.

On 21st August, approximately six weeks before Marie's birth, Felix wrote to Fanny as to how well Cécile had borne the journey from Frankfurt to Leipzig, having attended her sister Julie's wedding to Julius Schunck. Felix admitted himself to have been "in a state of nightmare" in case anything untoward occurred; but all went smoothly. Karl proved "a pattern of goodness, only receiving one slap, screaming loudly as a result, then slept. On waking, I kissed him to show that there was no ill will. As you will guess, with sausage, bread, sweets and wine packed in the luggage, we did not go hungry." Felix still had room in his thoughts to wonder how David was faring in London, asking about a book of songs by Julius Stern, social functions and the welfare of various visitors.

On 2nd October Felix announced the joyful tidings to Leah that, "at five o'clock this afternoon, Cécile was delivered of a daughter without too much difficulty and, thank God, both are well. Just now, having complained of hunger, Cécile is eating rolls and beef broth. I am too dazed to write properly. It has been scarcely an hour and a half, and yet today's mail is still supposed to bring the good news to you. Praise, thanks and glory to God that it all went well. I hope you are happy for us and thank heaven with us. Tell all my family right away. More tomorrow." Felix then added a most interesting postscript: "When it turned out to be a girl, Cécile said to me: 'Now even your mother will be happy with me, for this is what she wanted.' I do not know what I am writing." By this slip of the pen it becomes clear that Leah favoured females, certainly to the detriment of Felix, if not Paul, of which latter she may have been in awe, in view of his flair for finance. It is significant that this letter is not included in the 1862 compilation of Felix's letters translated by Lady Wallace.

In September 1840 Fanny, back from her Italian holiday, noted in her journal how "Cécile is as lovely as ever and the children are both well". A second son, Paul, was born on 18th January 1841, and the birth of this third child must have been particularly straightforward because all we learn is the comment written by Cécile to her cousin that, having been married for four years, she had given birth to three children. On 1st May 1843 a third son, Felix, was born. During the winter of 1843-44 his mother observed that "though a charming baby, and how well-grown, with me he seems fretful and more comfortable with his nurse". This child was always delicate and, in fact, passed away in 1852 at the age of nine, to be buried alongside his father in the family vault in Berlin.

However great Felix's frustration at his lack of activity in Berlin, love of his children was always paramount. In 1843 Felix wrote a letter to his eldest son, Karl, then five years old, thanking him for a letter he must have written. He asked him to greet "Mama, Marie, Paul and little Felix" and everyone they knew. A few words were written in capitals so that Karl could read them. Though the letter was especially written for Cécile's birthday, Mendelssohn showed equality towards his children by sharing her letter with them. On 6th February 1844 Felix wrote to Schleinitz in Leipzig: "The children's health seems to be improving, little by little, and, as soon as recovery is certain, I shall visit" after a whooping cough epidemic. However, Mendelssohn still had thoughts for the illness of Schleinitz's wife, expressing the hope that she, too, would soon recover from her illness. Yet a measles epidemic followed the whooping cough and, as little Felix was far more badly affected by this extra infection, Mendelssohn was summoned to Frankfurt, as the doctor predicted that the youngest child would not survive.

The Mendelssohns' fifth and last child, a daughter, Elisabeth (Lilli), was born on 19th September 1845. When, during the next year, Rebecka's youngest daughter Florentina (Flora) was born, the Italian nurse whom Cécile had engaged to care for Lilli was transferred back to her home to stay with the Dirichlets. Though Fanny was told that the girl was "quite nice", such a description is bland when compared with the letter written to Rebecka by Felix. "At a farewell meal she shared with the family, she was so upset at departing that I felt the need to talk volubly in her own language, as she could barely utter a word. When she called out her farewell phrases, she cried so much that I felt like doing the same. I thank God for the recovery of Rebecka and our little one, Felix, during the past two weeks. I, too, have felt unwell for the past fortnight but, four days ago, the doctor ceased his visits. Meat, wine and snoring should replace all I have lost by sighing, groaning and swearing, and we shall be in our own state again with everything right and bright."

Charles Horsley wrote of the Mendelssohn children as "admirably brought up, becoming most excellent members of society". He saw it as an advantage that none of them inherited their father's talent for music, citing the plight of Karl Mozart. Moritz Hauptmann, Horsley's former instructor, knew Wolfgang's son personally: "Though a sound and learned musician, he constantly complained of the want of success in his profession, giving as his reason the superlative greatness of his father, causing everyone to imagine it impossible that any scrap of the Mozartian mantle had not fallen onto the shoulders of his son." Of the Mendelssohn parents, Horsley wrote of their "extremes of temperament, meeting to mutual advantage. Cécile's calm, unexcitable temperament was precisely the reverse of her husband's. She was beautiful in person and accomplished in mind, devoted to husband and children." Horsley remembered their father, on the other hand, "crawling on the floor, whinnying like a pony or pulling along a toy ship on a rope, unmindful of his good clothes".

In 1846 Felix gave a synopsis of the routine his family maintained. The early mornings were given over to composing and, "at ten o'clock, Karl sits with me,

Chapter 28: "Dear, Good Children"

Figure 10. Pencil drawing of Mendelssohn family group.

reading and ciphering", as he called handwriting. At 5 p.m. Felix tried to instil into his son's head "some notion of geography and spelling". Felix spent time with Marie to teach her to play the piano: "Cécile was amused when, teaching her the scale of C major, I forgot the correct fingering, instructing Marie to turn her thumb over at E, rather than F." Like other children who play games relating to their parents' professions, so it was with the older Mendelssohn children. Felix wrote of Karl, Marie and Paul pretending to audition, "screeching and howling and reprimanding one another for the noise", as they must have heard their father do when auditioning singers. Writing to Charlotte Moscheles apologising for delay in correspondence on Cécile's behalf, he excused her on the grounds that "there is so much to manage and arrange with three little sopranos in the house. That is why you return your kind message through me."

As well as all the domestic tasks involved when looking after a family, Cécile made time to play with the children as much as Felix. "Here comes Cécile with Karl, the latter with a live crayfish that he sets to crawling on the floor, while Marie and Paul shriek with laughter. Even Felix looks about him intelligently with his blue eyes", even though still a baby. Cécile observed that, when the two elder children were little, "Karl, feeling himself too grown-up to be playing with his toy sheep on wheels, bequeathed him to Marie". From Interlaken in 1847 the mother wrote of two-year-old Lilli, evidently highly intelligent, talking of Albertine's fall in the cellar of their home in Berlin. But it is Karl, the eldest, of whom most is recorded. He was a great favourite with visitors who came to Leipzig; witness the time when, after Mendelssohn's sixth visit to London in 1840, Moscheles and Chorley returned with him to Leipzig. Moscheles invited the boy to watch him shave. It would not be until 1903 that King Gillette, an American travelling salesman, marketed his disposable razor blades and the safety razor, allowing the US government to order 3½ million razors and 36 million blades for the army in World War I. During the 1840s the aptly named cut-throat razor was the only implement in use, so care would have had to be taken by spectator and user. Karl was equally devoted to H. F. Chorley, his 'uncle Shorley'. The admiration was mutual, enough for the guest to compose a sonnet in which he called Karl "that blooming, bright-eyed boy with his infantile grace".

Another visitor, this time to Frankfurt, recollected the children. W. S. Rockstro shared a family lunch with the Mendelssohns. Felix was "full of fun, with a joke for each of the little ones: Karl seven, Marie six, and Paul nearly four". Two-year-old Felix must have been looked after by his nurse on that occasion; Lilli would make her appearance later that year. "Each member of the party was asked to cover the lower part of the face to represent some animal or bird. 'I am an eagle,' Papa began the game, placing his hands in a position that made the likeness absolutely striking. Cécile resembled a hare, Karl a roe-deer, Paul a bullfinch, and myself a setter." As Oscar Wilde was later to recall, "every father should know how to tell fairy tales to his children". Not only was Felix adept in recounting these, but also legends from

Chapter 28: "Dear, Good Children"

the past, many of which he set to music. Schumann remembered how Mendelssohn invented games for his children and their playmates, and drew "funny doodles" to amuse them.

As a child Felix had enjoyed theatricals, and a sketch exists of his taking part in a production of *Rumpelstiltskin,* by the Brothers Grimm. As an adult he regarded as "telepathic" the content of his sisters' letters when such incidents were mentioned. "This is the subject the children have been discussing for the past four days, as they have had the Grimms' stories read to them," Felix wrote. Another children's book, von Brentano's *Des Knaben Wunderhorn,* was equally popular. Felix set one of this collection of poems to music, though Mahler's equivalent would be the best known. The 1840s also saw Hans Christian Andersen's fairy tales published, matching those of 1812 by Wilhelm and Jakob Grimm in popularity with children.

Felix painted a portrait of his two elder children, about which the artist Bendemann commented that they were "too stiff", according to his biographer. Felix retorted that fear might have contributed to this. This is likely, especially if Karl and Marie had had it dinned into them, if not by Felix then certainly by their nursemaid, that they had to keep absolutely still and were not to move on any account. The same still applies when children have photographs taken today. Biographers constantly remind readers that Mendelssohn's sketches of people are never as convincing as his scenes from nature.

Felix loved other people's children equally well. On 7th February 1839 his uncle congratulated Sebastian Hensel on his letter as being "well written and in the proper style" – an encouraging response, unlike the catalogue of faults his own father had spluttered at Felix. Sebastian was thanked on behalf of the 15-month-old Karl for some chocolates, explaining that "he is too dumb to write himself, otherwise he would do so. Cécile also thanks you for her lovely presents. Have you taken any sleigh rides, as happens in Leipzig? I am pleased that you have seen an elephant. They are my favourite animals, so strong and powerful, yet so gentle, friendly and wise. Some day, you, too, must become so." In 1847, almost at the end of his life, Felix assessed his nephew's artistic potential: "If you are to become a professional artist you should contemplate nature lovingly, clearly, intimately and inwardly, studying all your life long and thoroughly taking account of the outer contour and inner structure that is formed in – say – a house, a tree, a mountain, as to how it should look if it is to appear beautiful." The picture, he continued, "should be produced initially in sepia or on a smoked plate to show how it should, or can, look. It would be good in any medium if only it testifies to your love of substance. [I hope] you will not mind this sermon from a screech owl, as I often am."

Felix wrote about Rebecka's two boys, Walter and Ernst. Of the latter, he wrote: "He is now at an age where he must be animated by conviction and enthusiasm" for a specific occupation. "I have confidence in him that he will not abuse a profession that he might later wish to reject or which might eventually become indifferent or boring [to him]. But it is all the same to me, whatever he may choose, or how high or low his path may be, if only he pursue it happily. It is his decision, and his alone, that will be valid...in which no one can assist or advise him... I believe he will...do well, whatever he decides to do." To Walter, his uncle wrote, as with Sebastian, regarding his art lessons: "You might have drawn me by this time; a horse or two; a skirmish; a siege; or Gregory at Canossa; or you might write. Tell me about what you eat or about what lessons you do; whether you have found the place where Cicero stood; or whether confetti can still be obtained on the Via Condotti and the Corso. You are now in the midst of the carnival and everything about Rome is interesting." Felix reminisced about his own Italian holiday when Rebecka's family made the same journey.

Since letters were passed around the large clan of Mendelssohn friends and relatives, Felix must have read of Sebastian Hensel's and the Dirichlet children's occupations when abroad. Rebecka wrote to Fanny saying how pleased she was that Sebastian had recovered from his dislocated elbow, sustained when falling from a tree: "This is better than falling through his exams," she joked, "for which I am convinced that credit must go not only to his teachers for his success, but to his parents especially. However, the blockhead must take care of himself, since what is the point of having such a good brain if he continues to act Punchinello with his acrobat's legs?" Of the young Dirichlets, Rebecka wrote of their yelling "Passa porto" whenever they entered a new location, imitating the officials. They played with children of another family when in Rome, waiting together when the weather was fine and playing indoors when not. "The children are really very good and most amusing," their mother wrote. One evening Walter tried to extinguish the lights in the downstairs passage with an 'avena', a reed pipe mentioned in Virgil's *Aeneid*. On another occasion they saw some camels, unique in Europe, except in a menagerie, "all crowded together and deprived of their freedom of movement", as Rebecka reported. "These camels seem to be phlegmatic and tame. None were standing, kneeling or lying down, but ruminating and staring at their visitors' queer faces." The Dirichlet family visited the Luminari carnival at Pisa, slept in luxurious accommodation at Perugia, "where even the children's quarters boasted red and white damask". Instead of taking Ernst for walks, Minna the maid visited the Uffizi Gallery with him when in Florence. The boys "shouted like mad when a bell rang in their lodgings. They got on well with the passengers on the crossing to Sicily, and this was mutual. They were enraptured at the smallness of the beds, though these were not to their mother's liking. Whilst in Rome, Felix's 'Children's Symphony' was performed for their amusement.

Whereas the original two Children's Symphonies were written for Rebecka and Paul, nothing appears to have been dedicated to Felix's own children, though others were to benefit from his musicianship. The Benecke children, Cécile's relatives, for whom Felix wrote his Op. 72, 'Six Children's Pieces', are an example. These

Chapter 28: "Dear, Good Children"

compositions were written whilst staying with this family at their home in Camberwell Green, south-east London – then a country village – in 1842. In this country, for no apparent reason, they are known as the 'Six Christmas Pieces', though Felix's seventh visit to London occurred in the summer. Jacob observes the "quick, ecstatic breathing" conveyed by some of the pieces, whilst broadcaster David Huckvale considers them "too advanced" for a child to play. Conversely, Roger Nichols declares them to be "not beyond any talented child pianist", though he defeats his own argument by adding that "it needs the calibre of Daniel Barenboim to fathom them". Incidentally, Marek claims that it was these so-called 'Christmas Pieces' that prompted Charles Dickens to write *A Christmas Carol* in 1843.

The Benecke children were responsible for an even better known piece, Mendelssohn's *Song without Words*, No. 6 of Book Five, Op. 62, the so-called 'Spring Song'. The alternative title is 'Camberwell Green', which, if the piece must have a title, makes far better sense. Frau Benecke, Cécile's aunt, whom the journalist F. G. Edwards is said to have interviewed in 1885, recalled how an excursion had been arranged to Windsor. Felix did not accompany the party, the reason being that Cécile thought "he wished to write something". On the family's return, Felix played his melody. "He was very fond of romping with the children, and they with him, and the quaver rests in the treble of this lied and the frequent staccato notes in the bass represent the constant withdrawal of hands from the pianoforte, in order to defend himself against the repeated attacks of the little ones, who, being alone with him, wanted to drag him away from the pianoforte and into the garden for a romp... The autographed manuscript is dated 1st June 1842, the day of the picnic," Edwards reported. During the same interview Edwards was informed of Felix's "childish traits", as he described Mendelssohn's behaviour. After a dinner, when the guests had included Benedict, Horsley and Moscheles, someone asked Felix for "some playing. 'Oh, yes, we shall have some playing,' Mendelssohn replied, and he at once marched the musicians off, not to play the pianoforte, but the game of hen and chickens in the garden. Horsley, who was not so young as the others [presumably this was William, the father], was in fits of laughter as he stood at the window watching the overgrown boys at their play, Mendelssohn being the life and soul of the game."

During the 1842 visit to London Felix played leapfrog with the Benecke children's tutor. As mentioned, Felix Moscheles recalled ball games, presumably in Regent's Park, near their home in Chester Place: "He could throw my ball farther than anyone else and he could run faster too, but, ...for all that, I could catch him. One of my achievements as a little boy in a black velveteen blouse was the impersonation of what we called 'the dead man' ('the dying man' would have been more correct). The dying man in the blouse was stretched full length, say, some three feet, on the Brussels carpet. Mendelssohn and my father would be at the piano, improvising a running accompaniment to my performance, and, between us, we illustrated musically and dramatically the thousand spasms of the expiring hero." The Benecke children were equally party to such improvisations at the piano. Edwards recorded how Felix had composed "a very amusing bear's dance, with the title 'The Real, Genuine, Warranted Bärentanz, as Performed with Unbounded Applause at the Denmark Hill Chamber Concerts and Dedicated, by Permission, to the Gooseberry-eaters of Castle Benecke, by their Humble Colleague and Servant, Felix Mendelssohn Bartholdy, usually called Peter Meffert'. The piece is on a rapidly reiterated pedal base [with] the lowest F on the pianoforte, each hand playing at the extreme ends of the keyboard," Edwards reported. "At the end is the direction 'da capo [repeat]', very often." Another instance of Felix imitating a bear's dance at the piano was recalled by Max Reger's wife. Her grandmother remembered how her two-year-old daughter (Reger's future mother-in-law) "sat on Mendelssohn's lap, whilst he pounded away at the piano keys. Asked why there was so much noise, Felix asked what else he could do when your Gustel wants to hear a bear dance."

It is a pity that such memoirs exist of other children's entertainments with Felix when they do not for his own children. In view of his constantly childlike pleasure in amusing them, who knows how many similar activities took place with his own brood? Sketches demonstrate how happy they were. As well as the sheep mentioned earlier, another drawing depicts the elder children looking at a picture book with their nurses, the tea table not yet cleared, on which cakes and biscuits remain. The sketch is dated 17th September 1844, when Felix was a baby and Lilli not yet born. But, as with the coach journey between Frankfurt and Leipzig of 1839, discipline was practised if considered appropriate. When, for example, little Paul struck his nurse and refused to obey a command, Cécile asked him to apologise, which he would not. Thereupon Felix slapped him, but he confided to his sisters how upset he had been in having to take such action. "I felt relieved when Paul appeared to have forgotten the incident the next day," he admitted.

From Bad Soden Felix wrote to Klingemann: "The children are as brown as Moors and play all day in the garden with Johann. I am watching them from the window", and he expressed joy at his family's health after his eighth visit to London in 1844. "I, too, have recovered from my fatigue after two days of sleeping and eating... We have early strawberries for breakfast. We have supper at half past eight in the evening and, by ten o'clock, we are all asleep." Though there were "no oranges, lemons or palms" at Bad Soden, he reminded Rebecka of the beautiful flowers, a sketch of which he enclosed that Cécile had painted. "There are also uncommonly good puddings and dumplings. If you do not think much of these, ask Walter, and he will side with the Germans, I know." As for the Mendelssohn children: "They ride on capricious donkeys and have to be watched and their hands held as they trot through the forest." Felix added: "I relish this peaceful life, without dress clothes, visiting cards, horses and carriages, but with donkeys,

Chapter 28: "Dear, Good Children"

flowers, music paper and sketchbooks." He added how Paul, though not yet four years old, "bargains with the woman who sells cherries".

It is clear that, now Sebastian had reached his teens, Fanny missed her nephews and nieces. She reported that Walter's pure white goat and the gardener's black and white, and grey animals, had all become mothers. "They appear to have copied their owners by producing males." As for her dietary decision: "I can consciously promise not to pollute my inside with food from any animal that has been part of the family. I disliked young goat [caporetto] in any case when I was in Italy." Sebastian, despite his deep voice, took pleasure in the young goats and Fanny joked that she was tempted to give Walter the market price for his when the time came for the herd to be culled. For Felix's children, Fanny had a tree planted for each of them. Rebecka, meanwhile, was pleased how satisfactorily her new nurse for Flora had become, having previously cared for Lilli. "You know by experience, dear Cécile, how seldom one likes the entourage of a baby. Your only compensation is that Lilli can devote more attention to her mother."

When Cécile and Felix had taken their holiday in Switzerland Felix expressed pleasure as to how well they had been looked after in Frankfurt. In 1847, when Cécile arranged a further Swiss holiday, the whole family travelled there. Albertine and Paul had stayed with them but were delayed at Mannheim, and throughout their journey to Berlin the children had kept asking, "Where is uncle now?" Albertine had sustained "an illness" at Mannheim and "the little one", presumably their youngest child, had experienced "an indisposition at the railway station". Felix, as ever, became anxious for news as the anticipated correspondence was delayed, and wrote: "The weather is more dreary than weeks past, not only on account of the thunderstorms, but in every respect." Felix and his family enjoyed "walking together, weather permitting", whilst "I completed a few sketches in Indian ink". Each morning the children took lessons with their father, as he explained to his old friend General von Webern: "They do writing, arithmetic and Latin with me. They daub landscapes during their free time and play draughts after tea. They ask 100 wise questions that no fool can answer. (People generally phrase this in reverse, but I believe my own words to be more accurate.) My regular reply is, and always will be – and this still vibrates in my ear [from my parents]: 'You cannot understand such things yet.' The happy and unalterable faces of my children have done me good in these days." Felix noticed a neglected hobby horse half covered with snow and had thought of writing a requiem for this unwanted toy. Apart from his Op. 80 String Quartet he was unable to put his mind to writing any music, as he confided to von Webern: "I have not been able to think of writing music. Whenever I try to do so, everything seems so empty and desolate [after Fanny's death]. It is only when the children come in that I feel better, and I can watch and listen to them for hours."

Felix had on several occasions considered finding a new home in a location that he enjoyed, and Cécile too, in 1845, told her husband that, before the spring arrived, they would have to look for somewhere suitable for the children's education. "Of the cities I know, their good and bad aspects are equally balanced. I do not mind where we live, so long as we can spend several winters together." In 1847 she told Albertine: "I am only sorry Felix does not want the children with us in Berlin", where they planned to return. "I think it would cheer him during the doubtless difficult days to come", during this unsettling time when Fanny had died and Leipzigerstrasse 3 would never be the same as formerly. "They [the children] should not be shuffled back and forth too much and the sooner they can be settled into their winter lodgings, the better." In fact, the Mendelssohns moved back to Leipzig after their Swiss vacation, and it was there, on 4th November, that Felix died. Albertine and Paul looked after Karl and Paul, young Felix having died in 1851, whilst Marie and Lilli were cared for by Mme. Jeanrenaud, when Cécile followed her husband and youngest son in 1852.

Chapter 29

The Special Relationship

Part I – Mendelssohn's Musical Life in Britain

Before 1829, when Mendelssohn paid his first visit to London, music in Britain was in a sorry state. The poet and essayist Charles Lamb had encapsulated this in a verse to amuse his publisher friend, Vincent Novello:

I would not give a fig to visit
Sebastian Batch, or Bach – which is it?

Having arrived in England, Felix felt compelled to write to Adolf Marx. "The musicians are worse than ours, for there is far more competition and, unlike the craftsmen, this makes them no better... In general, they have everything that can be produced by external means – practice facilities, money and the like – but everything spiritual is lacking. Everything is rough and clumsy; no liveliness, but only speed... The musicians worship Beethoven, but edit him; they worship Mozart, but are bored with him; they worship Haydn, but rush him to death." In a later letter Mendelssohn expressed bewilderment that, though access could be gained to the Royal Library, where Handel's manuscripts were preserved, "I have heard that none of the London musicians have taken the trouble to study them". An article in the *Literary Gazette* wrote of Felix's own appearance at a gathering: "A German gentleman with a long Christian name – far too long for any Christian to pronounce with impunity – made his debut by playing Weber's *Konzertstück*, but never once 'stuck' in his performance."

Music in the home could equally leave much to be desired: Fanny Horsley described the performance of a boy named Handford who sang "a ballad called 'The Sea' and the Scottish song 'Bonnie Breast-knots'", better known as a country dance. "In his first song, Handford went down in fifths in each verse", whilst his second solo caused Fanny to "leave the room, stopping my ears; otherwise, who knows what the consequences might have been, with all his rambling about – a burst blood vessel at least". A further letter described what could happen when the same family visited a festival in Birmingham: Sophie Horsley wrote in 1834 how "we heard from Mama yesterday. They sat with the lowest people, no better than [tantalisingly, the next word is illegible]. They fight for places and eat Banbury cakes and apples." How was it that such evident connoisseurs as the Horsley parents did not purchase tickets for a more salubrious part of the hall?

But not all was doom and gloom in the 19th-century English musical world. Even Felix praised the Philharmonic Society, which had been founded in 1813, as "outstanding; full of fire and strength. The basses and violins play quite splendidly." And so it should have done; among the patrons were some of the most celebrated musicians of the time, even remembered today. There was Johann Salomon, who had sponsored Haydn's visits to London and for whom his last 12 symphonies had been written; Muzio Clementi, the piano manufacturer, composer and teacher for that instrument; Sir George Smart, who also conducted at Covent Garden and who had been responsible for Weber's opera *Oberon* having been premiered in London. Apart from this prestigious orchestra, the 'City Concerts' had begun five years before Mendelssohn's first visit, followed by the Concert of Ancient Music, allowing London to have a thriving musical life. Musical festivals took place annually in provincial cities such as Birmingham, Leeds and Norwich. The oldest, which still continues, is the Three Choirs Festival, taking place in rotation in Gloucester, Hereford and Worcester Cathedrals. The oratorio was popular and had been since Handel's time. Whilst his works had pride of place with choral societies, these would be joined by Haydn's *Creation* and, later, those by Mendelssohn himself. On Friday 7th October 1836, for instance, the second performance ever of *St Paul* would be given at St Peter's Church, Liverpool, with Smart conducting and illustrious singers of the period engaged as soloists; concert tickets were sold out several days previously.

The patrons of the Philharmonic Society had invited Cherubini and Spontini to London, and had also donated £100 to Beethoven to help him during his last illness in 1827. Smart had undertaken to perform "a strange and peculiar work" of the composer – the 'Choral' Symphony. Yet, despite such a progressive approach, Smart delayed the first concert at which Mendelssohn's works were to be performed. Marek justifies such an attitude: "Perhaps he did not think the 1st Symphony good enough for his musicians, or, more likely, Felix, accustomed to success, became impatient and blamed the almost inevitable slowness at getting started on ill will." In a letter home Felix complained that Smart "brushed me off with excuses", calling the conductor "an intriguing, deceitful and untruthful man". Yet Smart's reluctance is comprehensible to anyone who knew the facts. Had he not called at Leipzigerstrasse 3 whilst in Berlin, on 16th October 1825, and heard Fanny and Felix playing the piano, giving Fanny a set of Maundy money on his departure? In other words, as far as Smart was concerned, the elder children of "this remarkable family" were destined to be nothing more than amateurs. Abraham would have intimated, as likely as not, that Felix was to work in the family bank, or take up a position with the Prussian government, whilst Fanny would be a wife and mother – the only course suitable for a woman. Smart had recommended "young Mendelssohn" to visit London when he was 16, but it was only four years later that his advice had been heeded. How could Smart know that, according to Abraham, Paris was the "be all and end all" for European culture, or of Felix's triumph with Bach's *St Matthew Passion*?

It was not until 25th May, towards the end of the 1828-29 concert season, that Felix made his debut as composer and conductor at the Argyll Rooms, Regent Street. The programme included his first mature symphony, sometimes known as his 13th String Symphony, in C minor. Though the work has been likened to Mozart's 40th Symphony and works by Beethoven, Herbert Kupferberg redresses the balance, pointing out its "drive and freshness". The third movement was, on this occasion, replaced by an orchestral arrangement of his scherzo from the Op. 20 String Octet. Despite Smart's reluctance to acknowledge Mendelssohn's worth, the 'Diary of a Dilettante' in *The Harmonicon* wrote: "He is the son of a rich banker in Berlin and, I believe, the grandson of the Jewish philosopher and elegant writer." Biographers and broadcasters so often eulogise Abraham's letters of introduction as responsible for Felix's welcome into London society, social and musical, but this assertion must be countered. More accurately, Felix's success can be attributed to the high reputation still prevalent that his grandfather, Moses Mendelssohn, had engendered.

The symphony was dedicated to the Philharmonic Society and, after its finale, Felix, who conducted from the piano, received enthusiastic applause. The next day he wrote to the secretary: "Its success must have been due to the playing of the orchestra and any indulgence I received cannot have been on account of any talent I may possess, but to my youth. The flattering reception I was given will encourage me to labour, so as to justify the hopes entertained of me." Music journals wrote lavishly of Mendelssohn's first appearance in London: "Through this work, Mendelssohn has gained a reputation and name more than sufficient to gratify that proud ambition...to grant him singular success." Words were "superfluous to describe the graceful, soothing, airy, sweet and fanciful qualities of his melodies. Those best fit to judge found the scherzo pre-eminent, having never been equalled, certainly not surpassed." A further performance of the symphony was given on 10th June at a concert organised by a Mr. Charles Nicholson, again at the Argyll Rooms, where the Regent Palace Hotel now stands. "Its great spirit, accuracy and effect" were reported. An encore had been requested at the first concert for the adagio, but Felix did not expect this at the present performance. Indeed, so impressed was the committee by his symphony that, on 29th November, as the result of a meeting, Felix was given honorary membership of the orchestra.

Though his parents detested their son's adopting music as a profession, they were shrewd enough to know how and when to take advantage of any perquisites that might accrue. Not only were they able to purchase pianos of superior quality at competitive prices through Felix's contacts, but they knew upon whom to call when funds were needed for charitable purposes. Thus Nathan Mendelssohn, wishing to raise money for the relief of floods that engulfed Silesia, asked his nephew to help. Schima Kaufman states that Felix's conscience was aroused by an incident from his boyhood. Whilst staying with his uncle, eight groschen were proffered to the bellows blower, so that Felix could play the organ at a Breslau church, but the money was refused. Whatever the truth of this anecdote, since no other Mendelssohn biography records it, Felix's endeavour to boost the coffers was prodigious. On 10th July 1829 he wrote home that his time was "almost exclusively taken up with arranging what would be called 'the most brilliant event of the season'". Members of the House of Lords were asked to help with publicity and any musician of consequence in London came forward to offer his services, almost all waiving their usual fee to appear at the concert. The most remarkable coup must have been Mmes. Sontag and Malibran singing together. No soloist was permitted, on account of there being so many applicants to perform; only ensembles took part and, indeed, many musicians were turned away. "Even so, the concert will last until the next day," Felix wrote. Blunt snipes that the agreement of the two prima donnas to perform together was not entirely altruistic. Sontag had asked Mendelssohn to accompany her at an entertainment. "This did not happen, due to Smart's malevolence." Mendelssohn must have therefore felt that Mme. Sontag owed him a favour and Malibran, not to be outdone and fearing she would lose face if she did not take part, swallowed her pride and agreed to sing in tandem with Sontag. "By request", the *Midsummer Night's Dream* Overture was performed, but the most significant item on the programme appears to have been the Concerto for Two Pianos that Moscheles had written for the occasion, for Mendelssohn and himself as soloists.

Although details of this piece are given in Chapter 20, 'Mendelssohn as soloist', no description can be found of any other item on the repertoire. So crowded was the concert hall that ladies sat among the bassoons and horns, whilst one was seen to have perched herself on the kettledrum. But such bizarre seating arrangements were not unique. At a concert organised by Moscheles during the previous year, a member of the audience was heard to remark that there were "more belles than bows in the orchestra". Nevertheless, not withstanding this strange circumstance, unanimous praise flowed from the musical press at this charity concert. "The whole concert was brilliant," wrote *The Athenaeum*, which eulogised Mendelssohn as "a truly remarkable man, one of the features of the occasion, putting Sontag and Malibran into the shade. His musical genius is almost transcendent. His love of, and interest in, music is unparalleled but, above all, his modesty blinds him to the success he has cultivated."

In a postscript to his uncle Nathan, Felix wrote: "Please excuse me for writing nothing but concert, concert, concert for, when my heart is full, my pen overflows and my feelings are absolutely justified." Yet, however self-effacing, he cannot have been unaware of his rise in credibility through this venture. He exhorted his family: "For God's sake, preserve my concert notices, as these are meant to amuse me at some future date, so do not burn them." This chance aside must lead a student of Mendelssohn to wonder just how many papers of his were burnt, contrary to myth.

In Scotland, Felix was introduced to musical notabilities of the time: "We hope to…see a bagpipe competition and Scottish folk dancing to amuse ourselves," he wrote home. "We also have engagements to dine with Mr. Findlay Dunn and to make music with Mr. Wood"; alas, neither of these personalities is covered by the usual reference books. However, Mendelssohn and Klingemann did meet "Mr. Thompson", whilst in Edinburgh. This was John Thompson, a Scottish classical composer whose works, which Mendelssohn admired, display a strong Schubertian influence. Fanny also wrote of Thompson that she liked him "best of all the Britons I know". Felix wrote of hearing "a marching tune that amused me. It sounds quite funny in F sharp major, which I intend to use, but do not know how or when." Though his Op. 28 Fantasy, sometimes known as the 'Scottish' Sonata, begins in F sharp minor, there is a part in the major key that sounds remarkably like a march, so it could have been here that the tune was employed.

After his coach accident (see Chapter 3 and part II of this chapter), Felix convalesced at the home of Sir Thomas Attwood, organist at St Paul's Cathedral and former pupil of Mozart. It was here that he discovered a manuscript of Weber's opera *Euryanthe*, which he studied meticulously. Felix had always had an intuition that there should have been a passage for brass in the score, but not until then did he realise that his erstwhile hunch had been correct. He had written to his family about Weber's "shabby treatment" when in London, but he need not have been so distressed. As the music critic Ernest Newman pointed out, having suffered from tuberculosis for some years, Weber had flouted medical advice and had insisted on coming to England to fulfil a lucrative commitment, so that his debt-ridden family could live more comfortably. Smart not only arranged for Weber's last opera, *Oberon*, to be performed, but found him accommodation with Herr Heinke, where Felix himself lodged. Here Weber had died in 1826, having lived practically rent-free. Newman wrote that Weber's wife Caroline complained how her husband "grumbled about anywhere payment was required. The only item that cost less in England than in his native Germany was the price of a haircut." This might have accounted for the fact that Germans who visited had longer hair than was fashionable in England. Perhaps, had Felix known the full story, he might not have felt such hostility towards Smart, since Weber had always been one of Mendelssohn's favourite composers.

During Mendelssohn's second visit to London, in 1832, admiration for him had continued. Sophie Horsley had noticed several English translations of his songs in Mori's music shop. Felix was taken aback by his own reception at a concert. "I was obliged to bow left and right and to shake hands with 200 people, including many ladies from abroad". It was only in England, of all the countries Felix had toured, "where I can share my musical ideas, who can look at a score and know how to play the piece". Elsewhere, "when the composition is finished, I have to lock it away in a trunk without anyone's having enjoyed it". In England Felix considered himself "spoilt", with so many friends around him who were skilled musicians. In Italy he had written: "Here, I miss someone with whom I can share everything openly, who can look at my music whilst it is in process of being written, making the task twice as pleasurable to me, with whom I can relax completely and from whom I can honestly learn, but, since trees do not grow all the way to heaven, as they say...I shall just have to hum to myself in Italy." How pleased, therefore, he must have felt when the Horsley family joined his circle of friends. Felix could call "any time" at their home, 1 High Row, Kensington Gravel Pits, where Notting Hill Gate tube station now stands, to discuss plans for his future compositions. It was here, according to Charles Horsley, that the seeds of Mendelssohn's "immortals" were sown – his *Fair Melusine* and *Hebrides* Overtures. This latter was performed at a Philharmonic concert, because the Argyll Rooms had been burnt down in 1830. The King's, (later Her Majesty's) Theatre was now the venue.

Felix wrote how "quaint" the piece sounded "among a variety of Rossini pieces. The audience received me and my work with extreme kindness and the work went admirably. This, despite the building having been so cold that ladies were advised to carry foot-muffs and the gentlemen to wear clogs. A further concert was to take place at Vaughan's Concert Rooms, but "I am sure you must be sick of hearing about so many concerts," he wrote to his family with his exasperating self-effacement. "I receive numbers of commissions from all sides, some so gratifying that I regret that I am unable to accept them in view of the time shortage," he was able to continue. A publisher had asked him for settings of the morning and evening service for the Church of England, which Felix planned to write on his return to Berlin. It was at this time that the first book of his 'Original Melodies for the pianoforte' was published.

Novello's, choosing to call them *Songs without Words*, caused these pieces to catch on with the public. Marek scorns their "having become too popular with freshly perfumed young lady pianists. " If such is the case, he is justified. It is a false notion that "anyone can play these trifles. Only when played by a top-class pianist, ideally a male, the muscles in whose hands can allow the requisite amount of control and deftness, will these melodies regain the reputation they deserve."

Of his G minor Piano Concerto that was performed at a concert, with Felix as soloist, Mendelssohn reported how "the audience went wild with joy and declared it my best work". *The Harmonicon* was evidently of the same mind, calling the composer "the most remarkable gentleman of the age". But, sadly, this halcyon period in Felix's life had to end. As described in Chapter 19, 'Conductor and Director', he was dragooned back to Berlin, at Abraham's instigation, in an attempt to replace Zelter as director of the Berlin Singakademie. "People buy from me what I write," Felix explained, "and for the present I can live from that, and I wish to continue to compose. Also, I must soon pay a third visit to London, and I have some very remarkable plans which I hope soon to finalise." On 7th February 1833 he told Attwood that, though he was working on his 'Italian' Symphony, this was "with difficulty, as I feel so depressed". With hindsight this mood is understandable, what with Abraham badgering him for an oratorio, if not an opera, and the possible delayed reaction of the Singakademie debacle. "Moscheles should not expect too much from me" as regards his commissions from the Philharmonic Society that he would conduct in the spring of 1833; "They will contain traces of moodiness which can only slowly be shaken off and by dint of an effort." Felix felt that he had never composed anything and had to learn anew such a skill.

"But, now that I have got into battle trim, my last things will sound far better." These "last things" comprised his 'Italian' Symphony, an aria for soprano, *Infelice* (published posthumously as Op. 90 and Op. 94 respectively) and his *Hebrides* Overture. Of the latter, *The Harmonicon* stated that the work would stay in the musical repertoire "for years to come", and so it has proved. This can be to Mendelssohn's disadvantage, since many of his other works are swamped in the popular imagination by the overture. For these commissions Felix was paid 720 Rheinthalers. The copyright would revert to him after two years and the orchestra would play these works "at all times". It was agreed by the Philharmonic committee that "Mr. Mendelssohn should have the privilege of publishing any arrangement as soon as seen fit after the first performance at a Philharmonic concert". Felix's letter confirmed "the great honour conferred upon me by such an arrangement". Stratton wryly comments: "This was the best piece of business to fall to the composer, the sum of 100 guineas being well worth accepting."

On arriving for his third visit to London, Felix fell into Klingemann's arms; neither did his friendship with Moscheles pall: "He is without envy, jealousy or miserable egotism, which is very cheering." He arranged to send Rebecka some songs "ready for Christmas" and, meanwhile, suggested he order his piano arrangement of the *Hebrides* Overture, though "I think that my Melusine [piano arrangement] will be the best thing I have ever done in this regard". He said he would send the score as soon as it had been completed. Abraham had opined that "a nation who had not produced its own composer cannot be said to be musical". English composers were, admittedly, few and far between during that period but, having accompanied his son on Felix's fourth visit to London that same year, his father was amazed how true his son's report was that more music could be heard in one day here than Berlin could produce in a week. Abraham would have been equally surprised as to how greatly his son's music was admired in London. On their return Felix thanked his father for accompanying him, especially in view of his lack of enthusiasm for England, his failing sight and, above all, his injured leg: "Though my advice, which you followed for the first time, proved unfortunate and caused us so much anxiety and unease, you never once reproached me. I am so pleased that you are in such good health and spirits."

During the years between his fourth and fifth visits to England, correspondence ricocheted back and forth between England and Germany. Felix wrote to Moscheles that he and Fanny would play a trio from "the big, grass-green volume" of his works. On 7th February 1834 Felix stated that his *Infelice* was finished: "I feel at home in Düsseldorf, with as much official corruption as I need and plenty of time to myself." He had "done a great deal of patching and polishing" on the variations on Weber's *Preciosa* that he and Moscheles had composed, "especially on those restless passages of mine". In the same letter Felix sought permission to dedicate his Op. 28 Fantasia (his 'Scottish' Sonata) to Moscheles, and his Op. 29 *Rondo brillant*. The purpose in quoting this otherwise banal anecdote is to point out the strange convention observed in musical etiquette: "I realise it is not good form to dedicate two pieces at once to a person but, despite this old piece of procedure, I have set my heart on flouting such a convention." Klingemann thanked Felix for composing a song to be sung at a party given by the Horsleys. He mentioned to the family how Felix had planned to visit England in the spring of 1835 – which, like his proposed visit of 1836, did not take place. Glimpses are discovered of English musical life during these years. Though Spohr's music was popular, Sophie Horsley, having heard his 2nd Symphony, liked it less on the second hearing, "though some parts are still fine". Mme. Stockhausen (née Margarethe Schmuck) sang "oratorio and lieder arias". Mme. Malibran sang 'Horns in the Woods', gaining "greater applause in the second part than Mme. Grisi" at a further recital. Malibran's husband, Bériot, also performed, "but not his own Violin Concerto, which I like better than anything he plays". Neither was William Horsley overlooked in the welter of correspondence. Mendelssohn congratulated him on his motet and asked him for further output. Whether Felix was being tactful, or stating an actual fact, he said that "it would take a great deal of practice" before the orchestra at Düsseldorf would be able to do justice to the work. "I hope, however, to have it performed some time during the year. The phrase 'One God' is worthy to be sung at any venue, including St. Paul's Cathedral. Other parts are beautiful and could be extended."

In order to make his long-promised fifth visit in 1837, Felix had to break off his honeymoon. The Birmingham Festival had begun in 1768 to raise funds for a local hospital; its last celebration was in 1912. Birmingham Town Hall would be graced by various illustrious musicians through the years. Singers included Mmes. Grisi, Malibran and Patti. Instrumentalists such as Paganini, Clara Schumann and Liszt performed. Saint-Saëns praised the singers selected by Elgar's friend William Stockley, when the French composer conducted his own compositions at the festival. Grieg, when conducting, had to stand on a stool because he was so small. In 1900, Elgar's *Dream of Gerontius* would receive its first, ill-starred performance at that venue. As far as the 1837 event was concerned Mendelssohn must be regarded as the most versatile participant. Not only did he direct *St Paul* but he gave an organ recital and took part as soloist in his 2nd (D minor) Piano Concerto at its premiere. Joseph Moore was in charge of the festival, and it was he who had invited Felix. Having made his wealth from the manufacture and sale of buttons, he appears to have been unable to come to terms with his rise in status. "He writes his letters on the borders of printed music festival programmes, which go post-free, and so do his letters, to cheat the post," Mendelssohn wrote in his honeymoon diary, disparagingly.

An even worse taste was left in Felix's mouth by the contumely between the Birmingham Festival committee and that of the Sacred Harmonic Society, which met at Exeter Hall, London. The latter, whose conductor, Joseph Surman, was a shoemaker, comprised workpeople who loved singing. A performance of *St Paul* had been given in May 1837 and its composer had agreed to conduct a further performance in September. However, on arriving in London, Felix received a letter from Moore, advising that a resolution had been passed "to prohibit Mendelssohn etc." from overseeing the performance until after the Birmingham Festival at the end of August. An article was printed in the London newspapers, which sided with Moore. This placed Felix in a quandary as to what to do next. Klingemann suggested that the most suitable person to approach was the journalist William Ayrton, "as he has a great knowledge of England and English customs in such matters". It was only later that Felix learnt that Ayrton himself had written the article, taking Moore's side against "the Exeter Hall people", as Mendelssohn called the Sacred Harmonic Society, of whom Moore and his cohorts were jealous. This annoyed Mendelssohn, who called the whole incident "unseemly". The problem was resolved by Felix taking no part in the London performance, except to congratulate the choir for their "beautiful manner" of presentation, according to Rockstro.

On 8th September Felix played the piano to Rosen and a young friend, Thomas Spring-Rice, whose descendant, Sir Cecil Spring-Rice, wrote the hymn 'I Vow to Thee, my Country', and whose wife would become a far-sighted, compassionate philanthropist. During the recital Samuel Wesley's daughter Eliza called, together with an unspecified lady, asking him to inscribe pieces that Felix had written for their autograph albums. Miss Wesley's album, now in the British Library, shows the nine-bar, four-part canon that Mendelssohn had dedicated to her. Samuel Wesley had been an early champion of Bach's music and, when Felix met him a month before he died, he was deeply moved at such a meeting.

The next day Charles Horsley came to breakfast, after which Felix played to him. Having then visited a gallery where one of John Horsley's pictures was exhibited, Felix played "fugues by Bach and others" at the organ of St. John's Church, in what is now Hyde Park but was then surrounded by fields. "The strange parson's wife, a bluestocking, came up to the organ and requested a psalm tune and annoyed Mrs. Horsley, who spoke sharply to her, because she found fault with Turle, the usual organist", whose psalm settings and anthems can still be heard today. Felix visited Novello with a view to engaging his daughter Clara to sing during the forthcoming Leipzig Gewandhaus season. "I wanted to send him three new things for 30 guineas. As he appeared churlish, I broke off the discussion and thought, 'I won't give you another chance.'"

Felix found time to write to Aloys Fuchs, expressing disappointment: "I am unable to send a Handel manuscript, not even in exchange for Beethoven. It is impossible even to prise a single sheet from the Royal Library. Other private collectors who do happen to possess any of his manuscripts have paid so dearly for them that they will not give them up at any price." But the Birmingham Festival was the chief item on Felix's agenda for the 1837 visit. In June, whilst on honeymoon, he and Cécile had read of the death of King William IV, which prompted the young bridegroom to hope the forthcoming festival would be, if not cancelled, at least postponed. Moore, then in his seventies, was as keen an impresario as ever and craved to play a part in boosting his city's prestige, the King's death or not. It was even mooted that the young Queen Victoria would attend, which, despite his melancholic mood, Felix thought "a capital idea", but this did not occur. This disappointment was lost on Mendelssohn. "If only I could let Birmingham be Birmingham and enjoy my life more than I do today," he grumbled to Hiller. "D... it!", as the genteel Lady Wallace translated his expletive; "you know what I mean, don't you?"

Whilst *St Paul* was the main feature of the Birmingham Festival of 1837, the *Midsummer Night's Dream* Overture and the premiere of Mendelssohn's 2nd Piano Concerto were performed. Smart conducted the soloist and orchestra and an Erard piano was provided. At an organ recital at the town hall, Stratton suggests that the E flat Prelude and Fugue, based on the chorale known as 'St Anne', must have been the first time a Birmingham audience had heard a work by Bach. Clara Novello and Mrs. Shaw were also asked to sing arias from the *St Matthew Passion*.

Unlike London audiences, who attended concerts to be seen, but particularly to gossip, those in Birmingham listened with rapt attention, whatever Mrs. Horsley might have said about "the lowest people" fighting for places at an earlier festival. Despite the adulation Mendelssohn received, he was always mindful of the fickleness of his audiences. He had learnt from Sigismund Neukomm's experience of 1834. On hearing his oratorio, he was pronounced 'King of Birmingham', but "now, his music is considered to be overvalued and written for effect merely... Such gratitude is not to be relied upon." He called Neukomm "a steady, true friend", having never met anyone who "combines such great integrity with calmness and refinement".

However, whilst Neukomm's music is rarely, if ever, heard, that of Mendelssohn is a different matter; even in 1837 people recognised his work as great music. When he was preparing to play his 2nd Piano Concerto "they prevented me for a long time from taking my seat at the instrument, and the offers bestowed on me from all sides confirmed my popularity". In a later letter, "many acquaintances flocked

Chapter 29: The Special Relationship

to the festival. One must be as cold-hearted as a fish not to be overwhelmed by the welcome I received."

Correspondence ensued with Novello's regarding an arrangement for a quintet of the new piano concerto, which could be rehearsed instead of the orthodox original if required. "The stringed instruments by which it was played in Birmingham are barely to be used now. Those I send are the correct ones," Felix explained. During the 1837 visit, Felix discussed with Klingemann a new oratorio to be performed at the Lower Rhine Festival at Düsseldorf two years hence: "I shall give further details at a later date. Meanwhile, I must stick to my present work plan," he wrote to his family. This path was pursued to the detriment of the proposed oratorio, which never materialised. It was eventually *Elijah* that saw the light of day as far into the future as 1846, and, even then, Mendelssohn was dissatisfied enough to revise it.

As far as the public was concerned Mendelssohn continued to be popular in England, as was proved by the English singer, George Sampson. Ferdinand David congratulated the guest on "coming to the right place" – Leipzig. "Mendelssohn dotes on you all." Sterndale Bennett, also present, concurred, saying that this was mutual. "Before I left England, all the young ladies were singing 'Es ist wahr?' ('Can it be?'). David began to imitate these singers "in a falsetto voice, with comic exaggeration and sentiment," Sampson recalled. "You play like an angel," Bennett retorted, "but you sing like – I will leave it to you." Sampson was then asked to sing the lied as it should be sung.

Despite Mendelssohn's earlier grouse with Novello's, this publishing house appears to have been the prominent publisher of his music. Letters auctioned in 1996 show Felix to have received £35 for his Op. 19 and Op. 38 books of *Songs without Words*. The English version of *St Paul* was "the most decisive step" in their becoming a company. Meticulous as ever, Mendelssohn made handwritten copies of the contracts, his instructions appearing on the fair copy of each. His facility with English was sufficiently advanced for him to write in this language, albeit with quite unnecessary apologies for the "trouble" his correspondent would be given in reading the script. Felix was "excessively obliged" for Novello's publishing his 'Piano Melodies'.

In 1840 Moore would invite Felix to conduct his *Hymn of Praise* at the Birmingham Festival. From 17th September Felix would stay in London for ten days, where a preliminary performance of his Symphony No. 2 was to take place, before availing himself of the now fully established railway to Birmingham. Meanwhile, on 17th January 1839 Felix had asked the Horsleys to introduce Ferdinand David to the music circles in London, explaining that not only was his friend from boyhood admired as a fine musician, but respected as a man. He had hoped to bring Cécile with him on his own visit of 1840 but, because the Mendelssohns' third child, Paul, was due in January 1841, doctors had advised against this. However, Felix was not without friends, for Chorley and Moscheles accompanied him to Birmingham.

Again, "Mendelssohn was the hero of the festival", his godson, Felix Moscheles was to write later. For the first chorus of the *Hymn of Praise*, the audience rose to their feet, causing contemporaries to assume that this would become a tradition, as with the 'Hallelujah!' Chorus from Handel's *Messiah*. Miss Charlotte Birch was the soprano soloist; John Braham, still going strong, sang the tenor role, other soloists being Mmes. Caradori and Knyvett. The festival included "a representation of Rossini's *The Thieving Magpie*, condensed into one act", as also a work by an abstruse composer, Gnecco. Mendelssohn's G minor Piano Concerto "served as an intermission". During the first half of a concert at the town hall, Felix played the organ to "a few close friends", which included improvisations on themes from Handel's *Jephtha*. During the second half, Mendelssohn's setting of Psalm 114 was performed.

Arriving for his seventh visit in 1842, Felix wrote to his family: "Having now slept away my weariness, I now feel well and fresh." Though ostensibly invited to conduct the Philharmonic Society concert season, Felix planned to dedicate his 'Scottish' Symphony to Queen Victoria. Though begun in 1829, the premiere had taken place in Leipzig only on 3rd March 1842. The first London performance occurred on 18th June, after which a strange incident was recorded in the newspapers. At the same concert, Sigismund Thalberg played a potpourri of themes from Bellini's *La Sonnambula*. Because he received applause equal to Mendelssohn's symphony, George MacFarren hissed Thalberg. At a subsequent concert, this provoked shouts of "Turn him out!" as MacFarren took his customary seat on the platform. However, apart from this contretemps, Mendelssohn and his music were as popular as ever. His *Hebrides* Overture had to be repeated by public demand. When his 2nd Piano Concerto was performed, with the composer again as soloist, "the orchestra played with a degree of enthusiasm that gave me more pleasure than I can say... The people make such a fuss of me that I am quite dumbfounded... They clapped and stamped for at least ten minutes."

The Philharmonic Society members gave Felix a dinner at Greenwich, "where I shall sail down the Thames and make speeches," he wrote in anticipation. "They speak of bringing out *Antigone* at Covent Garden, as soon as they can procure a tolerable translation." Even when he attended a concert at Exeter Hall, "where I had nothing to do", the reception was the same. Felix was surprised when, sauntering along with Klingemann, "such a clamorous clapping and stamping ensued". It was only when taking his seat, thinking that such noise "did not concern me", that he discovered the truth. When "Sir Robert Peel and Lord Wharncliffe next to me continued to applaud with the rest", Felix realised it was he whom the audience was applauding. "I bowed and thanked everyone. I was devilishly proud of my popularity in the presence of Peel. On leaving the concert hall, they gave me another cheer."

Chapter 29: The Special Relationship

On 22nd March 1843 Felix wrote to Horsley of his sadness at a rumour that the Philharmonic Society orchestra was to disband. Unaware of the reason, he did not know how to prevent such an occurrence. Fortunately, however, the rumour turned out, like so many, to be false. Mendelssohn was offered not only the chair of music at Edinburgh University, but the directorship of the Philharmonic Orchestra in London. Because of his appointment at the Prussian court he was unable to accept either of these prestigious posts. On 18th May of that year Klingemann wrote to Rebecka of how highly her brother's talents were regarded in Britain. Myles Birkett Foster, in his *History of the Philharmonic Society*, written in 1912 to commemorate its centenary the following year, observes: "Mendelssohn did much to cause the orchestra to rise, phoenix-like, from the ashes of its former state" during that period. Mendelssohn so much enjoyed his visits to London that it was a pleasure for him to mould the orchestra into a single entity. So strong was their team spirit that even Hans von Bülow, so often a detractor of Mendelssohn, had to admit his influence in this regard.

When invited to conduct the concert season of 1843-44, Felix explained that he wished only to remain in London for part of the schedule. He could not expect Cécile and the children to come with him, and, certainly, he refused to be away from them for so long, however grateful he might be for the honour bestowed upon him. He asked Rebecka not to breathe a word regarding this appointment: "*The Herald* is likely to repeat anything, even if you talk in your sleep," Felix joked. It was Sophie Horsley to whom the reason for his secrecy was divulged: "I cannot commit myself to conducting the concerts without first seeking sanction from the management, so that no one can take offence, as I recall having happened some years ago [referring to the Singakademie fiasco]. Therefore, I beg that nothing be advertised until firmer arrangements have been made to everyone's satisfaction."

Felix need not have worried. That concert season was considered "brilliant". Though that of 1842-43 had incurred a deficit amounting to £300, the current equivalent made a profit of £100. This was attributed, in no small part, to Mendelssohn's popularity, newspaper articles giving him the soubriquet 'the Pied Piper of London'. Several new works were performed. Sterndale Bennett made his debut with his Piano Concerto and, more durable, Beethoven's *Leonore* Overture No. 1 came into the London repertoire: "If this is not available in England, I can send a manuscript of the Second *Fidelio*," Felix had written. He also brought Gade's Symphony and "some other things that I can get here in Berlin or Leipzig, from which we can make our choice". Bennett was asked to give advice on the singers suitable to take part in the choral works that were planned. These included his own *First Walpurgisnacht*. Bennett's suggestions must have passed muster, for Felix wrote to Paul that the works were performed to an "unbelievable ovation". Beethoven's music to Kotzebue's almost forgotten play *The Ruins of Athens* received its London premiere, as also Schubert's *Fierrabras* Overture.

Nevertheless, one ill-starred venture must be noted. On 4th March Felix had asked Bennett if a rehearsal could be arranged during which hitherto untried works could be essayed; "if not, I shall be sorry but, in any case, I am bringing the score of Schubert's 9th Symphony." What more natural, Felix must have thought, than to introduce this masterpiece to London, when he remembered what a triumph it had been in Leipzig. Had Schumann not written to Ferdinand Schubert, the composer's brother, of "the great and sustained applause" after each movement? "All the musicians of the orchestra were moved and delighted", even after the first performance. Alas, London was not Leipzig, Felix was to discover. Unlike the Gewandhaus musicians, those of the Philharmonic Society found the symphony, especially the finale, puzzling, treating the work with "flippancy". The musicians behaved "so uproariously" that Mendelssohn's anger knew no bounds. Had he known the fact, Schubert's great work would not be given the credit it deserved in England until the 1850s, when Charles Hallé and August Manns would each ensure that it would enter the concert repertoire.

Not only did Mendelssohn abandon Schubert's 9th Symphony, he refused to allow his own *Ruy Blas* Overture to be performed in England during his lifetime. Indeed, George Anderson confided to his Philharmonic colleague, the journalist George Hogarth, that Mendelssohn had threatened to burn the score. However, Anderson was not to be thwarted. Since the Prince Consort admired Mendelssohn's music so much, he was asked if he might like to hear the overture. Thus, after 1849, when Cécile's permission was obtained, the overture received its first English performance, and "subsequently the work was regularly performed at Buckingham Palace and at Windsor Castle", Anderson being influential in this, as Master of the Queen's Music.

One of the longest-lasting consequences of the 1843-44 concert season was the emergence of a 13-year-old violinist. "The bearer of these lines," Felix wrote to Bennett on 10th March, "is one of my best and dearest friends and one of the most interesting people I have met for a long time. Of all the young talents that are now going about the world, I know no one who is to be compared with this violinist. Not only [am I aware of] the excellence of his performances, but the absolute certainty of his becoming a leading artist, if God grants him health and leaves him as he is at present." The Philharmonic Society had a strict rule that "no child prodigy" was to take the stage at any of their concerts, but, as Fanny Hensel had said, "Joseph Joachim is no child prodigy, but a musician". When he appeared on 25th May, the cognoscenti of London realised that Mendelssohn's boast was not an idle one. Joachim had already been invited to play on 22nd April for the Sacred Harmonic Society and on the 22nd May for the Melodists' Club. When, on the current occasion, Joachim began to play the solo part in Beethoven's Violin Concerto, even the *Midsummer Night's Dream* Overture was put into the shade. "No master could have performed better," wrote J. W. Davison of *The Times*. To Bennett, Mendelssohn had written: "Even the most difficult parts he can play at sight in string quartets, in the most masterly manner, and his accompanying in

Chapter 29: The Special Relationship

sonatas is, in my opinion, as perfect and remarkable as any I have heard." Joachim had, Felix explained, "excelled" in performing violin concertos by Vieuxtemps and Spohr. "Would you take him under your wing, be kind to him and tell him where he can hear good music; play to him, give him good advice and, for everything you do on his behalf, be sure I shall be as much indebted to you as possible." Though it is incessantly reported that Joachim became an intimate friend of Brahms, who wrote his Violin Concerto for him, it is Mendelssohn to whom Joachim's introduction to the world of European music must be attributed.

The fact that Joachim, who died in 1907, continued his musical career until almost the end of his life may have caused confusion. In his memoirs of 1937 Edward Speyer, a friend of Elgar, recalled how a Dutchman, having congratulated Joachim on a performance, added that, many years before, he had heard the violinist's father, 'the great Joseph', play. Joachim pointed out that his father had been a wood merchant and had never held a violin in his hand, let alone played one. It was Joachim himself whom the Dutchman had heard. Unconvinced, he was heard to mutter: "It is all wrong" as he left the room.

Mendelssohn, Thalberg and Moscheles took part in Bach's Concerto for Three Keyboards. As Thalberg did not like playing cadenzas, it had been agreed that none would be performed. However, during a pause in the orchestral part, encouraged by Thalberg, who broke this rule, Moscheles took the initiative. When the applause had subsided, "Mendelssohn began gently, gradually…rowing hither and thither until the storm became, at last, a hurricane of perfect octaves, which must have lasted for five minutes, bringing the cadenza to a close with an explosion of mechanical skill…that, neither before or since, that memorable Thursday afternoon has ever been approached. The effect on the audience was electric," Charles Horsley's memoirs record. "When the end came, rounds of cheers were given for the great artist, which sounded like salvos of artillery." All Felix said, when walking afterwards through Hyde Park, in response to Horsley's congratulations was: "I thought the audience would like some octaves, so I played them." Felix wrote to Paul, "The orchestra performed beyond all expectations, and all the reports are that there has not been such a season for many years."

Yet, despite his hectic schedule, musical and social, Mendelssohn made time to correct the errors in *Israel in Egypt*, to be published under the auspices of the Handel Society. His versatile mind also allowed him to contact Edward Buxton with a view to Schumann's cantata *Paradise and the Peri* being published. "Its melodies are worthy of its musical transcription [resulting from] the beautiful inspiration of your great poet [Tom] Moore. Schumann intends to visit England next year, when I am sure he and his work will be received as they so richly deserve." Sadly, the visit did not take place; the only privilege English audiences were given would result from the sterling work his widow Clara would undertake when promoting her late husband's music. It is only during these last few years that

Schumann's compositions have really come into their own; however, Mendelssohn's music has been heard regularly in this country.

Even if no one else saw to this, the Horsley family ensured its vogue throughout these years. A performance of his Op. 1 Piano Quartet "went better" than an earlier equivalent. At another concert Sophie played his "divine" concerto, and Klingemann wrote of a "new trio" heard at Kensington. Meanwhile, Felix thanked Novello for publishing settings he had composed for the Anglican service: "Whilst my Te Deum is not as I would wish, I do not consider it unworthy of being published, and any other such items I may write in the future will be better, when I am allowed quiet here in Berlin." Whilst Mendelssohn deprecated his standard of English, many Englishmen would be put to shame if attempting to speak or write in German. Again, he wrote to Novello: "Thank you for your kind behaviour in publishing my piano melodies, for which I am excessively obliged."

As with his fifth and sixth visits to England, the main reason for Mendelssohn's ninth, in 1846, was to direct his own work at the Birmingham Festival. For some time he had been contemplating an oratorio, possibly dealing with St. Peter, but "after careful consideration", as Rockstro reported, this "earlier project was shelved". Whilst the biographer believed that *Elijah* had "wider scope for musical and dramatic impact" than *Christus*, no one is in a position to verify this assertion. Only fragments exist of Mendelssohn's oratorio *Christus* (Op. 97), which are never heard and are, in fact, barely known, except among Mendelssohn connoisseurs. All Felix knew was that his present oratorio would be performed far better in an English city than in Berlin. Though *Elijah* is covered in Chapter 21, "A Handel and a half", a few anecdotes may add interest. At one rehearsal at the Hanover Square Rooms, before the 'Mendelssohn Special' train was hired to take musicians and press to Birmingham, music sheets were seen spread under the windows and observers would have heard copyists querying what should have been contained in gaps in the scores for the orchestral parts, some pages having been "lost". Though Felix's laughter would have mollified these operatives in Leipzig, the London copyists did not appreciate such humour. Eventually all was ready, and the party set off on what must have been an exciting journey on the still novel railway. Though Felix felt too exhausted to undertake any other task than to conduct the actual performance of *Elijah*, he had to replace Moscheles, through illness, at a rehearsal.

At ten o'clock one evening, despite being "tired enough", Felix analysed Mme. Grisi's singing and that of Mario and Lablache, who were to take part in items independent of Mendelssohn's Birmingham repertoire. After "lounging with their usual calm nonchalance, when they began to sing I immediately thanked God that they knew what they were doing. There was no question as to where the first crotchet should come in. Neither did the singers have any trouble with timing, and sang with purity. The fact that I felt no sympathy with their music is no fault of theirs." Neither was Mendelssohn scornful of musicians at the lowest end of the vocal echelon. At one rehearsal he noticed how a young chorister (named

Chapter 29: The Special Relationship

Humphreys) was "going through his part at the piano", as F. G. Edwards recounts. Tapping the boy on the shoulder, Felix rebuked him with the words "That is not how you play the piano", and showed Humphreys how the notes should be played.

Two days after his triumph, described elsewhere in this book, Felix wrote to Paul: "No work of mine ever went so admirably at its first performance, nor received such enthusiasm from musicians or audience. It was evident at its first performance in London that they liked it...but I must confess that I was far from anticipating that it would have such vigour and attractiveness in Birmingham. Had you been there during the whole hour and a half that it lasted, [you would know how] the 2,000 people in the hall concentrated on the subject that not the slightest sound could be heard from the audience, and I was able to sway the whole orchestra from the organ. How often during the performance I thought of you, but especially when the rain clouds came down, when they sang and played like furies. After the first part no fewer than four arias were encored – and not a single mistake. In the second half there were several, but not very important. A young English tenor, Charles Lockey, sang so beautifully that I was obliged to exercise great self-control in order not to be affected and to beat time steadily." In all there were 11 encores and, after each part, "musicians and audience vied with each other to augment the roar of the applause, which was deafening. In the end I grasped every hand that I could reach to thank everyone for their part in the performance." It is appropriate here to add a postscript. At the 50th anniversary performance the bass William Pountney, still singing in the oratorio in 1896, was sent a page of her father's original manuscript by Marie Benecke, Felix's elder daughter. A further anecdote that relates to the bestowal of a musical gift applies here also. Before Felix left Birmingham he presented a manuscript to a Miss Jenny Stephens, "a clever young pianist" and daughter of a festival committee member. Rather than being one of his own works, it was the score of a Chopin composition that this privileged young lady received.

Though *Elijah* had been such a triumph, Mendelssohn was still not satisfied with the work. Therefore, though he had written to Klingemann that two passages were being remodelled, a completely revised oratorio was presented on his tenth and final visit of 1847, at Exeter Hall. Performances took place originally on 16th, 23rd and 28th April, but so brilliantly successful were these that a fourth was hurriedly arranged for the 30th. So impressed had Mendelssohn been by a young chorister, William Hayman Cummings, drafted into service with other choristers from the Temple Church, that he was given Felix's visiting card. Cummings's claim to fame is his adaptation of a melody from *Festgesang*, to become known as 'Mendelssohn' and sung to the Christmas hymn 'Hark! The herald Angels sing'.

The Queen and Prince Albert attended the performance and, later, a concert at the same venue – "one of the best I can ever remember", as the Queen noted in her journal. "Michael Costa conducted admirably," she continued. The 'Scottish' Symphony was performed, but, for the Queen, the highlight was "that beautiful concerto...so full of feeling and soul" – Beethoven's 4th Piano Concerto, in which Felix was the soloist. This was "wonderful. He played entirely from memory, which, when doing so with the orchestra, must be very difficult. He is a wonderful genius and is deservedly an amazing favourite here." Having spoken with Costa and Mendelssohn during the interval, the Queen wrote of the latter as "so pleasant and amiable." Little did the royal couple, or anyone else, realise how exhausted Mendelssohn had become and how close the end of his life would be – as observed in Chapter 30, 'The spirit leaves its cage'.

Part II – 1829

Having discussed musical life in Britain until Mendelssohn's death in 1847, it is now appropriate to give details of his social life during the ten visits made thereto. Because so much occurred to this popular visitor in 1829, a whole section is needed to chronicle these fascinating events; part III outlines Mendelssohn's nine subsequent visits to England, between 1832 and 1847. The ideas and traditions of this land across the North Sea were never strange to Felix; the Mendelssohn parents imitated the fashionable habit of tea drinking, which, whilst the Netherlands claims to be the first European country to have adopted this social activity, it was England that really popularised the custom. Likewise, among the furniture at Leipzigerstrasse 3, pianos by the London firm of Broadwood were in evidence, and Felix was to follow this trait when in Leipzig.

As early as 1824 Ignaz Moscheles had advised Abraham that his elder son should visit London, then becoming the musical capital of Europe. When Klingemann had been posted there in 1828 by the Hanoverian Legation and Friedrich Rosen was pursuing his Oriental studies at the 'new' University of London, what more natural than that Felix, always full of curiosity for innovation, should yearn to explore this fascinating capital city – and to see his friends who had taken up residence there so comfortably? Klingemann's letters especially must have fuelled Felix's curiosity regarding London; "I have walked around the West End, the City, Westminster and Middlesex", part of which spread into what is now north-west London. "I eat classic mutton, half-cooked vegetables, praiseworthy apple pies and drink heavy port wine. I detest the dull, English Sunday. I argued with a miss as to whether she thought her appearance less appealing, or her meals less appetising, on Sundays compared with the rest of the week. She was still adamant that theatres were sinful" and were, therefore, closed on Sundays. Even in the comparatively free-spirited household of the Horsley family no letters were allowed to be written on Sundays. It is only recently that Sundays have become more relaxed. As late as the 1950s a children's playing field was closed in a north-country town, "because it's God's day" the querying child was informed.

Chapter 29: The Special Relationship

In view of Abraham's ban on Felix visiting Sicily, because it was "rife with bandits", as the father claimed, it is remarkable that this elder son was allowed to visit England in 1829. Klingemann regaled the family with newspaper accounts that resembled "the comedies of Aristophanes" that related to thieves and pickpockets – "between eighty and a hundred thousand, male and female". Yet, whatever hazards were to lurk in London's thoroughfares, there was no nonsense such as the prohibition of smoking, as the Berlin authorities had power to enact. Thus Felix was able to tell Klingemann that he would leave Berlin on 10th April to board the steamer, 'Attwood' in Hamburg, on the 18th, "to nestle down in your home, ready to fling myself into your arms" – as if Klingemann were his brother. Yet, despite his excitement, Felix had the thoughtfulness to ask if there were any messages to be forwarded whilst in Hamburg.

Having arrived there, "I do not know whether the good air or the local cooking make me constantly hungry. I am forever tripping over empty oyster shells", and he was fascinated by the red pails in which milk was carried: "Not at all German but, rather, a cross between London and Jerusalem." A relative of the poet Heine "flirted terribly with a young lady, kissing her and helping her on with her cloak". Had another young lady been "little less than a blonde, she would be quite pretty". Felix saw a German version of Auber's *La Muette di Portici*, "flirt a little with Cäcilie at the Lindenau home and, in all, gulp in the fresh air, converse with the oysters as well as the people and amuse myself as much as I like". As for music, Graun's *Death of Jesus* was performed in Hanover; "young Schwenke" had composed three chorales, to which he wished Felix to add a fourth "in four-part harmony". Felix had hoped "to tickle the organ at St Michael's Church with a few Bach pieces", but was forbidden this treat "unless I play quietly, as it is Holy Week. In this quiet time, all the theatres are closed and no concerts take place, though it is not too quiet a time for the people of Hamburg to parade their best clothes."

To Fanny, Felix gave details of Spohr's music that he had heard; he asked her to settle a query regarding Bach's *St Matthew Passion* and asked his father to send the scores of his Concerto for Two Pianos and Strings and his String Octet, both of which Klingemann had arranged to be performed once Mendelssohn had reached London. He also thanked her for sending Jean-Paul's *Flegeljahre* (*The Awkward Years*), a favourite among the author's novels with the Mendelssohn children.

The voyage across the English Channel – North Sea routes were not then in existence for tourists – was "not good". As Felix wrote to his family, the passengers experienced "contrary winds, dense fog and such a storm that all the passengers were ill". Mendelssohn's voyage had been anticipated to take two days, but this proved to be wishful thinking. "First the boat had to be repaired and, once the steamer arrived in London, we were obliged to cast anchor to avoid colliding with another ship. From Sunday morning until Monday evening I dragged myself from one fainting fit to another. I cursed…and scolded the steward with all my might… I felt disgusted with myself and everyone on the boat, but I decided to look on the bright side and noticed the moonlit sea and the hundreds of vessels gliding around us. We sailed up the Thames between green meadows and smoky towns, running a race with 20 steamers and soon getting ahead of all the others, finally beholding the awesome mass of London." Felix wrote that his thoughts were "so incoherent" that he would attempt a further letter "when the mail is sent to Rotterdam, four days hence". Meanwhile, "I must eat some dinner, something I have not done for four days – for I was very wretched. I must shave and, in short, be made to look human again." When Felix wrote again he had still not reorientated himself, feeling "quite giddy with everything around me. London is the most complicated monster on the face of the earth; it is fearful; it is mad. How can I compress into one letter what I have experienced during the past three days! Were I to keep a diary, I should have to see less of life, and this I do not wish. On the contrary, I want to take everything that offers itself. Things toss and whirl around me as if I were in a vortex and I am whirled around with them. Not in the last six months in Berlin have I seen so many contrasts, nor such variety, as in these past three days."

Felix lodged, as had Weber before him until his death in 1826, at 79 (later 103) Great Portland Street, London W1. His landlord, Herr Heinke, was a German ironmonger, whose wife made bread-and-butter puddings, which Felix particularly relished. He was fascinated "how the juice trickled into the basin when the lid was removed". Felix even asked that a store of these puddings could be placed in his room "to be eaten when arriving home at night" – a regular occurrence for this young man about town. There were two pianos in Felix's room, together with his silent keyboard with which he travelled, and on which he practised before rising each morning. "At night, the four-poster bed is so enormous that I can walk [myself] to sleep in it." Felix noted "the gay curtains, the quaint furniture, my breakfast tea, with dry toast, and the servant girl with curl-papers in her hair, who has just brought me my newly hemmed black cravat, who asks for further orders, whereupon I practise the English nod."

On the first morning in his new surroundings Felix reported: "A soft hand touched me very gently and stayed a whole hour, giving me all kinds of instruction as to whatever was agreeable, useful or advantageous to me." Moscheles had come to greet the new visitor to London. But, more often than not, Felix was to be seen at Klingemann's residence, 3 Bury Street, Hobart Place, SW1. Through this contact, and that of Moscheles, Felix met many important people and attended numerous official functions. For fashion-conscious Rebecka's benefit, Felix described the dress clothes he was expected to wear: "Olive gloves, long white trousers, brown silk waistcoat, blue overcoat and black cravat." At a coffee house "Of course, I read 'The Thunderer'", as *The Times* was then jocularly known. "Like any true Berliner, I first looked at the theatre news and noticed that, that evening, a performance of Rossini's *Otello* was to be given, with Mme. Malibran, which I was determined to attend, despite weariness and seasickness." So rushed were the two companions, Mendelssohn and Klingemann, that Felix could not find his

Chapter 29: The Special Relationship

"obligatory grey filigree stockings, so I had to borrow a pair from Klingemann. I was thus ready to face the genteel world" at the King's Theatre, "where I sat in the pit, having paid half a guinea" for the ticket. Though this amount is the equivalent of 55p in today's money, the sum should be multiplied by at least 120 to calculate its true value.

The theatre "is a large house, entirely decorated with crimson stuff, with six tiers of boxes, out of which the ladies can be seen bedecked with great white feathers and jewels of all kinds". On entering, the aroma of pomade with which the gentlemen anointed their hair and the ladies' perfume that assailed him gave Felix a headache. But, despite this, he was able to observe the trimmed whiskers of the gentlemen, "the crowded house, the very good orchestra conducted by Signor Spagnoletti. In December I shall give you an imitation of him. He is enough to make one die with laughter." The leading tenor's performance was "composed of flourishes, fraught with meaning. He shouts and forces his voice dreadfully and almost constantly sings a little too high" for his comfortable range. "However, when Malibran screams and rages almost disagreeably and the tenor drops his voice, so that the last bars are barely audible", the performance must have left something to be desired for this connoisseur of singing. "Malibran is a young woman, beautiful and splendidly made" – "with a gorgeous figure" is Marek's translation. "Bewigged, full of fire and power, and, at the same time, [she] enhances her coquettish role, partly with clever embellishments of her own invention; partly through imitation of Pasta", her operatic rival. "She takes up a harp and sings a whole scene like Mme. Pasta, even in that rambling passage at the end. Though she acts beautifully, she borders on the ridiculous and unpleasant so often, unfortunately, that, though I shall attend every performance in which Malibran takes part, this will not include *Otello*, for which Sontag is expected daily" to fill Malibran's role. Felix called Levasseur "a bear-bass" and Corlioni "a semi-bear tenor, both furiously applauded with hands and feet". Included in the evening's entertainment was "a divertissement of gymnastic and other absurdities, until 11.30, just as in Berlin. Though half dead with weariness, I held out until a quarter to one, when Malibran was despatched, gasping and screaming disgustingly. This was enough for me, and I went home." During the ballet in Bellini's *La Sonnambula*, Felix "had to keep hold of my seat, because I still felt the whole house was swaying to and fro. This giddy sensation has lasted for several days and it is only now that I can sleep undisturbed." Yet, despite this initial malaise, on 1st May Felix reported himself "in excellent health. London suits me very well. I have made many new acquaintances, received many new visitors, gulped down a few dinners, and plan many more." Among celebrities Felix met were Count Münster, the banker Goldschmidt and ambassador von Bülow, at whose residence a "diplomatic dinner" was given. "Feeling sick of fashionable entrées, conversation and trimmings, Mühlenfels [a German acquaintance living in London], Rosen and I came by a shop selling German sausages at two pence each" on the way home. Overcome by nostalgia for their homeland, and tempted by the appetising aroma coming from the shop, "we each bought a sausage and, moving to a less populated part of Great Portland Street, [we] devoured our purchases, at the same time attempting a song, but laughed so much that we could hardly sing. Mühlenfels led off in the bass, I sang tenor." Though Rosen's vocal compass was not mentioned, Felix observed him to be "quite wild at times".

Felix surmised that his family would not be concerned with the nobility he had met, forgetting, by accident or design, how his mother had yearned to cultivate such people. Some snippets of gossip seep through this sentiment. Leah must have felt discomforted on learning that Count Münster's wife was a princess and that the count himself was so bored with life that "he yawns at every other word he utters". Felix had arranged to attend a ball at the Duke of Devonshire's mansion, but, "for reasons too complicated to explain in writing", he was not able to experience this treat. Since, however, Count von Bülow assured him that he would be invited to another such event, "then what a letter you will receive".

And so he did, indeed, fulfil this promise: "Imagine me in an easy chair, shouting in French at a deaf duke, telling him stories about Berlin court life. Bülow's wife is so quiet that one cannot tell whether she is lost in thought, or merely bored." To Felix, Devonshire House resembled an Oriental scene. Though his own family lived in a mansion, everything in his environment was plain and austere. Felix therefore felt justified in describing the London residence: "The candelabra were hidden by huge wreaths of roses that seemed to grow, in an upside-down garden effect, from the ceiling. Dancing couples flowed into an adjacent hothouse, opened to spread the aroma of flowers through the palace. The tables were heaped with the fruits of all seasons. The young men flirted and waltzed very badly, while the older men lolled on the couches, engaged in tender conversation with the ladies." Further balls were given by the Marquesses of Lansdowne and Bute. Felix also paid calls on various bankers: Goldschmidt, Doxat, Sillem and Baring. He tended to find the female contingent of guests at these various houses somewhat artificial compared with his own sisters: "Imagine Fanny wearing maribou" (down from the West African stork of that name, used for trimming hats and cloaks). "Can you imagine Rebecka chatting to these English lambs, whom I would prefer to call camels or rhinoceros – lambs are too sweet – or how about Fanny conversing with these ladies over ice cream, whose sole response is: 'Chah-ming, chah-ming'."

Felix visited Westminster Abbey "two days after the fire", attended a lecture at the 'new' university and saw the British Museum Library. Mendelssohn was in the audience at a concert given by the violinist Cramer and at Mme. Sontag's debut in Handel's *Messiah*. He described the London streets: "On a new route to the City, green, yellow and red bills were stuck on the houses, with gigantic letters painted on them from top to bottom. Every minute I pass a church, a market place, a green square, a theatre. [I pass] glimpses of the Thames, on which steamers can go right

Chapter 29: The Special Relationship

through the town, under all the bridges, because a mechanism has been invented for lowering the large funnels and masts." The West India Docks had "a harbour as large as Hamburg's, treated like a pond with sluices, the ships not arranged singly, but in rows like regiments". Felix had taken a trip from St. Catherine's Dock to the West End and, on arriving in Piccadilly, he noticed the street name "painted in thick, black letters on white walls". To Adolf Marx the young visitor wrote saying he saw everything like a panorama... "Tall, brown houses made of bricks; signs in huge letters; sky-high chimneys and elegant shops; noblemen's palaces on one side and a graceful iron fence on the other, with a triumphal arch in the distance. In the wildest uproar, the dandies gallop by; the old lords ride slowly, children trot along on fillies. Splendid equipages with golden harnesses and velvet-clad servants wait for a mail coach, blocking the entrance with its elephantine horses. Then there are the dirty rented coaches all in a row, with beggars and rabble walking next to the duchesses, who look very English and cold, followed by powdered lackeys in sealskin breeches." Felix noticed "a man with a bell, reading letters aloud. Another is singing a new aria, with his hands cupped to receive the pennies. Another is playing a Scottish bagpipe. Most men lead a lady on each arm. Many faces are pressed to peer from the coaches. Six mail coaches, with passengers on top, race through, one after another. The shops are teeming but, through the iron fence work, one can see a broad, empty green meadow, with cows chewing the cud and, here and there, trees, which become denser, turning into woods. On the horizon one observes the white towers of Westminster soaring up into the blue sky. In the middle of the smartly dressed gentlemen, who are really ambitious dandies, there is one who walks deliberately and contentedly – namely, myself."

At the home of Sir Alexander Johnston, the Scottish geographer, a joke was played on Felix. He was asked to write a song in response to events in Ceylon (now Sri Lanka), "for the natives to celebrate their emancipation". In fact, the island did not become independent until 1948. In a list of Mendelssohn's works, Stratton included a song Felix wrote to commemorate the introduction of trial by jury and the abolition of slavery in what was then Ceylon. The words were written by the Scottish poet Allan Cunningham, and Stratton asserts that this was the commission Felix fulfilled for Johnston. Mendelssohn was also asked to write a song for the redoubtable Mme. Milder-Hauptmann – "an ukase", as he described her command. Though this should have been composed "straightaway, as you promised", Felix felt "my inner peace of mind is too disorientated to comply with this order, but I will try to torture something out of myself, be it a concert aria or some other thing". When it had been written, "I did not think it too bad. Goldschmidt worshipped it." This task had been undertaken "some time ago", and it might well be surmised that the prima donna never received the song. This theory arises because several other items of mail went astray at a similar time. Had the family received a song by Klingemann, for example? Had Marx received Felix's account of the concert in aid of the floods in Silesia?

These lapses in the delivery of letters, combined with Felix's crowded life in London, might have occasioned the criticisms he received from his home circle. Fanny suspected her brother of becoming too embroiled in London society; Devrient chided him for neglecting his music. To this riposte, having expressed his fury at such a slur, Felix replied: "Life and art are not two separate concepts and, if you are not afraid that I am not to become a Rossini or a John Bull, there is no reason to be afraid that this life will overwhelm me... I do not want you to think that I have changed. Really, Devrient, if ever I am to become better or worse, I will send you a special delivery letter. Until that time, do not worry." Nevertheless, Felix had to apologise for lapses in memory. Asked to look up someone called James, Felix had to admit the oversight, having never managed to meet the individual. Likewise, he had to ask his mother not to scold him for forgetting to send some seeds that he had promised: "In London, one forgets about the growing flowers. One smells them and puts them into one's buttonhole and forgets about them," he explained.

Felix visited an exhibition of paintings collected and assembled by 'the Earl of Grosvenor', as he called the Duke of Westminster. Of Titian's *The Age of Innocence* he mused: "The old fellow must have wondered quite a bit, whilst painting his young daughter, how the blonde child could have stood there so graceful, so poised, so charming, and slightly dishevelled, with an apple in her hand, thinking of nothing at all."

At a performance of *Hamlet* at Covent Garden, though Charles Kemble played the part well enough, Felix had far less praise for the production as a whole. "Whoever remarked that the English rarely understood Shakespeare was right. Hamlet's madness was demonstrated by Kemble wearing one yellow and one black trouser leg. He fell on his knees before the ghost to strike an attitude. He threw his applause-exciting high tone of voice at the end of every little phrase, behaving altogether like a John Bull Oxford student and not at all like a Danish Crown Prince. His acting was crazy and ruined the whole play... All that might pass, but that he should completely ignore Shakespeare's meaning as regards the proposed death of the King, by coolly skipping that scene where the King prays and Hamlet exits without having made up his mind to the deed – to me one of the finest passages in the play...treating the King in such a manner that he deserves to be shot down at once...constantly threatening him with his fist and shouting into his ear the words that should be quietly uttered – these things are unpardonable. Of course, Hamlet and Laertes do not jump into Ophelia's grave and wrestle there, for they never suspect why they should. And, at the end, when Hamlet falls down and says: 'The rest is silence', and I expect a flourish of trumpets, Horatio actually leaves the Prince, hurries down to the footlights and says: 'Ladies and gentlemen, tomorrow night, *The Devil's Elixir*.' Thus ended *Hamlet* in England. In the scene between the gravediggers, the old clown made wonderfully coarse jokes and sang his song very, very beautifully. Ophelia, on the contrary, sang quite madly at first and, while the others were talking, she murmured a low melody. The fencing and the exchange of rapiers was also done very nimbly. But what is all that? There is no poetry in England really."

From the specific to the general, Felix's view of London drama was jaundiced: "The plays are corrupted and spoilt by the inclusion of ridiculously bad artists and equally bad songs (commissioned by the more powerful elements in the theatre), exaggeration of pathos by actors, and the complete misunderstanding of the characters, notably the female ones, so much so that they are hardly recognisable or enjoyable. These productions are weak attempts to imitate those presented at French or German theatres. It cannot continue in this way. Things will have to change if truth is to be brought back. Though I hope this happens, I do not believe the present time and circumstances will make this possible."

Yet, though Felix revelled in all the activities London laid before him, he was most at home with the friends he had made in Germany. Debates in Klingemann's rooms often featured in his correspondence. Equally, he enjoyed excursions into what was then countryside with his friends. Once, unable to find a carriage, "I walked in the cool of the evening along the field path. Many musical ideas came to me, which I sang aloud. The whole sky was grey with a purple streak on the horizon, and the thick cloud of smoke lay behind me." A further outing was planned, "to a grassy village with trees, gardens and roses, to take breakfast with Mr. Richmond and his many daughters", who lived at Stamford Hill. "We shall walk through the fields, stay the night at the village inn, where we shall behave ourselves with devilish propriety, just like proper Londoners." Another outing was to the country village of Kilburn, where Moscheles was to give a party, the first after he and Charlotte had lost their first child. It might have been on that occasion that Felix met the London branch of the Rothschild family, who lived in that area. Nathan Meyer Rothschild, known to his friends as 'N M', who made his fortune in London trading bills of exchange, had two daughters, Hanna and Charlotte. The latter, an accomplished harpist, is claimed to have owned a harp of pure gold. As with other celebrities of the time, Mendelssohn was asked to compose a piano piece for the Rothschild family album, which still exists in the private collection, housed in the Rothschild home in Paris.

Mendelssohn's visit to Scotland was not a spur-of-the-moment whim. Even before he left Berlin, Felix invited Klingemann to accompany him: "I am looking forward to the oysters next August, when I shall search for folk music; to enjoy the lovely, fragrant countryside; to have a heart for the bare knees of the natives; and, altogether, to lead a right royal life, demolishing any obstacles, and to take a look at the Highlands when we travel to Scotland." The book *Mendelssohn in Scotland* by Jenkins and Visocchi covers the journey in minute detail. On the evening before the Scottish odyssey began, Felix wrote, whilst packing for the journey, "There is no point in writing anything sensible. Cramer, who has been in my room since 10.30 this morning, constantly plays arias to me and asks if he may also travel to the Isles of Krim, and is just now sitting at the piano improvising better than I have ever heard him before and has just slipped gently into F sharp, being drunk as a skunk." That same evening Johnston gave a farewell dinner for Felix at which a toast was given, not only to the Mendelssohn family but also to Germany, "to whom he attributed several of my own good qualities", as Felix jested to his parents. After the Mosel, gifts were exchanged. Felix received "a drinking song with canon" with which he reciprocated a score of his *Midsummer Night's Dream* Overture. Klingemann had also arranged a "going-away tea" at Bury Street to bid farewell to Rosen, "visiting the Rhine", and Mühlenfels, who was to return to Berlin. The piano manufacturer Collard was present, as also Isambard Kingdom Brunel, "the young architect [engineer] whose Thames tunnel project fell flat a while since".

Mendelssohn and Klingemann planned to leave for Scotland on 20th July, breaking their journey wherever it pleased them. "These vehicles go everywhere each day", as Felix observed of the stagecoaches. They aimed to reach Scotland in three days but, as Jenkins and Visocchi point out, this was ambitious. The distance of 400 miles, with stops every ten miles for the horses to be changed, would take far longer. Even to Stamford in Lincolnshire, less than halfway, would take 20 hours without breaks for meals or rest. A seat inside the coach would have cost £3.50 – half this price for an outside seat. Incidentally, this is from where the term 'outsider' originates, implying that passengers who travelled outside the coach were 'not one of us' in the more comfortable seats. Sadly, there is no record of the full journey north, though it is known that Mendelssohn and Klingemann stayed one night in York and another in Durham, where Felix sketched the cathedral.

Various London friends had invited the travellers to their country estates in Scotland. Johnston, a relative of the Duke of Argyll, would see to it that anyone Felix found useful would be introduced to him. An invitation was extended to the Isle of Islay, where Sir Walter Campbell had an estate. Felix called him "'the tyrant of the isles', whom one word from Johnston will tame", as he wrote to his family. Loch and Ben Lomond were on the itinerary, with Loch Katrine. Felix aimed to explore Cumberland, see a little of Ireland and Wales but, above all, to visit Staffa, "which sounds beautiful and looks so from the views I have seen from guidebooks".

On 28th July Felix told his family how he and Klingemann hoped to visit Sir Walter Scott at Abbotsford, having been given a letter of introduction from a friend in London. Scott's novels were the height of fashion throughout Western Europe, so it was regarded as nothing less than a duty to meet 'the wizard of the north', as the celebrated man of letters was known. Scott had moved to Cartley Holm, on the banks of the Tweed, in 1824, when he had been appointed Sheriff of Selkirk, renaming his residence Abbotsford. Klingemann gave his imagination full rein in an endeavour to placate Felix's family, writing of their flowery converse with the baronet. "In the evening we tremblingly wrote verse and music in a large album." Klingemann even translated a poem into English concerning the place where Scott lived and "the sage who has all knowledge of these riddles". What an anticlimax it must have been for the Mendelssohns, especially the social-climbing Leah, on reading Felix's postscript: "We found Sir Walter in the act of leaving

Figure 11. Pencil drawing by Mendelssohn of Durham Cathedral, 1829

Abbotsford, stared at him like fools and drove 80 miles, losing a whole day for the sake, at best, of a half-hour's superficial conversation. Melrose compensated us but little. We were out of humour with great men, with ourselves, with the world, with everything."

Felix wrote of reading his mail in Princes Street, where he and Klingemann must have lodged whilst in Edinburgh. "I have climbed onto Arthur's Seat and bathed in the neighbouring water, which tasted of salt", compared with the taste of lemonade at the Baltic spa, Bad Doberan. Then the journey to the Highlands began. Their itinerary included Stirling, where, in 1807, Thomas Telford had built a new road during his employment as an engineer with the Highlands Roads and Bridges Enterprise. The two travellers then visited Dunblane, Perth, Crieff, Dunkeld (where Felix sketched 'the rumbling bridge'), and Blair Atholl. At 'The Island Inn at Bridge of Tummel', Felix wrote of drinking whisky and eating pie (he used the English word), but his main concern involved the foul weather: "A storm is howling, blustering and whistling outside, a wild affair, causing the downstairs doors to slam and the shutters to fly open. The floors are so thin that the servants can be heard singing drunken songs and laughing. Dogs are barking and water is flying everywhere, but whether this is rain or the foaming stream is unclear, as both are raging. I poke the fire occasionally, causing it to spark, but, otherwise, the room is quite desolate." His meal there comprised "potato cakes and tea with honey," supplemented by the inevitable whisky, "brought by a maid, who appeared from the narrow, winding staircase. The beds have purple curtains. Shoes are worn instead of slippers. [One sees] little boys with their plaids, bare knees and colourful caps; waiters with their tartan; the people with their periwigs [who] all speak a jumble of incomprehensible Gaelic."

"Klingemann had the divine idea of writing poetry to accompany the drawings, from which some pretty things have resulted. We covered 21 English miles yesterday, [and we are now spending] a dismal, melancholy, rainy day. Earth and sky are wet through. We are trying to make shift as best we can, which, unlike yesterday, is not saying much. Klingemann says he does not find Scotland as bad a place as he was led to believe." Though Felix was fascinated by the "grey, cold and majestic landscape", he abhorred "the frequent black clouds and dreadful storms. When these abate, sunshine changes the heath into a thousand different colours, all so divinely gay and warmly lighted." Had Felix's whole stay in Scotland consisted of the blue skies and sunshine that he loved, might he have been able to create such masterpieces as his *Hebrides* Overture and 'Scottish' Symphony? (These compositions are covered in Chapter 16, 'Observer of nature and life').

Though, during the famed outing to Fingal's Cave from Oban, two ladies, daughters of Sir James, a local laird, appeared to care little for their mother's state of health, they, too, on the return journey by steamer, appeared with pale faces. This might well have arisen not only from the rough crossing but from "the stale

Chapter 29: The Special Relationship

ham, vegetables and herrings" that were served en route. Sir James ordered the captain to take the long way round to the mainland and, for those who did not complain about this high-handed attitude, wine was supplied, upon which, according to Klingemann, he and Felix "fell to". The latter had evidently recovered from his well-chronicled seasickness of the outward trip. Due to arrive back in Oban at 7 p.m., the steamer, 'Ben Lomond', did not reach Tobermory until eleven o'clock. The passengers had to remain, "where beds there were none", in the boat, "a strange boot" serving as a pillow for Felix. After such an adventure Mendelssohn and Klingemann must have appreciated the comparative comfort of the inn at Inverary, whence they travelled on their eventual return to Oban. "The landlord's daughter, with black curls, relieved me of my broken boots," Felix wrote. As she gazed out of the window Felix was reminded of a signboard, but whatever romantic picture he might have conceived was shattered by the way she "thumped the piano". It was at this inn that Mendelssohn described the herrings, "alive at nine o'clock, swimming around in the Atlantic, fried a quarter of an hour later, to be eaten for breakfast, accompanied by coffee". The Duke of Argyll's castle at Inverary could be seen through the trees. Pieces of wood could be seen, sawn into planks ready for shipbuilding, which "held a colloquy with their relatives bound for the navy, floating on the neighbouring water".

The coach from Inverary proved unroadworthy and another was made available, "said to be made of iron" but actually constructed of wood, as was realised when Felix knocked on its walls. It is evident that Mendelssohn and Klingemann, as town dwellers, not only loved but expected comfort. Therefore, it can only be imagined how they viewed the conditions at some of the inns at which they stayed on the journey back to 'civilisation'. In one, a fowl flew round the room; in another, the squealing of a pig was heard. In an inn near Loch Lomond "we slept close to the roof, so that, from sitting room to bedroom, we walked with umbrellas, cloaks and caps". He spoke of "the wretchedness, the inhospitable and comfortless attitude. We have endured ten days without meeting a single traveller." Whereas towns and cities were marked on the map, "only a few sheds, huddled together, appear to exist. A single entrance serves as door, window and chimney for people, animals, light and smoke. To any question, one receives a dry 'Naw'. Whisky is the only beverage known. No church, no street, no garden, rooms pitch-black in broad daylight. Children and fowls lie in the same straw. Many of the huts are without the roof, with unfurnished, crumbling walls and burnt ruins, and many that are occupied are sparsely scattered throughout the landscape."

To Droysen, Felix reported how Klingemann and he "are happy together and tramp the countryside as gaily as if the storms and rains do not exist, which all the newspapers, even those in Berlin, are reporting. We have weather that makes trees and rocks crash." A sudden gust blew from the mountains whilst Felix and Klingemann were in a boat on Loch Lomond. "The boat began to rock so frightfully that I began to take up my cloak and prepared to swim. All our belongings were thrown topsy-turvy." Having crossed the loch, the travellers were obliged to remain "with a cursing Englishman, half sportsman, half peasant, half gentleman and altogether insufferable, plus three others of the same calibre". The letter Felix was writing had "fluttered out of the sketchbook, so that we had to scramble about to rescue it. Just now, the innkeeper's wife is singing her child to sleep with a sweet melody in a minor key."

Of the scenery, Felix wrote of the "broad and wide [landscape], covered with dense vegetation. From all sides, cascades of water are running under the bridges. There is little corn, but much heather, with brown and red flowers; ravines, passes, crossroads, everything beautifully green; deep-blue water, but everywhere is stern and lonely. The state not only of bliss, but profound relief, can be imagined on reaching Glasgow." Felix wrote of new-laid eggs and "pork", as Klingemann had called the breakfast-time bacon, the herrings and the "beautiful rich cream", but there was more to this fine city than food. Glasgow had a university and a thriving population of almost 16,000. They dined "in the best commercial hotel", where Felix showed portraits of Fanny and Rebecka to people he met. A doctor thought how much the latter resembled Sappho, "especially in the chin". A dandy promised to learn German so that he could flirt with her and a musician saw "many beautiful traits" in Rebecka's face. "Unfortunately, he was half crazed, so do not set much store by this at all," Felix admonished.

The travellers were fascinated by the spirit of enterprise so apparent in Glasgow: "There are many steamboats, 40 of which start each day, and many tall chimneys are smoking. Coffee and sugar are always at hand and we can look back with equanimity at past disasters. The Highlands and the sea brew nothing but whisky and bad weather. Here it is different – smooth and comfortable – with the blue sky overhead and a good sofa beneath us." Of particular note to Klingemann was a "stupendous" cotton mill, where, "however maddening is its noise", he was still able to observe the habits and behaviour of the operatives. One woman had a wreath of cotton wound round her head; another's aching tooth was bound with thread. "Everything is poetry," he rhapsodised – even the fact that "little girls are employed from an early age".

Rather than the easterly route whence they travelled to Scotland, Felix and Klingemann returned in a westerly direction. They explored the Lake District, staying at Keswick and Kendal, and parted at Liverpool. Klingemann returned to London whilst Felix accepted the invitation to Coed Du ('Dark Wood'), the estate where the Taylor family lived in the summer, near Mold, North Wales. However, before embarking on this journey, a most unusual experience was recorded.

Curious about everything, Felix boarded the new railway that covered the 35 miles between Liverpool and Manchester. He found this "a bit intimidating" and could not see to the end of the larger of the two tunnels. In order to undertake this adventure, he had had to beg the train driver "with pleas and entreaties. A

Chapter 29: The Special Relationship

workman climbed onto the back and off we went at a speed of 15 miles an hour, with no horse and no engine, the carriage running on its own, the train gradually working itself up to the wildest speed as if it were quite imperceptibly [running] downhill. Two lamps were burning up front. The daytime disappeared. When the wind blew out the lamps, it became pitch-dark. For the first time in my life, I saw nothing, the train running faster and faster the whole while, chattering more loudly as it sped. It was a bit rough on my stomach." Halfway along, Felix noticed a coal fire where the workman stopped to relight the lamps.

"It was bitterly cold in the tunnel, but then the red, warm sunlight came streaming in from afar. I felt very invigorated as I stepped from the train; quite contented as I walked to the market buildings." Did anyone tell Mendelssohn that, apart from passengers on the Darlington-Stockton railway, opened four years previously, he must have been the first passenger to travel on the new railway? It was opened in 1830 by William Huskisson, Minister at the Board of Trade, who would be killed on this line.

The market hall in Liverpool was "a slight-framed building, but much larger than the cathedral. There are eight rows of stalls running along the centre, piled high with fruit, vegetables, meat, pastries loaded down, offering one a walk through alleyways of victuals." He observed the "crowds of people of all kinds – black, American, Italian, Welsh-speaking, naval officers, countless pretty cooks. In the middle hangs a huge clock; on the walls, maps of Liverpool. I got very adventurous and rode to Chester by coach". From there, Felix travelled to Holywell, in what was then Flintshire, to visit "my English family", whom he had first met in London.

In the coach a fellow passenger spoke about the loss of his son and invited Felix to visit his home, which he did. "He still does not know my name," he added. Whilst such a detail would not have signified had the new acquaintance done so, it proves just how modest Mendelssohn must have been, in view of the manner in which he had been fêted in the metropolis. After his visit to Coed Du, covered in Chapters 14 ('Flirting outrageously') and 16 ('Observer of nature and life'), Felix was invited to explore the principality further with a cousin of the Miss Taylors. The itinerary included Beddgelert, Llangollen, Snowdonia and other tourist attractions. Among his discoveries were a Roman citadel at the summit of a peak and a ruined abbey, the choir area of which had been converted into a stable and its altar into a kitchen, the whole "covered with lovely green trees". Nevertheless, "blue skies, and sun, which do so much to warm the heart [and which] are indispensable to me, do not exist here… A good day consists of being soaked through three times, wearing my cloak during the walk, and seeing the sun through the clouds once in a while. Storms have raged for four weeks, with howling winds and constant rain." When the Taylor cousin pointed out the place where "the fattest salmon may be caught", Felix had other matters on his mind, being engrossed in singing one of Fanny's songs, 'Hören mögt Ich' ('I would like to listen'). "I should never have growled or snapped at him had my thoughts not been so boorishly interrupted. These songs are more beautiful than can be described. I speak, God is my witness, as a sober judge."

Though Felix had planned to "see a little of Ireland", excited by scenes in pictures and calling them "the most beautiful in all Britain", the project did not materialise. Felix had hoped to see for himself the lakes of Killarney and visit Dublin. The crossing, he gauged, would take four hours. "Though such a short excursion, it will be well worth the trouble," he had assured his family. The steamer arriving at Holyhead had, in fact, taken 15 hours to cross the Irish Sea and the "absolutely heavenly landscape" would not tempt him to board the boat, having seen the disembarking passengers "with green faces, wet, weak and cursing". On the return coach journey to London "I was grumpy to all my unpleasant travelling companions and spoke not a word, but kept quiet, half dreaming, half reflecting, half grumbling".

Back in the place where Felix really confessed to feeling at ease, a misfortune occurred to him. As described in Chapter 3, 'Sound minds in frail bodies', the coach accident prevented Felix from attending Fanny's wedding on 3rd October 1829, to which he had looked forward with such excitement. Though the doctor's prescription comprised "fruit, soup and rice", more substantial nourishment was provided by friends who visited the sickroom. Lady Möller presented some "Dutch meringue"; Sir Thomas Attwood supplied a pheasant "covered with sweet-scented flowers"; and Benjamin Hawes, Member of Parliament for Lambeth in later years and a relative of Brunel, provided "some delicious grapes" for the invalid. "Old Horsley" of the Philharmonic Society "called with some compositions, which diverted me for an hour or two on the sofa". Frau Heinke, Felix's former landlady, insisted on cooking his favourite dishes, "sweetened bread, to be dipped in milk, cakes, fish and German broth", whilst Rosen visited regularly "and amused me highly. He noticed how we always recognised his knock and were thus always prepared for his visit, so, since then, he has always knocked once like a servant, another time like the milk girl and, this morning, like the postman. Once he had himself announced as Count Redern (superintendent of the Berlin Opera)."

During his confinement at Klingemann's residence George Hogarth, brother-in-law of Charles Dickens and a member of the Philharmonic Society, asked how Felix was faring. Yet it was Klingemann who not only saw to Felix's physical needs with infinite care but also stimulated the mind of his charge. "It altogether does so much good when people are friendly and stand by you, and it gives me the deepest pleasure to be able to say honestly that they do so here," Felix reported to his family.

As with a recovering convalescent, Felix grumbled about "the smoky hovel" of which he had "had enough", but this mood soon ebbed once he was able to leave his bed and venture out of doors. Everyone stepped out of their rooms to congratulate him on his recovery. The coachman took Felix's arm to assist him into

Chapter 29: The Special Relationship

the carriage for a ride around the West End of London – "Waterloo Place, Regent Street, Portland Place, New Road (Marylebone Road), Gloucester Place, Hyde Park, along Piccadilly" – before reaching Bury Street. Felix found London "indescribably beautiful, with everything shining so brilliantly that I was often blinded by red or yellow clothing and the bright shops. For the first time in my life I felt what health was like, for I have never been without it for so long." The green foliage of summer had been replaced by "red sticks", and he noticed how the blue sky, "pouring into every street crossing, contrasted with the red and brown chimney pots. Only the lawns are still green." Though "coals are the heaviest item on my bill", Felix's buoyant mood rarely left him until his final day in London, 29th November.

Since he was "still a wounded child", as he wrote, Felix planned to travel with the mail rather than hiring a private coach, but, more likely, this matter was settled by financial considerations. His injury, he reported, was "progressing at last, after eight weeks, but has still not healed completely. I can almost walk without my crutch, can sit properly in a chair and can dress practically all by myself. Occasionally, music makes its way into my head." Having spent five weeks "on my back in bed", Felix had still to take things "step by step, literally". He planned to rest, on the way home, in Brussels, Aachen "or wherever I like, catching the mail coach to Cologne, in which I shall travel in comfort". Klingemann read *Die Flegeljahre* aloud, whilst Felix studied "everything from the end of the 18th century", including Laurence Sterne, the dramatist Kotzebue and German authors. From the third week after his accident Felix had "fallen into a lazy apathy, which knows no bounds. I could sit on the sofa the whole day long and do nothing. I rarely rise before 1.30. For half an hour I sit alone in the twilight, looking into the fire and thinking of nothing at all. In Berlin this would have caused me to fall asleep. In London I am wide awake and content."

He wrote from Calais: "I feel as if my senses have taken leave of me, seeing the English white coast giving place to the black French landscape." En route to Ostend Felix planned to take in Ghent, Brussels, Aachen, Rotterdam and Amsterdam, where he would meet his father, who had made a business trip there. Half an hour from Ostend Felix saw "the lighthouse, white and bright, with a red light and a yellow one below it". Maastricht was the first place he heard German spoken since leaving Hamburg, apart from visitors to London. Here Felix experienced the pleasure of "a comfortable room, music paper and a beautiful trip by moonlight. The mail coach from Cologne will deliver my letter tonight and I will be following behind."

Part III – Later Visits to England

On 6th August 1830 Klingemann had written to Paul Mendelssohn before he set off for London, saying that his visit would be warmly welcomed as a highly respected member of the family bank. A bill had been presented to Parliament that would allow industrial and commercial interests to be given seats in the House of Commons and permit individuals who belonged to this newly established class to vote. Paul's presence would equally enhance both his own and the banking community's status. He wrote that Felix's sojourn in Britain of the previous year was now almost forgotten, since the 1829 Catholic Emancipation Act had taken precedence. (By this Act members of that faith were given the vote and the right to enter Parliament.) However, Klingemann's opinion would have to alter, in view of Felix's continued popularity and his nine subsequent visits across the North Sea. Indeed, very little is known of Paul Mendelssohn, in London or elsewhere, except that he joined his uncle Joseph Mendelssohn and his son Alexander, and married Albertine Heine, a cousin of the poet and a long-term friend of the Mendelssohn family.

As soon as Felix arrived for his second London trip in 1832 he was overwhelmed by his reception: "In this lovely country, where I find my friends again, I know myself to be well and among benevolent people... Of all the signs of recognition so far, which I shall remember with the greatest pleasure, [the most gratifying] occurred at a Philharmonic concert last Saturday. No sooner had I entered the concert hall than someone shouted from the orchestra: 'There's Mendelssohn', whereupon they all began yelling and clapping and, for a while, I did not know what to do. As soon as this was over, someone yelled: 'Welcome to him.' They struck up the same racket and I had to make my way through the hall...to make a bow... It was dearer to me than any [tangible] distinction. It shows that musicians are fond of me and are glad that I have come."

Of the various concerts Felix attended, he found a performance of Beethoven's 'Pastoral' Symphony "easy listening altogether". A further concert was given at Vaughan's Concert Rooms. The most significant anecdote from this outing is the confusion that arose from the pronunciation of the impresario's surname. "Please pronounce this name 'Von'," the Mendelssohn family were instructed. Whoever suggested this was evidently not conversant with German. The letter V is invariably pronounced as an F, the V sound being acquired by the letter W; thus 'Worn' would have been a more accurate rendering of the name.

Although Felix had met William Horsley, composer of glees and a member of the Philharmonic Society, in 1829, it was on this present visit that he really became acquainted with the family. Their home in Kensington welcomed many guests and, if one conversation is to serve as an example, a wide variety of topics were discussed at one session: "Our acquaintances, pictures, poems, trees, Berlin, the

Chapter 29: The Special Relationship

Mendelssohns, Kensington, beetles, statistics, summer, flowers, music and politics." Though the Miss Horsleys hoped "never to experience such a verbal marathon again" – it was on that occasion these "mental wanderings and conversational powers" were promulgated by Klingemann – Felix was able to marshal his intellect sufficiently to take such events in his stride. "We get on so happily and comfortably with one another," he reported. Of his social life as a whole, he informed his family: "Every afternoon and evening [I am] out with friends, making music and doing all manner of good things and discover many curiosities. I arrive home in the evening rather late, sleep for a long time, until Klingemann, Rosen and other friends arrive to take breakfast. We then talk politics, drink tea and eat tops and bottoms [sandwiches, perhaps?]."

Mendelssohn was made a member of the Literary Union, "where I can write, read the newspapers and eat as much as I please, though today I am dining with Moscheles and his family". In case his parents might have worried about his exciting life in London, Felix reminded them of a letter his father had written – "Enjoy your youth and your happiness," Abraham had entreated. "This I have done from the heart, and shall do, and I thank you all for it," Felix added. In case Leah or Abraham worried at the expense that might accrue, Felix ensured they knew of the generosity he experienced: "Cramer and Addison are very generous about paying and ordering more. What more can one need?" Later he wrote, not as tactfully as his parents might have wished, "It is very pleasant to feel oneself so much at home, when abroad." Yet Klingemann, ten years older than Felix, appears to have been disorientated by his younger companion's active life: "So much is happening here, I shall need a whole year to rest and recover from it," he added in a postscript, declaring that he had to forgo many social events undertaken by Felix, whose energy reminded the diplomat of "elastic rubber". After visiting Sir Thomas Attwood at Norwood he wrote: "Nothing has changed [since his 1829 visit]. Even the music is the same in the cabinet that remains in the position I recall it." His hosts were "kind, quiet and as attentive as before, as if the last three years have passed over them as peacefully as if half the world had not been uprooted during that period [through revolutions]. All that differs is that, in November 1829, there were fogs and blazing fires, whereas now, May, there is apple blossom, lilacs and all types of flowers in bloom. As I write the sun is shining, and I will go into the garden and perform some gymnastics and to smell the lilacs." Felix met Hauser, with whom, two years earlier, he had travelled through South Germany and Austria, "about which we reminisced, falling into each other's arms in friendship". On 15th June Felix wrote that he would soon be aboard the ship on his return home, "where I hope to find [that] nothing, and no one, has changed". Writing to the Horsley family Felix declared himself "confined to Berlin", as if he regretted the fact. Once he had boarded the boat, the scent had faded from the buttonhole that Mary Horsley had given him – "along with the memory". However, a sketch he had drawn was far longer-lasting. This described "what could be seen of the bedrooms from the outside window, the drawing-room and the shrub outside".

Felix's third visit to London, in 1833, was chiefly musical, and it was then that the premiere of his 'Italian' Symphony took place. Later in the year, accompanied this time by his father, his fourth London visit occurred. Before taking the plunge, Abraham still needed what were described as "inducements", but, once the journey began, his son was "mad with joy". Yet Abraham never did enjoy London as much as Paris, as he wrote to Leah. Whilst impressed by his walk along Oxford Street, Regent Street, Portland Place and Regent's Park, and the fact that London was the richest city known to him, "Paris is still the greatest" – but with no explanation as to how or why. To be fair, Abraham felt far from well during this visit. Though, for instance, he and his son were invited to dine with the Horsley family, this did not happen "on account of an old complaint; he even had hysterics", as Sophie recorded to her aunt. Abraham's eyesight was also failing. Though Wilfrid Blunt imagines that Abraham tended to exaggerate the London fogs, this is unfair.

Had Abraham lived today the cataracts that had formed in his eyes, rendering the lenses opaque, would have been straightforward to remove but, with the Mendelssohn family's negative attitude, such a condition must have terrified him and frustrated such a dominant, overweening personality. The Mendelssohns might well have heard how both Bach and Handel had completely lost whatever sight remained to them as the result of attempts to treat this condition. What a pity that nothing was known of a success story that occurred in 1846, when Charlotte and Emily Brontë escorted their father to Manchester, where a surgeon, Mr. Wilson, agreed to operate on the Rev. Brontë's left eye. Infection, he explained, might have occurred if both eyes had been treated. On returning to Howarth Parsonage, he was able to read and write in comfort. [This information is gratefully acknowledged to Miss Ann Dinsdale of the Brontë Society.] But, for Abraham, nothing was right. "Felix appears to find the yellow meadows green and the grey horizons blue," he wrote to his family. "At 9.14 a.m. the sun has enough power to colour the fog yellow," he reported on another occasion. "The fog itself resembles thick smoke during a major fire." In response to the "Fine morning" with which a barber greeted him, all Abraham could reply was "Is it?" Abraham wrote: "By midday, the fog was victorious", and, by four o'clock, Abraham was obliged to move his table nearer the window, "not to see what I was writing, but to see that I am writing. Felix will surely tell me that nowhere is the sun finer than in London." To make matters worse, Abraham had never troubled to learn English and could not, therefore, confide his feelings to anyone. Thus he wrote: "I conversed with Horsley in Italian. He can speak neither German nor French – and neither of us can speak Italian." Whereas the English have a reputation for stubbornness as regards any language but their own, this can be attributed equally to some Germans. Brahms reported in a letter, on meeting a Frenchman, that "we each keep silence – in French" when conversation was required.

Abraham, nevertheless, boasted of having learnt a few English phrases: "How do you do?" "Waiter, a mutton chop," and other such profundities. When Horsley visited the Mendelssohns' lodgings, Abraham reported: "I remarked on the number of horses I had seen in London, how well the charitable societies managed without government aid, and how well the children behaved at St. Paul's Cathedral." Twenty years hence Berlioz would make a similar comment. The Horsley family featured a great deal during this visit to London. Once, when Felix and Klingemann came to breakfast, "We had great fun being polite to one another, the ball of conversation being brilliantly kept up by the company." Subjects ranged through Mozart and his son, whom Felix had met in Milan two years earlier, to Shakespeare "and, of course, a few invectives about Berlin", as Sophie wrote. On another occasion, the book by Anthony Trollope's mother, Mrs. Frances Trollope, on her travels in America was debated. Isambard Brunel took one side; Marc, his father, who had lived in the United States, disagreed with the author's criticism of the customs and way of life she had witnessed.

On Fanny's Horsley's birthday, 1st July, Felix and his father were invited to dine with her family. "A little form was seen, wearing white trousers, a blue coat with gilt buttons, a brown waistcoat, a white cravat with a diamond pin, a fine face with a bright colour, black curly hair and dark eyes." Felix's hair had grown after the 'Spanish crop' of the previous year when, in Paris, he had had his hair cut in order not to be mistaken for Meyerbeer. Each guest received a buttonhole, or "nosegay", as Fanny Horsley described the flowers. Abraham's was accompanied by a card, with a message hoping that the souvenir attached to the coat would remain dear to him. Felix's posy comprised jasmine, a sprig of Mrs. Horsley's 'Empress Augusta' geraniums, and heliotrope. To celebrate Mary's wedding to Brunel, there were "wedding cakes decorated with white satin and sprigs of myrtle. Felix stuffed down a great and surprising quantity." Father and son "argued about German philosophy and the former, in unusually high spirits, laughed at his own jokes". Whilst Fanny and Abraham "talked pleasantly", the rest played "ghost". Whereas "Felix ran the faster, Dr. Rosen ran the more gracefully. Whilst the party tore about in fine form," Mary's fair hair "came undone and fell down her back". They then danced; "even Rosen danced, upon my word, extremely well. Felix whirled Fanny round with pirouettes and all sorts of follies."

Abraham and Felix had planned to leave London in September to stay at Dieppe for a fortnight, visiting a spa and returning home to see the new baby, Ernst Dirichlet, born to Rebecka, but, as with Felix four years earlier, a coach accident befell his father. Though Wilfrid Blunt states that this happened at Portsmouth dockyard, all other evidence gives London as the place of the accident. Such mishaps appear to have been frequent. At the time when Abraham was confined to bed he wrote to ask Leah to ensure that a young Englishman had everything he needed when visiting Berlin. "Kindness is your heritage from your mother," he pointed out. To bear out this philanthropic attitude the family contributed to a local hospital, where patients would be given better nursing care than might have been possible otherwise. At a similar time Mrs. Horsley and her eldest daughter Mary were in a vehicle that crashed into a wall. When three policemen came to investigate, the carriage was "on its last wheel". However, the only mishap that befell the mother and daughter was that their shoes had to be changed at a public house!

Like Felix, Abraham received many visitors bearing gifts: "Puddings, pies, grapes, pots of jam and marmalade, port with brandy and claret." But his recovery was aided especially by the diligent care to which this usually grudging patriarch had to admit: "Next to God and the doctor, I owe my life to one person whom I love more than anyone except for my wife," Abraham wrote to Leah. "I can never tell you how much he has done for me; what treasures of love, patience, kindness and the tenderest care [he has] lavished upon me." Whilst such solicitude was second nature to this sensitive young man (Felix), it appears that guilt played a part: "Had I not persuaded Papa to accompany me to London, this accident would not have occurred. I must therefore be held responsible for his injury, which would never have happened had he remained in Berlin." According to Charlotte Moscheles, Felix was "in a dreadful state of mind for the two worst days, saying he would not know how to cope, should his father's condition relapse".

The Miss Horsleys reported several occasions when Felix was not his usual exuberant self, and the lack of understanding can only be decried for such educated young women. "Once or twice he sank behind a cloud and, on foreseeing a further attack, he was given a very long poke to stir him up, [after] which his spirits rose and he went off quite elated." On a further visit, Felix was described as "in the glumps" when he had even neglected his usual immaculate appearance: "Though generous and big-hearted, he was dressed very badly, looking sadly in need of a piece of soap and a nail brush, which I have threatened so often to offer him. Dear, oh dear." When a book did not appear that Felix had promised for Fanny's birthday, Mrs. Horsley sent him a note that was "brief and cold". When he did arrive with the gift, Felix was "very cross, sitting in deep gloom, sighing all the time until he departed, and then went on apologising in a mumbling voice for ten minutes". A cab arrived to take Felix and Klingemann to bathe at Vauxhall: "They are nasty, indecent creatures. Men are sad, dirty pigs after all," Fanny dismissed the matter, forgetting that such relaxation would refresh Felix after such a long, painstaking vigil at his father's bedside.

However, there were instances of amusement – Felix imitated a drunken man – but the curiosities he had planned to experience were forgotten, on the whole, because of his father's illness. Klingemann had hoped to lure Felix to a lecture on philosophy at Cambridge with the 'carrot' that it would only take a day. Many excursions made by the Miss Horsleys, so amply described in their letters, did not include Felix. Despite so much enjoyment, a visit was paid to "old Mr. Mendelssohn" and his devoted son: "I had never seen Felix's face looking so

Chapter 29: The Special Relationship

pleased," Fanny reported, "as if in a blaze of light as he stood in the passage." As for Abraham: "The sufferer proved himself [to be] a very odd specimen. Had looks been exchanged, I would not have been able to control my muscles for laughter at such a bizarre spectacle. His poor little legs were just like two little sticks lying on the sofa, his flannel elastic drawers bound round his diminutive calves with red tape. He looked poorly, but talked a great deal. Had Mrs. Moscheles not been there I would have felt rather awful amongst men."

Once the time had arrived to return to Berlin, Abraham was in such high spirits that he decided to play a practical joke on the family. Instead of bringing Felix home, Abraham wrote, he was bringing a charming young Frenchman named Louis. After the anxiety and curiosity as to why Felix remained in England, the Mendelssohns' joy can only be imagined, for Abraham was not accompanied by the fictitious Louis but by Felix himself. Abraham had mellowed considerably by this period. At the sight of posters advertising the fact that a young child was missing, he wrote to Fanny Hensel and her husband: "The thought of it never leaves me. It is interwoven with my London life like a dark thread. Ach. That poor child, and all because the parents lost sight of him for possibly only half a minute." His grandfather hoped that no such misfortune would befall Sebastian, who had reached a similar age to the lost London child.

Felix had promised that, in 1837, he would conduct *St Paul* at the Birmingham Festival. However, when the time arrived for his fifth visit, he was not so keen to undertake the journey: "I find that the English fog, beef and porter has such a horribly bitter taste this time, and I used to like them so much." To Chorley Felix complained of "feeling fidgety". He had not heard from any of his family for five weeks, but this was a minor disappointment compared with his overwhelming one – having to leave his beloved Cécile after barely six months of marriage. The fact that she would give birth to their first child early the following year cannot have helped his anxiety. A further blow was the sudden death of Felix's dear friend Friedrich Rosen. Never in good health, the Oriental scholar had succumbed to blood poisoning, which, as antibiotics would not exist until the next century, his body could not survive. When Klingemann broke the news it was too late for Felix to bid farewell to their mutual friend. Though he had watched over Rosen at his bedside as often as possible, Felix had had to conduct *St Paul* at Exeter Hall, returning to find Rosen no longer alive.

Sophie Horsley had named Rosen "the nonpareil, not only of all Germans, but of all people". It was only his frail constitution that prevented his asking Sophie to marry him, which she would undoubtedly have gladly done. So many examples exist in her letters of her fondness and care for Rosen. Though Blunt states that Mendelssohn spent "a great deal" of time with the Horsley family, there is room for doubt. All the letters written or received at this period concerning the family have "disappeared". Though this can only be a conjecture, it might have been that Cécile had them burnt, along with other correspondence. A rift undoubtedly arose between Felix and the eldest daughter Mary after her marriage to Isambard Kingdom Brunel, as is evident from Mendelssohn's part of the honeymoon diary.

Brunel and his bride spent part of their honeymoon in Wales, returning to London via Devon. Such an apparently circuitous route might have allowed Brunel to display his fine railway projects in the west of England. When Felix visited their home in Duke Street, Westminster, he found Mary alone, "frightfully elegantly dressed", as if he found the over-ostentation uncomfortable. Worse was to come; when he dined at the Brunels' house one evening: "Everything is so elegant and artificial...that the likes of me began to feel quite sick in the stomach," Felix wrote, "What has happened to the Mary Horsley of old and to the former Isambard Brunel? Flown off into the world of grandeur, where there is room for everything but pleasure and concern for anyone; nothing was forthcoming from either of them, except for plenty of fish, poultry and the like. Beforehand, we had to wait awhile with the ladies and the baby, until the man of the house appeared with his father and Mr. Hawes and goodness knows who else, still engrossed in deepest conversation... Immediately after the feast we went into the elegant drawing room, in which stood a small organ, which I was expected to play. However, I took my hat and walked home alone through St. James's Park. There, in the darkness, I heard the retreat sounded on the trumpets and drums and could have almost wept, so moved was I." The only pleasant memory of that otherwise distasteful visit was seeing his father's portrait "between flowers on a small table".

Despite Felix's endeavours to make the best of his stay in England, he did not feel able to write any music, as he told Hiller, "but only to swear and long for my Cécile. What is the good of all the double counterpoint in the world, when she is not with me?" he groaned. "Chopin is supposed to be in London," Felix continued, "but has paid me no visit. He played beautifully at Broadwood's one evening, but then took himself off again. They say he is still very ill and miserable." As for the forthcoming festival, "Let Birmingham be Birmingham," he growled. On arrival Mr. Barker, Vice-Chairman of the festival committee, invited Felix to dine at his "fine house", which included "a beautiful garden with Arcadian plants", as he called the collection of orchids. The "fairly pleasant company" thought Germany "a dreadful country. I disagreed. Mr. Barker was on the first steamer that sailed from England up the Rhine. They had taken a cook and food with them because they could not eat the German stuff."

Back in London "old Souchay", Cécile's relative, gave Felix some gooseberries which, having been thrown into the coach, "became dreadfully crushed". Beforehand Klingemann had taken Felix to a hotel but, rather than being able to relax, he found the Exeter Hall committee waiting for him. "The President gave me a beautiful silver box, showed me the kind inscription and said: 'As a tobacconist, I have filled it with my best wares.'" However, rather than appreciating the snuff contained in the box, Felix had other matters on his mind: "Bewildered and flustered I thanked them, but would have liked to eat some of the

Chapter 29: The Special Relationship

many kinds of fine ham and sausage that lay on the table, but I could not, since the coach on which I had to travel to Dover left at midnight." Neither could he read a letter from Cécile that Klingemann had given him, "with many others". To add to his annoyance he discovered that the cape he had purchased in Birmingham, in order to sleep in comfort, had fallen from his "pocket".

Whereas the French and Belgian coaches were "detestable", travelling "round and round, rather than straight on, the German coaches are 100 times pleasanter, quieter and better". In Belgium the 'September Days' had been commemorated, marking the occasion when, in 1830, the country had been liberated from the Netherlands' rule. "'Trees of Liberty' were planted before each town hall." Having boarded the Rhine steamer, Felix rejoiced that he could lie down full length, "free from the rattle of the pavement". However, having slept soundly, Felix learnt that the boat would not reach Mainz for several hours. He therefore disembarked at Horchheim, where Joseph Mendelssohn lived. Asking the boatman to unload his luggage "onto the old, familiar path along the Rhine", Felix eventually arrived at Frankfurt at three o'clock in the afternoon, whence, reunited with Cécile, the couple reached Leipzig.

That evening Felix was due to conduct the first Gewandhaus concert of the 1837-38 season: "I found the trumpets and drums so noisy that, by the end of the evening, I own, I felt rather kaput." Later in the evening he told his friends: "I cannot begin to describe Birmingham but, when we are once more together, I will relate all the remarkable things that happened during those days." He admitted to Klingemann that, on rereading his part of the honeymoon diary that concerned his visit to England, "how out of sorts I must have appeared". Klingemann had tried to persuade his friend to take up residence in London but Felix had disagreed with 'A', who had planned to do so. His reason? "I fear I would take too much interest in matters averse to art." Despite the many temptations London offered, he still preferred to live in Germany, Felix declared. In Leipzig he ruled the musical world that he loved, had a blissful family life, a comfortable home, and not only the respect but the love of his musicians. There were to be, in any case, five further visits to London that Mendelssohn would make. It is worth mentioning Fanny's view. When, in 1838, Hensel exhibited his paintings in London, Fanny had grave misgivings about accompanying him: "I dread meeting acquaintances who might expect more from me than I am able to give," she wrote to Klingemann. "I do not want people to think me a prophetess or a heroine. I am a dwarf compared with such personages as Countess D", whose portrait her husband had painted. "I have never liked such meetings and I do not mean to begin now, in my old age [of 32 years]. Besides, the place is too big for me." Despite Felix's continued assurances that Fanny would feel comfortable in "that smoky old place", she was adamant in her attitude and never gave England the pleasure and privilege of meeting her.

Fortunately for England and her people, Felix never shared his sister's ambivalent attitude. When, therefore, in 1840 he was invited to conduct his *Hymn of Praise* at a further Birmingham Festival, he grasped the opportunity, together with "all the beautiful and splendid things" that were presented to him. Beforehand he and Cécile had "paced the room in sleeplessness" anticipating all the dreadful mishaps that might occur. Having arrived in London, he was able to recall such a period as being "like a troubled dream". All his friends were as loyal and welcoming as ever. Klingemann, the Moscheles and Horsley families, and the Miss Alexanders, despite their "elegant drawing room, with its new and fashionable furniture", and Abraham's portrait that Hensel had drawn "occupying its customary position". Felix remained eight days in London before travelling to Birmingham (discussed elsewhere in this book). Felix was obliged to report that "I stroll with Klingemann in the fields during the evening, to try to restore myself and to marshal my thoughts and impressions of this hectic life in London".

Later in the year Felix was able to convey his feelings to George Sampson when he visited Leipzig. "Dear old England," he sighed, "where the sun forgets to shine sometimes and, when it does shine, what land could be sweeter. The countryside on these occasions is like a beautiful picture." Felix even rhapsodised about the fog: "Despite the glowing sun of Italy, the pleasure of your smoky London seems to wrap itself around one like a friendly cloak." In 1841 Fanny Horsley married a physician named Seth Thompson, whom Felix had met whilst in Italy. Though they had planned to spend their honeymoon in Germany, the couple included neither Berlin nor Leipzig in their itinerary, which Felix termed "an injustice and a deficiency". Felix suggested a compromise, whereby they could meet in Dresden, 40 miles from each of these cities. There the Midsummer Fair would begin on 24th June, but, sadly, no information is extant as to whether or not this proposed meeting took place.

On his seventh visit not only was Felix invited to Buckingham Palace for the first time (as described in Chapter 23, 'The Highest In The Land'), but Cécile accompanied him to London. Of his mother, Charlotte, Felix Moscheles wrote that she was "lovely, this simple word telling [not only] of beauties of the intellect, but qualities of the heart", as well as physical attraction. The same word can be applied to Cécile, and, indeed, Charlotte Moscheles herself described her using the same term. She made a great impression on the literary celebrity, Samuel Rogers. Shaking hands with her, he begged Cécile to bring up her children to be as charming and to speak as good English as herself. Felix had written to the Horsley family of his wife's reading Oliver Goldsmith's novel *The Vicar of Wakefield* to learn English in preparation for the trip across the Channel. Sir Edward Bulwer Lytton, himself a novelist making his name, flirted with Cécile in a similar vein to Rogers; each were fascinated by her eyes, described as "violet-blue". It is not known how often Cécile accompanied her husband to the various functions organised for him, and it might be assumed that, as a rule, she remained with her relatives, the Benecke family, at Camberwell Green. A boat trip to Greenwich was planned for Felix by the Philharmonic Society, "with a fish supper and speeches". Indeed, fish

Chapter 29: The Special Relationship

appears to have played an important part in Mendelssohn's diet whilst in England. On one occasion, for instance, he wrote of enjoying "a fish supper at Lovegrove's in Blackfriars", and, on another, "after an onerous stint of concerts in London", repairing with the Benecke relatives to Ramsgate "to eat a few crabs". Felix also wrote of a gathering at which "Mrs. Butler" (formerly the actress Fanny Kemble) read from *Antony and Cleopatra* in Mendelssohn's honour: "We have always been on friendly terms since our first meeting 12 years ago [in Italy]. The reading...[was] too beautiful." Other guests included the portrait painter Winterhalter, the historian Grote, Sterndale Bennett and Moscheles. "A. M. Dupré sang an old French romance about an old beggar who was hungry and another about a young man who was losing his reason, with the refrain to the effect that the wind that comes over the mountain will drive me mad."

Not only did the couple visit London. Cécile and Felix travelled to Manchester in order to call on her Souchay relatives. It was whilst in this area that Felix still hankered after seeing Ireland but, as in 1829, the 12-hour crossing dissuaded him and "crushed all my ideas" on such a venture.

Again, in 1844, a similar pattern occurred as with Mendelssohn's earlier London odysseys: "My reception was unparalleled. I have not gone to bed before half past one each morning. Every hour of every day is crammed with engagements for the next three weeks." As Klingemann wrote to Felix's family: "He enjoys the lobsters, the pies and the ladies and never ceases to be astonished at the number of Englishmen he meets and the amount of English he hears spoken." He should have added that Mendelssohn could understand the language and reciprocate with equal fluency when speaking and listening. His love of fish was borne out in a letter to his nephew, Walter Dirichlet, in which he was advised to "eat all kinds of seafood". During this visit Klingemann was able to thank his guest for the "soft, warm, comfortable foot-rug" that was "spread on the floor with pride. The rug came at a very opportune time for, though my rooms have been decorated, my landlord, out of stinginess, did not provide a new carpet and this fits just nicely over the shabbier patches of the old one." He added how, though he wished to do so, "I do not have the moral courage to convert it into a waistcoat."

Felix dined with noblemen, bishops and other celebrities of the time. Among the latter were Dickens and Thackeray, who each pronounced him their favourite composer, which even cynics admit to have been genuine. Mendelssohn also met Charles Babbage, who did so much to promote the calculator, which became a forerunner of the computer. "He gives evening parties frequented by all the notables, Indian princes, Baron Gerlach, all the beauties of the season, Lord Ossulston and myself," Felix reported. During one of their meetings Felix spoke to Babbage about Gustav Dirichlet, to whom he was able later to pass on a pamphlet that this inventor had written. But it cannot be stressed too strongly that none of these invitations from "this mad, extraordinarily mad world" ever went to Felix's head. He was invariably touched when a stranger recognised him in the street and asked if he could shake hands with this illustrious musician.

Felix's "multifarious occupations" diverted his mind from homesickness, especially when he learnt that Cécile and the children were all well and that the country air at Bad Soden "was doing more good than all the medicines in the world". He hoped, nevertheless, that the labour of conducting the Philharmonic Society, the reason for his eighth visit, would prove fruitful and that he could fulfil his commitments as he wished. Klingemann noticed how "younger and fitter" Felix looked than on his previous visit of 1842. The reason can be clearly understood. The oppressive atmosphere of the Prussian court, and all its frustrations, no longer applied and Felix could settle once more in Leipzig where he belonged, and where his work was respected and appreciated as it deserved. Likewise in London, as Klingemann wrote to Fanny, "He has had many and great successes, about which he will be too modest to tell anyone." After a previous guest, "the Great B.", with his way of speaking, late hours, unpunctuality and other aggravations", Klingemann must have experienced real joy at Mendelssohn's presence at Bury Street. "It is no wonder that this kind feeling is mutual," Felix averred.

Felix's ninth and penultimate visit to England took place in 1846, principally to direct his new oratorio *Elijah*. As with his earlier visits, nothing had changed as regards the warmth and kindness with which his friends surrounded him. However, it was becoming apparent that, whilst he relished the hospitality awarded him and the high respect and honour conferred upon him, Felix was becoming thoroughly exhausted, mentally and emotionally as well as physically. On returning to Leipzig he confided his feelings to Fanny: "I cannot contemplate a journey, or anything else. Only to vegetate...like a bunch of flowers," he wrote on 23rd September. "I do nothing but eat, take walks and sleep all day and still wish for time to occupy myself in the same manner... I have been idle since the last note was played in Birmingham Town Hall. I was asked to go to Manchester for two concerts, but declined and went to London instead... Then I spent a day at Ostend because I felt sleepy and another at Cologne with the Seydlitzes, because I was too tired. Then four days at Horchheim, where uncle Joseph walked me around in the boiling sun through the vineyards for an hour and a half, taking me at such a pace that I was constantly on the point of telling him that I could not keep up, but I felt ashamed, so stopped up my mouth with warm, blue grapes. Then I stayed a day at Frankfurt because I was so weary and, ever since I have been in Leipzig, I have rested." Did Felix have a presentiment that his life might soon be coming to an end? On 8th November he wrote to Klingemann that, through their characters, Montaigne, Jean-Paul and Voltaire all say "that one can only have one true friend and, from my heart, I acknowledge that you fill that place". Was this Felix's way of bidding farewell to Klingemann? Yet, despite his evident need for rest, he paid his tenth and final visit to England in the spring of 1847. He noted that, since

Chapter 29: The Special Relationship

Klingemann's marriage to Sophie Rosen, "he has had his bachelor corners rubbed off", having become, as a result, "a pattern of patience and tolerance". Klingemann wrote to Rebecka about his guest, who "finds the spell of London working upon him, just as his own personality works upon the people he meets". Having scant success with Fanny, Felix tried to persuade Rebecka to visit London. She would be bound to enjoy the experience, since "it is not all Babbage and 'Rule, Britannia!' The lion is only allowed time for himself in the early mornings and late at night." As with Fanny, Felix's enthusiasm for the grand metropolis yielded no result with his younger sister.

Chapter 30

The Spirit Leaves its Cage

The musicologist Johann Christian Lobe recalled, during a conversation with Mendelssohn, his assertion that "he would never make old bones". For a man in his thirties, still handsome and, as far as anyone was aware, in the peak of health, such thoughts were surely inconceivable. Nevertheless, as Devrient noted, albeit with hindsight, changes in Mendelssohn's inner being were evident as far back as January 1846. "The fresh, youthful bloom had been replaced by a certain boredom and weariness with life. Everything that had to do with the organising of concerts burdened him unbearably." During his ninth visit to London later that year Klingemann noticed for the first time how Felix's hair had turned grey and that even conversation about music, or light-hearted banter, could not divert his gloomy mood. Rockstro, describing this same period, wrote in 1883: "There is no doubt that Mendelssohn's health was seriously, if not hopelessly, impaired. He worked himself almost to death in his superhuman aim for excellence."

On his visit of 1847, as an article in *The Musical Times* of 1861 reported, "he threw himself into all the musical and social engagements that he felt unable to refuse". However, as Max Müller remembered, "Mendelssohn had become much paler and felt things more intensely than hitherto". Once, for instance, at a gathering in honour of Mr. Gladstone that Ambassador Bunsen had organised, during a performance of Beethoven's 'Moonlight' Sonata, a lady's fan accompanied the music by opening and closing. When Felix could stand the jangling sound no longer he repeated the bar again and again, "following the movement of her fan" until the sound ceased. "He then went on playing as if nothing had happened." It was at this same tea party that he bade farewell to all his friends, hoping to visit them again in 1848. Julius Benedict begged him to stay for a further week on Mendelssohn's present visit. "Ach," he replied, "I believe I have already stayed too long here. One more week of this unremitting fatigue would kill me." As Stratton states: "The more his friends fêted him [the more] Mendelssohn was being killed with kindness…and that, had he been given more opportunity for repose, he might have lived longer. The sword was wearing out the scabbard." Mendelssohn's unquenchable spirit was always far too strong for his frail constitution.

With so much work to occupy him, Felix looked forward to a contented, fulfilled life once he reached Leipzig, yet even his efficient plans could go wrong. The homeward journey began propitiously enough, in the company of Klingemann and his new wife Sophie, as far as Ostend. What a pity they did not continue the route to Germany. As a diplomat, Klingemann would have been an ideal companion to untangle the ridiculous bureaucracy that befell the eminent musician. In the small town of Erbach, on the Belgian-German border, there was one individual who had never heard of Felix. This ill-educated but officious policeman, hoping, no doubt, for promotion, thought he had at last tracked down the Dr. Mendelssohn whom he was seeking. A strongbox had been stolen that contained incriminating documents relating to a sensational divorce instigated by the Countess Hatzfeldt. It had been rumoured that the political activist Ferdinand Lassalle had asked a colleague, the Dr. Mendelssohn in question, to steal the box, but he was later cleared of any complicity in the matter.

Though no photograph identification was available, with photography still in its infancy, Felix's travel documents were in pristine order, as usual. Nevertheless, he was delayed for a whole day whilst he was searched, unrecognised by this ignoramus. Felix was questioned and made to compile a long statement as to his precise whereabouts during the past months. Finding nothing suspicious with which to charge him, this Dr. Mendelssohn was allowed to continue his journey to Leipzig. In the peace of his home, with his loving wife and children around him, Mendelssohn might well have forgotten this incident, but an even more grievous blow assailed him.

Fanny never could be said to have sustained a strong constitution and, for the past three years, she had experienced severe nosebleeds, one of which was purported to have lasted 36 hours in the spring of 1847. On Friday 14th May, whilst rehearsing her brother's *First Walpurgisnacht* with her ladies' choir, her hands dropped suddenly into her lap from the piano keys. In order to bathe them in warm vinegar Fanny left the room, but, before returning, she collapsed. Her son Sebastian, then 16, rushed through the streets of Berlin to fetch the doctor, praying as he went that his mother's state of health would not be too serious and reassuring himself that nothing too severe could happen to her. But his sanguine thoughts were vain, for Fanny died at eleven o'clock that night, a brain haemorrhage having been diagnosed as the cause of her death.

When Felix heard the grim tidings "he gave a shriek and fell senseless to the floor", according to his first biographer, W. A. Lampadius. This "ruptured blood vessel in the head" was, according to Stratton, "due to the shock of hearing the news so suddenly that his second self no longer lived". This implies that Paul, who came to Leipzig to tell Felix and his family of this tragedy, might have been insensitive to the closeness between Fanny and Felix. Her death was so sudden that no warning could have been given. Paul made as great a speed as possible, when no telegrams or telephones existed. According to Kupferberg, Felix could face none of

Chapter 30: The Spirit Leaves its Cage

his immediate family, his widowed brother-in-law, his motherless nephew or any relatives of Paul or Rebecka. He left Julius Rietz to organise musical events. The only occasion to which he looked forward was the performance of *Elijah*, with Jenny Lind as the soprano soloist, due to take place in Vienna. "If my tears should interfere with my handwriting," he wrote to Hensel, "you must put this letter aside. There is nothing better we can do but to weep until our eyes are dry. We were happy together, but now life will be a grey, mournful affair. You made my sister happy all through her life. She deserved to be. I thank you for that today and will, as long as I breathe, and probably longer, not with mere words, but with bitter repentance, regret that I did not see her more; was not with her more."

On 19th May Felix wrote to Rebecka in a similar vein: "The only thing [that] helps a little is crying quite a lot, if only one could always do so. I cannot write or think of anything but Fanny." What is most moving, especially in view of the innuendos made by some biographers that there was more than a brother-sister relationship between Fanny and Felix, are the comforting words added by Cécile, the wife whom Mendelssohn loved and cherished so faithfully: "All day today I am standing in for Felix. I would like to console him, yet cannot. We speak of Fanny and reminisce together and ask God to help us bear the heavy blow that we have been dealt, without grumbling or sinful thoughts. Ever since yesterday, when the full news came to us, our spirits have crumpled and grown faint. After Hensel, you, dearest Rebecka, have suffered the greatest loss. In day-to-day life with Fanny, her beautiful soul lay open to you. You knew her best and the signs of her love accompanied you everywhere. My thoughts flow out to you. Oh, would that I could be with you at this time to lament and cry with you, that we were not so far apart. I have also lost a best friend. I knew well that she loved me; that I could count on her as on a solid rock and that she would never desert me; and I shall never again now see her beautiful eyes. God help us all."

Whey drinking had been prescribed for Felix and, on 24th May, Paul was also recommended to take this "cure". However, a more constructive antidote to the family's grief, Felix realised, would be to "occupy yourself with your children, for theirs are the only faces, and their words the only carefree words, that do one good". Yet, at the same time, "Now I find myself thinking, with every footstep I hear, every letter to be opened, that it might undo what cannot be undone, though, in my heart, I realise Fanny will not return. I cannot bear the company of others now, nor do I know what to tell them, nor do they know what to ask... I must now console Cécile, with whom I always enjoy every moment of conversation and must pull myself together when I am with her, so that she recovers from the terrible shock."

In order to try to alleviate her husband's sorrow Cécile, meanwhile, arranged with Paul a holiday in Felix's beloved Switzerland, staying at Baden en route. The resort "will be very quiet, as it is not yet the season for the baths and the accompanying social activity", Felix had written to Paul. Though the Swiss scenery had not changed since his last visit five years before, all Felix experienced was sleeplessness. The fine views could not tempt him to paint and the beautiful scenery of Lucerne, Thun and Interlaken reminded him only of times past, particularly of his boyhood holiday with Fanny. The only positive achievement was the Sixth String Quartet Op. 80, seen invariably by music critics as a requiem for his sister. "It shows a depth of expression and a sad passion," according to Stratton. Blunt calls it a "composition written in an agitated state of mind", having copied the phrase from Felix Moscheles.

The publisher Härtel came to Switzerland to discuss with Felix a project to print Fanny's works, but was told that "only when a precise accounting system was sent from Berlin could anything be agreed", despite Felix's expression of "charm" that this engraving might be put into effect. There was no shortage of visitors. Indeed, "Scarcely a day has passed lately without one, or several, but they all seem to be so empty and indifferent and I, no doubt, must appear the same to them... In the midst of all the phrases, enquiries and reports, I have only one thought – how short life is." The only exception to this view was H. F. Chorley, in Switzerland at the same time as the Mendelssohns. Chorley had wished to discuss a commission that Felix would conduct at Liverpool's new Philharmonic Hall. "I shall not live to see it," was the response. "I must have quiet, or I shall die."

Nevertheless, Felix still insisted on climbing the highest mountains and taking long walks, striding out so recklessly that his family could not catch up with him. Yet, once Paul had boarded the steamer for Berlin, depression could be observed. As Felix wrote to Rebecka: "The sky has become so dismal and rainy that I have only taken one walk since Paul returned home. We have a fire indoors and teeming rain outside and it is very cold. The weather is good for writing but not for gypsying, but I enjoy grim, rainy days that compel one to stay in the house. I shall force myself to be industrious in the hope that, later on, I shall become so from inclination and shall take pleasure in it." To that end Felix pursued his orderly routine, especially when teaching his children. He kept up to date with changes in musical trends. His tastes mellowed by comparison with his earlier jaundiced opinions of Rossini's and Donizetti's operas. He wrote of "the gay music" in the latter's *Daughter of the Regiment*, "full of a soldier's life. How strange it is," Felix reflected, "how accustomed one becomes to what one previously thought of as bad music." At Felix's request Chorley played finales from Verdi operas, notably *Ernani*, first produced in Milan in 1842. However, Mendelssohn was particularly fascinated by *Nabucco*, understandable in view of his lifelong interest in everything concerned with Judaism. Felix still yearned to compose an opera to be produced in Paris. Yet neither had his love of earlier music forsaken him. He complained, for instance, how ineptly Handel's organ concertos were played.

Literature still interested Felix also, as is evident from a comment to Paul on a book by the French author, Eugène Sue: "He relates everything together with the greatest precision." When Paul and Hensel returned to Germany, Felix decided to

Chapter 30: The Spirit Leaves its Cage

live with the family in Berlin: "It is almost impossible now to want to live among strangers," he confided to his brother. On returning to Berlin any hint of recovery as a result of his orderly Swiss holiday was not to last. On seeing Fanny's old rooms his health relapsed. Though, before Fanny's funeral, her coffin had been placed in the area in which the Sunday concerts took place, the piano had now been returned to its customary position and nothing had changed from his previous visit, when Fanny was alive. An Afghan rug was spread over the sofa as before and, even more poignant for Felix, the score of his *First Walpurgisnacht* could still be seen on the music stand of the piano. Felix never recovered from seeing this shrine to his beloved sister and mother figure.

Nevertheless, his thoughtfulness compelled Felix to enquire of Hensel as to his feelings and objectives for the future. The artist "talked wildly about the two of them [Felix and himself] journeying to the Orient, taking in Jerusalem en route, where we could study and try to unfathom the mysteries of early Christian art", Sebastian Hensel recorded in his memoir, *The Mendelssohn Family, 1729-1847*. What a pity such a trip never took place. Who knows what fine inspiration Hensel might have gained in his painting career, which would apply later to Holman Hunt in the same environment? Might Felix have felt himself able to complete his oratorio *Christus*, or compose other sacred works in this ideal ambience? Such fantasies are futile. Like Hensel, Germany was the only location in which Felix felt comfortable. He planned to live at Leipzigerstrasse 3, as he wrote to Dirichlet, "alongside those with whom I enjoyed my childhood and youth, whose memories, friendships and experiences are the same as my own, [in] one pleasant and united household, such as we have not had for a long time, living happily and independently of politics, which have swallowed up everything else".

Towards the end of his life doctors tried to prevent Felix playing any instrument in public, but no one could defy his sense of duty, nor his desire to compose. Von Fallersleben's *Commitatus* moved Felix so deeply that the poet confided how Mendelssohn's letter regarding this setting was stained by tears. Eichendorff's 'Night Song', believed to have been the last piece of Mendelssohn's music published in his lifetime, was chosen as a song setting, dedicated to his Leipzig friend Conrad Schleinitz. On 8th October 1847 Felix held a class at the Conservatorium, when he wrote specimen exercises for his students. The next day Moscheles and his wife suggested a walk in the Rosenthal Park, the scene of so many happy days with Schumann. He walked far more slowly than would ever have occurred to him on earlier occasions. All he wished was to reminisce about life in London. This must have revived his spirits, for Felix Moscheles described his godfather's mood as "almost gay" during the "excellent lunch" that he enjoyed afterwards.

But this rally was short-lived. That evening he called upon Livia Frege, begging her to sing in a forthcoming performance of *Elijah*, threatening to visit her each day until she agreed to this request. When she sang his 'Night Song', Felix shivered. "How weary it sounds," he sighed, "but it is just how I feel, grey on grey." Mme.

Frege was asked to perform the song again and again, after which he requested her to sing through the final quarter of *Elijah*, if she did not feel too fatigued. On returning to the room, having fetched materials to light the lamps, Mme. Frege found that Felix had collapsed. "An overwrought nervous system" was diagnosed, for which a saline draught was prescribed to act as a stimulant. Leeches were applied for "a stomach ailment", together with various other tonics and medicines, but nothing availed. On 25th October Felix wrote what is believed to have been his last letter, accepting Paul's invitation "with the utmost eagerness of heart" to live at Leipzigerstrasse 3. "Though, God be praised, my health is improving more and more, the idea of travelling to Vienna [for Jenny Lind's appearance in *Elijah*) is unthinkable. It is most unfortunate that they have made so many preparations and that my arrival should be put off a second time."

As for his move to Berlin, Felix could formulate no plans, since, like his trip to Vienna, the journey would have to be postponed, "at least until the end of November". Felix decided, however, to accept no further engagements, "even if one were not obliged to keep them – but one is". On 31st October Cécile wrote to Rebecka that Felix's condition "has remained stable for the past 15 days and he feels better, having been bled by the doctor today. Carus [the Mendelssohns' regular doctor] assures me that there is no cause for concern and Dr. Aarnt has said likewise." Despite these comforting words, Cécile added: "I am trying to achieve the impossible in keeping up my spirits, but this is too difficult."

Felix was able to take further walks with Moscheles and his wife, during which he spoke of the forthcoming performance of *Elijah* in Vienna and discussed at great length the future of the Leipzig Conservatorium. Once again, Felix lost consciousness, "speaking excitedly in English". According to Marek, Paul offered "to summon the whole medical faculty of Berlin". He is purported to have consulted Dr. Schönlein, "who could not attend, as he was looking after a princess at the time," Marek states. In view of Fanny's abhorrence of this physician, it is highly likely that he would have been the last doctor in whom Cécile or Felix would have shown faith. A further strange anecdote from Marek's biography is that Cécile called Paul back to Felix's room because she could not calm her husband: "Paul jokingly scolded Felix for making such a commotion." During the last days not only Cécile and Paul but Ferdinand David and Conrad Schleinitz kept vigil at Felix's bedside. Once Mendelssohn became lucid from his state of unconsciousness his wife reluctantly tried to rest, on doctor's orders. Cécile asked how Felix felt; "Tired. Very tired," was all he said.

In his reminiscences of Ferdinand David, Johann Eckardt wrote of how, like Mozart on his deathbed: "Felix pursed his lips, attempting to make musical sounds". In their chapter on Mendelssohn, J. and D. L. Thomas record how the noise of a passing carnival disturbed the peace of the sickroom. "Suddenly, the maestro raised his head and threw it back in a gesture well known to the bystanders. He had been summoned to conduct his first concert in the beyond." Paul stood at

Chapter 30: The Spirit Leaves its Cage

Figure 12. 'Altdeutsches Frühlingslied',
Mendelssohn's last known composition, 1847

his brother's bedside, "his hands clasped behind his back, motionless as a statue". Cécile bent towards her husband, either to hear something he was saying or, more likely, to proffer her last kiss to the man she loved so devotedly. Bulletins were issued, as in the case of royalty, giving news of Mendelssohn's state of health. Finally, however, an English student (possibly Rockstro), wrote home: "Mendelssohn passed away on 4th November at 9.24 p.m. and, on the two days following, mourners by the hundred crowded into the house to pay their final respects to the man they loved and no bar was given to their access."

On the following Sunday, at 4 p.m., the coffin was conveyed to the Church of St Paul for a funeral service. Moscheles had made an arrangement for wind band of Felix's *Song without Words* Op. 67, No. 3, later to be named 'Funeral March'. It is interesting to observe that the same melody is contained in Mahler's 4th Symphony. De Senlis, senior student at the Conservatorium, carried a cushion on which rested Mendelssohn's Order of Merit from the King of Prussia, with a silver crown to which each student had contributed. David, Hauptmann, Gade, Moscheles, Julius Rietz and Schumann carried the pall. The coffin was almost obliterated by flowers and palm leaves, and the procession constituted not only representatives from all the musical institutions in Leipzig but the whole spectrum of civic dignitaries. Paul led the family mourners and the coffin was placed on a catafalque with six candles. De Senlis placed the crown at Mendelssohn's feet and the choir sang three items, including 'Happy and Blest are They' from *St Paul*. Pastor Howard, who had married Cécile to Felix ten years previously, gave the sermon and the service ended with the choir singing the final chorus from Bach's *St Matthew Passion*. According to Paul, Cécile could not bear the ordeal of the service, but, once the congregation had departed, a solitary figure was observed, in deep mourning – Felix's widow, paying her final farewell to her husband and father of her children.

Mendelssohn was buried in the family vault in the Church of the Holy Trinity, Berlin, and his mortal remains were conveyed by rail from Leipzig to their final resting place. The train left at 10 p.m. and, at Dessau, Johann Schneider, having evidently forgotten his former hostility, had composed a song of farewell that his choir sang. At Köthen a chorale was sung by a choir conducted by Eduard Theile, and the mourners arrived in Berlin to commit the great composer's body to its final rest at dawn. The funeral service comprised a hymn composed by Grell, sung by the Singakademie Choir. Pastor Berduschek gave the funeral oration. The arrangement of Mendelssohn's 'Funeral March' was played, as in Leipzig, and the chorale 'Jesu my Joy' was sung as a finale. Thus the coffin, garlanded with ivy and laurel, was conveyed from the hearse, draped in black, to the family vault. Friends gave eulogies at the graveside, whilst women and children scattered flowers and the men threw earth into the grave.

Care must be taken when researching Mendelssohn's life, in view of so much myth attaching to his name. J. and D. L. Thomas write that Schumann carried a

Chapter 30: The Spirit Leaves its Cage

silver spade with which the earth was prepared for Felix's burial, but no one else records this incident. Likewise, Nathalie MacFarren, who translated Devrient's memoirs into English, claims that a Herr Grandieson informed her that the name 'Felix' did not appear on Mendelssohn's tombstone. This led Stratton to wonder why this name was ever given to him. However, Rockstro reproduces the simple superscription "Jakob Ludwig Felix Mendelssohn-Bartholdy, born 3rd February 1809, died 4th November 1847".

"By Fanny's death, our family was shattered. By Felix's, it is annihilated," Paul wrote later. Hensel's speciality was to sketch eminent people immediately after death, so what more natural than that Fanny and Felix were commemorated in this manner? In 1849 W. A. Lampadius wrote the first biography of Felix, to be joined in 1879 by Sebastian Hensel's memoirs, spanning the Mendelssohn family from the birth of Moses in 1729 to Felix's death in 1847.

On 7th November a concert was given at the Gewandhaus to replace that cancelled on the evening of Mendelssohn's death. The programme included Mendelssohn's own works during the first part, when Livia Frege was asked to perform his 'Night Song', sung "in a tear-choked voice". After the interval Beethoven's 'Choral' Symphony was given. In his usual state of health, 9.24 p.m. would have been the time when Felix looked forward to returning to his loving family. On the present occasion, musicians and audience must have reflected that, though not visible, their former director could have been with them in spirit.

Various causes have been propounded for Mendelssohn's death. A radio broadcaster suggested that a heart attack occurred, owing to the superhuman commitment he had given to composing *Elijah*. Clara Schumann remembered "the effects of three strokes, which came one after the other, during the course of a fortnight, just as had happened with his sister Fanny, as if she had drawn him after her". She recalled his saying: "I shall die like Fanny", which seems to have been a fixed idea with him. Klingemann, too, wrote of his friend having sustained "a series of strokes", whereas an article by R. Sterndale Bennett in *The Musical Times* (No. 48 of 1955) states that "a fit of apoplexy killed him". Grief at Fanny's loss must have had some bearing on her brother's demise. As Rockstro recalled: "The old wound reopened on Felix revisiting Fanny's former rooms, wearing his life away with a merciless rapidity." It is evident that Mendelssohn did, at various times have premonitions as to how short a time he might live. During his last visit to London this became more and more apparent. When Julius Benedict, noticing a Bible on a nearby table, asked Felix to quote his favourite passage, his answer was to read the words from Ecclesiastes: "Vanity of vanities; all is vanity"; and, wrote Benedict, "At that very moment, Mendelssohn looked extremely ancient." Even after his last farewell to the Queen and Prince Albert, he had complained of being "so tired that I can hardly raise my arm".

Though strokes may seem plausible in an analysis of how Mendelssohn died, no less an authority than the Heart and Stroke Association has given the verdict that such an ailment is far less likely to occur when an individual keeps fit, which Felix undoubtedly did, having revelled in so many athletic accomplishments. Research carried out in Denmark has shown, as publicised in an article in *The Times* of May 1995, that wine tends to prevent strokes or heart attacks. Wine played a regular part at the Mendelssohn family table. In any case, such conditions assail adults, whereas Mendelssohn's symptoms pursued him from youth. Dr. John O'Shea appears to be the most accurate in diagnosing how Felix died. In his book *Illnesses of Great Composers* he traces the cause to a "congenital aneurysm of the artery at the base of the brain", which occurred with several members of the family, beginning with Moses Mendelssohn, if not his ancestors. "In this condition, when the blood vessels dilate berry-like swellings form, known as 'berry aneurysms' on that account. These rupture, and, if severe bleeding is experienced, sudden death is imminent." Symptoms include fainting spells, due to congenitally weak blood vessels in the brain; falling asleep without warning; irritability, which could change his whole personality from one minute to the next, as friends reported; the strange phenomenon of speaking in a language other than his own when losing consciousness; and, above all, excruciating headaches that made him scream with pain. O'Shea also mentions clouded vision and stiffness of the neck muscles, from which Felix did suffer from time to time. Though high blood pressure was given as a cause of death, this cannot be ascertained, as the sphygmomanometer was not invented until 1876, almost 30 years after Mendelssohn's death. During his last illness Felix complained of his blood vessels "throbbing like hammers" and "each part of the body feeling as if playing chess, jumping over one another". His pulse rate was 40 beats to the minute and he felt "cold and clammy". He was "anxious and agitated, but not irrational".

Rockstro's remarks, albeit written with hindsight, are understandable. "'The curse of the Mendelssohns' was a phrase often used when a member of the family passed away unexpectedly, unable to reach their allotted 'three score years and ten' of the Old Testament. All around him failed to look fairly and squarely in the face. It is impossible to believe that those dear ones could have been really so blind to the truth." But is this too arbitrary a verdict? In view of the primitive state of medicine at the time, it is more likely that Felix's family and friends must have felt helpless and powerless to suggest any efficacious remedy, especially to someone who could not be persuaded to relax – which might have helped improve his health. After all, the most eminent physicians, treated even more like gods than today, found nothing seriously wrong, either with Felix or other members of the Mendelssohn family.

It is interesting to wonder what any composer, artist, poet or author who died young might have produced had they lived longer. Richard Strauss, Verdi and Vaughan Williams all created some of their most exciting works in their eighties. Conversely, it can be argued, Wordsworth and Sibelius, whilst living to a great age, each had the misfortune to run out of new and imaginative ideas whilst

Chapter 30: The Spirit Leaves its Cage

comparatively young. What about the unhappy circumstances of Liszt or Elgar? Having reached the mid-seventies in each case, both wished their life would end. Liszt had not only lost his looks and charismatic personality but had been forsaken by his children and grandchildren. Elgar pined for a world that had vanished and, "if anyone troubled about him at all, the present generation wanted his music – not the man himself", as Percy Young writes. It follows that genuine lovers of Mendelssohn need not grieve that he died so young. Not only did he create such a wide variety of music but he took every opportunity to prove himself to have possessed not only a multifaceted, but a loving and lovable personality. Medical analysis assists in allowing the Mendelssohn connoisseur in bearing the loss of this man of 38 years. Dr. Schönlein predicted that, had Felix sustained a further "attack", his life would have had no hope. The Leipzig physician to whom Charles Horsley had spoken was even more precise in his prognosis: whilst Felix's life could have been spared, "melancholy madness" would have resulted. Were this true, Mendelssohn's early death can only be seen as a blessing compared with this undignified state had he remained alive. As it was, all who had known him could remember the real person, full of vitality until almost the end of his life.

Tributes poured from many sources. Charles Horsley's first knowledge of the unbelievable circumstances was gleaned from *The Times* and Chorley's equivalent obituary in *The Athenaeum*. Not since Scott's death 15 years earlier, the latter pointed out, had so great an impact been made as when Mendelssohn passed away. "Our grief was great," Clara Schumann wrote in her diary, "for he was so dear to us, not only as an artist but as a man and a friend. His death is an irreparable loss to all who knew and loved him. He has been taken from earth in the full splendour of his powers. As an artist, he stands at the highest summit of his fame. Is it not happiness to die thus?" Clara took action whilst paying such a fine tribute. It was she who summoned Devrient from Dresden to comfort Cécile in her loss: "She received me with the friendliness of a sister," he recalled. "She wept in silence, but was calm and composed, as ever, thanking me for all the love and devotion I had shown to her Felix. She grieved that I must mourn for so faithful a friend and spoke of the love with which Felix had always recognised me. Long we spoke of him. It comforted her and she was loth for me to depart. She was most unpretentious in her sorrow, gentle and resigned to living for the care and education of their children, saying that God would surely help her and hoping that the boys would inherit some of their father's genius."

Hiller arrived during the week after Felix's death. Though their friendship had been severed, Cécile was able to tell him that, in Felix's last illness, he had spoken often of Hiller. "I witnessed the indelible marks of her sorrow," Hiller wrote later, "yet, though her eyes were full of tears, she showed admirable restraint." Cécile wrote to her sister-in-law how Hiller's visit had "fortified and sustained" her. "He has helped me to accept my loss with patience and resignation. How thankful I am, when waking each morning, to feel so well. Mother has written that she bows to the Almighty Will with fortitude worthy of the ancients." Rebecka wrote of how "the angels will help and preserve me", adding that a performance of Elijah had been given by the Berlin Singakademie as a requiem for Felix. Cécile received letters of condolence from the Kings of Prussia and Saxony, and from the Queen of England. Her reply described how deeply Felix's widow appreciated "your keen sympathy in the tragic loss that has just been inflicted upon me. If anything can console me for the cruel sorrow I have just experienced, it would be by the affection shown to me by Your Majesty and His Royal Highness, Prince Albert. Unfortunately, there is no human consolation in such a trial, but, thanks to the infinite mercy of God, I shall follow a path bare of all joy." Enclosed with Cécile's letter were some songs, including her late husband's 'Nachtlied' ('Night Song') – "a beautiful song, but very melancholy. It makes me feel quite sad."

Yet one mourner who wrote to Cécile appears to have shown not only self-indulgence but crass tactlessness. She expressed herself "numb with grief, as soon as I am obliged to hear or read anything about him. I become almost incapable of carrying out the great duty I have taken upon my shoulders. Everything seems dead to me. How happy, how blest did I feel, when I spoke to him. Seldom can there have been two people who understood and sympathised with each other, as we did." Thus Jenny Lind had written to Hans Christian Andersen. How thoughtless to write in this way to someone so completely in love with her, paying tribute with such eulogy to another man. How hurt this writer of fairy tales must have felt when learning of this prima donna's feelings, when all Jenny regarded Andersen as was her "dear brother". Meeting Clara and Robert Schumann in Vienna, Jenny had confided how thankful she was to God "for sending the purest and most refined artist into my life", forgetting how equally "pure and refined" the people were with whom she conversed. Even to Cécile, Jenny's thoughtlessness was witnessed. She expressed gratitude that she had been "loved and worshipped by someone not only exceptionally gifted, but noble and great. I hope that, one day, we shall be together again, and then we shall be happy for ever." Nothing about how Cécile must have felt at her untimely loss. Cécile can be forgiven for feeling not only painfully hurt, but, rarely for her usually gentle and forbearing personality, deeply angry at such selfish thoughts.

Flowers arrived from all quarters at the Leipzig home, filling the rooms with perfume. Not only did this apply to the commemoration of Felix's death, but to remember what would have been his 39th birthday, on the 3rd February 1848. Though she admitted herself to feeling well, Cécile excused herself to Wilhelm von Boguslawski for "resulting debts owing in correspondence" on account of a "long-standing indisposition". Indeed, she would be scarcely free from illness subsequently. Unlike Queen Victoria, who would grieve for almost 40 years at the death of Prince Albert, Cécile had barely six further years to live, passing away on 25th September 1853. She hoped that "God will give me the joy of bringing up the children of so much love and companionship, in a not unworthy manner";

Chapter 30: The Spirit Leaves its Cage

such a hope was unable to be fulfilled. Petitpierre writes of Cécile's bouts of depression and of her "suffering from a sort of anaemia", but no further details are forthcoming. Such a physical condition would not have been helped by the muddled state of her husband's business affairs. These were placed in the hands of various trustees. Though these persons are unnamed, it does not need a gambler to wager that Paul must have been the prime mover in their settlement. Felix had never made a will, believing, presumably, that ample time remained to him for his affairs to be put into order, despite his premonitions of an early death. It is interesting, however, to learn that, in an age when women were usually considered constitutionally incapable of coping with such 'male' subjects as finance, Felix had sighed to Cécile: "We shall never learn, my dear, to talk about business matters together." The plural might well have included Felix himself, whereas Cécile was a very shrewd businesswoman. It was she who kept a tight rein on the housekeeping (as has been seen in Chapter 27, 'At home with Cécile and Felix Mendelssohn').

Her business sense continued after her husband's death, as is glimpsed by random details. It was she who insisted on signing a document with Paul that allowed the children the full protection of, and entitlement to, Felix's inheritance. It was Cécile who constantly chivvied the trustees regarding the length of time taken by the law to settle such unfinished business. She even had the temerity to call such procedure "a singularly clumsy, German, way of behaving". It would be unfair to accuse Paul and his colleagues of deliberately prolonging the legal tangle into which the Mendelssohn estate had fallen. Rather, having been absorbed by a career in banking, he would have ensured that 'everything is done by the book', thus obeying the letter, rather than the spirit, of the law, since 'this is the way things must be done'. Any imagination he may have possessed as a young man might well have been muzzled by his years of discretion.

As regards the children, it was Droysen who recommended that Karl attend the school at which the historian von Ranke was principal. Ferdinand Ries and Niels Gade were asked to find a violin tutor "with patience" to instruct Marie; "Her piano playing makes progress," Cécile reported. Even on the fifth anniversary of Felix's death in 1852, despite her deterioration in health, Hiller noticed "the pleasant and natural chatter" of the children and "the gentle and charming way" in which Cécile "tried to moderate their liveliness". He considered his visit "a profoundly moving experience" and was "astonished" at the joy displayed by the children. What pleasure Felix would have received had he lived, and how well this would have been reciprocated. Yet, however much she strove for independence, Paul appears to have controlled his widowed sister-in-law's assets, even to the extent of her having to submit a budget of household expenses for his scrutiny and approval. On receiving, at last, the inventory of her husband's money, property and music, Cécile had to admit: "I do not in the least understand it, except for the last part. The extraordinary claims of the publishers have, in no way, diminished." A publisher at Koblenz, for example, claimed that a quantity of sacred music had been entrusted to him by Felix, on behalf of the King, who now wished to have the scores published. The proceeds, Cécile was told, would be given to a "Mendelssohn fund". Did his widow object? "I do not know the answer," she replied, "since Felix never gave an opinion on the matter." Various other of his compositions posed queries, details of which she was unaware, and neither could Paul shed any light thereon.

Yet there were occasions that allowed Cécile to enjoy herself during this period of gloom. Whilst at first she considered it her duty to remain in Berlin, despite the invitations from various friends to take a holiday with them, her doctor prescribed a complete change of air, not only for health reasons but to benefit from new surroundings.

In 1850, therefore, Cécile visited the spa town of Kreuznach and, the following year, she took a holiday at Schlangenbad. Here she dined with acquaintances, who enjoyed her own hospitality in return. An unnamed gentleman sent her six smoke-cured geese as a gift from Pomerania. The artist Jakob Becker wished to paint her portrait, and a kinsman, Charles Jeanrenaud de Bihl, offered to have a new house built for her. So expertly did Cécile discuss the plans that Jean Petitpierre believes that she could have qualified as an architect had she lived in a later generation. She was, equally, an early conservationist, asking that some larch trees should remain, rather than be destroyed when the house was built. On a visit to the Italian lakes Cécile expressed the hope that more trees would be planted.

In 1852 Cécile's godmother, her aunt Charlotte, passed away. This lady had inspired both love and respect with this loss, together with and the fifth anniversary of Felix's death coming at a similar date, his widow admitted, at last, how difficult she found life, having to cope with her day-to-day existence. To add to her personal burdens, times had been hard politically since 1848. Rather than having to dismiss a servant, Franz, his employer hoped that, during this time of revolution, he would have to be called up for military service. Though Albertine made everything as comfortable as if Felix himself were still present, Cécile elected to stay with her family in Frankfurt, but she still could not escape the rioting of revolutionaries, as she wrote to Paul. Stalls from the annual fair were used as barricades, and many townspeople were killed. Cécile expressed disgust at the sacking of Dresden, and exclaimed: "Does the progress of civilisation have to lead to such shameful war?" Berlin experienced similar insurrection. Cécile often complained of "being obscured by a dark veil" when considering her future. "My body is like a suit of armour." On 10th January 1853 she wrote what is said to have been her last letter, to her father's godmother, Julie Petitpierre. This consisted of reminiscences of times past, especially the immense garden at Leipzigerstrasse 3, where every bush reminded her of the "beautiful days now long gone. Yet, one is only travelling this life on a temporary basis, and there is no homeland."

Through the spring and summer Cécile's lungs deteriorated to such an extent that nothing could alleviate her condition. She passed away at her mother's home

Chapter 30: The Spirit Leaves its Cage

on 25th September of that year. At six o'clock that evening her aunt, Mme. Souchay, told her son of the "choking fits" her niece was experiencing. "I found her in an indescribable state. Taking both my hands, she begged me not to leave her. 'I have no one,' she pleaded. 'I do not want my mother to come in. She suffers too much when she sees my condition.'" On preparing to depart Mme. Souchay was called back, and her brother, a physician, Dr. Schmidt, was summoned. He advised, in view of the agony she was suffering, that Cécile should not be moved. Nevertheless, short of breath, she constantly begged for air. At 10 p.m. she was heard to reprimand her aunt for losing sleep the previous night and asking her to go home, but Mme. Souchay remained, as a storm had begun. Because Cécile had rallied, the doctor said it would be suitable to leave her alone. However, at five the next morning, relatives were summoned to her bedside. Having prayed for a peaceful end, her wish had been granted, as she had died in her sleep.

During Cécile's last moments of consciousness Paul, summoned from Berlin, recalled how she had held out her right hand, which he kissed. "Then, as if thinking of Felix, she lifted up her eyes for a long time, kissed her hand again and sent a greeting heavenward. She had greeted with a sublime, confident gesture her Christian husband, whom fate told her she was about to find shining in glory," Petitpierre recorded. When Hiller called the next day Mme. Jeanrenaud told him, "I have just this moment lost a daughter." Senator Souchay recalled how his niece had never complained, even when he had had to carry her upstairs when she suffered so much pain. "Today a rare flower has bowed her head," he wrote. "The gentle soul of Cécile has joined Felix in eternity." Wilhelm Hensel, as was his custom, made a drawing of his sister-in-law at her deathbed: "Her face looked haggard; her eyes were large," reported Sebastian Hensel, and, indeed, his father's sketch bears witness to this description. Cécile was buried in the Protestant cemetery in Frankfurt. A marble cross was placed at her graveside, bearing the date and place of birth and the date of her death, in letters of gilt. Though no explanation is extant as to why she was not buried along with her husband and youngest son in Berlin, this could well have been either her own or her family's choice.

To the children Marek pays short shrift, giving merely the dates on which they died, adding that "none of them were particularly gifted". Though Felix junior had little chance to exercise his potential, having lived to nine years of age, let readers judge how inaccurate Marek's verdict is. Both Marie and Lilli married distinguished academics, Victor Benecke and Adolf Wach respectively. Marie's husband was a relative of Cécile's, whose children were Marguerite, Eduard (whose body was never recovered from the Jungfrau after he had died whilst climbing that mountain), and Paul, the eldest, who became a professor of philology and, later, bursar of Magdalen College, Oxford. It was said of him that, during World War I, "he ruined his colleagues' digestions by his unnecessarily injurious economies." Lilli married an international lawyer who, representing many clients at courts of arbitration, was honoured by the King of Saxony. Their three sons followed in their father's profession and their daughter, Dora, married Karl's son, Albrecht Mendelssohn, as his second wife. One of the grandchildren, Maria Wach, lived to bequeath many Mendelssohn manuscripts and letters to the Bodleian Library, Oxford.

Of Karl, his mother had spoken of his "making only slow progress" as a boy, but it is evident that, once he and Paul were adopted by the family of Felix's brother, matters improved to an unprecedented degree. He was to become a professor of history at the Universities of Heidelberg and Freiburg-im-Breisgau, writing a history of Greece from 1453. He became a fellow of the Royal Geographical Society for his research on the pyramids, on which a definitive treatise of the time was compiled. Of his children, Albrecht was the most prominent, becoming a professor of jurisprudence and, like Paul Benecke, gravitating to Oxford University. In World War I he contributed leading articles on its causes and became a delegate at the Versailles Peace Conference of 1919. Albrecht became a specialist on the Dawes Plan, a commission promulgated by Senator Charles Gates Dawes of the United States to reconstruct the German economy and to ensure that reparation was made to the Allies. He edited the archives of the German Foreign Office but, once the Nazis came to power, was debarred of his professorship at the University of Hamburg. A position was therefore made for him at Oxford in 1933. A doctorate of law was awarded him by Harvard, where his book, *The War and German Society, The Testament of a Liberal*, was published. Herbert Kupferberg considers this the most concise and lucid analysis of the First World War. Albrecht, who died in 1936, wrote what Marek calls "a youthful opera", to which, sadly, no further reference has been discovered.

Paul, though originally gaining a degree in philology, became interested in science, for which he was awarded a doctorate from Heidelberg University. He fought at the Battle of Sadowa in 1866 as a non-commissioned officer and, having gained his commission, fought in the Franco-Prussian War of 1870-71. Between these periods of military achievement he joined the Hoffmann Laboratory to study chemistry and, later, he founded his own factory to experiment in modern dyeing methods, particularly aniline dyes. His Agfa Corporation became known throughout the industrial world, especially for films and cameras. It is, therefore, a Mendelssohn – a son of Felix – to whom credit must be given for what was to become a multinational empire. Sadly, however, Paul's overwork caused his death from a heart attack at a similar age to his father. His son, Otto, became a banker and Hugo, Otto's brother, was the last to bear the Mendelssohn name as a direct descendant of Felix. When Blunt wrote his biography *On Wings of Song*, Hugo still lived in Basle, Switzerland, where he collected family archives. The three daughters, according to Petitpierre, "did not manage to produce one Mendelssohn between them". Intermarriage became a cult among the family, producing "a galaxy of Céciles and a whole regiment of Felixes".

Of Albertine and Paul's five children, Ernst, the eldest, superseded his father as

Chapter 30: The Spirit Leaves its Cage

head of the Mendelssohn Bank, which he raised to even greater prestige, being honoured with the right to place 'von' in front of his name. When Ernst von Mendelssohn-Bartholdy died in 1919 he was believed to be the richest man in Berlin. Ernst and his cousin Robert, Joseph's grandson, donated Monet's painting *The Winter Garden* to Berlin's Museum of Modern Art.

After Fanny's death Wilhelm Hensel appeared to lose all interest in painting, although he had many commissions to complete, including, a picture for the Coronation Hall in Brunswick. He filled his time with politics, an interest which Fanny could never encourage him to pursue. He attended political clubs and meetings "and his desk was littered with newspapers", as his son Sebastian reported. Hensel died in 1861 as the result of injuries sustained whilst rescuing a little girl from a street accident. Gustav Dirichlet superseded the mathematician Professor Gauss at the University of Göttingen in the Netherlands. Though a few concerts took place at his home, nothing ever compared with those of Leipzigerstrasse 3. Indeed, Rebecka referred to these latter entertainments as "crumbs from our old feasts" in a letter to her nephew, Sebastian Hensel. Rebecka died in 1861 of a similar ailment to that of Felix and – probably – Fanny, Abraham, Moses and others of the Mendelssohn lineage. Her husband, Gustav, had died in 1855. Felix's brother Paul, despite "a long illness" (unexplained), survived until 1874, and his wife, Albertine, died five years later.

Of Joseph's children, Alexander succeeded his father at the Hamburg branch of the family bank. The luxury in which he lived is manifest by the fact that, when the Empress Augusta wanted a bath, it was Alexander Mendelssohn's family on whom she called for this rare item of domestic comfort. Alexander's sons, Robert and Franz, became joint heads of this branch of the bank. Robert, an amateur 'cellist, married an Italian singer, Giulietta Gordigiani, who gave birth to a daughter, Elinora, named after the actress Elinora Duse, in whose house the event occurred. Her own acting career is amply described by Herbert Kupferberg. Of Nathan's descendants, Arnold Mendelssohn is the best known, having written three operas and three symphonies amongst his compositions. He taught music theory at the Conservatories of Cologne and Frankfurt, but his greatest achievement was to have taught Paul Hindemith his craft. Other Mendelssohn descendants include Dr. Felix Gilbert, an academic of Princeton University, surviving as late as 1994, and a George H. de Mendelssohn, who became a president of the American Vox record company. Older readers will remember Felix Mendelssohn (1911-52), whose claim to be descended directly from his composer namesake leaves room for doubt. With his group, Felix Mendelssohn and his Hawaiian Serenaders, the latter Felix was wont to dress "in bright clothes", as his ancestor is supposed to have done. No one, however, of the popular music authorities questioned appears to know anything about this man of mystery.

Meanwhile, what became of Felix's intimate circle of friends? As is so often related, Robert Schumann died in a lunatic asylum at Endenich, near Bonn, in

1856. Having thrown himself into the Rhine, hoping to drown, some sailors, thinking he must have been drunk, as it was carnival time, fished him out, which caused him to be confined to the asylum. Clara survived him until 1896. Jenny Lind, having transferred her career from opera to oratorio at Mendelssohn's suggestion, lived in England until 1887, dying at Great Malvern. With her husband, Otto Goldschmidt, who had been a pupil of Felix at the Leipzig Conservatorium, she formed the Bach Choir, whose first performance in 1875 was the B minor Mass. Her main task, however, was to instigate the Mendelssohn Scholarship (see part IV of the Epilogue). When Klingemann died in 1862, the 20-year-old Arthur Sullivan wrote of him as "an upright and Christian gentleman". The diplomat's widow, Sophie, much younger, survived her husband, as did three of their five children. Fanny Horsley, who married the physician Seth Thompson, outlived Felix for only two years. When the Horsley letters were compiled by Rosamund Brunel Gotch in 1934, her 'biographical notes' give the information that, had she lived at that time, "a minor operation" would have remedied her ill health, but she gives no further explanation. Sophie's ambition to become a professional musician was never achieved, but she played a crucial part on behalf of the Mendelssohn family. As Mrs. Gotch writes: "She took Felix's whole family into her embrace – his wife, children, grandchildren, nephews, nieces, even cousins to an almost remote degree…for them, she was a 'universal aunt'." Sophie never married but, as well as the Mendelssohn clan, cared for her own sisters until her death in 1894. Sadly, nothing is known of the Miss Taylors, except for Anne's article on Felix in the first edition of Grove's *Dictionary of Music and Musicians*.

EPILOGUE

Retrospect

Part I: – The Pendulum of Fashion

Writing in 1883, Rockstro declared that, after his death, "the Mendelssohn cult was an historic fact". Though the biographer gives no explanation for this phenomenon, it is not difficult to find reasons. Before Queen Victoria shut herself away from 14th December 1861, when Prince Albert died, everything that pertained to Buckingham Palace and its occupants was copied implicitly throughout her realm. Since, therefore, Mendelssohn had been invited to play to the royal couple and even to accompany the Queen as she sang, there was no more to be said about the composer's peerless position, or the love of his music. England's most popular novelist, Charles Dickens, had acknowledged Mendelssohn as his favourite composer. A third seal was set upon his popularity when it was learnt that he had advised Jenny Lind not only to make her home in England but to transfer from opera to oratorio as a singer. Everything from soap and perfume to spectacle cases was marketed in her name, even before the circus impresario Phineas T. Barnum lured Miss Lind to the United States. It was only when she died in 1887 that Mendelssohn's popularity declined.

Newspapers continued not only to praise his music but to idealise his personality. Of *Elijah*, H. F. Chorley wrote that not only was the oratorio a sacred work for its time, but that it "will be suitable for our children and our children's children". Whereas Schumann and Wagner "only wrote critiques of other people's works", he continued, "Mendelssohn adds new beauties to what are regarded as the models of time." Rockstro followed this eulogy: "Of young composers coming to the front, there are none with reasonable prospect of carrying on the work of the departed genius. Mendelssohn, feeling the divine fire within him, stood forth as the champion of the art and did battle against the false partisans who, pretending to advance it, were, in reality, its bitterest enemies." Though he tactfully refrained from naming the composers he had in mind, Rockstro's arbitrary statement is not even worth debating when assessing the music created by composers contemporary with and subsequent to Mendelssohn.

The "Mendelssohn fever", as Stratton calls his popularity, did not concern his music solely but also his character. His music reflected his own "unfailing good manners" and his "ability to radiate a comfortable feeling to the company" with whom he came into contact. Not even the most censorious mama could reprimand her daughter when falling in love with this faultless paragon. The Rev. H. R. Haweis supported this feeling. In his book *Music and Morals* he stated that "the keen, piercing intellect, flashing with the summer lightning of sensibility and wit; that generous heart...that sweet humanity; that absolute devotion to all that was true and noble, coupled with an instinctive shrinking from all that was mean; that fierce scorn of a lie; that hatred of hypocrisy; that gentle, unassuming goodness" could all be seen in Mendelssohn's spirit. "In this age of art degradation," Haweis continued, "Mendelssohn towers above his contemporaries like a moral lighthouse in the midst of a dark and troubled sea. His light always shone strong and pure. The winds of heaven were about his head and the still, small voice was in his heart. In a lying generation, he was true. In an adulterous generation, he was pure. Neither popularity or gain could tempt him to sully the pages of his spotless inspiration with one meretricious effect or impure association."

This panegyric was written in 1871 and, though Haweis did not link such writing with an event of the previous year, Mendelssohn's popularity was enhanced beyond anyone's imagination. In 1870 a ground-breaking Education Act was passed, whereby everyone was given the opportunity to learn to read, allowing a whole new stratum of society to be made aware of Mendelssohn, through words and music. The Sacred Harmonic Society for working men continued to prosper, and, coupled with the 'tonic sol-fa' medium of music, many more people were given the means of singing and playing the piano than had been the case previously. The Crystal Palace concerts had begun in 1858, the 'Sunday Pops' four years later, encouraging people who might otherwise not have done so to listen to edifying music, which – by definition – would have included Mendelssohn's works. As a sample of what might be in the repertoire, W. S. Gilbert's quote from *The Mikado* is worth repeating: "Bach is woven with Spohr and Beethoven" at these entertainments.

A further aspect of Mendelssohn's popularity was his love of England. Chorley even forgot how Handel had made his home in London when he wrote: he was "unaware of any other fine visitor who loved England so well as did Mendelssohn", or who was "so honest and discriminating" in his appreciation of the country and her people. Yet such praise could well have had a stultifying effect on the reception of newer music, or that recently brought to light by earlier composers. *The Musical World* considered Schubert's *Fierrabras* Overture "not worth criticising". The music from Wagner's *Tannhäuser* was dismissed as "queer stuff", on which "criticism would be thrown away". Ironically, it was Mendelssohn who first brought these works to the fore.

Because of so much adulation, it was inevitable that adverse reaction had to follow. The English-speaking world found Mendelssohn's music to possess "the right mixture of decorous gaiety and decorous sentimentality", Marek writes in his book *Gentle Genius*, suiting the concept of "what a gentleman is and does. It could be taken at face value along with his personality." Once it was learnt how his domestic life resembled that of "the dear Queen and Prince Albert", Marek continues: "Mendelssohn could have written anything he chose and got away with it, so unshakable was his reputation as composer and perfect gentleman. His music was elevated far too highly. Listeners perceived profound meanings that were not there. Later, however, he was toppled from his high rock; his melodies, fluttering nonchalantly in the breeze, were harmless enough to be heard by the senior class at St. Timothy's Finishing School, without upsetting the emotional equilibrium of its pupils." After Berlioz and Wagner came onto the musical scene, "Mendelssohn's music…did not seem vital enough" to excite contemporary audiences.

Not only Marek gives Mendelssohn short shrift. Radcliffe passes off his *Songs without Words* as "sheltered from the disturbingly intense passion" displayed by Chopin or Schumann through their compositions. Radcliffe evidently forgets that these specific melodies were not written to excite audiences but to be heard quietly in a peaceful, domestic environment. This genre of Mendelssohn's music might well have been written with his own blissful family life in mind, whether as a bachelor at Leipzigerstrasse 3, as an idyllically happily married man in Leipzig, or as a guest, thoroughly at ease among his London friends. Did the Horsley or Taylor families yearn for the "breathtaking passion" that Mendelssohn could not achieve, according to his detractors? It is a pity that his *Songs without Words* were far too popular – and often too badly played – for the composer's good. They were churned out ad nauseam from the "leisured classes" in their drawing rooms, down to the pianists in the parlours of the lower strata. "Now, Melissa dear," an ambitious mother or fond aunt would exhort the young maiden, "why not play that delightful piece Miss Prout has just taught you – the one by that nice Mr. Mendelssohn?" Whilst poor Melissa's stumblings and embarrassed apologies might have been observed, it was far more likely that the older female element revelled in their own fantasies about Mendelssohn. Such a flight of fancy is not as bizarre as might first appear. Even Chorley, usually so loyal when championing Mendelssohn's music, was obliged to admit that, in order to achieve a pianistic coup, at least one of those melodies had to be included in the repertoire. Stratton complains of music libraries "groaning with diluted Mendelssohn imitations". Even otherwise highly original and worthy composers have come into this category. Anyone can be forgiven for thinking that Bizet's *Songs of the Rhine* are stablemates of Mendelssohn's *Songs without Words* or Tchaikovsky's *Chanson sans Paroles*. It is no wonder that such epithets as 'hackneyed' or 'superficial' are laid at Mendelssohn's door because of these melodies. Even music professors, who should know better, have been known to discourage their students from learning or performing them, as being "too easy".

It is a fact that only musicians of the highest calibre should attempt

Mendelssohn's works. This can be proved by an incident recorded by Ronald Pearsall in his book *Victorian Popular Music*. Whilst staying with the Lyttelton family at Hagley Hall, Worcestershire, a daughter of Gladstone remembered how "one evening, a piano sonata of Mendelssohn's was thundered out, to be followed by a Miss Glover attempting to sing some of his songs". Mendelssohn's choral music gave rise to a spate of oratorio writing but, again, not with the same success as *St Paul* or *Elijah* and his psalm settings. How many people know of Sir John Stainer's *Crucifixion*, except for the chorus 'God so Loved the World'? Can anyone answer quiz questions on Sterndale Bennett's *Woman of Samaria*, Spohr's *The Last Judgement* or Hiller's *Deborah* or *Jeremiah*? The only gleam in the oratorio repertoire of the 19th century, other than Mendelssohn's masterpieces, one can say without dispute, was Elgar's *Dream of Gerontius*, first performed at the 1900 Birmingham Festival, and even this was a failure at its first performance.

Because of Mendelssohn's waning popularity after his death, *Elijah* was condemned as "a Victorianism", too conservative for its time. Marek stresses its "smugness", due to "the English tradition", as if this were the composer's doing. Richard Hickox admits that far too many stodgy performances bear out this sentiment. Because, in his youth, the music director heard a performance by musicians who were able to do the work justice, he had "the thrill of his life". As early as 1872 Charles Horsley stated that the oratorio could be performed "with the greatest propriety...with scenery, costumes and dramatic action". Had Mendelssohn lived longer, he contended, such a production might have been staged. In fact, the baritone Sir Geraint Evans took part in such a performance at Llandaff Cathedral in the 1950s, playing the lead "in full costume".

According to Marek, "Mendelssohn is not at his best when dramatic, where he thunders weakly." Radcliffe blames his versatility for such shortcomings, seeing "the comparative ease and luxury" in which Felix is purported to have lived as assisting his musical faults. Yet these detractors are only taking the same view as Stratton had propounded 50 years earlier: "Mendelssohn's orchestral works are far less popular...because the public palate has become jaded, if not vitiated, by the pungent harmonies and gorgeous glitter of the later orchestral school." Yet even he has to contradict himself by admitting how the overtures "stand as the first of their order" and that the E minor Violin Concerto "has no rival, save that of Beethoven". It might be that musicologists, such as Radcliffe, distrust the sometimes too lavish adulation of Mendelssohn's contemporaries. When writing of the 1st movement of his 4th Organ Sonata of the set of six comprising Op. 65, John Gauntlett averred the "strong emotion, which must be concentrated. It must smite, sudden as the electric fluid; it must draw blood – and that is Mendelssohn... The movement has a heart-quivering march of the pedal from the lower E flat to the F", which Radcliffe dismisses as "a chromatic progression", chiding "the respectable Dr. Gauntlett" for reading far too much into a "merely mild and respectable" offering, which "does not deserve such an extravagant panegyric". Mendelssohn has,

Epilogue

likewise, got into musicianly hot water for his "inability" to compose an opera. His abhorrence of Victor Hugo's *Ruy Blas* is cited, having "disliked this example of lurid romanticism – the latest sensation".

This, and other librettos, caused Mendelssohn's reluctance to produce accompanying music for such works. The fact that Abraham Mendelssohn, supported by Devrient, exhorted Felix to achieve the goal of fine operas is overlooked. Because Felix "failed" to accomplish works of this genre, he is seen as "not having the right personality" for such an achievement. It is only in a Gluck biography that a counter-argument emerges: "If a composer is born into an earlier era, with an earlier style of composition, it is difficult for a musician to adapt to the new ideas." Having been born when the classical era still obtained, this might well have applied to Mendelssohn. Indeed, the more one considers his music the more remarkable was the gulf in musical styles that Mendelssohn embraced during his short lifespan. Had he lived more than his allotted 38 years, he might well have written an opera worthy of the name, having at last found a suitable heroine – Jenny Lind, for whom his *Lorelei* was begun. It must be remembered what a difficult birth Beethoven's *Fidelio* experienced; how Schubert's operas are only now being assessed as worthy of performance; how Brahms, Chopin, Bruckner and other composers of equal merit did not even attempt to write an opera. Finally, had Mendelssohn had the good fortune to work with librettists with as much empathy as did Mozart or Verdi, or, had he, like Wagner, written his own libretti, who knows what operatic triumphs he might have achieved?

As early as 1852 J. W. Davison wrote with regret how, in some musical circles, Mendelssohn was becoming "the object of pity and disparagement". As the century progressed his reputation had become "decidedly patchy", according to R. A. Streatfeild. Anything written by him was "ignored and forgotten, except for the few popular works that have survived his collapsed reputation". Indeed, Mendelssohn's and Schumann's careers were paralleled by those of Dives and Lazarus in the New Testament parable: Dives resembled "the self-indulgent Mendelssohn", whilst Lazarus (Schumann) was "reaping the glory" so unjustly given to his friend and contemporary. When the centenary of Mendelssohn's birth arrived in 1909 celebrations were of a very low key and, as far as the Paris Conservatoire was concerned, his music was not performed for many years after his death in 1847. However, other composers have suffered the same fate. In his youth, Mendelssohn deplored the state of neglect into which the music of Handel, Haydn and Mozart had fallen. Fortunately, there were exceptions against the decline of Mendelssohn's own reputation. Johannes Brahms, displeased with the "inanity" of such disparagement, was heard to murmur: "Yes. Yes. He was the last of the great masters." In 1865, Verdi's librettist, Arrigo Boito, called Mendelssohn "more than a musician...a thinker, a contemplator, a poet". Schumann regarded him as "the Mozart of the 19th century" and would refuse to sit in a room with anyone who decried the man or his music. To Liszt, Schumann stated that, whereas Meyerbeer was "a pygmy, who wrote for a small group of his followers, Mendelssohn wrote music for the whole world".

Chopin, on a visit to London, sniped that audiences wished the Philharmonic Orchestra to play works by Mozart, Beethoven and Mendelssohn and that a pianist "had to play" the latter's music to achieve success. Fortunately, however, Mendelssohn's music is now gaining a far better deserved position in the musical hierarchy. As Michael Kennedy states: "His craftsmanship, poetry, inventive orchestration and melodic freshness" are becoming recognised. How refreshing it was to hear a comment when a conversation occurred regarding this book; "Was Mendelssohn as early as that?" the speaker asked. "I thought he belonged to the 1880s, or thereabouts", so progressive did the speaker regard his music. Marek writes of his music as "faded", which can be understood when inferior performances are considered, or if all his music is lumped into the *Songs without Words* genre. Marek sees the music as "a reminder of vanished beauties. He knew how to make us feel good." Why not? His gibe is that some of Mendelssohn's music "smells of eau de Cologne". Yet, on a hot, sticky day, there is nothing more refreshing. The heady, 'sophisticated' fragrances just will not do. As for being "polite" via his music – a further criticism of Mendelssohn, – what is wrong with that? Mendelssohn's music has not faded, as some discerning musicologists are now coming to realise. To his connoisseurs, this has always been the case.

Part II: – 'Free Thought'

When, in 1849, W. A. Lampadius wrote Mendelssohn's first biography, Sterndale Bennett was prompted to plead for a more realistic pen portrait, to balance this "absurdly idealised" life history of his former friend and mentor. Schoolchildren of later generations might well have felt inadequate, realising that this apparently superhuman paragon could never be emulated. (There was even an article in a school magazine that rammed the young Mendelssohn down the throats of fellow pupils.) Yet such mawkish sentiment was far from the norm, even in his lifetime. When the Nazis came to power his image was so unutterably tarnished that his descendants were deprived of any honours earned; the Mendelssohn Bank was liquidated, and his own music was banned.

As has been observed in Chapter 17, 'Quest for an opera', Gasparo Spontini did all he could to inhibit the production of the young Mendelssohn's singspiel *Camacho's Wedding*, and, as late as 1841, this director of the Berlin Opera showed hostility towards Jewish influences on wholesome German music. At a theatre where *Antigone* was performed, Spontini opined to Heinrich Heine that music had been "spoilt" by the Jews. It was only when a beam of light revealed a lone figure sitting beneath the shadow of a pillar that Mendelssohn, who wrote the cantata,

Epilogue

was recognised by his protagonists, who must have then realised that he had heard their conversation. Heine was an ideal candidate for such a diatribe. Though born a Jew and acknowledging that he still adhered to his former faith, he wrote scurrilously about Judaism and its followers, showing particular antagonism towards Mendelssohn. "I feel malice towards the man," he wrote on 11th February 1846. "Because he pretends towards Christianity, I cannot forgive him… If I had the good fortune to be the grandson of Moses Mendelssohn, truly, I would not devote my talents to setting the piss of the Lamb of God to music." On another occasion Heine wrote how, in his opinion, Rossini's *Stabat Mater* was far more Christian than *St Paul*, adding that Mendelssohn had not been baptised until the age of 13.

Heine, for all his skill as the "great poet", as acknowledged by Fanny, via his *Travel Letters* from Italy, was unwilling to check his facts on this occasion. Felix was seven when his father, having been browbeaten by Leah's brother Jakob Bartholdy, had his family baptised into the Lutheran faith. Felix could do nothing about this change of religion. Being a free spirit (as observed in Chapter 11, "Glory to God alone"), he was as utterly sincere when composing music for the Christian Church as any other. As for the comparison between Rossini's *Stabat Mater* and *St Paul*, the latter resulted from such depression (see chapters relating thereto) that duty towards his earthly father took precedence over any spiritual intent. Had Felix been allowed to remember that he was the grandson of Moses, as opposed to the son of Abraham and Leah Mendelssohn, matters might well have proved of greater benefit to his music. Heine also took great delight that, in Paris, Mendelssohn's music had "experienced nothing but fiascos…whilst Rossini was the musical lion, whose sweet roar can still be heard". In fact, when Felix visited Paris for the final time, in 1831-32, Rossini was no longer composing.

During this latter visit Felix wrote home from Paris that he had an enemy, 'K' (probably Kalkbrenner), "who is ready to poison me from envy. At first he tried, by 1,000 intrigues, to prevent my playing altogether [at the Paris Conservatoire] but, when he heard that the Queen was actually to attend, he did everything within his power to get me out of the way." Despite such behaviour Felix did perform, for the first time in Paris, Beethoven's 4th Piano Concerto. "Happily, all the other members of the conservatoire…are my faithful allies, and so he [K] signally fails. He is the only musician here who acts unkindly towards me… It is always a very painful sensation to know that one is always in the company of a person who hates one, but who is careful not to show this outwardly." In 1834, writing to Julius Schubring, Felix was still "grieved" at the hostility 'K's family was demonstrating. "There is nothing more distressing than to have enemies, yet it seems impossible to avoid this. However much I aim to be on friendly terms, it is not always possible to do so."

It can be argued with justification that Mendelssohn did not do his own cause any good having learnt to be nothing but almost pathologically self-effacing, which might well have been regarded as false modesty by those who had no wish to understand him. His mother once remarked that Felix was "indifferent to praise", but, as this was so rare from his parents, he must have taken time to become accustomed to the adulation he would receive, from Leipzig and London especially. Neither was this attitude helped by his premonitions, whether true or imagined. He maintained that "a great gulf" existed between music conceived in the mind and that actually printed and which would reach an audience. This view caused many of his works to remain – as they still are – unpublished. Had Mendelssohn had his way, the public would have never been allowed to hear his Italian or Reformation Symphonies, his last two books of *Songs without Words*, or much sacred music, songs and chamber works. It is only latterly that his early singspiels and concertos have been published and there is still much music in manuscript to be explored and brought to light. As far as Mendelssohn was concerned his output reached Op. 77, whereas, since his death, his published works have been extended to Op. 121. He was equally despondent about works that did reach public audiences. Of his 'Scottish' Symphony, on which he was working, he told Ferdinand David that "it will be as good as I can make it, though whether it will be popular and played on a barrel organ I cannot tell". To George Sampson, as the English singer recalled, Felix declared: "Sadly, posterity will remember me for my little pieces, rather than for my larger efforts...[and] not as the master but the servant to earlier composers." To President Verkenius of Cologne he wrote: "I believe the present hostility to my music will prevail until the end of time in Berlin." In view of such depression, Felix might not have been surprised at the turn events would take in the 1930s when the Nazis came to power. Psychologists often tell their clients that, the greater the ill they think of themselves, the more likely others will think of them in a similar manner.

Neither did Mendelssohn enter any competitions for composers, and nor did he judge them. Stratton considers that this reluctance might have arisen from the incident Mendelssohn experienced during his first visit to London (detailed in part I of Chapter 24, 'Mendelssohn as music critic'). On 4th November 1834 Felix felt it necessary to explain his reason for expressing pride when publishing houses showed interest in future output: "I am only conveying this news, not from conceit, but because mother especially enjoys hearing such details." Max Müller showed crass misunderstanding of Mendelssohn; readers of his memoirs will assume that Fanny's death was the only blow he ever suffered. "He was so unaccustomed to suffering and distress that he could never recover from this unexpected loss." Yes, this was a grievous blow, but it was the end of a lifetime of sadness. From boyhood, Mendelssohn withheld his true feelings about his parents' short-sightedness regarding their elder son's art; likewise the annoyance caused by petty rules placed upon him in respect of money from the same source, or his depression when composing *St Paul* and his inability to find a suitable libretto for the opera that he so much yearned to write. And what about the frustration from the King of Prussia and the court officials that caused him such waste of time and creative energy? It is evident that Müller was totally unaware of Felix's full story.

Yet the above analysis, which attempts to play 'devil's advocate' in order to understand, defend or justify Mendelssohn's lack of popularity, cannot account for the unwarranted libels that attached to his name and music. Of the latter, H. E. Jacob declares that it did not die, but was murdered. The same can be said of Mendelssohn's character, for it was long before Hitler and his cohorts that Felix's name was (metaphorically speaking) dragged through the mud. As early as 1844, an anonymous letter appeared in an issue of the *Musical Examiner* by what the editor called "a certain clique in the profession". Having been invited to conduct six of that season's Philharmonic concerts in London, it was evident that the musicians were unused to the legendary discipline Mendelssohn expected (and received) from the Leipzig Gewandhaus Orchestra. However, this was only one grievance contained in the diatribe. Having been delayed at a Handel Society meeting, Mendelssohn, it was alleged, kept his musicians waiting for "over an hour" at a rehearsal. An "arbitrary demand" was disliked when a musician was threatened with dismissal and a viola player hissed Felix, upbraiding him in "vulgar and commonplace language". Further, a quartet by Ludwig Maurer was threatened with suppression, unless Heinrich Herz and Joseph Joachim replaced two less skilled musicians. "He was, however, reminded that he was the paid servant of the directors... We learn that Dr. Mendelssohn threatens not to return to this country, but we cannot give him such little credit for studying his own interests as to believe this to be true. At all events, we shall be glad to record an improvement in his private bearing towards his brother musicians." Fortunately, the letter was dismissed as "twaddle" and the claims were proved to be utterly false.

A further contumely based in London was the purported rivalry between Mendelssohn and Ludwig Spohr. Rather than express anger, Felix wrote to Charlotte Moscheles with "regret" that such a myth was countenanced: "I have never had the slightest idea of such competition... This pretended antagonism (imagined and started by heaven knows who) can in no way serve either of us, but must, rather, be detrimental to both... Even as a boy, I had the greatest respect for him in every aspect and, in my riper years, this feeling has never been weakened." So much, Felix averred, for what he called these "petty cockfights".

When Robert Schumann decided to give up the editorship of his *New Musical Journal* he hoped Mendelssohn would replace him but, as was his wont, Felix wanted nothing to do with such a task. Therefore, the only person whom Schumann thought suitable was his deputy, Franz Brendel. The new editor's main interest was the "music of the future", promulgated by Wagner and his disciples. Had healthy debate been encouraged among the readership by contributions from these sources, all might have been well. Instead, however, virulent articles were written, castigating the more traditional musical ideas. Wagner, one of the journal's main contributors, not content with this topic, expressed his views on anti-

Semitism and the way in which the Jews had "ruined" pure German music. Egged on by Heine, who had his own axe to grind on this subject, Wagner turned his thoughts into what became "a national issue", according to Kupferberg, especially against Mendelssohn, his music and the man. Wagner had become irrationally jealous of Felix and the luxurious lifestyle he was purported to lead – and the fabulous wealth that Wagner assumed permitted its indulgence.

In order to imitate this privileged life Wagner wore the finest clothes, ordered expensive perfumes from France and draped his rooms with satins and silks. Had not King Ludwig II of Bavaria adopted Wagner as his protégé and allowed the theatre to be built in Bayreuth, the composer of 'music dramas' might have continued to accumulate vast debts and been compelled to flee from creditors. What a contrast between this farcical lifestyle and that practised by Mendelssohn. As Felix wrote to Woldemar Frege: "What we most prefer is to be alone with our friends in the evening. These are the only moments in which I am truly happy." But Wagner had many grievances against Mendelssohn. His "classical clarity, form and tidiness" were out of fashion and Wagner still railed against the alleged loss of his own C major symphony by Mendelssohn (see Chapter 25, "'In paradise'"). Wagner accused Mendelssohn of jealousy at the "genius" of his opera *Rienzi* and his annoyance when Mme. Schröder-Devrient praised *The Flying Dutchman*. According to Wagner, Mendelssohn had expressed only "indifference" when his *Midsummer Night's Dream* music was praised; as for his *Ruy Blas* Overture, even Schumann was said to have expressed surprise at "this giddy piece, suitable only for the Paris public"; to Wagner, "operatic effects [were] spread through the work".

In 1850 a pamphlet appeared under the title *Judaism in Music*, with the author's pseudonym 'Freigedank' ('Free Thought'), which Jacob dismisses as consisting of "bogus social science". The author's main tenet was the manner in which Jews had ruined the "pure" music of Germany. The pamphlet was riddled with inconsistencies; no reason was put forward as to how the author's theories had been conceived; and neither could any cogent, rational points for debate be discovered. In 1868 the true identity of the author came to light: Richard Wagner, no less. A musicologist, Julius Kapp, was to give the reason for the revelation of his name. In 1850 Meyerbeer was still alive and very popular in Berlin and Dresden. As Meyerbeer was a Jew by birth, Wagner did not wish to cause offence, hoping that his own operas would be brought to the fore under the opera director's influence. However, *Judaism in Music* overlooked the sterling work of so many Jewish-born German instrumentalists, which would cause her orchestras to thrive and progress. Hermann Levy, son of a rabbi, had exhorted his musicians to give of their best and to present Wagner's operas as the composer would appreciate, during the Wagner Theatre, founded by an impresario named Naumann to tour European capitals. Neither did Wagner remember how many Jewish-born musicians had played an essential part, through their instrumental skill, in allowing German orchestras not only to thrive but improve. Beethoven could count upon many Jewish friends and

Weber, in producing his operas, worked in co-operation with John Abraham, the tenor who changed his surname to Braham.

However, Wagner's chief criticism was levelled at Mendelssohn – "an outsider, an interloper" but, first and foremost, "a minor composer". Jews, he maintained, had clung to ancient idiom in music, which, though popular in olden times, was now branded as "repulsive caricature". The sadness so often apparent in Mendelssohn's compositions demonstrated nothing more than the fact that, "as a Jew, he could not be a German". By patronising such musicians as Ferdinand David and Joseph Joachim, he had turned Leipzig "into a Jewish metropolis". Germans should have been given the places that these Jews had "usurped". In 1852 the Beethoven scholar Wilhelm von Lenz followed suit, taking up the cudgels against Mendelssohn. He wrote that the "Hebraic" tone of his music "prevented its universal acceptance".

In view of the foregoing, it is worth querying if either of these protagonists wrote the anonymous report of the Gewandhaus concert of 4th November 1846, where Schumann's 2nd Symphony was premiered. Mendelssohn was accused of playing "a Hebraic trick" when Rossini's *William Tell* Overture received "rapturous applause", putting Schumann's "pure German" music into the shade. Mendelssohn had, it was stated, engineered the spontaneous reception of the "foreign" piece in order to degrade the symphony. Be that as it may, *Judaism in Music* was translated into English in 1894 by William Ashton Ellis.

In 1855, when Wagner was invited to conduct the Philharmonic concert season in London, he complained that "this appalling Mendelssohn cult" still prevailed and called the various music critics "a bunch of Jews" – particularly J. W. Davison of *The Times* – for continuing to praise the dead composer's music. "This cold individual" had, Wagner contended, "been fit to join the Temperance Movement" on account of his "lack of passion and dramatic genius". Wagner related to his friend Ernst Kietz how, when "a very bad symphony" (the 'Italian') was performed, he had kept his gloves on "out of malice", removing them only when Weber's *Euryanthe* Overture was played in the same concert. Even his private life was dogged by the Mendelssohn cult, whilst in London. His friend Wesendonck, a Swiss silk merchant, had suggested Wagner visit a Herr Benecke, "a businessman" who lived at Denmark Hill, South-East London. Having made this "inconvenient journey, having to walk one German mile [two and a half English miles] into the country", his vexation can be imagined on discovering that the Herr Benecke was none other than a relative of Cécile Mendelssohn. The family "did not know what to do" with their guest, Wagner wrote in his autobiography, "except to praise my conducting of Mendelssohn's works and rewarding me with descriptions of Mendelssohn's abundant soul".

Not content to rail against Mendelssohn in *Judaism in Music* and *On Conducting*, he castigated anyone who had the effrontery to praise him in their memoirs. Wagner recalled with relish how Hiller had "boasted" of Mendelssohn quarrelling with him and how "he got rid of me" on his return to Leipzig from Berlin. Wagner had to return to the anonymity of a *nom de plume* – on this occasion, Wilhelm Drach – when, in 1869, Devrient's memoirs were written. Having learnt that many of Mendelssohn's friends and relatives still lived, he realised how little it would do to reveal the true name behind his vitriolic review of these recollections. Though a journalist, Paul Lindau, wrote articles against Wagner and his ideas, little notice was taken because, by that time, the Bayreuth festival had become so prestigious. Yet, with so much apparent popularity and a lifestyle that he had craved for so long, Wagner did not mellow. At the end of his life an article appeared in a Bayreuth newspaper entitled 'Know Thyself', in which Germany was advocated to follow Russia's example with regard to the Jews. These should be "cast out... They must not be turned out with gold vessels, as when they left Egypt, but with no shelter... They must descend into the Red Sea and never, never emerge therefrom." It is interesting to note that William Ellis, who collated Wagner's writings, omitted this article from his canon. Wagner's second wife Cosima was likewise to experience the onslaught of her husband's prejudices. In his autobiography, which was dictated to her, the statement is found: "Such an abomination deserves to remain in Hades – a suffering shade with bloodless face, as Thackeray reported in the 1840s." In fact, according to H. R. Haweis, Thackeray had remarked to the illustrator Richard Doyle that Mendelssohn's face made the novelist think of "how our Saviour" must have looked.

In 1912 Wagner's son-in-law, Houston Stewart Chamberlain, made great play of the letter written by the 12-year-old Felix whilst staying with Goethe in Weimar, in which he wrote of having received kisses from the elderly poet: "Goethe must have contaminated himself by making such familiar contact with a Jew-boy". Wagner's influence had become so pervasive that a later generation was to denigrate Mendelssohn's name – and his music – further. John F. Runciman of the *Saturday Review* wrote, in 1894, "Whatever Mendelssohn did not authorise was wrong" as far as the earlier "strange rules...canons of art" were concerned. Between 1888 and 1894 'Corno di Bassetto' wrote for *The Star* and *The World*, disclosing his true name – George Bernard Shaw – as music critic of the latter periodical. As a Wagner fanatic the journalist was obliged to carry on his predecessor's 'Mendelssohn bashing'. "Compare him with Bach, Handel, Haydn, Mozart, Beethoven and Wagner," he wrote "and then settle, if you can, what ought to be done with the fanatic who proclaims him 'a master'." Shaw viewed most of Mendelssohn's output as "elegantly superficial" and considered his oratorios "pompous". Indeed, it may be on Shaw's account that their performances dwindled during the 20th century. In the 1886-87 concert season there were 22 performances of *Elijah* and 20 of *St Paul*. There were only two performances of the latter during the 1926-27 calendar. "To *St Paul* on Saturday," Shaw wrote on 11th November 1889. "I shall go expressly to abuse it." He also said he would rather talk to a Sunday school teacher with no brains than attend a performance of *Elijah*. As for his 'Scottish' Symphony,

Shaw remarked, this resembled "someone in a dress suit and kid gloves, clean and *comme il faut*" – a quote taken, word for word, from Wagner himself.

Regarding what Shaw described as Mendelssohn's "oratorio-mongering", German musicologists directed their displeasure towards specific matters. In *St Paul* and *Elijah* "wrong" representations of the voice of God were brought to light. A journalist named Fink would have preferred "indefinite musical sounds" rather than the human voice. He likewise took exception to the phrase "I am Jesus of Nazareth, whom thou persecutest". He argued that "the Lord of Heaven is no longer Jesus of Nazareth", which, to Mendelssohn and Schubring, had "produced a hearty laugh". Though Fink is accurate in stating no such phrase appeared in Chapter 9, verse 5 of Acts of the Apostles, Mendelssohn and Schubring knew that it existed in Chapter 22, verse 8. The same arguments were produced as regards God's voice in *Elijah*. Widman found the application of wind instruments and soprano voice the least "convincing to depict the voice of the Almighty floating out of heaven". However, neither Fink nor Widman suggested a more suitable alternative to represent God's voice. Further criticism was levelled at Mendelssohn for "inventing a scene that did not exist". The First Book of Kings gives no clue as to how the widow's son died. "Thirst was chosen for the dramatic enhancement of the scene." On the subject of Mendelssohn's experience of sacred music, even the sycophantic Rockstro shows crass ignorance – certainly, lack of perception – when he writes: "What a curious upbringing Mendelssohn must have had... Such a method of singing [as that of the Papal Choir in Rome] is as familiar as the alphabet to the smallest choirboy." The fact remains that, to many brought up in Nonconformist churches, such a style of singing was not familiar.

Other biographers who purport to write sympathetically on their subject cast blemishes on Mendelssohn music through denigrating his character, however subtly. According to Stratton: "He lived far too much in a world of excitement to have a deep, contemplative nature." Whilst much of Mendelssohn's correspondence might not have become available to this erudite critic, there is no excuse for making such a remark when his music is heard. The 'Romantic Music' section of the Pelican *History of Music* should likewise have had impartial authors. It says: "Mendelssohn was restricted in his passions", as if this is something to be despised. No less a musician than Mozart declared, on the contrary: "Passions, whether violent or not, should never be expressed when they reach an unpleasant stage, and music, even in the most terrible situations, should never offend the ear. It should charm and should always remain music." Mendelssohn followed this advice implicitly, however greatly he is castigated by later proponents of musical lore.

As for George R. Marek, his readers can well be justified in wondering if the author of *Gentle Genius* has a hidden agenda concerning Mendelssohn. A few random sentences will serve to make this point. The word 'little' is used to excess when describing his early compositions. His piano pieces are "copper coin with which he dazzled his audiences". Some of his songs (no example given) "fall so far below the level of his best works that they detract from his total output". As with others, Marek takes Mendelssohn to task for his "inability" to write an opera: "He was not cut out to be a dramatic composer...having possessed a lack of the theatrical gift – a lack which he did not want to admit." Altogether, "his critical intelligence whispered to him that, good as he might be, he could not stand on the highest mountain top with his idols, Bach, Handel and Beethoven". As for his "hedonistic temperament, the praise given to him was far too densely woven not to cover him with a handsome and protective cloak against the real world. Too much was given to him, for which he was asked to pay little... He made light of the responsible task by producing too much in a short space. The changes in Mendelssohn's life were produced smoothly, and without shocks."

Former friends played their part in abusing Mendelssohn's character. In 1866 the widow of A. B. Marx published what R. Larry Todd calls "a highly partial account" of her late husband's friendship with Felix. "Not a day passed without our exchanging visits and unusual notes consisting of certain expressions and references that only we understood; musical passages and a crazy quilt of fantastic pictures." But, later: "Had he fallen away from me, or I from him? ... Had I even had it in my nature to do so, the latter would have been quite impossible to accomplish, for I had taken his side far too often, and far too decisively "[against Felix's parents]." "The feeling that I had been deserted by him was bitter wormwood, whose gall I was to taste for long years thereafter." Yet it was Marx who destroyed Mendelssohn's letters to him, which action is not consistent with the tone of these memoirs. Eduard Devrient appears also to have been less of a friend than is so often claimed. We learn, for instance, that "his constant activity...kept him composing incessantly. He called it 'doing his duty', but I felt that he would do his duty better if he wrote less and waited for the good hours of his inspiration, which now seemed to come even less frequently than before... He began to repeat himself voluntarily, copying the earlier masters, especially Sebastian Bach... I said this to him and he did not react sensitively, because he felt I was entirely wrong. Whatever idea came to him was quite good enough. If it seemed like Sebastian Bach, that was the way it would have to be... His drive to become active had become confused with his creative drive... I have not been able to change the opinion I formed at the time. Even with *Elijah*, the result is the same for me." Devrient evidently overlooked Abraham's love of Bach, which caused his son to be obliged to imitate the earlier composer. Neither did he take account of the constant harrying by the King of Prussia for music that no one else would even attempt to compose.

Yet the most unlikely source of adverse remarks derive from Clara and Robert Schumann. In his chapter on Mendelssohn, A. E. R. Dickinson tries to explain what he calls the "unexplained" rift between them. Schumann disliked Mendelssohn's "smugness" and "push"; Mendelssohn was irritated by his fellow musician's "amateurishness", his "Bohemian way of life" when younger and his "journalistic tendencies, known to have been decidedly tart". A further area of contumely must have been the 4th November 1846 Gewandhaus concert, which resulted in "such uncalled-for publicity. After that date, the director was reluctant to perform any newer work of Robert Schumann, until Clara and Cécile each persuaded him to reconsider the decision." Various unfriendly remarks can be discovered in diaries that the couple kept. As early as 3rd May 1832 Schumann wrote of Mendelssohn in Paris: "His tone and touch were poor. For the rest, he plays furiously, but only Beethoven and Mozart." On 9th October 1836: "Mendelssohn stamping in a furious rage." On 4th October 1837: "'He is not sincere with me,' said Clara this evening." On 14th November 1840: "Clara said to me that my attitude towards Mendelssohn seems to have changed... For years I have contributed to his elevation, more than almost anyone else... Jews remain Jews. They take their place at table ten times before it is the Christians' turn. The stones we supply to build their temple of fame, they then use to throw at us... We must act and work for ourselves too. Above all, let us approach more closely to the beautiful and true in art." Clara's entry for the next day admitted that she often felt the same, "but only out of deference to his art do I treat him with the old excessive courtesy. I shall follow your [Schumann's] advice and shall not abase myself too much before him [Felix], as I have so often done."

Mendelssohn had written of how the whole political system troubled him as regards Germany: "My country will either become enlightened in her ideas or the whole movement will have vanished, to be replaced by something far worse. If the status quo remains, Germany will be in danger of losing her finest characteristics – solidity, constancy and honourable perseverance – but gaining nothing to compensate... It is to be hoped that something better will ensue." It is fortunate that this prophet did not live to see what did happen once the National Socialists came to power in 1933. Not only would Mendelssohn's beloved homeland be defiled but his reputation would suffer, even more than hitherto. Jacob believes that the Nazis found it more difficult than they would admit to dissociate Mendelssohn's music from their ideology. The home-loving, peace-loving Germans had always enjoyed his compositions. His songs, Gisela Selden-Goth considers, were more German than many others: "Joys, sorrows, emotions and love of landscape are all represented in his lieder." Jakob Wassermann, in his book *The Way of a German and a Jew*, recounts a succinct account to demonstrate a point. A Danish gentleman was mystified by the present-day German attitude. "In Denmark," he stated, "Jews represent part of the aristocracy, with their irreproachable moral code and loyalty towards the country in which they had settled. What do the Germans want?" he asked. "Hatred," Wassermann was obliged to reply.

Wagner's writings were given a good airing during the Nazi period. For instance, a journalist named Franck had praised Mendelssohn's "good nature" and "self-sacrifice" on hearing how he had renounced the 3,000 thalers awarded by the Prussian court on returning from Berlin to Leipzig. No, Wagner countered, this had not been such a "beautiful" gesture. Von Falkenstein had arranged with the

King of Saxony for a Kapellmeistership for Mendelssohn to be granted via a "sub rosa" arrangement, with a salary to match. This would enhance the 1,000 thalers Felix received as Gewandhaus director, "plus his substantial private income. Secrecy had to be maintained to save embarrassment, since the budget was stretched to such a limit that the poor musicians of Dresden could not be paid adequately. But Mendelssohn's salary was far in excess of other kapellmeisters of the time. Had this been discovered, the disparity in remuneration would have been viewed with affront." Naturally, Franck viewed such assertions with astonishment, calling them "the most unusual example of false reputation". As has been described in Chapter 25, '"In paradise"', Mendelssohn was entrusted with money from the City's coffers to found the Leipzig Conservatorium, to the eternal credit of that establishment. Needless to say, Wagner made no acknowledgement of this fact; neither did he include the erection of the Bach monument in his writings, for which Mendelssohn had raised funds, nor the innumerable donations to charity. Such generosity would not have tallied with the self-seeking plutocrat that Mendelssohn was purported to have become.

Like Wagner before him Karl Blessinger wrote a pamphlet *Judaism in Music*, in which he wrote of "the three Jewish Ms": Mahler, Meyerbeer and Mendelssohn. Not content to vilify the latter especially, Mendelssohn's ancestors were also disparaged. Moses had "wormed his way into German society as the first step towards Jewish domination of the world". His daughters, Felix's aunts, "corrupted young Jewish intellectuals, spreading their perverted eroticism". The historian Heinrich Grätz called their salons "tents of the Midianites, where innocent young Jewish girls were lured into losing not only their virtue but their religion, by young Christian literati, who were distinguished by their selfishness, licentiousness and depravity". When Grätz's pamphlet was discovered, the text had been altered from the 18th-century original to imply that it was the Jewish hostesses who had enticed the fine specimens of Christian youth into their dens of wickedness. Johann Fichte had often visited Dorothea Veit's salon, and it was his words that Hitler twisted. In order for Jews to obtain civil rights, Fichte had said: "Each must have his head cut off, to be replaced by one which contained no Jewish ideas." Fichte's point was that such a drastic measure would be far simpler and more efficient than to wait for the due process of law to allow assimilation and emancipation of the time. Hitler took Fichte's writings literally, causing such of his henchmen as Blessinger to quote Grätz and his ilk.

Felix was the "the greatest cultural parasite" of the Mendelssohn family. He gained popularity solely on account of his father's financial acumen "and the machinations of international Jewish syndicates". Though his family had done "much damage to the entire German people", no explanation was given for this remark. A further assertion was that many compositions by Germans "had been lost through Jewish manipulation", citing Schumann's Violin Concerto as a prime example. As the work was not written until 1853, Mendelssohn can hardly be

Epilogue

blamed for its obscurity, but it is worth noting that Schumann's composition is purported to have been inspired by his late friend's Op. 64 Violin Concerto.

In 1934 Mendelssohn's music was banned altogether, and neither was any mention of it made in a textbook for music students published in 1936. German composers, including Carl Orff, were invited to replace his *Midsummer Night's Dream* music with something more suitable to the Nazi outlook. Though more than 45 composers obeyed this order, none of their results are ever heard of today. It was even rumoured that Shakespeare had been a German and that his drama had been translated into English. In his treatise on music in the Third Reich, Ernst Wolff relates how, during Sir Thomas Beecham's tour with the London Philharmonic Orchestra in 1936, General von Ribbentrop advised him that the 'Scottish' Symphony should not be performed and requested that something more "Aryan" be substituted. If this action were taken, Beecham and his half-Jewish secretary, Berta Geissmar, would be "protected". It should be explained that, at least in Britain, only the most far-seeing realised at that time how the Nazi regime operated. As a rule, most people, including Beecham, regarded such antics as no more than a huge joke. Beecham loved roaring around in a luxury, swastika-covered Mercedes, escorted by German officials. It was only later he was to witness the horrors perpetrated by his hosts.

During the tour Beecham asked the Mayor of Leipzig if a wreath of flowers might be laid at Mendelssohn's statue, erected in front of the Gewandhaus in 1892. Herr Gördeler thought such a gesture most fitting, but explained that he would be away from Leipzig on the evening of the concert. Imagine the reaction when, the next morning, the statue was found to have been dismantled, its pieces dumped in a cellar. It transpired that Herr Haake, the Deputy Mayor, had perpetrated this vandalism to curry favour with the authorities, whose party he supported. Though the press did all they could to vilify Mendelssohn's name, on this occasion there was complete silence. All realised that what Beecham had said was true: Mendelssohn had raised the orchestra to such a high standard that Leipzig had become known as "an international city of music".

Haake may well have read an article entitled 'Jewish Music and the Monument to a Jew', which advocated the removal of this statue because "it militated against the healthy interests of the German nation". The monument, it continued, had been erected by reason of "false piety" and such a structure was "inconsistent with the endeavour to expunge the damage wrought on our national heritage by Judaism". Such propaganda prompted the deputy mayor to obey an order from his Führer. This article was collated in 1963, with other such poison, into an anthology, *Music under the Third Reich*.

In 1920, because of the then rocketing inflation, the Mendelssohn Bank had opened a branch in Amsterdam, but this "eventually passed into history". The German parent bank flourished until, in 1938-39, it was liquidated and appropriated by a Herr Mannheimer, who, fate decreed, would suffer a heart attack in the following year. During this period, as Marek states, "any Mendelssohn descendants dispersed – some to America, some to Switzerland, some into oblivion". Percy Scholes adds England to this collection, and it is remarkable how often the name Mendelssohn is to be found, though some claim incorrectly to be descended from Felix's family.

In his *History of Germany*, written between 1875 and 1894, Triebsche acknowledges that Mendelssohn was "never truly happy, even in the most enchanting southern landscapes" of Italy. The French never understood his music and it was, indeed, "only by Britons – a German kin-race" – that his music was loved. Such a concept is simplistic. The United Kingdom comprises Celts, Danes and many other nationalities who have lived here for centuries, or who have made a home here in recent times. All play a part, when the mood takes them, in performing the music of Felix Mendelssohn. In other English-speaking countries this applies equally. America espoused his music, choral and orchestral, under German directors. When the Third Reich came into existence, nothing changed. Jews, too, wherever they live, regard Mendelssohn as "one of our greatest glories". It was overlooked by the Nazis that Moses Mendelssohn had become not only a true German but an international philosopher and thinker. His sons, Joseph and Abraham, had shown patriotism to Prussia at great risk to themselves during the war against Napoleon. Felix put German music on the map, both by composing and conducting and also by resurrecting earlier music, such as that of Bach. His sons, Karl and Paul, excelled themselves by application to historical studies and in industry. Other members of his family became brilliant academics and lawyers. A grandson, Ludwig Mendelssohn, was even killed fighting for Germany in the 1914-18 war. How much more proof is needed that the Mendelssohn family were "true" Germans?

But let this shameful narrative end with an amusing anecdote, recounted by the Czech author, Jiří Weil. A Nazi officer, too zealous for his own good, had been ordered to destroy a bust of Mendelssohn. He thus set about to demolish the representation of the man he considered to have possessed the longest nose. It was only later that the truth emerged. The maltreated sculpture was not that of Mendelssohn but of Wagner!

Part III: – Mendelssohn's Musical Legacy

Whilst in Vienna in 1830 Mendelssohn visited the graves of Beethoven and Schubert: "The grave is the end of all endeavour," he wrote to his family. "Genius must relinquish its labours to the world – and crawl into a corner and die." Fortunately, Mendelssohn's genius may be witnessed in so many instances, via later compositions that bear its influence. The first indication that such an idea can be proved arises from a letter written by Clara Schumann's stepbrother, Wilhelm Burgiel, as cited in Norman Lebrecht's *Book of Musical Anecdotes*. Whilst Schumann was still of sound mind, an angel visited him in a dream, carrying a piece of paper with a musical greeting, jointly, from Schubert and Mendelssohn. Several of Schumann's works bear the imprint of Mendelssohn's influence. Sometimes, indeed, it can be difficult, even for connoisseurs, to recognise who wrote which piece, when hearing some music for the first time.

Other contemporaries, such as Bizet, imitated Mendelssohn's style, however unconsciously (for example, in his *Songs of the Rhine*), and even Wagner, though loath to admit the fact, plagiarised Mendelssohn's musical ideas in some of his work.

W. S. Rockstro, writing in 1883, noted Mendelssohn's influence on the music of younger composers and Ray Longyear follows suit in his *Nineteenth-Century Romanticism in Music*. He describes the composer's style as being "like the trunk of a tree from which all branches spring". Such a tribute was even awarded by the Nazi historian Heinrich Triebsche. He reminded his readers how Mendelssohn "awoke the genre of oratorio to life for the Protestant Church. He gave the lied its deepest, almost solemn, expression. He educated the public towards the noble, truly German, art form of the symphony and the sonata." Since Mendelssohn, "known and beloved through Germany", began to conduct, "music, hitherto regarded as mere entertainment, regained esteem as the highest art. It is to him that Germans must be grateful...", Triebsche declares, "He led back our distinguished society to the old tradition of its national art." Not only did Mendelssohn resurrect the music of Bach, Handel and earlier composers, he brought to the fore works by Mozart, Haydn and Beethoven "that, for a long time, had not been relished" – or, Triebsche might have added, even known. But Mendelssohn cannot be considered as an antiquarian, for he was the first to play Schubert's music, notably his 9th Symphony, and works by Schumann, Wagner and other, lesser-known contemporaries. In fact, it can be cogently argued, in view of so many subtle hints in later music, it is Mendelssohn, not Wagner and his disciples, who is responsible for "the music of the future".

The word 'plagiarism' is used by Jean Petitpierre when describing Wagner's music. His Prelude to *Das Rheingold*, albeit at a slower tempo, and the dialogue between Brunnhilde and Siegmund are taken "almost without alteration" from Mendelssohn's *Fair Melusine* Overture. Idioms from the 'Scottish' Symphony can be heard in *Tristan und Isolde*. Cynics might well retort that, being a descendant of Mendelssohn's wife, "he would say that, wouldn't he?" However, several impartial musicologists have concurred with Petitpierre. There is a tiny passage in the *Hebrides Overture* that is imitated by a similar passage in *The Ride of the Valkyries*. The trumpets that begin the orchestral version of the *Wedding March* anticipate by a year a similar fanfare in Wagner's *Tannhäuser* orchestration. Stratton goes further:

"The string instrumentation in the *Wedding March* opened the doors for Wagner, Liszt and others to imitate this pattern in their future use of instrumentation."

Schumann's Fantasy for 'Cello reproduces, note for note, Mendelssohn's aria 'I waited for the Lord' from *St Paul*. Schumann's Arabesque, Op. 18, sounds, to the unwary, as if Mendelssohn had included it as one of his *Songs without Words*. It is noticeable that many of Mendelssohn's musical ideas appear in Schumann's string quartets, though, since these were dedicated to his friend, this could well have been deliberate. The first movement of the 'Scottish' Symphony, begun as early as 1829 but completed in 1841, can be recalled when listening to the first movement of Schumann's 3rd 'Rhenish' Symphony, depicting Cologne Cathedral and written in 1850.

Of later composers, Stratton sees Brahms as "Mendelssohn's legitimate successor". Having never met the earlier composer, Brahms admitted he would have "given everything" to have written the *Hebrides Overture*. Philip Radcliffe notices traces of Brahms in Mendelssohn's *Songs without Words*, but "never shirking the disturbing passion". Such extracts from biographies would be even more convincing had they cited Richard Strauss or our own Sir Edward Elgar as "legitimate successors" to Mendelssohn.

Strauss studied the earlier composer's work diligently, as can be heard from his early piano music. The highly respected conductor Norman del Mar wrote of the opera *Ariadne auf Naxos* that this, too, showed Mendelssohn's influence. Percy Young has made similar claims as regards Elgar's music. In Elgar's youth Mendelssohn was his hero, and he was influenced by *Elijah* far earlier than by any other music, as he admitted in 1878. His *Salve Regina* resembles 'Lord, Bow down thine Ear' from *Elijah*, and there are nuances of Mendelssohn's style in the early chamber music that Elgar wrote. Variation twelve of the *Enigma Variations* bears the signature of Mendelssohn's *Calm Sea and Prosperous Voyage* Overture. Young even goes so far as to trace some bars of the *Wedding March* in Elgar's *Cockaigne* Overture. Using Longfellow's *The Black Knight* and *The Saga of King Olaf*, Elgar "domesticated" the German choral ballads, as Young describes his work in this genre. Such German equivalents by the poet Uhland were set to music by Marschner, Humperdinck and other of Wagner's followers, in which Mendelssohn's influence can be observed, as well as in "the Nordic dialect of Gade, who was himself a weaker copy of Mendelssohn".

Although he lived until as late as 1920, Max Bruch gained great strength from Mendelssohn's music. Writing in 1900 he declared that, whilst Felix's *Midsummer Night's Dream* music "would ensure his immortality", Bruch's own favourite was the String Octet. It seems too much of a coincidence that, after visiting Scotland, Bruch was not influenced by the *Scottish* Symphony and the *Hebrides* Overture when writing his *Scottish Fantasy*. Likewise, his 1st Violin Concerto resembles that of Mendelssohn, whilst his chamber music can be regarded as a "watered-down version" of the earlier composer's works. Other European composers have also taken a leaf out of Mendelssohn's repertoire. The Russian composer Anton Arensky, who travelled throughout Europe, was inspired not only by Chopin but also by Mendelssohn. The same applied to Glazunov, who is sometimes called 'the Russian Mendelssohn'. Observers have seen Mendelssohn's influence – particularly through their choral works – on Bruckner and Dvořák. According to Radcliffe, such nuances can also be heard in Verdi's *Falstaff*, written in the early 1890s towards the end of his life. Another whose choral music bears Mendelssohn's stamp is Gabriel Fauré, whilst Saint-Säens is branded 'the French Mendelssohn'.

Of composers who did meet Mendelssohn, Gounod's music can bear witness to his influence, in such works as his oratorio *Mors et Vita*. As for Gade and Sterndale Bennett, Radcliffe asserts their "singular lack of individuality". The latter admitted he was "bowled over" by Mendelssohn's music. When he was appointed Principal at the Royal College of Music, Bennett's compositions were praised so highly precisely because he owed so much to his friend and mentor. In fact, it has been asserted that, were it not for Mendelssohn, neither Gade's nor Bennett's compositions would be heard today.

As Mel Cooper of Classic FM has declared, Mendelssohn "did more in his 38 years than most people accomplish in their allotted 70". As stated by Michael Kennedy in no less a musical institution than *The Oxford Companion to Music*, Mendelssohn was "generous to other musicians" (which puts paid completely to A. B. Marx's snipe of "having no time for anyone who had had to struggle to make his way"). He was "keen to raise public taste"; "an exceptional organist", doing much to revolutionise organ construction, especially in 19th-century England; "a superb pianist"; but also "an inspiring conductor".

Schumann could vouch for this latter tribute. Because of Mendelssohn, he found the work far more straightforward than would have otherwise applied on taking up the post in Düsseldorf, because Hiller, his predecessor, had maintained Mendelssohn's strict discipline with the musicians. This fine tradition was fostered not only there but on behalf of the Leipzig Gewandhaus Orchestra and the Conservatorium. Pupils were appointed to prestigious posts in Prague, Warsaw, Munich, Frankfurt and many other European orchestras. When Theodor Kullak and Julius Stern founded the Berlin Academy of Music, it was modelled on Leipzig's exemplary standard. Meanwhile, Leipzig went from strength to strength, with pupils such as Grieg, Delius and Arthur Sullivan to represent composition and Arthur Nikisch and Sir Adrian Boult to perpetuate the high reputation in conducting.

Gustav Mahler made his mark as a conductor through his performance of *St Paul* in Cassel, Germany, at the age of 25, in 1885. But, though *Paulus*, as it is known on the continent, is very popular there, *Elijah* is far more popular in the English-speaking world. It has been pointed out that the latter oratorio bridges the gulf that would have otherwise existed between *Messiah* and *The Dream of Gerontius*. According to Jacob, it "acts as a stepping-stone between Beethoven's

Christ on the Mount of Olives (now at last making a well-deserved comeback) and Wagner's *Parsifal*.

Chorley dismissed the choral music of Schumann and Wagner as "mere critiques of others' work", whereas that of Mendelssohn "added new beauties to what were recognised as the models for all time". Yet, sometimes, these "new beauties" went unacknowledged. At the 1846 premiere of *Elijah* in Birmingham, choristers were puzzled at the "startling dissonances" in the chorus 'Thanks be to God' and an extra rehearsal had to be called. It was on this occasion that Mendelssohn waived his fee, the money being given to Mr. Stimpson. The popularity of *Elijah* was enhanced, Blunt believes, by the painting by Ford Madox Brown *Elijah and the Widow's Son*, completed in 1868. Such a statement lacks credibility, for it was the oratorio that inspired the painting – not the reverse. Known as 'the oratorio of the 19th century', even the Chairman of the Players' Theatre made a joke about "breaking the back of Elijah" in a programme representing Victorian music hall. Boys were christened Elijah, as well as Felix. One Cornish tin miner's son was given the names 'Felix Mendelssohn' to accompany his surname.

Though Handel's oratorios remained popular from the 18th century, choral singing was enhanced by Mendelssohn's music in a later period. Choirs "wore out their lungs", even up to the 1950s, with anthems, psalm settings and oratorios. This applied throughout the choral spectrum, be it sacred or secular ensembles. Older readers may well recall with nostalgia seeing posters publicising such performances. Charities must have received, over the years, considerable funds through this type of entertainment for singers and audience alike. It is appropriate here to recount the popularity of Master Ernest Lough's recording of 'Hear my Prayer' in 1926, with the Temple Church Choir directed by Dr. George Thalben-Ball. This arose from the pleasure given to Mr. Justice Bankes by the anthem that the new choirmaster had prepared. Thalben-Ball replied that, as the recording industry had now become well established, a disc could be made that anyone, anywhere, could hear. The first pressing was made on 25th August 1927, to be re-recorded when required. If the singing was not up to the usual standard, words only would be recorded "in order for them to be heard, understood and meant". Presumably William Bartholomew's text was considered to be of far greater importance than Mendelssohn's setting.

However, the choir evidently passed muster because so popular did the record become that tickets had to be distributed to members of the congregation on a 'first come, first served' basis whenever the motet was sung. As for Master Lough, he was showered with inane remarks and shrouded in ridiculous rumours. He was said to have been chosen to sing whilst queuing outside the People's Palace Music Hall in the Mile End Road; he was invited to sing with a jazz band; and neither did such nonsense cease when he had become an adult and his sweet treble voice had matured into that of a baritone. He recalled that an hysterical female, on asking his name, accused Lough of wickedness. Did this shameful impostor not know that the sweet little boy whose name he was abusing had died and gone to heaven? In 1962, when the 'Golden Disc' was issued, having made a million copies, the inscription read "For 35 years of recording, in partnership with His Master's Voice". Royalties were given to the Temple Church and to charities of the Middle and Inner Temple, to which the Church is affiliated. What Miss Mounsey, for whom it was written, or Mendelssohn himself might have thought defies description.

Neither can Mendelssohn connoisseurs feel elated when hearing transcriptions of his music for completely unsuitable instruments. Liszt was one of the first to indulge in this practice, though, to be fair, Mendelssohn was not the only composer whose music suffered. Anything he fancied was 'transcribed' to show off his pianistic virtuosity, even to the extent of playing Beethoven's symphonies at the piano. Schubert, Schumann and others suffered the same fate, but, as regards Mendelssohn, Liszt's most flagrant abuse was on the Op. 34 set of songs, notably his most popular, 'On Wings of Song'. Others have arranged the melody for violin, and Queen Alexandra ordered that a musical box be given the tune as one of its repertoire. The unwarranted insolence of the concert pianist Frederic Lamond is difficult to countenance. At his 50th anniversary concert, Lamond included Mendelssohn's Op. 5 Capriccio for piano, written in 1825, the same year as the String Octet; but it was Liszt's transcription that was played – not Mendelssohn's original. Liszt, Lamond wrote in the concert programme, "improved" the piece, having "helped along" Mendelssohn's composition "by adding some overlapping arpeggio octaves". Whilst Mendelssohn "understood the technique of form to a remarkable degree" and the capriccio was "very mature for a boy of 16", Liszt's "improvements", especially to the first 20 bars, "enhanced the effect and gave to the climax vigour and brilliance".

In this sorry tale the virtuoso violinist Alberto Luigi Bianchi must be mentioned. It was whilst crossing a car park in Milan that his 1695 Amati viola was stolen. However, this unfortunate incident proved to be a blessing in disguise, for Bianchi's insurance pay-out allowed him to purchase the 1716 Stradivarius 'Colossus' violin, with which he has continued to tour the world. In 1992 his audiences were allowed to hear "Mendelssohn as he has never been played before", and a similar performance of the E minor Violin Concerto was given at the Chichester Festival two years later. This 'new' version caused screeds of print to be expended, whereby Bianchi's quest to track down this manuscript was brought to the attention of 'the great and the good' of the musical world. Originally the Mendelssohn Archive of Berlin staff had explained that, to protect rare manuscripts from the damage caused by Allied bombing, scores had been transferred to a castle in Silesia. Since no success was achieved on this visit, Bianchi learnt that perhaps a monastery at Grussau, Poland, would reveal the mystery. Still dissatisfied, the adventure continued to a library in Krakow, where the 'real' concerto was discovered. Mendelssohn, the virtuoso claimed, was "too sick to realise that changes had been made, possibly by Ferdinand David... The brilliance of the original idea was sadly lost. Because Itzhak Perlman has not played the fake for so long, when next he does so he will change to the real version." Had Bianchi realised the fact, he would have had no need to pursue such an odyssey, for the original can be studied from a manuscript at the Bodleian Library, Oxford.

The first English performance can be dated to May 1845, when an arrangement for violin and piano was published and was given at a lecture by a Mr. Lincoln, the violinist, accompanied by a then unnamed pianist, being a Herr Kreutzer. *The Athenaeum* hosted the lecture, but the *Musical Times* of July 1896 gives a different version. In this case, it was the Grand Duke of Baden who played the solo part, accompanied by "Mr. Henry Lincoln, at the Western Institution, 47 Leicester Square, London, in the year of its premiere, 1845". A full orchestral performance took place in the following year, with Camillo Sivori as soloist, and, in October 1847, barely a month before the composer's death, Joseph Joachim played what he would later call "the heart's jewel". The violin and piano arrangement appeared in 1860 and the full version, though advertised in 1858, was republished in 1862. Frederick Delius chose the concerto in 1888 to demonstrate violin technique, employing the first movement at a lecture in Danville, Virginia, where he taught for a year. (Gratitude is hereby expressed to Dr. Lionel Carley of the Delius Society for this information.) Another future composer was Jean Sibelius, who chose Mendelssohn's Violin Concerto to prove his ability as a virtuoso whilst studying in Vienna.

In view of the stringent recycling of paper ordered by the government during World War II, it is worth noting a performance in Stockport in 1942 with the Danish violinist Henry Holst as soloist, accompanied by the Liverpool Philharmonic under Malcolm Sargent. The unknown compiler of the programme notes sums up Mendelssohn's achievement when writing for violin – whether the 'fake' or 'true' version of his Op. 64: this work is "flawless in its scoring yet, at the same time, [it] allows the soloist to display to the greatest effect everything that can be achieved by his instrument. The soloist performs seemingly superhuman feats, without conveying a sense of struggle." The concerto has been recorded by many soloists worldwide, and it is worth repeating comments by some of its performers. Those from China and Japan seem to admire the work particularly. As for Western violinists, the same thoughts can be discerned. "The work is not meant for showing off... Every mistake shows", thereby becoming "a challenge" to Itzhak Perlman. He considers the concerto "a perfect pearl; a jigsaw puzzle, into which every piece fits together perfectly. The work has everything a musician requires." After his first public performance, Perlman deliberately refused to play the concerto for five more years. He made his first recording in 1972 and has added two more to the record catalogue to date. The German violinist Christian Tetzlaff pronounces the concerto "perfect, with just the right balance between form and melody". By contrast, he considers the Brahms equivalent to have "too much form", whereas the

Epilogue

Tchaikovsky work is "too much of a showpiece". Perceptive record reviewers can make equally pertinent observations. A review of 1997 compared the recordings of the Russian violinist Ivry Gitlis and the Belgian Arthur Grumiaux. Though the first revealed "Mendelssohn from the heart", the pleasure was "kept in check by a few technical shortcomings". After this 1968 recording, Grumiaux's 1960 version was said to possess "great poise and elegance…[and was] rounded and sensitive…showing a real sense of dignity".

When, in 1961, the Spanish 'cellist Pablo Casals was invited to play to President Kennedy at the White House, he included Mendelssohn's D minor Piano Trio Op. 49 in his recital. Though Mendelssohn is usually regarded as a romantic composer, Casals explained how much at ease he had felt "in the world of classicism, able to solve, …through the imaginative niche peculiarly his own, the most difficult problems of form, yet able to deal with both early and contemporary music". Others have reinforced this remark, noting how Mendelssohn's music spanned the whole range of styles from the 17th to the 19th centuries.

Mendelssohn's compositional techniques inspired other musicians to further development. In an article of July 1997 in the BBC *Music Magazine*, the Swedish trombonist Christian Lindberg explained how he had discovered a concerto by Ferdinand David for his instrument. Mendelssohn had apparently promised such a concerto for his friend but, when it was evident that this would be overlooked, David, "feeling sorry for the neglected instrument", wrote the piece himself, which Lindberg considered "resembled a military band", calling it "this terrible arrangement". He went back to the piano score "and orchestrated it as Mendelssohn would have done". Mendelssohn, having employed instruments that were rapidly becoming obsolete, had to transfer music originally written for the serpent and the ophicleide to more up-to-date equivalents. Such examples were witnessed in his *Calm Sea* and *Midsummer Night's Dream* Overtures, his 'War March of the Priests' from the music for *Athalie*, and orchestration in *Elijah*. Because of this earlier precept, Lindberg realised what an advantage this could be for later Mendelssohn students.

Another artistic concept can be found in the number of ballets inspired by Mendelssohn's music. Kupferberg gives examples of the 'Scottish' and 'Italian' Symphonies, the *Fair Melusine* Overture, the music from *Athalie*, the *First Walpurgisnacht*, the singspiel *Son and Stranger*, but, above all, the music for *A Midsummer Night's Dream* being applied to this art form. All these pieces were choreographed for the American Ballet Theatre and the New York City Ballet, where George Balanchine had been working for more than 20 years.

The latter instance of Mendelssohn's music was well represented in other productions. In the 1920s Max Reinhardt took a German version of Shakespeare's play on tour. When asked why the original English was not used, the impresario expressed "complete surprise" at the question, explaining that he did not wish his audiences to forgo the beauty of the German language. Mickey Rooney starred in a film version in 1939 and the Old Vic performed the English original at the Metropolitan Opera House in New York. To celebrate the 400th anniversary of Shakespeare's birth, the BBC gave a radio performance. On all these occasions, it was Mendelssohn's music that was played to complement the words.

Even though many people admit their "ignorance" of Mendelssohn's music, delight is invariably expressed when two exceptions are called to mind. The Wedding March, however out of fashion this has become with the establishment, is still as popular as ever with the general public. Even in Soviet Russia couples chose this music to enhance the wedding ceremony. Wilfrid Blunt cites a clergyman who set off a flurry of correspondence by advocating that, as a secular piece of music, the march should not be used at religious ceremonies. He was evidently anti-Mendelssohn, because a whole list of secular music can be compiled for use at weddings. Various arrangements have been made for the organ, including a slow version by Noel Rawsthorne, which, though pedestrian, is ideal for older couples to walk with dignity out of the ceremony. The other exception is Cummings's adaptation of Mendelssohn's melody in his *Festgesang* – the tune sung today to the Christmas hymn, 'Hark! The Herald Angels Sing', named 'Mendelssohn'.

It is remarkable, in view of the large number of tuneful melodies he wrote, how little of Mendelssohn's music has been adapted to popular songs. Some serious composers have suffered grievously in this regard – Chopin, Tchaikovsky, Ravel, even Brahms – but, apart from his Wedding March, a few bars of which are inserted into various songs that relate to weddings, Mendelssohn's work has escaped this abuse. The only exceptions appear to be Irving Berlin's *Mesmerising Mendelssohn Tune*, a ragtime version of his 'Spring Song', and a grisly Victorian ditty set to the tune of Heine's poem 'On Wings of Song'. This refers to the female singer's lover, who was hanged, a line of which runs: "And now they're erecting a gallows at one of Her Majesty's gaols." Other similarities have been noticed between Mendelssohn's E minor Violin Concerto and popular songs, but these appear to be coincidental rather than intentional on the songwriter's part. Sullivan's music appears to be the exception but, since he was the first musician to be awarded the British Mendelssohn Scholarship, which enabled him to study in Leipzig, such similarities might well have been a tribute to his predecessor and an expression of loyalty to his continuing influence at the Conservatorium and the Gewandhaus Orchestra. No less a musician than Busoni was found, at his death in 1924, to have been studying a book of Mendelssohn's *Songs without Words*, which remained on the music stand of his piano. In the present generation, Peter Maxwell Davies has admitted to admiring Mendelssohn. On a lighter note, the granddaughter of the 'English Waltz King', Archibald Joyce, records how he loved to play the composer's piano music, and some of his waltzes bear traces of Mendelssohn's style.

Street pianos (incorrectly known as barrel organs) reproduced Mendelssohn's music and, for a later generation, his so-called *Spring Song* can be heard from ice cream vans. By complete contrast, his Op. 19 No. 1, composed to commemorate the birth of his nephew, Sebastian Hensel, has been used as a hymn tune. Yet one of the most interesting results of Mendelssohn's musical legacy will remind readers of the proverb "many a true word is spoken in jest". On a favourite record to which 1950s children listened, Mendelssohn is mentioned. In the story of 'Sparky and his Magic Piano', the child 'hero' dreams of becoming a virtuoso pianist. All goes well until he announces his intention of playing one of Mendelssohn's *Songs without Words*. "No you will not," the piano interrupts him rudely... The piano (or the writer of the fantasy) might well have had the same thoughts as George Bernard Shaw. Despite so much criticism of Mendelssohn, on hearing a recital by the Polish virtuoso, Ignacy Paderewski, he had to admit, in order to discover flaws in a pianist's technique, "just wait until he has dazzled you with a Chopin polonaise, Liszt rhapsody or Schumann's Symphonic Studies, then ask him to play you ten bars of Mozart or Mendelssohn". In other words, rather than the latter's piano pieces being "too easy", they are, rather, too difficult for any but the best pianists to tackle.

The early Promenade concerts gave 'Mendelssohn nights' but, like evenings of Wagner's or Beethoven's works, these were consigned to the rubbish heap of time. The musical establishment has continued to belittle Mendelssohn's work. Whereas the first edition of Grove's *Dictionary of Music and Musicians* included a 60-page assessment of the composer, the number of pages has gradually dwindled. Musicologists, notably Philip Radcliffe, employ a subtle means of criticising his music. His *Songs without Words* are said to show "traces of Grieg and Brahms"; his Op. 54 *Variations sérieuses* is described as "Schumannesque". But the most absurd statement from this erudite biographer shows a complete lack of perception: a song from *Athalie* reminds Radcliffe of "a chorus from *The Pirates of Penzance*. For anyone unaware of the fact, when Mendelssohn died in 1847 Sullivan was, to quote Gilbert's libretto concerning the operetta's hero, "just a little boy of five" – so much for Mendelssohn's "plagiarism" from later composers! Yet bouquets can still be discovered amongst the brickbats. Despite the lack of 'Mendelssohn nights', the Promenade concert of 26th August 1996 commemorated the 150th anniversary of *Elijah*'s premiere. The next year, Wendy Thompson stated how Hans Werner Henze had been inspired, when writing his 8th Symphony, by Mendelssohn's *Midsummer Night's Dream* music, both of which were included in that concert. Even one of Mendelssohn's arch-critics, George R. Marek, has had to admit that "Mendelssohn is alive and, as far as one can prophesy, he is in no danger of oblivion".

Part IV: – Vivat Mendelssohn!

At the end of his life Mendelssohn was mourned at all levels, from King Ludwig I of Bavaria, who had hoped to appoint him to his court, to the humblest glee club by whom his songs were relished. Chopin had called Schumann's compositions "no music"; Schumann's dislike of Wagner – man and musician – had become a legend. When Brahms heard that a work of "that charlatan Liszt" was to be played at an otherwise "decent" concert, he had given vent to "ungentlemanly language". But, as far as the music of Mendelssohn was concerned, he admitted that he would have given anything to write the *Hebrides* Overture; likewise, Berlioz declared a similar view regarding the music to *A Midsummer Night's Dream*. Many visitors from abroad called at Mendelssohn's home and tributes were paid until long after his death. Julius Schubring wrote of his friend as "the finest we have", echoing the artist von Schwind's tribute to Schubert of 1828. When the composer Adolf Henselt received the Order of St. Vladimir from the Tsar in 1876, he declared how he prized his former friendship with Mendelssohn as being of equal importance to this rare honour. In a diary eventually published in 1949, Schumann had written that "if all Mendelssohn's friends were writers, each would have had something extraordinary and different to say of him and each would have had to fill a whole volume in so doing. It was as if, every day, he had been born anew." He was "a warrior of God, who had conquered", and his views were "the court of last appeal". His own self-criticism had been "the strictest and most conscientious I have ever met in an artist".

Schumann and his wife did not confine themselves simply to words. When Clara gave birth to her seventh child he was given Felix's name. As for Schumann, several sources record an incident that occurred when Liszt was invited to their home in Dresden to take part in a piano trio. Liszt arrived two hours later than expected, played very badly, considering the music "too Leipziger", and, to complete his demonstration of bad manners, praised Meyerbeer, saying that Mendelssohn's music was "as nothing" in comparison. Though Clara normally admired Liszt's musicianship, she felt sufficiently ashamed on this occasion to wish to leave the room. Her husband had no compunction in expressing his own feelings. Jumping to his feet, he seized Liszt by the shoulders, shouting at him: "Who do you think you are to dare to speak in that way about a master such as Mendelssohn!" Liszt asked Clara to assure her husband that he was the only person to be able to address him in such a manner. "Liszt grovelled his apologies", according to Elgar's friend Edward Speyer, "telling Mme. Schumann: 'I feel as if I am in the wrong place.'" The version given by Wagner, friendly with Liszt at the time, narrates how much argument was caused by "the wide gulf between the Meyerbeer and Mendelssohn camps", but he added that Liszt "had never been seen in such an expansive mood", whereas Schumann had "sulked in his bedroom" after

Epilogue

the fracas. Tributes were paid in equal profusion in Britain. Queen Victoria wrote, from Osborne House on 10th November 1847, in her journal of "our horrified and astonished distress" on hearing of Mendelssohn's death, calling him "the greatest genius since Mozart; a most amiable man, worshipped by those who knew him intimately, together with his most wonderfully beautiful music... We loved and esteemed the excellent man and revered his wonderful genius, whose intellect was too strong for his frail, delicate body... He was so modest and simple in his character." Mrs. Lucy Anderson, the first woman to play the piano in public in 1821 and who later taught the royal family to sing, passed the Queen some letters from Charlotte and Ignaz Moscheles, at which the sovereign was touched, as they concerned Mendelssohn's final days. "The loss of this great, good man is always to be remembered," they had written. Count Bunsen, then Prussian ambassador in London, presented a letter from King Friedrich Wilhelm IV to Queen Victoria regarding Mendelssohn's incomplete oratorio *Earth, Hell and Heaven*, known later as *Christus*. The Queen related to Bunsen how she had received a letter from Mendelssohn's "poor widow, who is so touching in her grief", and said that it was "incomprehensible" that the composer was no longer alive. He had just adapted a *Song without Words*, which the Queen and Prince Albert had so recently performed.

Further down the social scale, Sir Julius Benedict wrote: "Then came the sudden news of his death", having seen Mendelssohn barely six months earlier. "Always ready to oblige and please his friends; always amiable and charming – even under great provocation." Max Müller recorded that "on only one occasion, I recall Mendelssohn's anger. This was when he sent his precious album to be repaired but, on opening the package at Fanny's house, he jumped up and screamed. The blue skies and treetops had been cut off the top of an Italian sketch, as was the signature from many of the poems and letters."

"Fair as fair can be," Rockstro wrote of his former tutor at the Leipzig Conservatorium; "true as truth itself; noble in his aims; gentle in his ways; cultured in his tastes; masterly in his methods, yet so often belittled by those jealous of his fame or incapable of appreciating his genius... I believe there to have been no more engaging a personality in the whole gallery of musical celebrities... If civilisation is to continue his fame will endure, for rarely have so many worthy qualities existed in one nature." When his opera *Pierre Legrand* was being rehearsed, Louis Julien (who would later try to introduce the first Promenade concerts) declared, on hearing of Mendelssohn's death, that, if this happened to a genius, he would never compose anything more himself, and the opera was abandoned.

Meanwhile, Europe's largest cities vied one with another to pay tribute to Mendelssohn via performances of his music. Berlin, Frankfurt, Hamburg, Paris, Birmingham, Manchester and Dublin all played their part to this end. The performance of *Elijah* that Mendelssohn had planned took place in Vienna, but without Jenny Lind, overcome as she was by grief. However, she organised a performance of the oratorio by the Sacred Harmonic Society at Exeter Hall on

17th November 1847. The musicians wore black, with the music stands similarly draped. The conductor occupied a seat below Mendelssohn's usual position when at that venue, which was left vacant, with a score of the oratorio on the desk, together with a laurel wreath. Before the performance began, Handel's 'Death March' from *Saul* was played.

On the 20th of that month the Philharmonic Society of London proposed to Prince Albert that a statue be erected to represent Mendelssohn. So impressed were the royal couple by this idea that a donation of £50 was provided from Buckingham Palace, to match a like amount raised by the Philharmonic Society committee. A Mr. Bacon was commissioned to design the statue, and the sculpture was eventually cast in bronze by Messrs. Robinson & Cottam. The statue weighed one and a half tons and measured eight feet in height. On 4th May 1859 the statue was placed on the terrace outside the Crystal Palace, when a performance of *Elijah* was given, with a choir of 3,000 – the usual complement for the popular Handel festivals of the time. Gratitude is hereby given to the late Michael Gregory, a founder member of Friends of Mendelssohn, for an article from a contemporary *Illustrated London News*, which reported this information. Sadly, today, no one appears to know how, when or why this statue vanished.

As has been observed in Part II of this Epilogue, 'Free thought', a statue of Mendelssohn was erected in front of the Leipzig Gewandhaus in 1892, so wantonly dismantled on the night of 9th-10th November 1936. Fortunately, a replacement now stands proudly at the same location, commemorating the man who worked so unstintingly for the musicians of the city he loved, and who put Leipzig on the musical map for posterity.

Since Felix had left no will, it fell to Paul to manage his late brother's estate, but he adhered to the letter, as opposed to the spirit, of his remit with regard to Felix's unpublished manuscripts. He did not, therefore, take account of various factors in Mendelssohn's character. Felix often put a work aside when other commitments hampered him from completing a score. He also continually revised much of his music, "five or six times", as Schumann vouched. Thus he might well have brought them to the public had time permitted. Because he was so pathologically self-critical, it does not mean his work was inferior. Thus the public, had he had his way, would have been deprived of his 'Italian' and 'Reformation' Symphonies, quite apart from many other fine works. For anyone living in 1847, Mendelssohn's opus numbers reached to 77, whereas lists compiled by Stratton and Radcliffe stretch to Op. 121. Even today, however, many unnumbered works are still in manuscript. It is high time that someone be invited to catalogue the whole canon of Mendelssohn's works, as Köchel did for Mozart's manuscripts and Deutsch for those of Schubert, for example. Friends of Mendelssohn has this project as one of the objectives for which it has been formed.

Yet, despite Paul's task, Cécile had to contend with unwanted correspondence regarding her late husband's manuscripts. A Baron de Trémont, whom

Epilogue

Mendelssohn had met in Paris, sought permission to publish an E minor capriccio "in 6/8 time" for the instrumentation that comprised a string quartet. The Baron would make a contribution towards a Mendelssohn memorial. Cécile had no option but to reply that her hands were tied, as Paul was still overseeing her late husband's estate. She could only say that "musicians with special knowledge would decide which music was, or was not, fit for publication". Who these paragons were, and whoever would have the crass impudence to decide such matters, was not made clear. Such queries "lay in wait like ambushes" for this gentle woman, yet "she moved with perfect understanding through this labyrinth of special knowledge", according to Jean Petitpierre. There were pieces belonging to the Mendelssohn family, this biographer continues, that had remained unplayed. Then dispute arose regarding the revised score of *Elijah*. She hoped that Pauline Viardot would be able to sing the proposed French version and that "these paltry legal quibbles would be settled". In extenuation of Paul's attitude, it must be remembered that he might not have realised how ill Cécile had become despite the various "cures", which appeared to do nothing but cause "grimaces" to her face when applying them. In 1996 a collection of letters was auctioned at Sotheby's, giving details of these negotiations and the contracts signed by Cécile "and others". It was learnt from these that, on 25th November 1850, 14 manuscripts were permitted to be published, to be joined by 24 further scores two years later. In 1852 the 'Italian' Symphony could at last be heard by concert-goers: "incisive in its brilliant language, its orchestration both glows and scintillates" in its representation of "Italy's relaxed atmosphere, culture and history", as one critic has described this work. Further manuscripts were brought to public notice after Cécile's death in 1852, including Mendelssohn's 2nd Piano Concerto in 1857 and the incidental music for *Athalie* in 1859. In 1862 Julius Benedict found it "almost impossible" to catalogue Mendelssohn's works, as he found the project so confusing. However, despite his "most incomplete and imperfect" compilation, he believed that not only had he pleased the composer's surviving friends, but that his catalogue of works would be useful for biographers of the future. It was not until 1952 that Yehudi Menuhin discovered what Marek has called Mendelssohn's "little" Violin Concerto in D minor, dedicated to Eduard Rietz and written when Felix was 12. In 1961 a sterling effort was made to publish further works that had hitherto been considered "unfit for anyone to play or hear". Genuine Mendelssohn connoisseurs were thus able to judge for themselves what merit or otherwise these undiscovered compositions possess.

Musical scores were not the only fruit of Mendelssohn's active pen to receive publication. In February 1860 Felix's boyhood friend Johann Droysen, by then a respected historian, collaborated with Paul in circulating a notice to anyone who owned letters to or from Felix to send these to be compiled into a book for family and friends. This request resulted in the *Travel Letters* written between 1830 and 1832 being published in a two-volume edition by Hermann Mendelssohn, a cousin of the immediate family, in Leipzig. A further compilation was published by Paul and Felix's elder son Karl, comprising letters written between 1830 and 1847. A 'cheap' one-volume edition was published in the 1890s. The correspondence caused such a sensation that Mozart's and Beethoven's letters were also edited and published. Two years later, in 1865, Ludwig Nohl published collected material for his *Letters from Musicians*, which included further items relating to Mendelssohn. "An undiminished flood" followed, accompanied by memoirs by friends and contemporaries. These were withheld from publication by Paul, "executor of his late brother's estate and guardian of his two surviving sons", who, by that time, were of an age to exercise their own judgement as to what should be published on their father's behalf.

When Paul died in 1874 Felix's offspring "published with alacrity" these recollections, in exchange for funds that would allow a Mendelssohn Scholarship to be founded. Money was provided by the Prussian government and the 9,000 letters were housed in the Mendelssohn Archive in Dahlem, a suburb of Berlin. In 1861 Lady Grace Wallace, a former friend of Sir Walter Scott, had translated the published volumes into English. English-speaking readers would, thereby, glean "the most genuine impression of his character", as his letters "truly and faithfully mirrored his thoughts". Mendelssohn was still regarded in the English-speaking world as an idol, prompted, no doubt, by the fact that he had died so young and that his music was loved by the dear Queen and her beloved Albert, who passed away on 14th December 1861, causing his widow to grieve until her own death in 1901.

Whilst cataloguing Mendelssohn's works Benedict wrote how "the cautiousness of his representatives, in their desire to act in the same spirit as him [Mendelssohn], resisted publication of anything, among his papers, which might be unworthy of his name or his importance to the history of art". He had to admit that, nevertheless, "some documents that were censored might have caused great delight and enjoyment to the world". Rockstro also took the editors to task, especially regarding Lady Wallace's translation of the letters: her *Travel Letters* "give only a faint idea of the spirit which pervades the glowing pages" of his correspondence. Any elucidations she found necessary were of experiences "that would otherwise be shrouded in mystery". These painstaking tomes were followed by a further volume, *Letters of Goethe and Mendelssohn*, translated into English by M. E. von Glehn, of whom Sir George Grove was fond. The dedication by Karl Mendelssohn in the original German reads: "To Marie [his sister], in memory of our father and in gratitude for all the happiness we enjoyed through him". This book is far livelier and the English more readable than the often turgid efforts of Lady Wallace.

In 1945 came a contribution from the United States, where Gisela Selden-Goth compiled a further book of letters, chiefly from a musical standpoint. The time was right not only for Mendelssohn's music but his personality to be reassessed. "Had Hitler perused his correspondence," she opined, "he would have realised just how loyal a patriot Mendelssohn had been – as true a German as many of the Aryan heroes on whom he and his underlings doted so blatantly."

Apart from the large collection of family documents bequeathed to the Berlin archive, the actress Elinora Mendelssohn had informed Ms. Selden-Goth that a further archive had been donated by family members to the Public Library of New York. Yet, despite such a treasure trove, Peter Ward Jones, curator of the Music Department at the Bodleian Library, Oxford, believes he is responsible for "the largest collection in the world" of Mendelssohn material. This 'Mendelssohn collection', inherited from Maria Wach (Felix's granddaughter), has been added to, via purchases of other memorabilia. In 1997, to commemorate the 150th anniversary of Mendelssohn's death, an exhibition was held at that venue, for which a brochure was issued. Though comprehensive, as far as space was allocated, both the exhibition and its catalogue reveal only a minor part of the Mendelssohns' history, but enough to whet the appetite of any serious scholar or enthusiast of this remarkable family. Such artefacts include the silver goblet presented to Leah and Abraham on their 25th wedding anniversary by their children on 26th December 1829. The Berlin archive houses equally fascinating aspects of Mendelssohnia. What Marek calls Felix's "toilet kit" can be seen – the exquisitely crafted travelling case given to him by the St. Cecilia Society of Frankfurt when, in 1837, Felix conducted *St Paul* and replaced Johann Schelble as director during illness. At what is now 1 Goldschmidtstrasse, Leipzig, home of Cécile and Felix, period furniture can be viewed, together with the beautifully worked cushions and fire screens with which Cécile enhanced their comfortable home.

According to Marek, Dr. Rudolf Elvers had been working on the documents at the Berlin archive since the 1970s and, in 1986, his book *Mendelssohn – A Life in Letters* appeared, translated by Craig Tomlinson. As soon as anyone not conversant with the often quaint Americanisms becomes accustomed to such words and phrases, this book is of great interest, casting new light on Felix's life at home and work. The United States had fostered Mendelssohn's memory from the 1840s. As soon as news of his death reached that continent, America was "flooded", as Kupferberg terms the concept, with Mendelssohn clubs and societies. Such zeal was promulgated by German-speaking immigrants to the 'New World', with cities such as Boston, Chicago and Philadelphia marshalling their musicians to this end. In New York the Philharmonic Orchestra, which had invited Mendelssohn to conduct their 1844-45 concert season, mourned his death for 30 days, culminating in a memorial concert on 14th February 1848. Free to anyone who wished to attend, reports state that the audience consisted of 8,000 concert-goers. Each contingent of musicians and singers was represented and the repertoire included the Funeral March from Beethoven's 'Eroica' Symphony and items from Mozart's Requiem, *St Paul*, *Elijah* and the *Hymn of Praise*. Cécile, having studied the musical press, asked Paul to obtain a programme for this "tasteful occasion".

What Marek calls the "Sing-along-with-Mendelssohn craze" gravitated to schoolchildren. One example is recorded by Kupferberg, when a group of "more girls than boys" sang 'Be not Afraid' from *Elijah*; all he remembers is "the proliferation of blue jeans". There is no report of the choir's musical aptitude (or otherwise). Conversely, a 1970 performance of the oratorio was regarded as "first-rate". As regards orchestral music, Stephen Pettitt, in his biography of the legendary horn player Dennis Brain, recalls a concert in the Los Angeles area, "with a good local choir and strong orchestra" augmented by the woodwind section of the Los Angeles Philharmonic. Dennis's grandfather, Alfred Brain, had organised the proceedings and, despite prohibition, the supply of alcohol was "apparently endless". Arthur Bliss gave a dinner for musicians who had settled in the neighbourhood from war-torn Britain. Though Bliss had had a hangover as a result of this "merry evening", Brain "was beaming all over his face, playing the horn with complete confidence" during the performance. In the early 1970s the Mendelssohn Quartet paid a visit to England, scoring a particular success with the composer's Op. 44 No. 1 Quartet. Indeed, long before his chamber music was recognised and acknowledged, this ensemble paid particular attention thereto, and all three items in Op. 44 remain in their repertoire.

In Canada the Toronto Mendelssohn Choir still flourishes, together with the huge volume of sites devoted to Mendelssohn on the Internet. It is also the case, and it is to be warmly appreciated, that Mendelssohn's music is extremely popular in Japan and China where soloists have become household names through performing and recording works by Mendelssohn.

Mendelssohn's first biography was written by W. A. Lampadius in 1849. This was published in several editions, prompting other recollections and memoirs to follow. In 1855 Johann Christian Lobe, fresh from his success with *Goethe and his Circle*, published *Conversations with Mendelssohn*. This not only discussed Felix's musical ideas but gave shrewd insight into Mendelssohn's views on the arts in general and on politics. However, the most detailed memoir must be that written by Sebastian Hensel, using family letters and extracts from his mother's journal. The first draft of *The Family Mendelssohn, 1729-1847*, was completed in 1865 but, as surviving friends and relatives wished for a more comprehensive version, the two-volume edition was published, with an English translation by "Carl Klingemann and an American collaborator" (presumably Klingemann's son, as Mendelssohn's friend died in 1862 and Hensel's book appeared in the 1870s). Though Eric Werner calls the memoir "inaccurate" and Wilfrid Blunt calls it "misleading", much useful information can be gleaned therefrom for biographers of the future.

As Hensel explained, he aimed not only to relate the history of his forebears to anyone who might read his book, but also, of equal importance, he wished that "the middle classes understand the chronicle of this good middle-class family in Germany". No doubt, once Hensel's translation appeared, their English speaking equivalents would follow the same precepts. Sadly for students of the Mendelssohn family, Hensel considered some of his material "too sacred" and "too irrelevant" for inclusion. His parents' letters written during their courtship were omitted, for example. Perhaps Sebastian Hensel considered Leah's action too shameful in intercepting Fanny's declarations of love for his father.

Various biographies followed, some more trustworthy than others. W. S. Rockstro, writing in 1883, dismissed earlier examples as "mere reproductions" of Lampadius. Was he not, after all, "given the privilege" of studying under Mendelssohn's directorship in Leipzig! Cuthbert Hadden admitted that, during his lifetime, Mendelssohn "was praised too much" and, to bear out his point, quoted Lampadius wholesale: "Living in loose capitals and surrounded by unprincipled people, he was true to all his moral obligations and perfect in all his relationships – son, lover, husband, father and brother... He stood above them all...frank, transparent, honourable, noble, thorough, studious, earnest, religious, concentrating steadfastly on the highest and the best... Not one breath of scandal bedimmed his character." Ruskin weighed in with his eulogy: "He had the heart of a lark...had no enemies but plenty of friends." By comparison, Rockstro's effort is far more readable, but, even so, inaccuracies can be found. Having admitted that her book was written "con amore" ("with love"), Mme. Elise Polko receives short shrift for her collection of anecdotes, gathered at second-hand, if not more spuriously. Hugh Reginald Haweis describes this sentimental garland as "disfigured with enthusiasm"; Stratton calls it "unreliable", whilst R. Larry Todd considers the memoir "a freely embroidered biographical account". Another so-called biography – nothing more than a novel, in fact – was written by Schima Kaufman. *Mendelssohn – A Second Elijah* is spoilt for any serious Mendelssohn student by conversations adapted by the author from family letters. The only saving grace is derived from Ms. Kaufman's catalogue of Mendelssohn's works.

As might be guessed, in view of so much cloying sentiment regurgitated about Mendelssohn, two actual novels are in existence about him. *Charles Auchester* was written in 1853 by Elizabeth Sarah Sheppard, having been planned in 1846, when she "shared my literary secret" with a friend. An introduction to a 1928 edition gives a dramatis personae of the novel. Charles Auchester represents the author herself, which, when it is remembered that a female invented the character, is wholly unconvincing. Mendelssohn is represented by Le Chevalier Seraphael, who marries the Jenny Lind character. Other musical contemporaries decorate the story, Zelter having been portrayed as a wholly unbearable tyrant.

When Ms. Sheppard died at the age of 34, an obituary for *The Atlantic Monthly* described the pages of *Charles Auchester* as "literally drenched with beauty... Mendelssohn was almost a demigod, an unearthly being, so ethereal that he appears seen through the glamour of hero-worship." Chorley criticised the novel, according to Jessie Middleton, in "unfavourable and severe terms" in *The Athenaeum*; three closely printed columns were allowed for his review. Perhaps because her next novel, *Counterpoint*, was dedicated to Mrs. Disraeli in 1854, under the pseudonym 'E Berger', her Prime Minister husband wrote of *Charles Auchester*: "No greater book will ever be written about music and one day it will be recognised as the classic of the divine art." Had the novel been shorter than its 423 pages and had the hero appeared earlier than page 104, the book might have been more enjoyable than this "half-crazed book with no real story", as Chorley dismissed it.

The second novel, *Beyond Desire* by Pierre La Mure is a complete muddle from beginning to end (except for the introduction, which relates to Bach). The contents section mentions nothing about Mendelssohn's own musicianship, except for his bringing the *St Matthew Passion* to the public – and even this part of the novel is decidedly unreliable. The remainder of *Beyond Desire* chronicles Mendelssohn's entirely fictional sex life. His first encounter takes place with an actress who bears the unlikely name of Anna Skrumpnagel. Felix's aim was to lure her to London on Klingemann's behalf. He had been spirited there to protect him from creditors, having purchased a sable coat for the unfortunate Fräulein Skrumpnagel. Felix is then captivated by the Marchioness of Drossyth, lady-in-waiting to Queen Victoria, who eventually marries her groom and is debarred from society. But Mendelssohn's most important amour was Maria Salla, a cross between Maria Malibran and Maria Callas, as far as the reader can deduce. As may be imagined, in view of such 'goings-on', poor Cécile receives a very bad press, being made to resemble a tiresome puritan who understands nothing of her husband's libido.

As with *Charles Auchester*, nobody should rely on *Beyond Desire* for accurate information about Mendelssohn or his peers; a far more convincing novel could be written that would make the most pedantic enthusiast satisfied. Felix's life contains enough fact to avoid the need to conjure up such trashy fiction.

As far back as 1848 a Mendelssohn Scholarship was mooted in London. A performance of *Elijah* took place at Exeter Hall on 15th December of that year, with Miss Lind in the role that Mendelssohn had planned for her. "The most brilliant and aristocratic audience" crowded the hall, the *Musical World* reported. Proceeds, to be used for the proposed scholarship, amounted to £1,000. These funds were to be added to a similar project in Leipzig, but this never happened, and no explanation is to be found.

Though Marek gives Jenny Lind full credit for the project, other friends and musical colleagues gave assistance. Jenny had a great deal for which to thank Mendelssohn. Always almost pathologically afraid of strange venues and environments, Felix did everything in his power to smooth her path in this regard. In Vienna he had even asked his old friend Franz Hauser to "be friendly and helpful to her wherever and whenever you can, and to let her depend on you". Having reminisced with Hauser about their mutual friend, Jenny was able to recover her self-confidence, realising that the hall in Vienna was smaller than that of the Berlin Opera House and that her voice – with its beautiful high F sharp that Mendelssohn so admired – would carry.

With impeccable tact, Mendelssohn was able to negotiate the settlement of a contract that Jenny had omitted to honour during her opera season in London, of which Joan Bulman gives full details. All that she needed to pay in damages was £2,000 – a paltry sum when the unparalleled money she earned is taken into account. But the most important influence Miss Lind gained from Mendelssohn was her decision to switch from opera to oratorio – a far more suitable genre for her puritan personality. She and Mendelssohn often joked together. The pair understood one another to such an uncanny degree that the phrase "etc., etc." was often used, in either case, when each knew what the other was about to say. Though the Uppsala journalist had coined the sobriquet 'the Swedish nightingale' to describe Miss Lind, and though Queen Victoria had written of her "exquisite" voice, and though the Duke of Wellington greeted the prima donna as soon as he caught sight of her, the compliment she must have valued most came from Mendelssohn: "The greatest artist living. The greatest I have ever known." On another occasion he wrote: "One of ourselves; members of the invisible church; worshippers of everything wholesome and beautiful to the spirit. She pulls at the same rope [as myself, regarding the arts]... If all goes well with her in the world, it is as pleasant to me as if it went well with myself." To Hauser he had written: "Not a day passes without my rejoicing that we [Jenny and himself] both live in the same era."

Had Mendelssohn remained unmarried, Joan Bulman states, Jenny would have been able to reveal her true feelings towards him, but, as Cécile and Felix were idyllically happy as a married couple, Miss Lind's "puritan morals and rigid discipline" did not allow her to indulge in "forbidden fruit"; but who knows how her subconscious mind behaved? Friedrich Brockhaus noted, whilst lunching with the Mendelssohns, how Jenny – a guest on the same occasion – looked wistfully at the family, as if, as Brockhaus perceived, yearning to have children of her own. Unable to marry Mendelssohn, Jenny chose as a husband his former pupil, Otto Goldschmidt, who, when a student, had protested at the exorbitant ticket prices at an early Jenny Lind concert in Leipzig. He managed his wife's finances so carefully that no longer did her "lame duck" charities benefit from her largesse, nor were others allowed to squander her income so flagrantly as heretofore.

Despite any enthusiasm that might have been shown towards the proposed Mendelssohn Scholarship, the date on its trust deed, proffered by the Charity Commissioners, is given as 1st August 1871, "for the education of musical students of both sexes". A committee was formed, chaired by Cipriani Potter, a former pupil of Beethoven and still at that time a popular musician. Other names included Julius Benedict; J. W. Davison; John Gosse, whose anthems may still be heard; Charles Hallé; John Hullah (who popularised the 'tonic sol-fa' method of sight-reading); F. A. G. Ouseley, composer of hymn tunes and psalm settings; and Arthur Sullivan, the best remembered. When Sir George Grove joined the committee on 9th June 1874, members included Sir John Stainer of *Crucifixion* fame and Henry Leslie, the choirmaster whose best-known song was his setting of Edgar Allan Poe's poem, *Annabel Lee*, together with those already listed. With the financial acumen of Goldschmidt, who became treasurer, and the meticulous administration of Grove as secretary, there would be little likelihood of a repeat of Goldschmidt's discovery that a former secretary (name not given) had disappeared with the funds. Whether or not the date when Grove joined the committee is mere coincidence, in 1874 Goldschmidt "galvanised the committee into action", rousing them from what he called their "English comfort".

Jenny Lind had already founded a "stipendium" for Swedish students to win awards in order to study abroad, whose welfare she had watched with a personal, motherly interest. This personal care applied to winners of the Mendelssohn Scholarship, allowing her to show interest not only in a student's present mode of life but in a future career. Particularly did she pay attention to industry and moral behaviour, sending "forthright letters, ...which always bore fruit", as Joan Bulman relates, if she heard anything untoward regarding her charges. The first Mendelssohn Scholar was the 14-year-old Arthur Sullivan, who studied in Leipzig from July 1856 to September 1860. Miss Lind preferred male to female applicants, but became "furious" when a man was considered whom she thought to be "too old" for a scholarship. Though cynics might suggest that Jenny's aim was to turn male awardees into Mendelssohn clones, her reasoning was, more likely, based on economics. Whereas a man would pursue his musical career as long as he lived, females, she hoped, would marry and have a family.

On this point, it is interesting to note that, when Sir Hugh Allen had become principal of the Royal College of Music in the 1920s, he had considered nominating Elizabeth Maconchy for a Mendelssohn Scholarship, but decided against this, hoping that she would prefer to undertake marriage and motherhood instead. By contrast, in 1879, Maud Valerie White obtained a scholarship and was funded until February 1881. Up to 1952 only one further female, a Marie Wurm, became a Mendelssohn Scholar, from January 1884 to April 1887. Later scholars have included the composers Daniel Jones and Marc-Anthony Turnage, but no other names have graced the musical hierarchy, other than Sullivan.

When the German equivalent was founded, two scholarships were put into operation – one for composition; one for "practical musicianship". Elections took place on 1st October 1879, the first awardees being Engelbert Humperdinck, best known for his opera *Hansel and Gretel*, and, ironically, a pupil and friend of Wagner. Josef Kotek won the scholarship for "practical musicianship". A virtuoso violinist, Joachim appointed him to the High School in Berlin as a tutor, and he also became a friend of Tchaikovsky whilst staying with the composer in Switzerland. "Thus," Stratton concludes, "the memory of Mendelssohn will be kept in England and Germany. May the day be far distant when he will only be remembered for a scholarship." Mendelssohn prizes were awarded in other parts of Europe, according to Petitpierre, but no details are given from that source. It is known, however, that Frankfurt was one such location. When the Australian composer Percy Grainger was asked, whilst studying there, how he proposed to spend the money if he won this award, he said he aimed to travel to China to develop his musical ideas. Sadly, however, he did not win the Mendelssohn prize, so he would have to wait to achieve his ambition until a future date.

In 1909, the centenary of Mendelssohn's birth, any celebration that did take place was regarded as nothing more than a duty. However, in 1947, the anniversary of his death, recognition of Mendelssohn's music – and the man who composed it – began anew. Blunt recalls a newspaper cutting that related to a successful tour of the Toronto Mendelssohn Choir, headed: "Buffalo swept off feet by Mendelssohn". In London, Sir Thomas Beecham acknowledged the anniversary by giving a concert at Drury Lane on 2nd November 1947. The programme included the 2nd Piano Concerto and the *Midsummer Night's Dream* music. Whilst no mention was made of the piano soloist, a *Daily Telegraph* review acknowledged Dennis Brain's horn playing in the Nocturne, having "sounded the notes of a rare and lovely mellowness". Stephen Pettitt cites a recording for Columbia by Aubrey Brain of the same piece, with the BBC Symphony Orchestra conducted by "Dr Adrian Boult". It is worth observing here that, though biased, Jean Petitpierre's book *The Romance of the Mendelssohns*, originally written to commemorate the centenary of Felix's marriage, was republished in 1947. The author reproduced two pieces hitherto unknown to Mendelssohn connoisseurs – a sonata movement composed by Felix in 1822 and an allegretto written whilst on honeymoon in 1837. Petitpierre employed the latter piece in lectures on his book at Neuchâtel University, Switzerland and broadcasts from Lausanne and Paris.

In the 1950s other less illustrious, but decidedly perceptive, Mendelssohn enthusiasts helped to clear the thorny path of the anti-Mendelssohn wilderness. "Mendelssohn is on his own. The rest of the composers merely wrote music," an oboist from a provincial orchestra declared. Then there was the farmer who, having asked an uncle to help with haymaking, was told, "I can't", because he preferred to sit at home to listen to a broadcast of Mendelssohn's E minor Violin Concerto. But, whereas the English-speaking world had always loved Mendelssohn (apart from some curmudgeons of the musical establishment), the best news came from Germany. In 1959, the 150th anniversary of his birth, the authorities pronounced that Mendelssohn's music "is no longer under shrouds". At last, concert-goers could hear his compositions live, or listen to broadcasts and recordings. The German Post Office played their part in commemorating this anniversary by issuing various stamps, according to John Watson's book *Coins and Stamps in Music*. A 10 Pfennig issue showed the Leipzig Gewandhaus; the 25 Pfennig stamp showed a few bars of the 'Italian ' Symphony, whilst that for 40 Pfennigs reproduced Mendelssohn's signature. The Beethovenhalle in Bonn issued a sheet of paper that bore "the thin, delicate face of an aesthete, well versed in all the arts" – that of Mendelssohn. Not only were "grace and elegance" visible, but "above all, [it] provides us with some relief from the often oppressive greatness of the accepted masters. Mendelssohn's humanity shines through, allowing the spectator to feel no need of awe towards the music, or the man who wrote it." Whilst on this subject, it is relevant to mention a stamp that had been issued in 1949 to commemorate the centenary of the death of Conradin Kreutzer. It was, after all, Mendelssohn's dislike of Kreutzer's opera, based on Grillparzer's *Tale of the Beautiful Melusine*, that caused the overture to be written, Mendelssohn's own favourite of his works. As with so many of his compositions, this is far too rarely played, either at 'live' concerts or via the recording establishment, despite the constant campaigning of Friends of Mendelssohn for such neglect to be remedied.

Credit must here be given to Scotland's fine commemoration of the composer who put that country on the musical map. Each August a Mendelssohn Festival is held on the Isle of Mull and, at Tobermory, one hotel even has a Mendelssohn Room where guests can stay. Sadly, however, disappointment must be expressed as regards a further proposed project. Though the German Mendelssohn Scholarship was reinstated in 1964 (having been disbanded by the Nazis), and though Mendelssohn's home at Goldschmidtstrasse 1 in Leipzig has been converted into a study centre, to complement its museum status, in 1994 there had been discussion of a British branch, the International Mendelssohn Foundation of the United Kingdom, which was registered with the Charity Commissioners "the next day", according to one of its trustees. However, nothing has been heard of this organisation from anyone concerned therewith.

It was this lack of information and non-communication that caused Friends of Mendelssohn to be founded in 1997. Its aims include not only raising funds for any Mendelssohn project, at home or abroad, but also work of scholarship and research, which includes compiling programme notes for concerts and sleeve notes for recordings of his music and that of his contemporaries, when invited to do so. A further task, never accomplished, is to correct inaccuracies resulting from carelessly researched biographies or faulty memoirs, which broadcasters and others continue to disseminate. As a tribute to his sporting prowess (see chapter 4), Team Mendelssohn has also been formed. Members take part in unusual stunts, whereby money is raised for charities, on invitation.

Whereas, in 1901, Stratton wrote that "there is nothing further to write about Mendelssohn", Cuthbert Hadden, eight years later, gave a more positive view: "In an age which puts Wagner above Beethoven and prefers the passion of Tchaikovsky to the optimistic clarity of Haydn and Mozart...there is surely enough conflict and violence in life and in art without demanding more of it from Mendelssohn. When we want to be made unhappy by music, we can turn to others. In Mendelssohn, we shall find nothing that is not at once manly and refined, clever and pure, brilliant and solid", though reflection and contemplation can be found, to complement the exuberance and fun. The same concepts apply to the man as completely as his music and, with this in mind, it is hoped that Mendelssohn's *The Caged Spirit* has done justice to both Mendelssohn's music and the man himself.

BIBLIOGRAPHY

Compilations: letter collections, diaries, reminiscences, etc.

Elvers, R. R. (ed.), *Mendelssohn – A Life in Letters* (trans. by Craig Tomlinson) (Cassel, 1986)
Gotch, R. B. (ed.): *Mendelssohn and his Friends in Kensington: Letters from Sophy and Fanny Horsley to their Aunt, Lucy Callcott*; Humphrey Milford/Oxford University Press, 1934.
Mendelssohn, K., and Mendelssohn, P.: *Goethe and Mendelssohn: Correspondence between Composer and Dramatist, together with further Inclusions* (trans. by M. E. von Glehn); Macmillan & Co., 1874.
Mendelssohn, P., and Droysen, J. (eds.): *Travel Letters of Felix Mendelssohn, 1830-1832* (trans. by Lady Grace Wallace); Macmillan & Co., 1862.
Mendelssohn, P., and Droysen, J. (eds.): *Letters of Felix Mendelssohn, 1830-1847* (trans. by Lady Grace Wallace); Macmillan & Co., 1863.
Nichols, R.: *Mendelssohn Remembered*; Faber & Faber, 1996.
Sampson, G.: *A Day with Mendelssohn* [in the 'Days with the Great Composers' series]; Hodder & Stoughton, 19th century.
Selden-Goth, G. (ed.): *Letters of Felix Mendelssohn*; Vienna House, 1945.
Todd, R. L. (ed.): *Mendelssohn and his World: Essays and Reminiscences*; Princeton University Press, 1994.
Ward Jones, P. (ed.): *The Mendelssohns on Honeymoon: The 1837 Diary of Felix and Cécile Mendelssohn-Bartholdy, together with Letters to their Families*; The Clarendon Press, 1997.

Mendelssohn biographies

Blunt, W.: *On Wings of Song*; Hamish Hamilton, 1974.
Hensel, S.: *The Mendelssohn Family, 1729-1847* (trans. by C. Klingemann et al); Low, Marston, Searle & Rivington, 3rd edn., 1882.
Jacob, H. E.: *Mendelssohn and his Times* (trans. by R. and C. Winston); Barrie & Rockliff, 1963.

Jenkins, D., and Visocchi, M.: *Mendelssohn in Scotland*; Chappell & Co./Elm Tree Books, 1978.
Kaufman, S.: *Mendelssohn – A Second Elijah*; Tudor House Publishing Co., 1936.
Kupferberg, H.: *The Mendelssohns – Three Generations of Genius*; W. H. Allen/Howard & Wyndham Ltd, 1972.
Marek, G. R.: *Gentle Genius*; Robert Hale & Co., 1972.
Moszkowski, M.: *Mendelssohn*; publishers and date not known.
Petitpierre, J.: *The Romance of the Mendelssohns*; Dennis Dobson, 1937.
Radcliffe, P.: *Mendelssohn* [in the 'Master Musicians' series]; Dent & Sons, 1978.
Rockstro, W. S.: *Mendelssohn*; Sampson, Lowe, Marston & Co., 1883.
Stratton, S.: *Mendelssohn* [in the 'Master Musicians' series]; Dent & Sons, 1901.

Collective biographies of composers in which Mendelssohn appears

Hadden, C.: 'Mendelssohn: Singer of the Songs without Words', in *Master Musicians – A Book for Singers, Players and Listeners*; T. N. Foulis, 1909.
Kobbé, G.: 'Mendelssohn and his Cécile', in *Great Composers and their Loves*; George G. Harrap & Co., 1912.
O'Shea, J.: 'Mendelssohn', in *Illnesses of the Great Composers*; publisher and date not known.
Streatfeild, R. A.: 'Schumann and Mendelssohn', in *Modern Master Musicians*; Methuen & Co., 1900.

Reference books

Pike, E. R.: *Human Documents from the Age of Adam Smith*; David & Charles/Newton Abbot, 1971.
Pike E. R.: *Human Documents from the Age of the Forsytes*; David & Charles/Readers' Union, early 1970s.
Scholes, P. C.: *The Concise Oxford Dictionary of Music*; Oxford University Press, 1952 edition.

Fiction

La Mure, P.: *Beyond Desire* [see Introduction re J. S. Bach]; HarperCollins, 1956.
Sheppard, E. S.: *Charles Auchester*; Dent & Co., 1928 edition.

Peripheral reading

Brion, M.: *Schumann and the Romantic Age*; Collins, 1956.
Bulman, J.: *Jenny Lind*; Robert Cunningham, 1956.
Byrne, M.: *Robert Schumann* [in the 'Days with the Great Composers' series], Sampson & Lowe, 19th century.
Wagner, R.: *My Life* (trans. by C. Wagner); Cambridge University Press, 1983.
Young, P. M.: 'Elgar, O. M.: A Study of a Musician', in *The New Grove*; Oxford University Press, 1957.
Young, P. M.: *Sir George Grove;* Oxford University Press, 1960.

Various

Concert programmes; radio broadcasts; miscellaneous music dictionaries.
Personal communications, written and verbatim.

Index of Names and Compositions

Aachen: festivals at, 51, 331, 334, 373, 378, 457, 480; FMB meets Chopin in, 424
Aarnt, Dr. (Leipzig physician), 560
Abbt, Thomas, 15, 21
Abraham, John *see* Braham, John
Adam, Adolphe: *Le Postillon de Lonjumeau*, 411
Adams, Thomas, 344
Adelaide of Saxe-Meiningen, Queen Consort of King William IV: attends performance of *St Paul*, 359
Aeschylus, 72, 74, 297, 390, 395; *Oresteia*, 297, 395
Albert, Prince Consort of Queen Victoria, 280, 350, 366, 386, 398-9, 400, 525, 563, 566, 573, 575, 601, 602, 604; compositions of, 397; eulogy to FMB, 401
Alexander I, Tsar: Hensel's portrait of, 177
Alexandra, Queen Consort of King Edward VII: preference for 'On Wings of Song', 401, 595
Allegri, Gregorio, 94, 198, 408; *Miserere*, 136
Allen, Sir Hugh, 610
America, 545; emigration of Mendelssohn family to, 590; popularity of FMB's music in, 285, 590, 605
American Ballet Theatre, 597
American Vox, 571
Andersen, Hans Christian, 503, 566
Anderson, George, 522
Anderson, Lucy, 601
André, Julius, 344
Appel (pastor), 471
Aquinas, St. Thomas, 354
Arabian Nights' Entertainment, 74, 198, 387

Arensky, Anton, 593
Argyll, Duke of, 534, 536, 537
Aristophanes, 527; *The Wasps*, 297
Arnim, Bettina von (*née* Brentano), 150, 151, 242
Arnold, Matthew, 272
Arnold, Samuel, 115; edition of Handel's works edited by FMB, 115, 310-11, 312, 425, 430
Arnstein & Eskeles (bankers), 188
Athenaeum, The, 18, 35, 322, 350, 366, 376, 565, 596, 607; praise for FMB in, 512
Atlantic Monthly, The, 607
Attwood, Sir Thomas, 261, 441, 515, 540; FMB dedicates organ works to, 346; FMB visits, 57, 543
Auber, Daniel François Esprit, 276, 289, 414, 415; FMB criticises works of, 147, 293, 406; *La Muette di Portici*, 291, 527
Augsburg Confession tricentennial, 202, 238
Augusta, Empress, 545, 571
Augustus Frederick, Duke of Sussex, 16
Austen, Jane, 33, 250
Austin, Sarah, 82, 243
Ayrton, William, 114, 517
Bab, Julius, 480
Babbage, Charles, 551, 553
Bach, August Wilhelm, 114, 344
Bach, Carl Philipp Emmanuel, 303, 304
Bach, Johann Christian, 397
Bach, Johann Sebastian: hand span of, 34; eye surgery of, 58, 544; Mendelssohn family's appreciation of, 108, 109, 129, 181, 191, 273, 322; influence on FMB's compositional style, 106, 120, 273, 288, 354, 409, 428, 586; Zelter

studies, 107; fugues of, 126, 312, 340, 343, 346-7; manuscripts of, 131, 246, 379; Engelberg monks unaware of, 136, 345; reluctance to publish Bach's music in the eighteenth century, 303-4; nineteenth century revival of, 303-314, 317, 321, 323, 439, 443, 590, 591; FMB unable to play works of in Berne, 344; monument to Bach erected in Leipzig, 347-8, 450-1, 588; FMB compared with, 348, 358, 584; fugue on the name of, 350; performance of devotional works, 360-1; reception in Paris, 406; Rossini and, 416; in Leipzig, 437, 450; reception in England, 509, 517, 574; *Art of Fugue*, 303; B minor Mass, 198, 305, 313, 416, 572; *Brandenburg Concertos*, 303; cantatas, 308, 327; *Chaconne* (from Partita in D minor), 440; chorales, 222, 357; keyboard concertos, 102, 115, 119, 131, 154, 248, 343, 409, 426, 446, 523; organ works, 152, 331, 343, 346-7, 517, 518; *Prelude and Fugue* in E flat, 349, 518; *St John Passion*, 137, 308, 312, 361; *St Matthew Passion*, 132, 288, 304-9, 312, 314, 317, 323, 328, 351, 354, 448, 511, 518, 527, 562, 608; *Toccata and Fugue* in D minor, 345; violin concertos, 453, 486; *Well-Tempered Clavier*, 109, 131

Bach, Wilhelm Friedemann, 304

Bach, Wilhelm Friedrich Ernst: attends unveiling of Bach monument in Leipzig, 451

Bacon, Mr. (designer): designs London statue of FMB, 602

Bad Doberan, 76, 131, 536; cathedral at, 196; organ at, 344; spa at, 272

Bader, Adam: asked to sing in FMB's revival of the *St Matthew Passion*, 306-7

bagpipe: FMB hears, 276, 513, 531

Bahmer (family), 252

Baillot, Pierre Marie François de Sales, 419; performs quartet with FMB, 117

Baini, Abbate Giuseppe, 136

Balanchine, George, 597

Banck, Karl, 281

Bankes, Justice, 594

Banks, Joseph: visit to Staffa, 279

Barbarossa, Frederick, Holy Roman Emperor: palace at Monza, 92

Barenboim, Daniel, 505

Baring, Alexander, 1st Baron Ashburton, 530

Barker, Mr. (Vice-Chairman of Birmingham Festival), 548

Bärmann, Carl, 323

Bärmann, Heinrich Joseph, 318, 323; FMB's friendship with, 420

Barnum, Phineas T., 573

Bartholdy, Jakob (*earlier* Salomon), 97, 173; attitude to musicians, 105, 185; adoption of the surname 'Bartholdy', 176; death of, 176; role in the Mendelssohn family's conversion to Lutheranism, 191-2, 200, 356, 579

Bartholomew, William: paraphrase of 'Hear My Prayer', 204; presentation of opera libretto to FMB, 295; as librettist of *Elijah*, 353, 363, 594

Bathurst, Miss: tragic death of, 97

Baudissin, Wolf Graf, 446

Bauer, Albert, 59, 60, 194, 233, 351, 360, 459

Bax, Sir Arnold: *Tintagel*, 281

Bayreuth: opera house, 295, 324, 582; festival, 584

Becker, Carl: teaches organ at the Leipzig Conservatorium, 376

Becker, Jakob: offer to paint a portrait of Cécile Mendelssohn, 568

Becker, Nikolaus: FMB's dislike of 'The Rhine Song', 214-5

Beecham, Sir Thomas: encounters Nazi censorship of FMB's music 589; acknowledges centenary of FMB's death, 611

Beer, Jacob Judah Herz, 415

Beer, Mme., 229

Beethoven, Ludwig van, 23, 116-7, 149, 211, 321, 322, 327, 609, 612; FMB

lays flowers on the tomb of, 79, 420, 590; sketches and manuscripts of, 81, 112, 230, 328, 469, 518; and Dorothea von Ertmann, 91; meeting with Liszt, 105; influence on FMB, 106, 108-9, 110, 120, 273, 314, 586, 587; and Henriette Herz, 108; FMB sight-reads from a manuscript of, 125; Goethe and, 133-4, 272-3, 181; Zelter criticises, 148; FMB at the death of, 243; hurdy-gurdy arrangements of, 276; comparisons with FMB, 278, 287, 334, 511, 584; Tieck on, 296; FMB conducts music by, 315-6, 439, 443, 521; FMB on, 339-40, 409, 423, 432, 450; reception and performance of Beethoven's works in Paris, 406-7; philanthropy towards, 510; reception and performance in England, 509, 574, 578; Jewish friends of, 582; FMB promotes music of, 591; 'Adelaide', 131, 153; *Christ on the Mount of Olives*, 594; *Coriolan* Overture, 119-20; *Fidelio*, 207, 287, 306, 406, 418, 443, 469, 521, 577; *Glorreiche Augenblick*, 312; Incidental Music to *Egmont*, 317, 327; Incidental Music to *The Ruins of Athens*, 521; *Leonore* Overture No. 1, 521; *Leonore* Overture No. 3, 324, 332; *Missa Solemnis*, 312; Piano Concerto No. 1, 340; Piano Concerto No. 4, 52, 339, 526, 579; Piano Concerto No. 5, 'Emperor', 109, 339; Piano Sonata in C sharp minor, 'Moonlight', op. 27, No. 2, 91, 124, 340, 555; Piano Sonata in F minor, op. 57, 149, 155; Piano Sonata in A major, op. 101, 91, 421; String Quartet No.11 in F minor, op. 95, 243; String Quartet No. 15 in A minor, op. 132, 243; Symphony No. 2, 318; Symphony No. 3, 'Eroica', 265, 605; Symphony No. 4, 265; Symphony No. 5, 133-4, 265, 332; Symphony No. 6, 'Pastoral', 249, 281, 324, 427, 542; Symphony No. 8, 315, 317; Symphony No. 9, 'Choral', 131, 441, 510, 563;
Violin Concerto, 452-3, 486, 522, 576; Violin Sonata No. 9 in A major, 'Kreutzer', op. 47, 91, 340, 451

Bellini, Vincenzo, 244, 414, 423; *La Sonnambula*, 484, 520, 529; *Norma*, 454

Bendemann, Eduard, 165, 223, 470; paints portrait of FMB in Berlin, 331; supervises building of Bach monument in Leipzig, 451; critiques FMB's art, 503

Bendigan, Louise, 253

Benecke, Jette: FMB's dedication to, 284

Benecke, Marie *see* Mendelssohn, Marie

Benecke, Paul, 570

Benecke, Victor, 38, 569

Benedict, Sir Julius, 34, 110-11, 112, 132, 365-6, 387, 505, 555, 601, 609; describes FMB's piano playing, 337; catalogues FMB's works, 44, 228, 603, 604; FMB meets, 100; on the authorship of op. 19, 146; on FMB's style of conducting, 315-6; describes FMB's emotional state after Fanny death, 563

Bennett, Joseph, 361

Berduschek (pastor): gives FMB's funeral oration, 562

Berger, Ludwig: as FMB's music teacher, 41, 107-8, 261; FMB's dedication to, 114

Bériot, Charles Auguste de, 243, 451, 516; Violin Concerto, 516

Berk (musician in Vienna), 420

Berlin, Irving: *Mesmerising Mendelssohn Tune* (adaptation of 'Spring Song'), 598

Berlin: musical life of, 2, 125, 136, 151, 319, 320, 390, 432-3, 439, 515; treatment of Jews living in, 8, 200, 322; Flying Dutchman premiere, 261; FMB turns down professorship at Berlin University, 318, 320; selection of new director at Berlin Singakademie, 319-22; lack of recognition for FMB's music in, 323; Academy of Arts, 11, 319; Academy of Music, 377, 440, 593;

Academy of Sciences, 13, 70, 237; Cathedral, 217, 232, 310, 394, 432; Church of the Holy Trinity, 562; Institute of Church Music, 114; King's Theatre, 70, 131, 154, 265, 299, 529; Mendelssohn Archive, 45, 595, 604; Mendelssohn family's house, 69, 175, 259, 488; Observatory, 70; Opera House, 253, 321, 490, 608; Polytechnic, 24; Polytechnic Society, 26; Royal Theatre, xxiii; Singakademie, 52, 56, 59, 108, 114, 137, 148, 201, 222, 228, 238, 246, 247, 272, 301, 305, 308, 309, 310, 319-23, 344, 351, 371, 374, 412, 418, 429, 438, 514-5, 421, 562, 566; University, 76, 230, 259, 296, 318, 320, 409, 491

Berlioz, Hector, 94, 97, 116, 250, 303, 315, 341, 417, 422, 424, 453-4, 481, 545, 575; FMB on, 80, 422-3, 453; high regard for FMB's compositions, 263, 351, 423, 600; and the Dirichlet's nursemaids, 481; *Beatrice and Benedict*, 263; *Grande Messe des Morts*, 454; *Harold in Italy*, 275; *King Lear*, 263, 423, 453; *Les Francs-Juges*, 422; *Romeo and Juliet*, 263, 454; *Sardanapale*, 422; *Symphonie Fantastique*, 422

Berner, Friedrich Wilhelm, 115
Bernhard, Isaac, 9
Bernus, Franz, 217, 456-7
Bianchi, Luigi Alberto, 4; unearthing of an early draft of FMB's Violin Concerto, 452, 595-6
Biedermeier Era, 213
Bigot, Marie, 150, 419, 497; as piano teacher to FMB, 79, 111-2, 149; illness of, 149
Billing, Archibald, 244
Bilz-Planer, Natalie, 456
Birch-Pfeifer, Charlotte, 366, 434, 520
Birkett Foster, Myles: *History of the Philharmonic Society*, 521
Birmingham: Birmingham Festival, 51, 61, 144, 169, 239, 297, 341, 349, 359, 362-7, 443, 447, 475, 492, 496, 510, 516-20, 524-5, 547, 548, 549-50, 552, 576, 594; Town Hall, 349; pays tribute to FMB, 601

Bishop, David, 341
Bishop, Sir Henry: 'Home, Sweet Home', 104, 311; 'My Pretty Jane', 311; 'The Mistletoe Bough', 311
Bizet, Georges: *Songs of the Rhine*, 575, 591
Blas, Giles, 74
Blessinger, Karl: *Judaism in Music*, 588
Bliss, Arthur, 606
Blücher, Marshal Gebhard Leberecht von, 174
Blume, Heinrich, 300
Blumner, Herr. (benefactor), 375
Blunt, Wilfred, 3, 59, 60, 74, 108, 141, 148, 160, 176, 183, 241, 244, 245, 248, 252, 297, 298, 354, 389, 406, 415, 463, 468, 512, 544, 545, 547, 558, 594, 598, 606, 611; *On Wings of Song*, 37, 570
Boccaccio, Giovanni: *Decameron*, 74, 224
Böckh, Professor Philipp August, 232, 390, 491; as teacher of FMB, 45, 293, 296; birthday of, 229
Boguslawski, Wilhelm von, 326, 566; tutelage under FMB, 163, 172, 369-70; *Elfino*, 370
Böhme, Franz M., 376
Boito, Arrigo, 287; on FMB, 577
Bonaparte, Napoleon *see* Napoleon I, Emperor
Bonner (translator), 296
Borkhardt (tenor), 156
Botgerschreck, Mme. (Leipzig host), 342
Böttger, Professor Adolf: sends FMB libretto, 295
Botstein, Leon: on FMB's mode of composition, 351
Boult, Adrian, 593, 611
Braham, John, 233, 520; collaboration with Weber, 583
Brahms, Johannes, 285, 287, 309, 314, 334, 544, 577, 592, 598, 599, 600; on FMB, 281, 577; friendship with Joachim, 374, 451, 523; *Academic*

Festival Overture, 399; *German Requiem*, 334; 'Minnelied', 283; Violin Concerto, 453, 486, 523, 596
Brain, Alfred, 606
Brain, Aubrey, 611
Brain, Dennis, 606, 611
Brancusi, Constantine, 280
Braun, Alexander, 236
Braun, Friederike *see* Robert, Friederike
Breitkopf and Härtel (publisher), 39, 156, 185, 215, 311, 340, 443, 452
Brendel, Franz, 581
Brentano, Bernard von, 261
Brentano, Clemens, 172; *Des Knaben Wunderhorn*, 503
Breslau: FMB in, 115, 163, 263, 344, 372, 512
Breuer, Bernhard, 446
Brion, Marcel, 259, 426; *Schumann and the Romantic Age*, 428
Brisbane, Thomas: FMB meets, 421
Britten, Benjamin: *Peter Grimes*, 281
Broadley, Charles Bayles, 352-3
Broadwood (piano manufacturer), 337, 457, 526, 548
Brockhaus, Friedrich, 150, 455, 484, 494, 609
Bamberg, Hyam (Hermann), 9
Brontë, Charlotte, 58
Brontë, Emily, 544
Brontë, Patrick: successful eye operation carried out on, 544
Brown, Ford Madox: *Elijah and the Widow's Son*, 594
Browning, Robert, 295
Bruch, Max, 106, 592; Violin Concerto No. 1, 453, 486, 592; *Die Lorelei*, 287, 302; *Scottish Fantasy*, 592
Bruckner, Anton, 274, 577; influence of FMB on, 593
Brühl, Count Karl von, 299, 301
Brunel, Isambard Kingdom, 540; marriage of, 39, 249, 545, 547-8; FMB meets, 534, 545
Brunel, Marc Isambard, 545
Brutus, Marcus, 100

Buber, Franz: suicide of, 446
Bull, John, 532
Bulman, Joan, 37, 253, 254, 493, 609, 610
Bülow, Hans von, 338, 521
Bülow, Heinrich Freiherr von, 529-530
Bulwer-Lytton, Sir Edward, 550
Bünau-Grabau, Henriette, 148, 376
Bunsen, Baron Josias von, 94, 171, 185, 204, 296, 311, 312, 388, 396, 397, 421, 493, 555, 601
Burgiel, Wilhelm, 591
Burgmüller, Johann Friedrich, 228
Burgmüller, Norbert: FMB composes piece for funeral of, 228; symphonia performed in Düsseldorf, 327
Burney, Charles, 314
Burns, Robert, 74, 283
Bury, Miss, 465
Busoni, Ferruccio, 598
Butler, Mlle. (singer), 328
Butler, Samuel: *The Way of All Flesh*, 89
Buxton, Edward, 311, 354, 449, 492, 523
Byron, Lord George, 74, 85, 93, 283, 284, 421, 422-3; *Childe Harold*, 386; *Theramin*, 284
Cäcilie (journal), 47
Callcott, Lucy, 58, 162, 172, 249, 266, 329
Calderón de la Barca, Pedro: *Life is a Dream*, 122
Campbell, Sir Walter, 534
Candia, Cavaliere Giovanni Matteo di (Mario), 524
Caradori-Allan, Maria, 363-5, 520; requests that FMB alter the score of *Elijah*, 364
Carley, Lionel, 596
Caroline of Brunswick, Queen Consort of King George IV: emancipation to Italy, 92
Carus, Ernst August, 497, 498, 560
Casals, Pablo, 597
Caspar, Dr. Johann, 8, 44, 164; *Soldiers' Loves*, 297-8; *The Two Schoolmasters*, 298

Catalani, Angelica, 359
Catherine II, Empress of Russia, 12
Cavendish, William George Spencer, Sixth Duke of Devonshire, 102, 386, 530
Caxton, William, 239
Cellini, Benvenuto, 93
Cerito, Mme. (dancer), 200
Cervantes, Miguel de: *Don Quixote*, 131, 298-9; *The Gypsy Girl*, 343
Ceylon: FMB asked to write music for, 531
Chamberlain, Houston Stewart, 584
Chaos (newspaper), 133
Charles Augustus Bennet, Earl of Tankerville (Lord Ossulston), 551
Charles I, Duke of Brunswick, 15
Charles II, King, 358
Charles X, King of France, 211
Cherubini, Luigi, 81, 326, 327, 407, 417, 424, 510; FMB presented to, 79, 116-7, 265, 405; FMB on, 417, 419; *Ali Baba*, 419, 439; *Medea*, 172; *The Water Carrier*, 116
Chilton, Charles, 424
Chimanowsky, Marie *see* Szymanowska, Marie
Chissell, Joan, 342
Chladni, Professor Ernst, 122
Choir, The, 343
cholera epidemic, 58
Chopin, Fryderyk, 3, 80, 82, 111, 124, 174, 237, 287, 342, 343, 398, 428, 454, 525, 575, 577, 578, 593, 598, 599; FMB praises virtuosity of, 147, 424-5; FMB's meetings with 310, 424-5, 453; FMB criticises piano music of, 409; festival at Leipzig, 425; FMB requests autograph from, 425, 489; illness of, 548; on Schumann, 600; Piano Concerto No. 1, 424, 443
Chorley, Henry Fothergill, 125, 350, 366, 376, 422, 547, 607, 608; on FMB, 35, 106, 565, 573, 574, 575, 594; on personal appearance of FMB, 39; on Fanny Mendelssohn, 109, 146; on Jenny Lind, 253; makes English translation of *Son and Stranger*, 302; reports on the Brunswick Festival, 332-3; friendship with FMB, 345-6, 447, 502, 520, 558; *Modern German Music*, 106
Christian VII, King of Denmark, 16
Cicero, Marcus Tullius, 100, 127, 504
Citron, Marcia, 150
Clairbourg, Mme., 237
Claremont, 398-9
Clarus, Johann Christian August, 65
Classical Music Magazine, 151
Clementi, Muzio, 50, 107, 339, 407, 510
Clicquot, Barbe Nicole: promises FMB a yearly supply of champagne, 334, 480
Coburg-Gotha, Prince of, 400
Cohen, Rabbi Raphael, 16
Collard, Frederick William, 151, 342, 534
Cologne: music festivals at, 38, 51, 214, 310, 331-2, 425, 498; cathedral at, 277, 592
Columbus, Christopher, 93
Constant, Benjamin, 25, 118
Cook, Captain James, 279
Cook, Grattan: FMB grants wish to insert oboe solo into *Elijah*, 367
Cooper, James Fenimore: *Last of the Mohicans*, 454
Cooper, Mel, 593
Cooper, Mr. (Royal College of Arms), 348-9
Copernicus, Nicolaus, 421
Corlioni (tenor), 529
Cornelius, Peter von, 170, 228, 388
Costa, Sir Michael, 340, 525-6
Coventry's (publishers), 346
Cox, Revd J. E., describes FMB in concert, 338, 359
Cramer, Addison and Beale, 435
Cramer, Franz, 530
Cramer, Johann Baptist, 485, 533
Cranach, Lukas, 122
Crichton-Stuart, John, 2nd Marquess of Bute, 530
Cromwell, Oliver, 358
Cummings, William Hayman: setting of

Index of Names and Compositions

'Hark! The Herald Angels Sing', 239, 525, 598; FMB impressed by, 525
Cunningham, Allan, 531
Czerny, Karl, 303, 407
Da Ponte, Lorenzo, 287
Daguerre, Louis, 462
Dahms, Walter, 266
Daily Telegraph, 611
Damrosch, Leopold: founds New York Men's Chorus, 285
Dante, 44, 90, 109
Dautler, Mme. (singer), 327
D' Avanzi, Jacopo, 93
David, Félicien: *The Desert*, 379
David, Ferdinand, 37, 153, 154, 156, 169, 181, 250, 262, 295, 379-80, 381, 411, 413, 428, 431, 433, 455, 467, 519, 580, 583; friendship with FMB, 76, 247, 394, 488, 499, 519, 560, 562; conducts in tandem with FMB, 239-40; performs with FMB, 340, 414, 440, 455; as teacher to Joachim, 374, 453; at the Leipzig Conservatorium, 376; as leader of the Gewandhaus Orchestra, 394, 439; and FMB's Violin Concerto, 452-3, 485, 595-6; engagement of, 468; deputises for FMB as conductor, 498; Trombone Concerto, 597
David, Henri, 212
David, Jacques-Louis: *The Deluge*, 80; *Paris and Helen*, 80
David, King of Israel (Old Testament), 39, 129
Davison, J.W., 252-3, 332, 342, 423-4; on *Elijah*, 364; on Joseph Joachim, 522-3; on FMB's legacy, 577, 583; as member of the Mendelssohn Scholarship committee, 609
Davout, Marshal Louis Nicolas, 180
Dawes, Charles Gates: Dawes plan, 570
Debussy, Claude: *La Mer*, 281
Decker, Mme. (singer), 64, 434
Dehn (musicologist): request to FMB, 47
Delacroix, Eugène, 244
Delaroche, Paul, 198, 235
Delius, Frederick, 593, 596
Dessau, Duchess of *see* Friederike, Duchess of Anhalt-Dessau
Dessau: Moses Mendelssohn born in, 7; FMB performs in, 131; FMB visits with his father, 202; FMB visits Schubring in, 306; FMB mourned in, 562
Dessauer, Herr (relative of Mendelssohn), 200
Deutsch, Otto Erich, 602
Devonshire, Duke of *see* Cavendish, William George Spencer
Devrient, Eduard, 41, 42, 48, 52, 69, 74, 85, 120, 128, 148, 166, 171, 188, 209, 237, 291, 292, 298, 300, 320, 321-2, 326, 329, 355, 395, 459, 477, 532; on FMB, 35, 37, 38, 66, 111, 146, 174-5, 207, 218, 242, 301-2, 304, 307, 317, 463, 586; attempts to find a libretto for FMB to write an opera to, 48, 287-91, 302, 577; on the Mendelssohn home in Leipzig, 175; on Sophocles's *Antigone*, 296; on Spontini, 299; suggests public performance of the *St Matthew Passion*, 305; sings in FMB's revival of the *St Matthew Passion*, 306; applies for post at Berlin Singakademie, 321; leaves Berlin, 433-4, 488; on Cécile Mendelssohn, 462; recognises the demise in FMB's health, 555; comforts Cécile after the death of FMB, 565; *Memoirs*, 146, 301, 304, 312, 321, 563, 584
Devrient, Ludwig: unruly behaviour in a tavern, 480
Devrient, Thérèse (*née* Schlesinger), 69, 166, 171, 304, 307; describes mood of performers during FMB's revival of the *St Matthew Passion*, 304
Dibdin, Charles: 'All on the Downs the Fleet was moored' (FMB sings), 246, 250
Dickens, Charles, 540, 573; FMB meets, 74, 551; *A Christmas Carol*, 505
Dickinson, A. E. R.: describes rift between Schumann and FMB, 586

623

Diderot, Denis, 74
Diefenbach, Lorenz, 489
Dinsdale, Anne, 544
Dirichlet, Ernst Lejeune, 99, 503-4; birth of, 545
Dirichlet, Florentina (Flora), 507; birth of, 65, 90, 103, 500
Dirichlet, Gustav Peter Lejeune, 63, 94, 98-9, 102-103, 145, 180, 198, 199, 227, 236, 400, 481, 559; birth of daughter, 90, 500; early life of, 180; marriage to Rebecca Mendelssohn, 180, 222, 233; FMB expresses political concerns to, 217; on FMB, 491; FMB speaks to Babbage about, 551; gains professorship in Göttingen, 571; *Theory of Numbers*, 180
Dirichlet, Rebecka *see* Mendelssohn, Rebecca
Dirichlet, Walter Lejeune, 72, 98, 99, 198-9, 236, 503-4, 506, 507; birthday celebrations of, 225; FMB writes to, 504, 551
Disraeli, Benjamin, 201
Disraeli, Isaac, 201
Disraeli, Mary Anne, 607
Döhler, Théodore von, 151-2
Dolby, Charlotte Helen (*later* Sainton-Dolby), 366, 454
Döme, Christian, 17
Donizetti, Gaetano, 90, 244, 558; FMB's meets, 421-2; *Daughter of the Regiment*, 422, 558; *Lucia di Lammermoor*, 426, 432
Dorn, Heinrich: FMB attends concert given by, 153; praises FMB's setting of Ave Maria, 195
Douglas, Shipley: *Mephistopheles*, 267
Dowding, Air Chief Marshal Hugh Caswell, 265
Doxat (banker), 163, 167, 182, 530
Doyle, Richard: Thackeray describes FMB's face to, 39, 584
Doyle, Sir Arthur Conan, 39, 265
Dresden: treatment of Jews in, 7; festivals at, 228; FMB conducts in, 239, 308, 450; FMB promised kapellmeistership in, 395; riots in, 568
Drobisch, Johann Gottfried Traugott: FMB supports petition of, 445
Drouet, Louis François-Philippe, 433
Droysen, Johann Gustav, 123, 293, 537, 567; on FMB's youth, 71-2; Mendelssohns host birthday party for, 229; engagement of, 233; plans to collaborate with FMB, 293-4; on *St Paul*, 358; on *Antigone*, 390; compiles *Travel Letters*, 579, 603, 604
Du Maurier, George: *Trilby*, 493
Dunn, Findlay, 513
Dupré, A. M., 551
Dürer, Albrecht: celebrations for quartercentenary of death, 237-8, 272; Rebecka praises, 98
Dürrner, Johannes, 172
Duse, Elinora, 571
Dussek, Jan Ladislav: musical influence on FMB, 106
Düsseldorf: FMB at, 61, 72, 73, 74, 292, 323-31, 355, 384, 410, 425, 438, 439, 446, 456, 483, 487, 516, 593; FMB conducts in, 317, 323, 324, 332, 357, 358, 442, 519; protest by 'Die Schwarzen', 202; FMB's alleged liaison in, 252; 'Artist's Concerts' introduced in, 373
Dvořák, Antonín Leopold, 593
Dyck, Anthonis van, 83, 93, 386
Ecclesiastes: FMB quotes from, 563
Eckardt, Julius, 560
Eckermann, Johann Peter: *Dichtung und Wahrheit*, 137-8
Eckert, Carl, 264; FMB advises, 371, 430-1
Edinburgh: FMB in, 56, 195, 276, 513, 536; University of, 430; FMB offered professorship at, 521
Edward VII, King of England (*earlier* HRH The Prince of Wales), 386, 399, 401
Edwards, F. G., 505-6, 525; *The Story of Mendelssohn's Oratorio, Elijah*, 361
Egerton, Lord Francis, 386

Index of Names and Compositions

Eichendorff, Joseph von: FMB sets poetry of, 285, 456; *A Hunting Song*, 285, 485; *Night Song*, 559, 563, 566

Eichhorn, Johann Albrecht Friedrich: FMB criticises policies of, 215, 217, 395

Einstein, Alfred: criticises FMB's 'romantic' conception of the *St Matthew Passion*, 308

Elgar, Alice (*née* Roberts), 197, 463

Elgar, Sir Edward, 219, 271, 367, 449, 516, 523, 592, 600; visit to Rome, 197; old age of, 565; influence of FMB on music of, 592; *Cockaigne* Overture, 592; *The Dream of Gerontius*, 516, 576, 593; *Enigma Variations*, 592; *Salve Regina*, 592

Eliot, George: reaction to performance of *Elijah*, 366

Eliot, T. S., 10

Ellis, William Ashton, 583-4

Elsasser, Friedrich August, 198, 388; Paul Mendelssohn acquires painting by, 385

Elvers, Rudolf, 122, 159, 187, 244, 413, 417, 438, 605; *Mendelssohn – A Life in Letters*, 159, 605

Emmett, Mr. (music collector): requests FMB's opinion on the authenticity of a Bach manuscript, 379

Encke, Johann Franz, 70

Engelberg: FMB visits monastery in, 104, 136, 345

Erard, S. and J. B., FMB visits 81, 117; FMB's preference for pianos of, 341, 342, 518

Ertmann, Baroness Dorothea von: FMB meets, 90-1, 421

Ertmann, General Stephan von, 91, 421

Eskeles, Bernhard, 185, 188, 464; Henriette Mendelssohn refuses proposal of marriage from, 25

Esterhazy, Count *see* Nikolaus II, Prince of Esterhazy

Esterhazy, Prince *see* Nikolaus, Prince of Esterhazy *and* Paul Anton III, Prince of Esterhazy

Evans, Sir Geraint, 576

Ewers (publisher), 354

Eysenhart (pastor), 194

Ezra, Ibn, 14-15

Fairies: FMB's interest in the notion of, 60, 259, 260, 265-6, 269

Falkenstein, von (Leipzig councillor): FMB requests sponsorship for a music academy from, 375; rumour of financial arrangement with FMB in Dresden, 587-8

Fallersleben, August Heinrich Hoffmann von: visits FMB, 216, 217, 491; *Commitatus*, 559; *Das Lied der Deutschen*, 216

Fane, John, 11th Earl of Westmorland: FMB conducts works of, 392, 394, 433

Fasch, Johann Friedrich: sacred music of, 198

Fasch, Karl Friedrich Christian: founds Berlin Singakademie, 319

Fauré, Gabriel, 2; influence of FMB on choral music of, 593

Fay, Leontine: FMB's admiration for the acting of, 211, 212, 406

Ferdinand I, King of Austria: FMB attends coronation of, 383-4

Fétis, François Joseph: takes umbrage at comments made by FMB, 46-7

Fichte, Johann Gottlieb: Hitler distorts writings of, 588

Field, John, 107, 407

Field, Rachel: *All this and Heaven too*, 26

Figaro, Le, 318

Fleischer, Friedrich: FMB sends money to as a contribution towards the Bach monument, 451

Florence: FMB in, 87-90, 168, 184, 248, 504

Fodor, Josephine, 100; FMB meets, 422

folk music: FMB encounters, 273-6, 513, 533

Forkel, Johann Nikolaus: biography of J. S. Bach, 108, 287, 303

Foster, Stephen: on FMB's setting of *A Hunting Song*, 285

Fould, Benoit, 24, 25

Fouqué, Friedrich de la Motte, 55
Foy, General Maximilien Sébastien, 180; employment of Gustav Dirichlet, 180
Franck (journalist): defends FMB's reputation, 587-8
Franck (senator), 211, 212
Franck, César, 155, 371
Franck, Eduard, 155; FMB encourages, 371
Franck, Frau: FMB rebuffs, 372
Franck, Joseph, 155
Fränkel, Anna (*née* Halle), 72
Fränkel, David Hirschel: as teacher of Moses Mendelssohn, 8, 9, 12
Frankfurt: Abraham and Leah baptised in, xxii; FMB conducts in, 50, 308, 310, 357, 358, 442; Jewish ghetto in, 121; FMB married in, 165, 443, 468-71; commemorates invention of the printing press, 239; FMB on, 410; FMB plans to retire to, 456-7; FMB meets Cécile Jeanrenaud in, 460, 464-5; Mendelssohn family holiday in, 486, 490-1; Cécile Mendelssohn buried in, 569; FMB remembered in, 601
Franklin, Benjamin, 15
Franz, Robert: FMB criticises, 373
Frege, Livia (*née* Gerhard), 365, 488, 563; sings to FMB, 559-60
Frege, Woldemar, 186, 467, 488, 582
Freigedank, Karl, 582
Friederike, Duchess of Anhalt-Dessau (*earlier* Princess of Prussia), 185
Friedländer, Moses, xxi
Friedrich August I, King of Saxony: statue of, 450
Friedrich August II, King of Saxony, 239, 268, 311, 375, 385, 394, 395, 400, 433, 449-50, 566, 588
Friedrich Franz II, Duke of Mecklenburg-Schwerin, 434
Friedrich III, Kaiser, 263, 401
Friedrich The Great, King of Prussia *see* Friedrich August II
Friedrich Wilhelm III, King of Prussia, 299, 388
Friedrich Wilhelm IV, King of Prussia, 377, 382, 386, 387-8, 401, 454, 562, 601; commissions FMB, 52, 261; takes offence to FMB's comment, 297; FMB's appointment as court musical director to, 62, 66, 208, 375, 388-97, 451, 477, 580-1, 586; FMB on, 210; FMB dedicates *Elijah* to, 397; FMB writes to, 431
Friends of Mendelssohn, 602, 612
Fuchs, Aloys, 92, 187, 229, 312, 430, 441, 518; requests portrait of FMB, 37-8; requests that FMB set poetry of Vogl, 46; FMB meets, 79, 81, 420; book of Beethoven sketches, 81; FMB consults over new discoveries of Beethoven scores, 328; correspondence with FMB, 169, 187; chooses piano for FMB, 188, 230; sources music for FMB, 230, 328, 420-1, 463, 469
Fuchsius, Joseph von, 326
Fürst, Ignaz, 292, 326, 330, 356; FMB rejects libretto of, 289-90;
Gade, Niels Wilhelm, 66, 227, 562, 567, 592, 593; on *A Midsummer Night's Dream*, 262; replaces FMB as director of the Gewandhaus, 382, 432, 456; performs FMB's works, 413, 414; FMB praises, 431-2, 448; conducts at the premiere of FMB's Violin Concerto, 452; *Ossian* Overture, 448; Symphony No. 1, 431, 448, 521
Galileo Galilei, 88, 90
Gall, Franz Joseph: phrenology, 243
Gans, Eduard: as teacher to FMB, 72
Gans, Leopold, 156
Gans, Otto, 180, 230, 273
Garcia, Manuel, 253
Garcia, Maria Felicia *see* Malibran, Maria Felicia Garcia
Garden Times, The, 71
Garnett, F.: 'Great Musicians of Yesterday', 110
Gauntlett, John: supervises construction of Christ Church organ, 349; on FMB's organ sonatas, 576

Index of Names and Compositions

Gauss, Karl: anti-social manner of, 180; Dirichlet replaces at the University of Göttingen, 571

Gautier, Théophile, 423

Geern, Johann, 262

Geibel, Emmanuel von: libretto for *Die Lorelei*, 287, 291, 302

Geiger, Herr (friend of Jenny Lind), 335

Geissmar, Berta, 589

George II, King: Battle of Dettingen, 327

George III, King: patronage of J. C. Bach, 397

George IV, King, 5; divorce of, 92; Haydn praises, 397

Gerhardt, Livia *see* Frege, Livia

Gerlache, Baron of, 551

Gewandhaus Orchestra Statistics, 340

Gilbert & Sullivan: *HMS Pinafore*, 378; *The Mikado*, 574; *The Pirates of Penzance*, 297, 599

Gilbert, Dr. Felix, 571

Gilbert, William Schwenck, 574; *see also* Gilbert & Sullivan

Gillette, King C.: marketing of the disposable razor, 502

Giorgione, 89; *Girl with the Zither*, 135

Gitlis, Ivry: recording of FMB's Violin Concerto, 597

Giulio Romano: frescoes of, 196, 231

Gladstone, W. E.: FMB plays Beethoven for, 555

Glazunov, Alexander: FMB's influence on the music of, 593

Gleaner, The (periodical), 18

Glehn, M. E. von: *Letters of Goethe and Mendelssohn*, 160, 273, 604

Glover, Miss (amateur singer), 576

Gluck, Christoph Willibald Ritter von, 303, 577; FMB on, 74; Abraham Mendelssohn admires music of, 108, 287, 288; comparison with FMB, 285; treatise on music of, 420-1; Berlioz admires music of, 423; *Armide*, 411; *Iphigenia in Aulis*, 133, 395; 'Spring Thoughts', 399; *Telemaco*, 423

Gnecco, Francesco, 520

Goethe, August von, 123, 130, 139

Goethe, Johann Wolfgang von, 42, 90, 175, 200, 314, 345, 372, 419, 423; influence of Lessing on poetry of, 10; and the 'battle of Pantheism', 17; FMB sends translation to, 44-5; FMB inspired by poetry of, 48, 264, 267-8, 271, 272-3; death of, 49, 137; FMB and, 55, 114, 121-35, 141, 181, 184, 208, 242, 282, 344, 413; correspondence with Zelter, 60, 137; in Italy, 74, 85, 86, 87, 96, 100, 103; FMB critiques, 104; on Schubert, 108, 181; anti-Semitic sentiments of, 121; on Beethoven, 181; FMB's grief at the death of, 137, 227; biography of, 137-8; on Berliners, 162-3; on Scott, 276; on Bach, 303; compares the young FMB to Mozart, 340; criticises sermons of Krummacher, 361-2; statue of, 379; Houston Chamberlain criticises, 584; *Egmont*, 327; *Erlkönig*, 108; *Faust*, 39, 132, 134, 137, 154, 264, 267, 271; *Maiden's Lament*, 284; *Minnelied*, 283; *Suleika*, 490

Goethe, Ottilie von (*née* von Pogwisch), 55, 123, 125, 127, 132, 134, 138, 146, 200, 496; FMB and, 138-9

Goethe, Walther Wolfgang von, 127, 138, 230

Goldschmidt (banking house), 182, 529, 530, 609-10

Goldschmidt, Otto, 308, 531, 572; marriage to Jenny Lind, 254, 494; FMB teaches, 380; protests at rise in ticket prices, 454-5, 609

Goldsmith, Oliver: *The Vicar of Wakefield*, 74, 550

Gordigiani, Giulietta: marriage to Robert Mendelssohn, 571

Gosse, John: joins Mendelssohn Scolarship committee, 609

Gotch, Rosamund Brunel: *Mendelssohn and his Friends in Kensington*, 162, 249, 265, 572

Gounod, Charles, 435; with Fanny in

Rome, 154-5, 224, 424; on Bach, 154; influence of FMB on music of, 309, 593; FMB meets, 424; *Faust*, 154, 424; *Mors et Vita*, 593

Grabau *see* Bunau-Grabau, Henriette

Grabbe, Christian Dietrich: criticises Shakespeare, 208

Graf, Conrad, 187-8, 230

Grahl (friend of FMB), 321, 398

Grainger, Percy, 610

Grandieson, Herr, 563

Grant, Sir Robert: 'O Worship the King, All Glorious Above', 213

Grätz, Heinrich, writings distorted in the cause of anti-Semitism, 588

Graun, Carl Heinrich: *Death of Jesus*, 307, 351, 527

Green, Benny: on the birth of rock 'n' roll, 204

Gregory VII, Pope: Walk to Canossa, 504

Gregory XVI, Pope: festivities during the coronation of, 198, 199, 209, 227, 231, 234-5

Gregory, Michael, 602

Grell, Eduard: composes hymn for FMB's funeral service, 562

Gressini, Mme. (singer), 442

Grey, Charles, Second Earl of, 213

Grieffer, Karl: FMB requests meeting with, 292-3

Grieg, Edvard, 593, 599; conducting style, 516

Grillparzer, Franz: on Dorothea Mendelssohn, 23; Fanny sets text by, 107, 146; *Tale of the Beautiful Melusine*, 252, 265, 612; on fairy tales, 266

Grimm, Jakob and Wilhelm, 383, 388, 503; Fanny writes to, 217; Mendelssohn children enact the fairytales of, 259, 503; *Rumpelstiltskin*, 503

Grisi, Giulia, 387, 516, 524

Grosser, Fräulein (soprano): FMB angered by, 326

Grosvenor, Robert, Duke of Westminster, 2nd Earl of Grosvenor, 197, 532

Grote, George, 551

Grove, Sir George, 444, 604; on *A Midsummer Night's Dream*, 259, 260; translation of *Faust*, 264; on *St Paul*, 354; on *Elijah*, 361; on FMB's teaching, 377; joins Mendelssohn Scholarship committee, 609-10; *Dictionary of Music and Musicians*, 35, 354, 572, 599

Grumiaux, Arthur: recording of FMB's Violin Concerto, 597

Grund, Friedrich Wilhelm, 333

Guarneri, Giuseppe: Ferdinand David plays violin made by, 453

Gugenheim, Fromet *see* Mendelssohn, Fromet

Guizot, François: sleeps during performance of works by Prince Albert, 397

Gunton, Frederick: FMB praises, 350

Gusikov, Josef: FMB befriends, 431

Gustedt, Baroness Jenny von: on FMB's stay with Goethe, 129

Gutenberg, Johannes: anniversary of his invention of the printing press commemorated in Germany, 239-40, 445

Habeneck, François-Antoine: instructs FMB, 52, 318; FMB on, 318-9; FMB plays under, 339

Hadden, Cuthbert: on FMB, 34, 607; on the 'Bartholdy' appendage, 193; on the qualities of FMB's music, 612

Hake, Bruno: on Zelter, 369; on FMB as teacher, 370; on the Leipzig Conservatorium, 377; on Schumann, 428

Halévy, Jacques Fromenthal: on Cherubini, 117, 417; *The Jewess*, 415; *The Tempest*, 302

Halévy, Leon: teaches Latin to FMB, 415

Hallé, Charles: on FMB's pianistic abilities, 338; champions Schubert's 'Great' C major Symphony, 522; joins Mendelssohn Scholarship committee, 609

Index of Names and Compositions

Hamburg: Mendelssohns in, 13, 24, 25; proposal to buy the Mendelssohn home in, 18-9; branch of Mendelssohn bank in, 31-2, 571; smuggling in, 32, 173; music festival in, 333; measles epidemic in, 387; Paul Mendelssohn on, 427; St Michael's Church, 527; University of, 570

Hamm, Johann Valentin: *Millanollo Quick-Step*, 433

Handel, George Frideric, 114, 222, 281, 331, 360, 405, 430, 443, 457, 574, 584, 594, 602; FMB on, 47, 131, 309-11, 312, 375, 409, 419, 450, 475, 509, 577, 586; eye surgery of, 58, 544; influence on FMB, 106, 109, 354; edition of works compiled, 115, 425; FMB advises on performance of, 309; FMB edits music of, 310-11, 430, 523; comparison with Bach, 314; FMB on performances of works by, 320, 326-7, 331, 356, 558; FMB's memory for the music of, 382; Gottfried Weber on, 409; FMB's attempts to procure manuscripts of, 518; *Acis and Galatea*, 309, 328; *Alexander's Feast*, 309, 326, 327; Dettingen Te Deum, 309, 327; *Dixit Dominus*, 312, 469; *Israel in Egypt*, 310, 311, 324, 326, 523; *Jephtha*, 520; *Judas Maccabaeus*, 325, 326, 359, 366; *Messiah*, 232, 358, 360-1, 366, 520, 530, 593; *Saul*, 602; *Solomon*, 309, 331, 349; *Theodora*, 310; *Zadok the Priest*, 310

Handford (musically inept treble): Fanny Horsley describes performance of, 509

Handley, Hill, 250

Haake, Herr (Deputy Mayor of Leipzig): vandalises statue of FMB, 589

Hanover: tax against Jews abolished in, 7; insurrection in, 214; *Death of Jesus* performed in, 527

Hanslick, Eduard: on FMB's correspondence, 169; compilation of correspondence between Fuchs and FMB, 169, 187, 469

Hanstein, August: FMB writes prelude commemorating life of, 203, 243, 282, 442

Harmonicon (periodical): on FMB's coach accident, 57; on FMB and his works, 114, 117, 238, 341, 351, 511, 514, 515; on performance of a Mozart concerto by FMB and Moscheles, 343

Härtel, Louise (*née* Goring): FMB's mischievous letter to, 486

Härtel, Raymund: discusses a project to publish Fanny Mendelssohn's works with FMB, 156, 558

Haslinger, Tobias: FMB criticises verses of, 312; FMB sends music to, 420

Hasse, Johann Adolf, 344

Hatzfeldt, Countess Sophie von: divorce of, 556

Hauptmann, Moritz: transcription for FMB, 327; FMB recommends as music tutor, 374; at the Leipzig Conservatorium, 376, 381; reassures FMB, 413; conducts in Leipzig, 450; on Karl Mozart, 500; at FMB's funeral, 562

Hauser, Franz, 373; with FMB in Vienna, 79; FMB's concern over the health of, 172; FMB lodges with in Leipzig, 437; FMB travels Germany and Austria with, 543; FMB's request to, 608-9

Hawaiian Serenaders, Felix Mendelssohn and his, 571

Haweis, Hugh Reginald, on FMB, 574, 584; on Elise Polko's book, 607; *Music and Morals*, 574

Hawes, Benjamin, 39, 548; brings gift to FMB during an illness, 540

Hawes, Maria: FMB on, 365

Haydn, Franz Joseph, 79, 125, 230, 274, 510, 584, 612; promises to teach Mozart's son, 91; Zelter invites to Berlin, 108; FMB performs music by, 131, 133, 333, 351, 443, 450, 591; Ludwig Tieck on, 296; on Anna Milder-Hauptmann, 306; use of a baton when conducting, 315; praises

King George IV, 397; FMB on, 406-7, 423, 509, 577; Fuchs sends FMB manuscript of, 469; *The Creation*, 315, 326, 333, 334, 351, 360, 358, 510; *The Seasons*, 268, 450; String Quartet, op. 76, No. 3, 'Emperor', 349; Symphony No. 45, 'Farewell' 443; Symphony No. 82, 'The Bear', 317

Hazlitt, William: FMB reads works by, 74

Hebbel, Christian Friedrich: FMB sets verses of, 74

Hegel, Georg Wilhelm Friedrich: lectures to FMB in Berlin, 45, 293, 296; comment to FMB, 132; influence on FMB, 296; on Bach, 303; unseemly behaviour of, 307

Heidelberg: FMB on, 77, 217; FMB meets Anton Thibaut in, 77, 118-9, 305; Cécile Mendelssohn visits relatives in, 468; FMB on honeymoon in, 473; University of, 570

Heifetz, Jascha: acquires Guarneri violin, 453

Heine, Albertine *see* Mendelssohn, Albertine

Heine, Heinrich, 26, 149, 211, 343; on Dorothea Mendelssohn, 23; admiration for Rebecka Mendelssohn, 34; FMB on, 81; on Kalkbrenner, 82; in Boulogne, 82; meeting with Goethe in Weimar, 121-2; on Judaism, 191, 578-9; on FMB's Scottish Symphony, 278; on Fingal's Cave, 279; on rebellions in Germany, 290; criticism of FMB on religious grounds, 579, 582; 'On Wings of Song', 284, 598

Heine, Henriette (*née* Marcus), 66

Heinke, Gottlif Frederick: FMB lodges with in London, 513, 528; wife of, 540

Heller, Stefan, 423

Henning, Carl: Devrient deputises for, 298

Hensel, Fanny *see* Mendelssohn, Fanny

Hensel, Sebastian, 72, 73, 504, 569; defines the Mendelssohns' class status, 7, 182; on Fanny Mendelssohn, 33, 63-4, 65, 138, 145, 178-9; on Abraham Mendelssohn, 58, 107; on Leipzigerstrasse 3, 69, 259; on Rebecka Mendelssohn, 103; on FMB's sketches, 166; on the darker aspects of the Mendelssohn family, 187; confirmation of, 193-4; birth of, 223, 495, 599; birthdays of, 223-4; on FMB's 'Children's Symphonies', 230; musical ability of, 372-3; on Cécile Mendelssohn, 462; FMB encourages, 503; *The Mendelssohn Family, 1729-1847*, 559, 563, 606-7

Hensel, Wilhelm, 65, 89, 150, 207, 230, 232, 302, 385-6, 468, 488, 493; holiday to Italy, 62, 82-3, 85, 86-7, 92-4, 96-8, 101-3, 154-5, 167-8, 176-7, 197-8, 209-10, 221, 223-5, 231-2, 235; marriage to Fanny Mendelssohn, 69, 141-2, 156, 179, 210-11, 223, 233; portrait of Eduard Gans, 72; on FMB, 72; courtship with Fanny Mendelssohn, 74, 75, 141, 142, 149, 177-9; bachelorhood of, 177; portraits and sketches of FMB, 37, 145, 187, 563; sketches of the Mendelssohn family, 142, 178, 179, 550, 563, 569; encourages Fanny to compose, 151, 155-6, 385; in Paris, 186; declines request to listen to confessions, 194-5; FMB amused at verses of, 227; FMB writes 'one note role' for, 301; improvements in artistic technique, 385-6; sketches of the English royal family, 386; description of Queen Victoria's coronation, 386-8; deathbed sketch of Cécile Mendelssohn, 461-2; exhibits paintings in London, 549; after wife's death, 559, 571; death of, 571; *Miriam*, 386

Henselt, Adolf von: FMB introduces to Zelter, 169, 429; FMB's encouragement of, 429; receives commendation from Tsar, 600; Piano Concerto in F minor, op. 16, 429, 454

Henze, Hans Werner: symphony inspired

Index of Names and Compositions

by FMB's *A Midsummer Night's Dream*, 599
Herald, The: FMB on, 521
Hermann, Puzzi, 313
Hérold, Louis-Joseph-Ferdinand, 415
Hersh, R. C.: on FMB's *A Midsummer Night's Dream*, 262
Herz, Dr.: attempts to revive Moses Mendelssohn, 17-8
Herz, Henri: FMB and Fuchs visit, 81; music of, 252, 409, 418
Herz, Henriette (*née* Lemos), Henriette de: partner in salon, 22; on Dorothea Mendelssohn, 22; visits Schlegel, 23; suggestions linking her with Beethoven's 'Immortal Beloved', 108; on Fromet Mendelssohn, 174; attends performance of *Camacho's Wedding*, 300
Herz, Hofräthin: accident involving, 489
Heydemann, Albert Gustav: hiking holiday with FMB, 76-7, 118, 242, 409
Heyse, Karl Wilhelm Ludwig, 44-5, 75, 169, 293, 299, 415
Hickox, Richard: on *Elijah*, 365, 576
Hildebrandt, Theodor: paints portrait of FMB in Berlin, 331
Hill & Company (organ builders), 349
Hill, Corelli: invites FMB to conduct the New York Philharmonic Orchestra, 333-4
Hiller (Hebrew scholar), 14
Hiller (stonemason): works on Bach monument in Leipzig, 451
Hiller, Ferdinand, 72, 80, 92, 109, 172, 212, 227, 376, 417, 426, 475, 593; FMB champions music of, 52; on FMB, 56, 77-8, 82, 112, 259, 338, 342, 361, 405-6, 414, 422, 424, 460, 464, 470, 478; Abraham Mendelssohn on, 80; Hensel family visits, 92; on Fanny Mendelssohn, 109; on Jenny Lind, 254; praises FMB's musicianship, 338; FMB criticises music of, 409, 414; relationship with FMB, 414-5, 424-5, 441, 442, 444, 446, 447, 460, 478, 484-5, 565-6, 583-4; on Rossini, 417; on Chopin, 425; on Liszt, 427; on Cécile Jeanrenaud, 460, 477, 484, 567, 569; at FMB's wedding, 470-1; *Deborah*, 331, 424, 576; *The Destruction of Jerusalem*, 447; *Faust* Overture, 414; *Jeremiah*, 447, 576; Overture in D minor, 441
Hiller, Frau (Ferdinand Hiller's mother), 464
Hindemith, Paul, 372, 571
His Master's Voice (HMV), 595
Hitler, Adolf: anti-Semitism directed at FMB, 581, 588, 604-5
Hodson, Philip, 45
Hofer, Andreas, 290
Hoffmann, E. T. A.: biography of J.S. Bach, 303; FMB reads story by, 495; *The Devil's Elixir*, 532
Hofmeister, Friedrich: FMB sends music to, 185
Hogarth, George, 522, 540
Holland: Abraham Mendelssohn visits, 44, 179, 541; FMB on, 466
Holman, James: travels in Russia, 85
Holst, Henry: wartime performance of FMB's Violin Concerto, 596
Höltei, Karl von: as possible librettist, 267
Hölty, Ludwig Heinrich Christoph: *Hexenlied*, 267
Homer: Leah Mendelssohn reads 25, 33, 176; FMB reads, 74, 293; *Nausicaa*, 74; *Odyssey*, 293
Hood, Thomas, 86; 'November', 166
Horace: *Odes*, 415
Horsley, Charles Edward: on FMB, 36, 111, 343-4, 440, 484; FMB's meetings with, 37, 340, 517; on *St Paul*, 354-5; advises FMB, 364; as pupil of FMB, 374-5, 382; on FMB's family life, 500; on concert in London, 523; investigates cause of FMB's death, 565; on *Elijah*, 576
Horsley, Fanny, 59, 151, 172, 249-50, 266, 330, 374, 482, 495, 509, 542-3, 544-7; condemns anti-Semitism in Germany, 11; describes Abraham

Mendelssohn's recuperation, 58; on FMB, 161-2, 187, 246, 327-8, 329-30, 461; album of, 228-9, 265; attends baptism, 234; FMB's dedications to, 250, 284; plans to compose an opera, 289; arranges recital, 321; FMB attends birthday celebrations of, 545; marriage of, 550; marriage of, 550; death of, 572

Horsley, John Callcott: drawings of, 374, 517

Horsley, Mary (*later* Brunel), 151, 249-50, 266, 330, 374, 542-3, 544-7; marriage to Isambard Kingdom Brunel, 39, 548; FMB's rift with, 547-8; accident of, 545-6

Horsley, Sophie, 151, 172, 249-50, 266, 330, 374, 482, 513, 521, 542-3, 544-7; FMB's dedications to, 250, 484; on Friedrich Rosen, 547; describes festival in Birmingham, 510, 518; on Spohr, 516; performs concerto by FMB, 524

Horsley, William: FMB sends choral music to, 312; FMB writes to, 313, 320, 374, 418; attends FMB's dinner, 505; music of, 516, 540, 542; respect for the Sabbath, 526; FMB and his father visit family of, 544-7

Howard (pastor): conducts FMB's marriage ceremony, 471; speaks at FMB's funeral, 562

Hübner, Julius: supervises construction of the Bach monument in Leipzig, 451

Huckvale, David: on FMB's 'Six Christmas Pieces', 505

Hudson, Henry: on FMB's *A Midsummer Night's Dream*, 262

Hughes, Spike: on Toscanini's conducting of *A Midsummer Night's Dream*, 263

Hugo, Victor: *Ruy Blas*, 445, 577

Hullah, John: joins Mendelssohn Scolarship committee, 609

Humboldt, Alexander von, 26, 70, 388, 424; Joseph Mendelssohn helps, 24; and Gustav Dirichlet, 180; commissions FMB to write a cantata, 237-8

Hummel, Johann Nepomuk, 80, 109, 123, 154, 383, 412, 429; FMB's meetings with, 117-8; FMB impresses, 124, 126; FMB intimidated by, 125; Piano Concerto No. 3 in B minor, 126; Piano Sonata for four hands in A flat, 250; Piano Trio in G major, 115; *Rondo Favorri* for Piano in E flat, op. 11, 414; Septet No.1 in D minor, op. 74, 380

Humperdinck, Engelbert, 592; *Hansel and Gretel*, 610

Humphreys (chorister): FMB instructs, 524-5

Hunt, William Holman, 85, 559

Ignatius of Loyola: Titian's painting of, 197

Illustrated London News, 602

Immermann, Karl, 80; FMB meets, 48; falls out with FMB over opera libretto, 292; founds theatre, 326, 328; FMB falls out with, 326, 329; *Baron Munchhausen*, 74

Ingres, Jean-Auguste-Dominique, 97, 154, 155

Itzig, Benjamin Daniel: fosters greater understanding of Judaism, 16

Itzig, Henrietta *see* Henrietta Mendelssohn

Jacob, Heinrich Edward, 35, 144, 248, 293, 296, 298, 461, 467; on sketch of FMB, 38; on FMB's character, 119, 120, 195, 241, 246, 281, 463, 465, 498; on the relationship between FMB and Ottilie von Pogwisch, 138; on the affluence of the Mendelssohn family, 183; on FMB's music, 195, 203, 261, 267, 268, 271, 285, 289, 306, 317, 505, 581, 593-4; on the Leipzig Conservatorium, 376; on Wagner's pamphlet, 582; on FMB and the Nazis, 587; *Mendelssohn and his Times*, 2, 5, 461

Jacobi, Carl Gustav Jakob, 63; with the Dirichlets in Italy, 90, 199; pamphlet by, 216

Jacobi, Friedrich: slur against Lessing, 17

Jahn, Friedrich Ludwig: teaches FMB gymnastics, 72

Jahn, Otto: writings on FMB's works, 360
James, Sir (Scottish laird), 536
Jarocky, Professor Feliks: accompanies Chopin to convention, 237
Jean-Paul *see* Richter, Jean-Paul
Jeanrenaud, Cécile *see* Mendelssohn, Cécile
Jeanrenaud, Charles, 65, 172, 481, 497
Jeanrenaud, Elisabeth (*née* Souchay), 473, 491, 498; looks after FMB's children, 65, 508; gift to FMB, 74; sings at concert, 153; gives portrait of Cécile to FMB, 230-1; mistaken as object of FMB's affection, 460, 464; family heritage of, 461; on Cécile Mendelssohn, 462, 465, 471, 569; attitude to FMB, 463, 464, 467, 469
Jeanrenaud, Julie *see* Schunck, Julie
Jeanrenaud, Revd. (father of Cécile), 362, 460
Jenkins, D., *and* Visocchi, M., *Mendelssohn in Scotland*, 533, 534
Jesus, 39, 348, 360; as portrayed in *The Entombment*, 197; as portrayed in the *St Matthew Passion*, 306, 314; in FMB's oratorios, 585
Jette, Aunt *see* Mendelssohn, Henriette
Jews: repression of culture, 7-8, 11; assimilation into European society, 16-17, 18, 21, 22; respect for Moses Mendelssohn, 18; Passover, 21; anti-Semitism directed at, 69, 121, 200, 213, 235, 322, 578, 581-3, 587-90; conversions to Christianity, 191, 200; festivals of the, 200, 449; Berlin lootings of, 200; music of Jewish extraction, 203; influence of Saint-Simon on, 211
Joachim, Joseph, 227, 381, 414, 427, 451, 457, 581, 610; Fanny Mendelssohn on, 156, 374, 453, 522; on FMB's conducting, 316; on FMB's piano playing, 338; accompanies FMB to England, 365; FMB's influence on, 374, 451, 523, 583; awarded place at Leipzig Conservatorium, 377; and FMB's Violin Concerto, 453, 522, 596; FMB on, 522-3; confusion caused by lengthy career of, 523
Johannsen, Mlle. (companion of Jenny Lind), 334
Johnson, Dr. Samuel: on patriotism, 174; on MacPherson's translation of Ossian, 279; *Dictionary*, 9
Johnston, Sir Alexander Keith: gives climbing aid to FMB, 163; FMB at the house of, 531, 534
Jones, Daniel, 610
Jones, Peter Ward, 5, 605; on FMB's wedding and honeymoon, 470, 474; *The Mendelssohns on Honeymoon*, 470, 473
Joseph II, King of Austria, 17
Journal des Débats, 481
Joyce, Archibald, 598
Julien, Louis, 227, 601; *Pierre Legrand*, 601
Kaiser, Philipp Christoph: FMB visits, 131
Kalliwoda, Johann: FMB teaches, 380
Kalkbrenner, Friedrich Wilhelm, 151, 407; FMB meets, 82, 175, 345, 424; FMB on, 319, 417-8, 579
Kant, Immanuel, 15, 16; Moses Mendelssohn's and, 14; *Critique of Pure Reason*, 14
Kapp, Julius: on Wagner, 582
Karl August Grand Duke of Saxe-Weimar Eisenach, 128; FMB plays for, 125, 126
Kaselowsky, August Theodor: in Italy with the Hensels, 65, 99, 221, 229
Kastner, Karl Wilhelm Gottlob, 236
Kaufman, Schima, 80, 109, 118, 122, 237, 242, 248, 250, 260, 261, 292, 319, 344, 411, 512; *Mendelssohn – A Second Elijah*, 300, 607
Kelz, Johann Friedrich: receives advise from FMB, 371
Kemble, Charles, 102; FMB sees performance by, 532
Kemble, Fanny (*later* Butler), 551; Fanny Mendelssohn on, 102
Kennedy, John F., 597

Kennedy, Michael: on FMB's legacy, 578; on FMB's generosity, 593

Kermann, Herr (publicist), 426

Keudell, Robert von: interest in the music of Fanny Mendelssohn, 156, 435

Kiene, Mme. (sister of Marie Bigot), 150, 419, 497

Kiengel, Herr (friend of FMB), 492

Kiesewetter, Raphael, 172

Kietz, Ernst, 583

Kind, L. W.: attends to FMB after coach accident, 57

Kingdon-Ward, Martha, 238

Kirnberger, Johann: as teacher of Zelter, 107, 304

Kiss (sculptor), 434

Kistner (publishers), 47

Kistner, Friedrich, 438, 441

Klein, Bernhard, 319

Klingemann, Carl (son): translation of *The Family Mendelssohn*, 606

Klingemann, Carl, 69, 251, 276, 281, 309, 311, 312, 362, 396, 417, 483, 516, 517, 526, 531, 556, 608; friendship with FMB, 57, 60, 71, 73, 143, 207, 212-3, 216, 234, 243, 328, 329, 348, 365, 400, 457, 515, 519, 520, 540-1, 542-3, 545, 550, 552; on FMB, 61, 239, 266, 320, 341, 521, 524, 542, 551, 552, 555, 563; Fanny Mendelssohn and, 70, 151, 250, 387; visits the Hensels, 82; in Britain with FMB, 162-3, 179, 245, 247, 279-80, 513, 527-9, 533-8, 543-9, 551; on Gustav Dirichlet, 180; marriage to Sophie Rosen, 225, 552; FMB sets poetry of, 277, 284, 285; sends libretto to FMB, 293, 298-9; on performance of *St Paul*, 332; death of, 572; *Elves*, 265

Knaur, Immanuel August Hermann: involvement with Bach monument in Leipzig, 451

Knaurer (engraving artist), 39

Knyvett, Mme (singer), 520

Kobbé, Gustave, 460, 462, 469, 480

Köchel, Ludwig Ritter von, 469-70, 602

Kohlhaas, Michael, 290

Königsberg: unsuccessful performance of *St Matthew Passion* in, 308; University of, 9, 14

Kopisch, August, 434

Köpke (singer): sings both tenor and bass in performance of a piece by Fanny Mendelssohn, 148

Kördeler, Herr (Mayor of Leipzig), 589

Körner, Karl Theodor: FMB improvises on songs by, 127

Köstlin, Josephine *see* Lang, Josephine

Köstlin, Professor Karl, 169; FMB unable to attend child's christening, 234; marriage to Josephine Lang, 234, 251

Kotek, Josef: wins Mendelssohn Scholarship, 610

Kotzebue, August von, 293, 490, 541; *Rehbeck*, 78; *The Ruins of Athens*, 521

Krebs, Johann, 162, 483; FMB's grief on the death of, 162, 481

Kreutzer, Herr (pianist), 596

Kreutzer, Conradin: setting of 'La Colognaise', 215; stamp commemorates, 612; *Tale of the Beautiful Melusine*, 252, 265, 612

Kreutzer, Rodolphe: Beethoven's 'Kreutzer' Sonata, 91, 340, 451

Krummacher, Friedrich Wilhelm, 361-2

Kudelsky, Karl, 247

Kufferath, Johann Hermann: performance at a Gewandhaus concert, 440

Kugel, Joseph: FMB performs trio with, 112

Kuhe, Wilhelm: on FMB's performance as soloist in Beethoven's Piano Concerto No. 4, 340

Kuhlmann, Herr: FMB enjoys hospitality of, 334

Kullak, Theodor: founds Berlin Academy of music, 593

Kupferberg, Herbert: on Moses Mendelssohn, 10, 21; on Schlegel's *Lucinde*, 22; on Leah Mendelssohn, 25; on Henriette Mendelssohn, 25; on

Index of Names and Compositions

Rebecka Mendelssohn, 34; on FMB, 151, 200-1, 243, 252, 264, 300, 364, 389, 479, 511, 556-7, 597; on Fanny Mendelssohn, 151, 424; on the Mendelssohn family, 174; on Schumann, 259; on Wagner, 317, 582; on Jewish folklore, 324-5; on *St Paul*, 354; on Albrecht Mendelssohn, 570; on Elinore Duse, 571; on performance trends applied to FMB's music, 605, 606
La Mure, Pierre: *Beyond Desire*, 608
Lablache, Luigi, 387, 399, 524; singing feat of, 397-8
Lachner, Franz: FMB publicises symphony by, 441
Lafont, Charles Philippe, 147, 214
Lamartine, Alphonse: *Elegies*, 134
Lamb, Charles: on Bach, 509
Lamond, Frederic: on FMB's piano music, 203, 265, 449, 595
Lampadius, Wilhelm August, 556; on FMB's personal appearance, 35; on Fanny Mendelssohn, 109; on FMB's religious beliefs, 195; as first biographer of FMB, 563, 578, 606, 607
Landsberg, Ludwig: Fanny Mendelssohn meets in Rome, 154, 155
Landseer, Edward: on Marianne Skerrett, 397
Lang, Josephine (*later* Köstlin): marriage of, 234; FMB on, 251
Lanner, Joseph, 274
Lassalle, Ferdinand: involvement in the Hatzfeldt divorce, 556
Lassus, Orlando de, 197, 312, 326
Lattner, Konrad Philipp: sends librettos to FMB, 291; *Jean Beck*, 291; *Sakentale*, 291
Lavater, Johann Kaspar, 16; description of Moses Mendelssohn, 8, 10; challenges Moses Mendelssohn, 12
Leach, Rachel: on FMB's attitude to Fanny Mendelssohn's compositions, 149, 150
Lebrecht, Norman, on FMB's meeting with Mozart's son, 91; *Book of Musical Anecdotes*, 591
Léhar, Franz, 274

Leighton, Baron Frederic, 85
Leipzig: FMB on music in, 152, 390, 409, 442, 474, 522; archives destroyed in, 156; celebration of Gutenberg's invention, 239-40, 445; Mendelssohn Festival in, 251; FMB's memorial service in, 283; knowledge of Beethoven's works in, 340; Bach monument erected in, 347; Chopin Festival, 425; musical tradition of, 437, 439-40, 445-6, 450, 549, 589, 593; costs of living in, 482-3; FMB on the social life of, 492; statue of FMB in, 589, 602; Gewandhaus, 439; Leipzig Conservatorium, 51, 66, 375-9, 380, 382, 391-2, 395, 412, 494, 560, 588; University of, 188, 440;
Lejaune, Dr., 495
Lemos, Henriette *see* Herz, Henriette
Lenau, Nikolaus, 491
Lenz, Wilhelm von: anti-Semitism directed at FMB, 583
Leonardo da Vinci, 89
Leopold, Grand Duke of Baden, 596
Leslie, Henry, 609
Lessing, Gotthold Ephraim, 12, 21, 73, 444-5; Moses Mendelssohn defends, 10, 17; egalitarianism of, 10-11; on Moses Mendelssohn, 15; Abraham Mendelssohn defends, 19; *Antiquarian Letters*, 73; *Nathan the Wise*, 11, 26, 70, 330
Letters on the New Literature: Moses Mendelssohn edits, 10
Levasseur (bass), 529
Levin, Rahel *see* Varnhagen, Rahel
Levy (horn player in Vienna): request to FMB, 420
Levy, Hermann: on conducting, 315; conducts Wagner, 582
Levy, Isaac: on Moses Mendelssohn's translation of the Scriptures, 16
Levy, Sarah (*née* Itzig), 90; musical association with the Bach family, 304; bequeaths music to Berlin Singakademie, 322

Leyden, Lukas van, 119
Lichtenstein, Marie, 247-8
Liège: festival at, 51, 334, 354
Ligne, Prince Eugène de, 387
Lincoln, Henry, 596
Lind, Jenny, 37, 374; FMB and, 38, 253-4, 334-5, 340, 362, 364, 373, 457, 493-4, 557, 560, 573, 608-9; as potential *prima donna* in an opera, 157, 252, 293, 577; personal appearance and character of, 253, 263, 455; founds the London Bach Choir, 308, 380, 572; and the Aachen Festival, 334, 373-4; unable to perform role in *Elijah*, 363; after FMB's death, 367; performances in Leipzig, 454-5; marriage to Otto Goldschmidt, 455, 494, 609; after the death of FMB, 566, 572, 601; death of, 572, 573; fictional representation of, 607; performance in *Elijah*, 608; involvement in setting up the Mendelssohn Scholarship, 608, 610
Lindau, Paul: criticism of Wagner, 584
Lindberg, Christian: discovery of Ferdinand David's Trombone Concerto, 597
Lindblad, Adolf Fredrik: FMB's high regard for, 52; FMB's letters to, 56, 371; on FMB's Trumpet Overture, 272; songs of, 283, 371, 373
Lindenau, Leopold, 527
Lisle, Rouget de: death of, 210; *La Marseillaise*, 210
Liste, Anton: mountaineering prowess of, 131, 413
Liszt Adam: tours Europe with son, 105, 415
Liszt, Franz, 80, 156, 396, 577, 599; FMB on, 82, 92, 425-6, 427, 415, 425-7; childhood of, 105, 111, 116, 174, 407, 415; admiration for Maria Malibran, 244; comparisons with FMB, 287, 338, 339, 343, 484-5; preference for Erard pianos, 342; admiration for songs of Robert Franz, 373; performances by, 426-7; at the Mendelssohn home in Berlin, 435; in Leipzig, 437, 453, 454; in Italy with Hiller, 444; performs with FMB, 446; conducts Marx's *Moses*, 447; in Birmingham, 516; in old age, 565; influence of FMB's music on, 592; transcriptions of FMB's music, 595; Brahms on, 600; insults music of FMB, 600
Literary Gazette, 509
Liverpool: FMB's commission in, 156, 457, 558; FMB visits, 245, 538, 539; *St Paul* performed in, 358, 510; FMB's Violin Concerto performed in, 596; Philharmonic Hall, 156, 457, 558
Lobe, Johann Christian: on FMB, 35; conversations with FMB, 47; performance with the young FMB at Goethe's home, 125-6; FMB presages early death in conversation with, 555; *Conversations with Mendelssohn*, 606; *Goethe and his Circle*, 606
Lockey, Charles: FMB praises singing of, during performances of *Elijah*, 364, 365, 367, 525
London: FMB in, 4, 16, 47, 50, 52, 57-60, 62, 65, 74, 143, 144, 161-3, 175, 193, 197, 238, 243-7, 249-50, 252, 275, 319-20, 339, 348-50, 398-401, 429-30, 504-6, 509-33, 540-8, 550-3, 559, 574-5, 580-1, 583; writings of Moses Mendelssohn published in, 12; music in, 49, 120, 328, 379, 408, 410-11, 509-10, 515, 518; politics in, 212-3; *Elijah* performed in, 359, 365-7; Wilhelm Hensel in, 386-7; FMB on drama in, 532-3; statue of FMB erected in, 602; Argyll Rooms, 511, 514; Beethoven Rooms, 414; Buckingham Palace, 36, 65, 350, 397-401, 522, 550, 573, 602; Exeter Hall, 345-6, 349, 359, 365, 366, 517, 520, 525, 547, 548, 601-2, 608; Hanover Square Rooms, 249, 343, 524; Hyde Park, 340, 517, 523, 541; Literary Union Club, 161; Sacred Harmonic Society, 366, 517, 522, 574, 601; Regent Palace Hotel,

Index of Names and Compositions

511; Royal Academy of Music, 429; Royal Albert Hall, 367; Royal College of Arms, 348; Royal Library, 311, 469, 509, 518; University of, 526, 530; Vaughan's Concert Rooms, 514, 542; Westminster Abbey, 115, 310, 349, 356, 386, 430, 530

Longfellow, Henry Wadsworth: *Excelsior*, 104; *The Black Knight*, 592; *The Saga of King Olaf*, 592

Longyear, Ray, 106; *Nineteenth-Century Romanticism in Music*, 591

Lortzing, Albert: *Hans Sachs*, 239

Lotti, Antonio, 118

Lough, Ernest: recording of 'Hear my Prayer', 594-5

Louis Philippe, King of France, 210, 211

Louise, Queen Consort of King Friedrich Wilhelm III of Prussia, 461

Loveland, Kenneth: interpretation of the 'Scottish' Symphony, 277; on the *Hebrides* Overture, 281

Löwe, Carl: FMB performs work with, 261

Lower Rhine Festivals, 38, 202, 214, 323-6, 331-5, 373, 442, 456, 498

Lüdeke, Henry, 296

Ludwig I, King of Bavaria, 250, 383, 419, 600

Ludwig II, King of Bavaria: as Wagner's benefactor, 582

Luini, Bernardino, 93

Lully, Jean-Baptiste, 148

Lumley (Levy), Benjamin, 293

Luther, Martin: comparisons with Moses Mendelssohn, 15, 16, 23; statue unveiled in Wittenberg of, 121; FMB sets words of, 195; FMB composes music in honour of, 202, 238; FMB composes on hymn tune of, 238-9

Lützow, Baron Adolf: *Forest Hunt*, 399

Lvov, Count Alexis Feodorovich: purchases portrait of FMB by Hensel, 187

MacFarren, Nathalie, 563

MacFarren, Sir George, 279, 311, 340, 342; incident in London, 520; *Chevy Chase* Overture, 448-9; *Ma Cousine*, 449

MacKenzie, Richard, 114

Maconchy, Elizabeth, 610

Macpherson, James, 279

Magnus, Eduard, 264; portrait of FMB, 38; FMB reminisces with, 186; in Italy with the Hensels and Dirichlets, 225

Magnus, Gustav: hiking holiday with FMB, 76-7, 118, 242, 409; FMB meets in Leipzig, 415

Mahler, Gustav, 274, 314; conducts *St Paul*, 593; anti-Semitism directed at, 588; *Des Knaben Wunderhorn*, 503; Symphony No. 1, 238; Symphony No. 4, 562

Maimonides, Moses, 8, 15

Malibran, Maria Felicia Garcia, 253, 343, 451; FMB's admiration for, 81, 211, 243-4; performance at charity concert, 512; performances in England, 516, 528-9; fictional representation of, 608

Malthus, Thomas, 498

Manchester: FMB declines offer to conduct in, 53, 552; eye operation carried out in, 58, 544; Souchay family's business interests in, 461; FMB travels by rail from, 538-9; FMB and his wife visit, 551; after FMB's death, 601

Mannheimer, Herr (banker): buys Mendelssohn Bank, 589-90

Manns, August, 522

Mar, Norman del: on FMB's influence on Richard Strauss, 592

Marcello, Benedetto, 408

Marek, George R.: on FMB, 3, 5, 57, 72, 74, 141, 144, 191, 201, 202-3, 204, 207, 234, 241, 248, 296, 301, 326, 393, 424, 450, 451, 456, 462-3, 465, 469, 482, 471; on Moses Mendelssohn, 8, 14, 15, 16, 17, 21; on Ephraim Lessing, 10; on Frederick the Great, 12; on Leah Mendelssohn, 24, 41, 252, 292, 467; on Abraham Mendelssohn, 32, 41, 120, 174, 182; on Fanny Mendelssohn, 33, 141, 142, 144, 560;

on Rebecka Mendelssohn, 34; on FMB's musical works, 48, 239, 263, 275, 283, 284, 308, 361, 393, 452, 505, 510, 514, 575, 576, 578, 599, 603, 605; on Goethe and FMB, 130, 137; on FMB's letters, 160, 161, 163; on smuggling in Hamburg, 173; on unrest in Düsseldorf, 202; on Maria Malibran, 243; on the Horsleys, 250; on Jenny Lind, 253, 293, 363, 608; on FMB's part in the revival of the *St Matthew Passion*, 307; on Wilhelm Hensel, 385; on Dorothea von Ertmann, 421; on Cécile Mendelssohn, 461, 462, 463, 484, 496; on FMB's descendants, 569, 570, 590; attitude to FMB of, 489, 585-6; *Gentle Genius*, 2, 191, 389, 575, 585

Mariani, Luciano: Fanny Mendelssohn's admiration for, 432, 434

Mario *see* Candia, Cavaliere Giovanni Matteo di

Marschner, Heinrich: FMB sells music to, 185; FMB on *Hans Heiling*, 289, 302; FMB praises, 320; sets poetry of Uhland, 592; *Hans Heiling*, 214, 289

Marx, Adolf Bernhard: on Leah Mendelssohn, 33, 109, 176; friendship with FMB, 50, 71, 72, 79, 109, 242, 355, 396, 464; attitude of FMB's parents to, 108-9, 120, 148; on FMB, 109, 119-20, 176, 250, 337, 593; on Fanny Mendelssohn, 109, 337; on Paul Mendelssohn, 109-10; excitement at success of a Cherubini opera, 116; on a discussion with FMB about orchestration, 123; initial claims to authorship of *A Midsummer Night's Dream*, 260; on FMB's musical works, 265; on a performance of *Camacho's Wedding*, 299; and the music of Bach, 304, 305, 308; rift with FMB, 337, 338, 359-60, 430, 446-7, 586; asks FMB to write libretto to *Moses*, 359, 446-7; *Moses*, 359, 447

Marx, Karl, 290

Marx, Thérèse, 242, 260, 586

Mary, Queen of Scots, 276-7

Massow, Ludwig von, 388, 389, 391, 392-3, 395, 434

Mathis-Greyseman, M.: commissions FMB to write *Lauda Sion*, 334

Matthai, Heinrich: and the Leipzig Gewandhaus Orchestra, 439

Maupertuis, Pierre L. M. de: Moses Mendelssohn meets, 11

Maurer, Ludwig Wilhelm, 581

Maxwell-Davies, Peter: on FMB, 598

Mendel of Dessau, 7

Mendel, Marie *see* Mendheim, Marie

Mendel, Moses Ben *see* Mendelssohn, Moses

Mendel, Saul Ben, 8

Mendelssohn, Alexander: religion of, 24; and the Mendelssohn bank, 187, 571; sends gift to FMB, 330; visit to Frankfurt with FMB, 464

Mendelssohn, Arnold, 372, 571

Mendelssohn, Benjamin: FMB's correspondence with, 61, 187-8; FMB spends Christmas with, 230; receives gift for FMB, 330

Mendelssohn, Brendel *see* Mendelssohn, Dorothea

Mendelssohn, Dorothea (*later* Veit *then* Schlegel): on Moses Mendelssohn, 18; siblings of, 21; marriage to Simon Veit, 21, 141, 588; career and second marriage to Friedrich Schlegel, 22-3; conversion to Catholicism, 23, 177, 195; death of, 23; FMB's parents on, 42, 464, 467; correspondence of, 159; FMB and Cécile visit, 470, 474; attends FMB's wedding, 471; *Florentin*, 22

Mendelssohn, Dr.: FMB mistaken for, 556

Mendelssohn, Elinora, 571, 605

Mendelssohn, Franz, 481, 571

Mendelssohn, Fromet (*née* Gugenheim; FMB's grandmother): marriage to Moses Mendelssohn, 13, 21; death of daughter, 15; after husband's death, 25; death of, 25; frugality of, 174

Index of Names and Compositions

Mendelssohn, George H. de, 571
Mendelssohn, Henrietta (*née* Itzig): marriage to Nathan Mendelssohn, 26
Mendelssohn, Henrietta (*née* Meyer): marriage to Joseph Mendelssohn, 24
Mendelssohn, Henriette ('Tante Jette'): siblings of, 21, 22; in Paris, 23, 24, 25-6, 149, 218, 387; personality of, 25, 159; as potential governess to FMB, 42; and Fanny Mendelssohn, 74-5, 149, 177; Abraham Mendelssohn escorts to Berlin, 106, 116; on FMB, 128, 159, 163; correspondence of, 159; death of, 222
Mendelssohn, Hermann: publishes FMB's *Travel Letters*, 603
Mendelssohn, Joseph: early life, 17, 18, 21, 23-4; and the Mendelssohn Bank, 24, 32-3, 173, 174, 185, 590; writings of, 24; FMB translates Dante for, 44; FMB visits, 53, 77, 153, 186, 289, 409, 487, 549, 552; dinner given for, 230; and Paul Mendelssohn, 542
Mendelssohn, Marianne (*née* Seeligmann), 75, 165
Mendelssohn, Moses (FMB's grandfather), 174, 191, 192, 499, 563; childhood and adolescence, 7-9; personal appearance of, 8, 38; early career and studies of, 9-13, 173; marriage of, 13-14, 21-2, 69, 174; writings and prominence of, 14-17; death of, 17-18, 25, 63, 564, 571; legacy of, 18-19; relationship with son Joseph, 23-4; centenary of birth, 39; Sebastian Hensel studies writings of, 73; influence on FMB, 74, 200, 201, 202, 205, 238, 352, 444-5, 511, 579; and Zelter, 108; correspondence of, 159; anti-Semitic attacks on reputation, 588, 590; *Jerusalem, Europe and Mount Zion*, 17; *Morning Hours*, 17; *Phaedon, or the Immortality of the Soul*, 15
Mendelssohn, Nathan: childhood of, 11, 21, 26; life and career of, 26; FMB visits, 115, 344, 383; FMB helps organise charity concert, 342, 512-3; progeny of, 571
Mendelssohn, Robert, 571
Mendelssohn Bartholdy, Abraham (FMB's father): death of, 19, 357, 459, 571; siblings of, 21; courtship and marriage of, 24-5, 31-3; and Henriette Mendelssohn, 26; conversion to Lutheranism, 33, 191; attitude to children, 35, 46, 60, 71, 81, 110, 116, 120, 137, 175, 184-5, 168, 181, 184-5, 192, 202, 324-5; travel arrangements, 55; religious beliefs, 39, 192, 201, 498, 247; upbringing of children, 41-46, 106, 112, 115-6, 141, 149, 175, 183, 204, 221, 237, 338, 465; visit to London with FMB, 58, 229, 543-7; death of, 60-1; birthdays of, 62-3, 237; purchases house in Berlin, 69; family holiday, 74; visit to Paris with FMB and daughter Fanny, 79-80, 111-2, 116-8, 147, 149, 417; forbids FMB to visit Sicily, 85, 135, 184, 527; low opinion of music as a profession, 105, 176; and Zelter, 108, 122; musical tastes, 108-9, 586; and A.B. Marx, 120, 148; and Goethe, 121, 122, 129, 130, 137; and claims of FMB's incestuous relationship with daughter Fanny, 144; relationship with daughter Fanny, 149, 161; character of, 160, 174, 175-6, 182, 415, 547; and the Mendelssohn bank, 173-4, 383, 590; wealth of, 174, 177, 178; and Wilhelm Hensel, 178-9, 385; political views of, 207; silver wedding anniversary of, 232-3, 605; on Maria Malibran, 244; misattributes FMB's *A Midsummer Night's Dream*, 260; encourages FMB to compose an opera, 287, 288, 299-300, 577; on Karl Immermann, 292, 329; reservations over the revival of Bach's *St Matthew Passion*, 305; and FMB's application to the Berlin Singakademie, 319-20; on festival in Düsseldorf, 324; on von Winter's *The Power of Music*, 324; on

compositions of FMB's, 352, 356; on Handel and Haydn, 360-1; reaction to FMB's move to Leipzig, 438; on music in England, 515; failing eyesight of, 544

Mendelssohn Bartholdy, Albertine (née Heine), 170, 226, 502; FMB asks to be godmother, 172; husband Paul's wedding present to, 187; Fanny Mendelssohn and, 357, 489, 490; FMB invites to Leipzig, 498; with FMB and Cécile Mendelssohn in Switzerland, 507; as foster mother to FMB's children after the death of their parents, 508; marriage to Paul Mendelssohn, 542; after FMB's death, 568; death of, 571

Mendelssohn Bartholdy, Albrecht: life and career of, 570; *The War and German Society*, 570

Mendelssohn Bartholdy, Cécile (née Jeanrenaud; FMB's wife): personal appearance and character of, 41, 461-3, 470, 477, 500, 550, 608; honeymoon with FMB, 61, 166, 259, 471-4, 479, 518; relationship with FMB, 61-2, 74, 230, 241, 251, 252-4, 284, 411, 442, 468-70, 477-8, 493-4, 547-8, 557; health of, 65, 144, 239, 460, 497, 567, 603; on FMB, 65-6; marriage to FMB, 244, 443, 463-4; married life of, 74, 99, 141, 480-8, 491-2, 499, 502, 605, 609; Fanny Mendelssohn and, 144-5; religious practice of, 202-3; FMB dislikes portrait of, 230-1; FMB's gifts to, 232, 279, 425; FMB's correspondence to, 241, 463, 500, 547; family of, 362, 460-1; and Charles Horsley, 375; acts as interpreter, 444; trip to England with FMB, 400, 457, 550-1; courtship with and engagement to FMB, 459-60, 464-8, 469; artistic talent of, 463, 468, 483, 488-9; on Dorothea Mendelssohn, 470; wedding of, 470-1; meets FMB's family, 480; musical tastes, 489-90; pregnancy of, 495-7, 519-20; motherhood of, 497-500, 502; family life of, 505-8; gives permission for *Ruy Blas* to be performed, 522; during FMB's illness, 560, 562; at FMB's funeral, 562; after the death of FMB, 565-8, 602-3, 605; death of, 566, 568-9

Mendelssohn Bartholdy, Elisabeth (Lilli; FMB's daughter): birth of, 500; early childhood, 502, 507-8; marriage and family of, 569-70

Mendelssohn Bartholdy, Ernst von: career of, 570-1

Mendelssohn Bartholdy, Fanny (*later* Hensel; FMB's sister): birth of, 26, 32; personal appearance and character of, 33-4, 44, 70-1, 73, 152-3, 177-8, 186-7, 194, 215, 227, 356, 484, 530; on FMB's appearance, 35, 305; father Abraham's relationship with, 44, 74, 106, 110, 149, 161, 192, 222, 511; courtship with and marriage to Wilhelm Hensel, 50, 57, 69-70, 74-5, 141, 142, 177-9, 232-3, 540, 607; relationship with FMB, 51, 52, 106, 122, 129, 141-8, 150-2, 153, 156, 213, 222-3, 227, 241, 248, 264, 310, 394, 408; health of, 63, 64, 556; death of, 63-4, 145-6, 224, 269, 507-8, 556-7, 563; maternal instincts of, 65, 144, 480; on Eduard Gans, 72; trips to Italy, 79, 85, 86-7, 89-94, 96-9, 101-3, 154-5, 165, 167-8, 170, 171, 197-8, 209-10, 223-5, 231-2, 235-6, 480; visit to Paris for piano tuition, 79-80, 111-2, 116-8, 147, 149, 417; holiday to France, 82-3; musical compositions of, 106, 107, 146, 149-50, 152-4, 221, 225, 228, 484, 558; as pianist, 107, 109-10, 116, 129, 152-3, 424, 484, 540-1; and A.B. Marx, 109, 260, 337; FMB's champions the compositions of, 126-7, 146, 283, 289; on Goethe, 137-9; suggestions of incestuous relationship with FMB, 141, 144, 178, 557; comparisons with FMB, 146-8, 414, 484; musical performances of, 152-3,

154, 342, 516; organises concerts in Berlin, 155-6, 321, 434-5; von Keudell encourages, 156, 435; Fanny Horsley on, 162; relationship with sister Rebecka, 166, 225; on Kalkbrenner, 175, 417; anti-Semitism directed at, 200; holiday on the Baltic coast, 210-11; on developments in Berlin, 216-7, 394, 433, 489, 493; birth of son, 223; on FMB's compositions, 238, 262-3, 296, 332, 352, 357; on Delphine von Schauroth, 251; FMB's dedications to, 222, 284; suggests Niebelungen legend to FMB as source for opera libretto, 294; on Sophocles and Aeschylus, 297; on Nägeli's edition of the B minor mass, 305; on FMB's musical performances, 306-9, 310, 337, 394; on Joachim, 374, 453, 522; on the artist Elsasser, 385; painting gifted to, 386; on Wilhelm IV, 388; on Peter Cornelius, 388; and Gounod, 424; on Berlioz and FMB, 453-4; on FMB's engagement, 467-8; on Cécile Mendelssohn, 470, 499; suffers miscarriage, 472, 497; misses FMB's family, 507; enjoyment of opera, 490; on FMB in London, 532; misgivings over visiting London, 549; funeral of, 559; 'In Italy', 399; Piano Trio in D minor, 156, 228

Mendelssohn Bartholdy, Felix (FMB's son): birth of, 499; illness of, 500; life of, 502, 569; death of, 508

Mendelssohn Bartholdy, Felix: early years and upbringing, 31-5, 41-6, 69-73, 74-83, 175-6, 259-60; personal appearance of, 35-9, 66, 111, 126, 184, 305, 546, 563; work ethic of, 41-2, 47-53, 441-2; aversion to music journalism, 46-7, 405, 412-3, 581; relationship with sister Fanny, 51, 52, 106, 122, 129, 141-8, 150-2, 153, 156, 213, 222-3, 227, 241, 248, 264, 310, 394, 408; mental and physical health of, 55-63, 65-6, 555-6, 559-60; friendship with Goethe, 55, 114, 121-35, 139, 141, 181, 184, 208, 242, 267-8, 282, 344-5, 413; correspondence of, 56, 159-65, 166-9, 170-1, 172, 603-5; visit to Scotland, 56, 276-7, 279-81, 513, 533-8; in England, 57-8, 166-7, 212-3, 275-6, 319, 342-3, 397-401, 410-11, 495, 509-33, 538-541, 542-9, 549-53; in Italy, 65, 79, 85-9, 90-3, 94-6, 99-101, 135-6, 198-9, 208-9, 234-5, 248-9, 262, 268, 274, 309, 407-8, 421-3; first visit to Paris, 46, 79-80, 111-2, 116-8, 136-7, 147, 149, 164, 417; eating preferences of, 59, 76, 226, 479-80, 526, 528, 529-30, 538, 540, 545, 548, 550-1; relationship with father, 89, 91, 110, 112, 135, 137, 141, 160, 168, 181-2, 184-5, 192-3, 204, 221-2, 233, 237, 274, 352-3, 361, 415, 438, 459, 543, 579; in Switzerland, 103-4, 136, 218, 249, 413 (*see also* Switzerland); early musical development, 105-20, 148, 273; affluence of Mendelssohn family, 118, 174, 177, 178-9, 181-9; criticism of early compositions, 119, 260-1, 265; relations with women, 138-9, 236, 241-54, 334-5; relationship with sister Rebecka, 153-4, 248, 264, 329, 357, 466, 557; on music expressive powers, 169-72, 263, 274, 282-3; religious convictions, 191-7, 199-201, 202-3, 351, 360, 431, 579; sacred compositions, 195, 202, 351-67, 567-8; anti-Semitism directed at, 200, 201-2, 318, 578-9, 583-4, 587-90; influence of religious beliefs on compositions, 202-5; efforts to revive earlier composers, 202, 237, 303-314, 328, 420-1, 443, 448; political opinions, 207-9, 211-8, 587; posthumous reception of, 219, 285, 573-8, 580-90, 600-9, 611-12; as father, 231, 232, 379, 497-503, 506-8; marriage to Cécile Jeanrenaud, 244, 252-3, 459-60, 464-74, 477-84, 486-9, 491-2, 493-4;

attempts at opera, 287-302, 576-7; as conductor, 315-319, 323-4, 325, 331-4, 365-7, 440-6; application to Berlin Singakademie, 319-322; as pianist, 321, 337-43, 523, 385, 412, 455, 525-6; as Music Director at Düsseldorf, 325-30, 384, 410; as organist, 343-50; as musical director to King Friedrich Wilhelm IV, 375, 388-97, 451, 477, 580-1, 586; and the Leipzig Conservatorium, 375-8, 380-2, 456; visits to Buckingham Palace, 397-401, 522, 550, 573, 602; dislike of Parisian music, 405-7, 419, 425; friendship with Schumann, 427-9, 586-7; as director of the Leipzig Gewandhaus, 432, 437, 439-46, 448-50, 453-6, 549; in Leipzig, 437-57, 474, 477-81, 482-4, 486-9, 492-8, 549; death and funeral, 560-4; influence and legacy of, 564-5, 590-9, 609-11

Works Mentioned:

Antigone, op. 55, 47, 51, 295-7, 390, 434, 493, 520, 578

Antiphon et Responsorium, op. 121, 228

Athalie, op. 74, 51, 297, 393, 454, 597, 599, 603

Calm Sea and a Prosperous Voyage, op. 27, 50, 131, 272-3, 275, 426, 439, 592, 597

Camacho's Wedding, op. 10, 107, 131, 298-301, 307, 490, 578

Capriccio brillant, op. 22, 341-2

Capriccio in E minor, op. 81, no. 3, 602-3

Capriccio in F sharp minor, op. 5, 417, 595

'Cello Sonata No. 1 in B flat major, op. 45, 34, 51

Children's Pieces, op. 72, 504-5

Children's Symphonies, 230, 504

Christus (unfinished), op. 97, 157, 205, 360, 362, 524, 559, 601

Concerto for Two Pianos and Strings, 527

Elijah, op. 70, 51, 56, 66, 203, 205, 219, 253, 295, 334, 351, 355, 358, 361-7, 397, 492, 519, 524-5, 563, 573, 576, 584-5, 592-4

Fair Melusine, op. 32, 250, 252, 266-7, 272, 416, 438-9, 442, 514, 591

Fantasy, op. 28, 133, 282, 513, 516

First Walpurgisnacht, op. 60, 4, 48, 51, 63-4, 204, 259, 267-9, 447, 450, 521, 559

Hear My Prayer, 204-5, 353, 594

Hebrides Overture (*Fingal's Cave*), op. 26, 50, 56, 222, 250, 279-81, 416, 514, 515, 591, 592

Im Rührend Feierlich Tönes, 112

Infelice, op. 94, 275, 293, 515, 516

Jubi Domine, 114

Konzertstück in D minor, op. 113, 323

Konzertstück in F minor, op. 114, 323

Lauda Sion, op.73, 51, 334, 353-4

Lorelei (unfinished), op. 98, 252, 287, 289-91, 302

Midsummer Night's Dream Overture, op. 21, 52, 156, 185, 228, 259-65, 271-2, 392, 512, 518, 522, 597

Midsummer Night's Dream (incidental music), op. 61, 259-65, 334, 392, 400, 401, 423, 582, 589, 592, 597, 599, 600

Octet in E flat major, op. 20, 50, 107, 114, 126, 129, 185, 264-5, 271, 318, 511, 592

Oedipus at Colonus (incidental music), op. 93, 51, 297, 392, 454

Organ Sonatas, op. 65, 343, 346, 379, 576

Piano Concerto No. 1 in G minor, op. 25, 51, 52, 222, 251, 327, 383, 385, 426, 439, 453, 455, 514, 520

Piano Concerto No. 2 in D minor, op. 40, 144, 195, 341, 443, 516-7, 518-9, 520, 603

Piano Concerto in E minor (unfinished), 156, 452

Piano Fantasies, op. 16, 133, 245-6

Piano Quartet No. 1 in C minor, op. 1, 110, 112, 119, 130, 413, 524

Index of Names and Compositions

Piano Quartet No. 2 in F minor, op. 2, 119

Piano Quartet No. 3 in B minor, op. 3, 117, 265

Piano Sonata in G minor, op. 105, 126

Piano Trio No. 1 in D minor, op. 49, 342, 445, 484-5, 597

Piano Trio No. 2 in C sharp minor, op. 66, 354

Preludes and Fugues, op. 35, 203, 243, 282, 442

Preludes and Fugues (organ), op. 37, 346, 442

Psalms 2, 43, and 22, op. 78, 205, 352

Psalm 13, op. 96, 205, 352-3

Psalm 42, op. 42, 351, 473, 490

Psalm 95, op. 46, 394, 445

Psalm 98, op. 91, 205, 232

Psalm 114, op. 51, 195, 203, 205, 354, 450, 520

Psalm 115, op. 31, 48, 205, 222

Responsorium et hymnus, op. 121, 202, 204, 354, 524

Rondo brillant in E flat major, op. 29, 327, 516

Ruy Blas Overture, op. 95, 445, 522, 582

Serenade and Allegro Giocoso, op. 43, 342, 399

Seven Characteristic Pieces, op. 7, 114, 265

Son and Stranger, op. 89, 233, 301-2, 597

Sonata for Two Pianos, op. 34b, 111, 113

Songs, (various opp.), 107, 146, 152, 242, 267, 283-5, 288, 292, 314, 373, 398-9, 401, 456, 531, 559-60, 566, 585-7, 595, 598, 600

Songs to be Sung in the Open Air, op. 41, 284-5, 485, 490

Songs without Words, 46, 222, 282-3, 398-9, 485, 514, 575, 592, 598-9; Vol. I, op. 19, 86, 283, 519; Vol. II, op. 30, 223; Vol. III, op. 38, 442, 473, 519; Vol IV, op. 53, 484; Vol V, op. 62, 1, 62, 283, 449, 505; Vol VI, op. 67, 225, 250, 283, 454, 562; Vol VII, op. 85, 400, 580; Vol VIII, op. 102, 283, 580

St Paul, op. 36, 60-1, 147, 203-4, 227, 323, 351, 354-63, 398, 425, 442, 444, 460, 496, 510, 517-9, 576, 579, 580, 584-5, 592

String Quartet in E flat major, 46

String Quartet in E flat major, op.12, 50, 247

String Quartet in A minor, op.13, 52, 242-3

String Quartet in D major, op. 44, no. 1, 56, 445, 606

String Quartet in E minor, op. 44, no. 2, 56, 445, 473

String Quartet in E flat major, op. 44, no. 3, 56, 445

String Quartet in F minor, op. 80, 507, 558

String Quintet No. 1 in A major, op. 18, 49, 420

String Symphonies, 114, 115, 129, 511

Symphony No. 1 in C minor, op. 11, 511

Symphony No. 2 in B flat major, op. 52, (*Lobgesang*), 239, 317, 375, 445, 447, 484, 492-3, 519-20, 549

Symphony No. 3 in A minor, op. 56 ('Scottish'), 49, 50, 51, 277-9, 341, 398, 399, 424, 520, 536, 580, 584-5, 589, 591-2

Symphony No. 4 in A major, op. 90, ('Italian'), 49, 85, 155, 274-5, 277, 423, 515, 543, 583, 597, 602, 603

Symphony No. 5 in D minor, op. 107 ('Reformation'), 50, 52, 202, 238-9, 580, 602

Te Deum, 351, 354, 524

Three Sacred Pieces, op. 23, 195, 351-2

Three English Church Pieces, op. 69, 48, 202, 204

To the Artists (*Festival Song*), op. 68, 239-40, 331, 525, 598

Trumpet Overture, op. 101, 112, 227, 238, 272, 275, 324

Tu es Petrus, op. 111, 118, 195, 202, 204, 222, 351, 354, 524

Two Nephews or *The Uncle from Boston*, 76, 298

Variations concertantes, op. 17, 34, 228

Variations sérieuses, op. 54, 342, 599

Violin Concerto in D minor, 112-4, 603

Violin Concerto in E minor, op. 64, 279, 341, 394, 427, 451-3, 485-6, 576, 589, 592, 595-6

Violin Sonata in F minor, op. 4, 114, 115, 119

Mendelssohn Bartholdy, Karl Wolfgang Paul (FMB's son): birth and early years of, 65, 172, 231-2, 495, 497-503, 508, 567; compiles FMB's letters, 128, 477, 603-4; career of, 570, 590

Mendelssohn Bartholdy, Leah (*née* Salomon; FMB's mother): personal appearance and character of, 24, 33, 87, 109, 159, 168, 174, 175-7, 181, 182-4, 188, 305, 320, 383, 461, 462, 499, 530, 543; courtship and marriage of, 24-5, 31-3, 41, 173, 191, 201; birth of children, 26; as a mother, 33, 41-2, 45, 115-6, 122-3, 128, 141, 144, 146, 150, 163, 165, 168, 176-80, 209, 221, 292, 338, 342, 383, 392, 487; death of, 49-50, 62-3, 155, 170, 232, 353, 449, 489; Abraham admonishes, 55; health of, 55, 62, 331, 471, 489; FMB on, 60; in Switzerland, 75; relationship with daughter Fanny, 75, 142, 149, 150, 177-9, 607; complicit in change of family name, 105, 173, 181; appreciation of Bach, 106-7, 109, 181, 191; teaches piano to FMB, 107-8; FMB writes *The Maid of Andros* for, 131; correspondence of, 159, 164; and Henriette Mendelssohn, 159; receives plants, 172; during the annexing of Hamburg, 173-4; inheritance of, 176, 178; relationship with daughter Rebecka, 180; on husband Abraham, 182; attitude to Judaism, 201, 247; gift to Droysen, 229; silver wedding anniversary of, 232-3, 605; attitude to A. B. Marx, 260; on poetry of Immermann, 292; and the Berlin Singakademie, 305, 322; on FMB's appearance, 331; relatives in Vienna, 407, 417, 420; on Josef Gusikov, 431; attitude to Cécile Jeanrenaud, 464-5, 467-8, 474; absence at FMB's wedding, 471

Mendelssohn Bartholdy, Ludwig, 590

Mendelssohn Bartholdy, Marie (*later* Benecke; FMB's daughter), 500; FMB's portrait bequeathed to, 38; baptism of, 233; birth of, 499; FMB with, 502-3; after the deaths of her parents, 508; sends an FMB manuscript, 525; piano playing of, 567; marriage and children of, 569; Karl Mendelssohn's dedication to, 604

Mendelssohn Bartholdy, Paul (FMB's son): recovery from illness, 65; birth of, 239, 499; childhood of, 500-2, 506-8, 570; during mother's pregnancy, 519-20; career and offspring of, 570, 590

Mendelssohn Bartholdy, Paul (FMB's brother): after FMB's death, 2, 185, 462, 508, 562; during childhood, 26, 70, 76, 161, 171, 225-6, 305, 487; birth of, 32, 62, 191; personal appearance and character of, 34, 37, 175, 187, 215, 480, 491; musicianship of, 34, 71, 109, 228; favoured by parents, 42-44, 308, 499; relationship with FMB, 51, 55, 66, 74, 76, 109-10, 169, 183, 192, 216, 223, 225-6, 232, 389, 390, 471, 493, 556, 560-2; marriage and family of, 65, 155, 170; lack of biographical information regarding, 166, 187, 542; inheritance of Mendelssohn family home in Leipzig, 183, 393; oversees FMB's assets, 187, 567-8, 602-3; FMB acquires piano for, 187; FMB's dedications to, 34, 228, 230, 393, 504; attends baptism, 233; on popularity of FMB's *A Midsummer*

Night's Dream, 263; and the Mendelssohn Bank, 311, 542; as editor of FMB's correspondence, 329, 422, 477, 603-4; acquires painting, 385; represents FMB, 388, 456; on Liszt, 427; FMB invites to Leipzig, 498; holiday in Switzerland with FMB's family, 507, 557-8; invites FMB to live in Berlin, 560; on FMB's death, 563; and Cécile Mendelssohn after FMB's death, 568-9, 603, 605; progeny of, 570-1; death of, 571, 604

Mendelssohn Bartholdy, Rebecka (*later* Dirichlet; FMB's sister), 42, 44, 72-3, 109, 110, 144, 169, 170-1, 210, 216, 242, 246, 296, 310, 352, 388-9, 394, 429, 440, 466, 468, 470, 471, 481-2, 504, 507, 515, 530, 553, 571; character and talents of, 34, 151, 155, 331, 528, 538; health of, 64-5, 385, 471, 472, 497, 500; death of infant son, 64; in Italy, 90, 93-4, 98-9, 103, 165-6, 197, 198-200, 229, 234, 235-7, 481; birth of daughter, 90, 500; relationship with FMB, 153-4, 248, 264, 329, 357, 466, 557; marriage to Gustav Dirichlet, 180, 222, 233; aversion to the name 'Bartholdy', 200-1; birthdays of, 224-5, 228, 473; Fanny composes trio for, 228; FMB's dedications to, 230, 284, 504; friendship with Betty Pistor, 246-7; Chopin refuses to play for, 425; meets Cécile Jeanrenaud, 480; birth of son Ernst, 545; reaction to FMB's death, 566; death of, 571

Mendelssohn Brothers and Company: origins of 24, 177; Hamburg branch of, 31, 32, 173; honoured as *Bankers to the Tsar of All the Russias*, 33; success of, 182; name of, 185; after Abraham Mendelssohn's death, 187, 571; under Ernst von Mendelssohn-Bartholdy, 570-1; liquidation, 578, 589

Mendheim, Marie (*earlier* Mendel), 233

Menuhin, Yehudi: discovery of FMB's Violin Concerto in D minor, 112-4; 603

Menzel, Adolph von, 208

Mercadante, Saverio, 327

Mesmer, Otto, 34-5

Metternich, Prince Klemens, 274, 389, 407

Meyer, Henrietta *see* Mendelssohn, Henrietta

Meyer, Mendel, 25

Meyer, Nathan, 201

Meyer, Recha (*née* Mendelssohn): siblings of, 21; personality of, 22; life and career of, 25, 141

Meyerbeer, Giacomo, 80, 171, 415; FMB mistaken for, 201, 545; as director of the Berlin Opera House, 253, 388; FMB and, 391; FMB on *Robert le Diable*, 406; Jewish heritage of, 415; Schumann on, 577-8; Wagner's hypocrisy towards, 582; anti-Semitism directed at, 588; Liszt compares with FMB, 600; *Robert le Diable*, 99, 406

Michael (FMB's mountain guide), 487-8

Michelangelo, 89, 90; *Last Judgement*, 196

Middleton, Jessie, 607

Middleton, Richard, 308

Milan: FMB in, 48, 90-2, 262, 268, 421, 545; Fanny Mendelssohn in, 93; Souchay enterprises in, 461; Verdi's *Ernani* produced in, 558; violin stolen in, 595

Milder-Hauptmann, Anna: sings in FMB's revival of the *St Matthew Passion*, 306-7; FMB commissioned to write song for, 531

Millanolla (sisters), 433

Mills & Boon, 248

Milton, John, 74, 346

Minna (Mendelssohns' maid), 90, 97, 481, 504

Molique, Wilhelm Bernhardt, 442

Möller, Lady, 540

Monet, Claude: Ernst von Mendelssohn's donation of *The Winter Garden*, 571

Monsigny, Pierre-Alexandre, 345

Montaigne, Michel de, 162, 552
Montebello, Duke of, 101-2
Moore, Joseph: as manager of the Birmingham festival, 61, 239, 359, 362, 363, 364, 517, 518, 519; FMB on, 517
Moore, Thomas, 73, 283, 523; *Lalla Rookh*, 177, 449; *Travels of an Irish Gentleman in Search of Religion*, 73
Mori, M. (concert organiser), 341, 513
Morning Post, 343
Morris, Jan, 203
Moscheles, Charlotte (*née* Embden): on Moses Mendelssohn, 11; on Abraham Mendelssohn after his accident, 58; FMB's letters to, 73, 137, 492, 502, 581; at FMB's birthday celebrations, 227; on FMB's *Fair Melusine*, 266; attends rehearsal, 342; on Charles Broadley, 352-3; and Weimar, 412; death of child of, 533; on FMB in London, 546; Fanny Mendelssohn on, 547; Felix Moscheles on, 550; on Cécile Mendelssohn, 550; Queen Victoria reads letters of, 601
Moscheles, Felix: at FMB's birthday celebrations, 227; baptism of, 234; on FMB and Fanny Mendelssohn, 342; describes duets of FMB and his father, 343; on FMB at Buckingham palace, 400-1; FMB visits, 495; on FMB, 495, 505, 520, 558, 559
Moscheles, Ignaz: friendship with FMB, 11, 115, 169, 212, 234, 313, 321, 405, 409, 412, 418, 447, 483, 505, 515-6, 520, 528, 533, 543, 550, 551, 559, 560; compositions of, 234; as director of the Leipzig Conservatorium, 66, 382, 412, 494; as advisor to FMB's parents, 79, 116, 118, 120, 175, 526; on Fanny Mendelssohn, 109; on FMB, 115, 116, 146, 377-8, 515; on Malibran, 244; introduces FMB to the Horsley family, 249; as conductor, 266, 492; on FMB's 'Italian' Symphony, 275; arrangements of FMB's works, 283, 353, 562; familiarity with Bach's music, 303; FMB sends Beethoven manuscript to, 312; performs with FMB, 342-3, 446, 523; acts as intermediary, 352; sets psalms, 353; on *Elijah*, 364; dedication to Cécile Mendelssohn, 481; FMB gives financial advice to, 482-3; returns with FMB to Leipzig, 502; arranges concert, 512; composes with FMB, 516; FMB's dedication to, 516; FMB conducts for, 524; at FMB's funeral, 562; Queen Victoria reads letters of, 601; Concerto for Two Pianos, 342-3, 512; piano arrangement of *Der Freischütz*, 114; Duet for Two Pianos in G minor, 115; Six Songs, op. 97, 481
Möser, Carl, 114
Moser, Hans Joachim: on FMB's *First Walpurgisnacht*, 268
Moszkowski, Alexander, 3, 123, 141
Mounsey, Ann (*later* Bartholomew), 205, 353, 595
Mozart, Constanze, 462
Mozart, Franz Xavier Wolfgang: meeting with FMB in Italy, 91-2, 262, 268, 421, 545
Mozart, Karl Thomas: burden of father's reputation on, 500
Mozart, Leopold, 105, 230, 303; *Cassation in G for Orchestra and Toys* ('Toy Symphony'), 230
Mozart, Maria Anna, 105, 149
Mozart, Wolfgang Amadeus: as teacher of Thomas Attwood, 57, 346, 513; FMB performs works by, 91-2, 112, 124, 127, 133, 222, 237, 328, 340, 349, 412, 441, 446, 587, 591; FMB compares to son Franz Xavier, 92; FMB on, 94, 252, 409, 423, 450, 469-70, 545, 577; comparisons with FMB, 105-6, 111, 119, 126, 174, 278, 288-9, 317, 340, 428, 511, 560, 577, 584, 601; musical influence on FMB, 106, 314; Mendelssohn family's high regard for the works of, 109; as teacher of Hummel, 125; feminist theories

Index of Names and Compositions

regarding, 149; Fuchs provides autograph score of, 230, 469; music in Austria after the death of, 274; and Da Ponte, 287; Schumann distances Romantic music from, 303; on the organ, 303; FMB assesses an editions of music by, 313; reorchestrations of Handel works, 320, 328, 409; FMB discusses, 375; nineteenth century reception in Paris, 406-7; FMB's piano playing is compared with that of, 441; Jenny Lind sings arias by, 455; violin concertos of, 486; reception of music in England, 509, 578; on music and the emotions, 585; difficulties of performing the piano music of, 599; works catalogued, 602; correspondence published, 604; early twentieth century reception of, 612; 'Ave Verum Corpus', 416; Concerto for Two Pianos, K. 365, 343, 446; *Don Giovanni*, 92, 124, 127, 328, 341; *La Clemenza di Tito*, 227; *Lamentations*, 469-70; *Magic Flute*, 92, 155, 313; *Marriage of Figaro*, 124, 227, 332, 430; Piano Concerto No. 9, K. 271, 340; Piano Concerto No. 20, K. 466, 430, 441; Piano Concerto No. 24, K. 491, 443; *Requiem*, 137, 237, 605; Symphony No. 39, 237; Symphony No. 40, 237, 511; Symphony No. 41, 'Jupiter', 237, 313; *Zaide*, 443

Mühlenfels, Ludwig von, 529-30, 534

Müller, (soprano in Vienna), 79, 246, 248

Müller, F. Max: on gaps in FMB's biographical details, 4; on FMB, 4, 42, 71, 366, 469, 580-1, 601; on the upbringing of FMB and his siblings, 46; recollection of Abraham Mendelssohn, 71; completes Rosen's translation of the Rig Vedas, 73, 195; on concerts at the Mendelssohn home, 110, 427; on his stay with the Mendelssohns, 188; on performance in London of *Elijah*, 366; FMB advises to relinquish professional music, 370; on Schumann, 428; sings in concert at Gewandhaus, 469; notes FMB's decline in health, 555; *Auld Lang Syne* (memoirs), 4, 580

Müller, Gottfried: Fanny Mendelssohn recounts talk by, 236

Müller, Karl, 396

Müller, Wilhelm: Fanny Mendelssohn sets poem by, 146; 'Die Glückliche Fischerin', 146

Munich: Fanny Mendelssohn in, 64, 101, 146, 251; FMB in, 134, 143, 147, 169, 207, 223, 246, 250, 251, 318, 340-1, 345, 383, 419-20; FMB offered post in, 437

Münster, Ernst Graf zu, 529-30

Munthe, Judge, 254

Murray, John: inclusion of the Crown Inn at Mairingen into *Red Guides*, 487

Music Magazine (BBC), 597

Music under the Third Reich, 589

Musical Examiner, 581

Musical World, The: on FMB's upbringing, 41, 71; on concerts involving FMB, 268, 332, 359, 450, 608; analysis of *Elijah*, 361; defends FMB's reputation, 450; appraisal of Schubert's *Fierrabras* Overture, 574

Musset, Alfred de, 214

Nägeli (publisher): edition of Bach's B minor Mass, 305

Nägeli, Georg, 305

Naples: FMB in, 49, 99-101, 103, 135, 165, 168, 170, 184, 275, 421-2; Fanny Mendelssohn in, 101, 209-10; Rebecka Mendelssohn in, 103; insurrection in, 216; Spontini in, 299

Napoleon I, Emperor, 25, 31, 387, 590; and the 'Continental System', 32, 173; reparations after defeat of, 32, 112, 149; Countess Negri displays belongings of, 93; popularity in the Gulf of Spezia, 93; hypothetical discussion concerning, 101; proposed road, 104; Cherubini and, 116; Jakob Bartholdy writes book concerning, 176; Hensel's portrait of, 177; remains excavated, 210; Germany

following defeat of, 213; *Midnight Review*, 46, 283
Napoleon III, Emperor, 210-11
National Socialist (Nazi) Party: anti-Semitic slurs on FMB and his descendents, 2, 18, 570, 578, 580, 587, 589-90, 612; influence of Wagner on, 587; bans music of FMB, 589
Naumann, Emil: FMB refuses to teach, 372, 380
Naumann, Johann Gottlieb, 443
Naumann, Professor Carl Friedrich, 380
Neate, Charles, 233, 339
Negri (Countess): Hensel family's stay with, 93
Nesser, Franz, 372
Neue Zeitschrift für Musik, Die (New Musical Journal): Schumann edits, 445, 581
Neukomm, Count Sigismund Ritter von: FMB meets in Paris, 117; performance of music in Mainz, 240; FMB on, 320, 418-9, 518; and the *St Cecilia Society*, 475; *The Ten Commandments*, 418
Neumann, Johann, 238
New York: branch of the Mendelssohn Bank in, 32; FMB's invitation to, 333-4, 605; Gounod's *Faust* performed in, 424; documents relating to FMB donated to library in, 605; Metropolitan Opera House, 598; City Ballet, 597; Men's Chorus, 285; Philharmonic Orchestra, 278, 333, 605
Newman, Ernest, 513
Nicholas I, Tsar: commissions Wilhelm Hensel, 177
Nicholas, Grand Duke *see* Nicholas I, Tsar
Nichols, Roger, 400, 505
Nicholson, Charles, 511
Nikisch, Arthur, 593
Nikolaus II, Prince of Esterhazy, 415
Nikolaus, Prince of Esterhazy, 443
Nohl, Ludwig: *Letters from Musicians*, 604
Norwich, Viscount John Julius, 126
Nourrit, Adolphe, 406
Novello & Co: FMB sends music to, 146; fee for FMB's Piano Concerto No. 2, 195; as origin of the term *Songs Without Words*, 282-3, 485, 514; commissions FMB, 277; importance of FMB's *St Paul* to company, 519; FMB's association with, 519
Novello, Clara: FMB invites to Weimar, 138; FMB's comments on, 171; FMB engages, 332, 444, 518; replaces Jenny Lind in performance of *Elijah*, 367; Fanny Mendelssohn compares to Charlotte Birch, 434; and Hiller, 444
Novello, Vincent, 350, 354, 509, 517-8, 524
O'Shea, Dr. John: hypothesis as to the cause of FMB's death, 18, 55, 564; on FMB's physical stature, 35; on FMB's emotional development, 175; on FMB and women, 242; *Illnesses of Great Composers*, 55, 564
Oban: FMB in, 56, 279-80, 536-7
Oberhover, Herr (singer), 358
O'Connell, Daniel, 215-6
O'Connell, Morgan John, 215-6
Ohm, Georg: as teacher of Gustav Dirichlet, 180
Oldham, Edith, 361
Onslow, George: FMB dislikes, 130; on FMB's Trumpet Overture, 272; FMB's meeting with, 418
ophicleide: FMB's uses in *A Midsummer Night's Dream*, 272; FMB suggests to substitute harp, 453-4; FMB has to alter scores featuring, 597
Ossian (mythological poet), 279
Otho I, King of Greece, 385
Ouseley, Frederick Arthur Gore: joins Mendelssohn Scolarship committee, 609
Overbeck, Johann Friedrich, 170
Oxford Companion to Music, 593
Oxford: FMB rumoured to be performing in, 487; Bodleian Library, 159, 260, 281, 298, 308, 452, 469, 489, 570, 596, 605; Magdalen College, 569; University, 570

Index of Names and Compositions

Pacini, Giovanni: FMB attends performance of an opera by, 96

Paderewski, Ignacy, 599

Paganini, Niccolò, 91, 93, 214, 228, 425, 452, 516; FMB meets, 318; prevented from playing duets with FMB due to surgery, 340; violin concertos of, 486; *La Clochette*, 147

Palestrina, Giovanni, 94, 99, 197; FMB performances of music by, 136, 408; Zelter disapproves of, 148; FMB on, 409; Improperia, 198

Palma Vecchio: *Adoration of the Magi*, 93

Paperini (singer), 72

Parham, Lucy, 151

Paris: FMB in, 5, 46, 50, 52, 58, 79, 80-2, 85, 106, 111-2, 114, 116-8, 136-7, 147, 149, 164-5, 169, 172, 194, 201-2, 211-12, 227, 238, 265, 268, 318-9, 359, 405-7, 415, 417-9, 425-6, 579, 587; after the defeat of Napoleon, 32; music in, 49, 80, 82, 136, 232, 289, 297, 319, 405-7, 415, 417-8, 419, 579, 582; Académie Royale, 114, 407; Conservatoire, 46, 79, 116-7, 232, 265, 278, 318, 339, 371, 406-7, 417, 440, 577, 579; Louvre, 80; Père Lachaise, 80; Sorbonne, 15

Passman, Augusta von, 332

Pasta, Giuditta, 405, 529

Patti, Caterina, 516

Paul Anton III, Prince of Esterhazy, 384

Paul VIII, Pope: final illness of, 198-9

Paulze, Marie-Anne Pierette, 416

Pearsall, Ronald, 576; *Victorian Popular Music*, 576

Peel, Sir Robert: on Fingal's Cave, 280; applauds FMB, 520

Pendixon, Emma: George MacFarren dedicates *Ma Cousine* to, 449

Pereira, Baron Heinrich von, 185, 283, 420

Pereira-Arnstein, Baroness Henriette von, 46, 78-9, 91, 183-4, 420

Pereira-Arnstein, Flora von, 79

Pergolesi, Giovanni Battista, 197; *Stabat Mater*, 155

Perlman, Itzhak: on FMB's Violin Concerto, 596

Peters (publisher), 248, 312-3

Petitpierre, Jean: on FMB, 36, 172; on FMB's *A Midsummer Night's Dream*, 263; on FMB and Liszt, 427; on Cécile Mendelssohn, 461, 567, 568, 569, 603; account of FMB's honeymoon, 470; on the descendents of FMB and Cécile Mendelssohn, 570; accuses Wagner of plagiarism, 591; on scholarships awarded in FMB's name, 610; lectures on unpublished works of FMB, 611; *The Romance of the Mendelssohns*, 611

Petitpierre, Julie: Cécile Mendelssohn writes to, 568

Pettitt, Stephen, 606, 611

Petty-Fitzmaurice, Henry, 3rd Marquess of Lansdowne, 530

Philharmonic Society of London: FMB and, 266, 279, 520-3, 550, 552; commissions FMB, 275, 457, 515; Spohr conducts with a baton at a concert of, 315; possess Beethoven sketches, 328; Wagner conducts for, 448; FMB praises, 510; gives aid to composers, 510; FMB dedicates symphony to, 511; proposal to erect a statue in FMB's honour, 602

Piatti, Alfredo, 153, 156, 457

Picot, Mme. (milliner), 473

Piering, Herr (associate of Fuchs), 420-1

Pierson, Henry Hugh, 430

Pindar, 93

Pirani, Max, 375

Pistor, F. D. E. ('Betty'; *later* Rudorff): FMB's friendship with, 201, 301; FMB's dedication to and falling out with, 246-8; recalls FMB's revival of the *St Matthew Passion*, 304, 309

Planché, James Robinson: submits libretto to FMB, 294

Planer, Natalia: anti-Semitism of, 456

Platen, Count August Graf von, 130

Plato: Moses Mendelssohn's translation of, 12, 15; Moses Mendelssohn compared

with, 15; FMB reads works by, 72, 74; *The Immortality of the Soul*, 12
Pleasants, Henry: on Jenny Lind, 253, 363; *The Great Singers*, 253
Pleyel, Ignaz, 81, 111, 342, 424
Poe, Edgar Allan, 39; *Annabel Lee*, 609
Pogwisch, Ottilie von *see* Goethe, Ottilie von
Pogwisch, Ulrike von: FMB on, 55, 132, 138, 331; affair with Goethe, 123, 200; on Fanny Mendelssohn, 332
Poissl, Johann Nepomuk, 432
Polchau, Georg, 287, 328
Polko, Elise: on FMB, 125, 160, 250, 348, 461; authenticity of memoirs, 312, 607; sings under FMB, 332
Pope, Alexander: Moses Mendelssohn scrutinises *Essay on Man*, 11
Porsche, Karl Wilhelm August, 445
Potsdam: Sophocles's *Antigone* premiered in, 390; FMB performs in, 412, 454
Potter, Cipriani: chairs Mendelssohn Scholarship committee, 609
Pountney, William, 525
Pourtales, Count, 194-5
Praslin, Fanny Sebastiani, Duchesse de: Henriette Mendelssohn acts as governess to, 25, 116; murder of, 26, 218; songs presented to, 149
Praslin, Theobald, Duc de: marriage to Fanny Sebastiani, 25; murder of his wife, 26, 218
Punch, 297, 378, 491
Purcell, Henry: *Te Deum*, 47
Quarterly Musical Magazine and Review, 114
Queisser, Karl Traugott, 317
Racine, Jean Baptiste: *Athalie*, 297, 393
Radcliffe, Philip: on FMB, 71, 105, 300, 318; on FMB's musical works, 107, 228, 239, 288, 297, 334, 393, 473, 575, 576, 592, 599; on FMB's family, 163; compares FMB's song settings with those of other composers, 283-4; on FMB's influence on other composers, 593; cataloguing of FMB's works, 602

Radziwill, Prince Anton H.: FMB dedicates Piano Quartet to, 119; *Faust*, 442
Rameau, Jean-Philippe, 148
Ranke, Leopold von, 567
Raphael, 74, 81, 89, 109, 197, 212, 225, 296, 322, 386; *Assumption*, 197; *Entombment*, 197; *Fornarina*, 88; *Holy Family*, 80; *Loggia*, 196; *Transfiguration*, 177
Rau, Herr (musician in Vienna), 248, 420
Raupach, Ernst: FMB makes sketches on a libretto by, 294
Rawsthorne, Noel: arrangement of FMB's Wedding March, 598
Redern, Count Friedrich Wilhelm Graf von, 296, 301, 433, 434, 540
Reger, Elsa (*née* von Bagenski), 506
Reger, Max: influence of FMB on, 309; unearths works by Hiller, 447
Reich, Dr., 9
Reich, Nancy B.: posits feminist theory on FMB's relationship with his sister Fanny, 150, 153; discovers memoirs of Ernst Rudorff, 246
Reichardt, Johann Friedrich: settings of Goethe's poetry, 108; FMB praises song by, 313-4; comparison of Bach and Handel, 314; adapts cantata, 331
Reichenbach (Leipzig bank), 182
Reinecke, Carl: compares FMB's and Schumann's methods of teaching, 381
Reinhardt, Max, 262, 597
Rellstab, Ludwig: on an encounter with the young FMB, 124-5; as originator of the moniker 'Moonlight' to Beethoven's Piano Sonata op. 27 No. 2, 124; praises concerts conducted by FMB, 232, 321; on FMB's musical memory, 382
Rembrandt Harmenszoon van Rijn, 386
Reumont, Alfred von, 434
Reynolds, Sir Joshua, 353
Ribbentrop, Ulrich von: censors FMB's 'Scottish' Symphony, 589
Richardson, Joanna, 463
Richmond, Thomas, 243, 533

Richter, Jean-Paul: FMB and the novels of, 73, 162, 552; *Die Flegeljahre*, 527, 541

Riemer, Professor Friedrich Wilhelm: publishes Goethe's correspondence, 60; FMB on, 138, 162

Ries, Ferdinand, 475, 567; *The Robber Bride*, 133

Rietschel, Ernst Friedrich, 39

Rietz, Eduard, 161, 312, 317, 321, 420; death of, 49, 227; FMB's dedications to, 49, 112-4, 603; illness of, 117; FMB receives news of the death of, 227

Rietz, Julius, 154, 239, 346; FMB helps, 138, 456; performance by, 327; FMB performs works by, 448; FMB delegates to, 557; at FMB's funeral, 562

Righini, Vincenzo, 443

Rihm (composer), 441

Rimsky-Korsakov, Nikolai, 164

Rinck, Johann Christian, 344

Ritter, Carl: FMB studies under, 45; Heydemann imitates, 76

Rizzio, David, 277

Robert, Aulan, 86

Robert, Friederike (*née* Braun), 69; death of, 59, 86

Robert, Ludwig, 59, 69; suicide of, 86; FMB appraises libretto of, 289

Robinson, E. Stanley, 265

Roche, Henry, 382

Rocklitz, Friedrich, 124, 348, 438

Rockstro, William Smyth: on FMB's mode of composition, 112; on FMB's musical works, 114, 239, 339, 524; as biographer of FMB, 159-60, 380, 607; on FMB, 265, 326, 340, 389, 474, 479, 502, 585, 601; on the Mendelssohn family, 322; on performances by FMB, 340, 348, 349, 350, 441, 443, 454-5; on Moritz Hauptmann, 376; on meetings with FMB and the Leipzig Conservatorium, 378-82; on music in Berlin, 390; on Spohr, 414; on Cécile Mendelssohn, 461; on FMB's bad press in London, 517; on FMB's final illness and death, 555, 562, 563, 564; on FMB's legacy, 573, 591; on publications of his letters, 604; *Mendelssohn*, 378, 607

Rode, Pierre, 117

Rudorff, F. D. E. ('Betty') *see* Pistor, F. D. E.

Rogers, Samuel: Cécile Mendelssohn and, 550

Robinson & Cottam: cast London statue of FMB, 602

Romano, Guilio, 196, 231

Romberg, Bernhard Heinrich, 327

Rome: FMB in, 38, 46, 48-9, 72, 94-6, 103, 135-6, 170, 171, 182, 194, 195-6, 201, 208-9, 221-2, 226, 248, 312, 341, 408, 421, 423, 504; choral music in, 135-6, 197-8, 200, 232, 312, 360, 408, 585; Café Greco, 94-5, 423; French Academy, 97, 155, 165; Sistine Chapel, 96, 197, 198; Vatican, 99, 101, 199, 208; Villa Bartholdy, 96, 98, 176

Ronge, Johannes, 194

Rooney, Mickey, 597-8

Rosen, Friedrich, 162, 225, 330; on Moses Mendelssohn, 11; on Shakespeare, 70; translation of the Rig Vedas, 73, 195; death of, 73, 547; advises FMB on Bad Doberan, 131; discusses politics with FMB, 213; letter to FMB, 244; compares England and Germany, 482-3; FMB plays for, 517; in London, 526, 529-30, 534, 540, 543, 545

Rosen, Sophie (*later* Klingemann): marriage to Karl Klingemann, 162, 225, 552

Rossi, Salomon, 121

Rossini, Gioachino: performances of works by, 74, 330, 408, 514, 583; FMB on, 74, 92, 414, 415, 416, 532, 558; Abraham Mendelssohn on, 80; receives Order of Merit, 396; FMB's encounters with, 415-7, 464; Hiller on, 417; in Paris, 579; *Barber of Seville*, 80; *Otello*, 80, 405, 408, 528, 529; *William Tell*, 80, 281, 291, 583; *Stabat Mater*, 579; *The Thieving Magpie*, 520

Rothschild (family): comparisons with the Mendelssohns, 26, 111, 121, 174, 175; FMB meets, 188-9, 533; respect accorded to, 201; FMB declines invitation to ball held by, 464

Rothschild, Charlotte: wedding of, 464; as harpist, 533

Rothschild, Hanna, 533

Rothschild, Lionel Nathan de, 201, 416

Rothschild, Mayer Amschel (*earlier* Bauer): escape from Frankfurt ghetto, 121, 174; legacy of, 175

Rothschild, Nathan Mayer: Spohr seeks financial support from, 181; on financial success, 189

Rousseau, Jean Jacques, 80

Rouvroy, Claude Henri de, comte de Saint-Simon: Community of, 211-2

Rubens, Peter Paul, 197, 386

Rubinstein, Nikolai: piano playing compared with that of FMB, 343

Rückert, Friedrich, 388, 448

Rudorff, Ernst, 246

Rumford, Countess *see* Paulze, Marie-Anne Pierette

Runciman, John F., 584

Rungenhagen, Karl Friedrich: elected as director of the Berlin Singakademie in preference to FMB, 59, 319-22; as Zelter's deputy, 137, 309; as director of the Berlin Singakademie, 310, 374, 434

Ruskin, John, 10, 353; eulogy to FMB, 607

Rust, Wilhelm Karl, 131

Sachse (art dealer), 232

Sachse, Rudolf, 413

Sadie, Julie Anne: on Fanny Mendelssohn, 149-50

Sadie, Stanley: on FMB's compostional style, 106-7; on FMB's oratorios, 203

Sainton, Prosper, 454

Saint-Saëns, Camille, 106, 516, 593

Saint-Simon Community: beliefs of, 211-212

Salaman, Charles: on FMB's piano playing, 338

Saling, Fräulein, 131

Salomon, Bella (Babette) (*née* Itzig): rift with Jakob after his conversion from Judaism, 201; FMB and, 226; gives FMB a copy of Bach's *St Matthew Passion*, 304

Salomon, Jakob *see* Bartholdy, Jakob

Salomon, Johann, 510

Salomon, Leah *see* Mendelssohn, Leah

Samoilova, Countess Julia, 96

Sampson, George: on FMB's personal appearance and character, 36; visit to Leipzig, 36, 172, 181, 246, 259, 281-2, 314, 343, 428, 452, 483, 485-6, 519, 550, 580; on Schumann's personal appearance, 428; on Cécile Mendelssohn, 462

Sand, George, 92, 214

Sándor, Count, 384

Santini, Fortunato, 99, 309

Sappho: Rebecka Mendelssohn seen to resemble, 538

Sargent, Malcolm, 596

Saturday Review, 584

Saul, King of Israel (Old Testament), 129

Schadow, Gottfried von, 88, 121, 152, 153, 170, 292, 461, 465, 489

Schadow, Wilhelm von, 153, 170, 325, 326, 330, 425, 465, 473-4

Schauroth, Delphine von: FMB's involvement with, 143, 250-1, 419-20; FMB's dedication to, 251, 341; FMB shows composition to father of, 383

Schelble, Johann Nepomuk: FMB deputises for, 50, 414, 459, 605; admires FMB's improvisation, 112; FMB on, 222, 410; commissions FMB, 359; illness and death of, 442, 459-60, 605; FMB stays with, 464; the St Cecilia Society after, 475

Scheveningen: FMB in, 153, 170, 465, 466-7, 477

Schicht, Johann Gottfried, 122

Schikaneder, Emanuel, 313

Schiller, Friedrich von: influence of Lessing on, 10; FMB owns works of, 74; FMB

on, 104, 291; Goethe and, 122; criticism of, 208; FMB sets verses by, 239-40, 331; *The Maid of Orleans*, 299; *The Robber*, 433; *Wilhelm Tell*, 104, 291
Schinkel, Karl Friedrich, 388
Schirmer, Professor Johann Wilhelm, 194, 202
Schlegel, August Wilhelm von: translations of Shakespeare's plays, 12, 74, 259, 261, 264, 293
Schlegel, Caroline: dislike of sister-in-law Dorothea von Schlegel, 23
Schlegel, Dorothea *see* Mendelssohn, Dorothea
Schlegel, Friedrich Wilhelm von: marriage to Dorothea Mendelssohn, 22-3; *Lucinde*, 22
Schleiermacher, Friedrich, 23, 132, 137, 188, 193
Schleinitz, Heinrich Conrad: FMB and, 60-1, 169, 227, 312, 357-8, 377, 413, 415, 416, 438-9, 449, 464, 470, 500; sees Josef Gusikov perform in Leipzig, 431; FMB's dedication to, 559; during FMB's final illness, 560
Schlemmer, Fritz, 460, 473, 479
Schlesinger, Adolf Martin, 200, 304, 420
Schlesinger, Thérèse *see* Devrient, Thérèse
Schmidt, Dr., 569
Schmitt, Aloys: FMB plays at the house of, 112, 414; FMB compares an opera to those of, 289
Schnapper, Golde (*later* Rothschild), 121
Schneider, Johann Friedrich: FMB's uneasy friendship with, 131-2, 306, 440-1, 562
Schneider, Max: collects together FMB's portraits, 38
Schoenberg, Arnold, 274
Scholes, Percy: on von Döhler, 151-2; on Spontini, 299; on Romberg, 327; on the organ 'voluntary', 346; on Tamborini, 408; on von Henselt, 429; on Sterndale Bennett, 429; on Servais, 435; on the dispersal of the Mendelssohn family, 590
Scholz and Kuhnert, 480

Schön (minister), 216
Schönlein, Dr. Johann Lukas, 63, 560, 565
Schopenhauer, Adèle: on Goethe, 127; with FMB and Goethe, 128
Schopenhauer, Arthur, 127
Schröder (student): FMB visits the house of, 77, 118
Schröder-Devrient, Wilhelmine: performs Schubert's *Erlkönig*, 108; FMB gives dinner for, 227; historical obscurity of, 434; praises Wagner, 582
Schubert, Ferdinand: Schumann visits, 444; Schumann writes to, 522
Schubert, Franz Peter, 23, 595, 600; sets psalm translated by Moses Mendelssohn, 16; lieder of, 79, 314, 373; FMB lays flowers on the tomb of, 79, 420, 590; Abraham Mendelssohn disregards, 79, 116, 181, 417; sets Goethe, 108, 272-3, 283, 284; Vienna after the death of, 120, 274; FMB on, 181, 314; and Eichendorff, 285, 456; operas of, 287, 577; FMB promotes symphony of, 444, 522, 591; Deutsch catalogues the works of, 602; *Erlkonig*, 108, 426; *Fierrabras* Overture, 521, 574; Octet in F major, 271; Symphony No. 9, 'Great' in C major, 238, 444, 522, 591
Schubring, Julius: on FMB's childhood, 41-2, 45, 71, 188, 459; as librettist, 56, 355, 358, 360, 361-2, 365, 585; FMB's friendship with, 60, 71, 131-2, 169, 196, 204, 236, 271, 282, 306, 430, 474; on FMB's method of composition, 112, 191, 361; on FMB's religiosity, 193, 205; on FMB's musical works, 203, 272-3; FMB dissuades from setting Becker, 215; on FMB's translation, 221; on FMB and discordant sounds, 273; on Bach, 304, 307; on FMB in concert, 317; FMB admonishes, 355-6; FMB confides thoughts on contemporary music to, 439; eulogises FMB, 600

Schumacher (servant), 99, 481

Schumann, Clara (*née* Wieck), 146, 427; songs misattributed to husband Robert, 149; FMB on trio of, 151; troubled courtship of, 178, 483; piano practice disturbs husband Robert, 251, 465; and Jenny Lind, 254, 454, 566; on FMB as conductor, 316; on FMB as pianist, 338; Sterndale Bennett on, 430; performances in Leipzig, 443, 454, 455; performs with FMB, 446; FMB deputises for, 449; performs husband's Piano Concerto, 456; as hypothetical spouse of FMB, 462; fee for teaching piano, 482; marriage to Robert Schumann, 483; visit to FMB's home in Leipzig, 484; performance in Birmingham, 516; on FMB's failing health, 563; eulogy to FMB, 565; after husband's death, 572; and FMB's rift with Robert Schumann, 586-7; child named after FMB, 600; Piano Trio in G minor, op. 17, 228

Schumann, Robert: on the artist and society, 4; music journalism of, 46; studies as lawyer, 77, 118, 178, 483; FMB on, 111; on FMB's death, 171, 457; on FMB's letters, 172; marriage to Clara Wieck, 178, 443, 483; visits to FMB's home in Leipzig, 181, 428, 430, 437, 452, 484; setting of 'La Colognaise', 215; FMB's friendship with, 251, 427-9, 468-9, 559; on FMB's musical works, 259, 260, 266, 272, 428, 445, 578, 582, 602; lieder of, 284, 314, 373; operas of, 287, 295; on Bach, 303; on FMB as conductor, 316; on FMB's organ recital, 347; admires lieder of Robert Franz, 373; and the Leipzig Conservatorium, 376; as teacher, 381; on FMB as musician, 427-8, 577-8; personal appearance and character of, 428, 430; on Sterndale Bennett, 430; ambitions at the Gewandhaus, 432; discovery of Schubert symphony, 444, 522; on music in Leipzig, 445; serious injury to hand of, 449; on Joachim, 451; Berlioz and, 454; on Wagner, 456, 600; FMB promotes works by, 456, 523-4, 583, 591; on Cécile Mendelssohn, 461; on FMB as father, 503; at FMB's funeral, 562-3; suicide attempt and death of, 571-2; compositions compared with those of FMB, 573, 575, 577, 594; hands editorship to Brendel, 581-2; rift with FMB, 586-7; criticism of FMB's piano playing, 587; influence of FMB's music on, 591-2; in Düsseldorf, 593; Liszt's transcriptions of works by, 595; defends FMB's reputation 600-1; Chopin on, 600; child named after FMB, 600; *Andante and Variations* for two pianos, op. 46, 449; Arabesque, op. 18, 592; Fantasy for 'Cello, 592; *Genoveva*, 295; *Paradise and the Peri*, 449, 523; Piano Concerto, 456; Piano Quintet, op. 44, 449; Symphonic Studies, 599; Symphony No. 2, 456, 583; Symphony No. 3, 'Rhenish', 277, 592; Symphony No. 4, xxiii; Violin Concerto, 588-9

Schunck, Cornaille, 469

Schunck, Julie (*née* Jeanrenaud): at FMB's birthday celebrations, 227; FMB's dedication to, 284; compliments FMB's 'Maitrank', 480; wedding of, 499

Schunck, Julius, 499

Schüntze, Stefan: on Goethe's personality, 129

Schwarzen, Die: protest in Düsseldorf, 202

Schwencke, Johann Friedrich, 527

Schwind, Moritz von: tribute to Schubert, 600

Sciabatta, Mme. (contralto), 155, 434

Scotland: FMB's preparations for trip to, 142, 163, 167, 182; FMB in, 56, 276-7, 279-81, 513, 533-8; Mendelssohn Festival in, 612

Scott, Sir Walter: FMB meets, 73, 534-6; FMB owns works by, 74; FMB on, 99, 132; Goethe on, 132, 276; FMB inspired by, 276, 277; FMB sets verses of, 283; as potential source for a libretto, 295; death of, 565; as friend of Lady Wallace, 604; *Guy Mannering*, 59; *Waken, Lords and Ladies Gay*, 283

Scribe, Augustin Eugène: abortive collaboration with FMB, 293; libretto for *The Tempest* appropriated by Halévy, 302

Sebastiani, Fanny *see* Praslin, Fanny Sebastiani, Duchesse de

Sebastiani, General (also Baron) Horace François Bastien, 25, 180, 387

Seelmann, August, 430

Selden-Goth, Gisela: on FMB's personality and lifestyle, 3, 5, 241; on Abraham Mendelssohn, 45-6; translates FMB's correspondence into English, 160, 604-5; on FMB and Judaism, 203; on FMB's lieder, 587

Senlis, De: at FMB's funeral, 562

Serans, Mme., 155

Servais, Adrian François, 435

Sevigny, M.: Fanny Mendelssohn mistaken for the wife of, 144-5

Seydelmann, Karl, 330, 433

Shakespeare, William: translations of plays by, 12-3, 22, 74, 261; FMB's appreciation of, 70, 74, 208, 259-64, 295, 423, 532-3, 545; Berlioz and, 263; quartercentenary of birth commemorated, 263, 598; speculations concerning, 589; *A Midsummer Night's Dream*, 12, 227, 259-2, 597-8; *Hamlet*, 12, 70, 532-3; *King Lear*, 263, 462, 480; *The Tempest*, 12, 292-3, 302; *Macbeth*, 70, 224, 268, 386

Shaw, Alfred, 444

Shaw, George Bernard: attacks on FMB's reputation, 584-5, 599

Shaw, Mary (*née* Postone), 444, 518

Sheppard, Elizabeth Sarah: *Charles Auchester*, 607-8; *Counterpoint*, 607

Sibelius, Jean: ascribes colours to tonal areas, 123; in old age, 564; performs FMB's Violin Concerto, 596

Sicily: FMB forbidden to visit, 85, 135, 184, 274-5, 527; Wilhelm Hensel in, 102-3

Siepmann, Jeremy: on Chopin's first meeting with FMB, 237, 424; on the unreliability of Berlioz's memoirs, 422; *Chopin: The Reluctant Romantic*, 237, 398, 424

Silbermann, Gottfried, 472

Sillem, Jerôme, 530

Simrock, Nikolaus: FMB and, 39, 46, 52, 313, 353, 447, 485; edition of *The Magic Flute*, 313

Sivori, Camillo: as soloist in the English premiere of FMB's Violin Concerto, 596

Skelly, J.P., 141

Skerrett, Marianne, 397

Smart, Sir George: unfavourable assessment of FMB in Berlin, 116, 510-11; at a concert of FMB's, 339; conducts *St Paul*, 358-9, 510, 518; as patron to the London Philharmonic Society, 510; FMB on, 510, 512, 513; aids Weber during illness, 513

Socrates: Moses Mendelssohn compared with, 15, 18; bust of, in Moses Mendelssohn's house, 17-18

Sohl, Sophie, 332

Sontag, Henriette (*later* Countess Rossi): Rellstab arrested for insulting, 124; FMB on, 422; takes part in impromptu competition, 434; sings duet with Malibran, 512; performs in *Otello*, 529; in Handel's *Messiah*, 530

Sophocles: FMB on, 295; King Wilhelm IV introduced to plays of, 390; *Antigone*, 295, 296, 390, 493; *Oedipus at Colonus*, 51, 297

Sotheby's: FMB's letters auctioned by, 161, 195, 603

Souchay (family): business interests of, 461; in England, 548, 551

Souchay, Eduard: on FMB's piano playing, 338; on Cécile Mendelssohn, 463, 464, 569; recollections of, 470

Souchay, Marc André: on FMB, 36; conversation with FMB about music, 282; describes FMB playing the piano, 338

Souchay, Mme. (Cécile Jeanrenaud's aunt): cares for Cécile Mendelssohn during illness, 569

Souchay, Mme. (Cécile Jeanrenaud's grandmother): rescued from flooding, 492

Soult, Marshal Nicolas Jean de Dieu, 387

Spagnoletti, Paolo, 529

Speyer, Edward, 523, 600

Spinoza, Baruch, 15, 17

Spitta, Philipp: as biographer of Bach, 303

Spitzeder (artist), 154

Spohr, Ludwig: FMB's friendship with, 47, 51, 288, 413-4, 470, 581; FMB meets, 130-1, 413-4; compositional experiments of, 131; Nathan Rothschild declines to support, 181; FMB inspires, 266-7, 442; problems with Spontini, 300; and the use of a conductor's baton, 315; invitation to New York, 333-4; sets psalms, 353; declines court appointment, 392; FMB on, 392, 412, 414, 581; popularity in Leipzig, 439-40; rondo performed, 446; violin concertos of, 453, 486, 523; popularity in England, 516, 527, 574; *Daughter of the Air* Overture, 266-7, 442; *Die Kreuzfahrer*, 413; Double Quartet, op. 65, 271; *Jessonda*, 300, 413; *The Last Judgement*, 576; Symphony No. 2, 516; Quartet Concerto in A minor, op. 131, 413-4

Spontini, Gasparo, visits to salons of Henriette Mendelssohn, 25; Rellstab arrested for insulting, 124; Goethe discusses, 132; Chopin recognises, 237, 424; FMB on, 240, 411, 412; mixed accounts of, 299; criticises FMB's singspiel, 299-399, 578; dispute with Spohr, 300, 413; attempts to prevent staging of the *St Matthew Passion*, 306; on performance of the *St Matthew Passion*, 307; FMB deputises for, 316-7; Meyerbeer replaces, 388; gossip concerning, 473-4; Cécile Mendelssohn's admiration for, 489-90; invitation to London, 510; anti-Semitism of, 578; *La Vestale*, 25; *Olympe*, 117

Spring-Rice, Sir Cecil, 517

Spring-Rice, Thomas William, 517

Spurzheim, Johann Christoph: demonstrates phrenologic techniques, 243; examines FMB, 495

St Cecilia Society, 112, 222, 468, 490; FMB directs, 50, 414, 416, 442, 459, 464; FMB composes for, 114; FMB on, 152, 359, 410, 474, 475; wedding gift to FMB, 465, 605

Staël, Madame de: salons of, 23; visits salons of Dorothea Mendelssohn, 25; *Corinna*, 22

Staffa: Joseph Bank's visit to, 279; FMB visits, 280-1, 534; Fingal's Cave, 279-80, 536

Stainer, John: as member of the Mendelssohn Scholarship committee, 609; *Crucifixion*, 576, 609

Stanford, Charles Villiers: on FMB's meeting with Xavier Mozart, 91-2

Star, The, 584

Staudigl, Joseph, 364-5, 367

Steffens, Johanna (née Reichardt), 313

Stehelin, Martin: on FMB's inspiration for *Elijah*, 361

Steinberg, Michael, 192, 269, 388

Stephens, Jenny: FMB presents Chopin manuscript to, 525

Stern, Julius: FMB inquires after music of, 499; founds Berlin Academy of music, 593

Sterndale Bennett, Barry, 315, 430

Sterndale Bennett, Joan, 430

Sterndale Bennett, R., 563

Sterndale Bennett, Sir William: compliments Fanny Mendelssohn's song, 148; visit to FMB's home in Leipzig, 181, 246, 343, 430, 452, 486, 519; FMB confides in, 259-60; aids

FMB in editing Handel, 311, 430; career and life of, 429-30, 593; FMB's influence on, 432, 593; performs Piano Concerto, 442, 521; in London with FMB, 521-2, 551; enigmatic comment on Cécile Mendelssohn, 461; on Lampadius's biography of FMB, 578; Piano Concerto No. 1, 429, 430, 442, 521; *Woman of Samaria*, 576

Sterndale Bennett, T. C.: *Leanin'*, 430; *The Carol Singers*, 430

Sterne, Laurence: Moses Mendelssohn enjoys novels of, 9; FMB reads novels of, 541; *Tristram Shandy*, 9

Sternfeld, Herr (conductor), 185, 358

Stettin: first performance of FMB's *Midsummer Night's Dream* takes place in, 261; *St Matthew Passion* performed in, 308

Stiehler, Heinrich: FMB meets, 132, 134, 419; FMB dismisses painting by, 147; *Head of a Nymph*, 419; *The Young Fishergirl*, 419

Stimpson, Dr.: FMB performs benefit concert for, 367, 594

Stockhausen, Margarethe (*née* Schmuck), 516

Stockley, William, 516

Stöcklin, Paul: on the Leipzig Conservatorium, 376

Strasbourg: FMB and Cécile Mendelssohn visit, 472-3, 479

Stratton, Stephen: on FMB's childhood, 2, 34, 112; on intrusive writing about FMB, 4; on FMB's personal appearance and character, 37, 125, 241, 288, 350, 372, 378, 515, 574, 580, 585; on a drawing of FMB, 39; on love affair of FMB, 249, 252; on FMB and Planché, 294; on a performance of Beethoven's 'Emperor' Concerto, 339; on performances by FMB, 343, 359, 366, 518; on FMB as organist, 344, 349, 350; on FMB's compositions, 354, 355, 358-9, 364-5, 558, 576; on Spohr's autobiography, 413; catalogue of FMB's works, 531, 602; on FMB's demise, 555, 556; on FMB's name, 563; on FMB's legacy, 575, 591-2, 610, 612; on Elise Polko's memoirs, 607

Strauss (pastor), 352

Strauss, Johann, the Elder, 183, 274, 428, 472

Strauss, Richard: sets Eichendorff's poetry, 285, 456; lieder of, 314; in old age, 564; influence of FMB on, 592; *Ariadne auf Naxos*, 592; Four Last Songs, 456

Streatfeild, R. A., 577

Streckfuss, Adolph, 214

Streicher, Julius: pianos by, 123-4, 127, 129, 187, 333

Strohmeyer, Dr.: on FMB, 66, 241; *Memoirs of a Physician*, 241

Strong, Templeton: criticism of FMB's 'Scottish' Symphony, 278

Stuart, Mary *see* Mary, Queen of Scots

Stuntz, Joseph Hartmann, 432

Stuttaford, Dr. Thomas, 59

Sue, Eugène: FMB praises writing of, 74, 558

Sullivan, Arthur, 297, 593, 598; as Mendelssohn Scholar, 428, 599, 609; on Klingemann, 572; *see also* Gilbert & Sullivan

Summerville, Lady, 199

Suppé, Franz von, 274

Surman, Joseph, 517

Sutherland-Leveson-Gower, Harriet, Duchess of Sutherland, 386, 398

Switzerland: FMB in, 49, 59, 74-5, 103-4, 115, 136, 154, 164, 167, 171, 182, 208, 218, 228, 249, 291, 344-6, 393, 413, 507, 557-8; FMB's letters from, 160; Mendelssohn Archive in, 138, 159, 570; lithograph in Lausanne, 239; FMB on yodelling in, 273-4; FMB's plans to retire to, 456

Szymanowska, Marie, 123

Taglioni, Marie: Abraham Mendelssohn admires dancing of, 80; FMB on, 81, 82, 211, 406

Talbot, Henry Fox, 462
Tamburini, Antonio, 408
Tasso, Torquato: FMB on poems of, 74, 290; FMB's disappointment in Venice, 135; Rebecka Mendelssohn's sketch, 166; *Death of Clorinda*, 74; *Gerusalima Liberata*, 290
Taubert, Wilhelm, 208, 291, 372, 485; works by, 373, 434
Taylor, Anne: FMB stays with family of, 35, 71, 243, 245-6, 538; on FMB's personal appearance and character, 35-6, 111, 271; as contributor to Grove, 35, 572; FMB's dedication to, 133; and Betty Pistor, 247; FMB and cousin of, 539
Taylor, Bayard: meeting with FMB, 39, 334
Taylor, Honoria: FMB stays with family of, 35, 71, 243, 245-6, 538; FMB's dedication to, 133
Taylor, Suzanne (Susan): FMB stays with family of, 35, 71, 243, 245-6, 538; FMB's dedication to, 133
Taylor, Tom: publishes cartoon depicting FMB, 297
Tchaikovsky, Peter Ilyich, 598, 610, 612; *Chanson sans Paroles*, 575; Violin Concerto, 486, 596-7
Tea and Snow Times, The, 71
Telemachus, 86
Telemann, Georg Philipp: FMB recognises manuscript of, 312; on contrapuntal exercises, 369; in Leipzig, 437, 450
Telford, Thomas, 536
Tennyson, Alfred, 295, 463; *Maud*, 1
Tennyson, Emily (née Sellwood), 463
Terence: FMB's translation of *The Maid of Andros*, 44, 131, 221
Tetzlaff, Christian: on FMB's Violin Concerto, 596
Thackeray, William Makepeace: on FMB's personal appearance, 39, 584; admiration for FMB, 551
Thalben-Ball, George, 594
Thalberg, Sigismund, 151; piano playing of, compared with FMB, 338, 343; FMB performs with, 343, 523; arrangements by, 398; piano technique, 420; in FMB's correspondence, 420; FMB on, 426-7, 433; Clara Wieck performs work by, 443; FMB's attempt to emulate, 484; incident in London, 520
Theile, Eduard, 562
Therese, Queen Consort of Ludwig I of Bavaria, 385
Thibaut, Anton Friedrich Justus: FMB meets, 77, 118-9, 305
Thomas, J. & D.L., 242, 560, 562
Thompson, John, 513
Thompson, Seth, 550, 572
Thompson, Wendy, 341, 599
Thorwaldsen, Bertel, 248; statue of Goethe, 379; FMB meets, 421; honoured in Berlin, 434; death of, 493
Tieck, Ludwig: translations of Shakespeare's plays, 12, 74, 266; Goethe sees play by, 127; and *A Midsummer Night's Dream*, 261-4; declines FMB's offer to write libretto, 295; criticises FMB's music, 296; and *Antigone*, 296-7; translation of *Don Quixote*, 298-9; writes libretto to von Boguslawski's *Elfino*, 370; image on commemorative medallion, 390; on FMB's character, 396; *Eigensinn und Laune*, 194
Times, The, 59, 340, 564; on parliamentary debate concerning anti-Semitism in Britain, 213; Davison as music critic to, 252, 332, 583; on *St Paul*, 359; on *Elijah*, 364, 366; on Berlioz conducting the 'Italian' Symphony, 423; on Joachim, 522; FMB reads, 528; reports FMB's death, 565
Tinel, Edgar, 303
Titian: FMB on the paintings of, 81, 86, 89, 135, 197, 248, 532; works in the Brignole Palace, 93; *Age of Innocence*, 532; *Annunciation of the Blessed Virgin*,

86; *Assumption*, 135, 197; *Martyrdom of St Peter*, 135; portrait of St Ignatius Loyola, 197
Todd, R. Larry, 107, 452, 586, 607; *Unfinished Mendelssohn*, 107
Tolken, Herr, 238
Tomlinson, Craig, 605
Tork, Daniel, 315
Toscanini, Arturo, 262-3, 317
Tovey, Donald, 263
Trautwein (publisher), 137, 312
Trémont, Baron de (publisher), 602-3
Triebsche, Heinrich, 590, 591; *History of Germany*, 590
Trollope, Anthony, 245, 545
Trollope, Frances: *Domestic Manners of the Americans*, 545
Turle, James, 517
Turnage, Marc-Anthony, 610
Turner, Joseph Mallord William: painting of Fingal's cave, 279, 280
Uhland, Ludwig, 592
umbrellas: physics of, 104
Valentini (banker in Rome), 385
Van Dyck, Anthony, 83, 93, 386
Varnhagen von Ense, Karl August: dispute with Abraham Mendelssohn, 19
Varnhagen von Ense, Rahel (*née* Levin): partner in salon, 22; on Henriette Mendelssohn, 25; FMB on, 150-1, 242, 462-3; describes FMB's dancing, 236
Vaughan Williams, Ralph, 297, 564
Veit, Dorothea *see* Mendelssohn, Dorothea
Veit, Johannes, 21
Veit, Philipp, 21, 99, 170, 231
Veit, Simon, 21-2
Velten, Herr (musician): FMB's tribute to, 455-6
Venice: FMB in, 85-6, 96, 134-5, 185, 248; Church of St John and St Paul, 86, 198; St. Mark's Cathedral, 86
Venutelli, Mme., 154
Verdi, Giuseppe, 287, 288-9, 342, 462, 558, 564, 577; *Ernani*, 558; *Nabucco*, 558; *Falstaff*, 593

Verdi, Giuseppina, 462
Verhulst, Johannes Joseph Hermann: sets 'La Colognaise', 215; FMB and, 283, 443
Verkenius, Erich Heinrich Wilhelm: illness of, 58, 172; FMB corresponds with, 412, 580
Vernet, Horace: portrait of FMB, 38, 341; ball given by, 96, 341; FMB on, 194; letters sent to, 209
Vesuvius, Mount: FMB on, 101, 274; eruption of, 101, 333; Hensel family's climbs, 223-4
Viardot, Pauline (*née* Garcia), 451, 603
Victoria (Vittoria), Tomás Luis de, 119; *Passion according to St John*, 136
Victoria, Princess Royal, 263, 398, 401
Victoria, Queen: FMB meets, 5, 146, 398-401, 573; relation to Isaac Levy, 16; on FMB, 36-7, 65; FMB requests permission to dedicate 'Scottish' Symphony to, 278, 520; in Scotland, 280; attends concert, 340; on *Elijah*, 366; commissions Wilhelm Hensel, 386; coronation of, 386-7; and Marianne Skerrett, 397; and Luigi Lablache, 397; during childbirth, 498; planned trip to Birmingham, 518; after death of Prince Albert, 566; eulogy to FMB, 601; as depicted in *Beyond Desire*, 608; on Jenny Lind, 609
Vienna: Joseph Mendelssohn's society in, 24; Friends of Music, 52, 420; FMB in, 72, 78-9, 134, 183-4, 248, 274, 420-1, 590; music in, 116, 120, 303, 324, 407, 417, 420, 428, 439, 444, 596, 608; Congress of, 312; FMB postpones trip to, 560
Vieuxtemps, Henri François Joseph: violin concertos of, 486, 523
Viotti, Giovanni Battista: violin concertos of, 486
Virgil: *Aeneid*, 504
Voigt, Henriette, 414
Voigts, Friedrich: as librettist to FMB 70, 299, 300
Voltaire: FMB on, 162, 552

Voss, Johann Heinrich, 17, 74
Vuillermoz, Emile, 3
Wach, Adolf, 569
Wach, Maria, 570, 605
Wagner, Cosima, 448, 462
Wagner, Richard: as music critic, 46; on Beethoven's *Coriolan* Overture, 120; and Schlesinger, 200; FMB's involvement with, 261, 427, 591; influence of FMB in the music of, 267, 309, 591-2; on the *Hebrides* Overture, 281; librettos of, 287; attacks on FMB, 289, 317, 443-4, 450, 456, 480, 581-5, 587-8; comparisons with FMB, 289, 295, 575, 577, 612; on Böttger's libretto, 295; at Bayreuth, 324; pianos of, 342; honoured, 396; performs Spohr, 414; at farewell dinner, 433; accuses FMB, 443-4; on MacFarren's *Chevy Chase* Overture, 448; relation to Brockhaus, 455, 484; Schumann on, 456, 600; Chorley on, 573, 574, 594; anti-Semitism of, 581-2; statue vandalised, 590; at Promenade concerts, 599; on Liszt's contumely, 600-1; and Engelbert Humperdinck, 610; *The Flying Dutchman*, 261, 281, 434, 582; *Parsifal*, 238, 594; *Das Rheingold*, 267, 591; *Rienzi*, 582; *The Ring*, 295; Symphony in C major, 443, 582; *Tannhäuser*, 456, 574, 591; *Tristan und Isolde*, 296, 591; *Die Walküre*, 591; *Mein Leben*, 295, 450; *Essay On Conducting*, 317, 583; *Judaism in Music*, 582-3
Wahl, Saul (legend of), 324-5
Walerode, Herr (politician), 217
Wales: FMB in, 35, 71, 243, 245-6, 276, 538
Wallace, Lady Grace, 36, 160, 477, 499, 518, 604; *Travel Letters of Felix Mendelssohn, 1830-1832*, 604
Washington, George, 93
Wasielewski, Josef Wilhelm von, 378, 380, 381
Wasserman, Jakob: *The Way of a German and a Jew*, 587

Waterloo, Battle of, 174, 386
Watson, John, *Coins and Stamps in Music*, 611
Weber, Carl Maria von: musical influence on FMB, 106, 120, 261, 513; FMB meets, 110; FMB performs works by, 110-11, 133, 341, 342, 343, 412, 438-9, 509; Zelter on, 148; on Bach, 304; conducting of, 315, 317; and Bärmann, 318, 420; FMB on performances of operas by, 405, 411; Jenny Lind sings arias by, 455; in London, 510, 513, 528; and John Abraham, 583; *Euryanthe*, 250, 317, 513, 583; *Der Freischütz*, 110, 114, 148, 276, 405, 443; *Invitation to the Dance*, 250; *Jubilee* Overture, 383; *Konzertstück*, 341, 509; *Oberon*, 261, 294, 326, 327, 342, 411, 510, 513; *Preciosa*, 343, 516; *Ruler of the Spirits*, 438-9
Weber, Caroline von (*née* Brandt), 513
Weber, Gottfried, 409
Webern, Karl Emil von: friendship with FMB, 145, 507; visit to Frankfurt, 218; on FMB's relationship with his parents, 241
Weil, Jiří, 590
Weimar: FMB at, 55, 114, 117, 121, 123-34, 162, 192, 200, 221, 242, 282, 340, 344-5; Düsseldorf emulates, 326, 328; FMB advises Moscheles on, 412
Wellesley, Arthur, Duke of Wellington, 174, 387, 609
Wellington, Duke of *see* Wellesley, Arthur, Duke of Wellington
Werden, Professor, 346
Werner, Eric, 59, 244; on Friedrich Riemer, 60; on FMB's letters from Switzerland, 160; on Abraham Mendelssohn's depression, 182; on FMB's *First Walpurgisnacht*, 267; on FMB in Berlin, 322, 323; biography of FMB, 389; on *The Family Mendelssohn*, 606
Wesendonck, Otto, 583
Wesley, Charles, 239

Index of Names and Compositions

Wesley, Eliza: FMB's dedication to, 517
Wesley, Samuel, 344; FMB meets, 349, 517
Wessely, Hartwig, 18
Westminster, Duke of *see* Grosvenor, Robert
Westmorland, Earl of *see* Fane, John, 11th Earl of Westmorland
Wetton, Hilary Davan: on FMB's 'Italian' Symphony, 275, 277
Wharncliffe, Lord James Archibald, 520
White, Maud Valerie: awarded Mendelssohn Scholarship, 610
Whittaker, W. Gillies, 281
Wichmann, Ludwig, 253, 493
Widman (music critic): on *Elijah*, 585
Wieck, Clara *see* Schumann, Clara
Wilde, Oscar, 502
Wilhelm VIII, Duke of Brunswick, 333; festival of, 39, 332-3
Wilhelmssen (theologian), 193
Wilkins, Donald: *The Pifferone*, 275
William IV, King, 5, 16, 359; death of, 51, 518
Winckelmann, Johann Joachim: home in Italy, 98; birthday commemorated, 236-7
Windsor: Castle, 522; Chapel Royal, 353
Winter (nightwatchman), 493
Winter, Peter von: *The Power of Music*, 324
Winterhalter, Franz, 551
Wittmann, Franz Karl, 413
Wolff, Ernst, 294, 324, 485, 589
Wölfl, Joseph: Trio for two horns and piano, 112
Wood, Henry, 228
Wood, John Muir, 513
Wordsworth, William: on tourists in Scotland, 280; in old age, 564-5
Woringen (family): visit to Berlin, 152; daughter's marriage, 233; daughter at concert, 324; and Rebecka Mendelssohn, 480
Woringen, Franz Arnold von, 156, 323, 325

World, The, 584
Wranitzky, Paul: *Charon*, 126
Wurm, Marie: awarded Mendelssohn Scholarship, 610
Wycliffe, John, 16
Young, Percy: on Elgar, 271, 565, 592; on Jenny Lind, 367; on Wagner's Symphony in C major, 444; on Alice Elgar, 463
Zarek, Otto, 9
Zelter, Carl Friedrich: and Goethe, 44, 45, 49, 60, 108, 121, 127-8, 130, 134, 137, 267; death of, 49, 58, 114, 137, 227, 320; as mentor to FMB, 55, 81, 89, 106-8, 112-5, 121-7, 130-1, 134-6, 141, 165, 169, 172, 181, 198, 260, 276, 304, 322, 344-5, 351, 369, 413; as director of Berlin Singakademie, 59, 148, 305-8, 313-4, 319-21, 323, 374, 514; character, 60, 107, 116; and Abraham Mendelssohn, 108, 129, 175, 184; FMB's dedication to, 119; on FMB, 129, 131, 135, 221; Chopin sees at convention, 237; as curator of music, 246, 248, 304, 312; as pupil of Kirnberger, 304; FMB recommends von Henselt to, 429; fictional representation of, 607
Zelter, Doris, 121, 122, 127, 226, 242
Zollverein (Customs Union), 445-6
Zuccalmaglio, Anton von, 283
Zürich: FMB in, 487-8

ABOUT THE AUTHOR

As her pen-name suggests, Mary Allerton-North is a Yorkshire lass – her surname is the town of Northallerton the wrong way round; she has also written fiction, under the pseudonym Victoria Thirsk. Currently she lives in Reading with her psychoanalyst husband, to whom she has been married for over 40 years.

The author's interests encompass the 19th and early 20th centuries and all aspects of culture, and her hobbies include crossword puzzles, board games and quizzes (she has appeared on BBC TV's Mastermind). A member of the Georgian Group and the National Trust, Mary has also founded a voluntary group to help her local community, and the music appreciation society 'Friends of Mendelssohn', which, together with this biography, she hopes will allow his music and reputation to thrive.

A psychotherapist by profession, she has written this book – her first non-fiction work – as if Felix Mendelssohn and his family were her clients. With the research exhilarating her so much that she uses the phrase "life begins at 60", Mary aims to be responsible for further biographies. She also refuses to allow her very limited eyesight to prevent her leading a full and active life – inspired by her present biographical subject, Felix Mendelssohn.

www.ingramcontent.com/pod-product-compliance
Lightning Source LLC
Chambersburg PA
CBHW071327190426
43193CB00041B/889